THE DRAMATISED BIBLE

Marshall Pickering
Middlesex House, 34–42 Cleveland Street, London W1P 5FB

Bible Society
Stonehill Green, Westlea, Swindon SN5 7DG, England

First published in 1989 by Marshall Morgan & Scott Publications Ltd.(part of the Marshall
Pickering Holdings Group, a subsidiary of the Zondervan Corporation) and Bible Society.

British Library Cataloguing in Publication Data
The Dramatised Bible
  1. Bible   2. Drama   3. Liturgy
  I. Perry, Michael

  Marshall Pickering ISBN 0–551–01779–1
  Bible Society   ISBN 0–564–05135–7

Text set by Watermark, Hampermill Cottage, Watford WD1 4PL.

Printed and bound in Yugoslavia

The Dramatised Bible

Editor: Michael Perry

Good News Bible
New International Version
Jubilate Liturgical Psalms

MARSHALL PICKERING: BIBLE SOCIETY

Other books from the Jubilate group

Carols For Today
Carol Praise
Church Family Worship
Come Rejoice!
Coming Home
Hymns for Today's Church
Hymns for Today's Church (new editions)
Jesus Praise
Let's Praise!
Prom Praise Solos
The Wedding Book
Welcome Your King

Coming soon

Anthems for Today
Carol Praise for Children
Choir Carols for Today
Hymns 2000
Orchestral Carols
Orchestral Praise
Praise Today
Prayers for the People
Psalms for Today
Songs from the Psalms

CONTENTS

OLD TESTAMENT

NEW TESTAMENT

APPENDIX

INDEXES

To Helen and Simon,
for whom may the Book live
as it has for me.

Editor's Preface

The Dramatised Bible creates the opportunity for a vivid presentation of Bible narrative and teaching. Generations of ministers and teachers or youth and children's leaders have done it before—turned the Bible text into drama so that worshippers or students can become actively involved in its teaching. But publication has always been piecemeal. Episodes have been available previously in dramatised form (viz. the events leading up to Easter in various books, and the Christmas story in our *Church Family Worship* and *Carols for Today*) but never, so far as we are aware, all the Bible narrative.

It is remarkable how much of the Bible uses the device of 'reported speech' and so lends itself to dramatic presentation. For instance, we would not immediately think of the book Jeremiah in this way. And yet Jeremiah has a narrative form quite as amenable to dramatic presentation as, say, Genesis. It is the Hebrew tradition of story-telling which makes the task so inviting and the outcome so effective.

Old Testament precedent

We like to think that further encouragement is given to the exercise of dramatising the Bible for worship by one special discovery. It does appear that the Hebrew people in Temple worship used drama to rehearse the acts of God in their history—notably the crossing of the Red Sea and their deliverance from the slavery of Egypt. Such dramatic presentations were not entertainment—though they would have been marvellously *entertaining*. And they were far more than visual aids—though Hebrew faith did require each generation to recall, before the next, God's saving interventions, so that his mercy and his demands would not be forgotten. The Hebrew dramas had a teaching role, and they were acts of worship too—precedents of our own 'anamnesis', or calling to mind of the saving work of Christ in the drama we term, according to our Christian tradition, 'The Lord's Supper'/'The Holy Communion'/'The Eucharist'/'The Mass'.

Evidence for a more extended use of drama in Hebrew worship comes from the Psalms. We have only to look at Psalm 118 to see that it is neither a hymn nor merely a meditation. There are obvious character parts and choral parts. And there are even 'stage' instructions embedded in the text. For example, verse 27 "With palm branches in your hands march round the altar"—which, in some traditions, we blindly *sing* as though the psalm were homogeneous. It does not take much imagination to see that what we are dealing with is the script of a drama or the libretto of an opera, set in the context of a magnificent act of worship. Here the intending (and noble?) worshipper approaches the door of the Temple and asks to enter to give thanks for God's deliverance. The ministers/priests tell him righteousness is a prerequisite of an approach to God. And the drama progresses from there. Permeating the drama are the resonant choruses of the Hebrew liturgy:

Leader	Let Israel say:
All	His love endures for ever!
Leader	Let the House of Aaron say:
All	His love endures for ever!

ix

Leader	Let those who fear the Lord say:
All	His love endures for ever!

Finally, the worshipper is admitted ("Blessed is he who comes in the name of the Lord") and the celebration begins ("With branches in your hands . . ."). As long as we consider the Old Testament dour and prosaic its exciting suggestions for our own worship practice will be missed.

Other psalms are not so readily dramatised, especially those written to articulate the needs of individuals. Even so, it is surprising how many examples of reported speech there are among them. In *The Dramatised Bible* the division of parts has been made where the psalmist changes mood as the psalm moves from the the experience of one worshipper to that of another.

New Testament
The New Testament is full of vivid narrative. For the most part dramatising comes easily and is obviously appropriate. While we have not forced a dramatic pattern upon passages not amenable to such treatment, we have dramatised some of the teaching material where it might at first sight appear that only one voice is required. For instance, where Jesus' words are cast in the rabbinic style which preserved them through the oral period until they became written elements of the Gospels:

Teacher	Blessed are the poor in spirit:
Students	For theirs is the kingdom of heaven.

. . . the teaching of Jesus indeed—but thereafter used in catechetical pattern by the early Christians. We follow their very effective form of dramatising, and in this way recover its first freshness.

Much of the epistolary material is intentionally omitted from *The Dramatised Bible* as it is best left as straight prose to be read by a single voice. But there are exceptions; for instance, St Paul has his own style of 'question and answer':

Question	Is God unjust?
Answer	Not at all!

. . . positively *inviting* dramatisation!

Barriers broken
Much of the work of the Jubilate group has been in the interests of a clearer presentation of the facts of the faith in worship. Centrally within this context, *The Dramatised Bible* brings the text of Scripture to life. Using *The Dramatised Bible* means involving people in the recalling and recounting their salvation-history. The experience is memorable and challenging.

Those who listen to *The Dramatised Bible* are drawn into the presentation. As the story moves from voice to voice it is very difficult for attention to wander. Useful in all forms of church worship, *The Dramatised Bible* is especially an ideal focus for the 'word' aspect of all-age (so-called 'family') worship. Even young children, who naturally grow restive during a long and uneventful reading, find their interest and imagination caught up in the narrative as the scriptures are presented in dramatised form.

We confidently commend this book to churches, youth groups, schools, study groups, and all who work in the area of education. It may be that producers and presenters of religious programmes for radio and television will also find inspiration here. We happily anticipate that *The Dramatised Bible* will enrich our worship by granting us a clearer vision of God and a surer knowledge of the revelation of the eternal purpose for our world in Jesus Christ.

MICHAEL PERRY
Pentecost, 1989

Acknowledgements

As editor of *The Dramatised Bible* I gladly acknowledge the skills of the teams of experts who prepared the outstanding and now celebrated *Good News* and *New International* English texts of the Bible. I have appreciated the advice of the Reverend Kathleen Bowe upon the translation of my Liturgical Psalms, of the Reverend Robert Backhouse on all aspects of dramatisation and typesetting, and of Miss Janet Henderson on matters of copyright. My thanks go to my typist Ann, my secretary Bunty and my daughter Helen for their conscientious work on copy, proofs and indexes. I am grateful to the Church Pastoral Aid Society, The Bible Reading Fellowship, The Association of Christian Teachers, The Scripture Union, and to senior figures in the denominations, including the Anglican, Baptist, Roman Catholic, and United Reformed Churches for their encouragement and commendation. I am indebted to the friendly staff at Marshall Pickering and Bible Society, and applaud their proof-readers. I know that all who have co-operated in its production will find great satisfaction in the enthusiasm with which I am confident *The Dramatised Bible* will be received.

M.A.P.

Using *The Dramatised Bible*

Welcome to a new and powerful resource! If you are a minister, teacher, or leader, you will want to know how you can use this book to the greatest effect.

Realism

In designing *The Dramatised Bible* we have tried to be realistic about the pressure upon ministers, teachers, and leaders: on the whole they require a book that can be used spontaneously and without great forethought, preparation, or rehearsal. We suggest that each organisation using *The Dramatised Bible* eventually needs five copies because, on average, there are five characters to a script. Then, at a moment's notice, willing readers can be given a copy each, and invited to fill a character part. All characters are listed at the foot of each 'reading'.

Superfluous "Moses said"s and the like are already excised from the text (with the permission of the copyright-holders). While appropriate in prose, they are intrusive—sometimes even humorous—in drama. Usually in *The Dramatised Bible* they are left in at the beginning of the piece, in order to establish the character, and then omitted thereafter. Further phrases which for similar reasons might be thought to make performance stilted are enclosed in square brackets, [and]. But such phrases/sentences should not be omitted without considering the particular implications. To omit them may well enliven the drama, but it will require the cast to compensate for the omission. This can either be done visually—by turning to one of the other characters, or aurally—by a change of voice. The best solution will depend on the local circumstances, the initiative of the leader, and the ability of the participants. Hence, a rule of thumb might be—*only when consultation or rehearsal is possible omit phrases in square brackets.*

Shortening an episode

Square brackets have a different function when they enclose one or more paragraphs: they indicate where the 'reading' may sensibly be shortened. Unless a sermon/service/talk/discussion requires use of these longer sections they are best left out in the interests of lively presentation and greater impact upon an audience.

Psalms for the congregation or group

The Dramatised Bible contains forty psalms prepared for congregational or worship-group use. They are marked 'LIT' (Liturgical Version). These (but no other material) may be photo–copied freely in sufficient quantities for use by the whole congregation or local organisation, on condition that any item so used is marked '© The Dramatised Bible'.

Local reproduction

Applications for reproduction of material from *The Dramatised Bible* in the world outside North America may be addressed to The Copyright Secretary, Jubilate Hymns Ltd, 61 Chessel Avenue, Southampton, SO2 4DY (telephone 0703 630038). Jubilate's Agent in the United States of America is Hope Publishing Company, Carol Stream, Illinois 60188 (call 312–665–3200). Time should be allowed for reference by Jubilate to the proprietors of the *Good News Bible* or *New International Version*. For further information see: Legal Information (page xiv).

Audibility

Use of *The Dramatised Bible* has a very positive effect on the attention that a 'reading' is given by an audience—congregation, class, youth group or study group. It also makes the content of the 'reading' more memorable—not least to those who have participated. Much depends on audiblity; so care needs to be taken in larger buildings. In church, or in a school assembly hall, a dais holding a minimum of five people can be used to advantage. Where appropriate, a microphone with a wide field that will pick up all the speakers should be used; or separate microphones might be considered. This sort of preparation will enable the minister/leader to involve people whose voices are less clear and not so strong.

Casting

It is obviously important that a strong voice should be cast for any 'key' character, such as the frequent 'Narrator'. In a church service, this part can most usefully be given to the person who would have taken the scripture reading if it had not been dramatised, thus ensuring that no one feels usurped by what should be a welcome development in worship. It is worth noting that more male than female characters speak in the Bible. However, when using *The Dramatised Bible*, a good balance can still be obtained by employing female voices for narration, for the frequent anonymous '**Persons**', and in the teaching passages which divide into '**Voice 1**', '**Voice 2**' etc. Here it is good to have a contrast between the speakers.

Where **Voices 1–3**, **Persons 1–3** etc. are used, participants should stand together in a group. Where '**The Lord**', or '**God**', speaks as a prophetic utterance and not in direct conversation it is best for the reader to stand apart from the rest—even to be unseen.

Actions

There will be occasions—both formal and informal—when participants can add *actions* to a presentation from *The Dramatised Bible*. Then, prior agreement over what is to be done is a safeguard against unintended humorous accidents! And a rehearsal will be necessary unless the actors are very confident and experienced. At the rehearsal it is sensible to have someone watching who is able to assess the drama's impact on the proposed audience, and for the cast to listen and respond to that person's objective criticism. When actions are used in the context of large gatherings, visibility and audibility (especially when the speaker turns away from the audience) are of utmost importance. In seminar and class work, or in small groups, carefully prepared actions will add a startlingly fresh dynamic.

Finding your way around

The indexes to *The Dramatised Bible* are substantial, in order to be of maximum help to the teacher and minister. Suggestions for seasonal use of the liturgical psalms will be found on page 564 (Old Testament) and for simpler casting of the Christmas Readings on page 407 (New Testament). The *Index to Characters* gives ready access to remembered stories; the *Index to Selected Major Themes* offers a resource for the preacher or study group; and the *Index to Seasonal and Liturgical Material* provides the designer of services, conferences etc. with swift reference to the relevant passages. Finally, the *Index to Dramatised Versions* offers, at a glance, the full contents of *The Dramatised Bible* with the Bible version (in brackets) and reference, the title and the page number of each 'reading'—quickly answering the question: Is it in the book? The answer more often than not will be, "Yes!"

Legal Information

The Bible text used in this publication is that of:

(a) The *Good News Bible* (Today's English Version), British usage edition, published by The Bible Societies and Collins. Old Testament: copyright © American Bible Society 1976; New Testament: copyright © American Bible Society 1966, 1971, 1976. Used by permission.

(b) The *New International Version* copyright © 1973, 1978, 1984 by International Bible Society. Used with the permission of Hodder and Stoughton and (USA) of the Zondervan Corporation.

(c) The *Jubilate Liturgical Psalms* copyright © 1986, 1989 Michael Perry/ Jubilate Hymns; © 1986, 1989 Hope Publishing Company, Carol Stream, Illinois 60188.

The version being used in each dramatised reading is specified in the Index to Dramatised Versions (New Testament page 465).

OLD TESTAMENT

GENESIS

God's creation
From Genesis 1.1—2.4

Narrator	In the beginning, when God created the universe, the earth was formless and desolate. The raging ocean that covered everything was engulfed in total darkness, and the power of God was moving over the water. Then God commanded:
God	Let there be light.
Narrator	And light appeared. God was pleased with what he saw. Then he separated the light from the darkness, and he named the light:
God	Day.
Narrator	And the darkness:
God	Night.
Narrator	Evening passed and morning came—that was the first day. Then God commanded:
God	Let there be a dome to divide the water and to keep it in two separate places.
Narrator	And it was done. So God made a dome, and it separated the water under it from the water above it. He named the dome:
God	Sky.
Narrator	Evening passed and morning came—that was the second day. Then God commanded:
God	Let the water below the sky come together in one place, so that the land will appear—
Narrator	And it was done. He named the land:
God	Earth.
Narrator	And the water which had come together he named:
God	Sea.
Narrator	And God was pleased with what he saw. Then he commanded:
God	Let the earth produce all kinds of plants, those that bear grain and those that bear fruit.
Narrator	And it was done. So the earth produced all kinds of plants, and God was pleased with what he saw. Evening passed and morning came—that was the third day. Then God commanded:
God	Let lights appear in the sky to separate day from night and to show the time when days, years, and religious festivals begin; they will shine in the sky to give light to the earth.
Narrator	And it was done. So God made the two larger lights, the sun to rule over the day and the moon to rule over the night; he also

→

made the stars. He placed the lights in the sky to shine on the earth, to rule over the day and the night, and to separate light from darkness. And God was pleased with what he saw. Evening passed and morning came—that was the fourth day. Then God commanded:

God Let the water be filled with many kinds of living beings, and let the air be filled with birds.

Narrator So God created the great sea-monsters, all kinds of creatures that live in the water, and all kinds of birds. And God was pleased with what he saw. He blessed them all and told the creatures that live in the water to reproduce, and to fill the sea, and he told the birds to increase in number. Evening passed and morning came—that was the fifth day. Then God commanded:

God Let the earth produce all kinds of animal life: domestic and wild, large and small.

Narrator And it was done. So God made them all, and he was pleased with what he saw. Then God said:

God And now we will make human beings; they will be like us and resemble us. They will have power over the fish, the birds, and all animals, domestic and wild, large and small.

Narrator So God created human beings, making them to be like himself. He created them male and female, blessed them, and said:

God Have many children, so that your descendants will live all over the earth and bring it under their control. I am putting you in charge of the fish, the birds, and all the wild animals. I have provided all kinds of grain and all kinds of fruit for you to eat; but for all the wild animals and for all the birds I have provided grass and leafy plants for food.

Narrator And it was done. God looked at everything he had made, and he was very pleased. Evening passed and morning came—that was the sixth day. And so the whole universe was completed. By the seventh day God finished what he had been doing and stopped working. He blessed the seventh day and set it apart as a special day, because by that day he had completed his creation and stopped working. And that is how the universe was created.

Cast [This is] the word of the Lord.
All **Thanks be to God.**

Cast: **Narrator, God.**

The Garden of Eden
Genesis 2.4–24 [25]

Narrator 1 When the Lord God made the universe, there were no plants on the earth and no seeds had sprouted, because he had not sent any rain, and there was no one to cultivate the land; but water would come up from beneath the surface and water the ground.

Narrator 2	Then the Lord God took some soil from the ground and formed a man out of it; he breathed life-giving breath into his nostrils and the man began to live.
Narrator 1	Then the Lord God planted a garden in Eden, in the East, and there he put the man he had formed. He made all kinds of beautiful trees grow there and produce good fruit. In the middle of the garden stood the tree that gives life and the tree that gives knowledge of what is good and what is bad.
Narrator 2	A stream flowed in Eden and watered the garden; beyond Eden it divided into four rivers. The first river is the Pishon; it flows round the country of Havilah.
Narrator 1	Pure gold is found there and also rare perfume and precious stones.
Narrator 2	The second river is the Gihon; it flows round the country of Cush. The third river is the Tigris, which flows east of Assyria, and the fourth river is the Euphrates.
Narrator 1	Then the Lord God placed the man in the Garden of Eden to cultivate it and guard it:
God	You may eat the fruit of any tree in the garden, except the tree that gives knowledge of what is good and what is bad. You must not eat the fruit of that tree; if you do, you will die the same day. (PAUSE)
[Narrator 1	Then the Lord God said:]
God (musing)	It is not good for the man to live alone. I will make a suitable companion to help him.
Narrator 1	So he took some soil from the ground and formed all the animals and all the birds. Then he brought them to the man to see what he would name them; and that is how they all got their names. So the man named all the birds and all the animals; but not one of them was a suitable companion to help him.
Narrator 2	Then the Lord God made the man fall into a deep sleep, and while he was sleeping, he took out one of the man's ribs and closed up the flesh. He formed a woman out of the rib and brought her to him. Then the man said:
Man	At last, here is one of my own kind— Bone taken from my bone, and flesh from my flesh. 'Woman' is her name because she was taken out of man.
Narrator 2	That is why a man leaves his father and mother and is united with his wife, and they become one.
[Narrator 1	The man and the woman were both naked, but they were not embarrassed.]
Cast	[This is] the word of the Lord.
All	**Thanks be to God.**

Cast: **Narrator 1, Narrator 2** (can be the same as Narrator 1), **God, Man.**

3

Disobeying God
Genesis 3.1–24

Narrator	Now the snake was the most cunning animal that the Lord God had made. The snake asked the woman:
Snake	Did God really tell you not to eat fruit from any tree in the garden?
Narrator	The woman answered:
Woman	We may eat the fruit of any tree in the garden except the tree in the middle of it. God told us not to eat the fruit of that tree or even touch it; if we do, we will die.
Snake	That's not true; you will not die. God said that, because he knows that when you eat it you will be like God and know what is good and what is bad.
Narrator	The woman saw how beautiful the tree was and how good its fruit would be to eat, and she thought how wonderful it would be to become wise. So she took some of the fruit and ate it. Then she gave some to her husband, and he also ate it. As soon as they had eaten it they were given understanding and realized that they were naked; so they sewed fig leaves together and covered themselves. (PAUSE)
	That evening they heard the Lord God walking in the garden, and they hid from him among the trees. But the Lord God called out to the man.
God	Where are you?
Man	I heard you in the garden; I was afraid and hid from you, because I was naked.
God (to the Man)	Who told you that you were naked? Did you eat the fruit that I told you not to eat?
Man	The woman you put here with me gave me the fruit, and I ate it.
[Narrator	The Lord God asked the woman:
God (to the Woman)	Why did you do this?
Woman	The snake tricked me into eating it.
Narrator	Then the Lord God said to the snake:
God (to the Snake)	You will be punished for this; you alone of all the animals must bear this curse: From now on you will crawl on your belly, and you will have to eat dust as long as you live. I will make you and the woman hate each other; her offspring and yours will always be enemies. Her offspring will crush your head, and you will bite their heel.
Narrator	And he said to the woman:
God (to the Woman)	I will increase your trouble in pregnancy and your pain in giving birth. In spite of this, you will still have desire for your husband, yet you will be subject to him.

Narrator	And he said to the man:]
God (to the Man)	You listened to your wife and ate the fruit which I told you not to eat. Because of what you have done, the ground will be under a curse. You will have to work hard all your life to make it produce enough food for you. It will produce weeds and thorns, and you will have to eat wild plants. You will have to work hard and sweat to make the soil produce anything, until you go back to the soil from which you were formed. You were made from soil, and you will become soil again.
[Narrator	Adam named his wife Eve, because she was the mother of all human beings. And the Lord God made clothes out of animal skins for Adam and his wife, and he clothed them. (PAUSE) Then the Lord God said:
God	Now the man has become like one of us and has knowledge of what is good and what is bad. He must not be allowed to take fruit from the tree that gives life, eat it, and live for ever.]
Narrator	So the Lord God sent him out of the Garden of Eden and made him cultivate the soil from which he had been formed. Then at the east side of the garden he put living creatures and a flaming sword which turned in all directions. This was to keep anyone from coming near the tree that gives life.
Cast **All**	[This is] the word of the Lord. **Thanks be to God.**

Cast: **Narrator, Snake, Woman, God, Man.** (Please note the possibility of shortening this reading.)

Cain and Abel
From Genesis 4.1–16

Narrator	Adam's wife bore a son and named him Cain. Later she gave birth to another son, Abel. Abel became a shepherd, but Cain was a farmer. After some time, Cain brought some of his harvest and gave it as an offering to the Lord. Then Abel brought the first lamb born to one of his sheep, killed it, and gave the best parts of it as an offering. The Lord was pleased with Abel and his offering, but he rejected Cain and his offering. Cain became furious, and he scowled in anger. Then the Lord said to Cain:
The Lord	Why are you angry? Why that scowl on your face? If you had done the right thing, you would be smiling; but because you have done evil, sin is crouching at your door. It wants to rule you, but you must overcome it.
Narrator	Then Cain said to his brother Abel:
Cain	Let's go out in the fields.
Narrator	When they were out in the fields, Cain turned on his brother and killed him. (PAUSE) The Lord asked Cain:

The Lord	Where is your brother Abel?
Cain	I don't know. Am I supposed to take care of my brother?
The Lord	Why have you done this terrible thing? Your brother's blood is crying out to me from the ground, like a voice calling for revenge. You are placed under a curse and can no longer farm the soil. It has soaked up your brother's blood as if it had opened its mouth to receive it when you killed him. If you try to grow crops, the soil will not produce anything; you will be a homeless wanderer on the earth.
Cain (protesting)	This punishment is too hard for me to bear. You are driving me off the land and away from your presence. I will be a homeless wanderer on the earth, and anyone who finds me will kill me.
The Lord	No. If anyone kills you, seven lives will be taken in revenge.
Narrator	So the Lord put a mark on Cain to warn anyone who met him not to kill him. And Cain went away from the Lord's presence and lived in a land called 'Wandering', which is east of Eden.
Cast	[This is] the word of the Lord.
All	**Thanks be to God.**

Cast: **Narrator, The Lord, Cain.**

The descendants of Cain
Genesis 4.17–26

Narrator	Cain and his wife had a son and named him Enoch. Then Cain built a city and named it after his son. Enoch had a son named Irad, who was the father of Mehujael, and Mehujael had a son named Methushael, who was the father of Lamech. Lamech had two wives, Adah and Zillah. Adah gave birth to Jabal, who was the ancestor of those who raise livestock and live in tents. His brother was Jubal, the ancestor of all musicians who play the harp and the flute. Zillah gave birth to Tubal Cain, who made all kinds of tools out of bronze and iron. The sister of Tubal Cain was Naamah.
	Lamech said to his wives:
Lamech	Adah and Zillah, listen to me: I have killed a young man because he struck me. If seven lives are taken to pay for killing Cain, seventy-seven will be taken if anyone kills me.
Narrator	Adam and his wife had another son. [Eve said:]
Eve	God has given me a son to replace Abel, whom Cain killed.
Narrator	So she named him Seth. Seth had a son whom he named Enosh. It was then that people began using the Lord's holy name in worship.
Cast	[This is] the word of the Lord.
All	**Thanks be to God.**

Cast: **Narrator, Lamech, Eve.**

6

The wickedness of mankind
Genesis 6.1–8

Narrator When mankind had spread all over the world, and girls were being born, some of the heavenly beings saw that these girls were beautiful, so they took the ones they liked. Then the Lord said:

The Lord I will not allow people to live for ever; they are mortal. From now on they will live no longer than a hundred and twenty years.

Narrator In those days, and even later, there were giants on the earth who were descendants of human women and the heavenly beings. They were the great heroes and famous men of long ago.

When the Lord saw how wicked everyone on earth was and how evil their thoughts were all the time, he was sorry that he had ever made them and put them on the earth. He was filled with regret:

The Lord I will wipe out these people I have created, and also the animals
(bitterly) and the birds, because am sorry that I made any of them.

Narrator But the Lord was pleased with Noah.

Cast [This is] the word of the Lord.
All **Thanks be to God.**

Cast: **Narrator, The Lord.**

Noah and the flood
Genesis 6.9—7.16

Narrator 1 This is the story of Noah. He had three sons, Shem, Ham, and Japheth. Noah had no faults and was the only good man of his time. He lived in fellowship with God, but everyone else was evil in God's sight, and violence had spread everywhere. God looked at the world and saw that it was evil, for the people were all living evil lives. God said to Noah:

God I have decided to put an end to all mankind. I will destroy them completely, because the world is full of their violent deeds. Build a boat for yourself out of good timber; make rooms in it and cover it with tar inside and out. Make it 133 metres long, 22 metres wide, and 13 metres high. Make a roof for the boat and leave a space of 44 centimetres between the roof and the sides. Build it with three decks and put a door in the side. I am going to send a flood on the earth to destroy every living being. Everything on the earth will die, but I will make a covenant with you. Go into the boat with your wife, your sons, and their wives. Take into the boat with you a male and a female of every kind of animal and of every kind of bird, in order to keep them alive. Take along all kinds of food for you and for them.

Narrator 2 Noah did everything that God commanded. (PAUSE) The Lord said to Noah:

7

God	Go into the boat with your whole family; I have found that you are the only one in all the world who does what is right. Take with you seven pairs of each kind of ritually clean animal, but only one pair of each kind of unclean animal. Take also seven pairs of each kind of bird. Do this so that every kind of animal and bird will be kept alive to reproduce again on the earth. Seven days from now I am going to send rain that will fall for forty days and nights, in order to destroy all the living beings that I have made.
Narrator 1	And Noah did everything that the Lord commanded. Noah was six hundred years old when the flood came on the earth. He and his wife, and his sons and their wives, went into the boat to escape the flood. A male and a female of every kind of animal and bird, whether ritually clean or unclean, went into the boat with Noah, as God had commanded. Seven days later the flood came.
Narrator 2	When Noah was six hundred years old, on the seventeenth day of the second month all the outlets of the vast body of water beneath the earth burst open, all the floodgates of the sky were opened, and rain fell on the earth for forty days and nights. On that same day Noah and his wife went into the boat with their three sons, Shem, Ham, and Japheth, and their wives. With them went every kind of animal, domestic and wild, large and small, and every kind of bird. A male and a female of each kind of living being went into the boat with Noah, as God had commanded. Then the Lord shut the door behind Noah.

Cast	[This is] the word of the Lord.
All	**Thanks be to God.**

Cast: **Narrator 1, God, Narrator 2.**

The end of the flood
Genesis 7.17—8.19

Narrator 1	The flood continued for forty days, and the water became deep enough for the boat to float. The water became deeper, and the boat drifted on the surface. It became so deep that it covered the highest mountains; it went on rising until it was about seven metres above the tops of the mountains. Every living being on the earth died—every bird, every animal, and every person. Everything on earth that breathed died. The Lord destroyed all living beings on the earth—human beings, animals, and birds. The only ones left were Noah and those who were with him in the boat. The water did not start going down for a hundred and fifty days.
Narrator 2	God had not forgotten Noah and all the animals with him in the boat: he caused a wind to blow, and the water started going down. The outlets of the water beneath the earth and the floodgates of the sky were closed. The rain stopped, and the water gradually went down for a hundred and fifty days. On the seventeenth day of the seventh month the boat came to rest on a mountain in the Ararat range. The water kept going down, and on the first day of the tenth month the tops of the mountains appeared.

Narrator 1	After forty days Noah opened a window and sent out a raven. It did not come back, but kept flying around until the water was completely gone. Meanwhile, Noah sent out a dove to see if the water had gone down, but since the water still covered all the land, the dove did not find a place to alight. It flew back to the boat, and Noah reached out and took it in. He waited another seven days and sent out the dove again. It returned to him in the evening with a fresh olive leaf in its beak. So Noah knew that the water had gone down. Then he waited another seven days and sent out the dove once more; this time it did not come back.
Narrator 2	When Noah was 601 years old, on the first day of the first month, the water was gone. Noah removed the covering of the boat, looked round, and saw that the ground was getting dry. By the twenty-seventh day of the second month the earth was completely dry. God said to Noah:
God	Go out of the boat with your wife, your sons, and their wives. Take all the birds and animals out with you, so that they may reproduce and spread over all the earth.
Narrator 2	So Noah went out of the boat with his wife, his sons, and their wives. All the animals and birds went out of the boat in groups of their own kind.
Cast All	[This is] the word of the Lord. **Thanks be to God.**

Cast: **Narrator 1, Narrator 2, God.**

God's covenant with Noah
Genesis 8.20—9.17

Narrator	Noah built an altar to the Lord; he took one of each kind of ritually clean animal and bird, and burnt them whole as a sacrifice on the altar. The odour of the sacrifice pleased the Lord [and he said to himself]:
God (to himself)	Never again will I put the earth under a curse because of what man does; I know that from the time he is young his thoughts are evil. Never again will I destroy all living beings, as I have done this time. As long as the world exists, there will be a time for planting and a time for harvest. There will always be cold and heat, summer and winter, day and night.
Narrator	God blessed Noah and his sons:
God (to Noah)	Have many children, so that your descendants will live over all the earth. All the animals, birds, and fish will live in fear of you. They are all placed under your power. Now you can eat them, as well as green plants; I give them all to you for food. The one thing you must not eat is meat with blood still in it; I forbid this because the life is in the blood. If anyone takes human life, he will be punished. I will punish with death any animal that takes a human life. Man was made like God, so whoever murders a man will himself be killed by his fellow man.

→

9

You must have many children, so that your descendants will live all over the earth.

Narrator God said to Noah and his sons:

God I am now making my covenant with you and with your descendants, and with all living beings—all birds and all animals—everything that came out of the boat with you. With these words I make my covenant with you: I promise that never again will all living beings be destroyed by a flood; never again will a flood destroy the earth. As a sign of this everlasting covenant which I am making with you and with all living beings, I am putting my bow in the clouds. It will be the sign of my covenant with the world. Whenever I cover the sky with clouds and the rainbow appears, I will remember my promise to you and to all the animals that a flood will never again destroy all living beings. When the rainbow appears in the clouds, I will see it and remember the everlasting covenant between me and all living beings on earth. That is the sign of the promise which I am making to all living beings.

Cast [This is] the word of the Lord.
All **Thanks be to God.**

Cast: **Narrator, God.**

The Tower of Babylon
Genesis 11.1–9

Narrator At first, the people of the whole world had only one language and used the same words. As they wandered about in the East, they came to a plain in Babylonia and settled there. They said to one another:

Persons 1 and 2 Come on!

Person 1 Let's make bricks—

Person 2 And bake them hard.

Narrator They had bricks to build with and tar to hold them together. [They said:]

Person 1 Now let's build a city with a tower that reaches the sky, so that we can make a name for ourselves—

Person 2 And not be scattered all over the earth.

Narrator Then the Lord came down to see the city and the tower which those men had built, and he said:

The Lord (to himself) Now then, these are all one people and they speak one language; this is just the beginning of what they are going to do. Soon they will be able to do anything they want! Let us go down and mix up their language so that they will not understand one another.

Narrator	So the Lord scattered them all over the earth, and they stopped building the city. The city was called Babylon, because there the Lord mixed up the language of all the people, and from there he scattered them all over the earth.
Cast	[This is] the word of the Lord.
All	**Thanks be to God.**

Cast: **Narrator, Person 1, Person 2, The Lord.**

God's call to Abram, Abram in Egypt
Genesis 12.1–20

Narrator 1	The Lord said to Abram:
The Lord	Leave your country, your relatives, and your father's home, and go to a land that I am going to show you. I will give you many descendants, and they will become a great nation. I will bless you and make your name famous, so that you will be a blessing.
Narrator 2	I will bless those who bless you, But I will curse those who curse you. And through you I will bless all the nations.
Narrator 1	When Abram was seventy-five years old, he started out from Haran, as the Lord had told him to do; and Lot went with him. Abram took his wife Sarai, his nephew Lot, and all the wealth and all the slaves they had acquired in Haran, and they started out for the land of Canaan. (PAUSE)
Narrator 2	When they arrived in Canaan, Abram travelled through the land until he came to the sacred tree of Moreh, the holy place at Shechem—at that time the Canaanites were still living in the land. The Lord appeared to Abram [and said to him]:
The Lord	This is the country that I am going to give to your descendants.
Narrator 2	Then Abram built an altar there to the Lord, who had appeared to him. After that, he moved on south to the hill-country east of the city of Bethel and set up his camp between Bethel on the west and Ai on the east. There also he built an altar and worshipped the Lord. Then he moved on from place to place, going towards the southern part of Canaan.
Narrator 3	But there was a famine in Canaan, and it was so bad that Abram went farther south to Egypt, to live there for a while. When he was about to cross the border into Egypt, he said to his wife Sarai:
Abram	You are a beautiful woman. When the Egyptians see you, they will assume that you are my wife, and so they will kill me and let you live. Tell them that you are my sister; then because of you they will let me live and treat me well.
Narrator 3	When he crossed the border into Egypt, the Egyptians did see that his wife was beautiful. Some of the court officials saw her and told the king how beautiful she was; so she was taken to his palace.

→

Because of her the king treated Abram well and gave him flocks of sheep and goats, cattle, donkeys, slaves, and camels.

But because the king had taken Sarai, the Lord sent terrible diseases on him and on the people of his palace. Then the king sent for Abram [and asked him]:

King What have you done to me? Why didn't you tell me that she was your wife? Why did you say that she was your sister, and let me take her as my wife? Here is your wife; take her and get out!

Narrator 3 The king gave orders to his men, so they took Abram and put him out of the country, together with his wife and everything he owned.

Cast [This is] the word of the Lord.
All **Thanks be to God.**

Cast: **Narrator 1, The Lord, Narrator 2, Narrator 3, Abram, King.**

Abram and Lot separate
Genesis 13.1–18

Narrator 1 Abram went north out of Egypt to the southern part of Canaan with his wife and everything he owned, and Lot went with him. Abram was a very rich man, with sheep, goats, and cattle, as well as silver and gold. Then he left there and moved from place to place, going towards Bethel. He reached the place between Bethel and Ai where he had camped before and had built an altar. There he worshipped the Lord. (PAUSE)

Narrator 2 Lot also had sheep, goats, and cattle, as well as his own family and servants. And so there was not enough pasture land for the two of them to stay together, because they had too many animals. So quarrels broke out between the men who took care of Abram's animals and those who took care of Lot's animals.

Narrator 1 At that time the Canaanites and the Perizzites were still living in the land.

Then Abram said to Lot:

Abram We are relatives, and your men and my men shouldn't be quarrelling. So let's separate. Choose any part of the land you want. You go one way, and I'll go the other.

Narrator 1 Lot looked round and saw that the whole Jordan Valley, all the way to Zoar, had plenty of water, like the Garden of the Lord or like the land of Egypt. This was before the Lord had destroyed the cities of Sodom and Gomorrah. So Lot chose the whole Jordan Valley for himself and moved away towards the east. That is how the two men parted. Abram stayed in the land of Canaan.

Narrator 2 And Lot settled among the cities in the valley and camped near Sodom, whose people were wicked and sinned against the Lord.

Narrator 1 After Lot had left, the Lord said to Abram:

The Lord	From where you are, look carefully in all directions. I am going to give you and your descendants all the land that you see, and it will be yours for ever. I am going to give you so many descendants that no one will be able to count them all; it would be as easy to count all the specks of dust on earth! Now, go and look over the whole land, because I am going to give it all to you.
Narrator 2	So Abram moved his camp and settled near the sacred trees of Mamre at Hebron, and there he built an altar to the Lord.

Cast   [This is] the word of the Lord.
All   **Thanks be to God.**

Cast: **Narrator 1, Narrator 2, Abram, The Lord.**

Melchizedek blesses Abram
Genesis 14.17–24

Narrator	When Abram came back from his victory over Chedorlaomer and the other kings, the king of Sodom went out to meet him in the Valley of Shaveh—also called the King's Valley. And Melchizedek, who was king of Salem and also a priest of the Most High God, brought bread and wine to Abram and blessed him:
Melchizedek	May the Most High God, who made heaven and earth, bless Abram! May the Most High God, who gave you victory over your enemies, be praised!
Narrator	And Abram gave Melchizedek a tenth of all the loot he had recovered which belonged to the king of Sodom. (PAUSE) The king of Sodom said to Abram:
King (to Abram)	Keep the loot, but give me back all my people.
[Narrator	Abram answered:]
Abram (to King)	I solemnly swear before the Lord, the Most High God, Maker of heaven and earth, that I will not keep anything of yours, not even a thread or a sandal strap. Then you can never say, 'I am the one who made Abram rich.' I will take nothing for myself. I will accept only what my men have used. But let my allies, Aner, Eshcol, and Mamre, take their share.

Cast   [This is] the word of the Lord.
All   **Thanks be to God.**

Cast: **Narrator, Melchizedek, King, Abram.**

God's covenant with Abram
From Genesis 15.1–18

Narrator	Abram had a vision and heard the Lord say to him:
The Lord	Do not be afraid, Abram. I will shield you from danger and give you a great reward.

13

[Narrator	But Abram answered:]
Abram	Sovereign Lord, what good will your reward do me, since I have no children?
Narrator	The Lord took him outside and said:
The Lord	Look at the sky and try to count the stars; you will have as many descendants as that.
Narrator	Abram put his trust in the Lord, and because of this the Lord was pleased with him and accepted him. Then the Lord said to him:
The Lord	I am the Lord, who led you out of Ur in Babylonia, to give you this land as your own.
Abram	Sovereign Lord, how can I know that it will be mine?
The Lord	Bring me a cow, a goat, and a ram, each of them three years old, and a dove and a pigeon.
Narrator	Abram brought the animals to God, cut them in half, and placed the halves opposite each other in two rows. When the sun had set and it was dark, a smoking fire-pot and a flaming torch suddenly appeared and passed between the pieces of the animals. Then and there the Lord made a covenant with Abram:
The Lord	I promise to give you all this land from the border of Egypt to the River Euphrates.
Cast	[This is] the word of the Lord.
All	**Thanks be to God.**

Cast: **Narrator, The Lord, Abram.**

The three visitors
Genesis 18.1–15

Narrator	The Lord appeared to Abraham near the great trees of Mamre while he was sitting at the entrance to his tent in the heat of the day. Abraham looked up and saw three men standing nearby. When he saw them, he hurried from the entrance of his tent to meet them and bowed low to the ground:
Abraham	If I have found favour in your eyes, my lord, do not pass your servant by. Let a little water be brought, and then you may all wash your feet and rest under this tree. Let me get you something to eat, so you can be refreshed and then go on your way—now that you have come to your servant.
[Narrator	They answered:]
Man 1	Very well.
Man 2	Do as you say.
Narrator	So Abraham hurried into the tent to Sarah. [He said:]
Abraham	Quick, get three measures of fine flour and knead it and bake some bread.

Narrator	Then he ran to the herd and selected a choice, tender calf and gave it to a servant, who hurried to prepare it. He then brought some curds and milk and the calf that had been prepared, and set these before them. While they ate, he stood near them under a tree. [They asked him:]
Man 2	Where is your wife Sarah?
Abraham	There, in the tent.
[Narrator	Then the Lord said:]
The Lord	I will surely return to you about this time next year, and Sarah your wife will have a son.
Narrator	Now Sarah was listening at the entrance to the tent, which was behind him. Abraham and Sarah were already old and well advanced in years, and Sarah was past the age of childbearing. So Sarah laughed to herself:
Sarah (laughing)	After I am worn out and my master is old, will I now have this pleasure?
[Narrator	Then the Lord said to Abraham:]
The Lord	Why did Sarah laugh and say, 'Will I really have a child, now that I am old?' Is anything too hard for the Lord? I will return to you at the appointed time next year and Sarah will have a son.
[Narrator	Sarah was afraid, so she lied and said:]
Sarah	I did not laugh.
The Lord (slowly)	Yes . . . you *did* laugh.
Cast All	[This is] the word of the Lord. **Thanks be to God.**

Cast: **Narrator, Abraham, Man 1, Man 2, The Lord,** (Men 1 and 2 and the Lord can be the same), **Sarah.**

Abraham pleads for Sodom
Genesis 18.16–33 (NIV)

Narrator	When the three men whom Abraham saw got up to leave, they looked down towards Sodom, and Abraham walked along with them to see them on their way. And the Lord said to himself:
The Lord (thinking)	Shall I hide from Abraham what I am going to do? Abraham will surely become a great and powerful nation, and all nations on earth will be blessed through him. For I have chosen him, so that he will direct his children and his household after him to keep the way of the Lord by doing what is right and just, so that the Lord will bring about for Abraham what he has promised him.
[Narrator	Then the Lord said to Abraham:]
The Lord (to Abraham)	The outcry against Sodom and Gomorrah is so great and their sin so grievous that I will go down and see if what they have done is as bad as the outcry that has reached me. If not, I will know.

Narrator	The men turned away and went towards Sodom, but Abraham remained standing before the Lord. Then Abraham approached him and said:
Abraham	Will you sweep away the righteous with the wicked? What if there are fifty righteous people in the city? Will you really sweep it away and not spare the place for the sake of the fifty righteous people in it? Far be it from you to do such a thing—to kill the righteous with the wicked, treating the righteous and the wicked alike. Far be it from you! Will not the Judge of all the earth do right?
The Lord	If I find fifty righteous people in the city of Sodom, I will spare the whole place for their sake. (PAUSE)
Abraham	Now that I have been so bold as to speak to the Lord, though I am nothing but dust and ashes, what if the number of the righteous is five less than fifty? Will you destroy the whole city because of five people?
The Lord	If I find forty-five there I will not destroy it. (PAUSE)
Abraham	What if only forty are found there?
The Lord	For the sake of forty, I will not do it. (PAUSE)
Abraham	May the Lord not be angry, but let me speak. What if only thirty can be found there?
The Lord	I will not do it if I find thirty there. (PAUSE)
Abraham	Now that I have been so bold as to speak to the Lord, what if only twenty can be found there?
The Lord	For the sake of twenty, I will not destroy it. (PAUSE)
Abraham	May the Lord not be angry, but let me speak just once more. What if only ten can be found there?
The Lord	For the sake of ten, I will not destroy it.
Narrator	When the Lord had finished speaking with Abraham, he left, and Abraham returned home.
Cast	[This is] the word of the Lord.
All	**Thanks be to God.**

Cast: **Narrator, The Lord, Abraham.**

Abraham pleads for Sodom
Genesis 18.16–33 (GNB)

Narrator	When the men whom Abraham had seen left and went to a place where they could look down at Sodom, Abraham went with them to send them on their way. And the Lord said to himself:
The Lord (thinking)	I will not hide from Abraham what I am going to do. His descendants will become a great and mighty nation, and through

	him I will bless all the nations. I have chosen him in order that he may command his sons and his descendants to obey me and to do what is right and just. If they do, I will do everything for him that I have promised.
[Narrator	Then the Lord said to Abraham:]
The Lord (to Abraham)	There are terrible accusations against Sodom and Gomorrah, and their sin is very great. I must go down and see whether or not the accusations which I have heard are true.
Narrator	Then the two men left and went on towards Sodom, but the Lord remained with Abraham. Abraham approached the Lord and asked:
Abraham	Are you really going to destroy the innocent with the guilty? If there are fifty innocent people in the city, will you destroy the whole city? Won't you spare it in order to save fifty? Surely you won't kill the innocent with the guilty? That's impossible! You can't do that. If you did, the innocent would be punished along with the guilty. That is impossible. The judge of all the earth has to act justly.
The Lord	If I find fifty innocent people in Sodom, I will spare the whole city for their sake. (PAUSE)
Abraham	Please forgive my boldness in continuing to speak to you, Lord. I am only a man and have no right to say anything. But perhaps there will be only forty-five innocent people instead of fifty. Will you destroy the whole city because there are five too few?
The Lord	I will not destroy the city if I find forty-five innocent people. (PAUSE)
Abraham	Perhaps there will be only forty.
The Lord	I will not destroy it if there are only forty. (PAUSE)
Abraham	Please don't be angry, Lord, but I must speak again. What if there are only thirty?
The Lord	I will not do it if I find thirty. (PAUSE)
Abraham	Please forgive my boldness in continuing to speak to you, Lord. Suppose that only twenty are found?
The Lord	I will not destroy the city if I find twenty. (PAUSE)
Abraham	Please don't be angry, Lord, and I will speak just once more. What if only ten are found?
The Lord	I will not destroy it if there are only ten.
Narrator	After he had finished speaking with Abraham, the Lord went away, and Abraham returned home.
Cast	[This is] the word of the Lord.
All	**Thanks be to God.**

Cast: **Narrator, The Lord, Abraham.**

17

The sinfulness of Sodom
Genesis 19.1–11

Narrator	Two angels came to Sodom in the evening, Lot was sitting at the city gate. As soon as he saw them, he got up and went to meet them. He bowed down before them:
Lot	Sirs, I am here to serve you. Please come to my house. You can wash your feet and stay the night. In the morning you can get up early and go on your way.
[Narrator	But they answered:]
Angel	No, we will spend the night here in the city square.
Narrator	He kept on urging them, and finally they went with him to his house. Lot ordered his servants to bake some bread and prepare a fine meal for the guests. When it was ready, they ate it. (PAUSE)
	Before the guests went to bed, the men of Sodom surrounded the house. All the men of the city, both young and old, were there. They called out to Lot:
Man 1	Where are the men who came to stay with you tonight?
Man 2	Bring them out to us!
Narrator	The men of Sodom wanted to have sex with them.
	Lot went outside and closed the door behind him.
Lot	Friends, I beg you, don't do such a wicked thing! Look, I have two daughters who are still virgins. Let me bring them out to you, and you can do whatever you want with them. But don't do anything to these men; they are guests in my house, and I must protect them.
Man 1	Get out of our way, you foreigner!
Man 2	Who are you to tell us what to do?
Man 1	Out of our way, or we will treat you worse than them.
Narrator	They pushed Lot back and moved up to break down the door. But the two men inside reached out, pulled Lot back into the house, and shut the door. Then they struck all the men outside with blindness, so that they couldn't find the door.
Cast	[This is] the word of the Lord.
All	**Thanks be to God.**

Cast: **Narrator, Lot, Angel, Man 1, Man 2.**

Lot leaves Sodom, Sodom and Gomorrah are destroyed
Genesis 19.12–29

Narrator	The two angels who had come to Sodom said to Lot:
Angel 1	If you have anyone else here—sons, daughters, sons-in-law, or any other relatives living in the city—get them out of here, because we are going to destroy this place.
Angel 2	The Lord has heard the terrible accusations against these people and has sent us to destroy Sodom.
Narrator	Then Lot went to the men that his daughters were going to marry:
Lot	Hurry up and get out of here; the Lord is going to destroy this place.
Narrator	But they thought he was joking. (PAUSE)
	At dawn the angels tried to make Lot hurry:
Angels 1 and **2**	Quick!
Angel 1	Take your wife and your two daughters and get out, so that you will not lose your lives when the city is destroyed.
Narrator	Lot hesitated. The Lord, however, had pity on him; so the men took him, his wife, and his two daughters by the hand and led them out of the city. Then one of the angels said:
Angel 2	Run for your lives! Don't look back and don't stop in the valley. Run to the hills, so that you won't be killed.
[Narrator	But Lot answered:]
Lot	No, please don't make us do that, sir. You have done me a great favour and saved my life. But the hills are too far away; the disaster will overtake me, and I will die before I get there. Do you see that little town? It is near enough. Let me go over there—you can see it is just a small place—and I will be safe.
Angel 1	All right, I agree. I won't destroy that town. Hurry! Run! I can't do anything until you get there.
Narrator	Because Lot called it small, the town was named Zoar. (PAUSE)
	The sun was rising when Lot reached Zoar. Suddenly the Lord rained burning sulphur on the cities of Sodom and Gomorrah and destroyed them and the whole valley, along with all the people there and everything that grew on the land. But Lot's wife looked back and was turned into a pillar of salt. Early the next morning Abraham hurried to the place where he had stood in the presence of the Lord. He looked down at Sodom and Gomorrah and the whole valley and saw smoke rising from the land, like smoke from a huge furnace. But when God destroyed the cities of the valley where Lot was living, he kept Abraham in mind and allowed Lot to escape to safety.
Cast	[This is] the word of the Lord.
All	**Thanks be to God.**

Cast: **Narrator, Angel 1 Angel 2** (can be the same as Angel 1), **Lot.**

The origin of the Moabites and Ammonites
Genesis 19.30–38

Narrator	Because Lot was afraid to stay in Zoar, he and his two daughters moved up into the hills and lived in a cave. The elder daughter said to her sister:
Elder daughter	Our father is getting old, and there are no men in the whole world to marry us so that we can have children. Come on, let's make our father drunk, so that we can sleep with him and have children by him.
Narrator	That night they gave him wine to drink, and the elder daughter had intercourse with him. But he was so drunk that he didn't know it.
	The next day the elder daughter said to her sister:
Elder daughter	I slept with him last night; now let's make him drunk again tonight, and you sleep with him. Then each of us will have a child by our father.
Narrator	So that night they made him drunk, and the younger daughter had intercourse with him. Again he was so drunk that he didn't know it. In this way both of Lot's daughters became pregnant by their own father. The elder daughter had a son, whom she named Moab. He was the ancestor of the present-day Moabites. The younger daughter also had a son, whom she named Benammi. He was the ancestor of the present-day Ammonites.
Cast	[This is] the word of the Lord.
All	**Thanks be to God.**

Cast: **Narrator, Elder daughter.**

Abraham and Abimelech
Genesis 20.1–18

Narrator	Abraham moved from Mamre to the southern part of Canaan and lived between Kadesh and Shur. Later, while he was living in Gerar, he said that his wife Sarah was his sister. So King Abimelech of Gerar had Sarah brought to him. One night God appeared to him in a dream:
God	You are going to die, because you have taken this woman; she is already married.
Narrator	But Abimelech had not come near her:
Abimelech	Lord, I am innocent! Would you destroy me and my people? Abraham himself said that she was his sister, and she said the same thing. I did this with a clear conscience, and I have done no wrong.
[Narrator	God replied in the dream:]

God	Yes, I know that you did it with a clear conscience; so I kept you from sinning against me and did not let you touch her. But now, give the woman back to her husband. He is a prophet, and he will pray for you, so that you will not die. But if you do not give her back, I warn you that you are going to die, you and all your people.
Narrator	Early the next morning Abimelech called all his officials and told them what had happened, and they were terrified. Then Abimelech called Abraham:
Abimelech	What have you done to us? What wrong have I done to you to make you bring this disaster on me and my kingdom? No one should ever do what you have done to me. Why did you do it?
[Narrator	Abraham answered:]
Abraham	I thought that there would be no one here who has reverence for God and that they would kill me to get my wife. She really *is* my sister. She is the daughter of my father, but not of my mother, and I married her. So when God sent me from my father's house into foreign lands, I said to her, 'You can show how loyal you are to me by telling everyone that I am your brother.'
Narrator	Then Abimelech gave Sarah back to Abraham, and at the same time he gave him sheep, cattle, and slaves. [He said to Abraham:]
Abimelech	Here is my whole land; live anywhere you like.
Narrator	He said to Sarah:
Abimelech	I am giving your brother a thousand pieces of silver as proof to all who are with you that you are innocent; everyone will know that you have done no wrong.
Narrator	Because of what had happened to Sarah, Abraham's wife, the Lord had made it impossible for any woman in Abimelech's palace to have children. So Abraham prayed for Abimelech, and God healed him. He also healed his wife and his slave-girls, so that they could have children.
Cast	[This is] the word of the Lord.
All	**Thanks be to God.**

Cast: **Narrator, God, Abimelech, Abraham.**

The birth of Isaac
Genesis 21.1–8

Narrator	The Lord blessed Sarah, as he had promised, and she became pregnant and bore a son to Abraham when he was old. The boy was born at the time God had said he would be born. Abraham named him Isaac, and when Isaac was eight days old, Abraham circumcised him, as God had commanded. Abraham was a hundred years old when Isaac was born. Sarah said:
Sarah	God has brought me joy and laughter. Everyone who hears about it will laugh with me.

Narrator	Then she added:
Sarah	Who would have said to Abraham that Sarah would nurse children? Yet I have borne him a son in his old age.
Narrator	The child grew, and on the day that he was weaned, Abraham gave a great feast.
Cast	[This is] the word of the Lord.
All	**Thanks be to God.**

Cast: **Narrator, Sarah.**

Hagar and Ishmael are sent away
Genesis 21.9–21

Narrator	One day Ishmael, whom Hagar the Egyptian had borne to Abraham, was playing with Sarah's son Isaac. Sarah saw them and said to Abraham:
Sarah	Send this slave-girl and her son away. The son of this woman must not get any part of your wealth, which my son Isaac should inherit.
Narrator	This troubled Abraham very much, because Ishmael was also his son. But God said to Abraham:
God	Don't be worried about the boy and your slave Hagar. Do whatever Sarah tells you, because it is through Isaac that you will have the descendants I have promised. I will also give many children to the son of the slave-girl, so that they will become a nation. He too is your son.
Narrator	Early the next morning Abraham gave Hagar some food and a leather bag full of water. He put the child on her back and sent her away. She left and wandered about in the wilderness of Beersheba. When the water was all gone, she left the child under a bush and sat down about a hundred metres away. [She said to herself:]
Hagar	I can't bear to see my child die.
Narrator	While she was sitting there, the child began to cry. God heard the boy crying, and from heaven the angel of God spoke to Hagar:
Angel	What are you troubled about, Hagar? Don't be afraid. God has heard the boy crying. Get up, go and pick him up, and comfort him. I will make a great nation out of his descendants.
Narrator	Then God opened her eyes, and she saw a well. She went and filled the leather bag with water and gave some to the boy. God was with the boy as he grew up; he lived in the wilderness of Paran and became a skilful hunter. His mother found an Egyptian wife for him.
Cast	[This is] the word of the Lord.
All	**Thanks be to God.**

Cast: **Narrator, Sarah, God, Hagar, Angel.**

The agreement between Abraham and Abimelech
Genesis 21.22–34

Narrator	Abimelech went with Phicol, the commander of his army, and said to Abraham:
Abimelech	God is with you in everything you do. So make a vow here in the presence of God that you will not deceive me, my children, or my descendants. I have been loyal to you, so promise that you will also be loyal to me and to this country in which you are living.
[Narrator	Abraham said:]
Abraham	I promise.
Narrator	Abraham complained to Abimelech about a well which the servants of Abimelech had seized. Abimelech said:
Abimelech	I don't know who did this. You didn't tell me about it, and this is the first I have heard of it.
Narrator	Then Abraham gave some sheep and cattle to Abimelech, and the two of them made an agreement. Abraham separated seven lambs from his flock. [Abimelech asked him:]
Abimelech	Why did you do that?
Abraham	Accept these seven lambs. By doing this, you admit that I am the one who dug this well.
Narrator	And so the place was called Beersheba, because it was there that the two of them made a vow.
	After they had made this agreement at Beersheba, Abimelech and Phicol went back to Philistia. Then Abraham planted a tamarisk tree in Beersheba and worshipped the Lord, the Everlasting God. Abraham lived in Philistia for a long time.
Cast	[This is] the word of the Lord.
All	**Thanks be to God.**

Cast: **Narrator, Abimelech, Abraham.**

God commands Abraham to offer Isaac
Genesis 22.1–18

Narrator	God tested Abraham:
God	Abraham!
[Narrator	And Abraham answered:]
Abraham	Yes, here I am!
God	Take your son, your only son, Isaac, whom you love so much, and go to the land of Moriah. There on a mountain that I will show you, offer him as a sacrifice to me. (PAUSE)
Narrator	Early the next morning Abraham cut some wood for the sacrifice,

→

23

loaded his donkey, and took Isaac and two servants with him. They started out for the place that God had told him about. On the third day Abraham saw the place in the distance. Then he said to the servants:

Abraham   Stay here with the donkey. The boy and I will go over there and worship, and then we will come back to you.

Narrator   Abraham made Isaac carry the wood for the sacrifice, and he himself carried a knife and live coals for starting the fire. As they walked along together, Isaac said:

Isaac   Father!

Abraham   Yes, my son?

Isaac   I see that you have the coals and the wood, but where is the lamb for the sacrifice?

Abraham   God himself will provide one.

Narrator   And the two of them walked on together. (PAUSE)

When they came to the place which God had told him about, Abraham built an altar and arranged the wood on it. He tied up his son and placed him on the altar, on top of the wood. Then he picked up the knife to kill him. But the angel of the Lord called to him from heaven:

God   Abraham, Abraham!

Abraham   Yes, here I am.

God   Don't hurt the boy or do anything to him. Now I know that you honour and obey God, because you have not kept back your only son from me.

Narrator   Abraham looked round and saw a ram caught in a bush by its horns. He went and got it and offered it as a burnt-offering instead of his son. Abraham named that place:

Abraham   'The Lord Provides.'

Narrator   And even today people say:

Persons 1 and **2**   On the Lord's mountain he provides.

Narrator   The angel of the Lord called to Abraham from heaven a second time:

God   I make a vow by my own name—the Lord is speaking—that I will richly bless you. Because you did this and did not keep back your only son from me, I promise that I will give you as many descendants as there are stars in the sky or grains of sand along the seashore. Your descendants will conquer their enemies. All the nations will ask me to bless them as I have blessed your descendants—all because you obeyed my command.

Cast   [This is] the word of the Lord.
All   **Thanks be to God.**

Cast: **Narrator, God, Abraham, Isaac, Persons 1** and **2** (can be the same as Abraham and Isaac).

Sarah dies and Abraham buys a burial-ground
Genesis 23.1–20

Narrator	Sarah lived to be a hundred and twenty-seven years old. She died in Hebron in the land of Canaan, and Abraham mourned her death.
	He left the place where his wife's body was lying, went to the Hittites, and said:
Abraham	I am a foreigner living here among you; sell me some land, so that I can bury my wife.
[Narrator	They answered:]
Hittite 1	Listen to us, sir. We look upon you as a mighty leader.
Hittite 2	Bury your wife in the best grave that we have.
Hittite 1	Any of us would be glad to give you a grave, so that you can bury her.
Narrator	Then Abraham bowed before them.
Abraham	If you are willing to let me bury my wife here, please ask Ephron son of Zohar to sell me Machpelah Cave, which is near the edge of his field. Ask him to sell it to me for its full price, here in your presence, so that I can own it as a burial-ground.
Narrator	Ephron himself was sitting with the other Hittites at the meeting-place at the city gate. [He answered in the hearing of everyone there:]
Ephron	Listen, sir; I will give you the whole field and the cave that is in it. Here in the presence of my own people, I will give it to you, so that you can bury your wife.
Narrator	But Abraham bowed before the Hittites and spoke to Ephron, so that everyone could hear:
Abraham	May I ask you, please, to listen. I will buy the whole field. Accept my payment, and I will bury my wife there.
Ephron	Sir, land worth only four hundred pieces of silver—what is that between us? Bury your wife in it.
Narrator	Abraham agreed and weighed out the amount that Ephron had mentioned in the hearing of the people—four hundred pieces of silver, according to the standard weights used by the merchants.
	That is how the property which had belonged to Ephron at Machpelah, east of Mamre, became Abraham's. It included the field, the cave which was in it, and all the trees in the field up to the edge of the property. It was recognized as Abraham's property by all the Hittites who were there at the meeting.
	Then Abraham buried his wife Sarah in that cave in the land of Canaan. So the field which had belonged to the Hittites, and the cave in it, became the property of Abraham for a burial-ground.
Cast	[This is] the word of the Lord.
All	**Thanks be to God.**

Cast: **Narrator, Abraham, Hittite 1, Hittite 2, Ephron.**

A wife for Isaac
From Genesis 24.1–27 [28–53]

Narrator	Abraham was now very old, and the Lord had blessed him in everything he did. He said to his oldest servant, who was in charge of all that he had:
Abraham	I want you to make a vow in the name of the Lord, the God of heaven and earth, that you will not choose a wife for my son from the people here in Canaan. You must go back to the country where I was born and get a wife for my son Isaac from among my relatives.
[Narrator	But the servant asked:]
Servant	What if the girl will not leave home to come with me to this land? Shall I send your son back to the land you came from?
Abraham	Take care that you don't send my son back there! The Lord, the God of heaven, brought me from the home of my father and from the land of my relatives, and he solemnly promised me that he would give this land to my descendants. He will send his angel before you, so that you can get a wife there for my son. If the girl is not willing to come with you, you will be free from this promise. But you must not under any circumstances take my son back there.
Narrator	So the servant made a vow to do what Abraham had asked. (PAUSE) The servant, who was in charge of Abraham's property, took ten of his master's camels and went to the city where Nahor had lived in northern Mesopotamia. When he arrived, he made the camels kneel down at the well outside the city. It was late afternoon, the time when women came out to get water. He prayed:
Servant	Lord, God of my master Abraham, give me success today and keep your promise to my master. Here I am at the well where the young women of the city will be coming to get water. I will say to one of them, 'Please, lower your jar and let me have a drink.' If she says, 'Drink, and I will also bring water for your camels,' may she be the one that you have chosen for your servant Isaac. If this happens, I will know that you have kept your promise to my master.
Narrator	Before he had finished praying, Rebecca arrived with a water-jar on her shoulder. She was the daughter of Bethuel, who was the son of Abraham's brother Nahor and his wife Milcah. She was a very beautiful young girl and still a virgin. She went down to the well, filled her jar, and came back. The servant ran to meet her:
Servant	Please give me a drink of water from your jar.
Rebecca	Drink, sir.
Narrator	She quickly lowered her jar from her shoulder and held it while he drank. (PAUSE) [When he had finished, she said:]
Rebecca	I will also bring water for your camels and let them have all they want.

Narrator	She quickly emptied her jar into the animals' drinking-trough and ran to the well to get more water, until she had watered all his camels. The man kept watching her in silence, to see if the Lord had given him success. (PAUSE)
	When she had finished, the man took an expensive gold ring and put it in her nose and put two large gold bracelets on her arms:
Servant	Please tell me who your father is. Is there room in his house for my men and me to spend the night?
Rebecca	My father is Bethuel son of Nahor and Milcah. There is plenty of straw and fodder at our house, and there is a place for you to stay.
Narrator	Then the man knelt down and worshipped the Lord.
Servant	Praise the Lord, the God of my master Abraham, who has faithfully kept his promise to my master. The Lord has led me straight to my master's relatives.
[Narrator	The girl ran to her mother's house and told the whole story. Now Rebecca had a brother named Laban, and he ran outside to go to the well where Abraham's servant was. Laban had seen the nose-ring and the bracelets on his sister's arms and had heard her say what the man had told her. He went to Abraham's servant, who was standing by his camels at the well:
Laban	Come home with me. You are a man whom the Lord has blessed. Why are you standing out here? I have a room ready for you in my house, and there is a place for your camels.
Narrator	So the man went into the house, and Laban unloaded the camels and gave them straw and fodder. Then he brought water for Abraham's servant and his men to wash their feet. When food was brought, the man said:
Servant	I will not eat until I have said what I *have* to say.
Laban	Go on and speak.
Servant	I am the servant of Abraham. The Lord has greatly blessed my master and made him a rich man. My master made me promise with a vow to obey his command. He said, 'Do not choose a wife for my son from the girls in the land of Canaan. Instead, go to my father's people, to my relatives, and choose a wife for him.' And I asked my master, 'What if the girl will not come with me?' He answered, 'The Lord, whom I have always obeyed, will send his angel with you and give you success.' Now if you intend to fulfil your responsibility towards my master and treat him fairly, please tell me; if not, say so, and I will decide what to do.
Laban	Since this matter comes from the Lord, it is not for *us* to make a decision.
Bethuel	Here is Rebecca; take her and go. Let her become the wife of your master's son, as the Lord himself has said.

Narrator	When the servant of Abraham heard this, he bowed down and worshipped the Lord. Then he brought out clothing and silver and gold jewellery, and gave them to Rebecca. He also gave expensive gifts to her brother and to her mother.]

Cast	[This is] the word of the Lord.
All	**Thanks be to God.**

Cast: **Narrator, Abraham, Servant, Rebecca, [Laban, Bethuel** (can be the same as Laban)**].**

Rebecca and Isaac meet
Genesis 24.54–67

Narrator	Abraham's servant and the men with him ate and drank, and spent the night at Laban's house. When they got up in the morning, he said:
Servant	Let me go back to my master.
Narrator	But Rebecca's brother and her mother said:
Mother	Let the girl stay with us a week or ten days.
Brother	Then she may go.
Servant	Don't make us stay. The Lord has made my journey a success; let me go back to my master.
Brother	Let's call the girl and find out what she has to say.
Narrator	So they called Rebecca [and asked]:
Mother	Do you want to go with this man?
[Narrator	She answered:]
Rebecca	Yes.
Narrator	So they let Rebecca and her old family servant go with Abraham's servant and his men. And they gave Rebecca their blessing in these words:
Brother	May you, sister, become the mother of millions!
Mother	May your descendants conquer the cities of their enemies!
Narrator	Then Rebecca and her young women got ready and mounted the camels to go with Abraham's servant, and they all started out. (PAUSE) Isaac had come into the wilderness of 'The Well of the Living One Who Sees Me' and was staying in the southern part of Canaan. He went out in the early evening to take a walk in the fields and saw camels coming. When Rebecca saw Isaac, she got down from her camel and asked Abraham's servant:
Rebecca	Who is that man walking towards us in the field?
Servant	He is my master.
Narrator	So she took her scarf and covered her face. (PAUSE)

28

The servant told Isaac everything he had done. Then Isaac brought Rebecca into the tent that his mother Sarah had lived in, and she became his wife. Isaac loved Rebecca, and so he was comforted for the loss of his mother.

Cast	[This is] the word of the Lord.
All	**Thanks be to God.**

Cast: **Narrator, Servant, Mother, Brother, Rebecca.**

The story of Esau and Jacob
Genesis 25.19—34

Narrator   Abraham's son Isaac was forty years old when he married Rebecca. Because Rebecca had no children, Isaac prayed to the Lord for her. The Lord answered his prayer, and Rebecca became pregnant. She was going to have twins, and before they were born, they struggled against each other in her womb. She said:

Rebecca   Why should something like this happen to me?

Narrator   So she went to ask the Lord for an answer. The Lord said to her:

The Lord   Two nations are within you;
you will give birth to two rival peoples.
One will be stronger than the other;
the older will serve the younger.

Narrator   The time came for her to give birth, and she had twin sons. The first one was reddish, and his skin was like a hairy robe, so he was named Esau. The second one was born holding on tightly to the heel of Esau, so he was named Jacob. Isaac was sixty years old when they were born. (PAUSE)

The boys grew up, and Esau became a skilled hunter, a man who loved the outdoor life, but Jacob was a quiet man who stayed at home. Isaac preferred Esau, because he enjoyed eating the animals Esau killed, but Rebecca preferred Jacob. One day while Jacob was cooking some bean soup, Esau came in from hunting. He was hungry and said to Jacob:

Esau   I'm starving; give me some of that red stuff.

[Narrator   That is why he was called Edom. Jacob answered:]

Jacob   I will give it to you if you give me your rights as the first-born son.

Esau (hastily)   All right! I am about to die; what good will my rights do me then?

Jacob   First make a vow that you will give me your rights.

Narrator   Esau made the vow and gave his rights to Jacob. Then Jacob gave him some bread and some of the soup. He ate and drank and then got up and left. That was all Esau cared about his rights as the first-born son.

Cast	[This is] the word of the Lord.
All	**Thanks be to God.**

Cast: **Narrator, Rebecca, The Lord, Esau, Jacob.**

Isaac lives at Gerar
Genesis 26.1–25

Narrator There was another famine in the land besides the earlier one during the time of Abraham. Isaac went to Abimelech, king of the Philistines, at Gerar. The Lord had appeared to Isaac [and had said]:

The Lord Do not go to Egypt; stay in this land, where I tell you to stay. Live here, and I will be with you and bless you. I am going to give all this territory to you and to your descendants. I will keep the promise I made to your father Abraham. I will give you as many descendants as there are stars in the sky, and I will give them all this territory. All the nations will ask me to bless them as I have blessed your descendants. I will bless you, because Abraham obeyed me and kept all my laws and commands.

Narrator So Isaac lived at Gerar. When the men there asked about his wife, he said that she was his sister. He would not admit that she was his wife, because he was afraid that the men there would kill him to get Rebecca, who was very beautiful. When Isaac had been there for some time, King Abimelech looked down from his window and saw Isaac and Rebecca making love. Abimelech sent for Isaac and said:

Abimelech So she is your *wife*! Why did you say she was your *sister*?

[Narrator He answered:]

Isaac I thought I would be killed if I said she was my wife.

Abimelech What have you done to us? One of my men might easily have slept with your wife, and you would have been responsible for our guilt.

Narrator Abimelech warned all the people:

Abimelech Anyone who ill-treats this man or his wife will be put to death.

Narrator Isaac sowed seed in that land, and that year he harvested a hundred times as much as he had sown, because the Lord blessed him. He continued to prosper and became a very rich man. Because he had many herds of sheep and cattle and many servants, the Philistines were jealous of him. So they filled in all the wells which the servants of his father Abraham had dug while Abraham was alive. (PAUSE)

Then Abimelech said to Isaac:

Abimelech Leave our country. You have become more powerful than we are.

Narrator So Isaac left and set up his camp in the Valley of Gerar, where he stayed for some time. He dug once again the wells which had been dug during the time of Abraham and which the Philistines had stopped up after Abraham's death. Isaac gave the wells the same names that his father had given them. (PAUSE)

	Isaac's servants dug a well in the valley and found water. The shepherds of Gerar quarrelled with Isaac's shepherds:
Shepherd	This water belongs to us.
Narrator	So Isaac named the well:
[Isaac]	'Quarrel.'
Narrator	Isaac's servants dug another well, and there was a quarrel about that one also, so he named it:
[Isaac]	'Enmity.'
Narrator	He moved away from there and dug another well. There was no dispute about this one, so he named it:
[Isaac]	'Freedom.'
[Narrator	He said:]
Isaac	Now the Lord has given us freedom to live in the land, and we will be prosperous here.
Narrator	Isaac left and went to Beersheba. That night the Lord appeared to him:
The Lord	I am the God of your father Abraham. Do not be afraid; I am with you. I will bless you and give you many descendants because of my promise to my servant Abraham.
Narrator	Isaac built an altar there and worshipped the Lord. Then he set up his camp there, and his servants dug another well.
Cast	[This is] the word of the Lord.
All	**Thanks be to God.**

Cast: **Narrator, The Lord, Abimelech, Isaac, Shepherd.**

The agreement between Isaac and Abimelech
Genesis 26.26–33

Narrator	Abimelech came from Gerar with Ahuzzath his adviser and Phicol the commander of his army to see Isaac. So Isaac asked:
Isaac	Why have you now come to see me, when you were so unfriendly to me before and made me leave your country?
Abimelech	Now we know that the Lord is with you, and we think that there should be a solemn agreement between us.
Phicol	We want you to promise that you will not harm us, just as we did not harm you.
Adviser	We were kind to you and let you leave peacefully. Now it is clear that the Lord has blessed you.
Narrator	Isaac prepared a feast for them, and they ate and drank. Early next morning each man made his promise and sealed it with a vow. Isaac said good-bye to them, and they parted as friends.

$\rightarrow$

	On that day Isaac's servants came and told him about the well which they had dug:
Servant	We have found water.
Narrator	He named the well:
[Isaac]	'Vow.'
Narrator	That is how the city of Beersheba got its name.
Cast **All**	[This is] the word of the Lord. **Thanks be to God.**

Cast: **Narrator, Isaac, Abimelech, Phicol, Adviser, Servant.**

Isaac blesses Jacob
Genesis 27.1–41

Narrator	Isaac was now old and had become blind. He sent for his elder son Esau and said to him:
Isaac	My son!
Esau	Yes.
Isaac	You see that I am old and may die soon. Take your bow and arrows, go out into the country, and kill an animal for me. Cook me some of that tasty food that I like, and bring it to me. After I have eaten it, I will give you my final blessing before I die.
Narrator	While Isaac was talking to Esau, Rebecca was listening. So when Esau went out to hunt, she said to Jacob:
Rebecca	I have just heard your father say to Esau, 'Bring me an animal and cook it for me. After I have eaten it, I will give you my blessing in the presence of the Lord before I die.' Now, my son, listen to me and do what I say. Go to the flock and pick out two fat young goats, so that I can cook them and make some of that food your father likes so much. You can take it to him to eat, and he will give you his blessing before he dies.
[Narrator	But Jacob said to his mother:]
Jacob (to Rebecca)	You know that Esau is a hairy man, but I have smooth skin. Perhaps my father will touch me and find out that I am deceiving him; in this way I will bring a curse on myself instead of a blessing.
Rebecca	Let any curse against you fall on me, my son; just do as I say, and go and get the goats for me.
Narrator	So he went to get them and brought them to her, and she cooked the kind of food that his father liked. Then she took Esau's best clothes, which she kept in the house, and put them on Jacob. She put the skins of the goats on his arms and on the hairless part of his neck. She handed him the tasty food, together with the bread she had baked. (PAUSE) Then Jacob went to his father:

32

Jacob	Father!
Isaac	Yes. Which of my sons are you?
Jacob	I am your elder son Esau; I have done as you told me. Please sit up and eat some of the meat that I have brought you, so that you can give me your blessing.
Isaac	How did you find it so quickly, my son?
Jacob	The Lord your God helped me to find it.
Isaac	Please come closer so that I can touch you. Are you really Esau?
Narrator	Jacob moved closer to his father, who felt him:
Isaac (hesitating)	Your voice sounds like Jacob's voice, but your arms feel like Esau's arms.
Narrator	He did not recognize Jacob, because his arms were hairy like Esau's. He was about to give him his blessing, but asked again:
Isaac	Are you *really* Esau?
Jacob	I am.
Isaac	Bring me some of the meat. After I have eaten it, I will give you my blessing.
Narrator	Jacob brought it to him, and he also brought him some wine to drink. (PAUSE)
Isaac	Come closer and kiss me, my son.
Narrator	As he came up to kiss him, Isaac smelt his clothes—so he gave him his blessing:
Isaac	The pleasant smell of my son is like the smell of a field which the Lord has blessed. May God give you dew from heaven and make your fields fertile! May he give you plenty of corn and wine! May nations be your servants, and may peoples bow down before you. May you rule over all your relatives, and may your mother's descendants bow down before you. May those who curse you be cursed, and may those who bless you be blessed. (PAUSE)
Narrator	Isaac finished giving his blessing, and as soon as Jacob left, his brother Esau came in from hunting. He also cooked some tasty food and took it to his father.
Esau	Please, father, sit up and eat some of the meat that I have brought you, so that you can give me your blessing.
Isaac	Who are *you*?
Esau	Your elder son Esau.
Narrator	Isaac began to tremble and shake all over:
Isaac (aghast)	Who was it, then, who killed an animal and brought it to me? I ate it just before you came. I gave him my final blessing, and so it is his for ever.
Narrator	When Esau heard this, he cried out loudly and bitterly [and said]:

Esau	Give me your blessing also, father!
Isaac	Your brother came and deceived me. He has taken away your blessing.
Esau	This is the second time that he has cheated me. No wonder his name is Jacob. He took my rights as the first-born son, and now he has taken away my blessing. Haven't you saved a blessing for me?
Isaac	I have already made him master over you, and I have made all his relatives his slaves. I have given him corn and wine. Now there is nothing that I can do for you, my son!
Narrator	Esau continued to plead with his father:
Esau	Have you only one blessing, father? Bless me too, father!
Narrator	He began to cry. [Then Isaac said to him:]
Isaac	No dew from heaven for you, no fertile fields for you. You will live by your sword, but be your brother's slave. Yet when you rebel, you will break away from his control.
Narrator	Esau hated Jacob, because his father had given Jacob the blessing. [He thought:]
Esau (to himself)	The time to mourn my father's death is near; then I will kill Jacob.
Cast **All**	[This is] the word of the Lord. **Thanks be to God.**

Cast: **Narrator, Isaac, Esau, Rebecca, Jacob.**

Isaac sends Jacob to Laban
Genesis 27.46—28.9

Narrator	Rebecca said to Isaac:
Rebecca	I am sick and tired of Esau's foreign wives. If Jacob also marries one of these Hittite girls, I might as well die.
Narrator	Isaac called Jacob, greeted him, and said to him:
Isaac	Don't marry a Canaanite girl. Go instead to Mesopotamia, to the home of your grandfather Bethuel, and marry one of the girls there, one of your uncle Laban's daughters. May Almighty God bless your marriage and give you many children, so that you will become the father of many nations! May he bless you and your descendants as he blessed Abraham, and may you take possession of this land, in which you have lived and which God gave to Abraham!
Narrator	Isaac sent Jacob away to Mesopotamia, to Laban, who was the son of Bethuel the Aramean and the brother of Rebecca, the mother of Jacob and Esau.

Esau learnt that Isaac had blessed Jacob and sent him away to Mesopotamia to find a wife. He also learnt that when Isaac blessed him, he commanded him not to marry a Canaanite woman. He found out that Jacob had obeyed his father and mother and had gone to Mesopotamia. Esau then understood that his father Isaac did not approve of Canaanite women. So he went to Ishmael son of Abraham and married his daughter Mahalath, who was the sister of Nebaioth.

Cast	[This is] the word of the Lord.
All	**Thanks be to God.**

Cast: **Narrator, Rebecca, Isaac.**

Jacob's dream at Bethel
Genesis 28.10–22

Narrator	Jacob left Beersheba and started towards Haran. At sunset he came to a holy place and camped there. He lay down to sleep, resting his head on a stone. He dreamt that he saw a stairway reaching from earth to heaven, with angels going up and coming down on it. And there was the Lord standing beside him:
The Lord	I am the Lord, the God of Abraham and Isaac, I will give to you and to your descendants this land on which you are lying. They will be as numerous as the specks of dust on the earth. They will extend their territory in all directions, and through you and your descendants I will bless all the nations. Remember, I will be with you and protect you wherever you go, and I will bring you back to this land. I will not leave you until I have done all that I have promised you.
Narrator	Jacob woke up:
Jacob (startled)	The Lord is here! He is in this place, and I didn't know it!
Narrator	He was afraid.
Jacob (afraid)	What a terrifying place this is! It must be the house of God; it must be the gate that opens into heaven.
Narrator	Jacob got up early next morning, took the stone that was under his head, and set it up as a memorial. Then he poured olive-oil on it to dedicate it to God. He named the place Bethel. Then Jacob made a vow to the Lord:
Jacob	If you will be with me and protect me on the journey I am making and give me food and clothing, and if I return safely to my father's home, then you will be my God. This memorial stone which I have set up will be the place where you are worshipped, and I will give you a tenth of everything you give me.

Cast	[This is] the word of the Lord.
All	**Thanks be to God.**

Cast: **Narrator, The Lord, Jacob.**

Jacob arrives at Laban's home
Genesis 29.1–30

Narrator	Jacob continued on his journey and came to the land of the eastern peoples. There he saw a well in the field, with three flocks of sheep lying near it because the flocks were watered from that well. The stone over the mouth of the well was large. When all the flocks were gathered there, the shepherds would roll the stone away from the well's mouth and water the sheep. Then they would return the stone to its place over the mouth of the well. (PAUSE)
	Jacob asked the shepherds:
Jacob	My brothers, where are you from?
Shepherd 1	We're from Haran.
Jacob	Do you know Laban, Nahor's grandson?
Shepherds 1 & 2	Yes—
Shepherd 2	We know him.
Jacob	Is he well?
Shepherd 1	Yes, he is—
Shepherd 2	And here comes his daughter Rachel with the sheep.
Jacob	Look, the sun is still high; it is not time for the flocks to be gathered. Water the sheep and take them back to pasture.
Shepherd 2	We can't, until all the flocks are gathered and the stone has been rolled away from the mouth of the well.
Shepherd 1	Then we will water the sheep.
Narrator	While he was still talking with them, Rachel came with her father's sheep, for she was a shepherdess. When Jacob saw Rachel daughter of Laban, his mother's brother, and Laban's sheep, he went over and rolled the stone away from the mouth of the well and watered his uncle's sheep.
	Then Jacob kissed Rachel and began to weep aloud. He had told Rachel that he was a relative of her father and a son of Rebecca. So she ran and told her father. (PAUSE)
	As soon as Laban heard the news about Jacob, his sister's son, he hurried to meet him. He embraced him and kissed him and brought him to his home, and there Jacob told him all these things. Then Laban said to him:
Laban	You are my own flesh and blood. (PAUSE)
Narrator	After Jacob had stayed with him for a whole month, Laban said to him:
Laban	Just because you are a relative of mine, should you work for me for nothing? Tell me what your wages should be.

Narrator	Now Laban had two daughters; the name of the older was Leah, and the name of the younger was Rachel. Leah had weak eyes, but Rachel was lovely in form, and beautiful. Jacob was in love with Rachel [and said:]
Jacob	I'll work for you seven years in return for your younger daughter Rachel.
Laban	It's better that I give her to you than to some other man. Stay here with me.
Narrator	So Jacob served seven years to get Rachel, but they seemed like only a few days to him because of his love for her. (PAUSE)
	Then Jacob said to Laban:
Jacob	Give me my wife. My time is completed, and I want to lie with her.
Narrator	So Laban brought together all the people of the place and gave a feast. But when evening came, he took his daughter Leah and gave her to Jacob, and Jacob lay with her. And Laban gave his servant girl Zilpah to his daughter as her maidservant.
	When morning came, there was Leah! So Jacob said to Laban:
Jacob	What is this you have done to me? I served you for Rachel, didn't I? Why have you deceived me?
Laban	It is not our custom here to give the younger daughter in marriage before the older one. Finish this daughter's bridal week; then we will give you the younger one also . . . in return for another seven years of work.
Narrator	And Jacob did so. He finished out the week with Leah, and then Laban gave him his daughter Rachel to be his wife. Laban gave his servant girl Bilhah to his daughter Rachel as her maidservant. Jacob lay with Rachel also, and he loved Rachel more than Leah. And he worked for Laban another seven years.
Cast	[This is] the word of the Lord.
All	**Thanks be to God.**

Cast: **Narrator, Jacob, Shepherd 1, Shepherd 2** (can be the same as Shepherd 1), **Laban.**

The children born to Jacob
Genesis 29.31—30.24

Narrator	When the Lord saw that Leah was loved less than Rachel, he made it possible for her to have children, but Rachel remained childless. Leah became pregnant and gave birth to a son.
Leah	The Lord has seen my trouble, and now my husband will love me.
Narrator	So she named him Reuben. She became pregnant again and gave birth to another son.
Leah	The Lord has given me this son also, because he heard that I was not loved.

Narrator	So she named him Simeon. Once again she became pregnant and gave birth to another son.
Leah	Now my husband will be bound more tightly to me, because I have borne him three sons.
Narrator	So she named him Levi. Then she became pregnant again and gave birth to another son.
Leah	This time I will praise the Lord.
Narrator	So she named him Judah. Then she stopped having children. (PAUSE)
	But Rachel had not borne Jacob any children, and so she became jealous of her sister and said to Jacob:
Rachel	Give me children, or I will die.
Narrator	Jacob became angry with Rachel:
Jacob	I can't take the place of God. He is the one who keeps you from having children.
Rachel	Here is my slave-girl Bilhah; sleep with her, so that she can have a child for me. In this way I can become a mother through her.
Narrator	So she gave Bilhah to her husband, and he had intercourse with her. Bilhah became pregnant and bore Jacob a son. Rachel said:
Rachel	God has judged in my favour. He has heard my prayer and has given me a son.
Narrator	So she named him Dan. Bilhah became pregnant again and bore Jacob a second son. Rachel said:
Rachel	I have fought a hard fight with my sister, but I have won.
Narrator	So she named him Naphtali.
	When Leah realized that she had stopped having children, she gave *her* slave-girl Zilpah to Jacob as his wife. Then Zilpah bore Jacob a son. Leah said:
Leah	I have been lucky.
Narrator	So she named him Gad. Zilpah bore Jacob another son, and Leah said:
Leah	How happy I am! Now women will call me happy.
Narrator	So she named him Asher.
	During the wheat-harvest Reuben went into the fields and found mandrakes, which he brought to his mother Leah. Rachel said to Leah:
Rachel	Please give me some of your son's mandrakes.
Leah	Isn't it enough that you have taken away my husband? Now you are even trying to take away my son's mandrakes.
Rachel	If you will give me your son's mandrakes, you can sleep with Jacob tonight.

Narrator	When Jacob came in from the fields in the evening, Leah went out to meet him and said:
Leah	You are going to sleep with me tonight, because I have paid for you with my son's mandrakes.
Narrator	So he had intercourse with her that night.
	God answered Leah's prayer, and she became pregnant and bore Jacob a fifth son.
Leah	God has given me my reward, because I gave my slave to my husband.
Narrator	So she named her son Issachar. Leah became pregnant again and bore Jacob a sixth son.
Leah	God has given me a fine gift. Now my husband will accept me, because I have borne him six sons.
Narrator	So she named him Zebulun. Later she bore a daughter, whom she named Dinah.
	Then God remembered Rachel; he answered her prayer and made it possible for her to have children. She became pregnant and gave birth to a son:
Rachel	God has taken away my disgrace by giving me a son. May the Lord give me another son.
Narrator	So she named him Joseph.
Cast	[This is] the word of the Lord.
All	**Thanks be to God.**

Cast: **Narrator, Leah, Rachel, Jacob.**

Jacob's bargain with Laban
Genesis 30.25–43

Narrator 1	After the birth of Joseph, Jacob said to Laban:
Jacob	Let me go, so that I can return home. Give me my wives and children that I have earned by working for you, and I will leave. You know how well I have served you.
[Narrator 2	Laban said to him:]
Laban	Let me say this: I have learnt by divination that the Lord has blessed me because of you. Name your wages, and I will pay them.
Jacob	You know how I have worked for you and how your flocks have prospered under my care. The little you had before I came has grown enormously, and the Lord has blessed you wherever I went. Now it is time for me to look out for my own interests.
Laban	What shall I pay you?

Jacob	I don't want any wages. I will continue to take care of your flocks if you agree to this suggestion: Let me go through all your flocks today and take every black lamb and every spotted or speckled young goat. That is all the wages I want. In the future you can easily find out if I have been honest. When you come to check up on my wages, if I have any goat that isn't speckled or spotted or any sheep that isn't black, you will know that it has been stolen.
Laban	Agreed. We will do as you suggest.
Narrator 2	But that day Laban removed the male goats that had stripes or spots and all the females that were speckled and spotted or which had white on them; he also removed all the black sheep. He put his sons in charge of them, and then went away from Jacob with this flock as far as he could travel in three days. Jacob took care of the rest of Laban's flocks.
Narrator 1	Jacob got green branches of poplar, almond, and plane trees and stripped off some of the bark so that the branches had white stripes on them. He placed these branches in front of the flocks at their drinking-troughs. He put them there, because the animals mated when they came to drink. So when the goats bred in front of the branches, they produced young that were streaked, speckled, and spotted.
	Jacob kept the sheep separate from the goats and made them face in the direction of the streaked and black animals of Laban's flock.
Narrator 2	In this way he built up his own flock and kept it apart from Laban's.
Narrator 1	When the healthy animals were mating, Jacob put the branches in front of them at the drinking-troughs, so that they would breed among the branches. But he did not put the branches in front of the weak animals.
Narrator 2	Soon Laban had all the weak animals, and Jacob all the healthy ones.
Narrator 1	In this way Jacob became very wealthy. He had many flocks, slaves, camels, and donkeys.
Cast All	[This is] the word of the Lord. **Thanks be to God.**

Cast: **Narrator 1, Jacob, Narrator 2** (can be the same as Narrator 1), **Laban.**

Jacob flees from Laban
From Genesis 31.1–21

Narrator	Jacob heard that Laban's sons were saying:
Son 1	Jacob has taken everything that belonged to our father.
Son 2	All his wealth has come from what our father owned.
Narrator	He also saw that Laban was no longer as friendly as he had been earlier. Then the Lord said to him:

The Lord	Go back to the land of your fathers and to your relatives. I will be with you.
Narrator	So Jacob sent word to Rachel and Leah to meet him in the field where his flocks were [He said to them]:
Jacob	I have noticed that your father is not as friendly towards me as he used to be; but my father's God has been with me. You both know that I have worked for your father with all my strength. Yet he has cheated me and changed my wages ten times. But God did not let him harm me. Whenever Laban said, 'The speckled goats shall be your wages,' all the flocks produced speckled young. When he said, 'The striped goats shall be your wages,' all the flocks produced striped young. God has taken flocks away from your father and given them to me.
[Narrator	Rachel and Leah answered Jacob:]
Rachel	There is nothing left for us to inherit from our father.
Leah	He treats us like foreigners. He sold us, and now he has spent all the money he was paid for us.
Rachel	All this wealth which God has taken from our father belongs to us and to our children. Do whatever God has told you.
Narrator	So Jacob got ready to go back to his father in the land of Canaan. He put his children and his wives on the camels, and drove all his flocks ahead of him, with everything that he had acquired in Mesopotamia. Laban had gone to shear his sheep, and during his absence Rachel stole the household gods that belonged to her father. Jacob deceived Laban by not letting him know that he was leaving. He took everything he owned and left in a hurry. He crossed the River Euphrates and started for the hill-country of Gilead.
Cast	[This is] the word of the Lord.
All	**Thanks be to God.**

Cast: **Narrator, Son 1, Son 2, The Lord, Jacob, Rachel, Leah.**

Laban pursues Jacob
From Genesis 31.22–55

Narrator	Three days after Jacob had fled, Laban was told. He took his men with him and pursued Jacob for seven days until he caught up with him in the hill-country of Gilead. In a dream that night God came to Laban [and said to him]:
God	Be careful not to threaten Jacob in any way.
Narrator	Jacob had set up his camp on a mountain, and Laban set up his camp with his kinsmen in the hill-country of Gilead.
	[Laban said to Jacob:]

Laban (to Jacob)	Why did you deceive me and carry off my daughters like women captured in war? Why did you deceive me and slip away without telling me? If you had told me, I would have sent you on your way with rejoicing and singing to the music of tambourines and harps. You did not even let me kiss my grandchildren and my daughters good-bye. That was a foolish thing to do! I have the power to do you harm, but last night the God of your father warned me not to threaten you in any way. I know that you left because you were so anxious to get back home, but why did you steal my household gods?
[Narrator	Jacob answered:]
Jacob	I was afraid, because I thought that you might take your daughters away from me. But if you find that anyone here has your gods, he will be put to death. Here, with our men as witnesses, look for anything that belongs to you and take what is yours.
Narrator	Jacob did not know that Rachel had stolen Laban's gods. Laban went and searched Jacob's tent; then he went into Leah's tent, and the tent of the two slave-women, but he did not find his gods. Then he went into Rachel's tent. Rachel had taken the household gods and put them in a camel's saddlebag and was sitting on them. Laban searched through the whole tent, but did not find his household gods. Then Jacob lost his temper.
Jacob (angrily)	What crime have I committed? What law have I broken that gives you the right to hunt me down? Now that you have searched through all my belongings, what household article have you found that belongs to you? Put it out here where your men and mine can see it, and let them decide which one of us is right. I have been with you now for twenty years; your sheep and your goats have not failed to reproduce, and I have not eaten any rams from your flocks. Whenever a sheep was killed by wild animals, I always bore the loss myself. I didn't take it to you to show that it was not my fault. You demanded that I make good anything that was stolen during the day or during the night. Many times I suffered from the heat during the day and from the cold at night. I was not able to sleep. It was like that for the whole twenty years I was with you. For fourteen years I worked to win your two daughters—and six years for your flocks. And even then, you changed my wages ten times. If the God of my fathers, the God of Abraham and Isaac, had not been with me, you would have already sent me away empty-handed. But God has seen my trouble and the work I have done, and last night he gave his judgement.
Laban	These girls are my daughters; their children belong to me, and these flocks are mine. In fact, everything you see here belongs to me. But since I can do nothing to keep my daughters and their children, I am ready to make an agreement with you. Let us make a pile of stones to remind us of our agreement.

Narrator	So Jacob took a stone and set it up as a memorial. He told his men to gather some rocks and pile them up. Then they ate a meal beside the pile of rocks. Laban said to Jacob:
Laban	This pile of rocks will be a reminder for both of us.
[Narrator	That is why that place was named Galeed.]
Laban	May the Lord keep an eye on us while we are separated from each other.
[Narrator	So the place was also named Mizpah.]
Laban	If you ill-treat my daughters or if you marry other women, even though I don't know about it, remember that God is watching us. Here are the rocks that I have piled up between us, and here is the memorial stone. Both this pile and this memorial stone are reminders. I will never go beyond this pile to attack you, and you must never go beyond it or beyond this memorial stone to attack me. The God of Abraham and the God of Nahor will judge between us.
Narrator	Then, in the name of the God whom his father Isaac worshipped, Jacob solemnly vowed to keep this promise. He killed an animal, which he offered as a sacrifice on the mountain, and he invited his men to the meal. After they had eaten, they spent the night on the mountain. (PAUSE)
	Early the next morning Laban kissed his grandchildren and his daughters good-bye, and left to go back home.
Cast	[This is] the word of the Lord.
All	**Thanks be to God.**

Cast: **Narrator, God, Laban, Jacob.**

Jacob prepares to meet Esau
Genesis 32.[1–2] 3–21

[Narrator	As Jacob went on his way, some angels met him. When he saw them, he said:
Jacob	This is God's camp.
Narrator	So he called the place Mahanaim.]
Narrator	Jacob sent messengers ahead of him to his brother Esau in the country of Edom. He instructed them to say:
Jacob	I, Jacob, your obedient servant, report to my master Esau that I have been staying with Laban and that I have delayed my return until now. I own cattle, donkeys, sheep, goats, and slaves. I am sending you word, sir, in the hope of gaining your favour.
Narrator	When the messengers came back to Jacob, they said:
Messenger 1	We went to your brother Esau, and he is already on his way to meet you.

43

Messenger 2	He has four hundred men with him.
Narrator	Jacob was frightened and worried. He divided into two groups the people who were with him, and also his sheep, goats, cattle, and camels. [He thought:]
Jacob (thinking)	If Esau comes and attacks the first group, the other may be able to escape.
Narrator	Then Jacob prayed:
Jacob	God of my grandfather Abraham and God of my father Isaac, hear me! You told me, Lord, to go back to my land and to my relatives, and you would make everything go well for me. I am not worth all the kindness and faithfulness that you have shown me, your servant. I crossed the Jordan with nothing but a walking-stick, and now I have come back with these two groups. Save me, I pray, from my brother Esau. I am afraid—afraid that he is coming to attack us and destroy us all, even the women and children. Remember that you promised to make everything go well for me and to give me more descendants than anyone could count, as many as the grains of sand along the seashore.
Narrator	After spending the night there, Jacob chose from his livestock as a present for his brother Esau: two hundred female goats and twenty males, two hundred female sheep and twenty males, thirty milk camels with their young, forty cows and ten bulls, twenty female donkeys and ten males. He divided them into herds and put one of his servants in charge of each herd. He said to them:
Jacob	Go ahead of me, and leave a space between each herd and the one behind it.
Narrator	He ordered the first servant:
Jacob	When my brother Esau meets you and asks, 'Who is your master? Where are you going? Who owns these animals in front of you?' you must answer, 'They belong to your servant Jacob. He sends them as a present to his master Esau. Jacob himself is just behind us.'
Narrator	He gave the same order to the second, the third, and to all the others who were in charge of the herds:
Jacob	This is what you must say to Esau when you meet him. You must say, 'Yes, your servant Jacob is just behind us.'
[Narrator	Jacob was thinking:]
Jacob (thinking)	I will win him over with the gifts, and when I meet him, perhaps he will forgive me.
Narrator	He sent the gifts on ahead of him and spent that night in camp.
Cast	[This is] the word of the Lord.
All	**Thanks be to God.**

Cast: **Narrator, Jacob, Messenger 1, Messenger 2** (can be the same as Messenger 1).

Jacob wrestles at dawn
Genesis 32.22–30

Narrator	[That same night] Jacob got up, took his two wives, his two concubines, and his eleven children, and crossed the River Jabbok. After he had sent them across, he also sent across all that he owned, but he stayed behind, alone.
	Then a man came and wrestled with him until just before daybreak. When the man saw that he was not winning the struggle, he struck Jacob on the hip, and it was thrown out of joint. [The man said]:
Man	Let me go; daylight is coming.
Jacob	I won't, unless you bless me.
Man	What is your name?
Jacob	Jacob.
Man	Your name will no longer be Jacob. You have struggled with God and with men, and you have won; so your name will be Israel.
Jacob	Now tell me your name.
Man	Why do you want to know my name?
Narrator	Then he blessed Jacob. (PAUSE)
Jacob (amazed, to audience)	I have seen God face to face, and I am still alive!
Cast	[This is] the word of the Lord.
All	**Thanks be to God.**

Cast: **Narrator, Man, Jacob.**

God blesses Jacob at Bethel
Genesis 35.1–15

Narrator	God said to Jacob:
God	Go to Bethel at once, and live there. Build an altar there to me, the God who appeared to you when you were running away from your brother Esau.
Narrator	So Jacob said to his family and to all who were with him:
Jacob	Get rid of the foreign gods that you have; purify yourselves and put on clean clothes. We are going to leave here and go to Bethel, where I will build an altar to the God who helped me in the time of my trouble and who has been with me everywhere I have gone.
Narrator	So they gave Jacob all the foreign gods that they had and also the ear-rings that they were wearing. He buried them beneath the oak-tree near Shechem.

→

When Jacob and his sons started to leave, great fear fell on the people of the nearby towns, and they did not pursue them. Jacob came with all his people to Luz, which is now known as Bethel, in the land of Canaan. He built an altar there and named the place after the God of Bethel, because God had revealed himself to him there when he was running away from his brother. Rebecca's nurse Deborah died and was buried beneath the oak south of Bethel. So it was named 'Oak of Weeping'.

When Jacob returned from Mesopotamia, God appeared to him again and blessed him:

God   Your name is Jacob, but from now on it will be Israel.

[Narrator   So God named him Israel. And God said to him:]

God   I am Almighty God. Have many children. Nations will be descended from you, and you will be the ancestor of kings. I will give you the land which I gave to Abraham and to Isaac, and I will also give it to your descendants after you.

Narrator   Then God left him. There, where God had spoken to him, Jacob set up a memorial stone and consecrated it by pouring wine and olive oil on it. He named the place Bethel.

Cast   [This is] the word of the Lord.
All   **Thanks be to God.**

Cast: **Narrator, God, Jacob.**

The death of Rachel
Genesis 35.16–21

Narrator   Jacob and his family left Bethel and, when they were still some distance from Ephrath, the time came for Rachel to have her baby, and she was having difficult labour. When her labour pains were at their worst, the midwife said to her:

Midwife   Don't be afraid, Rachel; it's another boy.

Narrator   But she was dying, and as she breathed her last, she named her son Benoni, but his father named him Benjamin.

When Rachel died, she was buried beside the road to Ephrath, now known as Bethlehem. Jacob set up a memorial stone there, and it still marks Rachel's grave to this day. Jacob moved on and set up his camp on the other side of the tower of Eder.

Cast   [This is] the word of the Lord.
All   **Thanks be to God.**

Cast: **Narrator, Midwife.**

Joseph and his brothers
Genesis 37.1–36

Narrator   Jacob continued to live in the land of Canaan, where his father had lived, and this is the story of Jacob's family. Joseph, a young man of seventeen, took care of the sheep and goats with his brothers, the sons of Bilhah and Zilpah, his father's concubines. He brought bad reports to his father about what his brothers were doing.

Jacob loved Joseph more than all his other sons, because he had been born to him when he was old. He made a long robe with full sleeves for him. When his brothers saw that their father loved Joseph more than he loved them, they hated their brother so much that they would not speak to him in a friendly manner. (PAUSE)

One night Joseph had a dream, and when he told his brothers about it, they hated him even more:

Joseph   Listen to the dream I had. We were all in the field tying up sheaves of wheat, when my sheaf got up and stood up straight. Yours formed a circle round mine and bowed down to it.

Brother 1   Do you think you are going to be a king and rule over us?

Narrator   So they hated him even more because of his dreams and because of what he said about them. (PAUSE)

Then Joseph had another dream and told his brothers:

Joseph   I had another dream, in which I saw the sun, the moon, and eleven stars bowing down to me.

Narrator   He also told the dream to his father, and his father scolded him:

Jacob   What kind of a dream is that? Do you think that your mother, your brothers, and I are going to come and bow down to you?

Narrator   Joseph's brothers were jealous of him, but his father kept thinking about the whole matter. (PAUSE)

One day when Joseph's brothers had gone to Shechem to take care of their father's flock, Jacob said to Joseph:

Jacob   I want you to go to Shechem, where your brothers are taking care of the flock.

Joseph   I am ready.

Jacob   Go and see if your brothers are safe and if the flock is all right; then come back and tell me.

Narrator   So his father sent him on his way from the Valley of Hebron. (PAUSE)

Joseph arrived at Shechem and was wandering about in the country when a man saw him [and asked him]:

Man   What are you looking for?

Joseph	I am looking for my brothers, who are taking care of their flock. Can you tell me where they are?
Man	They have already left. I heard them say that they were going to Dothan.
Narrator	So Joseph went after his brothers and found them at Dothan. They saw him in the distance, and before he reached them, they plotted against him and decided to kill him.
Brother 1 (to brothers 2–4)	Here comes that dreamer.
Brother 2	Come on now, let's kill him and throw his body into one of the dry wells.
Brother 3	We can say that a wild animal killed him.
Brother 4	*Then* we will see what becomes of his dreams!
Narrator	Reuben heard them and tried to save Joseph:
Reuben	Let's not kill him. Just throw him into this well in the wilderness, but don't hurt him.
Narrator	He said this, planning to save him from them and send him back to his father. When Joseph came up to his brothers, they ripped off his long robe with full sleeves. Then they took him and threw him into the well, which was dry. (PAUSE)
	While they were eating, they suddenly saw a group of Ishmaelites travelling from Gilead to Egypt. Their camels were loaded with spices and resins. Judah said to his brothers:
Judah	What will we gain by killing our brother and covering up the murder? Let's sell him to these Ishmaelites. Then we won't have to hurt him; after all, he is our brother, our own flesh and blood.
Narrator	His brothers agreed, and when some Midianite traders came by, the brothers pulled Joseph out of the well and sold him for twenty pieces of silver to the Ishmaelites, who took him to Egypt. When Reuben came back to the well and found that Joseph was not there, he tore his clothes in sorrow. He returned to his brothers [and said]:
Reuben	The boy is not there! What am I going to do?
Narrator	Then they killed a goat and dipped Joseph's robe in its blood. They took the robe to their father [and said]:
Brother 3	We found this. Does it belong to your son?
Narrator	He recognized it.
Jacob	Yes, it is his! Some wild animal has killed him. My son Joseph has been torn to pieces!
Narrator	Jacob tore his clothes in sorrow and put on sackcloth. He mourned for his son a long time. All his sons and daughters came to comfort him, but he refused to be comforted:
Jacob	I will go down to the world of the dead still mourning for my son.

Narrator	So he continued to mourn for his son Joseph. (PAUSE)
	Meanwhile, in Egypt, the Midianites had sold Joseph to Potiphar, one of the king's officers, who was the captain of the palace guard.
Cast	[This is] the word of the Lord.
All	**Thanks be to God.**

Cast: **Narrator, Joseph, Brother 1, Jacob, Brother 2, Brother 3** (can be the same as Brother 2), **Brother 4, Man** (can be the same as Brother 3), **Reuben** (can be the same as Brother 1), **Judah** (can be the same as Brother 4).

Joseph, and Potiphar's wife
Genesis 39.1–23

Narrator	Now the Ishmaelites had taken Joseph to Egypt and sold him to Potiphar, one of the king's officers, who was the captain of the palace guard. The Lord was with Joseph and made him successful. He lived in the house of his Egyptian master, who saw that the Lord was with Joseph and had made him successful in everything he did. Potiphar was pleased with him and made him his personal servant; so he put him in charge of his house and everything he owned. From then on, because of Joseph the Lord blessed the household of the Egyptian and everything that he had in his house and in his fields. Potiphar handed over everything he had to the care of Joseph and did not concern himself with anything except the food he ate.
	Joseph was well-built and good-looking, and after a while his master's wife began to desire Joseph and asked him to go to bed with her. He refused:
Joseph	Look, my master does not have to concern himself with anything in the house, because I am here. He has put me in charge of everything he has. I have as much authority in this house as he has, and he has not kept back anything from me except you. How then could I do such an immoral thing and sin against God?
Narrator	Although she asked Joseph day after day, he would not go to bed with her.
	But one day when Joseph went into the house to do his work, none of the house servants was there. She caught him by his robe:
Wife	Come to bed with me.
Narrator	But he escaped and ran outside, leaving his robe in her hand. When she saw that he had left his robe and had run out of the house, she called to her house servants:
Wife	Look at this! This Hebrew that my husband brought to the house is insulting us. He came into my room and tried to rape me, but I screamed as loud as I could. When he heard me scream, he ran outside, leaving his robe beside me.
Narrator	She kept his robe with her until Joseph's master came home. Then she told him the same story:

Wife	That Hebrew slave that you brought here came into my room and insulted me. But when I screamed, he ran outside, leaving his robe beside me.
Narrator	Joseph's master was furious and had Joseph arrested and put in the prison where the king's prisoners were kept, and there he stayed. But the Lord was with Joseph and blessed him, so that the jailer was pleased with him. He put Joseph in charge of all the other prisoners and made him responsible for everything that was done in the prison. The jailer did not have to look after anything for which Joseph was responsible, because the Lord was with Joseph and made him succeed in everything he did.
Cast	[This is] the word of the Lord.
All	**Thanks be to God.**

Cast: **Narrator, Joseph, Wife.**

Joseph interprets the prisoners' dreams
Genesis 40.1–23

Narrator	[Some time later] the king of Egypt's wine steward and his chief baker offended the king. He was angry with these two officials and put them in prison in the house of the captain of the guard, in the same place where Joseph was being kept. They spent a long time in prison, and the captain assigned Joseph as their servant. (PAUSE)

One night there in prison the wine steward and the chief baker each had a dream, and the dreams had different meanings. (PAUSE)

When Joseph came to them in the morning, he saw that they were upset. [He asked them:] |
Joseph	Why do you look so worried today?
[**Narrator**	They answered:]
Baker	Each of us had a dream, and there is no one here to explain what the dreams mean.
Joseph	It is God who gives the ability to interpret dreams. Tell me your dreams.
Narrator	So the wine steward said:
Steward	In my dream there was a grapevine in front of me with three branches on it. As soon as the leaves came out, the blossoms appeared, and the grapes ripened. I was holding the king's cup; so I took the grapes and squeezed them into the cup and gave it to him.
Joseph	This is what it means: the three branches are three days. In three days the king will release you, pardon you, and restore you to your position. You will give him his cup as you did before when you were his wine steward. But please remember me when

everything is going well for you, and please be kind enough to mention me to the king and help me to get out of this prison. After all, I was kidnapped from the land of the Hebrews, and even here in Egypt I didn't do anything to deserve being put in prison.

Narrator When the chief baker saw that the interpretation of the wine steward's dream was favourable, he said to Joseph:

Baker I had a dream too; I was carrying three bread-baskets on my head. In the top basket there were all kinds of pastries for the king, and the birds were eating them.

Joseph This is what it means: the three baskets are three days. In three days the king will release you—and have your head cut off! Then he will hang your body on a pole, and the birds will eat your flesh.

Narrator On his birthday three days later the king gave a banquet for all his officials; he released his wine steward and his chief baker and brought them before his officials. He restored the wine steward to his former position, but he executed the chief baker. It all happened just as Joseph had said. (PAUSE)

But the wine steward never gave Joseph another thought—he forgot all about him.

Cast [This is] the word of the Lord.
All **Thanks be to God.**

Cast: **Narrator, Joseph, Baker, Steward.**

Joseph interprets the king's dreams
Genesis 41.1–44

Narrator [After two years had passed] the king of Egypt dreamt that he was standing by the River Nile, when seven cows, fat and sleek, came up out of the river and began to feed on the grass. Then seven other cows came up; they were thin and bony. They came and stood by the other cows on the river-bank, and the thin cows ate up the fat cows. Then the king woke up. He fell asleep again and had another dream. Seven ears of corn, full and ripe, were growing on one stalk. Then seven other ears of corn sprouted, thin and scorched by the desert wind, and the thin ears of corn swallowed the full ones. The king woke up and realized that he had been dreaming. In the morning he was worried, so he sent for all the magicians and wise men of Egypt. He told them his dreams, but no one could explain them to him.

Then the wine steward said to the king:

Steward I must confess today that I have done wrong. You were angry with the chief baker and me, and you put us in prison in the house of the captain of the guard. One night each of us had a dream, and the dreams had different meanings.

→

51

A young Hebrew was there with us, a slave of the captain of the guard. We told him our dreams, and he interpreted them for us. Things turned out just as he said: you restored me to my position, but you executed the baker.

Narrator   The king sent for Joseph, and he was immediately brought from the prison. After he had shaved and changed his clothes, he came into the king's presence. The king said to him:

King   I have had a dream, and no one can explain it. I have been told that you can interpret dreams.

[Narrator   Joseph answered:]

Joseph   *I* cannot, Your Majesty, but *God* will give a favourable interpretation.

King   I dreamt that I was standing on the bank of the Nile, when seven cows, fat and sleek, came up out of the river and began feeding on the grass. Then seven other cows came up which were thin and bony. They were the poorest cows I have ever seen anywhere in Egypt. The thin cows ate up the fat ones, but no one would have known it, because they looked just as bad as before. Then I woke up. I also dreamt that I saw seven ears of corn which were full and ripe, growing on one stalk. Then seven ears of corn sprouted, thin and scorched by the desert wind, and the thin ears of corn swallowed the full ones. I told the dreams to the magicians, but none of them could explain them to me.

Joseph   The two dreams mean the same thing; God has told you what he is going to do. The seven fat cows are seven years, and the seven full ears of corn are also seven years; they have the same meaning. The seven thin cows which came up later and the seven thin ears of corn scorched by the desert wind are seven years of famine.

It is just as I told you—God has shown you what he is going to do. There will be seven years of great plenty in all the land of Egypt. After that, there will be seven years of famine, and all the good years will be forgotten, because the famine will ruin the country. The time of plenty will be entirely forgotten, because the famine which follows will be so terrible. The repetition of your dream means that the matter is fixed by God and that he will make it happen in the near future.

Now you should choose some man with wisdom and insight and put him in charge of the country. You must also appoint other officials and take a fifth of the crops during the seven years of plenty. Order them to collect all the food during the good years that are coming, and give them authority to store up corn in the cities and guard it. The food will be a reserve supply for the country during the seven years of famine which are going to come on Egypt. In this way the people will not starve.

Narrator   The king and his officials approved this plan [and he said to them:]

King
(to officials)   We will never find a better man than Joseph, a man who has God's spirit in him.

[Narrator	The king said to Joseph:]
King (to Joseph)	God has shown you all this, so it is obvious that you have greater wisdom and insight than anyone else. I will put you in charge of my country, and all my people will obey your orders. Your authority will be second only to mine. I now appoint you governor over all Egypt.
Narrator	The king removed from his finger the ring engraved with the royal seal and put it on Joseph's finger. He put a fine linen robe on him, and placed a gold chain round his neck. He gave him the second royal chariot to ride in, and his guard of honour went ahead of him and cried out:
Guard	Make way! Make way!
Narrator	And so Joseph was appointed governor over all Egypt. [The king said to him]:
King	I am the king—and no one in all Egypt shall so much as lift a hand or a foot without your permission.
Cast	[This is] the word of the Lord.
All	**Thanks be to God.**

Cast: **Narrator, Steward, King, Joseph, Guard.**

Joseph's brothers go to Egypt to buy corn
Genesis 41.46—42.24

Narrator	Joseph was thirty years old when he began to serve the king of Egypt. He left the king's court and travelled all over the land. During the seven years of plenty the land produced abundant crops, all of which Joseph collected and stored in the cities. In each city he stored the food from the fields around it. There was so much corn that Joseph stopped measuring it—it was like the sand of the sea! (PAUSE)
	Before the years of famine came, Joseph had two sons by Asenath. He said:
Joseph	God has made me forget all my sufferings and all my father's family.
Narrator	So he named his first son:
Joseph	Manasseh.
Narrator	He also said:
Joseph	God has given me children in the land of my trouble.
Narrator	So he named his second son:
Joseph	Ephraim.
Narrator	The seven years of plenty that the land of Egypt had enjoyed came to an end, and the seven years of famine began, just as Joseph had said. There was famine in every other country, but

→

53

there was food throughout Egypt. When the Egyptians began to be hungry, they cried out to the king for food. So he ordered them to go to Joseph and do what he told them. The famine grew worse and spread over the whole country, so Joseph opened all the storehouses and sold corn to the Egyptians. People came to Egypt from all over the world to buy corn from Joseph, because the famine was severe everywhere.

When Jacob learnt that there was corn in Egypt, he said to his sons:

Jacob   Why don't you do something? I hear that there is corn in Egypt; go there and buy some to keep us from starving to death.

Narrator   So Joseph's ten half-brothers went to buy corn in Egypt, but Jacob did not send Joseph's full-brother Benjamin with them, because he was afraid that something might happen to him.

The sons of Jacob came with others to buy corn, because there was famine in the land of Canaan. Joseph, as governor of the land of Egypt, was selling corn to people from all over the world. So Joseph's brothers came and bowed down before him with their faces to the ground. When Joseph saw his brothers, he recognized them, but he acted as if he did not know them:

Joseph
(harshly)   Where do you come from?

Brother 1   We have come from Canaan—

Brother 2   To buy food.

Narrator   Although Joseph recognized his brothers they did not recognize him. He remembered the dreams he had dreamt about them and said:

Joseph   You are spies; you have come to find out where our country is weak.

Brothers
(protesting)   No, sir.

Brother 1   We have come as your slaves, to buy food.

Brother 2   We are all brothers.

Brother 3   We are not spies, sir, we are honest men.

Joseph   No! You have come to find out where our country is weak.

Brother 1   We *were* twelve brothers in all, sir—

Brother 2   Sons of the same man in the land of Canaan.

Brother 3   One brother is dead.

Brother 4   And the youngest is now with our father.

Joseph   It is just as I said. You are spies. This is how you will be tested: I swear by the name of the king that you will never leave unless your youngest brother comes here. One of you must go and get him. The rest of you will be kept under guard until the truth of what you say can be tested. Otherwise, as sure as the king lives, you are spies.

Narrator	Then he put them in prison for three days. On the third day Joseph said to them:
Joseph	I am a God-fearing man, and I will spare your lives on one condition. To prove that you are honest, one of you will stay in the prison where you have been kept; the rest of you may go and take back to your starving families the corn that you have bought. Then you must bring your youngest brother to me. This will prove that you have been telling the truth, and I will not put you to death.
Narrator	They agreed to this and said to one another:
Brother 1	Yes, now we are suffering the consequences of what we did to our brother.
Brother 2	We saw the great trouble he was in when he begged for help, but we would not listen.
Brother 3	That is why we are in this trouble now.
[Narrator	Reuben said:]
Reuben	I told you not to harm the boy, but you wouldn't listen. And now we are being paid back for his death.
Narrator	Joseph understood what they said, but they did not know it, because they had been speaking to him through an interpreter. Joseph left them and began to cry. When he was able to speak again, he came back, picked out Simeon, and had him tied up in front of them.
Cast	[This is] the word of the Lord.
All	**Thanks be to God.**

Cast: **Narrator, Joseph, Jacob, Brother 1, Brother 2, Brother 3, Brother 4, Reuben** (can be the same as Brother 4, OR Brothers 1–4 can be the same).

Joseph's brothers return to Canaan
Genesis 42.25–38

Narrator	Joseph gave orders to fill his brothers' packs with corn, to put each man's money back in his sack, and to give them food for the journey. This was done. The brothers loaded their donkeys with the corn they had bought, and then they left. At the place where they spent the night, one of them opened his sack to feed his donkey and found his money at the top of the sack.
	He called to his brothers:
Brother 1	My money has been returned to me. Here it is in my sack!
Narrator	Their hearts sank, and in fear they asked one another:
Reuben	What has God done to us?
Narrator	When they came to their father Jacob in Canaan, they told him all that had happened to them:

Brother 1	The governor of Egypt spoke harshly to us and accused us of spying against his country.
Brother 2	'We are not spies,' we answered, 'we are honest men. We were twelve brothers in all, sons of the same father. One brother is dead, and the youngest is still in Canaan with our father.'
Brother 3	The man answered, 'This is how I will find out if you are honest men: One of you will stay with me; the rest will take corn for your starving families and leave.'
Brother 2	'Bring your youngest brother to me. Then I will know that you are not spies, but honest men.'
Brother 4	'I will give your brother back to you, and you can stay here and trade.'
Narrator	Then when they emptied out their sacks, every one of them found his bag of money; and when they saw the money, they and their father Jacob were afraid. Their father said to them:
Jacob	Do you want to make me lose *all* my children? Joseph is gone; Simeon is gone; and now you want to take away Benjamin. *I* am the one who suffers!
Narrator	Reuben said to his father:
Reuben	If I do not bring Benjamin back to you, you can kill my two sons. Put him in my care, and I will bring him back.
Jacob	My son cannot go with you; his brother is dead, and he is the only one left. Something might happen to him on the way. I am an old man, and the sorrow you would cause me would kill me.
Cast	[This is] the word of the Lord.
All	**Thanks be to God.**

Cast: **Narrator, Brother 1, Brother 2, Brother 3, Brother 4, Reuben** (can be the same as Brother 4, OR Brothers 1–4 can be the same), **Jacob.**

Joseph's brothers return to Egypt with Benjamin
Genesis 43.1–34

Narrator	The famine in Canaan got worse, and when the family of Jacob had eaten all the corn which had been brought from Egypt, Jacob said to his sons:
Jacob	Go back and buy a little food for us.
Narrator	Judah said to him:
Judah	The man sternly warned us that we would not be admitted to his presence unless we had our brother with us. If you are willing to send our brother with us, we will go and buy food for you. If you are not willing, we will not go, because the man told us we would not be admitted to his presence unless our brother was with us.
Jacob	Why did you cause me so much trouble by telling the man that you had another brother?

Brother 1	The man kept asking about us and our family—
Brother 2	'Is your father still living?' 'Have you got another brother?'
Brother 3	We had to answer his questions.
Brother 4	How could we know that he would tell us to bring our brother with us?
Judah (to Jacob)	Send the boy with me, and we will leave at once. Then none of us will starve to death. I will pledge my own life, and you can hold me responsible for him. If I do not bring him back to you safe and sound, I will always bear the blame. If we had not waited so long, we could have been there and back twice by now.
Jacob	If that is how it has to be, then take the best products of the land in your packs as a present for the governor: a little resin, a little honey, spices, pistachio nuts, and almonds. Take with you also twice as much money, because you must take back the money that was returned in the top of your sacks. Maybe it was a mistake. Take your brother and return at once. May Almighty God cause the man to have pity on you, so that he will give Benjamin and your other brother back to you. As for me, if I must lose my children, I must lose them. (PAUSE)
Narrator	So the brothers took the gifts and twice as much money, and set out for Egypt with Benjamin. There they presented themselves to Joseph. When Joseph saw Benjamin with them, he said to the servant in charge of his house:
Joseph (to Servant)	Take these men to my house. They are going to eat with me at noon, so kill an animal and prepare it.
Narrator	The servant did as he was commanded and took the brothers to Joseph's house. As they were being brought to the house, they were afraid and thought:
Brother 1 (to other brothers)	We are being brought here because of the money that was returned in our sacks the first time.
Brother 2	They will suddenly attack us, take our donkeys, and make us his slaves.
Narrator	So at the door of the house, they said to the servant in charge:
Brother 1	If you please, sir, we came here once before to buy food.
Brother 2	When we set up camp on the way home, we opened our sacks, and each man found his money in the top of his sack—every bit of it.
Brother 3	We have brought it back to you.
Brother 4	We have also brought some more money with us to buy more food.
Brother 2	We do not know who put our money back in our sacks.
Narrator	The servant said:
Servant	Don't worry. Don't be afraid. Your God, the God of your father, must have put the money in your sacks for you. I received your payment.

Narrator	Then he brought Simeon to them. (PAUSE)
	The servant took the brothers into the house. He gave them water so that they could wash their feet, and he fed their donkeys. They got their gifts ready to present to Joseph when he arrived at noon, because they had been told that they were to eat with him. When Joseph got home, they took the gifts into the house to him and bowed down to the ground before him. He asked about their health and then said:
Joseph	You told me about your old father—how is he? Is he still alive and well?
Brother 1	Your humble servant, our father, is still alive and well.
Narrator	They knelt and bowed down before him. When Joseph saw his brother Benjamin, he said:
Joseph	So this is your youngest brother, the one you told me about. God bless you, my son.
Narrator	Then Joseph left suddenly, because his heart was full of tender feelings for his brother. He was about to break down, so he went to his room and cried. (PAUSE)
	After he had washed his face, he came out, and controlling himself, he ordered the meal to be served. Joseph was served at one table and his brothers at another. The Egyptians who were eating there were served separately, because they considered it beneath their dignity to eat with Hebrews. The brothers had been seated at table, facing Joseph, in the order of their age from the eldest to the youngest. When they saw how they had been seated, they looked at one another in amazement. Food was served to them from Joseph's table, and Benjamin was served five times as much as the rest of them. So they ate and drank with Joseph until they were drunk.
Cast	[This is] the word of the Lord.
All	**Thanks be to God.**

Cast: **Narrator, Jacob, Judah, Brother 1** (can be the same as Judah), **Brother 2, Brother 3, Brother 4** (Brothers 1–4 can be the same), **Joseph, Servant.**

The missing cup
Genesis 44.1—45.15, 25–26

Narrator	Joseph commanded the servant in charge of his house:
Joseph	Fill the men's sacks with as much food as they can carry, and put each man's money in the top of his sack. Put my silver cup in the top of the youngest brother's sack, together with the money for his corn.
Narrator	He did as he was told. Early in the morning the brothers were sent on their way with their donkeys. When they had gone only a short distance from the city, Joseph said to the servant in charge of his house:

Joseph	Hurry after those men. When you catch up with them, ask them, 'Why have you paid back evil for good? Why did you steal my master's silver cup? It is the one he drinks from, the one he uses for divination. You have committed a serious crime!'
Narrator	When the servant caught up with them, he repeated these words. They answered him:
Brother 1	What do you mean, sir, by talking like this?
Brother 2	We swear that we have done no such thing.
Brother 3	You know that we brought back to you from the land of Canaan the money we found in the top of our sacks. Why then should we steal silver or gold from your master's house?
Brother 4	Sir, if any one of us is found to have it, he will be put to death, and the rest of us will become your slaves.
Servant	I agree; but only the one who has taken the cup will become my slave, and the rest of you can go free.
Narrator	So they quickly lowered their sacks to the ground, and each man opened his sack. Joseph's servant searched carefully, beginning with the eldest and ending with the youngest, and the cup was found in Benjamin's sack. The brothers tore their clothes in sorrow, loaded their donkeys, and returned to the city. (PAUSE)
	When Judah and his brothers came to Joseph's house, he was still there. They bowed down before him, and Joseph said:
Joseph	What have you done? Didn't you know that a man in my position could find you out by practising divination?
Narrator	Judah answered:
Judah (to Joseph)	What can we say to you, sir? How can we argue? How can we clear ourselves? God has uncovered our guilt. All of us are now your slaves and not just the one with whom the cup was found.
Joseph	Oh, no! I would never do that! Only the one who had the cup will be my slave. The rest of you may go back safe and sound to your father.
Narrator	Judah went up to Joseph and said:
Judah	Please, sir, allow me to speak with you freely. [Don't be angry with me; you are like the king himself. Sir, you asked us, 'Have you got a father or another brother?' We answered, 'We have a father who is old and a younger brother, born to him in his old age. The boy's brother is dead, and he is the only one of his mother's children still alive; his father loves him very much.' Sir, you told us to bring him here, so that you could see him, and we answered that the boy could not leave his father; if he did, his father would die. Then you said, 'You will not be admitted to my presence again unless your youngest brother comes with you.'
	When we went back to our father, we told him what you had said. Then he told us to return and buy a little food. We answered, 'We cannot go; we will not be admittted to the man's presence unless

59

→

our youngest brother is with us. We can go only if our youngest brother goes also.' Our father said to us, 'You know that my wife Rachel bore me only two sons. One of them has already left me. He must have been torn to pieces by wild animals, because I have not seen him since he left. If you take this one from me now and something happens to him, the sorrow you would cause me would kill me, old as I am.'

And now, sir,] if I go back to my father without the boy, as soon as he sees that the boy is not with me, he will die. His life is wrapped up with the life of the boy, and he is so old that the sorrow we would cause him would kill him. What is more, I pledged my life to my father for the boy. I told him that if I did not bring the boy back to him, I would bear the blame all my life. And now, sir, I will stay here as your slave in place of the boy; let him go back with his brothers. How can I go back to my father if the boy is not with me? I cannot bear to see this disaster come upon my father.

Narrator Joseph was no longer able to control his feelings in front of his servants, so he ordered them all to leave the room. No one else was with him when Joseph told his brothers who he was. He cried with such loud sobs that the Egyptians heard it, and the news was taken to the king's palace. Joseph said to his brothers:

Joseph I am Joseph. Is my father still alive?

Narrator But when his brothers heard this, they were so terrified that they could not answer. [Then Joseph said to them:]

Joseph Please come closer. (PAUSE)

Narrator They did [and he said:]

Joseph I am your brother Joseph, whom you sold into Egypt. Now do not be upset or blame yourselves because you sold me here. It was really God who sent me ahead of you to save people's lives. This is only the second year of famine in the land; there will be five more years in which there will be neither ploughing nor reaping. God sent me ahead of you to rescue you in this amazing way and to make sure that you and your descendants survive. So it was not really you who sent me here, but God. He has made me the king's highest official. I am in charge of his whole country; I am the ruler of all Egypt.

Now hurry back to my father and tell him that this is what his son Joseph says: 'God has made me ruler of all Egypt; come to me without delay. You can live in the region of Goshen, where you can be near me—you, your children, your grandchildren, your sheep, your goats, your cattle, and everything else that you have. If you are in Goshen, I can take care of you. There will still be five years of famine; and I do not want you, your family, and your livestock to starve.'

Now all of you, and you too, Benjamin, can see that I am really Joseph. Tell my father how powerful I am here in Egypt and tell him about everything that you have seen. Then hurry and bring him here.

Narrator	He threw his arms round his brother Benjamin and began to cry; Benjamin also cried as he hugged him. Then, still weeping, he embraced each of his brothers and kissed them. After that, his brothers began to talk with him. (PAUSE)
	They left Egypt and went back home to their father Jacob in Canaan. They told him:
Brother 1	Joseph is still alive!
Brother 2	He is the ruler of all Egypt!
Cast	[This is] the word of the Lord.
All	**Thanks be to God.**

Cast: **Narrator, Joseph, Brother 1, Brother 2, Brother 3, Brother 4** (Brothers 1–4 can be the same), **Servant, Judah,** (can be the same as Brother 4).

Jacob and his family go to Egypt
Genesis 46.1–7, 28–30

Narrator	Jacob packed up all he had and went to Beersheba, where he offered sacrifices to the God of his father Isaac. God spoke to him in a vision at night and called:
God	Jacob, Jacob!
Narrator	He answered:
Jacob	Yes, here I am.
God	I am God, the God of your father. Do not be afraid to go to Egypt; I will make your descendants a great nation there. I will go with you to Egypt, and I will bring your descendants back to this land. Joseph will be with you when you die.
Narrator	Jacob set out from Beersheba. His sons put him, their small children, and their wives in the wagons which the king of Egypt had sent. They took their livestock and the possessions they had acquired in Canaan and went to Egypt. Jacob took all his descendants with him: his sons, his grandsons, his daughters, and his granddaughters. (PAUSE)
	Jacob sent Judah ahead to ask Joseph to meet them in Goshen. When they arrived, Joseph got into his chariot and went to Goshen to meet his father.
	When they met, Joseph threw his arms round his father's neck and cried for a long time. Jacob said to Joseph:
Jacob	I am ready to die, now that I have seen you and know that you are still alive.
Cast	[This is] the word of the Lord.
All	**Thanks be to God.**

Cast: **Narrator, God, Jacob.**

Jacob and his family in Egypt
Genesis 46.31—47.12

Narrator   Joseph said to his brothers and the rest of his father's family:

Joseph   I must go and tell the king that my brothers and all my father's family, who were living in Canaan, have come to me. I will tell him that you are shepherds and take care of livestock and that you have brought your flocks and herds and everything else that belongs to you. When the king calls for you and asks what your occupation is, be sure to tell him that you have taken care of livestock all your lives, just as your ancestors did. In this way he will let you live in the region of Goshen.

Narrator   Joseph said this because Egyptians will have nothing to do with shepherds.

So Joseph took five of his brothers and went to the king [He said:]

Joseph
(to King)   My father and my brothers have come from Canaan with their flocks, their herds, and all that they own. They are now in the region of Goshen.

Narrator   He then presented his brothers to the king. [The king asked them:]

King   What is your occupation?

Brother 1   We are shepherds, sir, just as our ancestors were.

Brother 2   We have come to live in this country, because in the land of Canaan the famine is so severe that there is no pasture for our flocks.

Brother 3   Please give us permission to live in the region of Goshen.

[Narrator   The king said to Joseph:]

King   Now that your father and your brothers have arrived, the land of Egypt is theirs. Let them settle in the region of Goshen, the best part of the land. And if there are any capable men among them, put them in charge of my own livestock.

Narrator   Then Joseph brought his father Jacob and presented him to the king. Jacob gave the king his blessing, [and the king asked him:]

King   How old are you?

Jacob   My life of wandering has lasted a hundred and thirty years. Those years have been few and difficult, unlike the long years of my ancestors in their wanderings.

Narrator   Jacob gave the king a farewell blessing and left. Then Joseph settled his father and his brothers in Egypt, giving them property in the best of the land near the city of Rameses, as the king had commanded. Joseph provided food for his father, his brothers, and all the rest of his father's family, including the very youngest.

Cast   [This is] the word of the Lord.
All   **Thanks be to God.**

Cast: **Narrator, Joseph, King, Brother 1, Brother 2, Brother 3** (can be the same as Brother 1, OR Brothers 1–3 can be the same), **Jacob.**

The famine
Genesis 47.13–26

Narrator	The famine was so severe that there was no food anywhere, and the people of Egypt and Canaan became weak with hunger. As they bought corn, Joseph collected all the money and took it to the palace. When all the money in Egypt and Canaan was spent, the Egyptians came to Joseph:
Egyptian 1	Give us food!
Egyptian 2	Don't let us die.
Egyptian 3	Do something!
Egyptian 1	Our money is all gone.
[Narrator	Joseph answered:]
Joseph	Bring your livestock; I will give you food in exchange for it if your money is all gone.
Narrator	So they brought their livestock to Joseph, and he gave them food in exchange for their horses, sheep, goats, cattle, and donkeys. That year he supplied them with food in exchange for all their livestock.
	They came to him the following year [and said]:
Egyptian 1	We will not hide the fact from you, sir, that our money is all gone and our livestock belongs to you.
Egyptian 2	There is nothing left to give you except our bodies and our lands.
Egyptian 3	Don't let us die. Do something!
Egyptian 1	Don't let our fields be deserted.
Egyptian 2	Buy us and our land in exchange for food.
Egyptian 3	We will be the king's slaves, and he will own our land.
Egyptian 1	Give us corn to keep us alive and seed to sow in our fields.
Narrator	Joseph bought all the land in Egypt for the king. Every Egyptian was forced to sell his land, because the famine was so severe; and all the land became the king's property. Joseph made slaves of the people from one end of Egypt to the other. The only land he did not buy was the land that belonged to the priests. They did not have to sell their lands, because the king gave them an allowance to live on. Joseph said to the people:
Joseph	You see, I have now bought you and your lands for the king. Here is seed for you to sow in your fields. At the time of harvest you must give one-fifth to the king. You can use the rest for seed and for food for yourselves and your families.
Egyptian 1	You have saved our lives.
Egyptian 2	You have been good to us, sir.
Egyptian 3	We will be the king's slaves.

Narrator	So Joseph made it a law for the land of Egypt that one-fifth of the harvest should belong to the king. This law still remains in force today. Only the lands of the priests did not become the king's property.
Cast	[This is] the word of the Lord.
All	**Thanks be to God.**

Cast: **Narrator, Egyptian 1, Egyptian 2, Egyptian 3, Joseph.**

Jacob's last request and blessing
Genesis 47.27—48.16 [17–22]

Narrator	The Israelites lived in Egypt in the region of Goshen, where they became rich and had many children. Jacob lived in Egypt for seventeen years, until he was a hundred and forty-seven years old. When the time drew near for him to die, he called for his son Joseph and said to him:
Jacob	Place your hand between my thighs and make a solemn vow that you will not bury me in Egypt. I want to be buried where my fathers are; carry me out of Egypt and bury me where they are buried.
[Narrator	Joseph answered:]
Joseph	I will do as you say.
[Narrator	Jacob said:]
Jacob	Make a vow that you will.
Narrator	Joseph made the vow, and Jacob gave thanks there on his bed. (PAUSE)
	Some time later Joseph was told that his father was ill. So he took his two sons, Manasseh and Ephraim, and went to see Jacob. When Jacob was told that his son Joseph had come to see him, he gathered his strength, sat up in bed and spoke to Joseph:
Jacob	Almighty God appeared to me at Luz in the land of Canaan and blessed me. He said to me, 'I will give you many children, so that your descendants will become many nations; I will give this land to your descendants as their possession for ever.'
Narrator	Jacob continued:
Jacob	Joseph, your two sons, who were born to you in Egypt before I came here, belong to me; Ephraim and Manasseh are just as much my sons as Reuben and Simeon. If you have any more sons, they will not be considered mine; the inheritance they get will come through Ephraim and Manasseh. I am doing this because of your mother Rachel. To my great sorrow she died in the land of Canaan, not far from Ephrath, as I was returning from Mesopotamia. I buried her there beside the road to Ephrath.
Narrator	Ephrath is now known as Bethlehem. When Jacob saw Joseph's sons, he asked:

Jacob	Who are these boys?
[Narrator	Joseph answered:]
Joseph	These are my sons, whom God has given me here in Egypt.
Jacob	Bring them to me so that I may bless them.
Narrator	Jacob's eyesight was failing because of his age, and he could not see very well. Joseph brought the boys to him, and he hugged them and kissed them.
Jacob (to Joseph)	I never expected to see you again, and now God has even let me see your children.
Narrator	Then Joseph took them from Jacob's lap and bowed down before him with his face to the ground.
	Joseph put Ephraim at Jacob's left and Manasseh at his right. But Jacob crossed his hands, and put his right hand on the head of Ephraim, even though he was the younger, and his left hand on the head of Manasseh, who was the elder. (PAUSE)
	Then he blessed Joseph:
Jacob	May the God whom my fathers Abraham and Isaac served bless these boys! May God, who has led me to this very day, bless them! May the angel, who has rescued me from all harm, bless them! May my name and the name of my fathers Abraham and Isaac live on through these boys! May they have many children, many descendants!
[Narrator	Joseph was upset when he saw that his father had put his right hand on Ephraim's head; so he took his father's hand to move it from Ephraim's head to the head of Manasseh:
Joseph	Not that way, father. This is the elder boy; put your right hand on his head.
Narrator	His father refused, saying:
Jacob	I know, my son, I know. Manasseh's descendants will also become a great people. But his younger brother will be greater than he, and his descendants will become great nations.
Narrator	So he blessed them that day, saying:
Jacob	The Israelites will use your names when they pronounce blessings. They will say, 'May God make you like Ephraim and Manasseh.'
Narrator	In this way Jacob put Ephraim before Manasseh. (PAUSE)
Jacob	As you see, I am about to die, but God will be with you and will take you back to the land of your ancestors. It is to you and not to your brothers that I am giving Shechem, that fertile region which I took from the Amorites with my sword and my bow.]
Cast	[This is] the word of the Lord.
All	**Thanks be to God.**

Cast: **Narrator, Jacob, Joseph.**

The death and burial of Jacob
Genesis 49.29—50.14

Narrator   Jacob commanded his sons:

Jacob   Now that I am going to join my people in death, bury me with my fathers in the cave that is in the field of Ephron the Hittite, at Machpelah, east of Mamre, in the land of Canaan. Abraham bought this cave and field from Ephron for a burial-ground. That is where they buried Abraham and his wife Sarah; that is where they buried Isaac and his wife Rebecca; and that is where I buried Leah. The field and the cave in it were bought from the Hittites. Bury me there.

Narrator   When Jacob had finished giving instructions to his sons, he lay down again and died.

Joseph threw himself on his father, crying and kissing his face. Then Joseph gave orders to embalm his father's body.

It took forty days, the normal time for embalming. The Egyptians mourned for him seventy days.

When the time of mourning was over, Joseph spoke to the king's officials:

Joseph   Please take this message to the king: 'When my father was about to die, he made me promise him that I would bury him in the tomb which he had prepared in the land of Canaan. So please let me go and bury my father, and then I will come back.'

Narrator   The king answered:

King   Go and bury your father, as you promised you would.

Narrator   So Joseph went to bury his father. All the king's officials, the senior men of his court, and all the leading men of Egypt went with Joseph. His family, his brothers, and the rest of his father's family all went with him. Only their small children and their sheep, goats, and cattle stayed in the region of Goshen. Men in chariots and men on horseback also went with him; it was a huge group.

When they came to the threshing-place at Atad east of the Jordan, they mourned loudly for a long time, and Joseph performed mourning ceremonies for seven days. When the citizens of Canaan saw those people mourning at Atad, they said:

Canaanite   What a solemn ceremony of mourning the Egyptians are holding!

Narrator   So Jacob's sons did as he had commanded them; they carried his body to Canaan and buried it in the cave at Machpelah, east of Mamre, in the field which Abraham had bought from Ephron the Hittite for a burial-ground. After Joseph had buried his father, he returned to Egypt with his brothers and all who had gone with him for the funeral.

Cast   [This is] the word of the Lord.
All   **Thanks be to God.**

Cast: **Narrator, Jacob, Joseph, King, Canaanite.**

Joseph's promise, and his death
Genesis 50.15–21 [22–26]

Narrator	After the death of their father, Joseph's brothers said:
Brother 1	What if Joseph still hates us?
Brother 2	And plans to pay us back for all the harm we did to him?
Narrator	So they sent a message to Joseph:
Brother 2	Before our father died, he told us to ask you, 'Please forgive the crime your brothers committed when they wronged you.'
Brother 1	Now please forgive us the wrong that we, the servants of your father's God, have done.
Narrator	Joseph cried when he received this message. Then his brothers themselves came and bowed down before him. [They said:]
Brother 1	Here we are before you—
Brother 2	As your slaves.
[Narrator	But Joseph said to them:]
Joseph	Don't be afraid; I can't put myself in the place of God. You plotted evil against me, but God turned it into good, in order to preserve the lives of many people who are alive today because of what happened. You have nothing to fear. I will take care of you and your children.
Narrator	So he reassured them with kind words that touched their hearts. (PAUSE) [Joseph continued to live in Egypt with his father's family; he was a hundred and ten years old when he died. He lived to see Ephraim's children and grandchildren. He also lived to receive the children of Machir son of Manasseh into the family. He said to his brothers:
Joseph	I am about to die, but God will certainly take care of you and lead you out of this land to the land he solemnly promised to Abraham, Isaac, and Jacob.
Narrator	Then Joseph asked his people to make a vow:
Joseph	Promise me, that when God leads you to that land, you will take my body with you.
Narrator	So Joseph died in Egypt at the age of a hundred and ten.]
Cast **All**	[This is] the word of the Lord. **Thanks be to God.**

Cast: **Narrator, Brother 1, Brother 2** (can be the same as Brother 1), **Joseph.**

EXODUS

The Israelites are treated cruelly in Egypt
Exodus 1.1–22

Narrator   The sons of Jacob who went to Egypt with him, each with his family, were Reuben, Simeon, Levi, Judah, Issachar, Zebulun, Benjamin, Dan, Naphtali, Gad, and Asher. The total number of these people directly descended from Jacob was seventy. His son Joseph was already in Egypt. In the course of time Joseph, his brothers, and all the rest of that generation died, but their descendants, the Israelites, had many children and became so numerous and strong that Egypt was filled with them. (PAUSE)

Then, a new king, who knew nothing about Joseph, came to power in Egypt. [He said to his people:]

King   These Israelites are so numerous and strong that they are a threat to us. In case of war they might join our enemies in order to fight against us, and might escape from the country. We must find some way to keep them from becoming even more numerous.

Narrator   So the Egyptians put slave-drivers over them to crush their spirits with hard labour. The Israelites built the cities of Pithom and Rameses to serve as supply centres for the king. But the more the Egyptians oppressed the Israelites, the more they increased in number and the further they spread through the land. The Egyptians came to fear the Israelites and made their lives miserable by forcing them into cruel slavery. They made them work on their building projects and in their fields, and they had no mercy on them.

Then the king of Egypt spoke to Shiphrah and Puah, the two midwives who helped the Hebrew women:

King
(brutally)   When you help the Hebrew women give birth, kill the baby if it is a boy; but if it is a girl, let it live.

Narrator   But the midwives feared God and so did not obey the king; instead, they let the boys live. So the king sent for the midwives [and asked them]:

King   Why are you doing this? Why are you letting the boys live?

Midwife 1   The Hebrew women are not like Egyptian women.

Midwife 2   They give birth easily, and their babies are born before either of us gets there. (PAUSE)

Narrator   Because the midwives feared God, he was good to them and gave them families of their own. And the Israelites continued to increase and become strong. Finally the king issued a command to all his people:

King	Take every new-born Hebrew boy and throw him into the Nile, but let all the girls live.
Cast	[This is] the word of the Lord.
All	**Thanks be to God.**

Cast: **Narrator, King, Midwife 1, Midwife 2.**

The birth of Moses
Exodus 2.1–10

Narrator 1	During the time when the king of Egypt had commanded that every new-born Hebrew boy was to be thrown into the Nile, a man from the tribe of Levi married a woman of his own tribe, and she bore him a son. When she saw what a fine baby he was, she hid him for three months. But when she could not hide him any longer, she took a basket made of reeds and covered it with tar to make it watertight. She put the baby in it and then placed it in the tall grass at the edge of the river. The baby's sister stood some distance away to see what would happen to him.
Narrator 2	The king's daughter came down to the river to bathe, while her servants walked along the bank. Suddenly she noticed the basket in the tall grass and sent a slave-girl to get it. The princess opened it and saw a baby boy. He was crying, and she felt sorry for him:
Princess	This is one of the Hebrew babies.
Narrator 1	Then his sister asked her:
Sister	Shall I go and call a Hebrew woman to act as a nurse?
Princess	Please do.
Narrator 2	So the girl went and brought the baby's *own mother*. (PAUSE)
	The princess told the woman:
Princess	Take this baby and nurse him for me, and I will pay you.
Narrator 1	So she took the baby and nursed him. (PAUSE)
Narrator 2	Later, when the child was old enough, she took him to the king's daughter, who adopted him as her own son. She said to herself:
Princess	I pulled him out of the water, and so I name him Moses.
Cast	[This is] the word of the Lord.
All	**Thanks be to God.**

Cast: **Narrator 1, Narrator 2, Princess, Sister.**

Moses escapes to Midian
Exodus 2.11–25

Narrator	When Moses had grown up, he went out to visit his people, the Hebrews, and he saw how they were forced to do hard labour. He even saw an Egyptian kill a Hebrew, one of Moses' own people. Moses looked all round, and when he saw that no one was watching, he killed the Egyptian and hid his body in the sand. The next day he went back and saw two Hebrew men fighting. He said to the one who was in the wrong:
Moses	Why are you beating up a fellow-Hebrew?
[Narrator	The man answered:]
Hebrew	Who made you our ruler and judge? Are you going to kill me just as you killed that Egyptian?
Narrator	Then Moses was afraid and said to himself:
Moses	People have found out what I have done.
Narrator	When the king heard about what had happened, he tried to have Moses killed, but Moses fled and went to live in the land of Midian. (PAUSE)
	One day, when Moses was sitting by a well, seven daughters of Jethro, the priest of Midian, came to draw water and fill the troughs for their father's sheep and goats. But some shepherds drove Jethro's daughters away. Then Moses went to their rescue and watered their animals for them.
	When they returned to their father, he asked:
Jethro	Why have you come back so early today?
Daughter	An Egyptian rescued us from the shepherds, and he even drew water for us and watered our animals.
Jethro	Where is he? Why did you leave the man out there? Go and invite him to eat with us.
Narrator	So Moses agreed to live there, and Jethro gave him his daughter Zipporah in marriage, who bore him a son. Moses said to himself:
Moses	I am a foreigner in this land, and so I name him Gershom. (PAUSE)
Narrator	Years later the king of Egypt died, but the Israelites were still groaning under their slavery and cried out for help. Their cry went up to God, who heard their groaning and remembered his covenant with Abraham, Isaac, and Jacob. He saw the slavery of the Israelites and was concerned for them.
Cast	[This is] the word of the Lord.
All	**Thanks be to God.**

Cast: **Narrator, Moses, Hebrew, Jethro, Daughter.**

Moses at the burning bush
From Exodus 3.1–15 (NIV)

Narrator	Moses was tending the flock of Jethro his father-in-law, the priest of Midian, and he led the flock to the far side of the desert and came to Horeb, the mountain of God. There the angel of the Lord appeared to him in flames of fire from within a bush. Moses saw that though the bush was on fire it did not burn up. So Moses thought:
Moses	I will go over and see this strange sight—why the bush does not burn up.
Narrator	When the Lord saw that he had gone over to look, God called to him from within the bush:
God	Moses! Moses!
[Narrator	And Moses said:]
Moses	Here I am!
God	Do not come any closer. Take off your sandals, for the place where you are standing is holy ground. (PAUSE) I am the God of your father, the God of Abraham, the God of Isaac and the God of Jacob.
Narrator	At this, Moses hid his face, because he was afraid to look at God.
God	I have indeed seen the misery of my people in Egypt. I have heard them crying out because of their slave-drivers, and I am concerned about their suffering. So I have come down to rescue them from the hand of the Egyptians and to bring them up out of that land into a good and spacious land, a land flowing with milk and honey. So now, go. I am sending you to Pharaoh to bring my people the Israelites out of Egypt.
[Narrator	But Moses said to God:]
Moses	Who am I, that I should go to Pharaoh and bring the Israelites out of Egypt?
God	I will be with you. And this will be the sign to you that it is I who have sent you: When you have brought the people out of Egypt, you will worship God on this mountain.
Moses	Suppose I go to the Israelites and say to them, 'The God of your fathers has sent me to you,' and they ask me, 'What is his name?' Then what shall I tell them?
[Narrator	God said to Moses:]
God (slowly)	I AM WHO I AM. This is what you are to say to the Israelites: 'I AM has sent me to you.'
[Narrator	Then the Lord said to Moses:]

God	Say to the Israelites, 'The Lord, the God of your fathers—the God of Abraham, the God of Isaac and the God of Jacob—has sent me to you.'
Cast	[This is] the word of the Lord.
All	**Thanks be to God.**

Cast: **Narrator, Moses, God.** (See also GNB extended version below.)

God calls Moses
From Exodus 3.1–15, 4.1–17 (GNB)

Narrator	One day while Moses was taking care of the sheep and goats of his father-in-law Jethro, the priest of Midian, he led the flock across the desert and came to Sinai, the holy mountain. There the angel of the Lord appeared to him as a flame coming from the middle of a bush. Moses saw that the bush was on fire but that it was not burning up [He thought]:
Moses	This is strange. Why isn't the bush burning up? I will go closer and see.
Narrator	When the Lord saw that Moses was coming closer, he called to him from the middle of the bush:
God	Moses! Moses!
Moses	Yes, here I am.
God	Do not come any closer. Take off your sandals, because you are standing on holy ground. I am the God of your ancestors, the God of Abraham, Isaac, and Jacob. (PAUSE)
Narrator	Moses covered his face, because he was afraid to look at God.
God	I have seen how cruelly my people are being treated in Egypt. Now I am sending you to the king of Egypt so that you can lead my people out of his country.
Moses	I am nobody. How can I go to the king and bring the Israelites out of Egypt?
God	I will be with you, and when you bring the people out of Egypt, you will worship me on this mountain. That will be the proof that I have sent you.
Moses	When I go to the Israelites and say to them, 'The God of your ancestors sent me to you,' they will ask me, 'What is his name?' So what can I tell them?
God (slowly)	I AM WHO I AM. This is what you must say to them: 'The one who is called I AM has sent me to you.'
	Tell the Israelites that I, the Lord, the God of their ancestors, the God of Abraham, Isaac, and Jacob, have sent you to them. This is my name for ever; this is what all future generations are to call me.

Moses	But suppose the Israelites do not believe me and will not listen to what I say. What shall I do if they say that you did not appear to me?
God	What are you holding?
Moses	A stick.
God	Throw it on the ground.
Narrator	When Moses threw it down, it turned into a snake, and he ran away from it.
God	Bend down and pick it up by the tail.
Narrator	So Moses bent down and caught it, and it became a stick again.
God	Do this to prove to the Israelites that the Lord, the God of their ancestors, the God of Abraham, Isaac, and Jacob, has appeared to you. (PAUSE)
	Put your hand inside your robe.
Narrator	Moses obeyed; and when he took his hand out, it was diseased, covered with white spots, like snow.
God	Put your hand inside your robe again.
Narrator	He did so, and when he took it out this time, it was healthy, just like the rest of his body.
God	If they will not believe you or be convinced by the first miracle, then this one will convince them. If in spite of these two miracles they still will not believe you, and if they refuse to listen to what you say, take some water from the Nile and pour it on the ground. The water will turn into blood.
Moses	No, Lord, don't send me. I have never been a good speaker, and I haven't become one since you began to speak to me. I am a poor speaker, slow and hesitant.
God	Who gives man his mouth? Who makes him deaf and dumb? Who gives him sight or makes him blind? It is I, the Lord. Now, go! I will help you to speak, and I will tell you what to say.
Moses	No, Lord, please send someone else.
God (angrily)	What about your brother Aaron, the Levite? I know that he can speak well. In fact, he is now coming to meet you and will be glad to see you. You can speak to him and tell him what to say. I will help both of you to speak, and I will tell you both what to do. He will be your spokesman and speak to the people for you. Then you will be like God, telling him what to say. Take this stick with you; for with it you will perform miracles.
Cast	[This is] the word of the Lord.
All	**Thanks be to God.**

Cast: **Narrator, Moses, God.** (See also NIV shorter version above.)

Moses returns to Egypt
Exodus 4.18–23, 29–31

Narrator   Moses went back to Jethro, his father-in-law [and said to him]:

Moses   Please let me go back to my relatives in Egypt to see if they are still alive.

Narrator   Jethro agreed and said good-bye to him. (PAUSE) While Moses was still in Midian, the Lord spoke to him:

The Lord   Go back to Egypt, for all those who wanted to kill you are dead.

Narrator   So Moses took his wife and his sons, put them on a donkey, and set out with them for Egypt, carrying the stick that God had told him to take. (PAUSE) Again the Lord spoke to Moses:

The Lord   Now that you are going back to Egypt, be sure to perform before the king all the miracles which I have given you the power to do. But I will make the king stubborn, and he will not let the people go. Then you must tell him that I, the Lord, say, 'Israel is my first-born son. I told you to let my son go, so that he might worship me, but you refused. Now I am going to kill your first-born son.'

Narrator   So Moses and Aaron went to Egypt and gathered all the Israelite leaders together. Aaron told them everything that the Lord had said to Moses, and then Moses performed all the miracles in front of the people. They believed, and when they heard that the Lord had come to them and had seen how they were being treated cruelly, they bowed down and worshipped.

Cast   [This is] the word of the Lord.
All   **Thanks be to God.**

Cast: **Narrator, Moses, The Lord.**

Moses and Aaron before the king of Egypt
Exodus 5.1–21

Narrator   Moses and Aaron went to the king of Egypt [and said]:

Moses   The Lord, the God of Israel, says, 'Let my people go—'

Aaron   So that they can hold a festival in the desert to honour me.'

Narrator   The king demanded:

King   Who is the *Lord*? Why should I listen to him and let Israel go? I do not know the Lord; and I will not let Israel go.

Aaron   The God of the Hebrews has revealed himself to us.

Moses   Allow us to travel three days into the desert to offer sacrifices to the Lord our God.

Aaron   If we don't do so, he will kill us with disease or by war.

[Narrator	The king said to Moses and Aaron:]
King (angrily)	What do you mean by making the people neglect their work? Get those slaves back to work! You people have become more numerous than the Egyptians. And now you want to stop working!
Narrator	That same day the king commanded the Egyptian slave drivers and the Israelite foremen:
King (meanly)	Stop giving the people straw for making bricks. Make them go and find it for themselves. But still require them to make the same number of bricks as before, not one brick less. They don't have enough work to do, and that is why they keep asking me to let them go and offer sacrifices to their God! Make these men work harder and keep them busy, so that they won't have time to listen to a pack of lies.
Narrator	The slave-drivers and the Israelite foremen went out and said to the Israelites:
Slave-driver 1	The king has said that he will not supply you with any more straw.
Slave-driver 2	He says that you must go and get it for yourselves wherever you can find it, but you must still make the same number of bricks.
Narrator	So the people went all over Egypt looking for straw. The slave-drivers kept trying to force them to make the same number of bricks every day as they had made when they were given straw. The Egyptian slave-drivers beat the Israelite foremen, whom they had put in charge of the work. They demanded:
Slave-driver 1	Why aren't you people making the same number of bricks that you made before?
Narrator	Then the foremen went to the king and complained:
Foreman 1	Why do you do this to us, Your Majesty?
Foreman 2	We are given no straw, but we are still ordered to make bricks!
Foreman 1	And now we are being beaten—
Foreman 2	It is *your* people that are at fault.
Narrator	The king answered:
King	You are lazy and don't want to work, and that is why you ask me to let you go and offer sacrifices to the Lord. Now get back to work! You will not be given any straw, but you must still make the same number of bricks.
Narrator	The foremen realized that they were in trouble when they were told that they had to make the same number of bricks every day as they had made before.
	As they were leaving, they met Moses and Aaron, who were waiting for them. They said to Moses and Aaron:
Foreman 1	The Lord has seen what you have done and will punish you for making the king and his officers hate us.

Foreman 2	You have given them an excuse to kill us.

Cast	[This is] the word of the Lord.
All	**Thanks be to God.**

Cast: **Narrator, Moses, Aaron,** (can be the same as Moses), **King, Slave-driver 1, Slave-driver 2** (can be the same as Slave-driver 1), **Foreman 1, Foreman 2** (can be the same as Foreman 1).

Moses complains to the Lord
Exodus 5.22—6.13

Narrator	Moses turned to the Lord:
Moses	Lord, why do you ill-treat your people? Why did you send me here? Ever since I went to the king to speak for you, he has treated them cruelly. And you have done nothing to help them!
[Narrator	Then the Lord said to Moses:]
The Lord	Now you are going to see what I will do to the king. I will force him to let my people go. In fact, I will force him to *drive* them out of his land. (PAUSE)
	I am the Lord. I appeared to Abraham, to Isaac, and to Jacob as Almighty God, but I did not make myself known to them by my holy name, the Lord. I also made my covenant with them, promising to give them the land of Canaan, the land in which they had lived as foreigners. Now I have heard the groaning of the Israelites, whom the Egyptians have enslaved, and I have remembered my covenant. So tell the Israelites that I say to them, 'I am the Lord; I will rescue you and set you free from your slavery to the Egyptians. I will raise my mighty arm to bring terrible punishment upon them, and I will save you. I will make you my own people, and I will be your God. You will know that I am the Lord your God when I set you free from slavery in Egypt. I will bring you to the land that I solemnly promised to give to Abraham, Isaac, and Jacob; and I will give it to you as your own possession. I am the Lord.'
Narrator	Moses told this to the Israelites, but they would not listen to him, because their spirit had been broken by their cruel slavery. Then the Lord said to Moses:
The Lord	Go and tell the king of Egypt that he must let the Israelites leave his land.
Moses	Even the Israelites will not listen to me, so why should the king? I am such a poor speaker.
The Lord	Tell the Israelites and the king of Egypt that I have ordered you to lead the Israelites out of Egypt.

Cast	[This is] the word of the Lord.
All	**Thanks be to God.**

Cast: **Narrator, Moses, The Lord.**

76

The Lord's command to Moses and Aaron
Exodus 6.28—7.13

Narrator	The Lord spoke to Moses in the land of Egypt:
The Lord	I AM THE LORD. Tell the king of Egypt everything I tell you.
Narrator	But Moses answered:
Moses	You know that I am such a poor speaker; why should the king listen to me?
The Lord	I am going to make you like God to the king, and your brother Aaron will speak to him as your prophet. Tell Aaron everything I command you, and he will tell the king to let the Israelites leave his country. But I will make the king stubborn, and he will not listen to you, no matter how many terrifying things I do in Egypt. Then I will bring severe punishment on Egypt and lead the tribes of my people out of the land. The Egyptians will then know that I AM THE LORD, when I raise my hand against them and bring the Israelites out of their country.
Narrator	Moses and Aaron did what the Lord commanded. At the time when they spoke to the king, Moses was eighty years old, and Aaron was eighty-three.
	The Lord said to Moses and Aaron:
The Lord	If the king demands that you prove yourselves by performing a miracle, tell Aaron to take his walking stick and throw it down in front of the king, and it will turn into a snake.
Narrator	So Moses and Aaron went to the king and did as the Lord had commanded. Aaron threw his stick down in front of the king and his officers, and it turned into a snake. Then the king called for his wise men and magicians, and by their magic they did the same thing. They threw down their sticks, and the sticks turned into snakes. But Aaron's stick swallowed theirs. The king, however, remained stubborn and, just as the Lord had said, the king would not listen to Moses and Aaron.
Cast	[This is] the word of the Lord.
All	**Thanks be to God.**

Cast: **Narrator, The Lord, Moses.**

Disasters strike Egypt—blood
Exodus 7.14–25

Narrator	The Lord spoke to Moses:
The Lord	The king is very stubborn and refuses to let the people go. So go and meet him in the morning when he goes down to the Nile. Take with you the walking stick that was turned into a snake, and wait for him on the bank of the river. Then say to the king, 'The Lord, the God of the Hebrews, sent me to tell you to let his people

→

go, so that they can worship him in the desert. But until now you have not listened. Now, Your Majesty, the Lord says that you will find out who he is by what he is going to do. Look, I am going to strike the surface of the river with this stick, and the water will be turned into blood. The fish will die, and the river will stink so much that the Egyptians will not be able to drink from it.'

[Narrator   The Lord said to Moses:]

The Lord   Tell Aaron to take his stick and hold it out over all the rivers, canals, and pools in Egypt. The water will become blood, and all over the land there will be blood, even in the wooden tubs and stone jars.

Narrator   Then Moses and Aaron did as the Lord commanded. In the presence of the king and his officers, Aaron raised his stick and struck the surface of the river, and all the water in it was turned into blood. The fish in the river died, and it smelt so bad that the Egyptians could not drink from it. There was blood everywhere in Egypt. Then the king's magicians did the same thing by means of their magic, and the king was as stubborn as ever. Just as the Lord had said, the king refused to listen to Moses and Aaron. Instead, he turned and went back to his palace without paying any attention even to this. All the Egyptians dug along the bank of the river for drinking water, because they were not able to drink water from the river.

Seven days passed after the Lord struck the river.

Cast   [This is] the word of the Lord.
All   **Thanks be to God.**

Cast: **Narrator, The Lord.**

Disasters strike Egypt—frogs
Exodus 8.1–15

Narrator   The Lord spoke to Moses:

The Lord   Go to the king and tell him that the Lord says, 'Let my people go, so that they can worship me. If you refuse, I will punish your country by covering it with frogs. The Nile will be so full of frogs that they will leave it and go into your palace, your bedroom, your bed, the houses of your officials and your people, and even into your ovens and baking pans. They will jump up on you, your people, and all your officials.'

[Narrator   The Lord said to Moses:]

The Lord   Tell Aaron to hold out his walking stick over the rivers, the canals, and the pools, and make frogs come up and cover the land of Egypt.

Narrator   So Aaron held it out over all the water, and the frogs came out and covered the land. But the magicians used magic, and they also made frogs come up on the land.

The king called for Moses and Aaron:

King Pray to the Lord to take away these frogs, and I will let your people go, so that they can offer sacrifices to the Lord.

[Narrator Moses replied:]

Moses I will be glad to pray for you. Just set the time when I am to pray for you, your officers, and your people. Then you will be rid of the frogs, and there will be none left except in the Nile.

King Pray for me tomorrow.

Moses I will do as you ask, and then you will know that there is no other god like the Lord, our God. You, your officials, and your people will be rid of the frogs, and there will be none left except in the Nile.

Narrator Then Moses and Aaron left the king, and Moses prayed to the Lord to take away the frogs which he had brought on the king. The Lord did as Moses asked, and the frogs in the houses, the courtyards, and the fields died. The Egyptians piled them up in great heaps, until the land stank with them. When the king saw that the frogs were dead, he became stubborn again and, just as the Lord had said, the king would not listen to Moses and Aaron.

Cast [This is] the word of the Lord.
All **Thanks be to God.**

Cast: **Narrator, The Lord, King, Moses.**

Disasters strike Egypt—gnats
Exodus 8.16–19

Narrator The Lord spoke to Moses:

The Lord Tell Aaron to strike the ground with his stick, and all over the land of Egypt the dust will change into gnats.

Narrator So Aaron struck the ground with his stick, and all the dust in Egypt was turned into gnats, which covered the people and the animals. The magicians tried to use *their* magic to make gnats appear, but they failed. There were gnats everywhere, and the magicians said to the king:

Magician God has done this!

Narrator But the king was stubborn and, just as the Lord had said, the king would not listen to Moses and Aaron.

Cast [This is] the word of the Lord.
All **Thanks be to God.**

Cast: **Narrator, The Lord, Magician.**

Disasters strike Egypt—flies
Exodus 8.20–32

Narrator   The Lord spoke to Moses:

The Lord   Early tomorrow morning go and meet the king as he goes to the river, and tell him that the Lord says, 'Let my people go, so that they can worship me. I warn you that if you refuse, I will punish you by sending flies on you, your officials, and your people. The houses of the Egyptians will be full of flies, and the ground will be covered with them. But I will spare the region of Goshen, where my people live, so that there will be no flies there. I will do this so that you will know that I, the Lord, am at work in this land. I will make a distinction between my people and your people. This miracle will take place tomorrow.'

Narrator   The Lord sent great swarms of flies into the king's palace and the houses of his officials. The whole land of Egypt was brought to ruin by the flies.

Then the king called for Moses and Aaron:

King   Go and offer sacrifices to your God here in *this* country.

Moses   It would not be right to do that, because the Egyptians would be offended by the animals that we sacrifice to the Lord our God. If we use animals that offend the Egyptians and sacrifice them where they can see us, they will stone us to death. We must travel three days into the desert to offer sacrifices to the Lord our God, just as he commanded us.

King   I will let you go to sacrifice to the Lord, your God, in the desert, if you do not go very far. Pray for me.

Moses   As soon as I leave, I will pray to the Lord that tomorrow the flies will leave you, your officials, and your people. But you must not deceive us again and prevent the people from going to sacrifice to the Lord.

Narrator   Moses left the king and prayed to the Lord, and the Lord did as Moses asked. The flies left the king, his officials, and his people; not one fly remained. But even this time the king became stubborn, and again he would not let the people go.

Cast   [This is] the word of the Lord.
All   **Thanks be to God.**

Cast: **Narrator, The Lord, King, Moses.**

Disasters strike Egypt—death of the animals
Exodus 9.1–7

Narrator   The Lord spoke to Moses:

The Lord   Go to the king and tell him that the Lord, the God of the Hebrews, says, 'Let my people go, so that they may worship me. If you again refuse to let them go, I will punish you by sending a terrible disease on all your animals—your horses, donkeys, camels, cattle, sheep, and goats. I will make a distinction between the animals of the Israelites and those of the Egyptians, and no animal that belongs to the Israelites will die. I, the Lord, have set tomorrow as the time when I will do this.'

Narrator The next day the Lord did as he had said, and all the animals of the Egyptians died, but not one of the animals of the Israelites died. The king asked what had happened and was told that none of the animals of the Israelites had died. But he was stubborn and would not let the people go.

Cast [This is] the word of the Lord.
All **Thanks be to God.**

Cast: **Narrator, The Lord.**

Disasters strike Egypt—boils
Exodus 9.8–12

Narrator The Lord spoke to Moses and Aaron:

The Lord Take a few handfuls of ashes from a furnace; Moses is to throw them into the air in front of the king. They will spread out like fine dust over all the land of Egypt, and everywhere they will produce boils that become open sores on the people and the animals.

Narrator So they got some ashes and stood before the king; Moses threw them into the air, and they produced boils that became open sores on the people and the animals. The magicians were not able to appear before Moses, because they were covered with boils, like all the other Egyptians. But the Lord made the king stubborn and, just as the Lord had said, the king would not listen to Moses and Aaron.

Cast [This is] the word of the Lord.
All **Thanks be to God.**

Cast: **Narrator, The Lord.**

Disasters strike Egypt—hail
Exodus 9.13–35

Narrator The Lord spoke to Moses:

The Lord Early tomorrow morning meet with the king and tell him that the Lord, the God of the Hebrews, says, 'Let my people go, so that they may worship me. This time I will punish not only your officials and your people, but I will punish you as well, so that you may know that there is no one like me in all the world. If I had raised my hand to strike you and your people with disease, you would have been completely destroyed. But to show you my power I have let you live so that my fame might spread over the whole world. Yet you are still arrogant and refuse to let my people

→

go. This time tomorrow I will cause a heavy hailstorm, such as Egypt has never known in all its history. Now give orders for your livestock and everything else you have in the open to be put under shelter. Hail will fall on the people and animals left outside unprotected, and they will all die.'

Narrator   Some of the king's officials were afraid because of what the Lord had said, and they brought their slaves and animals indoors for shelter. Others, however, paid no attention to the Lord's warning and left their slaves and animals out in the open.

Then the Lord said to Moses:

The Lord   Raise your hand toward the sky, and hail will fall over the whole land of Egypt—on the people, the animals, and all the plants in the fields.

Narrator   So Moses raised his stick toward the sky, and the Lord sent thunder and hail, and lightning struck the ground. The Lord sent a heavy hailstorm, with lightning flashing back and forth. It was the worst storm that Egypt had ever known in all its history. All over Egypt the hail struck down everything in the open, including all the people and all the animals. It beat down all the plants in the fields and broke all the trees. The region of Goshen, where the Israelites lived, was the only place where there was no hail.

The king sent for Moses and Aaron:

King   This time I have sinned; the Lord is in the right, and my people and I are in the wrong. Pray to the Lord! We have had enough of this thunder and hail! I promise to let you go; you don't have to stay here any longer.

Narrator   Moses said to him:

Moses   As soon as I go out of the city, I will lift up my hands in prayer to the Lord. The thunder will stop, and there will be no more hail, so that you may know that the earth belongs to the Lord. But I know that you and your officials do not yet fear the Lord God.

Narrator   The flax and the barley were ruined, because the barley was ripe, and the flax was budding. But none of the wheat was ruined, because it ripens later.

Moses left the king, went out of the city, and lifted up his hands in prayer to the Lord. The thunder, the hail, and the rain all stopped. When the king saw what had happened, he sinned again. He and his officials remained as stubborn as ever and, just as the Lord had foretold through Moses, the king would not let the Israelites go.

Cast   [This is] the word of the Lord.
All   **Thanks be to God.**

Cast: **Narrator, The Lord, King, Moses.**

Disasters strike Egypt—locusts
Exodus 10.1–20

Narrator	The Lord spoke to Moses:
The Lord	Go and see the king. I have made him and his officials stubborn in order that I may perform these miracles among them and in order that you may be able to tell your children and grandchildren how I made fools of the Egyptians when I performed the miracles. All of you will know that I am the Lord.
Narrator	So Moses and Aaron went to the king:
Moses	The Lord, the God of the Hebrews, says— How much longer will you refuse to submit to me? Let my people go, so that they may worship me. If you keep on refusing, then I will bring locusts into your country tomorrow.
Aaron	There will be so many that they will completely cover the ground. They will eat everything that the hail did not destroy, even the trees that are left. They will fill your palaces and the houses of all your officials and all your people. They will be worse than anything your ancestors ever saw.
Narrator	Then Moses turned and left.
	The king's officials said to him:
Official 1	How long is this man going to give us trouble?
Official 2	Let the Israelite men go, so that they can worship the Lord their God.
Official 1	Don't you realize that Egypt is ruined?
Narrator	So Moses and Aaron were brought back to the king [and he said to them:]
King	You may go and worship the Lord your God. But exactly *who* will go?
Moses	We will all go, including our children and our old people.
Aaron	We will take our sons and daughters, our sheep and goats, and our cattle, because we must hold a festival to honour the Lord.
King	I swear by the Lord that I will never let you take your women and children! It is clear that you are plotting to revolt. No! Only the men may go and worship the Lord if that is what you want.
Narrator	With that, Moses and Aaron were driven out of the king's presence.
	Then the Lord said to Moses:
The Lord	Raise your hand over the land of Egypt to bring the locusts. They will come and eat everything that grows, everything that has survived the hail.

Narrator	So Moses raised his stick, and the Lord caused a wind from the east to blow on the land all that day and all that night. By morning it had brought the locusts. They came in swarms and settled over the whole country. It was the largest swarm of locusts that had ever been seen or that ever would be seen again. They covered the ground until it was black with them; they ate everything that the hail had left, including all the fruit on the trees. Not a green thing was left on any tree or plant in all the land of Egypt.
	Then the king hurriedly called Moses and Aaron:
King	I have sinned against the Lord your God and against you. Now forgive my sin this once and pray to the Lord your God to take away this fatal punishment from me.
Narrator	Moses left the king and prayed to the Lord. And the Lord changed the east wind into a very strong west wind, which picked up the locusts and blew them into the Gulf of Suez. Not one locust was left in all Egypt.
(slowly)	But the Lord made the king stubborn, and he did not let the Israelites go.
Cast	[This is] the word of the Lord.
All	**Thanks be to God.**

Cast: **Narrator, The Lord, Moses, Aaron** (can be the same as Moses), **Official 1, Official 2, King.**

Disasters strike Egypt—darkness
Exodus 10.21–29

Narrator	The Lord spoke to Moses:
The Lord	Raise your hand towards the sky, and a darkness thick enough to be felt will cover the land of Egypt.
Narrator	Moses raised his hand towards the sky, and there was total darkness throughout Egypt for three days. The Egyptians could not see each other, and no one left his house during that time. But the Israelites had light where they were living.
	The king called Moses:
King	You may go and worship the Lord; even your women and children may go with you. But your sheep, goats, and cattle must stay here.
[Narrator	Moses answered:]
Moses	Then you would have to provide us with animals for sacrifices and burnt-offerings to offer to the Lord our God. No, we will take our animals with us; not one will be left behind. We ourselves must select the animals with which to worship the Lord our God. And until we get there, we will not know what animals to sacrifice to him.
Narrator	The Lord made the king stubborn, and he would not let them go. [He said to Moses:]

84

King	Get out of my sight! Don't let me ever see you again! On the day I do, you will die!
Moses (with emphasis)	You are right. You will never see me again.
Cast	[This is] the word of the Lord.
All	**Thanks be to God.**

Cast: **Narrator, The Lord, King, Moses.** (This overlaps the next reading.)

Moses announces the death of the first-born
Exodus 10.24–29, 11.4–8

Narrator	The king called Moses [and said]:
King	You may go and worship the Lord; even your women and children may go with you. But your sheep, goats, and cattle must stay here.
[Narrator	Moses answered:]
Moses	Then you would have to provide us with animals for sacrifices and burnt-offerings to offer to the Lord our God. No, we will take our animals with us; not one will be left behind. We ourselves must select the animals with which to worship the Lord our God. And until we get there, we will not know what animals to sacrifice to him.
Narrator	The Lord made the king stubborn, and he would not let them go. [He said to Moses:]
King	Get out of my sight! Don't let me ever see you again! On the day I do, you will die!
Moses	You are right. You will never see me again. The Lord says:
The Lord	At about midnight I will go through Egypt, and every first-born son in Egypt will die, from the king's son, who is heir to the throne, to the son of the slave-woman who grinds corn. The first-born of all the cattle will die also. There will be loud crying all over Egypt, such as there has never been before or ever will be again. But not even a dog will bark at the Israelites or their animals. Then you will know that I, the Lord, make a distinction between the Egyptians and the Israelites.
Moses	All your officials will come to me and bow down before me, and they will beg me to take all my people and go away. After that, I will leave.
Narrator	Then in great anger Moses left the king.
Cast	[This is] the word of the Lord.
All	**Thanks be to God.**

Cast: **Narrator, King, Moses, The Lord** (can be the same as Moses). (This overlaps the previous reading.)

Disaster will strike the first-born
Exodus 11.1–10

Narrator	The Lord spoke to Moses:
The Lord	I will send only one more punishment on the king of Egypt and his people. After that he will let you leave. In fact, he will drive all of you out of here. Now speak to the people of Israel and tell all of them to ask their neighbours for gold and silver jewellery.
Narrator	The Lord made the Egyptians respect the Israelites. Indeed, the officials and all the people considered Moses to be a very great man.
	Moses then said to the king:
Moses	The Lord says, 'At about midnight, I will go through Egypt, and every first-born son in Egypt will die, from the king's son, who is heir to the throne, to the son of the slave-woman, who grinds corn. The first-born of all the cattle will die also. There will be loud crying all over Egypt, such as there has never been before or ever will be again. But not even a dog will bark at the Israelites or their animals. Then you will know that I, the Lord, make a distinction between the Egyptians and the Israelites.'
[Narrator	Moses concluded by saying:]
Moses (angrily)	All your officials will come to me and bow down before me, and they will beg me to take all my people and go away. After that, I will leave.
Narrator	Then in great anger Moses left the king. (PAUSE)
	The Lord had said to Moses:
The Lord	The king will continue to refuse to listen to you, in order that I may do more of my miracles in Egypt.
Narrator	Moses and Aaron performed all these miracles before the king, but the Lord made him stubborn, and he would not let the Israelites leave his country.
Cast **All**	[This is] the word of the Lord. **Thanks be to God.**

Cast: **Narrator, The Lord, Moses.** (This overlaps the previous reading.)

The first Passover
Exodus 12.21–36

Narrator	Moses called for all the leaders of Israel [and said to them]:
Moses	Each of you is to choose a lamb or a young goat and kill it, so that your families can celebrate Passover. Take a sprig of hyssop, dip it in the bowl containing the animal's blood, and wipe the blood on the door-posts and the beam above the door of your house. Not one of you is to leave the house until morning. When the Lord

goes through Egypt to kill the Egyptians, he will see the blood on the beams and the door-posts and will not let the Angel of Death enter your houses and kill you. You and your children must obey these rules for ever. When you enter the land that the Lord has promised to give you, you must perform this ritual. When your children ask you, 'What does this ritual mean?' you will answer, 'It is the sacrifice of Passover to honour the Lord, because he passed over the houses of the Israelites in Egypt. He killed the Egyptians, but spared us.'

Narrator   The Israelites knelt down and worshipped. Then they went and did what the Lord had commanded Moses and Aaron. (PAUSE)

At midnight the Lord killed all the first-born sons in Egypt, from the king's son, who was heir to the throne, to the son of the prisoner in the dungeon; all the first-born of the animals were also killed. That night, the king, his officials, and all the other Egyptians were awakened. There was loud crying throughout Egypt, because there was not one home in which there was not a dead son. That same night the king sent for Moses and Aaron [and said]:

King   Get out, you and your Israelites! Leave my country; go and worship the Lord, as you asked. Take your sheep, goats and cattle, and leave. Also pray for a blessing on me.

Narrator   The Egyptians urged the people to hurry and leave the country:

Egyptian   We will all be dead if you don't leave.

Narrator   So the people filled their baking-pans with unleavened dough, wrapped them in clothing, and carried them on their shoulders. The Israelites had done as Moses had said, and had asked the Egyptians for gold and silver jewellery and for clothing. The Lord made the Egyptians respect the people and give them what they asked for. In this way the Israelites carried away the wealth of the Egyptians.

Cast   [This is] the word of the Lord.
All   **Thanks be to God.**

Cast: **Narrator, Moses, King, Egyptian.**

The pillar of cloud and the pillar of fire
Exodus 13.17—14.9

Narrator   When the king of Egypt let the people go, God did not take them by the road that goes up the coast to Philistia, although it was the shortest way. God thought:

The Lord   I do not want the people to change their minds and return to Egypt when they see that they are going to have to fight.

Narrator   Instead, he led them in a roundabout way through the desert towards the Red Sea. The Israelites were armed for battle.

→

Moses took the body of Joseph with him, as Joseph had made the Israelites solemnly promise to do. Joseph had said:

Joseph   When God rescues you, you must carry my body with you from this place.

Narrator   The Israelites left Sukkoth and camped at Etham on the edge of the desert. During the day the Lord went in front of them in a pillar of cloud to show them the way, and during the night he went in front of them in a pillar of fire to give them light, so that they could travel night and day. The pillar of cloud was always in front of the people during the day, and the pillar of fire at night.

Then the Lord said to Moses:

The Lord   Tell the Israelites to turn back and camp in front of Pi Hahiroth, between Migdol and the Red Sea, near Baal Zephon. The king will think that the Israelites are wandering about in the country and are closed in by the desert. I will make him stubborn, and he will pursue you, and my victory over the king and his army will bring me honour. Then the Egyptians will know that I am the Lord.

Narrator   The Israelites did as they were told.

When the king of Egypt was told that the people had escaped, he and his officials changed their minds:

King   What have we done?

Official 1   We have let the Israelites escape—

Official 2   And we have lost them as our slaves!

Narrator   The king got his war chariot and his army ready. He set out with all his chariots, including the six hundred finest, commanded by their officers. The Lord made the king stubborn, and he pursued the Israelites, who were leaving triumphantly. The Egyptian army, with all the horses, chariots, and drivers, pursued them and caught up with them where they were camped by the Red Sea near Pi Hahiroth and Baal Zephon.

Cast   [This is] the word of the Lord.
All   **Thanks be to God.**

Cast: **Narrator, The Lord, Joseph,** (preferably unseen, can be the same as Narrator), **King, Official 1, Official 2** (can be the same as Official 1 OR King and Official 1 and Official 2 can be the same) .

The Lord defeats the Egyptians
From Exodus 14.10—29

Narrator   When the Israelites saw the king and his army marching against them, they were terrified and cried out to the Lord for help. They said to Moses:

Israelite 1   Weren't there any graves in Egypt? Did you have to bring us out here in the desert to die?

Israelite 2	Look what you have done by bringing us out of Egypt! Didn't we tell you before we left that this would happen?
Israelite 3	We told you to leave us alone and let us go on being slaves of the Egyptians. It would be better to be slaves there than to die here in the desert.
[Narrator	Moses answered:]
Moses (firmly)	Don't be afraid! Stand your ground, and you will see what the Lord will do to save you today; you will never see these Egyptians again. The Lord will fight for you, and there is no need for you to do anything.
Narrator	The Lord said to Moses:
The Lord	Why are you crying out for help? Tell the people to move forward. Lift up your stick and hold it out over the sea. The water will divide, and the Israelites will be able to walk through the sea on dry ground. I will make the Egyptians so stubborn that they will go in after them, and I will gain honour by my victory over the king, his army, his chariots, and his drivers. When I defeat them, the Egyptians will know that I am the Lord.
Narrator	Moses held out his hand over the sea, and the Lord drove the sea back with a strong east wind. It blew all night and turned the sea into dry land. The water was divided, and the Israelites went through the sea on dry ground, with walls of water on both sides. The Egyptians pursued them and went after them into the sea with all their horses, chariots, and drivers. Just before dawn the Lord looked down from the pillar of fire and cloud at the Egyptian army and threw them into a panic. He made the wheels of their chariots get stuck, so that they moved with great difficulty. The Egyptians said:
Egyptian 1	The Lord is fighting for the Israelites against us.
Egyptian 2	Let's get out of here!
Narrator	The Lord said to Moses:
The Lord	Hold out your hand over the sea, and the water will come back over the Egyptians and their chariots and drivers.
Narrator	So Moses held out his hand over the sea, and at daybreak the water returned to its normal level. The Egyptians tried to escape from the water, but the Lord threw them into the sea. The water returned and covered the chariots, the drivers, and all the Egyptian army that had followed the Israelites into the sea; not one of them was left. But the Israelites walked through the sea on dry ground, with walls of water on both sides.
Cast	[This is] the word of the Lord.
All	**Thanks be to God.**

Cast: **Narrator, Israelite 1, Israelite 2, Israelite 3** (Israelites 1–3 can be the same), **Moses, The Lord, Egyptian 1, Egyptian 2** (can be the same as Egyptian 1).

Bitter water
Exodus 15.22–27

Narrator Moses led the people of Israel away from the Red Sea into the desert of Shur. For three days they walked through the desert, but found no water. Then they came to a place called Marah, but the water there was so bitter that they could not drink it. That is why it was named Marah. The people complained to Moses:

Israelite What are we going to drink?

Narrator Moses prayed earnestly to the Lord, and the Lord showed him a piece of wood, which he threw into the water; and the water became fit to drink. (PAUSE)

There the Lord gave them laws to live by, and there he also tested them. [He said:]

The Lord If you will obey me completely by doing what I consider right and by keeping my commands, I will not punish you with any of the diseases that I brought on the Egyptians. I am the Lord, the one who heals you.

Narrator Next they came to Elim, where there were twelve springs and seventy palm trees; there they camped by the water.

Cast [This is] the word of the Lord.
All **Thanks be to God.**

Cast: **Narrator, Israelite, The Lord.**

The manna and the quails
Exodus 16.1–35

Narrator The whole Israelite community set out from Elim, and on the fifteenth day of the second month after they had left Egypt, they came to the desert of Sin, which is between Elim and Sinai. There in the desert they all complained to Moses and Aaron:

Israelite 1 We wish that the Lord had killed us in Egypt.

Israelite 2 There we could at least sit down and eat meat and as much other food as we wanted.

Israelite 1 But you have brought us out into this desert to starve us all to death.

Narrator The Lord said to Moses:

The Lord Now I am going to make food rain down from the sky for all of you. The people must go out every day and gather enough for that day. In this way I can test them to find out if they will follow my instructions. On the sixth day they are to bring in twice as much as usual and prepare it.

Narrator So Moses and Aaron said to all the Israelites:

Aaron	This evening you will know that it was the Lord who brought you out of Egypt. In the morning you will see the dazzling light of the Lord's presence. He has heard your complaints against him—yes, against him, because we are only carrying out his instructions.
Narrator	Then Moses said:
Moses	It is the Lord who will give you meat to eat in the evening and as much bread as you want in the morning, because he has heard how much you have complained against him. When you complain against us, you are really complaining against the Lord.
[Narrator	Moses said to Aaron:]
Moses (to Aaron)	Tell the whole community to come and stand before the Lord, because he has heard their complaints.
Narrator	As Aaron spoke to the whole community, they turned towards the desert, and suddenly the dazzling light of the Lord appeared in a cloud. The Lord said to Moses:
The Lord	I have heard the complaints of the Israelites. Tell them that at twilight they will have meat to eat, and in the morning they will have all the bread they want. Then they will know that I, the Lord, am their God.
Narrator	In the evening a large flock of quails flew in, enough to cover the camp, and in the morning there was dew all round the camp. When the dew evaporated, there was something thin and flaky on the surface of the desert. It was as delicate as frost. When the Israelites saw it, they didn't know what it was and asked each other:
Israelites 1 and 2	What is it?
[Narrator	Moses said to them:]
Moses	This is the food that the Lord has given you to eat. The Lord has commanded that each of you is to gather as much of it as he needs, two litres for each member of his household.
Narrator	The Israelites did this, some gathering more, others less. When they measured it, those who gathered much did not have too much, and those who gathered less did not have too little. Each had gathered just what he needed.
	[Moses said to them:]
Moses	No one is to keep any of it for tomorrow.
Narrator	But some of them did not listen to Moses and saved part of it. The next morning it was full of worms and smelt rotten, and Moses was angry with them. Every morning each one gathered as much as he needed; and when the sun grew hot, what was left on the ground melted.
	On the sixth day they gathered twice as much food, four litres for each person. All the leaders of the community came and told Moses about it, and he said to them:

Moses	The Lord has commanded that tomorrow is a holy day of rest, dedicated to him. Bake today what you want to bake and boil what you want to boil. Whatever is left should be put aside and kept for tomorrow.
Narrator	As Moses had commanded, they kept what was left until the next day; it did not spoil or get worms in it.
Moses	Eat this today, because today is the Sabbath, a day of rest dedicated to the Lord, and you will not find any food outside the camp. You must gather food for six days, but on the seventh day, the day of rest, there will be none.
Narrator	On the seventh day some of the people went out to gather food, but they did not find any. Then the Lord said to Moses:
The Lord	How much longer will you people refuse to obey my commands? Remember that I, the Lord, have given you a day of rest, and that is why on the sixth day I will always give you enough food for two days. Everyone is to stay where he is on the seventh day and not leave his home.
Narrator	So the people did no work on the seventh day. The people of Israel called the food 'manna'. It was like a small white seed, and tasted like biscuits made with honey. [Moses said:]
Moses	The Lord has commanded us to save some manna, to be kept for our descendants, so that they can see the food which he gave us to eat in the desert when he brought us out of Egypt.
[Narrator	Moses said to Aaron:]
Moses (to Aaron)	Take a jar, put two litres of manna in it, and place it in the Lord's presence to be kept for our descendants.
Narrator	As the Lord had commanded Moses, Aaron put it in front of the Covenant Box, so that it could be kept. The Israelites ate manna for the next forty years, until they reached the land of Canaan, where they settled.
Cast	[This is] the word of the Lord.
All	**Thanks be to God.**

Cast: **Narrator, Israelite 1, Israelite 2** (can be the same as Israelite 1), **The Lord, Aaron, Moses.**

Water from the rock
Exodus 17.1–7

Narrator	The whole Israelite community left the desert of Sin, moving from one place to another at the command of the Lord. They made camp at Rephidim, but there was no water there to drink. They complained to Moses:
Israelite 1	Give us water to drink.
[Narrator	Moses answered:]
Moses	Why are you complaining? Why are you putting the Lord to the test?

Narrator	But the people were very thirsty and continued to complain to Moses.
Israelite 2	Why did you bring us out of Egypt?
Israelite 1	To kill us and our children and our livestock with thirst?
Narrator	Moses prayed earnestly to the Lord:
Moses	What can I do with these people? They are almost ready to stone me.
[Narrator	The Lord said to Moses:]
The Lord	Take some of the leaders of Israel with you, and go on ahead of the people. Take along the stick with which you struck the Nile. I will stand before you on a rock at Mount Sinai. Strike the rock, and water will come out of it for the people to drink.
Narrator	Moses did so in the presence of the leaders of Israel. The place was named Massah and Meribah, because the Israelites complained and put the Lord to the test when they asked:
Israelite 2	Is the Lord with us or not?
Cast	[This is] the word of the Lord.
All	**Thanks be to God.**

Cast: **Narrator, Israelite 1, Moses, Israelite 2** (can be the same as Israelite 1), **The Lord.**

War with the Amalekites
Exodus 17.8–16

Narrator	The Amalekites came and attacked the Israelites at Rephidim. Moses said to Joshua:
Moses	Pick out some men to go and fight the Amalekites tomorrow. I will stand on top of the hill holding the stick that God told me to carry.
Narrator	Joshua did as Moses commanded him and went out to fight the Amalekites, while Moses, Aaron, and Hur went up to the top of the hill. As long as Moses held up his arms, the Israelites won, but when he put his arms down, the Amalekites started winning. When Moses' arms grew tired, Aaron and Hur brought a stone for him to sit on, while they stood beside him and held up his arms, holding them steady until the sun went down. In this way Joshua totally defeated the Amalekites. The Lord said to Moses:
The Lord	Write an account of this victory, so that it will be remembered. Tell Joshua that I will completely destroy the Amalekites.
Narrator	Moses built an altar and named it:
Moses	'The Lord is my Banner'. Hold high the banner of the Lord! The Lord will continue to fight against the Amalekites for ever!
Cast	[This is] the word of the Lord.
All	**Thanks be to God.**

Cast: **Narrator, Moses, The Lord.**

Jethro visits Moses
Exodus 18.1–12

Narrator Moses' father-in-law Jethro, the priest of Midian, heard about everything that God had done for Moses and the people of Israel when he led them out of Egypt. So he came to Moses, bringing with him Moses' wife Zipporah, who had been left behind, and Gershom and Eliezer, her two sons. Moses had said:

Moses I have been a foreigner in a strange land.

Narrator So he had named one son: 'Gershom'.

He had also said:

Moses The God of my father helped me and saved me from being killed by the king of Egypt.

Narrator So he had named the other son: 'Eliezer'.

Jethro came with Moses' wife and her two sons into the desert where Moses was camped at the holy mountain. He had sent word to Moses that they were coming, so Moses went out to meet him, bowed before him, and kissed him. They asked about each other's health and then went into Moses' tent. Moses told Jethro everything that the Lord had done to the king and the people of Egypt in order to rescue the Israelites. He also told him about the hardships the people had faced on the way and how the Lord had saved them. When Jethro heard all this, he was happy:

Jethro Praise the Lord, who saved you from the king and the people of Egypt! Praise the Lord, who saved his people from slavery! Now I know that the Lord is greater than all the gods, because he did this when the Egyptians treated the Israelites with such contempt.

Narrator Then Jethro brought an offering to be burnt whole and other sacrifices to be offered to God; and Aaron and all the leaders of Israel went with him to eat the sacred meal as an act of worship.

Cast [This is] the word of the Lord.
All **Thanks be to God.**

Cast: **Narrator, Moses, Jethro.**

The appointment of judges
From Exodus 18.13–26

Narrator Moses was settling disputes among the people, and he was kept busy from morning till night. When Jethro saw everything that Moses had to do, he asked:

Jethro What is all this that you are doing for the people? Why are you doing this all alone, with people standing here from morning till night to consult you?

Narrator Moses answered:

Moses I must do this because the people come to me to learn God's will. When two people have a dispute, they come to me, and I decide which one of them is right, and I tell them God's commands and laws.

Jethro	You are not doing it the right way. You will wear yourself out and these people as well. This is too much for you to do alone. Now let me give you some good advice, and God will be with you. It is *right* for you to represent the people before God and bring their disputes to him. You *should* teach them God's commands and explain to them how they should live and what they should do. But in addition, you should choose some capable men and appoint them as leaders of the people. They must be God-fearing men who can be trusted and who cannot be bribed. Let them serve as judges for the people on a permanent basis. They can bring all the difficult cases to you, but they themselves can decide all the smaller disputes. That will make it easier for you, as they share your burden. If you do this, as God commands, you will not wear yourself out, and all these people can go home with their disputes settled.
Narrator	Moses took Jethro's advice and chose capable men from among all the Israelites. They served as judges for the people on a permanent basis, bringing the difficult cases to Moses but deciding the smaller disputes themselves.
Cast	[This is] the word of the Lord.
All	**Thanks be to God.**

Cast: **Narrator, Jethro, Moses.**

The Israelites at Mount Sinai
Exodus 19.2–13

Narrator	The people of Israel set up camp at the foot of Mount Sinai, and Moses went up the mountain to meet with God.
	The Lord called to him from the mountain and told him to say to the Israelites, Jacob's descendants:
The Lord	You saw what I, the Lord, did to the Egyptians and how I carried you as an eagle carries her young on her wings, and brought you here to me. Now, if you will obey me and keep my covenant, you will be my own people. The whole earth is mine, but you will be my chosen people, a people dedicated to me alone, and you will serve me as priests.
Narrator	So Moses went down and called the leaders of the people together and told them everything that the Lord had commanded him. Then all the people answered together:
Person(s)	We will do everything that the Lord has said!
Narrator	And Moses reported this to the Lord. (PAUSE) The Lord said to Moses:
The Lord	I will come to you in a thick cloud, so that the people will hear me speaking with you and will believe you from now on.
Narrator	Moses told the Lord what the people had answered, and the Lord said to him:
The Lord	Go to the people and tell them to spend today and tomorrow purifying themselves for worship. They must wash their clothes and be ready the day after tomorrow. On that day I will come down on Mount Sinai, where all the people can see me. Mark a

→

95

boundary round the mountain that the people must not cross, and tell them not to go up the mountain or even get near it. If anyone sets foot on it, he is to be put to death; he must either be stoned or shot with arrows, without anyone touching him. This applies to both men and animals; they must be put to death. But when the trumpet is blown, then the people are to go up the moutain.

Cast	[This is] the word of the Lord.
All	**Thanks be to God.**

Cast: **Narrator, The Lord, Person(s)** (two or more).

The Ten Commandments
From Exodus 19.14—20.21

Narrator	Moses came down the mountain and told the people to get ready for worship. On the morning of the third day there was thunder and lightning, a thick cloud appeared on the mountain, and a very loud trumpet blast was heard. All the people in the camp trembled with fear. Moses led them out of the camp to meet God, and they stood at the foot of the mountain. The whole of Mount Sinai was covered with smoke, because the Lord had come down on it in fire. The smoke went up like the smoke of a furnace, and all the people trembled violently. The sound of the trumpet became louder and louder. Moses spoke, and God answered him with thunder. The Lord came down on the top of Mount Sinai and called Moses to the top of the mountain. Moses went up and the Lord spoke to him:
The Lord	Go down and warn the people not to cross the boundary to come and look at me; if they do, many of them will die. Even the priests who come near me must purify themselves, or I will punish them.
[Narrator	Moses said to the Lord:]
Moses	The people cannot come up, because you commanded us to consider the mountain sacred and to mark a boundary round it.
The Lord	Go down and bring Aaron back with you. But the priests and the people must not cross the boundary to come up to me, or I will punish them.
Narrator	Moses then went down to the people and told them what the Lord had said. (PAUSE)
	God spoke, and these were his words:
The Lord	I am the Lord your God who brought you out of Egypt, where you were slaves.
	Worship no god but me.
	Do not make for yourselves images of anything in heaven or on earth or in the water under the earth. Do not bow down to any idol or worship it, because I am the Lord your God and I tolerate no rivals. I bring punishment on those who hate me and on their descendants down to the third and fourth generation. But I show my love to thousands of generations of those who love me and obey my laws.
	Do not use my name for evil purposes, for I, the Lord your God, will punish anyone who misuses my name.

Observe the Sabbath and keep it holy. You have six days in which to do your work, but the seventh day is a day of rest dedicated to me. On that day no one is to work—neither you, your children, your slaves, your animals, nor the foreigners who live in your country. In six days I, the Lord, made the earth, the sky, the sea, and everything in them, but on the seventh day I rested. That is why I, the Lord, blessed the Sabbath and made it holy.

Respect your father and your mother, so that you may live a long time in the land that I am giving you.

Do not commit murder.

Do not commit adultery.

Do not steal.

Do not accuse anyone falsely.

Do not desire another man's house; do not desire his wife, his slaves, his cattle, his donkeys, or anything else that he owns.

Narrator	When the people heard the thunder and the trumpet blast and saw the lightning and the smoking mountain, they trembled with fear and stood a long way off. They said to Moses:
Israelite 1	If *you* speak to us, we will listen.
Israelite 2	But we are afraid that if *God* speaks to us, we will die.
Moses	Don't be afraid; God has only come to test you and make you keep on obeying him, so that you will not sin.
Narrator	But the people continued to stand a long way off, and only Moses went near the dark cloud where God was.
Cast	[This is] the word of the Lord.
All	**Thanks be to God.**

Cast: **Narrator, The Lord, Moses, Israelite 1, Israelite 2** (can be the same as Israelite 1).

The covenant is sealed
Exodus 24.1–11

Narrator	The Lord spoke to Moses:
The Lord	Come up the mountain to me, you and Aaron, Nadab, Abihu, and seventy of the leaders of Israel; and while you are still some distance away, bow down in worship. You alone, and none of the others, are to come near me. The people are not even to come up the mountain.
Narrator	Moses went and told the people all the Lord's commands and all the ordinances, and all the people answered together:
Israelite(s)	We will do everything that the Lord has said.
Narrator	Moses wrote down all the Lord's commands. Early the next morning he built an altar at the foot of the mountain and set up twelve stones, one for each of the twelve tribes of Israel. Then he sent young men, and they burnt sacrifices to the Lord and sacrificed some cattle as fellowship-offerings. Moses took half the blood of the animals and put it in bowls; and the other half he threw against the altar. Then he took the book of the covenant, in

→

	which the Lord's commands were written, and read it aloud to the people. They said:
Israelite(s)	We will obey the Lord and do everything that he has commanded.
Narrator	Then Moses took the blood in the bowls and threw it on the people:
Moses	This is the blood that seals the covenant which the Lord made with you when he gave all these commands.
Narrator	Moses, Aaron, Nadab, Abihu, and seventy of the leaders of Israel went up the mountain and they saw the God of Israel. Beneath his feet was what looked like a pavement of sapphire, as blue as the sky. God did not harm these leading men of Israel; they saw God, and then they ate and drank together.
Cast	[This is] the word of the Lord.
All	**Thanks be to God.**

Cast: **Narrator, The Lord, Israelite(s)** (three or more), **Moses.**

Moses on Mount Sinai
Exodus 24.12–18

Narrator	The Lord spoke to Moses:
The Lord	Come up the mountain to me, and while you are here, I will give you two stone tablets which contain all the laws that I have written for the instruction of the people.
Narrator	Moses and his helper Joshua got ready, and Moses began to go up the holy mountain. Moses said to the leaders:
Moses	Wait here in the camp for us until we come back. Aaron and Hur are here with you; and so whoever has a dispute to settle can go to them.
Narrator	Moses went up Mount Sinai, and a cloud covered it. The dazzling light of the Lord's presence came down on the mountain. To the Israelites the light looked like a fire burning on top of the mountain. The cloud covered the mountain for six days, and on the seventh day the Lord called to Moses from the cloud. Moses went on up the mountain into the cloud. There he stayed for forty days and nights.
Cast	[This is] the word of the Lord.
All	**Thanks be to God.**

Cast: **Narrator, The Lord, Moses.**

Sabbath, the day of rest
Exodus 31.12–18

Narrator	The Lord commanded Moses to say to the people of Israel:
The Lord	Keep the Sabbath, my day of rest, because it is a sign between you and me for all time to come, to show that I, the Lord, have made you my own people. You must keep the day of rest, because it is sacred. Whoever does not keep it, but works on that day, is to be put to death. You have six days in which to do your work, but the

seventh day is a solemn day of rest dedicated to me. Whoever does any work on that day is to be put to death. The people of Israel are to keep this day as a sign of the covenant. It is a permanent sign between the people of Israel and me, because I, the Lord, made heaven and earth in six days, and on the seventh day I stopped working and rested.

Narrator When God had finished speaking to Moses on Mount Sinai, he gave him the two stone tablets on which God himself had written the commandments.

Cast [This is] the word of the Lord.
All **Thanks be to God.**

Cast: **Narrator, The Lord.**

The gold bull
Exodus 32.1–20

Narrator When the people saw that Moses had not come down from the mountain but was staying there a long time, they gathered round Aaron [and said to him:]

Israelite 1 We do not know what has happened to this man Moses, who led us out of Egypt—

Israelite 2 So make us a god to lead us.

Narrator Aaron said to them:

Aaron
(wearily) Take off the gold earrings which your wives, your sons, and your daughters are wearing, and bring them to me.

Narrator So all the people took off their gold earrings and brought them to Aaron. He took the earrings, melted them, poured the gold into a mould, and made a gold bull-calf.

The people said:

Israelites 1 and 2 Israel!

Israelite 1 This is our god—

Israelite 2 Who led us out of Egypt!

Narrator Then Aaron built an altar in front of the gold bull and announced:

Aaron Tomorrow there will be a festival to honour the Lord.

Narrator Early the next morning they brought some animals to burn as sacrifices and others to eat as fellowship offerings. The people sat down to a feast, which turned into an orgy of drinking and sex.

The Lord said to Moses:

The Lord Go back down at once, because your people, whom you led out of Egypt, have sinned and rejected me. They have already left the way that I commanded them to follow; they have made a bull-calf out of melted gold and have worshipped it and offered sacrifices

→

| | to it. They are saying that this is their god, who led them out of Egypt. I know how stubborn these people are. Now, don't try to stop me. I am angry with them, and I am going to destroy them. Then I will make you and your descendants into a great nation. |

Narrator   But Moses pleaded with the Lord his God:

Moses   Lord, why should you be so angry with your people, whom you rescued from Egypt with great might and power? Why should the Egyptians be able to say that you led your people out of Egypt, planning to kill them in the mountains and destroy them completely? Stop being angry; change your mind and do not bring this disaster on your people. Remember your servants Abraham, Isaac, and Jacob. Remember the solemn promise you made to them to give them as many descendants as there are stars in the sky and to give their descendants all that land you promised would be their possession for ever.

Narrator   So the Lord changed his mind and did not bring on his people the disaster he had threatened.

Moses went back down the mountain, carrying the two stone tablets with the commandments written on both sides. God himself had made the tablets and had engraved the commandments on them.

Joshua heard the people shouting [and said to Moses:]

Joshua
(to Moses)   I hear the sound of battle in the camp.

[Narrator   Moses said:]

Moses   That doesn't sound like a shout of victory or a cry of defeat; it's the sound of singing.

Narrator   When Moses came close enough to the camp to see the bull-calf and to see the people dancing, he was furious. There at the foot of the mountain, he threw down the tablets he was carrying and broke them. He took the bull-calf which they had made, melted it, ground it into fine powder, and mixed it with water. Then he made the people of Israel drink it.

Cast   [This is] the word of the Lord.
All   **Thanks be to God.**

Cast: **Narrator, Israelite 1, Israelite 2** (can be the same as Israelite 1), **Aaron, The Lord, Moses, Joshua.**

The Lord orders Israel to leave Mount Sinai
Exodus 33.1–6 [7–11]

Narrator   The Lord spoke to Moses:

The Lord   Leave this place, you and the people you brought out of Egypt, and go to the land that I promised to give to Abraham, Isaac, and Jacob and to their descendants. I will send an angel to guide you, and I will drive out the Canaanites, the Amorites, the Hittites, the

Perizzites, the Hivites, and the Jebusites. You are going to a rich and fertile land. But I will not go with you myself, because you are a stubborn people, and I might destroy you on the way.

Narrator When the people heard this, they began to mourn and did not wear jewellery any more. For the Lord had commanded Moses to say to them:

The Lord You are a stubborn people. If I were to go with you even for a moment, I would completely destroy you. Now take off your jewellery, and I will decide what to do with you.

Narrator So after they left Mount Sinai, the people of Israel no longer wore jewellery.

[Whenever the people of Israel set up camp, Moses would take the sacred Tent and put it up some distance away from the camp. It was called the Tent of the Lord's presence, and anyone who wanted to consult the Lord would go out to it. Whenever Moses went out there, the people would stand at the door of their tents and watch Moses until he entered it. After Moses had gone in, the pillar of cloud would come down and stay at the door of the Tent, and the Lord would speak to Moses from the cloud. As soon as the people saw the pillar of cloud at the door of the Tent, they would bow down. The Lord would speak with Moses face to face, just as a man speaks with a friend. Then Moses would return to the camp. But the young man who was his helper, Joshua son of Nun, stayed in the Tent.]

Cast [This is] the word of the Lord.
All **Thanks be to God.**

Cast: **Narrator, The Lord.**

The Lord promises to be with his people
Exodus 33.12–23

Narrator Moses spoke to the Lord:

Moses It is true that you have told me to lead these people to that land, but you did not tell me whom you would send with me. You have said that you know me well and are pleased with me. Now if you are, tell me your plans, so that I may serve you and continue to please you. Remember also that you have chosen this nation to be your own.

Narrator The Lord said:

The Lord I will go with you, and I will give you victory.

Moses If you do not go with us, don't make us leave this place. How will anyone know that you are pleased with your people and with me if you do not go with us? Your presence with us will distinguish us from any other people on earth.

The Lord I will do just as you have asked, because I know you very well and I am pleased with you.

[Narrator	Then Moses requested:]
Moses	Please, let me see the dazzling light of your presence.
The Lord	I will make all my splendour pass before you and in your presence I will pronounce my sacred name. I am the Lord, and I show compassion and pity on those I choose. I will not let you see my face, because no one can see me and stay alive, but here is a place beside me where you can stand on a rock. When the dazzling light of my presence passes by, I will put you in an opening in the rock and cover you with my hand until I have passed by. Then I will take my hand away, and you will see my back but not my face.
Cast	[This is] the word of the Lord.
All	**Thanks be to God.**

Cast: **Narrator, Moses, The Lord.**

The second set of stone tablets
Exodus 34.1–9

Narrator	The Lord spoke to Moses:
The Lord	Cut two stone tablets like the first ones, and I will write on them the words that were on the first tablets, which you broke. Be ready tomorrow morning, and come up Mount Sinai to meet me there at the top. No one is to come up with you; no one is to be seen on any part of the mountain; and no sheep or cattle are to graze at the foot of the mountain.
Narrator	So Moses cut two more stone tablets, and early the next morning he carried them up Mount Sinai, just as the Lord had commanded.
	The Lord came down in a cloud, stood with him there, and pronounced his holy name, the Lord. The Lord then passed in front of him and called out:
The Lord	I, the Lord, am a God who is full of compassion and pity, who is not easily angered and who shows great love and faithfulness. I keep my promise for thousands of generations and forgive evil and sin; but I will not fail to punish children and grandchildren to the third and fourth generation for the sins of their parents.
Narrator	Moses quickly bowed down to the ground and worshipped. [He said:]
Moses	Lord, if you really are pleased with me, I ask you to go with us. These people are stubborn, but forgive our evil and our sin, and accept us as your own people.
Cast	[This is] the word of the Lord.
All	**Thanks be to God.**

Cast: **Narrator, The Lord, Moses.**

LEVITICUS

The ordination of Aaron and his sons
From Leviticus 8.1–36

Narrator 1   The Lord spoke to Moses:

The Lord   Take Aaron and his sons to the entrance of the Tent of my presence and bring the priestly garments, the anointing oil, the young bull for the sin-offering, the two rams, and the basket of unleavened bread. Then call the whole community together there.

Narrator 1   Moses did as the Lord had commanded, and when the community had assembled, he spoke to them:

Moses   What I am now about to do is what the Lord has commanded.

Narrator 2   Moses brought Aaron and his sons forward and told them to take a ritual bath. He put the shirt and the robe on Aaron and the sash round his waist. He put the ephod on him and fastened it by putting its finely woven belt round his waist. He put the breast-piece on him and put the Urim and Thummim in it. He placed the turban on his head, and on the front of it he put the gold ornament, the sacred sign of dedication, just as the Lord had commanded him.

Narrator 1   Then Moses took the anointing oil and put it on the Tent of the Lord's presence and everything that was in it, and in this way he dedicated it all to the Lord. He took some of the oil and sprinkled it seven times on the altar and its equipment and on the basin and its base, in order to dedicate them to the Lord. He ordained Aaron by pouring some of the anointing oil on his head.

Narrator 2   Next, Moses brought the sons of Aaron forward and put shirts on them, put sashes round their waists, and tied caps on their heads, just as the Lord had commanded.

Narrator 1   Then Moses brought the young bull for the sin-offering, and Aaron and his sons put their hands on its head. Moses killed it and took some of the blood, and with his finger put it on the projections at the corners of the altar, in order to dedicate it. He then poured out the rest of the blood at the base of the altar. In this way he dedicated it and purified it.

Narrator 2   Next, Moses brought the ram for the burnt-offering, and Aaron and his sons put their hands on its head. Moses killed it and threw the blood on all four sides of the altar. This burnt-offering was a food-offering, and the smell was pleasing to the Lord.

Narrator 1   Then Moses brought the second ram, which was for the ordination of priests, and Aaron and his sons put their hands on its head.

Narrator 2   Moses killed it and took some of the blood and put it on the lobe of Aaron's right ear, on the thumb of his right hand, and on the big toe of his right foot.

Narrator 1	Then he brought Aaron's sons forward and put some of the blood on the lobes of their right ears, on the thumbs of their right hands, and on the big toes of their right feet. Moses then threw the rest of the blood on all four sides of the altar.
Narrator 2	Moses took some of the anointing oil and some of the blood that was on the altar and sprinkled them on Aaron and his sons and on their clothes. In this way he consecrated them and their clothes to the Lord.
Narrator 1	Moses said to Aaron and his sons:
Moses	You shall not leave the entrance of the Tent for seven days, until your ordination rites are completed. The Lord commanded us to do what we have done today, in order to take away your sin. You must stay at the entrance of the Tent day and night for seven days, doing what the Lord has commanded. If you don't, you will die. This is what the Lord has commanded me.
Narrator 1	So Aaron and his sons did everything that the Lord had commanded through Moses.
Cast	[This is] the word of the Lord.
All	**Thanks be to God.**

Cast: **Narrator 1, The Lord, Moses, Narrator 2.**

Aaron offers sacrifices
From Leviticus 9.2–24

Narrator	Moses spoke to Aaron:
Moses	Take a young bull and a ram without any defects and offer them to the Lord, the bull for a sin-offering and the ram for a burnt-offering. Then tell the people of Israel to take a male goat for a sin-offering, a one-year-old calf, and a one-year-old lamb without any defects for a burnt-offering, and a bull and a ram for a fellowship-offering. They are to sacrifice them to the Lord with the grain-offering mixed with oil. They must do this because the Lord will appear to them today.
Narrator	They brought to the front of the Tent everything that Moses had commanded, and the whole community assembled there to worship the Lord. [Moses said:]
Moses (to audience)	The Lord has commanded you to do all this, so that the dazzling light of his presence can appear to you.
Narrator	Then he said to Aaron:
Moses	Go to the altar and offer the sin-offering and the burnt-offering to take away your sins and the sins of the people. Present this offering to take away the sins of the people, just as the Lord commanded.
Narrator	Aaron went to the altar and killed the young bull which was for his own sin-offering. His sons brought him the blood, and he dipped

his finger in it, put some of it on the projections at the corners of the altar, and poured out the rest of it at the base of the altar.

When Aaron had finished all the sacrifices, he raised his hands over the people and blessed them, and then stepped down. Moses and Aaron went into the Tent of the Lord's presence, and when they came out, they blessed the people, and the dazzling light of the Lord's presence appeared to all the people. Suddenly the Lord sent a fire, and it consumed the burnt-offering and the fat parts on the altar. When the people saw it, they all shouted and bowed down with their faces to the ground.

Cast	[This is] the word of the Lord.
All	**Thanks be to God.**

Cast: **Narrator, Moses.**

Laws of holiness and justice
From Leviticus 19.1–37

Reader 1	The Lord told Moses to say to the community of Israel:
Readers 1 and **2**	Be holy, because I, the Lord your God, am holy.
Reader 2	Each of you must respect his mother and his father, and must keep the Sabbath, as I have commanded.
Readers 1 and **2**	I am the Lord your God.
Reader 3	Do not abandon me and worship idols; do not make gods of metal and worship them.
Readers 1 and **2**	I am the Lord your God.
Reader 1	When you harvest your fields, do not cut the corn at the edges of the fields, and do not go back to cut the ears of corn that were left. Do not go back through your vineyard to gather the grapes that were missed or to pick up the grapes that have fallen; leave them for poor people and foreigners.
Readers 1 and **2**	I am the Lord your God.
Reader 2	Do not steal or cheat or lie. Do not make a promise in my name if you do not intend to keep it; that brings disgrace on my name.
Readers 1 and **2**	I am the Lord your God.
Reader 3	Do not take advantage of anyone or rob him. Do not hold back the wages of someone you have hired, not even for one night. Do not curse a deaf man or put something in front of a blind man so as to make him stumble over it.
Readers 1 and **2**	Fear me; I am the Lord your God.
Reader 1	Be honest and just when you make decisions in legal cases; do not show favouritism to the poor or fear the rich. Do not spread lies about anyone, and when someone is on trial for his life, speak out if your testimony can help him.

Readers 1 and **2**	I am the Lord.
Reader 2	Do not bear a grudge against anyone, but settle your differences with him, so that you will not commit a sin because of him. Do not take revenge on anyone or continue to hate him, but love your neighbour as you love yourself.
Readers 1 and **2**	I am the Lord.
Reader 3	Do not go for advice to people who consult the spirits of the dead. If you do, you will be ritually unclean.
Readers 1 and **2**	I am the Lord your God.
Reader 2	Show respect for old people and honour them.
Readers 1 and **2**	Reverently obey me; I am the Lord.
Reader 3	Do not ill-treat foreigners who are living in your land. Treat them as you would a fellow-Israelite, and love them as you love yourselves. Remember that you were once foreigners in the land of Egypt.
Readers 1 and **2**	I am the Lord your God.
Reader 1	Do not cheat anyone by using false measures of length, weight, or quantity. Use honest scales, honest weights, and honest measures.
Readers 1 and **2**	I am the Lord your God, and I brought you out of Egypt. Obey all my laws and commands. I am the Lord.
Cast	[This is] the word of the Lord.
All	**Thanks be to God.**

Cast: **Reader 1, Reader 2, Reader 3.**

Laws about the harvest
From Leviticus 23.15–22; Deuteronomy 14.22–29, 16.9–12

Leviticus	Count seven full weeks from the day after the Sabbath on which you bring your sheaf of corn to present to the Lord. On the fiftieth day, the day after the seventh Sabbath, present to the Lord another new offering of corn. Each family is to bring two loaves of bread and present them to the Lord as a special gift. Each loaf shall be made of two kilogrammes of flour baked with yeast and shall be presented to the Lord as an offering of the first corn to be harvested . . . On that day do none of your daily work, but gather for worship. Your descendants are to observe this regulation for all time to come, no matter where they live.
Deuteronomy	Set aside a tithe—a tenth of all that your fields produce each year. Then go to the one place where the Lord your God has chosen to be worshipped; and there in his presence eat the tithes of your corn, wine, and olive-oil, and the first-born of your cattle and sheep. Do this so that you may learn to honour the Lord your God always . . . Do not neglect the Levites who live in your towns; they have no property of their own. At the end of every third year bring the tithe of all your crops and store it in your towns. This

food is for the Levites, since they own no property, and for the foreigners, orphans, and widows who live in your towns. They are to come and get all they need. Do this, and the Lord your God will bless you in everything you do.

Leviticus   When you harvest your fields, do not cut the corn at the edges of the fields, and do not go back to cut the ears of corn that were left; leave them for poor people and foreigners. The Lord is your God.

Deuteronomy   Count seven weeks from the time that you begin to harvest the corn, and then celebrate the Harvest Festival, to honour the Lord your God, by bringing him a freewill offering in proportion to the blessing he has given you. Be joyful in the Lord's presence, together with your children, your servants, and the Levites, foreigners, orphans, and widows who live in your towns. Do this at the one place of worship. Be sure that you obey these commands; do not forget that you were slaves in Egypt.

Cast	[This is] the word of the Lord.
All	**Thanks be to God.**

Cast: **Leviticus, Deuteronomy.**

NUMBERS

In the wilderness
From Numbers 10.33—11.32

Narrator	When the people left Sinai, the holy mountain, they travelled for three days. The Lord's Covenant Box always went ahead of them to find a place for them to camp. As they moved on from each camp, the cloud of the Lord was over them by day. Whenever the Covenant Box started out, Moses would say:
Moses	Arise, Lord; scatter your enemies and put to flight those who hate you!
Narrator	And whenever it stopped, he would say:
Moses	Return, Lord, to the thousands of families of Israel.
Narrator	The people began to complain to the Lord about their troubles. [When the Lord heard them, he was angry and sent fire on the people. It burnt among them and destroyed one end of the camp. The people cried out to Moses for help; he prayed to the Lord, and the fire died down. So the place was named Taberah, because there the fire of the Lord burnt among them.]
	There were some foreigners travelling with the Israelites. They had a strong craving for meat, and even the Israelites themselves began to complain:
Israelite 1	If only we could have some meat!
Israelite 2	In Egypt we used to eat all the fish we wanted, and it cost us nothing.
Israelite 1	Remember the cucumbers, the water-melons, the leeks, the onions, and the garlic we had?
Israelite 2	But now our strength is gone.
Israelite 1	There is nothing at all to eat—nothing but this manna day after day!
Narrator	Manna was like small seeds, whitish yellow in colour. It fell on the camp at night along with the dew. The next morning the people would go round and gather it, grind it or pound it into flour, and then boil it and make it into flat cakes. It tasted like bread baked with olive-oil. (PAUSE)
	Moses heard all the people complaining as they stood about in groups at the entrances of their tents. He was distressed because the Lord was angry with them, and he said to the Lord:
Moses (praying)	Why have you treated me so badly? Why are you displeased with me? Why have you given me the responsibility for all these people? I didn't create them or bring them to birth! Why should you ask me to act like a nurse and carry them in my arms like babies all the way to the land you promised to their ancestors? Where could I get enough meat for all these people? They keep

whining and asking for meat. I can't be responsible for all these people by myself; it's too much for me! If you are going to treat me like this, take pity on me and kill me, so that I won't have to endure your cruelty any longer.

[Narrator   The Lord said to Moses:]

The Lord   Assemble seventy respected men who are recognized as leaders of the people, bring them to me at the Tent of my presence, and tell them to stand there beside you. I will come down and speak with you there, and I will take some of the spirit I have given you and give it to them. Then they can help you to bear the responsibility for these people, and you will not have to bear it alone. Now tell the people, 'Purify yourselves for tomorrow; you will have meat to eat. The Lord has heard you whining and saying that you wished you had some meat and that you were better off in Egypt. Now the Lord will give you meat, and you will have to eat it.'

Moses   Here I am leading 600,000 people, and you say that you will give them meat? Could enough cattle and sheep be killed to satisfy them? Are all the fish in the sea enough for them?

The Lord   Is there a limit to my power? You will soon see whether what I have said will happen or not!

Narrator   So Moses went out and told the people what the Lord had said. He assembled seventy of the leaders and placed them round the Tent. Then the Lord came down in the cloud and spoke to him. He took some of the spirit he had given to Moses and gave it to the seventy leaders. When the spirit came on them, they began to shout like prophets, but not for long.

Joshua son of Nun, who had been Moses' helper since he was a young man, spoke up:

Joshua
(to Moses)   Stop them, sir!

Moses
(to Joshua)   Are you concerned about my interests? I wish that the Lord would give his spirit to all his people and make all of them shout like prophets!

Narrator   Then Moses and the seventy leaders of Israel went back to camp.

Suddenly the Lord sent a wind that brought quails from the sea, flying less than a metre above the ground. They settled on the camp and all round it for many kilometres in every direction. So all that day, all night, and all the next day, the people worked catching quails.

Cast   [This is] the word of the Lord.
All   **Thanks be to God.**

Cast: **Narrator, Moses,** Israelite 1, Israelite 2 (can be the same as Israelite 1), **The Lord, Joshua.**

Miriam is punished
Numbers 12.1–16

Narrator	Moses had married a Cushite woman, and Miriam and Aaron criticized him for it:
Miriam	Has the Lord spoken only through Moses?
Aaron	Hasn't he also spoken through us?
Narrator	The Lord heard what they said. Moses was a humble man, more humble than anyone else on earth.
	Suddenly the Lord spoke to Moses, Aaron, and Miriam:
The Lord	I want the three of you to come out to the Tent of my presence.
Narrator	They went, and the Lord came down in a pillar of cloud, stood at the entrance of the Tent, and called out:
The Lord (calling)	Aaron! (PAUSE) Miriam!
Narrator	The two of them stepped forward [and the Lord said:]
The Lord	Now hear what I have to say! When there are prophets among you, I reveal myself to them in visions and speak to them in dreams. It is different when I speak with my servant Moses; I have put him in charge of all my people Israel. So I speak to him face to face, clearly and not in riddles; he has even seen my form! How dare you speak against my servant Moses?
Narrator	The Lord was angry with them; and so as he departed and the cloud left the Tent, Miriam's skin was suddenly covered with a dreaded disease and turned as white as snow. When Aaron looked at her and saw that she was covered with the disease, he said to Moses:
Aaron	Please, sir, do not make us suffer this punishment for our foolish sin. Don't let her become like something born dead with half its flesh eaten away.
Narrator	So Moses cried out to the Lord:
Moses	O God, heal her!
[Narrator	The Lord answered:]
The Lord	If her father had spat in her face, she would have to bear her disgrace for seven days. So let her be shut out of the camp for a week, and after that she can be brought back in.
Narrator	Miriam was shut out of the camp for seven days, and the people did not move on until she was brought back in.
	Then they left Hazeroth and set up camp in the wilderness of Paran.
Cast	[This is] the word of the Lord.
All	**Thanks be to God.**

Cast: **Narrator, Miriam, Aaron, The Lord, Moses.**

The spies
From Numbers 13.1–33

Narrator	The Lord spoke to Moses:
The Lord	Choose one of the leaders from each of the twelve tribes and send them as spies to explore the land of Canaan, which I am giving to the Israelites.
Narrator	Moses obeyed, and from the wilderness of Paran he sent out leaders.
	[When Moses sent them out, he said to them:]
Moses	Go north from here into the southern part of the land of Canaan and then on into the hill-country. Find out what kind of country it is, how many people live there, and how strong they are. Find out whether the land is good or bad and whether the people live in open towns or in fortified cities. Find out whether the soil is fertile and whether the land is wooded. And be sure to bring back some of the fruit that grows there.
Commentator	It was the season when grapes were beginning to ripen.
Narrator	So the men went north and explored the land from the wilderness of Zin in the south all the way to Rehob, near Hamath Pass in the north. They went first into the southern part of the land and came to Hebron, where the clans of Ahiman, Sheshai, and Talmai, the descendants of a race of giants called the Anakim, lived.
Commentator	Hebron was founded seven years before Zoan in Egypt.
Narrator	They came to the Valley of Eshcol, and there they cut off a branch which had one bunch of grapes on it so heavy that it took two men to carry it on a pole between them. They also brought back some pomegranates and figs.
Commentator	That place was named the Valley of Eshcol because of the bunch of grapes the Israelites cut off there.
Narrator	After exploring the land for forty days, the spies returned to Moses, Aaron, and the whole community of Israel at Kadesh in the wilderness of Paran. They reported what they had seen and showed them the fruit they had brought:
Spy 1	We explored the land and found it to be rich and fertile.
Spy 2	Here is some of its fruit.
Spy 3	But the people who live there are powerful—
Spy 1	And their cities are very large and well fortified.
Spy 2	Even worse, we saw the descendants of the giants there.
Spy 3	Amalekites live in the southern part of the land.
Spy 1	Hittites, Jebusites, and Amorites live in the hill-country.
Spy 2	And Canaanites live by the Mediterranean Sea and along the River Jordan.

Narrator	Caleb silenced the people who were complaining against Moses:
Caleb	We should attack now and take the land; we are strong enough to conquer it.
Narrator	But the men who had gone with Caleb said:
Spy 1	No, we are not strong enough to attack them.
Spy 2	The people there are more powerful than we are.
Narrator	So they spread a false report among the Israelites about the land they had explored:
Spy 2	That land doesn't even produce enough to feed the people who live there.
Spy 1	Everyone we saw was very tall.
Spy 3	And we even saw giants there, the descendants of Anak.
Spy 2	We felt as small as grasshoppers.
Spy 1	And that is how we must have looked to *them*.
Cast	[This is] the word of the Lord.
All	**Thanks be to God.**

Cast: **Narrator, The Lord, Moses, Commentator, Spy 1, Spy 2, Spy 3, Caleb.**

The people complain
Numbers 14.1–10

Narrator	[All night long] the people cried out in distress and complained against Moses and Aaron:
Person 1	It would have been better to die in Egypt—
Person 2	Or even here in the wilderness!
Person 3	Why is the Lord taking us into that land?
Person 1	We will be killed in battle—
Person 2	And our wives and children will be captured.
Person 3	Wouldn't it be better to go back to Egypt? (PAUSE)
[Narrator	So they said to one another:]
Person 3	Let's choose a leader and go back to Egypt!
Narrator	Then Moses and Aaron bowed to the ground in front of all the people. And Joshua son of Nun and Caleb son of Jephunneh, two of the spies, tore their clothes in sorrow and said to the people:
Joshua	The land we explored is an excellent land.
Caleb	If the Lord is pleased with us, he will take us there and give us that rich and fertile land.
Joshua	Do not rebel against the Lord and don't be afraid of the people who live there. We will conquer them easily.

112

Caleb	The Lord is with us and has defeated the gods who protected them; so don't be afraid.
Narrator	The whole community was threatening to stone them to death, but suddenly the people saw the dazzling light of the Lord's presence appear over the tent.
Cast All	[This is] the word of the Lord. **Thanks be to God.**

Cast: **Narrator, Person 1, Person 2, Person 3, Joshua, Caleb.**

Moses prays for the people
Numbers 14.11–25

Narrator	The Lord spoke to Moses:
The Lord	How much longer will these people reject me? How much longer will they refuse to trust in me, even though I have performed so many miracles among them? I will send an epidemic and destroy them, but I will make you the father of a nation that is larger and more powerful than they are!
Narrator	But Moses said to the Lord:
Moses	You brought these people out of Egypt by your power. When the Egyptians hear what you have done to your people, they will tell it to the people who live in this land. These people have already heard that you, Lord, are with us, that you are plainly seen when your cloud stops over us, and that you go before us in a pillar of cloud by day and a pillar of fire by night. Now if you kill all your people, the nations who have heard of your fame will say that you killed your people in the wilderness because you were not able to bring them into the land you promised to give them. So now Lord, I pray, show us your power and do what you promised when you said, 'I, the Lord, am not easily angered, and I show great love and faithfulness and forgive sin and rebellion. Yet I will not fail to punish children and grandchildren to the third and fourth generation for the sins of their parents.' And now, Lord, according to the greatness of your unchanging love, forgive, I pray, the sin of these people, just as you have forgiven them ever since they left Egypt.
The Lord	I will forgive them, as you have asked. But I promise that as surely as I live and as surely as my presence fills the earth, none of these people will live to enter that land. They have seen the dazzling light of my presence and the miracles that I performed in Egypt and in the wilderness, but they have tried my patience over and over again and have refused to obey me. They will never enter the land which I promised to their ancestors. None of those who have rejected me will ever enter it. But because my servant Caleb has a different attitude and has remained loyal to me, I will bring him into the land which he explored, and his descendants will possess

$\longrightarrow$

the land in whose valleys the Amalekites and the Canaanites now live. Turn back tomorrow and go into the wilderness in the direction of the Gulf of Aqaba.

Cast	[This is] the word of the Lord.
All	**Thanks be to God.**

Cast: **Narrator, The Lord, Moses.**

The Lord punishes the people for complaining
Numbers 14.26–38

Narrator The Lord spoke to Moses and Aaron:

The Lord How much longer are these wicked people going to complain against me? I have heard enough of these complaints! Now give them this answer: 'I swear that as surely as I live, I will do to you just what you have asked. I, the Lord, have spoken. You will die and your corpses will be scattered across this wilderness. Because you have complained against me, none of you over twenty years of age will enter that land. I promised to let you live there, but not one of you will, except Caleb and Joshua. You said that your children would be captured, but I will bring them into the land that you rejected, and it will be their home. You will die here in this wilderness. Your children will wander in the wilderness for forty years, suffering for your unfaithfulness, until the last one of you dies. You will suffer the consequences of your sin for forty years, one year for each of the forty days you spent exploring the land. You will know what it means to have me against you! I swear that I will do this to you wicked people who have gathered together against me. Here in the wilderness every one of you will die. I, the Lord, have spoken!'

Narrator The men Moses had sent to explore the land brought back a false report which caused the people to complain against the Lord. And so the Lord struck them with a disease, and they died. Of the twelve spies only Joshua and Caleb survived.

Cast	[This is] the word of the Lord.
All	**Thanks be to God.**

Cast: **Narrator, The Lord.**

The first attempt to invade the land
Numbers 14.39–45

Narrator When Moses told the Israelites that the Lord had said they were to die in the wilderness, they mourned bitterly. Early the next morning they started out to invade the hill-country, saying:

Israelite 1 Now we are ready to go to the place which the Lord told us about.

Israelite 2 We admit that we have sinned.

Narrator But Moses said:

Moses	Then why are you disobeying the Lord now? You will not succeed! Don't go. The Lord is not with you, and your enemies will defeat you. When you face the Amalekites and the Canaanites, you will die in battle; the Lord will not be with you, because you have refused to follow him.
Narrator	Yet they still dared to go up into the hill-country, even though neither the Lord's Covenant Box nor Moses left the camp. Then the Amalekites and the Canaanites who lived there attacked and defeated them, and pursued them as far as Hormah.
Cast	[This is] the word of the Lord.
All	**Thanks be to God.**

Cast: **Narrator, Israelite 1, Israelite 2** (can be the same as Israelite 1), **Moses.**

The rebellion of Korah, Dathan, and Abiram
Numbers 16.1–22

Narrator	Korah son of Izhar, from the Levite clan of Kohath. rebelled against the leadership of Moses. He was joined by three members of the tribe of Reuben—Dathan and Abiram, the sons of Eliab, and On son of Peleth—and by 250 other Israelites, well-known leaders chosen by the community. They assembled before Moses and Aaron and said to them:
Rebel 1	You have gone too far!
Rebel 2	All the members of the community belong to the Lord, and the Lord is with all of us.
Rebel 3	Why, then, Moses, do you set yourself above the Lord's community?
Narrator	When Moses heard this, he threw himself on the ground and prayed. Then he said to Korah and his followers:
Moses	Tomorrow morning the Lord will show us who belongs to him; he will let the one who belongs to him, that is, the one he has chosen, approach him at the altar. Tomorrow morning you and your followers take firepans, put live coals and incense on them, and take them to the altar. Then we will see which of us the Lord has chosen. You Levites are the ones who have gone too far!
Narrator	Moses continued to speak to Korah:
Moses	Listen, you Levites! Do you consider it a small matter that the God of Israel has set you apart from the rest of the community, so that you can approach him, perform your service in the Lord's Tent, and minister to the community and serve them? He has let you and all the other Levites have this honour—and now you are trying to get the priesthood too! When you complain against Aaron, it is really against the Lord that you and your followers are rebelling.
Narrator	Then Moses sent for Dathan and Abiram, but they said:

Rebel 1	We will not come! Isn't it enough that you have brought us out of the fertile land of Egypt to kill us here in the wilderness?
Rebel 3	Do you also have to lord it over us?
Rebel 1	You certainly have not brought us into a fertile land or given us fields and vineyards as our possession, and now you are trying to deceive us.
Rebels 1 and **3**	We will not come!
Narrator	Moses was angry and said to the Lord:
Moses	Do not accept any offerings these men bring. I have not wronged any of them; I have not even taken one of their donkeys.
Narrator	Moses said to Korah:
Moses	Tomorrow you and your 250 followers must come to the Tent of the Lord's presence; Aaron will also be there. Each of you will take his firepan, put incense on it, and then present it at the altar.
Narrator	So every man took his firepan, put live coals and incense on it, and stood at the entrance of the Tent with Moses and Aaron. Then Korah gathered the whole community, and they stood facing Moses and Aaron at the entrance of the Tent. Suddenly the dazzling light of the Lord's presence appeared to the whole community, and the Lord said to Moses and Aaron:
The Lord	Stand back from these people, and I will destroy them immediately.
Narrator	But Moses and Aaron bowed down with their faces to the ground and said:
Moses	O, God, you are the source of all life. When one man sins, do you get angry with the whole community?
Cast All	[This is] the word of the Lord. **Thanks be to God.**

Cast: **Narrator, Rebel 1, Rebel 2, Rebel 3, Moses, The Lord.**

The Lord's judgement
Numbers 16.23–35; 41–48

Narrator	The Lord spoke to Moses:
The Lord	Say to the assembly, 'Move away from the tents of Korah, Dathan, and Abiram.'
Narrator	Moses got up and went to Dathan and Abiram, and the elders of Israel followed him. He warned the assembly:
Moses	Move back from the tents of these wicked men! Do not touch anything belonging to them, or you will be swept away because of all their sins.

Narrator	So they moved away from the tents of Korah, Dathan and Abiram. Dathan and Abiram had come out and were standing with their wives, children and little ones at the entrances to their tents. [Then Moses said:]
Moses	This is how you will know that the Lord has sent me to do all these things and that it was not my idea: If these men die a natural death and experience only what usually happens to men, then the Lord has not sent me. But if the Lord brings about something totally new, and the earth opens its mouth and swallows them, with everything that belongs to them, and they go down alive into the grave, then you will know that these men have treated the Lord with contempt.
Narrator	As soon as he finished saying all this, the ground under them split apart and the earth opened its mouth and swallowed them, with their households and all Korah's men and all their possessions. They went down alive into the grave, with everything they owned; the earth closed over them, and they perished and were gone from the community. At their cries, all the Israelites around them fled, shouting:
Israelite	The earth is going to swallow us too!
Narrator	And fire came out from the Lord and consumed the 250 men who were offering the incense. (PAUSE)
	The next day the whole Israelite community grumbled against Moses and Aaron:
Israelite	You have killed the Lord's people.
Narrator	But when the assembly gathered in opposition to Moses and Aaron and turned towards the Tent of Meeting, suddenly the cloud covered it and the glory of the Lord appeared. Then Moses and Aaron went to the front of the Tent of Meeting, and the Lord said to Moses:
The Lord	Get away from this assembly so that I can put an end to them at once.
Narrator	And they fell face down. Then Moses said to Aaron:
Moses	Take your censer and put incense in it, along with fire from the altar, and hurry to the assembly to make atonement for them. Wrath has come out from the Lord; the plague has started.
Narrator	So Aaron did as Moses said, and ran into the midst of the assembly. The plague had already started among the people, but Aaron offered the incense and made atonement for them. He stood between the living and the dead, and the plague stopped.
Cast	[This is] the word of the Lord.
All	**Thanks be to God.**

Cast: **Narrator, The Lord, Moses, Israelite.**

Aaron's stick
Numbers 17.1—18.7

Narrator	The Lord spoke to Moses:
The Lord	Tell the people of Israel to give you twelve sticks, one from the leader of each tribe. Write each man's name on his stick and then write Aaron's name on the stick representing Levi. There will be one stick for each tribal leader. Take them to the Tent of my presence and put them in front of the Covenant Box, where I meet you. Then the stick of the man I have chosen will sprout. In this way I will put a stop to the constant complaining of these Israelites against you.
Narrator	So Moses spoke to the Israelites, and each of their leaders gave him a stick, one for each tribe, twelve in all, and Aaron's stick was put with them. Moses then put all the sticks in the Tent in front of the Lord's Covenant Box.
	The next day, when Moses went into the Tent, he saw that Aaron's stick, representing the tribe of Levi, had sprouted. It had budded, blossomed, and produced ripe almonds! Moses took all the sticks and showed them to the Israelites. They saw what had happened, and each leader took his own stick back. The Lord said to Moses:
The Lord	Put Aaron's stick back in front of the Covenant Box. It is to be kept as a warning to the rebel Israelites that they will die unless their complaining stops.
Narrator	Moses did as the Lord commanded. The people of Israel said to Moses:
Israelite 1	Then that's the end of us!
Israelite 2	If anyone who even comes near the Tent must die, then we are all as good as dead!
Narrator	The Lord said to Aaron:
The Lord	You, your sons, and the Levites must suffer the consequences of any guilt connected with serving in the Tent of my presence; but only you and your sons will suffer the consequences of service in the priesthood. Bring in your relatives, the tribe of Levi, to work with you and help you while you and your sons are serving at the Tent. They are to fulfil their duties to you and their responsibilities for the Tent, but they must not have any contact with sacred objects in the Holy Place or with the altar. If they do, both they and you will be put to death. They are to work with you and fulfil their responsibilities for all the service in the Tent, but no unqualified person may work with you. You and your sons alone must fulfil the responsibilities for the Holy Place and the altar, so that my anger will not again break out against the people of Israel. I am the one who has chosen your relatives the Levites from among the Israelites as a gift to you. They are dedicated to me, so that they can carry out their duties in the Tent. But you and

your sons alone shall fulfil all the responsibilities of the priesthood that concern the altar and what is in the Most Holy Place. These things are your responsibility, because I have given you the gift of the priesthood. Any unqualified person who comes near the sacred objects shall be put to death.

Cast	[This is] the word of the Lord.
All	**Thanks be to God.**

Cast: **Narrator, The Lord, Israelite 1, Israelite 2** (can be the same as Israelite 1).

The Lord provides water
Numbers 20.1–13

Narrator	In the first month the whole community of Israel came to the wilderness of Zin and camped at Kadesh. There Miriam died and was buried.
	There was no water where they camped, so the people gathered round Moses and Aaron and complained:
Israelite 1	It would have been better if we had died in front of the Lord's Tent along with our fellow-Israelites.
Israelite 2	Why have you brought us out into this wilderness? Just so that we can die here with our animals?
Israelite 3	Why did you bring us out of Egypt into this miserable place where nothing will grow?
Israelite 1	There's no corn, no figs, no grapes, no pomegranates—
Israelite 2	There is not even any water to drink!
Narrator	Moses and Aaron moved away from the people and stood at the entrance of the Tent. They bowed down with their faces to the ground, and the dazzling light of the Lord's presence appeared to them.
	[The Lord said to Moses:]
The Lord	Take the stick that is in front of the Covenant Box, and then you and Aaron assemble the whole community. There in front of them all speak to that rock over there, and water will gush out of it. In this way you will bring water out of the rock for the people, for them and their animals to drink.
Narrator	Moses went and got the stick, as the Lord had commanded. He and Aaron assembled the whole community in front of the rock, and Moses said:
Moses (angrily)	Listen, you rebels! Do we have to get water out of this rock for you?
Narrator	Then Moses raised the stick and struck the rock twice with it, and a great stream of water gushed out, and all the people and animals drank. (PAUSE)
	But the Lord reprimanded Moses and Aaron:

119

The Lord	Because you did not have enough faith to acknowledge my holy power before the people of Israel, you will not lead them into the land that I promised to give them.
Narrator	This happened at Meribah, where the people of Israel complained against the Lord and where he showed them that he was holy.
Cast	[This is] the word of the Lord.
All	**Thanks be to God.**

Cast: **Narrator, Israelite 1, Israelite 2, Israelite 3** (can be the same as Israelite 1 OR Israelites 1–3 can be the same)**, The Lord, Moses.**

The king of Edom refuses to let Israel pass
Numbers 20.14–21

Narrator	Moses sent messengers from Kadesh to the king of Edom.
	[They said:]
Israelite 1	This message is from your kinsmen, the tribes of Israel.
Israelite 2	You know the hardships we have suffered, how our ancestors went to Egypt, where we lived many years. The Egyptians ill-treated our ancestors and us, and we cried to the Lord for help. He heard our cry and sent an angel, who led us out of Egypt.
Israelite 1	Now we are at Kadesh, a town at the border of your territory. Please permit us to pass through your land.
Israelite 2	We and our cattle will not leave the road or go into your fields or vineyards, and we will not drink from your wells.
Israelite 1	We will stay on the main road until we are out of your territory.
Narrator	But the Edomites answered:
Edomite 1	We *refuse* to let you pass through our country—
Edomite 2	If you try, we will march out and attack you!
[Narrator	The people of Israel said:]
Israelite 1	We will stay on the main road, and if we or our animals drink any of your water, we will pay for it.
Israelite 2	All we want is to pass through.
[Narrator	The Edomites repeated:]
Edomites 1 & 2	We refuse!
Narrator	And they marched out with a powerful army to attack the people of Israel. Because the Edomites would not let the Israelites pass through their territory, the Israelites turned and went another way.
Cast	[This is] the word of the Lord.
All	**Thanks be to God.**

Cast: **Narrator, Israelite 1, Israelite 2, Edomite 1, Edomite 2.**

The death of Aaron
Numbers 20.22–29

Narrator   The whole community of Israel left Kadesh and arrived at Mount Hor, on the border of Edom. There the Lord said to Moses and Aaron:

The Lord   Aaron is not going to enter the land which I promised to give to Israel; he is going to die, because the two of you rebelled against my command at Meribah. Take Aaron and his son Eleazar up Mount Hor, and there remove Aaron's priestly robes and put them on Eleazar. Aaron is going to die there.

Narrator   Moses did what the Lord had commanded. They went up Mount Hor in the sight of the whole community, and Moses removed Aaron's priestly robes and put them on Eleazar. There on the top of the mountain Aaron died, and Moses and Eleazar came back down. The whole community learnt that Aaron had died, and they all mourned for him for thirty days.

Cast   [This is] the word of the Lord.
All   **Thanks be to God.**

Cast: **Narrator, The Lord.**

The snake made of bronze
Numbers 21.4–9

Narrator   The Israelites left Mount Hor by the road that leads to the Gulf of Aqaba, in order to go round the territory of Edom. But on the way the people lost their patience and spoke against God and Moses. They complained:

Israelite 1   Why did you bring us out of Egypt to die in this desert, where there is no food or water?

Israelite 2   We can't stand any more of this miserable food!

Narrator   Then the Lord sent poisonous snakes among the people, and many Israelites were bitten and died. The people came to Moses and said:

Israelite 2   We sinned when we spoke against the Lord and against you.

Israelite 1   Now pray to the Lord to take these snakes away.

Narrator   So Moses prayed for the people. Then the Lord told Moses to make a metal snake and put it on a pole, so that anyone who was bitten could look at it and be healed. So Moses made a bronze snake and put it on a pole. Anyone who had been bitten would look at the bronze snake and be healed.

Cast   [This is] the word of the Lord.
All   **Thanks be to God.**

Cast: **Narrator, Israelite 1, Israelite 2** (can be the same as Israelite 1).

From Mount Hor to the Valley of the Moabites
Numbers 21.10–20

Narrator The Israelites moved on and camped at Oboth. After leaving that place, they camped at the ruins of Abarim in the wilderness east of Moabite territory. Then they camped in the Valley of Zered. From there they moved again and camped on the north side of the River Arnon, in the wilderness which extends into Amorite territory. The Arnon was the border between the Moabites and the Amorites. That is why The Book of the Lord's Battles speaks of:

Reader The town of Waheb in the area of Suphah, and the valleys; the River Arnon, and the slope of the valleys that extend to the town of Ar and towards the border of Moab.

Narrator From there they went on to a place called 'Wells', where the Lord said to Moses:

The Lord Bring the people together, and I will give them water.

Narrator At that time the people of Israel sang this song:

Singer(s) Wells, produce your water;
and we will greet it with a song—
the well dug by princes
and by leaders of the people,
dug with a royal sceptre
and with their sticks.

Narrator They moved from the wilderness to Mattanah, and from there they went on to Nahaliel, and from Nahaliel to Bamoth, and from Bamoth to the valley in the territory of the Moabites, below the top of Mount Pisgah, looking out over the desert.

Cast [This is] the word of the Lord.
All **Thanks be to God.**

Cast: **Narrator, Reader, The Lord, Singer(s).**

Victory over King Sihon and King Og
Numbers 21.21–35

Narrator The people of Israel sent messengers to the Amorite King Sihon [to say:]

Israelite 1 Let us pass through your land.

Israelite 2 We and our cattle will not leave the road and go into your fields or vineyards.

Israelite 1 And we will not drink water from your wells.

Israelite 2 We will stay on the main road until we are out of your territory.

Narrator But Sihon would not permit the people of Israel to pass through his territory. He gathered his army and went out to Jahaz in the wilderness and attacked the Israelites. But the Israelites killed many of the enemy in battle and occupied their land from the River Arnon north to the Jabbok, that is, to the Ammonites, because the Ammonite border was strongly defended. So the people of Israel captured all the Amorite cities, including Heshbon and all the surrounding towns, and settled in them. Heshbon was the capital city of the Amorite king Sihon, who had fought against the former king of Moab and had captured all his land as far as the River Arnon. That is why the poets sing:

Singers 1 and 2   Come to Heshbon, to King Sihon's city!
We want to see it rebuilt and restored.

Singer 1   Once from this city of Heshbon
Sihon's army went forth like a fire.

Singer 2   It destroyed the city of Ar in Moab
and devoured the hills of the upper Arnon.

Singer 1   How terrible for you, people of Moab!

Singer 2   You worshippers of Chemosh are brought to ruin!

Singer 1   Your god let the men become refugees,
and the women became captives of the Amorite king.

Singer 2   But now their descendants are destroyed,
[all the way from Heshbon to Dibon,
From Nashim to Nophah, near Medeba.]

Narrator   So the people of Israel settled in the territory of the Amorites, and Moses sent men to find the best way to attack the city of Jazer. The Israelites captured it and its surrounding towns and drove out the Amorites living there.

Then the Israelites turned and took the road to Bashan, and King Og of Bashan marched out with his army to attack them at Edrei. The Lord said to Moses:

The Lord   Do not be afraid of him. I will give you victory over him, all his people, and his land. Do to him what you did to Sihon, the Amorite king who ruled at Heshbon.

Narrator   So the Israelites killed Og, his sons, and all his people, leaving no survivors, and then they occupied his land.

Cast   [This is] the word of the Lord.
All   **Thanks be to God.**

Cast: **Narrator, Israelite 1, Israelite 2, Singer 1, Singer 2** (can be the same as Singer 1), **The Lord.**

The king of Moab sends for Balaam
Numbers 22.1–21

Narrator   The Israelites moved on and set up camp in the plains of Moab east of the Jordan and opposite Jericho. When the king of Moab, Balak son of Zippor, heard what the Israelites had done to the

→

	Amorites and how many Israelites there were, he and all his people became terrified. The Moabites said to the leaders of the Midianites:
Moabite	This horde will soon destroy everything round us, like a bull eating the grass in a pasture.
Narrator	So King Balak sent messengers to summon Balaam son of Beor, who was at Pethor near the River Euphrates in the land of Amaw. They brought him this message from Balak:
Balak	I want you to know that a whole nation has come from Egypt; its people are spreading out everywhere and threatening to take over our land. They outnumber us, so please come and put a curse on them for me. Then perhaps we will be able to defeat them and drive them out of the land. I know that when you pronounce a blessing, people are blessed, and when you pronounce a curse, they are placed under a curse.
Narrator	So the Moabite and Midianite leaders took with them the payment for the curse, went to Balaam, and gave him Balak's message. Balaam said to them:
Balaam	Spend the night here, and tomorrow I will report to you whatever the Lord tells me.
Narrator	So the Moabite leaders stayed with Balaam. (PAUSE)
	God came to Balaam and asked:
God	Who are these men that are staying with you?
Balaam	King Balak of Moab has sent them to tell me that a people who came from Egypt has spread out over the whole land. He wants me to curse them for him, so that he can fight them and drive them out.
God	Do not go with these men, and do not put a curse on the people of Israel, because they have my blessing.
Narrator	The next morning Balaam went to Balak's messengers [and said:]
Balaam	Go back home; the Lord has refused to let me go with you.
Narrator	So they returned to Balak and told him that Balaam had refused to come with them. Then Balak sent a larger number of leaders, who were more important than the first. They went to Balaam and gave him this message from Balak:
Balak	Please don't let anything prevent you from coming to me! I will reward you richly and do anything you say. Please come and curse these people for me.
[Narrator	But Balaam answered:]
Balaam	Even if Balak gave me all the silver and gold in his palace, I could not disobey the command of the Lord my God in even the smallest matter. But please stay the night, as the others did, so that I may learn whether or not the Lord has something else to tell me.
Narrator	That night God came to Balaam and said:

124

God	If these men have come to ask you to go with them, get ready to go, but do only what I tell you.
Narrator	So the next morning Balaam saddled his donkey and went with the Moabite leaders.
Cast	[This is] the word of the Lord.
All	**Thanks be to God.**

Cast: **Narrator, Moabite, Balak, Balaam, God.**

Balaam and his donkey
Numbers 22.22–35

Narrator	God was angry that Balaam was going, and as Balaam was riding along on his donkey, accompanied by his two servants, the angel of the Lord stood in the road to bar his way. When the donkey saw the angel standing there holding a sword, it left the road and turned into the fields. Balaam beat the donkey and brought it back on to the road. Then the angel stood where the road narrowed between two vineyards and had a stone wall on each side. When the donkey saw the angel, it moved over against the wall and crushed Balaam's foot against it. Again Balaam beat the donkey. Once more the angel moved ahead; he stood in a narrow place where there was no room at all to pass on either side. This time, when the donkey saw the angel, it lay down. Balaam lost his temper and began to beat the donkey with his stick. Then the Lord gave the donkey the power of speech, and it said to Balaam:
Donkey	What have I done to you? Why have you beaten me these three times?
[Narrator	Balaam answered:]
Balaam	Because you have made a fool of me! If I had a sword, I would kill you.
Donkey	Am I not the same donkey on which you have ridden all your life? Have I ever treated you like this before?
Balaam	No.
Narrator	Then the Lord let Balaam see the angel standing there with his sword; and Balaam threw himself face downwards on the ground. [The angel demanded:]
Angel	Why have you beaten your donkey three times like this? I have come to bar your way, because you should not be making this journey. But your donkey saw me and turned aside three times. If it hadn't, I would have killed you and spared the donkey.
Balaam	I have sinned. I did not know that you were standing in the road to oppose me; but now if you think it is wrong for me to go on, I will return home.

Angel	Go on with these men, but say only what I tell you to say.
Narrator	So Balaam went on with them.
Cast	[This is] the word of the Lord.
All	**Thanks be to God.**

Cast: **Narrator, Donkey, Balaam, Angel.**

Balaam and Balak
From Numbers 22.36–38, 23.28—24.12

Narrator	When Balak heard that Balaam was coming, he went to meet him at Ar, a city on the River Arnon at the border of Moab. Balak said to him:
Balak	Why didn't you come when I sent for you the first time? Did you think I wasn't able to reward you enough?
Narrator	Balaam answered:
Balaam	I came, didn't I? But now, what power have I got? I can say only what God tells me to say.
Narrator	Balak took Balaam to the top of Mount Peor overlooking the desert. By now Balaam knew that the Lord wanted him to bless the people of Israel, so he did not go to look for omens, as he had done before. He turned towards the desert and saw the people of Israel camped tribe by tribe. The spirit of God took control of him, and he uttered this prophecy:
Herald	The message of Balaam son of Beor, the words of the man who can see clearly, who can hear what God is saying.
Balaam	With staring eyes I see in a trance, a vision from Almighty God. The tents of Israel are beautiful, like long rows of palms or gardens beside a river, like aloes planted by the Lord or cedars beside the water. They will have abundant rainfall and plant their seed in well-watered fields. Their king shall be greater than Agag, and his rule shall be extended far and wide. God brought them out of Egypt; he fights for them like a wild ox. They devour their enemies, crush their bones, smash their arrows. The nation is like a mighty lion; when it is sleeping, no one dares wake it. Whoever blesses Israel will be blessed, and whoever curses Israel will be cursed.
Narrator	Balak clenched his fists in anger and said to Balaam:
Balak	I called you to *curse* my enemies, but three times now you have *blessed* them instead. Now go off home! I promised to reward you, but the Lord has kept you from getting the reward.

126

Balaam	I *told* the messengers you sent to me that even if you gave me all the silver and gold in your palace, I could not disobey the command of the Lord by doing anything of myself. I will say only what the Lord tells me to say.
Cast	[This is] the word of the Lord.
All	**Thanks be to God.**

Cast: **Narrator, Balak, Balaam, Herald** (can be the same as Balaam).

The daughters of Zelophehad
Numbers 27.1–11

Narrator	The daughters of Zelophehad went and stood before Moses, Eleazar the priest, the leaders, and the whole community at the entrance of the Tent of the Lord's presence [and said:]
Daughter 1	Our father died in the wilderness without leaving any sons.
Daughter 2	He was not among the followers of Korah, who rebelled against the Lord; he died because of his own sin.
Daughter 1	Just because he had no sons, why should our father's name disappear from Israel?
Daughter 2	Give us property among our father's relatives.
Narrator	Moses presented their case to the Lord, and the Lord said to him:
The Lord	What the daughters of Zelophehad request is right; give them property among their father's relatives. Let his inheritance pass on to them. Tell the people of Israel that whenever a man dies without leaving a son, his daughter is to inherit his property. If he has no daughter, his brothers are to inherit it. If he has no brothers, his father's brothers are to inherit it. If he has no brothers or uncles, then his nearest relative is to inherit it and hold it as his own property. The people of Israel are to observe this as a legal requirement, just as I, the Lord, have commanded you.
Cast	[This is] the word of the Lord.
All	**Thanks be to God.**

Cast: **Narrator, Daughter 1, Daughter 2, The Lord.**

Joshua is chosen as successor to Moses
Numbers 27.12– 23

Narrator	The Lord spoke to Moses:
The Lord	Go up the Abarim Mountains and look out over the land that I am giving to the Israelites. After you have seen it, you will die, as your brother Aaron did, because both of you rebelled against my command in the wilderness of Zin. When the whole community complained against me at Meribah, you refused to acknowledge my holy power before them.

Narrator	Meribah is the spring at Kadesh in the wilderness of Zin. (PAUSE)
	Moses prayed:
Moses	Lord God, source of all life, appoint, I pray, a man who can lead the people and can command them in battle, so that your community will not be like sheep without a shepherd.
Narrator	The Lord said to Moses:
The Lord	Take Joshua son of Nun, a capable man, and place your hands on his head. Make him stand in front of Eleazar the priest and the whole community, and there before them all proclaim him as your successor. Give him some of your own authority, so that the whole community of Israel will obey him. He will depend on Eleazar the priest, who will learn my will by using the Urim and Thummim. In this way Eleazar will direct Joshua and the whole community of Israel in all their affairs.
Narrator	Moses did as the Lord had commanded him. He made Joshua stand before Eleazar the priest and the whole community. As the Lord had commanded, Moses put his hands on Joshua's head and proclaimed him as his successor.
Cast	[This is] the word of the Lord.
All	**Thanks be to God.**

Cast: **Narrator, The Lord, Moses.**

128

DEUTERONOMY

Moses appoints judges
Deuteronomy 1.6–18

Moses speaks to the people

Moses When we were at Mount Sinai, the Lord our God spoke to us:

The Lord You have stayed long enough at this mountain. Break camp and move on. Go to the hill-country of the Amorites and to all the surrounding regions—to the Jordan Valley, to the hill-country and the lowlands, to the southern region, and to the Mediterranean coast. Go to the land of Canaan and on beyond the Lebanon Mountains as far as the great River Euphrates. All of this is the land which I, the Lord, promised to give to your ancestors, Abraham, Isaac, and Jacob, and to their descendants. Go and occupy it.

Moses While we were still at Mount Sinai, I told you:

Young Moses The responsibility for leading you is too much for me. I can't do it alone. The Lord your God has made you as numerous as the stars in the sky. May the Lord, the God of your ancestors, make you increase a thousand times more and make you prosperous, as he promised! But how can I alone bear the heavy responsibility for settling your disputes? Choose some wise, understanding, and experienced men from each tribe, and I will put them in charge of you.

Moses And you agreed that this was a good thing to do. So I took the wise and experienced leaders you chose from your tribes, and I placed them in charge of you. Some were responsible for a thousand people, some for a hundred, some for fifty, and some for ten. I also appointed other officials throughout the tribes.

At that time I instructed them:

Young Moses Listen to the disputes that come up among your people. Judge every dispute fairly, whether it concerns only your own people or involves foreigners who live among you. Show no partiality in your decisions; judge everyone on the same basis, no matter who he is. Do not be afraid of anyone, for the decisions you make come from God. If any case is too difficult for you, bring it to me, and I will decide it.

Moses At the same time I gave you instructions for everything else you were to do.

Cast [This is] the word of the Lord.
All **Thanks be to God.**

Cast: **Moses, The Lord, Young Moses.**

The spies are sent out from Kadesh Barnea
Deuteronomy 1.19–33

Moses speaks to the people

Moses	We did what the Lord our God commanded us. We left Mount Sinai and went through that vast and fearful desert on the way to the hill-country of the Amorites. When we reached Kadesh Barnea, I said:
Young Moses	You have now come to the hill-country of the Amorites, which the Lord our God, the God of our ancestors, is giving us. Look, there it is. Go and occupy it as he commanded. Do not hesitate or be afraid.
Moses	But you came to me and said:
Israelite 1	Let's send men ahead of us to spy out the land, so that they can tell us the best route to take and what kind of cities are there.
Moses	That seemed a good thing to do, so I selected twelve men, one from each tribe. They went into the hill-country as far as the Valley of Eshcol and explored it. They brought us back some fruit they found there, and reported that the land which the Lord our God was giving us was very fertile.
	But you rebelled against the command of the Lord your God, and you would not enter the land. You grumbled to one another:
Israelite 2	The Lord hates us.
Israelite 3	He brought us out of Egypt just to hand us over to these Amorites, so that they could kill us.
Israelite 2	Why should we go there?
Israelite 3	We are afraid. The men we sent tell us that the people there are stronger and taller than we are, and that they live in cities with walls that reach the sky.
Israelite 1	They saw giants there!
Young Moses	Don't be afraid of those people. The Lord your God will lead you, and he will fight for you, just as you saw him do in Egypt and in the desert. You saw how he brought you safely all the way to this place, just as a father would carry his son.
Moses	But in spite of what I said, you still would not trust the Lord, even though he always went ahead of you to find a place for you to camp. To show you the way, he went in front of you in a pillar of fire by night and in a pillar of cloud by day.
Cast	[This is] the word of the Lord.
All	**Thanks be to God.**

Cast: **Moses, Young Moses, Israelite 1, Israelite 2, Israelite 3.**

The Lord punishes Israel
Deuteronomy 1.34–45

Moses speaks to the people

Moses The Lord heard your complaints and became angry [and so he solemnly declared]:

The Lord Not one of you from this evil generation will enter the fertile land that I promised to give your ancestors. Only Caleb son of Jephunneh will enter it. He has remained faithful to me, and I will give him and his descendants the land that he has explored.

Moses Because of you the Lord also became angry with me [and said]:

The Lord Not even you, Moses, will enter the land. But strengthen the determination of your helper, Joshua son of Nun. He will lead Israel to occupy the land.

Moses Then the Lord said to all of us:

The Lord Your children, who are still too young to know right from wrong, will enter the land—the children you said would be seized by your enemies. I will give the land to them, and they will occupy it. But as for you people, turn round and go back into the desert along the road to the Gulf of Aqaba.

Moses You replied:

Israelite 1 Moses, we have sinned against the Lord—

Israelite 2 But now we will attack, just as the Lord our God commanded us.

Moses Then each one of you got ready to fight, thinking it would be easy to invade the hill-country. But the Lord said to me:

The Lord Warn them not to attack, for I will not be with them, and their enemies will defeat them.

Moses I told you what the Lord had said, but you paid no attention. You rebelled against him, and in your pride you marched into the hill-country. Then the Amorites who lived in those hills came out against you like a swarm of bees. They chased you as far as Hormah and defeated you there in the hill-country of Edom. So you cried out to the Lord for help, but he would not listen to you or pay any attention to you.

Cast [This is] the word of the Lord.
All **Thanks be to God.**

Cast: **Moses, The Lord, Israelite 1, Israelite 2.**

The years in the desert
From Deuteronomy 1.46—2.25

Moses speaks to the people

Moses
After we had stayed at Kadesh for a long time, we finally turned and went into the desert, along the road to the Gulf of Aqaba, as the Lord had commanded, and we spent a long time wandering about in the hill-country of Edom.

Then the Lord told me that we had spent enough time wandering about in those hills and that we should go north. He told me to give you the following instructions:

The Lord
You are about to go through the hill-country of Edom, the territory of your distant relatives, the descendants of Esau. They will be afraid of you, but you must not start a war with them, because I am not going to give you so much as a square metre of their land. I have given Edom to Esau's descendants. You may buy food and water from them.

Moses
Remember how the Lord your God has blessed you in everything that you have done. He has taken care of you as you wandered through this vast desert. He has been with you these forty years, and you have had everything you needed. (PAUSE)

So we moved on and left the road that goes from the towns of Elath and Eziongeber to the Dead Sea, and we turned north-east towards Moab. The Lord said to me:

The Lord
Don't trouble the people of Moab, the descendants of Lot, or start a war against them. I have given them the city of Ar, and I am not going to give you any of their land.

Moses
Then we crossed the River Zered as the Lord told us to do. This was thirty-eight years after we had left Kadesh Barnea. All the fighting men of that generation had died, as the Lord had said they would. The Lord kept on opposing them until he had destroyed them all.

After they had all died, the Lord said to us:

The Lord
Today you are to pass through the territory of Moab by way of Ar. You will then be near the land of the Ammonites, the descendants of Lot. Don't trouble them or start a war against them, because I am not going to give you any of the land that I have given them.

Moses
After we had passed through Moab, the Lord said to us:

The Lord
Now, start out and cross the River Arnon. I am placing in your power Sihon, the Amorite king of Heshbon, along with his land. Attack him, and begin occupying his land. From today on I will make people everywhere afraid of you. Everyone will tremble with fear at the mention of your name.

Cast
[This is] the word of the Lord.

All
Thanks be to God.

Cast: **Moses, The Lord.**

Israel defeats King Sihon and King Og
From Deuteronomy 2.26—3.8
Moses speaks to the people

Moses	I sent messengers from the desert of Kedemoth to King Sihon of Heshbon with the following offer of peace:
Messenger 1	Let us pass through your country.
Messenger 2	We will go straight through and not leave the road.
Messenger 1	We will pay for the food we eat and the water we drink.
Messenger 2	All we want to do is to pass through your country, until we cross the River Jordan into the land that the Lord our God is giving us.
Messenger 1	The descendants of Esau, who live in Edom, and the Moabites, who live in Ar, allowed us to pass through *their* territory.
Moses	But King Sihon would not let us pass through his country. The Lord your God had made him stubborn and rebellious, so that we could defeat him and take his territory, which we still occupy.
	Then the Lord said to me:
The Lord	Look, I have made King Sihon and his land helpless before you; take his land and occupy it.
Moses	Sihon came out with all his men to fight us near the town of Jahaz, but the Lord our God put him in our power.
	The Lord our God let us capture all the towns from Aroer, on the edge of the valley of the Amon, and the city in the middle of that valley, all the way to Gilead. No town had walls too strong for us.
	Next, we moved north towards the region of Bashan, and King Og came out with all his men to fight us near the town of Edrei.
	[But the Lord said to me:]
The Lord	Don't be afraid of him. I am going to give him, his men, and all his territory to you. Do the same to him as you did to Sihon the Amorite king who ruled in Heshbon.
Moses	So the Lord also placed King Og and his people in our power.
	At the same time we took from those two Amorite kings the land east of the River Jordan, from the River Arnon to Mount Hermon.
Cast	[This is] the word of the Lord.
All	**Thanks be to God.**

Cast: **Moses, Messenger 1, Messenger 2** (can be the same as Messenger 1), **The Lord.**

East of Jordan
From Deuteronomy 3.12—29
Moses speaks to the people

Moses	When we took possession of the land, I gave the following instructions:
Young Moses	The Lord our God has given you this land east of the Jordan to occupy. Now arm your fighting men and send them across the

→

	Jordan ahead of the other tribes of Israel, to help them to occupy their land. Only your wives, children, and livestock—I know you have a lot of livestock—will remain behind in the towns that I have assigned to you. Help your fellow-Israelites until they occupy the land that the Lord is giving them west of the Jordan and until the Lord lets them live there in peace, as he has already done here for you. After that, you may return to this land which I have assigned to you.
Moses	Then I instructed Joshua:
Young Moses	You have seen all that the Lord your God did to those two kings, Sihon and Og; and he will do the same to everyone else whose land you invade. Don't be afraid of them, for the Lord your God will fight for you.
Moses	At that time I earnestly prayed:
Young Moses (praying)	Sovereign Lord, I know that you have shown me only the beginning of the great and wonderful things you are going to do. There is no god in heaven or on earth who can do the mighty things that you have done! Let me cross the River Jordan, Lord, and see the fertile land on the other side, the beautiful hill-country and the Lebanon Mountains.
Moses	But because of you people the Lord was angry with me and would not listen. [Instead, he said:]
The Lord	That's enough! Don't mention this again! Go to the peak of Mount Pisgah and look to the north and to the south, to the east and to the west. Look carefully at what you see, because you will never go across the Jordan. Give Joshua his instructions. Strengthen his determination, because *he* will lead the people across to occupy the land that you see.
Moses	So we remained in the valley opposite the town of Bethpeor.
Cast	[This is] the word of the Lord.
All	**Thanks be to God.**

Cast: **Moses, Young Moses, The Lord.**

Moses gives the Ten Commandments
Deuteronomy 5.1–22

Moses speaks to the people

Moses	People of Israel, listen to all the laws that I am giving you today. Learn them and be sure that you obey them. At Mount Sinai the Lord our God made a covenant, not only with our fathers, but with all of us who are living today. There on the mountain the Lord spoke to you face-to-face from the fire. I stood between you and the Lord at that time to tell you what he said, because you were afraid of the fire and would not go up the mountain.

The Lord	I am the Lord your God, who rescued you from Egypt, where you were slaves. Worship no god but me.
	Do not make for yourselves images of anything in heaven or on earth or in the water under the earth. Do not bow down to any idol or worship it—
Voice	For I am the Lord your God and I tolerate no rivals. I bring punishment on those who hate me and on their descendants down to the third and fourth generation. But I show my love to thousands of generations of those who love me and obey my laws.
The Lord	Do not use my name for evil purposes—
Voice	For I, the Lord your God, will punish anyone who misuses my name.
The Lord	Observe the Sabbath and keep it holy, as I, the Lord your God, have commanded you.
Voice	You have six days in which to do your work, but the seventh day is a day of rest dedicated to me. On that day no one is to work— neither you, your children, your slaves, your animals, nor the foreigners who live in your country. Your slaves must rest just as you do. Remember that *you* were slaves in Egypt, and that I, the Lord your God, rescued you by my great power and strength. That is why I command you to observe the Sabbath.
The Lord	Respect your father and your mother, as I, the Lord your God, command you—
Voice	So that all may go well with you and so that you may live a long time in the land that I am giving you.
The Lord	Do not commit murder.
	Do not commit adultery.
	Do not steal.
	Do not accuse anyone falsely.
	Do not desire another man's wife; do not desire his house, his land, his slaves, his cattle, his donkeys, or anything else that he owns.
Moses	These are the commandments the Lord gave to all of you when you were gathered at the mountain. When he spoke with a mighty voice from the fire and from the thick clouds, he gave these commandments and no others.
	Then he wrote them on two stone tablets and gave them to me.
Cast	[This is] the word of the Lord.
All	**Thanks be to God.**

Cast: **Moses, The Lord, Voice** (can be the same as The Lord).

The people are afraid
Deuteronomy 5.23–33

Moses speaks to the people

Moses When the whole mountain was on fire and you heard the voice from the darkness, your leaders and the chiefs of your tribes came to me [and said]:

Leader 1 The Lord our God showed us his greatness and his glory when we heard him speak from the fire!

Leader 2 Today we have seen that it is possible for a man to continue to live, even though God has spoken to him.

Leader 3 But why should we risk death again?

Leader 2 That terrible fire will destroy us.

Leader 3 We are sure to die if we hear the Lord our God speak again.

Leader 1 Has any human being ever lived after hearing the living God speak from a fire?

Leader 2 Go back, Moses, and listen to everything that the Lord our God says.

Leader 3 Then return and tell us what he said to you. We will listen and obey.

Moses When the Lord heard this, he said to me:

The Lord I have heard what these people said, and they are right. If only they would always feel like this! If only they would always honour me and obey all my commands, so that everything would go well with them and their descendants for ever. Go and tell them to return to their tents. But you, Moses, stay here with me, and I will give you all my laws and commands. Teach them to the people, so that they will obey them in the land that I am giving them.

Moses People of Israel, be sure that you do everything that the Lord your God has commanded you. Do not disobey any of his laws. Obey them all, so that everything will go well with you and so that you will continue to live in the land that you are going to occupy.

Cast [This is] the word of the Lord.
All **Thanks be to God.**

Cast: **Moses, Leader 1, Leader 2, Leader 3, The Lord.**

The Great Commandment
Deuteronomy 6.1–9

Moses speaks to the people

Moses These are all the laws that the Lord your God commanded me to teach you. Obey them in the land that you are about to enter and occupy. As long as you live, you and your descendants are to honour the Lord your God and obey all his laws that I am giving you, so that you may live in that land a long time. Listen to them, people of Israel, and obey them! Then all will go well with you, and you will become a mighty nation and live in that rich and fertile land, just as the Lord, the God of our ancestors, has promised.

Voice Israel, remember this! The Lord—and the Lord alone—is our God. Love the Lord your God with all your heart, with all your soul, and with all your strength.

Moses Never forget these commands that I am giving you today. Teach them to your children. Repeat them when you are at home and when you are away, when you are resting and when you are working. Tie them on your arms and wear them on your foreheads as a reminder. Write them on the door-posts of your houses and on your gates.

Cast [This is] the word of the Lord.
All **Thanks be to God.**

Cast: **Moses, Voice.**

Passing on the faith
Deuteronomy 6.11–25

Moses speaks to the people

Moses When the Lord brings you into this land and you have all you want to eat, make certain that you do not forget the Lord who rescued you from Egypt, where you were slaves. Honour the Lord your God, worship only him, and make your promises in his name alone. Do not worship other gods, any of the gods of the peoples around you. If you do worship other gods, the Lord's anger will come against you like fire and will destroy you completely, because the Lord your God, who is present with you, tolerates no rivals.

Do not put the Lord your God to the test, as you did at Massah. Be sure that you obey all the laws that he has given you. Do what the Lord says is right and good, and all will go well with you. You will be able to take possession of the fertile land that the Lord promised your ancestors, and you will drive out your enemies, as he promised. →

137

In time to come your children will ask you:

Child   Why did the Lord our God command us to obey all these laws?

Moses   Then tell them:

Israelite   We were slaves of the king of Egypt, and the Lord rescued us by his great power. With our own eyes we saw him work miracles and do terrifying things to the Egyptians and to their king and to all his officials. He freed us from Egypt to bring us here and give us this land, as he had promised our ancestors he would. Then the Lord our God commanded us to obey all these laws and to honour him. If we do, he will always watch over our nation and keep it prosperous. If we faithfully obey everything that God has commanded us, he will be pleased with us.

Cast   [This is] the word of the Lord.
All   **Thanks be to God.**

Cast: **Moses, Child, Israelite.**

The people's disobedience
From Deuteronomy 9.1–29

Moses speaks to the people

Moses   Listen, people of Israel! Today you are about to cross the River Jordan and occupy the land belonging to nations greater and more powerful than you. Their cities are large, with walls that reach the sky. The people themselves are tall and strong; they are giants, and you have heard it said that no one can stand against them. But now you will see for yourselves that the Lord your God will go ahead of you like a raging fire. He will defeat them as you advance, so that you will drive them out and destroy them quickly, as he promised.

After the Lord your God has driven them out for you, do not say to yourselves that he brought you in to possess this land because you deserved it. No, the Lord is going to drive these people out for you because they are wicked. It is not because you are good and do what is right that the Lord is letting you take their land. He will drive them out because they are wicked and because he intends to keep the promise that he made to your ancestors, Abraham, Isaac, and Jacob.

Never forget how you made the Lord your God angry in the desert. From the day that you left Egypt until the day you arrived here, you have rebelled against him. Even at Mount Sinai you made the Lord angry—angry enough to destroy you. I went up the mountain to receive the stone tablets on which was written the covenant that the Lord had made with you. I stayed there forty days and nights and did not eat or drink anything. Then the Lord gave me the two stone tablets on which he had written with his own hand what he had said to you from the fire on the day that you were gathered there at the mountain.

Then the Lord said to me:

The Lord Go down the mountain at once, because your people, whom you led out of Egypt, have become corrupt and have done evil. They have already turned away from what I commanded them to do, and they have made an idol for themselves.

Moses So I turned and went down the mountain, carrying the two stone tablets on which the covenant was written. Flames of fire were coming from the mountain. I saw that you had already disobeyed the command that the Lord your God had given you, and that you had sinned against him by making yourselves a metal idol in the form of a bull-calf. So there in front of you I threw the stone tablets down and broke them to pieces. Then once again I lay face downwards in the Lord's presence for forty days and nights and did not eat or drink anything. I did this because you had sinned against the Lord and had made him angry. And I prayed:

Younger Moses Sovereign Lord, don't destroy your own people, the people you rescued and brought out of Egypt by your great strength and power. Remember your servants, Abraham, Isaac, and Jacob, and do not pay any attention to the stubbornness, wickedness, and sin of this people. Otherwise, the Egyptians will say that you were unable to take your people into the land that you had promised them. They will say that you took your people out into the desert to kill them, because you hated them. After all, these are the people whom you chose to be your own and whom you brought out of Egypt by your great power and might.

Cast [This is] the word of the Lord.
All **Thanks be to God.**

Cast: **Moses, The Lord, Younger Moses.**

Moses receives the Commandments again
Deuteronomy 10.1–5

Moses speaks to the people

Moses The Lord said to me:

The Lord Cut two stone tablets like the first ones and make a wooden box to put them in. Come up to me on the mountain, and I will write on those tablets what I wrote on the tablets that you broke, and then you are to put them in the box.

Moses	So I made a box of acacia-wood and cut two stone tablets like the first ones and took them up the mountain. Then the Lord wrote on those tablets the same words that he had written the first time, the Ten Commandments that he gave you when he spoke from the fire on the day you were gathered at the mountain. The Lord gave me the tablets, and I turned and went down the mountain. Then, just as the Lord had commanded, I put them in the box that I had made—and they have been there ever since.
Cast	[This is] the word of the Lord.
All	**Thanks be to God.**

Cast: **Moses, The Lord.**

Laws about harvest

From Deuteronomy 14.22–29, 16.9–12; Leviticus 23.15–21, 22

Leviticus	Count seven full weeks from the day after the Sabbath on which you bring your sheaf of corn to present to the Lord. On the fiftieth day, the day after the seventh Sabbath, present to the Lord another new offering of corn. Each family is to bring two loaves of bread and present them to the Lord as a special gift. Each loaf shall be made of two kilogrammes of flour baked with yeast and shall be presented to the Lord as an offering of the first corn to be harvested . . . On that day do none of your daily work, but gather for worship. Your descendants are to observe this regulation for all time to come, no matter where they live.
Deuteronomy	Set aside a tithe—a tenth of all that your fields produce each year. Then go to the one place where the Lord your God has chosen to be worshipped; and there in his presence eat the tithes of your corn, wine, and olive-oil, and the first-born of your cattle and sheep. Do this so that you may learn to honour the Lord your God always . . . Do not neglect the Levites who live in your towns; they have no property of their own. At the end of every third year bring the tithe of all your crops and store it in your towns. This food is for the Levites, since they own no property, and for the foreigners, orphans, and widows who live in your towns. They are to come and get all they need. Do this, and the Lord your God will bless you in everything you do.
Leviticus	When you harvest your fields, do not cut the corn at the edges of the fields, and do not go back to cut the ears of corn that were left; leave them for poor people and foreigners. The Lord is your God.
Deuteronomy	Count seven weeks from the time that you begin to harvest the corn, and then celebrate the Harvest Festival, to honour the Lord your God, by bringing him a freewill offering in proportion to the

blessing he has given you. Be joyful in the Lord's presence, together with your children, your servants, and the Levites, foreigners, orphans, and widows who live in your towns. Do this at the one place of worship. Be sure that you obey these commands; do not forget that you were slaves in Egypt.

Cast   [This is] the word of the Lord.
All   **Thanks be to God.**

Cast: **Leviticus, Deuteronomy.**

Harvest offerings
Deuteronomy 26.1–15

Moses speaks to the people

Moses   After you have occupied the land that the Lord your God is giving you and have settled there, each of you must place in a basket the first part of each crop that you harvest and you must take it with you to the one place of worship. Go to the priest in charge at that time and say to him:

Worshipper   I now acknowledge to the Lord my God that I have entered the land that he promised our ancestors to give us.

Moses   The priest will take the basket from you and place it before the altar of the Lord your God. Then, in the Lord's presence you will recite these words:

Worshipper   My ancestor was a wandering Aramean, who took his family to Egypt to live. They were few in number when they went there, but they became a large and powerful nation. The Egyptians treated us harshly and forced us to work as slaves. Then we cried out for help to the Lord, the God of our ancestors. He heard us and saw our suffering, hardship, and misery. By his great power and strength he rescued us from Egypt. He worked miracles and wonders, and caused terrifying things to happen. He brought us here and gave us this rich and fertile land. So now I bring to the Lord the first part of the harvest that he has given me.

Moses   Then set the basket down in the Lord's presence and worship there. Be grateful for the good things that the Lord your God has given you and your family; and let the Levites and the foreigners who live among you join in the celebration. Every third year give the tithe—a tenth of your crops—to the Levites, the foreigners, the orphans, and the widows, so that in every community they will have all they need to eat. When you have done this, say to the Lord:

Worshipper   None of the sacred tithe is left in my house; I have given it to the Levites, the foreigners, the orphans, and the widows, as you commanded me to do. I have not disobeyed or forgotten any of

$\rightarrow$

your commands concerning the tithe. I have not eaten any of it when I was mourning; I have not taken any of it out of my house when I was ritually unclean; and I have not given any of it as an offering for the dead. I have obeyed you, O Lord; I have done everything you commanded concerning the tithe. Look down from your holy place in heaven and bless your people Israel; bless also the rich and fertile land that you have given us, as you promised our ancestors.

Cast	[This is] the word of the Lord.
All	**Thanks be to God.**

Cast: **Moses, Worshipper.**

If you break the Covenant
Deuteronomy 29.22–29
Moses speaks to the people

Moses In future generations your descendants and foreigners from distant lands will see the disasters and sufferings that the Lord has brought on your land. The fields will be a barren waste, covered with sulphur and salt; nothing will be planted, and not even weeds will grow there. Your land will be like the cities of Sodom and Gomorrah, of Admah and Zeboiim, which the Lord destroyed when he was furiously angry. Then the whole world will ask:

Person 1 Why did the Lord do this to their land?

Person 2 What was the reason for his fierce anger?

Moses And the answer will be:

Interpreter It is because the Lord's people broke the covenant they had made with him, the God of their ancestors, when he brought them out of Egypt. They served other gods that they had never worshipped before, gods that the Lord had forbidden them to worship. And so the Lord became angry with his people and brought on their land all the disasters written in this book. The Lord became furiously angry, and in his great anger he uprooted them from their land and threw them into a foreign land, and there they are today.

Moses There are some things that the Lord our God has kept secret; but he has revealed his Law, and we and our descendants are to obey it for ever.

Cast	[This is] the word of the Lord.
All	**Thanks be to God.**

Cast: **Moses, Person 1, Person 2, Interpreter.**

142

If you keep the Covenant
From Deuteronomy 30.9–20

Moses speaks to the people

Moses The Lord will be as glad to make you prosperous as he was to make your ancestors prosperous, but you will have to obey him and keep all his laws that are written in this book of his teachings. You will have to turn to him with all your heart.

The command that I am giving you today is not too difficult or beyond your reach. It is not up in the sky. You do not have to ask:

Person 1 Who will go up and bring it down for us, so that we can hear it and obey it?

Moses Nor is it on the other side of the ocean. You do not have to ask:

Person 2 Who will go across the ocean and bring it to us, so that we may hear it and obey it?

Moses No, it is here with you. You know it and can quote it, so now obey it. (PAUSE)

Today I am giving you a choice between good and evil, between life and death. If you obey the commands of the Lord your God, which I give you today, if you love him, obey, and keep all his laws, then you will prosper and become a nation of many people. The Lord your God will bless you in the land that you are about to occupy. But if you disobey and refuse to listen, and are led away to worship other gods, you will be destroyed—I warn you here and now. You will not live long in that land across the Jordan that you are about to occupy. I am now giving you the choice between life and death, between God's blessing and God's curse, and I call heaven and earth to witness the choice you make. Choose life. Love the Lord your God, obey him and be faithful to him, and then you and your descendants will live long in the land that he promised to give your ancestors, Abraham, Isaac, and Jacob.

Cast [This is] the word of the Lord.
All **Thanks be to God.**

Cast: **Moses, Person 1, Person 2.**

Joshua becomes Moses' successor
Deuteronomy 31.1–8

Narrator Moses continued speaking to the people of Israel:

Moses I am now a hundred and twenty years old and am no longer able to be your leader. And besides this, the Lord has told me that I will not cross the Jordan. The Lord your God himself will go before you and destroy the nations living there, so that you can occupy their land; and Joshua will be your leader, as the Lord has said. The Lord will destroy those people, just as he defeated Sihon and Og, kings of the Amorites, and destroyed their country. The Lord will give you victory over them, and you are to treat them exactly

→

as I have told you. Be determined and confident. Do not be afraid of them. Your God, the Lord himself, will be with you. He will not fail you or abandon you.

Narrator Then Moses called Joshua and said to him in the presence of all the people of Israel:

Moses Be determined and confident; you are the one who will lead these people to occupy the land that the Lord promised to their ancestors. The Lord himself will lead you and be with you. He will not fail you or abandon you, so do not lose courage or be afraid.

Cast [This is] the word of the Lord.
All **Thanks be to God.**

Cast: **Narrator, Moses.**

The law is to be read every seven years
Deuteronomy 31.9–13

Narrator So Moses wrote down God's Law and gave it to the levitical priests, who were in charge of the Lord's Covenant Box, and to the leaders of Israel. He commanded them:

Moses At the end of every seven years, when the year that debts are cancelled comes round, read this aloud at the Festival of Shelters. Read it to the people of Israel when they come to worship the Lord your God at the one place of worship. Call together all the men, women, and children, and the foreigners who live in your towns, so that everyone may hear it and learn to honour the Lord your God and to obey his teachings faithfully. In this way your descendants who have never heard the Law of the Lord your God will hear it. And so they will learn to obey him as long as they live in the land that you are about to occupy across the Jordan.

Cast [This is] the word of the Lord.
All **Thanks be to God.**

Cast: **Narrator, Moses.**

The Lord's last instruction to Moses
From Deuteronomy 31.14–29

Narrator The Lord said to Moses:

The Lord You haven't much longer to live. Call Joshua and bring him to the Tent, so that I may give him his instructions.

Narrator Moses and Joshua went to the Tent, and the Lord appeared to them there in a pillar of cloud that stood by the door of the Tent. The Lord said to Moses:

The Lord You will soon die, and after your death the people will become unfaithful to me and break the covenant that I made with them. They will abandon me and worship the pagan gods of the land they are about to enter.

Narrator	Then the Lord spoke to Joshua son of Nun:
The Lord	Be confident and determined. You will lead the people of Israel into the land that I promised them, and I will be with you.
Narrator	Moses wrote God's Law in a book, taking care not to leave out anything. When he finished, he said to the levitical priests, who were in charge of the Lord's Covenant Box:
Moses	Take this book of God's Law and place it beside the Covenant Box of the Lord your God, so that it will remain there as a witness against his people. I know how stubborn and rebellious they are. They have rebelled against the Lord during my lifetime, and they will rebel even more after I am dead. Assemble all your tribal leaders and officials before me, so that I can tell them these things; I will call heaven and earth to be my witnesses against them. I know that after my death the people will become wicked and reject what I have taught them. And in time to come they will meet with disaster, because they will have made the Lord angry by doing what he has forbidden.
Cast	[This is] the word of the Lord.
All	**Thanks be to God.**

Cast: **Narrator, The Lord, Moses.**

Moses' final instructions
Deuteronomy 32.45–52

Narrator	When Moses had finished giving God's teachings to the people, he said:
Moses	Make sure you obey all these commands that I have given you today. Repeat them to your children, so that they may faithfully obey all God's teachings. These teachings are not empty words; they are your very life. Obey them and you will live long in that land across the Jordan that you are about to occupy.
Narrator	That same day the Lord spoke to Moses:
The Lord	Go to the Abarim Mountains in the land of Moab opposite the city of Jericho; climb Mount Nebo and look at the land of Canaan that I am about to give the people of Israel. You will die on that mountain as your brother Aaron died on Mount Hor, because both of you were unfaithful to me in the presence of the people of Israel. When you were at the waters of Meribah, near the town of Kadesh in the wilderness of Zin, you dishonoured me in the presence of the people. You will look at the land from a distance, but you will not enter the land that I am giving the people of Israel.
Cast	[This is] the word of the Lord.
All	**Thanks be to God.**

Cast: **Narrator, Moses, The Lord.**

The death of Moses
Deuteronomy 34.1–12

Narrator
Moses went up from the plains of Moab to Mount Nebo, to the top of Mount Pisgah east of Jericho, and there the Lord showed him the whole land: the territory of Gilead as far north as the town of Dan; the entire territory of Naphtali; the territories of Ephraim and Manasseh; the territory of Judah as far west as the Mediterranean Sea; the southern part of Judah; and the plain that reaches from Zoar to Jericho, the city of palm-trees. Then the Lord said to Moses:

The Lord
This is the land that I promised Abraham, Isaac, and Jacob I would give to their descendants. I have let you see it, but I will not let you go there.

Narrator
So Moses, the Lord's servant, died there in the land of Moab, as the Lord had said he would. The Lord buried him in a valley in Moab, opposite the town of Bethpeor, but to this day no one knows the exact place of his burial. Moses was a hundred and twenty years old when he died; he was as strong as ever, and his eyesight was still good. The people of Israel mourned for him for thirty days in the plains of Moab.

Joshua son of Nun was filled with wisdom, because Moses had appointed him to be his successor. The people of Israel obeyed Joshua and kept the commands that the Lord had given them through Moses. There has never been a prophet in Israel like Moses; the Lord spoke with him face to face. No other prophet has ever done miracles and wonders like those that the Lord sent Moses to perform against the king of Egypt, his officials, and the entire country. No other prophet has been able to do the great and terrifying things that Moses did in the sight of all Israel.

Cast [This is] the word of the Lord.
All **Thanks be to God.**

Cast: **Narrator, The Lord.**

JOSHUA

God commands Joshua to conquer Canaan
Joshua 1.1–18

Narrator After the death of the Lord's servant Moses, the Lord spoke to Moses' helper, Joshua son of Nun:

The Lord My servant Moses is dead. Get ready now, you and all the people of Israel, and cross the River Jordan into the land that I am giving them. As I told Moses, I have given you and all my people the entire land that you will be marching over. Your borders will reach from the desert in the south to the Lebanon Mountains in the north; from the great River Euphrates in the east, through the Hittite country, to the Mediterranean Sea in the west. Joshua, no one will be able to defeat you as long as you live. I will be with you as I was with Moses. I will always be with you; I will never abandon you. Be determined and confident, for you will be the leader of these people as they occupy this land which I promised their ancestors. Just be determined, be confident; and make sure that you obey the whole Law that my servant Moses gave you. Do not neglect any part of it and you will succeed wherever you go. Be sure that the book of the Law is always read in your worship. Study it day and night, and make sure that you obey everything written in it. Then you will be prosperous and successful. Remember that I have commanded you to be determined and confident!

Don't be afraid or discouraged, for I, the Lord your God, am with you wherever you go.

Narrator Then Joshua ordered the leaders to go through the camp and say to the people:

Leader Get some food ready, because in three days you are going to cross the River Jordan to occupy the land that the Lord your God is giving you.

Narrator Joshua said to the tribes of Reuben and Gad and to half the tribe of Manasseh:

Joshua Remember how Moses, the Lord's servant, told you that the Lord your God would give you this land on the east side of the Jordan as your home. Your wives, your children, and your livestock will stay here, but your soldiers, armed for battle, will cross over ahead of their fellow-Israelites in order to help them until they have occupied the land west of the Jordan that the Lord your God has given them. When he has given safety to all the tribes of Israel, then you may come back and settle here in your own land east of the Jordan, which Moses, the Lord's servant, gave to you.

Narrator They answered Joshua:

Person 1 We will do everything you have told us and will go wherever you send us.

Person 2	We will obey you, just as we always obeyed Moses.
Person 1	And may the Lord your God be with you as he was with Moses!
Person 2	Whoever questions your authority or disobeys any of your orders will be put to death.
Person 1	Be determined and confident!
Cast	[This is] the word of the Lord.
All	**Thanks be to God.**

Cast: **Narrator, The Lord, Leader, Joshua** (can be the same as Leader), **Person 1, Person 2** (can be the same as Person 1).

Joshua sends spies into Jericho
Joshua 2.1–24

Narrator	Joshua sent two spies from the camp at Acacia with orders to go and secretly explore the land of Canaan, especially the city of Jericho. When they came to the city, they went to spend the night in the house of a prostitute named Rahab. The king of Jericho heard that some Israelites had come that night to spy out the country, so he sent word to Rahab:
King of Jericho	The men in your house have come to spy out the whole country! Bring them out!
[Narrator	She answered:]
Rahab	Some men did come to my house, but I don't know where they were from. They left at sunset before the city gate was closed. I didn't find out where they were going, but if you start after them quickly, you can catch them.
Narrator	Now Rahab had taken the two spies up on the roof and hidden them under some stalks of flax that she had put there. The king's men left the city, and then the gate was shut. They went looking for the Israelite spies as far as the place where the road crosses the Jordan. (PAUSE)
	Before the spies settled down for the night, Rahab went up on the roof [and said to them:]
Rahab	I know that the Lord has given you this land. Everyone in the country is terrified of you. We have heard how the Lord dried up the Red Sea in front of you when you were leaving Egypt. We have also heard how you killed Sihon and Og, the two Amorite kings east of the Jordan. We were afraid as soon as we heard about it; we have all lost our courage because of you. The Lord your God is God in heaven above and here on earth. Now swear by him that you will treat my family as kindly as I have treated you, and give me some sign that I can trust you. Promise me that you will save my father and mother, my brothers and sisters, and all their families! Don't let us be killed!
[Narrator	The men said to her:]

Spy 1	May God take our lives if we don't do as we say!
Spy 2	If you do not tell anyone what we have been doing, we promise you that when the Lord gives us this land, we will treat you well.
Narrator	Rahab lived in a house built into the city wall, so she let the men down from the window by a rope. [She said:]
Rahab	Go into the hill-country, or the king's men will find you. Hide there for three days until they come back. After that you can go on your way.
Spy 1	We will keep the promise that you have made us give.
Spy 2	This is what you must do. When we invade your land, tie this red cord to the window you let us down from.
Spy 1	Get your father and mother, your brothers, and all your father's family together in your house.
Spy 2	If anyone goes out of the house, his death will be his own fault, and we will not be responsible; but if anyone in the house with you is harmed, then we *will* be responsible.
Spy 1	However, if you tell anyone what we have been doing, then we will not have to keep our promise which you have made us give you.
Narrator	She agreed and sent them away. When they had gone, she tied the red cord to the window. The spies went into the hills and hid. The king's men looked for them all over the countryside for three days, but they did not find them, so they returned to Jericho. Then the two spies came down from the hills, crossed the river, and went back to Joshua. They told him everything that had happened, and then said:
Spy 2	We are sure that the Lord has given us the whole country.
Spy 1	All the people there are terrified of us.
Cast All	[This is] the word of the Lord. **Thanks be to God.**

Cast: **Narrator, King of Jericho, Rahab, Spy 1, Spy 2.**

The people of Israel cross the Jordan
Joshua 3.1–17

Narrator	The morning after the spies had reported, Joshua and all the people of Israel got up early, left the camp at Acacia, and went to the Jordan, where they camped while waiting to cross it. Three days later the leaders went through the camp and said to the people:
Leader 1	When you see the priests carrying the Covenant Box of the Lord your God, break camp and follow them.
Leader 2	You have never been here before, so they will show you the way to go.

Leader 3	But do not get near the Covenant Box; stay about a kilometre behind it.
Narrator	Joshua said to the people:
Joshua	Purify yourselves, because tomorrow the Lord will perform miracles among you.
Narrator	Then he told the priests to take the Covenant Box and go with it ahead of the people. They did as he said. (PAUSE)
	The Lord said to Joshua:
The Lord	What I do today will make all the people of Israel begin to honour you as a great man, and they will realize that I am with you as I was with Moses. Tell the priests carrying the Covenant Box that when they reach the river, they must wade in and stand near the bank.
Narrator	Then Joshua said to the people:
Joshua	Come here and listen to what the Lord your God has to say. As you advance, he will surely drive out the Canaanites, the Hittites, the Hivites, the Perizzites, the Girgashites, the Amorites, and the Jebusites. You will know that the living God is among you when the Covenant Box of the Lord of all the earth crosses the Jordan ahead of you. Now choose twelve men, one from each of the tribes of Israel. When the priests who carry the Covenant Box of the Lord of all the earth put their feet in the water, the Jordan will stop flowing, and the water coming downstream will pile up in one place.
Narrator	It was harvest time, and the river was in flood. When the people left the camp to cross the Jordan, the priests went ahead of them, carrying the Covenant Box. As soon as the priests stepped into the river, the water stopped flowing and piled up, far upstream at Adam, the city beside Zarethan. The flow downstream to the Dead Sea was completely cut off, and the people were able to cross over near Jericho. While the people walked across on dry ground, the priests carrying the Lord's Covenant Box stood on dry ground in the middle of the Jordan until all the people had crossed over.
Cast	[This is] the word of the Lord.
All	**Thanks be to God.**

Cast: **Narrator, Leader 1, Leader 2, Leader 3** (Leaders 1–3 can be the same), **Joshua, The Lord.**

Memorial stones are set up
Joshua 4.1—5.1

Narrator 1	When the whole nation had crossed the Jordan, the Lord said to Joshua:
The Lord	Choose twelve men, one from each tribe, and command them to take twelve stones out of the middle of the Jordan, from the very

	place where the priests were standing. Tell them to carry these stones with them and to put them down where you camp tonight.
Narrator 2	Then Joshua called the twelve men he had chosen:
Joshua	Go into the Jordan ahead of the Covenant Box of the Lord your God. Each one of you take a stone on your shoulder, one for each of the tribes of Israel. These stones will remind the people of what the Lord has done. In the future, when your children ask what these stones mean to you, you will tell them that the water of the Jordan stopped flowing when the Lord's Covenant Box crossed the river. These stones will always remind the people of Israel of what happened here.
Narrator 1	The men followed Joshua's orders. As the Lord had commanded Joshua, they took twelve stones from the middle of the Jordan, one for each of the tribes of Israel, carried them to the camping place, and put them down there. Joshua also set up twelve stones in the middle of the Jordan, where the priests carrying the Covenant Box had stood.
Narrator 2	Those stones are still there.
Narrator 1	The priests stood in the middle of the Jordan until everything had been done that the Lord ordered Joshua to tell the people to do. This is what Moses had commanded.
Narrator 2	The people hurried across the river. When they were all on the other side, the priests with the Lord's Covenant Box went on ahead of the people. The men of the tribes of Reuben and Gad and of half the tribe of Manasseh, ready for battle, crossed ahead of the rest of the people, as Moses had told them to do. In the presence of the Lord about forty thousand men ready for war crossed over to the plain near Jericho.
Narrator 1	What the Lord did that day made the people of Israel consider Joshua a great man. They honoured him all his life, just as they had honoured Moses.
Narrator 2	Then the Lord told Joshua to command the priests carrying the Covenant Box to come up out of the Jordan. Joshua did so, and when the priests reached the river bank, the river began flowing once more and flooded its banks again.
Narrator 1	The people crossed the Jordan on the tenth day of the first month and made camp at Gilgal, east of Jericho. There Joshua set up the twelve stones taken from the Jordan. [He said to the people of Israel:]
Joshua	In the future, when your children ask you what these stones mean, you will tell them about the time when Israel crossed the Jordan on dry ground. Tell them that the Lord your God dried up the water of the Jordan for you until you had crossed, just as he dried up the Red Sea for us. Because of this everyone on earth will know how great the Lord's power is, and you will honour the Lord your God for ever.

Narrator 2	All the Amorite kings west of the Jordan and all the Canaanite kings along the Mediterranean Sea heard that the Lord had dried up the Jordan until the people of Israel had crossed it. They became afraid and lost their courage because of the Israelites.
Cast	[This is] the word of the Lord.
All	**Thanks be to God.**

Cast: **Narrator 1, The Lord, Narrator 2, Joshua.**

Joshua and the man with a sword
Joshua 5.13–15

Narrator	While Joshua was near Jericho, he suddenly saw a man standing in front of him, holding a sword. Joshua went up to him:
Joshua	Are you one of our soldiers, or an enemy?
[Narrator	The man answered:]
Commander	Neither. I am here as the commander of the Lord's army.
Narrator	Joshua threw himself on the ground in worship:
Joshua	I am your servant, sir. What do you want me to do?
Narrator	And the commander of the Lord's army told him:
Commander	Take your sandals off; you are standing on holy ground.
Narrator	And Joshua did as he was told.
Cast	[This is] the word of the Lord.
All	**Thanks be to God.**

Cast: **Narrator, Joshua, Commander.**

Joshua at Jericho
From Joshua 5.13—6.20 (combined selected reading)

Narrator	While Joshua was near Jericho, he suddenly saw a man standing in front of him, holding a sword. Joshua went up to him:
Joshua	Are you one of our soldiers, or an enemy?
[Narrator	The man answered:]
Commander	Neither. I am here as the commander of the Lord's army.
Narrator	Joshua threw himself on the ground in worship:
Joshua	I am your servant, sir. What do you want me to do?
Narrator	And the commander of the Lord's army told him:
Commander	Take your sandals off; you are standing on holy ground.
Narrator	And Joshua did as he was told. (PAUSE)

The gates of Jericho were kept shut and guarded to keep the Israelites out. No one could enter or leave the city. The Lord said to Joshua:

The Lord   I am putting into your hands Jericho, with its king and all its brave soldiers. You and your soldiers are to march round the city once a day for six days. Seven priests, each carrying a trumpet, are to go in front of the Covenant Box. On the seventh day you and your soldiers are to march round the city seven times while the priests blow the trumpets. Then they are to sound one long note. As soon as you hear it, all the men are to give a loud shout, and the city walls will collapse. Then the whole army will go straight into the city.

Narrator   Joshua called the priests and said to them:

Joshua   Take the Covenant Box, and seven of you go in front of it, carrying trumpets.

Narrator   Then he ordered his men to start marching round the city, with an advance guard going on ahead of the Lord's Covenant Box. At this time the trumpet was sounding. (PAUSE)

Joshua got up early the next morning, and for the second time the priests and soldiers marched round the city in the same order as the day before: first, the advance guard; next, the seven priests blowing the seven trumpets; then, the priests carrying the Lord's Covenant Box; and finally, the rearguard. All this time the trumpets were sounding. On this second day they again marched round the city once and then returned to camp. They did this for six days.

On the seventh day they got up at daybreak and marched seven times round the city in the same way—this was the only day that they marched round it seven times. The seventh time round, when the priests were about to sound the trumpets, Joshua ordered his men to shout, and he said:

Joshua   The Lord has given you the city!

Narrator   So the priests blew the trumpets. As soon as the men heard it, they gave a loud shout, and the walls collapsed. Then all the army went straight up the hill into the city and captured it.

Cast   [This is] the word of the Lord.
All   **Thanks be to God.**

Cast: **Narrator, Joshua, Commander, The Lord.** (See full readings in separate parts, pages 152 and below.)

The fall of Jericho
Joshua 6.1–20

Narrator 1   The gates of Jericho were kept shut and guarded to keep the Israelites out.

Narrator 2   No one could enter or leave the city.

Narrator 1   The Lord said to Joshua:

The Lord	I am putting into your hands Jericho, with its king and all its brave soldiers. You and your soldiers are to march round the city once a day for six days. Seven priests, each carrying a trumpet, are to go in front of the Covenant Box. On the seventh day you and your soldiers are to march round the city seven times while the priests blow the trumpets. Then they are to sound one long note. As soon as you hear it, all the men are to give a loud shout, and the city walls will collapse. Then the whole army will go straight into the city.
Narrator 2	Joshua called the priests:
Joshua	Take the Covenant Box, and seven of you go in front of it, carrying trumpets.
Narrator 2	Then he ordered his men to start marching round the city, with an advance guard going on ahead of the Lord's Covenant Box.
Narrator 1	So, just as Joshua had ordered, an advance guard started out ahead of the priests who were blowing trumpets; behind these came the priests who were carrying the Covenant Box, followed by a rearguard.
Narrator 2	All this time the trumpets were sounding. But Joshua had ordered his men not to shout, not to say a word until he gave the order. So he told this group of men to take the Lord's Covenant Box round the city once. Then they came back to camp and spent the night there.
Narrator 1	Joshua got up early the next morning, and for the second time the priests and soldiers marched round the city in the same order as the day before: first, the advance guard—
Narrator 2	Next, the seven priests blowing the seven trumpets—
Narrator 1	Then, the priests carrying the Lord's Covenant Box—
Narrator 2	And finally, the rearguard.
Narrator 1	All this time the trumpets were sounding.
Narrator 2	On this second day they again marched round the city once and then returned to camp. They did this for six days.
Narrator 1	On the seventh day they got up at daybreak and marched seven times round the city in the same way—this was the only day that they marched round it seven times.
Narrator 2	The seventh time round, when the priests were about to sound the trumpets, Joshua ordered his men to shout [and he said]:
Joshua	The Lord has given you the city! The city and everything in it must be totally destroyed as an offering to the Lord. Only the prostitute Rahab and her household will be spared, because she hid our spies. But you are not to take anything that is to be destroyed; if you do, you will bring trouble and destruction on the Israelite camp. Everything made of silver, gold, bronze, or iron is set apart for the Lord. It is to be put in the Lord's treasury.

Narrator 1	So the priests blew the trumpets.
Narrator 2	As soon as the men heard it, they gave a loud shout! (PAUSE) and the walls collapsed.
Narrator 1	Then all the army went straight up the hill into the city—
Narrators 1 and 2	And captured it.
Cast All	[This is] the word of the Lord. **Thanks be to God.**

Cast: **Narrator 1, Narrator 2, The Lord, Joshua.**

The rescue of Rahab
Joshua 6.22–27

Narrator 1	Joshua told the two men who had served as spies:
Joshua	Go into the prostitute's house and bring her and her family out, as you promised her.
Narrator 1	So they went and brought Rahab out, along with her father and mother, her brothers, and the rest of her family. They took them all, family and slaves, to safety near the Israelite camp.
Narrator 2	Then they set fire to the city and burnt it to the ground, along with everything in it, except the things made of gold, silver, bronze, and iron, which they took and put in the Lord's treasury.
Narrator 1	But Joshua spared the lives of the prostitute Rahab and all her relatives, because she had hidden the two spies that he had sent to Jericho.
Narrator 2	Her descendants have lived in Israel to this day.
Narrator 1	At that time Joshua issued a solemn warning:
Joshua	Anyone who tries to rebuild the city of Jericho will be under the Lord's curse. Whoever lays the foundation will lose his eldest son; whoever builds the gates will lose his youngest.
Narrator 2	So the Lord was with Joshua—
Narrators 1 and 2	And his fame spread through the whole country.
Cast All	[This is] the word of the Lord. **Thanks be to God.**

Cast: **Narrator 1, Joshua, Narrator 2.**

Achan's sin (i)
Joshua 7.1–15

Narrator 1 The Lord's command to Israel not to take from Jericho anything that was to be destroyed was not obeyed. A man named Achan disobeyed that order, and so the Lord was furious with the Israelites.

Narrator 2 Achan was the son of Carmi and grandson of Zabdi, and belonged to the clan of Zerah, a part of the tribe of Judah.

Narrator 1 Joshua sent some men from Jericho to Ai, a city east of Bethel, near Bethaven, with orders to go and explore the land. When they had done so, they reported back to Joshua:

Man 1 There is no need for everyone to attack Ai.

Man 2 Send only about two or three thousand men.

Man 1 Don't send the whole army up there to fight—

Man 2 It is not a large city.

Narrator 1 So about three thousand Israelites made the attack.

Narrator 2 But they were forced to retreat. The men of Ai chased them from the city gate as far as some quarries and killed about thirty-six of them on the way down the hill. Then the Israelites lost their courage and were afraid.

Narrator 1 Joshua and the leaders of Israel tore their clothes in grief, threw themselves to the ground before the Lord's Covenant Box, and lay there till evening, with dust on their heads to show their sorrow. And Joshua said:

Joshua Sovereign Lord! Why did you bring us across the Jordan at all? To hand us over to the Amorites? To destroy us? Why didn't we just stay on the other side of the Jordan? What can I say, O Lord, now that Israel has retreated from the enemy? The Canaanites and everyone else in the country will hear about it. They will surround us and kill every one of us! And then what will you do to protect your honour?

Narrator 2 The Lord said to Joshua:

The Lord Get up! Why are you lying on the ground like this? Israel has sinned! They have broken the agreement with me that I ordered them to keep. They have taken some of the things condemned to destruction. They stole them, lied about it, and put them with their own things. This is why the Israelites cannot stand against their enemies. They retreat from them because they themselves have now been condemned to destruction! I will not stay with you any longer unless you destroy the things you were ordered not to take! Get up! Purify the people and get them ready to come before me. Tell them to be ready tomorrow, because I, the Lord God of Israel, have this to say: 'Israel, you have in your possession some things that I ordered you to destroy! You cannot stand

156

against your enemies until you get rid of these things!' So tell them that in the morning they will be brought forward, tribe by tribe. The tribe that I pick out will then come forward, clan by clan. The clan that I pick out will come forward, family by family. The family that I pick out will come forward, man by man. The one who is then picked out and found with the condemned goods will be burnt, along with his family and everything he owns, for he has brought terrible shame on Israel and has broken my covenant.

Cast	[This is] the word of the Lord.
All	**Thanks be to God.**

Cast: **Narrator 1, Narrator 2, Man 1, Man 2** (can be the same as Man 1), **Joshua, The Lord.**

Achan's sin (ii)
Joshua 7.16–26

Narrator 1   Early on the morning after the Lord had spoken Joshua brought Israel forward, tribe by tribe, and the tribe of Judah was picked out.

Narrator 2   He brought the tribe of Judah forward, clan by clan, and the clan of Zerah was picked out.

Narrator 1   Then he brought the clan of Zerah forward, family by family, and the family of Zabdi was picked out.

Narrator 2   He then brought Zabdi's family forward, man by man, and Achan, the son of Carmi and grandson of Zabdi, was picked out. Joshua said to him:

Joshua   My son, tell the truth here before the Lord, the God of Israel, and confess. Tell me now what you have done. Don't try to hide it from me.

Narrator 2   Achan answered:

Achan   It's true. I have sinned against the Lord, Israel's God, and this is what I did. Among the things we seized I saw a beautiful Babylonian cloak, about two kilogrammes of silver, and a bar of gold weighing over half a kilogramme. I wanted them so much that I took them. You will find them buried inside my tent, with the silver at the bottom.

Narrator 1   So Joshua sent some men, who ran to the tent and found that the condemned things really were buried there, with the silver at the bottom. They brought them out of the tent, took them to Joshua and all the Israelites, and laid them down in the presence of the Lord.

Narrator 2   Joshua, along with all the people of Israel, seized Achan, the silver, the cloak, and the bar of gold, together with Achan's sons and daughters, his cattle, donkeys, and sheep, his tent, and everything else he owned; and they took them to Trouble Valley.

And Joshua said:

Joshua	Why have you brought such trouble on us? The Lord will now bring trouble on you!
Narrator 1	All the people then stoned Achan to death:
Narrator 2	They also stoned and burnt his family and possessions.
Narrator 1	They put a huge pile of stones over him, which is there to this day.
Narrator 2	That is why that place is still called—
Narrators 1 and 2	Trouble Valley.
Narrator 2	Then the Lord was no longer furious.
Cast All	[This is] the word of the Lord. **Thanks be to God.**

Cast: **Narrator 1, Narrator 2, Joshua, Achan.**

The capture and destruction of Ai
Joshua 8.1–23

Narrators 1 and 2	The Lord said to Joshua:
The Lord	Take all the soldiers with you and go on up to Ai. Don't be afraid or discouraged. I will give you victory over the king of Ai; his people, city, and land will be yours. You are to do to Ai and its king what you did to Jericho and its king, but this time you may keep its goods and livestock for yourselves. Prepare to attack the city by surprise from the rear.
Narrator 1	So Joshua got ready to go to Ai with all his soldiers.
Narrator 2	He picked out thirty thousand of his best troops and sent them out at night with these orders:
Joshua	Hide on the other side of the city, but not too far away from it; be ready to attack. My men and I will approach the city. When the men of Ai come out against us, we will turn and run, just as we did the first time. They will pursue us until we have led them away from the city. They will think that we are running away from them, as we did before. Then you will come out of hiding and capture the city. The Lord your God will give it to you. After you have taken the city, set it on fire, just as the Lord has commanded. These are your orders.
Narrator 1	So Joshua sent them out, and they went to their hiding place and waited there, west of Ai, between Ai and Bethel. Joshua spent the night in camp.
Narrator 2	Early in the morning Joshua got up and called the soldiers together. Then he and the leaders of Israel led them to Ai.
Narrator 1	The soldiers with him went towards the main entrance to the city and set up camp on the north side, with a valley between themselves and Ai. He took about five thousand men and put

Narrator 2

them in hiding west of the city, between Ai and Bethel. The soldiers were arranged for battle with the main camp north of the city and the rest of the men to the west. Joshua spent the night in the valley. (PAUSE)

Narrator 2
When the king of Ai saw Joshua's men, he acted quickly. He and all his men went out towards the Jordan Valley to fight the Israelites at the same place as before, not knowing that he was about to be attacked from the rear.

Narrator 1
Joshua and his men pretended that they were retreating, and ran away towards the barren country.

Narrator 2
All the men in the city had been called together to go after them, and as they pursued Joshua, they kept getting farther away from the city.

Narrator 1
Every man in Ai went after the Israelites, and the city was left wide open, with no one to defend it.

Narrator 2
Then the Lord spoke to Joshua:

The Lord
Point your spear at Ai; I am giving it to you.

Narrator 1
Joshua did as he was told, and as soon as he lifted his hand, the men who had been hiding got up quickly, ran into the city and captured it. They immediately set the city on fire.

Narrator 2
When the men of Ai looked back, they saw the smoke rising to the sky. There was no way for them to escape, because the Israelites who had run towards the barren country now turned round to attack them.

Narrator 1
When Joshua and his men saw that the others had taken the city and that it was on fire, they turned round and began killing the men of Ai. The Israelites in the city now came down to join the battle.

Narrator 2
So the men of Ai found themselves completely surrounded by Israelites, and they were all killed. No one got away, and no one lived through it except the king of Ai. He was captured and taken to Joshua.

Cast   [This is] the word of the Lord.
All   **Thanks be to God.**

Cast: **Narrator 1, Narrator 2** (can be the same as Narrator 1), **The Lord, Joshua.**

The Gibeonites deceive Joshua
Joshua 9.1–27

Narrator
The victories of Israel became known to all the kings west of the Jordan—in the hills, in the foothills, and all along the coastal plain of the Mediterranean Sea as far north as Lebanon; these were the kings of the Hittites, the Amorites, the Canaanites, the Perizzites, the Hivites, and the Jebusites. They all came together and joined forces to fight against Joshua and the Israelites.

→

159

But the people of Gibeon, who were Hivites, heard what Joshua had done to Jericho and Ai, and they decided to deceive him. They went and got some food and loaded their donkeys with worn-out sacks and patched-up wineskins. They put on ragged clothes and worn-out sandals that had been mended. The bread they took with them was dry and mouldy. Then they went to the camp at Gilgal and said to Joshua and the men of Israel:

Gibeonite 1	We have come from a distant land.
Gibeonite 2	We want you to make a treaty with us.
Narrator	But the men of Israel said:
Israelite 1	Why should we make a treaty with you?
Israelite 2	Maybe you live nearby.
Narrator	They said to Joshua:
Gibeonites 1 and 2	We are at your service.
Narrator	Joshua asked them:
Joshua	Who are you? Where do you come from?
Narrator	Then they told him this story:
Gibeonite 1	We have come from a very distant land, sir, because we have heard of the Lord your God.
Gibeonite 2	We have heard about everything that he did in Egypt and what he did to the two Amorite kings east of the Jordan: King Sihon of Heshbon and King Og of Bashan, who lived in Ashtaroth.
Gibeonite 1	Our leaders and all the people that live in our land told us to get some food ready for a journey and to go and meet you. We were told to put ourselves at your service and ask you to make a treaty with us.
Gibeonite 2	Look at our bread. When we left home with it and started out to meet you, it was still warm. But look! Now it is dry and mouldy.
Gibeonite 1	When we filled these wineskins, they were new, but look! They are torn.
Gibeonite 2	Our clothes and sandals are worn out from the long journey.
Narrator	The men of Israel accepted some food from them, but did not consult the Lord about it. Joshua made a treaty of friendship with the people of Gibeon and allowed them to live. The leaders of the community of Israel gave their solemn promise to keep the treaty. (PAUSE)

Three days after the treaty had been made, the Israelites learnt that these people did indeed live nearby. So the people of Israel started out and three days later arrived at the cities where these people lived: Gibeon, Chephirah, Beeroth, and Kiriath Jearim. But the Israelites could not kill them, because their leaders had made a solemn promise to them in the name of the Lord, Israel's

God. All the people complained to the leaders about this, but they answered:

Israelite 1   We have made our solemn promise to them in the name of the Lord God of Israel. Now we cannot harm them.

Israelite 2   We must let them live because of our promise; if we don't, God will punish us.

Israelite 1   Let them live, but they will have to cut wood and carry water for us.

Narrator   This was what the leaders suggested.

Joshua ordered the people of Gibeon to be brought to him, and he asked them:

Joshua   Why did you deceive us and tell us that you were from far away, when you live right here? Because you did this, God has condemned you. Your people will always be slaves, cutting wood and carrying water for the sanctuary of my God.

Narrator   They answered:

Gibeonite 1   We did it, sir, because we learnt that it was really true that the Lord your God had commanded his servant Moses to give you the whole land and to kill the people living in it as you advanced.

Gibeonite 2   We did it because we were terrified of you; we were in fear of our lives. Now we are in your power; do with us what you think is right.

Narrator   So this is what Joshua did: he protected them and did not allow the people of Israel to kill them. But at the same time he made them slaves, to cut wood and carry water for the people of Israel and for the Lord's altar. To this day they have continued to do this work in the place where the Lord has chosen to be worshipped.

Cast   [This is] the word of the Lord.
All   **Thanks be to God.**

Cast: **Narrator, Gibeonite 1, Gibeonite 2, Israelite 1, Israelite 2, Joshua.**

The Amorites are defeated
Joshua 10.1–15

Narrator   Adonizedek, the king of Jerusalem, heard that Joshua had captured and totally destroyed Ai and had killed its king, just as he had done to Jericho and its king. He also heard that the people of Gibeon had made peace with the Israelites and were living among them. The people of Jerusalem were greatly alarmed at this because Gibeon was as large as any of the cities that had a king; it was larger than Ai, and its men were good fighters. So Adonizedek sent the following message to King Hoham of Hebron, King Piram of Jarmuth, King Japhia of Lachish, and to King Debir of Eglon:

Adonizedek	Come and help me attack Gibeon, because its people have made peace with Joshua and the Israelites.
Narrator	These five Amorite kings, the kings of Jerusalem, Hebron, Jarmuth, Lachish, and Eglon, joined forces, surrounded Gibeon, and attacked it.
	The men of Gibeon sent word to Joshua at the camp in Gilgal:
Gibeonite 1	Do not abandon us, sir!
Gibeonite 2	Come at once and help us!
Gibeonites 1 and 2	Save us!
Gibeonite 1	All the Amorite kings in the hill-country have joined forces and have attacked us!
Narrator	So Joshua and his whole army, including the best troops, started out from Gilgal. The Lord said to Joshua:
The Lord	Do not be afraid of them. I have already given you the victory. Not one of them will be able to stand against you.
Narrator	All night Joshua and his army marched from Gilgal to Gibeon, and they made a surprise attack on the Amorites. The Lord made the Amorites panic at the sight of Israel's army. The Israelites slaughtered them at Gibeon and pursued them down the mountain pass at Beth Horon, keeping up the attack as far south as Azekah and Makkedah. While the Amorites were running down the pass from the Israelite army, the Lord made large hailstones fall down on them all the way to Azekah. More were killed by the hailstones than by the Israelites.
	On the day that the Lord gave the men of Israel victory over the Amorites, Joshua spoke to the Lord. In the presence of the Israelites he said:
Joshua	Sun, stand still over Gibeon; moon, stop over Aijalon Valley.
Narrator	The sun stood still and the moon did not move until the nation had conquered its enemies. This is written in The Book of Jashar. The sun stood still in the middle of the sky and did not go down for a whole day. Never before, and never since, has there been a day like it, when the Lord obeyed a human being. The Lord fought on Israel's side!
	After this, Joshua and his army went back to the camp at Gilgal.
Cast All	[This is] the word of the Lord. **Thanks be to God.**

Cast: **Narrator, Adonizedek, Gibeonite 1, Gibeonite 2, The Lord, Joshua.**

Joshua captures the five Amorite kings
Joshua 10.16–27

Narrator   The five Amorite kings had escaped and were hiding in the cave at Makkedah. Someone found them, and Joshua was told where they were hiding. [He said.]

Joshua   Roll some big stones in front of the entrance to the cave. Place some guards there, but don't stay there yourselves. Keep on after the enemy and attack them from the rear; don't let them get to their cities! The Lord your God has given you victory over them.

Narrator   Joshua and the men of Israel slaughtered them, although some managed to find safety inside their city walls and were not killed. Then all of Joshua's men came back safe to him at the camp at Makkedah.

No one in the land dared even to *speak* against the Israelites.

Then Joshua said:

Joshua   Open the entrance to the cave and bring those five kings out to me.

Narrator   So the cave was opened, and the kings of Jerusalem, Hebron, Jarmuth, Lachish, and Eglon were brought out and taken to Joshua. Joshua then called all the men of Israel to him and ordered the officers who had gone with him to come and put their feet on the necks of the kings. They did so. Then Joshua said to his officers:

Joshua   Don't be afraid or discouraged. Be determined and confident because this is what the Lord is going to do to all your enemies.

Narrator   Then Joshua killed the kings and hanged them on five trees, where their bodies stayed until evening. At sunset Joshua gave orders, and their bodies were taken down and thrown into the same cave where they had hidden earlier. Large stones were placed at the entrance to the cave, and they are still there.

Cast   [This is] the word of the Lord.
All   **Thanks be to God.**

Cast: **Narrator, Joshua.**

Ephraim and West Manasseh request more land
Joshua 17.14–18

Narrator   The descendants of Joseph said to Joshua:

Person 1   Why have you given us only one part of the land to possess as our own?

Person 2   There are very many of us because the Lord has blessed us.

Narrator   Joshua answered:

Joshua	If there are so many of you and the hill-country of Ephraim is too small for you, then go into the forests and clear ground for yourselves in the land of the Perizzites and the Rephaim.
Person 2	The hill-country is not big enough for us—
Person 1	But the Canaanites in the plains have iron chariots, both those who live in Beth Shan and its surrounding towns and those who live in the Valley of Jezreel.
Narrator	Joshua said to the tribes of Ephraim and West Manasseh:
Joshua	There are indeed many of you, and you are very powerful. You shall have more than one share. The hill-country will be yours. Even though it is a forest, you will clear it and take possession of it from one end to the other. As for the Canaanites, you will drive them out, even though they do have iron chariots and are a strong people.
Cast	[This is] the word of the Lord.
All	**Thanks be to God.**

Cast: **Narrator, Person 1, Person 2, Joshua.**

The division of the rest of the land
Joshua 18.1–10

Narrator	After they had conquered the land, the entire community of Israel assembled at Shiloh and set up the Tent of the Lord's presence. There were still seven tribes of the people of Israel who had not yet been assigned their share of the land. So Joshua said to the people of Israel:
Joshua	How long are you going to wait before you go in and take the land that the Lord, the God of your ancestors, has given you? Let me have three men from each tribe. I will send them out over the whole country to map out the territory that they would like to have as their possession. Then they are to come back to me. The land will be divided among them in seven parts; Judah will stay in its territory in the south, and Joseph in its territory in the north. Write down a description of these seven divisions and bring it to me. Then I will draw lots to consult the Lord our God for you. The Levites, however, will not receive a share of the land with the rest of you, because their share is to serve as the Lord's priests. And of course, the tribes of Gad, Reuben, and East Manasseh have already received their land east of the Jordan, which Moses, the Lord's servant, gave to them.
Narrator	The men went on their way to map out the land after Joshua had given them these instructions:
Joshua	Go all over the land and map it out, and come back to me. And then here in Shiloh I will consult the Lord for you by drawing lots.
Narrator	So the men went all over the land and set down in writing how they divided it into seven parts, making a list of the towns. Then

they went back to Joshua in the camp at Shiloh. Joshua drew lots to consult the Lord for them, and assigned each of the remaining tribes of Israel a certain part of the land.

Cast	[This is] the word of the Lord.
All	**Thanks be to God.**

Cast: **Narrator, Joshua.**

Israel takes possession of the land
Joshua 21.43—22.9

Narrator The Lord gave to Israel all the land that he had solemnly promised their ancestors he would give them. When they had taken possession of it, they settled down there. The Lord gave them peace throughout the land, just as he had promised their ancestors. Not one of all their enemies had been able to stand against them, because the Lord gave the Israelites the victory over all their enemies. The Lord kept every one of the promises that he had made to the people of Israel.

Then Joshua called together the people of the tribes of Reuben, Gad, and East Manasseh. [He said to them:]

Joshua You have done everything that Moses the Lord's servant ordered you to do and you have obeyed all my commands. All this time you have never once deserted your fellow-Israelites. You have been careful to obey the commands of the Lord your God. Now, as he promised, the Lord your God has given your fellow-Israelites peace. So go back home to the land which you claimed for your own, the land on the east side of the Jordan, that Moses, the Lord's servant, gave you. Make sure you obey the law that Moses commanded you: love the Lord your God, do his will, obey his commandments, be faithful to him, and serve him with all your heart and soul.

Narrator Joshua sent them home with his blessing [and with these words]:

Joshua You are going back home very rich, with a lot of livestock, silver, gold, bronze, iron, and many clothes. Share with your fellow-tribesmen what you took from your enemies.

Narrator Then they left for home (PAUSE).

Moses had given land east of the Jordan to one half of the tribe of Manasseh, but to the other half Joshua had given land west of the Jordan, along with the other tribes.

So the people of the tribes of Reuben, Gad, and East Manasseh went back home. They left the rest of the people of Israel at Shiloh in the land of Canaan and started out for their own land, the land of Gilead, which they had taken as the Lord had commanded them through Moses.

Cast	[This is] the word of the Lord.
All	**Thanks be to God.**

Cast: **Narrator, Joshua.**

The altar by the Jordan
From Joshua 22.10–33

Narrator	When the tribes of Reuben, Gad, and East Manasseh arrived at Geliloth, still on the west side of the Jordan, they built a large, impressive altar there by the river. The rest of the people of Israel were told:
Persons 1 and 2	Listen!
Person 1	The people of the tribes of Reuben, Gad, and East Manasseh have built an altar at Geliloth.
Person 2	On our side of the Jordan!
Narrator	When the people of Israel heard this, the whole community came together at Shiloh to go to war against the eastern tribes.
	Then the people of Israel sent Phinehas, the son of Eleazar the priest, to the people of the tribes of Reuben, Gad, and East Manasseh in the land of Gilead. Ten leading men went with Phinehas, one from each of the western tribes and each one the head of a family among the clans. They came to the land of Gilead, to the people of Reuben, Gad, and East Manasseh, and speaking for the whole community of the Lord, they said to them:
Leader 1	Why have you done this evil thing against the God of Israel?
Leader 2	You have rebelled against the Lord by building this altar for yourselves! You are no longer following him!
Leader 1	Remember our sin at Peor, when the Lord punished his own people with an epidemic? We are still suffering because of that. Wasn't that sin enough?
Leader 2	Are you going to refuse to follow him now?
Leader 1	If you rebel against the Lord today, he will be angry with everyone in Israel tomorrow. Now then, if your land is not fit to worship in, come over into the Lord's land, where his Tent is.
Leader 2	Claim some land among us. But don't rebel against the Lord or make rebels out of us by building an altar in addition to the altar of the Lord our God.
Leader 3	Remember how Achan son of Zerah refused to obey the command about the things condemned to destruction; the whole community of Israel was punished for that. Achan was not the only one who died because of his sin.
Narrator	The people of the tribes of Reuben, Gad, and East Manasseh answered the heads of the families of the western tribes:
Person 3	The Mighty One is God!
Persons 4 and 5	He is the Lord!
Person 3	The Mighty One is God!

Persons 4 and 5	He is the Lord!
Person 4	He knows why we did this, and we want you to know too!
Person 5	If we rebelled and did not keep faith with the Lord, do not let us live any longer!
Person 3	If we disobeyed the Lord and built our own altar to burn sacrifices on or to use for grain-offerings or fellowship-offerings, let the Lord himself punish us.
Person 4	No! We did it because we were afraid that in the future your descendants would say to ours, 'What do you have to do with the Lord, the God of Israel?'
Narrator	Phinehas the priest and the ten leading men of the community who were with him, the heads of families of the western tribes, heard what the people of the tribes of Reuben, Gad, and East Manasseh had to say, and they were satisfied. Phinehas, the son of Eleazar the priest, said to them:
Phinehas	Now we know that the Lord is with us. You have not rebelled against him, and so you have saved the people of Israel from the Lord's punishment.
Narrator	Then Phinehas and the leaders left the people of Reuben and Gad in the land of Gilead and went back to Canaan, to the people of Israel, and reported to them. The Israelites were satisfied and praised God. They no longer talked about going to war to devastate the land where the people of Reuben and Gad had settled.
Cast	[This is] the word of the Lord.
All	**Thanks be to God.**

Cast: **Narrator, Person 1, Person 2** (can be the same as Person 1), **Person 3, Person 4, Person 5** (can be the same as Person 4), **Leader 1, Leader 2, Leader 3** (Leaders 1–3 can be the same), **Phinehas.**

Joshua speaks to the people at Shechem
From Joshua 24:14–25

[Narrator	Joshua said:]
Joshua	Now then, honour the Lord and serve him sincerely and faithfully. Get rid of the gods which your ancestors used to worship in Mesopotamia and in Egypt, and serve only the Lord. If you are not willing to serve him, decide today whom you will serve, the gods your ancestors worshipped in Mesopotamia or the gods of the Amorites, in whose land you are now living. As for my family and me, we will serve the Lord.
[Narrator	The people replied:]
Person 1	We would never leave the Lord to serve other gods!
Person 2	The Lord our God brought our fathers and us out of slavery in Egypt—

Person 3	And we saw the miracles that he performed.
Person 2	He kept us safe wherever we went among all the nations through which we passed.
Person 3	As we advanced into this land, the Lord drove out all the Amorites who lived here.
Person 1	So *we also* will serve the Lord; he is our God.
Joshua	But you may not be *able* to serve the Lord. He is a holy God and will not forgive your sins. He will tolerate no rivals, and if you leave him to serve foreign gods, he will turn against you and punish you. He will destroy you, even though he was good to you before.
Person 1	No—
Persons 2 and **3**	We *will* serve the Lord!
Joshua (firmly)	You are your own witnesses to the fact that you have chosen to serve the Lord.
Persons 1 and **2**	Yes—
Person 3	We are witnesses.
Joshua (demanding)	Then get rid of those foreign gods that you have, and pledge your loyalty to the Lord, the God of Israel.
Person 1	We will serve the Lord our God.
Person 2	We will obey his commands.
Narrator	So Joshua made a covenant for the people that day.
Cast	[This is] the word of the Lord.
All	**Thanks be to God.**

Cast: [**Narrator**], **Joshua, Person 1, Person 2, Person 3** (Persons 1–3 can be the same).

JUDGES

The tribes of Judah and Simeon capture Adonibezek
Judges 1.1–7

Narrator   After Joshua's death the people of Israel asked the Lord:

Person 1   Which of our tribes should be the first to go and attack the Canaanites?

Narrator   The Lord answered:

The Lord   The tribe of Judah will go first. I am giving them control of the land.

Narrator   The people of Judah said to the people of Simeon:

Person 2   Go with us into the territory assigned to us, and we will fight the Canaanites together.

Person 3   Then we will go with you into the territory assigned to you.

Narrator   So the tribes of Simeon and Judah went into battle together. The Lord gave them victory over the Canaanites and the Perizzites, and they defeated ten thousand men at Bezek. They found Adonibezek there and fought against him. He ran away, but they chased him, caught him, and cut off his thumbs and big toes. Adonibezek said:

Adonibezek   Seventy kings with their thumbs and big toes cut off have picked up scraps under my table. God has now done to me what I did to them.

Narrator   He was taken to Jerusalem, where he died.

Cast   [This is] the word of the Lord.
All   **Thanks be to God.**

Cast: **Narrator, Person 1, The Lord, Person 2, Person 3** (can be the same as Person 2), **Adonibezek**.

Deborah and Barak
Judges 4.1—5.3

Narrator 1   After Ehud died, the people of Israel sinned against the Lord again. So the Lord let them be conquered by Jabin, a Canaanite king who ruled in the city of Hazor. The commander of his army was Sisera, who lived at Harosheth-of-the-Gentiles. Jabin had nine hundred iron chariots, and he ruled the people of Israel with cruelty and violence for twenty years. Then the people of Israel cried out to the Lord for help.

Narrator 2   Now Deborah, the wife of Lappidoth, was a prophet, and she was serving as a judge for the Israelites at that time. She used to sit under a certain palm-tree between Ramah and Bethel in the hill-

→

	country of Ephraim, and the people of Israel would go there for her decisions. One day she sent for Barak son of Abinoam from the city of Kedesh in Naphtali and said to him:
Deborah	The Lord, the God of Israel, has given you this command:
The Lord	Take ten thousand men from the tribes of Naphtali and Zebulun and lead them to Mount Tabor. I will bring Sisera, the commander of Jabin's army, to fight against you at the River Kishon. He will have his chariots and soldiers, but I will give you victory over him.
Narrator 1	Then Barak replied:
Barak (to Deborah)	I will go if you go with me, but if you don't go with me, *I* won't go either.
Deborah	All right, I will go with you, but you won't get any credit for the victory, because the Lord will hand Sisera over to a woman.
Narrator 1	So Deborah set off for Kedesh with Barak. (PAUSE)
	Barak called the tribes of Zebulun and Naphtali to Kedesh, and ten thousand men followed him. Deborah went with him.
Narrator 2	In the meantime Heber the Kenite had set up his tent close to Kedesh near the oak-tree at Zanannim. He had moved away from the other Kenites, the descendants of Hobab, the brother-in-law of Moses.
Narrator 1	When Sisera learnt that Barak had gone up to Mount Tabor, he called out his nine hundred iron chariots and all his men, and sent them from Harosheth-of-the-Gentiles to the River Kishon. Then Deborah said to Barak:
Deborah	Go! The Lord is leading you! Today he has given you victory over Sisera.
Narrator 1	So Barak went down from Mount Tabor with his ten thousand men. When Barak attacked with his army, the Lord threw Sisera into confusion together with all his chariots and men. Sisera got down from his chariot and fled on foot. Barak pursued the chariots and the army to Harosheth-of-the-Gentiles, and Sisera's whole army was killed. Not a man was left.
Narrator 2	Sisera ran away to the tent of Jael, the wife of Heber the Kenite, because King Jabin of Hazor was at peace with Heber's family. Jael went out to meet Sisera and said to him:
Jael (to Sisera)	Come in, sir; come into my tent. Don't be afraid.
Narrator 2	So he went in, and she hid him behind a curtain. [He said to her:]
Sisera	Please give me a drink of water; I'm thirsty.
Narrator 2	She opened a leather bag of milk, gave him a drink, and hid him again.
Sisera (to Jael)	Stand at the door of the tent, and if anyone comes and asks you if someone is here, say no.

Narrator 2	Sisera was so tired that he fell sound asleep. Then Jael took a hammer and a tent-peg, went up to him quietly, and killed him by driving the peg right through the side of his head and into the ground.
Narrator 1	When Barak came looking for Sisera, Jael went out to meet him:
Jael	Come here! I'll show you the man you're looking for.
Narrator 1	So he went in with her, and there was Sisera on the ground, dead, with the tent-peg through his head.
Narrator 2	That day God gave the Israelites victory over Jabin, the Canaanite king. They pressed harder and harder against him until they destroyed him.
Narrator 1	On that day Deborah and Barak son of Abinoam sang this song:
Deborah and **Barak**	Praise the Lord!
Barak	The Israelites were determined to fight.
Deborah	The people gladly volunteered.
Barak	Listen, you kings! Pay attention, you rulers!
Deborah	I will sing, I will play music to Israel's God, the Lord.
Cast	[This is] the word of the Lord.
All	**Thanks be to God.**

Cast: **Narrator 1, Narrator 2,** (can be the same as Narrator 1), **Deborah, The Lord** (can be the same as Deborah), **Barak, Jael, Sisera.**

Gideon
Judges 6.[1–10] 11–24

The people cry out to the Lord (Judges 6.1–10)

[Narrator	Once again the people of Israel sinned against the Lord, so he let the people of Midian rule them for seven years. The Midianites were stronger than Israel, and the people of Israel hid from them in caves and other safe places in the hills.
	Whenever the Israelites sowed any seed, the Midianites would come with the Amalekites and the desert tribes and attack them. They would camp on the land and destroy the crops as far south as the area round Gaza. They would take all the sheep, cattle, and donkeys, and leave nothing for the Israelites to live on. They would come with their cattle and tents, as thick as locusts. They and their camels were too many to count. They came and devastated the land, and Israel was helpless against them.
	Then the people of Israel cried out to the Lord for help against the Midianites, and he sent them a prophet who brought them this message from the Lord, the God of Israel:

171

The Lord	I brought you out of slavery in Egypt. I rescued you from the Egyptians and from the people who fought against you here in this land. I drove them out as you advanced, and I gave you their land. I told you that I am the Lord your God and that you should not worship the gods of the Amorites, whose land you are now living in. But you did not listen to me.]

God calls Gideon (Judges 6.11–24)

Narrator	[Then] the Lord's angel came to the village of Ophrah and sat under the oak tree that belonged to Joash, a man of the clan of Abiezer. His son Gideon was threshing some wheat secretly in a winepress, so that the Midianites would not see him. The Lord's angel appeared to him there [and said:]
Angel	The Lord is with you, brave and mighty man!
[Narrator	Gideon said to him:]
Gideon	If I may ask, sir, why has all this happened to us if the Lord is with us? What about all the wonderful things that our fathers told us the Lord used to do—how he brought them out of Egypt? The Lord has abandoned us and left us to the mercy of the Midianites.
Narrator	Then the Lord ordered him:
The Lord	Go with all your great strength and rescue Israel from the Midianites. I myself am sending you.
Gideon	But Lord, how can *I* rescue Israel? My clan is the weakest in the tribe of Manasseh, and I am the least important member of my family.
The Lord	You can do it because I will help you. You will crush the Midianites as easily as if they were only one man.
Gideon	If you are pleased with me, give me some *proof* that you are really the Lord. Please do not leave until I bring you an offering of food.
Angel	I will stay until you come back.
Narrator	So Gideon went into his house and cooked a young goat and used ten kilogrammes of flour to make bread without any yeast. He put the meat in a basket and the broth in a pot, brought them to the Lord's angel under the oak-tree, and gave them to him. The angel ordered him:
Angel	Put the meat and the bread on this rock, and pour the broth over them.
Narrator	Gideon did so. (PAUSE)
	Then the Lord's angel reached out and touched the meat and the bread with the end of the stick he was holding. Fire came out of the rock and burnt up the meat and the bread. Then the angel disappeared.
	Gideon then realized that it was the Lord's angel he had seen, and he said in terror:

172

Judges	Sovereign Lord! I have seen your angel face to face!
Narrator	But the Lord said to him:
The Lord	Peace. Don't be afraid. You will not die.
Narrator	Gideon built an altar to the Lord there and named it:
Gideon	'The Lord is Peace'.
Cast	[This is] the word of the Lord.
All	**Thanks be to God.**

Cast: **Narrator, The Lord, Angel** (can be the same as The Lord), **Gideon.**

Gideon tears down the altar
Judges 6.25–32

Narrator	[That night] the Lord told Gideon:
The Lord	Take your father's bull and another bull seven years old, tear down your father's altar to Baal, and cut down the symbol of the goddess Asherah, which is beside it. Build a well-constructed altar to the Lord your God on top of this mound. Then take the second bull and burn it whole as an offering, using for firewood the symbol of Asherah you have cut down.
Narrator	So Gideon took ten of his servants and did what the Lord had told him. He was too afraid of his family and the people of the town to do it by day, so he did it at night. (PAUSE)
	When the people of the town got up early the next morning, they found that the altar to Baal and the symbol of Asherah had been cut down, and that the second bull had been burnt on the altar that had been built there. They asked each other:
Person 1	Who did this?
Narrator	They investigated and found out that Gideon son of Joash had done it. Then they said to Joash:
Person 2	Bring your son out here, so that we can kill him!
Person 1	He tore down the altar to Baal and cut down the symbol of Asherah beside it.
Narrator	But Joash said to all those who confronted him:
Joash	Are you standing up for Baal? Are you defending him? Anyone who stands up for him will be killed before morning. If Baal is a god, let him defend him*self*. It is *his* altar that was torn down.
Narrator	From then on Gideon was known as Jerubbaal, because Joash said, 'Let Baal defend himself; it is his altar that was torn down.'
Cast	[This is] the word of the Lord.
All	**Thanks be to God.**

Cast: **Narrator, The Lord, Person 1, Person 2** (can be the same as Person 1), **Joash.**

Gideon and the fleece
Judges 6.33–40

Narrator   All the Midianites, the Amalekites, and the desert tribes assembled, crossed the River Jordan, and camped in the Valley of Jezreel. The spirit of the Lord took control of Gideon, and he blew a trumpet to call the men of the clan of Abiezer to follow him. He sent messengers throughout the territory of both parts of Manasseh to call them to follow him. He sent messengers to the tribes of Asher, Zebulun, and Naphtali, and they also came to join him. Then Gideon said to God:

Gideon   You say that you have decided to use me to rescue Israel. Well, I am putting some wool on the ground where we thresh the wheat. If in the morning there is dew only on the wool but not on the ground, then I will know that you are going to use me to rescue Israel.

Narrator   That is exactly what happened. When Gideon got up early the next morning, he squeezed the wool and wrung enough dew out of it to fill a bowl with water. Then Gideon said to God:

Gideon   Don't be angry with me; let me speak just once more. Please let me make one more test with the wool. This time let the wool be dry, and the ground be wet.

Narrator   That night God did that very thing. The next morning the wool was dry, but the ground was wet with dew.

Cast   [This is] the word of the Lord.
All   **Thanks be to God.**

Cast: **Narrator, Gideon.**

Gideon chooses his men
Judges 7.1–8

Narrator   One day Gideon and all his men got up early and camped beside the Spring of Harod. The Midianite camp was in the valley to the north of them by Moreh Hill. The Lord said to Gideon:

The Lord   The men you have are too many for me to give them victory over the Midianites. They might think that they had won by themselves, and so give me no credit. Announce to the people, 'Anyone who is afraid should go back home, and we will stay here at Mount Gilead.'

Narrator   So twenty-two thousand went back, but ten thousand stayed. (PAUSE)

Then the Lord said to Gideon:

The Lord   You still have too many men. Take them down to the water, and I will separate them for you there. If I tell you a man should go with you, he will go. If I tell you a man should not go with you, he will not go.

Narrator	Gideon took the men down to the water [and the Lord said to him]:
The Lord	Separate everyone who laps up the water with his tongue like a dog, from everyone who gets down on his knees to drink.
Narrator	There were three hundred men who scooped up water in their hands and lapped it; all the others got down on their knees to drink. [The Lord said to Gideon:]
The Lord	I will rescue you and give you victory over the Midianites with the three hundred men who lapped the water. Tell everyone else to go home.
Narrator	So Gideon sent all the Israelites home, except the three hundred, who kept all the supplies and trumpets. The Midianite camp was below them in the valley.
Cast	[This is] the word of the Lord.
All	**Thanks be to God.**

Cast: **Narrator, The Lord.**

Gideon defeats the Midianites
Judges 7.9–21

Narrator	The Lord commanded Gideon:
The Lord	Get up and attack the camp; I am giving you victory over it. But if you are afraid to attack, go down to the camp with your servant Purah. You will hear what they are saying, and then you will have the courage to attack.
Narrator	So Gideon and his servant Purah went down to the edge of the enemy camp. The Midianites, the Amalekites, and the desert tribesmen were spread out in the valley like a swarm of locusts, and they had as many camels as there were grains of sand on the seashore. (PAUSE) When Gideon arrived, he heard a man telling a friend about a dream. He was saying:
Man	I dreamt that a loaf of barley bread rolled into our camp and hit a tent. The tent collapsed and lay flat on the ground.
Narrator	His friend replied:
Friend (awestruck)	It's the sword of the Israelite, Gideon son of Joash! It can't mean anything else! God has given him victory over Midian and our whole army!
Narrator	When Gideon heard about the man's dream and what it meant, he fell to his knees and worshipped the Lord. Then he went back to the Israelite camp [and said]:
Gideon	Get up! The Lord is giving you victory over the Midianite army!
Narrator	He divided his three hundred men into three groups and gave each man a trumpet and a jar with a torch inside it. [He told them:]

175

Gideon	When I get to the edge of the camp, watch me, and do what I do. When my group and I blow our trumpets, then you blow yours all round the camp and shout, 'For the Lord and for Gideon!'
Narrator	Gideon and his hundred men came to the edge of the camp a short while before midnight, just after the guard had been changed. Then they blew the trumpets and broke the jars they were holding, and the other two groups did the same. They all held the torches in their left hands, the trumpets in their right, and shouted:
Gideon, Soldiers 1 & 2	A sword for the Lord and for Gideon!
Narrator	Every man stood in his place round the camp, and the whole enemy army ran away yelling.
Cast	[This is] the word of the Lord.
All	**Thanks be to God.**

Cast: **Narrator, The Lord, Man, Friend, Gideon, Soldiers 1 and 2** (can be replaced by whole cast except for Narrator).

The final defeat of the Midianites
Judges 8.1–28

Narrator	Then the men of Ephraim said to Gideon:
Man 1	Why didn't you call us when you went to fight the Midianites?
Man 2	Why did you treat us like this?
Narrator	They complained bitterly about it. [But he said:]
Gideon	What I was able to do is nothing compared with what you have done. Even the little that you men of Ephraim did is worth more than what my whole clan has done. After all, through the power of God you killed the two Midianite chiefs, Oreb and Zeeb. What have I done to compare with that?
Narrator	When he said this, they were no longer so angry. By this time Gideon and his three hundred men had come to the River Jordan and had crossed it. They were exhausted, but were still pursuing the enemy. When they arrived at Sukkoth, he said to the men of the town:
Gideon	Please give my men some loaves of bread. They are exhausted, and I am pursuing Zebah and Zalmunna, the Midianite kings.
Narrator	But the leaders of Sukkoth said:
Leader 1	Why should we give your army any food?
Leader 2	You haven't captured Zebah and Zalmunna yet.
Gideon	All right! When the Lord has handed Zebah and Zalmunna over to me, I will beat you with thorns and briars from the desert!

Narrator	Gideon went on to Penuel and made the same request of the people there, but the men of Penuel gave the same answer as the men of Sukkoth. So he said to them:
Gideon	I am going to come back safe and sound, and when I do, I will tear your tower down!
Narrator	Zebah and Zalmunna were at Karkor with their army. Of the whole army of desert tribesmen, only about 15,000 were left; 120,000 soldiers had been killed.
	Gideon went along the road by the edge of the desert, east of Nobah and Jogbehah, and attacked the army by surprise. The two Midianite kings, Zebah and Zalmunna, ran away, but he pursued them and captured them, and caused their whole army to panic.
	When Gideon was returning from the battle by way of Heres Pass, he captured a young man from Sukkoth and questioned him. The young man wrote down for Gideon the names of the seventy-seven leading men of Sukkoth. Then Gideon went to the men of Sukkoth and said:
Gideon	Remember when you refused to help me? You said that you couldn't give any food to my exhausted army because I hadn't captured Zebah and Zalmunna yet. Well, here they are!
Narrator	He then took thorns and briars from the desert and used them to punish the leaders of Sukkoth. He also tore down the tower at Penuel and killed the men of that city.
	Then Gideon asked Zebah and Zalmunna:
Gideon	What about the men you killed at Tabor?
[Narrator	They answered:]
Zebah	They looked like you—
Zalmunna	Every one of them like the son of a king.
Gideon (bitterly)	They were my brothers, my own mother's sons. I solemnly swear that if you had not killed them, I would not kill you.
Narrator	Then he said to Jether, his eldest son:
Gideon	Go ahead, kill them!
Narrator	But the boy did not draw his sword. He hesitated, because he was still only a boy.
	Then Zebah and Zalmunna said to Gideon:
Zebah	Come on, kill us yourself.
Zalmunna	It takes a man to do a man's job.
Narrator	So Gideon killed them and took the ornaments that were on the necks of their camels. After that, the Israelites said to Gideon:
Person 1	Be our ruler—you and your descendants after you.
Person 2	You have saved us from the Midianites.

Narrator	Gideon answered:
Gideon	I will not be your ruler, nor will my son. The Lord will be your ruler. (PAUSE)
[Narrator	But he went on to say:]
Gideon	Let me ask one thing of you. Every one of you give me the earrings you took.
Narrator	The Midianites, like other desert people, wore gold earrings.
	[The people answered:]
Person 1	We'll be glad to give them to you.
Narrator	They spread out a cloth, and everyone put on it the earrings that he had taken. The gold earrings that Gideon received weighed nearly twenty kilogrammes, and this did not include the ornaments, necklaces, and purple clothes that the kings of Midian wore, nor the collars that were round the necks of their camels. Gideon made an idol from the gold and put it in his home town, Ophrah. All the Israelites abandoned God and went there to worship the idol. It was a trap for Gideon and his family.
	So Midian was defeated by the Israelites and was no longer a threat. The land was at peace for forty years, until Gideon died.
Cast	[This is] the word of the Lord.
All	**Thanks be to God.**

Cast: **Narrator, Man 1, Man 2** (can be the same as Man 1), **Gideon, Leader 1 Leader 2,** (can be the same as Leader 1), **Zebah, Zalmunna, Person 1, Person 2** (can be the same as Person 1).

Abimelech (i)
From Judges 9.1–21

Narrator	Gideon's son Abimelech went to the town of Shechem, where all his mother's relatives lived, and told them to ask the men of Shechem:
Person 1	Which would you prefer? To be governed by all seventy of Gideon's sons or by just one man?
Person 2	Remember that Abimelech is your own flesh and blood.
Narrator	His mother's relatives talked to the men of Shechem about this for him, and the men of Shechem decided to follow Abimelech because he was their relative. They gave him seventy pieces of silver from the temple of Baal-of-the-Covenant, and with this money he hired a bunch of worthless scoundrels to join him. He went to his father's house at Ophrah, and there on the top of a single stone he killed his seventy brothers, Gideon's sons. But Jotham, Gideon's youngest son, hid and was not killed. Then all the men of Shechem and Bethmillo got together and went to the sacred oak-tree at Shechem, where they made Abimelech king.
	When Jotham heard about this, he went and stood on top of Mount Gerizim and shouted out to them:

Jotham	Listen to me, you men of Shechem, and God may listen to you! Once upon a time the trees got together to choose a king for themselves. They said to the olive-tree:
Tree(s)	Be our king.
Jotham	The olive-tree answered:
Olive-tree	In order to govern you, I would have to stop producing my oil, which is used to honour gods and men.
Jotham	Then the trees said to the fig-tree:
Tree(s)	You come and be our king.
Jotham	But the fig-tree answered:
Fig-tree	In order to govern you, I would have to stop producing my good sweet fruit.
Jotham	So the trees then said to the grapevine:
Tree(s)	You come and be our king.
Jotham	But the vine answered:
Vine	In order to govern you, I would have to stop producing my wine, that makes gods and men happy.
Jotham	So then all the trees said to the thorn-bush:
Tree(s)	You come and be our king.
Jotham	The thorn-bush answered:
Thorn-bush	If you really want to make me your king, then come and take shelter in my shade. If you don't, fire will blaze out of my thorny branches and burn up the cedars of Lebanon.
Jotham	Now then, were you really honest and sincere when you made Abimelech king? Did you respect Gideon's memory and treat his family properly, as his actions deserved? Now then, if what you did today to Gideon and his family was sincere and honest, then be happy with Abimelech and let him be happy with you. But if not, may fire blaze out from Abimelech and burn up the men of Shechem and Bethmillo. May fire blaze out from the men of Shechem and Bethmillo and burn Abimelech up.
Narrator	Then because he was afraid of his brother Abimelech, Jotham ran away and went to live at Beer.
Cast	[This is] the word of the Lord.
All	**Thanks be to God.**

Cast: **Narrator, Person 1, Person 2** (can be the same as Person 1), **Jotham, Tree(s), Olive-tree, Fig-tree, Vine, Thorn-bush.**

Abimelech (ii)
From Judges 9.22–41

Narrator   Abimelech ruled Israel for three years. Then God made Abimelech and the men of Shechem hostile to each other, and they rebelled against him. This happened so that Abimelech and the men of Shechem, who encouraged him to murder Gideon's seventy sons, would pay for their crime. The men of Shechem put men in ambush against Abimelech on the mountain-tops, and they robbed everyone who passed their way. Abimelech was told about this.

Then Gaal son of Ebed came to Shechem with his brothers, and the men of Shechem put their confidence in him. They all went out into their vineyards and picked the grapes, made wine from them, and held a festival. They went into the temple of their god, where they ate and drank and spoke scornfully of Abimelech. Gaal said:

Gaal   What kind of men are we in Shechem? Why are we serving Abimelech? Who is he, anyway? The son of Gideon! And Zebul takes orders from him, but why should we serve him? Be loyal to your ancestor Hamor, who founded your clan! I wish I were leading this people! I would get rid of Abimelech! l would say to him, 'Reinforce your army, come on out and fight!'

Narrator   Zebul, the ruler of the city, became angry when he heard what Gaal had said. He sent messengers to Abimelech at Arumah:

Zebul   Gaal son of Ebed and his brothers have come to Shechem, and they are not going to let you into the city. Now then, you and your men should move by night and hide in the fields. Get up tomorrow morning at sunrise and make a sudden attack on the city. Then when Gaal and his men come out against you, hit them as hard as you can!

Narrator   So Abimelech and all his men made their move at night and hid outside Shechem in four groups. When Abimelech and his men saw Gaal come out and stand at the city gate, they got up from their hiding places. Gaal saw them [and said to Zebul]:

Gaal   Look! There are men coming down from the mountain-tops!

Zebul (wearily)   Those are not men. They are just shadows on the mountains.

Gaal   Look! There *are* men coming down the crest of the mountain and one group is coming along the road from the oak-tree of the fortune-tellers!

Zebul   Where is all your big talk now? You were the one who asked why we should serve this man Abimelech. These are the men you were treating so scornfully. Go on out now and fight them.

Narrator   Gaal led the men of Shechem out and fought Abimelech. Gaal

180

fled, and Abimelech pursued him. Many were wounded, even at the city gate. Abimelech lived in Arumah, and Zebul drove Gaal and his brothers out of Shechem, so that they could no longer live there.

Cast	[This is] the word of the Lord.
All	**Thanks be to God.**

Cast: **Narrator, Gaal, Zebul.**

Jephthah
Judges 10.10—11.11

Narrator	The Israelites cried out to the Lord:
Israelite 1	We have sinned against you.
Israelite 2	We left you, our God, and worshipped the Baals.
Narrator	The Lord gave them this answer:
The Lord	The Egyptians, the Amorites, the Ammonites, the Philistines, the Sidonians, the Amalekites, and the Maonites oppressed you in the past, and you cried out to me. Did I not save you from them? But you still left me and worshipped other gods, so I am not going to rescue you again. Go and cry out to the gods you have chosen. Let them rescue you when you get into trouble.
Narrator	But the people of Israel said to the Lord:
Israelite 1	We have sinned.
Israelite 2	Do whatever you like, but please, save us today.
Narrator	So they got rid of their foreign gods and worshipped the Lord; and he became troubled over Israel's distress. (PAUSE)
	Then the Ammonite army prepared for battle and made camp in Gilead. The men of Israel came together and camped at Mizpah in Gilead. There the people and the leaders of the Israelite tribes asked one another:
Israelite 1	Who will lead the fight against the Ammonites?
Israelite 2	Whoever does will be the leader of everyone in Gilead.
Narrator	Jephthah, a brave soldier from Gilead, was the son of a prostitute. His father Gilead had other sons by his wife, and when they grew up, they forced Jephthah to leave home. They said to him:
Israelite 1	You will not inherit anything from our father; you are the son of another woman.
Narrator	Jephthah fled from his brothers and lived in the land of Tob. There he attracted a group of worthless men, and they went round with him.
	It was some time later that the Ammonites went to war against Israel. When this happened, the leaders of Gilead went to bring Jephthah back from the land of Tob. They said:

Israelite 2	Come and lead us.
Israelite 1	So that we can fight the Ammonites.
Narrator	But Jephthah answered:
Jephthah	You hated me so much that you forced me to leave my father's house. Why come to me now that you're in trouble?
Israelite 1	We are turning to you now because we want you to go with us and fight the Ammonites—
Israelite 2	And lead all the people of Gilead.
Jephthah	If you take me back home to fight the Ammonites and the Lord gives me victory, I will be your ruler.
Israelites 1 and 2	We agree.
Israelite 2	The Lord is our witness.
Narrator	So Jephthah went with the leaders of Gilead, and the people made him their ruler and leader. Jephthah stated his terms at Mizpah in the presence of the Lord.
Cast	[This is] the word of the Lord.
All	**Thanks be to God.**

Cast: **Narrator, Israelite 1, Israelite 2, The Lord, Jephthah.**

Jephthah defeats Ammon
From Judges 11.12–33

Narrator	Jephthah sent messengers to the king of Ammon to say:
Messenger 1	What is your quarrel with us?
Messenger 2	Why have you invaded our country?
Narrator	The king of Ammon answered Jephthah's messengers:
King	When the Israelites came out of Egypt, they took away my land from the River Arnon to the River Jabbok and the River Jordan. Now you must give it back peacefully.
Narrator	Jephthah sent messengers back to the king of Ammon with the answer:
Jephthah	It is not true that Israel took away the land of Moab or the land of Ammon. For three hundred years Israel has occupied Heshbon and Aroer, and the towns round them, and all the cities on the banks of the River Arnon. Why haven't you taken them back in all this time? No, I have not done you any wrong. You are doing wrong by making war on me. The Lord is the judge. He will decide today between the Israelites and the Ammonites.
Narrator	But the king of Ammon paid no attention to this message from Jephthah. (PAUSE)

Then the spirit of the Lord came upon Jephthah. He went through Gilead and Manasseh and returned to Mizpah in Gilead and went on to Ammon. Jephthah promised the Lord:

Jephthah   If you give me victory over the Ammonites, I will burn as an offering the first person that comes out of my house to meet me, when I come back from the victory. I will offer that person to you as a sacrifice.

Narrator   So Jephthah crossed the river to fight the Ammonites, and the Lord gave him victory. He struck at them from Aroer to the area round Minnith, twenty cities in all, and as far as Abel Keramim. There was a great slaughter, and the Ammonites were defeated by Israel.

Cast   [This is] the word of the Lord.
All   **Thanks be to God.**

Cast: **Narrator, Messenger 1, Messenger 2** (can be the same as Messenger 1), **King, Jephthah.**

Jephthah's daughter
From Judges 11.30–40

Narrator   Jephthah promised the Lord:

Jephthah   If you give me victory over the Ammonites I will burn as an offering the first person that comes out of my house to meet me when I come back from the victory. I will offer that person to you as a sacrifice.

Narrator   And the Lord gave him victory. (PAUSE) When Jephthah went back home to Mizpah, there was his daughter coming out to meet him, dancing and playing the tambourine. She was his only child. When he saw her, he tore his clothes in sorrow:

Jephthah   Oh, my daughter! You are breaking my heart! Why must it be you that causes me pain? I have made a solemn promise to the Lord, and I cannot take it back!

[Narrator   She said to him:]

Daughter   If you have made a promise to the Lord, do what you said you would do to me, since the Lord has given you revenge on your enemies, the Ammonites. (PAUSE) Do this one thing for me. Leave me alone for two months, so that I can go with my friends to wander in the mountains and grieve that I must die a virgin.

Narrator   He told her to go and sent her away for two months. She and her friends went up into the mountains and grieved because she was going to die unmarried and childless. After two months she came back to her father. He did what he had promised the Lord, and she died still a virgin. (PAUSE)

This was the origin of the custom in Israel that the young women would go away for four days every year to grieve for the daughter of Jephthah of Gilead.

Cast   [This is] the word of the Lord.
All   **Thanks be to God.**

Cast: **Narrator, Jephthah, Daughter.** (This reading overlaps with the previous one.)

Jephthah and the Ephraimites
Judges 12.1–7

Narrator	The men of Ephraim prepared for battle; they crossed the River Jordan to Zaphon and said to Jephthah:
Man 1	Why did you cross the border to fight the Ammonites without calling us to go with you?
Man 2	We'll burn the house down over your head!
Narrator	But Jephthah said to them:
Jephthah	My people and I had a serious quarrel with the Ammonites. I did call you, but you would not rescue me from them. When I saw that you were not going to, I risked my life and crossed the border to fight them, and the Lord gave me victory over them. So why are you coming to fight me now?
Narrator	Then Jephthah brought all the men of Gilead together, fought the men of Ephraim and defeated them.
[Commentator	The Ephraimites had said, 'You Gileadites in Ephraim and Manasseh, you are deserters from Ephraim!']
Narrator	In order to keep the Ephraimites from escaping, the Gileadites captured the places where the Jordan could be crossed. When any Ephraimite who was trying to escape asked permission to cross, the men of Gilead would ask:
Man 1	Are you an Ephraimite?
Narrator	If he said:
Man 2	No.
Narrator	They would tell him to say 'Shibboleth'. But he would say:
Man 2	'Sibboleth'—
Narrator	Because he could not pronounce it correctly. Then they would seize him and kill him there at one of the crossings of the Jordan. At that time forty-two thousand of the Ephraimites were killed.

Jephthah led Israel for six years. Then he died and was buried in his home town in Gilead. |
| **Cast** | [This is] the word of the Lord. |
| **All** | **Thanks be to God.** |

Cast: **Narrator, Man 1, Man 2, Jephthah, Commentator** (can be the same as Narrator).

The birth of Samson
Judges 13.1–25

Narrator	The Israelites sinned against the Lord again, and he let the Philistines rule them for forty years.
	At that time there was a man named Manoah from the town of Zorah. He was a member of the tribe of Dan. His wife had never been able to have children. The Lord's angel appeared to her and said:
Angel	You have never been able to have children, but you will soon be pregnant and have a son. Take care not to drink any wine or beer, or eat any forbidden food; and after your son is born, you must never cut his hair, because from the day of his birth he will be dedicated to God as a Nazirite. He will begin the work of rescuing Israel from the Philistines.
Narrator	Then the woman went and said to her husband:
Wife	A man of God has come to me, and he looked as frightening as the angel of God. I didn't ask him where he came from, and he didn't tell me his name. But he did tell me that I would become pregnant and have a son. He told me not to drink any wine or beer, or eat any forbidden food, because the boy is to be dedicated to God as a Nazirite as long as he lives.
Narrator	Then Manoah prayed to the Lord:
Manoah	Please, Lord, let the man of God that you sent come back to us and tell us what we must do with the boy when he is born.
Narrator	God did what Manoah asked, and his angel came back to the woman while she was sitting in the fields. Her husband Manoah was not with her, so she ran at once and said to him:
Wife	Look! The man who came to me the other day has appeared to me again.
Narrator	Manoah got up and followed his wife. He went to the man [and asked]:
Manoah	Are you the man who was talking to my wife?
Angel	Yes.
Manoah	When your words come true, what must the boy do? What kind of a life must he lead?
Angel	Your wife must be sure to do everything that I have told her. She must not eat anything that comes from the grapevine; she must not drink any wine or beer, or eat any forbidden food. She must do everything that I have told her.
Narrator	Manoah did not know that it was the Lord's angel [so he said to him]:
Manoah	Please do not go yet. Let us cook a young goat for you.

Angel	If I do stay, I will not eat your food. But if you want to prepare it, burn it as an offering to the Lord.
Manoah	Tell us your name, so that we can honour you when your words come true.
Angel	Why do you want to know my name? It is a name of wonder.
Narrator	So Manoah took a young goat and some grain, and offered them on the rock altar to the Lord who works wonders.
	While the flames were going up from the altar, Manoah and his wife saw the Lord's angel go up towards heaven in the flames. Manoah realized then that the man had been the Lord's angel, and he and his wife threw themselves face downwards on the ground. They never saw the angel again.
	[Manoah said to his wife:]
Manoah (to wife)	We are sure to die, because we have seen God!
Wife	If the Lord had wanted to kill us, he would not have accepted our offerings; he would not have shown us all this or told us such things now.
Narrator	The woman gave birth to a son and named him Samson. The child grew and the Lord blessed him. And the Lord's power began to strengthen him while he was between Zorah and Eshtaol in the Camp of Dan.
Cast	[This is] the word of the Lord.
All	**Thanks be to God.**

Cast: **Narrator, Angel, Wife, Manoah.**

Samson and the girl from Timnah
Judges 14.1–20

Narrator	One day Samson went down to Timnah, where he noticed a certain Philistine girl. He went back home and said to his father and mother:
Samson	There is a Philistine girl down at Timnah who has caught my attention. Get her for me; I want to marry her.
[Narrator	But his mother and father asked him:]
Mother	Why do you have to go to those heathen Philistines to get a wife?
Father	Can't you find a girl in our own clan, among all our people?
Narrator	But Samson said to his father:
Samson	She is the one I want you to get for me. I like her.
Narrator	His parents did not know that it was the Lord who was leading Samson to do this, for the Lord was looking for a chance to fight the Philistines. At this time the Philistines were ruling Israel. (PAUSE)

So Samson went down to Timnah with his father and mother. As they were going through the vineyards there, he heard a young lion roaring. Suddenly the power of the Lord made Samson strong, and he tore the lion apart with his bare hands, as if it were a young goat. But he did not tell his parents what he had done.

Then he went and talked to the girl, and he liked her. A few days later Samson went back to marry her. On the way he left the road to look at the lion he had killed, and he was surprised to find a swarm of bees and some honey inside the dead body. He scraped the honey out into his hands and ate it as he walked along. Then he went to his father and mother and gave them some. They ate it, but Samson did not tell them that he had taken the honey from the dead body of a lion.

His father went to the girl's house, and Samson gave a banquet there. This was a custom among the young men. When the Philistines saw him, they sent thirty young men to stay with him. Samson said to them:

Samson	Let me ask you a riddle. I'll bet each one of you a piece of fine linen and a change of fine clothes that you can't tell me its meaning before the seven days of the wedding feast are over.
Man 1	Tell us your riddle.
Man 2	Let's hear it.
Samson (slowly)	Out of the eater came something to eat; out of the strong came something sweet.
Narrator	Three days later they had still not solved the riddle.
	On the fourth day they said to Samson's wife:
Man 1	Trick your husband into telling us what the riddle means.
Man 2	If you don't, we'll set fire to your father's house and burn you with it.
Man 1	You two invited us so that you could rob us, didn't you?
Narrator	So Samson's wife went to him in tears and said:
Wife	You don't love me! You just hate me! You asked my friends a riddle and didn't tell me what it means!
Samson	Look, I haven't even told my father and mother. Why should I tell you?
Narrator	She cried about it for the whole seven days of the feast. But on the seventh day he told her what the riddle meant, for she nagged him about it so much. Then she told the Philistines. (PAUSE)
	So on the seventh day, before Samson went into the bedroom, the men of the city said to him:
Man 1	What could be sweeter than honey?
Man 2	What could be stronger than a lion?
Narrator	Samson replied:

Samson (rhyming)	If you hadn't been ploughing with my cow, you wouldn't know the answer now.
Narrator	Suddenly the power of the Lord made him strong, and he went down to Ashkelon, where he killed thirty men, stripped them, and gave their fine clothes to the men who had solved the riddle. After that, he went back home, furious about what had happened, and his wife was given to the man that had been his best man at the wedding.
Cast **All**	[This is] the word of the Lord. **Thanks be to God.**

Cast: **Narrator, Samson, Mother, Father, Man 1, Man 2, Wife.**

Samson and the foxes
Judges 15.1–8

Narrator	Samson went to visit his wife during the wheat harvest and took her a young goat. He said to her father:
Samson	I want to go to my wife's room.
Narrator	But he wouldn't let him go in. [He said to Samson:]
Father	I really thought that you hated her, so I gave her to your friend. But her younger sister is prettier, anyway. You can have her, instead.
Samson (angrily)	This time I'm not going to be responsible for what I do to the Philistines!
Narrator	So he went and caught three hundred foxes. Two by two, he tied their tails together and put torches in the knots. Then he set fire to the torches and turned the foxes loose in the Philistine cornfields. In this way he burnt up not only the corn that had been harvested but also the corn that was still in the fields, and the olive orchards as well. When the Philistines asked who had done this, they learnt that Samson had done it because his father-in-law, a man from Timnah, had given Samson's wife to a friend of Samson's. So the Philistines went and burnt the woman to death and burnt down her father's house. Samson told them:
Samson	So this is how you act! I swear that I won't stop until I pay you back!
Narrator	He attacked them fiercely and killed many of them. Then he went and stayed in the cave in the cliff at Etam.
Cast **All**	[This is] the word of the Lord. **Thanks be to God.**

Cast: **Narrator, Samson, Father.**

Samson defeats the Philistines
Judges 15.9—16.3

Narrator	The Philistines came and made camp in Judah, and attacked the town of Lehi. The men of Judah asked them:
Man 1	Why are you attacking us?
Narrator	They answered:
Philistine	We came to take Samson prisoner and to treat him as he treated us.
Narrator	So three thousand men of Judah went to Samson in the cave in the cliff at Etam:
Man 1	Don't you know that the Philistines are our rulers?
Man 2	What have you done to us?
[Narrator	He answered:]
Samson	I did to them just what they did to me.
Man 2	We have come here to tie you up, so that we can hand you over to them.
Samson	Give me your word that you won't kill me yourselves.
Man 1	All right, we are only going to tie you up and hand you over to them.
Man 2	We won't kill you.
Narrator	So they tied him up with two new ropes and brought him back from the cliff. (PAUSE)
	When he got to Lehi, the Philistines came running towards him, shouting at him. Suddenly the power of the Lord made him strong, and he broke the ropes round his arms and hands as if they were burnt thread. Then he found the jaw-bone of a donkey that had recently died. He bent down and picked it up, and killed a thousand men with it. (PAUSE)
	So Samson sang:
Samson	With the jaw-bone of a donkey I killed a thousand men; with the jaw-bone of a donkey I piled them up in piles.
Narrator	After that, he threw the jaw-bone away. The place where this happened was named Ramath Lehi.
	Then Samson became very thirsty, so he called to the Lord:
Samson	You gave me this great victory; am I now going to die of thirst and be captured by these heathen Philistines?
Narrator	Then God opened a hollow place in the ground there at Lehi, and water came out of it. Samson drank it and began to feel much better. So the spring was named Hakkore; it is still there at Lehi.
	Samson led Israel for twenty years while the Philistines ruled the land. (PAUSE)

→

One day Samson went to the Philistine city of Gaza, where he met a prostitute and went to bed with her. The people of Gaza found out that Samson was there, so they surrounded the place and waited for him all night long at the city gate. They were quiet all night, thinking to themselves:

Person 1 (furtively)	We'll wait until daybreak.
Person 2	And then we'll kill him.
Narrator	But Samson stayed in bed only until midnight. Then he got up and took hold of the city gate and pulled it up—doors, posts, lock, and all. He put them on his shoulders and carried them all the way to the top of the hill overlooking Hebron.
Cast **All**	[This is] the word of the Lord. **Thanks be to God.**

Cast: **Narrator, Man 1, Philistine, Man 2, Samson, Person 1, Person 2.**

Samson and Delilah
Judges 16.4–22

Narrator	Samson fell in love with a woman named Delilah, who lived in the Valley of Sorek. The five Philistine kings went to her and said:
Philistine 1	Trick Samson into telling you why he is so strong and how we can overpower him.
Philistine 2	Tie him up, and make him helpless.
Philistine 3	Each one of us will give you eleven hundred pieces of silver.
Narrator	So Delilah said to Samson:
Delilah	Please tell me what makes you so strong. If someone wanted to tie you up and make you helpless, how could he do it?
Samson	If they tie me up with seven new bowstrings that are not dried out, I'll be as weak as anybody else.
Narrator	So the Philistine kings brought Delilah seven new bowstrings that were not dried out, and she tied Samson up. She had some men waiting in another room, so she shouted:
Delilah	Samson! The Philistines are coming!
Narrator	But he snapped the bowstrings just as thread breaks when fire touches it. So they still did not know the secret of his strength. (PAUSE) [Delilah said to Samson:]
Delilah	Look, you've been making a fool of me and not telling me the truth. Please tell me how someone could tie you up.
Samson	If they tie me with new ropes that have never been used, I'll be as weak as anybody else.

190

Narrator	So Delilah got some new ropes and tied him up. Then she shouted:
Delilah	Samson! The Philistines are coming!
Narrator	The men were waiting in another room. But he snapped the ropes off his arms like thread. [Delilah said to Samson:]
Delilah	You're still making a fool of me and not telling me the truth. Tell me how someone could tie you up.
Samson	If you weave my seven locks of hair into a loom, and make it tight with a peg, I'll be as weak as anybody else.
Narrator	Delilah then lulled him to sleep, took his seven locks of hair, and wove them into the loom. She made it tight with a peg and shouted:
Delilah	Samson! The Philistines are coming!
Narrator	But he woke up and pulled his hair loose from the loom. [So she said to him:]
Delilah	How can you say you love me, when you don't mean it? You've made a fool of me three times, and you still haven't told me what makes you so strong.
Narrator	She kept on asking him, day after day. He got so sick and tired of her nagging him about it that he finally told her the truth.
Samson	My hair has never been cut. I have been dedicated to God as a Nazirite from the time I was born. If my hair were cut, I would lose my strength and be as weak as anybody else.
Narrator	When Delilah realized that he had told her the truth, she sent a message to the Philistine kings [and said]:
Delilah	Come back just once more. He has told me the truth.
Narrator	Then they came and brought the money with them. Delilah lulled Samson to sleep in her lap and then called a man, who cut off Samson's seven locks of hair. Then she began to torment him, for he had lost his strength. Then she shouted:
Delilah	Samson! The Philistines are coming!
Narrator	He woke up and thought:
Samson	I'll get loose and go free, as always.
Narrator	He did not know that the Lord had left him. The Philistines captured him and put his eyes out. They took him to Gaza, chained him with bronze chains, and put him to work grinding at the mill in the prison. But his hair started growing again.
Cast	[This is] the word of the Lord.
All	**Thanks be to God.**

Cast: **Narrator, Philistine 1, Philistine 2, Philistine 3** (can be the same as Philistine 1, OR Philistines 1–3 can be the same), **Delilah, Samson.**

Samson's death and victory
Judges 16.23–30 [31]

Narrator   The Philistine kings met together to celebrate and offer a great sacrifice to their god Dagon. They sang:

Philistine 1   Our god has given us victory over our enemy Samson!

Narrator   They were enjoying themselves, so they said:

Philistine 1   Call Samson.

Philistine 2   Let's make him entertain us!

Narrator   When they brought Samson out of the prison, they made him entertain them and made him stand between the pillars. When the people saw him, they sang praise to their god:

Philistine 3   Our god has given us victory over our enemy, who devastated our land—

Philistine 2   And killed so many of us!

Narrator   Samson said to the boy who was leading him by the hand:

Samson   Let me touch the pillars that hold up the building. I want to lean on them.

Narrator   The building was crowded with men and women. All five Philistine kings were there, and there were about three thousand men and women on the roof, watching Samson entertain them. (PAUSE)

Then Samson prayed:

Samson   Sovereign Lord, please remember me; please, God, give me my strength just once more, so that with this one blow I can get even with the Philistines for putting out my two eyes.

Narrator   So Samson took hold of the two middle pillars holding up the building. Putting one hand on each pillar, he pushed against them and shouted:

Samson   Let me die with the Philistines!

Narrator   He pushed with all his might, and the building fell down on the five kings and everyone else. Samson killed more people at his death than he had killed during his life.

[His brothers and the rest of his family came down to get his body. They took him back and buried him between Zorah and Eshtaol in the tomb of his father Manoah. He had been Israel's leader for twenty years.]

Cast   [This is] the word of the Lord.
All   **Thanks be to God.**

Cast: **Narrator, Philistine 1, Philistine 2, Philistine 3** (Philistines 1–3 can be the same), **Samson.**

Micah's idols
Judges 17.1–13

Narrator

There was once a man named Micah, who lived in the hill-country of Ephraim. He said to his mother:

Micah

When someone stole those eleven hundred pieces of silver from you, you put a curse on the thief. I heard you do it. Look, I have the money. I am the one who took it.

[Narrator

His mother said:]

Mother

May the Lord bless you, my son!

Narrator

He gave the money back to his mother [and she said]:

Mother
(to audience)

To stop the curse from falling on my son, I myself am solemnly dedicating the silver to the Lord.

(to Micah)

It will be used to make a wooden idol covered with silver. So now I will give the pieces of silver back to you.

Narrator

Then he gave them back to his mother. She took two hundred of the pieces of silver and gave them to a metal-worker, who made an idol, carving it from wood and covering it with the silver. It was placed in Micah's house.

This man Micah had his own place of worship. He made some idols and an ephod, and appointed one of his sons as his priest. There was no king in Israel at that time; everyone did just as he pleased. (PAUSE)

At that same time there was a young Levite who had been living in the town of Bethlehem in Judah. He left Bethlehem to find somewhere else to live. While he was travelling, he came to Micah's house in the hill-country of Ephraim. Micah asked him:

Micah
(to Levite)

Where do you come from?

Levite

I am a Levite from Bethlehem in Judah. I am looking for somewhere to live.

Micah

Stay with me. Be my adviser and priest, and I will give you ten pieces of silver a year, some clothes, and your food.

Narrator

The young Levite agreed to stay with Micah and became like a son to him. Micah appointed him as his priest, and he lived in Micah's home.

Micah
(to audience)

Now that I have a Levite as my priest, I know that the Lord will make things go well for me.

Cast   [This is] the word of the Lord.
All   **Thanks be to God.**

Cast: **Narrator, Micah, Mother, Levite.**

Micah and the tribe of Dan
Judges 18.1–31

Narrator	There was no king in Israel at that time. In those days the tribe of Dan was looking for territory to claim and occupy because they had not yet received any land of their own among the tribes of Israel. So the people of Dan chose five qualified men out of all the families in the tribe and sent them from the towns of Zorah and Eshtaol with instructions to explore the land. When they arrived in the hill-country of Ephraim, they stayed at Micah's house. While they were there, they recognized the accent of the young Levite [so they went up to him and asked]:
Man 1	What are you doing here?
Man 2	Who brought you here?
Levite	I have an arrangement with Micah, who pays me to serve as his priest.
Man 3	Please ask God if we are going to be successful on our journey.
[Narrator	The priest answered:]
Levite	You have nothing to worry about. The Lord is taking care of you on this journey.
Narrator	So the five men left and went to the town of Laish. They saw how safely the people there were living, like the Sidonians. They were a peaceful, quiet people, with no disputes with anyone; they had all they needed. They lived far away from the Sidonians and had no dealings with any other people. When the five men returned to Zorah and Eshtaol, their countrymen asked them what they had found out. They replied:
Man 1	Come on. Let's attack Laish.
Man 2	We saw the land, and it's very good.
Man 3	Don't stay here doing nothing; hurry!
Man 1	Go on in and take it over!
Man 3	When you get there, you will find that the people don't suspect a thing.
Man 2	It is a big country; it has everything a person could want—
Man 1	And God has given it to you.
Narrator	So six hundred men from the tribe of Dan left Zorah and Eshtaol, ready for battle. They went up and made camp west of Kiriath Jearim in Judah. That is why the place is still called Camp of Dan. They went on from there and came to Micah's house in the hill-country of Ephraim. Then the five men who had gone to explore the country round Laish said to their companions:
Man 1	Did you know that here in one of these houses there is a wooden idol covered with silver?

194

Man 2	There are also other idols and an ephod.
Man 3	What do you think we should do?
Narrator	So they went into Micah's house, where the young Levite lived, and asked the Levite how he was getting on. Meanwhile the six hundred soldiers from Dan, ready for battle, were standing at the gate. The five spies went straight on into the house and took the wooden idol covered with silver, the other idols, and the ephod, while the priest stayed at the gate with the six hundred armed men. (PAUSE)
	When the men went into Micah's house and took the sacred objects, the priest asked them:
Levite	What are you doing?
Man 1	Keep quiet.
Man 3	Don't say a word.
Man 2	Come with us and be our priest and adviser.
Man 1	Wouldn't you rather be a priest for a whole Israelite tribe than for the family of one man?
Narrator	This made the priest very happy, so he took the sacred objects and went along with them. (PAUSE) They turned round and started off, with their children, their livestock, and their belongings going ahead. They had travelled a good distance from the house when Micah called his neighbours out for battle. They caught up with the men from Dan and shouted at them. The men from Dan turned round and asked Micah:
Man 1	What's the matter?
Man 2	Why all this mob?
[Narrator	Micah answered:]
Micah	What do you mean, 'What's the matter?' You take my priest and the gods that I made, and walk off! What have I got left?
Narrator	The men from Dan said:
Man 1	You had better not say anything else unless you want these men to get angry and attack you.
Man 3	Then you and your whole family would die.
Narrator	Then they went on. Micah saw that they were too strong for him, so he turned and went back home. (PAUSE) After the men from Dan had taken the priest and the things that Micah had made, they went and attacked Laish, that town of peaceful, quiet people which was in the same valley as Bethrehob. They killed the inhabitants and burnt the town. There was no one to save them, because Laish was a long way from Sidon, and they had no dealings with any other people. The men from Dan rebuilt the town and settled down there. They changed its name from

$\rightarrow$

Laish to Dan, after their ancestor Dan, the son of Jacob. The men from Dan set up the idol to be worshipped, and Jonathan, the son of Gershom and grandson of Moses, served as a priest for the tribe of Dan, and his descendants served as their priests until the people were taken away into exile. Micah's idol remained there all the time that the Tent where God was worshipped remained at Shiloh.

Cast	[This is] the word of the Lord.
All	**Thanks be to God.**

Cast: **Narrator, Man 1, Man 2, Levite, Man 3, Micah.**

The Levite and his concubine (i)
Judges 19.1–21

Narrator In the days before Israel had a king, there was a Levite living far back in the hill-country of Ephraim. He took a girl from Bethlehem in Judah to be his concubine, but she became angry with him, went back to her father's house in Bethlehem, and stayed there four months. Then the man decided to go after her and try to persuade her to return to him. He took his servant and two donkeys with him. The girl showed the Levite into the house, and when her father saw him, he gave him a warm welcome. The father insisted that he stay, and so he stayed for three days. The couple had their meals and spent the nights there. On the morning of the fourth day they woke up early and got ready to go. But the girl's father said to the Levite:

Father Have something to eat first. It will do you good. You can go later.

Narrator So the two men sat down and ate and drank together. Then the girl's father said to him:

Father Please spend the night here and enjoy yourself.

Narrator The Levite got up to go, but the father urged him to stay, so he spent another night there. Early in the morning of the fifth day he started to leave, but the girl's father said:

Father Eat something, please. Wait until later in the day.

Narrator So the two men ate together. (PAUSE)

When the man, his concubine, and the servant once more started to leave, the father said:

Father Look, it's almost evening now; you might as well stay all night. It will be dark soon; stay here and have a good time. Tomorrow you can get up early for your journey and go home.

Narrator But the man did not want to spend another night there, so he and his concubine started on their way, with their servant and two donkeys with pack saddles. It was late in the day when they came near Jebus—

[Commentator That is, Jerusalem]

Narrator	So the servant said to his master:
Servant	Why don't we stop and spend the night here in this Jebusite city?
Narrator	But his master said:
Levite	We're not going to stop in a city where the people are not Israelites. We'll pass on and go a little farther and spend the night at Gibeah or Ramah.
Narrator	So they went past Jebus and continued on their way. It was sunset when they came to Gibeah in the territory of the tribe of Benjamin. They turned off the road to go and spend the night there. They went into the city and sat down in the square, but no one offered to take them home for the night.
	While they were there, an old man came by at the end of a day's work in the fields. He was originally from the hill-country of Ephraim, but he was now living in Gibeah.
[Commentator	The other people there were from the tribe of Benjamin.]
Narrator	The old man noticed the traveller in the city square and asked him:
Old man	Where do you come from? Where are you going?
Narrator	The Levite answered:
Levite	We have been to Bethlehem in Judah, and now we are on our way home deep in the hill-country of Ephraim. No one will put us up for the night, even though we have fodder and straw for our donkeys, as well as bread and wine for my concubine and me and for my servant. We have everything we need.
Old man	You are welcome in my home! I'll take care of you; you don't have to spend the night in the square.
Narrator	So he took them home with him and fed their donkeys. His guests washed their feet and had a meal.
Cast	[This is] the word of the Lord.
All	**Thanks be to God.**

Cast: **Narrator, Father, [Commentator,] Servant, Levite, Old man.**

The Levite and his concubine (ii)
Judges 19.22–30

Narrator	The old man and his guests were enjoying themselves when all of a sudden some sexual perverts from the town surrounded the house and started beating on the door. They said to the old man:
Man 1	Bring out that man that came home with you!
Man 2	We want to have sex with him!
Narrator	But the old man went outside and said to them:

Old man	No, my friends! Please! Don't do such an evil, immoral thing! This man is my guest. Look! Here is his concubine and my own daughter, who is a virgin. I'll bring them out now, and you can have them. Do with them whatever you want. But don't do such an awful thing to this man!
Narrator	But the men would not listen to him. So the Levite took his concubine and put her outside with them. They raped her and abused her all night long and didn't stop until morning.
	At dawn the woman came and fell down at the door of the old man's house, where her husband was. She was still there when daylight came. Her husband got up that morning, and when he opened the door to go on his way, he found his concubine lying in front of the house with her hands reaching for the door. [He said:]
Levite	Get up. Let's go.
Narrator	But there was no answer. So he put her body across the donkey and started on his way home. When he arrived, he went into the house and got a knife. He took his concubine's body, cut it into twelve pieces, and sent one piece to each of the twelve tribes of Israel. Everyone who saw it said:
Person 1	We have never heard of such a thing!
Person 2	Nothing like this has ever happened since the Israelites left Egypt!
Person 1	We have to do something about this! What will it be?
Cast	[This is] the word of the Lord.
All	**Thanks be to God.**

Cast: **Narrator, Man 1, Man 2, Old man, Levite, Person 1, Person 2.**

Israel prepares for war
Judges 20.1–17

Narrator	All the people of Israel from Dan in the north to Beersheba in the south, as well as from the land of Gilead in the east, gathered in one body in the Lord's presence at Mizpah. The leaders of all the tribes of Israel were present at this gathering of God's people, and there were 400,000 foot-soldiers. Meanwhile the people of Benjamin heard that all the other Israelites had gathered at Mizpah. [The Israelites asked:]
Person 1	Tell us, how was this crime committed?
Narrator	The Levite whose concubine had been murdered answered:
Levite	My concubine and I went to Gibeah in the territory of Benjamin to spend the night. The men of Gibeah came to attack me and surrounded the house at night. They intended to kill me; instead they raped my concubine, and she died. I took her body, cut it in pieces, and sent one piece to each of the twelve tribes of Israel.

These people have committed an evil and immoral act among us. All of you here are Israelites. What are we going to do about this?

Narrator All the people stood up together and said:

Person 1 None of us, whether he lives in a tent or in a house, will go home.

Person 2 This is what we will do: we will draw lots and choose some men to attack Gibeah.

Person 1 One tenth of the men in Israel will provide food for the army—

Person 2 And the others will go and punish Gibeah for this immoral act that they have committed in Israel.

Narrator So all the men in Israel assembled with one purpose—to attack the town.

The Israelite tribes sent messengers all through the territory of the tribe of Benjamin to say:

Messenger 1 What is this crime that you have committed?

Messenger 2 Now hand over those perverts in Gibeah, so that we can kill them and remove this evil from Israel.

Narrator But the people of Benjamin paid no attention to the other Israelites. From all the cities of Benjamin they came to Gibeah to fight against the other people of Israel. They called out twenty-six thousand soldiers from their cities that day. Besides these, the citizens of Gibeah gathered seven hundred specially chosen men who were left-handed. Every one of them could sling a stone at a strand of hair and never miss. The rest of the Israelite tribes gathered 400,000 trained soldiers.

Cast [This is] the word of the Lord.
All **Thanks be to God.**

Cast: **Narrator, Person 1, Levite, Person 2, Messenger 1, Messenger 2** (can be the same as Messenger 1).

The war against the Benjaminites
Judges 20.18–36

Narrator The Israelites went to the place of worship at Bethel, and there they asked God:

Person 1 Which tribe should attack the Benjaminites first?

Narrator The Lord answered:

The Lord The tribe of Judah.

Narrator So the Israelites started out the next morning and made camp near the city of Gibeah. They went to attack the army of Benjamin, and placed the soldiers in position facing the city. The army of Benjamin came out of the city, and before the day was over they had killed twenty-two thousand Israelite soldiers. Then the Israelites went to the place of worship and mourned in the presence of the Lord until evening. They asked him:

Person 2	Should we go again into battle against our brothers the Benjaminites?
[Narrator	The Lord answered:]
The Lord	Yes.
Narrator	So the Israelite army was encouraged, and they placed their soldiers in the same position as they had been the day before. They marched against the army of Benjamin a second time. And for the second time the Benjaminites came out of Gibeah, and this time they killed eighteen thousand trained Israelite soldiers. (PAUSE) Then all the people of Israel went up to Bethel and mourned. They sat there in the Lord's presence and did not eat until evening. They offered fellowship sacrifices and burnt some sacrifices whole—all in the presence of the Lord. God's Covenant Box was there at Bethel in those days, and Phinehas, the son of Eleazar and grandson of Aaron, was in charge of it. The people asked the Lord:
Person 1	Should we go out to fight our brothers the Benjaminites again?
Person 2	Or should we give up?
[Narrator	The Lord answered:]
The Lord	Fight. Tomorrow I will give you victory over them.
Narrator	So the Israelites put some soldiers in hiding round Gibeah. Then for the third successive day they marched against the army of Benjamin and placed their soldiers in battle position facing Gibeah, as they had done before. The Benjaminites came out to fight and were led away from the city. As before, they began killing some Israelites in the open country on the road to Bethel and on the road to Gibeah. They killed about thirty Israelites. The Benjaminites said:
Benjaminites 1 and 2	We've beaten them.
Benjaminite 2	Just as we did before.
Narrator	But the Israelites had *planned* to retreat and lead them away from the city on to the roads. So when the main army of the Israelites pulled back and regrouped at Baaltamar, the men surrounding Gibeah suddenly rushed out of their hiding places in the rocky country round the city. Ten thousand men, specially chosen out of all Israel, attacked Gibeah, and the fighting was hard. The Benjaminites had not realized that they were about to be destroyed. The Lord gave Israel victory over the army of Benjamin. The Israelites killed 25,000 of the enemy that day, and the Benjaminites realized they were defeated.
Cast	[This is] the word of the Lord.
All	**Thanks be to God.**

Cast: **Narrator, Person 1, The Lord, Person 2** (can be the same as Person 1), **Benjaminite 1, Benjaminite 2** (can be the same as Benjaminite 1).

Wives for the tribe of Benjamin
Judges 21.1–25

Narrator   When the Israelites had gathered at Mizpah, they had made a solemn promise to the Lord:

Person 1   None of us will allow a Benjaminite to marry a daughter of ours.

Narrator   So now the people of Israel went to Bethel and sat there in the presence of God until evening. Loudly and bitterly they mourned:

Person 1   Lord God of Israel, why has this happened?

Person 2   Why is the tribe of Benjamin about to disappear from Israel?

Narrator   Early the next morning the people built an altar there, offered fellowship sacrifices and burnt some sacrifices whole. [They asked:]

Person 3   Is there any group out of all the tribes of Israel that did not go to the gathering in the Lord's presence at Mizpah?

[Commentator   They had taken a solemn oath that anyone who had not gone to Mizpah would be put to death.]

Narrator   The people of Israel felt sorry for their brothers the Benjaminites [and said]:

Person 1   Today Israel has lost one of its tribes.

Person 2   What shall we do to provide wives for the men of Benjamin who are left?

Person 3   We have made a solemn promise to the Lord that we will not give them any of our daughters.

Narrator   When they asked if there was some group out of the tribes of Israel that had not gone to the gathering at Mizpah, they found out that no one from Jabesh in Gilead had been there; at the roll call of the army no one from Jabesh had responded. So the assembly sent twelve thousand of their bravest men with the orders:

Person 3   Go and kill everyone in Jabesh, including the women and children. Kill all the males, and also every woman who is not a virgin.

Narrator   Among the people in Jabesh they found four hundred young virgins, so they brought them to the camp at Shiloh, which is in the land of Canaan.

Then the whole assembly sent word to the Benjaminites who were at the Rock of Rimmon and offered to end the war. The Benjaminites came back, and the other Israelites gave them the girls from Jabesh whom they had not killed. But there were not enough of them.

The people felt sorry for the Benjaminites because the Lord had

$\rightarrow$

broken the unity of the tribes of Israel. So the leaders of the gathering said:

Person 1 There are no more women in the tribe of Benjamin. What shall we do to provide wives for the men who are left?

Person 2 Israel must not lose one of its twelve tribes.

Person 1 We must find a way for the tribe of Benjamin to survive, but we cannot allow them to marry our daughters, because we have put a curse on anyone of us who allows a Benjaminite to marry one of our daughters.

Person 3 The yearly festival of the Lord at Shiloh is coming soon.

[Commentator Shiloh is north of Bethel, south of Lebonah, and east of the road between Bethel and Shechem.]

Narrator They said to the Benjaminites:

Person 3 Go and hide in the vineyards and watch. When the girls of Shiloh come out to dance during the festival, you come out of the vineyards.

Person 2 Each of you take a wife by force from among the girls and take her back to the territory of Benjamin with you.

Person 3 If their fathers or brothers come to you and protest, you can say: 'Please let us keep them, because we did not take them from you in battle to be our wives. And since you did not give them to us, you are not guilty of breaking your promise.'

Narrator The Benjaminites did this; each of them chose a wife from the girls who were dancing at Shiloh and carried her away. Then they went back to their own territory, rebuilt their towns, and lived there. At the same time the rest of the Israelites left, and every man went back to his own tribe and family and to his own property.

Narrator and There was no king in Israel at that time. Everyone did just as he
Commentator pleased.

Cast [This is] the word of the Lord.
All **Thanks be to God.**

Cast: **Narrator, Person 1, Person 2, Person 3** (Persons 1–3 can be the same), **Commentator** (can be the same as Narrator).

RUTH

Naomi and Ruth return to Bethlehem
Ruth 1.6–22

Narrator Naomi heard that the Lord had blessed his people by giving them a good harvest; so she got ready to leave Moab with her daughters-in-law. They started out together to go back to Judah, but on the way she said to them:

Naomi Go back home and stay with your mothers. May the Lord be as good to you as you have been to me and to those who have died. And may the Lord make it possible for each of you to marry again and have a home.

Narrator So Naomi kissed them good-bye. But they started crying [and said to her]:

Ruth and **Orpah** No!

Orpah We will go with you to your people.

Naomi You must go back, my daughters. Why do you want to come with me? Do you think I could have sons again for you to marry? Go back home, for I am too old to get married again. Even if I thought there was still hope, and so got married tonight and had sons, would you wait until they had grown up? Would this keep you from marrying someone else? No, my daughters, you know that's impossible. The Lord has turned against me, and I feel very sorry for you.

Narrator Again they started crying. Then Orpah kissed her mother-in-law good-bye and went back home, but Ruth held on to her. [So Naomi said to her:]

Naomi
(to Ruth) Ruth, your sister-in-law has gone back to her people and to her god. Go back home with her.

[Narrator But Ruth answered:]

Ruth Don't ask me to leave you! Let me go with you. Wherever you go, I will go; wherever you live, I will live. Your people will be my people, and your God will be my God. Wherever you die, I will die, and that is where I will be buried. May the Lord's worst punishment come upon me if I let anything but death separate me from you!

Narrator When Naomi saw that Ruth was determined to go with her, she said nothing more. (PAUSE)

They went on until they came to Bethlehem. When they arrived, the whole town got excited, and the women there exclaimed:

Women Is this really Naomi?

Naomi Don't call me *Naomi*; call me *Marah*, because Almighty God has made my life bitter. When I left here, I had plenty, but the Lord

→

has brought me back without a thing. Why call me Naomi when the Lord Almighty has condemned me and sent me trouble?

Narrator   This, then, was how Naomi came back from Moab with Ruth, her Moabite daughter-in-law. The barley harvest was just beginning when they arrived in Bethlehem.

Cast   [This is] the word of the Lord.
All   **Thanks be to God.**

Cast: **Narrator, Naomi, Ruth, Orpah** (can be the same as Ruth)**, Women** (two or more).

Ruth works in the field of Boaz
Ruth 2.1–23

Narrator   Naomi had a relative named Boaz, a rich and influential man who belonged to the family of her husband Elimelech. One day Ruth said to Naomi:

Ruth   Let me go to the fields to gather the corn that the harvest workers leave. I am sure to find someone who will let me work with him.

Naomi   Go ahead, my daughter.

Narrator   So Ruth went out to the fields and walked behind the workers, picking up the corn which they left. It so happened that she was in a field that belonged to Boaz.

Some time later Boaz himself arrived from Bethlehem and greeted the workers:

Boaz   The Lord be with you!

Men 1 and 2   The Lord bless you!

Narrator   Boaz asked the man in charge:

Boaz   Who is that young woman?

Man 2   She is the foreign girl who came back from Moab with Naomi. She asked me to let her follow the workers and pick up the corn. She has been working since early morning and has just now stopped to rest for a while under the shelter.

Narrator   Then Boaz spoke to Ruth:

Boaz (to Ruth)   Let me give you some advice. Don't pick up corn anywhere except in this field. Work with the women here; watch them to see where they are reaping and stay with them. I have ordered my men not to molest you. And whenever you are thirsty, go and drink from the water jars that they have filled.

Narrator   Ruth bowed down with her face touching the ground:

Ruth   Why should you be so concerned about me? Why should you be so kind to a foreigner?

Boaz   I have heard about everything that you have done for your mother-in-law since your husband died. I know how you left your father and mother and your own country and how you came to live among a people you had never known before. May the Lord reward you for what you have done. May you have a full reward from the Lord God of Israel, to whom you have come for protection!

Ruth   You are very kind to me, sir. You have made me feel better by speaking gently to me, even though I am not the equal of one of your servants.

Narrator   At meal-time Boaz said to Ruth:

Boaz   Come and have a piece of bread, and dip it in the sauce.

Narrator   So she sat with the workers, and Boaz passed some roasted grain to her. She ate until she was satisfied, and she still had some food left over. After she had left to go on picking up corn, Boaz ordered the workers:

Boaz   Let her pick it up even where the bundles are lying, and don't say anything to stop her. Besides that, pull out some corn from the bundles and leave it for her to pick up.

Narrator   So Ruth went on gathering corn in the field until evening, and when she had beaten it out, she found she had nearly ten kilogrammes. She took the corn back into town and showed her mother-in-law how much she had gathered. She also gave her the food left over from the meal. (PAUSE)

Naomi asked her:

Naomi   Where did you gather all this? Whose field have you been working in? May God bless the man who took an interest in you!

Narrator   So Ruth told Naomi that she had been working in a field belonging to a man named Boaz.

Naomi
(exclaiming)   May the Lord bless Boaz! The Lord always keeps his promises to the living and the dead. That man is a close relative of ours, one of those responsible for taking care of us.

Ruth   Best of all, he told me to keep picking up corn with his workers until they finish the harvest.

Naomi   Yes, my daughter, it will be better for you to work with the women in Boaz' field. You might be molested if you went to someone else's field.

Narrator   So Ruth worked with them and gathered corn until all the barley and wheat had been harvested. And she continued to live with her mother-in-law.

Cast   [This is] the word of the Lord.
All   **Thanks be to God.**

Cast: **Narrator, Ruth, Naomi, Boaz, Man 1, Man 2.**

Ruth finds a husband
Ruth 3.1–18

Narrator   [Some time later] Naomi said to Ruth:

Naomi   I must find a husband for you, so that you will have a home of your own. Remember that this man Boaz, whose women you have been working with, is our relative. Now listen. This evening he will be threshing the barley. So wash yourself, put on some perfume, and get dressed in your best clothes. Then go where he is threshing, but don't let him know you are there until he has finished eating and drinking. Be sure to notice where he lies down, and after he falls asleep, go and lift the covers and lie down at his feet. He will tell you what to do.

Narrator   Ruth answered:

Ruth   I will do everything you say.

Narrator   So Ruth went to the threshing-place and did just what her mother-in-law had told her. When Boaz had finished eating and drinking, he was in a good mood. He went to the pile of barley and lay down to sleep. Ruth slipped over quietly, lifted the covers and lay down at his feet. During the night he woke up suddenly, turned over, and was surprised to find a woman at his feet.

Boaz   Who are you?

Ruth   It's Ruth, sir. Because you are a close relative, you are responsible for taking care of me. So please marry me.

Boaz   The Lord bless you. You are showing even greater family loyalty in what you are doing now than in what you did for your mother-in-law. You might have gone looking for a young man, either rich or poor, but you didn't. Now don't worry, Ruth. I will do everything you ask; as everyone in town knows, you are a fine woman. It is true that I am a close relative and am responsible for you, but there is a man who is a closer relative than I am. Stay here the rest of the night, and in the morning we will find out whether or not he will take responsibility for you. If so, well and good; if not, then I swear by the living Lord that I will take the responsibility. Now lie down and stay here till morning.

Narrator   So she lay there at his feet, but she got up before it was light enough for her to be seen, because Boaz did not want anyone to know that she had been there. Boaz said to her:

Boaz   Take off your cloak and spread it out here.

Narrator   She did, and he poured out nearly twenty kilogrammes of barley and helped her to lift it on her shoulder. Then she returned to the town with it. When she arrived home, her mother-in-law asked her:

Naomi   How did you get on, my daughter?

Narrator   Ruth told her everything that Boaz had done for her. [She added:]

Ruth	He told me I must not come back to you empty-handed, so he gave me all this barley.
Narrator	Naomi said to her:
Naomi	Now be patient, Ruth, until you see how this all turns out. Boaz will not rest today until he settles the matter.
Cast	[This is] the word of the Lord.
All	**Thanks be to God.**

Cast: **Narrator, Naomi, Ruth, Boaz.**

Boaz marries Ruth
Ruth 4.1–22

Narrator	Boaz went to the meeting place at the town gate and sat down there. Then Elimelech's nearest relative, the man whom Boaz had mentioned, came by, and Boaz called to him:
Boaz	Come over here, my friend, and sit down.
Narrator	So he went over and sat down. Then Boaz got ten of the leaders of the town and asked them to sit down there too. When they were seated, he said to his relative:
Boaz	Now that Naomi has come back from Moab, she wants to sell the field that belonged to our relative Elimelech, and I think you ought to know about it. Now then, if you want it, buy it in the presence of these men sitting here. But if you don't want it, say so, because the right to buy it belongs first to you and then to me.
[Narrator	The man said:]
Man	I will buy it.
Boaz	Very well, but if you buy the field from Naomi, then you are also buying Ruth, the Moabite widow, so that the field will stay in the dead man's family.
Man	In that case I will give up my right to buy the field, because it would mean that my own children would not inherit it. You buy it; I would rather not.
Narrator	Now in those days, to settle a sale or an exchange of property, it was the custom for the seller to take off his sandal and give it to the buyer. In this way the Israelites showed that the matter was settled. So when the man said to Boaz, 'You buy it,' he took off his sandal and gave it to Boaz. Then Boaz spoke to the leaders and all the others there:
Boaz	You are all witnesses today that I have bought from Naomi everything that belonged to Elimelech and to his sons Chilion and Mahlon. In addition, Ruth the Moabite, Mahlon's widow, becomes my wife. This will keep the property in the dead man's family, and his family line will continue among his people and in his town. You are witnesses to this today.

Narrator	The leaders and the others said:
Leader 1	Yes, we are witnesses.
Leader 2	May the Lord make your wife become like Rachel and Leah, who bore many children to Jacob.
Leader 3	May you become rich in the clan of Ephrath and famous in Bethlehem.
Leader 1	May the children that the Lord will give you by this young woman make your family like the family of Perez, the son of Judah and Tamar.
Narrator	So Boaz took Ruth home as his wife. The Lord blessed her, and she became pregnant and had a son. The women said to Naomi:
Woman 1	Praise the Lord! He has given you a grandson today to take care of you.
Woman 2	May the boy become famous in Israel!
Woman 1	Your daughter-in-law loves you, and has done more for you than seven sons.
Woman 2	And now she has given you a grandson, who will bring new life to you and give you security in your old age.
Narrator	Naomi took the child, held him close, and took care of him. The women of the neighbourhood named the boy Obed. They told everyone:
Women 1 and 2	A son has been born to Naomi!
Narrator	Obed became the father of Jesse, who was the father of David. This is the family line from Perez to David: Perez, Hezron, Ram, Amminadab, Nahshon, Salmon, Boaz, Obed, Jesse, David.
Cast	[This is] the word of the Lord.
All	**Thanks be to God.**

Cast: **Narrator, Boaz, Man, Leader 1, Leader 2** (can be the same as Leader 1), **Leader 3, Woman 1, Woman 2.**

1 SAMUEL

The birth of Samuel
From 1 Samuel 1.1–20

Narrator　There was a certain man from the hill-country of Ephraim, whose name was Elkanah. Year after year this man went up from his town to worship and sacrifice to the Lord Almighty at Shiloh. Whenever the day came for Elkanah to sacrifice, he would give his wife Hannah a double portion of the meat because he loved her, and the Lord had closed her womb. But whenever Hannah went up to the house of the Lord she wept and would not eat. Elkanah her husband would say to her:

Elkanah　Hannah, why are you weeping? Why don't you eat? Why are you downhearted? Don't I mean more to you than ten sons?

Narrator　Once when they had finished eating and drinking in Shiloh, Hannah stood up. Now Eli the priest was sitting on a chair by the doorpost of the Lord's temple. In bitterness of soul Hannah wept much and prayed to the Lord. And she made a vow:

Hannah　O Lord Almighty, if you will only look upon your servant's misery and remember me, and not forget your servant but give her a son, then I will give him to the Lord for all the days of his life.

Narrator　As she kept on praying to the Lord, Eli observed her mouth. Hannah was praying in her heart, and her lips were moving but her voice was not heard. Eli thought she was drunk [and said to her:]

Eli (severely)　How long will you keep on getting drunk? Get rid of your wine.

Hannah (sadly)　Not so, my lord. I am a woman who is deeply troubled. I have not been drinking wine or beer; I was pouring out my soul to the Lord. Do not take your servant for a wicked woman; I have been praying here out of my great anguish and grief.

Narrator　Eli answered:

Eli (with compassion)　Go in peace, and may the God of Israel grant you what you have asked of him.

Hannah (pleased)　May your servant find favour in your eyes.

Narrator　Then she went her way and ate something, and her face was no longer downcast. Early the next morning they arose and worshipped before the Lord and then went back to their home. Hannah conceived and gave birth to a son. She named him:

Hannah (slowly)　Samuel—

| Narrator | [Saying:] |
| Hannah | Because I asked the Lord for him. |

| Cast | [This is] the word of the Lord. |
| All | **Thanks be to God.** |

Cast: **Narrator, Elkanah, Hannah, Eli.**

Samuel's dedication
1 Samuel 1.21—2.11

Narrator	The time came again for Elkanah and his family to go to Shiloh and offer to the Lord the yearly sacrifice and the special sacrifice he had promised. But this time Hannah did not go. [She told her husband:]
Hannah (to Elkanah)	As soon as the child is weaned, I will take him to the house of the Lord, where he will stay all his life.
[Narrator	Elkanah answered:]
Elkanah	All right, do whatever you think best; stay at home until you have weaned him. And may the Lord make your promise come true.
Narrator	So Hannah stayed at home and nursed her child. (PAUSE)
	After she had weaned him, she took him to Shiloh, taking along a three-year-old bull, ten kilogrammes of flour, and a leather bag full of wine. She took Samuel, young as he was, to the house of the Lord at Shiloh. After they had killed the bull, they took the child to Eli. [Hannah said to him:]
Hannah	Excuse me, sir. Do you remember me? I am the woman you saw standing here, praying to the Lord. I asked him for this child, and he gave me what I asked for. So I am dedicating him to the Lord. As long as he lives, he will belong to the Lord.
Narrator	Then they worshipped the Lord there. [Hannah prayed:
Hannah	The Lord has filled my heart with joy; how happy I am because of what he has done! I laugh at my enemies; how joyful I am because God has helped me!
	No one is holy like the Lord; there is none like him, no protector like our God.
	Stop your loud boasting; silence your proud words. For the Lord is a God who knows, and he judges all that people do.
	The bows of strong soldiers are broken, but the weak grow strong.
	The people who once were well fed now hire themselves out to get food,

but the hungry are hungry no more.
The childless wife has borne seven children,
but the mother of many is left with none.

The Lord kills and restores to life;
he sends people to the world of the dead
and brings them back again.
He makes some men poor and others rich;
he humbles some and makes others great.

He lifts the poor from the dust
and raises the needy from their misery.
He makes them companions of princes
and puts them in places of honour.
The foundations of the earth belong to the Lord;
on them he has built the world.

He protects the lives of his faithful people,
but the wicked disappear in darkness;
a man does not triumph by his own strength.

The Lord's enemies will be destroyed;
he will thunder against them from heaven.
The Lord will judge the whole world;
he will give power to his king,
he will make his chosen king victorious.]

Narrator Elkanah went back home to Ramah, but the boy Samuel stayed in Shiloh and served the Lord under the priest Eli.

Cast [This is] the word of the Lord.
All **Thanks be to God.**

Cast: **Narrator, Hannah, Elkanah.**

The sons of Eli
1 Samuel 2.12—26

Narrator The sons of Eli were scoundrels. They paid no attention to the Lord or to the regulations concerning what the priests could demand from the people. Instead, when a man was offering his sacrifice, the priest's servant would come with a three-pronged fork. While the meat was still cooking, he would stick the fork into the cooking-pot, and whatever the fork brought out belonged to the priest. All the Israelites who came to Shiloh to offer sacrifices were treated like this. In addition, even before the fat was taken off and burnt, the priest's servant would come and say to the man offering the sacrifice:

Servant Give me some meat for the priest to roast; he won't accept boiled meat from you, only raw meat.

Narrator If the man answered:

Man Let us do what is right and burn the fat first; then take what you want—

Narrator	The priest's servant would say:
Servant	No! Give it to me now! If you don't, I will have to take it by force!
Narrator	This sin of the sons of Eli was extremely serious in the Lord's sight, because they treated the offerings to the Lord with such disrespect.
	In the meantime the boy Samuel continued to serve the Lord, wearing a sacred linen apron. Each year his mother would make a little robe and take it to him when she accompanied her husband to offer the yearly sacrifice. Then Eli would bless Elkanah and his wife, and say to Elkanah:
Eli	May the Lord give you other children by this woman to take the place of the one you dedicated to him.
Narrator	After that they would go back home. The Lord did bless Hannah, and she had three more sons and two daughters. The boy Samuel grew up in the service of the Lord. Eli was now very old. He kept hearing about everything his sons were doing to the Israelites and that they were even sleeping with the women who worked at the entrance to the Tent of the Lord's presence. So he said to them:
Eli	Why are you doing these things? Everybody tells me about the evil you are doing. Stop it, my sons! This is an awful thing the people of the Lord are talking about! If a man sins against another man, God can defend him; but who can defend a man who sins against the Lord?
Narrator	But they would not listen to their father, for the Lord had decided to kill them. The boy Samuel continued to grow and to gain favour both with the Lord and with men.
Cast	[This is] the word of the Lord.
All	**Thanks be to God.**

Cast: **Narrator, Servant, Man, Eli.**

The Lord calls Samuel
1 Samuel 3.1–10

Narrator	The boy Samuel ministered before the Lord under Eli. In those days the word of the Lord was rare; there were not many visions. One night Eli, whose eyes were becoming so weak that he could barely see, was lying down in his usual place. The lamp of God had not yet gone out, and Samuel was lying down in the temple of the Lord, where the ark of God was. Then the Lord called Samuel. Samuel answered:
Samuel	Here I am.
Narrator	And he ran to Eli [and said:]
Samuel (to Eli)	Here I am; you called me.
[Narrator	But Eli said:]

212

Eli	*I* did not call; go back and lie down.
Narrator	So he went and lay down. Again the Lord called:
The Lord	Samuel!
Narrator	And Samuel got up and went to Eli [and said:]
Samuel	Here I am; you called me.
Eli	My son, I did *not* call; go back and lie down.
Narrator	Now Samuel did not yet know the Lord: The word of the Lord had not yet been revealed to him. The Lord called Samuel a third time, and Samuel got up and went to Eli [and said:]
Samuel	Here I am; you called me.
Narrator	Then Eli realized that the Lord was calling the boy. So Eli told Samuel:
Eli	Go and lie down, and if he calls you, say, 'Speak, Lord, for your servant is listening.'
Narrator	So Samuel went and lay down in his place. The Lord came and stood there, calling as at the other times:
The Lord	Samuel! Samuel!
Narrator	Then Samuel said:
Samuel	Speak, for your servant is listening.
Cast	[This is] the word of the Lord.
All	**Thanks be to God.**

Cast: **Narrator, Samuel** (as a boy), **Eli, The Lord.**

The Lord's message to Eli
1 Samuel 3.11–21

Narrator	The Lord said to Samuel:
The Lord	Some day I am going to do something to the people of Israel that is so terrible that everyone who hears about it will be stunned. On that day I will carry out all my threats against Eli's family, from beginning to end. I have already told him that I am going to punish his family for ever because his sons have spoken evil things against me. Eli knew they were doing this, but he did not stop them. So I solemnly declare to the family of Eli that no sacrifice or offering will ever be able to remove the consequences of this terrible sin.
Narrator	Samuel stayed in bed until morning; then he got up and opened the doors of the house of the Lord. He was afraid to tell Eli about the vision. Eli called him:
Eli	Samuel, my boy!
[Narrator	Samuel answered:]

Samuel	Yes, sir!
Eli	What did the Lord tell you? Don't keep anything from me. God will punish you severely if you don't tell me everything he said.
Narrator	So Samuel told him everything; he did not keep anything back.
Eli (sadly)	He is the Lord; he will do whatever seems best to him.
Narrator	As Samuel grew up, the Lord was with him and made everything that Samuel said come true. So all the people of Israel, from one end of the country to the other, knew that Samuel was indeed a prophet of the Lord. The Lord continued to reveal himself at Shiloh, where he had appeared to Samuel and had spoken to him. And when Samuel spoke, all Israel listened.
Cast	[This is] the word of the Lord.
All	**Thanks be to God.**

Cast: **Narrator, The Lord, Eli, Samuel** (as a boy).

The capture of the Covenant Box
1 Samuel 4.1–11

Narrator	The Philistines gathered to go to war against Israel, so the Israelites set out to fight them. The Israelites set up their camp at Ebenezer and the Philistines at Aphek. The Philistines attacked, and after fierce fighting they defeated the Israelites and killed about four thousand men on the battlefield. When the survivors came back to camp, the leaders of Israel said:
Leader 1	Why did the Lord let the Philistines defeat us today?
Leader 2	Let's go and bring the Lord's Covenant Box from Shiloh, so that he will go with us and save us from our enemies.
Narrator	So they sent messengers to Shiloh and fetched the Covenant Box of the Lord Almighty, who is enthroned above the winged creatures. And Eli's two sons, Hophni and Phinehas, came along with the Covenant Box. (PAUSE)
	When the Covenant Box arrived, the Israelites gave such a loud shout of joy that the earth shook. The Philistines heard the shouting [and said:]
Philistine 1	Listen to all that shouting in the Hebrew camp!
Philistines 2 and 3	What does it mean?
Narrator	When they found out that the Lord's Covenant Box had arrived in the Hebrew camp, they were afraid:
Philistine 1	A god has come into their camp!
Philistine 2	We're lost!
Philistine 3	Nothing like this has ever happened to us before!
Philistine 1	Who can save us from those powerful gods?

Philistine 2	They are the gods who slaughtered the Egyptians in the desert!
Philistine 3	Be brave, Philistines!
Philistine 1	Fight like men—
Philistine 2	Or we will become slaves to the Hebrews, just as they were our slaves.
Philistine 1	So fight like men!
Narrator	The Philistines fought hard and defeated the Israelites, who went running to their homes. There was a great slaughter: thirty thousand Israelite soldiers were killed. God's Covenant Box was captured, and Eli's sons, Hophni and Phinehas, were both killed.
Cast	[This is] the word of the Lord.
All	**Thanks be to God.**

Cast: **Narrator, Leader 1, Leader 2** (can be the same as Leader 1), **Philistine 1, Philistine 2, Philistine 3.**

The death of Eli
1 Samuel 4.12–22

Narrator	A man from the tribe of Benjamin ran all the way from the battlefield to Shiloh and arrived there the same day. To show his grief, he had torn his clothes and put earth on his head. Eli, who was very anxious about the Covenant Box, was sitting on a seat beside the road, staring. The man spread the news throughout the town, and everyone cried out in fear. Eli heard the noise [and asked]:
Eli	What is all this noise about?
Narrator	The man hurried to Eli to tell him the news. Eli was now ninety-eight years old and almost completely blind. [The man said:]
Man	I have escaped from the battle and have run all the way here today.
Eli	What happened, my son?
Man	Israel ran away from the Philistines; it was a terrible defeat for us! Besides that, your sons Hophni and Phinehas were killed, and God's Covenant Box was captured!
Narrator	When the man mentioned the Covenant Box, Eli fell backwards from his seat beside the gate. He was so old and fat that the fall broke his neck, and he died. He had been a leader in Israel for forty years.
	Eli's daughter-in-law, the wife of Phinehas, was pregnant, and it was almost time for her baby to be born. When she heard that God's Covenant Box had been captured and that her father-in-law and her husband were dead, she suddenly went into labour and gave birth. As she was dying, the women helping her said to her:
Woman 1	Be brave!

Woman 2	You have a son!
Narrator	But she paid no attention and did not answer. She named the boy Ichabod, explaining:
Wife	God's glory has left Israel.
Narrator	Referring to the capture of the Covenant Box and the death of her father-in-law and her husband, she said:
Wife	God's glory has left Israel, because God's Covenant Box has been captured.
Cast	[This is] the word of the Lord.
All	**Thanks be to God.**

Cast: **Narrator, Eli, Man, Woman 1, Woman 2** (can be the same as Woman 1), **Wife.**

The Covenant Box among the Philistines
1 Samuel 5.1–12

Narrator	After the Philistines captured the Covenant Box, they carried it from Ebenezer to their city of Ashdod, took it into the temple of their god Dagon, and set it up beside his statue. Early next morning the people of Ashdod saw that the statue of Dagon had fallen face downwards on the ground in front of the Lord's Covenant Box. So they lifted it up and put it back in its place. Early the *following* morning they saw that the statue had again fallen down in front of the Covenant Box. This time its head and both its arms were broken off and were lying in the doorway; only the body was left. That is why even today the priests of Dagon and all his worshippers in Ashdod step over that place and do not walk on it. The Lord punished the people of Ashdod severely and terrified them. He punished them and the people in the surrounding territory by causing them to have tumours. When they saw what was happening, they said:
Person 1	The God of Israel is punishing us and our god Dagon.
Person 2	We can't let the Covenant Box stay here any longer.
Narrator	So they sent messengers and called together all five of the Philistine kings and asked them:
Person 1	What shall we do with the Covenant Box of the God of Israel?
[Narrator	They answered:]
Philistine	Take it over to Gath.
Narrator	So they took it to Gath, another Philistine city. But after it arrived there, the Lord punished that city too and caused a great panic. He punished them with tumours which developed in all the people of the city, young and old alike. So they sent the Covenant Box to Ekron, another Philistine city; but when it arrived there, the people cried out:

Person 3	They have brought the Covenant Box of the God of Israel here, in order to kill us all!
Narrator	So again they sent for all the Philistine kings [and said]:
Person 3	Send the Covenant Box of Israel back to its own place, so that it won't kill us and our families.
Narrator	There was panic throughout the city because God was punishing them so severely. Even those who did not die developed tumours and the people cried out to their gods for help.
Cast	[This is] the word of the Lord.
All	**Thanks be to God.**

Cast: **Narrator, Person 1, Person 2** (can be the same as Person 1), **Philistine, Person 3.**

The return of the Covenant Box
1 Samuel 6.1–16

Narrator	After the Lord's Covenant Box had been in Philistia for seven months, the people called the priests and the magicians [and asked]:
Person 1	What shall we do with the Covenant Box of the Lord?
Person 2	If we send it back where it belongs, what shall we send with it?
[Narrator	They answered:]
Priest	If you return the Covenant Box of the God of Israel, you must, of course, send with it a gift to him to pay for your sin.
Magician	The Covenant Box must not go back without a gift. In this way you will be healed, and you will find out why he has kept on punishing you.
Person 1	What gift shall we send him?
Magician	Five gold models of tumours and five gold mice, one of each for each Philistine king. The same plague was sent on all of you and on the five kings. You must make these models of the tumours and of the mice that are ravaging your country.
Priest	And you must give honour to the God of Israel. Perhaps he will stop punishing you, your gods, and your land. Why should you be stubborn, as the king of Egypt and the Egyptians were? Don't forget how God made fools of them until they let the Israelites leave Egypt. So prepare a new wagon and two cows that have never been yoked; hitch them to the wagon and drive their calves back to the barn. Take the Lord's Covenant Box, put it on the wagon.
Magician	And place in a box beside it the gold models that you are sending to him as a gift to pay for your sins.
Priest	Start the wagon on its way and let it go by itself. Then watch it go; if it goes towards the town of Beth Shemesh, this means that it is the God of the Israelites who has sent this terrible disaster on us.

→

217

But if it doesn't, then we will know that he did not send the plague; it was only a matter of chance.

Narrator They did what they were told: they took two cows and hitched them to the wagon, and shut the calves in the barn. They put the Covenant Box in the wagon, together with the box containing the gold models of the mice and of the tumours. The cows started off on the road to Beth Shemesh and headed straight towards it, without turning off the road. They were mooing as they went. The five Philistine kings followed them as far as the border of Beth Shemesh. (PAUSE)

The people of Beth Shemesh were harvesting wheat in the valley, when suddenly they looked up and saw the Covenant Box. They were overjoyed at the sight. The wagon came to a field belonging to a man named Joshua, who lived in Beth Shemesh, and it stopped there near a large rock. The people chopped up the wooden wagon and killed the cows and offered them as a burnt-sacrifice to the Lord. The Levites lifted off the Covenant Box of the Lord and the box with the gold models in it, and placed them on the large rock. Then the people of Beth Shemesh offered burnt-sacrifices and other sacrifices to the Lord. The five Philistine kings watched them do this and then went back to Ekron that same day.

Cast [This is] the word of the Lord.
All **Thanks be to God.**

Cast: **Narrator, Person 1, Person 2** (can be the same as Person 1), **Priest, Magician.**

The Covenant Box at Kiriath Jearim
1 Samuel 6.18—7.1

Narrator The large rock in the field of Joshua of Beth Shemesh, on which they placed the Lord's Covenant Box, is still there as a witness to what happened. The Lord killed seventy of the men of Beth Shemesh because they looked inside the Covenant Box. And the people mourned because the Lord had caused such a great slaughter among them. So the men of Beth Shemesh said:

Man 1 Who can stand before the Lord, this holy God?

Man 2 Where can we send him to get him away from us?

Narrator They sent messengers to the people of Kiriath Jearim to say:

Messenger 1 The Philistines have returned the Lord's Covenant Box.

Messenger 2 Come down and fetch it.

Narrator So the people of Kiriath Jearim fetched the Lord's Covenant Box and took it to the house of a man named Abinadab, who lived on a hill. They consecrated his son Eleazar to be in charge of it.

Cast [This is] the word of the Lord.
All **Thanks be to God.**

Cast: **Narrator, Man 1, Man 2** (can be the same as Man 1), **Messenger 1, Messenger 2** (can be the same as Messenger 1).

Samuel rules Israel
1 Samuel 7.2–14

Narrator	The Covenant Box of the Lord stayed in Kiriath Jearim a long time, some twenty years. During this time all the Israelites cried to the Lord for help. Samuel said to the people of Israel:
Samuel	If you are going to turn to the Lord with all your hearts, you must get rid of all the foreign gods and the images of the goddess Astarte. Dedicate yourselves completely to the Lord and worship only him, and he will rescue you from the power of the Philistines.
Narrator	So the Israelites got rid of their idols of Baal and Astarte, and worshipped only the Lord. Then Samuel sent for all the Israelites to meet at Mizpah, saying:
Samuel	I will pray to the Lord for you there.
Narrator	So they all gathered at Mizpah. They drew some water and poured it out as an offering to the Lord and fasted that whole day. [They said:]
Israelite	We have sinned against the Lord.
Narrator	It was at Mizpah that Samuel settled disputes among the Israelites. When the Philistines heard that the Israelites had gathered at Mizpah, the five Philistine kings started out with their men to attack them. The Israelites heard about it and were afraid, and said to Samuel:
Israelite	Keep praying to the Lord our God to save us from the Philistines.
Narrator	Samuel killed a young lamb and burnt it whole as a sacrifice to the Lord. Then he prayed to the Lord to help Israel, and the Lord answered his prayer. While Samuel was offering the sacrifice, the Philistines moved forward to attack; but just then the Lord thundered from heaven against them. They became completely confused and fled in panic. The Israelites marched out from Mizpah and pursued the Philistines almost as far as Bethcar, killing them along the way. Then Samuel took a stone, set it up between Mizpah and Shen, and said:
Samuel	The Lord has helped us all the way.
Narrator	And he named it:
Samuel	'Stone of Help'.
Narrator	So the Philistines were defeated, and the Lord prevented them from invading Israel's territory as long as Samuel lived. All the cities which the Philistines had captured between Ekron and Gath were returned to Israel, and so Israel got back all its territory. And there was peace also between the Israelites and the Canaanites.
Cast	[This is] the word of the Lord.
All	**Thanks be to God.**

Cast: **Narrator, Samuel, Israelite.**

219

The people ask for a king
1 Samuel 7.15—8.22

Narrator   Samuel ruled Israel as long as he lived. Every year he would go round to Bethel, Gilgal, and Mizpah, and in these places he would settle disputes. Then he would go back to his home in Ramah, where also he would serve as judge. In Ramah he built an altar to the Lord. When Samuel grew old, he made his sons judges in Israel. The elder son was named Joel and the younger one Abijah; they were judges in Beersheba. But they did not follow their father's example; they were interested only in making money, so they accepted bribes and did not decide cases honestly. Then all the leaders of Israel met together and went to Samuel in Ramah.

Leader   Look, Samuel, you are getting old and your sons don't follow your example. So then, appoint a king to rule over us, so that we will have a king, as other countries have.

Narrator   Samuel was displeased with their request for a king; so he prayed to the Lord, and the Lord said:

The Lord   Listen to everything the people say to you. You are not the one they have rejected; I am the one they have rejected as their king. Ever since I brought them out of Egypt, they have turned away from me and worshipped other gods; and now they are doing to you what they have always done to me. So then, listen to them, but give them strict warnings and explain how their kings will treat them.

Narrator   Samuel told the people who were asking him for a king everything that the Lord had said to him:

Samuel   This is how your king will treat you. He will make soldiers of your sons; some of them will serve in his war chariots, others in his cavalry, and others will run before his chariots. He will make some of them officers in charge of a thousand men, and others in charge of fifty men. Your sons will have to plough his fields, harvest his crops, and make his weapons and the equipment for his chariots. Your daughters will have to make perfumes for him and work as his cooks and his bakers. He will take your best fields, vineyards, and olive-groves, and give them to his officials. He will take a tenth of your corn and of your grapes for his court officers and other officials. He will take your servants and your best cattle and donkeys, and make them work for him. He will take a tenth of your flocks. And you yourselves will become his slaves. When that time comes, you will complain bitterly because of your king, whom you yourselves chose, but the Lord will not listen to your complaints.

Narrator   The people paid no attention to Samuel:

Person 1   No! We want a king—

Person 2   So that we will be like other nations—

Person 1	With our own king to rule us—
Person 2	And lead us out to war and fight our battles.
Narrator	Samuel listened to everything they said and then went and told the Lord. The Lord answered:
The Lord	Do what they want and give them a king.
Narrator	Then Samuel told all the men of Israel to go back home.
Cast	[This is] the word of the Lord.
All	**Thanks be to God.**

Cast: **Narrator, Leader, The Lord, Samuel, Person 1, Person 2** (can be the same as Leader, OR both Person 1 and Person 2 can be the same as Leader).

Saul meets Samuel
1 Samuel 9.1—10.1

Narrator	There was a wealthy and influential man named Kish, from the tribe of Benjamin; he was the son of Abiel and grandson of Zeror, and belonged to the family of Becorath, a part of the clan of Aphiah. He had a son named Saul, a handsome man in the prime of life. Saul was a head taller than anyone else in Israel and more handsome as well. Some donkeys belonging to Kish had wandered off, so he said to Saul:
Kish	Take one of the servants with you and go and look for the donkeys.
Narrator	They went through the hill-country of Ephraim and the region of Shalishah, but did not find them; so they went on through the region of Shaalim, but the donkeys were not there. Then they went through the territory of Benjamin, but still did not find them. When they came into the region of Zuph, Saul said to his servant:
Saul	Let's go back home, or my father might stop thinking about the donkeys and start worrying about us.
[Narrator	The servant answered:]
Servant (respectfully)	Wait! In this town there is a holy man who is highly respected because everything he says comes true. Let's go to him, and maybe he can tell us where we can find the donkeys.
Saul	If we go to him, what can we give him? There is no food left in our packs, and we haven't anything to give him, have we?
Servant	I have a small silver coin. I can give him that, and then he will tell us where we can find them.
Saul	A good idea! Let's go.
Narrator	So they went to the town where the holy man lived. As they were going up the hill to the town, they met some girls who were coming out to draw water. [They asked the girls:]

Servant	Is the seer in town?
[Narrator	At that time a prophet was called a seer, and so whenever someone wanted to ask God a question, he would say, 'Let's go to the seer.' The girls answered:]
Girls 1 and 2	Yes, he is.
Girl 1	In fact, he is just ahead of you.
Girl 2	If you hurry, you will catch up with him.
Girl 1	As soon as you go into the town, you will find him.
Girl 2	He arrived in town today because the people are going to offer a sacrifice on the altar on the hill.
Girl 1	The people who are invited won't start eating until he gets there, because he has to bless the sacrifice first.
Girl 2	If you go now, you will find him before he goes up the hill to eat.
Narrator	So Saul and his servant went on to the town, and as they were going in, they saw Samuel coming out towards them on his way to the place of worship. Now on the previous day the Lord had said to Samuel:
The Lord	Tomorrow about this time I will send you a man from the tribe of Benjamin; anoint him as ruler of my people Israel, and he will rescue them from the Philistines. I have seen the suffering of my people and have heard their cries for help.
Narrator	When Samuel caught sight of Saul, the Lord said to him:
The Lord	This is the man I told you about. He will rule my people.
Narrator	Then Saul went over to Samuel, who was near the gate:
Saul	Tell me, where does the seer live?
[Narrator	Samuel answered:]
Samuel	I *am* the seer. Go on ahead of me to the place of worship. Both of you are to eat with me today. Tomorrow morning I will answer all your questions and send you on your way. As for the donkeys that were lost three days ago, don't worry about them; they have already been found. But who is it that the people of Israel want so much? It is you—you and your father's family.
Saul	I belong to the tribe of Benjamin, the smallest tribe in Israel, and my family is the least important one in the tribe. Why, then, do you talk like this to me?
Narrator	Then Samuel led Saul and his servant into the large room and gave them a place at the head of the table where the guests, about thirty in all, were seated. Samuel said to the cook:
Samuel	Bring the piece of meat I gave you, which I told you to set aside.
Narrator	So the cook brought the choice piece of the leg and placed it before Saul.

Samuel	Look, here is the piece that was kept for you. Eat it. I saved it for you to eat at this time with the people I invited.
Narrator	So Saul ate with Samuel that day. When they went down from the place of worship to the town, they made up a bed for Saul on the roof, and he slept there. (PAUSE)
	At dawn Samuel called to Saul on the roof:
Samuel	Get up, and I will send you on your way.
Narrator	Saul got up, and he and Samuel went out to the street together. When they arrived at the edge of the town, Samuel said to Saul:
Samuel	Tell the servant to go on ahead of us.
Narrator	The servant left, and Samuel continued:
Samuel	Stay here a minute, and I will tell you what God has said.
Narrator	Then Samuel took a jar of olive-oil and poured it on Saul's head, kissed him, and said:
Samuel	The Lord anoints you as ruler of his people Israel. You will rule his people and protect them from all their enemies.
Cast	[This is] the word of the Lord.
All	**Thanks be to God.**

Cast: **Narrator, Kish, Saul** (younger than his father, Kish), **Servant, Girl 1, Girl 2, The Lord, Samuel.**

Samuel and Saul
1 Samuel 10.1–2, 9–16

Narrator	Samuel said to Saul:
Samuel	This is the proof to you that the Lord has chosen you to be the ruler of his people: When you leave me today, you will meet two men near Rachel's tomb at Zelzah in the territory of Benjamin. They will tell you that the donkeys you were looking for have been found.
Narrator	When Saul turned to leave Samuel, God gave Saul a new nature. And everything Samuel had told him happened that day. When Saul and his servant arrived at Gibeah, a group of prophets met him. Suddenly the spirit of God took control of him, and he joined in their ecstatic dancing and shouting. People who had known him before saw him doing this and asked one another:
Person 1	What has happened to the son of Kish?
Person 2	Has Saul become a prophet?
Narrator	A man who lived there asked:
Man	How about these other prophets—who do you think their fathers are?
Narrator	This is how the saying originated, 'Has even Saul become a prophet?' (PAUSE) →

223

When Saul finished dancing and shouting, he went to the altar on the hill. Saul's uncle saw him and the servant, and he asked them:

Uncle	Where have you been?
Narrator	Saul answered:
Saul	Looking for the donkeys. When we couldn't find them, we went to see Samuel.
Uncle	And what did he tell you?
Saul	He told us that the animals had been found.
Narrator	But he did not tell his uncle what Samuel had said about becoming king.
Cast	[This is] the word of the Lord.
All	**Thanks be to God.**

Cast: **Narrator, Samuel, Person 1, Person 2, Man** (can be the same as Person 1), **Uncle, Saul.**

Saul is acclaimed as king
1 Samuel 10.17–27

Narrator	Samuel called the people together for a religious gathering at Mizpah [and said to them]:
Samuel	The Lord, the God of Israel, says:
The Lord	I brought you out of Egypt and rescued you from the Egyptians and all the other peoples who were oppressing you. I am your God, the one who rescues you from all your troubles and difficulties, but today you have rejected me and have asked me to give you a king.
Samuel	Very well, then, gather yourselves before the Lord by tribes and by clans.
Narrator	Then Samuel made each tribe come forward, and the Lord picked the tribe of Benjamin. Then Samuel made the families of the tribe of Benjamin come forward, and the family of Matri was picked out. Then the men of the family of Matri came forward, and Saul son of Kish was picked out. They looked for him, but when they could not find him, they asked the Lord:
Person 1	Is there still someone else?
[Narrator	The Lord answered:]
The Lord	Saul is over there, hiding behind the supplies.
Narrator	So they ran and brought Saul out to the people, and they could see that he was a head taller than anyone else. Samuel said to the people:
Samuel	Here is the man the Lord has chosen! There is no one else among us like him.
[Narrator	All the people shouted:]
Persons 1 and 2	Long live the king!
Narrator	Samuel explained to the people the rights and duties of a king,

and then wrote them in a book, which he deposited in a holy place. Then he sent everyone home. Saul also went back home to Gibeah. Some powerful men, whose hearts God had touched, went with him. But some worthless people said:

Person 2   How can this fellow do us any good?

Narrator   They despised Saul and did not bring him any gifts.

Cast   [This is] the word of the Lord.
All   **Thanks be to God.**

Cast: **Narrator, Samuel, The Lord,** (can be the same as Samuel), **Person 1, Person 2.**

Saul rescues Israel
1 Samuel 11.1–15

Narrator   About a month after Saul had been acclaimed as king, King Nahash of Ammon led his army against the town of Jabesh in the territory of Gilead and besieged it. The men of Jabesh said to Nahash:

Man 1   Make a treaty with us—

Man 2   And we will accept you as our ruler.

[Narrator   Nahash answered:]

King   I will make a treaty with you on one condition: I will put out everyone's right eye and so bring disgrace on all Israel.

Narrator   The leaders of Jabesh said:

Leader 1   Give us seven days to send messengers throughout the land of Israel.

Leader 2   If no one will help us, then we will surrender to you.

Narrator   The messengers arrived at Gibeah, where Saul lived, and when they told the news, the people started crying in despair. Saul was just coming in from the field with his oxen [and he asked:]

Saul   What's wrong? Why is everyone crying?

Narrator   They told him what the messengers from Jabesh had reported. When Saul heard this, the spirit of God took control of him, and he became furious. He took two oxen, cut them in pieces, and sent messengers to carry the pieces throughout the land of Israel with this warning:

Saul   Whoever does not follow Saul and Samuel into battle will have this done to his oxen!

Narrator   The people of Israel were afraid of what the Lord might do, and all of them, without exception, came out together. Saul gathered them at Bezek: there were 300,000 from Israel and 30,000 from Judah. They said to the messengers from Jabesh:

Saul   Tell your people that before noon tomorrow they will be rescued.

Narrator	When the people of Jabesh received the message, they were overjoyed—and said to Nahash:
Person 1 (cunningly)	Tomorrow we will surrender to you—
Person 2 (cunningly)	And you can do with us whatever you wish.
Narrator	That night Saul divided his men into three groups, and at dawn they rushed into the enemy camp and attacked the Ammonites. By noon they had slaughtered them. The survivors scattered, each man running off by himself. Then the people of Israel said to Samuel:
Person 1	Where are the people who said that Saul should not be our king?
Person 2	Hand them over to us—
Persons 1 and **2**	We'll kill them!
Saul	No one will be put to death today, for this is the day the Lord rescued Israel.
Narrator	And Samuel said to them:
Samuel	Let us all go to Gilgal and once more proclaim Saul as your king.
Narrator	So they all went to Gilgal, and there at the holy place they proclaimed Saul king. They offered fellowship-sacrifices, and Saul and all the people of Israel celebrated the event.
Cast	[This is] the word of the Lord.
All	**Thanks be to God.**

Cast: **Narrator, Man 1, Man 2, King, Leader 1, Leader 2, Saul, Person 1, Person 2, Samuel.** (Man 1, Leader 1, Person 1 can be the same; Man 2, Leader 2, Person 2 can be the same).

Samuel's farewell
1 Samuel 12.1–15

Narrator	Samuel said to the people of Israel:
Samuel	I have done what you asked me to do. I have given you a king to rule you, and now you have him to lead you. As for me, I am old and grey, and my sons are with you. I have been your leader from my youth until now. Here I am. If I have done anything wrong, accuse me now in the presence of the Lord and the king he has chosen. Have I taken anybody's cow or anybody's donkey? Have I cheated or oppressed anyone? Have I accepted a bribe from anyone? If I have done any of these things, I will pay back what I have taken.
Narrator	The people answered:
Person 1	No, you have not cheated us or oppressed us.
Person 2	You have not taken anything from anyone.
Narrator	Samuel replied:

Samuel	The Lord and the king he has chosen are witnesses today that you have found me to be completely innocent.
Persons 1 and **2**	Yes, the Lord is our witness.
Samuel	The Lord is the one who chose Moses and Aaron and who brought your ancestors out of Egypt. Now stand where you are, and I will accuse you before the Lord by reminding you of all the mighty actions the Lord did to save you and your ancestors. When Jacob and his family went to Egypt and the Egyptians oppressed them, your ancestors cried to the Lord for help, and he sent Moses and Aaron, who brought them out of Egypt and settled them in this land. But the people forgot the Lord their God, and so he let the Philistines and the king of Moab and Sisera, commander of the army of the city of Hazor, fight against your ancestors and conquer them. Then they cried to the Lord for help:
Person 1	We have sinned, because we turned away from you, Lord, and worshipped the idols of Baal and Astarte.
Person 2	Rescue us from our enemies, and we will worship you!
Samuel	And the Lord sent Gideon, Barak, Jephthah, and finally me. Each of us rescued you from your enemies, and you lived in safety. But when you saw that King Nahash of Ammon was about to attack you, you rejected the Lord as your king and said to me:
[Persons 1 and **2]**	We want a king to rule us.
Samuel	Now here is the king you chose; you asked for him, and now the Lord has given him to you. All will go well with you if you honour the Lord your God, serve him, listen to him, and obey his commands, and if you and your king follow him. But if you do not listen to the Lord but disobey his commands, he will be against you and your king.
Cast	[This is] the word of the Lord.
All	**Thanks be to God.**

Cast: **Narrator, Samuel, Person 1, Person 2.**

Samuel's sign
1 Samuel 12.16–25

Narrator	Samuel said:
Samuel	Stand where you are, and you will see the great thing which the Lord is going to do. It's the dry season, isn't it? But I will pray, and the Lord will send thunder and rain. When this happens, you will realize that you committed a great sin against the Lord when you asked him for a king.
Narrator	So Samuel prayed, and on that same day the Lord sent thunder and rain. Then all the people became afraid of the Lord and of Samuel:

Person 1	Please, sir, pray to the Lord your God for us, so that we won't die.
Person 2	We now realize that, besides all our other sins, we have sinned by asking for a king.
Samuel	Don't be afraid. Even though you have done such an evil thing, do not turn away from the Lord, but serve him with all your heart. Don't go after false gods; they cannot help you or save you, for they are not real. The Lord has made a solemn promise, and he will not abandon you, for he has decided to make you his own people. As for me, the Lord forbid that I should sin against him by no longer praying for you. Instead, I will teach you what is good and right for you to do. Obey the Lord and serve him faithfully with all your heart. Remember the great things he has done for you. But if you continue to sin, you and your king will be destroyed.
Cast	[This is] the word of the Lord.
All	**Thanks be to God.**

Cast: **Narrator, Samuel, Person 1, Person 2.**

War against the Philistines
1 Samuel 13.5–14

Narrator	The Philistines assembled to fight the Israelites; they had thirty thousand war chariots, six thousand horsemen, and as many soldiers as there are grains of sand on the seashore. They went to Michmash, east of Bethaven, and camped there. Then they launched a strong attack against the Israelites, putting them in a desperate situation. Some of the Israelites hid in caves and holes or among the rocks or in pits and wells; others crossed the River Jordan into the territories of Gad and Gilead. Saul was still at Gilgal, and the people with him were trembling with fear. He waited seven days for Samuel, as Samuel had instructed him to do, but Samuel still had not come to Gilgal. The people began to desert Saul, so he said to them:
Saul	Bring me the burnt-sacrifices and the fellowship-sacrifices.
Narrator	He offered a burnt-sacrifice, and just as he was finishing, Samuel arrived. Saul went out to meet him and welcome him, but Samuel said:
Samuel	What have you done?
Saul	The people were deserting me, and you had not come when you said you would; besides that, the Philistines are gathering at Michmash. So I thought, 'The Philistines are going to attack me here in Gilgal, and I have not tried to win the Lord's favour.' So I felt I had to offer a sacrifice.
Samuel	That was a foolish thing to do. You have not obeyed the command the Lord your God gave you. If you had obeyed, he would have let

you and your descendants rule over Israel for ever. But now your rule will not continue. Because you have disobeyed him, the Lord will find the kind of man he wants and make him ruler of his people.

Cast	[This is] the word of the Lord.
All	**Thanks be to God.**

Cast: **Narrator, Saul, Samuel.**

Jonathan's daring deed
1 Samuel 14.1–15

Narrator	One day Jonathan said to the young man who carried his weapons:
Jonathan	Let's go across to the Philistine camp.
Narrator	But Jonathan did not tell his father Saul, who was camping under a pomegranate-tree in Migron, not far from Gibeah; he had about six hundred men with him. The men did not know that Jonathan had left. (PAUSE)
	In the pass of Michmash, which Jonathan had to go through to get over to the Philistine camp, there were two large jagged rocks, one on each side of the pass: one was called Bozez and the other Seneh. One was on the north side of the pass, facing Michmash, and the other was on the south side, facing Geba. Jonathan said to the young man:
Jonathan	Let's cross over to the camp of those heathen Philistines. Maybe the Lord will help us; if he does, nothing can keep him from giving us the victory, no matter how few of us there are.
[Narrator	The young man answered:]
Young man	Whatever you want to do, I'm with you.
Jonathan	All right. We will go across and let the Philistines see us. If they tell us to wait for them to come to us, then we will stay where we are. But if they tell us to go to them, then we will, because that will be the sign that the Lord has given us victory over them.
Narrator	So they let the Philistines see them [and the Philistines said:]
Philistine 1	Look! Some Hebrews are coming out of the holes they have been hiding in!
Narrator	Then they called out to Jonathan and the young man:
Philistine 1	Come on up here!
Philistine 2 (taunting)	We have something to tell you!
Jonathan (to young man)	Follow me. The Lord has given Israel victory over them.

Narrator	Jonathan climbed up out of the pass on his hands and knees, and the young man followed him. Jonathan attacked the Philistines and knocked them down, and the young man killed them. In that first slaughter Jonathan and the young man killed about twenty men in an area of about a quarter of a hectare. All the Philistines in the countryside were terrified; the raiders and the soldiers in the camp trembled with fear; the earth shook, and there was great panic.
Cast	[This is] the word of the Lord.
All	**Thanks be to God.**

Cast: **Narrator, Jonathan, Young man, Philistine 1, Philistine 2** (can be the same as Philistine 1).

The defeat of the Philistines
1 Samuel 14.16–23

Narrator	Saul's men on watch at Gibeah in the territory of Benjamin saw the Philistines running in confusion. So Saul said to his men:
Saul	Count the soldiers and find out who is missing.
Narrator	They did so and found that Jonathan and the young man who carried his weapons were missing. Saul said to Ahijah the priest:
Saul	Bring the ephod here.
Narrator	On that day Ahijah was carrying it in front of the people of Israel. As Saul was speaking to the priest, the confusion in the Philistine camp got worse and worse, so Saul said to him:
Saul	There's no time to consult the Lord!
Narrator	Then he and his men marched into battle against the Philistines, who were fighting each other in complete confusion. Some Hebrews, who had been on the Philistine side and had gone with them to the camp, changed sides again and joined Saul and Jonathan. Others, who had been hiding in the hills of Ephraim, heard that the Philistines were running away, so they also joined in and attacked the Philistines, fighting all the way beyond Bethaven. The Lord saved Israel that day.
Cast	[This is] the word of the Lord.
All	**Thanks be to God.**

Cast: **Narrator, Saul.**

Events after the battle
1 Samuel 14.24–46

Narrator	The Israelites were weak with hunger that day, because Saul, with a solemn oath, had given the order:
Saul	A curse be on anyone who eats any food today before I take revenge on my enemies.

Narrator	So nobody had eaten anything all day. They all came into a wooded area and found honey everywhere. The woods were full of honey, but no one ate any of it because they were all afraid of Saul's curse. But Jonathan had not heard his father threaten the people with a curse; so he reached out with the stick he was carrying, dipped it in a honeycomb, and ate some honey. At once he felt much better. But one of the men said:
Man	We are all weak with hunger, but your father threatened us and said, 'A curse be on anyone who eats any food today.'
Narrator	Jonathan answered:
Jonathan	What a terrible thing my father has done to our people! See how much better I feel because I ate some honey! How much better it would have been today if our people had eaten the food they took when they defeated the enemy. Just think how many more Philistines they would have killed!
Narrator	That day the Israelites defeated the Philistines, fighting all the way from Michmash to Aijalon. By this time the Israelites were very weak with hunger, and so they rushed over to what they had captured from the enemy, took sheep and cattle, slaughtered them on the spot, and ate the meat with the blood still in it. Saul was told:
Man	Look, the people are sinning against the Lord by eating meat with the blood in it.
Narrator	Saul cried out:
Saul	You are traitors! Roll a big stone over here to me.
Narrator	Then he gave another order:
Saul	Go among the people and tell them all to bring their cattle and sheep here. They are to slaughter them and eat them here; they must not sin against the Lord by eating meat with blood in it.
Narrator	So that night they all brought their cattle and slaughtered them there. Saul built an altar to the Lord, the first one that he built. (PAUSE) Saul said to his men:
Saul	Let's go down and attack the Philistines in the night, plunder them until dawn, and kill them all.
Narrator	They answered:
Man	Do whatever you think best.
Narrator	But the priest said:
Priest	Let's consult God first.
Narrator	So Saul asked God:
Saul	Shall I attack the Philistines? Will you give us victory?
Narrator	But God did not answer that day. Then Saul said to the leaders of the people:

Saul	Come here and find out what sin was committed today. I promise by the living Lord, who gives Israel victory, that the guilty one will be put to death, even if he is my son Jonathan.
Narrator	But no one said anything. [Then Saul said to them:]
Saul	All of you stand over there, and Jonathan and I will stand over here.
[Narrator	They answered:]
Man	Do whatever you think best.
Narrator	Saul said to the Lord, the God of Israel:
Saul	Lord, why have you not answered me today? Lord, God of Israel, answer me by the sacred stones. If the guilt is Jonathan's or mine, answer by the Urim; but if it belongs to your people Israel, answer by the Thummim.
Narrator	The answer indicated Jonathan and Saul; and the people were cleared. [Then Saul said:]
Saul	Decide between my son Jonathan and me.
Narrator	And Jonathan was indicated. [Then Saul asked Jonathan:]
Saul (to Jonathan)	What have you done?
[Narrator	Jonathan answered:]
Jonathan	I ate a little honey with the stick I was holding. Here I am—I am ready to die.
Saul	May God strike me dead if you are not put to death!
Narrator	But the people said to Saul:
Person 1	Will Jonathan, who won this great victory for Israel, be put to death?
Persons 1 and 2	No!
Person 2	We promise by the living Lord that he will not lose even a hair from his head.
Person 1	What he did today was done with God's help.
Narrator	So the people saved Jonathan from being put to death. (PAUSE) After that, Saul stopped pursuing the Philistines, and they went back to their own territory.
Cast	[This is] the word of the Lord.
All	**Thanks be to God.**

Cast: **Narrator, Saul, Man, Jonathan, Priest, Person 1** (can be the same as Priest), **Person 2** (can be the same as Man).

War against the Amalekites
1 Samuel 15.1–9

Narrator   Samuel said to Saul:

Samuel   I am the one whom the Lord sent to anoint you king of his people Israel. Now listen to what the Lord Almighty says. He is going to punish the people of Amalek because their ancestors opposed the Israelites when they were coming from Egypt. Go and attack the Amalekites and completely destroy everything they have. Don't leave a thing; kill all the men, women, children, and babies; the cattle, sheep, camels, and donkeys.

Narrator   Saul called his forces together and inspected them at Telem: there were 200,000 soldiers from Israel and 10,000 from Judah. Then he and his men went to the city of Amalek and waited in ambush in a dry river-bed. He sent a warning to the Kenites, a people whose ancestors had been kind to the Israelites when they came from Egypt:

Saul   Go away and leave the Amalekites, so that I won't kill you along with them.

Narrator   So the Kenites left. (PAUSE)

Saul defeated the Amalekites, fighting all the way from Havilah to Shur, east of Egypt; he captured King Agag of Amalek alive and killed all the people. (PAUSE) But Saul and his men spared Agag's life and did not kill the best sheep and cattle, the best calves and lambs, or anything else that was good; they destroyed only what was useless or worthless.

Cast   [This is] the word of the Lord.
All   **Thanks be to God.**

Cast: **Narrator, Samuel, Saul.**

Saul is rejected as king
1 Samuel 15.10–31; 34–35

Narrator   The Lord said to Samuel:

The Lord   I am sorry that I made Saul king; he has turned away from me and disobeyed my commands.

Narrator   Samuel was angry, and all night long he pleaded with the Lord. Early the following morning he went off to find Saul. He heard that Saul had gone to the town of Carmel, where he had built a monument to himself, and then had gone on to Gilgal. Samuel went up to Saul. Saul greeted him:

Saul   The Lord bless you, Samuel! I have obeyed the Lord's command.

[Narrator   Samuel asked:]

Samuel   Why, then, do I hear cattle mooing and sheep bleating?

Saul	My men took them from the Amalekites. They kept the best sheep and cattle to offer as a sacrifice to the Lord your God, and the rest we have destroyed completely . . .
Samuel (interrupting)	Stop, and I will tell you what the Lord said to me last night.
Saul	Tell me.
Samuel	Even though you consider yourself of no importance, you are the leader of the tribes of Israel. The Lord anointed you king of Israel, and he sent you out with orders to destroy those wicked people of Amalek. He told you to fight until you had killed them all. Why, then, did you not obey him? Why did you rush to seize the loot, and so do what displeases the Lord?
Saul (assertively)	I did obey the Lord. I went out as he told me to, brought back King Agag, and killed all the Amalekites. But my men did not kill the best sheep and cattle that they captured; instead, they brought them here to Gilgal to offer as a sacrifice to the Lord your God.
Samuel	Which does the Lord prefer: obedience or offerings and sacrifices? It is better to obey him than to sacrifice the best sheep to him. Rebellion against him is as bad as witchcraft, and arrogance is as sinful as idolatry. Because you rejected the Lord's command, he has rejected you as king. (PAUSE)
Saul (contritely)	Yes, I have sinned. I disobeyed the Lord's command and your instructions. I was afraid of my men and did what they wanted. But now I beg you, forgive my sin and go back with me, so that I can worship the Lord.
Samuel	I will not go back with you. You rejected the Lord's command, and he has rejected you as king of Israel.
Narrator	Then Samuel turned to leave, but Saul caught hold of his cloak, and it tore. Samuel said to him:
Samuel	The Lord has torn the kingdom of Israel away from you today and given it to someone who is a better man than you. Israel's majestic God does not lie or change his mind. He is not a man—he does not change his mind. (PAUSE)
[Narrator	Saul replied:]
Saul	I have sinned. But at least show me respect in front of the leaders of my people and all Israel. Go back with me so that I can worship the Lord your God.
Narrator	So Samuel went back with him, and Saul worshipped the Lord.
	Then Samuel went to Ramah, and King Saul went home to Gibeah. As long as Samuel lived, he never again saw the king; but he grieved over him. The Lord was sorry that he had made Saul king of Israel.
Cast	[This is] the word of the Lord.
All	**Thanks be to God.**

Cast: **Narrator, The Lord, Saul, Samuel.**

David is anointed king
1 Samuel 16.1–13

Narrator	The Lord said to Samuel:
The Lord	How long will you go on grieving over Saul? I have rejected him as king of Israel. But now get some olive-oil and go to Bethlehem, to a man named Jesse, because I have chosen one of his sons to be king.
[Narrator	Samuel asked:]
Samuel	How can I do that? If Saul hears about it, he will kill me!
The Lord	Take a calf with you and say that you are there to offer a sacrifice to the Lord. Invite Jesse to the sacrifice, and I will tell you what to do. You will anoint as king the man I tell you to.
Narrator	Samuel did what the Lord told him to do and went to Bethlehem, where the city leaders came trembling to meet him [and asked]:
Leader	Is this a peaceful visit, seer?
Samuel	Yes. I have come to offer a sacrifice to the Lord. Purify yourselves and come with me.
Narrator	Samuel *also* told Jesse and his sons to purify themselves, and he invited *them* to the sacrifice. (PAUSE)
	When they arrived, Samuel saw Jesse's son Eliab [and said to himself:]
Samuel (to himself)	This man standing here in the Lord's presence is surely the one he has chosen.
[Narrator	But the Lord said to him:]
The Lord	Pay no attention to how tall and handsome he is. I have rejected him, because I do not judge as man judges. Man looks at the outward appearance, but I look at the heart.
Narrator	Then Jesse called his son Abinadab and brought him to Samuel. But Samuel said:
Samuel	No, the Lord hasn't chosen him either.
Narrator	Jesse then brought Shammah.
Samuel	No, the Lord hasn't chosen him either.
Narrator	In this way Jesse brought seven of his sons to Samuel. [And Samuel said to him:]
Samuel	No, the Lord hasn't chosen any of these. (PAUSE) Have you any more sons?
[Narrator	Jesse answered:]
Jesse	There is still the youngest, but he is out taking care of the sheep.
Samuel	Tell him to come here. We won't offer the sacrifice until he comes.
Narrator	So Jesse sent for him. He was a handsome, healthy young man, and his eyes sparkled. [The Lord said to Samuel:]

235

The Lord	This is the one—anoint him!
Narrator	Samuel took the olive-oil and anointed David in front of his brothers. Immediately the spirit of the Lord took control of David and was with him from that day on.
Cast	[This is] the word of the Lord.
All	**Thanks be to God.**

Cast: **Narrator, The Lord, Samuel, Leader, Jesse.**

David in Saul's court
1 Samuel 16.14–23

Narrator	The Lord's spirit left Saul, and an evil spirit sent by the Lord tormented him. His servants said to him:
Servant 1	We know that an evil spirit sent by God is tormenting you.
Servant 2	So give us the order, sir, and we will look for a man who knows how to play the harp.
Servant 1	Then when the evil spirit comes on you, the man can play his harp, and you will be all right again.
[Narrator	Saul ordered them:]
Saul	Find me a man who plays well and bring him to me.
Servant 1	Jesse, of the town of Bethlehem, has a son who is a good musician.
Servant 2	He is also a brave and handsome man, a good soldier, and an able speaker. The Lord is with him.
Narrator	So Saul sent messengers to Jesse to say:
Saul	Send me your son David, the one who takes care of the sheep.
Narrator	Jesse sent David to Saul with a young goat, a donkey loaded with bread, and a leather bag full of wine. David came to Saul and entered his service. Saul liked him very much and chose him as the man to carry his weapons. Then Saul sent a message to Jesse:
Saul	I like David. Let him stay here in my service.
Narrator	From then on, whenever the evil spirit sent by God came on Saul, David would get his harp and play it. The evil spirit would leave, and Saul would feel better and be all right again.
Cast	[This is] the word of the Lord.
All	**Thanks be to God.**

Cast: **Narrator, Servant 1, Servant 2** (can be the same as Servant 1)**, Saul.**

Goliath challenges the Israelites
1 Samuel 17.1–11

Narrator	The Philistines gathered for battle in Socoh, a town in Judah; they camped at a place called Ephes Dammim, between Socoh and

Azekah. Saul and the Israelites assembled and camped in the Valley of Elah, where they got ready to fight the Philistines. The Philistines lined up on one hill and the Israelites on another, with a valley between them. A man named Goliath, from the city of Gath, came out from the Philistine camp to challenge the Israelites. He was nearly three metres tall and wore bronze armour that weighed about fifty-seven kilogrammes and a bronze helmet. His legs were also protected by bronze armour, and he carried a bronze javelin slung over his shoulder. His spear was as thick as the bar on a weaver's loom, and its iron head weighed about seven kilogrammes. A soldier walked in front of him carrying his shield. Goliath stood and shouted at the Israelites:

Goliath   What are you doing there, lined up for battle? I am a Philistine, you slaves of Saul! Choose one of your men to fight me. If he wins and kills me, we will be your slaves; but if I win and kill him, you will be our slaves. Here and now I challenge the Israelite army. I dare you to pick someone to fight me!

Narrator   When Saul and his men heard this, they were terrified.

Cast   [This is] the word of the Lord.
All   **Thanks be to God.**

Cast: **Narrator, Goliath.**

David in Saul's camp
1 Samuel 17.12–40

Narrator   David was the son of Jesse, who was an Ephrathite from Bethlehem in Judah. Jesse had eight sons, and at the time Saul was king, he was already a very old man. His three eldest sons had gone with Saul to war. The eldest was Eliab, the next was Abinadab, and the third was Shammah. David was the youngest son, and while the three eldest brothers stayed with Saul, David would go back to Bethlehem from time to time, to take care of his father's sheep.

Goliath challenged the Israelites every morning and evening for forty days.

One day Jesse said to David:

Jesse   Take ten kilogrammes of this roasted grain and these ten loaves of bread, and hurry with them to your brothers in the camp. And take these ten cheeses to the commanding officer. Find out how your brothers are getting on and bring back something to show that you saw them and that they are well. King Saul, your brothers, and all the other Israelites are in the Valley of Elah fighting the Philistines.

Narrator   David got up early the next morning, left someone else in charge of the sheep, took the food, and went as Jesse had told him to. He arrived at the camp just as the Israelites were going out to their battle line, shouting the war-cry. The Philistine and the Israelite

→

armies took up positions for battle, facing each other. David left the food with the officer in charge of the supplies, ran to the battle line, went to his brothers, and asked how they were getting on. As he was talking to them, Goliath came forward and challenged the Israelites as he had done before. And David heard him. When the Israelites saw Goliath, they ran away in terror. They said to each other:

Man 1	Look at him!
Man 2	Listen to his challenge!
Man 1	King Saul has promised to give a big reward to the man who kills him.
Man 2	The king will also give him his daughter to marry—
Man 1	And will not require his father's family to pay taxes.
Narrator	David spoke to the men who were near him:
David	What will the man get who kills this Philistine and frees Israel from this disgrace? After all, who *is* this heathen Philistine to defy the army of the living God?
Narrator	They told him what would be done for the man who killed Goliath.
	Eliab, David's eldest brother, heard David talking to the men. He was angry with David:
Eliab	What are you doing here? Who is taking care of those sheep of yours out there in the wilderness? You cheeky brat, you! You just came to watch the fighting!
David	Now what have I done? Can't I even ask a question?
Narrator	David turned to another man and asked him the same question, and every time he asked, he got the same answer. (PAUSE)
	Some men heard what David had said, and they told Saul, who sent for him. David said to Saul:
David	Your Majesty, no one should be afraid of this Philistine! I will go and fight him.
[Narrator	Saul answered:]
Saul	No. How could *you* fight him? You're just a boy, and he has been a soldier all his life!
David	Your Majesty, I take care of my father's sheep. Whenever a lion or a bear carries off a lamb, I go after it, attack it, and rescue the lamb. And if the lion or bear turns on me, I grab it by the throat and beat it to death. I have killed lions and bears, and I will do the same to this heathen Philistine, who has defied the army of the living God. The Lord has saved me from lions and bears; he will save me from this Philistine.
Saul	All right. Go, and the Lord be with you.
Narrator	He gave his own armour to David for him to wear: a bronze

helmet, which he put on David's head, and a coat of armour. David strapped Saul's sword over the armour and tried to walk, but he couldn't, because he wasn't used to wearing them.

David I can't fight with all this. I'm not used to it.

Narrator So he took it all off. (PAUSE)

He took his shepherd's stick and then picked up five smooth stones from the stream and put them in his bag. With his catapult ready, he went out to meet Goliath.

Cast [This is] the word of the Lord.
All **Thanks be to God.**

Cast: **Narrator, Jesse, Man 1, Man 2, David, Eliab** (can be the same as Man 1), **Saul.**

David defeats Goliath
From 1 Samuel 17.40–50

Narrator David took his shepherd's stick and then picked up five smooth stones from the stream and put them in his bag. With his catapult ready, he went out to meet Goliath. *The Philistine started walking towards David, with his shield-bearer walking in front of him. He kept coming closer, and when he got a good look at David, he was filled with scorn for him because he was just a nice, good-looking boy. [He said to David:]

Goliath What's that stick for? Do you think I'm a dog?

Narrator He called down curses from his god on David. He challenged David:

Goliath Come on, I will give your body to the birds and animals to eat.

[Narrator David answered:]

David You are coming against me with sword, spear, and javelin, but I come against you in the name of the Lord Almighty, the God of the Israelite armies, which you have defied. This very day the Lord will put you in my power; I will defeat you and cut off your head. And I will give the bodies of the Philistine soldiers to the birds and animals to eat. Then the whole world will know that Israel has a God, and everyone here will see that the Lord does not need swords or spears to save his people. He is victorious in battle, and he will put all of you in our power.

Narrator Goliath started walking towards David again, and David ran quickly towards the Philistine battle line to fight him. He put his hand into his bag and took out a stone, which he slung at Goliath. It hit him on the forehead and broke his skull, and Goliath fell face downwards on the ground. And so, without a sword, David defeated and killed Goliath with a catapult and a stone!

Cast [This is] the word of the Lord.
All **Thanks be to God.**

Cast: **Narrator, Goliath, David** (*indicates where this reading follows from the previous one).

David is presented to Saul
1 Samuel 17.55—18.5

Narrator	When Saul saw David going out to fight Goliath, he asked Abner, the commander of his army:
Saul	Abner, whose son is he?
[Narrator	Abner answered:]
Abner	I have no idea, Your Majesty.
Saul	Then go and find out!
Narrator	So when David returned to camp after killing Goliath, Abner took him to Saul. David was still carrying Goliath's head. Saul asked him:
Saul	Young man, whose son are you?
[Narrator	David answered:]
David	I am the son of your servant Jesse from Bethlehem.
Narrator	Saul and David finished their conversation. After that, Saul's son Jonathan was deeply attracted to David and came to love him as much as he loved himself. Saul kept David with him from that day on and did not let him go back home. Jonathan swore eternal friendship with David because of his deep affection for him. He took off the robe he was wearing and gave it to David, together with his armour and also his sword, bow, and belt. David was successful in all the missions on which Saul sent him, and so Saul made him an officer in his army. This pleased all of Saul's officers and men.
Cast	[This is] the word of the Lord.
All	**Thanks be to God.**

Cast: **Narrator, Saul, Abner, David.**

Saul becomes jealous of David
1 Samuel 18.6–16

Narrator	As David was returning after killing Goliath and as the soldiers were coming back home, women from every town in Israel came out to meet King Saul. They were singing joyful songs, dancing, and playing tambourines and lyres. In their celebration the women sang:
Women 1 and **2**	Saul has killed thousands, but David tens of thousands.
Narrator	Saul did not like this, and he became very angry:
Saul	For David they claim tens of thousands, but only thousands for me. They will be making him *king* next!
Narrator	And so he was jealous and suspicious of David from that day on. (PAUSE)

The next day an evil spirit from God suddenly took control of Saul, and he raved in his house like a madman. David was playing the harp, as he did every day, and Saul was holding a spear. Saul said to himself:

Saul (angrily)	I'll pin him to the wall.
Narrator	And he threw the spear at him twice; but David dodged each time. (PAUSE)

Saul was afraid of David because the Lord was with David but had abandoned him. So Saul sent him away and put him in command of a thousand men. David led his men in battle and was successful in all he did, because the Lord was with him. Saul noticed David's success and became even more afraid of him. But everyone in Israel and Judah loved David because he was such a successful leader.

Cast	[This is] the word of the Lord.
All	**Thanks be to God.**

Cast: **Narrator, Woman 1, Woman 2** (can be the same as Woman 1), **Saul.**

David marries Saul's daughter
From 1 Samuel 18.17–30

Narrator	Saul said to David:
Saul	Here is my elder daughter Merab. I will give her to you as your wife on condition that you serve me as a brave and loyal soldier, and fight the Lord's battles.
Narrator	Saul was thinking that in this way the Philistines would kill David, and he would not have to do it himself. [David answered:]
David	Who am I and what is my family that I should become the king's son-in-law?
Narrator	But when the time came for Merab to be given to David, she was given instead to a man named Adriel from Meholah. Saul's daughter Michal, however, fell in love with David, and when Saul heard of this, he was pleased:
Saul (to himself)	I'll give Michal to David; I will use her to trap him, and he will be killed by the Philistines.
Narrator	So for the second time Saul said to David:
Saul	You will be my son-in-law.
Narrator	He ordered his officials to speak privately to David and tell him:
Official 1	The king is pleased with you, and all his officials like you.
Official 2	Now is a good time for you to marry his daughter.
[Narrator	So they told David this, and he answered:]
David	It's a great honour to become the king's son-in-law, too great for someone poor and insignificant like me.

Narrator	The officials told Saul what David had said, and Saul ordered them to tell David:
Official 1	All the king wants from you as payment for the bride is a hundred dead Philistines—
Official 2	As revenge on his enemies.
Narrator	This was how Saul planned to have David killed by the Philistines. Saul's officials reported to David what Saul had said, and David was delighted with the thought of becoming the king's son-in-law. Before the day set for the wedding, David and his men went and killed two hundred Philistines so that he might become his son-in-law. So Saul had to give his daughter Michal in marriage to David. (PAUSE)
	Saul realized clearly that the Lord was with David and also that his daughter Michal loved him. So he became even more afraid of David and was his enemy as long as he lived. The Philistine armies would come and fight, but in every battle David was more successful than any of Saul's other officers. As a result David became very famous.
Cast	[This is] the word of the Lord.
All	**Thanks be to God.**

Cast: **Narrator, Saul, David, Official 1, Official 2.**

David is persecuted by Saul
1 Samuel 19.1–18

Narrator	Saul told his son Jonathan and all his officials that he planned to kill David. But Jonathan was very fond of David [and so he said to him]:
Jonathan	My father is trying to kill you. Please be careful tomorrow morning; hide in some secret place and stay there. I will go and stand by my father in the field where you are hiding, and I will speak to him about you. If I find out anything, I will let you know.
Narrator	Jonathan praised David to Saul:
Jonathan	Sir, don't do wrong to your servant David. He has never done you any wrong; on the contrary, everything he has done has been a great help to you. He risked his life when he killed Goliath, and the Lord won a great victory for Israel. When you saw it, you were glad. Why, then, do you now want to do wrong to an innocent man and kill David for no reason at all?
Narrator	Saul was convinced by what Jonathan said and made a vow in the Lord's name that he would not kill David. So Jonathan called David and told him everything; then he took him to Saul, and David served the king as he had before.
	War with the Philistines broke out again. David attacked them and defeated them so thoroughly that they fled.

One day an evil spirit from the Lord took control of Saul. He was sitting in his house with his spear in his hand, and David was there, playing his harp. Saul tried to pin David to the wall with his spear, but David dodged, and the spear stuck in the wall. David ran away and escaped.

That same night Saul sent some men to watch David's house and kill him the next morning. Michal, David's wife, warned him:

Michal	If you don't get away tonight, tomorrow you will be dead.
Narrator	She let him down from a window, and he ran away and escaped. Then she took the household idol, laid it on the bed, put a pillow made of goats'-hair at its head, and put a cover over it. When Saul's men came to get David, Michal told them that he was ill. But Saul sent them back to see David for themselves. He ordered them:
Saul	Carry him here in his bed, and I will kill him.
Narrator	They went inside and found the household idol in the bed and the goats'-hair pillow at its head. Saul asked Michal:
Saul	Why have you tricked me like this and let my enemy escape?
Michal	He said he would kill me if I didn't help him to escape.
Narrator	David escaped and went to Samuel in Ramah and told him everything that Saul had done to him. Then he and Samuel went to Naioth and stayed there.
Cast	[This is] the word of the Lord.
All	**Thanks be to God.**

Cast: **Narrator, Jonathan, Michal, Saul.**

Jonathan helps David (i)
1 Samuel 20.1–17

Narrator	David fled from Naioth in Ramah and went to Jonathan. He asked:
David	What have I done? What crime have I committed? What wrong have I done to your father to make him want to kill me?
Narrator	Jonathan answered:
Jonathan	God forbid that you should die! My father tells me everything he does, important or not, and he would not hide this from me. It isn't true!
David	Your father knows very well how much you like me, and he has decided not to let you know what he plans to do, because you would be deeply hurt. I swear to you by the living Lord that I am only a step away from death!
Jonathan	I'll do anything you want.

David	Tomorrow is the New Moon Festival, and I am supposed to eat with the king. But if it's all right with you, I will go and hide in the fields until the evening of the day after tomorrow. If your father notices that I am not at table, tell him that I begged your permission to hurry home to Bethlehem, since it's the time for the annual sacrifice there for my whole family. If he says, 'All right,' I will be safe; but if he becomes angry, you will know that he is determined to harm me. Please do me this favour, and keep the sacred promise you made to me. But if I'm guilty, kill me yourself! Why take me to your father to be killed?
Jonathan	Don't even think such a thing! If I knew for certain that my father was determined to harm you, wouldn't I tell you? (PAUSE)
David	Who will let me know if your father answers you angrily?
Jonathan	Let's go out to the fields.
Narrator	So they went, and Jonathan talked to David:
Jonathan	May the Lord God of Israel be our witness! At this time tomorrow and on the following day I will question my father. If his attitude towards you is good, I will send you word. If he intends to harm you, may the Lord strike me dead if I don't let you know about it and get you safely away. May the Lord be with you as he was with my father! And if I remain alive, please keep your sacred promise and be loyal to me; but if I die, show the same kind of loyalty to my family for ever. And when the Lord has completely destroyed all your enemies, may our promise to each other still be unbroken. If it is broken, the Lord will punish you.
Narrator	Once again Jonathan made David promise to love him, for Jonathan loved David as much as he loved himself.
Cast	[This is] the word of the Lord.
All	**Thanks be to God.**

Cast: **Narrator, David, Jonathan.**

Jonathan helps David (ii)
1 Samuel 20.18–24

Narrator	Jonathan said to David:
Jonathan	Since tomorrow is the New Moon Festival, your absence will be noticed even more; so go to the place where you hid the other time, and hide behind the pile of stones there. I will then shoot three arrows at it, as though it were a target. Then I will tell my servant to go and find them. And if I tell him:
Voice	Look, the arrows are on this side of you; get them!
Jonathan	That means that you are safe and can come out. I swear by the living Lord that you will be in no danger. But if I tell him:
Voice	The arrows are on the other side of you.

Jonathan	Then leave, because the Lord is sending you away. As for the promise we have made to each other, the Lord will make sure that we will keep it for ever.
Narrator	So David hid in the fields.
Cast	[This is] the word of the Lord.
All	**Thanks be to God.**

Cast: **Narrator, Jonathan, Voice.**

Jonathan helps David (iii)
1 Samuel 20.24–34

Narrator	At the New Moon Festival, King Saul came to the meal and sat in his usual place by the wall. Abner sat next to him, and Jonathan sat opposite him. David's place was empty, but Saul said nothing that day, because he thought:
Saul (thinking)	Something has happened to him, and he is not ritually pure.
Narrator	On the following day, the day after the New Moon Festival, David's place was still empty, and Saul asked Jonathan:
Saul	Why didn't David come to the meal either yesterday or today?
[Narrator	Jonathan answered:]
Jonathan	He begged me to let him go to Bethlehem. 'Please let me go,' he said, 'because our family is celebrating the sacrificial feast in town, and my brother ordered me to be there. So then, if you are my friend, let me go and see my relatives.' That is why he isn't in his place at your table.
Narrator	Saul was furious with Jonathan and said to him:
Saul (angrily)	You . . . Now I know you are taking sides with David and are disgracing yourself and that mother of yours! Don't you realize that as long as David is alive, you will never be king of this country? Now go and bring him here—he must die!
Jonathan	Why should he die? What has he done?
Narrator	At that, Saul threw his spear at Jonathan to kill him, and Jonathan realized that his father was really determined to kill David. Jonathan got up from the table in a rage and ate nothing that day—the second day of the New Moon Festival. He was deeply distressed about David, because Saul had insulted him.
Cast	[This is] the word of the Lord.
All	**Thanks be to God.**

Cast: **Narrator, Saul, Jonathan.**

Jonathan helps David (iv)
1 Samuel 20.35–42

Narrator [The following morning] Jonathan went to the fields to meet David, as they had agreed. He took a young boy with him and said to him:

Jonathan Run and find the arrows I'm going to shoot.

Narrator The boy ran, and Jonathan shot an arrow beyond him. When the boy reached the place where the arrow had fallen, Jonathan shouted to him:

Jonathan The arrow is further on! Don't just stand there! Hurry up!

Narrator The boy picked up the arrow and returned to his master, not knowing what it all meant; only Jonathan and David knew. Jonathan gave his weapons to the boy and told him to take them back to the town.

After the boy had left, David got up from behind the pile of stones, fell on his knees and bowed with his face to the ground three times. Both he and Jonathan were crying as they kissed each other; David's grief was even greater than Jonathan's. Then Jonathan said to David:

Jonathan God be with you. The Lord will make sure that you and I, and your descendants and mine, will for ever keep the sacred promise we have made to each other.

Narrator Then David left, and Jonathan went back to the town.

Cast [This is] the word of the Lord.
All **Thanks be to God.**

Cast: **Narrator, Jonathan.**

David flees from Saul
From 1 Samuel 21.1–11 [12–15]

Narrator David went to the priest Ahimelech in Nob. Ahimelech came out trembling to meet him and asked:

Ahimelech Why did you come here all by yourself?

[Narrator David answered:]

David I am here on the king's business. He told me not to let anyone know what he sent me to do. As for my men, I have told them to meet me at a certain place. Now, then, what supplies have you got? Give me five loaves of bread or anything else you have.

Ahimelech I haven't any ordinary bread, only sacred bread.

Narrator So the priest gave David the sacred bread, because the only bread he had was the loaves offered to God, which had been removed from the sacred table and replaced by fresh bread. David said to Ahimelech:

246

David	Have you got a spear or a sword you can give me? The king's orders made me leave in such a hurry that I didn't have time to get my sword or any other weapon.
Ahimelech	I have the sword of Goliath the Philistine, whom you killed in the Valley of Elah; it is behind the ephod, wrapped in a cloth. If you want it, take it—it's the only weapon here.
David	Give it to me. There is not a better sword anywhere! (PAUSE)
Narrator	So David left, fleeing from Saul, and went to King Achish of Gath. The king's officials said to Achish:
Official 1	Isn't this David, the king of his country?
Official 2	This is the man about whom the women sang, as they danced, 'Saul has killed thousands, but David has killed tens of thousands.'
[Narrator	Their words made a deep impression on David, and he became very much afraid of King Achish. So whenever they were around, David pretended to be insane and acted like a madman when they tried to restrain him; he would scribble on the city gates and dribble down his beard. So Achish said to his officials:
Achish	Look! The man is mad! Why did you bring him to me? Haven't I got enough madmen already? Why bring another one to annoy me with his daft actions right here in my own house?]
Cast	[This is] the word of the Lord.
All	**Thanks be to God.**

Cast: **Narrator, Ahimelech, David, Official 1, Official 2** (can be the same as Official 1), **[Achish].**

The slaughter of the priests
1 Samuel 22.1–23

Narrator	David fled from the city of Gath and went to a cave near the town of Adullam. When his brothers and the rest of the family heard that he was there, they joined him. People who were oppressed or in debt or dissatisfied went to him, about four hundred men in all, and he became their leader. (PAUSE)
	David went on from there to Mizpah in Moab and said to the king of Moab:
David	Please let my father and mother come and stay with you until I find out what God is going to do for me.
Narrator	So David left his parents with the king of Moab, and they stayed there as long as David was hiding in the cave. Then the prophet Gad came to David and said:
Prophet	Don't stay here; go at once to the land of Judah.
Narrator	So David left and went to the forest of Hereth. (PAUSE)
	One day Saul was in Gibeah, sitting under a tamarisk-tree on a hill, with his spear in his hand, and all his officers were standing

→

	round him. He was told that David and his men had been found, and he said to his officers:
Saul	Listen, men of Benjamin! Do you think that David will give fields and vineyards to all of you, and make you officers in his army? Is that why you are plotting against me? Not one of you told me that my own son had made an alliance with David. No one is concerned about me or tells me that David, one of my own men, is at this moment looking for a chance to kill me, and that my son has encouraged him!
Narrator	Doeg was standing there with Saul's officers, and he said:
Doeg	I saw David when he went to Ahimelech son of Ahitub in Nob. Ahimelech asked the Lord what David should do, and then he gave David some food and the sword of Goliath the Philistine.
Narrator	So King Saul sent for the priest Ahimelech and all his relatives, who were also priests in Nob, and they came to him. Saul said to Ahimelech:
Saul	Listen, Ahimelech!
Ahimelech	At your service, sir.
Saul	Why are you and David plotting against me? Why did you give him some food and a sword, and consult God for him? Now he has turned against me and is waiting for a chance to kill me!
Ahimelech	David is the most faithful officer you have! He is your own son-in-law, captain of your bodyguard, and highly respected by everyone in the royal court. Yes, I consulted God for him, and it wasn't the first time. As for plotting against you, Your Majesty must not accuse me or anyone else in my family. I don't know anything about this matter!
Saul (angrily)	Ahimelech, you and all your relatives must die.
Narrator	Then he said to the guards standing near him:
Saul	Kill the Lord's priests! They conspired with David and did not tell me that he had run away, even though they knew it all along.
Narrator	But the guards refused to lift a hand to kill the Lord's priests. So Saul said to Doeg:
Saul	You kill them!
Narrator	And Doeg killed them all. On that day he killed eighty-five priests who were qualified to carry the ephod. Saul also ordered all the other inhabitants of Nob, the city of priests, to be put to death: men and women, children and babies, cattle, donkeys, and sheep—they were all killed.
	But Abiathar, one of Ahimelech's sons, escaped, and went and joined David. He told him how Saul had slaughtered the priests of the Lord. David said to him:

David	When I saw Doeg there that day, I knew that he would be sure to tell Saul. So I am responsible for the death of all your relatives. Stay with me and don't be afraid. Saul wants to kill both you and me, but you will be safe with me.
Cast	[This is] the word of the Lord.
All	**Thanks be to God.**

Cast: **Narrator, David, Prophet, Saul, Doeg, Ahimelech.**

David saves the town of Keilah
1 Samuel 23.1–13

Narrator	David heard that the Philistines were attacking the town of Keilah and were stealing the newly-harvested corn. So he asked the Lord:
David	Shall I go and attack the Philistines?
[Narrator	The Lord answered:]
The Lord	Yes. Attack them and save Keilah.
Narrator	But David's men said to him:
Man 1	We have enough to be afraid of here in Judah.
Man 2	It will be much worse if we go to Keilah and attack the Philistine forces!
Narrator	So David consulted the Lord again, and the Lord said to him:
The Lord	Go and attack Keilah, because I will give you victory over the Philistines.
Narrator	So David and his men went to Keilah and attacked the Philistines; they killed many of them and took their livestock. And that was how David saved the town. (PAUSE)
	When Abiathar son of Ahimelech escaped and joined David in Keilah, he took the ephod with him. Saul was told that David had gone to Keilah, and he said:
Saul (with cunning voice)	God has put him in my power. David has trapped himself by going into a walled town with fortified gates.
Narrator	So Saul called his troops to war, to march against Keilah and besiege David and his men. (PAUSE)
	When David heard that Saul was planning to attack him, he said to the priest Abiathar:
David	Bring the ephod here.
Narrator	Then David prayed:
David	Lord, God of Israel, I have heard that Saul is planning to come to Keilah and destroy it on account of me, your servant. Will the

$\rightarrow$

citizens of Keilah hand me over to Saul? Will Saul really come, as I have heard? Lord, God of Israel, I beg you to answer me!

Narrator	The Lord answered:
The Lord	Saul will come.
David	And will the citizens of Keilah hand my men and me over to Saul?
The Lord	They will.
Narrator	So David and his men—about six hundred in all—left Keilah at once and kept on the move. When Saul heard that David had escaped from Keilah, he gave up his plan.
Cast	[This is] the word of the Lord.
All	**Thanks be to God.**

Cast: **Narrator, David, The Lord, Man 1, Man 2** (can be the same as Man 1), **Saul.**

David in the hill-country
1 Samuel 23.14–29

Narrator	David stayed in hiding in the hill-country, in the wilderness near Ziph. Saul was always trying to find him, but God did not hand David over to him. David saw that Saul was out to kill him. David was at Horesh, in the wilderness near Ziph. Jonathan went to him there and encouraged him with assurances of God's protection:
Jonathan	Don't be afraid. My father Saul won't be able to harm you. He knows very well that you are the one who will be the king of Israel and that I will be next in rank to you.
Narrator	The two of them made a sacred promise of friendship to each other. David stayed at Horesh, and Jonathan went home.
	Some people from Ziph went to Saul at Gibeah [and said]:
Person 1	David is hiding in our territory at Horesh on Mount Hachilah, in the southern part of the Judaean wilderness.
Person 2	We know, Your Majesty, how much you want to capture him.
Person 1	So come to our territory, and we will make sure that you catch him.
[Narrator	Saul answered:]
Saul	May the Lord bless you for being so kind to me! Go and make sure once more; find out for certain where he is and who has seen him there. I hear that he is very cunning. Find out exactly the places where he hides, and be sure to bring back a report to me straight away. Then I will go with you, and if he is still in the region, I will hunt him down, even if I have to search the whole land of Judah.
Narrator	So they left and returned to Ziph ahead of Saul. David and his men were in the wilderness of Maon, in a desolate valley in the southern part of the Judaean wilderness. Saul and his men set out to look for David, but he heard about it and went to a rocky hill in

the wilderness of Maon and stayed there. When Saul heard about this, he went after David. Saul and his men were on one side of the hill, separated from David and his men, who were on the other side. They were hurrying to get away from Saul and his men, who were closing in on them and were about to capture them. Just then a messenger arrived and said to Saul:

Messenger   Come back at once! The Philistines are invading the country!

Narrator   So Saul stopped pursuing David and went to fight the Philistines. That is why that place is called Separation Hill. David left and went to the region of Engedi, where he stayed in hiding.

Cast   [This is] the word of the Lord.
All   **Thanks be to God.**

Cast: **Narrator, Jonathan, Person 1, Person 2, Saul, Messenger.**

David spares Saul's life
1 Samuel 24.1–22

Narrator   When Saul came back from fighting the Philistines, he was told that David was in the wilderness near Engedi. Saul took three thousand of the best soldiers in Israel and went looking for David and his men east of Wild Goat Rocks. He came to a cave close to some sheep pens by the road and went in to relieve himself. It happened to be the very cave in which David and his men were hiding far back in the cave. They said to him:

Man 1 (loud whisper)   This is your chance!

Man 2 (loud whisper)   The Lord has told you that he would put your enemy in your power and you could do to him whatever you wanted to.

Narrator   David crept over and cut off a piece of Saul's robe without Saul's knowing it. But then David's conscience began to trouble him, and he said to his men:

David   May the Lord keep me from doing any harm to my master, whom the Lord chose as king! I must not harm him in the least, because he is the king chosen by the Lord!

Narrator   So David convinced his men that they should not attack Saul. (PAUSE)

Saul got up, left the cave, and started on his way. Then David went out after him and called to him:

David   Your Majesty!

Narrator   Saul turned round, and David bowed down to the ground in respect [and said]:

David   Why do you listen to people who say that I am trying to harm you? You can see for yourself that just now in the cave the Lord put you in my power. Some of my men told me to kill you, but I felt sorry for you and said that I would not harm you in the least, because you are the one whom the Lord chose to be king. Look, my father,

→

look at the piece of your robe I am holding! I could have killed you, but instead I only cut this off. This should convince you that I have no thought of rebelling against you or of harming you. You are hunting me down to kill me, even though I have not done you any wrong. May the Lord judge which one of us is wrong! May he punish you for your action against me, for I will not harm you in the least. You know the old saying, 'Evil is done only by evil men.' And so I will not harm you. Look at what the king of Israel is trying to kill! Look at what he is chasing! A dead dog, a flea! The Lord will judge, and he will decide which one of us is wrong. May he look into the matter, defend me, and save me from you.

[Narrator	When David had finished speaking, Saul said:]
Saul	Is that really you, David my son?
Narrator	Saul started crying. [Then he said to David:]
Saul	You are right, and I am wrong. You have been so good to me, while I have done such wrong to you! Today you have shown how good you are to me, because you did not kill me, even though the Lord put me in your power. How often does a man catch his enemy and then let him get away unharmed? The Lord bless you for what you have done to me today! Now I am sure that you will be king of Israel and that the kingdom will continue under your rule. But promise me in the Lord's name that you will spare my descendants, so that my name and my family's name will not be completely forgotten.
Narrator	David promised that he would. Then Saul went back home, and David and his men went back to their hiding place.
Cast	[This is] the word of the Lord.
All	**Thanks be to God.**

Cast: **Narrator, Man 1, Man 2** (can be the same as Man 1), **David, Saul** (at the back of the audience).

David and Abigail
From 1 Samuel 25.1–42

Narrator	David went to the wilderness of Paran. There was a man of the clan of Caleb named Nabal, who was from the town of Maon, and who owned land near the town of Carmel. He was a very rich man, the owner of three thousand sheep and one thousand goats. His wife Abigail was beautiful and intelligent, but he was a mean, bad-tempered man.
	Nabal was shearing his sheep in Carmel, and David, who was in the wilderness, heard about it, so he sent ten young men with orders to go to Carmel, find Nabal, and give him his greetings. He instructed them to say to Nabal:
David	David sends you greetings, my friend, with his best wishes for you, your family, and all that is yours. He heard that you were shearing your sheep, and he wants you to know that your shepherds have been with us and we did not harm them. Nothing that belonged

to them was stolen all the time they were at Carmel. Just ask them, and they will tell you. We have come on a feast day, and David asks you to receive us kindly. Please give what you can to us your servants and to your dear friend David.

Narrator David's men delivered this message to Nabal in David's name. Then they waited there, and Nabal finally answered:

Nabal David? Who is he? I've never heard of him! The country is full of runaway slaves nowadays! I'm not going to take my bread and water, and the animals I have slaughtered for my shearers, and give them to men who come from I don't know where!

Narrator David's men went back to him and told him what Nabal had said. He ordered:

David Buckle on your swords!

Narrator And they all did. David also buckled on his sword and left with about four hundred of his men, leaving two hundred behind with the supplies.

One of Nabal's servants said to Nabal's wife Abigail:

Servant Have you heard? David sent some messengers from the wilderness with greetings for our master, but he insulted them. Yet they were very good to us; they never bothered us, and all the time we were with them in the fields, nothing that belonged to us was stolen. They protected us day and night the whole time we were with them looking after our flocks. Please think this over and decide what to do. This could be disastrous for our master and all his family. He is so pigheaded that he won't listen to anybody!

Narrator Abigail quickly collected two hundred loaves of bread, two leather bags full of wine, five roasted sheep, seventeen kilogrammes of roasted grain, a hundred bunches of raisins, and two hundred cakes of dried figs, and loaded them on donkeys. Then she said to the servants:

Abigail You go on ahead and I will follow you.

Narrator But she said nothing to her husband. (PAUSE)

She was riding her donkey round a bend on a hillside when suddenly she met David and his men coming towards her. David had been thinking:

David
(musing) Why did I ever protect that fellow's property out here in the wilderness? Not a thing that belonged to him was stolen, and this is how he pays me back for the help I gave him! May God strike me dead if I don't kill every last one of those men before morning!

Narrator When Abigail saw David, she quickly dismounted and threw herself on the ground at David's feet, and said to him:

Abigail Please, sir, listen to me! Let me take the blame. Please, don't pay any attention to Nabal, that good-for-nothing! He is exactly what his name means—a fool! I wasn't there when your servants arrived, sir. It is the Lord who has kept you from taking revenge and killing your enemies. And now I swear to you by the living

→

Lord that your enemies and all who want to harm you will be punished like Nabal. Please, sir, accept this present I have brought you, and give it to your men. Please forgive me, sir, for any wrong I have done. The Lord will make you king, and your descendants also, because you are fighting his battles; and you will not do anything evil as long as you live. If anyone should attack you and try to kill you, the Lord your God will keep you safe, as a man guards a precious treasure. As for your enemies, however, he will throw them away as a man hurls stones with his catapult. And when the Lord has done all the good things he has promised you and has made you king of Israel, then you will not have to feel regret or remorse, sir, for having killed without cause or for having taken your own revenge. And when the Lord has blessed you, sir, please do not forget me.

David Praise the Lord, the God of Israel, who sent you today to meet me! Thank God for your good sense and for what you have done today in keeping me from the crime of murder and from taking my own revenge. The Lord has kept me from harming you. But I swear by the living God of Israel that if you had not hurried to meet me, all of Nabal's men would have been dead by morning!

Narrator Then David accepted what she had brought him and said to her:

David Go back home and don't worry. I will do what you want.

Narrator Abigail went back to Nabal, who was at home having a feast fit for a king. He was drunk and in a good mood, so she did not tell him anything until the next morning. Then, after he had sobered up, she told him everything. He suffered a stroke and was completely paralysed. Some ten days later the Lord struck Nabal and he died. (LONG PAUSE)

David sent a proposal of marriage to Abigail. His servants went to her at Carmel and said to her:

Servant David sent us to take you to him to be his wife.

Narrator Abigail bowed down to the ground:

Abigail I am his servant, ready to wash the feet of his servants.

Narrator She rose quickly and mounted her donkey. Accompanied by her five maids, she went with David's servants and became his wife.

Cast [This is] the word of the Lord.
All **Thanks be to God.**

Cast: **Narrator, David, Nabal, Servant, Abigail.**

David spares Saul's life again
1 Samuel 26.1–25

Narrator Some men from Ziph came to Saul at Gibeah and told him that David was hiding on Mount Hachilah at the edge of the Judaean wilderness. Saul went at once with three thousand of the best soldiers in Israel to the wilderness of Ziph to look for David, and camped by the road on Mount Hachilah. David was still in the wilderness, and when he learnt that Saul had come to look for him, he sent spies and found out that Saul was indeed there. He went at once and located the exact place where Saul and Abner son of Ner, commander of Saul's army, slept. Saul slept inside the camp, and his men camped round him. Then David asked Ahimelech the Hittite, and Abishai the brother of Joab:

David Which of you two will go to Saul's camp with me?

Narrator Abishai answered:

Abishai *I* will.

Narrator So that night David and Abishai entered Saul's camp and found Saul sleeping in the centre of the camp with his spear stuck in the ground near his head. Abner and the troops were sleeping round him. Abishai said to David:

Abishai God has put your enemy in your power tonight. Now let me plunge his own spear through him and pin him to the ground with just one blow—I won't have to strike twice!

David You must not harm him! The Lord will certainly punish whoever harms his chosen king.

By the living Lord, I know that the Lord himself will kill Saul, either when his time comes to die a natural death or when he dies in battle. The Lord forbid that I should try to harm the one whom the Lord has made king! Let's take his spear and his water jar, and go.

Narrator So David took the spear and the water jar from just beside Saul's head, and he and Abishai left. No one saw it or knew what had happened or even woke up—they were all sound asleep, because the Lord had sent a heavy sleep on them all. (PAUSE)

Then David crossed over to the other side of the valley to the top of the hill, a safe distance away, and shouted to Saul's troops and to Abner:

David (calling) Abner! Can you hear me?

[Narrator Abner asked:]

Abner (calling) Who is that shouting and waking up the king?

David (calling) Abner, aren't you the greatest man in Israel? So why aren't you protecting your master, the king? Just now someone entered the camp to kill your master. You failed in your duty, Abner! I swear by the living Lord that all of you deserve to die, because you have →

not protected your master, whom the Lord made king. Look! Where is the king's spear? Where is the water jar that was beside his head?

Narrator Saul recognized David's voice [and asked]:

Saul (calling) David, is that you, my son?

David (calling) Yes, Your Majesty. (PAUSE)

Why, sir, are you still pursuing me, your servant? What have I done? What crime have I committed? (PAUSE)

Your Majesty, listen to what I have to say. If it is the Lord who has turned you against me, an offering to him will make him change his mind; but if men have done it, may the Lord's curse fall on them. For they have driven me out from the Lord's land to a country where I can only worship foreign gods. Don't let me be killed on foreign soil, away from the Lord. Why should the king of Israel come to kill a flea like me? Why should he hunt me down like a wild bird?

Saul (calling) I have done wrong. Come back, David, my son! I will never harm you again, because you have spared my life tonight. I have been a fool! I have done a terrible thing!

David (calling) Here is your spear, Your Majesty. Let one of your men come over and get it. The Lord rewards those who are faithful and righteous. Today he put you in my power, but I did not harm you, whom the Lord made king. Just as I have spared your life today, may the Lord do the same to me and free me from all troubles!

Saul (calling) God bless you, my son! You will succeed in everything you do!

Narrator So David went on his way, and Saul returned home.

Cast [This is] the word of the Lord.
All **Thanks be to God.**

Cast: **Narrator, David, Abishai, Abner** (at the back of the audience), **Saul** (at the back of the audience).

David among the Philistines
1 Samuel 27.1—28.2

Narrator David said to himself:

David One of these days Saul will kill me. The best thing for me to do is to escape to Philistia. Then Saul will give up looking for me in Israel, and I will be safe.

Narrator So David and his six hundred men went over at once to Achish son of Maoch, king of Gath. David and his men settled there in Gath with their families. David had his two wives with him, Ahinoam from Jezreel, and Abigail, Nabal's widow, from Carmel. When Saul heard that David had fled to Gath, he gave up trying to find him.

David said to Achish:

David	If you are my friend, let me have a small town to live in. There is no need, sir, for me to live with you in the capital city.
Narrator	So Achish gave him the town of Ziklag, and for this reason Ziklag has belonged to the kings of Judah ever since. David lived in Philistia for sixteen months. (PAUSE)
	During that time David and his men would attack the people of Geshur, Girzi, and Amalek, who had been living in the region a very long time. He would raid their land as far as Shur, all the way down to Egypt, killing all the men and women and taking the sheep, cattle, donkeys, camels, and even the clothes. Then he would come back to Achish, who would ask him:
Achish	Where did you go on a raid this time?
Narrator	David would tell him that he had gone to the southern part of Judah or to the territory of the clan of Jerahmeel or to the territory where the Kenites lived. David would kill everyone, men and women, so that no one could go back to Gath and report what he and his men had really done. This is what David did the whole time he lived in Philistia. But Achish trusted David [and said to himself]:
Achish (craftily)	He is hated so much by his own people the Israelites that he will have to serve me all his life.
Narrator	Some time later, the Philistines gathered their troops to fight Israel, and Achish said to David:
Achish	Of course you understand that you and your men are to fight on my side.
David	Of course. I am your servant, and you will see for yourself what I can do.
Achish	Good! I will make you my permanent bodyguard.
Cast	[This is] the word of the Lord.
All	**Thanks be to God.**

Cast: **Narrator, David, Achish.**

Saul consults a medium
1 Samuel 28.3–25

Narrator	Now Samuel had died, and all the Israelites had mourned for him and had buried him in his own city of Ramah. Saul had forced all the fortune-tellers and mediums to leave Israel.
	The Philistine troops assembled and camped near the town of Shunem; Saul gathered the Israelites and camped at Mount Gilboa. When Saul saw the Philistine army, he was terrified, and so he asked the Lord what to do. But the Lord did not answer him at all, either by dreams or by the use of Urim and Thummim or by prophets. Then Saul ordered his officials:
Saul	Find me a woman who is a medium, and I will go and consult her.

[Narrator	They answered:]
Official	There is one in Endor.
Narrator	So Saul disguised himself; he put on different clothes, and after dark he went with two of his men to see the woman. He said to her:
Saul	Consult the spirits for me and tell me what is going to happen. Call up the spirit of the man I name.
[Narrator	The woman answered:]
Woman	Surely you know what King Saul has done, how he forced the fortune-tellers and mediums to leave Israel. Why, then, are you trying to trap me and get me killed?
Narrator	Then Saul made a sacred vow:
Saul (slowly)	By the living Lord I promise that you will not be punished for doing this.
Woman	Whom shall I call up for you?
Saul	Samuel.
Narrator	When the woman saw Samuel, she screamed:
Woman	Why have you tricked me? You are King Saul!
Saul	Don't be afraid! What do you see?
Woman	I see a spirit coming up from the earth.
Saul	What does it look like?
Woman	It's an old man coming up. He is wearing a cloak.
Narrator	Then Saul knew that it was Samuel, and he bowed to the ground in respect. Samuel said to Saul:
Samuel	Why have you disturbed me? Why did you make me come back?
Saul	I am in great trouble! The Philistines are at war with me, and God has abandoned me. He doesn't answer me any more, either by prophets or by dreams. And so I have called you, for you to tell me what I must do.
Samuel	Why do you call me when the Lord has abandoned you and become your enemy? The Lord has done to you what he told you through me: he has taken the kingdom away from you and given it to David instead. You disobeyed the Lord's command and did not completely destroy the Amalekites and all they had. That is why the Lord is doing this to you now. He will hand you and Israel over to the Philistines. Tomorrow you and your sons will join me, and the Lord will also hand the army of Israel over to the Philistines.
Narrator	At once Saul fell down and lay stretched out on the ground, terrified by what Samuel had said. He was weak, because he had not eaten anything all day and all night. The woman went over to him and saw that he was terrified, so she said to him:

Woman	Please, sir, I risked my life by doing what you asked. Now please do what I ask. Let me prepare some food for you. You must eat so that you will be strong enough to travel.
Narrator	Saul refused and said he would not eat anything. But his officers also urged him to eat. He finally gave in, got up from the ground, and sat on the bed. The woman quickly killed a calf which she had been fattening. Then she took some flour, prepared it, and baked some bread without yeast. She set the food before Saul and his officers, and they ate it. And they left that same night.
Cast	[This is] the word of the Lord.
All	**Thanks be to God.**

Cast: **Narrator, Saul, Official, Woman, Samuel** (can be Woman with voice disguised as Samuel).

David is rejected by the Philistines
1 Samuel 29.1–11

Narrator	The Philistines brought all their troops together at Aphek, while the Israelites camped at the spring in the Valley of Jezreel. The five Philistine kings marched out with their units of a hundred and of a thousand men; David and his men marched in the rear with King Achish. The Philistine commanders saw them and asked:
Philistine 1	What are these Hebrews doing here?
Narrator	Achish answered:
Achish	This is David, an official of King Saul of Israel. He has been with me for quite a long time now. He has done nothing I can find fault with since the day he came over to me.
Narrator	But the Philistine commanders were angry with Achish:
Philistine 1	Send that fellow back to the town you gave him.
Philistine 2	Don't let him go into battle with us; he might turn against us during the fighting.
Philistine 1	What better way is there for him to win back his master's favour than by the death of our men?
Philistine 2	After all, this is David, the one about whom the women sang, as they danced, 'Saul has killed thousands, but David has killed tens of thousands.'
Narrator	Achish called David and said to him:
Achish	I swear by the living God of Israel that you have been loyal to me; and I would be pleased to let you go with me and fight in this battle. I have not found any fault in you from the day you came over to me. But the other kings don't approve of you. So go back home in peace, and don't do anything that would displease them.
Narrator	David answered:

David	What have I done wrong, sir? If, as you say, you haven't found any fault in me since the day I started serving you, why shouldn't I go with you, my master and king, and fight your enemies?
Achish	I agree. I consider you as loyal as an angel of God. But the other kings have said that you can't go with us into battle. So then, David, tomorrow morning all of you who left Saul and came over to me will have to get up early and leave as soon as it's light.
Narrator	So David and his men started out early the following morning to go back to Philistia, and the Philistines went on to Jezreel.
Cast	[This is] the word of the Lord.
All	**Thanks be to God.**

Cast: **Narrator, Philistine 1, Achish, Philistine 2, David.**

The war against the Amalekites
1 Samuel 30.1–30

Narrator	David and his men arrived back at Ziklag. The Amalekites had raided southern Judah and attacked Ziklag. They had burnt down the town and captured all the women; they had not killed anyone, but had taken everyone with them when they left. When David and his men arrived, they found that the town had been burnt down and that their wives, sons, and daughters had been carried away. David and his men started crying and did not stop until they were completely exhausted. Even David's two wives, Ahinoam and Abigail, had been taken away.
	David was now in great trouble, because his men were all very bitter about losing their children, and they were threatening to stone him; but the Lord his God gave him courage. David said to the priest Abiathar son of Ahimelech:
David	Bring me the ephod.
Narrator	Abiathar brought it to him. David asked the Lord:
David	Shall I go after those raiders? And will I catch them?
[Narrator	He answered:]
The Lord	Go after them; you will catch them and rescue the captives.
Narrator	So David and his six hundred men started out, and when they arrived at the brook of Besor, some of them stayed there. David continued on his way with four hundred men; the other two hundred men were too tired to cross the brook and so stayed behind. The men with David found an Egyptian boy out in the country and brought him to David. They gave him some food and water, some dried figs, and two bunches of raisins. After he had eaten, his strength returned; he had not had anything to eat or drink for three full days. [David asked him:]

David	Who is your master, and where are you from?
[Narrator	He answered:]
Boy	I am an Egyptian, the slave of an Amalekite. My master left me behind three days ago because I was ill. We had raided the territory of the Cherethites in the southern part of Judah and the territory of the clan of Caleb, and we burnt down Ziklag.
David	Will you lead me to those raiders?
Boy	I will if you promise me in God's name that you will not kill me or hand me over to my master.
Narrator	And he led David to them. (PAUSE)
	The raiders were scattered all over the place, eating, drinking, and celebrating because of the enormous amount of loot they had captured from Philistia and Judah. At dawn the next day David attacked them and fought until evening. Except for four hundred young men who mounted camels and got away, none of them escaped. David rescued everyone and everything the Amalekites had taken, including his two wives; nothing at all was missing. David got back all his men's sons and daughters, and all the loot the Amalekites had taken. He also recovered all the flocks and herds; his men drove all the livestock in front of them and said:
Men 1 and 2	This belongs to David!
Narrator	Then David went back to the two hundred men who had been too weak to go with him and had stayed behind at the brook of Besor. They came forward to meet David and his men, and David went up to them and greeted them warmly. But some mean and worthless men who had gone with David said:
Man 1	They didn't go with us, and so we won't give them any of the loot.
Man 2	They can take their wives and children and go away.
Narrator	But David answered:
David	My brothers, you can't do this with what the Lord has given us! He kept us safe and gave us victory over the raiders. No one can agree with what you say! All must share alike: whoever stays behind with the supplies gets the same share as the one who goes into battle.
Narrator	David made this a rule, and it has been followed in Israel ever since. (PAUSE)
	When David returned to Ziklag, he sent part of the loot to his friends, the leaders of Judah, with the message:
David	Here is a present for you from the loot we took from the Lord's enemies.

Narrator	He sent it to the people in Bethel, to the people in Ramah in the southern part of Judah, and to the people in the towns of Jattir, Aroer, Siphmoth, Eshtemoa, and Racal; to the clan of Jerahmeel, to the Kenites, and to the people in the towns of Hormah, Borashan, Athach, and Hebron. He sent it to all the places where he and his men had roamed.
Cast	[This is] the word of the Lord.
All	**Thanks be to God.**

Cast: **Narrator, David, The Lord, Boy, Man 1, Man 2.**

The death of Saul and his sons
1 Samuel 31.1–6

Narrator	The Philistines fought a battle against the Israelites on Mount Gilboa. Many Israelites were killed there, and the rest of them, including King Saul and his sons, fled. But the Philistines caught up with them and killed three of Saul's sons, Jonathan, Abinadab, and Malchishua. The fighting was heavy round Saul, and he himself was hit by enemy arrows and badly wounded. He said to the young man carrying his weapons:
Saul	Draw your sword and kill me, so that these godless Philistines won't gloat over me and kill me.
Narrator	But the young man was too terrified to do it. So Saul took his own sword and threw himself on it. The young man saw that Saul was dead, so he too threw himself on his own sword and died with Saul. And that is how Saul, his three sons, and the young man died; all of Saul's men died that day.
Cast	[This is] the word of the Lord.
All	**Thanks be to God.**

Cast: **Narrator, Saul.**

2 SAMUEL

David learns of Saul's death
2 Samuel 1.1–16

Narrator After Saul's death David came back from his victory over the Amalekites and stayed in Ziklag for two days. The next day a young man arrived from Saul's camp. To show his grief, he had torn his clothes and put earth on his head. He went to David and bowed to the ground in respect. David asked him:

David Where have you come from?

Young man I have escaped from the Israelite camp.

David Tell me what happened.

Young man Our army ran away from the battle, and many of our men were killed. Saul and his son Jonathan were also killed.

David (alarmed) How do you know that Saul and Jonathan are dead?

Young man I happened to be on Mount Gilboa, and I saw that Saul was leaning on his spear and that the chariots and horsemen of the enemy were closing in on him. Then he turned round, saw me, and called to me. I answered, 'Yes, sir!' He asked who I was, and I told him that I was an Amalekite. Then he said, 'Come here and kill me! I have been badly wounded, and I'm about to die.' So I went up to him and killed him, because I knew that he would die anyway as soon as he fell. Then I took the crown from his head and the bracelet from his arm, and I have brought them to you, sir.

Narrator David tore his clothes in sorrow, and all his men did the same. They grieved and mourned and fasted until evening for Saul and Jonathan and for Israel, the people of the Lord, because so many had been killed in battle.

[David asked the young man who had brought him the news:]

David Where are you from?

Young man I'm an Amalekite, but I live in your country.

David (angrily) How is it that you dared to kill the Lord's chosen king?

Narrator Then David called one of his men [and said]:

David Kill him!

Narrator The man struck the Amalekite and mortally wounded him. [And David said to the Amalekite:]

David You brought this on yourself. You condemned yourself when you admitted that you killed the one whom the Lord chose to be king.

Cast [This is] the word of the Lord.
All **Thanks be to God.**

Cast: **Narrator, David, Young man.**

David laments for Saul and Jonathan
2 Samuel 1.17–27

Narrator	David sang this lament for Saul and his son Jonathan, and ordered it to be taught to the people of Judah. [It is recorded in The Book of Jashar.]
David	On the hills of Israel our leaders are dead!
Person 1	The bravest of our soldiers have fallen!
David	Do not announce it in Gath—
Person 2	Or in the streets of Ashkelon.
David	Do not make the women of Philistia glad—
Person 1	Do not let the daughters of pagans rejoice.
David	May no rain or dew fall on Gilboa's hills—
Person 2	May its fields be always barren!
David	For the shields of the brave lie there in disgrace—
Person 1	The shield of Saul is no longer polished with oil.
David	Jonathan's bow was deadly—
Person 2	The sword of Saul was merciless.
David	Striking down the mighty—
Person 1	Killing the enemy.
David	Saul and Jonathan, so wonderful and dear—
Person 2	Together in life, together in death.
David	Swifter than eagles—
Person 1	Stronger than lions.
David	Women of Israel, mourn for Saul!
Person 2	He clothed you in rich scarlet dresses and adorned you with jewels and gold.
David	The brave soldiers have fallen—
Person 1	They were killed in battle.
David	Jonathan lies dead in the hills. (PAUSE)
	I grieve for you, my brother Jonathan; how dear you were to me! How wonderful was your love for me, better even than the love of women.
Person 2	The brave soldiers have fallen, their weapons abandoned and useless.
Cast	[This is] the word of the Lord.
All	**Thanks be to God.**

Cast: **Narrator, David, Person 1, Person 2.**

David is made king of Judah
2 Samuel 2.1–7

Narrator	David asked the Lord:
David	Shall I go and take control of one of the towns of Judah?
Narrator	The Lord answered:
The Lord	Yes.
David	Which one?
The Lord	Hebron.
Narrator	So David went to Hebron, taking with him his two wives Ahinoam, who was from Jezreel, and Abigail, Nabal's widow, who was from Carmel. He also took his men and their families, and they settled in the towns round Hebron. Then the men of Judah came to Hebron and anointed David as king of Judah. (PAUSE)
	When David heard that the people of Jabesh in Gilead had buried Saul, he sent some men there with the message:
David	May the Lord bless you for showing your loyalty to your king by burying him. And now may the Lord be kind and faithful to you. I too will treat you well because of what you have done. Be strong and brave! Saul your king is dead, and the people of Judah have anointed me as their king.
Cast	[This is] the word of the Lord.
All	**Thanks be to God.**

Cast: **Narrator, David, The Lord.**

War between Israel and Judah
2 Samuel 2.12—3.1

Narrator	Abner and the officials of Ishbosheth went from Mahanaim to the city of Gibeon. Joab, whose mother was Zeruiah, and David's other officials met them at the pool, where they all sat down, one group on one side of the pool and the other group on the opposite side. Abner said to Joab:
Abner	Let's get some of the young men from each side to fight an armed contest.
[Narrator	Joab answered:]
Joab	All right.
Narrator	So twelve men, representing Ishbosheth and the tribe of Benjamin, fought twelve of David's men. Each man caught his opponent by the head and plunged his sword into his opponent's side, so that all twenty-four of them fell down dead together. And so that place in Gibeon is called Field of Swords. Then a furious battle broke out, and Abner and the Israelites were defeated by David's men. The three sons of Zeruiah were there: Joab, Abishai,

→

	and Asahel. Asahel, who could run as fast as a wild deer, started chasing Abner, running straight for him. Abner looked back [and said]:
Abner (calling)	Is that you, Asahel?
Asahel (calling)	Yes.
Abner	Stop chasing me! Run after one of the soldiers and take what he has.
Narrator	But Asahel kept on chasing him. [Once more Abner said to him:]
Abner	Stop chasing me! Why force me to kill you? How could I face your brother Joab?
Narrator	But Asahel would not give up; so Abner, with a backward thrust of his spear, struck him through the belly so that the spear came out at his back. Asahel dropped to the ground dead, and everyone who came to the place where he was lying stopped and stood there. But Joab and Abishai started out after Abner, and at sunset they came to the hill of Ammah, which is to the east of Giah on the road to the wilderness of Gibeon. The men from the tribe of Benjamin gathered round Abner again and took their stand on the top of a hill. Abner called out to Joab:
Abner (calling)	Do we have to go on fighting for ever? Can't you see that in the end there will be nothing but bitterness? We are your fellow-countrymen. How long will it be before you order your men to stop chasing us?
[Narrator	Joab answered:]
Joab (calling)	I swear by the living God that if you had not spoken, my men would have kept on chasing you until tomorrow morning.
Narrator	Then Joab blew the trumpet as a signal for his men to stop pursuing the Israelites; and so the fighting stopped. Abner and his men marched through the Jordan Valley all that night; they crossed the River Jordan, and after marching all the next morning, they arrived back at Mahanaim.
	When Joab gave up the chase, he gathered all his men and found that nineteen of them were missing, in addition to Asahel. David's men had killed 360 of Abner's men from the tribe of Benjamin. Joab and his men took Asahel's body and buried it in the family tomb at Bethlehem. Then they marched all night and at dawn arrived back at Hebron. The fighting between the forces supporting Saul's family and those supporting David went on for a long time. As David became stronger and stronger, his opponents became weaker and weaker.
Cast	[This is] the word of the Lord.
All	**Thanks be to God.**

Cast: **Narrator, Abner, Joab, Asahel.** (Note: During the course of this narrative, distances between speakers change).

Abner joins David
From 2 Samuel 3.6–21

Narrator	As the fighting continued between David's forces and the forces loyal to Saul's family, Abner became more and more powerful among Saul's followers.
	One day Ishbosheth, son of Saul, accused Abner of sleeping with Saul's concubine Rizpah, the daughter of Aiah. This made Abner furious:
Abner (angrily)	Do you think that I would betray Saul? Do you really think I'm serving Judah? From the very first I have been loyal to the cause of your father Saul, his brothers, and his friends, and I have saved you from being defeated by David; yet today you find fault with me about a woman! The Lord promised David that he would take the kingdom away from Saul and his descendants and would make David king of both Israel and Judah, from one end of the country to the other. Now may God strike me dead if I don't make this come true!
Narrator	Ishbosheth was so afraid of Abner that he could not say a word. (PAUSE)
	Abner sent messengers to David, who at that time was at Hebron, to say:
Abner	Who is going to rule this land? Make an agreement with me, and I will help you win all Israel over to your side.
Narrator	David answered:
David	Good! I will make an agreement with you on one condition: you must bring Saul's daughter Michal to me when you come to see me.
Narrator	Abner went to the leaders of Israel and said to them:
Abner	For a long time you have wanted David to be your king. Now here is your chance. Remember that the Lord has said:
[The Lord]	I will use my servant David to rescue my people Israel from the Philistines and from all their other enemies.
Narrator	When Abner came to David at Hebron with twenty men, David gave a feast for them. Abner told David:
Abner	I will go now and win all Israel over to Your Majesty. They will accept you as king, and then you will get what you have wanted and will rule over the whole land.
Narrator	David gave Abner a guarantee of safety and sent him on his way.
Cast	[This is] the word of the Lord.
All	**Thanks be to God.**

Cast: **Narrator, Abner, David, [The Lord].**

Joab murders Abner
2 Samuel 3.22–30

Narrator [Just then] David's men and Joab returned from a raid and brought with them a great deal of plunder. But Abner was no longer with David in Hebron, because David had sent him away, and he had gone in peace.

When Joab and all the soldiers with him arrived, he was told that Abner son of Ner had come to the king and that the king had sent him away and that he had gone in peace. So Joab went to the king:

Joab What have you done? Look, Abner came to you. Why did you let him go? Now he is gone! You know Abner son of Ner; he came to deceive you and observe your movements and find out everything you are doing.

Narrator Joab then left David and sent messengers after Abner, and they brought him back from the well of Sirah. But David did not know it. Now when Abner returned to Hebron, Joab took him aside into the gateway, as though to speak with him privately. And there, to avenge the blood of his brother Asahel, Joab stabbed him in the stomach, and he died. Later, when David heard about this, he said:

David I and my kingdom are for ever innocent before the Lord concerning the blood of Abner son of Ner. May his blood fall upon the head of Joab and upon all his father's house! May Joab's house never be without someone who has a running sore or leprosy or who leans on a crutch or who falls by the sword or who lacks food.

Narrator Joab and his brother Abishai murdered Abner because he had killed their brother Asahel in the battle of Gibeon.

Cast [This is] the word of the Lord.
All **Thanks be to God.**

Cast: **Narrator, Joab, David.**

Abner is buried
2 Samuel 3.31–39

Narrator David ordered Joab and his men to tear their clothes, wear sackcloth, and mourn for Abner. And at the funeral King David himself walked behind the coffin. Abner was buried at Hebron, and the king wept aloud at the grave, and so did all the people. David sang this lament for Abner:

David Why did Abner have to die like a fool?
His hands were not tied,
and his feet were not bound;
he died like someone killed by criminals!

Narrator	And the people wept for him again. All day long the people tried to get David to eat something, but he made a solemn promise:
David	May God strike me dead if I eat anything before the day is over!
Narrator	They took note of this and were pleased. Indeed, everything the king did pleased the people. All David's people and all the people in Israel understood that the king had no part in the murder of Abner. The king said to his officials:
David	Don't you realize that this day a great leader in Israel has died? Even though I am the king chosen by God, I feel weak today. These sons of Zeruiah are too violent for me. May the Lord punish these criminals as they deserve!
Cast	[This is] the word of the Lord.
All	**Thanks be to God.**

Cast: **Narrator, David.**

Ishbosheth is murdered
From 2 Samuel 4.1–12

Narrator	When Saul's son Ishbosheth heard that Abner had been killed in Hebron, he was afraid, and all the people of Israel were alarmed. Ishbosheth had two officers who were leaders of raiding parties, Baanah and Rechab, sons of Rimmon, from Beeroth in the tribe of Benjamin. Rechab and Baanah set out for Ishbosheth's house and arrived there about noon, while he was taking his midday rest. The woman at the door had become drowsy while she was sifting wheat and had fallen asleep, so Rechab and Baanah slipped in. Once inside, they went to Ishbosheth's bedroom, where he was sound asleep, and killed him. Then they cut off his head, took it with them, and walked all night through the Jordan Valley. They presented the head to King David at Hebron:
Rechab	Here is the head of Ishbosheth, the son of your enemy Saul, who tried to kill you.
Baanah	Today the Lord has allowed Your Majesty to take revenge on Saul and his descendants.
[Narrator	David answered them:]
David	I make a vow by the living Lord, who has saved me from all dangers! The messenger who came to me at Ziklag and told me of Saul's death thought he was bringing good news. I seized him and had him put to death. That was the reward I gave him for his good news! How much worse it will be for evil men who murder an innocent man asleep in his own house! I will now take revenge on you for murdering him and will wipe you off the face of the earth!

Narrator	David gave the order, and his soldiers killed Rechab and Baanah and cut off their hands and feet, which they hung up near the pool in Hebron. They took Ishbosheth's head and buried it in Abner's tomb there at Hebron.
Cast	[This is] the word of the Lord.
All	**Thanks be to God.**

Cast: **Narrator, Rechab, Baanah, David.**

David becomes king of Israel and Judah
2 Samuel 5.1–12

Narrator 1	All the tribes of Israel came to David at Hebron and said to him:
Person 1	We are your own flesh and blood.
Person 2	In the past, even when Saul was still our king, you led the people of Israel in battle, and the Lord promised you that you would lead his people and be their ruler.
Narrator 2	So all the leaders of Israel came to King David at Hebron. He made a sacred alliance with them, they anointed him, and he became king of Israel. David was thirty years old when he became king, and he ruled for forty years. He ruled in Hebron over Judah for seven and a half years, and in Jerusalem over all Israel and Judah for thirty-three years.
Narrator 1	The time came when King David and his men set out to attack Jerusalem. The Jebusites, who lived there, thought that David would not be able to conquer the city, and so they said to him:
Jebusite 1	You will never get in here—
Jebusite 2	Even the blind and the crippled could keep you out.
Narrator 2	But David did capture their fortress of Zion, and it became known as David's City.
Narrator 1	That day David said to his men:
David	Does anybody here hate the Jebusites as much as I do? Enough to kill them? Then go up through the water tunnel and attack those poor blind cripples.
Narrator 1	That is why it is said, 'The blind and the crippled cannot enter the Lord's house.'
Narrator 2	After capturing the fortress, David lived in it and named it David's City. He built the city round it, starting at the place where land was filled in on the east side of the hill. He grew stronger all the time, because the Lord God Almighty was with him.

Narrator 1	King Hiram of Tyre sent a trade mission to David; he provided him with cedar logs and with carpenters and stonemasons to build a palace. And so David realized that the Lord had established him as king of Israel and was making his kingdom prosperous for the sake of his people.
Cast	[This is] the word of the Lord.
All	**Thanks be to God.**

Cast: **Narrator 1, Narrator 2** (can be the same as Narrator 1), **Person 1, Person 2** (can be the same as Person 1), **Jebusite 1, Jebusite 2** (can be the same as Jebusite 1), **David.**

Victory over the Philistines
2 Samuel 5.17–25

Narrator	The Philistines were told that David had been made king of Israel, so their army set out to capture him. When David heard of it, he went down to a fortified place. The Philistines arrived at the Valley of Rephaim and occupied it.
	David asked the Lord:
David	Shall I attack the Philistines? Will you give me the victory?
[Narrator	The Lord answered:]
The Lord	Yes, attack! I will give you the victory!
Narrator	So David went to Baal Perazim and there he defeated the Philistines. [He said:]
David (victoriously)	The Lord has broken through my enemies like a flood.
Narrator	And so that place is called Baal Perazim. When the Philistines fled, they left their idols behind, and David and his men carried them away. Then the Philistines went back to the Valley of Rephaim and occupied it again. Once more David consulted the Lord, who answered:
The Lord	Don't attack them from here, but go round and get ready to attack them from the other side, near the balsam-trees. When you hear the sound of marching in the tree-tops, then attack because I will be marching ahead of you to defeat the Philistine army.
Narrator	David did what the Lord had commanded, and was able to drive the Philistines back from Geba all the way to Gezer.
Cast	[This is] the word of the Lord.
All	**Thanks be to God.**

Cast: **Narrator, David, The Lord.**

The Covenant Box is brought to Jerusalem
2 Samuel 6.1–23

Narrator 1	Once more David called together the best soldiers in Israel, a total of thirty thousand men, and led them to Baalah in Judah, in order to bring from there God's Covenant Box, bearing the name of the Lord Almighty, who is enthroned above the winged creatures.

Narrator 2	They took it from Abinadab's home on the hill and placed it on a new cart. Uzzah and Ahio, sons of Abinadab, were guiding the cart, with Ahio walking in front.
Narrator 1	David and all the Israelites were dancing and singing with all their might to honour the Lord. They were playing harps, lyres, drums, rattles, and cymbals.
Narrator 2	As they came to the threshing-place of Nacon the oxen stumbled, and Uzzah reached out and took hold of the Covenant Box.
Narrator 1	At once the Lord God became angry with Uzzah and killed him because of his irreverence.
Narrator 2	Uzzah died there beside the Covenant Box, and so that place has been called Perez Uzzah ever since. David was furious because the Lord had punished Uzzah in anger.
Narrator 1	Then David was afraid of the Lord and said:
David	How can I take the Covenant Box with me now?
Narrator 1	So he decided not to take it with him to Jerusalem; instead, he turned off the road and took it to the house of Obed Edom, a native of the city of Gath. It stayed there three months, and the Lord blessed Obed Edom and his family. (PAUSE)
Narrator 2	King David heard that because of the Covenant Box the Lord had blessed Obed Edom's family and all that he had; so he fetched the Covenant Box from Obed's house to take it to Jerusalem with a great celebration.
Narrator 1	After the men carrying the Covenant Box had gone six steps, David made them stop while he offered the Lord a sacrifice of a bull and a fattened calf.
Narrator 2	David, wearing only a linen cloth round his waist, danced with all his might to honour the Lord. And so he and all the Israelites took the Covenant Box up to Jerusalem with shouts of joy and the sound of trumpets.
Narrator 1	As the Box was being brought into the city, Michal, Saul's daughter, looked out of the window and saw King David dancing and jumping around in the sacred dance, and she was disgusted with him.
Narrator 2	They brought the Box and put it in its place in the Tent that David had set up for it. Then he offered sacrifices and fellowship-offerings to the Lord. When he had finished offering the sacrifices, he blessed the people in the name of the Lord Almighty and distributed food to them all. He gave each man and woman in Israel a loaf of bread, a piece of roasted meat, and some raisins. Then everyone went home.
Narrator 1	Afterwards, when David went home to greet his family, Michal came out to meet him.
Michal	The king of Israel made a big name for himself today! He exposed himself like a fool in the sight of the servant-girls of his officials!
Narrator 1	David answered:

David	I was dancing to honour the Lord, who chose me instead of your father and his family to make me the leader of his people Israel. And I will go on dancing to honour the Lord, and will disgrace myself even more. You may think I am nothing, but those girls will think highly of me!
Narrator 2 (wrily)	Michal, Saul's daughter, never had any children.
Cast	[This is] the word of the Lord.
All	**Thanks be to God.**

Cast: **Narrator 1, Narrator 2, David, Michal.**

Nathan's message to David
2 Samuel 7.1–17

Narrator	King David was settled in his palace, and the Lord kept him safe from all his enemies. Then the king said to the prophet Nathan:
David	Here I am living in a house built of cedar, but God's Covenant Box is kept in a tent!
Narrator	Nathan answered:
Nathan	Do whatever you have in mind, because the Lord is with you.
Narrator (slowly)	But that night the Lord said to Nathan:
The Lord	Go and tell my servant David that I say to him, 'You are not the one to build a temple for me to live in. From the time I rescued the people of Israel from Egypt until now, I have never lived in a temple; I have travelled round living in a tent. In all my travelling with the people of Israel I never asked any of the leaders that I appointed why they had not built me a temple made of cedar.'

So tell my servant David that I, the Lord Almighty, say to him, 'I took you from looking after sheep in the fields and made you the ruler of my people Israel. I have been with you wherever you have gone, and I have defeated all your enemies as you advanced. I will make you as famous as the greatest leaders in the world. I have chosen a place for my people Israel and have settled them there, where they will live without being oppressed any more. Ever since they entered this land, they have been attacked by violent people, but this will not happen again. I promise to keep you safe from all your enemies and to give you descendants. When you die and are buried with your ancestors, I will make one of your sons king and will keep his kingdom strong. He will be the one to build a temple for me, and I will make sure that his dynasty continues for ever. I will be his father, and he will be my son. When he does wrong, I will punish him as a father punishes his son. But I will not withdraw my support from him as I did from Saul, whom I removed so that |

→

	you could be king. You will always have descendants, and I will make your kingdom last for ever. Your dynasty will never end.'
Narrator	Nathan told David everything that God had revealed to him.
Cast	[This is] the word of the Lord.
All	**Thanks be to God.**

Cast: **Narrator, David, Nathan, The Lord.**

David and Mephibosheth
2 Samuel 9.1–13

Narrator	One day David asked:
David	Is there anyone left of Saul's family? If there is, I would like to show him kindness for Jonathan's sake.
Narrator	There was a servant of Saul's family named Ziba, and he was told to go to David. The king asked:
David	Are you Ziba?
[Narrator	He answered:]
Ziba	At your service, sir.
David	Is there anyone left of Saul's family to whom I can show loyalty and kindness, as I promised God I would?
Ziba	There is still one of Jonathan's sons. He is crippled.
David	Where is he?
Ziba	At the home of Machir son of Ammiel in Lodebar.
Narrator	So King David sent for him. (PAUSE)
	When Mephibosheth, the son of Jonathan and grandson of Saul, arrived, he bowed down before David in respect. David said:
David	Mephibosheth.
[Narrator	And he answered:]
Mephibosheth	At your service, sir.
David	Don't be afraid. I will be kind to you for the sake of your father Jonathan. I will give you back all the land that belonged to your grandfather Saul, and you will always be welcome at my table.
Narrator	Mephibosheth bowed again:
Mephibosheth	I am no better than a dead dog, sir! Why should you be so good to me?
Narrator	Then the king called Ziba, Saul's servant:
David	I am giving Mephibosheth, your master's grandson, everything that belonged to Saul and his family. You, your sons, and your servants will farm the land for your master Saul's family and bring

	in the harvest, to provide food for them. But Mephibosheth himself will always be a guest at my table.
[Commentator	Ziba had fifteen sons and twenty servants.
Narrator	Ziba answered:]
Ziba	I will do everything Your Majesty commands.
Narrator	So Mephibosheth ate at the king's table, just like one of the king's sons. Mephibosheth had a young son named Mica. (PAUSE)
	All the members of Ziba's family became servants of Mephibosheth. So Mephibosheth, who was crippled in both feet, lived in Jerusalem, eating all his meals at the king's table.
Cast	[This is] the word of the Lord.
All	**Thanks be to God.**

Cast: **Narrator, David, Ziba, Mephibosheth, [Commentator].**

David defeats the Ammonites and the Syrians
2 Samuel 10.1–14 [15–19]

Narrator	King Nahash of Ammon died, and his son Hanun became king. King David said:
David	I must show loyal friendship to Hanun, as his father Nahash did to me.
Narrator	So David sent messengers to express his sympathy. (PAUSE)
	When they arrived in Ammon, the Ammonite leaders said to the king:
Ammonite	Do you think that it is in your father's honour that David has sent these men to express sympathy to you? Of course not! He has sent them here as spies to explore the city, so that he can conquer us!
Narrator	Hanun seized David's messengers, shaved off one side of their beards, cut off their clothes at the hips, and sent them away. They were too ashamed to return home. When David heard about what had happened, he sent word that they should stay in Jericho and not return until their beards had grown again. (PAUSE)
	The Ammonites realized that they had made David their enemy, so they hired twenty thousand Syrian soldiers from Bethrehob and Zobah, twelve thousand men from Tob, and the king of Maacah with a thousand men. David heard of it and sent Joab against them with the whole army. The Ammonites marched out and took up their position at the entrance to Rabbah, their capital city, while the others, both the Syrians and the men from Tob and Maacah, took up their position in the open countryside.
	Joab saw that the enemy troops would attack him in front and from the rear, so he chose the best of Israel's soldiers and put them in position facing the Syrians. He placed the rest of his troops under the command of his brother Abishai, who put them in position facing the Ammonites. Joab said to him:

Joab	If you see that the Syrians are defeating me, come and help me, and if the Ammonites are defeating you, I will go and help you. Be strong and courageous! Let's fight hard for our people and for the cities of our God. And may the Lord's will be done!
Narrator	Joab and his men advanced to attack, and the Syrians fled. When the Ammonites saw the Syrians running away, they fled from Abishai and retreated into the city. Then Joab turned back from fighting the Ammonites and went back to Jerusalem.
	[The Syrians realized that they had been defeated by the Israelites, so they called all their troops together. King Hadadezer sent for the Syrians who were on the east side of the River Euphrates, and they came to Helam under the command of Shobach, commander of the army of King Hadadezer of Zobah. When David heard of it, he gathered the Israelite troops, crossed the River Jordan, and marched to Helam, where the Syrians took up their position facing him. The fighting began, and the Israelites drove the Syrian army back. David and his men killed seven hundred Syrian chariot drivers and forty thousand horsemen, and they wounded Shobach, the enemy commander, who died on the battlefield. When the kings who were subject to Hadadezer realized that they had been defeated by the Israelites, they made peace with them and became their subjects. And the Syrians were afraid to help the Ammonites any more.]
Cast	[This is] the word of the Lord.
All	**Thanks be to God.**

Cast: **Narrator, David, Ammonite, Joab.**

David and Bathsheba
2 Samuel 11.1–27

Narrator	[The following spring] at the time of the year when kings usually go to war, David sent out Joab with his officers and the Israelite army; they defeated the Ammonites and besieged the city of Rabbah. But David himself stayed in Jerusalem. (PAUSE)
	One day, late in the afternoon, David got up from his nap and went to the palace roof. As he walked about up there, he saw a woman having a bath. She was very beautiful. So he sent a messenger to find out who she was, and learnt that she was Bathsheba, the daughter of Eliam and the wife of Uriah the Hittite. David sent messengers to fetch her; they brought her to him and he made love to her. Then she went back home. Afterwards she discovered that she was pregnant and sent a message to David to tell him. David then sent a message to Joab:
David	Send me Uriah the Hittite.
Narrator	So Joab sent him to David. (PAUSE)
	When Uriah arrived, David asked him if Joab and the troops were well, and how the fighting was going. Then he said to Uriah:

David	Go home and rest a while.
Narrator	Uriah left, and David sent a present to his home. But Uriah did not go home; instead he slept at the palace gate with the king's guards. When David heard that Uriah had not gone home, he asked him:
David	You have just returned after a long absence; why didn't you go home?
[Narrator	Uriah answered:]
Uriah	The men of Israel and Judah are away at the war, and the Covenant Box is with them; my commander Joab and his officers are camping out in the open. How could I go home, eat and drink, and sleep with my wife? By all that's sacred, I swear that I could never do such a thing!
David	Then stay here the rest of the day, and tomorrow I'll send you back.
Narrator	So Uriah stayed in Jerusalem that day and the next. David invited him to supper and made him drunk. But again that night Uriah did not go home; instead he slept on his blanket in the palace guardroom. (PAUSE)
	The next morning David wrote a letter to Joab and sent it by Uriah [He wrote]:
David	Put Uriah in the front line, where the fighting is heaviest, then retreat and let him be killed.
Narrator	So while Joab was besieging the city, he sent Uriah to a place where he knew the enemy was strong. The enemy troops came out of the city and fought Joab's forces; some of David's officers were killed, and so was Uriah. (PAUSE)
	Then Joab sent a report to David telling him about the battle, and he instructed the messenger:
Joab	After you have told the king all about the battle, he may get angry and ask you, 'Why did you go so near the city to fight them? Didn't you realize that they would shoot arrows from the walls? Don't you remember how Abimelech son of Gideon was killed? It was at Thebez, where a woman threw a millstone down from the wall and killed him. Why, then, did you go so near the wall?' If the king asks you this, tell him, 'Your officer Uriah was also killed.'
Narrator	So the messenger went to David and told him what Joab had commanded him to say [He said]:
Messenger	Our enemies were stronger than we were and came out of the city to fight us in the open, but we drove them back to the city gate. Then they shot arrows at us from the wall, and some of Your Majesty's officers were killed; (PAUSE) your officer Uriah was also killed.
Narrator	David said to the messenger:

David	Encourage Joab and tell him not to be upset, since you never can tell who will die in battle. Tell him to launch a stronger attack on the city and capture it.(PAUSE)
Narrator	When Bathsheba heard that her husband had been killed, she mourned for him. When the time of mourning was over, David sent for her to come to the palace; she became his wife and bore him a son.
Narrator (deliberately)	But the Lord was not pleased with what David had done.
Cast	[This is] the word of the Lord.
All	**Thanks be to God.**

Cast: **Narrator, David, Uriah, Joab, Messenger.**

Nathan's message and David's repentance
2 Samuel 12.1–15

Narrator	The Lord sent the prophet Nathan to David. Nathan went to him and said:
Nathan	There were two men who lived in the same town; one was rich and the other poor. The rich man had many cattle and sheep, while the poor man had only one lamb, which he had bought. He took care of it, and it grew up in his home with his children. He would feed it with some of his own food, let it drink from his cup, and hold it in his lap. The lamb was like a daughter to him. One day a visitor arrived at the rich man's home. The rich man didn't want to kill one of his own animals to prepare a meal for him; instead, he took the poor man's lamb and cooked a meal for his guest.
[Narrator	David was very angry with the rich man:]
David (angrily)	I swear by the living Lord that the man who did this ought to die! For having done such a cruel thing, he must pay back four times as much as he took.
Nathan (pointedly)	*You* are that man. And this is what the Lord God of Israel says: 'I made you king of Israel and rescued you from Saul. I gave you his kingdom and his wives; I made you king over Israel and Judah. If this had not been enough, I would have given you twice as much. Why, then, have you disobeyed my commands? Why did you do this evil thing? You had Uriah killed in battle; you let the Ammonites kill him, and then you took his wife! Now, in every generation some of your descendants will die a violent death because you have disobeyed me and have taken Uriah's wife. I swear to you that I will cause someone from your own family to bring trouble on you. You will see it when I take your wives from you and give them to another man; and he will have intercourse with them in broad daylight. You sinned in secret, but I will make this happen in broad daylight for all Israel to see.'
David (sadly)	I have sinned against the Lord.

278

Nathan	The Lord forgives you; you will not die. But because you have shown such contempt for the Lord in doing this, your child will die.
Narrator	Then Nathan went home.
Cast All	[This is] the word of the Lord. **Thanks be to God.**

Cast: **Narrator, Nathan, David.**

David's son dies
From 2 Samuel 12.15–25

Narrator	The Lord caused the child that Uriah's wife had borne to David to become very ill. David prayed to God that the child would get well. He refused to eat anything, and every night he went into his room and spent the night lying on the floor. His court officials went to him and tried to make him get up, but he refused and would not eat anything with them. (PAUSE) A week later the child died, and David's officials were afraid to tell him the news. [They said:]
Official 1 (to Official 2)	While the child was living, David wouldn't answer when we spoke to him.
Official 2	How can we tell him that his child is *dead?*
Official 1	He might do himself some harm!
Narrator	When David noticed them whispering to each other, he realized that the child had died. So he asked them:
David	Is the child dead?
Officials 1 and 2	Yes—
Official 2	He is.
Narrator	David got up from the floor, had a bath, combed his hair, and changed his clothes. Then he went and worshipped in the house of the Lord. When he returned to the palace, he asked for food and ate it as soon as it was served. His officials said to him:
Official 2	We don't understand this.
Official 1	While the child was alive, you wept for him and would not eat:
Official 2	But as soon as he died, you got up and ate!
David	Yes. I did fast and weep while he was still alive. I thought that the Lord might be merciful to me and not let the child die. But now that he is dead, why should I fast? Could I bring the child back to life? I will some day go to where he is, but he can never come back to me.
Narrator	Then David comforted his wife Bathsheba. She bore a son, whom David named Solomon. The Lord loved the boy and commanded the prophet Nathan to name the boy Jedidiah, because the Lord loved him.
Cast All	[This is] the word of the Lord. **Thanks be to God.**

Cast: **Narrator, Official 1, Official 2** (can be the same as Official 1), **David.**

David captures Rabbah
2 Samuel 12.26–31

Narrator Joab continued his campaign against Rabbah, the capital city of Ammon, and was about to capture it. He sent messengers to David to report:

Joab I have attacked Rabbah and have captured its water supply. Now gather the rest of your forces, attack the city and take it yourself. I don't want to get the credit for capturing it.

Narrator So David gathered his forces, went to Rabbah, attacked it, and conquered it. From the head of the idol of the Ammonite god Molech, David took a gold crown which weighed about thirty-five kilogrammes and had a jewel in it. David took the jewel and put it in his own crown. He also took a large amount of loot from the city and put its people to work with saws, iron hoes, and iron axes, and forced them to work at making bricks. He did the same to the people of all the other towns of Ammon. Then he and his men returned to Jerusalem.

Cast [This is] the word of the Lord.
All **Thanks be to God.**

Cast: **Narrator, Joab.**

Amnon and Tamar
2 Samuel 13.1–22

Narrator David's son Absalom had a beautiful unmarried sister named Tamar. Amnon, another of David's sons, fell in love with her. He was so much in love with her that he became ill, because it seemed impossible for him to have her; as a virgin, she was kept from meeting men. But he had a friend, a very shrewd man named Jonadab, the son of David's brother Shammah. Jonadab said to Amnon:

Jonadab You are the king's son, yet day after day I see you looking sad. What's the matter?

Narrator Amnon answered:

Amnon I'm in love with Tamar, the sister of my half-brother Absalom.

Jonadab Pretend that you are ill and go to bed. When your father comes to see you, say to him, 'Please ask my sister Tamar to come and feed me. I want her to prepare the food here where I can see her, and then serve it to me herself.'

Narrator So Amnon pretended that he was ill and went to bed. King David went to see him, and Amnon said to him:

Amnon Please let Tamar come and make a few cakes here where I can see her, and then serve them to me herself.

Narrator So David sent word to Tamar in the palace:

David	Go to Amnon's house and prepare some food for him.
Narrator	She went there and found him in bed. She took some dough, prepared it, and made some cakes there where he could see her. Then she baked the cakes and emptied them out of the pan for him to eat, but he wouldn't.
Amnon	Send everyone away.
Narrator	And they all left. Then he said to her:
Amnon	Bring the cakes here to my bed and serve them to me yourself.
Narrator	She took the cakes and went over to him. As she offered them to him, he grabbed her:
Amnon(roughly)	Come to bed with me!
[Narrator	She replied:]
Tamar (urgently)	No. Don't force me to do such a degrading thing! That's awful! How could I ever hold up my head in public again? And you—you would be completely disgraced in Israel. Please, speak to the king, and I'm sure that he will give me to you.
Narrator	But he would not listen to her; and since he was stronger than she was, he overpowered her and raped her.
	Then Amnon was filled with a deep hatred for her; he hated her now even more than he had loved her before. [He said to her:]
Amnon	Get out!
Tamar	No. To send me away like this is a greater crime than what you just did!
Narrator	But Amnon would not listen to her; he called in his personal servant:
Amnon	Get this woman out of my sight! Throw her out and lock the door!
Narrator	The servant put her out and locked the door.
	Tamar was wearing a long robe with full sleeves, the usual clothing for an unmarried princess in those days. She sprinkled ashes on her head, tore her robe, and with her face buried in her hands went away crying. When her brother Absalom saw her, he asked:
Absalom	Has Amnon molested you? Please, sister, don't let it upset you so much. He is your half-brother, so don't tell anyone about it.
Narrator	So Tamar lived in Absalom's house, sad and lonely. (PAUSE)
	When King David heard what had happened, he was furious. And Absalom hated Amnon so much for having raped his sister Tamar that he would no longer even speak to him.
Cast	[This is] the word of the Lord.
All	**Thanks be to God.**

Cast: **Narrator, Jonadab, Amnon, David, Tamar, Absalom.**

Absalom's revenge
2 Samuel 13.23–39

Narrator	[Two years later] Absalom was having his sheep sheared at Baal Hazor, near the town of Ephraim, and he invited all the king's sons to be there. He went to King David and said:
Absalom	Your Majesty, I am having my sheep sheared. Will you and your officials come and take part in the festivities?
[Narrator	The king answered:]
David	No, my son. It would be too much trouble for you if we all went.
Narrator	Absalom insisted, but the king would not give in, and he asked Absalom to leave. [But Absalom said:]
Absalom	Well, then, will you at least let my brother Amnon come?
David	Why should he?
Narrator	But Absalom kept on insisting until David finally let Amnon and all his other sons go with Absalom. (PAUSE)
	Absalom prepared a banquet fit for a king and instructed his servants:
Absalom	Notice when Amnon has had too much to drink, and then when I give the order, kill him. Don't be afraid. I will take the responsibility myself. Be brave and don't hesitate!
Narrator	So the servants followed Absalom's instructions and killed Amnon. All the rest of David's sons mounted their mules and fled.
	While they were on their way home, David was told:
Person	Absalom has killed all your sons—not one of them is left!
Narrator	The king stood up, tore his clothes in sorrow, and threw himself to the ground. The servants who were there with him tore their clothes also. But Jonadab, the son of David's brother Shammah, said:
Jonadab	Your Majesty, they *haven't* killed all your sons. Only Amnon is dead. You could tell by looking at Absalom that he had made up his mind to do this from the time that Amnon raped his sister Tamar. So don't believe the news that all your sons are dead; only Amnon was killed.
Narrator	In the meantime Absalom had fled.
	Just then the soldier on sentry duty saw a large crowd coming down the hill on the road from Horonaim. He went to the king and reported what he had seen. Jonadab said to David:
Jonadab	Those are your sons coming, just as I said they would.
Narrator	As soon as he finished saying this, David's sons came in; they started crying, and David and his officials also wept bitterly. (PAUSE)

Absalom fled and went to the king of Geshur, Talmai son of Ammihud, and stayed there three years. David mourned a long time for his son Amnon; but when he got over Amnon's death, he was filled with longing for his son Absalom.

Cast	[This is] the word of the Lord.
All	**Thanks be to God.**

Cast: **Narrator, Absalom, David, Person, Jonadab.**

Joab arranges for Absalom's return
2 Samuel 14.1–24

Narrator   Joab knew that King David missed Absalom very much, so he sent for a clever woman who lived in Tekoa. When she arrived, he said to her:

Joab   Pretend that you are in mourning; put on your mourning clothes, and don't comb your hair. Act like a woman who has been in mourning for a long time. Then go to the king and say to him what I tell you to say.

Narrator   Then Joab told her what to say. The woman went to the king and bowed down to the ground in respect:

Woman   Help me, Your Majesty!

[Narrator   He asked her:]

David   What do you want?

Woman   I am a poor widow, sir. My husband is dead. Sir, I had two sons, and one day they got into a quarrel out in the fields, where there was no one to separate them, and one of them killed the other. And now, sir, all my relatives have turned against me and are demanding that I hand my son over to them, so that they can kill him for murdering his brother. If they do this, I will be left without a son. They will destroy my last hope and leave my husband without a son to keep his name alive.

David   Go back home, and I will take care of the matter.

Woman   Your Majesty, whatever you do, my family and I will take the blame; you and the royal family are innocent.

David   If anyone threatens you, bring him to me, and he will never trouble you again.

Woman   Your Majesty, please pray to the Lord your God, so that my relative who is responsible for avenging the death of my son will not commit a greater crime by killing my other son.

David   I promise by the living Lord that your son will not be harmed in the least.

Woman   Please, Your Majesty, let me say just one more thing.

David   All right.

Woman	Why have you done such a wrong to God's people? You have not allowed your own son to return from exile, and so you have condemned yourself by what you have just said. We will all die; we are like water spilt on the ground, which can't be gathered again. Even God does not bring the dead back to life, but the king can at least find a way to bring a man back from exile. Now, Your Majesty, the reason I have come to speak to you is that the people threatened me, and so I said to myself that I would speak to you in the hope that you would do what I ask. I thought you would listen to me and save me from the one who is trying to kill my son and me and so remove us from the land God gave his people. I said to myself that your promise, sir, would make me safe, because the king is like God's angel and can distinguish good from evil. May the Lord your God be with you!
David	I'm going to ask you a question, and you must tell me the whole truth.
Woman	Ask me anything, Your Majesty.
David	Did Joab put you up to this?
Woman	I swear by all that is sacred, Your Majesty . . . (HESITATE) that there is no way to avoid answering your question. It was indeed your officer Joab who told me what to do and what to say. But he did it in order to straighten out this whole matter. Your Majesty is as wise as the angel of God and knows everything that happens.
Narrator	Later on the king said to Joab:
David	I have decided to do what you want. Go and get the young man Absalom and bring him back here.
Narrator	Joab threw himself to the ground in front of David in respect:
Joab	God bless you, Your Majesty! Now I know that you are pleased with me, because you have granted my request.
Narrator	Then he got up and went to Geshur and brought Absalom back to Jerusalem. The king, however, gave orders that Absalom should not live in the palace:
David	I don't want to see him.
Narrator	So Absalom lived in his own house and did not appear before the king.
Cast	[This is] the word of the Lord.
All	**Thanks be to God.**

Cast: **Narrator, Joab, Woman, David.**

Absalom is reconciled to David
2 Samuel 14.25–33

Narrator	There was no one in Israel as famous for his good looks as Absalom; he had no defect from head to foot. His hair was very thick, and he had to cut it once a year, when it grew too long and heavy. It would weigh more than two kilogrammes according to the royal standard of weights. Absalom had three sons and one daughter named Tamar, a very beautiful woman.
	Absalom lived two years in Jerusalem without seeing the king. Then he sent for Joab, to ask him to go to the king for him; but Joab would not come. Again Absalom sent for him, and again Joab refused to come. So Absalom said to his servants:
Absalom	Look, Joab's field is next to mine, and it has barley growing in it. Go and set fire to it.
Narrator	So they went and set the field on fire.
	Joab went to Absalom's house and demanded:
Joab	Why did your servants set fire to my field?
Absalom	Because you wouldn't come when I sent for you. I wanted you to go to the king and ask him from me: 'Why did I leave Geshur and come here? It would have been better for me to have stayed there.' (PAUSE)
	I want you to arrange for me to see the king, and if I'm guilty, then let him put me to death.
Narrator	So Joab went to King David and told him what Absalom had said. The king sent for Absalom, who went to him and bowed down to the ground in front of him. The king welcomed him with a kiss.
Cast	[This is] the word of the Lord.
All	**Thanks be to God.**

Cast: **Narrator, Absalom, Joab.**

Absalom plans rebellion
2 Samuel 15.1–12

Narrator	Absalom provided a chariot and horses for himself, and an escort of fifty men. He would get up early and go and stand by the road at the city gate. Whenever someone came there with a dispute that he wanted the king to settle, Absalom would call him over and ask him where he was from. And after the man had told him what tribe he was from, Absalom would say:
Absalom	Look, the law is on your side, but there is no representative of the king to hear your case.
Narrator	And he would add:

Absalom	How I wish I were a judge! Then anyone who had a dispute or a claim could come to me, and I would give him justice.
Narrator	When the man approached Absalom to bow down before him, Absalom would reach out, take hold of him, and kiss him. Absalom did this with every Israelite who came to the king for justice, and so he won their loyalty.
	After four years Absalom said to King David:
Absalom	Sir, let me go to Hebron and keep a promise I made to the Lord. While I was living in Geshur in Syria, I promised the Lord that if he would take me back to Jerusalem, I would worship him in Hebron. [The king said:]
David	Go in peace.
Narrator	So Absalom went to Hebron. But he sent messengers to all the tribes of Israel to say:
Absalom	When you hear the sound of trumpets, shout, 'Absalom has become king at Hebron!'
Narrator	There were two hundred men who at Absalom's invitation had gone from Jerusalem with him; they knew nothing of the plot and went in all good faith. And while he was offering sacrifices, Absalom also sent to the town of Gilo for Ahithophel, who was one of King David's advisers. The plot against the king gained strength, and Absalom's followers grew in number.
Cast	[This is] the word of the Lord.
All	**Thanks be to God.**

Cast: **Narrator, Absalom, David.**

David flees from Jerusalem (i)
2 Samuel 15.13–23

Narrator	A messenger reported to David:
Messenger	The Israelites are pledging their loyalty to Absalom.
Narrator	So David said to all his officials who were with him in Jerusalem:
David	We must get away at once if we want to escape from Absalom! Hurry! Or else he will soon be here and defeat us and kill everyone in the city!
Narrator	They answered:
Official 1	Yes, Your Majesty—
Official 2	We are ready to do whatever you say.
Narrator	So the king left, accompanied by all his family and officials, except for ten concubines, whom he left behind to take care of the palace. As the king and all his men were leaving the city, they stopped at the last house. All his officials stood next to him as the royal bodyguard passed by in front of him. The six hundred soldiers

	who had followed him from Gath also passed by, and the king said to Ittai, their leader:
David	Why are *you* going with us? Go back and stay with the new king. You are a foreigner, a refugee away from your own country. You have lived here only a short time, so why should I make you wander round with me? I don't even know where I'm going. Go back and take your fellow-countrymen with you—and may the Lord be kind and faithful to you.
[Narrator	But Ittai answered:]
Ittai	Your Majesty, I swear to you in the Lord's name that I will always go with you wherever you go, even if it means death.
David	Fine! March on!
Narrator	So Ittai went on with all his men and their dependants. The people cried loudly as David's followers left.
Cast	[This is] the word of the Lord.
All	**Thanks be to God.**

Cast: **Narrator, Messenger, David, Official 1, Official 2** (can be the same as Official 1), **Ittai.**

David flees from Jerusalem (ii)
2 Samuel 15.23-27

Narrator	The king crossed the brook of Kidron, followed by his men, and together they went out towards the wilderness.
	Zadok the priest was there, and with him were the Levites, carrying the sacred Covenant Box. They set it down and didn't pick it up again until all the people had left the city. The priest Abiathar was there too. Then the king said to Zadok:
David	Take the Covenant Box back to the city. If the Lord is pleased with me, some day he will let me come back to see it and the place where it stays. But if he isn't pleased with me—well, then, let him do to me what he wishes.
[Narrator	And he went on to say to Zadok:]
David	Look, take your son Ahimaaz and Abiathar's son Jonathan and go back to the city in peace. Meanwhile, I will wait at the river crossings in the wilderness until I receive news from you.
Narrator	So Zadok and Abiathar took the Covenant Box back into Jerusalem and stayed there. David went on up the Mount of Olives weeping; he was barefoot and had his head covered as a sign of grief. All who followed him covered their heads and wept also. When David was told that Ahithophel had joined Absalom's rebellion, he prayed:
David	Please, Lord, turn Ahithophel's advice into nonsense!

Narrator	When David reached the top of the hill, where there was a place of worship, his trusted friend Hushai the Archite met him with his clothes torn and with earth on his head. David said to him:
David	You will be of no help to me if you come with me, but you can help me by returning to the city and telling Absalom that you will now serve him as faithfully as you served his father. And do all you can to oppose any advice that Ahithophel gives. The priests Zadok and Abiathar will be there; tell them everything you hear in the king's palace. They have their sons Ahimaaz and Jonathan with them, and you can send them to me with all the information you gather.
Narrator	So Hushai, David's friend, returned to the city just as Absalom was arriving.
Cast	[This is] the word of the Lord.
All	**Thanks be to God.**

Cast: **Narrator, David.**

David and Ziba
2 Samuel 16.1–4

Narrator	When David had gone a little beyond the top of the Mount of Olives, he was suddenly met by Ziba, the servant of Mephibosheth, who had with him a couple of donkeys loaded with two hundred loaves of bread, a hundred bunches of raisins, a hundred bunches of fresh fruit, and a leather bag full of wine. King David asked him:
David	What are you going to do with all that?
[Narrator	Ziba answered:]
Ziba	The donkeys are for Your Majesty's family to ride, the bread and the fruit are for the men to eat, and the wine is for them to drink when they get tired in the wilderness.
David	Where is Mephibosheth, the grandson of your master Saul?
Ziba	He is staying in Jerusalem, because he is convinced that the Israelites will now restore to him the kingdom of his grandfather Saul.
David	Everything that belonged to Mephibosheth is yours.
Ziba	I am your servant. May I always please Your Majesty!
Cast	[This is] the word of the Lord.
All	**Thanks be to God.**

Cast: **Narrator, David, Ziba.**

David and Shimei
2 Samuel 16.5–14

Narrator	When King David arrived at Bahurim, one of Saul's relatives, Shimei son of Gera, came out to meet him, cursing him as he came. Shimei started throwing stones at David and his officials, even though David was surrounded by his men and his bodyguard. Shimei cursed him [and said]:
Shimei	Get out! Get out! Murderer! Criminal! You took Saul's kingdom, and now the Lord is punishing you for murdering so many of Saul's family. The Lord has given the kingdom to your son Absalom, and you are ruined, you murderer!
Narrator	Abishai, whose mother was Zeruiah, said to the king:
Abishai	Your Majesty, why do you let this dog curse you? Let me go over there and cut off his head!
Narrator	The king said to Abishai and his brother Joab:
David (to Abishai)	This is none of your business. If he curses me because the Lord told him to, who has the right to ask why he does it?
[**Narrator**	And David said to Abishai and to all his officials:]
David	My own *son* is trying to kill me; so why should you be surprised at this Benjaminite? The Lord told him to curse; so leave him alone and let him do it. Perhaps the Lord will notice my misery and give me some blessings to take the place of his curse.
Narrator	So David and his men continued along the road. Shimei kept up with them, walking on the hillside; he was cursing and throwing stones and earth at them as he went. The king and all his men were worn out when they reached the Jordan, and there they rested.
Cast	[This is] the word of the Lord.
All	**Thanks be to God.**

Cast: **Narrator, Shimei, Abishai, David.**

Absalom in Jerusalem
2 Samuel 16.15–23

Narrator	[Meanwhile] Absalom and all the men of Israel came to Jerusalem, and Ahithophel was with him. Then Hushai the Arkite, David's friend, went to Absalom and said to him:
Hushai	Long live the king! Long live the king!
Narrator	Absalom asked Hushai:
Absalom	Is this the love you show your friend? Why didn't you go with your friend?
[**Narrator**	Hushai said to Absalom:]

289

Hushai	No, the one chosen by the Lord, by these people and by all the men of Israel—his I will be, and I will remain with him. Furthermore, whom should I serve? Should I not serve the son? Just as I served your father, so I will serve *you*.
Narrator	Absalom said to Ahithophel:
Absalom	Give us your advice. What should we do?
[Narrator	Ahithophel answered:]
Ahithophel (to Absalom)	Lie with your father's concubines whom he left to take care of the palace. Then all Israel will hear that you have made yourself an offence to your father's nostrils, and the hands of everyone with you will be strengthened.
Narrator	So they pitched a tent for Absalom on the roof, and he lay with his father's concubines in the sight of all Israel. Now in those days the advice Ahithophel gave was like that of one who enquires of God. That was how both David and Absalom regarded all of Ahithophel's advice.
Cast **All**	[This is] the word of the Lord. **Thanks be to God.**

Cast: **Narrator, Hushai, Absalom, Ahithophel.**

Hushai misleads Absalom
2 Samuel 17.1–14

Narrator	[Not long after that] Ahithophel said to Absalom:
Ahithophel	Let me choose twelve thousand men, and tonight I will set out after David. I will attack him while he is tired and discouraged. He will be frightened, and all his men will run away. I will kill only the king and then bring back all his men to you, like a bride returning to her husband. You want to kill only one man; the rest of the people will be safe.
Narrator	This seemed like good advice to Absalom and all the Israelite leaders. Absalom said:
Absalom	Now call Hushai, and let us hear what he has to say.
Narrator	When Hushai arrived, Absalom said to him:
Absalom	This is the advice that Ahithophel has given us; shall we follow it? If not, you tell us what to do.
[Narrator	Hushai answered:]
Hushai	The advice Ahithophel gave you this time is no good. You know that your father David and his men are hard fighters and that they are as fierce as a mother bear robbed of her cubs. Your father is an experienced soldier and does not stay with his men at night. Just now he is probably hiding in a cave or some other place. As soon as David attacks your men, whoever hears about it will say that your men have been defeated. Then even the bravest men, as

fearless as lions, will be afraid because everyone in Israel knows that your father is a great soldier and that his men are hard fighters. My advice is that you bring all the Israelites together from one end of the country to the other, as many as the grains of sand on the sea-shore, and that you lead them personally in battle. We will find David wherever he is, and attack him before he knows what's happening. Neither he nor any of his men will survive. If he retreats into a city, our people will all bring ropes and just pull the city into the valley below. Not a single stone will be left there on top of the hill.

Narrator	Absalom and all the Israelites said:
Absalom	Hushai's advice is better than Ahithophel's.
Narrator	The Lord had decided that Ahithophel's good advice would not be followed, so that disaster would come on Absalom.
Cast	[This is] the word of the Lord.
All	**Thanks be to God.**

Cast: **Narrator, Ahithophel, Absalom, Hushai.**

David is warned and escapes
2 Samuel 17.15–22 [23–29]

Narrator	Hushai told the priests Zadok and Abiathar what advice he had given to Absalom and the Israelite leaders and what advice Ahithophel had given. Hushai added:
Hushai	Quick, now! Send a message to David not to spend the night at the river crossings in the wilderness, but to cross the Jordan at once, so that he and his men won't all be caught and killed.
Narrator	Abiathar's son Jonathan and Zadok's son Ahimaaz were waiting at the spring of Enrogel, on the outskirts of Jerusalem, because they did not dare to be seen entering the city. A servant-girl would regularly go and tell them what was happening, and then they would go and tell King David. But one day a boy happened to see them, and he told Absalom; so they hurried off to hide in the house of a certain man in Bahurim. He had a well near his house, and they got down into it. The man's wife took a covering, spread it over the opening of the well and scattered grain over it, so that no one would notice anything. Absalom's officials came to the house and asked the woman:
Official	Where are Ahimaaz and Jonathan?
[Narrator	She answered:]
Woman	They crossed the river.
Narrator	The men looked for them but could not find them, and so they returned to Jerusalem. After they left, Ahimaaz and Jonathan came up out of the well and went and reported to King David. They told him what Ahithophel had planned against him and said:

291

Jonathan	Hurry up and cross the river.
Narrator	So David and his men started crossing the Jordan, and by daybreak they had all gone across.
[Narrator	When Ahithophel saw that his advice had not been followed, he saddled his donkey and went back to his own city. After putting his affairs in order, he hanged himself. He was buried in the family grave.
	David had reached the town of Mahanaim by the time Absalom and the Israelites had crossed the Jordan. Absalom and his men camped in the land of Gilead.
	When David arrived at Mahanaim, he was met by Shobi son of Nahash, from the city of Rabbah in Ammon, and by Machir son of Ammiel, from Lodebar, and by Barzillai, from Rogelim in Gilead. They brought bowls, clay pots, and bedding, and also food for David and his men: wheat, barley, meal, roasted grain, beans, peas, honey, cheese, cream, and some sheep. They knew that David and his men would be hungry, thirsty, and tired in the wilderness.]
Cast	[This is] the word of the Lord.
All	**Thanks be to God.**

Cast: **Narrator, Hushai, Official, Woman, Jonathan.**

Absalom is defeated and killed
2 Samuel 18.1–18

Narrator	King David brought all his men together, divided them into units of a thousand and of a hundred, and placed officers in command of them. Then he sent them out in three groups, with Joab and Joab's brother Abishai and Ittai from Gath, each in command of a group. And the king said to his men:
David	I will go with you myself.
Man 1	You mustn't go with us.
Man 2	It won't make any difference to the enemy if the rest of us turn and run, or even if half of us are killed; but you are worth ten thousand of us.
Man 1	It will be better if you stay here in the city and send us help.
David	I will do whatever you think best.
Narrator	Then David stood by the side of the gate as his men marched out in units of a thousand and of a hundred.
	He gave orders to Joab, Abishai, and Ittai:
David	For my sake don't harm the young man Absalom.
Narrator	And all the troops heard David give this command to his officers. (PAUSE)

David's army went out into the countryside and fought the Israelites in the forest of Ephraim. The Israelites were defeated by David's men; it was a terrible defeat, with twenty thousand men killed that day. The fighting spread over the countryside, and more men died in the forest than were killed in battle. Suddenly Absalom met some of David's men. Absalom was riding a mule, and as it went under a large oak-tree, Absalom's head got caught in the branches. The mule ran on and Absalom was left hanging in mid air. One of David's men saw him and reported to Joab:

Man 2 Sir, I saw Absalom hanging in an oak-tree!

Narrator Joab answered:

Joab If you saw him, why didn't you kill him on the spot? I myself would have given you ten pieces of silver and a belt.

[Narrator But the man answered:]

Man 2 Even if you gave me a thousand pieces of silver, I wouldn't lift a finger against the king's son. We all heard the king command you and Abishai and Ittai, 'For my sake don't harm the young man Absalom.' But if I had disobeyed the king and killed Absalom, the king would have heard about it—he hears about everything—and you would not have defended me.

Narrator Joab said:

Joab I'm not going to waste any more time with you.

Narrator He took three spears and plunged them into Absalom's chest while he was still alive, hanging in the oak-tree. Then ten of Joab's soldiers closed in on Absalom and finished killing him. Joab ordered the trumpet to be blown to stop the fighting, and his troops came back from pursuing the Israelites. They took Absalom's body, threw it into a deep pit in the forest, and covered it with a huge pile of stones. All the Israelites fled, each man to his own home.

During his lifetime Absalom had built a monument for himself in King's Valley, because he had no son to keep his name alive. So he named it after himself, and to this day it is known as Absalom's Monument.

Cast [This is] the word of the Lord.
All **Thanks be to God.**

Cast: **Narrator, David, Man 1, Man 2** (can be the same as Man 1)**, Joab.**

David is told of Absalom's death
2 Samuel 18.19–33

Narrator Ahimaaz son of Zadok said to Joab:

Ahimaaz Let me run to the king with the good news that the Lord has saved him from his enemies.

[Narrator Joab said:]

Joab	No, today you will not take any good news. Some other day you may do so, but not today, for the King's son is dead.
Narrator	Then he said to his Sudanese slave:
Joab	Go and tell the king what you have seen.
Narrator	The slave bowed and ran off.
	[Ahimaaz insisted:]
Ahimaaz	I don't care what happens; please let me take the news also.
Joab	Why do you want to do it, my son? You will get no reward for it.
Ahimaaz	Whatever happens, I want to go.
Joab	Then go.
Narrator	So Ahimaaz ran off down the road through the Jordan Valley, and soon he passed the slave. David was sitting in the space between the inner and outer gates of the city. The watchman went up to the top of the wall and stood on the roof of the gateway; he looked out and saw a man running alone. He called down and told the king, and the king said:
David	If he is alone, he is bringing good news.
Narrator	The runner came nearer and nearer. Then the watchman saw another man running alone, and he called down to the gatekeeper:
Watchman (calling)	Look! There's another man running!
David	This one also is bringing good news.
Watchman (calling)	I can see that the first man runs like Ahimaaz.
David	He's a good man, and he is bringing good news.
Narrator	Ahimaaz called out a greeting to the king, threw himself down to the ground before him [and said:]
Ahimaaz	Praise the Lord your God, who has given you victory over the men who rebelled against Your Majesty!
David (anxiously)	Is the young man Absalom safe?
Ahimaaz	Sir, when your officer Joab sent me, I saw a great commotion, but I couldn't tell what it was.
David	Stand over there.
Narrator	He went over and stood there. Then the Sudanese slave arrived and said to the king:
Slave	I have good news for Your Majesty! Today the Lord has given you victory over all who rebelled against you!
David	Is the young man Absalom safe?

Slave	I wish that what has happened to him would happen to all your enemies, sir, and to all who rebel against you.
Narrator	The king was overcome with grief. He went up to the room over the gateway and wept. As he went, he cried:
David	O my son! My son Absalom! Absalom, my son! If only I had died in your place, my son! Absalom, my son!
Cast All	[This is] the word of the Lord. **Thanks be to God.**

Cast: **Narrator, Ahimaaz, Joab, David, Watchman, Slave.**

Joab reprimands David
2 Samuel 19.1–8

Narrator	Joab was told that King David was weeping and mourning for Absalom. And so the joy of victory was turned into sadness for all David's troops that day, because they heard that the king was mourning for his son. They went back into the city quietly, like soldiers who are ashamed because they are running away from battle. The king covered his face and cried loudly:
David	O my son! My son Absalom! Absalom, my son!
Narrator	Joab went to the king's house and said to him:
Joab	Today you have humiliated your men—the men who saved your life and the lives of your sons and daughters and of your wives and concubines. You oppose those who love you and support those who hate you! You have made it clear that your officers and men mean nothing to you. I can see that you would be quite happy if Absalom were alive today and all of us were dead. Now go and reassure your men. I swear by the Lord's name that if you don't, not one of them will be with you by tomorrow morning. That would be the worst disaster you have suffered in all your life.
Narrator	Then the king got up, and went and sat near the city gate. His men heard that he was there, and they all gathered round him.
Cast All	[This is] the word of the Lord. **Thanks be to God.**

Cast: **Narrator, David, Joab.**

David starts back to Jerusalem
2 Samuel 19.8–18

Narrator	All the Israelites had fled, each man to his own home. All over the country they started quarrelling among themselves:
Israelite 1	King David saved us from our enemies.

295

Israelite 2	He rescued us from the Philistines. But now he has fled from Absalom and left the country.
Israelite 1	We anointed Absalom as our king, but he has been killed in battle.
Israelite 2	So why doesn't somebody try to bring King David back?
Narrator	The news of what the Israelites were saying reached King David. So he sent the priests Zadok and Abiathar to ask the leaders of Judah:
David	Why should you be the last to help bring the king back to his palace? You are my relatives, my own flesh and blood; why should you be the last to bring me back?
Narrator	David also told them to say to Amasa:
David	You are my relative. From now on I am putting you in charge of the army in place of Joab. May God strike me dead if I don't!
Narrator	David's words won the complete loyalty of all the men of Judah, and they sent him word to return with all his officials. (PAUSE)
	On his way back the king was met at the River Jordan by the men of Judah, who had come to Gilgal to escort him across the river. At the same time the Benjaminite Shimei, son of Gera from Bahurim, hurried to the Jordan to meet King David. He had with him a thousand men from the tribe of Benjamin. And Ziba, the servant of Saul's family, also came with his fifteen sons and twenty servants, and they arrived at the Jordan before the king. They crossed the river to escort the royal party across and to do whatever the king wanted.
Cast	[This is] the word of the Lord.
All	**Thanks be to God.**

Cast: **Narrator, Israelite 1, Israelite 2, David.**

David shows kindness
2 Samuel 19.18–39

Narrator	As the king was getting ready to cross the river Jordan, Shimei threw himself down in front of him and said:
Shimei	Your Majesty, please forget the wrong I did that day you left Jerusalem. Don't hold it against me or think about it any more. I know, sir, that I have sinned, and this is why I am the first one from the northern tribes to come and meet Your Majesty today.
Narrator	Abishai son of Zeruiah spoke up:
Abishai	Shimei should be put to death because he cursed the one whom the Lord chose as king.
Narrator	But David said to Abishai and his brother Joab:
David	Who asked your opinion? Are you going to give me trouble? I am the one who is king of Israel now, and no Israelite will be put to death today.

Narrator	And he said to Shimei:
David	I give you my word that you will not be put to death.
Narrator	Then Mephibosheth, Saul's grandson, came down to meet the king. He had not washed his feet, trimmed his beard, or washed his clothes from the time the king left Jerusalem until he returned victorious. When Mephibosheth arrived from Jerusalem to meet the king, the king said to him:
David	Mephibosheth, you didn't go with me. Why not?
Narrator	He answered:
Mephibosheth	As you know, Your Majesty, I am crippled. I told my servant to saddle my donkey so that I could ride along with you, but he betrayed me. He lied about me to Your Majesty, but you are like God's angel, so do what seems right to you. All my father's family deserved to be put to death by Your Majesty, but you gave me the right to eat at your table. I have no right to ask for any more favours from Your Majesty.
David	You don't have to say anything more. I have decided that you and Ziba will share Saul's property.
Mephibosheth	Let Ziba have it all. It's enough for me that Your Majesty has come home safely.
Narrator	Barzillai, from Gilead, had also come down from Rogelim to escort the king across the Jordan. Barzillai was a very old man, eighty years old. He was very rich and had supplied the king with food while he was staying at Mahanaim. The king said to him:
David	Come with me to Jerusalem, and I will take care of you.
Narrator	But Barzillai answered:
Barzillai	I haven't long to live; why should I go with Your Majesty to Jerusalem? I am already eighty years old, and nothing gives me pleasure any more. I can't taste what I eat and drink, and I can't hear the voices of singers. I would only be a burden to Your Majesty. I don't deserve such a great reward. So I will go just a little way with you beyond the Jordan. Then let me go back home and die near my parents' grave. Here is my son Chimham, who will serve you; take him with you, Your Majesty, and do for him as you think best.
David	I will take him with me and do for him whatever you want. And I will do for you anything you ask.
Narrator	Then David and all his men crossed the Jordan. He kissed Barzillai and gave him his blessing, and Barzillai went back home.
Cast	[This is] the word of the Lord.
All	**Thanks be to God.**

Cast: **Narrator, Shimei, Abishai, David, Mephibosheth, Barzillai.**

Judah and Israel argue over the king
2 Samuel 19.40–43

Narrator	When the king had crossed the river Jordan, escorted by all the men of Judah and half the men of Israel, he went on to Gilgal, and Chimham went with him. Then all the Israelites went to the king and said to him:
Israelite 1	Your Majesty!
Israelite 2	Why did our brothers, the men of Judah, think they had the right to take you away and escort you, your family, and your men across the Jordan?
Narrator	The men of Judah answered:
Judaean 1 (indignantly)	We did it because the king is one of us.
Judaean 2	Why should this make you angry?
Judaean 1	He hasn't paid for our food nor has he given us anything.
Israelite 1	We have ten times as many claims on King David as you have, even if he is one of you.
Israelite 2	Why do you look down on us? Don't forget that we were the first to talk about bringing the king back!
Narrator	But the men of Judah were more violent in making their claims than the men of Israel.
Cast	[This is] the word of the Lord.
All	**Thanks be to God.**

Cast: **Narrator, Israelite 1, Israelite 2** (can be the same as Israelite 1), **Judaean 1, Judaean 2** (can be the same as Judaean 1).

Sheba rebels against David
From 2 Samuel 20.1–26

Narrator	Now a troublemaker named Sheba son of Bicri, a Benjaminite, happened to be there when King David had crossed the river Jordan. He sounded the trumpet and shouted:
Sheba	We have no share in David, no part in Jesse's son! Every man to his tent, O Israel!
Narrator	So all the men of Israel deserted David to follow Sheba son of Bicri. But the men of Judah stayed by their king all the way from the Jordan to Jerusalem. When David returned to his palace in Jerusalem, he took the ten concubines he had left to take care of the palace and put them in a house under guard. He provided for them, but did not lie with them. They were kept in confinement till the day of their death, living as widows. Then the king said to Amasa:

David	Summon the men of Judah to come to me within three days, and be here yourself.
Narrator	But when Amasa went to summon Judah, he took longer than the time the king had set for him. David said to Abishai:
David	Now Sheba son of Bicri will do us more harm than Absalom did. Take your master's men and pursue him, or he will find fortified cities and escape from us.
Narrator	So Joab's men and the Kerethites and Pelethites and all the mighty warriors went out under the command of Abishai. They marched out from Jerusalem to pursue Sheba son of Bicri.
	While they were at the great rock in Gibeon, Amasa came to meet them. Joab was wearing his military tunic, and strapped over it at his waist was a belt with a dagger in its sheath. As he stepped forward, it dropped out of its sheath. Joab said to Amasa:
Joab (cunningly)	How are you, my brother?
Narrator	Then Joab took Amasa by the beard with his right hand to kiss him. Amasa was not on his guard against the dagger in Joab's hand, and Joab plunged it into him. Without being stabbed again, Amasa died. Then Joab and his brother Abishai pursued Sheba son of Bicri. Sheba passed through all the tribes of Israel to Abel Beth Maacah and through the entire region of the Berites, who gathered together and followed him. All the troops with Joab came and besieged Sheba in Abel Beth Maacah. They built a siege ramp up to the city, and it stood against the outer fortifications. While they were battering the wall to bring it down, a wise woman called from the city:
Woman	Listen! Listen! Tell Joab to come here so that I can speak to him.
Narrator	He went towards her.
Woman (to Joab)	Are you Joab?
Joab (to woman)	I am.
Woman	Listen to what your servant has to say.
Joab	I'm listening.
Woman	Long ago they used to say, 'Get your answer at Abel,' and that settled it. We are the peaceful and faithful in Israel. You are trying to destroy a city that is a mother in Israel. Why do you want to swallow up the Lord's inheritance?
Joab	Far be it from me! Far be it from me to swallow up or destroy! That is not the case. A man named Sheba son of Bicri, from the hill country of Ephraim, has lifted up his hand against the king, against David. Hand over this one man, and I'll withdraw from the city.
Woman	His head will be thrown to you from the wall.

Narrator	Then the woman went to all the people with her wise advice, and they cut off the head of Sheba son of Bicri and threw it to Joab. So he sounded the trumpet, and his men dispersed from the city, each returning to his home. And Joab went back to the king in Jerusalem.
	Joab was over Israel's entire army; Benaiah son of Jehoiada was over the Kerethites and Pelethites; Adoniram was in charge of forced labour; Jehoshaphat son of Ahilud was recorder; Sheva was secretary; Zadok and Abiathar were priests; and Ira the Jairite was David's priest.
Cast	[This is] the word of the Lord.
All	**Thanks be to God.**

Cast: **Narrator, Sheba, David, Joab, Woman.**

Saul's descendants are put to death
2 Samuel 21.1–9

Narrator	During David's reign there was a severe famine which lasted for three full years. So David consulted the Lord about it, and the Lord said:
The Lord	Saul and his family are guilty of murder; he put the people of Gibeon to death.
Commentator	The people of Gibeon were not Israelites; they were a small group of Amorites whom the Israelites had promised to protect, but Saul had tried to destroy them because of his zeal for the people of Israel and Judah.
Narrator	So David summoned the people of Gibeon:
David	What can I do for you? I want to make up for the wrong that was done to you, so that you will bless the Lord's people.
Person 1	Our quarrel with Saul and his family can't be settled with silver or gold.
Person 2	Nor do we want to kill any Israelite.
David	What, then, do you think I should do for you?
Person 1	Saul wanted to destroy us and leave none of us alive anywhere in Israel. So hand over seven of his male descendants.
Person 2	And we will hang them before the Lord at Gibeah, the town of Saul, the Lord's chosen king.
David	I will hand them over.
Narrator	But because of the sacred promise that he and Jonathan had made to each other, David spared Jonathan's son Mephibosheth, the grandson of Saul. However, he took Armoni and Mephibosheth, the two sons that Rizpah the daughter of Aiah had borne to Saul; he also took the five sons of Saul's daughter Merab,

300

whom she had borne to Adriel son of Barzillai, who was from Meholah. David handed them over to the people of Gibeon, who hanged them on the mountain before the Lord—and all seven of them died together.

Cast	[This is] the word of the Lord.
All	**Thanks be to God.**

Cast: **Narrator, The Lord, Commentator** (can be the same as The Lord), **David, Person 1, Person 2.**

David's last words
2 Samuel 23.1–7

Narrator   David son of Jesse was the man whom God made great, whom the God of Jacob chose to be king, and who was the composer of beautiful songs for Israel. These are David's last words:

David   The spirit of the Lord speaks through me;
his message is on my lips.
The God of Israel has spoken;
the protector of Israel said to me:

Voice of God   The king who rules with justice,
who rules in obedience to God,
is like the sun shining on a cloudless dawn,
the sun that makes the grass sparkle after rain.

David   And that is how God will bless my descendants,
because he has made an eternal covenant with me,
an agreement that will not be broken,
a promise that will not be changed.
That is all I desire; that will be my victory,
and God will surely bring it about.
But godless men are like thorns that are thrown away;
no one can touch them with bare hands.
You must use an iron tool or a spear;
they will be burnt completely.

Cast	[This is] the word of the Lord.
All	**Thanks be to God.**

Cast: **Narrator, David, Voice of God.**

David's famous soldiers
From 2 Samuel 23.8–17 [18–39]

Narrator 1   These were the brave deeds of the three famous soldiers: the first was Josheb Basshebeth from Tachemon, who was the leader of The Three; he fought with his spear against eight hundred men and killed them all in one battle.

Narrator 2   The second of the famous three was Eleazar son of Dodo, of the clan of Ahoh. One day he and David challenged the Philistines who had gathered for battle. The Israelites fell back, but he stood

→

	his ground and fought the Philistines until his hand was so stiff that he could not let go of his sword. The Lord won a great victory that day. After it was over, the Israelites returned to where Eleazar was and stripped the armour from the dead.
Narrator 3	The third of the famous three was Shammah son of Agee, from Harar. The Philistines had gathered at Lehi, where there was a field of peas. The Israelites fled from the Philistines, but Shammah stood his ground in the field, defended it, and killed the Philistines. The Lord won a great victory that day.
Narrator 1	Near the beginning of harvest time three of 'The Thirty' went down to the cave of Adullam, where David was, while a band of Philistines was camping in the Valley of Rephaim. At that time David was on a fortified hill, and a group of Philistines had occupied Bethlehem. David felt homesick and said:
David	How I wish someone would bring me a drink of water from the well by the gate at Bethlehem!
Narrator 2	The three famous soldiers forced their way through the Philistine camp, drew some water from the well, and brought it back to David. But he would not drink it; instead he poured it out as an offering to the Lord and said:
David	Lord, I could never drink this! It would be like drinking the blood of these men who risked their lives!
Narrator 2	So he refused to drink it.
Narrator 3	Those were the brave deeds of the three famous soldiers.
[Narrator 1	Joab's brother Abishai (their mother was Zeruiah) was the leader of The Famous Thirty. He fought with his spear against three hundred men and killed them, and became famous among The Thirty. He was the most famous of The Thirty and became their leader, but he was not as famous as The Three.
Narrator 2	Benaiah son of Jehoiada, from Kabzeel, was another famous soldier; he did many brave deeds, including killing two great Moabite warriors. He once went down into a pit on a snowy day and killed a lion. He also killed an Egyptian, a huge man who was armed with a spear. Benaiah attacked him with his club, snatched the spear from the Egyptian's hand, and killed him with it. Those were the brave deeds of Benaiah, who was one of The Thirty. He was outstanding among them, but was not as famous as The Three. David put him in charge of his bodyguard.
Narrator 1	There were thirty-seven famous soldiers in all.]
Cast	[This is] the word of the Lord.
All	**Thanks be to God.**

Cast: **Narrator 1, Narrator 2, Narrator 3, David.**

David takes a census
2 Samuel 24.1–25

Narrator   The Lord was angry with Israel once more, and he made King David bring trouble on them [The Lord said to him]:

The Lord   Go and count the people of Israel and Judah.

Narrator   So David gave orders to Joab, the commander of his army:

David   Go with your officers through all the tribes of Israel from one end of the country to the other, and count the people. I want to know how many there are.

Narrator   But Joab answered the king:

Joab   Your Majesty, may the Lord your God make the people of Israel a hundred times more numerous than they are now, and may you live to see him do it. But why does Your Majesty want to do this?

Narrator   But the king made Joab and his officers obey his order; they left his presence and went out to count the people of Israel. They crossed the Jordan and camped south of Aroer, the city in the middle of the valley, in the territory of Gad. From there they went north to Jazer, and on to Gilead and to Kadesh, in Hittite territory. Then they went to Dan, and from Dan they went west to Sidon. Then they went south to the fortified city of Tyre, on to all the cities of the Hivites and the Canaanites, and finally to Beersheba, in the southern part of Judah. So after nine months and twenty days they returned to Jerusalem, having travelled through the whole country. They reported to the king the total number of men capable of military service: 800,000 in Israel and 500,000 in Judah.

But after David had taken the census, his conscience began to trouble him, and he said to the Lord:

David   I have committed a terrible sin in doing this! Please forgive me. I have acted foolishly.

Narrator   The Lord said to Gad, David's prophet:

The Lord   Go and tell David that I am giving him three choices. I will do whichever he chooses.

Narrator   The next morning, after David got up, Gad went to him. He told him what the Lord had said [and asked]:

Gad   Which is it to be? Three years of famine in your land or three months of running away from your enemies or three days of an epidemic in your land? Now think it over, and tell me what answer to take back to the Lord.

David
(hesitating)   I am in a desperate situation! But I don't want to be punished by men. Let the Lord himself be the one to punish us, for he is merciful.

Narrator   So the Lord sent an epidemic on Israel, which lasted from that morning until the time that he had chosen. From one end of the

$\rightarrow$

country to the other seventy thousand Israelites died. When the Lord's angel was about to destroy Jerusalem, the Lord changed his mind about punishing the people and said to the angel who was killing them:

The Lord   Stop! That's enough!

Narrator   The angel was by the threshing-place of Araunah, a Jebusite. (PAUSE)

David saw the angel who was killing the people, and said to the Lord:

David   I am the guilty one. I am the one who did wrong. What have these poor people done? You should punish me and my family.

Narrator   That same day Gad went to David [and said to him]:

Gad   Go up to Araunah's threshing-place and build an altar to the Lord.

Narrator   David obeyed the Lord's command and went as Gad had told him. Araunah looked down and saw the king and his officials coming up to him. He threw himself on the ground in front of David [and asked]:

Araunah   Your Majesty, why are you here?

David   To buy your threshing-place and build an altar for the Lord, in order to stop the epidemic.

Araunah   Take it, Your Majesty, and offer to the Lord whatever you wish. Here are these oxen to burn as an offering on the altar; here are their yokes and the threshing-boards to use as fuel.

Narrator   Araunah gave it all to the king [and said to him]:

Araunah   May the Lord your God accept your offering.

David   No, I will pay you for it. I will not offer to the Lord my God sacrifices that have cost me nothing.

Narrator   And he bought the threshing-place and the oxen for fifty pieces of silver. Then he built an altar to the Lord and offered burnt-offerings and fellowship-offerings. The Lord answered his prayer, and the epidemic in Israel was stopped.

Cast   [This is] the word of the Lord.
All   **Thanks be to God.**

Cast: **Narrator, The Lord, David, Joab, Gad, Araunah.**

1 KINGS

Solomon is made king
1 Kings 1.11–52

Narrator	Nathan went to Bathsheba, Solomon's mother, and asked her:
Nathan	Haven't you heard that Haggith's son Adonijah has made himself king? And King David doesn't know anything about it! If you want to save your life and the life of your son Solomon, I would advise you to go at once to King David and ask him, 'Your Majesty, didn't you solemnly promise me that my son Solomon would succeed you as king? How is it, then, that Adonijah has become king?'
[Narrator	And Nathan added:]
Nathan	Then, while you are still talking with King David, I will come in and confirm your story.
Narrator	So Bathsheba went to see the king in his bedroom. He was very old, and Abishag, the girl from Shunem, was taking care of him. Bathsheba bowed low before the king [and he asked]:
David	What do you want?
Bathsheba	Your Majesty, you made me a solemn promise in the name of the Lord your God that my son Solomon would be king after you. But Adonijah has already become king, and you don't know anything about it. He has offered a sacrifice of many bulls, sheep, and fattened calves, and he invited your sons, and Abiathar the priest, and Joab the commander of your army to the feast, but he did not invite your son Solomon. Your Majesty, all the people of Israel are looking to you to tell them who is to succeed you as king. If you don't, as soon as you are dead my son Solomon and I will be treated as traitors.
Narrator	She was still speaking, when Nathan arrived at the palace. The king was told that the prophet was there, and Nathan went in and bowed low before the king:
Nathan	Your Majesty, have you announced that Adonijah would succeed you as king? This very day he has gone and offered a sacrifice of many bulls, sheep, and fattened calves. He invited all your sons, Joab the commander of your army, and Abiathar the priest, and just now they are feasting with him and shouting, 'Long live King Adonijah!' But he did not invite me, sir, or Zadok the priest, or Benaiah, or Solomon. Did Your Majesty approve all this and not even tell your officials who is to succeed you as king?
David	Ask Bathsheba to come back in.
Narrator	She came and stood before him. [Then he said to her:]

305

David (to Bathsheba)	I promise you by the living Lord, who has rescued me from all my troubles, that today I will keep the promise I made to you in the name of the Lord, the God of Israel, that your son Solomon would succeed me as king.
Narrator	Bathsheba bowed low:
Bathsheba	May my lord the king live for ever!
Narrator	Then King David sent for Zadok, Nathan, and Benaiah. [When they came in, he said to them:]
David	Take my court officials with you; let my son Solomon ride my own mule, and escort him down to the spring of Gihon, where Zadok and Nathan are to anoint him as king of Israel. Then blow the trumpet and shout, 'Long live King Solomon!' Follow him back here when he comes to sit on my throne. He will succeed me as king, because he is the one I have chosen to be the ruler of Israel and Judah.
[Narrator	Benaiah answered:]
Benaiah	It shall be done, and may the Lord your God confirm it. As the Lord has been with Your Majesty, may he also be with Solomon, and make his reign even more prosperous than yours.
Narrator	So Zadok, Nathan, Benaiah, and the royal bodyguard put Solomon on King David's mule, and escorted him to the spring of Gihon. Zadok took the container of olive-oil which he had brought from the Tent of the Lord's presence, and anointed Solomon. They blew the trumpet, and all the people shouted:
Persons 1–3	Long live King Solomon!
Narrator	Then they all followed him back, shouting for joy and playing flutes, making enough noise to shake the ground. As Adonijah and all his guests were finishing the feast, they heard the noise. [And when] Joab heard the trumpet [he asked]:
Joab	What's the meaning of all that noise in the city?
Narrator	Before he finished speaking, Jonathan, the son of the priest Abiathar, arrived. Adonijah said:
Adonijah	Come in. You're a good man—you must be bringing good news.
[Narrator	Jonathan answered:]
Jonathan	I'm afraid not. His Majesty King David has made Solomon king. He sent Zadok, Nathan, Benaiah, and the royal bodyguard to escort him. They made him ride on the king's mule, and Zadok and Nathan anointed him as king at the spring of Gihon. Then they went into the city, shouting for joy, and the people are now in an uproar. That's the noise you just heard. Solomon is now the king. What is more, the court officials went in to pay their respects to His Majesty King David, and said:
[Person 1*]	May your God make Solomon even more famous than you.
[Person 2*]	And may Solomon's reign be even more prosperous than yours.

Narrator	Then King David bowed in worship on his bed and prayed:
David*	Let us praise the Lord, the God of Israel, who has today made one of my descendants succeed me as king, and has let me live to see it!
Narrator	Then Adonijah's guests were afraid, and they all got up and left, each going his own way. Adonijah, in great fear of Solomon, went to the Tent of the Lord's presence and took hold of the corners of the altar. King Solomon was told that Adonijah was afraid of him and that he was holding on to the corners of the altar and had said:
[Adonijah*]	First, I want King Solomon to swear to me that he will not have me put to death.
Narrator	Solomon replied:
Solomon	If he is loyal, not even a hair on his head will be touched; but if he is not, he will die.
Narrator	King Solomon then sent for Adonijah and had him brought down from the altar. Adonijah went to the king and bowed low before him [and the king said to him]:
Solomon	You may go home.
Cast **All**	[This is] the word of the Lord. **Thanks be to God.**

Cast: **Narrator, Nathan, David, Bathsheba, Benaiah, Person 1, Person 2, Person 3** (Persons 1–3 can be the same), **Joab, Adonijah, Jonathan, Solomon.** (*Speakers preferably unseen here.)

The death of David
From 1 Kings 2.1–12

Narrator	When David was about to die, he called his son Solomon and gave him his last instructions:
David	My time to die has come. Be confident and determined, and do what the Lord your God orders you to do. Obey all his laws and commands, as written in the Law of Moses, so that wherever you go you may prosper in everything you do. If you obey him, the Lord will keep the promise he made when he told me that my descendants would rule Israel as long as they were careful to obey his commands faithfully with all their heart and soul.
Narrator	David died and was buried in David's City. He had been king of Israel for forty years, ruling seven years in Hebron and thirty-three years in Jerusalem. Solomon succeeded his father David as king, and his royal power was firmly established.
Cast **All**	[This is] the word of the Lord. **Thanks be to God.**

Cast: **Narrator, David.**

The death of Adonijah
1 Kings 2.13–25 (with introduction from 1 Kings 1.1–4)

Narrator	When King David was a very old man, although his servants covered him with blankets, he could not keep warm. So his officials said to him:
Official	Your Majesty, let us find a young woman to stay with you and take care of you. She will lie close to you and keep you warm.
Narrator	A search was made all over Israel for a beautiful girl, and in Shunem they found such a girl named Abishag, and brought her to the king. She was very beautiful, and waited on the king and took care of him.
	Adonijah, whose mother was Haggith, went to Bathsheba, who was Solomon's mother. [Bathsheba asked:]
Bathsheba	Is this a friendly visit?
Adonijah	It is. I have something to ask of you.
Bathsheba	What is it?
Adonijah	You know that I should have become king and that everyone in Israel expected it. But it happened differently, and my brother became king, because it was the Lord's will. And now I have one request to make; please do not refuse me.
Bathsheba	What is it?
Adonijah	Please ask King Solomon—I know he won't refuse you—to let me have Abishag, the girl from Shunem, as my wife.
Bathsheba	Very well, I will speak to the king for you.
Narrator	So Bathsheba went to the king to speak to him on behalf of Adonijah. The king stood up to greet his mother and bowed to her. Then he sat on his throne and had another one brought in on which she sat at his right. [She said:]
Bathsheba	I have a small favour to ask of you; please do not refuse me.
Solomon	What is it, mother? I will not refuse you.
Bathsheba	Let your brother Adonijah have Abishag as his wife.
Solomon	Why do you ask me to give Abishag to him? You might as well ask me to give him the throne too. After all, he is my elder brother, and Abiathar the priest and Joab are on his side!
Narrator	Then Solomon made a solemn promise in the Lord's name:
Solomon	May God strike me dead if I don't make Adonijah pay with his life for asking this! The Lord has firmly established me on the throne of my father David; he has kept his promise and given the kingdom to me and my descendants. I swear by the living Lord that Adonijah will die this very day!
Narrator	So King Solomon gave orders to Benaiah, who went out and killed Adonijah.

Cast	[This is] the word of the Lord.
All	**Thanks be to God.**

Cast: **Narrator, Official, Bathsheba, Adonijah, Solomon.**

Abiathar's banishment and Joab's death
1 Kings 2.26–35

Narrator	King Solomon said to Abiathar the priest:
Solomon	Go to your country home in Anathoth. You deserve to die, but I will not have you put to death now, for you were in charge of the Lord's Covenant Box while you were with my father David, and you shared in all his troubles.
Narrator	Then Solomon dismissed Abiathar from serving as a priest of the Lord, and so he made what the Lord had said in Shiloh about the priest Eli and his descendants come true. Joab, who had conspired against Solomon, heard what had happened. So he fled to the Tent of the Lord's presence and took hold of the corners of the altar. When the news reached King Solomon that Joab had fled to the Tent and was by the altar, Solomon sent a messenger to Joab to ask him why he had fled to the altar. Joab answered that he had fled to the Lord because he was afraid of Solomon. So King Solomon sent Benaiah to kill Joab. He went to the Tent of the Lord's presence and said to Joab:
Benaiah	The king orders you to come out.
[Narrator	Joab answered:]
Joab	No, I will die here.
Narrator	Benaiah went back to the king and told him what Joab had said. Solomon answered:
Solomon	Kill him and bury him. Then neither I nor any other of David's descendants will any longer be held responsible for what Joab did when he killed innocent men. The Lord will punish Joab for those murders, which he committed without my father David's knowledge. Joab killed two innocent men who were better men than he: Abner, commander of the army of Israel, and Amasa, commander of the army of Judah. The punishment for their murders will fall on Joab and on his descendants for ever. But the Lord will always give success to David's descendants who sit on his throne.
Narrator	So Benaiah went to the Tent of the Lord's presence and killed Joab, and he was buried at his home in the open country. The king made Benaiah commander of the army in Joab's place and put Zadok the priest in Abiathar's place.
Cast	[This is] the word of the Lord.
All	**Thanks be to God.**

Cast: **Narrator, Solomon, Benaiah, Joab.**

The death of Shimei
From 1 Kings 2.36–46

Narrator	King Solomon sent for Shimei:
Solomon	Build a house for yourself here in Jerusalem. Live in it and don't leave the city. If you ever leave and go beyond the brook of Kidron, you will certainly die—and you yourself will be to blame.
[Narrator	Shimei answered:]
Shimei	Very well, your Majesty, I will do what you say.
Narrator	So he lived in Jerusalem a long time. (PAUSE)
	Three years later, however, two of Shimei's slaves ran away to the king of Gath, Achish son of Maacah. When Shimei heard that they were in Gath, he saddled his donkey and went to King Achish in Gath, to find his slaves. He found them and brought them back home. When Solomon heard what Shimei had done, he sent for him:
Solomon	I made you promise in the Lord's name not to leave Jerusalem. And I warned you that if you ever did, you would certainly die. Did you not agree to it and say that you would obey me? Why, then, have you broken your promise and disobeyed my command? You know very well all the wrong that you did to my father David. The Lord will punish you for it. But he will bless me and he will make David's kingdom secure for ever.
Narrator	Then the king gave orders to Benaiah, who went out and killed Shimei. Solomon was now in complete control.
Cast	[This is] the word of the Lord.
All	**Thanks be to God.**

Cast: **Narrator, Solomon, Shimei.**

Solomon prays for wisdom
From 1 Kings 3.5–15

Narrator	The Lord appeared to Solomon in a dream [and asked him]:
The Lord	What would you like me to give you?
Narrator	Solomon answered:
Solomon	You always showed great love for my father David, your servant, and he was good, loyal, and honest in his relations with you. And you have continued to show him your great and constant love by giving him a son who today rules in his place. O Lord God, you have let me succeed my father as king, even though I am very young and don't know how to rule. Here I am among the people you have chosen to be your own, a people who are so many that they cannot be counted. So give me the wisdom I need to rule your people with justice and to know the difference between good and evil. Otherwise, how would I ever be able to rule this great people of yours?

Narrator	The Lord was pleased that Solomon had asked for this [and so he said to him]:
The Lord	Because you have asked for the wisdom to rule justly, instead of long life for yourself or riches or the death of your enemies, I will do what you have asked. I will give you more wisdom and understanding than anyone has ever had before or will ever have again. I will also give you what you have not asked for: all your life you will have wealth and honour, more than that of any other king. And if you obey me and keep my laws and commands, as your father David did, I will give you a long life.
Narrator	Solomon woke up and realized that God had spoken to him in the dream.
Cast	[This is] the word of the Lord.
All	**Thanks be to God.**

Cast: **Narrator, The Lord, Solomon.**

Solomon judges a difficult case
1 Kings 3.16–28

Narrator	One day two women came and presented themselves before King Solomon. [One of them said:]
Woman 1	Your Majesty, this woman and I live in the same house, and I gave birth to a baby boy at home while she was there. Two days after my child was born she also gave birth to a baby boy. Only the two of us were there in the house—no one else was present. Then one night she accidentally rolled over on her baby and smothered it. She got up during the night, took my son from my side while I was asleep, and carried him to her bed; then she put the dead child in my bed. The next morning, when I woke up and was going to feed my baby, I saw that it was dead. I looked at it more closely and saw that it was not my child.
[Narrator	But the other woman said:]
Woman 2	No! The living child is mine, and the dead one is yours!
Woman 1	No! The dead child is yours, and the living one is mine!
Narrator	And so they argued before the king. (PAUSE)
	Then King Solomon said:
Solomon	Each of you claims that the living child is hers and that the dead child belongs to the other one.
Narrator	He sent for a sword (PAUSE) [and when it was brought, he said]:
Solomon	Cut the living child in two and give each woman half of it.
Narrator	The real mother's heart was full of love for her son:
Woman 1	Please, Your Majesty, don't kill the child! Give it to her!
[Narrator	But the other woman said:]

Woman 2 (callously)	Don't give it to either of us; go ahead and cut it in two. (PAUSE)
Solomon	Don't kill the child! Give it to the first woman—she is its real mother.
Narrator	When the people of Israel heard of Solomon's decision, they were all filled with deep respect for him, because they knew then that God had given him the wisdom to settle disputes fairly.
Cast	[This is] the word of the Lord.
All	**Thanks be to God.**

Cast: **Narrator, Woman 1, Woman 2, Solomon.**

Solomon prepares to build the Temple
1 Kings 5.1–12

Narrator	King Hiram of Tyre had always been a friend of David's, and when he heard that Solomon had succeeded his father David as king he sent ambassadors to him. Solomon sent back this message to Hiram:
Solomon	You know that because of the constant wars my father David had to fight against the enemy countries all round him, he could not build a temple for the worship of the Lord his God until the Lord had given him victory over all his enemies. But now the Lord my God has given me peace on all my borders. I have no enemies, and there is no danger of attack. The Lord promised my father David:
[The Lord]	Your son, whom I will make king after you, will build a temple for me.
Solomon	And I have now decided to build that temple for the worship of the Lord my God. So send your men to Lebanon to cut down cedars for me. My men will work with them, and I will pay your men whatever you decide. As you well know, my men don't know how to cut down trees as well as yours do.
Narrator	Hiram was extremely pleased when he received Solomon's message [and he said]:
Hiram	Praise the Lord today for giving David such a wise son to succeed him as king of that great nation!
Narrator	Then Hiram sent Solomon the following message:
Hiram	I have received your message and I am ready to do what you ask. I will provide the cedars and the pine-trees. My men will bring the logs down from Lebanon to the sea, and will tie them together in rafts to float them down the coast to the place you choose. There my men will untie them, and your men will take charge of them. On your part, I would like you to supply the food for my men.

Narrator	So Hiram supplied Solomon with all the cedar and pine logs that he wanted, and Solomon provided Hiram with two thousand tons of wheat and four hundred thousand litres of pure olive-oil every year to feed his men. The Lord kept his promise and gave Solomon wisdom. There was peace between Hiram and Solomon, and they made a treaty with each other.
Cast	[This is] the word of the Lord.
All	**Thanks be to God.**

Cast: **Narrator, Solomon, The Lord** (can be the same as Solomon)**, Hiram.**

The Covenant Box is brought to the Temple
From 1 Kings 8.1–13

Narrator 1	King Solomon summoned all the leaders of the tribes and clans of Israel to come to him in Jerusalem in order to take the Lord's Covenant Box from Zion, David's City, to the Temple.
Narrator 2	The Levites and the priests also moved the Tent of the Lord's presence and all its equipment to the Temple.
Narrator 1	Then the priests carried the Covenant Box into the Temple and put it in the Most Holy Place, beneath the winged creatures. Their outstretched wings covered the box and the poles it was carried by.
Narrator 2	There was nothing inside the Covenant Box except the two stone tablets which Moses had placed there at Mount Sinai, when the Lord made a covenant with the people of Israel as they were coming from Egypt.
Narrator 1	As the priests were leaving the Temple, it was suddenly filled with a cloud shining with the dazzling light of the Lord's presence, and they could not go back in to perform their duties.
Narrator 2	Then Solomon prayed:
Solomon	You, Lord, have placed the sun in the sky, yet you have chosen to live in clouds and darkness. Now I have built a majestic temple for you, a place for you to live in for ever.
Cast	[This is] the word of the Lord.
All	**Thanks be to God.**

Cast: **Narrator 1, Narrator 2, Solomon.**

Solomon's address to the people
1 Kings 8.14–21

Narrator	As the people stood in the Temple, King Solomon turned to face them, and he asked God's blessing on them. He said:
Solomon	Praise the Lord God of Israel! He has kept the promise he made to my father David [when he said]:

313

The Lord	From the time I brought my people out of Egypt, I have not chosen any city in all the land of Israel in which a temple should be built where I would be worshipped. But I chose you, David, to rule my people.
Narrator	And Solomon continued:
Solomon	My father David planned to build a temple for the worship of the Lord God of Israel, but the Lord said to him:
The Lord	You were right in wanting to build a temple for me, but *you* will never build it. It is your son, your own son, who will build my temple.
Solomon	And now the Lord has kept his promise. I have succeeded my father as king of Israel, and I have built the Temple for the worship of the Lord God of Israel. I have also provided a place in the Temple for the Covenant Box containing the stone tablets of the covenant which the Lord made with our ancestors when he brought them out of Egypt.
Cast	[This is] the word of the Lord.
All	**Thanks be to God.**

Cast: **Narrator, Solomon, The Lord** (preferably unseen).

The final prayer
1 Kings 8.54–66

Narrator	After Solomon had finished praying to the Lord in the Temple, he stood up in front of the altar, where he had been kneeling with uplifted hands. In a loud voice he asked God's blessings on all the people assembled there.
Solomon	Praise the Lord who has given his people peace, as he promised he would. He has kept all the generous promises he made through his servant Moses. May the Lord our God be with us, as he was with our ancestors; may he never leave us, or abandon us; may he make us obedient to him, so that we will always live as he wants us to live, and keep all the laws and commands he gave our ancestors. May the Lord our God remember at all times this prayer and these petitions I have made to him. May he always be merciful to the people of Israel and to their king, according to their daily needs. And so all the nations of the world will know that the Lord alone is God—there is no other. May you, his people, always be faithful to the Lord our God, obeying all his laws and commands, as you do today.
Narrator	Then King Solomon and all the people there offered sacrifices to the Lord. He sacrificed 22,000 head of cattle and 120,000 sheep as fellowship-offerings. And so the king and all the people dedicated the Temple. That same day he also consecrated the central part of the courtyard, the area in front of the Temple, and then he offered there the sacrifices burnt whole, the grain-offerings, and the fat of the animals for the fellowship-offerings.

He did this because the bronze altar was too small for all these offerings. There at the Temple, Solomon and all the people of Israel celebrated the Festival of Shelters for seven days. There was a huge crowd of people from as far away as Hamath Pass in the north and the Egyptian border in the south. On the eighth day Solomon sent the people home. They all praised him and went home happy because of all the blessings that the Lord had given his servant David and his people Israel.

Cast	[This is] the word of the Lord.
All	**Thanks be to God.**

Cast: **Narrator, Solomon.**

God appears to Solomon again
1 Kings 9.1–9

Narrator   After King Solomon had finished building the Temple and the palace and everything else he wanted to build, the Lord appeared to him again, as he had in Gibeon. [The Lord said to him:]

The Lord   I have heard your prayer. I consecrate this Temple which you have built as the place where I shall be worshipped for ever. I will watch over it and protect it for all time. If you will serve me in honesty and integrity, as your father David did, and if you obey my laws and do everything I have commanded you, I will keep the promise I made to your father David when I told him that Israel would always be ruled by his descendants. But if you or your descendants stop following me, if you disobey the laws and commands I have given you, and worship other gods, then I will remove my people Israel from the land that I have given them. I will also abandon this Temple which I have consecrated as the place where I am to be worshipped. People everywhere will ridicule Israel and treat her with contempt. This Temple will become a pile of ruins, and everyone who passes by will be shocked and amazed. [They will ask:]

Person 1   Why did the Lord do this to this land and this Temple?

[The Lord   People will answer:]

Person 2   It is because they abandoned the Lord their God, who brought their ancestors out of Egypt.

Person 3   They gave their allegiance to other gods and worshipped them.

Person 1   That is why the Lord has brought this disaster on them.

Cast	[This is] the word of the Lord.
All	**Thanks be to God.**

Cast: **Narrator, The Lord, Person 1, Person 2, Person 3** (Persons 1–3 can be the same).

Solomon's agreement with Hiram
1 Kings 9.10–14

Narrator   It took Solomon twenty years to build the Temple and his palace. King Hiram of Tyre had provided him with all the cedar and pine and with all the gold he wanted for this work. After it was finished, King Solomon gave Hiram twenty towns in the region of Galilee. Hiram went to see them, and he did not like them. So he said to Solomon:

Hiram   So these, my brother, are the towns you have given me!

Narrator   For this reason the area is still called Cabul. Hiram had sent Solomon more than four thousand kilogrammes of gold.

Cast   [This is] the word of the Lord.
All   **Thanks be to God.**

Cast: **Narrator, Hiram**

The visit of the queen of Sheba
1 Kings 10.1–13

Narrator   The queen of Sheba heard of Solomon's fame, and she travelled to Jerusalem to test him with difficult questions. She brought with her a large group of attendants, as well as camels loaded with spices, jewels, and a large amount of gold. When she and Solomon met, she asked him all the questions that she could think of. He answered them all; there was nothing too difficult for him to explain. The queen of Sheba heard Solomon's wisdom and saw the palace he had built. She saw the food that was served at his table, the living quarters for his officials, the organization of his palace staff and the uniforms they wore, the servants who waited on him at feasts, and the sacrifices he offered in the Temple. It left her breathless and amazed. She said to King Solomon:

Queen   What I heard in my own country about you and your wisdom is true! But I couldn't believe it until I had come and seen it all for myself. But I didn't hear even half of it; your wisdom and wealth are much greater than what I was told. How fortunate are your wives! And how fortunate your servants, who are always in your presence and are privileged to hear your wise sayings! Praise the Lord your God! He has shown how pleased he is with you by making you king of Israel. Because his love for Israel is eternal, he has made you their king so that you can maintain law and justice.

Narrator   She presented to King Solomon the gifts she had brought: more than four thousand kilogrammes of gold and a very large amount of spices and jewels. The amount of spices she gave him was by far the greatest that he ever received at any time.

[Commentator]	Hiram's fleet, which had brought gold from Ophir, also brought from there a large amount of juniper wood and jewels. Solomon used the wood to build railings in the Temple and the palace, and also to make harps and lyres for the musicians. It was the finest juniper wood ever imported into Israel; none like it has ever been seen again.
Narrator	King Solomon gave the queen of Sheba everything she asked for, besides all the other customary gifts that he had generously given her. Then she and her attendants returned to the land of Sheba.
Cast	[This is] the word of the Lord.
All	**Thanks be to God.**

Cast: **Narrator, Queen, Commentator** (can be the same as Narrator).

Solomon turns away from God
From 1 Kings 11.1–13

Narrator	Solomon loved many foreign women. Besides the daughter of the king of Egypt he married Hittite women and women from Moab, Ammon, Edom, and Sidon. He married them even though the Lord had commanded the Israelites not to intermarry with these people, because they would cause the Israelites to give their loyalty to other gods. Solomon married seven hundred princesses and also had three hundred concubines. They made him turn away from God, and by the time he was old they had led him into the worship of foreign gods. He was not faithful to the Lord his God, as his father David had been. He worshipped Astarte the goddess of Sidon, and Molech the disgusting god of Ammon. He sinned against the Lord and was not true to him as his father David had been. On the mountain east of Jerusalem he built a place to worship Chemosh, the disgusting god of Moab, and a place to worship Molech, the disgusting god of Ammon. He also built places of worship where all his foreign wives could burn incense and offer sacrifices to their own gods. Even though the Lord, the God of Israel, had appeared to Solomon twice and had commanded him not to worship foreign gods, Solomon did not obey the Lord, but turned away from him. So the Lord was angry with Solomon and said to him:
The Lord	Because you have deliberately broken your covenant with me and disobeyed my commands, I promise that I will take the kingdom away from you and give it to one of your officials. However, for the sake of your father David I will not do this in your lifetime, but during the reign of your son. And I will not take the whole kingdom away from him; instead, I will leave him one tribe for the sake of my servant David and for the sake of Jerusalem, the city I have made my own.
Cast	[This is] the word of the Lord.
All	**Thanks be to God.**

Cast: **Narrator, The Lord.**

Solomon's enemies
1 Kings 11.14–25

Narrator	The Lord caused Hadad, of the royal family of Edom, to turn against Solomon. Long before this, when David had conquered Edom, Joab the commander of his army had gone there to bury the dead. He and his men remained in Edom six months, and during that time they killed every male in Edom except Hadad and some of his father's Edomite servants, who escaped to Egypt. At that time Hadad was just a child. They left Midian and went to Paran, where some other men joined them. Then they travelled to Egypt and went to the king, who gave Hadad some land and a house and provided him with food. Hadad won the friendship of the king, and the king gave his sister-in-law, the sister of Queen Tahpenes, to Hadad in marriage. She bore him a son, Genubath, who was brought up by the queen in the palace, where he lived with the king's sons. When the news reached Hadad in Egypt that David had died and that Joab the commander of the army was dead, Hadad said to the king:
Hadad	Let me go back to my own country.
[Narrator	The king asked:]
King	Why? Have I failed to give you something? Is that why you want to go back home?
[Narrator	Hadad answered the king:]
Hadad	Just let me go.
Narrator	And he went back to his country. (PAUSE) As king of Edom, Hadad was an evil, bitter enemy of Israel. God also caused Rezon son of Eliada to turn against Solomon. Rezon had fled from his master, King Hadadezer of Zobah, and had become the leader of a gang of outlaws.
[Commentator]	This happened after David had defeated Hadadezer and had slaughtered his Syrian allies.
Narrator	Rezon and his men went and lived in Damascus, where his men made him king of Syria. He was an enemy of Israel during the lifetime of Solomon.
Cast	[This is] the word of the Lord.
All	**Thanks be to God.**

Cast: **Narrator, Hadad, King, Commentator** (can be the same as Narrator).

God's promise to Jeroboam
From 1 Kings 11.26–43

Narrator	A man who turned against King Solomon was one of his officials, Jeroboam son of Nebat, from Zeredah in Ephraim. His mother was a widow named Zeruah. This is the story of the revolt. Solomon was filling in the land on the east side of Jerusalem and

repairing the city walls. Jeroboam was an able young man, and when Solomon noticed how hard he worked, he put him in charge of all the forced labour in the territory of the tribes of Manasseh and Ephraim.

One day, as Jeroboam was travelling from Jerusalem, the prophet Ahijah, from Shiloh, met him alone on the road in the open country. Ahijah took off the new robe he was wearing and tore it into twelve pieces.

Ahijah	Take ten pieces for yourself, Jeroboam, because the Lord, the God of Israel, says to you:
[The Lord]	I am going to take the kingdom away from Solomon, and I will give you ten tribes. Solomon will keep one tribe, for the sake of my servant David and for the sake of Jerusalem, the city I have chosen to be my own from the whole land of Israel. I am going to do this because Solomon has rejected me and has worshipped foreign gods. But I will not take the whole kingdom away from Solomon, and I will keep him in power as long as he lives. I will take the kingdom away from Solomon's son and will give you ten tribes, but I will let Solomon's son keep one tribe, so that I will always have a descendant of my servant David ruling in Jerusalem, the city I have chosen as the place where I am worshipped. Jeroboam, I will make you king of Israel, and you will rule over all the territory that you want. If you obey me completely, live by my laws, and win my approval by doing what I command, as my servant David did, I will always be with you. I will make you king of Israel and will make sure that your descendants rule after you, just as I have done for David. Because of Solomon's sin I will punish the descendants of David, but not for all time.
Narrator	And so Solomon tried to kill Jeroboam, but he escaped to King Shishak of Egypt and stayed there until Solomon's death. Everything else that Solomon did, his career and his wisdom, are all recorded in The History of Solomon. He was king in Jerusalem over all Israel for forty years. He died and was buried in David's City, and his son Rehoboam succeeded him as king.
Cast	[This is] the word of the Lord.
All	**Thanks be to God.**

Cast: **Narrator, Ahijah, The Lord** (can be the same as Ahijah).

The northern tribes revolt
1 Kings 12.1–24

Narrator	Rehoboam went to Shechem, where all the people of northern Israel had gathered to make him king. When Jeroboam son of Nebat, who had gone to Egypt to escape from King Solomon, heard this news, he returned from Egypt. The people of the northern tribes sent for him, and then they all went together to Rehoboam [and said to him]:

319

Person 1	Your father Solomon treated us harshly and placed heavy burdens on us.
Person 2	If you make these burdens lighter and make life easier for us, we will be your loyal subjects.
[Narrator	Rehoboam replied:]
Rehoboam	Come back in three days and I will give you my answer.
Narrator	So they left. (PAUSE) King Rehoboam consulted the older men who had served as his father Solomon's advisers:
Rehoboam	What answer do you advise me to give these people?
[Narrator	They replied:]
Senior adviser 1	If you want to serve this people well, give a favourable answer to their request—
Senior adviser 2	And they will always serve you loyally.
Narrator	But Rehoboam ignored the advice of the older men and went instead to the young men who had grown up with him and who were now his advisers. [He asked:]
Rehoboam	What do *you* advise me to do? What shall I say to the people who are asking me to make their burdens lighter?
[Narrator	They replied:]
Junior adviser 1	This is what you should tell them: 'My little finger is thicker than my father's waist!'
Junior adviser 2	Tell them, 'My father placed heavy burdens on you; I will make them even heavier. He beat you with a whip; I'll flog you with a horsewhip!' (PAUSE)
Narrator	Three days later Jeroboam and all the people returned to King Rehoboam, as he had instructed them. The king ignored the advice of the older men and spoke harshly to the people, as the younger men had advised:
Rehoboam	My father placed heavy burdens on you; I will make them even heavier. He beat you with a whip; I'll flog you with a horsewhip!
Narrator	It was the will of the Lord to bring about what he had spoken to Jeroboam son of Nebat through the prophet Ahijah from Shiloh. This is why the king did not pay any attention to the people.
	When the people saw that the king would not listen to them, they shouted:
Person 1	Down with David and his family!
Person 2	What have they ever done for us?
Persons 1 and 2	Men of Israel, let's go home!
Person 2	Let Rehoboam look out for himself!
Narrator	So the people of Israel rebelled, leaving Rehoboam as king only of the people who lived in the territory of Judah. Then King

Rehoboam sent Adoniram, who was in charge of the forced labour, to go to the Israelites, but they stoned him to death. At this, Rehoboam hurriedly got into his chariot and escaped to Jerusalem. Ever since that time the people of the northern kingdom of Israel have been in rebellion against the dynasty of David. When the people of Israel heard that Jeroboam had returned from Egypt, they invited him to a meeting of the people and made him king of Israel. Only the tribe of Judah remained loyal to David's descendants. When Rehoboam arrived in Jerusalem, he called together 180,000 of the best soldiers from the tribes of Judah and Benjamin. He intended to go to war and restore his control over the northern tribes of Israel. But God told the prophet Shemaiah to give this message to Rehoboam and to all the people of the tribes of Judah and Benjamin:

Shemaiah   Do not attack your own brothers, the people of Israel. Go home, all of you. What has happened is my will.

Narrator   They all obeyed the Lord's command and went back home.

Cast   [This is] the word of the Lord.
All   **Thanks be to God.**

Cast: **Narrator, Person 1, Person 2, Rehoboam, Senior adviser 1, Senior adviser 2** (can be the same as Senior adviser 1)**, Junior adviser 1, Junior adviser 2, Shemaiah.**

Jeroboam turns away from the Lord
1 Kings 12.25–31

Narrator   King Jeroboam of Israel fortified the town of Shechem in the hill-country of Ephraim and lived there for a while. Then he left and fortified the town of Penuel. He said to himself:

Jeroboam
(thinking)   As things are now, if my people go to Jerusalem and offer sacrifices to the Lord in the Temple there, they will transfer their allegiance to King Rehoboam of Judah and will kill me.

Narrator   After thinking it over, he made two bull-calves of gold and said to his people:

Jeroboam (to
the people)   You have been going long enough to Jerusalem to worship. People of Israel, here are your gods who brought you out of Egypt!

Narrator   He placed one of the gold bull-calves in Bethel and the other in Dan. And so the people sinned, going to worship in Bethel and in Dan. Jeroboam also built places of worship on hilltops, and he chose priests from families who were not of the tribe of Levi.

Cast   [This is] the word of the Lord.
All   **Thanks be to God.**

Cast: **Narrator, Jeroboam.**

Worship at Bethel is condemned
1 Kings 12.32—13.10

Narrator	Jeroboam instituted a religious festival on the fifteenth day of the eighth month, like the festival in Judah. On the altar in Bethel he offered sacrifices to the gold bull-calves he had made, and he placed there in Bethel the priests serving at the places of worship he had built. And on the fifteenth day of the eighth month, the day that he himself had set, he went to Bethel and offered a sacrifice on the altar in celebration of the festival he had instituted for the people of Israel. At the Lord's command a prophet from Judah went to Bethel and arrived there as Jeroboam stood at the altar to offer the sacrifice. Following the Lord's command, the prophet denounced the altar:
Prophet	O altar, altar, this is what the Lord says: A child, whose name will be Josiah, will be born to the family of David. He will slaughter on you the priests serving at the pagan altars who offer sacrifices on you, and he will burn human bones on you.
[Narrator	And the prophet went on to say:]
Prophet	This altar will fall apart, and the ashes on it will be scattered. Then you will know that the Lord has spoken through me.
Narrator	When King Jeroboam heard this, he pointed at him [and ordered]:
Jeroboam	Seize that man!
Narrator	At once the king's arm became paralysed so that he couldn't pull it back. The altar suddenly fell apart and the ashes spilt to the ground, as the prophet had predicted in the name of the Lord. [King Jeroboam said to the prophet:]
Jeroboam (to the Prophet)	Please pray for me to the Lord your God, and ask him to heal my arm!
Narrator	The prophet prayed to the Lord, and the king's arm was healed. [Then the king said to the prophet:]
Jeroboam	Come home with me and have something to eat. I will reward you for what you have done.
Prophet	Even if you gave me half your wealth, I would not go with you or eat or drink anything with you. The Lord has commanded me not to eat or drink a thing, and not to return home the same way I came.
Narrator	So he did not go back the same way he had come, but by another road.
Cast	[This is] the word of the Lord.
All	**Thanks be to God.**

Cast: **Narrator, Prophet, Jeroboam.**

The old prophet of Bethel
1 Kings 13.11–34

Narrator	There was an old prophet living in Bethel. His sons came and told him what the prophet from Judah had done in Bethel that day and what he had said to King Jeroboam. The old prophet asked them:
Old prophet	Which way did he go when he left?
Narrator	They showed him the road and he told them to saddle his donkey for him. They did so, and he rode off down the road after the prophet from Judah and found him sitting under an oak. [He asked:]
Old prophet	Are you the prophet from Judah?
Young prophet	I am.
Old prophet	Come home and have a meal with me.
Young prophet	I can't go home with you or accept your hospitality. And I won't eat or drink anything with you here, because the Lord has commanded me not to eat or drink a thing, and not to return home the same way I came.
Old prophet	I, too, am a prophet just like you, and at the Lord's command an angel told me to take you home with me and offer you my hospitality.
Narrator	But the old prophet was lying. So the prophet from Judah went home with the old prophet and had a meal with him. As they were sitting at the table, the word of the Lord came to the old prophet, and he cried out to the prophet from Judah:
Old prophet	The Lord says that you disobeyed him and did not do what he commanded. Instead, you returned and ate a meal in a place he had ordered you not to eat in. Because of this you will be killed, and your body will not be buried in your family grave.
Narrator	After they had finished eating, the old prophet saddled the donkey for the prophet from Judah, who rode off. On the way, a lion met him and killed him. His body lay on the road, and the donkey and the lion stood beside it. Some men passed by and saw the body on the road, with the lion standing near by. They went on into Bethel and reported what they had seen.
Narrator	When the old prophet heard about it, he said:
Old prophet	That is the prophet who disobeyed the Lord's command! And so the Lord sent the lion to attack and kill him, just as the Lord said he would.
Narrator	Then he said to his sons:
Old prophet	Saddle my donkey for me.
Narrator	They did so, and he rode off and found the prophet's body lying on the road, with the donkey and the lion still standing by it. The →

	lion had not eaten the body or attacked the donkey. The old prophet picked up the body, put it on the donkey, and brought it back to Bethel to mourn over it and bury it. He buried it in his own family grave, and he and his sons mourned over it, saying:
Old prophet	Oh my brother, my brother!
Narrator	After the burial, the prophet said to his sons:
Old prophet	When I die, bury me in this grave and lay my body next to his. The words that he spoke at the Lord's command against the altar in Bethel and against all the places of worship in the towns of Samaria will surely come true.
Narrator	King Jeroboam of Israel still did not turn from his evil ways, but continued to choose priests from ordinary families to serve at the altars he had built. He ordained as priest anyone who wanted to be one. This sin on his part brought about the ruin and total destruction of his dynasty.
Cast	[This is] the word of the Lord.
All	**Thanks be to God.**

Cast: **Narrator, Old prophet, Young prophet.**

The death of Jeroboam's son
1 Kings 14.1–18

Narrator	King Jeroboam's son Abijah fell ill. Jeroboam said to his wife:
Jeroboam	Disguise yourself so that no one will recognize you, and go to Shiloh, where the prophet Ahijah lives, the one who said I would be king of Israel. Take him ten loaves of bread, some cakes, and a jar of honey. Ask him what is going to happen to our son, and he will tell you.
Narrator	So she went to Ahijah's home in Shiloh. Old age had made Ahijah blind. The Lord had told him that Jeroboam's wife was coming to ask him about her son, who was ill. And the Lord told Ahijah what to say. When Jeroboam's wife arrived, she pretended to be someone else. But when Ahijah heard her coming in the door, he said:
Ahijah	Come in. I know you are Jeroboam's wife. Why are you pretending to be someone else? I have bad news for you. Go and tell Jeroboam that this is what the Lord, the God of Israel, says to him:
The Lord	I chose you from among the people and made you the ruler of my people Israel. I took the kingdom away from David's descendants and gave it to you. But you have not been like my servant David, who was completely loyal to me, obeyed my commands, and did only what I approve of. You have committed far greater sins than those who ruled before you. You have rejected me and have aroused my anger by making idols and metal images to worship. Because of this I will bring disaster on your dynasty and will kill all

your male descendants, young and old alike. I will get rid of your family; they will be swept away like dung. Any members of your family who die in the city will be eaten by dogs, and any who die in the open country will be eaten by vultures. I, the Lord, have spoken.

Narrator And Ahijah went on to say to Jeroboam's wife:

Ahijah Now go back home. As soon as you enter the town your son will die. All the people of Israel will mourn for him and bury him. He will be the only member of Jeroboam's family who will be properly buried, because he is the only one with whom the Lord, the God of Israel, is pleased. The Lord is going to place a king over Israel who will put an end to Jeroboam's dynasty. The Lord will punish Israel, and she will shake like a reed shaking in a stream. He will uproot the people of Israel from this good land which he gave to their ancestors, and he will scatter them beyond the River Euphrates, because they have aroused his anger by making idols of the goddess Asherah. The Lord will abandon Israel because Jeroboam sinned and led the people of Israel into sin.

Narrator Jeroboam's wife went back to Tirzah. Just as she entered her home, the child died. The people of Israel mourned for him and buried him, as the Lord had said through his servant, the prophet Ahijah.

Cast [This is] the word of the Lord.
All **Thanks be to God.**

Cast: **Narrator, Jeroboam, Ahijah, The Lord** (can be the same as Ahijah).

Elijah and the drought
1 Kings 17.1–7

Narrator A prophet named Elijah, from Tishbe in Gilead, said to King Ahab:

Elijah In the name of the Lord, the living God of Israel, whom I serve, I tell you that there will be no dew or rain for the next two or three years until I say so.

Narrator Then the Lord said to Elijah:

The Lord Leave this place and go east and hide yourself near the brook of Cherith, east of the Jordan. The brook will supply you with water to drink, and I have commanded ravens to bring you food there.

Narrator So Elijah obeyed the Lord's command, and went and stayed by the brook of Cherith. He drank water from the brook, and ravens brought him bread and meat every morning and every evening. After a while the brook dried up because of the lack of rain.

Cast [This is] the word of the Lord.
All **Thanks be to God.**

Cast: **Narrator, Elijah, The Lord.**

Elijah and the widow in Zarephath
1 Kings 17.8–16

Narrator	The Lord said to Elijah:
The Lord	Now go to the town of Zarephath, near Sidon, and stay there. I have commanded a widow who lives there to feed you.
Narrator	So Elijah went to Zarephath, and as he came to the gate of the town, he saw a widow gathering firewood.
	[He said to her:]
Elijah	Please bring me a drink of water.
[Narrator	As she was going to get it, he called out:]
Elijah (calling)	And please bring me some bread, too.
[Narrator	She answered:]
Widow	By the living Lord your God I swear that I haven't got any bread. All I have is a handful of flour in a bowl and a drop of olive-oil in a jar. I came here to gather some firewood to take back home and prepare what little I have for my son and me. That will be our last meal, and then we will starve to death.
Elijah	Don't worry. Go ahead and prepare your meal. But first make a small loaf from what you have and bring it to me, and then prepare the rest for you and your son. For this is what the Lord, the God of Israel, says:
[The Lord]	The bowl will not run out of flour or the jar run out of oil before the day that I, the Lord, send rain.
Narrator	The widow went and did as Elijah had told her, and all of them had enough food for many days. As the Lord had promised through Elijah, the bowl did not run out of flour nor did the jar run out of oil.
Cast	[This is] the word of the Lord.
All	**Thanks be to God.**

Cast: **Narrator, The Lord, Elijah, Widow.**

The widow's son
1 Kings 17.17–24

Narrator	[Some time later] the son of the widow in Zarephath fell ill; he got worse and worse, and finally he died. [She said to Elijah:]
Widow	Man of God, why did you do this to me? Did you come here to remind God of my sins and so cause my son's death?
[Narrator	Elijah said:]
Elijah	Give the boy to me.

326

Narrator	He took the boy from her arms, carried him upstairs to the room where he was staying, and laid him on the bed. Then he prayed aloud:
Elijah	O Lord my God, why have you done such a terrible thing to this widow? She has been kind enough to take care of me, and now you kill her son!
Narrator	Then Elijah stretched himself out on the boy three times and prayed:
Elijah	O Lord my God, restore this child to life!
Narrator	The Lord answered Elijah's prayer; the child started breathing again and revived. Elijah took the boy back downstairs to his mother [and said to her]:
Elijah	Look, your son is alive!
[Narrator	She answered:]
Widow	Now I *know* that you are a man of God and that the Lord really speaks through you!
Cast	[This is] the word of the Lord.
All	**Thanks be to God.**

Cast: **Narrator, Widow, Elijah.**

Elijah and Ahab
1 Kings 18.1–19

Narrator	In the third year of the drought, the Lord said to Elijah:
The Lord	Go and present yourself to King Ahab, and I will send rain.
Narrator	So Elijah started out. The famine in Samaria was at its worst, so Ahab called in Obadiah, who was in charge of the palace.
Commentator	Obadiah was a devout worshipper of the Lord, and when Jezebel was killing the Lord's prophets, Obadiah took a hundred of them, hid them in caves in two groups of fifty, and provided them with food and water.
Narrator	Ahab said to Obadiah:
Ahab	Let us go and look at every spring and every river-bed in the land to see if we can find enough grass to keep the horses and mules alive. Maybe we won't have to kill any of our animals.
Narrator	They agreed on which part of the land each one would explore, and set off in different directions. As Obadiah was on his way, he suddenly met Elijah. He recognized him and bowed low before him:
Obadiah	Is it really you, sir?
Elijah	Yes, I'm Elijah. Go and tell your master the king that I am here.

Obadiah	What have I done that you want to put me in danger of being killed by King Ahab? By the living Lord, your God, I swear that the king has made a search for you in every country in the world. Whenever the ruler of a country reported that you were not in his country, Ahab would require that ruler to swear that you could not be found. And now you want me to go and tell him that you are here? What if the spirit of the Lord carries you off to some unknown place as soon as I leave? Then, when I tell Ahab that you are here, and he can't find you, he will put me to death. Remember that I have been a devout worshipper of the Lord ever since I was a boy. Haven't you heard that when Jezebel was killing the prophets of the Lord I hid a hundred of them in caves, in two groups of fifty, and supplied them with food and water? So how can you order me to go and tell the king that you are here? He will kill me!
Elijah	By the living Lord, whom I serve, I promise that I will present myself to the king today.
Narrator	So Obadiah went to King Ahab and told him, and Ahab set off to meet Elijah. When Ahab saw him, he said:
Ahab	So there you are—the worst troublemaker in Israel!
Elijah	I'm not the troublemaker. You are—you and your father. You are disobeying the Lord's commands and worshipping the idols of Baal. Now order all the people of Israel to meet me at Mount Carmel. Bring along the prophets of Baal and the prophets of the goddess Asherah who are supported by Queen Jezebel.
Cast	[This is] the word of the Lord.
All	**Thanks be to God.**

Cast: **Narrator, The Lord, Commentator** (can be the same as Narrator), **Ahab, Obadiah, Elijah.**

Elijah and the prophets of Baal
1 Kings 18.20–39

Narrator	Ahab summoned all the Israelites and the prophets of Baal to meet at Mount Carmel. Elijah went up to the people:
Elijah (to the people)	How much longer will it take you to make up your minds? If the Lord is God, worship him; but if Baal is God, worship him!
Narrator	But the people didn't say a word.
Elijah	I am the only prophet of the Lord still left, but there are 450 prophets of Baal. Bring two bulls; let the prophets of Baal take one, kill it, cut it in pieces, and put it on the wood—but don't light the fire. I will do the same with the other bull. Then let the prophets of Baal pray to their god, and I will pray to the Lord, and the one who answers by sending fire—he is God.
Narrator	The people shouted their approval. (PAUSE) Then Elijah said to the prophets of Baal:

Elijah (to Prophets)	Since there are so many of you, you take a bull and prepare it first. Pray to your god, but don't set fire to the wood.
Narrator	They took the bull that was brought to them, prepared it, and prayed to Baal until noon. [They shouted:]
Prophets (shouting)	Answer us, Baal!
Narrator	They kept dancing round the altar they had built. But no answer came. (PAUSE) At noon Elijah started making fun of them:
Elijah	Pray louder! He is a god! Maybe he is day-dreaming or relieving himself, or perhaps he's gone on a journey! Or maybe he's sleeping, and you've got to wake him up!
Narrator	So the prophets prayed louder and cut themselves with knives and daggers, according to their ritual, until blood flowed. They kept on ranting and raving until the middle of the afternoon; but no answer came, not a sound was heard. (PAUSE) Then Elijah said to the people:
Elijah (to the people)	Come closer to me.
Narrator	And they all gathered round him. He set about repairing the altar of the Lord which had been torn down. He took twelve stones, one for each of the twelve tribes named after the sons of Jacob, the man to whom the Lord had given the name Israel. With these stones he rebuilt the altar for the worship of the Lord. He dug a trench round it, large enough to hold almost fourteen litres of water. Then he placed the wood on the altar, cut the bull in pieces, and laid it on the wood. [He said:]
Elijah	Fill four jars with water and pour it on the offering and the wood.
Narrator	They did so. (PAUSE) [And he said:]
Elijah	Do it again.
Narrator	And they did. (PAUSE) [He said:]
Elijah	Do it once more.
Narrator	And they did. The water ran down round the altar and filled the trench. (PAUSE) At the hour of the afternoon sacrifice the prophet Elijah approached the altar:
Elijah	O Lord, the God of Abraham, Isaac, and Jacob, prove now that you are the God of Israel and that I am your servant and have done all this at your command. Answer me, Lord, answer me, so that this people will know that you, the Lord, are God, and that you are bringing them back to yourself.
Narrator	The Lord sent fire down, and it burnt up the sacrifice, the wood, and the stones, scorched the earth and dried up the water in the

$\rightarrow$

trench. When the people saw this, they threw themselves on the ground [and exclaimed:]

Person 1
(exclaiming)   The Lord is God!

Person 2
(exclaiming)   The Lord alone is God!

Cast   [This is] the word of the Lord.
All   **Thanks be to God.**

Cast: **Narrator, Elijah, Prophets** (2 or more), **Person 1, Person 2.**

The end of the drought
1 Kings 18.41–46

Narrator   Elijah said to King Ahab:

Elijah   Now, go and eat. I hear the roar of rain approaching.

Narrator   While Ahab went to eat, Elijah climbed to the top of Mount Carmel, where he bowed down to the ground, with his head between his knees. He said to his servant:

Elijah   Go and look towards the sea.

Narrator   The servant went (PAUSE) and returned [saying:]

Servant   I didn't see anything.

Narrator   Seven times in all Elijah told him to go and look. The seventh time he returned . . . [and said:]

Servant   I saw a little cloud no bigger than a man's hand, coming up from the sea.

Elijah   Go to King Ahab and tell him to get into his chariot and go back home before the rain stops him. (PAUSE)

Narrator   In a little while the sky was covered with dark clouds, the wind began to blow, and heavy rain began to fall. Ahab got into his chariot and started back to Jezreel. The power of the Lord came on Elijah; he fastened his clothes tight round his waist and ran ahead of Ahab all the way to Jezreel.

Cast   [This is] the word of the Lord.
All   **Thanks be to God.**

Cast: **Narrator, Elijah, Servant.**

Elijah on Mount Sinai
1 Kings 19.1–18

Narrator   King Ahab told his wife Jezebel everything that Elijah had done and how he had put all the prophets of Baal to death. She sent a message to Elijah:

330

Jezebel	May the gods strike me dead if by this time tomorrow I don't do the same thing to you that you did to the prophets.
Narrator	Elijah was afraid, and fled for his life; he took his servant and went to Beersheba in Judah.
	Leaving the servant there, Elijah walked a whole day into the wilderness. He stopped and sat down in the shade of a tree and wished he would die:
Elijah	It's too much, Lord. Take away my life; I might as well be dead!
Narrator	He lay down under the tree and fell asleep. (PAUSE) Suddenly, an angel touched him:
Angel	Wake up and eat.
Narrator	He looked round, and saw a loaf of bread and a jar of water near his head. He ate and drank, and lay down again. The Lord's angel returned and woke him up a second time:
Angel	Get up and eat, or the journey will be too much for you.
Narrator	Elijah got up, ate and drank, and the food gave him enough strength to walk forty days to Sinai, the holy mountain. There he went into a cave to spend the night. (PAUSE)
	Suddenly the Lord spoke to him:
The Lord	Elijah, what are you doing here?
Elijah	Lord God Almighty, I have always served you—you alone. But the people of Israel have broken their covenant with you, torn down your altars, and killed all your prophets. I am the only one left—and they are trying to kill me!
The Lord	Go out and stand before me on top of the mountain.
Narrator	Then the Lord passed by and sent a furious wind that split the hills and shattered the rocks—but the Lord was not in the wind. The wind stopped blowing, and then there was an earthquake—but the Lord was not in the earthquake. After the earthquake there was a fire—but the Lord was not in the fire. And after the fire, there was the soft whisper of a voice. (PAUSE)
	When Elijah heard it, he covered his face with his cloak and went out and stood at the entrance of the cave. [A voice said to him:]
The Lord	Elijah, what are you doing here?
Elijah	Lord God Almighty, I have always served you—you alone. But the people of Israel have broken their covenant with you, torn down your altars, and killed all your prophets. I am the only one left—and they are trying to kill me.
The Lord	Return to the wilderness near Damascus, then enter the city and anoint Hazael as king of Syria; anoint Jehu son of Nimshi as king of Israel, and anoint Elisha son of Shaphat from Abel Meholah to succeed you as prophet. Anyone who escapes being put to death by Hazael will be killed by Jehu, and anyone who escapes Jehu will be killed by Elisha. Yet I will leave seven thousand people alive in

→

Israel—all those who are loyal to me and have not bowed to Baal or kissed his idol.

Cast	[This is] the word of the Lord.
All	**Thanks be to God.**

Cast: **Narrator, Jezebel, Elijah, Angel, The Lord.**

The call of Elisha
1 Kings 19.19–21

Narrator	Elijah left Sinai and found Elisha ploughing with a team of oxen; there were eleven teams ahead of him, and he was ploughing with the last one. Elijah took off his cloak and put it on Elisha. Elisha then left his oxen, ran after Elijah [and said]:
Elisha	Let me kiss my father and mother goodbye, and then I will go with you.
[Narrator	Elijah answered:]
Elijah	All right, go back. I'm not stopping you!
Narrator	Then Elisha went to his team of oxen, killed them, and cooked the meat, using the yoke as fuel for the fire. He gave the meat to the people, and they ate it. Then he went and followed Elijah as his helper.
Cast	[This is] the word of the Lord.
All	**Thanks be to God.**

Cast: **Narrator, Elisha, Elijah.**

War with Syria
1 Kings 20.1–22

Narrator	King Benhadad of Syria gathered all his troops and, supported by thirty-two other rulers with their horses and chariots, he marched up, laid siege to Samaria, and launched attacks against it. He sent messengers into the city to King Ahab of Israel [to say]:
Messenger 1 (to Ahab)	King Benhadad demands that you surrender to him your silver and gold—
Messenger 2	Your women and the strongest of your children.
Narrator	Ahab answered:
Ahab (to Messengers 1 and 2)	Tell my lord, King Benhadad, that I agree; he can have me and everything I own.
Narrator	Later the messengers came back to Ahab with another demand from Benhadad:
Messenger 1	I sent you word that you were to hand over to me your silver and gold, your women and your children.

Messenger 2	Now, however, I will send my officers to search your palace and the homes of your officials, and to take everything they consider valuable.
Messenger 1	They will be there about this time tomorrow.
Narrator	King Ahab called in all the leaders of the country and said:
Ahab (to Persons 1 and 2)	You see that this man wants to ruin us. He sent me a message demanding my wives and children, my silver and gold, and I agreed.
Narrator	The leaders and the people answered:
Person 1	Don't pay any attention to him.
Person 2	Don't give in.
[Narrator	So Ahab replied to Benhadad's messengers:]
Ahab (to Messengers 1 and 2)	Tell my lord the king that I agreed to his first demand, but I cannot agree to the second.
Narrator	The messengers left and then returned with another message from Benhadad:
Messenger 1	I will bring enough men to destroy this city of yours and carry off the rubble in their hands.
Messenger 2	May the gods strike me dead if I don't!
[Narrator	King Ahab answered:]
Ahab	Tell King Benhadad that a real soldier does his boasting *after* a battle, not before it.
Narrator	Benhadad received Ahab's answer as he and his allies, the other rulers, were drinking in their tents. He ordered his men to get ready to attack the city, so they moved into position. (PAUSE) Meanwhile, a prophet went to King Ahab:
Prophet	The Lord says, 'Don't be afraid of that huge army! I will give you victory over it today, and you will know that I am the Lord.'
Ahab	Who will lead the attack?
Prophet	The Lord says that the young soldiers under the command of the district governors are to do it.
Ahab	Who will command the main force?
Prophet	You.
Narrator	So the king called out the young soldiers who were under the district commanders, 232 in all. Then he called out the Israelite army, a total of seven thousand men. The attack began at noon, as Benhadad and his thirty-two allies were getting drunk in their tents. The young soldiers advanced first. Scouts sent out by Benhadad reported to him that a group of soldiers was coming out of Samaria. [He ordered:]

333

Benhadad	Take them alive, no matter whether they are coming to fight or to ask for peace.
Narrator	The young soldiers led the attack, followed by the Israelite army, and each one killed the man he fought. The Syrians fled, with the Israelites in hot pursuit, but Benhadad escaped on horseback, accompanied by some of the cavalry. King Ahab took to the field, captured the horses and chariots, and inflicted a severe defeat on the Syrians. Then the prophet went to King Ahab:
Prophet	Go back and build up your forces, and make careful plans, because the king of Syria will attack again next spring.
Cast	[This is] the word of the Lord.
All	**Thanks be to God.**

Cast: **Narrator, Messenger 1, Messenger 2** (can be the same as Messenger 1), **Ahab, Person 1, Person 2, Prophet, Benhadad.**

The second Syrian attack
1 Kings 20.23–34

Narrator	King Benhadad's officials said to him:
Official 1	The gods of Israel are mountain gods, and that is why the Israelites defeated us. But we will certainly defeat them if we fight them in the plains.
Official 2	Now, remove the thirty-two rulers from their commands and replace them with field commanders.
Official 1	Then call up an army as large as the one that deserted you, with the same number of horses and chariots.
Official 2	We will fight the Israelites in the plains, and this time we will defeat them.
Narrator	King Benhadad agreed and followed their advice. The following spring he called up his men and marched with them to the city of Aphek to attack the Israelites. The Israelites were called up and equipped; they marched out and camped in two groups facing the Syrians. The Israelites looked like two small flocks of goats compared with the Syrians, who spread out over the countryside. A prophet went to King Ahab [and said]:
Prophet	This is what the Lord says, 'Because the Syrians say that I am a god of the hills and not of the plains, I will give you victory over their huge army, and you and your people will know that I am the Lord.'
Narrator	For seven days the Syrians and the Israelites stayed in their camps, facing each other. On the seventh day they started fighting, and the Israelites killed a hundred thousand Syrians. The survivors fled into the city of Aphek, where the city walls fell on twenty-seven thousand of them. (PAUSE) Benhadad also escaped into the city and took refuge in the back room of a house. His officials went to him and said:

Official 1	We have heard that the Israelite kings are merciful.
Official 2	Give us permission to go to the king of Israel with sackcloth round our waists and ropes round our necks.
Official 1	Maybe he will spare your life.
Narrator	So they wrapped sackcloth round their waists and ropes round their necks and went to Ahab:
Official 1	Your servant Benhadad pleads with you for his life.
[Narrator	Ahab answered:]
Ahab	Is he still alive? Good! He's like a brother to me!
Narrator	Benhadad's officials were watching for a good sign, and when Ahab said 'brother', they took it up at once:
Official 1	As you say, Benhadad is your brother!
Ahab	Bring him to me.
Narrator	When Benhadad arrived, Ahab invited him to get in the chariot with him. [Benhadad said to him:]
Benhadad	I will restore to you the towns my father took from your father, and you may set up a commercial centre for yourself in Damascus, just as my father did in Samaria.
Ahab	On these terms, then, I will set you free.
Narrator	He made a treaty with him and let him go.
Cast	[This is] the word of the Lord.
All	**Thanks be to God.**

Cast: **Narrator, Official 1, Official 2** (can be the same as Official 1), **Prophet, Ahab, Benhadad.**

A prophet condemns Ahab
1 Kings 20.35–43

Narrator	At the Lord's command a member of a group of prophets ordered a fellow-prophet to hit him. But he refused [so he said to him]:
Prophet	Because you have disobeyed the Lord's command, a lion will kill you as soon as you leave me.
Narrator	And as soon as he left, a lion came along and killed him. Then this same prophet went to another man [and said]:
Prophet	Hit me!
Narrator	This man did so; he hit him a hard blow and hurt him. The prophet bandaged his face with a cloth, to disguise himself, and went and stood by the road, waiting for the king of Israel to pass. As the king was passing by, the prophet called out to him:
Prophet (calling)	Your Majesty! (PAUSE)

→

I was fighting in the battle when a soldier brought a captured enemy to me and said, 'Guard this man; if he escapes, you will pay for it with your life or else pay a fine of three thousand pieces of silver.' But I got busy with other things, and the man escaped.

[Narrator	The king answered:]
Ahab	You have pronounced your own sentence, and you will have to pay the penalty.
Narrator	The prophet tore the cloth from his face, and at once the king recognized him as one of the prophets. [The prophet then said to the king:]
Prophet (firmly)	This is the word of the Lord: 'Because you allowed the man to escape whom I had ordered to be killed, you will pay for it with your life, and your army will be destroyed for letting his army escape.'
Narrator	The king went back home to Samaria, worried and depressed.
Cast	[This is] the word of the Lord.
All	**Thanks be to God.**

Cast: **Narrator, Prophet, Ahab.**

Naboth's vineyard
1 Kings 21.1–29

Narrator	Near King Ahab's palace in Jezreel there was a vineyard owned by a man named Naboth. One day Ahab said to Naboth:
Ahab	Let me have your vineyard; it is close to my palace, and I want to use the land for a vegetable garden. I will give you a better vineyard for it, or, if you prefer, I will pay you a fair price.
[Narrator	Naboth replied:]
Naboth	I inherited this vineyard from my ancestors. The Lord forbid that I should let you have it!
Narrator	Ahab went home, depressed and angry over what Naboth had said to him. He lay down on his bed, facing the wall, and would not eat. His wife Jezebel went to him [and asked]:
Jezebel	Why are you so depressed? Why won't you eat?
Ahab	Because of what Naboth said to me. I offered to buy his vineyard, or, if he preferred, to give him another one for it, but he told me that I couldn't have it!
Jezebel	Well, are you the king or aren't you? Get out of bed, cheer up and eat. I will get you Naboth's vineyard!
Narrator	Then she wrote some letters, signed them with Ahab's name, sealed them with his seal, and sent them to the officials and leading citizens of Jezreel. [The letters said:]

Jezebel	Proclaim a day of fasting, call the people together, and give Naboth the place of honour. Get a couple of scoundrels to accuse him to his face of cursing God and the king. Then take him out of the city and stone him to death.
Narrator	The officials and leading citizens of Jezreel did what Jezebel had commanded. They proclaimed a day of fasting, called the people together, and gave Naboth the place of honour. The two scoundrels publicly accused him of cursing God and the king, and so he was taken outside the city and stoned to death. The message was sent to Jezebel: 'Naboth has been put to death.' (PAUSE)
	As soon as Jezebel received the message, she said to Ahab:
Jezebel	Naboth is dead. Now go and take possession of the vineyard which he refused to sell to you.
Narrator	At once Ahab went to the vineyard to take possession of it. (PAUSE)
	Then the Lord said to Elijah, the prophet from Tishbe:
The Lord	Go to King Ahab of Samaria. You will find him in Naboth's vineyard, about to take possession of it. Tell him that I, the Lord, say to him: 'After murdering the man, are you taking over his property as well?' Tell him that this is what I say: 'In the very place that the dogs licked up Naboth's blood they will lick up your blood!'
Narrator	When Ahab saw Elijah, he said:
Ahab	Have you caught up with me, my enemy?
Elijah	Yes, I have. You have devoted yourself completely to doing what is wrong in the Lord's sight. So the Lord says to you:
[The Lord]	I will bring disaster on you. I will do away with you and get rid of every male in your family, young and old alike. Your family will become like the family of King Jeroboam son of Nebat and like the family of King Baasha son of Ahijah, because you have stirred up my anger by leading Israel into sin.
Elijah	And concerning Jezebel, the Lord says that dogs will eat her body in the city of Jezreel. Any of your relatives who die in the city will be eaten by dogs, and any who die in the open country will be eaten by vultures.
Commentator	There was no one else who had devoted himself so completely to doing wrong in the Lord's sight as Ahab—all at the urging of his wife Jezebel. He committed the most shameful sins by worshipping idols as the Amorites had done, whom the Lord had driven out of the land as the people of Israel advanced.
Narrator	When Elijah finished speaking, Ahab tore his clothes, took them off, and put on sackcloth. He refused food, slept in the sackcloth, and went about gloomy and depressed. (PAUSE)
	The Lord said to the prophet Elijah:

The Lord	Have you noticed how Ahab has humbled himself before me? Since he has done this, I will not bring disaster on him during his lifetime; it will be during his son's lifetime that I will bring disaster on Ahab's family.
Cast	[This is] the word of the Lord.
All	**Thanks be to God.**

Cast: **Narrator, Ahab, Naboth, Jezebel, The Lord, Elijah, Commentator** (can be the same as Narrator).

The prophet Micaiah warns Ahab
1 Kings 22.1–28

Narrator	There was peace between Israel and Syria for two years, but in the third year King Jehoshaphat of Judah went to see King Ahab of Israel. Ahab asked his officials:
Ahab	Why is it that we have not done anything to get back Ramoth in Gilead from the king of Syria? It belongs to us!
[Narrator	And Ahab asked Jehoshaphat:]
Ahab (to Jehoshaphat)	Will you go with me to attack Ramoth?
[Narrator	Jehoshaphat answered:]
Jehoshaphat	I am ready when you are, and so are my soldiers and my cavalry. But first let's consult the Lord.
Narrator	So Ahab called in the prophets, about four hundred of them [and asked them]:
Ahab	Should I go and attack Ramoth, or not?
Prophet 1	Attack it.
Prophet 2	The Lord will give you victory.
[Narrator	But Jehoshaphat asked:]
Jehoshaphat	Isn't there another prophet through whom we can consult the Lord?
[Narrator	Ahab answered:]
Ahab	There is one more, Micaiah son of Imlah. But I hate him, because he never prophesies anything good for me; it's always something bad.
Jehoshaphat	You shouldn't say that!
Narrator	Then Ahab called in a court official and told him to go and fetch Micaiah at once. The two kings, dressed in their royal robes, were sitting on their thrones at the threshing-place just outside the gate of Samaria, and all the prophets were prophesying in front of them. One of them, Zedekiah son of Chenaanah, made iron horns and said to Ahab:

Prophet 1	This is what the Lord says: 'With these you will fight the Syrians and totally defeat them.'
Narrator	All the other prophets said the same thing:
Prophet 2	March against Ramoth and you will win. The Lord will give you victory.
Narrator	Meanwhile, the official who had gone to get Micaiah said to him:
Official (firmly)	All the other prophets have prophesied success for the king, and you had better do the same.
[Narrator	But Micaiah answered:]
Micaiah	By the living Lord I promise that I will say what he tells me to!
Narrator	Micaiah appeared before King Ahab [and the king asked him:]
Ahab	Micaiah, should King Jehoshaphat and I go and attack Ramoth, or not?
Narrator	Micaiah answered:
Micaiah (casually)	Attack! Of course you'll win. The Lord will give you victory.
Ahab (frustrated)	When you speak to me in the name of the Lord, tell the truth! How many times do I have to tell you that?
Micaiah (sadly)	I can see the army of Israel scattered over the hills like sheep without a shepherd. And the Lord said:
[The Lord]	These men have no leader; let them go home in peace.
[Narrator	Ahab said to Jehoshaphat:]
Ahab (crossly to Jehoshaphat)	Didn't I tell you that he never prophesies anything good for me? It's always something bad!
[Narrator	Micaiah went on:]
Micaiah	Now listen to what the Lord says! I saw the Lord sitting on his throne in heaven, with all his angels standing beside him. The Lord asked:
The Lord	Who will deceive Ahab so that he will go and be killed at Ramoth?
Micaiah	Some of the angels said one thing, and others said something else, until a spirit stepped forward, approached the Lord, and said:
A spirit	I will deceive him.
[Micaiah	The Lord asked:]
The Lord	How?
A spirit	I will go and make all Ahab's prophets tell lies.
The Lord	Go and deceive him. You will succeed.
[Narrator	And Micaiah concluded:]

Micaiah	This is what has happened. The Lord has made these prophets of yours lie to you. But he himself has decreed that you will meet with disaster!
Narrator	Then the prophet Zedekiah went up to Micaiah and slapped his face:
Zedekiah (angrily)	Since when did the Lord's spirit leave me and speak to you?
Micaiah (severely)	You will find out when you go into some back room to hide.
[**Narrator**	Then King Ahab ordered one of his officers:]
Ahab (to Official)	Arrest Micaiah and take him to Amon, the governor of the city, and to Prince Joash. Tell them to throw him in prison and to put him on bread and water until I return safely.
Micaiah (exclaiming)	If you return safely, then the Lord has not spoken through me!
(to all)	Listen, everyone, to what I have said!
Cast	[This is] the word of the Lord.
All	**Thanks be to God.**

Cast: **Narrator, Ahab, Jehoshaphat, Prophet 1, Prophet 2, Official, Micaiah, The Lord, A spirit, Zedekiah.**

The death of Ahab
From 1 Kings 22.29–40

Narrator	King Ahab of Israel and King Jehoshaphat of Judah went to attack the city of Ramoth in Gilead. Ahab said to Jehoshaphat:
Ahab	As we go into battle, I will disguise myself, but you wear your royal garments.
Narrator	So the king of Israel went into battle in disguise. The king of Syria had ordered his thirty-two chariot commanders to attack no one else except the king of Israel. So when they saw King Jehoshaphat, they all thought that he was the king of Israel, and they turned to attack him. But when he cried out, they realized that he was not the king of Israel, and they stopped their attack. By chance, however, a Syrian soldier shot an arrow which struck King Ahab between the joints of his armour. He cried out to his chariot driver:
Ahab	I'm wounded! Turn round and pull out of the battle!
Narrator	While the battle raged on, King Ahab remained propped up in his chariot, facing the Syrians. The blood from his wound ran down and covered the bottom of the chariot, and at evening he died. Near sunset the order went out through the Israelite ranks:
Commander	Every man go back to his own country and city!

Narrator So died King Ahab. His body was taken to Samaria and buried. Everything else that King Ahab did, including an account of his palace decorated with ivory and all the cities he built, is recorded in The History of the Kings of Israel. At his death his son Ahaziah succeeded him as king.

Cast [This is] the word of the Lord.
All **Thanks be to God.**

Cast: **Narrator, Ahab, Commander.**

2 KINGS

Elijah and King Ahaziah
2 Kings 1.1–18

Narrator	After the death of King Ahab of Israel, the country of Moab rebelled against Israel. King Ahaziah of Israel fell off the balcony on the roof of his palace in Samaria and was seriously injured. So he sent some messengers to consult Baalzebub, the god of the Philistine city of Ekron, in order to find out whether or not he would recover. But an angel of the Lord commanded Elijah, the prophet from Tishbe, to go and meet the messengers of King Ahaziah and ask them:
Elijah	Why are you going to consult Baalzebub, the god of Ekron? Is it because you think there is no god in Israel? Tell the king that the Lord says, 'You will not recover from your injuries; you will die!'
Narrator	Elijah did as the Lord commanded, and the messengers returned to the king. He asked:
King	Why have you come back?
[Narrator	They answered:]
Messenger 1	We were met by a man who told us to come back and tell you that the Lord says to you, 'Why are you sending messengers to consult Baalzebub, the god of Ekron?'
Messenger 2	'Is it because you think there is no god in Israel?'
Messenger 3	'You will not recover from your injuries; you will die!'
King	What did the man look like?
Messenger 1	He was wearing a cloak made of animal skins—
Messenger 2	Tied with a leather belt.
King (exclaiming)	It's Elijah!
Narrator	Then he sent an officer with fifty men to get Elijah. The officer found him sitting on a hill [and said to him]:
Messenger 1	Man of God, the king orders you to come down.
Elijah	If I am a man of God, may fire come down from heaven and kill you and your men!
Narrator	At once fire came down and killed the officer and his men. The king sent another officer with fifty men, who went up to Elijah:

Messenger 2	Man of God, the king orders you to come down at once!
Elijah	If I am a man of God, may fire come down from heaven and kill you and your men!
Narrator	At once fire came down and killed the officer and his men.
	Once more the king sent an officer with fifty men. He went up the hill, fell on his knees in front of Elijah, and pleaded:
Messenger 3	Man of God, be merciful to me and my men. Spare our lives! The two other officers and their men were killed by fire from heaven; but please be merciful to me!
Narrator	The angel of the Lord said to Elijah:
Angel	Go down with him, and don't be afraid.
Narrator	So Elijah went with the officer to the king and said to him:
Elijah	This is what the Lord says: 'Because you sent messengers to consult Baalzebub, the god of Ekron—as if there were no god in Israel to consult—you will not get well; you will die!'
Narrator	Ahaziah died, as the Lord had said through Elijah. Ahaziah had no sons, so his brother Joram succeeded him as king in the second year of the reign of Jehoram son of Jehoshaphat, king of Judah. Everything else that King Ahaziah did is recorded in The History of the Kings of Israel.
Cast	[This is] the word of the Lord.
All	**Thanks be to God.**

Cast: **Narrator, Elijah, King, Messenger 1, Messenger 2, Messenger 3** (Messengers 1, 2, and 3 *cannot* be the same), **Angel.**

Elijah is taken up to heaven
2 Kings 2.1–15

Narrator	The time came for the Lord to take Elijah up to heaven in a whirlwind. Elijah and Elisha set out from Gilgal, and on the way Elijah said to Elisha:
Elijah	Now stay here; the Lord has ordered me to go to Bethel.
Elisha	I swear by my loyalty to the living Lord and to you that I will not leave you.
Narrator	So they went on to Bethel (PAUSE). A group of prophets who lived there went to Elisha and asked him:
Prophet 1	Do you know that the Lord is going to take your master away from you today?
Elisha	Yes, I know. But let's not talk about it.
Narrator	Then Elijah said to Elisha:

Elijah	Now stay here; the Lord has ordered me to go to Jericho.
Elisha	I swear by my loyalty to the living Lord and to you that I will not leave you.
Narrator	So they went on to Jericho. (PAUSE)
	A group of prophets who lived there went to Elisha and asked him:
Prophet 2	Do you know that the Lord is going to take your master away from you today?
Elisha	Yes, I know. But let's not talk about it.
Narrator	Then Elijah said to Elisha:
Elijah	Now stay here; the Lord has ordered me to go to the River Jordan.
[Narrator	But Elisha answered:]
Elisha	I swear by my loyalty to the living Lord and to you that I will not leave you.
Narrator	So they went on, and fifty of the prophets followed them to the Jordan. Elijah and Elisha stopped by the river, and the fifty prophets stood a short distance away. Then Elijah took off his cloak, rolled it up, and struck the water with it; the water divided, and he and Elisha crossed to the other side on dry ground. [There, Elijah said to Elisha:]
Elijah	Tell me what you want me to do for you before I am taken away.
Elisha	Let me receive the share of your power that will make me your successor.
Elijah	That is a difficult request to grant. But you will receive it if you see me as I am being taken away from you; if you don't see me, you won't receive it.
Narrator	They kept talking as they walked on; then suddenly a chariot of fire pulled by horses of fire came between them, and Elijah was taken up to heaven by a whirlwind. Elisha saw it and cried out to Elijah:
Elisha	My father, my father! Mighty defender of Israel! You are gone!
Narrator	And he never saw Elijah again. (PAUSE)
	In grief, Elisha tore his cloak in two. Then he picked up Elijah's cloak that had fallen from him, and went back and stood on the bank of the Jordan. He struck the water with Elijah's cloak [and said]:
Elisha	Where is the Lord, the God of Elijah?
Narrator	Then he struck the water again, and it divided, and he walked over to the other side. The fifty prophets from Jericho saw him [and said]:
Prophets 1 and **2**	The power of Elijah is on Elisha!
Cast	[This is] the word of the Lord.
All	**Thanks be to God.**

Cast: **Narrator, Elijah, Elisha, Prophet 1, Prophet 2.**

344

The prophets search for Elijah
2 Kings 2.15–18

Narrator	The fifty prophets from Jericho saw Elisha strike the water so that it divided, and walk over to the other side [and they said:]
Prophet 1 (amazed)	The power of Elijah is on Elisha!
Narrator	They went to meet him and bowed down before him [and said:]
Prophet 2	There are fifty of us here, all strong men. Let us go and look for your master. Maybe the spirit of the Lord has carried him away and left him on some mountain or in some valley.
Narrator	Elisha answered:
Elisha	No, you must not go.
Narrator	But they insisted until he gave in and let them go. (PAUSE) The fifty of them went and looked high and low for Elijah for three days, but didn't find him. Then they returned to Elisha, who had waited at Jericho, and he said to them:
Elisha	Didn't I tell you not to go?
Cast All	[This is] the word of the Lord. **Thanks be to God.**

Cast: **Narrator, Prophet 1, Prophet 2, Elisha.**

Miracles of Elisha
2 Kings 2.19–25

Narrator	Some men from Jericho went to Elisha:
Man 1	As you know, sir, this is a fine city.
Man 2	But the water is bad and causes miscarriages.
Narrator	Elisha ordered:
Elisha	Put some salt in a new bowl, and bring it to me.
Narrator	They brought it to him, and he went to the spring, and threw the salt in the water. [He said:]
Elisha	This is what the Lord says: 'I make this water pure, and it will not cause any more deaths or miscarriages.'
Narrator	And that water has been pure ever since, just as Elisha said it would be. (PAUSE)
	Elisha left Jericho to go to Bethel, and on the way some boys came out of a town and made fun of him. They shouted:

Boys 1 and **2**	Get out of here—
Boy 2	Baldy!
Narrator	Elisha turned round, glared at them, and cursed them in the name of the Lord. Then two she-bears came out of the woods and tore the boys to pieces. Elisha went on to Mount Carmel, and later returned to Samaria.
Cast	[This is] the word of the Lord.
All	**Thanks be to God.**

Cast: **Narrator, Man 1, Man 2** (can be the same as Man 1), **Elisha, Boy 1, Boy 2.**

War between Israel and Moab
2 Kings 3.1–27

Narrator	In the eighteenth year of the reign of King Jehoshaphat of Judah, Joram son of Ahab became king of Israel, and he ruled in Samaria for twelve years. He sinned against the Lord, but he was not as bad as his father or his mother Jezebel; he pulled down the image his father had made for the worship of Baal. Yet, like King Jeroboam son of Nebat before him, he led Israel into sin, and would not stop. King Mesha of Moab bred sheep, and every year he gave as tribute to the king of Israel 100,000 lambs, and the wool from 100,000 sheep. But when King Ahab of Israel died, Mesha rebelled against Israel. At once King Joram left Samaria and gathered all his troops. He sent word to King Jehoshaphat of Judah:
Joram	The king of Moab has rebelled against me; will you join me in war against him?
Narrator	King Jehoshaphat replied:
Jehoshaphat	I will. I am at your disposal, and so are my men and my horses. What route shall we take for the attack?
Joram	We will go the long way, through the wilderness of Edom.
Narrator	So King Joram and the kings of Judah and Edom set out. After marching for seven days, they ran out of water, and there was none left for the men or the pack-animals. [King Joram exclaimed:]
Joram (exclaiming)	We're done for! The Lord has put the three of us at the mercy of the king of Moab!
Jehoshaphat	Is there a prophet here through whom we can consult the Lord?
Narrator	An officer of King Joram's forces answered:
Officer	Elisha son of Shaphat is here. He was Elijah's assistant.
Jehoshaphat	He is a true prophet.

Narrator	So the three kings went to Elisha. (PAUSE)
	Elisha said to the king of Israel:
Elisha	Why should I help you? Go and consult those prophets that your father and mother consulted.
[Narrator	Joram replied:]
Joram	No! It is the Lord who has put us three kings at the mercy of the king of Moab.
Elisha	By the living Lord, whom I serve, I swear that I would have nothing to do with you if I didn't respect your ally King Jehoshaphat of Judah. Now get me a musician.
Narrator	As the musician played his harp, the power of the Lord came on Elisha [and he said]:
Elisha	This is what the Lord says: 'Dig ditches all over this dry stream bed. Even though you will not see any rain or wind, this stream bed will be filled with water, and you, your livestock, and your pack-animals will have plenty to drink.'
[Narrator	And Elisha continued:]
Elisha	But this is an easy thing for the Lord to do; he will also give you victory over the Moabites. You will conquer all their beautiful fortified cities; you will cut down all their fruit-trees, stop all their springs, and ruin all their fertile fields by covering them with stones.
Narrator	The next morning, at the time of the regular morning sacrifice, water came flowing from the direction of Edom, and covered the ground. (PAUSE)
	When the Moabites heard that the three kings had come to attack them, all the men who could bear arms, from the oldest to the youngest, were called out and stationed at the border. When they got up the following morning, the sun was shining on the water, making it look as red as blood. [They exclaimed:]
Moabite 1	It's blood!
Moabite 2	The three enemy armies must have fought and killed each other!
Moabite 1	Let's go and loot their camp!
Narrator	But when they reached the camp, the Israelites attacked them and drove them back. The Israelites kept up the pursuit, slaughtering the Moabites and destroying their cities. As they passed a fertile field, every Israelite would throw a stone on it until finally all the fields were covered; they also stopped up the springs and cut down the fruit-trees. At last only the capital city of Kir Heres was left, and the slingers surrounded it and attacked it. When the king of Moab realized that he was losing the battle, he took seven hundred swordsmen with him and tried to force his way through the enemy lines and escape to the king of Syria, but he failed. So he took his eldest son, who was to succeed him as king, and offered him on the city wall as a sacrifice to the god of Moab. The

347 →

Israelites were terrified and so they drew back from the city and returned to their own country.

Cast	[This is] the word of the Lord.
All	**Thanks be to God.**

Cast: **Narrator, Joram, Jehoshaphat, Officer, Elisha, Moabite 1, Moabite 2** (can be the same as Moabite 1).

Elisha helps a poor widow
2 Kings 4.1–7

Narrator	The widow of a member of a group of prophets went to Elisha [and said]:
Widow	Sir, my husband has died! As you know, he was a God-fearing man, but now a man he owed money to has come to take away my two sons as slaves in payment for my husband's debt.
Elisha	What shall I do for you? Tell me, what have you got at home?
Widow	Nothing at all, except a small jar of olive-oil.
Elisha	Go to your neighbours and borrow as many empty jars as you can. Then you and your sons go into the house, close the door, and start pouring oil into the jars. Set each one aside as soon as it is full.
Narrator	So the woman went into her house with her sons, closed the door, took the small jar of olive-oil, and poured oil into the jars as her sons brought them to her. When they had filled all the jars, she asked if there were any more. One of her sons answered:
Son	That was the last one.
Narrator	And the olive-oil stopped flowing. (PAUSE) She went back to Elisha, the prophet, who said to her:
Elisha	Sell the olive-oil and pay all your debts, and there will be enough money left over for you and your sons to live on.
Cast	[This is] the word of the Lord.
All	**Thanks be to God.**

Cast: **Narrator, Widow, Elisha, Son.**

Elisha and the rich woman from Shunem
2 Kings 4.8–37

Narrator	One day Elisha went to Shunem, where a rich woman lived. She invited him to a meal, and from then on every time he went to Shunem he would have his meals at her house. She said to her husband:
Woman	I am sure that this man who comes here so often is a holy man. Let's build a small room on the roof, put a bed, a table, a chair, and a lamp in it, and he can stay there whenever he visits us.

Narrator	One day Elisha returned to Shunem and went up to his room to rest. He told his servant Gehazi to go and call the woman. When she came, he said to Gehazi:
Elisha	Ask her what I can do for her in return for all the trouble she has had in providing for our needs. Maybe she would like me to go to the king or the army commander and put in a good word for her.
Narrator	She answered:
Woman	I have all I need here among my own people.
Narrator	Elisha asked Gehazi:
Elisha	What can I do for her then?
[Narrator	He answered:]
Gehazi	Well, she has no son, and her husband is an old man.
Elisha	Tell her to come here.
Narrator	She came and stood in the doorway, and Elisha said to her:
Elisha	By this time next year you will be holding a son in your arms.
Woman (exclaiming)	Oh! Please, sir, don't lie to me. You are a man of God!
Narrator	But, as Elisha had said, at about that time the following year she gave birth to a son. (PAUSE)
	Some years later, at harvest time, the boy went out one morning to join his father, who was in the field with the harvest workers. Suddenly he cried out to his father:
Boy	My head hurts! My head hurts!
Narrator	The father said to the servant:
Father	Carry the boy to his mother.
Narrator	The servant carried the boy back to his mother, who held him in her lap until noon, at which time he died. She carried him up to Elisha's room, put him on the bed and left, closing the door behind her. Then she called her husband and said to him:
Woman	Send a servant here with a donkey. I need to go to the prophet Elisha. I'll be back as soon as I can.
Father	Why do you have to go today? It's neither a Sabbath nor a New Moon Festival.
Woman	Never mind.
Narrator	Then she had the donkey saddled, and ordered the servant:
Woman	Make the donkey go as fast as it can, and don't slow down, unless I tell you to.
Narrator	So she set out, and went to Mount Carmel, where Elisha was. (PAUSE)

→

Elisha saw her coming while she was still some distance away, and said to his servant Gehazi:

Elisha Look—there comes the woman from Shunem! Hurry to her and find out if everything is all right with her, her husband, and her son.

Narrator She told Gehazi that everything was all right, but when she came to *Elisha* she bowed down before him and took hold of his feet. Gehazi was about to push her away [but Elisha said:]

Elisha
(to Gehazi) Leave her alone. Can't you see she's deeply distressed? And the Lord has not told me a thing about it.

[Narrator The woman said to him:]

Woman
(distressed) Sir, did I ask you for a son? Didn't I tell you not to raise my hopes?

Narrator Elisha turned to Gehazi [and said:]

Elisha
(to Gehazi) Hurry! Take my stick and go. Don't stop to greet anyone you meet, and if anyone greets you, don't take time to answer. Go straight to the house and hold my stick over the boy.

Woman
(to Elisha) I swear by my loyalty to the living Lord and to you that I will not leave you!

Narrator So the two of them started back together. Gehazi went on ahead and held Elisha's stick over the child, but there was no sound or any other sign of life. So he went back to meet Elisha:

Gehazi The boy didn't wake up. (PAUSE)

Narrator When Elisha arrived, he went alone into the room and saw the boy lying dead on the bed. He closed the door and prayed to the Lord. Then he lay down on the boy, placing his mouth, eyes, and hands on the boy's mouth, eyes, and hands. As he lay stretched out over the boy, the boy's body started to get warm. Elisha got up, walked about the room, and then went back and again stretched himself over the boy. The boy sneezed seven times, and then opened his eyes. Elisha called Gehazi and told him to call the boy's mother. [When] she came in [he said to her:]

Elisha
(to Woman) Here's your son.

Narrator She fell at Elisha's feet, with her face touching the ground; then she took her son and left.

Cast [This is] the word of the Lord.
All **Thanks be to God.**

Cast: **Narrator, Woman, Elisha, Gehazi, Boy, Father.**

Two more miracles of Elisha
2 Kings 4.38—44

Narrator	Once, when there was a famine throughout the land, Elisha returned to Gilgal. While he was teaching a group of prophets, he told his servant to put a big pot on the fire and make some stew for them. One of them went out in the fields to get some herbs. He found a wild vine, and picked as many gourds as he could carry. He brought them back and sliced them up into the stew, not knowing what they were. The stew was poured out for the men to eat, but as soon as they tasted it they exclaimed to Elisha:
Prophet	It's poisoned!
Narrator	And they wouldn't eat it. Elisha asked for some meal, and threw it into the pot:
Elisha	Pour out some more stew for them.
Narrator	And then there was nothing wrong with it. (PAUSE)
	Another time, a man came from Baal Shalishah, bringing Elisha twenty loaves of bread made from the first barley harvested that year, and some freshly-cut ears of corn. Elisha told his servant to feed the group of prophets with this, but he answered:
Man	Do you think this is enough for a hundred men?
Elisha	Give it to them to eat, because the Lord says that they will eat and still have some left over.
Narrator	So the servant set the food before them, and, as the Lord had said, they all ate and there was still some left over.
Cast	[This is] the word of the Lord.
All	**Thanks be to God.**

Cast: **Narrator, Prophet, Elisha, Man.**

Naaman is cured
2 Kings 5.1–14 [15]

Narrator	Naaman, the commander of the Syrian army, was highly respected and esteemed by the king of Syria, because through Naaman the Lord had given victory to the Syrian forces. He was a great soldier, but he suffered from leprosy. In one of their raids against Israel, the Syrians had carried off a little Israelite girl, who became a servant of Naaman's wife. One day she said to her mistress:
Girl	I wish that my master could go to the prophet who lives in Samaria! He would cure him of his disease.
Narrator	When Naaman heard of this, he went to the king and told him what the girl had said. The king said:
King of Syria	Go to the king of Israel (PAUSE) and take this letter to him.

Narrator	So Naaman set out, taking thirty thousand pieces of silver, six thousand pieces of gold, and ten changes of fine clothes. The letter that he took read:
King of Syria	This letter will introduce my officer Naaman. I want you to cure him of his disease.
Narrator	When the king of Israel read the letter, he tore his clothes in dismay:
King of Israel (exclaiming)	How can the king of Syria expect me to cure this man? Does he think that I am God, with the power of life and death? It's plain that he is trying to start a quarrel with me!
Narrator	When the prophet Elisha heard what had happened, he sent word to the king:
Elisha	Why are you so upset? Send the man to *me*, and I'll show him that there is a prophet in Israel!
Narrator	So Naaman went with his horses and chariot, and stopped at the entrance to Elisha's house. Elisha sent a servant out to tell him to go and wash himself seven times in the River Jordan, and he would be completely cured of his disease. But Naaman left in a rage:
Naaman (angrily)	I thought that he would at least come out to me, pray to the Lord his God, wave his hand over the diseased spot, and cure me! Besides, aren't the rivers Abana and Pharpar, back in Damascus, better than any river in Israel? I could have washed in them and been cured!
Narrator	His servants went up to him [and said]:
Servant 1	Sir, if the prophet had told you to do something difficult, you would have done it.
Servant 2	Now why can't you just wash yourself, as he said, and be cured?
Narrator	So Naaman went down to the Jordan, dipped himself in it seven times, as Elisha had instructed, and he was completely cured. His flesh became firm and healthy, like that of a child. [He returned to Elisha with all his men and said:
Naaman	Now I know that there is no god but the God of Israel; so please, sir, accept a gift from me.]
Cast	[This is] the word of the Lord.
All	**Thanks be to God.**

Cast: **Narrator, Girl, King of Syria, King of Israel, Elisha, Naaman, Servant 1, Servant 2** (can be the same as Servant 1).

Naaman's gift
2 Kings 5.15–27

Narrator	Naaman, when he was cured, returned to Elisha with all his men and said:
Naaman	Now I know that there is no god but the God of Israel; so please, sir, accept a gift from me.

Narrator	Elisha answered:
Elisha	By the living Lord, whom I serve, I swear that I will not accept a gift.
Narrator	Naaman insisted that he accept it, but he would not. So Naaman said:
Naaman	If you won't accept my gift, then let me have two mule-loads of earth to take home with me, because from now on I will not offer sacrifices or burnt-offerings to any god except the Lord. So I hope that the Lord will forgive me when I accompany my king to the temple of Rimmon, the god of Syria, and worship him. Surely the Lord will forgive me!
Elisha	Go in peace.
Narrator	Naaman left. He had gone only a short distance, when Elisha's servant Gehazi said to himself:
Gehazi	My master has let Naaman get away without paying a thing! He should have accepted what that Syrian offered him. By the living Lord, I will run after him and get something from him.
Narrator	So he set off after Naaman. When Naaman saw a man running after him, he got down from his chariot to meet him.
Naaman	Is something wrong?
Gehazi	No, but my master sent me to tell you that just now two members of the group of prophets in the hill-country of Ephraim arrived, and he would like you to give them three thousand pieces of silver and two changes of fine clothes.
Naaman	Please take six thousand pieces of silver.
Narrator	Naaman insisted on it, tied up the silver in two bags, gave them and two changes of fine clothes to two of his servants, and sent them on ahead of Gehazi. When they reached the hill where Elisha lived, Gehazi took the two bags and carried them into the house. Then he sent Naaman's servants back. (PAUSE)
	He went back into the house, and Elisha asked him:
Elisha	Where have you been?
Gehazi (hesitantly)	Oh, nowhere, sir.
Elisha	Wasn't I there in spirit when the man got out of his chariot to meet you? This is no time to accept money and clothes, olive-groves and vineyards, sheep and cattle, or servants! And now Naaman's disease will come upon you, and you and your descendants will have it for ever!
Narrator	When Gehazi left, he had the disease—his skin was as white as snow.
Cast	[This is] the word of the Lord.
All	**Thanks be to God.**

Cast: **Narrator, Naaman, Elisha, Gehazi.**

The recovery of the axe-head
2 Kings 6.1–7

Narrator	One day the group of prophets that Elisha was in charge of complained to him:
Prophet 1	The place where we live is too small! Give us permission to go to the Jordan and cut down some trees, so that we can build a place to live.
[Narrator	Elisha answered:]
Elisha	All right.
Narrator	One of them urged him to go with them; he agreed, and they set out together. When they arrived at the Jordan, they began to work. As one of them was cutting down a tree, suddenly his iron axe-head fell in the water. [He exclaimed to Elisha:]
Prophet 2 (exclaiming)	What shall I do, sir? It was a borrowed axe!
Elisha	Where did it fall?
Narrator	The man showed him the place, and Elisha cut off a stick, threw it in the water, and made the axe-head float.
Elisha (firmly)	Take it out.
Narrator	And the man bent down and picked it up.
Cast	[This is] the word of the Lord.
All	**Thanks be to God.**

Cast: **Narrator, Prophet 1, Elisha, Prophet 2.**

The Syrian army is defeated
2 Kings 6.8–23

Narrator	The king of Syria was at war with Israel. He consulted his officers and chose a place to set up his camp. But Elisha sent word to the king of Israel, warning him not to go near that place, because the Syrians were waiting in ambush there. So the king of Israel warned the men who lived in that place, and they were on guard. This happened several times. The Syrian king became greatly upset over this; he called in his officers:
King of Syria	Which one of you is on the side of the king of Israel?
[Narrator	One of them answered:]
Officer	No one is, Your Majesty. The prophet Elisha tells the king of Israel what you say even in the privacy of your own room.
King of Syria	Find out where he is, and I will capture him. (PAUSE)
Narrator	When he was told that Elisha was in Dothan, he sent a large force there with horses and chariots. They reached the town at night

and surrounded it. Early the next morning Elisha's servant got up, went out of the house, and saw the Syrian troops with their horses and chariots surrounding the town. He went back to Elisha:

Servant
(exclaiming)   We are doomed, sir! What shall we do?

Elisha   Don't be afraid. We have more on our side than they have on theirs.

[Narrator   Then Elisha prayed:]

Elisha
(praying)   O, Lord, open his eyes and let him see!

Narrator   The Lord answered his prayer, and Elisha's servant looked up and saw the hillside covered with horses and chariots of fire all round Elisha. (PAUSE)

When the Syrians attacked, Elisha prayed:

Elisha   O Lord, strike these men blind!

Narrator   The Lord answered his prayer and struck them blind. Then Elisha went to them [and said]:

Elisha   You are on the wrong road; this is not the town you are looking for. Follow me, and I will lead you to the man you are after.

Narrator   And he led them to Samaria. As soon as they had entered the city, Elisha prayed:

Elisha   Open their eyes, Lord, and let them see.

Narrator   The Lord answered his prayer; he restored their sight, and they saw that they were inside Samaria. When the king of Israel saw the Syrians, he asked Elisha:

King of Israel
(excitedly)   Shall I kill them, sir? Shall I kill them?

Elisha   No, not even soldiers you had captured in combat would you put to death. Give them something to eat and drink, and let them return to their king.

Narrator   So the king of Israel provided a great feast for them; and after they had eaten and drunk, he sent them back to the king of Syria. From then on the Syrians stopped raiding the land of Israel.

Cast   [This is] the word of the Lord.
All   **Thanks be to God.**

Cast: **Narrator, King of Syria, Officer, Servant, Elisha, King of Israel.**

The siege of Samaria
2 Kings 6.24—7.2

Narrator   King Benhadad of Syria led his entire army against Israel and laid siege to the city of Samaria. As a result of the siege the food shortage in the city was so severe that a donkey's head cost eighty pieces of silver, and two hundred grammes of vegetables cost five pieces of silver. The king of Israel was walking by on the city wall when a woman cried out:

Woman   Help me, Your Majesty!

Narrator   He replied:

King of Israel   If the Lord won't help you, what help can I provide? Have I got any wheat or wine? What's your trouble?

Woman   The other day this woman here suggested that we eat my child, and then eat her child the next day. So we cooked my son and ate him. The next day I told her that we would eat her son, but she had hidden him!

Narrator   Hearing this, the king tore his clothes in dismay, and the people who were close to the wall could see that he was wearing sackcloth under his clothes.

King of Israel
(exclaiming)   May God strike me dead if Elisha is not beheaded before the day is over!

Narrator   And he sent a messenger to get Elisha. (PAUSE)

Meanwhile, Elisha was at home with some elders who were visiting him. Before the king's messenger arrived, Elisha said to the elders:

Elisha   That murderer is sending someone to kill me! Now, when he gets here, shut the door and don't let him come in. The king himself will be just behind him.

Narrator   He had hardly finished saying this, when the king arrived [and said]:

King of Israel   It's the Lord who has brought this trouble on us! Why should I wait any longer for him to do something?

Elisha   Listen to what the Lord says! By this time tomorrow you will be able to buy in Samaria three kilogrammes of the best wheat or six kilogrammes of barley for one piece of silver.

Narrator   The personal attendant of the king said to Elisha:

Attendant   That can't happen—not even if the Lord himself were to send grain at once!

Elisha   You will see it happen, but you will never eat any of the food.

Cast   [This is] the word of the Lord.
All   **Thanks be to God.**

Cast: **Narrator, Woman, King of Israel, Elisha, Attendant.**

The siege is lifted
2 Kings 7.3–20

Narrator	There were four men with leprosy at the entrance of the city gate of Samaria. They said to each other:
Man 1	Why stay here until we die?
Man 2	If we say, 'We'll go into the city'—the famine is there, and we will die.
Man 1	And if we stay here, we will die.
Man 2	Let's go over to the camp of the Syrians, and surrender.
Man 1	If they spare us, we live; if they kill us, then we die.
Narrator	At dusk they got up and went to the camp of the Syrians. When they reached the edge of the camp, not a man was there, for the Lord had caused the Syrians to hear the sound of chariots and horses and a great army, so that they said to one another:
Syrian	Look, the king of Israel has hired the Hittite and Egyptian kings to attack us!
Narrator	So they got up and fled in the dusk and abandoned their tents and their horses and donkeys. They left the camp as it was and ran for their lives. (PAUSE)
	The men who had leprosy reached the edge of the camp and entered one of the tents. They ate and drank, and carried away silver, gold and clothes, and went off and hid them. They returned and entered another tent and took some things from it and hid them also. [Then they said to each other:]
Man 1	We're not doing right.
Man 2	This is a day of good news and we are keeping it to ourselves.
Man 1	If we wait until daylight, punishment will overtake us.
Man 2	Let's go at once and report this to the royal palace.
Narrator	So they went and called out to the city gatekeepers [and told them]:
Man 1 (calling)	We went into the Syrian camp and not a man was there.
Man 2	Not a sound of anyone.
Man 1	Only tethered horses and donkeys.
Man 2	And the tents were left just as they were.
Narrator	The gatekeepers shouted the news, and it was reported within the palace. The king got up in the night and said to his officers:
King	I will tell you what the Syrians have done to us. They know we are starving; so they have left the camp to hide in the countryside, thinking, 'They will surely come out, and then we will take them alive and get into the city.'

Narrator	One of his officers answered:
Officer	Make some men take five of the horses that are left in the city. Their plight will be like that of all the Israelites left there—yes, they will only be like these Israelites who are doomed. So let us send them to find out what happened.
Narrator	So they selected two chariots with their horses, and the king sent them after the Syrian army. He commanded the drivers:
King	Go and find out what has happened.
Narrator	They followed them as far as the Jordan, and they found the whole road strewn with the clothing and equipment the Syrians had thrown away in their headlong flight. So the messengers returned and reported to the king. Then the people went out and plundered the camp of the Syrians. So a measure of flour sold for a shekel, and two measures of barley sold for a shekel, as the Lord had said. Now the king had put the officer on whose arm he leaned in charge at the gate, and the people trampled him in the gateway, and he died, just as the man of God had foretold when the king came down to his house. It happened as the man of God had said to the king:
Voice of Elisha	About this time tomorrow, a measure of flour will sell for a shekel and two measures of barley for a shekel at the gate of Samaria.
Narrator	The officer had said to the man of God:
Voice of Officer	Look, even if the Lord should open the floodgates of the heavens, could this happen?
Narrator	The man of God had replied:
Voice of Elisha	You will see it with your own eyes, but you will not eat any of it!
Narrator	And that is exactly what happened to him, for the people trampled him in the gateway, and he died.
Cast All	[This is] the word of the Lord. **Thanks be to God.**

Cast: **Narrator, Man 1, Man 2, Syrian, King, Officer, Voice of Elisha** (as if from a distance), **Voice of Officer** (as if from a distance—can be the same as Officer).

Elisha and King Benhadad of Syria
From 2 Kings 8.7–15

Narrator	Elisha went to Damascus at a time when King Benhadad of Syria was ill. When the king was told that Elisha was there, he said to Hazael, one of his officials:
Benhadad	Take a gift to the prophet, and ask him to consult the Lord to find out whether or not I am going to get well.
Narrator	So Hazael loaded forty camels with all kinds of the finest products of Damascus and went to Elisha. Hazael met him:

Hazael	Your servant King Benhadad has sent me to ask you whether or not he will recover from his illness.
[Narrator	Elisha answered:]
Elisha	The Lord has revealed to me that he will die; but go to him and tell him that he will recover from his illness.
Narrator	Then Elisha stared at him with a horrified look on his face until Hazael became ill at ease. Suddenly Elisha burst into tears.
Hazael	Why are you crying, sir?
Elisha	Because I know the horrible things you will do against the people of Israel.
Hazael	How could I ever be that powerful? I'm a nobody!
Elisha	The Lord has shown me that you will be king of Syria.
Narrator	Hazael went back to Benhadad [who asked him]:
Benhadad	What did Elisha say?
Hazael	He told me that you would certainly get well.
Narrator	But on the following day Hazael took a blanket, soaked it in water, and smothered the king. And Hazael succeeded Benhadad as king of Syria.
Cast	[This is] the word of the Lord.
All	**Thanks be to God.**

Cast: **Narrator, Benhadad, Hazael, Elisha.**

Jehu is anointed king of Israel
2 Kings 9.1–13

Narrator	The prophet Elisha called one of the young prophets:
Elisha	Get ready and go to Ramoth in Gilead. Take this jar of olive-oil with you, and when you get there look for Jehu, the son of Jehoshaphat and grandson of Nimshi. Take him to a private room away from his companions, pour this olive-oil on his head, and say, 'The Lord proclaims that he anoints you king of Israel.' Then leave there as fast as you can.
Narrator	So the young prophet went to Ramoth, where he found the army officers in a conference. He said:
Young prophet	Sir, I have a message for you.
Narrator	Jehu asked:
Jehu	Which one of us are you speaking to?
Young prophet	To you, sir.
Narrator	Then the two of them went indoors, and the young prophet poured the olive-oil on Jehu's head and said to him:
Young prophet	The Lord, the God of Israel, proclaims:

[The Lord]	I anoint you king of my people Israel. You are to kill your master the king, that son of Ahab, so that I may punish Jezebel for murdering my prophets and my other servants. All Ahab's family and descendants are to die; I will get rid of every male in his family, young and old alike. I will treat his family as I did the families of King Jeroboam of Israel and of King Baasha of Israel. Jezebel will not be buried; her body will be eaten by dogs in the territory of Jezreel.
Narrator	After saying this, the young prophet left the room and fled. (PAUSE) Jehu went back to his fellow-officers, who asked him:
Officer 1	Is everything all right?
Officer 2	What did that crazy fellow want with you?
Narrator	Jehu answered:
Jehu	You know what he wanted.
Officer 2	No we don't!
Officer 1	Tell us what he said!
Jehu	He told me that the Lord proclaims: 'I anoint you king of Israel.'
Narrator	At once Jehu's fellow-officers spread their cloaks at the top of the steps for Jehu to stand on, blew trumpets, and shouted:
Officers 1 and **2**	Jehu is king!
Cast **All**	[This is] the word of the Lord. **Thanks be to God.**

Cast: **Narrator, Elisha, Young prophet, Jehu, [The Lord** (preferably unseen)**], Officer 1, Officer 2.**

King Joram of Israel is killed
2 Kings 9.14–26

Narrator	Jehu plotted against King Joram, who was in Jezreel, where he had gone to recover from the wounds which he had received in the battle at Ramoth against King Hazael of Syria. So Jehu said to his fellow-officers:
Jehu	If you are with me, make sure that no one slips out of Ramoth to go and warn the people in Jezreel.
Narrator	Then he got into his chariot and set off for Jezreel. Joram had still not recovered, and King Ahaziah of Judah was there, visiting him. A guard on duty in the watch-tower at Jezreel saw Jehu and his men approaching. He called out:
Guard (calling)	I see some men riding up!
Narrator	Joram replied:
Joram	Send a horseman to find out if they are friends or enemies.
Narrator	The messenger rode out to Jehu [and said to him]:

Messenger	The king wants to know if you come as a friend.
[Narrator	Jehu answered:]
Jehu	That's none of your business! Fall in behind me.
Narrator	The guard on the watch-tower reported that the messenger had reached the group but was not returning. Another messenger was sent out, who asked Jehu the same question. [Again Jehu answered:]
Jehu	That's none of your business! Fall in behind me.
Narrator	Once more the guard reported that the messenger had reached the group but was not returning [and he added]:
Guard (calling)	The leader of the group is driving his chariot like a madman, just like Jehu!
[Narrator	King Joram ordered:]
Joram	Get my chariot ready.
Narrator	It was done, and he and King Ahaziah rode out, each in his own chariot, to meet Jehu. They met him at the field which had belonged to Naboth. [Joram asked him:]
Joram	Are you coming in peace?
[Narrator	Jehu answered:]
Jehu	How can there be peace when we still have all the witchcraft and idolatry that your mother Jezebel started?
Joram	It's treason, Ahaziah!
Narrator	Joram turned his chariot round and fled. Jehu drew his bow, and with all his strength shot an arrow that struck Joram in the back and pierced his heart. Joram fell dead in his chariot, and Jehu said to his aide Bidkar:
Jehu	Get his body and throw it in the field that belonged to Naboth. Remember that when you and I were riding together behind King Joram's father Ahab, the Lord spoke these words against Ahab:
[The Lord]	I saw the murder of Naboth and his sons yesterday. And I promise that I will punish you here in this same field.
Narrator	Jehu ordered his aide:
Jehu	Take Joram's body, and throw it in the field that belonged to Naboth, so as to fulfil the Lord's promise.
Cast	[This is] the word of the Lord.
All	**Thanks be to God.**

Cast: **Narrator, Jehu, Guard** (from a distance), **Joram, Messenger, [The Lord** (preferably unseen)].

Queen Jezebel is killed
2 Kings 9.30–37

Narrator	Jehu arrived in Jezreel. Jezebel, having heard what had happened, put on eyeshadow, arranged her hair, and stood looking down at the street from a window in the palace. As Jehu came through the gate, she called out:
Jezebel (calling)	You Zimri! You assassin! Why are you here?
Narrator	Jehu looked up and shouted:
Jehu (shouting)	Who is on my side?
Narrator	Two or three palace officials looked down at him from a window, and Jehu said to them:
Jehu	Throw her down!
Narrator	They threw her down, and her blood spattered the wall and the horses. Jehu drove his horses and chariot over her body, entered the palace, and had a meal. Only then did he say:
Jehu	Take that damned woman and bury her; after all, she is a king's daughter.
Narrator	But the men who went to bury her found nothing except her skull, and the bones of her hands and feet. When they reported this to Jehu, he said:
Jehu	This is what the Lord said would happen, when he spoke through his servant Elijah:
[Elijah]	Dogs will eat Jezebel's body in the territory of Jezreel. Her remains will be scattered so that no one will be able to identify them.
Cast	[This is] the word of the Lord.
All	**Thanks be to God.**

Cast: **Narrator, Jezebel, Jehu, [Elijah** (preferably unseen)**]**.

The descendants of Ahab are killed
2 Kings 10.1–11

Narrator	There were seventy descendants of King Ahab living in the city of Samaria. Jehu wrote a letter and sent copies to the rulers of the city, to the leading citizens, and to the guardians of Ahab's descendants. The letter read:
Jehu	You are in charge of the king's descendants and you have at your disposal chariots, horses, weapons, and fortified cities. So then, as soon as you receive this letter, you are to choose the best qualified of the king's descendants, make him king, and fight to defend him.
Narrator	The rulers of Samaria were terrified.

Ruler	How can we oppose Jehu, when neither King Joram nor King Ahaziah could?
Narrator	So the officer in charge of the palace and the official in charge of the city, together with the leading citizens and the guardians, sent this message to Jehu:
Officer	We are your servants and we are ready to do anything you say. But we will not make anyone king; do whatever you think best.
Narrator	Jehu wrote them another letter:
Jehu	If you are with me, and are ready to follow my orders, bring the heads of King Ahab's descendants to me at Jezreel by this time tomorrow.
Narrator	The seventy descendants of King Ahab were under the care of the leading citizens of Samaria, who were bringing them up. When Jehu's letter was received, the leaders of Samaria killed all seventy of Ahab's descendants, put their heads in baskets, and sent them to Jehu at Jezreel. When Jehu was told that the heads of Ahab's descendants had been brought, he ordered them to be piled up in two heaps at the city gate and to be left there until the following morning. In the morning, he went out to the gate and said to the people who were there:
Jehu	I was the one who plotted against King Joram and killed him; you are not responsible for that. But who killed all these? This proves that everything that the Lord said about the descendants of Ahab will come true. The Lord has done what he promised through his prophet Elijah.
Narrator	Then Jehu put to death all the other relatives of Ahab living in Jezreel, and all his officers, close friends, and priests; not one of them was left alive.
Cast	[This is] the word of the Lord.
All	**Thanks be to God.**

Cast: **Narrator, Jehu, Ruler, Officer.**

The relatives of King Ahaziah are killed
2 Kings 10.12–17

Narrator	Jehu left Jezreel to go to Samaria. On the way, at a place called 'Shepherds' Camp,' he met some relatives of the late King Ahaziah of Judah and asked them:
Jehu	Who are you?
Narrator	They answered:
Relative 1	Ahaziah's relatives.
Relative 2	We are going to Jezreel to pay our respects to the children of Queen Jezebel—
Relative 1	And to the rest of the royal family.

Narrator	Jehu ordered his men:
Jehu	Take them alive!
Narrator	They seized them, and he put them to death near a pit there. There were forty-two people in all, and not one of them was left alive. (PAUSE)
	Jehu started out again, and on his way he was met by Jonadab son of Rechab. Jehu greeted him and said:
Jehu	You and I think alike. Will you support me?
Jonadab	I will.
Jehu	Give me your hand, then.
Narrator	They clasped hands, and Jehu helped him up into the chariot:
Jehu	Come with me and see for yourself how devoted I am to the Lord.
Narrator	And they rode on together to Samaria. When they arrived there, Jehu killed all of Ahab's relatives, not sparing even one. This is what the Lord had told Elijah would happen.
Cast All	[This is] the word of the Lord. **Thanks be to God.**

Cast: **Narrator, Jehu, Relative 1, Relative 2, Jonadab.**

The worshippers of Baal are killed
2 Kings 10.18–29 [30–31]

Narrator	Jehu called the people of Samaria together:
Jehu	King Ahab served the god Baal a little, but I will serve him much more. Call together all the prophets of Baal, all his worshippers, and all his priests. No one is excused; I am going to offer a great sacrifice to Baal, and whoever is not present will be put to death.
Commentator	This was a trick on the part of Jehu by which he meant to kill all the worshippers of Baal.
Jehu (announcing)	Proclaim a day of worship in honour of Baal!
Narrator	The proclamation was made, and Jehu sent word throughout all the land of Israel. All who worshipped Baal came; not one of them failed to come. They all went into the temple of Baal, filling it from one end to the other. Then Jehu ordered the priest in charge of the sacred robes to bring the robes out and give them to the worshippers. After that, Jehu himself went into the temple with Jonadab son of Rechab and said to the people there:
Jehu	Make sure that only worshippers of Baal are present and that no worshipper of the Lord has come in.
Narrator	Then he and Jonadab went in to offer sacrifices and burnt-offerings to Baal. He had stationed eighty men outside the temple and had instructed them:

Jehu (quietly)	You are to kill all these people; anyone who lets one of them escape will pay for it with his life!
Narrator	As soon as Jehu had presented the offerings, he said to the guards and officers:
Jehu	Go in and kill them all; don't let anyone escape!
Narrator	They went in with drawn swords, killed them all, and dragged the bodies outside. Then they went on into the inner sanctuary of the temple, brought out the sacred pillar that was there, and burnt it.
	So they destroyed the sacred pillar and the temple, and turned the temple into a latrine—which it still is today. (PAUSE)
	That was how Jehu wiped out the worship of Baal in Israel. But he imitated the sin of King Jeroboam, who led Israel into the sin of worshipping the gold bull-calves he set up in Bethel and in Dan.
	[The Lord said to Jehu:
The Lord	You have done to Ahab's descendants everything I wanted you to do. So I promise you that your descendants, down to the fourth generation, will be kings of Israel.
Narrator	But Jehu did not obey with all his heart the law of the Lord, the God of Israel; instead, he followed the example of Jeroboam, who led Israel into sin.]
Cast	[This is] the word of the Lord.
All	**Thanks be to God.**

Cast: **Narrator, Jehu, Commentator, [The Lord].**

Queen Athaliah of Judah
2 Kings 11.1–21

Narrator	As soon as King Ahaziah's mother Athaliah learnt of her son's murder, she gave orders for all the members of the royal family to be killed. Only Ahaziah's son Joash escaped. He was about to be killed with the others, but was rescued by his aunt Jehosheba, who was King Jehoram's daughter and Ahaziah's half-sister. She took him and his nurse into a bedroom in the Temple and hid him from Athaliah, so that he was not killed. For six years Jehosheba took care of the boy and kept him hidden in the Temple, while Athaliah ruled as queen.
	But in the seventh year Jehoiada the priest sent for the officers in charge of the royal bodyguard and of the palace guards, and told them to come to the Temple, where he made them agree under oath to what he planned to do. He showed them King Ahaziah's son Joash, and gave them the following orders:
Jehoiada	When you come on duty on the Sabbath, one third of you are to guard the palace; another third are to stand guard at the Sur Gate, and the other third are to stand guard at the gate behind the other guards. The two groups that go off duty on the Sabbath are

→

365

to stand guard at the Temple to protect the king. You are to guard King Joash with drawn swords and stay with him wherever he goes. Anyone who comes near you is to be killed.

Narrator The officers obeyed Jehoiada's instructions and brought their men to him—those going off duty on the Sabbath and those going on duty. He gave the officers the spears and shields that had belonged to King David and had been kept in the Temple, and he stationed the men with drawn swords all round the front of the Temple, to protect the king. Then Jehoiada led Joash out, placed the crown on his head, and gave him a copy of the laws governing kingship. Then Joash was anointed and proclaimed king. The people clapped their hands and shouted:

Persons 1 and 2
(clapping) Long live the king!

Narrator Queen Athaliah heard the noise being made by the guards and the people, so she hurried to the Temple, where the crowd had gathered. There she saw the new king standing by the column at the entrance of the Temple, as was the custom. He was surrounded by the officers and the trumpeters, and the people were all shouting joyfully and blowing trumpets. Athaliah tore her clothes in distress and shouted:

Queen Athaliah Treason! Treason!

Narrator Jehoiada did not want Athaliah killed in the temple area, so he ordered the army officers:

Jehoiada Take her out between the rows of guards, and kill anyone who tries to rescue her.

Narrator They seized her, took her to the palace, and there at the Horse Gate they killed her. (PAUSE)

The priest Jehoiada made King Joash and the people enter into a covenant with the Lord that they would be the Lord's people; he also made a covenant between the king and the people.

Then the people went to the temple of Baal and tore it down; they smashed the altars and the idols, and killed Mattan, the priest of Baal, in front of the altars. Jehoiada put guards on duty at the Temple, and then he, the officers, the royal bodyguard, and the palace guards escorted the king from the Temple to the palace, followed by all the people. Joash entered by the Guard Gate and took his place on the throne. All the people were filled with happiness, and the city was quiet, now that Athaliah had been killed in the palace. Joash became king of Judah at the age of seven.

Cast [This is] the word of the Lord.
All **Thanks be to God.**

Cast: **Narrator, Jehoiada, Person 1, Person 2, Queen Athaliah.**

The death of Elisha
2 Kings 13.14–20

Narrator The prophet Elisha fell ill with a fatal disease, and as he lay dying King Jehoash of Israel went to visit him [As he wept he exclaimed]:

Jehoash
(weeping) My father, my father! You have been the mighty defender of Israel!

[Narrator Elisha ordered him:]

Elisha
(with effort) Get a bow and some arrows.

Narrator Jehoash got them, and Elisha told him to get ready to shoot. The king did so, and Elisha placed his hands on the king's hands. Then, following the prophet's instructions, the king opened the window that faced towards Syria.

Elisha Shoot the arrow!

Narrator As soon as the king shot the arrow, the prophet exclaimed:

Elisha You are the Lord's arrow, with which he will win victory over Syria. You will fight the Syrians in Aphek until you defeat them.

Narrator Then Elisha told the king to take the other arrows and strike the ground with them. The king struck the ground three times, and then stopped. This made Elisha angry, and he said to the king:

Elisha You should have struck five or six times, and then you would have won complete victory over the Syrians; but now you will defeat them only three times.

Narrator Elisha died and was buried.

Cast [This is] the word of the Lord.
All **Thanks be to God.**

Cast: **Narrator, Jehoash, Elisha.**

King Amaziah of Judah
2 Kings 14.1–16

Narrator In the second year of the reign of Jehoash son of Jehoahaz as king of Israel, Amaziah son of Joash became king of Judah at the age of twenty-five, and he ruled in Jerusalem for twenty-nine years. His mother was Jehoaddin, from Jerusalem. He did what was pleasing to the Lord, but he was not like his ancestor King David; instead, he did what his father Joash had done. He did not tear down the pagan places of worship, and the people continued to offer sacrifices and burn incense there. As soon as Amaziah was firmly in power, he executed the officials who had killed his father, the king. However, he did not kill their children but followed what the Lord had commanded in the Law of Moses:

Lawyer   Parents are not to be put to death for crimes committed by their children, and children are not to be put to death for crimes committed by their parents; a person is to be put to death only for a crime he himself has committed.

Narrator   Amaziah killed ten thousand Edomite soldiers in Salt Valley; he captured the city of Sela in battle and called it Joktheel, the name it still has. Then Amaziah sent messengers to King Jehoash of Israel, challenging him to fight. But King Jehoash sent back the following reply:

Jehoash   Once a thorn bush on the Lebanon Mountains sent a message to a cedar: 'Give your daughter in marriage to my son.' A wild animal passed by and trampled the bush down. Now Amaziah, you have defeated the Edomites, and you are filled with pride. Be satisfied with your fame and stay at home. Why stir up trouble that will only bring disaster on you and your people?

Narrator   But Amaziah refused to listen, so King Jehoash marched out with his men and fought against him at Beth Shemesh in Judah. Amaziah's army was defeated, and all his soldiers fled to their homes. Jehoash took Amaziah prisoner, advanced on Jerusalem, and tore down the city wall from Ephraim Gate to the Corner Gate, a distance of nearly two hundred metres. He took all the silver and gold he could find, all the temple equipment and all the palace treasures, and carried them back to Samaria. He also took hostages with him. Everything else that Jehoash did, including his bravery in the war against King Amaziah of Judah, is recorded in The History of the Kings of Israel. Jehoash died and was buried in the royal tombs in Samaria, and his son Jeroboam II succeeded him as king.

Cast   [This is] the word of the Lord.
All   **Thanks be to God.**

Cast: **Narrator, Lawyer, Jehoash.**

The Assyrians threaten Jerusalem
From 2 Kings 18.13–37

Narrator   In the fourteenth year of the reign of King Hezekiah, Sennacherib, the emperor of Assyria, attacked the fortified cities of Judah and conquered them. Hezekiah sent a message to Sennacherib, who was in Lachish:

Hezekiah   I have done wrong; please stop your attack, and I will pay whatever you demand.

Narrator   The emperor's answer was that Hezekiah should send him ten thousand kilogrammes of silver and a thousand kilogrammes of gold. Hezekiah sent him all the silver in the Temple and in the palace treasury; he also stripped the gold from the temple doors and the gold with which he himself had covered the doorposts, and he sent it all to Sennacherib. The Assyrian emperor sent a large army from Lachish to attack Hezekiah at Jerusalem; it was commanded by his three highest officials. When they arrived at Jerusalem, they occupied the road where the cloth-makers work, by the ditch that brings water from the upper pond. Then they sent for King Hezekiah, and three of his officials went out to meet them: Eliakim son of Hilkiah, who was in charge of the palace; Shebna, the court secretary; and Joah son of Asaph, who was in charge of the records. One of the Assyrian officials told them that the emperor wanted to know what made King Hezekiah so confident. He demanded:

Official Do you think that words can take the place of military skill and might? Who do you think will help you rebel against Assyria? You are expecting Egypt to help you, but that would be like using a reed as a walking-stick—it would break and jab your hand. That is what the king of Egypt is like when anyone relies on him.

Narrator The Assyrian official went on:

Official Or will you tell me that you are relying on the Lord your God? It was the Lord's shrines and altars that Hezekiah destroyed, when he told the people of Judah and Jerusalem to worship only at the altar in Jerusalem. I will make a bargain with you in the name of the emperor. I will give you two thousand horses if you can find that many men to ride them! You are no match for even the lowest ranking Assyrian official, and yet you expect the Egyptians to send you chariots and horsemen! Do you think I have attacked your country and destroyed it without the Lord's help? The Lord himself told me to attack it and destroy it.

Narrator Then Eliakim, Shebna, and Joah told the official:

Eliakim Speak Aramaic to us, sir. We understand it.

Shebna Don't speak Hebrew; all the people on the wall are listening.

Official Do you think you and the king are the only ones the emperor sent me to say all these things to? No, I am also talking to the people who are sitting on the wall.

Narrator Then the official stood up and shouted in Hebrew:

Official Listen to what the emperor of Assyria is telling you! He warns you not to let Hezekiah deceive you. Hezekiah can't save you. And don't let him persuade you to rely on the Lord. Don't think that the Lord will save you, and that he will stop our Assyrian army from capturing your city. Don't listen to Hezekiah. The emperor of Assyria commands you to come out of the city and surrender. You will all be allowed to eat grapes from your own vines, and figs from your own trees, and to drink water from your own wells—until the emperor resettles you in a country much like your own, where there are vineyards to give wine and there is corn for making bread; it is a land of olives, olive-oil, and honey. If you do what he commands, you will not die, but live. Don't let Hezekiah fool you into thinking that the Lord will rescue you. Did the gods of any other nations save their countries from the emperor of Assyria? Where are they now, the gods of Hamath and Arpad? Where are the gods of Sepharvaim, Hena, and Ivvah? Did anyone

→

save Samaria? When did any of the gods of all these countries ever save their country from our emperor? Then what makes you think the Lord can save Jerusalem?

Narrator The people kept quiet, just as King Hezekiah had told them to; they did not say a word. Then Eliakim, Shebna, and Joah tore their clothes in grief, and went and reported to the king what the Assyrian official had said.

Cast [This is] the word of the Lord.
All **Thanks be to God.**

Cast: **Narrator, Hezekiah, Official, Eliakim, Shebna** (can be the same as Eliakim).

The King asks Isaiah's advice
2 Kings 19.1–19

Narrator As soon as King Hezekiah heard the report of what the Assyrian official had said, he tore his clothes in grief, put on sackcloth, and went to the Temple of the Lord. He sent Eliakim, the official in charge of the palace, Shebna, the court secretary, and the senior priests to the prophet Isaiah son of Amoz. They also were wearing sackcloth. This is the message which he told them to give Isaiah:

Hezekiah Today is a day of suffering; we are being punished and are in disgrace. We are like a woman who is ready to give birth, but is too weak to do it. The Assyrian emperor has sent his chief official to insult the living God. May the Lord your God hear these insults and punish those who spoke them. So pray to God for those of our people who survive.

Narrator When Isaiah received King Hezekiah's message, he sent back this answer:

Isaiah The Lord tells you not to let the Assyrians frighten you with their claims that he cannot save you. The Lord will cause the emperor to hear a rumour that will make him go back to his own country, and the Lord will have him killed there.

Narrator The Assyrian official learnt that the emperor had left Lachish and was fighting against the nearby city of Libnah; so he went there to consult him. Word reached the Assyrians that the Egyptian army, led by King Tirhakah of Sudan, was coming to attack them. When the emperor heard this, he sent a letter to King Hezekiah of Judah:

Sennacherib The god you are trusting in has told you that you will not fall into my hands, but don't let that deceive you. You have heard what an Assyrian emperor does to any country he decides to destroy. Do you think that you can escape? My ancestors destroyed the cities of Gozan, Haran, and Rezeph, and killed the people of Betheden who lived in Telassar, and none of their gods could save them. Where are the kings of the cities of Hamath, Arpad, Sepharvaim, Hena, and Ivvah?

Narrator	King Hezekiah took the letter from the messengers and read it. Then he went to the Temple, placed the letter there in the presence of the Lord, and prayed:
Hezekiah	O Lord, the God of Israel, enthroned above the winged creatures, you alone are God, ruling all the kingdoms of the world. You created the earth and the sky. Now, Lord, look at what is happening to us. Listen to all the things that Sennacherib is saying to insult you, the living God. We all know, Lord, that the emperors of Assyria have destroyed many nations, made their lands desolate, and burnt up their gods—which were no gods at all, only images of wood and stone made by human hands. Now, Lord our God, rescue us from the Assyrians, so that all the nations of the world will know that only you, O Lord, are God.
Cast	[This is] the word of the Lord.
All	**Thanks be to God.**

Cast: **Narrator, Hezekiah, Isaiah, Sennacherib.**

Isaiah's message to King Hezekiah
2 Kings 19.20–37

Narrator	Isaiah sent a message telling King Hezekiah that in answer to the king's prayer the Lord had said:
The Lord	The city of Jerusalem laughs at you, Sennacherib, and despises you. Whom do you think you have been insulting and ridiculing? You have been disrespectful to *me*, the holy God of Israel. You sent your messengers to boast to me that with all your chariots you had conquered the highest mountains of Lebanon. You boasted that there you cut down the tallest cedars and the finest cypress-trees and that you reached the deepest parts of the forests. You boasted that you dug wells and drank water in foreign lands and that the feet of your soldiers tramped the River Nile dry. Have you never heard that I planned all this long ago? And now I have carried it out. I gave you the power to turn fortified cities into piles of rubble. The people who lived there were powerless; they were frightened and stunned. They were like grass in a field or weeds growing on a roof when the hot east wind blasts them. But I know everything about you, what you do and where you go. I know how you rage against me. I have received the report of that rage and that pride of yours, and now I will put a hook through your nose and a bit in your mouth, and take you back by the same road you came.
Narrator	Then Isaiah said to King Hezekiah:
Isaiah	This is a sign of what will happen. This year and next you will have only wild grain to eat, but the following year you will be able to sow your corn and harvest it, and plant vines and eat grapes. Those in Judah who survive will flourish like plants that send roots deep into the ground and produce fruit. There will be people in Jerusalem and on Mount Zion who will survive, because the Lord

→

371

	is determined to make this happen. This is what the Lord has said about the Assyrian emperor:
The Lord	He will not enter this city or shoot a single arrow against it. No soldiers with shields will come near the city, and no siege-mounds will be built round it. He will go back by the same road he came, without entering this city. I, the Lord, have spoken. I will defend this city and protect it, for the sake of my own honour and because of the promise I made to my servant David.
Narrator	That night an angel of the Lord went to the Assyrian camp and killed 185,000 soldiers. At dawn the next day, there they lay, all dead! Then the Assyrian emperor Sennacherib withdrew and returned to Nineveh. One day, when he was worshipping in the temple of his god Nisroch, two of his sons, Adrammelech and Sharezer, killed him with their swords, and then escaped to the land of Ararat. Another of his sons, Esarhaddon, succeeded him as emperor.
Cast	[This is] the word of the Lord.
All	**Thanks be to God.**

Cast: **Narrator, The Lord, Isaiah.**

King Hezekiah's illness and recovery
2 Kings 20.1–11

Narrator	King Hezekiah fell ill and almost died. The prophet Isaiah son of Amoz went to see him and said to him:
Isaiah	The Lord tells you that you are to put everything in order, because you will not recover. Get ready to die.
Narrator	Hezekiah turned his face to the wall and prayed:
Hezekiah	Remember, Lord, that I have served you faithfully and loyally, and that I have always tried to do what you wanted me to.
Narrator	And he began to cry bitterly. Isaiah left the king, but before he had passed through the central courtyard of the palace the Lord told him to go back to Hezekiah, ruler of the Lord's people, and say to him:
The Lord	I, the Lord, the God of your ancestor David, have heard your prayer and seen your tears. I will heal you, and in three days you will go to the Temple. I will let you live fifteen years longer. I will rescue you and this city of Jerusalem from the emperor of Assyria. I will defend this city, for the sake of my own honour and because of the promise I made to my servant David.
Narrator	Then Isaiah told the king's attendants to put on his boil a paste made of figs, and he would get well. King Hezekiah asked:
Hezekiah	What is the sign to prove that the Lord will heal me and that three days later I will be able to go to the Temple?
Narrator	Isaiah replied:

Isaiah	The Lord will give you a sign to prove that he will keep his promise. Now, would you prefer the shadow on the stairway to go forward ten steps or go back ten steps?
Hezekiah	It's easy to make the shadow go forward ten steps! Make it go back ten steps.
Narrator	Isaiah prayed to the Lord, and the Lord made the shadow go back ten steps on the stairway set up by King Ahaz.
Cast	[This is] the word of the Lord.
All	**Thanks be to God.**

Cast: **Narrator, Isaiah, Hezekiah, The Lord.**

Messengers from Babylonia
2 Kings 20.12–21

Narrator	The king of Babylonia, Merodach Baladan, the son of Baladan, heard that King Hezekiah had been ill, so he sent him a letter and a present. Hezekiah welcomed the messengers and showed them his wealth—his silver and gold, his spices and perfumes, and all his military equipment. There was nothing in his storerooms or anywhere in his kingdom that he did not show them. Then the prophet Isaiah went to King Hezekiah and asked:
Isaiah	Where did these men come from and what did they say to you?
[Narrator	Hezekiah answered:]
Hezekiah (vaguely)	They came from a very distant country . . . from Babylonia.
Isaiah	What did they see in the palace?
Hezekiah (proudly)	They saw everything. There is nothing in the storerooms that I didn't show them.
[Narrator	Isaiah then said to the king:]
Isaiah (firmly)	The Lord Almighty says that a time is coming when everything in your palace, everything that your ancestors have stored up to this day, will be carried off to Babylonia. Nothing will be left. Some of your own direct descendants will be taken away and made eunuchs to serve in the palace of the king of Babylonia.
Narrator	King Hezekiah understood this to mean that there would be peace and security during his lifetime [so he replied]:
Hezekiah	The message you have given me from the Lord is good. (PAUSE)
Narrator	Everything else that King Hezekiah did, his brave deeds, and an account of how he built a reservoir and dug a tunnel to bring water into the city, are all recorded in The History of the Kings of Judah. Hezekiah died, and his son Manasseh succeeded him as king.
Cast	[This is] the word of the Lord.
All	**Thanks be to God.**

Cast: **Narrator, Isaiah, Hezekiah.**

King Manasseh of Judah
2 Kings 21.1–18

Narrator Manasseh was twelve years old when he became king of Judah, and he ruled in Jerusalem for fifty-five years. His mother was Hephzibah. Following the disgusting practices of the nations whom the Lord had driven out of the land as his people advanced, Manasseh sinned against the Lord. He rebuilt the pagan places of worship that his father Hezekiah had destroyed; he built altars for the worship of Baal and made an image of the goddess Asherah, as King Ahab of Israel had done. Manasseh also worshipped the stars. He built pagan altars in the Temple, the place that the Lord had said was where he should be worshipped. In the two courtyards of the Temple he built altars for the worship of the stars. He sacrificed his son as a burnt-offering. He practised divination and magic and consulted fortune-tellers and mediums. He sinned greatly against the Lord and stirred up his anger. He placed the symbol of the goddess Asherah in the Temple, the place about which the Lord had said to David and his son Solomon:

The Lord Here in Jerusalem, in this Temple, is the place that I have chosen out of all the territory of the twelve tribes of Israel as the place where I am to be worshipped. And if the people of Israel will obey all my commands and keep the whole Law that my servant Moses gave them, then I will not allow them to be driven out of the land that I gave to their ancestors.

Narrator But the people of Judah did not obey the Lord, and Manasseh led them to commit even greater sins than those committed by the nations whom the Lord had driven out of the land as his people advanced. Through his servants the prophets the Lord said:

The Lord King Manasseh has done these disgusting things, things far worse than what the Canaanites did; and with his idols he has led the people of Judah into sin. So I, the Lord God of Israel, will bring such a disaster on Jerusalem and Judah that everyone who hears about it will be stunned. I will punish Jerusalem as I did Samaria, as I did King Ahab of Israel and his descendants. I will wipe Jerusalem clean of its people, as clean as a plate that has been wiped and turned upside down. I will abandon the people who survive, and will hand them over to their enemies, who will conquer them and plunder their land. I will do this to my people because they have sinned against me and have stirred up my anger from the time their ancestors came out of Egypt to this day.

Narrator Manasseh killed so many innocent people that the streets of Jerusalem were flowing with blood; he did this in addition to leading the people of Judah into idolatry, causing them to sin against the Lord. Everything else that Manasseh did, including the sins he committed, is recorded in The History of the Kings of Judah. Manasseh died and was buried in the palace garden, the garden of Uzza, and his son Amon suceeded him as king.

Cast	[This is] the word of the Lord.
All	**Thanks be to God.**

Cast: **Narrator, The Lord.**

The book of the Law is discovered (i)
From 2 Kings 22.1–13

Narrator   Josiah was eight years old when he became king of Judah, and he ruled in Jerusalem for thirty-one years. Josiah did what was pleasing to the Lord; he followed the example of his ancestor King David, strictly obeying all the laws of God. In the eighteenth year of his reign, King Josiah sent the court secretary Shaphan to the Temple with the order:

Josiah   Go to the High Priest Hilkiah and get a report on the amount of money that the priests on duty at the entrance to the Temple have collected from the people. Tell him to give the money to the men who are in charge of the repairs in the Temple. They are to pay the carpenters, the builders, and the masons.

Narrator   Shaphan delivered the king's order to Hilkiah, and Hilkiah told him that he had found *the book of the Law* in the Temple. Hilkiah gave him the book, and Shaphan read it. Then he went back to the king and reported:

Shaphan   Your servants have taken the money that was in the Temple and have handed it over to the men in charge of the repairs.

[Narrator   And then he said:]

Shaphan
(uncertainly)   I have here a *book* that Hilkiah gave me.

Narrator   And he read it aloud to the king.

When the king heard the book being read, he tore his clothes in dismay, and gave the following order to Hilkiah the priest, to Ahikam son of Shaphan, to Achbor son of Micaiah, to Shaphan, the court secretary, and to Asaiah, the king's attendant:

Josiah   Go and consult the Lord for me and for all the people of Judah about the teachings of this book. The Lord is angry with us because our ancestors have not done what this book says must be done.

Cast	[This is] the word of the Lord.
All	**Thanks be to God.**

Cast: **Narrator, Josiah, Shaphan.**

The book of the Law is discovered (ii)
2 Kings 22.14–20

Narrator   Hilkiah, Ahikam, Achbor, Shaphan, and Asaiah went to consult a woman named Huldah, a prophet who lived in the newer part of Jerusalem.

Commentator   Her husband Shallum, the son of Tikvah and grandson of Harhas, was in charge of the temple robes.

Narrator   They described to her what had happened, and she told them to go back to the king and give him the following message from the Lord:

The Lord   I am going to punish Jerusalem and all its people, as written in the book that the king has read. They have rejected me and have offered sacrifices to other gods, and so have stirred up my anger by all they have done. My anger is aroused against Jerusalem, and it will not die down. As for the king himself, this is what I, the Lord God of Israel, say: You listened to what is written in the book, and you repented and humbled yourself before me, tearing your clothes and weeping, when you heard how I threatened to punish Jerusalem and its people. I will make it a terrifying sight, a place whose name people will use as a curse. But I have heard your prayer, and the punishment which I am going to bring on Jerusalem will not come until after your death. I will let you die in peace.

Narrator   The men returned to King Josiah with this message.

Cast   [This is] the word of the Lord.
All   **Thanks be to God.**

Cast: **Narrator, Commentator, The Lord.**

Josiah does away with pagan worship
From 2 Kings 23.1–23

Narrator   King Josiah summoned all the leaders of Judah and Jerusalem, and together they went to the Temple, accompanied by the priests and the prophets and all the rest of the people, rich and poor alike. Before them all, the king read aloud the whole book of the covenant which had been found in the Temple. He stood by the royal column and made a covenant with the Lord to obey him, to keep his laws and commands with all his heart and soul, and to put into practice the demands attached to the covenant, as written in the book. And all the people promised to keep the covenant. Then Josiah ordered the High Priest Hilkiah, his assistant priests, and the guards on duty at the entrance to the Temple to bring out of the Temple all the objects used in the worship of Baal, of the goddess Asherah, and of the stars. The king burnt all these objects outside the city near the valley of the Kidron, and then had the ashes taken to Bethel. He removed from office the priests that the kings of Judah had ordained to offer sacrifices on the pagan altars in the cities of Judah and places near Jerusalem—all the priests who offered sacrifices to Baal, to the sun, the moon, the planets, and the stars. He removed from the Temple the symbol of the goddess Asherah, took it out of the city to the valley of the Kidron, burnt it, pounded its ashes to dust, and scattered it over the public burial-ground. He destroyed the living-quarters in the Temple occupied by the temple prostitutes.

Commentator It was there that women wove robes used in the worship of Asherah.

Narrator He also tore down the altars dedicated to the goat-demons near the gate built by Joshua, the city governor, which was to the left of the main gate as one enters the city. King Josiah also desecrated Topheth, the pagan place of worship in the Valley of Hinnom, so that no one could sacrifice his son or daughter as a burnt-offering to the god Molech. He also removed the horses that the kings of Judah had dedicated to the worship of the sun, and he burnt the chariots used in this worship.

Commentator These were kept in the temple courtyard, near the gate and not far from the living-quarters of Nathan Melech, a high official.

Narrator Josiah also tore down the place of worship in Bethel which had been built by King Jeroboam son of Nebat, who led Israel into sin. Then Josiah looked round and saw some tombs there on the hill; he had the bones taken out of them and burnt on the altar. In this way he desecrated the altar, doing what the prophet had predicted long before during the festival as King Jeroboam was standing by the altar. King Josiah looked round and saw the tomb of the prophet who had made this prediction. [He asked:]

Josiah Whose tomb is that?

Narrator The people of Bethel answered:

Person 1 It is the tomb of the prophet who came from Judah.

Person 2 And predicted these things that you have done to this altar.

Josiah Leave it as it is. His bones are not to be moved.

Narrator So his bones were not moved, neither were those of the prophet who had come from Samaria. In every city of Israel King Josiah tore down all the pagan places of worship which had been built by the kings of Israel, who thereby aroused the Lord's anger. Then he returned to Jerusalem. King Josiah ordered the people to celebrate the Passover in honour of the Lord their God, as written in the book of the covenant. No Passover like this one had ever been celebrated by any of the kings of Israel or of Judah, since the time when judges ruled the nation. Now at last, in the eighteenth year of the reign of Josiah, the Passover was celebrated in Jerusalem.

Cast [This is] the word of the Lord.
All **Thanks be to God.**

Cast: **Narrator, Commentator, Josiah, Person 1, Person 2.**

Other changes made by Josiah
2 Kings 23.24–30

Narrator In order to enforce the laws written in the book that the High Priest Hilkiah had found in the Temple, King Josiah removed from Jerusalem and the rest of Judah all the mediums and fortune-tellers, and all the household gods, idols, and all other pagan objects of worship. There had never been a king like him before, who served the Lord with all his heart, mind, and strength, obeying all the Law of Moses; nor has there been a king like him since. But the Lord's fierce anger had been aroused against Judah by what King Manasseh had done, and even now it did not die down:

The Lord I will do to Judah what I have done to Israel: I will banish the people of Judah from my sight, and I will reject Jerusalem, the city I chose, and the Temple, the place I said was where I should be worshipped.

Narrator Everything else that King Josiah did is recorded in The History of the Kings of Judah. While Josiah was king, King Neco of Egypt led an army to the River Euphrates to help the emperor of Assyria. King Josiah tried to stop the Egyptian army at Megiddo and was killed in battle. His officials placed his body in a chariot and took it back to Jerusalem, where he was buried in the royal tombs. The people of Judah chose Josiah's son Joahaz and anointed him king.

Cast [This is] the word of the Lord.
All **Thanks be to God.**

Cast: **Narrator, The Lord.**

Judah in exile
2 Kings 25.22–30

Narrator 1 King Nebuchadnezzar of Babylonia made Gedaliah, the son of Ahikam and grandson of Shaphan, governor of Judah, and placed him in charge of all those who had not been taken away to Babylonia. When the Judaean officers and soldiers who had not surrendered heard about this, they joined Gedaliah at Mizpah. These officers were Ishmael son of Nethaniah, Johanan son of Kareah, Seraiah son of Tanhumeth, from the town of Netophah, and Jezaniah from Maacah.

Gedaliah I give you my word that there is no need for you to be afraid of the Babylonian officials. Settle in this land, serve the king of Babylonia, and all will go well with you.

Narrator 1 But in the seventh month of that year, Ishmael, the son of Nethaniah and grandson of Elishama, a member of the royal family, went to Mizpah with ten men, attacked Gedaliah and killed him. He also killed the Israelites and Babylonians who were there with him. Then all the Israelites, rich and poor alike,

→

together with the army officers, left and went to Egypt, because they were afraid of the Babylonians.

Narrator 2 In the year that Evilmerodach became king of Babylonia, he showed kindness to King Jehoiachin of Judah by releasing him from prison. This happened on the twenty-seventh day of the twelfth month of the thirty-seventh year after Jehoiachin had been taken away as prisoner. Evilmerodach treated him kindly, and gave him a position of greater honour than he gave the other kings who were exiles with him in Babylonia. So Jehoiachin was permitted to change from his prison clothes and to dine at the king's table for the rest of his life. Each day, for as long as he lived, he was given a regular allowance for his needs.

Cast [This is] the word of the Lord.
All **Thanks be to God.**

Cast: **Narrator 1 Gedaliah, Narrator 2.**

1 CHRONICLES

David becomes king of Israel and Judah
1 Chronicles 11.1–9

Chronicler   The people of Israel went to David at Hebron [and said to him]:

Israelite 1   We are your own flesh and blood.

Israelite 2   In the past, even when Saul was still our king, you led the people of Israel in battle—

Israelite 1   And the Lord your God promised you that you would lead his people and be their ruler.

Chronicler   So all the leaders of Israel came to King David at Hebron. He made a sacred alliance with them, they anointed him, and he became king of Israel, just as the Lord had promised through Samuel. King David and all the Israelites went and attacked the city of Jerusalem. It was then known as Jebus, and the Jebusites, the original inhabitants of the land, were still living there. The Jebusites told David he would never get inside the city, but David captured their fortress of Zion, and it became known as 'David's City.' David said:

David   The first man to kill a Jebusite will be commander of the army!

Chronicler   Joab, whose mother was Zeruiah, led the attack and became commander. Because David went to live in the fortress, it came to be called 'David's City.' He rebuilt the city, starting at the place where land was filled in on the east side of the hill, and Joab restored the rest of the city. David grew stronger and stronger, because the Lord Almighty was with him.

Cast   [This is] the word of the Lord.
All   **Thanks be to God.**

Cast: **Chronicler, Israelite 1, Israelite 2** (can be the same as Israelite 1), **David.**

David refuses to drink
1 Chronicles 11.15–19

Chronicler   One day, three of the thirty leading soldiers went to a rock where David was staying near the cave of Adullam, while a band of Philistines was camping in the Valley of Rephaim. At that time David was on a fortified hill, and a group of Philistines had occupied Bethlehem. David got homesick and said:

David   How I wish someone would bring me a drink of water from the well by the gate in Bethlehem!

Chronicler   The three famous soldiers forced their way through the Philistine camp, drew some water from the well, and brought it back to

David. But he would not drink it; instead he poured it out as an offering to the Lord:

David I could never drink this! It would be like drinking the blood of these men who risked their lives!

Chronicler So he refused to drink it. (PAUSE)

These were the brave deeds of the three famous soldiers.

Cast [This is] the word of the Lord.
All **Thanks be to God.**

Cast: **Chronicler, David.**

The Covenant Box is removed from Kiriath Jearim
1 Chronicles 13.1–14

Chronicler King David consulted with all the officers in command of units of a thousand men and units of a hundred men. Then he announced to all the people of Israel:

David If you give your approval and if it is the will of the Lord our God, let us send messengers to the rest of our countrymen and to the priests and Levites in their towns, and tell them to assemble here with us. Then we will go and fetch God's Covenant Box, which was ignored while Saul was king.

Chronicler The people were pleased with the suggestion and agreed to it. (PAUSE)

So David assembled the people of Israel from all over the country, from the Egyptian border in the south to Hamath Pass in the north, in order to bring the Covenant Box from Kiriath Jearim to Jerusalem. David and the people went to the city of Baalah, that is, to Kiriath Jearim, in the territory of Judah, to fetch the Covenant Box of God, which bears the name of the Lord enthroned above the winged creatures. At Abinadab's house they brought out the Covenant Box and put it on a new cart. Uzzah and Ahio guided the cart, while David and all the people danced with all their might to honour God. They sang and played musical instruments—harps, drums, cymbals, and trumpets. (PAUSE)

As they came to the threshing-place of Chidon, the oxen stumbled, and Uzzah stretched out his hand and took hold of the Covenant Box. At once the Lord became angry with Uzzah and killed him for touching the box. He died there in God's presence, and so that place has been called Perez Uzzah ever since. David was furious because the Lord had punished Uzzah in anger. (PAUSE)

Then David was afraid of God [and said]:

David How can I take the Covenant Box with me now?

Chronicler So David did not take it with him to Jerusalem. Instead, he left it at

→

the house of a man named Obed Edom, a native of the city of Gath. It stayed there three months, and the Lord blessed Obed Edom's family and everything that belonged to him.

Cast	[This is] the word of the Lord.
All	**Thanks be to God.**

Cast: **Chronicler, David.**

Victory over the Philistines
1 Chronicles 14.8–17

Chronicler	When the Philistines heard that David had now been made king over the whole country of Israel, their army went out to capture him. So David marched out to meet them. The Philistines arrived at the Valley of Rephaim and began plundering. David asked God:
David	Shall I attack the Philistines? Will you give me the victory?
Chronicler	The Lord answered:
The Lord	Yes, attack! I will give you the victory!
Chronicler	So David attacked them at Baal Perazim and defeated them. He said:
David	God has used me to break through the enemy army like a flood.
Chronicler	So that place is called Baal Perazim. When the Philistines fled, they left their idols behind, and David gave orders for them to be burnt. (PAUSE)
	Soon the Philistines returned to the valley and started plundering it again. Once more David consulted God, who answered:
The Lord	Don't attack them from here, but go round and get ready to attack them from the other side, near the balsam-trees. When you hear the sound of marching in the tree-tops, then attack, because I will be marching ahead of you to defeat the Philistine army.
Chronicler	David did what God had commanded, and so he drove the Philistines back from Gibeon all the way to Gezer. David's fame spread everywhere, and the Lord made every nation afraid of him.
Cast	[This is] the word of the Lord.
All	**Thanks be to God.**

Cast: **Chronicler, David, The Lord.**

A song of praise
1 Chronicles 16.8–36

Chronicler	Give thanks to the Lord, proclaim his greatness; tell the nations what he has done. Sing praise to the Lord;

382

tell the wonderful things he has done.
Be glad that we belong to him;
let all who worship him rejoice!
Go to the Lord for help,
and worship him continually.
You descendants of Jacob, God's servant,
descendants of Israel, whom God chose,
remember the miracles that God performed
and the judgements that he gave.
The Lord is our God;
his commands are for all the world.
Never forget God's covenant,
which he made to last for ever,
the covenant he made with Abraham,
the promise he made to Isaac.
The Lord made a covenant with Jacob,
one that will last for ever:

The Lord   I will give you the land of Canaan.
It will be your own possession.

Chronicler   God's people were few in number,
strangers in the land of Canaan.
They wandered from country to country,
from one kingdom to another.
But God let no one oppress them;
to protect them, he warned the kings:

The Lord   Don't harm my chosen servants;
do not touch my prophets.

Chronicler   Sing to the Lord, all the world!
Proclaim every day the good news that he has saved us.
Proclaim his glory to the nations, his mighty deeds to all peoples.
The Lord is great and is to be highly praised;
he is to be honoured more than all the gods.
The gods of all other nations are only idols,
but the Lord created the heavens.
Glory and majesty surround him,
power and joy fill his Temple.

Praise the Lord, all people on earth,
praise his glory and might.
Praise the Lord's glorious name;
bring an offering and come into his Temple.
Bow down before the Holy One when he appears;
tremble before him, all the earth!
The earth is set firmly in place and cannot be moved.
Be glad, earth and sky!
Tell the nations that the Lord is king.
Roar, sea, and every creature in you;
be glad, fields, and everything in you!
The trees in the woods will shout for joy,
when the Lord comes to rule the earth.

$\rightarrow$

Give thanks to the Lord, because he is good;
his love is eternal.

Say to him:

Worshipper 1   Save us, O God our Saviour:

Worshipper 2   Gather us together.

Worshipper 1   Rescue us from the nations—

Worshipper 2   So that we may be thankful and praise your holy name.

Worshippers   Praise the Lord, the God of Israel!
1 and 2   Praise him now and for ever!

Chronicler   Then all the people said:

Worshippers
1 and 2   Amen!

Chronicler   And they praised the Lord.

Cast   [This is] the word of the Lord.
All   **Thanks be to God.**

Cast: **Chronicler, The Lord, Worshipper 1, Worshipper 2** (can be the same as Worshipper 1).

Nathan's message to David
1 Chronicles 17.1–15

Chronicler   King David was now living in his palace. One day he sent for the prophet Nathan and said to him:

David   Here I am living in a house built of cedar, but the Lord's Covenant Box is kept in a tent!

Chronicler   Nathan answered:

Nathan   Do whatever you have in mind, because God is with you.

Chronicler   But that night God said to Nathan:

The Lord   Go and tell my servant David that I say to him: You are not the one to build a temple for me to live in. From the time I rescued the people of Israel from Egypt until now, I have never lived in a temple; I have always lived in tents and moved from place to place. In all my travelling with the people of Israel I never asked any of the leaders that I appointed why they had not built me a temple made of cedar. So tell my servant David that I, the Lord Almighty, say to him, I took you from looking after sheep in the fields and made you the ruler of my people Israel. I have been with you wherever you have gone, and I have defeated all your enemies as you advanced. I will make you as famous as the greatest leaders in the world. I have chosen a place for my people Israel and have settled them there, where they will live without being oppressed any more. Ever since they entered this land they have been attacked by violent people, but this will not happen again. I promise to defeat all your enemies and to give you descendants. When you die and are buried with your ancestors, I will make one of your sons king and will keep his kingdom strong. He will be the one to build a temple for me, and I will make sure that his dynasty continues for ever. I will be his father and he will be my son. I will not withdraw my support from him as I did from Saul, whom I removed so that you could be king. I will put him in charge of my people and my kingdom for ever. His dynasty will never end.

Chronicler   Nathan told David everything that God had revealed to him.

Cast   [This is] the word of the Lord.
All   **Thanks be to God.**

Cast: **Chronicler, David, Nathan, The Lord.**

David's prayer of thanksgiving
1 Chronicles 17.16–27

Chronicler   King David went into the Tent of the Lord's presence, sat down, and prayed:

David   I am not worthy of what you have already done for me, Lord God, nor is my family. Yet now you are doing even more; you have made promises about my descendants in the years to come, and you, Lord God, are already treating me like a great man. What more can I say to you! You know me well, and yet you honour me, your servant. It was your will and purpose to do this for me and to show me my future greatness. Lord, there is none like you; we have always known that you alone are God. There is no other nation on earth like Israel, whom you rescued from slavery to make them your own people. The great and wonderful things you did for them spread your fame throughout the world. You rescued your people from Egypt and drove out other nations as your people advanced. You have made Israel your own people for ever, and you, Lord, have become their God.

And now, O Lord, fulfil for all time the promise you made about me and my descendants, and do what you said you would. Your fame will be great, and people will for ever say:

Persons 1 and **2**   The Lord Almighty is God over Israel.

David   And you will preserve my dynasty for all time. I have the courage to pray this prayer to you, my God, because you have revealed all this to me, your servant, and have told me that you will make my descendants kings. You, Lord, are God, and you have made this wonderful promise to me. I ask you to bless my descendants so that they will continue to enjoy your favour. You, Lord, have blessed them, and your blessing will rest on them for ever.

Cast   [This is] the word of the Lord.
All   **Thanks be to God.**

Cast: **Chronicler, David, Person 1, Person 2** (can be the same as Person 1).

David defeats the Ammonites
1 Chronicles 19.1–15

Chronicler King Nahash of Ammon died, and his son Hanun became king. King David said:

David I must show loyal friendship to Hanun, as his father Nahash did to me.

Chronicler So David sent messengers to express his sympathy. (PAUSE)

When they arrived in Ammon and called on King Hanun, the Ammonite leaders said to the king:

Leader 1 Do you think that it is in your father's honour that David has sent these men to express sympathy to you? Of course not!

Leader 2 He has sent them here as spies to explore the land, so that he can conquer it!

Chronicler Hanun seized David's messengers, shaved off their beards, cut off their clothes at the hips, and sent them away. They were too ashamed to return home. When David heard what had happened, he sent word for them to stay in Jericho and not return until their beards had grown again.

King Hanun and the Ammonites realized that they had made David their enemy, so they paid thirty-four thousand kilogrammes of silver to hire chariots and charioteers from Upper Mesopotamia and from the Syrian states of Maacah and Zobah. The thirty-two thousand chariots they hired and the army of the king of Maacah came and camped near Medeba. The Ammonites too came out from all their cities and got ready to fight.

When David heard what was happening, he sent out Joab and the whole army. The Ammonites marched out and took up their position at the entrance to Rabbah, their capital city, and the kings who had come to help took up their position in the open countryside.

Joab saw that the enemy troops would attack him in front and from the rear, so he chose the best of Israel's soldiers and put them in position facing the Syrians. He placed the rest of his troops under the command of his brother Abishai, who put them in position facing the Ammonites. [Joab said to him:]

Joab If you see that the Syrians are defeating me, come and help me, and if the Ammonites are defeating you, I will go and help you. Be strong and courageous! Let's fight hard for our people and for the cities of our God. And may the Lord's will be done.

Chronicler Joab and his men advanced to attack, and the Syrians fled. When the Ammonites saw the Syrians running away, they fled from Abishai and retreated into the city. Then Joab went back to Jerusalem.

Cast [This is] the word of the Lord.
All **Thanks be to God.**

Cast: **Chronicler, David, Leader 1, Leader 2, Joab.**

David takes a census
1 Chronicles 21.1–13

Chronicler	Satan wanted to bring trouble on the people of Israel, so he made David decide to take a census. David gave orders to Joab and the other officers:
David	Go through Israel, from one end of the country to the other, and count the people. I want to know how many there are.
Chronicler	Joab answered:
Joab	May the Lord make the people of Israel a hundred times more numerous than they are now! Your Majesty, they are all your servants. Why do you want to do this and make the whole nation guilty?
Chronicler	But the king made Joab obey the order. Joab went out, travelled through the whole country of Israel, and then returned to Jerusalem. He reported to King David the total number of men capable of military service: 1,100,000 in Israel, and 470,000 in Judah. Because Joab disapproved of the king's command, he did not take any census of the tribes of Levi and Benjamin. God was displeased with what had been done, so he punished Israel. David said to God:
David	I have committed a terrible sin in doing this! Please forgive me. I have acted foolishly.
Chronicler	Then the Lord said to Gad, David's prophet:
The Lord	Go and tell David that I am giving him three choices. I will do whichever he chooses.
Chronicler	Gad went to David, told him what the Lord had said, and asked:
Gad	Which is it to be? Three years of famine? Or three months of running away from the armies of your enemies? Or three days during which the Lord attacks you with his sword and sends an epidemic on your land, using his angel to bring death throughout Israel? What answer shall I give the Lord?
Chronicler	David replied to Gad:
David	I am in a desperate situation! But I don't want to be punished by men. Let the Lord himself be the one to punish me, because he is merciful.
Cast	[This is] the word of the Lord.
All	**Thanks be to God.**

Cast: **Chronicler, David, Joab, The Lord, Gad.**

The Lord answers David's prayer
1 Chronicles 21.14—22.1

Chronicler The Lord sent an epidemic on the people of Israel, and seventy thousand of them died. Then he sent an angel to destroy Jerusalem, but he changed his mind and said to the angel:

The Lord Stop! That's enough!

Chronicler The angel was standing by the threshing-place of Araunah, a Jebusite. David saw the angel standing in mid air, holding his sword in his hand, ready to destroy Jerusalem. Then David and the leaders of the people—all of whom were wearing sackcloth—bowed low, with their faces touching the ground. David prayed:

David O God, I am the one who did wrong. I am the one who ordered the census. What have these poor people done? Lord, my God, punish me and my family, and spare your people.

Chronicler The angel of the Lord told Gad to command David to go and build an altar to the Lord at Araunah's threshing-place. David obeyed the Lord's command and went, as Gad had told him to. There at the threshing-place Araunah and his four sons were threshing wheat, and when they saw the angel, the sons ran and hid. As soon as Araunah saw King David approaching, he left the threshing-place and bowed low, with his face touching the ground. David said to him:

David Sell me your threshing-place, so that I can build an altar to the Lord, to stop the epidemic. I'll give you the full price.

Araunah Take it, Your Majesty, and do whatever you wish. Here are these oxen to burn as an offering on the altar, and here are the threshing-boards to use as fuel, and wheat to give as an offering. I give it all to you.

David No, I will pay you the full price. I will not give as an offering to the Lord something that belongs to you, something that costs me nothing.

Chronicler And he paid Araunah six hundred gold coins for the threshing-place. He built an altar to the Lord there and offered burnt-offerings and fellowship-offerings. He prayed, and the Lord answered him by sending fire from heaven to burn the sacrifices on the altar. The Lord told the angel to put his sword away, and the angel obeyed. David saw by this that the Lord had answered his prayer, so he offered sacrifices on the altar at Araunah's threshing-place.

The Tent of the Lord's presence which Moses had made in the wilderness, and the altar on which sacrifices were burnt were still at the place of worship at Gibeon at this time; but David was not able to go there to worship God, because he was afraid of the sword of the Lord's angel. So David said:

David	This is where the Temple of the Lord God will be. Here is the altar where the people of Israel are to offer burnt-offerings.
Cast	[This is] the word of the Lord.
All	**Thanks be to God.**

Cast: **Chronicler, The Lord, David, Araunah.**

David's preparations for building the Temple
From 1 Chronicles 22.2—23.1

Chronicler	King David gave orders for all the foreigners living in the land of Israel to assemble, and he put them to work. Some of them prepared stone blocks for building the Temple. He supplied a large amount of iron for making nails and clamps for the wooden gates, and so much bronze that no one could weigh it. He arranged for the people of Tyre and Sidon to bring him a large number of cedar logs. David thought:
David	The Temple that my son Solomon is to build must be splendid and world-famous. But he is young and inexperienced, so I must make preparations for it.
Chronicler	So David got large amounts of the materials ready before he died. He sent for his son Solomon and commanded him to build a temple for the Lord, the God of Israel:
David	My son, I wanted to build a temple to honour the Lord my God. But the Lord told me that I had killed too many people and fought too many wars. And so, because of all the bloodshed I have caused, he would not let me build a temple for him. He did, however, make me a promise. [He said:]
[The Lord]	You will have a son who will rule in peace, because I will give him peace from all his enemies. His name will be Solomon, because during his reign I will give Israel peace and security. He will build a temple for me. He will be my son, and I will be his father. His dynasty will rule Israel for ever.
[Chronicler	David continued:]
David	Now, my son, may the Lord your God be with you, and may he keep his promise to make you successful in building a temple for him. And may the Lord your God give you insight and wisdom so that you may govern Israel according to his Law. If you obey all the laws which the Lord gave to Moses for Israel, you will be successful. Be determined and confident, and don't let anything make you afraid. Now begin the work, and may the Lord be with you.
Chronicler	David commanded all the leaders of Israel to help Solomon. [He said]:
David	The Lord your God has been with you and given you peace on all sides. He let me conquer all the people who used to live in this land, and they are now subject to you and to the Lord. Now serve

$\rightarrow$

the Lord your God with all your heart and soul. Start building the Temple, so that you can place in it the Covenant Box of the Lord and all the other sacred objects used in worshipping him.

Chronicler   When David was very old, he made his son Solomon king of Israel.

Cast   [This is] the word of the Lord.
All   **Thanks be to God.**

Cast: **Chronicler, David, [The Lord** (preferably unseen)**].**

David's instructions for the Temple
1 Chronicles 28.1–21

Chronicler   King David commanded all the officials of Israel to assemble in Jerusalem. So all the officials of the tribes, the officials who administered the work of the kingdom, the leaders of the clans, the supervisors of the property and livestock that belonged to the king and his sons—indeed all the palace officials, leading soldiers, and important men—gathered in Jerusalem. David stood before them and addressed them:

David   My countrymen, listen to me. I wanted to build a permanent home for the Covenant Box, the footstool of the Lord our God. I have made preparations for building a temple to honour him, but he has forbidden me to do it, because I am a soldier and have shed too much blood. The Lord, the God of Israel, chose me and my descendants to rule Israel for ever. He chose the tribe of Judah to provide leadership, and out of Judah he chose my father's family. From all that family it was his pleasure to take me and make me king over all Israel. He gave me many sons, and out of them all he chose Solomon to rule over Israel, the Lord's kingdom. The Lord said to me:

[The Lord]   Your son Solomon is the one who will build my Temple. I have chosen him to be my son, and I will be his father. I will make his kingdom last for ever if he continues to obey carefully all my laws and commands as he does now.

David   So now, my people, in the presence of our God and of this assembly of all Israel, the Lord's people, I charge you to obey carefully everything that the Lord our God has commanded us, so that you may continue to possess this good land and so that you may hand it on to succeeding generations for ever.

Chronicler   And to Solomon he said:

David   My son, I charge you to acknowledge your father's God and to serve him with an undivided heart and a willing mind. He knows all our thoughts and desires. If you go to him, he will accept you; but if you turn away from him, he will abandon you for ever. You must realize that the Lord has chosen you to build his holy Temple. Now do it—and do it with determination.

Chronicler	David gave Solomon the plans for all the temple buildings, for the storerooms and all the other rooms, and for the Most Holy Place, where sins are forgiven. He also gave him the plans for all he had in mind for the courtyards and the rooms around them, and for the storerooms for the temple equipment and the gifts dedicated to the Lord. David also gave him the plans for organizing the priests and Levites to perform their duties, to do the work of the Temple, and to take care of all the temple utensils. He gave instructions as to how much silver and gold was to be used for making the utensils, for each lamp and lampstand, for the silver tables, and for each gold table on which were placed the loaves of bread offered to God. He also gave instructions as to how much pure gold was to be used in making forks, bowls, and jars, how much silver and gold in making dishes, and how much pure gold in making the altar on which incense was burnt and in making the chariot for the winged creatures that spread their wings over the Lord's Covenant Box. King David said:
David	All this is contained in the plan written according to the instructions which the Lord himself gave me to carry out.
Chronicler	King David said to his son Solomon:
David	Be confident and determined. Start the work and don't let anything stop you. The Lord God, whom I serve, will be with you. He will not abandon you, but he will stay with you until you finish the work to be done on his Temple. The priests and the Levites have been assigned duties to perform in the Temple. Workmen with every kind of skill are eager to help you, and all the people and their leaders are at your command.
Cast	[This is] the word of the Lord.
All	**Thanks be to God.**

Cast: **Chronicler, David, [The Lord** (preferably unseen)**]**.

Gifts for building the Temple
1 Chronicles 29.1–9

Chronicler	King David announced to the whole assembly:
David	My son Solomon is the one whom God has chosen, but he is still young and lacks experience. The work to be done is tremendous, because this is not a palace for men but a temple for the Lord God. I have made every effort to prepare materials for the Temple— gold, silver, bronze, iron, timber, precious stones and gems, stones for mosaics, and quantities of marble. Over and above all this that I have provided, I have given silver and gold from my personal property because of my love for God's Temple. I have given more than a hundred tons of the finest gold and almost two hundred and forty tons of pure silver for decorating the walls of the Temple and for all the objects which the craftsmen are to make. Now who else is willing to give a generous offering to the Lord?

Chronicler	Then the heads of the clans, the officials of the tribes, the commanders of the army, and the administrators of the royal property volunteered to give the following for the work on the Temple: more than 170 tons of gold, over 340 tons of silver, almost 620 tons of bronze, and more than 3,400 tons of iron. Those who had precious stones gave them to the temple treasury, which was administered by Jehiel of the Levite clan of Gershon. The people had given willingly to the Lord, and they were happy that so much had been given. King David also was extremely happy.
Cast	[This is] the word of the Lord.
All	**Thanks be to God.**

Cast: **Chronicler, David.**

David praises God
1 Chronicles 29.9–20

Chronicler	[*The people had given willingly to the Lord for the building of the Temple, and they were happy that so much had been given. King David also was extremely happy.] There in front of the whole assembly King David praised the Lord:
David	Lord God of our ancestor Jacob, may you be praised for ever and ever! You are great and powerful, glorious, splendid, and majestic. Everything in heaven and earth is yours, and you are king, supreme ruler over all. All riches and wealth come from you; you rule everything by your strength and power; and you are able to make anyone great and strong. Now, our God, we give you thanks, and we praise your glorious name.
	Yet my people and I cannot really give you anything, because everything is a gift from you, and we have only given back what is yours already. You know, O Lord, that we pass through life like exiles and strangers, as our ancestors did. Our days are like a passing shadow, and we cannot escape death. O Lord, our God, we have brought together all this wealth to build a temple to honour your holy name, but it all came from you and all belongs to you. I know that you test everyone's heart and are pleased with people of integrity. In honesty and sincerity I have willingly given all this to you, and I have seen how your people who are gathered here have been happy to bring offerings to you. Lord God of our ancestors Abraham, Isaac, and Jacob, keep such devotion for ever strong in your people's hearts and keep them always faithful to you. Give my son Solomon a wholehearted desire to obey everything that you command and to build the Temple for which I have made these preparations.
Chronicler	Then David commanded the people:
David	Praise the Lord your God!

Chronicler   And the whole assembly praised the Lord, the God of their ancestors, and they bowed low and gave honour to the Lord and also to the king.

Cast   [This is] the word of the Lord.
All   **Thanks be to God.**

Cast: **Chronicler, David.** (*Please note: this section overlaps with the previous reading.)

2 CHRONICLES

Solomon's preparations for building the Temple
2 Chronicles 2.1–16

Chronicler   King Solomon decided to build a temple where the Lord would be worshipped, and also to build a palace for himself. He put seventy thousand men to work transporting materials, and eighty thousand men to work quarrying stone. There were three thousand six hundred men responsible for supervising the work. Solomon sent a message to King Hiram of Tyre:

Solomon   Do business with me as you did with my father, King David, when you sold him cedar logs for building his palace. I am building a temple to honour the Lord my God. It will be a holy place where my people and I will worship him by burning incense of fragrant spices, where we will present offerings of sacred bread to him continuously, and where we will offer burnt-offerings every morning and evening, as well as on Sabbaths, New Moon Festivals, and other holy days honouring the Lord our God. He has commanded Israel to do this for ever. I intend to build a great temple, because our God is greater than any other god. Yet no one can really build a temple for God, because even all the vastness of heaven cannot contain him. How then can I build a temple that would be anything more than a place to burn incense to God?

Now send me a man with skill in engraving, in working gold, silver, bronze, and iron, and in making blue, purple and red cloth. He will work with the craftsmen of Judah and Jerusalem whom my father David selected. I know how skilful your woodmen are, so send me cedar, cypress, and juniper logs from Lebanon. I am ready to send my men to assist yours in preparing large quantities of timber, because this temple I intend to build will be large and magnificent. As provisions for your workmen, I will send you two thousand tons of wheat, two thousand tons of barley, four hundred thousand litres of wine, and four hundred thousand litres of olive-oil.

Chronicler   King Hiram sent Solomon a letter in reply [He wrote]:

Hiram   Because the Lord loves his people, he has made you their king. Praise the Lord God of Israel, Creator of heaven and earth! He has given King David a wise son, full of understanding and skill, who now plans to build a temple for the Lord and a palace for himself. I am sending you a wise and skilful master craftsman named Huram. His mother was a member of the tribe of Dan and his father was a native of Tyre. He knows how to make things out of gold, silver, bronze, iron, stone, and wood. He can work with blue, purple, and red cloth, and with linen. He can do all sorts of engraving and can follow any design suggested to him. Let him work with your craftsmen and with those who worked for your father, King David. So now send us the wheat, barley, wine, and olive-oil that you promised. In the mountains of Lebanon we will cut down all the cedars you need, bind them together in rafts, and float them by sea as far as Joppa. From there you can take them to Jerusalem.

Cast	[This is] the word of the Lord.
All	**Thanks be to God.**

Cast: **Chronicler, Solomon, Hiram.**

The glory of the Lord
2 Chronicles 5.11–14

Chronicler	All the priests present, regardless of the group to which they belonged, had consecrated themselves. And all the Levite musicians—Asaph, Heman, and Jeduthun, and the members of their clans—were wearing linen clothing. The Levites stood near the east side of the altar with cymbals and harps, and with them were a hundred and twenty priests playing trumpets. The singers were accompanied in perfect harmony by trumpets, cymbals, and other instruments, as they praised the Lord, singing:
Singer 1	Praise the Lord because he is good—
Singer 2	And his love is eternal.
Chronicler	As the priests were leaving the Temple, it was suddenly filled with a cloud shining with the dazzling light of the Lord's presence, and they could not continue the service of worship.
Cast	[This is] the word of the Lord.
All	**Thanks be to God.**

Cast: **Chronicler, Singer 1, Singer 2** (can be the same as Singer 1).

Solomon's address to the people
2 Chronicles 6.1–11

Chronicler	King Solomon prayed:
Solomon	Lord, you have chosen to live in clouds and darkness. Now I have built a majestic temple for you, a place for you to live in for ever.
Chronicler	All the people of Israel were standing there. The king turned to face them and asked God's blessing on them. He said:
Solomon	Praise the Lord God of Israel! He has kept the promise he made to my father David when he said to him:

[The Lord]	From the time I brought my people out of Egypt until now, I did not choose any city in the land of Israel as the place to build a temple where I would be worshipped, and I did not choose anyone to lead my people Israel. But now I have chosen Jerusalem as the place where I will be worshipped, and you, David, to rule my people.
Chronicler	And Solomon continued:
Solomon	My father David planned to build a temple for the worship of the Lord God of Israel, but the Lord said to him:
[The Lord]	You were right in wanting to build a temple for me, but you will never build it. It is your son, your own son, who will build my temple.
Solomon	Now the Lord has kept his promise: I have succeeded my father as king of Israel, and I have built a temple for the worship of the Lord God of Israel. I have placed in the Temple the Covenant Box, which contains the stone tablets of the covenant which the Lord made with the people of Israel.
Cast	[This is] the word of the Lord.
All	**Thanks be to God.**

Cast: **Chronicler, Solomon, [The Lord** (preferably unseen)**]**.

Solomon's prayer (i)
2 Chronicles 6.12–21

Chronicler	In the presence of the people Solomon went and stood in front of the altar and raised his arms in prayer.
[Commentator]	Solomon had made a bronze platform and put it in the middle of the courtyard. It was 2.2 metres square and 1.3 metres high. He mounted this platform, knelt down where everyone could see him, and raised his hands towards heaven.
Chronicler	Solomon prayed:
Solomon	Lord God of Israel, in all heaven and earth there is no god like you. You keep your covenant with your people and show them your love when they live in wholehearted obedience to you. You have kept the promise you made to my father David; today every word has been fulfilled. Now, Lord God of Israel, keep the other promise you made to my father when you told him that there would always be one of his descendants ruling as king of Israel, provided that they carefully obeyed your Law just as he did. So now, Lord God of Israel, let everything come true that you promised to your servant David.
	But can you, O God, really live on earth among men and women? Not even all heaven is large enough to hold you, so how can this Temple that I have built be large enough? Lord my God, I am your servant. Listen to my prayer and grant the requests I make to you. Watch over this Temple day and night. You have

promised that this is where you will be worshipped, so hear me when I face this Temple and pray. Hear my prayers and the prayers of your people Israel when they face this place and pray. In your home in heaven hear us and forgive us.

Cast	[This is] the word of the Lord.
All	**Thanks be to God.**

Cast: **Chronicler, [Commentator], Solomon.**

Solomon's prayer (ii)
2 Chronicles 6.22–31

Voice 1   When a person is accused of wronging another and is brought to your altar in this Temple to take an oath that he is innocent—

Voice 2   O Lord, listen in heaven and judge your servants. Punish the guilty one as he deserves and acquit the one who is innocent.

Voice 1   When your people Israel are defeated by their enemies because they have sinned against you and then when they turn to you and come to this Temple, humbly praying to you for forgiveness—

Voice 2   Listen to them in heaven. Forgive the sins of your people and bring them back to the land which you gave to them and to their ancestors.

Voice 1   When you hold back the rain because your people have sinned against you and then when they repent and face this Temple, humbly praying to you—

Voice 2   O Lord, listen to them in heaven and forgive the sins of your servants, the people of Israel, and teach them to do what is right. Then, O Lord, send rain on this land of yours, which you gave to your people as a permanent possession.

Voice 1   When there is famine in the land or an epidemic or the crops are destroyed by scorching winds or swarms of locusts, or when your people are attacked by their enemies, or when there is disease or sickness among them—

Voice 2   Listen to their prayers.

Voice 1   If any of your people Israel, out of heartfelt sorrow, stretch out their hands in prayer towards this Temple—

Voice 2   Hear their prayer. Listen to them in your home in heaven and forgive them. You alone know the thoughts of the human heart. Deal with each person as he deserves, so that your people may honour you and obey you all the time they live in the land which you gave to our ancestors.

Cast	[This is] the word of the Lord.
All	**Thanks be to God.**

Cast: **Voice 1, Voice 2.**

Solomon's prayer (iii)
2 Chronicles 6.32–40

Voice 1   When a foreigner who lives in a distant land hears how great and powerful you are and how you are always ready to act, and then comes to pray at this Temple—

Voice 2   Listen to his prayer. In heaven, where you live, hear him and do what he asks you to do, so that all the peoples of the world may know you and obey you, as your people Israel do. Then they will know that this Temple I have built is where you are to be worshipped.

Voice 1   When you command your people to go into battle against their enemies and they pray to you, wherever they are, facing this city which you have chosen and this Temple which I have built for you—

Voice 2   Listen to their prayers. Hear them in heaven and give them victory.

Voice 1   When your people sin against you—and there is no one who does not sin—and in your anger you let their enemies defeat them and take them as prisoners to some other land, even if that land is far away—

Voice 2   Listen to your people's prayers.

Voice 1   If there in that land they repent and pray to you, confessing how sinful and wicked they have been—

Voice 2   Hear their prayers, O Lord.

Voice 1   If in that land they truly and sincerely repent and pray to you as they face towards this land which you gave to our ancestors, this city which you have chosen, and this Temple which I have built for you—

Voice 2   Then listen to their prayers. In your home in heaven hear them and be merciful to them and forgive all the sins of your people.

     Now, O my God—

Voices 1 and **2**   Look on us and listen to the prayers offered in this place.

Cast   [This is] the word of the Lord.
All   **Thanks be to God.**

Cast: **Voice 1, Voice 2.**

God appears to Solomon again
2 Chronicles 7.11–22

Chronicler   After King Solomon had finished the Temple and the palace, successfully completing all his plans for them, the Lord appeared to him at night [He said to him]:

The Lord I have heard your prayer, and I accept this Temple as the place where sacrifices are to be offered to me. Whenever I hold back the rain or send locusts to eat up the crops or send an epidemic on my people, if they pray to me and repent and turn away from the evil they have been doing, then I will hear them in heaven, forgive their sins, and make their land prosperous again. I will watch over this Temple and be ready to hear all the prayers that are offered here, because I have chosen it and consecrated it as the place where I will be worshipped for ever. I will watch over it and protect it for all time. If you serve me faithfully as your father David did, obeying my laws and doing everything I have commanded you, I will keep the promise I made to your father David when I told him that Israel would always be ruled by his descendants. But if you and your people ever disobey the laws and commands I have given you, and worship other gods, then I will remove you from the land that I gave you, and I will abandon this Temple that I have consecrated as the place where I am to be worshipped. People everywhere will ridicule it and treat it with contempt.

The Temple is now greatly honoured, but then everyone who passes by it will be amazed and will ask:

Person 1 Why did the Lord do this to this land and this Temple?

The Lord People will answer:

Person 2 It is because they abandoned the Lord their God, who brought their ancestors out of Egypt.

Person 3 They gave their allegiance to other gods and worshipped *them*.

Person 2 That is why the Lord has brought this disaster on them.

Cast [This is] the word of the Lord.
All **Thanks be to God.**

Cast: **Chronicler, The Lord, Person 1, Person 2, Person 3** (can be the same as Person 2).

The visit of the Queen of Sheba
2 Chronicles 9.1–12

Chronicler The queen of Sheba heard of King Solomon's fame, and she travelled to Jerusalem to test him with difficult questions. She brought with her a large group of attendants, as well as camels loaded with spices, jewels, and a large amount of gold. When she and Solomon met, she asked him all the questions that she could think of. He answered them all; there was nothing too difficult for him to explain. The queen of Sheba heard Solomon's wisdom and saw the palace he had built. She saw the food that was served at his table, the living-quarters for his officials, the organization of his palace staff and the uniforms they wore, the clothing of the servants who waited on him at feasts, and the sacrifices he offered in the Temple. It left her breathless and amazed [She said to the king]:

Queen (amazed)	What I heard in my own country about you and your wisdom is true! I did not believe what they told me until I came and saw for myself. I had not heard of even half your wisdom. You are even wiser than people say. How fortunate are the men who serve you, who are always in your presence and are privileged to hear your wise sayings! Praise the Lord your God! He has shown how pleased he is with you by making you king, to rule in his name. Because he loves his people Israel and wants to preserve them for ever, he has made you their king so that you can maintain law and justice.
Chronicler	She presented to King Solomon the gifts she had brought: more than four thousand kilogrammes of gold and a very large amount of spices and jewels. There have never been any other spices as fine as those that the queen of Sheba gave to King Solomon.
[Commentator]	The men of King Hiram and of King Solomon who brought gold from Ophir also brought juniper wood and jewels. Solomon used the wood to make stairs for the Temple and for his palace, and to make harps and lyres for the musicians.Nothing like that had ever been seen before in the land of Judah.
Chronicler	King Solomon gave the queen of Sheba everything she asked for. This was in addition to what he gave her in exchange for the gifts she brought to him. Then she and her attendants returned to the land of Sheba.
Cast	[This is] the word of the Lord.
All	**Thanks be to God.**

Cast: **Chronicler, Queen, [Commentator].**

The northern tribes revolt
From 2 Chronicles 10.1–19

Chronicler	Rehoboam went to Shechem, where all the people of northern Israel had gathered to make him king. When Jeroboam son of Nebat, who had gone to Egypt to escape from King Solomon, heard this news, he returned home. The people of the northern tribes sent for him, and they all went together to Rehoboam [and said to him]:
Person 1	Your father placed heavy burdens on us.
Person 2	If you make these burdens lighter and make life easier for us, we will be your loyal subjects.
Chronicler	Rehoboam replied:
Rehoboam	Give me three days to consider the matter. Then come back.
Chronicler	So the people left. King Rehoboam consulted the older men who had served as his father Solomon's advisers:
Rehoboam	What answer do you advise me to give these people?

Senior adviser	If you are kind to these people and try to please them by giving a considerate answer, they will always serve you loyally.
Chronicler	But he ignored the advice of the older men and went instead to the young men who had grown up with him and who were now his advisers:
Rehoboam	What do you advise me to do? What shall I say to the people who are asking me to make their burdens lighter?
Young adviser 1	This is what you should tell them: 'My little finger is thicker than my father's waist.'
Young adviser 2	Tell them, 'My father placed heavy burdens on you; I will make them even heavier.'
Young adviser 1	'He beat you with a whip; I'll flog you with a horsewhip!'
Chronicler	Three days later Jeroboam and all the people returned to King Rehoboam, as he had instructed them. The king ignored the advice of the older men and spoke harshly to the people, as the younger men had advised:
Rehoboam	My father placed heavy burdens on you; I will make them even heavier. He beat you with a whip; I'll flog you with a horsewhip!
Chronicler	When the people saw that the king would not listen to them, they shouted:
Person 1	Down with David and his family!
Person 2	What have they ever done for us?
Persons 1 and **2**	Men of Israel, let's go home!
Person 1	Let Rehoboam look out for himself!
Chronicler	So the people of Israel rebelled, leaving Rehoboam as king only of the people who lived in the territory of Judah. Then King Rehoboam sent Adoniram, who was in charge of the forced labour, to go to the Israelites, but they stoned him to death. At this, Rehoboam hurriedly got into his chariot and escaped to Jerusalem. Ever since that time the people of the northern kingdom of Israel have been in rebellion against the dynasty of David.
Cast	[This is] the word of the Lord.
All	**Thanks be to God.**

Cast: **Chronicler, Person 1, Person 2** (can be the same as Person 1), **Rehoboam, Senior adviser, Young adviser 1, Young adviser 2** (can be the same as Young adviser 1).

An Egyptian invasion of Judah
2 Chronicles 12.1–12

Chronicler	As soon as Rehoboam had established his authority as king, he and all his people abandoned the Law of the Lord. In the fifth year of Rehoboam's reign their disloyalty to the Lord was

→

punished. King Shishak of Egypt attacked Jerusalem with an army of twelve hundred chariots, sixty thousand horsemen, and more soldiers than could be counted, including Libyan, Sukkite, and Sudanese troops. He captured the fortified cities of Judah and advanced as far as Jerusalem.

Shemaiah the prophet went to King Rehoboam and the Judaean leaders who had gathered in Jerusalem to escape Shishak [He said to them]:

Shemaiah	This is the Lord's message to you—
The Lord	You have abandoned me, so now I have abandoned you to Shishak.
Chronicler	The king and the leaders admitted that they had sinned:
Rehoboam	What the Lord is doing is just.
Chronicler	When the Lord saw this, he spoke again to Shemaiah:
The Lord	Because they admit their sin, I will not destroy them. But when Shishak attacks, they will barely survive. Jerusalem will not feel the full force of my anger, but Shishak will conquer them, and they will learn the difference between serving me and serving earthly rulers.
Chronicler	King Shishak came to Jerusalem and took the treasures from the Temple and from the palace. He took everything, including the gold shields that King Solomon had made. To replace them, Rehoboam made bronze shields and entrusted them to the officers responsible for guarding the palace gates. Every time the king went to the Temple, the guards carried the shields and then returned them to the guardroom. Because he submitted to the Lord, the Lord's anger did not completely destroy him, and things went well for Judah.
Cast	[This is] the word of the Lord.
All	**Thanks be to God.**

Cast: **Chronicler, Shemaiah, The Lord, Rehoboam.**

Abijah's war with Jeroboam
2 Chronicles 13.1–17

Chronicler	In the eighteenth year of the reign of King Jeroboam of Israel, Abijah became king of Judah, and he ruled for three years in Jerusalem. His mother was Micaiah daughter of Uriel, from the city of Gibeah.
	War broke out between Abijah and Jeroboam. Abijah raised an army of 400,000 soldiers, and Jeroboam opposed him with an army of 800,000.
	The armies met in the hill-country of Ephraim. King Abijah went up Mount Zemaraim and called out to Jeroboam and the Israelites:

Abijah	Listen to me! Don't you know that the Lord, the God of Israel, made an unbreakable covenant with David, giving him and his descendants kingship over Israel for ever? Jeroboam son of Nebat rebelled against Solomon, his king. Later he gathered together a group of worthless scoundrels, and they forced their will on Rehoboam son of Solomon, who was too young and inexperienced to resist them. Now you propose to fight against the royal authority that the Lord gave to David's descendants. You have a huge army and have with you the gold bull-calves that Jeroboam made to be your gods. You drove out the Lord's priests, the descendants of Aaron, and you drove out the Levites. In their place you appointed priests in the same way that other nations do. Anybody who comes along with a bull or seven sheep can get himself consecrated as a priest of those so-called gods of yours.
	But we still serve the Lord our God and have not abandoned him. Priests descended from Aaron perform their duties, and Levites assist them. Every morning and every evening they offer him incense and animal sacrifices burnt whole. They present the offerings of bread on a table that is ritually clean, and every evening they light the lamps on the gold lampstand. We do what the Lord has commanded, but you have abandoned him. God himself is our leader and his priests are here with trumpets, ready to blow them and call us to battle against you. People of Israel, don't fight against the Lord, the God of your ancestors! You can't win!
Chronicler	Meanwhile Jeroboam had sent some of his troops to ambush the Judaean army from the rear, while the rest faced them from the front. The Judaeans looked round and saw that they were surrounded. They cried to the Lord for help, and the priests blew the trumpets. The Judaeans gave a loud shout, and led by Abijah, they attacked; God defeated Jeroboam and the Israelite army. The Israelites fled from the Judaeans, and God let the Judaeans overpower them. Abijah and his army dealt the Israelites a crushing defeat.
Cast	[This is] the word of the Lord.
All	**Thanks be to God.**

Cast: **Chronicler, Abijah.**

King Asa defeats the Sudanese
2 Chronicles 14.1–13

Chronicler	King Abijah died and was buried in the royal tombs in David's City. His son Asa succeeded him as king, and under Asa the land enjoyed peace for ten years. Asa pleased the Lord, his God, by doing what was right and good. He removed the foreign altars and the pagan places of worship, broke down the sacred stone columns, and cut down the symbols of the goddess Asherah. He commanded the people of Judah to do the will of the Lord, the God of their ancestors, and to obey his teachings and commands.

→

	Because he abolished the pagan places of worship and the incense-altars from all the cities of Judah, the kingdom was at peace under his rule. He built fortifications for the cities of Judah during this time, and for several years there was no war, because the Lord gave him peace. He said to the people of Judah:

Asa Let us fortify the cities by building walls and towers, and gates that can be shut and barred. We have control of the land because we have done the will of the Lord our God. He has protected us and given us security on every side.

Chronicler And so they built and prospered. King Asa had an army of 300,000 men from Judah, armed with shields and spears, and 280,000 men from Benjamin, armed with shields and bows. All of them were brave, well-trained men.

A Sudanese named Zerah invaded Judah with an army of a million men and three hundred chariots and advanced as far as Mareshah. Asa went out to fight him, and both sides took up their positions in the Valley of Zephathah near Mareshah. Asa prayed to the Lord his God:

Asa O Lord, you can help a weak army as easily as a powerful one. Help us now, O Lord our God, because we are relying on you, and in your name we have come out to fight against this huge army. Lord, you are our God; no one can hope to defeat you.

Chronicler The Lord defeated the Sudanese army when Asa and the Judaean army attacked them. They fled, and Asa and his troops pursued them as far as Gerar.

Cast [This is] the word of the Lord.
All **Thanks be to God.**

Cast: **Chronicler, Asa.**

Asa's reforms
From 2 Chronicles 15.1–15

Chronicler The spirit of God came upon Azariah son of Oded, and he went to meet King Asa [He called out]:

Azariah Listen to me, King Asa, and all you people of Judah and Benjamin! The Lord is with you as long as you are with him. If you look for him, he will let you find him, but if you turn away, he will abandon you. For a long time Israel lived without the true God, without priests to teach them, and without a law. But when trouble came, they turned to the Lord, the God of Israel. They searched for him and found him. In those days no one could come and go in safety, because there was trouble and disorder in every land. One nation oppressed another nation, and one city oppressed another city, because God was bringing trouble and distress on them. But you must be strong and not be discouraged. The work that you do will be rewarded.

Chronicler	When Asa heard the prophecy that Azariah son of Oded had spoken, he was encouraged. He did away with all the idols in the land of Judah and Benjamin and all the idols in the cities he had captured in the hill-country of Ephraim. He also repaired the altar of the Lord that stood in the temple courtyard.
	In a loud voice the people took an oath in the Lord's name that they would keep the covenant, and then they shouted and blew trumpets. All the people of Judah were happy because they had made this covenant with all their heart. They took delight in worshipping the Lord, and he accepted them and gave them peace on every side.
Cast	[This is] the word of the Lord.
All	**Thanks be to God.**

Cast: **Chronicler, Azariah.**

More about King Asa of Judah
From 2 Chronicles 16.1–14

Chronicler	In the thirty-sixth year of the reign of King Asa of Judah, King Baasha of Israel invaded Judah and started to fortify Ramah in order to cut off all traffic in and out of Judah. So Asa took silver and gold from the treasuries of the Temple and the palace and sent it to Damascus, to King Benhadad of Syria, with this message:
Asa	Let us be allies, as our fathers were. This silver and gold is a present for you. Now break your alliance with King Baasha of Israel so that he will have to pull his troops out of my territory.
Chronicler	Benhadad agreed to Asa's proposal and sent his commanding officers and their armies to attack the cities of Israel. They captured Ijon, Dan, Abel Beth Maacah, and all the cities of Naphtali where supplies were stored. When King Baasha heard what was happening, he stopped fortifying Ramah and abandoned the work. Then King Asa gathered men from throughout Judah and ordered them to carry off the stones and timber that Baasha had been using at Ramah, and they used them to fortify the cities of Geba and Mizpah. (PAUSE)
	At that time the prophet Hanani went to King Asa [and said]:
Hanani	Because you relied on the king of Syria instead of relying on the Lord your God, the army of the king of Israel has escaped from you. Didn't the Sudanese and the Libyans have large armies with many chariots and horsemen? But because you relied on the Lord, he gave you victory over them. The Lord keeps close watch over the whole world, to give strength to those whose hearts are loyal to him. You have acted foolishly, and so from now on you will always be at war.
Chronicler	This made Asa so angry with the prophet that he had him put in chains. It was at this same time that Asa began treating some of the people cruelly. (PAUSE) $\rightarrow$

In the thirty-ninth year that Asa was king, he was crippled by a severe foot disease; but even then he did not turn to the Lord for help, but to doctors. Two years later he died and was buried in the rock tomb which he had carved out for himself in David's City. They used spices and perfumed oils to prepare his body for burial, and they built a huge bonfire to mourn his death.

Cast	[This is] the word of the Lord.
All	**Thanks be to God.**

Cast: **Chronicler, Asa, Hanani.**

The prophet Micaiah warns Ahab
2 Chronicles 18.1–27

Chronicler	When King Jehoshaphat of Judah became rich and famous, he arranged a marriage between a member of his family and the family of King Ahab of Israel. A number of years later Jehoshaphat went to the city of Samaria to visit Ahab. To honour Jehoshaphat and those with him, Ahab had a large number of sheep and cattle slaughtered for a feast. He tried to persuade Jehoshaphat to join him in attacking the city of Ramoth in Gilead.
Ahab	Will you go with me to attack Ramoth?
[Chronicler	Jehoshaphat replied:]
Jehoshaphat	I am ready when you are, and so is my army. We will join you. (PAUSE) But first let's consult the Lord.
Chronicler	So Ahab called in the prophets, about four hundred of them [and asked them:]
Ahab	Should I go and attack Ramoth, or not?
Prophet 1	Attack it.
Prophet 2	God will give you victory.
[Chronicler	But Jehoshaphat asked Ahab:]
Jehoshaphat	Isn't there another prophet through whom we can consult the Lord?
Ahab (petulantly)	There is one more, Micaiah son of Imlah. But I hate him because he never prophesies anything good for me; it's always something bad.
Jehoshaphat	You shouldn't say that!
Chronicler	So King Ahab called in a court official and told him to go and fetch Micaiah at once. The two kings, dressed in their royal robes, were sitting on their thrones at the threshing-place just outside the gate of Samaria, and all the prophets were prophesying in front of them. One of them, Zedekiah son of Chenaanah, made iron horns and said to Ahab:
Zedekiah	This is what the Lord says: With these you will fight the Syrians and totally defeat them.

Chronicler	All the other prophets said the same thing:
Prophet 1	March against Ramoth and you will win.
Prophet 2	The Lord will give you victory.
Chronicler	Meanwhile, the official who had gone to fetch Micaiah said to him:
Official (firmly)	All the other prophets have prophesied success for the king, and you had better do the same.
[**Chronicler**	But Micaiah answered:]
Micaiah	By the living Lord, I will say what my God tells me to!
Chronicler	When he appeared before King Ahab, the king asked him:
Ahab	Micaiah, should King Jehoshaphat and I go and attack Ramoth, or not?
Micaiah (casually)	Attack! Of course you'll win. The Lord will give you victory.
Ahab (angrily)	When you speak to me in the name of the Lord, tell the truth! How many times do I have to tell you that?
Micaiah (sadly)	I can see the army of Israel scattered over the hills like sheep without a shepherd. And the Lord said:
[**The Lord**]	These men have no leader—let them go home in peace.
Chronicler	Ahab said to Jehoshaphat:
Ahab (sulkily)	I told you that he never prophesies anything good for me; it's always something bad!
Micaiah	Now listen to what the Lord says! I saw the Lord sitting on his throne in heaven, with all his angels standing beside him. The Lord asked:
[**The Lord**]	Who will deceive Ahab so that he will go and get killed at Ramoth?
Micaiah	Some of the angels said one thing, and others said something else, until a spirit stepped forward, approached the Lord, and said:
[**A spirit**]	I will deceive him.
[**Micaiah**	The Lord asked:]
[**The Lord**]	How?
[**Micaiah**	The spirit replied:]
[**A spirit**]	I will go and make all Ahab's prophets tell lies.
[**Micaiah**	The Lord said:]
[**The Lord**]	Go and deceive him. You will succeed.
[**Chronicler**	And Micaiah concluded:]
Micaiah	This is what has happened. The Lord has made these prophets of yours lie to you. But he himself has decreed that you will meet with disaster!

407

Chronicler	Then the prophet Zedekiah went up to Micaiah and slapped his face.
Zedekiah	Since when did the Lord's spirit leave me and speak to you?
Micaiah	You will find out when you go into some back room to hide.
Chronicler	Then King Ahab ordered one of his officers:
Ahab	Arrest Micaiah and take him to Amon, the governor of the city, and to Prince Joash. Tell them to throw him in prison and to put him on bread and water until I return safely.
Micaiah (firmly, to Ahab)	If you return safely, then the Lord has not spoken through me!
Cast	[This is] the word of the Lord.
All	**Thanks be to God.**

Cast: **Chronicler, Ahab, Jehoshaphat, Prophet 1, Prophet 2** (can be the same as Prophet 1), **Zedekiah, Official, Micaiah, [The Lord], [A spirit].**

The death of Ahab
2 Chronicles 18.28–34

Chronicler	King Ahab of Israel and King Jehoshaphat of Judah went to attack the city of Ramoth in Gilead. Ahab said to Jehoshaphat:
Ahab	As we go into battle, I will disguise myself, but you wear your royal garments.
Chronicler	So the king of Israel went into battle in disguise. (PAUSE) The king of Syria had ordered his chariot commanders to attack no one else except the king of Israel. So when they saw King Jehoshaphat, they all thought that he was the king of Israel, and they turned to attack him. But Jehoshaphat gave a shout, and the Lord God rescued him and turned the attack away from him. The chariot commanders saw that he was not the king of Israel, so they stopped pursuing him. By chance, however, a Syrian soldier shot an arrow which struck King Ahab between the joints of his armour.
Ahab	I'm wounded! Turn round and pull out of the battle!
Chronicler	While the battle raged on, King Ahab remained propped up in his chariot, facing the Syrians. At sunset he died.
Cast	[This is] the word of the Lord.
All	**Thanks be to God.**

Cast: **Chronicler, Ahab.**

A prophet reprimands Jehoshaphat
2 Chronicles 19.1–3

Chronicler	King Jehoshaphat of Judah returned safely to his palace in Jerusalem. A prophet, Jehu son of Hanani, went to meet the king [and said to him]:

Jehu	Do you think it is right to help those who are wicked and to take the side of those who hate the Lord? What you have done has brought the Lord's anger on you. But even so, there is *some* good in you. You have removed all the symbols of the goddess Asherah which people worshipped, and you have tried to follow God's will.
Cast	[This is] the word of the Lord.
All	**Thanks be to God.**

Cast: **Chronicler, Jehu.** (This reading would normally be linked with the next.)

Jehoshaphat's reforms
2 Chronicles 19.4–11

Chronicler	Even though King Jehoshaphat lived in Jerusalem, he travelled regularly among the people, from Beersheba in the south to the edge of the hill-country of Ephraim in the north, in order to call the people back to the Lord, the God of their ancestors. He appointed judges in each of the fortified cities of Judah and instructed them:
Jehoshaphat	Be careful in pronouncing judgement; you are not acting on human authority, but on the authority of the Lord, and he is with you when you pass sentence. Honour the Lord and act carefully, because the Lord our God does not tolerate fraud or partiality or the taking of bribes.
Chronicler	In Jerusalem Jehoshaphat appointed Levites, priests, and some of the leading citizens as judges in cases involving a violation of the Law of the Lord or legal disputes between inhabitants of the city. He gave them the following instructions:
Jehoshaphat	You must perform your duties in reverence for the Lord, faithfully obeying him in everything you do. Whenever your fellow-citizens from any of the cities bring before you a case of homicide or any other violation of a law or commandment, you must instruct them carefully how to conduct themselves during the trial, so that they do not become guilty of sinning against the Lord. Unless you do, you and your fellow-citizens will feel the force of the Lord's anger. But if you do your duty, you will not be guilty. Amariah the High Priest will have final authority in all religious cases, and Zebadiah son of Ishmael, governor of Judah, will have final authority in all civil cases. The Levites have the responsibility of seeing that the decisions of the courts are carried out. Be courageous and carry out these instructions, and may the Lord be on the side of the right!
Cast	[This is] the word of the Lord.
All	**Thanks be to God.**

Cast: **Chronicler, Jehoshaphat.**

War against Edom
From 2 Chronicles 20.1–30

Chronicler   The armies of Moab and Ammon, together with their allies, the Meunites, invaded Judah. Some messengers came and announced to King Jehoshaphat:

Messenger   A large army from Edom has come from the other side of the Dead Sea to attack you. They have already captured Engedi.

Chronicler   Jehoshaphat was frightened and prayed to the Lord for guidance. Then he gave orders for a fast to be observed throughout the country. From every city of Judah people hurried to Jerusalem to ask the Lord for guidance, and they and the people of Jerusalem gathered in the new courtyard of the Temple. King Jehoshaphat went and stood before them and prayed aloud:

Jehoshaphat   O Lord God of our ancestors, you rule in heaven over all the nations of the world. You are powerful and mighty, and no one can oppose you. You are our God.

When your people Israel moved into this land, you drove out the people who were living here and gave the land to the descendants of Abraham, your friend, to be theirs for ever. They have lived here and have built a temple to honour you, knowing that if any disaster struck them to punish them—a war, an epidemic, or a famine—then they could come and stand in front of this Temple where you are worshipped. They could pray to you in their trouble, and you would hear them and rescue them. Now the people of Ammon, Moab, and Edom have attacked us. When our ancestors came out of Egypt, you did not allow them to enter those lands, so our ancestors went round them and did not destroy them. This is how they repay us—they come to drive us out of the land that you gave us. You are our God! Punish them, for we are helpless in the face of this large army that is attacking us. We do not know what to do, but we look to you for help.

Chronicler   All the men of Judah, with their wives and children, were standing there at the Temple. The spirit of the Lord came upon a Levite who was present in the crowd. His name was Jahaziel son of Zechariah:

Jahaziel   Your Majesty and all you people of Judah and Jerusalem, the Lord says that you must not be discouraged or be afraid to face this large army. The battle depends on God, not on you. Attack them tomorrow as they come up the pass at Ziz. You will meet them at the end of the valley that leads to the wild country near Jeruel. You will not have to fight this battle. Just take up your positions and wait; you will see the Lord give you victory. People of Judah and Jerusalem, do not hesitate or be afraid. Go out to battle, and the Lord will be with you!

Chronicler   Then King Jehoshaphat bowed low, with his face touching the ground, and all the people bowed with him and worshipped the Lord.

Early the next morning the people went out to the wild country near Tekoa. As they were starting out, Jehoshaphat addressed them with these words:

Jehoshaphat   Men of Judah and Jerusalem! Put your trust in the Lord your God, and you will stand firm. Believe what his prophets tell you, and you will succeed.

Chronicler   After consulting with the people, the king ordered some musicians to put on the robes they wore on sacred occasions and to march ahead of the army, singing:

Musician 1   Praise the Lord!

Musician 2   His love is eternal!

Chronicler   When they began to sing, the Lord threw the invading armies into a panic. The Ammonites and the Moabites attacked the Edomite army and completely destroyed it, and then they turned on each other in savage fighting. When the Judaean army reached a tower that was in the desert, they looked towards the enemy and saw that they were all lying on the ground, dead. Not one had escaped. Jehoshaphat led his troops back to Jerusalem in triumph, because the Lord had defeated their enemies. When they reached the city, they marched to the Temple, to the music of harps and trumpets. Every nation that heard how the Lord had defeated Israel's enemies was terrified, so Jehoshaphat ruled in peace, and God gave him security on every side.

Cast   [This is] the word of the Lord.
All   **Thanks be to God.**

Cast: **Chronicler, Messenger, Jehoshaphat, Jahaziel, Musician 1, Musician 2** (can be the same as Messenger; Musician 1 and Musician 2 can also be the same).

Queen Athaliah of Judah
2 Chronicles 22.10—23.15

Chronicler 1   As soon as King Ahaziah's mother Athaliah learnt of her son's murder, she gave orders for all the members of the royal family of Judah to be killed. Ahaziah had a half-sister, Jehosheba, who was married to a priest named Jehoiada. She secretly rescued one of Ahaziah's sons, Joash, took him away from the other princes who were about to be murdered and hid him and a nurse in a bedroom at the Temple. By keeping him hidden, she saved him from death at the hands of Athaliah. For six years he remained there in hiding, while Athaliah ruled as queen.

Chronicler 2   After waiting six years Jehoiada the priest decided that it was time to take action. He made a pact with five army officers: Azariah son of Jeroham, Ishmael son of Jehohanan, Azariah son of Obed, Maaseiah son of Adaiah, and Elishaphat son of Zichri. They travelled to all the cities of Judah and brought back with them to Jerusalem the Levites and all the heads of the clans.

→

411

	They all gathered in the Temple, and there they made a covenant with Joash, the king's son. Jehoiada said to them:
Jehoiada	Here is the son of the late king! He is now to be king, as the Lord promised that King David's descendants would be. This is what we will do. When the priests and Levites come on duty on the Sabbath, one third of them will guard the temple gates, another third will guard the royal palace, and the rest will be stationed at the Foundation Gate. All the people will assemble in the temple courtyard. No one is to enter the temple buildings except the priests and the Levites who are on duty. They may enter, because they are consecrated, but the rest of the people must obey the Lord's instructions and stay outside. The Levites are to stand guard round the king, with their swords drawn, and are to stay with the king wherever he goes. Anyone who tries to enter the Temple is to be killed.
Chronicler 2	The Levites and the people of Judah carried out Jehoiada's instructions. The men were not dismissed when they went off duty on the Sabbath, so the commanders had available both those coming on duty and those going off. Jehoiada gave the officers the spears and shields that had belonged to King David and had been kept in the Temple. He stationed the men with drawn swords all round the front of the Temple, to protect the king. Then Jehoiada led Joash out, placed the crown on his head, and gave him a copy of the laws governing kingship. And so he was made king. Jehoiada the priest and his sons anointed Joash, and everyone shouted:
Persons 1 and **2**	Long live the king!
Chronicler 2	Athaliah heard the people cheering for the king, so she hurried to the Temple, where the crowd had gathered. There she saw the new king at the temple entrance, standing by the column reserved for kings and surrounded by the army officers and the trumpeters. All the people were shouting joyfully and blowing trumpets, and the temple musicians with their instruments were leading the celebration. She tore her clothes in distress and shouted:
Athaliah	Treason! Treason!
Chronicler 2	Jehoiada did not want Athaliah killed in the temple area, so he called out the army officers and said:
Jehoiada	Take her out between the rows of guards, and kill anyone who tries to rescue her.
Chronicler 1	They seized her, took her to the palace, and there at the Horse Gate they killed her.
Cast	[This is] the word of the Lord.
All	**Thanks be to God.**

Cast: **Chronicler 1, Chronicler 2, Jehoiada, Person 1, Person 2, Athaliah.**

King Joash of Judah
2 Chronicles 24.1–14

Chronicler 1   Joash became king of Judah at the age of seven, and he ruled in Jerusalem for forty years. His mother was Zibiah from the city of Beersheba. He did what was pleasing to the Lord as long as Jehoiada the priest was alive. Jehoiada chose two wives for King Joash, and they bore him sons and daughters.

Chronicler 2   After he had been king for a while, Joash decided to have the Temple repaired. He ordered the priests and the Levites to go to the cities of Judah and collect from all the people enough money to make the annual repairs on the Temple. He told them to act promptly, but the Levites delayed, so he called in Jehoiada, their leader [and demanded]:

Joash   Why haven't you seen to it that the Levites collect from Judah and Jerusalem the tax which Moses, the servant of the Lord, required the people to pay for support of the Tent of the Lord's presence?

Commentator   The followers of Athaliah, that corrupt woman, had damaged the Temple and had used many of the sacred objects in the worship of Baal.

Chronicler 1   The king ordered the Levites to make a box for contributions and to place it at the temple gate. They sent word throughout Jerusalem and Judah for everyone to bring to the Lord the tax which Moses, God's servant, had first collected in the wilderness. This pleased the people and their leaders, and they brought their tax money and filled the box with it. Every day the Levites would take the box to the royal official who was in charge of it. Whenever it was full, the royal secretary and the High Priest's representative would take the money out and return the box to its place. And so they collected a large sum of money.

Chronicler 2   The king and Jehoiada would give the money to those who were in charge of repairing the Temple, and they hired stonemasons, carpenters, and metalworkers to make the repairs. All the workmen worked hard, and they restored the Temple to its original condition, as solid as ever. When the repairs were finished, the remaining gold and silver was given to the king and Jehoiada, who used it to have bowls and other utensils made for the Temple.

Cast   [This is] the word of the Lord.
All   **Thanks be to God.**

Cast: **Chronicler 1, Chronicler 2, Joash, Commentator.**

Jehoiada's policies are reversed
2 Chronicles 24.14–22

Chronicler 1   As long as Jehoiada was alive, sacrifices were offered regularly at the Temple. After reaching the very old age of a hundred and

→

thirty, he died. They buried him in the royal tombs in David's City in recognition of the service he had done for the people of Israel, for God, and for the Temple.

Chronicler 2 But once Jehoiada was dead, the leaders of Judah persuaded King Joash to listen to *them* instead. So the people stopped worshipping in the Temple of the Lord, the God of their ancestors, and began to worship idols and the images of the goddess Asherah.

Chronicler 1 Their guilt for these sins brought the Lord's anger on Judah and Jerusalem. The Lord sent prophets to warn them to return to him, but the people refused to listen. Then the spirit of God took control of Zechariah son of Jehoiada the priest. He stood where the people could see him and called out:

Zechariah The Lord God asks why you have disobeyed his commands and are bringing disaster on yourselves! You abandoned him, so he has abandoned you!

Chronicler 2 King Joash joined in a conspiracy against Zechariah, and on the king's orders the people stoned Zechariah in the temple courtyard. The king forgot about the loyal service that Zechariah's father Jehoiada had given him, and he had Zechariah killed. As Zechariah was dying, he called out:

Zechariah May the Lord see what you are doing and punish you!

Cast [This is] the word of the Lord.
All **Thanks be to God.**

Cast: **Chronicler 1, Chronicler 2, Zechariah.**

King Amaziah of Judah
2 Chronicles 25.1–4

Chronicler Amaziah became king at the age of twenty-five, and he ruled in Jerusalem for twenty-nine years. His mother was Jehoaddin from Jerusalem. He did what was pleasing to the Lord, but did it reluctantly. As soon as he was firmly in power, he executed the officials who had murdered his father. He did not, however, execute their children, but followed what the Lord had commanded in the Law of Moses:

The Lord Parents are not to be put to death for crimes committed by their children, and children are not to be put to death for crimes committed by their parents; a person is to be put to death only for a crime he himself has committed.

Cast [This is] the word of the Lord.
All **Thanks be to God.**

Cast: **Chronicler, The Lord.**

War against Edom
2 Chronicles 25.5–16

Chronicler	King Amaziah organized all the men of the tribes of Judah and Benjamin into army units, according to the clans they belonged to, and placed officers in command of units of a thousand men and units of a hundred men. This included all men twenty years of age or older, 300,000 in all. They were picked troops, ready for battle, skilled in using spears and shields. In addition, he hired 100,000 soldiers from Israel at a cost of about 3,400 kilogrammes of silver. But a prophet went to the king [and said to him]:
Prophet	Don't take these Israelite soldiers with you. The Lord is not with these men from the Northern Kingdom. You may think that they will make you stronger in battle, but it is God who has the power to give victory or defeat, and he will let your enemies defeat you.
[Chronicler	Amaziah asked the prophet:]
Amaziah	But what about all that silver I have already paid for them?
Prophet	The Lord can give you back more than that!
Chronicler	So Amaziah sent the hired troops away and told them to go home. At this they went home, bitterly angry with the people of Judah. (PAUSE)
	Amaziah summoned up his courage and led his army to the Valley of Salt. There they fought and killed ten thousand Edomite soldiers and captured another ten thousand. They took the prisoners to the top of the cliff at the city of Sela and threw them off, so that they were killed on the rocks below.
	Meanwhile the Israelite soldiers that Amaziah had not allowed to go into battle with him attacked the Judaean cities between Samaria and Beth Horon, killed three thousand men, and captured quantities of loot.
	When Amaziah returned from defeating the Edomites, he brought their idols back with him, set them up, worshipped them, and burnt incense to them. This made the Lord angry, so he sent a prophet to Amaziah. The prophet demanded:
Prophet	Why have you worshipped foreign gods that could not even save their own people from your power?
[Chronicler	Amaziah interrupted:]
Amaziah (interrupting)	Since when have we made you adviser to the king? Stop talking, or I'll have you killed!
Chronicler	The prophet stopped, but not before saying:
Prophet	Now I know that God has decided to destroy you because you have done all this and have ignored my advice.
Cast	[This is] the word of the Lord.
All	**Thanks be to God.**

Cast: **Chronicler, Prophet, Amaziah.**

War against Israel
2 Chronicles 25.17–28

Chronicler	King Amaziah of Judah and his advisers plotted against Israel. He then sent a message to King Jehoash of Israel, who was the son of Jehoahaz and grandson of Jehu, challenging him to fight. Jehoash sent this answer to Amaziah:
Jehoash	Once, a thorn bush in the Lebanon Mountains sent a message to a cedar: 'Give your daughter in marriage to my son.' A wild animal passed by and trampled the bush down. Now Amaziah, you boast that you have defeated the Edomites, but I advise you to stay at home. Why stir up trouble that will only bring disaster on you and your people?
Chronicler	But Amaziah refused to listen. It was God's will for Amaziah to be defeated, because he had worshipped the Edomite idols. So King Jehoash of Israel went into battle against King Amaziah of Judah. They met at Beth Shemesh in Judah, the Judaean army was defeated, and the soldiers fled to their homes. Jehoash captured Amaziah and took him to Jerusalem. There he tore down the city wall from Ephraim Gate to the Corner Gate, a distance of nearly two hundred metres. He took back to Samaria as loot all the gold and silver in the Temple, the temple equipment guarded by the descendants of Obed Edom, and the palace treasures. He also took hostages with him.
	King Amaziah of Judah outlived King Jehoash of Israel by fifteen years.
Commentator	All the other things that Amaziah did from the beginning to the end of his reign are recorded in The History of the Kings of Judah and Israel. Ever since the time when he rebelled against the Lord, there had been a plot against him in Jerusalem. Finally he fled to the city of Lachish, but his enemies followed him there and killed him. His body was carried to Jerusalem on a horse, and he was buried in the royal tombs in David's City.
Cast	[This is] the word of the Lord.
All	**Thanks be to God.**

Cast: **Chronicler, Jehoash, Commentator.**

King Uzziah's downfall
From 2 Chronicles 26.16–23

Chronicler	After King Uzziah became powerful, his pride led to his downfall. He was unfaithful to the Lord his God, and entered the Temple of the Lord to burn incense on the altar of incense. Azariah the priest with eighty other courageous priests of the Lord followed him in. They confronted him:
Azariah	It is not right for you, Uzziah, to burn incense to the Lord. That is for the priests and descendants of Aaron, who have been

consecrated to burn incense. Leave the sanctuary for you have been unfaithful; and you will not be honoured by the Lord God.

Chronicler Uzziah who had a censer in his hand ready to burn incense, became angry. While he was raging at the priests, in their presence before the incense altar in the Lord's Temple, leprosy broke out on his forehead. When Azariah the chief priest and all the other priests looked at him, they saw that he had leprosy on his forehead, so they hurried him out. Indeed, he himself was eager to leave, because the Lord had afflicted him.

King Uzziah had leprosy until the day he died. He lived in a separate house—leprous, and excluded from the Temple of the Lord. Uzziah rested with his fathers and was buried near them in a field for burial that belonged to the kings, for people said:

Persons 1 and **2**
(in awed tones) He had leprosy!

Cast [This is] the word of the Lord.
All **Thanks be to God.**

Cast: **Chronicler, Azariah, Person 1, Person 2** (can be the same as Person 1).

The Prophet Oded
From 2 Chronicles 28.8–15

Chronicler Even though the Judaeans were their fellow-countrymen, the Israelite army captured 200,000 women and children as prisoners and took them back to Samaria, along with large amounts of loot. A man named Oded, a prophet of the Lord, lived in the city of Samaria. He met the returning Israelite army with its Judaean prisoners as it was about to enter the city, and he said:

Oded The Lord God of your ancestors was angry with Judah and let you defeat them, but now he has heard of the vicious way you slaughtered them. And now you intend to make the men and women of Jerusalem and Judah your slaves. Don't you know that you also have committed sins against the Lord your God? Listen to me! These prisoners are your brothers and sisters. Let them go, or the Lord will punish you in his anger.

Chronicler Four of the leading men of the Northern Kingdom also opposed the actions of the army. They said:

Leader 1 Don't bring those prisoners here!

Leader 2 We have already sinned against the Lord—

Leader 3 and made him angry enough to punish us.

Leader 4 Now you want to do something that will increase our guilt.

Chronicler So then the army handed the prisoners and the loot over to the people and their leaders, and the four men were appointed to provide the prisoners with clothing from the captured loot. They gave them clothes and sandals to wear, gave them enough to eat

→

and drink, and put olive-oil on their wounds. Those who were too weak to walk were put on donkeys, and all the prisoners were taken back to Judaean territory at Jericho, the city of palm-trees. Then the Israelites returned home to Samaria.

Cast	[This is] the word of the Lord.
All	**Thanks be to God.**

Cast: **Chronicler, Oded, Leader 1, Leader 2, Leader 3** (can be the same as Leader 2), **Leader 4** (can be the same as Leader 2), (Leaders 1–4 can be the same).

King Hezekiah of Judah
From 2 Chronicles 29.1–17

Chronicler Hezekiah became king of Judah at the age of twenty-five, and he ruled in Jerusalem for twenty-nine years. His mother was Abijah, the daughter of Zechariah. Following the example of his ancestor King David, he did what was pleasing to the Lord. (PAUSE)

In the first month of the year after Hezekiah became king, he reopened the gates of the Temple and had them repaired. He assembled a group of priests and Levites in the east courtyard of the Temple and spoke to them there:

Hezekiah You Levites are to consecrate yourselves and purify the Temple of the Lord, the God of your ancestors. Remove from the Temple everything that defiles it. Our ancestors were unfaithful to the Lord our God and did what was displeasing to him. They abandoned him and turned their backs on the place where he dwells. They closed the doors of the Temple, let the lamps go out, and failed to burn incense or offer burnt-offerings in the Temple of the God of Israel. Because of this the Lord has been angry with Judah and Jerusalem, and what he has done to them has shocked and frightened everyone. You know this very well. Our fathers were killed in battle, and our wives and children have been taken away as prisoners. I have now decided to make a covenant with the Lord, the God of Israel, so that he will no longer be angry with us. My sons, do not lose any time. You are the ones that the Lord has chosen to burn incense to him and to lead the people in worshipping him.

Chronicler The Levites all made themselves ritually clean. Then, as the king had commanded them to do, they began to make the Temple ritually clean, according to the Law of the Lord. The priests went inside the Temple to purify it, and they carried out into the temple courtyard everything that was ritually unclean. From there the Levites took it all outside the city to the valley of the Kidron. The work was begun on the first day of the first month, and by the eighth day they had finished it all, including the entrance room to the Temple. Then they worked for the next eight days, until the sixteenth of the month, preparing the Temple for worship.

Cast	[This is] the word of the Lord.
All	**Thanks be to God.**

Cast: **Chronicler, Hezekiah.**

The Temple is rededicated
From 2 Chronicles 29.18–36

Chronicler   The Levites made the following report to King Hezekiah:

Levite 1   We have completed the ritual purification of the whole Temple, including the altar for burnt-offerings, the table for the sacred bread, and all their equipment.

Levite 2   We have also brought back all the equipment which King Ahaz took away during those years he was unfaithful to God, and we have rededicated it.

Levite 1   It is all in front of the Lord's altar.

Chronicler   Without delay King Hezekiah assembled the leading men of the city, and together they went to the Temple. As an offering to take away the sins of the royal family and of the people of Judah and to purify the Temple, they took seven bulls, seven sheep, seven lambs, and seven goats. The king told the priests, who were descendants of Aaron, to offer the animals as sacrifices on the altar. The priests killed the bulls first, then the sheep, and then the lambs, and sprinkled the blood of each sacrifice on the altar. Finally they took the goats to the king and to the other worshippers, who laid their hands on them. Then the priests killed the goats and poured their blood on the altar as a sacrifice to take away the sin of all the people, for the king had commanded burnt-offerings and sin-offerings to be made for all Israel.

Then King Hezekiah and all the people knelt down and worshipped God. The king and the leaders of the nation told the Levites to sing to the Lord the songs of praise that were written by David and by Asaph the prophet. So everyone sang with great joy as they knelt and worshipped God. And so worship in the Temple was begun again. King Hezekiah and the people were happy, because God had helped them to do all this so quickly.

Cast   [This is] the word of the Lord.
All   **Thanks be to God.**

Cast: **Chronicler, Levite 1, Levite 2** (can be the same as Levite 1).

Preparations for Passover
2 Chronicles 30.1–12

Chronicler   The people had not been able to celebrate the Passover Festival at the proper time, in the first month, because not enough priests were ritually clean and not many people had assembled in Jerusalem. So King Hezekiah, his officials, and the people of Jerusalem agreed to celebrate it in the second month, and the king sent word to all the people of Israel and Judah. He took special care to send letters to the tribes of Ephraim and Manasseh, inviting them to come to the Temple in Jerusalem to celebrate the Passover in honour of the Lord, the God of Israel. The king and

→

the people were pleased with their plan, so they invited all the Israelites, from Dan in the north to Beersheba in the south, to come together in Jerusalem and celebrate the Passover according to the Law, in larger numbers than ever before. Messengers went out at the command of the king and his officials through all Judah and Israel [with the following invitation:]

Messenger 1 People of Israel, you have survived the Assyrian conquest of the land. Now return to the Lord, the God of Abraham, Isaac, and Jacob, and he will return to you. Do not be like your ancestors and your fellow-Israelites who were unfaithful to the Lord their God. As you can see, he punished them severely. Do not be stubborn as they were, but obey the Lord. Come to the Temple in Jerusalem, which the Lord your God has made holy for ever, and worship him so that he will no longer be angry with you.

Messenger 2 If you return to the Lord, then those who have taken your relatives away as prisoners will take pity on them and let them come back home. The Lord your God is kind and merciful, and if you return to him, he will accept you.

Chronicler The messengers went to every city in the territory of the tribes of Ephraim and Manasseh, and as far north as the tribe of Zebulun, but people laughed at them and ridiculed them. Still, there were some from the tribes of Asher, Manasseh, and Zebulun who were willing to come to Jerusalem. God was also at work in Judah and united the people in their determination to obey his will by following the commands of the king and his officials.

Cast [This is] the word of the Lord.
All **Thanks be to God.**

Cast: **Chronicler, Messenger 1, Messenger 2.**

Passover is celebrated
From 2 Chronicles 30.13–22

Chronicler A great number of people gathered in Jerusalem in the second month to celebrate the Festival of Unleavened Bread. They took all the altars that had been used in Jerusalem for offering sacrifices and burning incense and threw them into the valley of the Kidron. And on the fourteenth day of the month they killed the lambs for the Passover sacrifice. The priests and Levites who were not ritually clean were so ashamed that they dedicated themselves to the Lord, and now they could sacrifice burnt-offerings in the Temple. They took their places in the Temple according to the instructions in the Law of Moses, the man of God. The Levites gave the blood of the sacrifices to the priests, who sprinkled it on the altar. [Because many of the people were not ritually clean, they could not kill the Passover lambs, so the Levites did it for them, and dedicated the lambs to the Lord. In addition, many of those who had come from the tribes of Ephraim, Manasseh, Issachar, and Zebulun had not performed the ritual of purification, and so they were observing Passover improperly.] King Hezekiah offered this prayer for them:

Hezekiah   O Lord, the God of our ancestors, in your goodness forgive those who are worshipping you with all their heart, even though they are not ritually clean.

Chronicler   The Lord answered Hezekiah's prayer; he forgave the people and did not harm them. For seven days the people who had gathered in Jerusalem celebrated the Festival of Unleavened Bread with great joy, and day after day the Levites and the priests praised the Lord with all their strength. Hezekiah praised the Levites for their skill in conducting the worship of the Lord.

Cast   [This is] the word of the Lord.
All   **Thanks be to God.**

Cast: **Chronicler, Hezekiah.**

At the Festival of Unleavened Bread
From 2 Chronicles 30.26—31.21

Chronicler 1   The city of Jerusalem was filled with joy, because nothing like the Festival of Unleavened Bread had happened since the days of King Solomon, the son of David. The priests and the Levites asked the Lord's blessing on the people. In his home in heaven God heard their prayers and accepted them.

Chronicler 2   After the festival ended, all the people of Israel went to every city in Judah and broke the stone pillars, cut down the symbols of the goddess Asherah, and destroyed the altars and the pagan places of worship. They did the same thing throughout the rest of Judah, and the territories of Benjamin, Ephraim, and Manasseh; then they all returned home.

Chronicler 1   King Hezekiah re-established the organization of the priests and Levites, under which they each had specific duties. In addition, the king told the people of Jerusalem to bring the offerings to which the priests and the Levites were entitled, so that they could give all their time to the requirements of the Law of the Lord. As soon as the order was given, the people of Israel brought gifts of their finest corn, wine, olive-oil, honey, and other farm produce, and they also brought the tithes of everything they had.

Chronicler 2   The gifts started arriving in the third month and continued to pile up for the next four months. When King Hezekiah and his officials saw how much had been given, they praised the Lord and praised his people Israel. The king spoke to the priests and the Levites about these gifts, and Azariah the High Priest, a descendant of Zadok, said to him:

Azariah   Since the people started bringing their gifts to the Temple, there has been enough to eat and a large surplus besides. We have all this because the Lord has blessed his people.

Chronicler 1	Throughout all Judah, King Hezekiah did what was right and what was pleasing to the Lord his God. He was successful, because everything he did for the Temple or in observance of the Law, he did in a spirit of complete loyalty and devotion to his God.
Cast	[This is] the word of the Lord.
All	**Thanks be to God.**

Cast: **Chronicler 1, Chronicler 2, Azariah.**

The Assyrians threaten Jerusalem
From 2 Chronicles 31.20—32.23

Chronicler	Throughout all Judah, King Hezekiah did what was right and what was pleasing to the Lord his God. He was successful, because everything he did for the Temple or in observance of the Law, he did in a spirit of complete loyalty and devotion to his God.
	After these events, in which King Hezekiah served the Lord faithfully, Sennacherib, the emperor of Assyria, invaded Judah. He besieged the fortified cities and gave orders for his army to break their way through the walls. When Hezekiah saw that Sennacherib intended to attack Jerusalem also, he and his officials decided to cut off the supply of water outside the city in order to prevent the Assyrians from having any water when they got near Jerusalem. The officials led a large number of people out and stopped up all the springs, so that no more water flowed out of them. The king strengthened the city's defences by repairing the wall, building towers on it, and building an outer wall. In addition, he repaired the defences built on the land that was filled in on the east side of the old part of Jerusalem. He also had a large number of spears and shields made. He placed all the men in the city under the command of army officers and ordered them to assemble in the open square at the city gate. He said to them:
Hezekiah	Be determined and confident, and don't be afraid of the Assyrian emperor or of the army he is leading. We have more power on our side than he has on his. He has human power, but we have the Lord our God to help us and to fight our battles.
Chronicler	The people were encouraged by these words of their king. Some time later, while Sennacherib and his army were still at Lachish, he sent the following message to Hezekiah and the people of Judah who were with him in Jerusalem:
Sennacherib	I, Sennacherib, Emperor of Assyria, ask what gives you people the confidence to remain in Jerusalem under siege. Hezekiah tells you that the Lord your God will save you from our power, but Hezekiah is deceiving you and will let you die of hunger and thirst. He is the one who destroyed the Lord's shrines and altars and then told the people of Judah and Jerusalem to worship and burn incense at one altar only. Don't you know what my ancestors and I have done to the people of other nations? Did the gods of any other nation save their people from the emperor of Assyria?

422

When did any of the gods of all those countries ever save their country from us? Then what makes you think that your god can save you? Now don't let Hezekiah deceive you or mislead you like that. Don't believe him! No god of any nation has ever been able to save his people from any Assyrian emperor. So certainly this god of yours can't save you!

Chronicler The Assyrians shouted this in Hebrew in order to frighten and discourage the people of Jerusalem who were on the city wall, so that it would be easier to capture the city. They talked about the God of Jerusalem in the same way that they talked about the gods of the other peoples, idols made by human hands. Then King Hezekiah and the prophet Isaiah son of Amoz prayed to God and cried out to him for help, and the Lord rescued King Hezekiah and the people of Jerusalem from the power of Sennacherib, the emperor of Assyria, and also from their other enemies. He let the people live in peace with all the neighbouring countries. Many people came to Jerusalem, bringing offerings to the Lord and gifts to Hezekiah, so that from then on all the nations held Hezekiah in honour.

Cast [This is] the word of the Lord.
All **Thanks be to God.**

Cast: **Chronicler, Hezekiah, Sennacherib.** (This reading overlaps with the previous one.)

King Manasseh of Judah
2 Chronicles 33.1–13

Chronicler Manasseh was twelve years old when he became king of Judah, and he ruled in Jerusalem for fifty-five years. Following the disgusting practices of the nations whom the Lord had driven out of the land as his people advanced, Manasseh sinned against the Lord. He rebuilt the pagan places of worship that his father Hezekiah had destroyed. He built altars for the worship of Baal, made images of the goddess Asherah, and worshipped the stars. He built pagan altars in the Temple, the place that the Lord had said was where he should be worshipped for ever. In the two courtyards of the Temple he built altars for the worship of the stars. He sacrificed his sons in the Valley of Hinnom as burnt-offerings. He practised divination and magic and consulted fortune-tellers and mediums. He sinned greatly against the Lord and stirred up his anger. He placed an image in the Temple, the place about which God had said to David and his son Solomon:

The Lord Here in Jerusalem, in this Temple, is the place that I have chosen out of all the territory of the twelve tribes of Israel as the place where I am to be worshipped. And if the people of Israel will obey all my commands and keep the whole Law that my servant Moses gave them, then I will not allow them to be driven out of the land that I gave to their ancestors.

Chronicler Manasseh led the people of Judah to commit even greater sins than those committed by the nations whom the Lord had driven

→

423

out of the land as his people advanced. Although the Lord warned Manasseh and his people, they refused to listen. So the Lord let the commanders of the Assyrian army invade Judah. They captured Manasseh, stuck hooks in him, put him in chains, and took him to Babylon. In his suffering he became humble, turned to the Lord his God, and begged him for help. God accepted Manasseh's prayer and answered it by letting him go back to Jerusalem and rule again. This convinced Manasseh that the Lord was God.

Cast	[This is] the word of the Lord.
All	**Thanks be to God.**

Cast: **Chronicler, The Lord.**

The book of the law is discovered
From 2 Chronicles 34.1–21 [22–31]

Chronicler Josiah was eight years old when he became king of Judah, and he ruled in Jerusalem for thirty-one years. He did what was pleasing to the Lord; he followed the example of his ancestor King David, strictly obeying all the laws of God. In the eighteenth year of his reign, after he had purified the land and the Temple by ending pagan worship, King Josiah sent three men to repair the Temple of the Lord God: Shaphan son of Azaliah, Maaseiah, the governor of Jerusalem, and Joah son of Joahaz, a high official.

The money that the Levite guards had collected in the Temple was handed over to Hilkiah the High Priest. This money was then handed over to the three men in charge of the temple repairs, and they gave it to the carpenters and the builders to buy the stones and the timber used to repair the buildings that the kings of Judah had allowed to decay.

While the money was being taken out of the storeroom, Hilkiah found the book of the Law of the Lord, the Law that God had given to Moses. [He said to Shaphan:]

Hilkiah
  (to Shaphan) I have found the book of the Law here in the Temple.

Chronicler He gave Shaphan the book. Shaphan took it to the king [and reported]:

Shaphan We have done everything that you commanded. We have taken the money that was kept in the Temple and handed it over to the workmen and their supervisors. (PAUSE)

I have here a book that Hilkiah gave me.

Chronicler He read it aloud to the king. When the king heard the book being read, he tore his clothes in dismay and gave the following order to Hilkiah, to Ahikam son of Shaphan, to Abdon son of Micaiah, to Shaphan, the court secretary and to Asaiah, the king's attendant:

Josiah Go and consult the Lord for me and for the people who still

424

remain in Israel and Judah. Find out about the teachings of this book. The Lord is angry with us because our ancestors have not obeyed the word of the Lord and have not done what this book says must be done.

[Chronicler   At the king's command, Hilkiah and the others went to consult a woman named Huldah, a prophet who lived in the newer part of Jerusalem. They described to her what had happened, and she told them to go back to the king and give him the following message from the Lord:

The Lord   I am going to punish Jerusalem and all its people with the curses written in the book that was read to the king. They have rejected me and have offered sacrifices to other gods, and so have stirred up my anger by all they have done. My anger is aroused against Jerusalem, and it will not die down. As for the king himself, this is what I, the Lord God of Israel, say—'You listened to what is written in the book, and you repented and humbled yourself before me, tearing your clothes and weeping, when you heard how I threatened to punish Jerusalem and its people. I have heard your prayer, and the punishment which I am going to bring on Jerusalem will not come until after your death. I will let you die in peace.'

Chronicler   The men returned to King Josiah with this message. (PAUSE)

King Josiah summoned all the leaders of Judah and Jerusalem, and together they went to the Temple, accompanied by the priests and the Levites and all the rest of the people, rich and poor alike. Before them all, the king read aloud the whole book of the covenant, which had been found in the Temple. He stood by the royal column and made a covenant with the Lord to obey him, to keep his laws and commands with all his heart and soul, and to put into practice the demands attached to the covenant, as written in the book.]

Cast   [This is] the word of the Lord.
All   **Thanks be to God.**

Cast: **Chronicler, Hilkiah, Shaphan, Josiah, The Lord.**

The end of Josiah's reign
2 Chronicles 35.20–27

Chronicler   After King Josiah had done all that he did for the Temple, King Neco of Egypt led an army to fight at Carchemish on the River Euphrates. Josiah tried to stop him, but Neco sent Josiah this message:

Neco   This war I am fighting does not concern you, King of Judah. I have not come to fight you, but to fight my enemies, and God has told me to hurry. God is on my side, so don't oppose me, or he will destroy you.

Chronicler   But Josiah was determined to fight. He refused to listen to what

→

God was saying through King Neco, so he disguised himself and went into battle on the plain of Megiddo. (PAUSE)

During the battle King Josiah was struck by Egyptian arrows. He ordered his servants:

Josiah   Take me away—I'm badly hurt!

Chronicler   They lifted him out of his chariot, placed him in a second chariot which he had there, and took him to Jerusalem. There he died and was buried in the royal tombs. All the people of Judah and Jerusalem mourned his death.

Commentator   The prophet Jeremiah composed a lament for King Josiah. It has become a custom in Israel for the singers, both men and women, to use this song when they mourn for him. The song is found in the collection of laments. Everything that Josiah did—his devotion to the Lord, his obedience to the Law, and his history from beginning to end—is all recorded in The History of the Kings of Israel and Judah.

Cast   [This is] the word of the Lord.
All   **Thanks be to God.**

Cast: **Chronicler, Neco, Josiah, Commentator** (can be the same as Chronicler).

EZRA

Cyrus commands the Jews to return
Ezra 1.1–11

Narrator 1   In the first year that Cyrus of Persia was emperor, the Lord made what he had said through the prophet Jeremiah come true. He prompted Cyrus to issue the following command and send it out in writing to be read aloud everywhere in his empire:

Cyrus   This is the command of Cyrus, Emperor of Persia. The Lord, the God of Heaven, has made me ruler over the whole world and has given me the responsibility of building a temple for him in Jerusalem in Judah. May God be with all of you who are his people. You are to go to Jerusalem and rebuild the Temple of the Lord, the God of Israel, the God who is worshipped in Jerusalem. If any of his people in exile need help to return, their neighbours are to give them this help. They are to provide them with silver and gold, supplies and pack animals, as well as offerings to present in the Temple of God in Jerusalem.

Narrator 2   Then the heads of the clans of the tribes of Judah and Benjamin, the priests and Levites, and everyone else whose heart God had moved got ready to go and rebuild the Lord's Temple in Jerusalem. All their neighbours helped them by giving them many things: silver utensils, gold, supplies, pack animals, other valuables, and offerings for the Temple.

Narrator 1   Cyrus gave them back the bowls and cups that King Nebuchadnezzar had taken from the Temple in Jerusalem and had put in the temple of his gods. He handed them over to Mithredath, chief of the royal treasury, who made an inventory of them for Sheshbazzar, the governor of Judah, as follows:

Gold bowls for offerings—

Narrator 2   30

Narrator 1   Silver bowls for offerings—

Narrator 2   1,000

Narrator 1   Other bowls—

Narrator 2   29

Narrator 1   Small gold bowls—

Narrator 2   30

Narrator 1   Small silver bowls—

Narrator 2   410

Narrator 1   Other utensils—

Narrator 2	1,000. In all there were 5,400 gold and silver bowls and other articles which Sheshbazzar took with him when he and the other exiles went from Babylon to Jerusalem.
Cast	[This is] the word of the Lord.
All	**Thanks be to God.**

Cast: **Narrator 1, Cyrus, Narrator 2.**

The rebuilding of the Temple begins
Ezra 3.7–13

Narrator 1	The people of Israel gave money to pay the stonemasons and the carpenters and gave food, drink, and olive-oil to be sent to the cities of Tyre and Sidon in exchange for cedar-trees from Lebanon, which were to be brought by sea to Joppa. All this was done with the permission of Cyrus, emperor of Persia.
Narrator 2	So in the second month of the year after they came back to the site of the Temple in Jerusalem, they began work. Zerubbabel, Joshua, and the rest of their fellow-countrymen, the priests, and the Levites—
Commentator	In fact all the exiles who had come back to Jerusalem—
Narrator 2	Joined in the work. All the Levites twenty years of age or older were put in charge of the work of rebuilding the Temple.
Narrator 1	The Levite Jeshua and his sons and relatives, and Kadmiel and his sons—
Commentator	The clan of Hodaviah—
Narrator 1	Joined together in taking charge of the rebuilding of the Temple.
Commentator	They were helped by the Levites of the clan of Henadad.
Narrator 2	When the men started to lay the foundation of the Temple, the priests in their robes took their places with trumpets in their hands, and the Levites of the clan of Asaph stood there with cymbals. They praised the Lord according to the instructions handed down from the time of King David. They sang the Lord's praises, repeating the refrain:
Singers 1 and **2**	The Lord is good.
Singer 1	And his love for Israel is eternal.
Narrator 1	Everyone shouted with all his might, praising the Lord, because the work on the foundation of the Temple had been started.
Narrator 2	Many of the older priests, Levites, and heads of clans had seen the first Temple, and as they watched the foundation of this Temple being laid, they cried and wailed.
Narrator 1	But the others who were there shouted for joy.

Narrator 2	No one could distinguish between the joyful shouts and the crying, because the noise they made was so loud that it could be heard far and wide.

Cast	[This is] the word of the Lord.
All	**Thanks be to God.**

Cast: **Narrator 1, Narrator 2, Commentator, Singer 1, Singer 2** (can be the same as Commentator).

Opposition to the rebuilding of the Temple
Ezra 4.1–5

Narrator	The enemies of the people of Judah and Benjamin heard that those who had returned from exile were rebuilding the Temple of the Lord, the God of Israel. So they went to see Zerubbabel and the heads of the clans and said:
Enemy 1	Let us join you in building the Temple.
Enemy 2	We worship the same God you worship, and we have been offering sacrifices to him ever since Esarhaddon, emperor of Assyria, sent us here to live.
Narrator	Zerubbabel, Joshua, and the heads of the clans said to them:
Zerubbabel	We don't need your help to build a temple for the Lord our God.
Joshua	We will build it ourselves, just as Cyrus, emperor of Persia, commanded us.
Narrator	Then the people who had been living in the land tried to discourage and frighten the Jews and keep them from building. They also bribed Persian government officials to work against them. They kept on doing this throughout the reign of Cyrus and into the reign of Darius.

Cast	[This is] the word of the Lord.
All	**Thanks be to God.**

Cast: **Narrator, Enemy 1, Enemy 2** (can be the same as Enemy 1), **Zerubbabel, Joshua** (can be the same as Enemy 1).

Opposition to the rebuilding of Jerusalem
From Ezra 4.6–23

Narrator	Rehum, the governor, and Shimshai, the secretary of the province, wrote the following letter to Artaxerxes about Jerusalem:
Rehum	To Emperor Artaxerxes from his servants, the men of West Euphrates. We want Your Majesty to know that the Jews who came here from your other territories have settled in Jerusalem and are rebuilding that evil and rebellious city. They have begun to rebuild the walls and will soon finish them. Your Majesty, if this city is rebuilt and its walls are completed, the people will stop paying taxes, and your royal revenues will decrease. Now,

→

because we are under obligation to Your Majesty, we do not want to see this happen, and so we suggest that you order a search to be made in the records your ancestors kept. If you do, you will discover that this city has always been rebellious and that from ancient times it has given trouble to kings and to rulers of provinces. Its people have always been hard to govern. This is why the city was destroyed. We therefore are convinced that if this city is rebuilt and its walls are completed, Your Majesty will no longer be able to control the province of West Euphrates.

Narrator   The emperor sent this answer:

Emperor   The letter which you sent has been translated and read to me. I gave orders for an investigation to be made, and it has indeed been found that from ancient times Jerusalem has revolted against royal authority and that it has been full of rebels and troublemakers. Powerful kings have reigned there and have ruled over the entire province of West Euphrates, collecting taxes and revenue. Therefore you are to issue orders that those men are to stop rebuilding the city until I give further commands. Do this at once, so that no more harm may be done to my interests.

Narrator   As soon as this letter from Artaxerxes was read to Rehum, Shimshai, and their associates, they hurried to Jerusalem and forced the Jews to stop rebuilding the city.

Cast   [This is] the word of the Lord.
All   **Thanks be to God.**

Cast: **Narrator, Rehum, Emperor.**

Work on the Temple begins again
Ezra 4.24—5.17

Narrator   Work on the Temple had been stopped and had remained at a standstill until the second year of the reign of Darius, emperor of Persia. At that time two prophets, Haggai and Zechariah son of Iddo, began to speak in the name of the God of Israel to the Jews who lived in Judah and Jerusalem. When Zerubbabel son of Shealtiel and Joshua son of Jehozadak heard their messages, they began to rebuild the Temple in Jerusalem, and the two prophets helped them. Almost at once Tattenai, governor of West Euphrates, Shethar Bozenai, and their fellow-officials came to Jerusalem and demanded:

Tattenai   Who gave you orders to build this Temple and equip it?

Narrator   They also asked for the names of all the men who were helping to build the Temple. But God was watching over the Jewish leaders, and the Persian officials decided to take no action until they could write to Darius and receive a reply. This is the report that they sent to the emperor:

Official	To Emperor Darius, may you rule in peace. Your Majesty should know that we went to the province of Judah and found that the Temple of the great God is being rebuilt with large stone blocks and with wooden beams set in the wall. The work is being done with great care and is moving ahead steadily. We then asked the leaders of the people to tell us who had given them authority to rebuild the Temple and to equip it. We also asked them their names so that we could inform you who the leaders of this work are. They answered:
Leader 1	We are servants of the God of heaven and earth, and we are rebuilding the Temple which was originally built and equipped many years ago by a powerful king of Israel.
Leader 2	Because our ancestors made the God of Heaven angry, he let them be conquered by King Nebuchadnezzar of Babylonia, a king of the Chaldean dynasty.
Leader 1	The Temple was destroyed, and the people were taken into exile in Babylonia.
Leader 3	Then in the first year of the reign of King Cyrus as emperor of Babylonia, Cyrus issued orders for the Temple to be rebuilt.
Leader 2	He restored the gold and silver temple utensils which Nebuchadnezzar had taken from the Temple in Jerusalem and had placed in the temple in Babylon.
Leader 3	Cyrus handed these utensils over to a man named Sheshbazzar, whom he appointed governor of Judah.
Leader 1	The emperor told him to take them and return them to the Temple in Jerusalem, and to rebuild the Temple where it had stood before.
Leader 2	So Sheshbazzar came and laid its foundation; construction has continued from then until the present, but the Temple is still not finished.
Official	Now, if it please Your Majesty, let a search be made in the royal records in Babylon to find whether or not Cyrus gave orders for this Temple in Jerusalem to be rebuilt, and then inform us what your will is in this matter.
Cast	[This is] the word of the Lord.
All	**Thanks be to God.**

Cast: **Narrator, Tattenai, Official, Leader 1, Leader 2, Leader 3** (Leaders 1–3 can be the same).

Cyrus' order is rediscovered
Ezra 6.1–12

Narrator	Darius the emperor issued orders for a search to be made in the royal records that were kept in Babylon. But it was in the city of Ecbatana in the province of Media that a scroll was found, containing the following record:

Reader	In the first year of his reign Cyrus the emperor commanded that the Temple in Jerusalem be rebuilt as a place where sacrifices are made and offerings are burnt. The Temple is to be twenty-seven metres high and twenty-seven metres wide. The walls are to be built with one layer of wood on top of every three layers of stone. All expenses are to be paid by the royal treasury. Also the gold and silver utensils which King Nebuchadnezzar brought to Babylon from the Temple in Jerusalem are to be returned to their proper place in the Jerusalem Temple.
Narrator	Then Darius sent the following reply:
Darius	To Tattenai, governor of West Euphrates, Shethar Bozenai, and your fellow-officials in West Euphrates.
	Stay away from the Temple and do not interfere with its construction. Let the governor of Judah and the Jewish leaders rebuild the Temple of God where it stood before. I hereby command you to help them rebuild it. Their expenses are to be paid promptly out of the royal funds received from taxes in West Euphrates, so that the work is not interrupted. Day by day, without fail, you are to give the priests in Jerusalem whatever they tell you they need: young bulls, sheep, or lambs to be burnt as offerings to the God of Heaven, or wheat, salt, wine, or olive-oil. This is to be done so that they can offer sacrifices that are acceptable to the God of Heaven and pray for his blessing on me and my sons. [I further command that if anyone disobeys this order, a wooden beam is to be torn out of his house, sharpened at one end, and then driven through his body. And his house is to be made a rubbish heap.] May the God who chose Jerusalem as the place where he is to be worshipped overthrow any king or nation that defies this command and tries to destroy the Temple there. I, Darius, have given this order. It is to be fully obeyed.
Cast	[This is] the word of the Lord.
All	**Thanks be to God.**

Cast: **Narrator, Reader, Darius.**

The document which Artaxerxes gave to Ezra
From Ezra 7.11–28

Narrator	Artaxerxes, the emperor of Persia, gave the following document to Ezra, the priest and scholar, who had a thorough knowledge of the laws and commands which the Lord had given to Israel:
Artaxerxes	From Artaxerxes the emperor to Ezra the priest, scholar in the Law of the God of Heaven.
	I command that throughout my empire all the Israelite people, priests, and Levites that so desire be permitted to go with you to Jerusalem. I, together with my seven counsellors, send you to investigate the conditions in Jerusalem and Judah in order to see how well the Law of your God, which has been entrusted to you, is being obeyed. You are to take with you the gold and silver

offerings which I and my counsellors desire to give to the God of Israel, whose Temple is in Jerusalem. You are also to take all the silver and gold which you collect throughout the province of Babylon and the offerings which the Israelite people and their priests give for the Temple of their God in Jerusalem. You are to spend this money carefully and buy bulls, rams, lambs, corn, and wine and offer them on the altar of the Temple in Jerusalem. And anything else which you need for the Temple, you may get from the royal treasury. I command all the treasury officials in the province of West Euphrates to provide promptly for Ezra, the priest and scholar in the Law of the God of Heaven, everything he asks you for. You must be careful to provide everything which the God of Heaven requires for his Temple, and so make sure that he is never angry with me or with those who reign after me.

You, Ezra, using the wisdom which your God has given you, are to appoint administrators and judges to govern all the people in West Euphrates who live by the Law of your God. You must teach that Law to anyone who does not know it. If anyone disobeys the laws of your God or the laws of the empire, he is to be punished promptly: by death or by exile or by confiscation of his property or by imprisonment.

Narrator Ezra said:

Ezra Praise the Lord, the God of our ancestors! He has made the emperor willing to honour in this way the Temple of the Lord in Jerusalem. By God's grace I have won the favour of the emperor, of his counsellors, and of all his powerful officials; the Lord my God has given me courage, and I have been able to persuade many of the heads of the clans of Israel to return with me.

Cast [This is] the word of the Lord.
All **Thanks be to God.**

Cast: **Narrator, Artaxerxes, Ezra.**

Ezra learns of intermarriages with non-Jews
From Ezra 9.1–15

Ezra Some of the leaders of the people of Israel came and told me that the people, the priests, and the Levites had not kept themselves separate from the people in the neighbouring countries. They were doing the same disgusting things that those people did. Jewish men were marrying foreign women, and so God's holy people had become contaminated. The leaders and officials were the chief offenders. When I heard this, I tore my clothes in despair, tore my hair and my beard, and sat down crushed with grief. I sat there grieving until the time for the evening sacrifice to be offered, and people began to gather round me—all those who were frightened because of what the God of Israel had said about the sins of those who had returned from exile.

→

When the time came for the evening sacrifice, I got up from where I had been grieving, and still wearing my torn clothes, I knelt in prayer and stretched out my hands to the Lord my God:

Young Ezra   O God, I am too ashamed to raise my head in your presence. Our sins pile up, high above our heads; they reach as high as the heavens. From the days of our ancestors until now, we, your people, have sinned greatly. Because of our sins we, our kings, and our priests have fallen into the hands of foreign kings, and we have been slaughtered, robbed, and carried away as prisoners. We have been totally disgraced, as we still are today. Now for a short time, O Lord our God, you have been gracious to us and have let some of us escape from slavery and live in safety in this holy place. You have freed us from slavery and given us new life. We were slaves, but you did not leave us in slavery. You made the emperors of Persia favour us and permit us to go on living and to rebuild your Temple, which was in ruins, and to find safety here in Judah and Jerusalem.

But now, O God, what can we say after all that has happened? We have again disobeyed the commands that you gave us through your servants, the prophets. Lord God of Israel, you are just, but you have let us survive. We confess our guilt to you; we have no right to come into your presence.

Cast   [This is] the word of the Lord.
All   **Thanks be to God.**

Cast: **Ezra, Young Ezra.**

The plan for ending mixed marriages
Ezra 10.1–17

Narrator   While Ezra was bowing in prayer in front of the Temple, weeping and confessing the sins of the people, a large group of Israelites—men, women, and children—gathered round him, weeping bitterly. Then Shecaniah son of Jehiel, of the clan of Elam, said to Ezra:

Shecaniah   We have broken faith with God by marrying foreign women, but even so there is still hope for Israel. Now we must make a solemn promise to our God that we will send these women and their children away. We will do what you and the others who honour God's commands advise us to do. We will do what God's Law demands. It is your responsibility to act. We are behind you, so go ahead and get it done.

Narrator   So Ezra began by making the leaders of the priests, of the Levites, and of the rest of the people take an oath that they would do what Shecaniah had proposed. Then he went from in front of the Temple into the living-quarters of Jehohanan son of Eliashib, and spent the night there grieving over the unfaithfulness of the exiles. He did not eat or drink anything.

A message was sent throughout Jerusalem and Judah that all those who had returned from exile were to meet in Jerusalem by order of the leaders of the people. If anyone failed to come within three days, all his property would be confiscated, and he would lose his right to be a member of the community. Within the three days, on the twentieth day of the ninth month, all the men living in the territory of Judah and Benjamin came to Jerusalem and assembled in the temple square. It was raining hard, and because of the weather and the importance of the meeting everyone was trembling.

Ezra the priest stood up and spoke to them:

Ezra You have been faithless and have brought guilt on Israel by marrying foreign women. Now then, confess your sins to the Lord, the God of your ancestors, and do what pleases him. Separate yourselves from the foreigners living in our land and get rid of your foreign wives.

Narrator The people shouted in answer:

Persons 1 and 2 We will do whatever you say.

Narrator But they added:

Person 1 The crowd is too big, and it's raining hard. We can't stand here in the open like this.

Person 2 This isn't something that can be done in one or two days, because so many of us are involved in this sin.

Person 1 Let our officials stay in Jerusalem and take charge of the matter.

Person 2 Then let anyone who has a foreign wife come at a set time, together with the leaders and the judges of his city.

Person 1 In this way God's anger over this situation will be turned away.

Narrator No one was opposed to the plan except Jonathan son of Asahel and Jahzeiah son of Tikvah, who had the support of Meshullam and of Shabbethai, a Levite.

The returned exiles accepted the plan, so Ezra the priest appointed men from among the heads of the clans and recorded their names. On the first day of the tenth month they began their investigation, and within the next three months they investigated all the cases of men with foreign wives.

Cast [This is] the word of the Lord.
All **Thanks be to God.**

Cast: **Narrator, Shecaniah, Ezra, Person 1, Person 2** (can be the same as Person 1).

NEHEMIAH

This is the account of what Nehemiah son of Hacaliah accomplished

Nehemiah's concern for Jerusalem
Nehemiah 1.1–11

Old Nehemiah　In the month of Kislev in the twentieth year that Artaxerxes was emperor of Persia, I, Nehemiah, was in Susa, the capital city. Hanani, one of my brothers, arrived from Judah with a group of other men, and I asked them about Jerusalem and about our fellow-Jews who had returned from exile in Babylonia. They told me that those who had survived and were back in the homeland were in great difficulty and that the foreigners who lived near by looked down on them. They also told me that the walls of Jerusalem were still broken down and that the gates had not been restored since the time they were burnt. When I heard all this, I sat down and wept. (PAUSE)

For several days I mourned and did not eat. I prayed to God:

Young Nehemiah　Lord God of Heaven! You are great, and we stand in fear of you. You faithfully keep your covenant with those who love you and do what you command. Look at me, Lord, and hear my prayer, as I pray day and night for your servants, the people of Israel. I confess that we, the people of Israel, have sinned. My ancestors and I have sinned. We have acted wickedly against you and have not done what you commanded. We have not kept the laws which you gave us through Moses, your servant. Remember now what you told Moses:

[The Lord]　If you people of Israel are unfaithful to me, I will scatter you among the other nations. But then if you turn back to me and do what I have commanded you, I will bring you back to the place where I have chosen to be worshipped, even though you are scattered to the ends of the earth.

Young Nehemiah　Lord, these are your servants, your own people. You rescued them by your great power and strength. Listen now to my prayer and to the prayers of all your other servants who want to honour you. Give me success today and make the emperor merciful to me.

Old Nehemiah　In those days I was the emperor's wine steward.

Cast　[This is] the word of the Lord.
All　**Thanks be to God.**

Cast: **Old Nehemiah, Young Nehemiah, The Lord** (can be the same as Young Nehemiah).

Nehemiah talks to the Emperor
Nehemiah 2.1–8

Old Nehemiah One day, when Emperor Artaxerxes was dining, I took the wine to him. He had never seen me look sad before, so he asked:

Emperor Why are you looking so sad? You aren't ill, so it must be that you're unhappy.

Old Nehemiah I was startled and answered:

Young Nehemiah May Your Majesty live for ever! How can I help looking sad when the city where my ancestors are buried is in ruins and its gates have been destroyed by fire?

Emperor What is it that you want?

Old Nehemiah I prayed to the God of Heaven, and then I said to the emperor:

Young Nehemiah If Your Majesty is pleased with me and is willing to grant my request, let me go to the land of Judah, to the city where my ancestors are buried, so that I can rebuild the city.

Old Nehemiah The emperor, with the empress sitting at his side, approved my request. He asked me how long I would be gone and when I would return, and I told him. (PAUSE)

Then I asked him to grant me the favour of giving me letters to the governors of West Euphrates Province, instructing them to let me travel to Judah. I asked also for a letter to Asaph, keeper of the royal forests, instructing him to supply me with timber for the gates of the fort that guards the Temple, for the city walls, and for the house I was to live in. The emperor gave me all I asked for, because God was with me.

Cast [This is] the word of the Lord.
All **Thanks be to God.**

Cast: **Old Nehemiah, Emperor, Young Nehemiah.**

Nehemiah goes to Jerusalem
Nehemiah 2.9–20

Old Nehemiah The emperor sent some army officers and a troop of horsemen with me, and I made the journey to West Euphrates. There I gave the emperor's letters to the governors. But Sanballat, from the town of Beth Horon, and Tobiah, an official in the province of Ammon, heard that someone had come to work for the good of the people of Israel, and they were highly indignant. I went on to Jerusalem, and for three days I did not tell anyone what God had inspired me to do for Jerusalem. Then in the middle of the night I got up and went out, taking a few of my companions with me. The only animal we took was the donkey that I rode on. It was still night as I left the city through the Valley Gate on the west and went south past Dragon's Fountain to the Rubbish Gate. As I

→

went, I inspected the broken walls of the city and the gates that had been destroyed by fire. Then on the east side of the city I went north to the Fountain Gate and the King's Pool. The donkey I was riding could not find any path through the rubble, so I went down into the valley of the Kidron and rode along, looking at the wall. Then I returned the way I had come and went back into the city through the Valley Gate. None of the local officials knew where I had been or what I had been doing. So far I had not said anything to any of my fellow-Jews—the priests, the leaders, the officials, or anyone else who would be taking part in the work. But now I said to them:

Young Nehemiah See what trouble we are in because Jerusalem is in ruins and its gates are destroyed! Let's rebuild the city walls and put an end to our disgrace.

Old Nehemiah And I told them how God had been with me and helped me, and what the emperor had said to me. They responded:

Persons 1 and 2 Let's start rebuilding!

Old Nehemiah And they got ready to start the work. (PAUSE) When Sanballat, Tobiah, and an Arab named Geshem heard what we were planning to do, they laughed at us and said:

Sanballat What do you think you're doing?

Tobiah Are you going to rebel against the emperor?

Young Nehemiah The God of Heaven will give us success. We are his servants, and we are going to start building. But you have no right to any property in Jerusalem, and you have no share in its traditions.

Cast [This is] the word of the Lord.
All **Thanks be to God.**

Cast: **Old Nehemiah, Young Nehemiah, Person 1, Person 2** (can be the same as Person 1), **Sanballat, Tobiah** (can be the same as Sanballat).

Nehemiah overcomes opposition to his work
Nehemiah 4.1–23

Old Nehemiah When Sanballat heard that we Jews had begun rebuilding the wall, he was furious and began to ridicule us in front of his companions and the Samaritan troops:

Sanballat What do these miserable Jews think they're doing? Do they intend to rebuild the city? Do they think that by offering sacrifices they can finish the work in one day? Can they make building-stones out of heaps of burnt rubble?

Old Nehemiah Tobiah was standing there beside him, and he added:

Tobiah What kind of wall could *they* ever build? Even a *fox* could knock it down!

Old Nehemiah I prayed:

Young Nehemiah	Listen to them mocking us, O God! Let their ridicule fall on their own heads. Let them be robbed of everything they have, and let them be taken as prisoners to a foreign land. Don't forgive the evil they do and don't forget their sins, for they have insulted us who are building.
Old Nehemiah	So we went on rebuilding the wall, and soon it was half its full height, because the people were eager to work. (PAUSE)
	Sanballat, Tobiah, and the people of Arabia, Ammon, and Ashdod heard that we were making progress in rebuilding the wall of Jerusalem and that the gaps in the wall were being closed, and they were very angry. So they all plotted together to come and attack Jerusalem and create confusion, but we prayed to our God and kept men on guard against them day and night.
	The people of Judah had a song they sang:
Person 1	We grow weak carrying burdens—
Person 2	There's so much rubble to take away.
Person 1	How can we build the wall today?
Old Nehemiah	Our enemies thought we would not see them or know what was happening until they were already upon us, killing us and putting an end to our work. But time after time Jews who were living among our enemies came to warn us of the plans our enemies were making against us. So I armed the people with swords, spears, and bows, and stationed them by clans behind the wall, wherever it was still unfinished. I saw that the people were worried, so I said to them and to their leaders and officials:
Young Nehemiah	Don't be afraid of our enemies. Remember how great and terrifying the Lord is, and fight for your fellow-countrymen, your children, your wives, and your homes.
Old Nehemiah	Our enemies heard that we had found out what they were plotting, and they realized that God had defeated their plans. Then all of us went back to rebuilding the wall. (PAUSE)
	From then on half my men worked and half stood guard, wearing coats of armour and armed with spears, shields, and bows. And our leaders gave their full support to the people who were rebuilding the wall. Even those who carried building materials worked with one hand and kept a weapon in the other, and everyone who was building kept a sword strapped to his waist. The man who was to sound the alarm on the bugle stayed with me. I told the people and their officials and leaders:
Young Nehemiah	The work is spread out over such a distance that we are widely separated from one another on the wall. If you hear the bugle, gather round me. Our God will fight for us.
Old Nehemiah	So every day, from dawn until the stars came out at night, half of us worked on the wall, while the other half stood guard with spears. (PAUSE)

→

During this time I told the men in charge that they and all their helpers had to stay in Jerusalem at night, so that we could guard the city at night as well as work in the daytime. I didn't take off my clothes even at night, neither did any of my companions nor my servants nor my bodyguard. And we all kept our weapons to hand.

Cast	[This is] the word of the Lord.
All	**Thanks be to God.**

Cast: **Old Nehemiah, Sanballat, Tobiah, Young Nehemiah, Person 1, Person 2** (can be the same as Person 1).

Oppression of the poor
Nehemiah 5.1–13

Old Nehemiah　　Many of the people, both men and women, began to complain against their fellow-Jews [Some said]:

Woman 1　　We have large families, we need corn to keep us alive.

[Old Nehemiah　　Others said:]

Man 1　　We have had to mortgage our fields and vineyards and houses to get enough corn to keep us from starving.

[Old Nehemiah　　Still others said:]

Man 2　　We had to borrow money to pay the royal tax on our fields and vineyards.

Woman 2　　We are of the same race as our fellow-Jews. Aren't our children just as good as theirs? But we have to make slaves of our children.

Man 1　　Some of our daughters have already been sold as slaves.

Woman 1　　We are helpless because our fields and vineyards have been taken away from us.

Old Nehemiah　　When I heard their complaints, I was angry and decided to act. I denounced the leaders and officials of the people and told them:

Young Nehemiah　　You are oppressing your brothers!

Old Nehemiah　　I called a public assembly to deal with the problem and said:

Young Nehemiah　　As far as we have been able, we have been buying back our Jewish brothers who had to sell themselves to foreigners. Now you are forcing your own brothers to sell themselves to you, their fellow-Jews!

Old Nehemiah　　The leaders were silent and could find nothing to say. Then I said:

Young Nehemiah　　What you are doing is wrong! You ought to obey God and do what's right. Then you would not give our enemies, the Gentiles, any reason to ridicule us. I have let the people borrow money and corn from me, and so have my companions and the men who work for me. Now let's give up all our claims to repayment. Cancel all the debts they owe you—money or corn or wine or olive-oil. And give them back their fields, vineyards, olive-groves, and houses at once!

Old Nehemiah	The leaders replied:
Leader 1	We'll do as you say.
Leader 2	We'll give the property back and not try to collect the debts.
Old Nehemiah	I called in the priests and made the leaders swear in front of them to keep the promise they had just made. Then I took off the sash I was wearing round my waist and shook it out.
Young Nehemiah	This is how God will shake any of you who don't keep your promise. God will take away your houses and everything you own, and will leave you with nothing.
Old Nehemiah	Everyone who was present said:
Women 1 and **2**, **Men 1** and **2**, **Leaders 1** and **2**	Amen!
Old Nehemiah	And praised the Lord. And the leaders kept their promise.
Cast	[This is] the word of the Lord.
All	**Thanks be to God.**

Cast: **Old Nehemiah, Woman 1, Man 1, Man 2** (can be the same as Man 1), **Woman 2** (can be the same as Woman 1), **Young Nehemiah, Leader 1, Leader 2** (can be the same as Leader 1).

Plots against Nehemiah
Nehemiah 6.1–16

Old Nehemiah	Sanballat, Tobiah, Geshem, and the rest of our enemies heard that we had finished building the wall and that there were no gaps left in it, although we still had not set up the gates in the gateways. So Sanballat and Geshem sent me a message, suggesting that I meet with them in one of the villages in the Plain of Ono. This was a trick of theirs to try to harm me. I sent messengers to say to them:
Young Nehemiah	I am doing important work and can't go down there. I am not going to let the work stop just to go and see you.
Old Nehemiah	They sent me the same message four times, and each time I sent them the same reply. Then Sanballat sent one of his servants to me with a fifth message, this one in the form of an unsealed letter. It read:
Sanballat	Geshem tells me that a rumour is going round among the neighbouring peoples that you and the Jewish people intend to revolt and that this is why you are rebuilding the wall. He also says you plan to make yourself king and that you have arranged for some prophets to proclaim in Jerusalem that you are the king of Judah. His Majesty is certain to hear about this, so I suggest that you and I meet to talk the situation over.
Old Nehemiah	I sent a reply to him:
Young Nehemiah	Nothing of what you are saying is true. You have made it all up yourself.

441

Old Nehemiah	They were trying to frighten us into stopping work. I prayed:
Young Nehemiah	But now, God, make me strong!
Old Nehemiah	About this time I went to visit Shemaiah, the son of Delaiah and grandson of Mehetabel, who was unable to leave his house. He said to me:
Shemaiah	You and I must go and hide together in the Holy Place of the Temple and lock the doors, because they are coming to kill you. Any night now they will come to kill you.
Young Nehemiah	I'm not the kind of man that runs and hides. Do you think I would try to save my life by hiding in the Temple? I won't do it.
Old Nehemiah	When I thought it over, I realized that God had not spoken to Shemaiah, but that Tobiah and Sanballat had bribed him to give me this warning. They hired him to frighten me into sinning, so that they could ruin my reputation and humiliate me. I prayed:
Young Nehemiah	God, remember what Tobiah and Sanballat have done and punish them. Remember that woman Nodiah and all the other prophets who tried to frighten me.
Old Nehemiah	After fifty-two days of work the entire wall was finished on the twenty-fifth day of the month of Elul. When our enemies in the surrounding nations heard this, they realized that they had lost face, since everyone knew that the work had been done with God's help.
Cast	[This is] the word of the Lord.
All	**Thanks be to God.**

Cast: **Old Nehemiah, Young Nehemiah, Sanballat, Shemaiah.**

Ezra reads the law to the people
Nehemiah 8.1–12 (Version A: with lists of names)

Narrator	By the seventh month the people of Israel were all settled in their towns. On the first day of that month they all assembled in Jerusalem, in the square just inside the Water Gate. They asked Ezra, the priest and scholar of the Law which the Lord had given Israel through Moses, to get the book of the Law. So Ezra brought it to the place where the people had gathered—men, women, and the children who were old enough to understand. There in the square by the gate he read the Law to them from dawn until noon, and they all listened attentively.
	Ezra was standing on a wooden platform that had been built for the occasion. The following men stood at his right:
Secretary	Mattithiah, Shema, Anaiah, Uriah, Hilkiah, and Maaseiah;
Narrator	And the following stood at his left:
Secretary	Pedaiah, Mishael, Malchijah, Hashum, Hashbaddanah, Zechariah, and Meshullam.

Narrator	As Ezra stood there on the platform high above the people, they all kept their eyes fixed on him. As soon as he opened the book, they all stood up. Ezra said:
Ezra	Praise the Lord, the great God!
Narrator	All the people raised their arms in the air and answered:
People	Amen! Amen!
Narrator	They knelt in worship, with their faces to the ground. Then they rose and stood in their places, and the following Levites explained the Law to them:
Secretary	Jeshua, Bani, Sherebiah, Jamin, Akkub, Shabbethai, Hodiah, Maaseiah, Kelita, Azariah, Jozabad, Hanan, and Pelaiah.
Narrator	They gave an oral translation of God's Law and explained it so that the people could understand it. (PAUSE)
	When the people heard what the Law required, they were so moved that they began to cry. So Nehemiah, who was the governor, Ezra, the priest and scholar of the Law, and the Levites who were explaining the Law told all the people:
Ezra	This day is holy to the Lord your God, so you are not to mourn or cry. Now go home and have a feast. Share your food and wine with those who haven't enough. Today is holy to our Lord, so don't be sad. The joy that the Lord gives you will make you strong.
Narrator	The Levites went about calming the people and telling them not to be sad on such a holy day. So all the people went home and ate and drank joyfully and shared what they had with others, because they understood what had been read to them.
Cast	[This is] the word of the Lord.
All	**Thanks be to God.**

Cast: **Narrator, Secretary, Ezra, People** (two or more). (The inclusion of the names adds a humorous element, provided the casting is right.)

Ezra reads the law to the people
From Nehemiah 8.1–12 (Version B: omitting lists of names)

Narrator	By the seventh month the people of Israel were all settled in their towns. On the first day of that month they all assembled in Jerusalem, in the square just inside the Water Gate. They asked Ezra, the priest and scholar of the Law which the Lord had given Israel through Moses, to get the book of the Law. So Ezra brought it to the place where the people had gathered—men, women, and the children who were old enough to understand. There in the square by the gate he read the Law to them from dawn until noon, and they all listened attentively.
	Ezra was standing on a wooden platform that had been built for the occasion. Six men stood at his right, and seven stood at his left.

→

443

As Ezra stood there on the platform high above the people, they all kept their eyes fixed on him. As soon as he opened the book, they all stood up. Ezra said:

Ezra Praise the Lord, the great God!

Narrator All the people raised their arms in the air and answered:

People Amen! Amen!

Narrator They knelt in worship, with their faces to the ground. Then they rose and stood in their places, and the Levites explained the Law to them. They gave an oral translation of God's Law and explained it so that the people could understand it. (PAUSE)

When the people heard what the Law required, they were so moved that they began to cry. So Nehemiah, who was the governor, Ezra, the priest and scholar of the Law, and the Levites who were explaining the Law told all the people:

Ezra This day is holy to the Lord your God, so you are not to mourn or cry. Now go home and have a feast. Share your food and wine with those who haven't enough. Today is holy to our Lord, so don't be sad. The joy that the Lord gives you will make you strong.

Narrator The Levites went about calming the people and telling them not to be sad on such a holy day. So all the people went home and ate and drank joyfully and shared what they had with others, because they understood what had been read to them.

Cast [This is] the word of the Lord.
All **Thanks be to God.**

Cast: **Narrator, Ezra, People** (two or more).

The Festival of Shelters
Nehemiah 8.13–18

Nehemiah The heads of the clans, together with the priests and the Levites, went to Ezra to study the teachings of the Law. They discovered that the Law, which the Lord gave through Moses, ordered the people of Israel to live in temporary shelters during the Festival of Shelters. So they gave the following instructions and sent them all through Jerusalem and the other cities and towns:

Leader 1 Go out to the hills and get branches from pines, olives, myrtles, palms, and other trees—

Leader 2 To make shelters according to the instructions written in the Law.

Nehemiah So the people got branches and built shelters on the flat roofs of their houses, in their yards, in the temple courtyard, and in the public squares by the Water Gate and by the Ephraim Gate. All the people who had come back from captivity built shelters and lived in them. This was the first time it had been done since the days of Joshua son of Nun, and everybody was excited and happy. From the first day of the festival to the last they read a part of God's Law every day. They celebrated for seven days, and on the eighth day there was a closing ceremony, as required in the Law.

Cast	[This is] the word of the Lord.
All	**Thanks be to God.**

Cast: **Nehemiah, Leader 1, Leader 2** (can be the same as Leader 1).

Nehemiah's reforms (i)
Nehemiah 13.15–22

Old Nehemiah I saw people in Judah pressing juice from grapes on the Sabbath. Others were loading corn, wine, grapes, figs, and other things on their donkeys and taking them into Jerusalem; I warned them not to sell anything on the Sabbath. Some men from the city of Tyre were living in Jerusalem, and they brought fish and all kinds of goods into the city to sell to our people on the Sabbath. I reprimanded the Jewish leaders:

Young Nehemiah Look at the evil you're doing! You're making the Sabbath unholy. This is exactly why God punished your ancestors when he brought destruction on this city. And yet you insist on bringing more of God's anger down on Israel by profaning the Sabbath.

Old Nehemiah So I gave orders for the city gates to be shut at the beginning of every Sabbath, as soon as evening began to fall, and not to be opened again until the Sabbath was over. I stationed some of my men at the gates to make sure that nothing was brought into the city on the Sabbath. Once or twice merchants who sold all kinds of goods spent Friday night outside the city walls. I warned them:

Young Nehemiah It's no use waiting out there for morning to come. If you try this again, I'll use force against you.

Old Nehemiah From then on they did not come back on the Sabbath. I ordered the Levites to purify themselves and to go and guard the gates to make sure that the Sabbath was kept holy.

Cast	[This is] the word of the Lord.
All	**Thanks be to God.**

Cast: **Old Nehemiah, Young Nehemiah.**

Nehemiah's reforms (ii)
Nehemiah 13.23–30

Old Nehemiah I discovered that many of the Jewish men had married women from Ashdod, Ammon, and Moab. Half their children spoke the language of Ashdod or some other language and didn't know how to speak our language. I reprimanded the men, called down curses on them, beat them, and pulled out their hair. Then I made them take an oath in God's name that never again would they or their children intermarry with foreigners. [I said:]

Young Nehemiah	It was foreign women that made King Solomon sin. He was a man who was greater than any of the kings of other nations. God loved him and made him king over all Israel, and yet he fell into this sin. Are we then to follow your example and disobey our God by marrying foreign women?
Old Nehemiah	Joiada was the son of Eliashib the High Priest, but one of Joiada's sons married the daughter of Sanballat, from the town of Beth Horon, so I made Joiada leave Jerusalem.
(in prayer)	Remember, O God, how those people defiled both the office of priest and the covenant you made with the priests and the Levites.
	I purified the people from everything foreign; I prepared regulations for the priests and the Levites so that each one would know his duty; I arranged for the wood used for burning the offerings to be brought at the proper times, and for the people to bring their offerings of the first corn and the first fruits that ripened.
Cast	[This is] the word of the Lord.
All	**Thanks be to God.**

Cast: **Old Nehemiah, Young Nehemiah.**

446

ESTHER

Queen Vashti defies King Xerxes
From Esther 1.1–22

Narrator 1	From his royal throne in Persia's capital city of Susa, King Xerxes ruled over 127 provinces, all the way from India to Sudan.
Narrator 2	In the third year of his reign he gave a banquet for all his officials and administrators. The armies of Persia and Media were present, as well as the governors and noblemen of the provinces.
Narrator 1	The king gave a banquet for all the men in the capital city of Susa, rich and poor alike. It lasted a whole week and was held in the gardens of the royal palace. The courtyard there was decorated with blue and white cotton curtains, tied by cords of fine purple linen to silver rings on marble columns. Couches made of gold and silver had been placed in the courtyard, which was paved with white marble, red feldspar, shining mother-of-pearl, and blue turquoise. Drinks were served in gold cups, no two of them alike, and the king was generous with the royal wine. There were no limits on the drinks; the king had given orders to the palace servants that everyone could have as much as he wanted.
Narrator 2	Meanwhile, inside the royal palace Queen Vashti was giving a banquet for the women.
Narrator 1	On the seventh day of his banquet the king was drinking and feeling merry, so he called in the seven eunuchs who were his personal servants, Mehuman, Biztha, Harbona, Bigtha, Abagtha, Zethar, and Carkas. He ordered them to bring in Queen Vashti, wearing her royal crown. The queen was a beautiful woman, and the king wanted to show off her beauty to the officials and all his guests. But when the servants told Queen Vashti of the king's command, she refused to come.
Narrators 1 & 2	This made the king furious.
Narrator 2	Now it was the king's custom to ask for expert opinion on questions of law and order, so he called for his advisers, who would know what should be done. He said to them:
King	I, King Xerxes, sent my servants to Queen Vashti with a command, and she refused to obey it! What does the law say that we should do with her?
Narrator 1	Then his servant Memucan declared to the king and his officials:
Memucan	Queen Vashti has insulted not only the king but also his officials— in fact, every man in the empire! Every woman in the empire will begin to look down on her husband as soon as she hears what the queen has done. They'll say:

447

Woman 1	King Xerxes commanded Queen Vashti to come to him—
Women 1 and **2**	And she refused!
Memucan	When the wives of the royal officials of Persia and Media hear about the queen's behaviour they will be telling their husbands about it before the day is out. Wives everywhere will have no respect for their husbands, and husbands will be angry with their wives. If it please Your Majesty, issue a royal proclamation that Vashti may never again appear before the king. Order it to be written into the laws of Persia and Media, so that it can never be changed. Then give her place as queen to some better woman. When your proclamation is made known all over this huge empire, every woman will treat her husband with proper respect, whether he's rich or poor.
Narrator 1	The king and his officials liked this idea, and the king did what Memucan suggested.
Narrator 2	To each of the royal provinces he sent a message in the language and the system of writing of that province, saying that every husband should be the master of his home and speak with final authority.
Cast	[This is] the word of the Lord.
All	**Thanks be to God.**

Cast: **Narrator 1, Narrator 2, King, Memucan, Woman 1, Woman 2** (can be the same as Woman 1).

Esther wins favour
Esther 2.1–9

Narrator	After the king's anger had cooled down, he kept thinking about what Vashti had done and about his proclamation against her. So some of the king's advisers who were close to him suggested:
Adviser 1	Why don't you make a search to find some beautiful young virgins?
Adviser 2	You can appoint officials in every province of the empire and order them to bring all these beautiful young girls to your harem here in Susa, the capital city.
Adviser 1	Put them in the care of Hegai, the eunuch who is in charge of your women, and let them be given a beauty treatment. Then take the girl you like best and make her queen in Vashti's place.
Narrator	The king thought this was good advice, so he followed it. (PAUSE)
	There in Susa lived a Jew named Mordecai son of Jair; he was from the tribe of Benjamin and was a descendant of Kish and Shimei. When King Nebuchadnezzar of Babylon took King Jehoiachin of Judah into exile from Jerusalem, along with a group of captives, Mordecai was among them. He had a cousin, Esther, whose Hebrew name was Hadassah; she was a beautiful girl, and had a good figure. At the death of her parents, Mordecai

had adopted her and brought her up as his own daughter. When the king had issued his new proclamation and many girls were being brought to Susa, Esther was among them. She too was put in the royal palace in the care of Hegai, who had charge of the harem. Hegai liked Esther, and she won his favour.

Cast	[This is] the word of the Lord.
All	**Thanks be to God.**

Cast: **Narrator, Adviser 1, Adviser 2** (can be the same as Adviser 1).

Esther becomes Queen and Mordecai saves the king's life
Esther 2.15–23

Narrator 1   The time came for Esther to go to the king—

Narrator 2   Esther—the daughter of Abihail and the cousin of Mordecai, who had adopted her as his daughter.

Narrator 3   Esther—admired by everyone who saw her.

Narrator 1   When her turn came, she wore just what Hegai, the eunuch in charge of the harem, advised her to wear.

Narrator 2   So in Xerxes' seventh year as king, in the tenth month, the month of Tebeth, Esther was brought to King Xerxes in the royal palace.

Narrator 3   The king liked her more than any of the other girls, and more than any of the others she won his favour and affection.

Narrator 1   He placed the royal crown on her head and made her queen in place of Vashti.

Narrator 2   Then the king gave a banquet in Esther's honour and invited all his officials and administrators. He proclaimed a holiday for the whole empire and distributed gifts worthy of a king. (PAUSE)

Narrator 3   Meanwhile Mordecai had been appointed by the king to an administrative position.

Narrator 1   As for Esther, she had still not let it be known that she was Jewish.

Narrator 2   Mordecai had told her not to tell anyone, and she obeyed him in this, just as she had obeyed him when she was a little girl under his care.

Narrator 3   During the time that Mordecai held office in the palace, Bigthana and Teresh, two of the palace eunuchs who guarded the entrance to the king's rooms, became hostile to King Xerxes and plotted to assassinate him.

Narrator 1   Mordecai learnt about it and told Queen Esther, who then told the king what Mordecai had found out.

Narrator 2   There was an investigation, and it was discovered that the report was true, so both men were hanged on the gallows. (PAUSE)

Narrator 3	The king ordered an account of this to be written down in the official records of the empire.
Cast	[This is] the word of the Lord.
All	**Thanks be to God.**

Cast: **Narrator 1, Narrator 2, Narrator 3.**

Haman plots to destroy the Jews
From Esther 3.1–15

Narrator 1	King Xerxes promoted a man named Haman to the position of prime minister. Haman was the son of Hammedatha, a descendant of Agag. The king ordered all the officials in his service to show their respect for Haman by kneeling and bowing to him.
Narrator 2	They all did so, except for Mordecai, who refused to do it. The other officials in the royal service asked him why he was disobeying the king's command; day after day they urged him to give in, but he would not listen to them. He explained:
Mordecai	I am a Jew, and I cannot bow to Haman.
Narrator 2	So they told Haman about this, wondering if he would tolerate Mordecai's conduct.
Narrator 1	Haman was furious when he realized that Mordecai was not going to kneel and bow to him, and when he learnt that Mordecai was a Jew, he decided to do more than punish Mordecai alone. He made plans to kill every Jew in the whole Persian Empire. So Haman told the king:
Haman	There is a certain race of people scattered all over your empire and found in every province. They observe customs that are not like those of any other people. Moreover, they do not obey the laws of the empire, so it is not in your best interests to tolerate them. If it please Your Majesty, issue a decree that they are to be put to death. If you do, I guarantee that I will be able to put silver into the royal treasury for the administration of the empire.
Narrator 1	The king took off his ring, which was used to stamp proclamations and make them official, and gave it to the enemy of the Jewish people, Haman son of Hammedatha, the descendant of Agag. The king told him:
King	The people and their money are yours; do as you like with them.
Narrator 1	So on the thirteenth day of the first month Haman called the king's secretaries and dictated a proclamation to be translated into every language and system of writing used in the empire and to be sent to all the rulers, governors, and officials.
Narrator 2	It was issued in the name of King Xerxes and stamped with his ring.
Narrator 1	Runners took this proclamation to every province of the empire.

Narrator 2	It contained the instructions that on a single day, the thirteenth day of Adar, all Jews—young and old, women and children—were to be killed. They were to be slaughtered without mercy and their belongings were to be taken.
Narrator 1	The contents of the proclamation were to be made public in every province, so that everyone would be prepared when that day came.
Narrator 2	At the king's command the decree was made public in the capital city of Susa, and runners carried the news to the provinces.
Narrator 1	The king and Haman sat down and had a drink while the city of Susa was being thrown into confusion.
Cast	[This is] the word of the Lord.
All	**Thanks be to God.**

Cast: **Narrator 1, Narrator 2** (can be the same as Narrator 1), **Mordecai, Haman, King.**

Mordecai asks for Esther's help
Esther 4.1–17

Narrator 1	When Mordecai learnt that Haman had persuaded the king to decree that all the Jews in the empire should be killed, he tore his clothes in anguish. Then he dressed in sackcloth, covered his head with ashes, and walked through the city, wailing loudly and bitterly, until he came to the entrance of the palace. He did not go in because no one wearing sackcloth was allowed inside. Throughout all the provinces, wherever the king's proclamation was made known, there was loud mourning among the Jews. They fasted, wept and wailed, and most of them put on sackcloth and lay in ashes.
Narrator 2	When Esther's servant-girls and eunuchs told her what Mordecai was doing, she was deeply disturbed. She sent Mordecai some clothes to put on instead of the sackcloth, but he would not accept them. Then she called Hathach, one of the palace eunuchs appointed as her servant by the king, and told him to go to Mordecai and find out what was happening and why.
Narrator 1	Hathach went to Mordecai in the city square at the entrance of the palace. Mordecai told him everything that had happened to him and just how much money Haman had promised to put into the royal treasury if all the Jews were killed. He gave Hathach a copy of the proclamation that had been issued in Susa, ordering the destruction of the Jews. Mordecai asked him to take it to Esther, explain the situation to her, and ask her to go and plead with the king and beg him to have mercy on her people.
Narrator 2	Hathach did this, and Esther gave him this message to take back to Mordecai:
Esther	If anyone, man or woman, goes to the inner courtyard and sees the king without being summoned, that person must die. That is the law; everyone, from the king's advisers to the people in the

$\rightarrow$

provinces, knows that. There is only one way to get round this law: if the king holds out his gold sceptre to someone, then that person's life is spared. But it has been a month since the king sent for me.

Narrator 1 When Mordecai received Esther's message, he sent her this warning:

Mordecai Don't imagine that you are safer than any other Jew just because you are in the royal palace. If you keep quiet at a time like this, help will come from heaven to the Jews, and they will be saved, but you will die and your father's family will come to an end. Yet who knows—maybe it was for a time like this that you were made queen!

Narrator 2 Esther sent Mordecai this reply:

Esther Go and gather all the Jews in Susa together; hold a fast and pray for me. Don't eat or drink anything for three days and nights. My servant-girls and I will be doing the same. After that, I will go to the king, even though it is against the law. If I must die for doing it, I will die.

Narrator 1 Mordecai then left and did everything that Esther had told him to do.

Cast [This is] the word of the Lord.
All **Thanks be to God.**

Cast: **Narrator 1, Narrator 2, Esther, Mordecai.**

Esther invites the king and Haman to a banquet
Esther 5.1–8

Narrator Esther put on her royal robes and went and stood in the inner court-yard of the palace, facing the throne room. The king was inside, seated on the royal throne, facing the entrance. When the king saw Queen Esther standing outside, she won his favour, and he held out to her the gold sceptre. She then came up and touched the tip of it.

The king asked:

King What is it, Queen Esther? Tell me what you want, and you shall have it—even if it is half my empire.

Esther If it please Your Majesty, I would like you and Haman to be my guests tonight at a banquet I am preparing for you.

Narrator The king then ordered Haman to come quickly, so that they could be Esther's guests. So the king and Haman went to Esther's banquet. Over the wine the king asked her:

King Tell me what you want, and you shall have it. I will grant your request, even if you ask for half my empire.

Esther If Your Majesty is kind enough to grant my request, I would like you and Haman to be my guests tomorrow at another banquet that I will prepare for you. At that time I will tell you what I want.

Cast [This is] the word of the Lord.
All **Thanks be to God.**

Cast: **Narrator, King, Esther.**

Haman plots to kill Mordecai
Esther 5.9–14

Narrator When Haman left Queen Esther's banquet he was happy and in a good mood. But then he saw Mordecai at the entrance of the palace, and when Mordecai did not rise or show any sign of respect as he passed, Haman was furious with him. But he controlled himself and went home. Then he invited his friends to his house and asked his wife Zeresh to join them. He boasted to them how rich he was, how many sons he had, how the king had promoted him to high office, and how much more important he was than any of the king's other officials. Haman went on:

Haman What is more, Queen Esther gave a banquet for no one but the king and me, and we are invited back tomorrow. But none of this means a thing to me as long as I see that Jew Mordecai sitting at the entrance of the palace.

Narrator So his wife and all his friends suggested:

Wife/friend Why don't you have a gallows built, twenty-two metres tall?* Tomorrow morning you can ask the king to have Mordecai hanged on it, and then you can go to the banquet happy.

Narrator Haman thought this was a good idea, so he had the gallows built.

Cast [This is] the word of the Lord.
All **Thanks be to God.**

Cast: **Narrator, Haman, Wife/friend.** (* OR 'seventy-five feet high'—NIV.)

The king honours Mordecai
Esther 6.1–13

Narrator The king could not get to sleep, so he ordered the official records of the empire to be brought and read to him. The part they read included the account of how Mordecai had uncovered a plot to assassinate the king—the plot made by Bigthana and Teresh, the two palace eunuchs who had guarded the king's rooms. The king asked:

King How have we honoured and rewarded Mordecai for this?

Narrator His servants answered:

Servant Nothing has been done for him.

King Are any of my officials in the palace?

Narrator Now Haman had just entered the courtyard; he had come to ask the king to have Mordecai hanged on the gallows that was now ready. So the servants answered:

Servant Haman is here, waiting to see you.

King Show him in.

Narrator	So Haman came in, and the king said to him:
King	There is someone I wish very much to honour. What should I do for this man?
Narrator	Haman thought to himself:
Haman (to himself)	Now who could the king want to honour so much? Me, of course.
[Narrator	So he answered the king:]
Haman (to the King)	Order royal robes to be brought for this man—robes that you yourself wear. Order a royal ornament to be put on your own horse. Then get one of your highest noblemen to dress the man in these robes and lead him, mounted on the horse, through the city square. Let the nobleman announce as they go:
[Nobleman]	See how the king rewards a man he wishes to honour!
King (urgently)	Hurry and get the robes and the horse, and provide these honours for Mordecai the Jew. Do everything for him that you have suggested. You will find him sitting at the entrance of the palace.
Narrator	So Haman got the robes and the horse, and he put the robes on Mordecai. Mordecai got on the horse, and Haman led him through the city square, announcing to the people as they went:
Haman (miserably)	See how the king rewards a man he wishes to honour!
Narrator	Mordecai then went back to the palace entrance while Haman hurried home, covering his face in embarrassment. He told his wife and all his friends everything that had happened to him. Then she and those wise friends of his said to him:
Wife/friend	You are beginning to lose power to Mordecai. He is a Jew, and you cannot overcome him. He will certainly defeat you.
Cast	[This is] the word of the Lord.
All	**Thanks be to God.**

Cast: **Narrator, King, Servant, Haman, [Nobleman], Wife/friend.**

Haman is put to death
Esther 6.14—7.10

Narrator	While Haman and his wife and friends were still talking, the palace eunuchs arrived in a hurry to take Haman to Esther's banquet. And so the king and Haman went to eat with Esther for a second time. Over the wine the king asked her again:
King	Now, Queen Esther, what do you want? Tell me and you shall have it. I'll even give you half the empire.
Narrator	Queen Esther answered:

Esther	If it please Your Majesty to grant my humble request, my wish is that I may live and that my people may live. My people and I have been sold for slaughter. If it were nothing more serious than being sold into slavery, I would have kept quiet and not bothered you about it; but we are about to be destroyed—exterminated!
Narrator	Then King Xerxes asked Queen Esther:
King	Who dares to do such a thing? Where is this man?
Esther (slowly)	Our enemy, our persecutor, is this evil man Haman!
Narrator	Haman stared at the king and queen in terror. The king got up in a fury, left the room, and went outside to the palace gardens. Haman could see that the king was determined to punish him for this, so he stayed behind to beg Queen Esther for his life. He had just thrown himself down on Esther's couch to beg for mercy, when the king came back into the room from the gardens. Seeing this, the king cried out:
King	Is this man going to rape the queen right here in front of me, in my own palace?
Narrator	The king had no sooner said this than the eunuchs covered Haman's head. Then one of them, who was named Harbonah, said:
Harbonah	Haman even went so far as to build a gallows at his house so that he could hang Mordecai, who saved Your Majesty's life. And it's twenty-two metres tall!*
King	Hang Haman on it!
Narrator	So Haman was hanged on the gallows that he had built for Mordecai. Then the king's anger cooled down.
Cast	[This is] the word of the Lord.
All	**Thanks be to God.**

Cast: **Narrator, King, Esther, Harbonah.** (* or 'seventy-five feet high'—NIV.)

The Jews are told to fight back
From Esther 8.[1–2], 3–17

[Narrator 1	King Xerxes gave Queen Esther all the property of Haman, the enemy of the Jews. Esther told the king that Mordecai was related to her, and from then on Mordecai was allowed to enter the king's presence.
Narrator 2	The king took off his ring with his seal on it (which he had taken back from Haman) and gave it to Mordecai. Esther put Mordecai in charge of Haman's property.]
Narrator 1	Then Esther spoke to the king again, throwing herself at his feet and crying. She begged him to do something to stop the evil plot that Haman, the descendant of Agag, had made against the Jews. The king held out the gold sceptre to her, so she stood up and said:

Esther	If it please Your Majesty, and if you care about me and if it seems right to you, please issue a proclamation to prevent Haman's orders from being carried out—those orders that the son of Hammedatha the descendant of Agag gave for the destruction of all the Jews in the empire. How can I endure it if this disaster comes on my people, and my own relatives are killed?
Narrator 1	King Xerxes then said to Queen Esther and Mordecai, the Jew:
King	Look, I have hanged Haman for his plot against the Jews, and I have given Esther his property. But a proclamation issued in the king's name and stamped with the royal seal cannot be revoked. You may, however, write to the Jews whatever you wish; and you may write it in my name and stamp it with the royal seal.
Narrator 1	This happened on the twenty-third day of the third month, the month of Sivan.
Narrator 2	Mordecai called the king's secretaries and dictated letters to the Jews and to the governors, administrators, and officials of all the 127 provinces from India to Sudan. The letters were written to each province in its own language and system of writing and to the Jews in their language and system of writing.
Narrator 1	Mordecai had the letters written in the name of King Xerxes, and he stamped them with the royal seal. They were delivered by riders mounted on fast horses from the royal stables.
Narrator 2	These letters explained that the king would allow the Jews in every city to organize themselves for self-defence. If they were attacked by armed men of any nationality in any province they could fight back. At the king's command the riders mounted royal horses and rode off at top speed.
Narrator 1	The decree was also made public in Susa, the capital city.
Narrator 2	Mordecai left the palace, wearing royal robes of blue and white, a cloak of fine purple linen, and a magnificent gold crown. Then the streets of Susa rang with cheers and joyful shouts. For the Jews there was joy and relief, happiness and a sense of victory.
Narrator 1	In every city and province, wherever the king's proclamation was read, the Jews held a joyful holiday with feasting and happiness.
Cast	[This is] the word of the Lord.
All	**Thanks be to God.**

Cast: **Narrator 1, Narrator 2** (can be the same as Narrator 1), **Esther, King.**

JOB

Satan tests Job
Job 1.1–12

Narrator	There was a man named Job, living in the land of Uz, who worshipped God and was faithful to him. He was a good man, careful not to do anything evil. He had seven sons and three daughters, and owned seven thousand sheep, three thousand camels, one thousand head of cattle, and five hundred donkeys. He also had a large number of servants and was the richest man in the East.
	Job's sons used to take it in turns to give a feast, to which all the others would come, and they always invited their three sisters to join them. The morning after each feast, Job would get up early and offer sacrifices for each of his children in order to purify them. He always did this because he thought that one of them might have sinned by insulting God unintentionally. (PAUSE)
	When the day came for the heavenly beings to appear before the Lord, Satan was there among them. The Lord asked him:
The Lord	What have you been doing?
Satan(casually)	I have been walking here and there, roaming round the earth.
The Lord	Did you notice my servant Job? There is no one on earth as faithful and good as he is. He worships me and is careful not to do anything evil.
Satan	Would Job worship you if he got nothing out of it? You have always protected him and his family and everything he owns. You bless everything he does, and you have given him enough cattle to fill the whole country. But now suppose you take away everything he has—he will curse you to your face!
The Lord	All right, everything he has is in your power, but you must not hurt Job himself.
Narrator	So Satan left.
Cast	[This is] the word of the Lord.
All	**Thanks be to God.**

Cast: **Narrator, The Lord, Satan.**

Job's children and wealth are destroyed
Job 1.13–22

Narrator	One day when Job's children were having a feast at the home of their eldest brother, a messenger came running to Job:

Servant 1	We were ploughing the fields with the oxen, and the donkeys were in a nearby pasture. Suddenly the Sabeans attacked and stole them all. They killed every one of your servants except me. I am the only one who escaped to tell you.
Narrator	Before he had finished speaking, another servant came:
Servant 2	Lightning struck the sheep and the shepherds and killed them all. I am the only one who escaped to tell you.
Narrator	Before he had finished speaking, another servant came:
Servant 3	Three bands of Chaldean raiders attacked us, took away the camels, and killed all your servants except me. I am the only one who escaped to tell you.
Narrator	Before he had finished speaking, another servant came:
Servant 4	Your children were having a feast at the home of your eldest son, when a storm swept in from the desert. It blew the house down and killed them all. I am the only one who escaped to tell you.
Narrator	Then Job stood up and tore his clothes in grief. He shaved his head and threw himself face downwards on the ground. [He said:]
Job	I was born with nothing, and I will die with nothing. The Lord gave, and now he has taken away. May his name be praised!
Narrator	In spite of everything that had happened, Job did not sin by blaming God.
Cast All	[This is] the word of the Lord. **Thanks be to God.**

Cast: **Narrator, Servant 1, Servant 2, Servant 3, Servant 4, Job.**

Satan tests Job again
Job 2.1–10

Narrator	When the day came for the heavenly beings to appear before the Lord again, Satan was there among them. The Lord asked him:
The Lord	Where have you been?
[Narrator	Satan answered:]
Satan (casually)	I have been walking here and there, roaming round the earth.
The Lord	Did you notice my servant Job? There is no one on earth as faithful and good as he is. He worships me and is careful not to do anything evil. You persuaded me to let you attack him for no reason at all, but Job is still as faithful as ever.
Satan	A man will give up everything in order to stay alive. But now suppose you hurt his body—he will curse you to your face!
The Lord	All right, he is in your power, but you are not to kill him.

Narrator	Then Satan left the Lord's presence and made sores break out all over Job's body. Job went and sat by the rubbish heap and took a piece of broken pottery to scrape his sores. His wife said to him:
Wife	You are still as faithful as ever, aren't you? Why don't you curse God and die?
Job (replying)	You are talking nonsense! When God sends us something good, we welcome it. How can we complain when he sends us trouble?
Narrator	In spite of everything he suffered, Job said nothing against God.
Cast	[This is] the word of the Lord.
All	**Thanks be to God.**

Cast: **Narrator, The Lord, Satan, Wife, Job.**

Job and his friends—the dialogue
From Job 2.11—42.6

Narrator	Three of Job's friends were Eliphaz, from the city of Teman, Bildad, from the land of Shuah, and Zophar, from the land of Naamah. When they heard how much Job had been suffering, they decided to go and comfort him. While they were still a long way off they saw Job, but did not recognize him. When they did, they began to weep and wail, tearing their clothes in grief and throwing dust into the air and on their heads. Then they sat there on the ground with him for seven days and nights without saying a word, because they saw how much he was suffering.
	Finally Job broke the silence and cursed the day on which he had been born.
Job (crying out to God)	O God, put a curse on the day I was born; put a curse on the night when I was conceived! Turn that day into darkness, God. Never again remember that day; never again let light shine on it.
(musing)	I wish I had died in my mother's womb or died the moment I was born. If I had died then, I would be at rest now, sleeping like the kings and rulers who rebuilt ancient palaces. In the grave wicked men stop their evil, and tired workmen find rest at last. Even prisoners enjoy peace, free from shouts and harsh commands. Everyone is there, the famous and the unknown, and slaves at last are free. Why let men go on living in misery? Why give light to men in grief? They wait for death, but it never comes; they prefer a grave to any treasure. I have no peace, no rest, and my troubles never end.

Eliphaz (to Job)	Job, will you be annoyed if I speak? I can't keep quiet any longer. You have taught many people and given strength to feeble hands. You worshipped God, and your life was blameless; and so you should have confidence and hope. (PAUSE)
(naïvely)	Think back now. Name a single case where a righteous man met with disaster. Evil does not grow in the soil, nor does trouble grow out of the ground. No indeed! Man brings trouble on himself, as surely as sparks fly up from a fire. If I were you, I would turn to God and present my case to him. We cannot understand the great things he does, and to his miracles there is no end. Happy is the person whom God corrects! Do not resent it when he rebukes you. God bandages the wounds he makes; his hand hurts you, and his hand heals. Time after time he will save you from harm; when famine comes, he will keep you alive. God will rescue you from slander; he will save you when destruction comes. (PAUSE)
(pleading)	Job, we have learnt this by long study. It is true, so now accept it.
Job (to Eliphaz)	If my troubles and griefs were weighed on scales, they would weigh more than the sands of the sea, so my wild words should not surprise you. Almighty God has pierced me with arrows, and their poison spreads through my body. God has lined up his terrors against me. Why won't God give me what I ask? Why won't he answer my prayer? If only he would go ahead and kill me! I know that God is holy; I have never opposed what he commands. I have no strength left to save myself; there is nowhere I can turn for help. In trouble like this I need loyal friends— whether I've forsaken God or not. But you, my friends, you deceive me like streams that go dry when no rain comes. (PAUSE)
(resigned)	All right, teach me; tell me my faults. I will be quiet and listen to you. Honest words are convincing, but you are talking nonsense. Look me in the face. I won't lie. You have gone far enough. Stop being unjust. Don't condemn me. I'm in the right.

(looking up)	But you think I am lying—
	you think I can't tell right from wrong.
(to God, in prayer)	Remember, O God, my life is only a breath; my happiness has already ended.
(to God, angrily)	I can't be quiet!
	I am angry and bitter.
	I have to speak.
	Why do you keep me under guard?
	Do you think I am a sea-monster?
	Are you harmed by my sin, you jailer?
	Why use me for your target-practice?
	Am I so great a burden to you?
	Can't you ever forgive my sin?
	Can't you pardon the wrong I do?
	Soon I will be in my grave,
	and I'll be gone when you look for me.
Bildad (to Job)	Are you finally through with your windy speech?
	God never twists justice;
	he never fails to do what is right.
	Your children must have sinned against God,
	and so he punished them as they deserved.
	But turn now and plead with Almighty God.
	If you are so honest and pure,
	then God will come and help you.
(to Eliphaz)	Evil men sprout like weeds in the sun,
	like weeds that spread all through the garden.
	Their roots wrap round the stones
	and hold fast to every rock.
	But then pull them up—
	no one will ever know they were there.
	Yes, that's all the joy evil men have;
	others now come and take their places.
	But God will never abandon the faithful
	or ever give help to evil men.
Job (to Bildad)	Yes, I've heard all that before.
	But how can a man win his case against God?
	How can anyone argue with him?
	He can ask a thousand questions
	that no one could ever answer.
	God is so wise and powerful;
	no man can stand up against him.
	God passes by, but I cannot see him.
	He takes what he wants, and no one can stop him;
	no one dares ask him, 'What are you doing?'
	So how can I find words to answer God?
	Though I am innocent, all I can do
	is beg for mercy from God my judge.
	Yet even then, if he lets me speak,
	I can't believe he would listen to me.

→

461

He sends storms to batter and bruise me
without any reason at all.
He won't let me get my breath;
he has filled my life with bitterness.
Should I try force? Try force on God?
Should I take him to court? Could anyone make him go?
I am innocent and faithful, but my words sound guilty,
and everything I say seems to condemn me.

(musing)   I am innocent, but I no longer care.
I am sick of living. Nothing matters;
innocent or guilty, God will destroy us.

(bitterly)   When an innocent man suddenly dies,
God laughs.
God gave the world to the wicked.
He made all the judges blind.
And if God didn't do it, who did?

(despairing) If God were human, I could answer him;
we could go to court to decide our quarrel.
But there is no one to step between us—
no one to judge both God and me.

(to God,
angrily)   Stop punishing me, God!
Keep your terrors away!
I am not afraid. I am going to talk
because I know my own heart.

(to God,
quietly
pleading)   Listen to my bitter complaint.
Don't condemn me, God.
Tell me! What is the charge against me?
Is it right for you to be so cruel?
To despise what you yourself have made?
And then to smile on the schemes of wicked men?
Do you see things as we do?
Is your life as short as ours?

Your hands formed and shaped me,
and now those same hands destroy me.
Remember that you made me from clay;
are you going to crush me back to dust?
You gave my father strength to beget me;
you made me grow in my mother's womb.
You formed my body with bones and sinews
and covered the bones with muscles and skin.
You have given me life and constant love,
and your care has kept me alive.

(to God,
petulantly) But now I know that all that time
you were secretly planning to harm me.
You were watching to see if I would sin,
so that you could refuse to forgive me.
As soon as I sin, I'm in trouble with you,
but when I do right, I get no credit.
I am miserable and covered with shame.

(to God, exasperated)	Why, God, did you let me be born?
	I should have died before anyone saw me.
	To go from the womb straight to the grave
	would have been as good as never existing.
	Isn't my life almost over? Leave me alone!
	Let me enjoy the time I have left.
	I am going soon and will never come back—
	going to a land that is dark and gloomy,
	a land of darkness, shadows, and confusion,
	where the light itself is darkness.

Zophar

(to Bildad and Eliphaz)	Will no one answer all this nonsense?
	Does talking so much put a man in the right?

(to Job)	Job, do you think we can't answer you?
	That your mocking words will leave us speechless?
	You claim that what you say is true;
	you claim you are pure in the sight of God.
	How I wish God would answer you!
	He would tell you there are many sides to wisdom;
	there are things too deep for human knowledge.
	God is punishing you less than you deserve.

(patronizingly)	Put your heart right, Job. Reach out to God.
	Put away evil and wrong from your home.
	Then face the world again, firm and courageous.
	Then all your troubles will fade from your memory,
	like floods that are past and remembered no more.
	Your life will be brighter than sunshine at noon,
	and life's darkest hours will shine like the dawn.

Job

(sarcastically)	Yes, you are the voice of the people.
	When you die, wisdom will die with you.
	But I have as much sense as you have;
	I am in no way inferior to you;
	everyone knows all that you have said.

(to audience)	Even my friends laugh at me now;
	they laugh, although I am righteous and blameless;
	but there was a time when God answered my prayers.

(to friends)	You have no troubles, and yet you make fun of me;
	you hit a man who is about to fall.
	But thieves and godless men live in peace,
	though their only god is their own strength.
	Everything you say, I have heard before.
	I understand it all; I know as much as you do.
	I'm not your inferior.
	But my dispute is with God, not you;
	I want to argue my case with him.
	You cover up your ignorance with lies;
	you are like doctors who can't heal anyone.
	Say nothing, and someone may think you are wise!
	I've lost all hope, so what if God kills me?

→

I am going to state my case to him.
It may even be that my boldness will save me,
since no wicked man would dare to face God.

(to God)   Now listen to my words of explanation.
I am ready to state my case,
because I know I am in the right.
Are you coming to accuse me, God?
If you do, I am ready to be silent and die.
Let me ask for two things;
agree to them, and I will not try to hide from you:
   stop punishing me, and
     don't crush me with terror.

Speak first, O God, and I will answer.
Or let me speak, and you answer me.
What are my sins? What wrongs have I done?
What crimes am I charged with?
Why do you avoid me?
Why do you treat me like an enemy?
Are you trying to frighten me? I'm nothing but a leaf;
you are attacking a piece of dry straw.

(musing)   We are all born weak and helpless.
All lead the same short, troubled life.
We grow and wither as quickly as flowers;
we disappear like shadows.
There is hope for a tree that has been cut down;
it can come back to life and sprout.
Even though its roots grow old,
and its stump dies in the ground,
with water it will sprout like a young plant.
But a man dies, and that is the end of him;
he dies, and where is he then?
Like rivers that stop running,
and lakes that go dry,
people die, never to rise.
They will never wake up while the sky endures;
they will never stir from their sleep.

(to God)   Water will wear down rocks,
and heavy rain will wash away the soil;
so you destroy man's hope for life.
You overpower a man and send him away for ever;
his face is twisted in death.
His sons win honour, but he never knows it,
nor is he told when they are disgraced.
He feels only the pain of his own body
and the grief of his own mind.

Eliphaz   Empty words, Job! Empty words!
(patronizingly) No wise man would talk as you do
or defend himself with such meaningless words.
If you had your way, no one would fear God;
no one would pray to him.

Your wickedness is evident by what you say;
you are trying to hide behind clever words.
There is no need for *me* to condemn you;
you are condemned by every word you speak. (PAUSE)

(calmly)   Do you think you were the first man born?
Were you there when God made the mountains?
Did you overhear the plans God made?
Does human wisdom belong to you alone?
There is nothing *you* know that *we* don't know.
We learnt our wisdom from grey-haired men—
men born before your father.

God offers you comfort; why still reject it?
We have spoken for him with calm, even words.
But you are excited and glare at us in anger.
You are angry with God and denounce him.
Can any man be really pure?
Can anyone be right with God?
A wicked man who oppresses others
will be in torment as long as he lives.
That is the fate of the man
who shakes his fist at God
and defies the Almighty.
That man is proud and rebellious;
he stubbornly holds up his shield
and rushes to fight against God.

Job
(to Eliphaz)   I have heard words like that before;
the comfort you give is only torment.
Are you going to keep on talking for ever?
Do you always have to have the last word?
If you were in my place and I in yours,
I could say everything you are saying.
I could shake my head wisely
and drown you with a flood of words.
I could strengthen you with advice
and keep talking to comfort you.

(to God)   You have worn me out, God;
you have let my family be killed.
You have seized me; you are my enemy.
I am skin and bones,
and people take that as proof of my guilt.

(musing)   People sneer at me;
they crowd round me and slap my face.
God has handed me over to evil men.
I was living in peace,
but God took me by the throat
and battered me and crushed me.
God uses me for target-practice
and shoots arrows at me from every side—
arrows that pierce and wound me;
and even then he shows no pity.

→

He wounds me again and again;
he attacks like a soldier gone mad with hate.
I have cried until my face is red,
and my eyes are swollen and circled with shadows,
but I am not guilty of any violence,
and my prayer to God is sincere.

(to the
ground)

O Earth, don't hide the wrongs done to me!
Don't let my call for justice be silenced!
There *is* someone in heaven
to stand up for me and take my side.
My friends scorn me;
my eyes pour out tears to God.
I want someone to plead with God for me,
as a man pleads for his friend.

(to God)

I am being honest, God. Accept my word.
There is no one else to support what I say.
You have closed their minds to reason;
don't let them triumph over me now.

(musing)

Those who claim to be honest are shocked,
and they all condemn me as godless.
Those who claim to be respectable
are more and more convinced they are right.

My days have passed; my plans have failed;
my hope is gone.
But my friends say night is daylight;
they say that light is near,
but I know I remain in darkness.
My only hope is the world of the dead,
where I will lie down to sleep in the dark.

Bildad
(frustrated)

Job, can't people like you ever be quiet?
If you stopped to listen, we could talk to you.

(deliberately)

The wicked man's light will still be put out;
its flame will never burn again.
His steps were firm, but now he stumbles;
he falls—a victim of his own advice.
He walks into a net, and his feet are caught;
a trap catches his heels and holds him.
On the ground a snare is hidden;
a trap has been set in his path.
He has no descendants, no survivors.
From east to west, all who hear of his fate
shudder and tremble with fear.
That is the fate of evil men,
the fate of those who care nothing for God.

Job
(to Bildad)

Why do you keep tormenting me with words?
Time after time you insult me
and show no shame for the way you abuse me.
Even if I have done wrong,
how does that hurt *you*?

466

You think you are better than I am,
and regard my troubles as proof of my guilt.
Can't you see it is *God* who has done this?
He has set a trap to catch me.
I protest against his violence,
but no one is listening;
no one hears my cry for justice.
God has blocked the way, and I can't get through;
he has hidden my path in darkness.

(to friends)   You are my friends! Take pity on me!
The hand of God has struck me down.
Why must you persecute me as God does?
Haven't you tormented me enough?
My courage failed because you said,
'How can we torment him?'
You looked for some excuse to attack me.
But now, be afraid of the sword—
the sword that brings God's wrath on sin,
so that you will know there is one who judges.

Zophar (crossly)   Job, you upset me. Now I'm impatient to answer.
What you have said is an insult,
but I know how to reply to you.
Surely you know that from ancient times,
when man was first placed on earth,
no wicked man has been happy for long.
He may grow great, towering to the sky,
so great that his head reaches the clouds,
but he will be blown away like dust.
His body used to be young and vigorous,
but soon it will turn to dust.
He will have to give up all he has worked for;
he will have no chance to enjoy his wealth,
because he oppressed and neglected the poor
and seized houses someone else had built.
At the height of his success
all the weight of misery will crush him.

Let him eat all he wants!
God will punish him in fury and anger.
Heaven reveals this man's sin,
and the earth gives testimony against him.
All his wealth will be destroyed
in the flood of God's anger.
This is the fate of wicked men,
the fate that God assigns to them.

Job
(patiently,
to friends)   Listen to what I am saying;
that is all the comfort I ask from you.
Give me a chance to speak and then,
when I am through, sneer if you like.
My quarrel is not with mortal men;
I have good reason to be impatient.

→

Why does God let evil men live,
let them grow old and prosper?
They have children and grandchildren,
and live to watch them all grow up.
God does not bring disaster on *their* homes;
they never have to live in terror.
Yes, all their cattle breed
and give birth without trouble.
Their children run and play like lambs
and dance to the music of harps and flutes.
They live out their lives in peace
and quietly die without suffering.

The wicked tell God to leave them alone;
they don't want to know his will for their lives.
They think there is no need to serve God
nor any advantage in praying to him.
They claim they succeed by their own strength,
though their way of thinking I can't accept.
Was a *wicked* man's light ever put out?
Did one of *them* ever meet with disaster?
Did God ever punish the *wicked* in anger
and blow them away like straw in the wind,
or like dust carried away in a storm?

(to Bildad)   You claim God punishes a child for the sins of his father.
No! Let God punish the sinners themselves;
let him show that he does it because of *their* sins.
Let sinners bear their *own* punishment;
let *them* feel the wrath of Almighty God.

(to Zophar)   Haven't you talked with people who travel?
Don't you know the reports they bring back?
On the day God is angry and punishes,
it is the wicked man who is always spared.
There is no one to accuse a wicked man
or pay him back for all he has done.
When he is carried to the graveyard,
to his well-guarded tomb,
thousands join the funeral procession,
and even the earth lies gently on his body.
And you! You try to comfort me with nonsense!
Every answer you give is a lie!

Eliphaz (to Job)   Is there any man, even the wisest,
who could ever be of use to God?
Does your doing right *benefit* God,
or does your being good *help* him at all?
It is not because you stand in awe of God
that he reprimands you and brings you to trial.
No, it's because you have sinned so much;
it's because of all the evil you do.
Doesn't God live in the highest heavens
and look down on the stars, even though they are high?

And yet you ask, 'What does God know?
He is hidden by clouds—how can he judge us?'
You think the thick clouds keep him from seeing,
as he walks on the dome of the sky.
Are you determined to walk in the paths
that evil men have always followed?

(persuasively)   Now, Job, make peace with God
and stop treating him like an enemy;
if you do, then he will bless you.
Accept the teaching he gives;
keep his words in your heart.
Yes, you must humbly return to God
and put an end to all the evil
that is done in your house.
When you pray, he will answer you,
and you will keep the vows you made.
You will succeed in all you do,
and light will shine on your path.
God brings down the proud
and saves the humble.
He will rescue you if you are innocent,
if what you do is right.

Job (musing   I still rebel and complain against God;
wearily)   I can't hold back my groaning.
How I wish I knew where to find him,
and knew how to go where he is.
I would state my case before him
and present all the arguments in my favour.
I want to know what he would say
and how he would answer me. (PAUSE)

(to Eliphaz)   Would God use all his strength against me?
No, he would listen as I spoke.
I am honest; I could reason with God;
he would declare me innocent once and for all.
I have searched in the east, but God is not there;
I have not found him when I searched in the west.
God has been at work in the north and the south,
but still I have not seen him.
Yet God knows every step I take;
if he tests me, he will find me pure.
I follow faithfully the road he chooses,
and never wander to either side.
I always do what God commands;
I follow his will, not my own desires.
There *are* men who reject the light;
they don't understand it or go where it leads.
At dawn the murderer gets up
and goes out to kill the poor,
and at night he steals.
The adulterer waits for twilight to come;
he covers his face so that no one can see him.

→

At night thieves break into houses,
but by day they hide and avoid the light.
They fear the light of day,
but darkness holds no terror for them.

Zophar
(precisely)

The wicked man is swept away by floods.
As snow vanishes in heat and drought,
so a sinner vanishes from the land of the living.
God may let him live secure,
but keeps an eye on him all the time.
For a while the wicked man prospers,
but then he withers like a weed,
like an ear of corn that has been cut off.

Bildad
(airily)

God is powerful; all must stand in awe of him;
he keeps his heavenly kingdom in peace.
Can anyone count the angels who serve him?
Is there any place where God's light does not shine?
Can anyone be righteous or pure in God's sight?
In his eyes even the moon is not bright,
nor the stars pure.
Then what about man, that worm, that insect?
What is man worth in God's eyes?

Job
(to friends,
with irony)

What a fine help you are to me—
poor, weak man that I am!
You give such good advice
and share your knowledge with a fool like me!
Who do you think will hear all your words?
Who inspired you to speak like this?

Bildad
(continuing
airily)

The spirits of the dead tremble
in the waters under the earth.
The world of the dead lies open to God;
no covering shields it from his sight.
God stretched out the northern sky
and hung the earth in empty space.
It is God who fills the clouds with water
and keeps them from bursting with the weight.
But these are only hints of his power,
only the whispers that we have heard.
Who can know how truly great God is?

Job(protesting)

I swear by the living Almighty God,
who refuses me justice and makes my life bitter—
as long as God gives me breath,
my lips will never say anything evil,
my tongue will never tell a lie.
I will never say that you men are right;
I will insist on my innocence to my dying day.
I will never give up my claim to be right;
my conscience is clear.

Zophar

This is how Almighty God
punishes wicked, violent men.

They may have many sons,
but all will be killed in war;
their children never have enough to eat.
One last time they will lie down rich,
and when they wake up, they will find their wealth gone.
Terror will strike like a sudden flood;
a wind in the night will blow them away.
God said to men,
'To be wise, you must have reverence for the Lord.
To understand, you must turn from evil.'

Job (musing) If only my life could once again
be as it was when God watched over me.
God was always with me then
and gave me light as I walked through the darkness.
Those were the days when I was prosperous,
and the friendship of God protected my home.
Everyone who saw me or heard of me
had good things to say about what I had done.

I always expected to live a long life
and to die at home in comfort.

(brightening) When I gave advice, people were silent
and listened carefully to what I said;
I smiled on them when they had lost confidence;
my cheerful face encouraged them.
I took charge and made the decisions;
I led them as a king leads his troops,
and gave them comfort in their despair.

(sadly) But men younger than I am make fun of me now!
Now they come and laugh at me;
I am nothing but a joke to them.
Because God has made me weak and helpless,
they turn against me with all their fury.
My dignity is gone like a puff of wind,
and my prosperity like a cloud.

(deliberately) Now I am about to die;
there is no relief for my suffering.
At night my bones all ache;
the pain that gnaws me never stops.
God seizes me by my collar
and twists my clothes out of shape.
He throws me down in the mud;
I am no better than dirt.

(to God) I call to you, O God, but you never answer;
and when I pray, you pay no attention.
You are treating me cruelly;
you persecute me with all your power.

(musing) I hoped for happiness and light,
but trouble and darkness came instead.

→

471

God knows everything I do;
he sees every step I take.

(to audience)   I swear I have never acted wickedly
and never tried to deceive others.
Let God weigh me on honest scales,
and he will see how innocent I am.
I have never refused to help the poor;
never have I let widows live in despair
or let orphans go hungry while I ate.
All my life I have taken care of them.
I have never trusted in riches
or taken pride in my wealth.
I have never been glad when my enemies suffered,
or pleased when they met with disaster;
I never sinned by praying for their death.
Will no one listen to what I am saying?
I swear that every word is true.
Let Almighty God answer me.

Narrator   Because Job was convinced of his own innocence, the three men
gave up trying to answer him. But a bystander named Elihu could
not control his anger any longer, because Job was justifying
himself and blaming God. He was also angry with Job's three
friends. They could find no way to answer Job, and this made it
appear that God was in the wrong. Because Elihu was the
youngest one there, he had waited until everyone finished
speaking. When he saw that the three men could not answer Job,
he was angry and began to speak:

Elihu (to Job's
friends)   I am young, and you are old,
so I was afraid to tell you what I think.
I told myself that you ought to speak,
that you older men should share your wisdom.
But it is the spirit of Almighty God
that comes to men and gives them wisdom.
It is not growing old that makes men wise
or helps them to know what is right.
So now I want you to listen to me;
let me tell you what I think.
I listened patiently while you were speaking
and waited while you searched for wise phrases.
I paid close attention and heard you fail;
you have not disproved what Job has said.
How can you claim you have discovered wisdom?
God must answer Job, for you have failed.
Job was speaking to you, not to me,
but I would never answer as you did.

(to Job)   Words have failed them, Job;
they have no answer for you.
Now this is what I heard *you* say:
'I am not guilty; I have done nothing wrong.
I am innocent and free from sin.

But God finds excuses for attacking me
and treats me like an enemy.
He binds chains on my feet;
he watches every move I make.'
But I tell you, Job, you are wrong.
God is greater than any man.
Why do you accuse God
of never answering a man's complaints?
Although God speaks again and again,
no one pays *attention* to what he says.

(to friends)   Job claims that he is innocent,
that God refuses to give him justice.
He asks, 'How could I lie and say I am wrong?
I am fatally wounded, but I am sinless.'
Have you ever seen anyone like this man Job?
He never shows *respect* for God.
Job, have you confessed your sins to God
and promised not to sin again?
Have you asked God to show you your faults,
and have you agreed to stop doing evil?
Since you object to what God does,
can you expect him to do what you want?

(to friends)   Any sensible person will surely agree;
any wise man who hears me will say
that Job is speaking from ignorance
and that nothing he says makes sense.
Think through everything that Job says;
you will see that he talks like an evil man.
To his sins he adds rebellion;
in front of us all he mocks God.

(to Job)   It is not right, Job, for you to say
that you are innocent in God's sight,
or to ask God, 'How does my sin affect you?
What have I gained by not sinning?'

(persuasively)   Job, you say you can't see God;
but wait patiently—your case is before him.
You think that God does not punish,
that he pays little attention to sin.
It is useless for you to go on talking;
it is clear you don't know what you are saying.

Those who are godless keep on being angry,
and even when punished, they don't pray for help.
They die while they are still young,
worn out by a life of disgrace.
But God *teaches* men through suffering
and *uses* distress to open their eyes. (PAUSE)

Remember how great is God's power;
he is the greatest teacher of all.
No one can tell God what to do

→

or accuse him of doing evil.
He has always been praised for what he does;
you also must praise him.
Everyone has seen what he has done;
but we can only watch from a distance.
We cannot fully know his greatness
or count the number of his years.

(looking up)   Thunder announces the approaching storm,
and the cattle know it is coming.
The storm makes my heart beat wildly.

(to friends   Listen, all of you, to the voice of God,
and to Job)   to the thunder that comes from his mouth.
He sends the lightning across the sky,
from one end of the earth to the other.
Then the roar of his voice is heard,
the majestic sound of thunder,
and all the while the lightning flashes.
At God's command amazing things happen,
wonderful things that we can't understand.

(to Job)   Pause a moment, Job, and listen!

Narrator
(slowly and
deliberately)   Then out of the storm the Lord spoke to Job:

The Lord   Who are you to question my wisdom
(to Job)   with your ignorant, empty words?
Stand up now like a man
and answer the questions I ask you.

Were you there when I made the world?
If you know so much, tell me about it.
Who decided how large it would be?
Who stretched the measuring-line over it?
Do you know all the answers?
What holds up the pillars that support the earth?
Who laid the corner-stone of the world?
In the dawn of that day, the stars sang together,
and the heavenly beings shouted for joy.
Who closed the gates to hold back the sea
when it burst from the womb of the earth?
It was *I* who covered the sea with clouds
and wrapped it in darkness.
I marked a boundary for the sea
and kept it behind bolted gates.
I told it, 'So far and no farther!
Here your powerful waves must stop.'

Job, have you ever in all your life
commanded a day to dawn?
Have you been to the springs in the depths of the sea?
Have you walked on the floor of the ocean?
Has anyone ever shown you the gates

that guard the dark world of the dead?
Have you any idea how big the world is?
Answer me if you know.
Do you know where the light comes from
or what the source of darkness is?
Do you find food for lions to eat,
and satisfy hungry young lions
when they hide in their caves,
or lie in wait in their dens?
Who is it that feeds the ravens
when they wander about hungry,
when their young cry to me for food?
Do you know when mountain-goats are born?
Have you watched wild deer give birth?
Who gave the wild donkeys their freedom?
Who turned them loose and let them roam?

Was it you, Job, who made horses so strong
and gave them their flowing manes?
Does a hawk learn from you how to fly
when it spreads its wings towards the south?
Does an eagle wait for your command
to build its nest high in the mountains?

Job, you challenged Almighty God;
will you give up now, or will you answer?

Job

I spoke foolishly, Lord. What can I answer?
I will not try to say anything else.
I have already said more than I should.

Narrator
(slowly and
deliberately)

Then out of the storm the Lord spoke to Job once again:

The Lord

Stand up now like a man,
and answer my questions.
Are you trying to prove that I am unjust—
to put me in the wrong and yourself in the right?
Are you as strong as I am?
Can your voice thunder as loud as mine?
If so, stand up in your honour and pride;
clothe yourself with majesty and glory.

Narrator

Then Job answered the Lord:

Job (humbly)

I know, Lord, that you are all-powerful;
that you can do everything you want.
You ask how I dare question your wisdom
when I am so very ignorant.
I talked about things I did not understand,
about marvels too great for me to know.
You told me to listen while you spoke
and to try to answer your questions.
Then I knew only what others had told me,
but now I have seen you with my own eyes.

So I am ashamed of all I have said
and repent in dust and ashes.

Cast	[This is] the word of the Lord.
All	**Thanks be to God.**

Cast: **Narrator, Job, Eliphaz, Bildad, Zophar, Elihu** (a younger person), **The Lord.**

Conclusion
Job 42.7–12

Narrator	After the Lord had finished speaking to Job, he said to Eliphaz:
The Lord	I am angry with you and your two friends, because you did not speak the truth about me, as my servant Job did. Now take seven bulls and seven rams to Job and offer them as a sacrifice for yourselves. Job will pray for you, and I will answer his prayer and not disgrace you as you deserve. You did not speak the truth about me as he did.
Narrator	Eliphaz, Bildad, and Zophar did what the Lord had told them to do, and the Lord answered Job's prayer.
	Then, after Job had prayed for his three friends, the Lord made him prosperous again and gave him twice as much as he had had before. All Job's brothers and sisters and former friends came to visit him and feasted with him in his house. They expressed their sympathy and comforted him for all the troubles the Lord had brought on him. Each of them gave him some money and a gold ring.
	The Lord blessed the last part of Job's life even more than he had blessed the first.
Cast	[This is] the word of the Lord.
All	**Thanks be to God.**

Cast: **Narrator, The Lord.**

PSALMS

True happiness
Psalm 1.1–6

Voice 1   Happy are those who reject the advice of evil men,
who do not follow the example of sinners
or join those who have no use for God.

Voice 2   Instead, they find joy in obeying the Law of the Lord,
and they study it day and night.
They are like trees that grow beside a stream,
that bear fruit at the right time,
and whose leaves do not dry up.
They succeed in everything they do.

Voice 1   But evil men are not like this at all;
they are like straw that the wind blows away.
Sinners will be condemned by God
and kept apart from God's own people.

Voice 2   The righteous are guided and protected by the Lord—

Voice 1   But the evil are on the way to their doom.

Cast [This is] the word of the Lord.   **All** Glory to the Father, and to the Son, and to the Holy Spirit:
All   Thanks be to God.   OR   as it was in the beginning, is now, and shall be for ever. Amen.

Cast: **Voice 1** (happy voice), **Voice 2** (serious voice).

God's chosen king
Psalm 2.1–12

Psalmist   Why do the nations plan rebellion?
Why do people make their useless plots?

Their kings revolt,
their rulers plot together against the Lord
and against the king he chose [They say]:

Ruler 1   Let us free ourselves from their rule—

Ruler 2   Let us throw off their control.

Psalmist   From his throne in heaven the Lord laughs
and mocks their feeble plans.
Then he warns them in anger
and terrifies them with his fury:

The Lord   On Zion, my sacred hill, I have installed my king.
The king says:

The King   I will announce what the Lord has declared.
He said to me:

The Lord	You are my son; today I have become your father. Ask, and I will give you all the nations; the whole earth will be yours. You will break them with an iron rod; you will shatter them in pieces like a clay pot.
Psalmist	Now listen to this warning, you kings; learn this lesson, you rulers of the world: Serve the Lord with fear; tremble and bow down to him; or else his anger will be quickly aroused, and you will suddenly die. Happy are all who go to him for protection.

Cast [This is] the word of the Lord. **All** **Glory to the Father, and to the Son, and to the Holy Spirit:**
All **Thanks be to God.**   OR   **as it was in the beginning, is now, and shall be for ever. Amen.**

Cast: **Psalmist, Ruler 1, Ruler 2** (can be same as Ruler 1), **The Lord, The King.**

A morning prayer for help
Psalm 3.1–8

Worshipper 1	I have so many enemies, Lord, so many who turn against me!
	They talk about me and say:
Enemy	God will not help him.
Worshipper 1	But you, O Lord, are always my shield from danger; you give me victory and restore my courage.
Worshipper 2	I call to the Lord for help, and from his sacred hill he answers me. I lie down and sleep, and all night long the Lord protects me. I am not afraid of the thousands of enemies who surround me on every side.
Worshipper 1	Come, Lord!
Worshipper 2	Save me, my God!
Worshipper 1	You punish all my enemies and leave them powerless to harm me.
Worshippers 1 and 2	Victory comes from the Lord— may he bless his people.

Cast [This is] the word of the Lord. **All** **Glory to the Father, and to the Son, and to the Holy Spirit:**
All **Thanks be to God.**   OR   **as it was in the beginning, is now, and shall be for ever. Amen.**

Cast: **Worshipper 1, Enemy, Worshipper 2.**

An evening prayer for help
Psalm 4.1–8

Worshipper
(praying)

Answer me when I pray,
O God, my defender!
When I was in trouble, you helped me.
Be kind to me now and hear my prayer.

The Lord

How long will you people insult me?
How long will you love what is worthless
and go after what is false?

Worshipper

Remember that the Lord has chosen the righteous for his own,
and he hears me when I call to him.

Teacher

Tremble with fear and stop sinning;
think deeply about this,
when you lie in silence on your beds.
Offer the right sacrifices to the Lord,
and put your trust in him.

Worshipper

There are many who pray:

Person 1

Give us more blessings, O Lord.

Person 2

Look on us with kindness!

Worshipper

But the joy that you have given me
is more than they will ever have
with all their corn and wine.

(praying)

When I lie down, I go to sleep in peace;
you alone, O Lord, keep me perfectly safe.

Cast [This is] the word of the Lord. **All Glory to the Father, and to the Son, and to the Holy Spirit:**
All Thanks be to God. OR **as it was in the beginning, is now, and shall be for ever. Amen.**

Cast: **Worshipper, The Lord** (preferably unseen), **Teacher, Person 1, Person 2** (can be the same as Person 1).

God's glory and our dignity
Psalm 8.1–9

Voices 1–3

O Lord, our Lord,
your greatness is seen in all the world!

Voice 1

Your praise reaches up to the heavens.

Voice 2

It is sung by children and babies.

Voice 3

You are safe and secure from all your enemies;
you stop anyone who opposes you.

Voice 1

When I look at the sky, which you have made,
at the moon and the stars, which you set in their places—
what is man, that you think of him;
mere man, that you care for him?

Voice 3	Yet you made him inferior only to yourself; you crowned him with glory and honour. You appointed him ruler over everything you made; you placed him over all creation—
Voice 2	Sheep and cattle, and the wild animals too; the birds and the fish and the creatures in the seas.
Voices 1–3	O Lord, our Lord, your greatness is seen in all the world!

Cast [This is] the word of the Lord. **All Glory to the Father, and to the Son, and to the Holy Spirit:**
All Thanks be to God. OR **as it was in the beginning, is now, and shall be for ever. Amen.**

Cast: **Voice 1, Voice 2** (soprano voice)**, Voice 3.**

God and humanity
Psalm 8.1–9 (LIT)

Leader	O Lord, our Lord:
All	**how great is your name in all the world!**
All (group 1)	**Your glory fills the skies.**
All (group 2)	**Your praise is sung by children.**
All (group 3)	**You silence your enemies.**
Leader	I look at the sky your hands have made, the moon and stars you put in place:
All	**Who are we that you care for us?**
Leader	You made us less than gods:
All	**to crown us with glory and honour.**
Leader	You put us in charge of creation:
All (group 1)	**the beasts of the field.**
All (group 2)	**the birds of the air.**
All (group 3)	**the fish of the sea.**
Leader	O Lord, our Lord,
All	**how great is your name in all the world!**
All	**Glory to the Father, and to the Son, and to the Holy Spirit:** **as it was in the beginning, is now, and shall be for ever. Amen.**

Cast: **Leader, All** (group 1 – two or more persons/part of congregation)**, All** (group 2 – two or more persons/part of congregation)**, All** (group 3 – two or more persons/part of congregation)

Thanksgiving to God for his justice
Psalm 9.1–20

Worshipper 1	I will praise you, Lord, with all my heart; I will tell of all the wonderful things you have done. I will sing with joy because of you. I will sing praise to you, Almighty God.
Worshipper 2	My enemies turn back when you appear;

they fall down and die.
You are fair and honest in your judgements,
and you have judged in my favour.

Worshipper 1 You have condemned the heathen
and destroyed the wicked;
they will be remembered no more.

Worshipper 2 Our enemies are finished for ever;
you have destroyed their cities,
and they are completely forgotten.

Teacher 1 But the Lord is king for ever;
he has set up his throne for judgement.
He rules the world with righteousness;
he judges the nations with justice.

Teacher 2 The Lord is a refuge for the oppressed,
a place of safety in times of trouble.

Worshipper 1 Those who know you, Lord, will trust you;
you do not abandon anyone who comes to you.

Worshippers 1 and 2 Sing praise to the Lord, who rules in Zion!

Teachers 1 and 2 Tell every nation what he has done!

Teacher 2 God remembers those who suffer;
he does not forget their cry,
and he punishes those who wrong them.

Worshipper 1 Be merciful to me, O Lord!
See the sufferings my enemies cause me!
Rescue me from death, O Lord,
that I may stand before the people of Jerusalem
and tell them all the things for which I praise you.
I will rejoice because you saved me.

Teacher 1 The heathen have dug a pit and fallen in;
they have been caught in their own trap.
The Lord has revealed himself by his righteous judgements,
and the wicked are trapped by their own deeds.

Teacher 2 Death is the destiny of all the wicked,
of all those who reject God.
The needy will not always be neglected;
the hope of the poor will not be crushed for ever.

Worshipper 2 Come, Lord! Do not let men defy you!
Bring the heathen before you
and pronounce judgement on them.

Worshipper 1 Make them afraid, O Lord;
make them know that they are only mortal beings.

Cast [This is] the word of the Lord. **All Glory to the Father, and to the Son, and to the Holy Spirit:**
All Thanks be to God. OR **as it was in the beginning, is now, and shall be for ever. Amen.**

Cast: **Worshipper 1, Worshipper 2, Teacher 1, Teacher 2.**

481

A prayer for justice
Psalm 10.1–18

Worshipper Why are you so far away, O Lord?
Why do you hide yourself when we are in trouble?

Voice 1 The wicked are proud and persecute the poor;
catch them in the traps they have made.

Voice 2 The wicked man is proud of his evil desires;
the greedy man curses and rejects the Lord.

Voice 1 A wicked man does not care about the Lord;
in his pride he thinks that God doesn't matter.

Voice 2 A wicked man succeeds in everything.

Voice 1 He cannot understand God's judgements;
he sneers at his enemies.

Voice 2 He says to himself:

Wicked man I will never fail;
I will never be in trouble.

Voice 1 His speech is filled with curses, lies, and threats;
he is quick to speak hateful, evil words.

Voice 2 He hides himself in the villages,
waiting to murder innocent people.

Voice 1 He spies on his helpless victims;
he waits in his hiding place like a lion.

Voice 2 He lies in wait for the poor;
he catches them in his trap and drags them away.

Voice 1 The helpless victims lie crushed;
brute strength has defeated them.

Voice 2 The wicked man says to himself:

Wicked man God doesn't care!
He has closed his eyes and will never see me!

Worshipper O Lord, punish those wicked men!
Remember those who are suffering!

How can a wicked man despise God
and say to himself:

Wicked man He will not punish me!

Worshipper But you do see; you take notice of trouble and suffering
and are always ready to help.
The helpless man commits himself to you;
you have always helped the needy.

Break the power of wicked and evil men;
punish them for the wrong they have done
until they do it no more.

Voice 1   The Lord is king for ever and ever.

Voice 2   Those who worship other gods
                      will vanish from his land.

                      You will listen, O Lord, to the prayers of the lowly;
                      you will give them courage.
                      You will hear the cries of the oppressed and the orphans;
                      you will judge in their favour,
                      so that mortal men may cause terror no more.

Cast [This is] the word of the Lord.   **All** **Glory to the Father, and to the Son, and to the Holy Spirit:**
All   **Thanks be to God.**   **OR**   **as it was in the beginning, is now, and shall be for ever. Amen.**

Cast: **Worshipper, Voice 1, Voice 2** (can be the same as Voice 1), **Wicked man.**

Confidence in the Lord
Psalm 11.1–7

Worshipper 1   In the Lord I take refuge.
                      How then can you say to me:

Adviser   Flee like a bird to your mountain.
                      For look, the wicked bend their bows;
                      they set their arrows against the strings
                      to shoot from the shadows
                      at the upright in heart.
                      When the foundations are being destroyed,
                      what can the righteous do?

Worshipper 1   The Lord is in his holy temple;
                      the Lord is on his heavenly throne.
                      He observes the sons of men;
                      his eyes examine them.

Worshipper 2   The Lord examines the righteous;
                      but the wicked and those who love violence
                      his soul hates.

Worshipper 1   On the wicked he will rain fiery coals and burning sulphur;
                      a scorching wind will be their lot.

Worshipper 2   For the Lord is righteous,
                      he loves justice.

Worshipper 1   Upright men will see his face.

Cast [This is] the word of the Lord.   **All** **Glory to the Father, and to the Son, and to the Holy Spirit:**
All   **Thanks be to God.**   **OR**   **as it was in the beginning, is now, and shall be for ever. Amen.**

Cast: **Worshipper 1, Adviser, Worshipper 2.**

A prayer for help
Psalm 12.1–8

Worshippers 1 and 2	Help us, Lord!
Worshipper 1	There is not a good man left; honest men can no longer be found.
Worshipper 2	All of them lie to one another; they deceive each other with flattery.
Worshipper 1	Silence those flattering tongues, O Lord!
Worshipper 2	Close those boastful mouths that say:
Person 1 (boasting)	With our words we get what we want.
Person 2 (boasting)	We will say what we wish, and no one can stop us.
Worshipper 1	The Lord says:
The Lord	But now I will come, because the needy are oppressed and the persecuted groan in pain. I will give them the security they long for.
Worshipper 1	The promises of the Lord can be trusted; they are as genuine as silver refined seven times in the furnace.
Worshipper 2	Wicked men are everywhere, and everyone praises what is evil.
Worshippers 1 and 2	Keep us always safe, O Lord, and preserve us from such people.

Cast [This is] the word of the Lord. **All Glory to the Father, and to the Son, and to the Holy Spirit:**
All   Thanks be to God.   OR   **as it was in the beginning, is now, and shall be for ever. Amen.**

Cast: **Worshipper 1, Worshipper 2** (can be the same as Worshipper 1) **Person 1, Person 2, The Lord.**

A prayer for help
Psalm 13.1–6

Worshipper 1	How much longer will you forget me, Lord? For ever?
Worshipper 2	How much longer will you hide yourself from me?
Worshipper 1	How long must I endure trouble?
Worshipper 2	How long will sorrow fill my heart day and night?
Worshipper 1	How long will my enemies triumph over me?
Worshipper 2	Look at me, O Lord my God, and answer me. Restore my strength; don't let me die.
Worshipper 1	Don't let my enemies say:

Enemies
1 and **2** We have defeated him.

Worshipper 1 Don't let them gloat over my downfall.

Worshipper 2 I rely on your constant love.

Worshipper 1 I will be glad, because you will rescue me.

Worshipper 2 I will sing to you, O Lord,
    because you have been good to me.

Cast [This is] the word of the Lord. **All** **Glory to the Father, and to the Son, and to the Holy Spirit:**
All **Thanks be to God.**   OR   **as it was in the beginning, is now, and shall be for ever. Amen.**

Cast: **Worshipper 1, Worshipper 2, Enemy 1, Enemy 2** (can be the same as Enemy 1).

Wickedness and ignorance
Psalm 14.1–7

Voice 1 Fools say to themselves:

Fool(s) There is no God.

Voice 1 They are all corrupt,
    and they have done terrible things;
    there is no one who does what is right. (PAUSE)

Voice 2 The Lord looks down from heaven at mankind
    to see if there are any who are wise,
    any who worship him.
    But they have all gone wrong;
    they are all equally bad.

Voice 1 Not one of them does what is right,
    not a single one.

Voice 2 The Lord asks:

The Lord Don't they know?
    Are all these evildoers ignorant?
    They live by robbing my people,
    and they never pray to me.

Voice 2 But then they will be terrified,
    for God is with those who obey him.

Voice 1 Evildoers frustrate the plans of the humble man,
    but the Lord is his protection.

Voice 2 How I pray that victory
    will come to Israel from Zion.

Voice 1 How happy the people of Israel will be
    when the Lord makes them prosperous again!

Cast [This is] the word of the Lord. **All** **Glory to the Father, and to the Son, and to the Holy Spirit:**
All **Thanks be to God.**   OR   **as it was in the beginning, is now, and shall be for ever. Amen.**

Cast: **Voice 1, Fool(s), Voice 2** (can be the same as Voice 1), **The Lord.**

What God requires
Psalm 15.1–5

Enquirer 1	Lord, who may enter your Temple?
Enquirer 2	Who may worship on Zion, your sacred hill?
Voice 1	A person who obeys God in everything and always does what is right, whose words are true and sincere, and who does not slander others.
Voice 2	He does no wrong to his friends nor spreads rumours about his neighbours.
Voice 1	He despises those whom God rejects, but honours those who obey the Lord.
Voice 2	He always does what he promises, no matter how much it may cost.
Voice 1	He makes loans without charging interest and cannot be bribed to testify against the innocent.
Voices 1 and **2**	Whoever does these things will always be secure.

Cast [This is] the word of the Lord. **All** Glory to the Father, and to the Son, and to the Holy Spirit:
All **Thanks be to God.** OR **as it was in the beginning, is now, and shall be for ever. Amen.**

Cast: **Enquirer 1, Enquirer 2** (can be the same as Enquirer 1), **Voice 1, Voice 2.**

A prayer of confidence
Psalm 16.1–11

Voice 1	Protect me, O God; I trust in you for safety. (PAUSE) I say to the Lord:
Voice 2	You are my Lord; all the good things I have come from you.
Voice 3	How excellent are the Lord's faithful people! My greatest pleasure is to be with them.
Voice 1	Those who rush to other gods bring many troubles on themselves.
Voice 3	I will not take part in their sacrifices; I will not worship their gods.
Voice 2	You, Lord, are all I have, and you give me all I need; my future is in your hands. How wonderful are your gifts to me; how good they are!
Voice 3	I praise the Lord, because he guides me, and in the night my conscience warns me. (PAUSE)

Voice 2	I am always aware of the Lord's presence; he is near, and nothing can shake me. And so I am thankful and glad, and I feel completely secure, because you protect me from the power of death.
Voice 1	I have served you faithfully, and you will not abandon me to the world of the dead.
Voice 2	You will show me the path that leads to life.
Voices 1–3	Your presence fills me with joy—
Voice 3	And brings me pleasure for ever.

Cast [This is] the word of the Lord. **All** Glory to the Father, and to the Son, and to the Holy Spirit:
All Thanks be to God.   OR   as it was in the beginning, is now, and shall be for ever. Amen.

Cast: **Voice 1, Voice 2, Voice 3.**

God's glory and law
Psalm 19.1–14

Voice 1	How clearly the sky reveals God's glory!
Voice 2	How plainly it shows what he has done!
Voice 1	Each day announces it to the following day—
Voice 2	Each night repeats it to the next.
Voice 1	No speech or words are used, no sound is heard; yet their message goes out to all the world and is heard to the ends of the earth.
Voice 3	God made a home in the sky for the sun; it comes out in the morning like a happy bridegroom, like an athlete eager to run a race. It starts at one end of the sky and goes across to the other. Nothing can hide from its heat.
Voice 1	The law of the Lord is perfect; it gives new strength.
Voice 2	The commands of the Lord are trustworthy, giving wisdom to those who lack it.
Voice 1	The laws of the Lord are right, and those who obey them are happy.
Voice 2	The commands of the Lord are just and give understanding to the mind.
Voice 1	Reverence for the Lord is good; it will continue for ever.
Voice 2	The judgements of the Lord are just; they are always fair.

Voice 1	They are more desirable than the finest gold—
Voice 2	They are sweeter than the purest honey.
Voice 1	They give knowledge to me, your servant; I am rewarded for obeying them.
Voice 3	No one can see his own errors; deliver me, Lord, from hidden faults! Keep me safe, also, from wilful sins; don't let them rule over me. Then I shall be perfect and free from the evil of sin.
Voices 1 and **2**	May my words and my thoughts be acceptable to you, O Lord, my refuge and my redeemer!

Cast [This is] the word of the Lord. **All Glory to the Father, and to the Son, and to the Holy Spirit:**
All   Thanks be to God.   OR   **as it was in the beginning, is now, and shall be for ever. Amen.**

Cast: **Voice 1, Voice 2, Voice 3** (can be the same as Voice 2).

A prayer for victory
Psalm 20. 1–9

Voice 1	May the Lord answer you when you are in trouble!
Voice 2	May the God of Jacob protect you!
Voice 1	May he send you help from his Temple and give you aid from Mount Zion.
Voice 2	May he accept all your offerings and be pleased with all your sacrifices.
Voice 1	May he give you what you desire and make all your plans succeed.
Voice 2	Then we will shout for joy over your victory and celebrate your triumph by praising our God.
Voices 1 and **2**	May the Lord answer all your requests.
Voice 3	Now I know that the Lord gives victory to his chosen king; he answers him from his holy heaven and by his power gives him great victories.
Voice 1	Some trust in their war-chariots—
Voice 2	And others in their horses—
Voices 1–3	But we trust in the power of the Lord our God.
Voice 3	Such people will stumble and fall, but we will rise and stand firm.
Voice 1	Give victory to the king, O Lord—
Voice 2	Answer us when we call.

Cast [This is] the word of the Lord. **All Glory to the Father, and to the Son, and to the Holy Spirit:**
All   Thanks be to God.   OR   **as it was in the beginning, is now, and shall be for ever. Amen.**

Cast: **Voice 1, Voice 2, Voice 3** (regal voice).

A cry of anguish and a song of praise
Psalm 22.1–31

Lonely person   My God, my God, why have you abandoned me?
I have cried desperately for help,
but still it does not come.
During the day I call to you, my God,
but you do not answer;
I call at night,
but get no rest.

Singer   You are enthroned as the Holy One,
the one whom Israel praises.
Our ancestors put their trust in you;
they trusted you, and you saved them.
They called to you and escaped from danger;
they trusted you and were not disappointed.

Despised person   But I am no longer a man; I am a worm,
despised and scorned by everyone!
All who see me jeer at me;
they stick out their tongues and shake their heads.
They say:

Accuser 1   You relied on the Lord.
Why doesn't he save you?

Accuser 2   If the Lord likes you,
why doesn't he help you?

Lonely person   It was you who brought me safely through birth,
and when I was a baby, you kept me safe.
I have relied on you since the day I was born,
and you have always been my God.
Do not stay away from me!
Trouble is near,
and there is no one to help.

Despised person   Many enemies surround me like bulls;
they are all round me,
like fierce bulls from the land of Bashan.
They open their mouths like lions,
roaring and tearing at me.

Lonely person   My strength is gone,
gone like water spilt on the ground.
All my bones are out of joint;
my heart is like melted wax.
My throat is as dry as dust,
and my tongue sticks to the roof of my mouth.
You have left me for dead in the dust.

Despised person	A gang of evil men is round me; like a pack of dogs they close in on me; they tear at my hands and feet. All my bones can be seen. My enemies look at me and stare. They gamble for my clothes and divide them among themselves. O Lord, don't stay away from me! Come quickly to my rescue! Save me from the sword; save my life from these dogs. Rescue me from these lions; I am helpless before these wild bulls.
Lonely person	I will tell my people what you have done; I will praise you in their assembly:
Singer	Praise him, you servants of the Lord! Honour him, you descendants of Jacob! Worship him, you people of Israel! He does not neglect the poor or ignore their suffering; he does not turn away from them, but answers when they call for help.
Lonely person	In the full assembly I will praise you for what you have done; in the presence of those who worship you I will offer the sacrifices I promised.
Despised person	The poor will eat as much as they want; those who come to the Lord will praise him. May they prosper for ever!
Lonely person	All nations will remember the Lord. From every part of the world they will turn to him; all races will worship him. The Lord is king, and he rules the nations.
Despised person	All proud men will bow down to him; all mortal men will bow down before him.
Lonely person	Future generations will serve him; men will speak of the Lord to the coming generation. People not yet born will be told:
Cast	The Lord saved his people.

Cast [This is] the word of the Lord.   **All Glory to the Father, and to the Son, and to the Holy Spirit:**
All Thanks be to God.   OR   **as it was in the beginning, is now, and shall be for ever. Amen.**

Cast: **Lonely person, Singer, Despised person, Accuser 1, Accuser 2** (can be the same as Accuser 1).

The Lord our shepherd
Psalm 23.1–6

Voices 1–3   The Lord is my shepherd;
I have everything I need.

Voice 1   He lets me rest in fields of green grass
and leads me to quiet pools of fresh water.
He gives me new strength.
He guides me in the right paths,
as he has promised.

Voice 2   Even if I go through the deepest darkness,
(prayerfully)   I will not be afraid, Lord,
for you are with me.
Your shepherd's rod and staff protect me.

Voice 3   You prepare a banquet for me,
where all my enemies can see me;
you welcome me as an honoured guest
and fill my cup to the brim.

Voices 1 and **2**   I know that your goodness and love will be with me all my life—

Voice 3   And your house will be my home as long as I live.

Cast [This is] the word of the Lord.   **All** Glory to the Father, and to the Son, and to the Holy Spirit:
All   Thanks be to God.   OR   as it was in the beginning, is now, and shall be for ever. Amen.

Cast: **Voice 1, Voice 2, Voice 3.**

The great king
Psalm 24.1–10 (LIT)

Leader   The earth is the Lord's, and everything in it:
All   **the world, and all who live here.**

Leader   He founded it upon the seas:
All   **and established it upon the waters.**

Enquirer   Who has the right to go up the Lord's hill; who may enter his holy temple?
All   **Those who have clean hands and a pure heart,**
who do not worship idols
or swear by what is false.

Leader   They receive blessing continually from the Lord:
All   **and righteousness from the God of their salvation.**

Leader   Such are the people who seek for God:
All   **who enter the presence of the God of Jacob.**

Director   Fling wide the gates, open the ancient doors:
All   **that the king of glory may come in.**

→

Enquirer	Who is the king of glory?
All	**The Lord, strong and mighty,**
	the Lord mighty in battle.
Director	Fling wide the gates, open the ancient doors:
All	**that the king of glory may come in.**
Enquirer	Who is he, this king of glory?
All	**The Lord almighty, he is the king of glory.**
All	**Glory to the Father, and to the Son, and to the Holy Spirit:**
	as it was in the beginning, is now, and shall be for ever. Amen.

Cast: **Leader, All** (two or more persons/congregation), **Enquirer, Director.**

A prayer of praise
Psalm 27.1–14

Worshipper 1	The Lord is my light and my salvation;
	I will fear no one.
	The Lord protects me from all danger;
	I will never be afraid.
	When evil men attack me and try to kill me,
	they stumble and fall.
	Even if a whole army surrounds me,
	I will not be afraid;
	even if enemies attack me,
	I will still trust God. (PAUSE)
Worshipper 2	I have asked the Lord for one thing;
	one thing only do I want:
	to live in the Lord's house all my life,
	to marvel there at his goodness,
	and to ask for his guidance.
Worshipper 1	In times of trouble he will shelter me;
	he will keep me safe in his Temple
	and make me secure on a high rock.
	So I will triumph over my enemies around me.
	With shouts of joy I will offer sacrifices in his Temple;
	I will sing, I will praise the Lord.
Worshipper 2	Hear me, Lord, when I call to you!
	Be merciful and answer me!
	When you said:
The Lord	Come and worship me.
Worshipper 1	I answered:
Worshipper 2	I will come, Lord;
	don't hide yourself from me!
Worshipper 1	Don't be angry with me;
	don't turn your servant away.

You have been my help;
don't leave me, don't abandon me,
O God, my saviour.

My father and mother may abandon me,
but the Lord will take care of me.

Worshipper 2 Teach me, Lord, what you want me to do,
and lead me along a safe path,
because I have many enemies.
Don't abandon me to my enemies,
who attack me with lies and threats.

Worshipper 1 I know that I will live to see the Lord's goodness
in this present life.

**Worshippers
1 and 2** Trust in the Lord.

Worshipper 2 Have faith, do not despair.

**Worshippers
1 and 2** Trust in the Lord.

Cast [This is] the word of the Lord. **All Glory to the Father, and to the Son, and to the Holy Spirit:**
All **Thanks be to God.** OR **as it was in the beginning, is now, and shall be for ever. Amen.**

Cast: **Worshipper 1, Worshipper 2, The Lord.**

A prayer of thanksgiving
Psalm 30.1–12

Worshipper 1 I praise you, Lord, because you have saved me
and kept my enemies from gloating over me.
I cried to you for help, O Lord my God,
and you healed me;
you kept me from the grave.
I was on my way to the depths below,
but you restored my life.

Worshipper 2 Sing praise to the Lord,
all his faithful people!
Remember what the Holy One has done,
and give him thanks!

Worshipper 1 His anger lasts only a moment,
his goodness for a lifetime.

Worshipper 2 Tears may flow in the night,
but joy comes in the morning.

I felt secure and said to myself:

Worshipper 3 I will never be defeated.

Worshipper 2 You were good to me, Lord;
you protected me like a mountain fortress.

→

493

But then you hid yourself from me, and I was afraid.

I called to you, Lord; I begged for your help:

Worshipper 3 What will you gain from my death?
What profit from my going to the grave?
Are dead people able to praise you?
Can they proclaim your unfailing goodness?
Hear me, Lord, and be merciful!
Help me, Lord!

Worshipper 2 You have changed my sadness into a joyful dance;
you have taken away my sorrow
and surrounded me with joy.
So I will not be silent;
I will sing praise to you.

Worshipper 1 Lord, you are my God,
I will give you thanks for ever.

Cast [This is] the word of the Lord. **All Glory to the Father, and to the Son, and to the Holy Spirit:**
All Thanks be to God.   OR   **as it was in the beginning, is now, and shall be for ever. Amen.**

Cast: **Worshipper 1, Worshipper 2, Worshipper 3.**

Confession and forgiveness
Psalm 32.1–11

Worshipper 1 Happy are those whose sins are forgiven,
whose wrongs are pardoned.
Happy is the one whom the Lord does not accuse of doing wrong
and who is free from all deceit.

Worshipper 2 When I did not confess my sins,
I was worn out from crying all day long.
Day and night you punished me, Lord;
my strength was completely drained,
as moisture is dried up by the summer heat.

Then I confessed my sins to you;
I did not conceal my wrongdoings.
I decided to confess them to you,
and you forgave all my sins.

Worshipper 1 So all your loyal people should pray to you in times of need;
when a great flood of trouble comes rushing in,
it will not reach them.

Worshipper 2 You are my hiding place;
you will save me from trouble.
I sing aloud of your salvation,
because you protect me.

The Lord says:

The Lord I will teach you the way you should go;
I will instruct you and advise you.

494

	Don't be stupid like a horse or a mule, which must be controlled with a bit and bridle to make it submit.
Worshipper 2	The wicked will have to suffer, but those who trust in the Lord are protected by his constant love.
Worshipper 1	You that are righteous, be glad and rejoice because of what the Lord has done. You that obey him:
Worshippers 1 and 2	Shout for joy!

Cast [This is] the word of the Lord. **All** Glory to the Father, and to the Son, and to the Holy Spirit:
All Thanks be to God. OR as it was in the beginning, is now, and shall be for ever. Amen.

Cast: **Worshipper 1** (bright voice), **Worshipper 2** (serious voice), **The Lord**.

A song of praise
From Psalm 33.1–22 (LIT)

Leader	Sing joyfully to the Lord, you righteous:
All	**it is right that his people should praise him.**
Leader	Praise the Lord with the harp:
All (group 1)	**make music to him on the strings.**
Leader	Sing to the Lord a new song:
All (group 2)	**play skilfully, and shout for joy.**
Leader	For the word of the Lord is right and true:
All	**and all his work is faithfulness.**
Leader	The Lord loves righteousness and justice:
All (group 1)	**his endless love fills the earth.**
Leader	By the word of the Lord the skies were formed:
All (group 2)	**his breath created moon and stars.**
Leader	Let all the earth fear the Lord:
All	**the people of the world revere him.**
Leader	For he spoke, and it came to be:
All (group 1)	**he commanded, and all was made.**
Leader	The Lord holds back the nations:
All (group 2)	**he thwarts their evil intent.**
Leader	God's purposes are sure:
All	**his plans endure for ever.**
Leader	Happy is the nation whose God is the Lord:
All (group 1)	**happy the people he makes his own.**
Leader	The eyes of the Lord are on those who fear him:
All (group 2)	**who trust in his unfailing love.**

→

Leader	We wait in hope for the Lord:
All (group 1)	**he is our help and shield.**
Leader	In him our hearts rejoice:
All (group 2)	**we trust his holy name.**
Leader	May your constant love be with us, Lord:
All	**as we put our hope in you.**
All	**Glory to the Father, and to the Son, and to the Holy Spirit: as it was in the beginning, is now, and shall be for ever. Amen.**

Cast: **Leader, All** (group 1 – two or more persons/part of congregation), **All** (group 2 – two or more persons/part of congregation).

A prayer for help
From Psalm 35.9–28

Worshipper	I will be glad because of the Lord; I will be happy because he saved me. With all my heart I will say to the Lord:
New person	There is no one like you. You will protect the weak from the strong, the poor from the oppressor.
Worshipper	Evil men testify against me and accuse me of crimes I know nothing about. They pay me back evil for good, and I sink in despair.

How much longer, Lord, will you just look on?
Rescue me from their attacks;
save my life from these lions!
Then I will thank you in the assembly of your people;
I will praise you before them all.

Don't let my enemies, those liars,
gloat over my defeat.

Don't let those who hate me for no reason
smirk with delight over my sorrow.

They do not speak in a friendly way;
instead they invent all kinds of lies about peace-loving people.
They accuse me, shouting:

Enemies 1 and **2**	We saw what you did!
Worshipper	But you, O Lord, have seen this. So don't be silent, Lord; don't keep yourself far away! Rouse yourself, O Lord, and defend me; rise up, my God, and plead my cause. You are righteous, O Lord, so declare me innocent; don't let my enemies gloat over me. Don't let them say to themselves:

Enemy 1	We are rid of him!
Enemy 2	That's just what we wanted!
Worshipper	May those who gloat over my suffering be completely defeated and confused; may those who claim to be better than I am be covered with shame and disgrace.
	May those who want to see me acquitted shout for joy and say again and again:
Friend 1	How great is the Lord!
Friend 2	He is pleased with the success of his servant.
Worshipper	Then I will proclaim your righteousness, and I will praise you all day long.

Cast [This is] the word of the Lord. **All** **Glory to the Father, and to the Son, and to the Holy Spirit:**
All **Thanks be to God.** OR **as it was in the beginning, is now, and shall be for ever. Amen.**

Cast: **Worshipper, New person, Enemy 1, Enemy 2** (can be the same as Enemy 1), **Friend 1, Friend 2** (can be the same as Friend 1).

Our wickedness and God's goodness
Psalm 36.1–12

Psalmist	Sin speaks to the wicked man deep in his heart; he rejects God and has no reverence for him. Because he thinks so highly of himself, he thinks that God will not discover his sin and condemn it. His speech is wicked and full of lies; he no longer does what is wise and good. He makes evil plans as he lies in bed; nothing he does is good, and he never rejects anything evil.
Worshipper 1	Lord, your constant love reaches the heavens; your faithfulness extends to the skies.
Worshipper 2	Your righteousness is towering like the mountains; your justice is like the depths of the sea. Men and animals are in your care.
Worshipper 1	How precious, O God, is your constant love! We find protection under the shadow of your wings.
Worshipper 2	We feast on the abundant food you provide; you let us drink from the river of your goodness. You are the source of all life, and because of your light we see the light.
Worshipper 1	Continue to love those who know you and to do good to those who are righteous.
Worshipper 2	Do not let proud men attack me or wicked men make me run away.

Psalmist	See where evil men have fallen. There they lie, unable to rise.

Cast	[This is] the word of the Lord.	**All**	**Glory to the Father, and to the Son, and to the Holy Spirit:**
All	**Thanks be to God.**	OR	**as it was in the beginning, is now, and shall be for ever. Amen.**

Cast: **Psalmist, Worshipper 1, Worshipper 2.**

The goodness of God
From Psalm 36.5–9 (LIT)

Leader 1 **All** (group 1)	Your love, O Lord, reaches the heavens: **your faithfulness extends to the skies.**
Leader 2 **All** (group 2)	Your righteousness is towering like the mountains: **your justice is like the great deep.**
Leader 1 **All** (group 1)	How precious is your love, O God: **we find shelter beneath your wings!**
Leader 2 **All** (group 2)	We feast on the food you provide: **we drink from the river of your goodness:**
Leader 1 **All**	For with you is the fountain of life: **in your light we see light.**
All	**Glory to the Father, and to the Son, and to the Holy Spirit:** **as it was in the beginning, is now, and shall be for ever. Amen.**

Cast: **Leader 1, Leader 2** (can be the same as Leader 1), **All** (group 1—two or more persons/part of congregation), **All** (group 2—two or more persons/part of congregation).

Confessions
Psalm 39.1–13

Psalmist	I said:
Young psalmist	I will be careful what I do and will not let my tongue make me sin; I will not say anything while evil men are near.
Psalmist	I kept quiet, not saying a word, not even about anything good! But my suffering only grew worse, and I was overcome with anxiety. The more I thought, the more troubled I became; I could not keep from asking:
Young psalmist	Lord, how long will I live? When will I die? Tell me how soon my life will end. How short you have made my life! In your sight my lifetime seems nothing. Indeed every living man is no more than a puff of wind, no more than a shadow.

All he does is for nothing;
he gathers wealth, but doesn't know who will get it. (PAUSE)

What, then, can I hope for, Lord?
I put my hope in you.
Save me from all my sins,
and don't let fools laugh at me.
I will keep quiet, I will not say a word,
for you are the one who made me suffer like this.
Don't punish me any more!
I am about to die from your blows.
You punish a man's sins by your rebukes,
and like a moth you destroy what he loves.
Indeed a man is no more than a puff of wind!

Psalmist   Hear my prayer, Lord,
and listen to my cry;
come to my aid when I weep.
Like all my ancestors
I am only your guest for a little while.
Leave me alone so that I may have some happiness
before I go away and am no more.

Cast [This is] the word of the Lord. **All** **Glory to the Father, and to the Son, and to the Holy Spirit:**
All   **Thanks be to God.**   OR   **as it was in the beginning, is now, and shall be for ever. Amen.**

Cast: **Psalmist, Young psalmist.**

A song of praise (i)
From Psalm 40.1–3 (LIT)

Leader   I waited patiently for the Lord:
All   **he turned and heard my cry.**

Leader   He pulled me out of the slimy pit:
All   **out of the mud and mire.**

Leader   He set my feet upon a rock:
All   **and made my step secure.**

Leader   He put a new song in my mouth:
All   **a hymn of praise to God.**

All   **Many will see it and fear;**
and put their trust in the Lord.

All   **Glory to the Father, and to the Son, and to the Holy Spirit:**
as it was in the beginning, is now, and shall be for ever. Amen.

Cast: **Leader, All** (two or more persons/congregation).

A song of praise (ii)
From Psalm 40.4–16 (LIT)

Leader 1   Happy are those who trust in God:
All   **who do not worship idols.**   →

Leader 1	Sacrifice and offering you do not desire:
All	**but you want my ears to be open.**
Leader 2	So I said, 'Lord I come:
All	**obedient to your word.'**
Leader 2	I delight to do your will, O God:
All	**and keep your teaching in my heart.**
Leader 2	I'll tell the world your saving news:
All	**you know my lips will not be sealed.**
Leader 2	I have not hid your righteousness:
All	**but speak of your salvation, Lord.**
Leader 2	I do not hide your faithful love:
All	**but share your mercy with them all.**
Leader 1	May all who come to you be glad—
Leader 2	May all who know your saving power for ever say:
All	**How great is the Lord!**
All	**Glory to the Father, and to the Son, and to the Holy Spirit: as it was in the beginning, is now, and shall be for ever. Amen.**

Cast: **Leader 1, Leader 2, All** (two or more persons/congregation).

The prayer for health
Psalm 41.1–13

Worshipper 1	Happy are those who are concerned for the poor; the Lord will help them when they are in trouble.
Worshipper 2	The Lord will protect them and preserve their lives; he will make them happy in the land:
Worshipper 1	He will not abandon them to the power of their enemies.
Worshipper 2	The Lord will help them when they are sick and will restore them to health.
Worshipper 1	I said:
Worshipper 2	I have sinned against you, Lord; be merciful to me and heal me.
Worshipper 1	My enemies say cruel things about me. They want me to die and be forgotten.
Worshipper 2	Those who come to see me are not sincere; they gather bad news about me and then go out and tell it everywhere.
Worshipper 1	All who hate me whisper to each other about me, they imagine the worst about me. They say:
Enemy	He is fatally ill; he will never leave his bed again.

Worshipper 1	Even my best friend, the one I trusted most,
	the one who shared my food,
	has turned against me.
Worshipper 2	Be merciful to me, Lord, and restore my health,
	and I will pay my enemies back.
	They will not triumph over me,
	and I will know that you are pleased with me.
	You will help me, because I do what is right;
	you will keep me in your presence for ever.
Worshipper 1	Praise the Lord, the God of Israel!
Worshipper 2	Praise him now and for ever!
Cast/All	Amen! Amen!

Cast [This is] the word of the Lord. **All** **Glory to the Father, and to the Son, and to the Holy Spirit:**
All   **Thanks be to God.**   OR   **as it was in the beginning, is now, and shall be for ever. Amen.**

Cast: **Worshipper 1, Worshipper 2, Enemy.**

Prayers in exile
Psalm 42.1–11

Worshipper 1	As a deer longs for a stream of cool water,
	so I long for you, O God.
	I thirst for you, the living God;
	when can I go and worship in your presence?
	Day and night I cry,
	and tears are my only food;
	all the time my enemies ask me:
Enemies	Where is your God?
Worshipper 2	My heart breaks when I remember the past,
	when I went with the crowds to the house of God
	and led them as they walked along,
	a happy crowd, singing and shouting praise to God. (PAUSE)
Worshipper 1	Why am I so sad?
Worshipper 2	Why am I so troubled?
Worshippers 1 and 2	I will put my hope in God,
	and once again I will praise him,
	my saviour and my God.
Worshipper 2	Here in exile my heart is breaking,
	and so I turn my thoughts to him.
	He has sent waves of sorrow over my soul;
	chaos roars at me like a flood,
	like waterfalls thundering down to the Jordan
	from Mount Hermon and Mount Mizar.
Worshipper 1	May the Lord show his constant love during the day,
	so that I may have a song at night,
	a prayer to the God of my life.

Worshipper 2	To God, my defender, I say:
Worshipper 1	Why have you forgotten me? Why must I go on suffering from the cruelty of my enemies?
Worshipper 2	I am crushed by their insults, as they keep on asking me:
Enemies	Where is your God?
Worshipper 1	Why am I so sad?
Worshipper 2	Why am I so troubled?
Worshippers 1 and 2	I will put my hope in God, and once again I will praise him, my saviour and my God.

Cast [This is] the word of the Lord. **All Glory to the Father, and to the Son, and to the Holy Spirit:**
All Thanks be to God. OR **as it was in the beginning, is now, and shall be for ever. Amen.**

Cast: **Worshipper 1, Enemies** (two or more), **Worshipper 2** .

God is with us
Psalm 46.1–11

Psalmist	God is our refuge and strength, an ever present help in trouble.
Worshipper 1	Therefore we will not fear:
Worshipper 2	Though the earth give way and the mountains fall into the heart of the sea—
Worshipper 3	Though its waters roar and foam and the mountains quake with their surging.
Psalmist	There is a river whose streams make glad the city of God, the holy place where the Most High dwells. God is within her, she will not fall; God will help her at break of day. Nations are in uproar, kingdoms fall; he lifts his voice, the earth melts.
Worshipper 1	The Lord Almighty is with us.
Worshippers 2 and 3	The God of Jacob is our fortress.
Psalmist	Come and see the works of the Lord, the desolations he has brought on the earth. He makes wars cease to the ends of the earth; he breaks the bow and shatters the spear, he burns the shields with fire.
The Lord	Be still, and know that I am God; I will be exalted among the nations, I will be exalted in the earth.

Psalmist	The Lord Almighty is with us.
Worshippers **1–3**	The God of Jacob is our fortress.

Cast [This is] the word of the Lord. **All Glory to the Father, and to the Son, and to the Holy Spirit:**
All   Thanks be to God.   OR   **as it was in the beginning, is now, and shall be for ever. Amen.**

Cast: **Psalmist, Worshipper 1** (can be the same as Psalmist), **Worshipper 2, Worshipper 3, The Lord**
(preferably unseen).

God is with us
From Psalm 46.1–11 (LIT)

Leader	God is our refuge and strength:
All	**an ever-present help in trouble.**
Leader	Therefore we will not fear:
All (group 1)	**though the earth should shake,**
All (group 2)	**though the mountains fall into the sea,**
All (group 1)	**though the waters surge and foam,**
All (group 2)	**though the mountains shake and roar.**
All	**The Lord Almighty is with us:** **the God of Jacob is our fortress.**
Leader	There is a river whose streams make glad the city of God: the holy place where the Most High dwells.
All (group 1)	**God is within her, she will not fall:**
All (group 2)	**God will help her at break of day.**
Leader	Nations are in uproar, kingdoms fall:
All	**God lifts his voice—the earth melts away.**
All (group 1)	**The Lord Almighty is with us:**
All (group 2)	**the God of Jacob is our fortress.**
Leader	Come and see what God has done:
All	**his devastation on the earth!**
Leader	He stops the wars throughout the world:
All (group 1)	**he breaks the bow and shatters the spear—**
All (group 2)	**he sets the shield on fire.**
Voice of God	Be still, and know that I am God: I will be exalted over the nations, I will be exalted over the earth.
All	**The Lord Almighty is with us:** **the God of Jacob is our fortress.**
All	**Glory to the Father, and to the Son, and to the Holy Spirit:** **as it was in the beginning, is now, and shall be for ever. Amen.**

Cast: **Leader, All** (group 1—two or more persons/part of congregation), **All** (group 2—two or more persons/part of congregation), **Voice of God**.

The supreme ruler
From Psalm 47.1–9 (LIT)

Leader	Clap your hands, all you nations:
All	**shout to God with cries of joy.**
Leader	How awesome is the Lord most high:
All (group 1)	**the King who rules the whole wide earth!**
Leader	God has ascended to his throne:
All (group 2)	**with shouts of joy and sound of trumpets.**
Leader	Sing praises to our God, sing praises:
All (group 1)	**sing praises to our King, sing praises.**
Leader	For God is King of all the earth:
All (group 2)	**sing to him a psalm of praise.**
Leader	God is seated on his throne:
All (group 1)	**he rules the nations of the world.**
Leader	The leaders of the nations come:
All (group 2)	**as subjects of our holy God.**
Leader	The lords of earth belong to God:
All	**he reigns supreme.**
All	**Glory to the Father, and to the Son, and to the Holy Spirit: as it was in the beginning, is now, and shall be for ever. Amen.**

Cast: **Leader, All** (group 1—two or more persons/part of congregation), **All** (group 2—two or more persons/part of congregation).

The city of God
Psalm 48.1–14

Worshipper	Great is the Lord, and most worthy of praise, in the city of our God, his holy mountain.
Psalmist	It is beautiful in its loftiness, the joy of the whole earth. Like the utmost heights of Zaphon is Mount Zion, the city of the Great King. God is in her citadels; he has shown himself to be her fortress.
	When the kings joined forces, when they advanced together, they saw her and were astounded; they fled in terror. Trembling seized them there, pain like that of a woman in labour.
Worshipper	You destroyed them like ships of Tarshish shattered by an east wind.

504

Psalmist	As we have heard, so have we seen in the city of the Lord Almighty, in the city of our God: God makes her secure for ever.
Worshipper	Within your temple, O God, we meditate on your unfailing love. Like your name, O God, your praise reaches to the ends of the earth; your right hand is filled with righteousness. Mount Zion rejoices, the villages of Judah are glad because of your judgments.
Psalmist	Walk about Zion, go round her, count her towers, consider well her ramparts, view her citadels, that you may tell of them to the next generation.
Worshipper	For this God is our God for ever and ever; he will be our guide even to the end.

Cast [This is] the word of the Lord. **All** **Glory to the Father, and to the Son, and to the Holy Spirit:**
All **Thanks be to God.** OR **as it was in the beginning, is now, and shall be for ever. Amen.**

Cast: **Worshipper, Psalmist.**

True worship
Psalm 50.1–23

Worshipper 1	The Almighty God, the Lord, speaks; he calls to the whole earth from east to west.
Worshipper 2	God shines from Zion, the city perfect in its beauty.
Worshippers 1 and 2	Our God is coming, but not in silence:
Worshipper 1	A raging fire is in front of him—
Worshipper 2	A furious storm is round him.
Worshipper 1	He calls heaven and earth as witnesses to see him judge his people. He says:
God	Gather my faithful people to me, those who made a covenant with me by offering a sacrifice.
Worshipper 1	The heavens proclaim that God is righteous—
Worshipper 2	That he himself is judge.
God	Listen, my people, and I will speak; I will testify against you, Israel.

$\rightarrow$

I am God, your God.
I do not reprimand you because of your sacrifices
and the burnt-offerings you always bring me.
And yet I do not need bulls from your farms
or goats from your flocks;
all the animals in the forest are mine
and the cattle on thousands of hills.
All the wild birds are mine
and all living things in the fields.

If I were hungry, I would not ask you for food,
for the world and everything in it is mine.
Do I eat the flesh of bulls
or drink the blood of goats?
Let the giving of thanks be your sacrifice to God,
and give the Almighty all that you promised.
Call to me when trouble comes;
I will save you,
and you will praise me.

Worshipper 2   But God says to the wicked:

God

Why should you recite my commandments?
Why should you talk about my covenant?
You refuse to let me correct you;
you reject my commands.
You become the friend of every thief you see
and you associate with adulterers.

You are always ready to speak evil;
you never hesitate to tell lies.
You are ready to accuse your own brothers
and to find fault with them.
You have done all this, and I have said nothing,
so you thought that I was like you.
But now I reprimand you
and make the matter plain to you.

Listen to this, you that ignore me,
or I will destroy you,
and there will be no one to save you.
Giving thanks is the sacrifice that honours me,
and I will surely save all who obey me.

Cast [This is] the word of the Lord. **All Glory to the Father, and to the Son, and to the Holy Spirit:**
All Thanks be to God. OR **as it was in the beginning, is now, and shall be for ever. Amen.**

Cast: **Worhipper 1, Worshipper 2, God.**

Prayers for forgiveness
Psalm 51.1–19

Penitent 1   Be merciful to me, O God,
                because of your constant love.

Sinner 1   Because of your great mercy
                wipe away my sins!

Sinner 2   Wash away all my evil
                and make me clean from my sin!

Sinner 1   I recognize my faults;
                I am always conscious of my sins.

Sinner 2   I have sinned against *you*—only against *you*—
                and done what you consider evil.
                So you are right in judging me;
                you are justified in condemning me.

Sinner 1   I have been evil from the day I was born;
                from the time I was conceived, I have been sinful.

Penitent 1   Sincerity and truth are what you require:
                fill my mind with your wisdom.

Sinner 1   Remove my sin, and I will be clean;
                wash me, and I will be whiter than snow.

Penitent 2   Let me hear the sounds of joy and gladness;
                and though you have crushed me and broken me,
                I will be happy once again.

Sinner 2   Close your eyes to my sins
                and wipe out all my evil.

Penitent 1   Create a pure heart in me, O God,
                and put a new and loyal spirit in me.

Penitent 2   Do not banish me from your presence;
                do not take your holy spirit away from me.

Penitent 1   Give me again the joy that comes from your salvation,
                and make me willing to obey you.
                Then I will teach sinners your commands,
                and they will turn back to you.

Sinner 1   Spare my life, O God, and save me,
                and I will gladly proclaim your righteousness.

Penitent 1   Help me to speak, Lord,
                and I will praise you.

Sinner 2   You do not want sacrifices,
                or I would offer them;
                you are not pleased with burnt-offerings.

Sinner 1   My sacrifice is a humble spirit, O God;
                you will not reject a humble and repentant heart.

Penitent 1   O God, be kind to Zion and help her;
rebuild the walls of Jerusalem.
Then you will be pleased with proper sacrifices
and with our burnt-offerings;
and bulls will be sacrificed on your altar.

Cast [This is] the word of the Lord.   **All** **Glory to the Father, and to the Son, and to the Holy Spirit:**
All   **Thanks be to God.**   OR   **as it was in the beginning, is now, and shall be for ever. Amen.**

Cast: **Penitent 1, Sinner 1, Sinner 2, Penitent 2**

Prayer for the help of God's Spirit
From Psalm 51.6–12 and Psalm 143.6–10 (LIT)

Leader   O Lord, I spread my hands out to you:
All   **I thirst for you like dry ground.**

Leader   Teach me to do your will, for you are my God:
All   **let your good Spirit lead me in safety.**

Leader   You require sincerity and truth in me:
All   **fill my mind with your wisdom.**

Leader   Create in me a pure heart, O God:
All   **and renew a faithful spirit in me.**

Leader   Do not cast me from your presence:
All   **or take your Holy Spirit from me.**

Leader   Give me again the joy of your salvation:
All   **and make me willing to obey.**

All   **Glory to the Father, and to the Son, and to the Holy Spirit:**
as it was in the beginning, is now, and shall be for ever. Amen.

Cast: **Leader, All** (two or more persons/congregation). (Verses from Psalms 51 and 143 have been grouped together to make provision for an occasion when the person and work of the Holy Spirit is being considered.)

God's judgement and grace
Psalm 52.1–9

Psalmist   Why do you boast, great man, of your evil?
God's faithfulness is eternal.
You make plans to ruin others;
your tongue is like a sharp razor.
You are always inventing lies.
You love evil more than good
and falsehood more than truth.
You love to hurt people with your words, you liar!

So God will ruin you for ever;
he will take hold of you and snatch you from your home;
he will remove you from the world of the living.
Righteous people will see this and be afraid;
then they will laugh at you and say:

Righteous person 1	Look, here is a man who did not depend on God for safety.
Righteous person 2	He trusted instead in his great wealth.
Righteous person 1	He looked for security in being wicked.
Worshipper	But I am like an olive-tree growing in the house of God; I trust in his constant love for ever and ever. I will always thank you, God, for what you have done; in the presence of your people I will proclaim that you are good.

Cast [This is] the word of the Lord. **All** Glory to the Father, and to the Son, and to the Holy Spirit:
All Thanks be to God. OR as it was in the beginning, is now, and shall be for ever. Amen.

Cast: **Psalmist, Righteous person 1, Righteous person 2** (can be the same as Righteous person 1), **Worshipper.**

Wickedness and ignorance
Psalm 53.1–6

Psalmist	Fools say to themselves:
Fool(s)	There is no God.
Psalmist	They are all corrupt, and they have done terrible things; there is no one who does what is right. (PAUSE)
	God looks down from heaven at mankind to see if there are any who are wise, any who worship him. But they have all turned away; they are all equally bad. Not one of them does what is right, not a single one. (PAUSE) [God asks:]
God	Don't they know? Are these evildoers ignorant? They live by robbing my people, and they never pray to me.
Psalmist	But then they will be terrified, as they have never been before, for God will scatter the bones of the enemies of his people. God has rejected them, and so Israel will totally defeat them.
Worshipper	How I pray that victory will come to Israel from Zion.

→

509

How happy the people of Israel will be
when God makes them prosperous again!

**Psalmist and
Worshipper**   Amen.

Cast [This is] the word of the Lord.   **All** Glory to the Father, and to the Son, and to the Holy Spirit:
All   Thanks be to God.   OR   as it was in the beginning, is now, and shall be for ever. Amen.

Cast: **Psalmist, Fool(s), God, Worshipper.**

A prayer for deliverance
Psalm 60.1–12

Worshipper 1   You have rejected us, God, and defeated us;
you have been angry with us—but now turn back to us.

Worshipper 2   You have made the land tremble, and you have cut it open;
now heal its wounds, because it is falling apart.

Worshipper 1   You have made your people suffer greatly;
we stagger around as though we were drunk.

Worshipper 3   You have warned those who show you reverence,
so that they might escape destruction.

Worshipper 2   Save us by your might; answer our prayer,
so that the people you love may be rescued. (PAUSE)

Worshipper 3   From his sanctuary God has said:

God   In triumph I will divide Shechem
and distribute the Valley of Sukkoth to my people.
Gilead is mine, and Manasseh too;
Ephraim is my helmet
and Judah my royal sceptre.
But I will use Moab as my wash-basin
and I will throw my sandals on Edom,
as a sign that I own it.
Did the Philistines think they would shout in triumph over me?

Worshipper 3   Who, O God, will take me into the fortified city?
Who will lead me to Edom?

Worshipper 1   Have you really rejected us?
Aren't you going to march out with our armies?

Worshipper 2   Help us against the enemy;
human help is worthless.

Worshipper 3   With God on our side we will win;
he will defeat our enemies.

Cast [This is] the word of the Lord.   **All** Glory to the Father, and to the Son, and to the Holy Spirit:
All   Thanks be to God.   OR   as it was in the beginning, is now, and shall be for ever. Amen.

Cast: **Worshipper 1, Worshipper 2, Worshipper 3, God.**

A prayer for protection
Psalm 64.1–10

Worshipper 1	I am in trouble, God—listen to my prayer!
Worshipper 2	I am afraid of my enemies—save my life!
Worshipper 1	Protect me from the plots of the wicked, from mobs of evil men.
Worshipper 2	They sharpen their tongues like swords and aim cruel words like arrows.
Worshipper 1	They are quick to spread their shameless lies; they destroy good men with cowardly slander.
Worshipper 2	They encourage each other in their evil plots; they plan where to place their traps.
Worshipper 1	They say:
Evil person(s)	No one can see them.
Worshipper 2	They make evil plans and say:
Evil person(s)	We have planned a perfect crime.
Worshipper 1 (thoughtfully)	The heart and mind of man are a mystery. (PAUSE)
Worshipper 2	But God shoots his arrows at them, and suddenly they are wounded. He will destroy them because of those words.
Worshipper 1	All who see them will shake their heads.
Worshipper 2	They will all be afraid; they will think about what God has done and tell about his deeds.
Worshipper 1	All righteous people will rejoice because of what the Lord has done. They will find safety in him;
Worshippers 1 and 2	All good people will praise him.

Cast [This is] the word of the Lord.   **All Glory to the Father, and to the Son, and to the Holy Spirit:**
All   Thanks be to God.   OR   **as it was in the beginning, is now, and shall be for ever. Amen.**

Cast: **Worshipper 1, Worshipper 2, Evil person(s).**

Praise for the harvest
From Psalm 65.1–13 (LIT)

Leader 2	O God, it is right for us to praise you, because you answer our prayers:
Leader 1	You care for the land and water it:
All (group 1)	**and make it rich and fertile.**

→

Leader 2	You fill the running streams with water:
All (group 2)	**and irrigate the land.**
Leader 1	You soften the ground with showers:
All (group 1)	**and make the young crops grow.**
Leader 2	You crown the year with goodness:
All (group 2)	**and give us a plentiful harvest.**
Leader 1	The pastures are filled with flocks:
All (group 1)	**the hillsides are clothed with joy.**
Leader 2	The fields are covered with grain:
All	**they shout for joy and sing.**
All	**Glory to the Father, and to the Son, and to the Holy Spirit:**
	as it was in the beginning, is now, and shall be for ever. Amen.

Cast: **Leader 2, Leader 1, All** (group 1—two or more persons/part of congregation), **All** (group 2—two or more persons/part of congregation).

A song of praise and thanksgiving
Psalm 66.1–20

Psalmist	Praise God with shouts of joy, all people!
	Sing to the glory of his name;
	offer him glorious praise!
	Say to God:
Worshipper 1	How wonderful are the things you do!
	Your power is so great
	that your enemies bow down in fear before you.
	Everyone on earth worships you;
	they sing praises to you,
	they sing praises to your name.
Psalmist	Come and see what God has done,
	his wonderful acts among us.
	He changed the sea into dry land;
	our ancestors crossed the river on foot.
	There we rejoiced because of what he did.
	He rules for ever by his might
	and keeps his eyes on the nations.
	Let no rebels rise against him.
	Praise our God, all nations;
	let your praise be heard.
	He has kept us alive
	and has not allowed us to fall.
Worshipper 1	You have put us to the test, God;
	as silver is purified by fire
	so you have tested us.
	You let us fall into a trap
	and placed heavy burdens on our backs.
	You let our enemies trample over us;

we went through fire and flood,
but now you have brought us to a place of safety.

Worshipper 2   I will bring burnt-offerings to your house;
I will offer you what I promised.
I will give you what I said I would
when I was in trouble.
I will offer sheep to be burnt on the altar;
I will sacrifice bulls and goats,
and the smoke will go up to the sky.

Worshipper 3   Come and listen, all who honour God,
and I will tell you what he has done for me.
I cried to him for help;
I praised him with songs.
If I had ignored my sins,
the Lord would not have listened to me.
But God has indeed heard me;
he has listened to my prayer.

Worshipper 2   I praise God,
because he did not reject my prayer
or keep back his constant love from me.

Cast [This is] the word of the Lord.   **All** Glory to the Father, and to the Son, and to the Holy Spirit:
All   Thanks be to God.   OR   as it was in the beginning, is now, and shall be for ever. Amen.

Cast: **Psalmist, Worshipper 1, Worshipper 2, Worshipper 3.**

A song of praise and thanksgiving
From Psalm 66.1–20 (LIT)

Leader   Praise your God with shouts of joy:
All   **all the earth sing praise to him.**

Leader   Sing the glory of his name:
All (group 1)   **offer him your highest praise.**

Leader   Say to him: How great you are:
All (group 2)   **wonderful the things you do!**

Leader   All your enemies bow down:
All (group 3)   **all the earth sings praise to you.**

Leader   Come and see what God has done:
All (group 1)   **causing mortal men to fear;**
All (group 2)   **how he turned the sea to land,**
All (group 3)   **led his people safely through.**

Leader   We rejoice at what he does—
All (group 1)   **ruling through eternity,**
All (group 2)   **watching over all the world,**
All (group 3)   **keeping every rebel down.**

→

Leader	Praise our God, O nations, praise:
All (group 1)	**let the sound of praise be heard!**
All (group 2)	**God sustains our very lives:**
All (group 3)	**keeps our feet upon the way.**

Leader	Once, you tested us, O God—
All (group 1)	**silver purified by fire—**

Leader	Let us fall into a trap,
All (group 2)	**placed hard burdens on our backs—**

Leader	Sent us through the flame and flood:
All (group 3)	**now you bring us safely home.**

Leader	I will come to worship you:
All (group 1)	**bring to you my offering,**
All (group 2)	**give you what I said I would,**
All (group 3)	**when the troubles threatened me.**

Leader	All who love and honour God:
All (group 1)	**come and listen, while I tell**
All (group 2)	**what great things he did for me**
All (group 3)	**when I cried to him for help,**
All (group 1)	**when I praised him with my songs,**
All (group 2)	**when my heart was free from sin,**
All (group 3)	**then he listened to my prayer.**

Leader	Praise the Lord who heard my cry:
All	**God has shown his love to me!**

All	**Glory to the Father, and to the Son, and to the Holy Spirit:** **as it was in the beginning, is now, and shall be for ever. Amen.**

Cast: **Leader, All** (group 1—two or more persons/part of congregation), **All** (group 2—two or more persons/part of congregation), **All** (group 3—two or more persons/part of congregation).

A song of thanksgiving
Psalm 67.1–7 (LIT)

Leader 1	May God be gracious to us and bless us:
All (group 1)	**and make his face to shine upon us.**

Leader 2	Let your ways be known upon earth:
All (group 2)	**your saving grace to every nation.**

Leaders 1 and 2	Let the peoples praise you, O God:
All	**let the peoples praise you.**

Leader 1	Let the nations be glad:
All (group 1)	**and sing aloud for joy.**

Leader 2	Because you judge the peoples justly:
All (group 2)	**and guide the nations of the earth.**

Leaders 1 and 2	Let the peoples praise you, O God:
All	**let all the peoples praise you.**

Leader 1	Then the land will yield its harvest:
All (group 1)	**and God, our God, will bless us.**
Leader 2	God will bless us:
All (group 2)	**and people will fear him**
All	**to the ends of the earth.**
All	**Glory to the Father, and to the Son, and to the Holy Spirit:** **as it was in the beginning, is now, and shall be for ever. Amen.**

Cast: **Leader 1, All** (group 1—two or more persons/part of congregation), **Leader 2, All** (group 2—two or more persons/part of congregation).

A national song of triumph
From Psalm 68.1–35

Psalmist	God rises up and scatters his enemies. Those who hate him run away in defeat. As smoke is blown away, so he drives them off; as wax melts in front of the fire, so do the wicked perish in God's presence. But the righteous are glad and rejoice in his presence; they are happy and shout for joy.
Leader	Sing to God, sing praises to his name; prepare a way for him who rides on the clouds. His name is the Lord—be glad in his presence!
Psalmist	God, who lives in his sacred Temple, cares for orphans and protects widows. He gives the lonely a home to live in and leads prisoners out into happy freedom, but rebels will have to live in a desolate land.
Worshipper	O God, when you led your people, when you marched across the desert, the earth shook, and the sky poured down rain, because of the coming of the God of Sinai, the coming of the God of Israel. You caused abundant rain to fall and restored your worn-out land; your people made their home there; in your goodness you provided for the poor. The Lord gave the command, and many women carried the news:
Woman	Kings and their armies are running away!
Psalmist	With his many thousands of mighty chariots the Lord comes from Sinai into the holy place. He goes up to the heights, taking many captives with him; he receives gifts from rebellious men. The Lord God will live there.

Leader	Praise the Lord, who carries our burdens day after day; he is the God who saves us. Our God is a God who saves; he is the Lord, our Lord, who rescues us from death.
Worshipper	O God, your march of triumph is seen by all, the procession of God, my king, into his sanctuary.
Onlooker 1	The singers are in front.
Onlooker 2	The musicians are behind.
Onlooker 3	In between are the girls beating the tambourines.
Leader	Praise God in the meeting of his people; praise the Lord, all you descendants of Jacob!
Onlooker 1	First comes Benjamin, the smallest tribe.
Onlooker 2	Then the leaders of Judah with their group—
Onlooker 3	Followed by the leaders of Zebulun and Naphtali.
Leader	Sing to God, kingdoms of the world, sing praise to the Lord, to him who rides in the sky, the ancient sky. Listen to him shout with a mighty roar. Proclaim God's power; his majesty is over Israel, his might is in the skies.
Worshipper	How awesome is God as he comes from his sanctuary— the God of Israel! He gives strength and power to his people.
Cast	Praise God!

Cast [This is] the word of the Lord. **All** Glory to the Father, and to the Son, and to the Holy Spirit:
All Thanks be to God. OR as it was in the beginning, is now, and shall be for ever. Amen.

Cast: **Psalmist, Leader, Worshipper, Woman** (can be the same as Worshipper), **Onlooker 1, Onlooker 2, Onlooker 3.**

The prayer of an older person
Psalm 71.1–24

Senior person 1	Lord, I have come to you for protection; never let me be defeated!
Senior person 2	Because you are righteous, help me and rescue me. Listen to me and save me!
Senior person 1	Be my secure shelter and a strong fortress to protect me; you are my refuge and defence.

Senior person 2   My God, rescue me from wicked men,
from the power of cruel and evil men.
Sovereign Lord, I put my hope in you;
I have trusted in you since I was young.
I have relied on you all my life;
you have protected me since the day I was born.
I will always praise you.

Senior person 1   My life has been an example to many,
because you have been my strong defender.
All day long I praise you
and proclaim your glory.
Do not reject me now that I am old;
do not abandon me now that I am feeble.
My enemies want to kill me;
they talk and plot against me.
They say:

Enemy 1   God has abandoned him.

Enemy 2   Let's go after him and catch him.

Enemy 3   There is no one to rescue him.

Senior person 1   Don't stay so far away, O God;
my God, hurry to my aid!
May those who attack me
be defeated and destroyed.
May those who try to hurt me
be shamed and disgraced.
I will always put my hope in you;
I will praise you more and more.
I will tell of your goodness;
all day long I will speak of your salvation,
though it is more than I can understand.
I will praise your power, Sovereign Lord;
I will proclaim your goodness, yours alone.

Senior person 2   You have taught me ever since I was young,
and I still tell of your wonderful acts.
Now that I am old and my hair is grey,
do not abandon me, O God!
Be with me while I proclaim your power and might
to all generations to come.

Senior person 1   Your righteousness, God, reaches the skies.
You have done great things;
there is no one like you.
You have sent troubles and suffering on me,
but you will restore my strength;
you will keep me from the grave.
You will make me greater than ever;
you will comfort me again.

Senior person 2   I will indeed praise you with the harp;
I will praise your faithfulness, my God.

→

517

On my harp I will play hymns to you,
the Holy One of Israel.
I will shout for joy as I play for you;
with my whole being I will sing
because you have saved me.
I will speak of your righteousness all day long,
because those who tried to harm me
have been defeated and disgraced.

Cast [This is] the word of the Lord. **All Glory to the Father, and to the Son, and to the Holy Spirit:**
All Thanks be to God. OR **as it was in the beginning, is now, and shall be for ever. Amen.**

Cast: **Senior person 1, Senior person 2, Enemy 1, Enemy 2** (can be the same as Enemy 1)**, Enemy 3.**

God, the Judge
Psalm 75.1–10

Worshippers 1 and 2	We give thanks to you, O God, we give thanks to you!
Worshipper 1	We proclaim how great you are and tell of the wonderful things you have done.
Worshipper 2	God says:
God	I have set a time for judgement, and I will judge with fairness. Though every living creature tremble and the earth itself be shaken, I will keep its foundations firm. I tell the wicked not to be arrogant; I tell them to stop their boasting.
Worshipper 2	Judgement does not come from the east or from the west, from the north or from the south; it is God who is the judge, condemning some and acquitting others.
Worshipper 1	The Lord holds a cup in his hand, filled with the strong wine of his anger. He pours it out, and all the wicked drink it; they drink it down to the last drop.
Worshipper 2	But I will never stop speaking of the God of Jacob or singing praises to him. He will break the power of the wicked, but the power of the righteous will be increased.

Cast [This is] the word of the Lord. **All Glory to the Father, and to the Son, and to the Holy Spirit:**
All Thanks be to God. OR **as it was in the beginning, is now, and shall be for ever. Amen.**

Cast: **Worshipper 1, Worshipper 2, God.**

Comfort in time of distress
Psalm 77.1–20

Worshipper 1　I cry aloud to God;
I cry aloud, and he hears me.
In times of trouble I pray to the Lord;
all night long I lift my hands in prayer,
but I cannot find comfort.

Worshipper 2　When I think of God, I sigh;
when I meditate, I feel discouraged.

He keeps me awake all night;
I am so worried that I cannot speak.
I think of days gone by
and remember years of long ago.
I spend the night in deep thought;
I meditate, and this is what I ask myself:

Thinker　Will the Lord always reject us?
Will he never again be pleased with us?
Has he stopped loving us?
Does his promise no longer stand?
Has God forgotten to be merciful?
Has anger taken the place of his compassion?

Worshipper 2　Then I said:

Thinker　What hurts me most is this—
that God is no longer powerful.

Worshipper 2　I will remember your great deeds, Lord;
I will recall the wonders you did in the past.
I will think about all that you have done;
I will meditate on all your mighty acts.

Worshipper 1　Everything you do, O God, is holy.
No god is as great as you.
You are the God who works miracles;
you showed your might among the nations.
By your power you saved your people,
the descendants of Jacob and of Joseph.

Worshipper 2　When the waters saw you, O God, they were afraid,
and the depths of the sea trembled.

Worshipper 1　The clouds poured down rain;
thunder crashed from the sky,
and lightning flashed in all directions.

Worshipper 2　The crash of your thunder rolled out,
and flashes of lightning lit up the world;
the earth trembled and shook.

Worshipper 1　You walked through the waves;
you crossed the deep sea,
but your footprints could not be seen.

Worshipper 2   You led your people like a shepherd,
with Moses and Aaron in charge.

Cast [This is] the word of the Lord.   **All** Glory to the Father, and to the Son, and to the Holy Spirit:
All   Thanks be to God.   OR   as it was in the beginning, is now, and shall be for ever. Amen.

Cast: **Worshipper 1, Worshipper 2, Thinker.**

A prayer for restoration
From Psalm 80.1–19 (LIT)

Leader 1   Hear us, O Shepherd of Israel, leader of your flock.

Leader 2   Hear us from your throne above the cherubim.

Leader 3   Shine forth, awaken your strength, and come to save us.
All   **Bring us back, O God, and save us,**
make your face to shine upon us.

Leader 1   O Lord God almighty, how long will you be angry with your
people's prayers?

Leader 2   You have given us sorrow to eat and tears to drink.

Leader 3   You have made us a source of contention to our neighbours, and
our enemies insult us.
All   **Bring us back, O God, and save us,**
make your face to shine upon us.

Leader 1   Return to us, O God Almighty, look down from heaven and see.

Leader 2   Look on this vine that you planted with your own hand, this child
you raised for yourself.

Leader 3   Let your hand rest upon the people you have chosen, then we will
not turn away from you; revive us, and we shall praise your name.
All   **Bring us back, O God, and save us,**
make your face to shine upon us.

All   Glory to the Father, and to the Son, and to the Holy Spirit:
as it was in the beginning, is now, and shall be for ever. Amen.

Cast: **Leader 1, Leader 2, Leader 3** (can be the same as Leader 1), **All** (two or more persons/congregation).

A song for a festival
Psalm 81.1–16

Psalmist   Shout for joy to God our defender;
sing praise to the God of Jacob!
Start the music and beat the tambourines;
play pleasant music on the harps and the lyres.
Blow the trumpet for the festival,
when the moon is new and when the moon is full.
This is the law in Israel,
an order from the God of Jacob.
He gave it to the people of Israel

when he attacked the land of Egypt. (PAUSE)
I hear an unknown voice saying:

Voice of God   I took the burdens off your backs;
I let you put down your loads of bricks.
When you were in trouble, you called to me, and I saved you.
From my hiding-place in the storm, I answered you.
I put you to the test at the springs of Meribah.
Listen, my people, to my warning;
Israel, how I wish you would listen to me!
You must never worship another god.
I am the Lord your God,
who brought you out of Egypt.
Open your mouth, and I will feed you.

But my people would not listen to me;
Israel would not obey me.
So I let them go their stubborn ways
and do whatever they wanted.

How I wish my people would listen to me;
how I wish they would obey me!
I would quickly defeat their enemies
and conquer all their foes.
Those who hate me would bow in fear before me;
their punishment would last for ever.
But I would feed you with the finest wheat
and satisfy you with wild honey.

Cast [This is] the word of the Lord.   **All Glory to the Father, and to the Son, and to the Holy Spirit:**
All   **Thanks be to God.**   OR   **as it was in the beginning, is now, and shall be for ever. Amen.**

Cast: **Psalmist, Voice of God.**

God, the supreme ruler
Psalm 82.1–8

Psalmist   God presides in the heavenly council;
in the assembly of the gods he gives his decision:

God   You must stop judging unjustly;
you must no longer be partial to the wicked!
Defend the rights of the poor and the orphans;
be fair to the needy and the helpless.
Rescue them from the power of evil men.

How ignorant you are! How stupid!
You are completely corrupt,
and justice has disappeared from the world.
I said:

Voice of God   You are gods,
all of you are sons of the Most High.

God   But you will die like men;
your life will end like that of any prince.

| Psalmist | Come, O God, and rule the world;
all the nations are yours. |

Cast [This is] the word of the Lord. **All** Glory to the Father, and to the Son, and to the Holy Spirit:
All Thanks be to God. OR as it was in the beginning, is now, and shall be for ever. Amen.

Cast: **Psalmist, God, Voice of God** (can be the same as God).

A prayer for the defeat of Israel's enemies
Psalm 83.1–18

Worshipper 1   O God, do not keep silent;
do not be still, do not be quiet!
Look! Your enemies are in revolt,
and those who hate you are rebelling.
They are making secret plans against your people;
they are plotting against those you protect.
They say:

Enemies 1 and **2**   Come, let us destroy their nation—

Enemy 2   So that Israel will be forgotten for ever.

Worshipper 1   They agree on their plan
and form an alliance against you:
the people of Edom and the Ishmaelites;
the people of Moab and the Hagrites;
the people of Gebal, Ammon, and Amalek,
and of Philistia and Tyre.
Assyria has also joined them
as a strong ally of the Ammonites and Moabites,
the descendants of Lot.

Worshipper 2   Do to them what you did to the Midianites,
and to Sisera and Jabin at the River Kishon.
You defeated them at Endor,
and their bodies rotted on the ground.
Do to their leaders what you did to Oreb and Zeeb;
defeat all their rulers as you did Zebah and Zalmunna,
who said:

Zebah and **Zalmunna**   We will take for our own
the land that belongs to God.

Worshipper 2   Scatter them like dust, O God,
like straw blown away by the wind.
As fire burns the forest,
as flames set the hills on fire,
chase them away with your storm
and terrify them with your fierce winds.
Cover their faces with shame, O Lord,
and make them acknowledge your power.
May they be defeated and terrified for ever;
may they die in complete disgrace.

Worshippers 1 and 2	May they know that you alone are the Lord, supreme ruler over all the earth.

Cast [This is] the word of the Lord. **All** **Glory to the Father, and to the Son, and to the Holy Spirit:**
All   **Thanks be to God.**   OR   **as it was in the beginning, is now, and shall be for ever. Amen.**

Cast: **Worshipper 1, Enemy 1, Enemy 2** (can be the same as Enemy 1)**, Worshipper 2, Zebah, Zalmunna**
(can be the same as Zebah).

Longing for God's House
Psalm 84.1–12

Worshipper 1	How I love your Temple, Lord Almighty! How I want to be there!
Worshipper 2	I long to be in the Lord's Temple. With my whole being I sing for joy to the living God.
Worshipper 1	Even the sparrows have built a nest, and the swallows have their own home; they keep their young near your altars, Lord Almighty, my king and my God.
Worshipper 2	How happy are those who live in your Temple, always singing praise to you.
Worshipper 1	How happy are those whose strength comes from you, who are eager to make the pilgrimage to Mount Zion. As they pass through the dry valley of Baca, it becomes a place of springs; the autumn rain fills it with pools. They grow stronger as they go; they will see the God of gods on Zion.
Worshipper 2	Hear my prayer, Lord God Almighty. Listen, O God of Jacob! Bless our king, O God, the king you have chosen.
Worshipper 1	One day spent in your Temple is better than a thousand anywhere else.
Worshipper 2	I would rather stand at the gate of the house of my God than live in the homes of the wicked.
Worshipper 1	The Lord is our protector and glorious king, blessing us with kindness and honour. He does not refuse any good thing to those who do what is right.
Worshippers 1 and 2	Almighty Lord, how happy are those who trust in you!

Cast [This is] the word of the Lord. **All** **Glory to the Father, and to the Son, and to the Holy Spirit:**
All   **Thanks be to God.**   OR   **as it was in the beginning, is now, and shall be for ever. Amen.**

Cast: **Worshipper 1, Worshipper 2.**

A prayer for the nation's welfare
Psalm 85.1–13

Worshipper 1 Lord, you have been merciful to your land;
you have made Israel prosperous again.
You have forgiven your people's sins
and pardoned all their wrongs.
You stopped being angry with them
and held back your furious rage.

Worshipper 2 Bring us back, O God our saviour,
and stop being displeased with us!
Will you be angry with us for ever?
Will your anger *never* cease?
Make us strong again,
and we, your people, will praise you.
Show us your constant love, O Lord,
and give us your saving help.

Psalmist I am listening to what the Lord God is saying;
he promises peace to us, his own people,
if we do not go back to our foolish ways.
Surely he is ready to save those who honour him,
and his saving presence will remain in our land.

Worshippers 1 and 2 Love and faithfulness will meet;
righteousness and peace will embrace.

Worshipper 1 Man's loyalty will reach up from the earth—

Psalmist And God's righteousness will look down from heaven.

Worshipper 2 The Lord will make us prosperous,
and our land will produce rich harvests.

Psalmist Righteousness will go before the Lord
and prepare the path for him.

Cast [This is] the word of the Lord. **All Glory to the Father, and to the Son, and to the Holy Spirit:**
All Thanks be to God. OR **as it was in the beginning, is now, and shall be for ever. Amen.**

Cast: **Worshipper 1, Worshipper 2, Psalmist.**

In praise of Jerusalem
Psalm 87.1–7

Psalmist The Lord built his city on the sacred hill;
more than any other place in Israel
he loves the city of Jerusalem.
Listen, city of God,
to the wonderful things he says about you:

The Lord I will include Egypt and Babylonia
when I list the nations that obey me;
I will number among the inhabitants of Jerusalem
the people of Philistia, Tyre, and Sudan.

Psalmist	Of Zion it will be said that all nations belong there and that the Almighty will make her strong. The Lord will write a list of the peoples and include them all as citizens of Jerusalem. They dance and sing:
Dancer(s)	In Zion is the source of all our blessings.

Cast [This is] the word of the Lord. **All Glory to the Father, and to the Son, and to the Holy Spirit:**
All Thanks be to God. OR **as it was in the beginning, is now, and shall be for ever. Amen.**

Cast: **Psalmist, The Lord, Dancer(s).**

A national hymn; God's promise to David
Psalm 89.1–52

Worshipper 1	O Lord, I will always sing of your constant love; I will proclaim your faithfulness for ever. I know that your love will last for all time, that your faithfulness is as permanent as the sky. You said:
The Lord	I have made a covenant with the man I chose; I have promised my servant David, 'A descendant of yours will always be king; I will preserve your dynasty for ever.'
Worshipper 2	The heavens sing of the wonderful things you do; the holy ones sing of your faithfulness, Lord. No one in heaven is like you, Lord; none of the heavenly beings is your equal. You are feared in the council of the holy ones; and all of them stand in awe of you.
Worshipper 1	Lord God Almighty, none is as mighty as you; in all things you are faithful, O Lord. You rule over the powerful sea; you calm its angry waves. You crushed the monster Rahab and killed it; with your mighty strength you defeated your enemies. Heaven is yours, the earth also; you made the world and everything in it. You created the north and the south; Mount Tabor and Mount Hermon sing to you for joy. How powerful you are! How great is your strength! Your kingdom is founded on righteousness and justice; love and faithfulness are shown in all you do.
Worshippers 1 and 2	How happy are the people who worship you with songs, who live in the light of your kindness!

→

Because of you they rejoice all day long,
and they praise you for your goodness.

Worshipper 2 You give us great victories;
in your love you make us triumphant.
You, O Lord, chose our protector;
you, the Holy God of Israel, gave us our king.

In a vision long ago you said to your faithful servants:

The Lord I have given help to a famous soldier;
I have given the throne to one I chose from the people.
I have made my servant David king
by anointing him with holy oil.
My strength will always be with him,
my power will make him strong.
His enemies will never succeed against him;
the wicked will not defeat him.
I will crush his foes
and kill everyone who hates him.
I will love him and be loyal to him;
I will make him always victorious.
I will extend his kingdom
from the Mediterranean to the River Euphrates.
He will say to me:

David You are my father and my God;
you are my protector and saviour.

The Lord I will make him my first-born son,
the greatest of all kings.
I will always keep my promise to him,
and my covenant with him will last for ever.
His dynasty will be as permanent as the sky;
a descendant of his will always be king.

But if his descendants disobey my law
and do not live according to my commands,
if they disregard my instructions
and do not keep my commandments,
then I will punish them for their sins;
I will make them suffer for their wrongs.
But I will not stop loving David
or fail to keep my promise to him.
I will not break my covenant with him
or take back even one promise I made him.

Once and for all I have promised by my holy name:
I will never lie to David.
He will always have descendants,
and I will watch over his kingdom as long as the sun shines.
It will be as permanent as the moon,
that faithful witness in the sky.

Worshipper 1 But you are angry with your chosen king;
you have deserted and rejected him.

You have broken your covenant with your servant
and thrown his crown in the mud.
You have torn down the walls of his city
and left his forts in ruins.
All who pass by steal his belongings;
all his neighbours laugh at him.
You have given the victory to his enemies;
you have made them all happy.
You have made his weapons useless
and let him be defeated in battle.
You have taken away his royal sceptre
and hurled his throne to the ground.
You have made him old before his time
and covered him with disgrace.

Worshipper 2   Lord, will you hide yourself for ever?
How long will your anger burn like fire?
Remember how short my life is;
remember that you created all of us mortal!
Who can live and never die?
How can man keep himself from the grave?

Worshipper 1   Lord, where are the former proofs of your love?
Where are the promises you made to David?
Don't forget how I, your servant, am insulted,
how I endure all the curses of the heathen.
Your enemies insult your chosen king, O Lord!
They insult him wherever he goes.

Worshippers
  1 and 2   Praise the Lord for ever!

Cast/All   Amen! Amen!

Cast [This is] the word of the Lord. **All** **Glory to the Father, and to the Son, and to the Holy Spirit:**
All **Thanks be to God.**   OR   **as it was in the beginning, is now, and shall be for ever. Amen.**

Cast: **Worshipper 1, The Lord, Worshipper 2, David** (can be the same as The Lord).

The sovereignty of God
Psalm 90.1–17

Worshipper 1   O Lord, you have always been our home.
Before you created the hills
or brought the world into being,
you were eternally God,
and will be God for ever.

Worshipper 2   You tell us to return to what we were;
you change us back to dust.
A thousand years to you are like one day;
they are like yesterday, already gone,
like a short hour in the night.

Worshipper 1 You carry us away like a flood;
we last no longer than a dream.
We are like weeds that sprout in the morning,
that grow and burst into bloom,
then dry up and die in the evening.

Worshipper 2 We are destroyed by your anger;
we are terrified by your fury.
You place our sins before you,
our secret sins where you can see them.

Worshipper 1 Our life is cut short by your anger;
it fades away like a whisper.
Seventy years is all we have—
eighty years, if we are strong;
yet all they bring us is trouble and sorrow;
life is soon over, and we are gone.

Worshipper 2 Who has felt the full power of your anger?
Who knows what fear your fury can bring?
Teach us how short our life is,
so that we may become wise.

Worshipper 1 How much longer will your anger last?
Have pity, O Lord, on your servants!
Fill us each morning with your constant love,
so that we may sing and be glad all our life.

Worshipper 2 Give us now as much happiness
as the sadness you gave us during all our years of misery.

Worshipper 1 Let us, your servants, see your mighty deeds.

Worshipper 2 Let our descendants see your glorious might.

**Worshippers
1 and 2** Lord our God, may your blessings be with us.

Worshipper 1 Give us success in all we do!

Cast [This is] the word of the Lord. **All** Glory to the Father, and to the Son, and to the Holy Spirit:
All Thanks be to God.   OR   as it was in the beginning, is now, and shall be for ever. Amen.

Cast: **Worshipper 1, Worshipper 2.**

God, our protector
Psalm 91.1–16

Voice 1 Whoever goes to the Lord for safety,
whoever remains under the protection of the Almighty,
can say to him:

Supplicant You are my defender and protector.
You are my God; in you I trust.

Voice 1
(to Supplicant) He will keep you safe from all hidden dangers
and from all deadly diseases.

Voice 2 (to Supplicant)	He will cover you with his wings; you will be safe in his care; his faithfulness will protect and defend you.
Voice 1	You need not fear any dangers at night or sudden attacks during the day or the plagues that strike in the dark or the evils that kill in daylight.
Voice 2	A thousand may fall dead beside you, ten thousand all round you, but you will not be harmed. You will look and see how the wicked are punished.
Voice 1	You have made the Lord your defender, the Most High your protector, and so no disaster will strike you, no violence will come near your home.
Voice 2	God will put his angels in charge of you to protect you wherever you go. They will hold you up with their hands to keep you from hurting your feet on the stones.
Voice 1	You will trample down lions and snakes, fierce lions and poisonous snakes. (PAUSE) God says:
God	I will save those who love me, and will protect those who acknowledge me as Lord. When they call to me, I will answer them; when they are in trouble, I will be with them. I will rescue them and honour them. I will reward them with long life; I will save them.

Cast [This is] the word of the Lord.   **All** **Glory to the Father, and to the Son, and to the Holy Spirit:**
All   **Thanks be to God.**   OR   **as it was in the beginning, is now, and shall be for ever. Amen.**

Cast: **Voice 1, Supplicant, Voice 2, God.**

God, the king
Psalm 93.1–5

Psalmist	The Lord is king. He is clothed with majesty and strength. The earth is set firmly in place and cannot be moved.
Worshipper 1	Your throne, O Lord, has been firm from the beginning, and you existed before time began.
Worshipper 2	The ocean depths raise their voice, O Lord; they raise their voice and roar.

Psalmist	The Lord rules supreme in heaven, greater than the roar of the ocean, more powerful than the waves of the sea.
Worshipper 1	Your laws are eternal, Lord, and your Temple is holy indeed—
Worshippers 1 and 2	For ever and ever.

Cast [This is] the word of the Lord. **All Glory to the Father, and to the Son, and to the Holy Spirit:**
All Thanks be to God.   OR   **as it was in the beginning, is now, and shall be for ever. Amen.**

Cast: **Psalmist, Worshipper 1, Worshipper 2** (can be the same as Worshipper 1).

God is king
From Psalm 93.1–5 (LIT)

Leader **All** (group 1)	The Lord reigns, robed in majesty: **he arms himself with power.**
Leader **All** (group 2)	The earth is firmly set in place: **it never can be moved.**
Leader **All** (group 1)	Your throne was founded long ago: **before all time began.**
Leader **All** (group 2)	The oceans raise their voice, O Lord: **and lift their roaring waves.**
Leader **All** (group 1)	The Lord is mightier than the sea: **he rules supreme on high.**
Leader **All** (group 2)	His laws stand firm through endless days: **his praise for evermore.**
All	Amen.
All	**Glory to the Father, and to the Son, and to the Holy Spirit: as it was in the beginning, is now, and shall be for ever. Amen.**

Cast: **Leader, All** (group 1—two or more persons/part of congregation), **All** (group 2—two or more persons/part of congregation).

God, the judge of all
Psalm 94.1–23

Worshipper 1	Lord, you are a God who punishes: reveal your anger! You are the judge of all men: rise and give the proud what they deserve! How much longer will the wicked be glad? How much longer, Lord? How much longer will criminals be proud and boast about their crimes?

They crush your people, Lord;
they oppress those who belong to you.
They kill widows and orphans,
and murder the strangers who live in our land.

They say:

Criminal   The Lord does not see us;
the God of Israel does not notice.

Prophet   My people, how can you be such stupid fools?
When will you ever learn?
God made our ears—can't he hear?
He made our eyes—can't he see?
He scolds the nations—won't he punish them?
He is the teacher of all men—hasn't he any knowledge?
The Lord knows what they think;
he knows how senseless their reasoning is.

Worshipper 2   Lord, how happy is the person you instruct,
the one to whom you teach your law!
You give him rest from days of trouble
until a pit is dug to trap the wicked.

Prophet   The Lord will not abandon his people;
he will not desert those who belong to him.
Justice will again be found in the courts,
and all righteous people will support it.

Worshipper 1   Who stood up for me against the wicked?
Who took my side against the evildoers?
If the Lord had not helped me,
I would have gone quickly to the land of silence.

I said:

**Young
worshipper**   I am falling.

Worshipper 2   But your constant love, O Lord, held me up. (PAUSE)
Whenever I am anxious and worried,
you comfort me and make me glad.

Worshipper 1   You have nothing to do with corrupt judges,
who make injustice legal,
who plot against good men
and sentence the innocent to death.

Worshipper 2   But the Lord defends me;
my God protects me.

Prophet   He will punish them for their wickedness
and destroy them for their sins;
the Lord our God will destroy them.

Cast [This is] the word of the Lord.   **All Glory to the Father, and to the Son, and to the Holy Spirit:**
All   Thanks be to God.   OR   **as it was in the beginning, is now, and shall be for ever. Amen.**

Cast: **Worshipper 1, Criminal, Prophet, Worshipper 2, Young worshipper** (can be the same as Worshipper 1).

A song of praise
Psalm 95.1–11

Psalmist

Come, let us praise the Lord!
Let us sing for joy to God, who protects us!
Let us come before him with thanksgiving
and sing joyful songs of praise.
For the Lord is a mighty God,
a mighty king over all the gods.
He rules over the whole earth,
from the deepest caves to the highest hills.
He rules over the sea, which he made;
the land also, which he himself formed.

Come, let us bow down and worship him;
let us kneel before the Lord, our Maker!

**Worshippers
1 and 2**

He is our God;
we are the people he cares for,
the flock for which he provides.

Psalmist

Listen today to what he says:

The Lord

Don't be stubborn, as your ancestors were at Meribah,
as they were that day in the desert at Massah.
There they put me to the test and tried me,
although they had seen what I did for them.
For forty years I was disgusted with those people.
I said, 'How disloyal they are!
They refuse to obey my commands.'
I was angry and made a solemn promise:
'You will never enter the land
where I would have given you rest.'

Cast [This is] the word of the Lord. **All Glory to the Father, and to the Son, and to the Holy Spirit:**
All Thanks be to God.   OR   **as it was in the beginning, is now, and shall be for ever. Amen.**

Cast: **Psalmist, Worshippers 1 and 2, The Lord.**

Invitation to worship
From Psalm 95.1–7 (LIT)

Leader 1

Come, let's joyfully praise our God,
acclaiming the Rock of our salvation.

Leader 2

Come before him with thanksgiving,
and greet him with melody.

**All (group 1)
All (group 2)**

**Our God is a great God:
a king above all other gods!**

**All (group 1)
All (group 2)**

**The depths of the earth are in his hands:
the mountain peaks belong to him.**

**All (group 1)
All (group 2)**

**The sea is his—he made it!
his hands have fashioned all the earth.**

Leader 1	Come, bow down to worship him.
Leader 2	Kneel before the Lord who made us.
All (groups 1 & 2)	**We are his people: the sheep of his flock.**
Leader 1	Let us trust in him today.
Leader 2	Please listen to his voice!
All	**Glory to the Father, and to the Son, and to the Holy Spirit: as it was in the beginning, is now, and shall be for ever. Amen.**

Cast: **Leader 1**, **Leader 2**, **All** (group 1—two or more persons/part of congregation), **All** (group 2—two or more persons/part of congregation).

God, the supreme king
Psalm 96.1–13

Leader 1	Sing a new song to the Lord!
Leader 2	Sing to the Lord, all the world!
Leader 3	Sing to the Lord, and praise him!
Leader 1	Proclaim every day the good news that he has saved us.
Leader 2	Proclaim his glory to the nations—
Leader 3	His mighty deeds to all peoples.
Worshipper 1	The Lord is great and is to be highly praised;
Worshipper 2	He is to be honoured more than all the gods.
Worshipper 1	The gods of all other nations are only idols, but the Lord created the heavens.
Worshippers 1 and 2	Glory and majesty surround him; power and beauty fill his Temple.
Leader 1	Praise the Lord, all people on earth—
Leader 2	Praise his glory and might.
Leader 3	Praise the Lord's glorious name—
Leader 1	Bring an offering and come into his Temple.
Leader 2	Bow down before the Holy One when he appears;
Leader 3	Tremble before him, all the earth!
Leader 1	Say to all the nations:
Cast/All	The Lord is king!
Worshipper 1	The earth is set firmly in place and cannot be moved.
Worshipper 2	He will judge the peoples with justice.
Leader 1	Be glad, earth and sky!
Leader 2	Roar, sea, and every creature in you!

Leader 3	Be glad, fields, and everything in you!
Worshipper 1	The trees in the woods will shout for joy when the Lord comes to rule the earth.
Worshipper 2	He will rule the peoples of the world with justice and fairness.

Cast [This is] the word of the Lord. **All** **Glory to the Father, and to the Son, and to the Holy Spirit:**
All **Thanks be to God.** OR **as it was in the beginning, is now, and shall be for ever. Amen.**

Cast: **Leader 1, Leader 2, Leader 3, Worshipper 1, Worshipper 2** (Worshippers 1 and 2 can be within or behind the congregation/audience).

God, the supreme king
From Psalm 96.1–13 (LIT)

Leader **All** (group 1)	Sing to the Lord a new song: **sing to the Lord, all the earth.**
Leader **All** (group 2)	Sing to the Lord, praise his name: **proclaim his salvation each day.**
Leader **All** (group 1)	Declare his glory among the nations: **his marvellous deeds among the peoples.**
Leader **All** (group 2)	Great is the Lord, and worthy of praise: **honour him above all gods.**
Leader **All** (group 1)	Splendour and majesty surround him: **power and beauty fill his temple.**
Leader **All** (group 2)	Praise the Lord all people on earth: **praise his glory and might.**
Leader **All** (group 1)	Give him the glory due to his name: **bring an offering into his temple.**
Leader **All** (group 2)	Worship the Lord in his beauty and holiness: **tremble before him all the earth.**
Leader **All**	Say to the nations: **The Lord is king!**
Leader **All** (group 1)	Let the heavens rejoice and the earth be glad: **let all creation sing for joy.**
Leader **All** (group 2)	For God shall come to judge the world: **and rule the people with his truth.**
All	**Glory to the Father, and to the Son, and to the Holy Spirit:** **as it was in the beginning, is now, and shall be for ever. Amen.**

Cast: **Leader, All** (group 1—two or more persons/part of congregation), **All** (group 2—two or more persons/part of congregation).

God, the supreme ruler
From Psalm 97.1–12 (LIT)

Leader		The Lord is king:
All		**the Lord is king!**
Leader		Let the whole wide earth rejoice:
All (group 1)		**let the islands all be glad.**
Leader		Thunder-clouds encircle him:
All (group 2)		**truth and justice are his throne.**
Leader		Fire shall go before the Lord:
All (group 3)		**burning up his enemies.**
Leader		Lightning strikes the darkened world:
All (group 1)		**all the people see and fear.**
Leader		Mountains melt before our God:
All (group 2)		**he is Lord of all the earth.**
Leader		Skies proclaim his righteousness:
All (group 3)		**nations see his glory now.**
Leader		Idol-worshippers are shamed:
All (group 1)		**gods bow down before the Lord.**
Leader		Let Jerusalem rejoice:
All (group 2)		**in your faithful judgements, Lord!**
Leader		Sovereign of the universe:
All (group 3)		**mightier still than all the gods!**
Leader		Yet you help your saints, O Lord:
All (group 1)		**saving them from wicked men.**
Leader		Light will shine upon the good:
All (group 2)		**gladness fill the righteous heart.**
Leader		Now recall what God has done:
All (group 3)		**thank him,**
All (group 2)		**praise him,**
All		**and rejoice!**
All		**Glory to the Father, and to the Son, and to the Holy Spirit:** **as it was in the beginning, is now, and shall be for ever. Amen.**

Cast: **Leader, All** (group 1—two or more persons/part of congregation), **All** (group 2—two or more persons/part of congregation) **All,** (group 3—two or more persons/part of congregation).

God, the ruler of the world
From Psalm 98.1–9 (LIT)

Leader		Sing to the Lord a new song:
All		**for he has done marvellous things.**
Leader		His right hand and his holy arm:
All		**have brought a great triumph to us.** →

All (group 1)	**He lets his salvation be known:**
All (group 2)	**his righteousness shines in the world.**
All (group 1)	**To us he continues his love:**
All (group 2)	**his glory is witnessed by all.**
Leader	Shout for joy to the Lord, all the earth:
All	**and burst into jubilant song.**
All (group 1)	**Make music to God with the harp:**
All (group 2)	**with songs and the sound of your praise.**
All (group 1)	**With trumpets and blast of the horn:**
All (group 2)	**sing praises to God as your king.**
Leader	Let rivers and streams clap their hands:
All	**the mountains together sing praise.**
Leader	The Lord comes to judge the whole earth:
All	**in righteousness God rules the world.**
All	**Glory to the Father, and to the Son, and to the Holy Spirit: as it was in the beginning, is now, and shall be for ever. Amen.**

Cast: **Leader, All** (group 1—two or more persons/part of congregation), **All** (group 2—two or more persons/part of congregation).

God, the supreme king
From Psalm 99.1–9 (LIT)

Leader 1	The Lord reigns:
All (group 1)	**let the nations tremble!**
Leader 2	He sits enthroned on high:
All (group 2)	**let the earth shake!**
Leader 1	Great is the Lord our God:
All (group 1)	**exalted over all the world.**
Leader 2	Let the nations praise his awesome name, and say:
All (group 2)	**God is holy!**
Leader 1	Praise the Lord our God, and worship at his feet:
All (group 1)	**God is holy!**
Leader 2	Exalt the Lord our God, and worship on his holy mountain:
All	**The Lord our God is holy!**
All	**Glory to the Father, and to the Son, and to the Holy Spirit: as it was in the beginning, is now, and shall be for ever. Amen.**

Cast: **Leader 1, Leader 2, All** (group 1—two or more persons/part of congregation), **All** (group 2—two or more persons/part of congregation).

A hymn of praise
From Psalm 100.1–5 (LIT)

Leader	Rejoice in the Lord, all the earth:
All	**worship the Lord with gladness.**

Leader	Remember the Lord is our God:
All	**we are his flock and he made us.**
Leader	Come to his temple with praise:
All	**enter his gates with thanksgiving.**
Leader	The love of the Lord will not fail:
All	**God will be faithful for ever.**
All	**Glory to the Father, and to the Son, and to the Holy Spirit:** **as it was in the beginning, is now, and shall be for ever. Amen.**

Cast: **Leader, All** (two or more persons/congregation).

The love of God
From Psalm 103.1–22 (LIT)

Leader	Praise the Lord, my soul:
All	**all my being, praise his holy name!**
Leader	Praise the Lord, my soul:
All	**and do not forget how generous he is.**
All (group 1)	**He forgives all my sins:**
All (group 2)	**and heals all my diseases.**
All (group 1)	**He keeps me from the grave:**
All (group 2)	**and blesses me with love and mercy.**
Leader	The Lord is gracious and compassionate:
All (group 1)	**slow to become angry,**
All (group 2)	**and full of constant love.**
All (group 1)	**He does not keep on rebuking:**
All (group 2)	**he is not angry for ever.**
All (group 1)	**He does not punish us as we deserve:**
All (group 2)	**or repay us for our wrongs.**
All (group 1)	**As far as the east is from the west:**
All (group 2)	**so far does he remove our sins from us.**
Leader	As kind as a Father to his children:
All (group 1)	**so kind is the Lord to those who honour him.**
Leader	Praise the Lord, all his creation:
All	**praise the Lord, my soul!**
All	**Glory to the Father, and to the Son, and to the Holy Spirit:** **as it was in the beginning, is now, and shall be for ever. Amen.**

Cast: **Leader, All** (group 1—two or more persons/part of congregation), **All** (group 2—two or more persons/part of congregation).

In praise of the Creator
From Psalm 104.1–4, 29–30 (LIT)

Leader	O Lord our God, you are very great:
All	**you are clothed with splendour and majesty.**

→

All (group 1)	**You make winds your messengers:**
All (group 2)	**and flashes of fire your servants.**
All (group 1)	**How many are your works:**
All (group 2)	**the earth is full of your creatures!**
Leader	When you hide your face, they are afraid:
All (group 1)	**when you take away their breath, they die.**
Leader	When you send your Spirit they are created:
All	**and you renew the face of the earth.**
All	**Glory to the Father, and to the Son, and to the Holy Spirit:**
	as it was in the beginning, is now, and shall be for ever. Amen.

Cast: **Leader, All** (group 1—two or more persons/part of congregation), **All** (group 2—two or more persons/part of congregation). (See also choral version below.)

Praise the Lord, my soul
From Psalm 104.1–34 (choral version)

All	O Lord, our God, how great you are!
Light people	You are clothed with majesty and glory, you cover yourself with light.
Sky people	You spread out the heavens like a tent and build your home on the waters above; you use the clouds as your chariot and ride on the wings of the wind.
Light people	You use the winds as your messengers and flashes of lightning as your servants.
Deep voices	You have set the earth firmly on its foundations, and it will never be moved.
Water people	You placed the ocean over it like a robe, and the water covered the mountains.
Deep voices	When you rebuked the waters—
Water people	They fled!
Deep voices	They rushed when they heard the shout of your command.
Water people	They flowed over the mountains and into the valleys, to the place you had made for them.
Deep voices	You set a boundary they can never pass, to keep them from covering the earth again.
Water people	You make springs flow in the valleys, and rivers run between the hills.
Animals	They provide water for the wild animals; there the wild donkeys quench their thirst.
Birds	In the trees near by, the birds make their nests and sing.

538

Sky people	From the sky you send rain on the hills, and the earth is filled with your blessings.
Animals	You make grass grow for the cattle—
Man	And plants for man to use, so that he can grow crops—
Woman	And produce wine to make him happy.
Man	Olive-oil—
Woman	To make him cheerful.
Man	And bread—
Woman	To give him strength.
Deep voices	The cedars of Lebanon—
Water people	Get plenty of rain—
Deep voices	The Lord's own trees which he planted.
Birds	There the birds build their nests, the storks nest in the fir trees.
Animals	The wild goats live in the high mountains, and the rock-badgers hide in the cliffs.
Light people	You created the moon to mark the months; the sun knows the time to set.
Deep voices	You made the night, and in the darkness—
Animals	All the wild animals come out. The young lions roar while they hunt, looking for the food that God provides.
Light people	When the sun rises—
Animals	They go back and lie down in their dens.
Man & **woman**	Then people go out to do their work and keep working until evening.
All	Lord, you made so many things! How wisely you made them all! The earth is filled with your creatures.
Water people	There is the ocean, large and wide—
Animals	Where countless creatures live, large and small alike.
Man	The ships sail on it—
Animals	And in it plays—
Deep voices	Leviathan—
Animals	The sea-monster which you made.
Woman	All of them depend on you to give them food when they need it.
Man	You give it to them and they eat it.

All	You provide food and they are satisfied.
Man	When you turn away they are afraid.
All	When you take away their breath (PAUSE) they die—
Man	And go back to the dust from which they came.
Woman	But when you give them breath—
All	They are created.
Woman	You give new life to the earth.
Light people	May the glory of God last for ever!
Animals	May the Lord be happy with what he has made!
Deep voices	He looks at the earth and it trembles: he touches the mountains—
Sky and water people	And they pour out smoke.
Man	I will sing to the Lord all my life.
Woman	As long as I live I will sing praises to my God.
All	May he be pleased with our song!

Cast [This is] the word of the Lord. **All Glory to the Father, and to the Son, and to the Holy Spirit:**
All   Thanks be to God.   OR   **as it was in the beginning, is now, and shall be for ever. Amen.**

Cast: **Light people, Sky people, Deep voices, Water people, Animals, Birds, Man, Woman.** (This reading is arranged for choral speaking. Properties—such as torches/lamps for light people, blue cloth for sky and water people, costumes for animals—can be used by children. See also short version above).

God and his people
From Psalm 105.1–45 (LIT)

Leader 1	Give thanks to the Lord, praise his name:
All (group 1)	**tell the nations what he has done.**
Leader 2	Sing to him, sing praise to him:
All (group 2)	**tell of all his wonderful deeds.**
Leader 1	Glory in his holy name:
All (group 1)	**let all who worship him rejoice.**
Leader 2	Go to the Lord for help:
All (group 2)	**and worship him for ever.**
Leader 1	Remember the wonders he does:
All (group 1)	**the miracles he performs.**
Leader 2	He is the Lord our God:
All (group 2)	**he judges the whole wide earth.**
Leader 1	He keeps his word and covenant:
All (group 1)	**for a thousand generations.**

Leader 2	The covenant he made with Abraham:
All (group 2)	**the oath he swore to Israel.**
Leader 1	He brought them out of Egypt:
All (group 1)	**and none of them was lost.**
Leader 2	He gave a cloud for covering:
All (group 2)	**a pillar of fire by night.**
Leader 1	He gave them bread from heaven:
All (group 1)	**and water from the rock.**
Leader 2	He brought his people out rejoicing:
All (group 2)	**his chosen ones with shouts of joy.**
All	**Praise the Lord!**
All	**Glory to the Father, and to the Son, and to the Holy Spirit: as it was in the beginning, is now, and shall be for ever. Amen.**

Cast: **Leader 1, All** (group 1—two or more persons/part of congregation), **Leader 2, All** (group 2—two or more persons/part of congregation).

In praise of God's goodness
From Psalm 107.1–31 (LIT)

Leader	Give thanks to the Lord, for he is good:
All	**his love endures for ever.**
Leader	Repeat these words in praise to the Lord:
All (group 1)	**all those he has redeemed.**
Leader	Some sailed the ocean in ships:
All (group 2)	**they earned their way on the seas.**
Leader	They saw what the Lord can do:
All (group 3)	**his wonderful deeds in the deep.**
Leader	For he spoke and stirred up a storm:
All (group 1)	**and lifted high the waves.**
Leader	Their ships were thrown in the air:
All (group 2)	**and plunged into the depths.**
Leader	Their courage melted away:
All (group 3)	**they reeled like drunken men.**
Leader	They came to the end of themselves:
All (group 1)	**and cried to the Lord in their trouble.**
Leader	He brought them out of distress:
All (group 2)	**and stilled the raging storm.**
Leader	They were glad because of the calm:
All (group 3)	**he brought them safely to harbour.**

→

541

Leader	Let them give thanks to the Lord:
All	**for his unfailing love.**

All	**Glory to the Father, and to the Son, and to the Holy Spirit:**
	as it was in the beginning, is now, and shall be for ever. Amen.

Cast: **Leader, All** (group 1—two or more persons/part of congregation), **All** (group 2—two or more persons/part of congregation), **All** (group 3—two or more persons/part of congregation).

The Lord and his chosen king
Psalm 110.1–7

Psalmist	The Lord said to my lord, the king,
The Lord	Sit here at my right
	until I put your enemies under your feet.
Psalmist	From Zion the Lord will extend your royal power.
	He says:
The Lord	Rule over your enemies.
Psalmist	On the day you fight your enemies,
	your people will volunteer.
	Like the dew of early morning
	your young men will come to you on the sacred hills. (PAUSE)
	The Lord made a solemn promise and will not take it back:
The Lord	You will be a priest for ever
	in the priestly order of Melchizedek.
Psalmist	The Lord is at your right side;
	when he becomes angry, he will defeat kings.
	He will pass judgement on the nations
	and fill the battlefield with corpses;
	he will defeat kings all over the earth.
	The king will drink from the stream by the road,
	and strengthened, he will stand victorious.

Cast [This is] the word of the Lord.   **All Glory to the Father, and to the Son, and to the Holy Spirit:**
All   Thanks be to God.   OR   **as it was in the beginning, is now, and shall be for ever. Amen.**

Cast: **Psalmist, The Lord.**

In praise of the Lord
From Psalm 111.1–10 (LIT)

Leader 1	Praise the Lord:
All	**praise the Lord!**
Leader 2	With my whole heart I will thank the Lord: in the company of his
	people. Great are the works of the Lord:
All	**those who marvel seek them.**

Leader 2	Glorious and majestic are his deeds:
All	**his goodness lasts for ever.**
Leader 2	He reminds us of his works of grace:
All	**he is merciful and kind.**
Leader 2	He sustains those who fear him:
All	**he keeps his covenant always.**
Leader 2	All he does is right and just:
All	**all his words are faithful.**
Leader 2	They will last for ever and ever:
All	**and be kept in faith and truth.**
Leader 1	He provided redemption for his people, and made an eternal covenant with them:
All	**holy and awesome is his name!**
Leader 1	The fear of the Lord is the beginning of wisdom; he gives understanding to those who obey:
All	**to God belongs eternal praise!**
All	**Glory to the Father, and to the Son, and to the Holy Spirit: as it was in the beginning, is now, and shall be for ever. Amen.**

Cast: **Leader 1, Leader 2,** (can be the same as Leader 1), **All** (two or more persons/congregation).

In praise of the Lord's goodness
From Psalm 113.1–9 (LIT)

Leaders 1 and 2	Praise the Lord:
All	**praise the Lord!**
Leader 2	You servants of the Lord, praise his name:
All	**let the name of the Lord be praised, both now and for evermore!**
Leader 1	From the rising of the sun to the place where it sets:
All	**the name of the Lord be praised!**
Leader 2	The Lord is exalted above the earth:
All	**his glory over the heavens.**
Leader 1	Who is like the Lord our God?
All	**He is throned in the heights above—**
Leader 2	Yet he bends down:
All	**he stoops to look at our world.**
Leader 1	He raises the poor from the dust:
All	**and lifts the needy from their sorrow.**
Leader 2	He honours the childless wife in her home:
All	**he makes her happy, the mother of children.**

→

| Leaders 1 and 2 | Praise the Lord: |
| **All** | **Amen.** |

| All | **Glory to the Father, and to the Son, and to the Holy Spirit:**
as it was in the beginning, is now, and shall be for ever. Amen. |

Cast: **Leader 1, Leader 2, All** (two or more persons/congregation).

A Passover song
Psalm 114.1–8

Psalmist	When the people of Israel left Egypt, when Jacob's descendants left that foreign land, Judah became the Lord's holy people, Israel became his own possession.
Worshipper 1	The Red Sea looked and ran away; the River Jordan stopped flowing.
Worshipper 2	The mountains skipped like goats; the hills jumped about like lambs.
Enquirer 1	What happened, Sea, to make you run away?
Enquirer 2	And you, O Jordan, why did you stop flowing?
Enquirer 1	You mountains, why did you skip like goats?
Enquirer 2	You hills, why did you jump about like lambs?
Psalmist	Tremble, earth, at the Lord's coming, at the presence of the God of Jacob, who changes rocks into pools of water and solid cliffs into flowing springs.

Cast [This is] the word of the Lord. **All** Glory to the Father, and to the Son, and to the Holy Spirit:
All Thanks be to God. OR as it was in the beginning, is now, and shall be for ever. Amen.

Cast: **Psalmist, Worshipper 1, Worshipper 2, Enquirer 1, Enquirer 2.**

The one true God
Psalm 115.1–18

Psalmist	To you alone, O Lord, to you alone, and not to us, must glory be given because of your constant love and faithfulness. (PAUSE)
Worshipper 1	Why should the nations ask us:
Enquirer	Where is your God?
Worshipper 1	Our God is in heaven; he does whatever he wishes. *Their* gods are made of silver and gold, formed by human hands.
Worshipper 2	They have mouths, but cannot speak, and eyes, but cannot see.

Worshipper 1	They have ears, but cannot hear, and noses, but cannot smell.
Worshipper 2	They have hands, but cannot feel, and feet, but cannot walk; they cannot make a sound.
Psalmist	May all who made them and who trust in them become like the idols they have made. (PAUSE)
	Trust in the Lord, you people of Israel—
Worshippers 1 and 2	He helps you and protects you.
Psalmist	Trust in the Lord, you priests of God—
Priests 1 and 2	He helps you and protects you.
Psalmist	Trust in the Lord, all you that worship him—
Worshippers 1 and 2	He helps you and protects you.
Psalmist	The Lord remembers us and will bless us; he will bless the people of Israel and all the priests of God. He will bless everyone who honours him, the great and the small alike.
Priest 1	May the Lord give you children— you and your descendants!
Priest 2	May you be blessed by the Lord, who made heaven and earth!
Psalmist	Heaven belongs to the Lord alone, but he gave the earth to man. The Lord is not praised by the dead, by any who go down to the land of silence. But we, the living, will give thanks to him now and for ever.
Worshippers and Priests	Praise the Lord!

Cast [This is] the word of the Lord. **All** Glory to the Father, and to the Son, and to the Holy Spirit:
All Thanks be to God. OR as it was in the beginning, is now, and shall be for ever. Amen.

Cast: **Psalmist, Worshipper 1, Enquirer, Worshipper 2, Priest 1** (can be the same as Enquirer), **Priest 2** (can be the same as Priest 1).

A testimony of salvation
Psalm 116.1–19

Psalmist	I love the Lord, because he hears me; he listens to my prayers. He listens to me every time I call to him.

545

→

	The danger of death was all round me; the horrors of the grave closed in on me; I was filled with fear and anxiety. Then I called to the Lord,
Young Psalmist	I beg you, Lord, save me!
Psalmist	The Lord is merciful and good; our God is compassionate. The Lord protects the helpless; when I was in danger, he saved me. Be confident, my heart, because the Lord has been good to me.
	The Lord saved me from death; he stopped my tears and kept me from defeat. And so I walk in the presence of the Lord in the world of the living. I kept on believing, even when I said:
Young Psalmist	I am completely crushed.
Psalmist	Even when I was afraid and said:
Young Psalmist (bitterly)	No one can be trusted. (PAUSE)
Psalmist	What can I offer the Lord for all his goodness to me? I will bring a wine-offering to the Lord, to thank him for saving me. In the assembly of all his people I will give him what I have promised. (PAUSE)
	How painful it is to the Lord when one of his people dies! I am your servant, Lord; I serve you, just as my mother did.
	You have saved me from death. I will give you a sacrifice of thanksgiving and offer my prayer to you. In the assembly of all your people, in the sanctuary of your Temple in Jerusalem, I will give you what I have promised.
Psalmist and **Young** **Psalmist**	Praise the Lord!

Cast [This is] the word of the Lord.   **All** **Glory to the Father, and to the Son, and to the Holy Spirit:**
All   **Thanks be to God.**   OR   **as it was in the beginning, is now, and shall be for ever. Amen.**

Cast: **Psalmist, Young Psalmist.**

Praising God, who saves from death
From Psalm 116.1–19 (LIT)

Leader	I love the Lord because he heard my voice:
All (group 1)	**the Lord in mercy listened to my prayers.**
Leader	Because the Lord has turned his ear to me:
All (group 2)	**I'll call on him as long as I shall live.**
Leader	The cords of death entangled me around:
All (group 3)	**the horrors of the grave came over me.**
Leader	But then I called upon the Lord my God:
All (group 1)	**I said to him: 'O Lord, I beg you, save!'**
Leader	The Lord our God is merciful and good:
All (group 2)	**the Lord protects the simple-hearted ones.**
Leader	The Lord saved me from death and stopped my tears:
All (group 3)	**he saved me from defeat and picked me up.**
Leader	And so I walk before him all my days:
All (group 1)	**and live to love and praise his holy name.**
Leader	What shall I give the Lord for all his grace?
All (group 2)	**I'll take his saving cup, and pay my vows.**
Leader	Within the congregation of his saints:
All (group 3)	**I'll offer him my sacrifice of praise.**
Leader	Praise the Lord:
All	**Amen, amen!**
All	**Glory to the Father, and to the Son, and to the Holy Spirit: as it was in the beginning, is now, and shall be for ever. Amen.**

Cast: **Leader, All** (group 1—two or more persons/part of congregation), **All,** (group 2—two or more persons/part of congregation), **All** (group 3—two or more persons/part of congregation).

In praise of the Lord
From Psalm 117.1–2 (LIT)

Leader	Praise the Lord, all you nations:
All (group 1)	**praise him, all you people!**
Leader	Great is his love towards us:
All (group 2)	**his faithfulness shall last for ever.**
Leader	Praise the Lord:
All	**Amen.**
All	**Glory to the Father, and to the Son, and to the Holy Spirit: as it was in the beginning, is now, and shall be for ever. Amen.**

Cast: **Leader, All** (group 1—two or more persons/part of congregation), **All** (group 2—two or more persons/part of congregation).

A prayer of thanks for victory
Psalm 118.1–29

Leader	Give thanks to the Lord, because he is good, and his love is eternal. (PAUSE)
	Let the people of Israel say:
Worshippers 1 and **2**	His love is eternal.
Leader	Let the priests of God say:
Priests 1 and **2**	His love is eternal.
Leader	Let all who worship him say:
Worshippers and **Priests**	His love is eternal.
Worshipper 1	In my distress I called to the Lord; he answered me and set me free.
Worshipper 2	The Lord is with me, I will not be afraid; what can anyone do to me?
Worshipper 1	It is the Lord who helps me, and I will see my enemies defeated.
Worshipper 2	It is better to trust in the Lord than to depend on man.
Worshipper 1	It is better to trust in the Lord than to depend on human leaders.
	Many enemies were round me—
Worshipper 2	But I destroyed them by the power of the Lord!
Worshipper 1	They were round me on every side—
Worshipper 2	But I destroyed them by the power of the Lord!
Worshipper 1	They swarmed round me like bees, but they burnt out as quickly as a fire among thorns.
Worshipper 2	By the power of the Lord I destroyed them.
Worshipper 1	I was fiercely attacked and was being defeated—
Worshipper 2	But the Lord helped me.
Worshipper 1	The Lord makes me powerful and strong—
Worshippers 1 and **2**	He has saved me. (PAUSE)
Victor (at a distance)	Listen to the glad shouts of victory in the tents of God's people:
Worshippers 1 and **2**	The Lord's mighty power has done it!

Victor (at a distance)	His power has brought us victory— his mighty power in battle!
Worshipper 1	I will not die; instead, I will live and proclaim what the Lord has done.
Worshipper 2	He has punished me severely, but he has not let me die.
Victor (at a distance)	Open to me the gates of the Temple; I will go in and give thanks to the Lord!
Priest 1	This is the gate of the Lord; only the righteous can come in.
Victor (closer)	I praise you, Lord, because you heard me, because you have given me victory.
Leader	The stone which the builders rejected as worthless turned out to be the most important of all.
Priests 1 and **2**	This was done by the Lord; what a wonderful sight it is!
Leader	This is the day of the Lord's victory: let us be happy, let us celebrate!
Worshippers **1** and **2**	Save us, Lord, save us!
Worshippers and **Priests**	Give us success, O Lord!
Priest 1	May God bless the one who comes in the name of the Lord!
Priest 2	From the Temple of the Lord we bless you.
Worshippers **1** and **2**	The Lord is God; he has been good to us.
Leader	With branches in your hands, start the festival and march round the altar.
Victor (near cast)	You are my God, and I give you thanks; I will proclaim your greatness.
Leader	Give thanks to the Lord, because he is good—
Victor, **Worshippers** and **Priests**	And his love is eternal!

Cast [This is] the word of the Lord. **All Glory to the Father, and to the Son, and to the Holy Spirit:**
All Thanks be to God. OR **as it was in the beginning, is now, and shall be for ever. Amen.**

Cast: **Leader, Worshipper 1, Worshipper 2, Priest 1, Priest 2, Victor** (The Victor should begin at the back of the audience/congregation—or outside a door—and move forward in two stages as indicated).

Thanking God for victory
From Psalm 118.1–29 (LIT)

Leader	Give thanks to the Lord, for he is good:
All	**his love endures for ever.**
Leader	All those who fear the Lord shall say:
All	**His love endures for ever.**
Worshipper	Open for me the gates of the temple; I will go in and give thanks to the Lord.
Leader	This is the gate of the Lord, only the righteous can come in.
Worshipper	I will give thanks because you heard me; you have become my salvation.
Choir	The stone which the builders rejected as worthless turned out to be the most important of all:
All (group 1)	**The Lord has done this—**
All (group 2)	**what a wonderful sight it is!**
Choir	This is the day of the Lord's victory—let us be happy, let us celebrate:
All (group 1)	**O Lord save us—**
All (group 2)	**O Lord, grant us success.**
Leader	May God bless the one who comes in the name of the Lord:
All (group 1)	**The Lord is God—**
All (group 2)	**he has been good to us!**
Choir	From the temple of the Lord, we bless you.
Director (in matter-of-fact tone)	With branches in your hands, start the procession and march round the altar:
All (group 1)	**You are my God and I will give you thanks.**
All (group 2)	**You are my God, and I will exalt you.**
Leader	Give thanks to the Lord, for he is good:
All	**His love endures for ever.**
All	**Glory to the Father, and to the Son, and to the Holy Spirit:** **as it was in the beginning, is now, and shall be for ever. Amen.**

Cast: **Leader, Worshipper, Choir, Director** (can be the same as Leader), **All** (group 1—two or more persons/part of congregation), **All** (group 2—two or more persons/part of congregation).

The Lord, our protector
Psalm 121.1–8

Pilgrim	I look to the mountains; where will my help come from? (PAUSE) My help will come from the Lord, who made heaven and earth.
Adviser 1	He will not let you fall; your protector is always awake.

Adviser 2	The protector of Israel never dozes or sleeps.
Adviser 1	The Lord will guard you; he is by your side to protect you.
Adviser 2	The sun will not hurt you during the day, nor the moon during the night.
Adviser 1	The Lord will protect you from all danger; he will keep you safe.
Adviser 2	He will protect you as you come and go now and for ever.

Cast [This is] the word of the Lord. **All Glory to the Father, and to the Son, and to the Holy Spirit:**
All Thanks be to God. OR **as it was in the beginning, is now, and shall be for ever. Amen.**

Cast: **Pilgrim, Adviser 1, Adviser 2.**

In praise of Jerusalem
Psalm 122.1–9

Psalmist	I was glad when they said to me:
Worshippers **1 and 2**	Let us go to the Lord's house.
Psalmist	And now we are here, standing inside the gates of Jerusalem! (PAUSE)
	Jerusalem is a city restored in beautiful order and harmony. This is where the tribes come, the tribes of Israel, to give thanks to the Lord according to his command. Here the kings of Israel sat to judge their people. (PAUSE)
	Pray for the peace of Jerusalem:
Worshipper 1	May those who love you prosper.
Worshipper 2	May there be peace inside your walls and safety in your palaces.
Psalmist	For the sake of my relatives and friends I say to Jerusalem:
Worshippers **1 and 2**	Peace be with you!
Psalmist	For the sake of the house of the Lord our God I pray for your prosperity.

Cast [This is] the word of the Lord. **All Glory to the Father, and to the Son, and to the Holy Spirit:**
All Thanks be to God. OR **as it was in the beginning, is now, and shall be for ever. Amen.**

Cast: **Psalmist, Worshipper 1, Worshipper 2.**

In praise of Jerusalem
From Psalm 122.1–8 (LIT)

Leader	I was glad when they said to me:
All	**let us go to the house of the Lord!**
Leader	Pray for the peace of Jerusalem:
All (group 1)	**may those who love our land be blessed.**
Leader	May there be peace in your homes:
All (group 2)	**and safety for our families.**
Leader	For the sake of those we love we say:
All	**Let there be peace!**
All	**Glory to the Father, and to the Son, and to the Holy Spirit:**
	as it was in the beginning, is now, and shall be for ever. Amen.

Cast: **Leader**, **All** (group 1, preferabley male voices—two or more persons/part of congregation), **All** (group 2, preferably female voices—two or more persons/part of congregation).

God, the protector of his people
Psalm 124.1–8

Leader	What if the Lord had not been on our side?
	Answer, O Israel!
Worshipper 1	If the Lord had not been on our side
	when our enemies attacked us,
Worshipper 2	Then they would have swallowed us alive
	in their furious anger against us;
Worshipper 3	Then the flood would have carried us away,
Worshipper 2	The water would have covered us,
Worshipper 3	The raging torrent would have drowned us.
Leader	Let us thank the Lord,
	who has not let our enemies destroy us.
Worshipper 1	We have escaped like a bird from a hunter's trap.
Worshipper 2	The trap is broken, and we are free!
Cast	Our help comes from the Lord,
	who made heaven and earth.

Cast [This is] the word of the Lord.   **All Glory to the Father, and to the Son, and to the Holy Spirit:**
All   Thanks be to God.   OR   **as it was in the beginning, is now, and shall be for ever. Amen.**

Cast: **Leader, Worshipper 1, Worshipper 2, Worshipper 3.**

God, the protector of his people
Psalm 124.1–8 (LIT)

Leader	If the Lord had not been on our side—now let Israel say:
All	**If the Lord had not been on our side—**
All (group 1)	**when enemies attacked us,**
All (group 2)	**when their anger flared against us,**
All (group 3)	**they would have swallowed us alive.**
All (group 1)	**The flood would have engulfed us,**
All (group 2)	**the torrent would have swept over us,**
All (group 3)	**the waters would have have drowned us.**
Leader	Praise the Lord:
All (group 1)	**who has not given us up to their teeth.**
All (group 2)	**We have escaped like a bird from the snare:**
All (group 3)	**the snare is broken and we are free.**
Leader	Our help is in the name of the Lord:
All	**who made heaven and earth.**
All	**Glory to the Father, and to the Son, and to the Holy Spirit:**
	as it was in the beginning, is now, and shall be for ever. Amen.

Cast: **Leader, All** (group 1—two or more persons/part of congregation), **All** (group 2—two or more persons/part of congregation), **All** (group 3—two or more persons/part of congregation).

A prayer for deliverance
Psalm 126.1–6

Worshipper 1	When the Lord brought us back to Jerusalem, it was like a dream!
Worshipper 2	How we laughed, how we sang for joy!
Worshipper 1	Then the other nations said about us:
Person(s)	The Lord did great things for them.
Worshipper 1	Indeed he did great things for us!
Worshippers 1 and 2	How happy we were!
Exile 1	Lord, make us prosperous again, just as the rain brings water back to dry river-beds.
Exile 2	Let those who wept as they sowed their seed, gather the harvest with joy!
Psalmist	Those who wept as they went out carrying the seed will come back singing for joy, as they bring in the harvest.

Cast [This is] the word of the Lord. **All Glory to the Father, and to the Son, and to the Holy Spirit:**
All Thanks be to God. OR **as it was in the beginning, is now, and shall be for ever. Amen.**

Cast: **Worshipper 1, Worshipper 2, Person(s), Exile 1, Exile 2, Psalmist** (can be the same as Worshipper 1).

A prayer for deliverance
From Psalm 126.1–6 (LIT)

Leader   When the Lord brought us back from slavery:
All (group 1)   **we were like those who dream.**

Leader   Our mouths were filled with laughter:
All (group 2)   **our tongues with songs of joy.**

Leader   Then those around us said, 'The Lord has done great things for them':
All (group 1)   **The Lord has done great things for us, and we are filled with joy.**

Leader   Those who sow in tears
All (group 2)   **shall reap with songs of joy.**

All   **Glory to the Father, and to the Son, and to the Holy Spirit: as it was in the beginning, is now, and shall be for ever. Amen.**

Cast: **Leader, All** (group 1—two or more persons/part of congregation), **All** (group 2—two or more persons/part of congregation).

The reward of obedience to the Lord
Psalm 128.1–6

Psalmist   Happy are those who obey the Lord, who live by his commands.

Teacher 1   Your work will provide for your needs; you will be happy and prosperous.

Teacher 2   Your wife will be like a fruitful vine in your home—

Teacher 1   And your sons will be like young olive-trees round your table.

Psalmist   A man who obeys the Lord will surely be blessed like this.

Priest 1   May the Lord bless you from Zion!

Priest 2   May you see Jerusalem prosper all the days of your life!

Priest 1   May you live to see your grandchildren!

Priests 1 and **2**   Peace be with Israel!

Cast [This is] the word of the Lord.   **All Glory to the Father, and to the Son, and to the Holy Spirit:**
All Thanks be to God.   OR   **as it was in the beginning, is now, and shall be for ever. Amen.**

Cast: **Psalmist, Teacher 1, Teacher 2** (can be the same as Psalmist), **Priest 1, Priest 2.**

The reward of obedience to the Lord
From Psalm 128.1–6 (LIT)

Leader	The pilgrims' song:
All (group 1)	**Blessed are those who fear the Lord,**
All (group 2)	**who walk in his ways.**
Leader	You will eat the fruit of your work; blessings and prosperity will be yours:
All (group 1)	**Blessed are those who fear the Lord,**
All (group 2)	**who walk in his ways.**
Leader	Your wife will be like a fruitful vine within your house; your children will be like young olive trees around your table:
All (group 1)	**Blessed are those who fear the Lord,**
All (group 2)	**who walk in his ways.**
Leader	May the Lord bless you all the days of your life; may you have prosperity; may you live to see your children's children:
All	**Peace be with you.**
All	**Glory to the Father, and to the Son, and to the Holy Spirit: as it was in the beginning, is now, and shall be for ever. Amen.**

Cast: **Leader, All** (group 1—two or more persons/part of congregation), **All** (group 2—two or more persons/part of congregation).

A psalm about Israel's enemies
Psalm 129.1–8

Leader	Israel, tell us how your enemies have persecuted you ever since you were young.
Israel	Ever since I was young, my enemies have persecuted me cruelly, but they have not overcome me. They cut deep wounds in my back and made it like a ploughed field. But the Lord, the righteous one, has freed me from slavery.
Leader	May everyone who hates Zion be defeated and driven back. May they all be like grass growing on the house-tops, which dries up before it can grow; no one gathers it up or carries it away in bundles. No one who passes by will say:
Person 1	May the Lord bless you!
Person 2	We bless you in the name of the Lord.

Cast [This is] the word of the Lord. **All Glory to the Father, and to the Son, and to the Holy Spirit:**
All Thanks be to God. OR **as it was in the beginning, is now, and shall be for ever. Amen.**

Cast: **Leader, Israel, Person 1, Person 2** (can be the same as Person 1).

A prayer for help
Psalm 130.1–8

Supplicant From the depths of my despair I call to you, Lord.
Hear my cry, O Lord;
listen to my call for help!

Psalmist If you kept a record of our sins,
who could escape being condemned?
But you forgive us,
so that we should stand in awe of you.

Supplicant I wait eagerly for the Lord's help,
and in his word I trust.
I wait for the Lord
more eagerly than watchmen wait for the dawn—

Cast Than watchmen wait for the dawn.

Psalmist Israel, trust in the Lord,
because his love is constant
and he is always willing to save.
He will save his people Israel
from all their sins.

Cast [This is] the word of the Lord. **All** Glory to the Father, and to the Son, and to the Holy Spirit:
All Thanks be to God. OR as it was in the beginning, is now, and shall be for ever. Amen.

Cast: **Supplicant, Psalmist.**

In praise of the Temple
Psalm 132.1–18

Psalmist Lord, do not forget David
and all the hardships he endured.
Remember, Lord, what he promised,
the vow he made to you, the Mighty God of Jacob:

David I will not go home or go to bed;
I will not rest or sleep,
until I provide a place for the Lord,
a home for the Mighty God of Jacob.

Psalmist In Bethlehem we heard about the Covenant Box,
and we found it in the fields of Jearim.

We said:

Person 1 Let us go to the Lord's house.

Person 2 Let us worship before his throne.

Psalmist Come to the Temple, Lord, with the Covenant Box,
the symbol of your power,
and stay here for ever.
May your priests do always what is right;
may your people shout for joy!

You made a promise to your servant David;
do not reject your chosen king, Lord.
You made a solemn promise to David—
a promise you will not take back:

The Lord   I will make one of your sons king,
and he will rule after you.
If your sons are true to my covenant
and to the commands I give them,
their sons, also, will succeed you for all time as kings.

Psalmist   The Lord has chosen Zion;
he wants to make it his home:

The Lord   This is where I will live for ever;
this is where I want to rule.
I will richly provide Zion with all she needs;
I will satisfy her poor with food.
I will bless her priests in all they do,
and her people will sing and shout for joy.
Here I will make one of David's descendants a great king;
here I will preserve the rule of my chosen king.
I will cover his enemies with shame,
but his kingdom will prosper and flourish.

Cast [This is] the word of the Lord. **All** **Glory to the Father, and to the Son, and to the Holy Spirit:**
All   **Thanks be to God.**   OR   **as it was in the beginning, is now, and shall be for ever. Amen.**

Cast: **Psalmist, David, Person 1, Person 2** (can be the same as Person 1), **The Lord.**

A call to praise the Lord
From Psalm 134.1–3 (LIT)

Leader   You servants of the Lord,
who stand in his temple at night:
All (group 1)   **praise the Lord!**

Leader   Lift your hands in prayer to the Lord:
All (group 2)   **in his sanctuary, praise the Lord!**

Leader   May the Lord who made the heaven and earth bless you from Zion:
All   **Amen!**

All   **Glory to the Father, and to the Son, and to the Holy Spirit:**
as it was in the beginning, is now, and shall be for ever. Amen.

Cast: **Leader, All** (group 1—two or more persons/part of congregation), **All** (group 2—two or more persons/part of congregation).

A hymn of praise
Psalm 135.1–21

Psalmist   Praise the Lord!

Praise his name, you servants of the Lord,
who stand in the Lord's house,
in the Temple of our God.
Praise the Lord, because he is good;
sing praises to his name, because he is kind.
He chose Jacob for himself,
the people of Israel for his own.

Worshipper   I know that our Lord is great,
greater than all the gods.
He does whatever he wishes
in heaven and on earth,
in the seas and in the depths below.
He brings storm clouds from the ends of the earth;
he makes lightning for the storms,
and he brings out the wind from his storeroom.

[Psalmist   In Egypt he killed all the first-born
of men and animals alike.
There he performed miracles and wonders
to punish the king and all his officials.
He destroyed many nations
and killed powerful kings:
Sihon, king of the Amorites,
Og, king of Bashan,
and all the kings in Canaan.
He gave their lands to his people;
he gave them to Israel.] (PAUSE)

Worshipper   Lord, you will always be proclaimed as God;
all generations will remember you.

Psalmist   The Lord will defend his people;
he will take pity on his servants.

The gods of the nations are made of silver and gold;
they are formed by human hands.
They have mouths, but cannot speak,
and eyes, but cannot see.
They have ears, but cannot hear;
they are not even able to breathe.

Worshipper   May all who made them and who trust in them
become like the idols they have made!

Psalmist   Praise the Lord, people of Israel!

Worshipper   Praise him, you priests of God!

Psalmist   Praise the Lord, you Levites!

Psalmist and
  Worshipper   Praise him, all you that worship him!

Worshipper	Praise the Lord in Zion, in Jerusalem, his home.

Psalmist and Worshipper	Praise the Lord!

Cast [This is] the word of the Lord. **All** Glory to the Father, and to the Son, and to the Holy Spirit:
All   Thanks be to God.   OR   as it was in the beginning, is now, and shall be for ever. Amen.

Cast: **Psalmist, Worshipper.**

A hymn of thanksgiving
From Psalm 136.1–26 (LIT)

Leader 1 **All** (group 1)	Give thanks to God, for he is good: **his love shall last for ever!**
Leader 2 **All** (group 2)	Give thanks to him, the God of gods: **his love shall last for ever!**
Leader 3 **All** (group 3)	Give thanks to him, the Lord of lords: **his love shall last for ever!**
Leader 1 **All** (group 1)	For God alone works miracles: **his love shall last for ever!**
Leader 2 **All** (group 2)	The skies were made at his command: **his love shall last for ever!**
Leader 3 **All** (group 3)	He spread the seas upon the earth: **his love shall last for ever!**
Leader 1 **All** (group 1)	He made the stars to shine at night: **his love shall last for ever!**
Leader 2 **All** (group 2)	He made the sun to shine by day: **his love shall last for ever!**
Leader 3 **All** (group 3)	He brought us out from slavery: **his love shall last for ever!**
Leader 1 **All** (group 1)	He leads us onward by his grace: **his love shall last for ever!**
Leader 2 **All** (group 2)	He saves us from our enemies: **his love shall last for ever!**
Leader 3 **All**	Give thanks to God, for he is good: **his love shall last for ever!**

All	**Glory to the Father, and to the Son, and to the Holy Spirit:** **as it was in the beginning, is now, and shall be for ever. Amen.**

Cast: **Leader 1, Leader 2, Leader 3, All** (group 1—two or more persons/part of congregation), **All** (group 2—two or more persons/part of congregation), **All** (group 3—two or more persons/part of congregation). (This reading should not be used with a congregation unless it is divided into three parts.)

A lament of Israelites in exile
From Psalm 137.1–8

Israelite 1	By the rivers of Babylon we sat down; there we wept when we remembered Zion.
Israelite 2	On the willows near by we hung up our harps.
Israelite 1	Those who captured us told us to sing; they told us to entertain them:
Enemies	Sing us a song about Zion.
Israelite 1	How can we sing a song to the Lord in a foreign land?
Israelite 2	May I never be able to play the harp again if I forget you, Jerusalem!
Israelite 1	May I never be able to sing again if I do not remember you, if I do not think of you as my greatest joy!
Israelite 2	Remember, Lord, what the Edomites did the day Jerusalem was captured. Remember how they kept saying:
Enemies	Tear it down to the ground!
Israelites 1 and **2**	Babylon!
Israelite 1	You will be destroyed.

Cast [This is] the word of the Lord. **All** Glory to the Father, and to the Son, and to the Holy Spirit:
All   Thanks be to God.   OR   as it was in the beginning, is now, and shall be for ever. Amen.

Cast: **Israelite 1, Israelite 2, Enemies** (two or more).

Prayer for the help of God's Spirit
From Psalm 143.6–10, and Psalm 51.6–12 (LIT)

Leader **All**	O Lord, I spread my hands out to you: **I thirst for you like dry ground.**
Leader **All**	Teach me to do your will, for you are my God: **let your good Spirit lead me in safety.**
Leader **All**	You require sincerity and truth in me: **fill my mind with your wisdom.**
Leader **All**	Create in me a pure heart, O God: **and renew a faithful spirit in me.**
Leader **All**	Do not cast me from your presence: **or take your Holy Spirit from me.**

Leader	Give me again the joy of your salvation:
All	**and make me willing to obey.**

All	**Glory to the Father, and to the Son, and to the Holy Spirit:**
	as it was in the beginning, is now, and shall be for ever. Amen.

Cast: **Leader, All** (two or more persons/congregation). (Psalms 143 and 51 have been grouped together to make provision for an occasion when the person and work of the Holy Spirit is being considered.)

In praise of God the almighty
From Psalm 147.1–20 (LIT)

Leader	O praise the Lord, sing out to God:
All	**such praise is right and good.**

Leader	The Lord restores Jerusalem:
All (group 1)	**he brings the exiles home.**

Leader	He heals all those with broken hearts:
All (group 2)	**he bandages their wounds.**

Leader	He counts the number of the stars:
All (group 3)	**he calls them each by name.**

Leader	How great and mighty is the Lord:
All (group 1)	**immeasurably wise!**

Leader	He raises up the humble ones:
All (group 2)	**and brings the mighty down.**

Leader	Sing hymns of triumph to his name:
All (group 3)	**make music to our God!**

Leader	He spreads the clouds across the sky:
All (group 1)	**he showers the earth with rain.**

Leader	He sends the animals their food:
All (group 2)	**he feeds the hungry birds.**

Leader	His true delight is not the strong:
All (group 3)	**but those who trust his love.**

Leader	Extol the Lord, Jerusalem:
All (group 1)	**let Zion worship God!**

Leader	For God shall keep your people safe:
All (group 2)	**and bring your harvest home.**

Leader	He gives commandment to the earth:
All (group 3)	**his will is quickly done.**

Leader	He spreads like wool the falling snow:
All (group 1)	**how cold the frosty air!**

Leader	He sends the wind, the warming rain:
All (group 2)	**and melts the ice away.**

Leader	His laws he gives to Israel:
All (group 3)	**and Judah hears his word.**

→

Leader	He does not favour other lands:
All	**so, praise the Lord. Amen!**

All	**Glory to the Father, and to the Son, and to the Holy Spirit:**
	as it was in the beginning, is now, and shall be for ever. Amen.

Cast: **Leader, All** (group 1—two or more persons/part of congregation), **All** (group 2—two or more persons/part of congregation), **All** (group 3—two or more persons/part of congregation).

Let the universe praise God!
From Psalm 148.1–14 (LIT)

All	**Praise the Lord!**
Leader 1	Praise the Lord from the heavens:
All (group 1)	**praise him in the heights above.**
Leader 2	Praise him, all his angels:
All (group 2)	**praise him, all his heavenly host.**
Leader 1	Praise him, sun and moon:
All (group 1)	**praise him, all you shining stars.**
Leader 2	Let them praise the name of the Lord:
All	**Praise the Lord!**
Leader 1	Praise the Lord from the earth:
All (group 1)	**praise him, great sea creatures.**
Leader 2	Praise him, storms and clouds:
All (group 2)	**praise him, mountains and hills.**
Leader 1	Praise him, fields and woods:
All (group 1)	**praise him, animals and birds.**
Leader 2	Praise him, rulers and nations:
All (group 2)	**praise him, old and young.**
Leader 1	Let them praise the name of the Lord:
All	**Praise the Lord! Amen.**
All	**Glory to the Father, and to the Son, and to the Holy Spirit:**
	as it was in the beginning, is now, and shall be for ever. Amen.

Cast: **Leader 1, Leader 2, All** (group 1—two or more persons/part of congregation), **All** (group 2—two or more persons/part of congregation).

A hymn of praise
Psalm 149.1–9 (LIT)

Leader	Praise the Lord:
All	**praise the Lord!**
Leader	Sing a new song to the Lord:
All	**let the people shout his name!**
Leader	Praise your maker, Israel:
All (group 1)	**hail, your king, Jerusalem.**

562

Leader	Sing and dance to honour him:
All (group 2)	**praise him with the strings and drums.**
Leader	God takes pleasure in his saints:
All (group 1)	**crowns the meek with victory.**
Leader	Rise, you saints, in triumph now:
All (group 2)	**sing the joyful night away!**
Leader	Shout aloud and praise your God!
All (group 1)	**Hold aloft the two-edged sword!**
Leader	Let the judgement now begin:
All (group 2)	**kings shall fail and tyrants die.**
Leader	Through his people, by his word:
All	**God shall have the victory!**
Leader	Praise the Lord!
All	**Praise the Lord!**
All	**Glory to the Father, and to the Son, and to the Holy Spirit: as it was in the beginning, is now, and shall be for ever. Amen.**

Cast: **Leader, All** (group 1—two or more persons/part of congregation), **All** (group 2—two or more persons/part of congregation).

A hymn of praise
Psalm 149.1–9

Cast	Praise the Lord!
Leader 1	Sing a new song to the Lord; praise him in the assembly of his faithful people!
Leader 2	Be glad, Israel, because of your Creator; rejoice, people of Zion, because of your king!
Leader 1	Praise his name with dancing; play drums and harps in praise of him.
Psalmist	The Lord takes pleasure in his people; he honours the humble with victory.
Leader 1	Let God's people rejoice in their triumph and sing joyfully all night long.
Leader 2	Let them shout aloud as they praise God, with sharp swords in their hands to defeat the nations and to punish the peoples; to bind their kings in chains, their leaders in chains of iron; to punish the nations as God has commanded.
Psalmist	This is the victory of God's people.
Cast	Praise the Lord!

Cast [This is] the word of the Lord.	**All** Glory to the Father, and to the Son, and to the Holy Spirit:
All Thanks be to God. OR	as it was in the beginning, is now, and shall be for ever. Amen.

Cast: **Leader 1, Leader 2, Psalmist.**

Praise the Lord

From Psalm 150.1–6 (LIT)

Leader	Praise the Lord!
All (group 1)	**praise God in his sanctuary:**
All (group 2)	**praise his strength beyond the skies.**

| **All** (group 1) | **Praise him for his acts of power:** |
| **All** (group 2) | **praise him for his surpassing greatness.** |

| **All** (group 1) | **Praise him with the sounding of the trumpet:** |
| **All** (group 2) | **praise him with the harp and lyre.** |

| **All** (group 1) | **Praise him with tambourine and dancing:** |
| **All** (group 2) | **praise him with the strings and flute.** |

| **All** (group 1) | **Praise him with the clash of cymbals:** |
| **All** (group 2) | **praise him with resounding cymbals.** |

| Leader | Let everything that has breath praise the Lord: |
| **All** | **Praise the Lord!** |

| **All** | **Glory to the Father, and to the Son, and to the Holy Spirit:** |
| | **as it was in the beginning, is now, and shall be for ever. Amen.** |

Cast: **Leader, All** (group 1—two or more persons/part of congregation), **All** (group 2—two or more persons/part of congregation).

PROVERBS

The value of Proverbs
Proverbs 1.1–19

Announcer The proverbs of Solomon, son of David and king of Israel:

Here are proverbs that will help you to recognize wisdom and good advice, and understand sayings with deep meaning. They can teach you how to live intelligently and how to be honest, just, and fair. They can make an inexperienced person clever and teach young men how to be resourceful. These proverbs can even add to the knowledge of wise men and give guidance to the educated, so that they can understand the hidden meanings of proverbs and the problems that wise men raise. (PAUSE)

Teacher To have knowledge, you must first have reverence for the Lord. Stupid people have no respect for wisdom and refuse to learn.

Pay attention to what your father and mother tell you, my son. Their teaching will improve your character as a handsome turban or a necklace improves your appearance.

When sinners tempt you, my son, don't give in. Suppose they say:

Sinner 1 Come on; let's find someone to kill!

Sinner 2 Let's attack some innocent people for the fun of it!

Sinner 1 They may be alive and well when we find them, but they'll be dead when we're through with them!

Sinner 2 We'll find all kinds of riches and fill our houses with loot!

Sinner 1 Come and join us, and we'll all share what we steal.

Teacher Don't go with people like that, my son. Stay away from them. They can't wait to do something bad. They're always ready to kill. It does no good to spread a net when the bird you want to catch is watching, but men like that are setting a trap for themselves, a trap in which they will die. Robbery always claims the life of the robber—this is what happens to anyone who lives by violence.

Cast [This is] the word of the Lord.
All **Thanks be to God.**

Cast: **Announcer, Teacher, Sinner 1, Sinner 2.**

Wisdom calls
Proverbs 1.20—2.8

Teacher Listen! Wisdom is calling out in the streets and market-places, calling loudly at the city gates and wherever people come together:

Wisdom (to audience)	Foolish people! How long do you want to be foolish? How long will you enjoy pouring scorn on knowledge? Will you never learn? Listen when I reprimand you; I will give you good advice and share my knowledge with you. I have been calling you, inviting you to come, but you would not listen. You paid no attention to me. You have ignored all my advice and have not been willing to let me correct you. So when you get into trouble, I will laugh at you. I will mock you when terror strikes—when it comes on you like a storm, bringing fierce winds of trouble, and you are in pain and misery. Then you will call for wisdom, but I will not answer. You may look for me everywhere, but you will not find me. You have never had any use for knowledge and have always refused to obey the Lord. You have never wanted my advice or paid any attention when I corrected you. So then, you will get what you deserve, and your own actions will make you sick.
Teacher	Inexperienced people die because they reject wisdom. Stupid people are destroyed by their own lack of concern.
Wisdom	But whoever listens to me will have security. He will be safe, with no reason to be afraid.
(to an individual)	Learn what I teach you, my son, and never forget what I tell you to do. Listen to what is wise and try to understand it. Yes, beg for knowledge; plead for insight. Look for it as hard as you would for silver or some hidden treasure. If you do, you will know what it means to fear the Lord and you will succeed in learning about God.
Teacher	It is the Lord who gives wisdom; from him come knowledge and understanding. He provides help and protection for righteous, honest men. He protects those who treat others fairly, and guards those who are devoted to him.
Cast	[This is] the word of the Lord.
All	**Thanks be to God.**

Cast: **Teacher, Wisdom.**

Advice to young men
From Proverbs 3.5–26

Teacher 1	Trust in the Lord with all your heart. Never rely on what you think you know. Remember the Lord in everything you do, and he will show you the right way. Never let yourself think that you are wiser than you are; simply obey the Lord and refuse to do wrong. Honour the Lord by making him an offering from the best of all that your land produces. If you do, your barns will be filled with grain, and you will have too much wine to be able to store it all.
Teacher 2	When the Lord corrects you, my son, pay close attention and take it as a warning. The Lord corrects those he loves, as a father corrects a son of whom he is proud. Those who become wise are happy; wisdom will give them life.

Singer(s)	The Lord created the earth by his wisdom; by his knowledge he set the sky in place. His wisdom caused the rivers to flow and the clouds to give rain to the earth.
Teacher 2	Hold on to your wisdom and insight, my son. Never let them get away from you. They will provide you with life—a pleasant and happy life. You can go safely on your way and never even stumble. You will not be afraid when you go to bed, and you will sleep soundly through the night. You will not have to worry about sudden disasters, such as come on the wicked like a storm.
Teacher 1	The Lord will keep you safe. He will not let you fall into a trap.
Cast All	[This is] the word of the Lord. **Thanks be to God.**

Cast: **Teacher 1, Teacher 2** (can be the same as Teacher 1), **Singer(s).**

The benefits of wisdom
From Proverbs 4.1–27

Teacher	Listen to what your father teaches you, my sons. Pay attention, and you will have understanding. What I am teaching you is good, so remember it all. When I was only a little boy, my parents' only son, my father would teach me:
Father	Remember what I say and never forget it. Do as I tell you, and you will live. Get wisdom and insight! Do not forget or ignore what I say. Do not abandon wisdom, and she will protect you; love her, and she will keep you safe. Getting wisdom is the most important thing you can do. Whatever else you get, get insight. Love wisdom, and she will make you great. Embrace her, and she will bring you honour. She will be your crowning glory.
Teacher	Listen to me, my son. Take seriously what I am telling you, and you will live a long life. I have taught you wisdom and the right way to live. Nothing will stand in your way if you walk wisely, and you will not stumble when you run. Always remember what you have learnt. Your education is your life—guard it well. Do not go where evil men go. Do not follow the example of the wicked.
Father	The road the righteous travel is like the sunrise, getting brighter and brighter until daylight has come. The road of the wicked, however, is dark as night. They fall, but cannot see what they have stumbled over.
Teacher	Be careful how you think; your life is shaped by your thoughts. Never say anything that isn't true. Have nothing to do with lies and misleading words. Look straight ahead with honest confidence; don't hang your head in shame. Plan carefully what you do, and whatever you do will turn out right. Avoid evil and walk straight ahead. Don't go one step off the right way.
Cast All	[This is] the word of the Lord. **Thanks be to God.**

Cast: **Teacher, Father.**

Warnings
Proverbs 6.1–19

Teacher
Have you promised to be responsible for someone else's debts, my son? Have you been caught by your own words, trapped by your own promises? Well then, my son, you are in that man's power, but this is how to get out of it: hurry to him, and beg him to release you. Don't let yourself go to sleep or even stop to rest. Get out of the trap like a bird or a deer escaping from a hunter.

Lazy people should learn a lesson from the way ants live. They have no leader, chief, or ruler, but they store up their food during the summer, getting ready for winter. How long is the lazy man going to lie in bed? When is he ever going to get up? [He says:]

Lazy person
(yawning)
I'll just take a short nap. I'll fold my hands and rest a while.

Teacher
(furtively)
But while he sleeps, poverty will attack him like an armed robber. (PAUSE)

(normally)
Worthless, wicked people go around telling lies. They wink and make gestures to deceive you, all the while planning evil in their perverted minds, stirring up trouble everywhere. Because of this, disaster will strike them without warning, and they will be fatally wounded.

There are seven things that the Lord hates and cannot tolerate:

Speaker 1
A proud look

Speaker 2
A lying tongue

Speaker 3
Hands that kill innocent people

Speaker 1
A mind that thinks up wicked plans

Speaker 2
Feet that hurry off to do evil

Speaker 3
A witness who tells one lie after another

Speaker 1
And a man who stirs up trouble among friends.

Cast
[This is] the word of the Lord.
All
Thanks be to God.

Cast: **Teacher, Lazy person, Speaker 1, Speaker 2, Speaker 3** (the 'Speaker' section can be mimed effectively—with up to seven speakers).

Women to avoid
Proverbs 7.4–27

Teacher
Treat wisdom as your sister, and insight as your closest friend. They will keep you away from other men's wives, from women with seductive words.

Storyteller	Once I was looking out of the window of my house, and I saw many inexperienced young men, but noticed one foolish fellow in particular. He was walking along the street near the corner where a certain woman lived. He was passing near her house in the evening after it was dark. And then she met him; she was dressed like a prostitute and was making plans. She was a bold and shameless woman who always walked the streets or stood waiting at a corner, sometimes in the streets, sometimes in the market-place. She threw her arms round the young man, kissed him and looked him straight in the eye:
Woman (seductively)	I made my offerings today and have the meat from the sacrifices. So I came out looking for you. I wanted to find you, and here you are! I've covered my bed with sheets of coloured linen from Egypt. I've perfumed it with myrrh, aloes, and cinnamon. Come on! Let's make love all night long. We'll be happy in each other's arms. My husband isn't at home. He's gone away on a long journey. He took plenty of money with him and won't be back for two weeks.
Storyteller	So she tempted him with her charms, and he gave in to her smooth talk. Suddenly he was going with her like an ox on the way to be slaughtered, like a deer prancing into a trap where an arrow would pierce its heart. He was like a bird going into a net—he did not know that his life was in danger.
Teacher	Now then, my sons, listen to me. Pay attention to what I say. Do not let such a woman win your heart; don't go wandering after her. She has been the ruin of many men and caused the death of too many to count. If you go to her house, you are on the way to the world of the dead. It is a short cut to death.
Cast	[This is] the word of the Lord.
All	**Thanks be to God.**

Cast: **Teacher, Storyteller** (can be the same as Teacher), **Woman.**

In praise of wisdom (i)
From Proverbs 8.1–21

Teacher	Listen! Wisdom is calling out. Reason is making herself heard. On the hilltops near the road and at the cross-roads she stands. At the entrance to the city, beside the gates, she calls:
Wisdom	I appeal to you, mankind; I call to everyone on earth. Are you immature? Learn to be mature. Are you foolish? Learn to have sense. Listen to my excellent words; all I tell you is right. Choose my instruction instead of silver; choose knowledge rather than the finest gold.
	To honour the Lord is to hate evil; I hate pride and arrogance, evil ways and false words. I make plans and carry them out. I have understanding, and I am strong. I help kings to govern and rulers to make good laws. Every ruler on earth governs with my help, statesmen and noblemen alike. I love those who love me; whoever

→

looks for me can find me. I have riches and honour to give, prosperity and success. I walk the way of righteousness; I follow the paths of justice, giving wealth to those who love me, filling their houses with treasures.

Cast	[This is] the word of the Lord.
All	**Thanks be to God.**

Cast: **Teacher, Wisdom.**

In praise of wisdom (ii)
From Proverbs 8.1–3, 22–36

Teacher Listen! Wisdom is calling out. Reason is making herself heard. On the hilltops near the road and at the cross-roads she stands. At the entrance to the city, beside the gates, she calls:

Wisdom The Lord created me first of all, the first of his works, long ago. I was made in the very beginning, at the first, before the world began. I was born before the oceans, when there were no springs of water. I was born before the mountains, before the hills were set in place, before God made the earth and its fields or even the first handful of soil. I was there when he set the sky in place, when he stretched the horizon across the ocean, when he placed the clouds in the sky, when he opened the springs of the ocean and ordered the waters of the sea to rise no further than he said. I was there when he laid the earth's foundations. I was beside him like an architect, I was his daily source of joy, always happy in his presence—happy with the world and pleased with the human race.

The man who listens to me will be happy— the man who stays at my door every day, waiting at the entrance to my home. The man who finds me finds life, and the Lord will be pleased with him. The man who does not find me hurts himself; anyone who hates me loves death.

Cast	[This is] the word of the Lord.
All	**Thanks be to God.**

Cast: **Teacher, Wisdom.**

Wisdom and Stupidity
From Proverbs 9.1–18

Teacher Wisdom has built her house and made seven pillars for it. She has had an animal killed for a feast, mixed spices in the wine, and laid the table. She has sent her servant-girls to call out from the highest place in the town:

Wisdom
(kindly) Come, eat my food and drink the wine that I have mixed. Leave the company of ignorant people, and live. Follow the way of knowledge. (PAUSE)

Teacher	If you correct a conceited man, you will only be insulted. If you reprimand an evil man, you will only get hurt. Never correct a conceited man; he will hate you for it. But if you correct a wise man, he will respect you. Anything you say to a wise man will make him wiser. Whatever you tell a righteous man will add to his knowledge.
	To be wise you must first have reverence for the Lord. If you know the Holy One, you have understanding. Wisdom will add years to your life. You are the one who will profit if you have wisdom, and if you reject it, you are the one who will suffer.
	Stupidity is like a loud, ignorant, shameless woman. She sits at the door of her house or on a seat in the highest part of the town, and calls out to people passing by, who are minding their own business:
Stupidity	Come in, ignorant people!
Teacher	To the foolish man she says:
Stupidity	Stolen water is sweeter. Stolen bread tastes better.
Teacher	Her victims do not know that the people die who go to her house, that those who have already entered are now deep in the world of the dead.
Cast	[This is] the word of the Lord.
All	**Thanks be to God.**

Cast: **Teacher, Wisdom, Stupidity.**

The capable wife
Proverbs 31.10–31

Man	How hard it is to find a capable wife!
Woman 1	She is worth far more than jewels!
Man	Her husband puts his confidence in her, and he will never be poor. As long as she lives, she does him good and never harm.
Woman 2	She keeps herself busy making wool and linen cloth.
Woman 1	She brings home food from out-of-the-way places, as merchant ships do.
Woman 2	She gets up before daylight to prepare food for her family and to tell her servant-girls what to do.
Woman 1	She looks at land and buys it, and with money she has earned she plants a vineyard.
Woman 2	She is a hard worker, strong and industrious.
Woman 1	She knows the value of everything she makes, and works late into the night.
Woman 2	She spins her own thread and weaves her own cloth.

Woman 1	She is generous to the poor and needy.
Child	She doesn't worry when it snows, because her family has warm clothing.
Woman 2	She makes bedspreads and wears clothes of fine purple linen.
Man	Her husband is well known, one of the leading citizens.
Woman 1	She makes clothes and belts, and sells them to merchants.
Woman 2	She is strong and respected and not afraid of the future.
Woman 1	She speaks with gentle wisdom.
Man	She is always busy and looks after her family's needs.
Child	Her children show their appreciation, and her husband praises her.
	He says:
Man	Many women are good wives, but you are the best of them all.
Woman 2	Charm is deceptive and beauty disappears, but a woman who honours the Lord should be praised.
Man	Give her credit for all she does.
Cast	She deserves the respect of everyone.
Cast **All**	[This is] the word of the Lord. **Thanks be to God.**

Cast: **Man, Woman 1, Woman 2, Child.**

ECCLESIASTES

Life is useless
Ecclesiastes 1.1–18

Announcer These are the words of the Philosopher, David's son, who was king in Jerusalem.

Philosopher
(protesting) It is useless, useless. Life is useless, all useless. You spend your life working, labouring, and what do you have to show for it? Generations come and generations go, but the world stays just the same. The sun still rises, and it still goes down, going wearily back to where it must start all over again. The wind blows south, the wind blows north—round and round and back again. Every river flows into the sea, but the sea is not yet full. The water returns to where the rivers began, and starts all over again. Everything leads to weariness—a weariness too great for words. Our eyes can never see enough to be satisfied; our ears can never hear enough. What has happened before will happen again. What has been done before will be done again. There is nothing new in the whole world. They say:

Person(s) Look, here is something new!

Philosopher But no, it has all happened before, long before we were born. No one remembers what has happened in the past, and no one in days to come will remember what happens between now and then. (PAUSE)

(deliberately) I, the Philosopher, have been king over Israel in Jerusalem. I determined that I would examine and study all the things that are done in this world. God has laid a miserable fate upon us. I have seen everything done in this world, and I tell you, it is all useless. It is like chasing the wind. You can't straighten out what is crooked; you can't count things that aren't there. I told myself:

Young Philosopher I have become a great man, far wiser than anyone who ruled Jerusalem before me. I know what wisdom and knowledge really are.

Philosopher I was determined to learn the difference between knowledge and foolishness, wisdom and madness. But I found out that I might as well be chasing the wind. The wiser you are, the more worries you have; the more you know, the more it hurts.

Cast [This is] the word of the Lord.
All **Thanks be to God.**

Cast: **Announcer, Philosopher, Person(s), Young Philosopher.**

Work and worry
Ecclesiastes 2.11–17 [18–26]

Philosopher I thought about all that I had done and how hard I had worked doing it, and I realized that it didn't mean a thing. It was like chasing the wind—of no use at all. After all, a king can only do what previous kings have done.

So I started thinking about what it meant to be wise or reckless or foolish. Oh, I know:

Reader Wisdom is better than foolishness, just as light is better than darkness. Wise men can see where they are going, and fools can not.

Philosopher But I also know that the same fate is waiting for us all. I thought to myself:

Young Philosopher I will suffer the same fate as fools. So what have I gained from being so wise? (PAUSE) Nothing. Not a thing.

Philosopher No one remembers wise men, and no one remembers fools. In days to come, we will all be forgotten. We must all die—wise and foolish alike.

So life came to mean nothing to me, because everything in it had brought me nothing but trouble. It had all been useless; I had been chasing the wind.

[Nothing that I had worked for and earned meant a thing to me, because I knew that I would have to leave it to my successor, and he might be wise, or he might be foolish—who knows? Yet he will own everything I have worked for, everything my wisdom has earned for me in this world. It is all useless. So I came to regret that I had worked so hard. You work for something with all your wisdom, knowledge, and skill, and then you have to leave it all to someone who hasn't had to work for it. It is useless, and it isn't right! You work and worry your way through life, and what do you have to show for it? As long as you live, everything you do brings nothing but worry and heartache. Even at night your mind can't rest. It is all useless.

The best thing a man can do is to eat and drink and enjoy what he has earned. And yet, I realized that even this comes from God. How else could you have anything to eat or enjoy yourself at all? God gives wisdom, knowledge, and happiness to those who please him, but he makes sinners work, earning and saving, so that what they get can be given to those who please him. It is all useless. It is like chasing the wind.]

Cast [This is] the word of the Lord.
All **Thanks be to God.**

Cast: **Philosopher, Reader, Young Philosopher.**

A time for everything
Ecclesiastes 3.1–15

Philosopher	Everything that happens in this world happens at the time God chooses. He sets . . .
Singer 1	the time for birth
Singer 1A	and the time for death,
Singer 2	the time for planting
Singer 2A	and the time for pulling up,
Singer 3	the time for killing
Singer 3A	and the time for healing,
Singer 4	the time for tearing down
Singer 4A	and the time for building.
Philosopher	He sets . . .
Singer 1	the time for sorrow
Singer 1A	and the time for joy,
Singer 2	the time for mourning
Singer 2A	and the time for dancing,
Singer 3	the time for making love
Singer 3A	and the time for not making love,
Singer 4	the time for kissing
Singer 4A	and the time for not kissing.
Philosopher	He sets . . .
Singer 1	the time for finding
Singer 1A	and the time for losing,
Singer 2	the time for saving
Singer 2A	and the time for throwing away,
Singer 3	the time for tearing
Singer 3A	and the time for mending,
Singer 4	the time for silence
Singer 4A	and the time for talk.
Philosopher	He sets . . .
Singer 1	the time for love
Singer 1A	and the time for hate,
Singer 2	the time for war
Singer 2A	and the time for peace.
Philosopher	[What do we gain from all our work? I know the heavy burdens that God has laid on us. He has set the right time for everything. He has given us a desire to know the future, but never gives us the satisfaction of fully understanding what he does. So I realized that all we can do is to be happy and do the best we can while we are still alive. All of us should eat and drink and enjoy what we have worked for. It is God's gift.]

→

I know that everything God does will last for ever. You can't add anything to it or take anything away from it. And one thing God does is to make us stand in awe of him. Whatever happens or can happen has already happened before. God makes the same thing happen again and again.

Cast	[This is] the word of the Lord.
All	**Thanks be to God.**

Cast: **Philosopher, Singer 1, Singer 1A, Singer 2, Singer 2A, Singer 3, Singer 3A, Singer 4, Singer 4A** (Singers 1, 1A; 2, 2A; 3, 3A; 4, 4A; should have contrasting voices).

SONG OF SONGS

The First Song
Song of Songs 1.1—2.7

Announcer	The most beautiful of songs, by Solomon.
The Woman (to The Man)	Your lips cover me with kisses; your love is better than wine. There is a fragrance about you; the sound of your name recalls it. No woman could help loving you. Take me with you, and we'll run away; be my king and take me to your room. We will be happy together, drink deep, and lose ourselves in love. No wonder all women love you!
(to audience)	Women of Jerusalem, I am dark but beautiful, dark as the desert tents of Kedar, but beautiful as the curtains in Solomon's palace. Don't look down on me because of my colour, because the sun has tanned me. My brothers were angry with me and made me work in the vineyard. I had no time to care for myself.
(to The Man)	Tell me, my love, Where will you lead your flock to graze? Where will they rest from the noonday sun? Why should I need to look for you among the flocks of the other shepherds?
The Man (to The Woman)	Don't you know the place, loveliest of women? Go and follow the flock; find pasture for your goats near the tents of the shepherds.
(musing)	You, my love, excite men as a mare excites the stallions of Pharaoh's chariots. Your hair is beautiful upon your cheeks and falls along your neck like jewels. But we will make for you a chain of gold with ornaments of silver.
The Woman (to audience)	My king was lying on his couch, and my perfume filled the air with fragrance. My lover has the scent of myrrh as he lies upon my breasts. My lover is like the wild flowers that bloom in the vineyards at Engedi.

The Man (to The Woman)	How beautiful you are, my love; how your eyes shine with love!
The Woman (to The Man)	How handsome you are, my dearest; how you delight me! The green grass will be our bed; the cedars will be the beams of our house. and the cypress-trees the ceiling. I am only a wild flower in Sharon, a lily in a mountain valley.
The Man (to The Woman)	Like a lily among thorns is my darling among women.
The Woman (to audience)	Like an apple-tree among the trees of the forest, so is my dearest compared with other men. I love to sit in its shadow, and its fruit is sweet to my taste. He brought me to his banqueting hall and raised the banner of love over me. Restore my strength with raisins and refresh me with apples! I am weak from passion. His left hand is under my head, and his right hand caresses me.
(to Women 2 and 3, OR to audience)	Promise me, women of Jerusalem; swear by the swift deer and the gazelles that you will not interrupt our love.

Cast: **Announcer, The Woman, The Man.** (Women 2 and 3 appear later).

The Second Song
Song of Songs 2.8—3.5

The Woman (to audience)	I hear my lover's voice. He comes running over the mountains, racing across the hills to me. My lover is like a gazelle, like a young stag. There he stands beside the wall. He looks in through the window and glances through the lattice. My lover speaks to me.
The Man (to The Woman)	Come then, my love; my darling, come with me. The winter is over; the rains have stopped; in the countryside the flowers are in bloom. This is the time for singing; the song of doves is heard in the fields. Figs are beginning to ripen; the air is fragrant with blossoming vines. Come then, my love;

my darling, come with me.
You are like a dove that hides
in the crevice of a rock.
Let me see your lovely face
and hear your enchanting voice.

[(singing) Catch the foxes, the little foxes,
before they ruin our vineyard in bloom.]

The Woman My lover is mine, and I am his.
(to audience) He feeds his flock among the lilies
until the morning breezes blow
and the darkness disappears.

(to The Man) Return, my darling, like a gazelle,
like a stag on the mountains of Bether.

(to audience) Asleep on my bed,
night after night I dreamt of the one I love;
I was looking for him, but couldn't find him.
I went wandering through the city,
through its streets and alleys.
I looked for the one I love.
I looked, but couldn't find him.
The watchmen patrolling the city saw me.
I asked them—

(calling) 'Have you found my lover?'
As soon as I left them, I found him.
I held him and wouldn't let him go
until I took him to my mother's house,
to the room where I was born.

(to Women Promise me, women of Jerusalem;
2 and 3, OR swear by the swift deer and the gazelles
to audience) that you will not interrupt our love.

Cast: **The Woman, The Man.** (Women 2 and 3 appear later).

The Third Song
Song of Songs 3.6—5.1

The Woman What is this coming from the desert
(to audience) like a column of smoke,
fragrant with incense and myrrh,
the incense sold by the traders?
Solomon is coming, carried on his throne;
sixty soldiers form the bodyguard,
the finest soldiers in Israel.
All of them are skilful with the sword;
they are battle-hardened veterans.
Each of them is armed with a sword,
on guard against a night attack.

→

King Solomon is carried on a throne
made of the finest wood.
Its posts are covered with silver;
over it is cloth embroidered with gold.
Its cushions are covered with purple cloth,
lovingly woven by the women of Jerusalem.
Women of Zion, come and see King Solomon.
He is wearing the crown
that his mother placed on his head on his wedding day,
on the day of his gladness and joy.

The Man (to
The Woman)

How beautiful you are, my love!
How your eyes shine with love behind your veil.
Your hair dances, like a flock of goats
bounding down the hills of Gilead.
Your teeth are as white as sheep
that have just been shorn and washed.
Not one of them is missing;
they are all perfectly matched.
Your lips are like a scarlet ribbon;
how lovely they are when you speak.
Your cheeks glow behind your veil.
Your neck is like the tower of David,
round and smooth,
with a necklace like a thousand shields hung round it.
Your breasts are like gazelles,
twin deer feeding among lilies.

(musing)

I will stay on the hill of myrrh,
the hill of incense,
until the morning breezes blow
and the darkness disappears.

(to The
Woman)

How beautiful you are, my love;
how perfect you are!

(musing)

Come with me from the Lebanon Mountains,
my bride;
come with me from Lebanon.
Come down from the top of Mount Amana,
from Mount Senir and Mount Hermon,
where the lions and leopards live.

(to The
Woman)

The look in your eyes, my sweetheart and bride,
and the necklace you are wearing
have stolen my heart.
Your love delights me,
my sweetheart and bride.
Your love is better than wine;
your perfume more fragrant than any spice.
The taste of honey is on your lips, my darling;
your tongue is milk and honey for me.
Your clothing has all the fragrance of Lebanon.

(to audience)	My sweetheart, my bride, is a secret garden, a walled garden, a private spring; there the plants flourish. They grow like an orchard of pomegranate-trees and bear the finest fruits. There is no lack of henna and nard, of saffron, calamus, and cinnamon, or incense of every kind. Myrrh and aloes grow there with all the most fragrant perfumes. Fountains water the garden, streams of flowing water, brooks gushing down from the Lebanon Mountains.
The Woman (calling)	Wake up, North Wind. South Wind, blow on my garden; fill the air with fragrance.
(to The Man)	Let my lover come to his garden and eat the best of its fruits.
The Man (to The Woman)	I have entered my garden, my sweetheart, my bride. I am gathering my spices and myrrh; I am eating my honey and honeycomb; I am drinking my wine and milk.
Women 2 and **3**	Eat, lovers, and drink until you are drunk with love!

Cast: **The Woman, The Man, Woman 2, Woman 3** (can be the same as Woman 2).

The Fourth Song
Song of Songs 5.2—6.3

The Woman (to audience)	While I slept, my heart was awake. I dreamt my lover knocked at the door.
The Man (to The Woman)	Let me come in, my darling, my sweetheart, my dove.
(musing)	My head is wet with dew, and my hair is damp from the mist.
The Woman (musing)	I have already undressed; why should I get dressed again? I have washed my feet; why should I get them dirty again?
(to audience)	My lover put his hand to the door, and I was thrilled that he was near. I was ready to let him come in. My hands were covered with myrrh, my fingers with liquid myrrh, as I grasped the handle of the door.

→

I opened the door for my lover,
but he had already gone. (PAUSE)

(musing) How I wanted to hear his voice!
I looked for him, but couldn't find him;
I called to him, but heard no answer.

(to audience) The watchmen patrolling the city found me;
they struck me and bruised me;
the guards at the city wall tore off my cape.

(to Women 2 and 3) Promise me, women of Jerusalem,
that if you find my lover,
you will tell him I am weak from passion.

Woman 2 Most beautiful of women,
is your lover different from everyone else?

Woman 3 What is there so wonderful about him
that we should give you our promise?

The Woman
(to Women 2 and 3)
My lover is handsome and strong;
he is one in ten thousand.
His face is bronzed and smooth;
his hair is wavy,
black as a raven.
His eyes are as beautiful
as doves by a flowing brook,
doves washed in milk and standing by the stream.
His cheeks are as lovely as a garden
that is full of herbs and spices.
His lips are like lilies,
wet with liquid myrrh.
His hands are well-formed,
and he wears rings set with gems.
His body is like smooth ivory,
with sapphires set in it.
His thighs are columns of alabaster
set in sockets of gold.
He is majestic, like the Lebanon Mountains
with their towering cedars.
His mouth is sweet to kiss;
everything about him enchants me.
This is what my lover is like,
women of Jerusalem.

Woman 2 (to
The Woman)
Most beautiful of women,
where has your lover gone?

Woman 3 (to
The Woman)
Tell us which way your lover went,
so that we can help you find him.

The Woman
(musing)
My lover has gone to his garden,
where the balsam-trees grow.
He is feeding his flock in the garden
and gathering lilies.

My lover is mine, and I am his;
he feeds his flock among the lilies.

Cast: **The Woman, The Man, Woman 2, Woman 3.**

The Fifth Song
Songs of Songs 6.4—8.4

The Man (to The Woman)	My love, you are as beautiful as Jerusalem, as lovely as the city of Tirzah, as breathtaking as these great cities. Turn your eyes away from me; they are holding me captive. Your hair dances, like a flock of goats bounding down the hills of Gilead. Your teeth are as white as a flock of sheep that have just been washed. Not one of them is missing; they are all perfectly matched. Your cheeks glow behind your veil.
(to audience)	Let the king have sixty queens, eighty concubines, young women without number! But I love only one, and she is as lovely as a dove. She is her mother's only daughter, her mother's favourite child. All women look at her and praise her; queens and concubines sing her praises. Who *is* this whose glance is like the dawn? She is beautiful and bright, as dazzling as the sun or the moon.
(musing)	I have come down among the almond-trees to see the young plants in the valley, to see the new leaves on the vines and the blossoms on the pomegranate-trees.
(to The Woman)	I am trembling; you have made me as eager for love as a chariot driver is for battle.
Woman 2	Dance, dance, girl of Shulam.
Woman 3	Let us watch you as you dance.
The Woman	Why do you want to watch me as I dance between the rows of onlookers?
The Man (to The Woman)	What a wonderful girl you are! How beautiful are your feet in sandals. The curve of your thighs is like the work of an artist. A bowl is there,

→

583

A sheaf of wheat is there.
surrounded by lilies.
Your breasts are like twin deer,
like two gazelles.
Your neck is like a tower of ivory.
Your eyes are like the pools in the city of Heshbon,
near the gate of that great city.
Your nose is as lovely as the tower of Lebanon
that stands guard at Damascus.
Your head is held high like Mount Carmel.
Your braided hair shines like the finest satin;
its beauty could hold a king captive.

How pretty you are, how beautiful;
how complete the delights of your love.
You are as graceful as a palm-tree,
and your breasts are clusters of dates.

(musing)	I will climb the palm-tree and pick its fruit.
(to The Woman)	To me your breasts are like bunches of grapes, your breath like the fragrance of apples, and your mouth like the finest wine.
The Woman (to audience)	Then let the wine flow straight to my lover, flowing over his lips and teeth. I belong to my lover, and he desires me.
(to The Man)	Come, darling, let's go out to the countryside and spend the night in the villages. We will get up early and look at the vines to see whether they've started to grow, whether the blossoms are opening and the pomegranate-trees are in bloom. There I will give you my love. You can smell the scent of mandrakes, and all the pleasant fruits are near our door. Darling, I have kept for you the old delights and the new.
(musing)	I wish that you were my brother, that my mother had nursed you at her breast. Then, if I met you in the street, I could kiss you and no one would mind. I would take you to my mother's house, where you could teach me love. I would give you spiced wine, my pomegranate wine to drink. (PAUSE)
(to The Man)	Your left hand is under my head, and your right hand caresses me.
(to Women 2 and 3)	Promise me, women of Jerusalem, that you will not interrupt our love.

Cast: **The Man, The Woman, Woman 2, Woman 3.**

The Sixth Song
Song of Songs 8.5–14

Woman 2 (to
  Woman 3 OR
  to audience)

Who is this coming from the desert,
arm in arm with her lover?

The Woman
  (to The Man)

Under the apple-tree I woke you,
in the place where you were born.
Close your heart to every love but mine;
hold no one in your arms but me.

  (to audience)

Love is as powerful as death;
passion is as strong as death itself.
It bursts into flame
and burns like a raging fire.
Water cannot put it out;
no flood can drown it.
But if anyone tried to buy love with his wealth,
contempt is all he would get.

[Brother 1
  (to audience)

We have a young sister,
and her breasts are still small.

Brother 2
  (to audience)

What will we do for her
when a young man comes courting?

Brother 1
  (to audience)

If she is a wall,
we will build her a silver tower.

Brother 2
  (to audience)

But if she is a gate,
we will protect her with panels of cedar.

The Woman
  (to audience)

I am a wall,
and my breasts are its towers.
My lover knows that with him
I find contentment and peace.]

The Man
  (to audience)

Solomon has a vineyard
in a place called Baal Hamon.
There are farmers who rent it from him;
each one pays a thousand silver coins.
Solomon is welcome to his thousand coins,
and the farmers to two hundred as their share;
I have a vineyard of my own!

  (*to The
  Woman)

Let me hear your voice from the garden, my love;
my companions are waiting to hear you speak.

The Woman
  (to The Man)

Come to me, my lover, like a gazelle,
like a young stag on the mountains where spices grow.

Cast: **Woman 2, The Woman, [Brother 1, Brother 2], The Man.** (*at this point, The Woman and The Man can move away and out in opposite directions).

Full cast for The Song of Songs: **Announcer, The Woman, The Man, Woman 2, Woman 3, [Brother 1, Brother 2].**

ISAIAH

God reprimands his people
Isaiah 1.1–9

Narrator   This book [of Isaiah] contains the messages about Judah and Jerusalem which God revealed to Isaiah son of Amoz during the time when Uzziah, Jotham, Ahaz, and Hezekiah were kings of Judah.

Isaiah   The Lord said:

The Lord   Earth and sky, listen to what I am saying! The children I brought up have rebelled against me. Cattle know who owns them, and donkeys know where their master feeds them. But that is more than my people Israel know. They don't understand at all.

Isaiah   You are doomed, you sinful nation, you corrupt and evil people! Your sins drag you down! You have rejected the Lord, the holy God of Israel, and have turned your backs on him. Why do you keep on rebelling? Do you want to be punished even more? Israel, your head is already covered with wounds, and your heart and mind are sick. From head to foot there is not a healthy spot on your body. You are covered with bruises and sores and open wounds. Your wounds have not been cleaned or bandaged. No ointment has been put on them.

Your country has been devastated, and your cities have been burnt to the ground. While you look on, foreigners take over your land and bring everything to ruin. Jerusalem alone is left, a city under siege—as defenceless as a watchman's hut in a vineyard or a shed in a cucumber field. If the Lord Almighty had not let some of the people survive, Jerusalem would have been totally destroyed, just as Sodom and Gomorrah were.

Cast   [This is] the word of the Lord.
All   **Thanks be to God.**

Cast: **Narrator, Isaiah, The Lord.**

God reprimands his city
Isaiah 1.10–20

Isaiah   Jerusalem, your rulers and your people are like those of Sodom and Gomorrah. Listen to what the Lord is saying to you. Pay attention to what our God is teaching you:

The Lord   Do you think I want all these sacrifices you keep offering to me? I have had more than enough of the sheep you burn as sacrifices and of the fat of your fine animals. I am tired of the blood of bulls and sheep and goats. Who asked you to bring me all this when you come to worship me? Who asked you to do all this tramping about in my Temple? It's useless to bring your offerings. I am disgusted with the smell of the incense you burn. I cannot stand your New Moon Festivals, your Sabbaths, and your religious gatherings; they are all corrupted by your sins. I hate your New Moon Festivals and holy days; they are a burden that I am tired of bearing.

When you lift your hands in prayer, I will not look at you. No matter how much you pray, I will not listen, for your hands are covered with blood. Wash yourselves clean. Stop all this evil that I see you doing. Yes, stop doing evil and learn to do right. See that justice is done—help those who are oppressed, give orphans their rights, and defend widows.

Isaiah   The Lord says:

The Lord   Now, let's settle the matter. You are stained red with sin, but I will wash you as clean as snow. Although your stains are deep red, you will be as white as wool. If you will only obey me, you will eat the good things the land produces. But if you defy me, you are doomed to die. (PAUSE) I, the Lord, have spoken!

Cast   [This is] the word of the Lord.
All   **Thanks be to God.**

Cast: **Isaiah, The Lord.**

The sinful city
Isaiah 1.21–31

Isaiah   The city that once was faithful is behaving like a whore! At one time it was filled with righteous men, but now only murderers remain. Jerusalem, you were once like silver, but now you are worthless; you were like good wine, but now you are only water. Your leaders are rebels and friends of thieves; they are always accepting gifts and bribes. They never defend orphans in court or listen when widows present their case. So now, listen to what the Lord Almighty, Israel's powerful God, is saying:

The Lord   I will take revenge on you, my enemies, and you will cause me no more trouble. I will take action against you. I will purify you just as metal is refined, and will remove all your impurity. I will give you rulers and advisers like those you had long ago. Then Jerusalem will be called the righteous, faithful city.

Isaiah   Because the Lord is righteous, he will 'save Jerusalem and everyone there who repents. But he will crush everyone who sins and rebels against him; he will kill everyone who forsakes him. You will be sorry that you ever worshipped trees and planted sacred gardens. You will wither like a dying oak, like a garden that no one waters. Just as straw is set on fire by a spark, so powerful

→

men will be destroyed by their own evil deeds, and no one will be able to stop the destruction.

Cast	[This is] the word of the Lord.
All	**Thanks be to God.**

Cast: **Isaiah, The Lord.**

Everlasting peace
Isaiah 2.1–5

Narrator	This is the message which God gave to Isaiah son of Amoz about Judah and Jerusalem:
Isaiah	In days to come the mountain where the Temple stands will be the highest one of all, towering above all the hills. Many nations will come streaming to it, and their people will say—
Person 1	Let us go up the hill of the Lord, to the Temple of Israel's God.
Person 2	He will teach us what he wants us to do.
Person 1	We will walk in the paths he has chosen. For the Lord's teaching comes from Jerusalem.
Person 2	From Zion he speaks to his people.
Isaiah	He will settle disputes among great nations. They will hammer their swords into ploughs and their spears into pruning-knives. Nations will never again go to war, never prepare for battle again. Now, descendants of Jacob, let us walk in the light which the Lord gives us!
Cast	[This is] the word of the Lord.
All	**Thanks be to God.**

Cast: **Narrator, Isaiah, Person 1, Person 2.**

Isaiah calls out to God
Isaiah 2.6–22

Voice 1	O God, you have forsaken your people, the descendants of Jacob!
Voice 2	The land is full of magic practices from the east and from Philistia.
Voice 3	The people follow foreign customs.
Voice 1	Their land is full of silver and gold, and there is no end to their treasures.

Voice 2	Their land is full of horses, and there is no end to their chariots.
Voice 3	Their land is full of idols, and they worship objects that they have made with their own hands.
Voice 1	Everyone will be humiliated and disgraced.
Voices 1–3	Do not forgive them, Lord!
Voice 1	They will hide in caves in the rocky hills or dig holes in the ground to try to escape from the Lord's anger and to hide from his power and glory!
Voice 2	A day is coming when human pride will be ended and human arrogance destroyed. Then the Lord alone will be exalted.
Voice 3	On that day the Lord Almighty will humble everyone who is powerful, everyone who is proud and conceited.
Voice 1	He will destroy the tall cedars of Lebanon and all the oaks in the land of Bashan.
Voice 2	He will level the high mountains and hills, every high tower, and the walls of every fortress.
Voice 3	He will sink even the largest and most beautiful ships. Human pride will be ended, and human arrogance will be destroyed. Idols will completely disappear.
Voices 1–3	The Lord alone will be exalted on that day.
Voice 1	People will hide in caves in the rocky hills or dig holes in the ground to try to escape from the Lord's anger and to hide from his power and glory, when he comes to shake the earth.
Voice 2	When that day comes, they will throw away the gold and silver idols they have made, and abandon them to the moles and the bats.
Voice 3	When the Lord comes to shake the earth, people will hide in holes and caves in the rocky hills to try to escape from his anger and to hide from his power and glory.
Voices 1–3	Put no more confidence in mortal men.
Voice 1	What are they worth?
Cast	[This is] the word of the Lord.
All	**Thanks be to God.**

Cast: **Voice 1, Voice 2, Voice 3.**

The Lord judges his people
Isaiah 3.1—15

Isaiah	The Lord, the Almighty Lord, is about to take away from Jerusalem and Judah everything and everyone that the people depend on. He is going to take away their food and their water, their heroes and their soldiers, their judges and their prophets, their fortune-tellers and their statesmen, their military and

→

589

civilian leaders, their politicians and everyone who uses magic to control events. The Lord will let the people be governed by immature *boys*. Everyone will take advantage of everyone else. Young people will not respect their elders, and worthless people will not respect their superiors.

A time will come when the members of a clan will choose one of their number and say to him:

Person   You at least have something to wear, so be our leader in this time of trouble.

Isaiah   But he will answer:

Man   Not me! I can't help you. I haven't any food or clothes either. Don't make me your leader!

Isaiah   Yes, Jerusalem is doomed! Judah is collapsing! Everything they say and do is against the Lord; they openly insult God himself. Their prejudices will be held against them. They sin as openly as the people of Sodom did. They are doomed, and they have brought it on themselves. Righteous men will be happy, and things will go well for them. They will be able to enjoy what they have worked for. But evil men are doomed; what they have done to others will now be done to them. Money-lenders oppress my people, and their creditors cheat them. My people, your leaders are misleading you, so that you do not know which way to turn. (PAUSE)

The Lord is ready to state his case; he is ready to judge his people. The Lord is bringing the elders and leaders of his people to judgement. He makes this accusation:

The Lord   You have plundered vineyards, and your houses are full of what you have taken from the poor. You have no right to crush my people and take advantage of the poor. (PAUSE)

I, the Sovereign Lord Almighty, have spoken!

Cast   [This is] the word of the Lord.
All   **Thanks be to God.**

Cast: **Isaiah, Person, Man, The Lord.**

A warning to the women of Jerusalem
Isaiah 3.16—4.1

Isaiah   The Lord said:

The Lord   Look how proud the women of Jerusalem are! They walk along with their noses in the air. They are always flirting. They take dainty little steps, and the bracelets on their ankles jingle. But I will punish them—I will shave their heads and leave them bald.

Isaiah   A day is coming when the Lord will take away from the women of Jerusalem everything they are so proud of—the ornaments they wear on their ankles, on their heads, on their necks, and on their wrists. He will take away their veils and their hats; the magic charms they wear on their arms and at their waists; the rings they wear on their fingers and in their noses; all their fine robes, gowns, cloaks, and purses; their revealing garments, their linen handkerchiefs, and the scarves and long veils they wear on their heads. Instead of using perfumes, they will stink; instead of fine belts, they will wear coarse ropes; instead of having beautiful hair, they will be bald; instead of fine clothes, they will be dressed in rags; their beauty will be turned to shame!

The men of the city, yes, even the strongest men, will be killed in war. The city gates will mourn and cry, and the city itself will be like a woman sitting destitute on the ground. In that day seven women will take hold of one man and say:

Woman 1   We will eat our own food and provide our own clothes—

Woman 2   Only let us be called by your name.

Women 1 and **2**   Take away our disgrace!

Cast   [This is] the word of the Lord.
All   **Thanks be to God.**

Cast: **Isaiah, The Lord, Woman 1, Woman 2.**

The song of the vineyard
Isaiah 5.1–7

Isaiah   Listen while I sing you this song, a song of my friend and his vineyard:

Singer   My friend had a vineyard on a very fertile hill.
He dug the soil and cleared it of stones;
he planted the finest vines.
He built a tower to guard them,
dug a pit for treading the grapes.
He waited for the grapes to ripen,
but every grape was sour.

Isaiah   So now my friend says:

Friend   You people who live in Jerusalem and Judah, judge between my vineyard and me. Is there anything I failed to do for it? Then why did it produce sour grapes and not the good grapes I expected? This is what I am going to do to my vineyard; I will take away the hedge round it, break down the wall that protects it, and let wild animals eat it and trample it down. I will let it be overgrown with weeds. I will not prune the vines or hoe the ground; instead I will let briars and thorns cover it. I will even forbid the clouds to let rain fall on it.

Isaiah   Israel is the vineyard of the Lord Almighty; the people of Judah are the vines he planted. He expected them to do what was good,

→

but instead they committed murder. He expected them to do what was right, but their victims cried out for justice.

Cast	[This is] the word of the Lord.
All	**Thanks be to God.**

Cast: **Isaiah, Singer** (can be the same as Isaiah), **Friend.**

The evil that people do
Isaiah 5.8–30

Isaiah You are doomed! You buy more houses and fields to add to those you already have. Soon there will be nowhere for anyone else to live, and you alone will live in the land. I have heard the Lord Almighty say:

The Lord All these big, fine houses will be empty ruins. The grapevines growing on ten hectares of land will yield only eight litres of wine. A hundred and eighty litres of seed will produce only eighteen litres of corn.

Isaiah You are doomed! You get up early in the morning to start drinking, and you spend long evenings getting drunk. At your feasts you have harps and tambourines and flutes—and wine. But you don't understand what the Lord is doing, and so you will be carried away as prisoners. Your leaders will starve to death, and the common people will die of thirst. The world of the dead is hungry for them, and it opens its mouth wide. It gulps down the nobles of Jerusalem along with the noisy crowd of common people.

Everyone will be disgraced, and all who are proud will be humbled. But the Lord Almighty shows his greatness by doing what is right, and he reveals his holiness by judging his people. In the ruins of the cities lambs will eat grass and young goats will find pasture.

You are doomed! You are unable to break free from your sins. (PAUSE)

You say:

Person 1 Let the Lord hurry up and do what he says he will, so that we can see it.

Person 2 Let Israel's holy God carry out his plans; let's see what he has in mind.

Isaiah You are doomed! You call evil good and call good evil. You turn darkness into light and light into darkness. You make what is bitter sweet, and what is sweet you make bitter.

You are doomed! You think you are wise, so very clever.

You are doomed! Heroes of the wine bottle! Brave and fearless when it comes to mixing drinks! But for just a bribe you let guilty men go free, and you prevent the innocent from getting justice.

592

So now, just as straw and dry grass shrivel and burn in the fire, your roots will rot and your blossoms will dry up and blow away, because you have rejected what the Lord Almighty, Israel's holy God, has taught us. The Lord is angry with his people and has stretched out his hand to punish them. The mountains will shake, and the bodies of those who die will be left in the streets like rubbish. Yet even then the Lord's anger will not be ended, but his hand will still be stretched out to punish.

The Lord gives a signal to call for a distant nation. He whistles for them to come from the ends of the earth. And here they come, swiftly, quickly! None of them grows tired; none of them stumbles. They never doze or sleep. Not a belt is loose; not a sandal strap is broken. Their arrows are sharp, and their bows are ready to shoot. Their horses' hooves are as hard as flint, and their chariot-wheels turn like a whirlwind. The soldiers roar like lions that have killed an animal and are carrying it off where no one can take it away from them. When that day comes, they will roar over Israel as loudly as the sea. Look at this country! Darkness and distress! The light is swallowed by darkness.

Cast	[This is] the word of the Lord.
All	**Thanks be to God.**

Cast: **Isaiah, The Lord, Person 1, Person 2** (can be the same as Person 1).

God calls Isaiah to be a prophet
Isaiah 6.1–8 (GNB)

Isaiah　In the year that King Uzziah died, I saw the Lord. He was sitting on his throne, high and exalted, and his robe filled the whole Temple. Round him flaming creatures were standing, each of which had six wings. Each creature covered its face with two wings, and its body with two, and used the other two for flying. They were calling out to each other:

Creature 1　Holy, holy, holy!

Creature 2　The Lord Almighty is holy!

Creatures 1 & 2　His glory fills the world.

Isaiah　The sound of their voices made the foundation of the Temple shake, and the Temple itself was filled with smoke.

I said:

Young Isaiah　There is no hope for me! I am doomed because every word that passes my lips is sinful, and I live among a people whose every word is sinful. And yet, with my own eyes, I have seen the King, the Lord Almighty!

Isaiah　Then one of the creatures flew down to me, carrying a burning coal that he had taken from the altar with a pair of tongs. He touched my lips with the burning coal and said:

Creature 1	This has touched your lips, and now your guilt is gone, and your sins are forgiven.
Isaiah	Then I heard the Lord say:
The Lord	Whom shall I send? Who will be our messenger?
Isaiah	I answered:
Young Isaiah	I will go! Send me!
Cast All	[This is] the word of the Lord. **Thanks be to God.**

Cast: **Isaiah, Creature 1, Creature 2, Young Isaiah, The Lord.** (See also extended version of this reading below, or the continuation of this version on page 595).

God calls Isaiah to be a prophet
Isaiah 6.1–9 [9–12] (NIV)

Isaiah	In the year that King Uzziah died, I saw the Lord seated on a throne, high and exalted, and the train of his robe filled the Temple. Above him were seraphs, each with six wings: With two wings they covered their faces, with two they covered their feet, and with two they were flying. And they were calling to one another:
Seraphs 1 [and 2]	Holy, holy, holy is the Lord Almighty—
Seraph 2	The whole earth is full of his glory.
Isaiah	At the sound of their voices the the doorposts and thresholds shook and the temple was filled with smoke. I cried:
Young Isaiah	Woe to me! I am ruined! For I am a man of unclean lips, and I live among a people of unclean lips, and my eyes have seen the King, the Lord Almighty.
Isaiah	Then one of the seraphs flew to me with a live coal in his hand, which he had taken with tongs from the altar. With it he touched my mouth and said:
Seraph 1	See, this has touched your lips; your guilt is taken away and your sin atoned for.
Isaiah	Then I heard the voice of the Lord saying:
The Lord	Whom shall I send? And who will go for us?
Isaiah	And I said:
Young Isaiah	Here am I. Send me!
Isaiah	He said:
The Lord	Go! [And tell this people, 'Be ever hearing, but never understanding; be ever seeing, but never perceiving.'

> Make the heart of this people calloused;
> make their ears dull
> and close their eyes.
> Otherwise they might see with their eyes,
> hear with their ears,
> understand with their hearts,
> and turn and be healed.

Isaiah Then I said:

Young Isaiah For how long, O Lord?

Isaiah And he answered:

The Lord Until the cities lie ruined
and without inhabitant,
until the houses are left deserted
and the fields ruined and ravaged,
until the Lord has sent everyone far away
and the land is utterly forsaken.]

Cast [This is] the word of the Lord.
All **Thanks be to God.**

Cast: **Isaiah, Seraph 1, Seraph 2, Young Isaiah, The Lord.** (This reading overlaps with the one below.)

Isaiah's commission
Isaiah 6.9–13

Isaiah The Lord told me to go and give the people this message:

The Lord No matter how much you listen, you will not understand. No matter how much you look, you will not know what is happening.

Isaiah Then he said to me:

The Lord Make the minds of these people dull, their ears deaf, and their eyes blind, so that they cannot see or hear or understand. If they did, they might turn to me and be healed.

Isaiah I asked:

Young Isaiah How long will it be like this, Lord?

Isaiah He answered:

The Lord Until the cities are ruined and empty—until the houses are uninhabited—until the land itself is a desolate waste. I will send the people far away and make the whole land desolate. Even if one person out of ten remains in the land, he too will be destroyed; he will be like the stump of an oak-tree that has been cut down.

Isaiah The stump represents a new beginning for God's people.

Cast [This is] the word of the Lord.
All **Thanks be to God.**

Cast: **Isaiah, The Lord, Young Isaiah.** (This reading follows on from that on pages 593–594.)

A message for King Ahaz
Isaiah 7.1–9

Narrator   When King Ahaz, the son of Jotham and grandson of Uzziah, ruled Judah, war broke out. Rezin, king of Syria, and Pekah son of Remaliah, king of Israel, attacked Jerusalem, but were unable to capture it.

When word reached the king of Judah that the armies of Syria were already in the territory of Israel, he and all his people were so terrified that they trembled like trees shaking in the wind.

The Lord said to Isaiah:

The Lord   Take your son Shear Jashub, and go to meet King Ahaz. You will find him on the road where the cloth makers work, at the end of the ditch that brings water from the upper pool. Tell him to keep alert, to stay calm, and not to be frightened or disturbed. The anger of King Rezin and his Syrians and of King Pekah is no more dangerous than the smoke from two smouldering sticks. Syria, together with Israel and its king, has made a plot. They intend to invade Judah, terrify the people into joining their side, and then put Tabeel's son on the throne.

But I, the Lord, declare that this will never happen. Why? Because Syria is no stronger than Damascus, its capital city, and Damascus is no stronger than King Rezin. As for Israel, within sixty-five years it will be too shattered to survive as a nation. Israel is no stronger than Samaria, its capital city, and Samaria is no stronger than King Pekah.

(deliberately)   If your faith is not enduring, you will not endure.

Cast   [This is] the word of the Lord.
All   **Thanks be to God.**

Cast: **Narrator, The Lord.**

The sign of Immanuel
Isaiah 7.10–14

Narrator   The Lord spoke to Ahaz, the King of Judah:

The Lord   Ask the Lord your God for a sign, whether in the deepest depths or in the highest heights.

Narrator   But Ahaz said:

Ahaz   I will not ask; I will not put the Lord to the test.

Narrator   Then Isaiah said:

Isaiah   Hear now, you house of David! Is it not enough to try the patience of men? Will you try the patience of my God also? Therefore the Lord himself will give you a sign:

The virgin will be with child
and will give birth to a son,
and will call him Immanuel.

Cast	[This is] the word of the Lord.
All	**Thanks be to God.**

Cast: **Narrator, The Lord, Ahaz, Isaiah.** (See also Appendix: Christmas Readings, New Testament page 405.)

Isaiah's son as a sign to the people
Isaiah 8.1–4

Isaiah	The Lord said to me:
The Lord	Isaiah, take a large piece of writing material and write on it in large letters:
	'Quick Loot, Fast Plunder.'
	Get two reliable men, the priest Uriah and Zechariah son of Jeberechiah, to serve as witnesses.
Isaiah	Some time later my wife became pregnant. When our son was born, the Lord said to me:
The Lord	Name him 'Quick-Loot-Fast-Plunder.' Before the boy is old enough to say 'Mummy' and 'Daddy,' all the wealth of Damascus and all the loot of Samaria will be carried off by the king of Assyria.
Cast	[This is] the word of the Lord.
All	**Thanks be to God.**

Cast: **Isaiah, The Lord.**

The King of Assyria is coming
Isaiah 8.5–10

Isaiah	The Lord spoke to me again.
The Lord	Because the people have rejected the quiet waters from the brook of Shiloah, and tremble before King Rezin and King Pekah, I, the Lord, will bring the emperor of Assyria and all his forces to attack Judah. They will advance like the flood waters of the River Euphrates, overflowing all its banks. They will sweep through Judah in a flood, rising shoulder high and covering everything.
Isaiah	God is with us! His outspread wings protect the land. Gather together in fear, you nations! Listen, you distant parts of the earth. Get ready to fight, but be afraid! Yes, get ready, but be afraid! Make your plans! But they will never succeed. Talk as much as you like! But it is all useless, because God is with us.
Cast	[This is] the word of the Lord.
All	**Thanks be to God.**

Cast: **Isaiah, The Lord.**

The Lord warns the Prophet
Isaiah 8.11–15

Isaiah With his great power the Lord warned me not to follow the path which the people were following:

The Lord Do not join in the schemes of the people and do not be afraid of the things that they fear. Remember that I, the Lord Almighty, am holy; I am the one you must fear. Because of my awesome holiness I am like a stone that people stumble over; I am like a trap that will catch the people of the kingdoms of Judah and Israel and the people of Jerusalem. Many will stumble; they will fall and be crushed. They will be caught in a trap.

Cast [This is] the word of the Lord.
All **Thanks be to God.**

Cast: **Isaiah, The Lord.**

Isaiah's warning against consulting the dead
Isaiah 8.16–20

Isaiah You, my disciples are to guard and preserve the messages that God has given me. The Lord has hidden himself from his people, but I trust him and place my hope in him.

Here I am with the children the Lord has given me. The Lord Almighty, whose throne is on Mount Zion, has sent us as living messages to the people of Israel. But people will tell you to ask for messages from fortune-tellers and mediums, who chirp and mutter [They will say]:

Person 1 After all, people *should* ask for messages from the spirits.

Person 2 They should consult the dead on behalf of the living.

Isaiah You are to answer them:

Disciple Listen to what the *Lord* is teaching you! Don't listen to *mediums*— what they tell you will do you no good.

Cast [This is] the word of the Lord.
All **Thanks be to God.**

Cast: **Isaiah, Person 1, Person 2** (can be the same as Person 1), **Disciple.**

The future King
Isaiah 9.2–7

Voice 1 The people who walked in darkness have seen a great light.

Voice 2 They lived in a land of shadows, but now light is shining on them.

Voice 3 You have given them great joy, Lord; you have made them happy.

Voice 1	They rejoice in what you have done, as people rejoice when they harvest their corn—
Voice 2	Or when they divide captured wealth.
Voice 3	For you have broken the yoke that burdened them—
Voice 1	And the rod that beat their shoulders.
Voice 2	You have defeated the nation that oppressed and exploited your people, just as you defeated the army of Midian long ago.
Voice 3	The boots of the invading army and all their bloodstained clothing will be destroyed by fire. (PAUSE)
Voice 1	A child is born to us!
Voice 2	A son is given to us!
Voice 3	And he will be our ruler.
Voice 1	He will be called—
Voice 2	'Wonderful Counsellor'
Voice 3	'Mighty God'
Voice 2	'Eternal Father'
Voice 3	'Prince of Peace'.
Voice 1	His royal power will continue to grow.
Voice 2	His kingdom will always be at peace.
Voice 3	He will rule as King David's successor, basing his power on right and justice, from now until the end of time.
Voices 1–3 (with flourish)	The Lord Almighty is determined to do all this!
Cast	[This is] the word of the Lord.
All	**Thanks be to God.**

Cast: **Voice 1, Voice 2, Voice 3.** (See also Appendix: Christmas Readings, New Testament page 405.)

The Lord will punish Israel
From Isaiah 9.8—10.3

Isaiah	The Lord has pronounced judgement on the kingdom of Israel, on the descendants of Jacob. All the people of Israel, everyone who lives in the city of Samaria, will know that he has done this. Now they are proud and arrogant [They say]:
Person 1	The brick buildings have fallen down, but we will replace them with stone buildings.
Person 2	The beams of sycomore wood have been cut down, but we will replace them with the finest cedar.
Isaiah	The Lord has stirred up their enemies to attack them. Syria on the east and Philistia on the west have opened their mouths to devour Israel. Yet even so the Lord's anger is not ended; his hand is still stretched out to punish.

→

The people of Israel have not repented; even though the Lord Almighty has punished them, they have not returned to him. In a single day the Lord will punish Israel's leaders and its people; he will cut them off, head and tail. The old and honourable men are the head—and the tail is the prophets whose teachings are lies! Those who lead these people have misled them and totally confused them.

You are doomed! You make unjust laws that oppress my people. That is how you prevent the poor from having their rights and from getting justice. That is how you take the property that belongs to widows and orphans. What will you do when God punishes you? What will you do when he brings disaster on you from a distant country? Where will you run to find help? Where will you hide your wealth?

Cast	[This is] the word of the Lord.
All	**Thanks be to God.**

Cast: **Isaiah, Person 1, Person 2.**

The Emperor of Assyria as the instrument of God
Isaiah 10.5–19

Isaiah	The Lord said:
The Lord	Assyria! I use Assyria like a club to punish those with whom I am angry. I sent Assyria to attack a godless nation, people who have made me angry. I sent them to loot and steal and trample on the people like dirt in the streets. But the Assyrian emperor has his own violent plans in mind. He is determined to destroy many nations [He boasts]:
Emperor (boastfully)	Every one of my commanders is a king! I conquered the cities of Calno and Carchemish, the cities of Hamath and Arpad. I conquered Samaria and Damascus. I stretched out my hand to punish those kingdoms that worship idols, idols more numerous than those of Jerusalem and Samaria. I have destroyed Samaria and all its idols, and I will do the same to Jerusalem and the images that are worshipped there.
[Isaiah	But the Lord says:]
The Lord	When I finish what I am doing on Mount Zion and in Jerusalem, I will punish the emperor of Assyria for all his boasting and all his pride.
[Isaiah	The emperor of Assyria boasts:]
Emperor (boastfully)	I have done it all myself. I am strong and wise and clever. I wiped out the boundaries between nations and took the supplies they had stored. Like a bull I have trampled on the people who live there. The nations of the world were like a bird's nest, and I gathered their wealth as easily as gathering eggs. Not a wing fluttered to scare me off; no beak opened to scream at me!

[Isaiah	But the Lord says:]
The Lord	Can an axe claim to be greater than the man who uses it? Is a saw more important than the man who saws with it? A club doesn't lift up a man; a man lifts up a club.
Isaiah	The Lord Almighty is going to send disease to punish those who are now well-fed. In their bodies there will be a fire that burns and burns. God, the light of Israel, will become a fire. Israel's holy God will become a flame, which in a single day will burn up everything, even the thorns and thistles. The rich forests and farmlands will be totally destroyed, in the same way that a fatal sickness destroys a man. There will be so few trees left that even a child will be able to count them.
Cast	[This is] the word of the Lord.
All	**Thanks be to God.**

Cast: **Isaiah, The Lord, Emperor.**

A few will come back
Isaiah 10.20–27

Isaiah	A time is coming when the people of Israel who have survived will no longer rely on the nation that almost destroyed them. They will truly put their trust in the Lord, Israel's holy God. A few of the people of Israel will come back to their mighty God. Even though now there are as many people of Israel as there are grains of sand by the sea, only a few will come back. Destruction is in store for the people, and it is fully deserved. Yes, throughout the whole country the Sovereign Lord Almighty will bring destruction, as he said he would. The Sovereign Lord Almighty says to his people who live in Zion:
The Lord	Do not be afraid of the Assyrians, even though they oppress you as the Egyptians used to do. In only a little while I will finish punishing you, and then I will destroy them. I, the Lord Almighty, will beat them with my whip as I beat the people of Midian at the Rock of Oreb. I will punish Assyria as I punished Egypt. When that time comes, I will free you from the power of Assyria, and their yoke will no longer be a burden on your shoulders.
Cast	[This is] the word of the Lord.
All	**Thanks be to God.**

Cast: **Isaiah, The Lord.**

The peaceful kingdom
Isaiah 11.1–9

Isaiah	The royal line of David is like a tree that has been cut down; but just as new branches sprout from a stump, so a new king will arise from among David's descendants.
Singer 1	The spirit of the Lord will give him wisdom, and the knowledge and skill to rule his people.
Singer 2	He will know the Lord's will and have reverence for him, and find pleasure in obeying him.
Singer 1	He will not judge by appearance or hearsay.
Singer 2	He will judge the poor fairly and defend the rights of the helpless.
Singer 1	At his command the people will be punished, and evil persons will die.
Singers 1 and 2	He will rule his people with justice and integrity. (PAUSE)
Singer 1	Wolves and sheep will live together in peace,
Singer 2	And leopards will lie down with young goats.
Singer 1	Calves and lion cubs will feed together, and little children will take care of them.
Singer 2	Cows and bears will eat together, and their calves and cubs will lie down in peace.
Singer 1	Lions will eat straw as cattle do.
Singer 2	Even a baby will not be harmed if it plays near a poisonous snake.
Singer 1	On Zion, God's sacred hill, there will be nothing harmful or evil.
Singers 1 and 2	The land will be as full of knowledge of the Lord as the seas are full of water.
Cast	[This is] the word of the Lord.
All	**Thanks be to God.**

Cast: **Isaiah, Singer 1, Singer 2.**

A hymn of thanksgiving
Isaiah 12.1–6

Isaiah	A day is coming when people will sing:
Singer 1	I praise you, Lord! You were angry with me, but now you comfort me and are angry no longer.
Singer 2	God is my saviour; I will trust him and not be afraid.

Singer 3	The Lord gives me power and strength; he is my saviour.
Singers 1–3	As fresh water brings joy to the thirsty, so God's people rejoice when he saves them. (PAUSE)
Isaiah	A day is coming when people will sing:
Singer 1	Give thanks to the Lord! Call for him to help you!
Singer 2	Tell all the nations what he has done!
Singer 3	Tell them how great he is!
Singer 1	Sing to the Lord because of the great things he has done.
Singer 2	Let the whole world hear the news.
Singer 3	Let everyone who lives in Zion shout and sing!
Singers 1–3	Israel's holy God is great, and he lives among his people.
Cast	[This is] the word of the Lord.
All	**Thanks be to God.**

Cast: **Isaiah, Singer 1, Singer 2, Singer 3.**

The Day of the Lord
Isaiah 13.6–13

Isaiah	Howl in pain! The day of the Lord is near, the day when the Almighty brings destruction. Everyone's hands will hang limp, and everyone's courage will fail. They will all be terrified and overcome with pain, like the pain of a woman in labour. They will look at each other in fear, and their faces will burn with shame. The day of the Lord is coming—that cruel day of his fierce anger and fury. The earth will be made a wilderness, and every sinner will be destroyed. Every star and every constellation will stop shining, the sun will be dark when it rises, and the moon will give no light. The Lord says:
The Lord	I will bring disaster on the earth and punish all wicked people for their sins. I will humble everyone who is proud and punish everyone who is arrogant and cruel. Those who survive will be scarcer than gold. I will make the heavens tremble, and the earth will be shaken out of its place on that day when I, the Lord Almighty, show my anger.
Cast	[This is] the word of the Lord.
All	**Thanks be to God.**

Cast: **Isaiah, The Lord.**

The return from exile
Isaiah 14.1–21

Isaiah

The Lord will once again be merciful to his people Israel and choose them as his own. He will let them live in their own land again, and foreigners will come and live there with them. Many nations will help the people of Israel to return to the land which the Lord gave them, and there the nations will serve Israel as slaves. Those who once captured Israel will now be captured by Israel, and the people of Israel will rule over those who once oppressed them.

The Lord will give the people of Israel relief from their pain and suffering, and from the hard work they were forced to do. When he does this, they are to mock the king of Babylonia and say:

Israelite 1

The cruel king has fallen!

Israelite 2

He will never oppress anyone again! The Lord has ended the power of the evil rulers who angrily oppressed the peoples and never stopped persecuting the nations they had conquered.

Israelite 1

Now at last the whole world enjoys rest and peace, and everyone sings for joy.

Israelite 2

The cypress-trees and the cedars of Lebanon rejoice over the fallen king, because there is no one to cut them down, now that he is gone!

Israelite 3

The world of the dead is getting ready to welcome the king of Babylonia.

Israelite 4

The ghosts of those who were powerful on earth are stirring about.

Israelite 3

The ghosts of kings are rising from their thrones. They all call out to him:

Ghost 1

Now you are as weak as we are!

Ghosts 1 and 2

You are one of us!

Ghost 2

You used to be honoured with the music of harps, but now here you are in the world of the dead.

Ghost 1

You lie on a bed of maggots and are covered with a blanket of worms.

Israelite 1

King of Babylonia, bright morning star, you have fallen from heaven!

Israelite 2

In the past you conquered nations, but now you have been thrown to the ground.

Israelite 1

You were determined to climb up to heaven and to place your throne above the highest stars.

Israelite 2

You thought you would sit like a king on that mountain in the north where the gods assemble.

Israelite 1	You said you would climb to the tops of the clouds and be like the Almighty.
Israelite 2	But instead, you have been brought down to the deepest part of the world of the dead.
Israelite 3	The dead will stare and gape at you. They will ask:
Ghost 1	Is this the man who shook the earth and made kingdoms tremble?
Ghost 2	Is this the man who destroyed cities and turned the world into a desert?
Ghost 1	Is this the man who never freed his prisoners or let them go home?
Israelite 4	All the kings of the earth lie in their magnificent tombs—
Israelite 3	But you have no tomb, and your corpse is thrown out to rot. It is covered by the bodies of soldiers killed in battle, thrown with them into a rocky pit, and trampled down.
Israelite 4	Because you ruined your country and killed your own people, you will not be buried like other kings.
Israelite 3	None of your evil family will survive.
Israelites 3 and 4	Let the slaughter begin!
Israelite 3	The sons of this king will die because of their ancestors' sins.
Israelite 4	None of them will ever rule the earth or cover it with cities.
Cast All	[This is] the word of the Lord. **Thanks be to God.**

Cast: **Isaiah, Israelite 1, Israelite 2, Israelite 3, Israelite 4, Ghost 1, Ghost 2.**

God will destroy Babylon
Isaiah 14.22–27

Isaiah	The Lord Almighty says:
The Lord	I will attack Babylon and bring it to ruin. I will leave nothing— no children, no survivors at all. I, the Lord, have spoken. I will turn Babylon into a marsh, and owls will live there. I will sweep Babylon with a broom that will sweep everything away. I, the Lord Almighty, have spoken.
Isaiah	The Lord Almighty has sworn an oath:
The Lord	What I have planned will happen. What I have determined to do will be done. I will destroy the Assyrians in my land of Israel and trample upon them on my mountains. I will free my people from the Assyrian yoke and from the burdens they have had to bear. This is my plan for the world, and my arm is stretched out to punish the nations.

Isaiah	The Lord Almighty is determined to do this; he has stretched out his arm to punish, and no one can stop him.
Cast **All**	[This is] the word of the Lord. **Thanks be to God.**

Cast: **Isaiah, The Lord.**

Moab's hopeless situation
From Isaiah 16.1–14

Isaiah	From the city of Sela in the desert, the people of Moab send a lamb as a present to the one who rules in Jerusalem. They wait on the banks of the River Arnon and move aimlessly to and fro, like birds driven from their nest. They say to the people of Judah:
Moabite 1	Tell us what to do.
Moabite 2	Protect us like a tree that casts a cool shadow in the heat of noon, and let us rest in your shade.
Moabite 1	We are refugees; hide us where no one can find us.
Moabite 2	Let us stay in your land.
Moabites 1 & 2	Protect us from those who want to destroy us.
Commentator	Oppression and destruction will end, and those who are devastating the country will be gone. Then one of David's descendants will be king, and he will rule the people with faithfulness and love. He will be quick to do what is right, and he will see that justice is done.
Isaiah	The people of Judah say:
Judaean 1	We have heard how proud the people of Moab are.
Judaean 2	We know that they are arrogant and conceited, but their boasts are empty.
Isaiah	That is the message the Lord gave earlier about Moab. And now the Lord says:
The Lord	In exactly three years, Moab's great wealth will disappear. Of its many people, only a few will survive, and they will be weak.
Cast **All**	[This is] the word of the Lord. **Thanks be to God.**

Cast: **Isaiah, Moabite 1, Moabite 2, Commentator** (can be the same as Isaiah), **Judaean 1, Judaean 2, The Lord.**

God will punish Syria and Israel
From Isaiah 17.1–11

Isaiah	The Lord said:
The Lord	Damascus will not be a city any longer; it will be only a pile of ruins. The cities of Syria will be deserted for ever. They will be a

pasture for sheep and cattle, and no one will drive them away. Israel will be defenceless, and Damascus will lose its independence. Those Syrians who survive will be in disgrace like the people of Israel. I, the Lord Almighty, have spoken.

Isaiah The Lord said:

The Lord A day is coming when Israel's greatness will come to an end, and its wealth will be replaced by poverty. Israel will be like a field where the corn has been cut and harvested, as desolate as a field in the valley of Rephaim when it has been picked bare. Only a few people will survive, and Israel will be like an olive-tree from which all the olives have been picked except two or three at the very top, or a few that are left on the lower branches. I, the Lord God of Israel, have spoken.

Isaiah When that day comes, people will turn for help to their Creator, the holy God of Israel. They will no longer rely on the altars they made with their own hands, or trust in their own handiwork—symbols of the goddess Asherah and altars for burning incense.

Israel, you have forgotten the God who rescues you and who protects you like a mighty rock. Instead, you plant sacred gardens in order to worship a foreign god. But even if they sprouted and blossomed the very morning you planted them, there would still be no harvest. There would be only trouble and incurable pain.

Cast [This is] the word of the Lord.
All **Thanks be to God.**

Cast: **Isaiah, The Lord.**

God will punish Sudan
Isaiah 18.1–7

Isaiah Beyond the rivers of Sudan there is a land where the sound of wings is heard. From that land ambassadors come down the Nile in boats made of reeds. Go back home, swift messengers! Take a message back to your land divided by rivers, to your strong and powerful nation, to your tall and smooth-skinned people, who are feared all over the world.

Listen, everyone who lives on earth! Look for a signal flag to be raised on the tops of the mountains! Listen for the blowing of the bugle! The Lord said to me:

The Lord I will look down from heaven as quietly as the dew forms in the warm nights of harvest time, as serenely as the sun shines in the heat of the day. Before the grapes are gathered, when the blossoms have all fallen and the grapes are ripening, the enemy will destroy the Sudanese as easily as a knife cuts branches from a vine. The corpses of their soldiers will be left exposed to the birds and the wild animals. In summer the birds will feed on them, and in winter, the animals.

Isaiah	A time is coming when the Lord Almighty will receive offerings from this land divided by rivers, this strong and powerful nation, this tall and smooth-skinned people, who are feared all over the world. They will come to Mount Zion, where the Lord Almighty is worshipped.
Cast	[This is] the word of the Lord.
All	**Thanks be to God.**

Cast: **Isaiah, The Lord.**

God will punish Egypt
Isaiah 19.1–12

Isaiah	This is a message about Egypt.
	The Lord is coming to Egypt, riding swiftly on a cloud. The Egyptian idols tremble before him, and the people of Egypt lose their courage. The Lord says:
The Lord	I will stir up civil war in Egypt and turn brother against brother and neighbour against neighbour. Rival cities will fight each other, and rival kings will struggle for power. I am going to frustrate the plans of the Egyptians and destroy their morale. They will ask their idols to help them, and they will go and consult mediums and ask the spirits of the dead for advice. I will hand the Egyptians over to a tyrant, to a cruel king who will rule them. I, the Lord Almighty, have spoken.
Isaiah	The water will be low in the Nile, and the river will gradually dry up. The channels of the river will stink as they slowly go dry. Reeds and rushes will wither, and all the crops sown along the banks of the Nile will dry up and be blown away. Everyone who earns his living by fishing in the Nile will groan and cry; their hooks and their nets will be useless. Those who make linen cloth will be in despair; weavers and skilled workmen will be broken and depressed.
	The leaders of the city of Zoan are fools! Egypt's wisest men give stupid advice! How dare they tell the king that they are successors to the ancient scholars and kings? King of Egypt, where are those clever advisers of yours? Perhaps they can tell you what plans the Lord Almighty has for Egypt.
Cast	[This is] the word of the Lord.
All	**Thanks be to God.**

Cast: **Isaiah, The Lord.**

A vision of the fall of Babylon
Isaiah 21.1–10

Isaiah	This is a message about Babylonia. Like a whirlwind sweeping across the desert, disaster will come from a terrifying land. I have seen a vision of cruel events, a vision of betrayal and destruction:

Commander	Army of Elam, attack! Army of Media, lay siege to the cities! God will put an end to the suffering which Babylon has caused.
Isaiah	What I saw and heard in the vision has filled me with terror and pain, pain like that of a woman in labour. My head is spinning, and I am trembling with fear. I had been longing for evening to come, but it has brought me nothing but terror. In the vision a banquet is ready; rugs are spread for the guests to sit on. They are eating and drinking. Suddenly the command rings out:
Commander	Officers! Prepare your shields!
Isaiah	Then the Lord said to me:
The Lord	Go and post a sentry, and tell him to report what he sees. If he sees men coming on horseback, two by two, and men riding on donkeys and camels, he is to observe them carefully.
Isaiah	The sentry calls out:
Sentry	Sir, I have been standing guard at my post day and night.
Isaiah	Suddenly, here they come! Men on horseback, two by two. The sentry gives the news:
Sentry	Babylon has fallen! All the idols they worshipped lie shattered on the ground.
Isaiah	My people Israel, you have been threshed like wheat, but now I have announced to you the good news that I have heard from the Lord Almighty, the God of Israel.
Cast	[This is] the word of the Lord.
All	**Thanks be to God.**

Cast: **Isaiah, Commander, The Lord, Sentry.**

Messages about Edom, Arabia and Jerusalem
Isaiah 21.11—22.4, 12–14

Announcer	This is a message about Edom.
Isaiah	Someone calls to me from Edom:
Edomite	Sentry, how soon will the night be over? Tell me how soon it will end.
Isaiah	I answer, 'Morning is coming, but night will come again. If you want to ask again, come back and ask.' (PAUSE)
Announcer	This is a message about Arabia:
Isaiah	You people of Dedan, whose caravans camp in the barren country of Arabia, give water to the thirsty people who come to you. You people of the land of Tema, give food to the refugees. People are fleeing to escape from swords that are ready to kill them, from bows that are ready to shoot, from all the dangers of war.

Then the Lord said to me: |

The Lord	In exactly one year the greatness of the tribes of Kedar will be at an end. The bowmen are the bravest men of Kedar, but few of them will be left. I, the Lord God of Israel, have spoken. (PAUSE)
Announcer	This is a message about the Valley of Vision.
Isaiah	What is happening? Why are all the people of the city celebrating on the roofs of the houses? The whole city is in an uproar, filled with noise and excitement.
	Your men who died in this war did not die fighting. All your leaders ran away and were captured before they shot a single arrow. Now leave me alone to weep bitterly over all those of my people who have died. Don't try to comfort me.
	The Sovereign Lord Almighty was calling you then to weep and mourn, to shave your heads and wear sackcloth. Instead, you laughed and celebrated. You killed sheep and cattle to eat, and you drank wine. You said:
Jew 1	We might as well eat and drink!
Jew 2	Tomorrow we'll be dead.
Isaiah	The Sovereign Lord Almighty himself spoke to me and said:
The Lord	This evil will never be forgiven them as long as they live. (PAUSE) I, the Sovereign Lord Almighty, have spoken!
Cast	[This is] the word of the Lord.
All	**Thanks be to God.**

Cast: **Announcer, Isaiah** (can be the same as Announcer), **Edomite, The Lord, Jew 1, Jew 2** (can be the same as Jew 1).

A warning to Shebna
Isaiah 22.15–25

Isaiah	The Sovereign Lord Almighty told me to go to Shebna, the manager of the royal household, and say to him:
Voice of Isaiah	Who do you think you are? What right have you to carve a tomb for yourself out of the rocky hillside? You may be important, but the Lord will pick you up and throw you away. He will pick you up like a ball and throw you into a much larger country. You will die there beside the chariots you were so proud of. You are a disgrace to your master's household. The Lord will remove you from office and bring you down from your high position.
Isaiah	The Lord said to Shebna:
The Lord	When that happens, I will send for my servant Eliakim son of Hilkiah. I will put your official robe and belt on him and give him all the authority you have had. He will be like a father to the people of Jerusalem and Judah. I will give him complete authority under the king, the descendant of David. He will have the keys of office; what he opens, no one will shut, and what he shuts, no one will open. I will fasten him firmly in place like a peg, and he will be a source of honour to his whole family.

But all his relatives and dependants will become a burden to him. They will hang on him like pots and bowls hanging from a peg! When that happens, the peg that was firmly fastened will work loose and fall. And that will be the end of everything that was hanging on it.

Isaiah
(with flourish)   The Lord has spoken!

Cast   [This is] the word of the Lord.
All   **Thanks be to God.**

Cast: **Isaiah, Voice of Isaiah, The Lord.**

A hymn of praise
Isaiah 25.1–5

Singer 1   Lord, you are my God;
I will honour you and praise your name.

Singer 2   You have done amazing things;
you have faithfully carried out the plans you made long ago.

Singer 1   You have turned cities into ruins
and destroyed their fortifications.

Singer 2   The palaces which our enemies built
are gone for ever.

Singer 1   The people of powerful nations will praise you;
you will be feared in the cities of cruel nations.

Singer 2   The poor and the helpless have fled to you
and have been safe in times of trouble.

Singer 1   You give them shelter from storms
and shade from the burning heat.

Singer 2   Cruel men attack like a winter storm,
like drought in a dry land.
But you, Lord, have silenced our enemies.

Singer 1   You silence the shouts of cruel men,
as a cloud cools a hot day.

Cast   [This is] the word of the Lord.
All   **Thanks be to God.**

Cast: **Singer 1, Singer 2.**

God prepares a banquet
Isaiah 25.6–9

Isaiah   Here on Mount Zion the Lord Almighty will prepare a banquet for all the nations of the world—a banquet of the richest food and the finest wine. Here he will suddenly remove the cloud of sorrow that has been hanging over all the nations. The Sovereign Lord will destroy death for ever! He will wipe away the tears from

→

everyone's eyes and take away the disgrace his people have suffered throughout the world. The Lord himself has spoken! When it happens, everyone will say:

Believers 1 and 2	He is our God!
Believer 1	We have put our trust in him, and he has rescued us.
Believers 1 and 2	He is the Lord!
Believer 2	We have put our trust in him, and now we are happy and joyful because he has saved us.

Cast	[This is] the word of the Lord.
All	**Thanks be to God.**

Cast: **Isaiah, Believer 1, Believer 2.**

God will give his people victory
Isaiah 26.1–8

Isaiah	A day is coming when the people will sing this song in the land of Judah:
Singer 1	Our city is strong! God himself defends its walls!
Singer 2	Open the city gates and let the faithful nation enter, the nation whose people do what is right.
Singer 3	You, Lord, give perfect peace to those who keep their purpose firm and put their trust in you.
Singer 1	Trust in the Lord for ever; he will always protect us.
Singer 2	He has humbled those who were proud; he destroyed the strong city they lived in, and sent its walls crashing into the dust.
Singer 3	Those who were oppressed walk over it now and trample it under their feet.
Singer 1	Lord, you make the path smooth for good men; the road they travel is level.
Singers 2 and 3	We follow your will and put our hope in you; you are all that we desire.

Cast	[This is] the word of the Lord.
All	**Thanks be to God.**

Cast: **Isaiah, Singer 1, Singer 2, Singer 3.**

Restoration
Isaiah 27.2–6

Isaiah   The Lord will say of his pleasant vineyard:

The Lord   I watch over it and water it continually. I guard it night and day so that no one will harm it. I am no longer angry with the vineyard. If only there were thorns and briars to fight against, then I would burn them up completely. But if the enemies of my people want my protection, let them make peace with me. Yes, let them make peace with me.

Isaiah   In days to come the people of Israel, the descendants of Jacob, will take root like a tree, and they will blossom and bud. The earth will be covered with the fruit they produce.

Cast   [This is] the word of the Lord.
All   **Thanks be to God.**

Cast: **Isaiah, The Lord.**

Isaiah and the drunken prophets of Judah
From Isaiah 28.7–13

Isaiah   The prophets and the priests are so drunk that they stagger. They have drunk so much wine and liquor that they stumble in confusion. The prophets are too drunk to understand the visions that God sends, and the priests are too drunk to decide the cases that are brought to them. They complain about me [They say]:

Priest 1   Who does that man think he's teaching?

Priest 2   Who needs his message?

Priest 1   It's only good for babies that have just been weaned!

Priest 2   He is trying to teach us letter by letter, line by line, lesson by lesson.

Isaiah   If you won't listen to me, then God will use foreigners speaking some strange-sounding language to teach you a lesson. He offered rest and comfort to all of you, but you refused to listen to him. That is why the Lord is going to teach you letter by letter, line by line, lesson by lesson. Then you will stumble with every step you take. You will be wounded, trapped, and taken prisoner.

Cast   [This is] the word of the Lord.
All   **Thanks be to God.**

Cast: **Isaiah, Priest 1, Priest 2.**

A cornerstone for Zion
Isaiah 28.14–22

Isaiah   Now you arrogant men who rule here in Jerusalem over this people, listen to what the Lord is saying. You boast that you have

→

made a treaty with death and reached an agreement with the world of the dead. You are certain that disaster will spare you when it comes, because you depend on lies and deceit to keep you safe. This, now, is what the Sovereign Lord says:

The Lord I am placing in Zion a foundation that is firm and strong. In it I am putting a solid cornerstone on which are written the words, 'Faith that is firm is also patient.' Justice will be the measuring-line for the foundation, and honesty will be its plumb-line.

Isaiah Hailstorms will sweep away all the lies you depend on, and floods will destroy your security. The treaty you have made with death will be abolished, and your agreement with the world of the dead will be cancelled. When disaster sweeps down, you will be overcome. It will strike you again and again, morning after morning. You will have to bear it day and night. Each new message from God will bring new terror! You will be like the man in the proverb, who tries to sleep in a bed too short to stretch out on, with a blanket too narrow to wrap himself in. The Lord will fight as he did at Mount Perazim and in the valley of Gibeon, in order to do what he intends to do—strange as his actions may seem. He will complete his work, his mysterious work.

Don't laugh at the warning I am giving you! If you do, it will be even harder for you to escape. I have heard the Lord Almighty's decision to destroy the whole country.

Cast [This is] the word of the Lord.
All **Thanks be to God.**

Cast: **Isaiah, The Lord.**

Disregarded warnings
Isaiah 29.9–14

Isaiah Go ahead and be stupid! Go ahead and be blind! Get drunk without any wine! Stagger without drinking a drop! The Lord has made you drowsy, ready to fall into a deep sleep. The prophets should be the eyes of the people, but God has blindfolded them. The meaning of every prophetic vision will be hidden from you; it will be like a sealed scroll. If you take it to someone who knows how to read and ask him to read it to you, he will say he can't because it is sealed. If you give it to someone who can't read and ask him to read it to you, he will answer that he doesn't know how. The Lord said:

The Lord These people claim to worship me, but their words are meaningless, and their hearts are somewhere else. Their religion is nothing but human rules and traditions, which they have simply memorized. So I will startle them with one unexpected blow after another. Those who are wise will turn out to be fools, and all their cleverness will be useless.

Cast [This is] the word of the Lord.
All **Thanks be to God.**

Cast: **Isaiah, The Lord.**

Hope for the future
Isaiah 29.15—24

Isaiah   Those who try to hide their plans from the Lord are doomed! They carry out their schemes in secret and think no one will see them or know what they are doing. They turn everything upside down. Which is more important, the potter or the clay? Can something a man has made say to him:

Thing   You didn't make me?

Isaiah   Or can it say to him:

Thing   You don't know what you are doing?

Isaiah   As the saying goes, before long the dense forest will become farmland, and the farmland will go back to forest.

When that day comes, the deaf will be able to hear a book being read aloud, and the blind, who have been living in darkness, will open their eyes and see. Poor and humble people will once again find the happiness which the Lord, the holy God of Israel, gives. It will be the end of those who oppress others and show contempt for God. Every sinner will be destroyed. God will destroy those who slander others, those who prevent the punishment of criminals, and those who tell lies to keep honest men from getting justice. So now the Lord, the God of Israel, who rescued Abraham from trouble, says:

The Lord   My people, you will not be disgraced any longer, and your faces will no longer be pale with shame. When you see the children that I will give you, then you will acknowledge that I am the holy God of Israel. You will honour me and stand in awe of me. Foolish people will learn to understand, and those who are always grumbling will be glad to be taught.

Cast   [This is] the word of the Lord.
All   **Thanks be to God.**

Cast: **Isaiah, Thing, The Lord.**

The disobedient people
From Isaiah 30.8—18

Isaiah   God told me to write down in a book what the people are like, so that there would be a permanent record of how evil they are. They are always rebelling against God, always lying, always refusing to listen to the Lord's teachings. They tell the prophets to keep quiet.

Person 1   Don't talk to us about what's right.

Person 2   Tell us what we want to hear.

Person 1   Let us keep our illusions.

Person 3   Get out of our way and stop blocking our path.

Person 2	We don't want to hear about your holy God of Israel.
Isaiah	But this is what the holy God of Israel says:
The Lord	You ignore what I tell you and rely on violence and deceit. You are guilty. You are like a high wall with a crack running down it; suddenly you will collapse. You will be shattered like a clay pot, so badly broken that there is no piece big enough to pick up hot coals with, or to scoop water from a cistern.
Isaiah	The Sovereign Lord, the holy God of Israel, says to the people:
The Lord	Come back and quietly trust in me. Then you will be strong and secure.
Isaiah	But you refuse to do it! And yet the Lord is waiting to be merciful to you. He is ready to take pity on you because he always does what is right. Happy are those who put their trust in the Lord.
Cast	[This is] the word of the Lord.
All	**Thanks be to God.**

Cast: **Isaiah, Person 1, Person 2, Person 3, The Lord.**

God will bless his people
Isaiah 30.19–26

Isaiah	You people who live in Jerusalem will not weep any more. The Lord is compassionate, and when you cry to him for help, he will answer you. The Lord will make you go through hard times, but he himself will be there to teach you, and you will not have to search for him any more. If you wander off the road to the right or the left, you will hear his voice behind you saying:
The Lord	Here is the road. Follow it.
Isaiah	You will take your idols plated with silver and your idols covered with gold, and will throw them away like filth, shouting:
Person	Out of my sight!
Isaiah	Whenever you sow your seeds, the Lord will send rain to make them grow and will give you a rich harvest, and your livestock will have plenty of pasture. The oxen and donkeys that plough your fields will eat the finest and best fodder. On the day when the forts of your enemies are captured and their people are killed, streams of water will flow from every mountain and every hill. The moon will be as bright as the sun, and the sun will be seven times brighter than usual, like the light of seven days in one. This will all happen when the Lord bandages and heals the wounds he has given his people.
Cast	[This is] the word of the Lord.
All	**Thanks be to God.**

Cast: **Isaiah, The Lord, Person.**

God will protect Jerusalem
Isaiah 31.1–9

Isaiah Those who go to Egypt for help are doomed! They are relying on Egypt's vast military strength—horses, chariots, and soldiers. But they do not rely on the Lord, the holy God of Israel, or ask him for help. He knows what he is doing! He sends disaster. He carries out his threats to punish evil men and those who protect them. The Egyptians are not gods—they are only human. Their horses are not supernatural. When the Lord acts, the strong nation will crumble, and the weak nation it helped will fall. Both of them will be destroyed. The Lord said to me:

The Lord No matter how shepherds yell and shout, they can't scare away a lion from an animal that it has killed; in the same way, there is nothing that can keep me, the Lord Almighty, from protecting Mount Zion. Just as a bird hovers over its nest to protect its young, so I, the Lord Almighty, will protect Jerusalem and defend it.

Isaiah The Lord said:

The Lord People of Israel, you have sinned against me and opposed me. But now, come back to me! A time is coming when all of you will throw away the sinful idols you made out of silver and gold. Assyria will be destroyed in war, but not by human power. The Assyrians will run from battle, and their young men will be made slaves. Their emperor will run away in terror, and the officers will be so frightened that they will abandon their battle flags.

Isaiah The Lord has spoken—the Lord who is worshipped in Jerusalem and whose fire burns there for sacrifices.

Cast [This is] the word of the Lord.
All **Thanks be to God.**

Cast: **Isaiah, The Lord.**

The Lord warns the people
From Isaiah 33.10–16

Isaiah The Lord says to the nations:

The Lord Now I will act. I will show how powerful I am. You make worthless plans and everything you do is useless. My spirit is like a fire that will destroy you. You will crumble like rocks burnt to make lime, like thorns burnt to ashes. Let everyone near and far hear what I have done and acknowledge my power.

Isaiah The sinful people of Zion are trembling with fright. They say:

Jew 1 God's judgement is like a fire that burns for ever.

Jew 2 Can any of us survive a fire like that?

Isaiah	You can survive if you say and do what is right. Don't use your power to cheat the poor and don't accept bribes. Don't join with those who plan to commit murder or to do other evil things. Then you will be safe; you will be as secure as if you were in a strong fortress. You will have food to eat and water to drink.
Cast	[This is] the word of the Lord.
All	**Thanks be to God.**

Cast: **Isaiah, The Lord, Jew 1, Jew 2.**

The Road of Holiness
Isaiah 35.1–10

Voice 1	The desert will rejoice, and flowers will bloom in the wilderness.
Voice 2	The desert will sing and shout for joy; it will be as beautiful as the Lebanon Mountains and as fertile as the fields of Carmel and Sharon.
Voice 3	Everyone will see the Lord's splendour, see his greatness and power.
Voice 1	Give strength to hands that are tired and to knees that tremble with weakness.
Voice 2	Tell everyone who is discouraged:
Voice 3	Be strong and don't be afraid! God is coming to your rescue, coming to punish your enemies.
Voice 1	The blind will be able to see, and the deaf will hear.
Voice 2	The lame will leap and dance, and those who cannot speak will shout for joy.
Voice 1	Streams of water will flow through the desert.
Voice 2	The burning sand will become a lake—
Voice 3	And dry land will be filled with springs.
Voice 1	Where jackals used to live—
Voice 2	Marsh grass and reeds will grow.
Voice 1	There will be a highway there, called—
Voice 3	'The Road of Holiness.'
Voice 1	No sinner will ever travel that road.
Voice 2	No fools will mislead those who follow it.
Voice 1	No lions will be there.
Voice 3	No fierce animals will pass that way.
Voice 1	Those whom the Lord has rescued will travel home by that road.

Voice 2	They will reach Jerusalem with gladness, singing and shouting for joy.
Voice 3	They will be happy for ever, for ever free from sorrow and grief.
Cast	[This is] the word of the Lord.
All	**Thanks be to God.**

Cast: **Voice 1, Voice 2, Voice 3.**

The Assyrians threaten Jerusalem
From Isaiah 36.1–22

Narrator	In the fourteenth year that Hezekiah was king of Judah, Sennacherib, the emperor of Assyria, attacked the fortified cities of Judah and captured them. Then he ordered his chief official to go from Lachish to Jerusalem with a large military force to demand that King Hezekiah should surrender. The official occupied the road where the clothmakers work, by the ditch that brings water from the upper pond. Three Judaeans came out to meet him: the official in charge of the palace, Eliakim son of Hilkiah; the court secretary, Shebna; and the official in charge of the records, Joah son of Asaph. The Assyrian official told them that the emperor wanted to know what made King Hezekiah so confident [He demanded]:
Official	Do you think that words can take the place of military skill and might? Who do you think will help you rebel against Assyria? You are expecting Egypt to help you, but that would be like using a reed as a walking-stick—it would break and jab your hand. That is what the king of Egypt is like when anyone relies on him.
Narrator	The Assyrian official went on:
Official	Or will you tell me that you are relying on the Lord your God? It was the Lord's shrines and altars that Hezekiah destroyed when he told the people of Judah and Jerusalem to worship at one altar only. I will make a bargain with you in the name of the emperor. I will give you two thousand horses if you can find that many men to ride them. You are no match for even the lowest ranking Assyrian official, and yet you expect the Egyptians to send you chariots and cavalry. Do you think I have attacked your country and destroyed it without the Lord's help? The Lord himself told me to attack it and destroy it.
Narrator	Then Eliakim, Shebna, and Joah said to the official:
Eliakim	Speak Aramaic to us. We understand it. Don't speak Hebrew; all the people on the wall are listening.
Narrator	He replied:
Official	Do you think you and the king are the only ones the emperor sent me to say all these things to? No, I am also talking to the people who are sitting on the wall.

Narrator	Then the official stood up and shouted in Hebrew:
Official	Listen to what the emperor of Assyria is telling you. He warns you not to let Hezekiah deceive you. Hezekiah can't save you. And don't let him persuade you to rely on the Lord. Don't think that the Lord will save you and that he will stop our Assyrian army from capturing your city. Don't listen to Hezekiah! The emperor of Assyria commands you to come out of the city and surrender. You will all be allowed to eat grapes from your own vines and figs from your own trees, and to drink water from your own wells—until the emperor resettles you in a country much like your own, where there are vineyards to give wine and there is corn for making bread. Don't let Hezekiah fool you into thinking that the Lord will rescue you. Did the gods of any other nations save their countries from the emperor of Assyria? Where are they now, the gods of Hamath and Arpad? Where are the gods of Sepharvaim? Did anyone save Samaria? When did any of the gods of all these countries ever save their country from our emperor? Then what makes you think the Lord can save Jerusalem?
Narrator	The people kept quiet, just as King Hezekiah had told them to; they did not say a word. Then Eliakim, Shebna, and Joah tore their clothes in grief and went and reported to the king what the Assyrian official had said.
Cast	[This is] the word of the Lord.
All	**Thanks be to God.**

Cast: **Narrator, Official, Eliakim.**

The king asks Isaiah's advice
Isaiah 37.1–7

Narrator	As soon as King Hezekiah heard that the emperor of Assyria was demanding the surrender of Jerusalem, he tore his clothes in grief, put on sackcloth, and went to the Temple of the Lord. He sent Eliakim, the official in charge of the palace, Shebna, the court secretary, and the senior priests to the prophet Isaiah son of Amoz. They also were wearing sackcloth. This is the message which he told them to give to Isaiah:
Hezekiah	Today is a day of suffering; we are being punished and are in disgrace. We are like a woman who is ready to give birth, but is too weak to do it. The Assyrian emperor has sent his chief official to insult the living God. May the Lord your God hear these insults and punish those who spoke them. So pray to God for those of our people who survive.
Narrator	When Isaiah received King Hezekiah's message, he sent back this answer:
Isaiah	The Lord tells you not to let the Assyrians frighten you by their

claims that he cannot save you. The Lord will cause the emperor to hear a rumour that will make him go back to his own country, and the Lord will have him killed there.

Cast	[This is] the word of the Lord.
All	**Thanks be to God.**

Cast: **Narrator, Hezekiah, Isaiah.**

The Assyrians send another threat
Isaiah 37.8–20

Narrator The Assyrian emperor's chief official learnt that the emperor had left Lachish and was fighting against the nearby city of Libnah; so he went there to consult him. Word reached the Assyrians that the Egyptian army, led by King Tirhakah of Sudan, was coming to attack them. When the emperor heard this, he sent a letter to King Hezekiah of Judah [to say to him]:

Emperor The god you are trusting in has told you that you will not fall into my hands, but don't let that deceive you. You have heard what an Assyrian emperor does to any country he decides to destroy. Do you think that you can escape? My ancestors destroyed the cities of Gozan, Haran, and Rezeph, and killed the people of Betheden who lived in Telassar, and none of their gods could save them. Where are the kings of the cities of Hamath, Arpad, Sepharvaim, Hena, and Ivvah?

Narrator King Hezekiah took the letter from the messengers and read it. Then he went to the Temple, and placed the letter there in the presence of the Lord. [He prayed:]

Hezekiah Almighty Lord, God of Israel, enthroned above the winged creatures, you alone are God, ruling all the kingdoms of the world. You created the earth and the sky. Now, Lord, hear us and look at what is happening to us. Listen to all the things that Sennacherib is saying to insult you, the living God. We all know, Lord, that the emperors of Assyria have destroyed many nations, made their lands desolate, and burnt up their gods—which were no gods at all, only images of wood and stone made by human hands. Now, Lord our God, rescue us from the Assyrians, so that all the nations of the world will know that you alone are God.

Cast	[This is] the word of the Lord.
All	**Thanks be to God.**

Cast: **Narrator, Emperor, Hezekiah.**

Isaiah's message to the king
From Isaiah 37.21–35

Narrator Isaiah sent a message telling King Hezekiah that in answer to the king's prayer the Lord had said:

The Lord	The city of Jerusalem laughs at you, Sennacherib, and despises you. Whom do you think you have been insulting and ridiculing? You have been disrespectful to me, the holy God of Israel. You sent your servants to boast to me that with all your chariots you had conquered the highest mountains of Lebanon. You boasted that there you cut down the tallest cedars and the finest cypress-trees, and that you reached the deepest parts of the forests. You boasted that you dug wells and drank water in foreign lands, and that the feet of your soldiers tramped the River Nile dry.
	Have you never heard that I planned all this long ago? And now I have carried it out. I gave you the power to turn fortified cities into piles of rubble. The people who lived there were powerless; they were frightened and stunned. They were like grass in a field or weeds growing on a roof when the hot east wind blasts them.
	But I know everything about you, what you do and where you go. I know how you rage against me. I have received the report of that rage and that pride of yours, and now I will put a hook through your nose and a bit in your mouth and will take you back by the road on which you came.
Narrator	Then Isaiah said to King Hezekiah:
Isaiah	This is a sign of what will happen. This year and next you will have only wild grain to eat, but the following year you will be able to sow your corn and harvest it, and plant vines and eat grapes. Those in Judah who survive will flourish like plants that send roots deep into the ground and produce fruit. There will be people in Jerusalem and on Mount Zion who will survive, because the Lord Almighty is determined to make this happen.
	This is what the Lord has said about the Assyrian emperor:
The Lord	He will not enter this city or shoot a single arrow against it. No soldiers with shields will come near the city, and no siege-mounds will be built round it. He will go back by the road on which he came, without entering this city. I, the Lord, have spoken. I will defend this city and protect it, for the sake of my own honour and because of the promise I made to my servant David.
Cast	[This is] the word of the Lord.
All	**Thanks be to God.**

Cast: **Narrator, The Lord, Isaiah.**

King Hezekiah's illness and recovery
Isaiah 38.1–20

Narrator	King Hezekiah fell ill and almost died. The prophet Isaiah son of Amoz went to see him [and said to him:]
Isaiah	The Lord tells you that you are to put everything in order because you will not recover. Get ready to die.
Narrator	Hezekiah turned his face to the wall [and prayed]:

Hezekiah	Remember, Lord, that I have served you faithfully and loyally, and that I have always tried to do what you wanted me to.
Narrator	And he began to cry bitterly. Then the Lord commanded Isaiah to go back to Hezekiah and say to him:
The Lord	I, the Lord, the God of your ancestor David, have heard your prayer and seen your tears; I will let you live fifteen years longer. I will rescue you and this city of Jerusalem from the emperor of Assyria, and I will continue to protect the city.
Narrator	Isaiah told the king to put a paste made of figs on his boil, and he would get well. Then King Hezekiah asked:
Hezekiah	What is the sign to prove that I will be able to go to the Temple?
Narrator	Isaiah replied:
Isaiah	The Lord will give you a sign to prove that he will keep his promise. On the stairway built by King Ahaz, the Lord will make the shadow go back ten steps.
Narrator	And the shadow moved back ten steps. (PAUSE)
	After Hezekiah recovered from his illness, he wrote this song of praise:
Hezekiah (to audience)	I thought that in the prime of life I was going to the world of the dead, never to live out my life. I thought that in this world of the living I would never again see the Lord or any living person. My life was cut off and ended, like a tent that is taken down, like cloth that is cut from a loom. I thought that God was ending my life. All night I cried out with pain, as if a lion were breaking my bones. I thought that God was ending my life. My voice was thin and weak, and I moaned like a dove. My eyes grew tired from looking to heaven.
(praying)	Lord, rescue me from all this trouble.
(to audience)	What can I say? The Lord has done this. My heart is bitter, and I cannot sleep.
(praying)	Lord, I will live for you, for you alone; heal me and let me live. My bitterness will turn into peace. You save my life from all danger; you forgive all my sins. No one in the world of the dead can praise you; the dead cannot trust in your faithfulness. It is the living who praise you, as I praise you now.

→

623

Fathers tell their children how faithful you are.
Lord, you have healed me.
We will play harps and sing your praise,
sing praise in your Temple as long as we live.

Cast	[This is] the word of the Lord.
All	**Thanks be to God.**

Cast: **Narrator, Isaiah, Hezekiah, The Lord** (can also be Isaiah).

Messengers from Babylonia
Isaiah 39.1–8

Narrator	The king of Babylonia, Merodach Baladan, son of Baladan, heard that King Hezekiah had been ill, so he sent him a letter and a present. Hezekiah welcomed the messengers and showed them his wealth—his silver and gold, his spices and perfumes, and all his military equipment. There was nothing in his storerooms or anywhere in his kingdom that he did not show them.

Then the prophet Isaiah went to King Hezekiah [and asked:] |
Isaiah	Where did these men come from and what did they say to you?
[Narrator	Hezekiah answered:]
Hezekiah	They came from a very distant country, from Babylonia.
Isaiah	What did they see in the palace?
Hezekiah (proudly)	They saw everything. There is nothing in the storerooms that I didn't show them.
[Narrator	Isaiah then told the king:]
Isaiah (severely)	The Lord Almighty says that a time is coming when everything in your palace, everything that your ancestors have stored up to this day, will be carried off to Babylonia. Nothing will be left. Some of your own direct descendants will be taken away and made eunuchs to serve in the palace of the king of Babylonia.
Narrator	King Hezekiah understood this to mean that there would be peace and security during his lifetime, so he replied:
Hezekiah	The message you have given me from the Lord is good.
Cast	[This is] the word of the Lord.
All	**Thanks be to God.**

Cast: **Narrator, Isaiah, Hezekiah.**

Words of hope
Isaiah 40.1–11

The Lord	Comfort my people—
Isaiah (with flourish)	Says our God.
The Lord	Comfort them! Encourage the people of Jerusalem. Tell them they have suffered long enough and their sins are now forgiven. I have punished them in full for all their sins.
Isaiah	A voice cries out:
Voice	Prepare in the wilderness a road for the Lord! Clear the way in the desert for our God! Fill every valley; level every mountain. The hills will become a plain, and the rough country will be made smooth. Then the glory of the Lord will be revealed, and all mankind will see it. The Lord himself has promised this.
Isaiah	A voice cries out:
Voice	Proclaim a message!
Isaiah	What message shall I proclaim?
Voice	Proclaim that all mankind are like grass; they last no longer than wild flowers. Grass withers and flowers fade, when the Lord sends the wind blowing over them. People are no more enduring than grass.
Isaiah	Yes, grass withers and flowers fade, but the word of our God endures for ever. (PAUSE)
Voice	Jerusalem, go up on a high mountain and proclaim the good news! Call out with a loud voice, Zion; announce the good news! Speak out and do not be afraid. Tell the towns of Judah that their God is coming!
Isaiah	The Sovereign Lord is coming to rule with power, bringing with him the people he has rescued. He will take care of his flock like a shepherd; he will gather the lambs together and carry them in his arms; he will gently lead their mothers.
Cast	[This is] the word of the Lord.
All	**Thanks be to God.**

Cast: **The Lord, Isaiah, Voice.**

Israel's incomparable God
Isaiah 40.12–31

Voice 1   Can anyone measure the ocean by handfuls
or measure the sky with his hands?

Voice 2   Can anyone hold the soil of the earth in a cup
or weigh the mountains and hills on scales?

Voice 3   Can anyone tell the Lord what to do?

Voice 1   Who can teach him or give him advice?

Voice 2   With whom does God consult
in order to know and understand
and to learn how things should be done?

Voice 3   To the Lord the nations are nothing,
no more than a drop of water;
the distant islands are as light as dust.

Voice 1   All the animals in the forests of Lebanon
are not enough for a sacrifice to our God,
and its trees are too few to kindle the fire.

Voice 2   The nations are nothing at all to him.

Voice 1   To whom can God be compared?

Voice 2   How can you describe what he is like?

Voice 3   He is not like an idol that workmen make,
that metalworkers cover with gold
and set in a base of silver.
The man who cannot afford silver or gold
chooses wood that will not rot.
He finds a skilful craftsman
to make an image that won't fall down.

Voice 1   Do you not know?

Voice 2   Were you not told long ago?

Voice 3   Have you not heard how the world began?

Voice 1   It was made by the one who sits on his throne
above the earth and beyond the sky;
the people below look as tiny as ants.

Voice 2   He stretched out the sky like a curtain,
like a tent in which to live.

Voice 3   He brings down powerful rulers
and reduces them to nothing.

Voice 1   They are like young plants,
just set out and barely rooted.

Voice 2   When the Lord sends a wind,
they dry up and blow away like straw.

Voice 1	To whom can the holy God be compared?
Voice 2	Is there anyone else like him?
Voice 3	Look up at the sky! Who created the stars you see?
Voice 1	The one who leads them out like an army, he knows how many there are and calls each one by name!
Voice 2	His power is so great— not one of them is ever missing!
Voice 1	Israel, why then do you complain that the Lord doesn't know your troubles or care if you suffer injustice?
Voice 2	Don't you know? Haven't you heard? The Lord is the everlasting God; he created all the world.
Voice 1	He never grows tired or weary.
Voice 2	No one understands his thoughts.
Voice 3	He strengthens those who are weak and tired.
Voice 1	Even those who are young grow weak—
Voice 2	Young men can fall exhausted.
Voice 3	But those who trust in the Lord for help will find their strength renewed.
Voice 1	They will rise on wings like eagles.
Voice 2	They will run and not get weary.
Voice 3	They will walk and not grow weak.
Cast	[This is] the word of the Lord.
All	**Thanks be to God.**

Cast: **Voice 1, Voice 2, Voice 3.**

The Lord's servant
Isaiah 42.1–9

Isaiah	The Lord says:
The Lord	Here is my servant, whom I strengthen—the one I have chosen, with whom I am pleased. I have filled him with my spirit, and he will bring justice to every nation. He will not shout or raise his voice or make loud speeches in the streets. He will not break off a bent reed or put out a flickering lamp. He will bring lasting justice to all. He will not lose hope or courage; he will establish justice on the earth. Distant lands eagerly wait for his teaching.
Isaiah	God created the heavens and stretched them out; he fashioned the earth and all that lives there; he gave life and breath to all its people. And now the Lord God says to his servant:

The Lord I, the Lord, have called you and given you power to see that justice is done on earth. Through you I will make a covenant with all peoples; through you I will bring light to the nations. You will open the eyes of the blind and set free those who sit in dark prisons. I alone am the Lord your God. No other god may share my glory; I will not let idols share my praise. The things I predicted have now come true. Now I will tell you of new things even before they begin to happen.

Cast [This is] the word of the Lord.
All **Thanks be to God.**

Cast: **Isaiah, The Lord.**

Escape from Babylon
Isaiah 43.14–21

Isaiah Israel's holy God, the Lord who saves you, says:

The Lord To save you, I will send an army against Babylon; I will break down the city gates, and the shouts of her people will turn into crying. I am the Lord, your holy God. I created you, Israel, and I am your king.

Isaiah Long ago the Lord made a road through the sea, a path through the swirling waters. He led a mighty army to destruction, an army of chariots and horses. Down they fell, never to rise, snuffed out like the flame of a lamp! But the Lord says:

The Lord Do not cling to events of the past or dwell on what happened long ago. Watch for the new thing I am going to do. It is happening already— you can see it now! I will make a road through the wilderness and give you streams of water there. Even the wild animals will honour me; jackals and ostriches will praise me when I make rivers flow in the desert to give water to my chosen people. They are the people I made for myself, and they will sing my praises!

Cast [This is] the word of the Lord.
All **Thanks be to God.**

Cast: **Isaiah, The Lord.**

The Lord is the only God
Isaiah 44.1–8

Isaiah The Lord says:

The Lord Listen now, Israel, my servant, my chosen people, the descendants of Jacob. I am the Lord who created you; from the time you were born, I have helped you. Do not be afraid; you are my servant, my chosen people whom I love. I will give water to the thirsty land and make streams flow on the dry ground. I will pour out my spirit on your children and my blessing on your descendants. They will thrive like well-watered grass, like willows by streams of running water.

	One by one, people will say:
[Person(s)]	I am the Lord's.
The Lord	They will come to join the people of Israel. Each one will mark the name of the Lord on his arm and call himself one of God's people.
Isaiah	The Lord, who rules and protects Israel, the Lord Almighty, has this to say:
The Lord	I am the first, the last, the only God; there is no other god but me. Could anyone else have done what I did? Who could have predicted all that would happen from the very beginning to the end of time? Do not be afraid, my people! You know that from ancient times until now I have predicted all that would happen, and you are my witnesses. Is there any other god? Is there some powerful god I never heard of?
Cast	[This is] the word of the Lord.
All	**Thanks be to God.**

Cast: **Isaiah, The Lord, [Persons(s)].**

Idolatry is ridiculed
Isaiah 44.9–20

Isaiah	All those who make idols are worthless, and the gods they prize so highly are useless. Those who worship these gods are blind and ignorant—and they will be disgraced. It's no good making a metal image to worship as a god! Everyone who worships it will be humiliated. The people who make idols are human beings and nothing more. Let them come and stand trial—they will be terrified and will suffer disgrace.
	The metalworker takes a piece of metal and works with it over a fire. His strong arm swings a hammer to pound the metal into shape. As he works, he gets hungry, thirsty, and tired.
	The carpenter measures the wood. He outlines a figure with chalk, carves it out with his tools, and makes it in the form of a man, a handsome human figure, to be placed in his house. He might cut down cedars to use, or choose oak or cypress wood from the forest. Or he might plant a laurel-tree and wait for the rain to make it grow. A man uses part of a tree for fuel and part of it for making an idol.
(with irony)	With one part he builds a fire to warm himself and bake bread; with the other part he makes a god and worships it! With some of the wood he makes a fire; he roasts meat, eats it, and is satisfied. He warms himself [and says]:
Idol-worshipper	How nice and warm! What a beautiful fire!
Isaiah (with irony)	The rest of the wood he makes into an *idol*, and then he bows down and *worships* it. He *prays* to it [and says]:

Idol-worshipper (stupidly)	You are my god—save me!
Isaiah	Such people are too stupid to know what they are doing. They close their eyes and their minds to the truth. The maker of idols hasn't the wit or the sense to say:
Idol-worshipper (reflectively)	Some of the wood I burnt up. I baked some bread on the embers and I roasted meat and ate it. And the rest of the wood I made into an idol. Here I am bowing down to a block of wood!
Isaiah	It makes as much sense as eating ashes. His foolish ideas have so misled him that he is beyond help. He won't admit to himself that the idol he holds in his hand is not a god at all.
Cast All	[This is] the word of the Lord. **Thanks be to God.**

Cast: **Isaiah, Idol-worshipper.**

The Lord, the creator and saviour
Isaiah 44.21–26 [26–28]

Isaiah	The Lord says:
The Lord	Israel, remember this; remember that you are my servant. I created you to be my servant, and I will never forget you. I have swept your sins away like a cloud. Come back to me; I am the one who saves you.
Isaiah	Shout for joy, you heavens! Shout, deep places of the earth! Shout for joy, mountains, and every tree of the forest! The Lord has shown his greatness by saving his people Israel.
The Lord	I am the Lord, your saviour; I am the one who created you. I am the Lord, the Creator of all things. I alone stretched out the heavens; when I made the earth, no one helped me. I make fools of fortune-tellers and frustrate the predictions of astrologers. The words of the wise I refute and show that their wisdom is foolishness. But when my servant makes a prediction, when I send a messenger to reveal my plans, I make those plans and predictions come true.
	[I tell Jerusalem that people will live there again, and the cities of Judah that they will be rebuilt. Those cities will rise from the ruins. With a word of command I dry up the ocean. I say to Cyrus, 'You are the one who will rule for me; you will do what I want you to do: you will order Jerusalem to be rebuilt and the Temple foundations to be laid.']
Cast All	[This is] the word of the Lord. **Thanks be to God.**

Cast: **Isaiah, The Lord.**

The Lord appoints Cyrus
Isaiah 45.1–8

Isaiah   The Lord has chosen Cyrus to be king! He has appointed him to conquer nations; he sends him to strip kings of their power; the Lord will open the gates of cities for him. To Cyrus the Lord says:

The Lord   I myself will prepare your way, levelling mountains and hills. I will break down bronze gates and smash their iron bars. I will give you treasures from dark, secret places; then you will know that I am the Lord, and that the God of Israel has called you by name. I appoint you to help my servant Israel, the people that I have chosen. I have given you great honour, although you do not know me.

I am the Lord; there is no other god. I will give you the strength you need, although you do not know me. I do this so that everyone from one end of the world to the other may know that I am the Lord and that there is no other god. I create both light and darkness; I bring both blessing and disaster. I, the Lord, do all these things. I will send victory from the sky like rain; the earth will open to receive it and will blossom with freedom and justice. (PAUSE) I, the Lord, will make this happen.

Cast   [This is] the word of the Lord.
All   **Thanks be to God.**

Cast: **Isaiah, The Lord.**

The Lord of creation and history
Isaiah 45.9–19

Isaiah   Does a clay pot dare to argue with its maker, a pot that is like all the others? Does the clay ask the potter what he is doing? Does the pot complain that its maker has no skill? Does anyone dare to say to his parents:

Child
(impudently)   Why did you make me like this?

Isaiah   The Lord, the holy God of Israel, the one who shapes the future, says:

The Lord   You have no right to question me about my children or to tell me what I ought to do! I am the one who made the earth and created mankind to live there. By my power I stretched out the heavens; I control the sun, the moon, and the stars.

[I myself have stirred Cyrus to action to fulfil my purpose and put things right. I will straighten every road that he travels. He will rebuild my city, Jerusalem, and set my captive people free. No one has hired him or bribed him to do this.]

Isaiah   The Lord Almighty has spoken. (PAUSE)

The Lord says to Israel:

The Lord	The wealth of Egypt and Sudan will be yours, and the tall men of Seba will be your slaves; they will follow you in chains. They will bow down to you and confess:
Tall man	God is with you—he alone is God. The God of Israel, who saves his people, is a God who conceals himself. Those who make idols will all be ashamed; all of them will be disgraced. But Israel is saved by the Lord, and her victory lasts for ever; her people will never be disgraced.
Isaiah	The Lord created the heavens—he is the one who is God! He formed and made the earth—he made it firm and lasting. He did not make it a desolate waste, but a place for people to live in. It is he who says:
The Lord	I am the Lord, and there is no other god. I have not spoken in secret or kept my purpose hidden. I did not require the people of Israel to look for me in a desolate waste. (PAUSE) I am the Lord, and I speak the truth; I make known what is right.
Cast	[This is] the word of the Lord.
All	**Thanks be to God.**

Cast: **Isaiah, Child, The Lord, Tall man.**

God is Lord of the future
From Isaiah 48.1–11

Isaiah	Listen to this, people of Israel, you that are descended from Judah: You swear by the name of the Lord and claim to worship the God of Israel—but you don't mean a word you say. And yet you are proud to say that you are citizens of the holy city and that you depend on Israel's God, whose name is the Lord Almighty.
	The Lord says to Israel:
The Lord	Long ago I predicted what would take place; then suddenly I made it happen. I knew that you would prove to be stubborn, as rigid as iron and unyielding as bronze. And so I predicted your future long ago, announcing events before they took place, to prevent you from claiming that your idols and images made them happen.
	In order that people will praise my name, I am holding my anger in check; I am keeping it back and will not destroy you. I have tested you in the fire of suffering, as silver is refined in a furnace. But I have found that you are worthless. What I do is done for my own sake—I will not let my name be dishonoured or let anyone else share the glory that should be mine and mine alone.
Cast	[This is] the word of the Lord.
All	**Thanks be to God.**

Cast: **Isaiah, The Lord.**

632

The Lord's plan for his people
Isaiah 48.17–22

Isaiah	The holy God of Israel, the Lord who saves you, says:
The Lord	I am the Lord your God, the one who wants to teach you for your own good and direct you in the way you should go.
	If only you had listened to my commands! Then blessings would have flowed for you like a stream that never goes dry! Victory would have come to you like the waves that roll on the shore. Your descendants would be as numerous as grains of sand, and I would have made sure they were never destroyed.
Isaiah	Go out from Babylon, go free! Shout the news gladly; make it known everywhere:
Herald	The Lord has saved his servant Israel!
Isaiah	When the Lord led his people through a hot, dry desert, they did not suffer from thirst. He made water come from a rock for them; he split the rock open, and water flowed out.
The Lord	There is no safety for sinners—
Isaiah (with flourish)	Says the Lord.
Cast	[This is] the word of the Lord.
All	**Thanks be to God.**

Cast: **Isaiah, The Lord, Herald.**

Israel, a light to the nations
Isaiah 49.1–7

The Servant	Listen to me, distant nations, you people who live far away! Before I was born, the Lord chose me and appointed me to be his servant. He made my words as sharp as a sword. With his own hand he protected me. He made me like an arrow, sharp and ready for use. He said to me:
The Lord	Israel, you are my servant; because of you, people will praise me.
The Servant	I said:
[Young Servant]	I have worked, but how hopeless it is! I have used up my strength, but have accomplished nothing.
The Servant	Yet I can trust the Lord to defend my cause; he will reward me for what I do.
	Before I was born, the Lord appointed me; he made me his servant to bring back his people, to bring back the scattered people of Israel. The Lord gives me honour; he is the source of my strength. The Lord said to me:

The Lord	I have a greater task for you, my servant. Not only will you restore to greatness the people of Israel who have survived, but I will also make you a light to the nations—so that all the world may be saved.
Isaiah	Israel's holy God and saviour says to the one who is deeply despised, who is hated by the nations and is the servant of rulers:
The Lord	Kings will see you released and will rise to show you their respect; princes also will see it, and they will bow low to honour you.
Isaiah	This will happen because the Lord has chosen his servant; the holy God of Israel keeps his promises.
Cast All	[This is] the word of the Lord. **Thanks be to God.**

Cast: **The Servant, The Lord, Young Servant** (can be the same as Servant), **Isaiah.**

The restoration of Jerusalem
Isaiah 49.8–16

Isaiah	The Lord says to his people:
The Lord	When the time comes to save you, I will show you favour and answer your cries for help. I will guard and protect you and through you make a covenant with all peoples. I will let you settle once again in your land that is now laid waste. I will say to the prisoners, 'Go free!' and to those who are in darkness, 'Come out to the light!'
Isaiah	They will be like sheep that graze on the hills; they will never be hungry or thirsty. Sun and desert heat will not hurt them, for they will be led by one who loves them. He will lead them to springs of water.
The Lord	I will make a highway across the mountains and prepare a road for my people to travel. My people will come from far away, from the north and the west, and from Aswan in the south.
Isaiah	Sing, heavens! Shout for joy, earth! Let the mountains burst into song! The Lord will comfort his people; he will have pity on his suffering people. (PAUSE) But the people of Jerusalem said:
Person(s)	The Lord has abandoned us! He has forgotten us.
Isaiah	So the Lord answers:
The Lord	Can a woman forget her own baby and not love the child she bore? Even if a mother should forget her child, I will never forget you. Jerusalem, I can never forget you! I have written your name on the palms of my hands.
Cast All	[This is] the word of the Lord. **Thanks be to God.**

Cast: **Isaiah, The Lord, Person(s).**

The Lord's deliverance
From Isaiah 51.4–16

Isaiah   The Lord says:

The Lord   Listen to me, my people, listen to what I say: I give my teaching to the nations; my laws will bring them light. I will come quickly and save them; the time of my victory is near. I myself will rule over the nations. Distant lands wait for me to come; they wait with hope for me to save them. Look up at the heavens; look at the earth! The heavens will disappear like smoke; the earth will wear out like old clothing, and all its people will die like flies. But the deliverance I bring will last for ever; my victory will be final.

Listen to me, you that know what is right, who have my teaching fixed in your hearts. Do not be afraid when people taunt and insult you; they will vanish like moth-eaten clothing! But the deliverance I bring will last for ever; my victory will endure for all time.

Isaiah   Wake up, Lord, and help us! Use your power and save us; use it as you did in ancient times. It was you that cut the sea-monster Rahab to pieces. It was you also who dried up the sea and made a path through the water, so that those you were saving could cross. Those whom you have rescued will reach Jerusalem with gladness, singing and shouting for joy. They will be happy for ever, for ever free from sorrow and grief.

The Lord   I am the one who strengthens you. Why should you fear mortal man, who is no more enduring than grass? Have you forgotten the Lord who made you, who stretched out the heavens and laid the earth's foundations? Why should you live in constant fear of the fury of those who oppress you, of those who are ready to destroy you? Their fury can no longer touch you. I am the Lord your God; I stir up the sea and make its waves roar. My name is the Lord Almighty! I stretched out the heavens and laid the earth's foundations; I say to Jerusalem, 'You are my people! I have given you my teaching, and I protect you with my hand.'

Cast   [This is] the word of the Lord.
All   **Thanks be to God.**

Cast: **Isaiah, The Lord.**

The end of Jerusalem's suffering
Isaiah 51.17–23

Isaiah   Jerusalem, wake up! Rouse yourself and get up! You have drunk the cup of punishment that the Lord in his anger gave you to drink; you drank it down, and it made you stagger. There is no one to lead you, no one among your people to take you by the hand. A double disaster has fallen on you: your land has been devastated by war, and your people have starved. There is no one to show you sympathy. At the corner of every street your people

635

→

collapse from weakness; they are like deer caught in a hunter's net. They have felt the force of God's anger.

You suffering people of Jerusalem, you that stagger as though you were drunk, the Lord your God defends you [and says]:

The Lord I am taking away the cup that I gave you in my anger. You will no longer have to drink the wine that makes you stagger. I will give it to those who oppressed you, to those who made you lie down in the streets and trampled on you as if you were dirt.

Cast [This is] the word of the Lord.
All **Thanks be to God.**

Cast: **Isaiah, The Lord.**

God will rescue Jerusalem
Isaiah 52.1–12

Isaiah Jerusalem, be strong and great again!
Holy city of God, clothe yourself with splendour!
The heathen will never enter your gates again.
Shake yourself free, Jerusalem!
Rise from the dust and sit on your throne!
Undo the chains that bind you,
captive people of Zion!

The Sovereign Lord says to his people:

The Lord When you became slaves, no money was paid for you; in the same way nothing will be paid to set you free. When you went to live in Egypt as foreigners, you did so of your own free will; Assyria, however, took you away by force and paid nothing for you. And now in Babylonia the same thing has happened: you are captives, and nothing was paid for you. Those who rule over you boast and brag and constantly show contempt for me. In time to come you will acknowledge that I am God and that I have spoken to you.

Isaiah How wonderful it is to see
a messenger coming across the mountains,
bringing good news, the news of peace!
He announces victory and says to Zion,

Messenger Your God is king!

Isaiah Those who guard the city are shouting,
shouting together for joy!
They can see with their own eyes
the return of the Lord to Zion!

Break into shouts of joy,
you ruins of Jerusalem!
The Lord will rescue his city
and comfort his people.
The Lord will use his holy power;
he will save his people,

and all the world will see it.
Make sure you leave Babylonia,
all you that carry the temple equipment!
Touch no forbidden thing;
keep yourselves holy and leave.
This time you will not have to leave in a hurry;
you will not be trying to escape.
The Lord your God will lead you
and protect you on every side.

Cast	[This is] the word of the Lord.
All	**Thanks be to God.**

Cast: **Isaiah, The Lord, Messenger.**

The suffering servant
Isaiah 52.13—53.12

Isaiah	The Lord says:
The Lord	My servant will succeed in his task; he will be highly honoured. Many people were shocked when they saw him; he was so disfigured that he hardly looked human. But now many nations will marvel at him, and kings will be speechless with amazement. They will see and understand something they had never known.
Isaiah	The people reply:
Person 1	Who would have believed what we now report?
Person 2	Who could have seen the Lord's hand in this?
Person 1	It was the will of the Lord that his servant should grow like a plant taking root in dry ground.
Person 2	He had no dignity or beauty to make us take notice of him.
Person 1	There was nothing attractive about him—
Person 2	Nothing that would draw us to him.
Person 1	We despised him and rejected him.
Person 2	He endured suffering and pain.
Person 1	No one would even look at him—
Person 2	We ignored him as if he were nothing.
Person 3	But he endured the suffering that should have been ours—
Person 1	The pain that we should have borne.
Person 2	All the while we thought that his suffering was punishment sent by God.
Person 3	But because of our sins he was wounded—
Person 2	Beaten because of the evil we did.

Person 3	We are healed by the punishment he suffered—
Person 1	Made whole by the blows he received.
Persons 1–3	All of us were like sheep that were lost—
Person 2	Each of us going his own way.
Person 3	But the Lord made the punishment fall on him—
Persons 1 and 2	The punishment all of us deserved.
Person 1	He was treated harshly, but endured it humbly—
Person 3	He never said a word.
Person 1	Like a lamb about to be slaughtered—
Person 2	Like a sheep about to be sheared—
Person 3	He never said a word.
Person 1	He was arrested and sentenced and led off to die—
Person 2	And no one cared about his fate.
Person 3 (slowly)	He was put to death for the sins of our people.
Person 1	He was placed in a grave with evil men.
Person 2	He was buried with the rich—
Person 1	Even though he had never committed a crime—
Person 3	Or ever told a lie.
Isaiah	The Lord says:
The Lord	It was my will that he should suffer; his death was a sacrifice to bring forgiveness. And so he will see his descendants; he will live a long life, and through him my purpose will succeed. After a life of suffering, he will again have joy; he will know that he did not suffer in vain. My devoted servant, with whom I am pleased, will bear the punishment of many and for his sake I will forgive them. And so I will give him a place of honour, a place among great and powerful men. He willingly gave his life and shared the fate of evil men. He took the place of many sinners and prayed that they might be forgiven.
Cast	[This is] the word of the Lord.
All	**Thanks be to God.**

Cast: **Isaiah, The Lord, Person 1, Person 2, Person 3** (Persons 1–3 can be the same).

The Lord's love for Israel
Isaiah 54.6–10

Isaiah   Israel, you are like a young wife, deserted by her husband and deeply distressed. But the Lord calls you back to him and says:

The Lord   For one brief moment I left you; with deep love I will take you back. I turned away angry for only a moment, but I will show you my love for ever.

Isaiah
(with flourish)   So says the Lord who saves you.

The Lord   In the time of Noah I promised never again to flood the earth. Now I promise not to be angry with you again; I will not reprimand or punish you. The mountains and hills may crumble, but my love for you will never end; I will keep for ever my promise of peace.

Cast   [This is] the word of the Lord.
All   **Thanks be to God.**

Cast: **Isaiah, The Lord.**

God's offer of mercy
Isaiah 55.1–11 [12–13]

Isaiah   The Lord says:

The Lord   Come, everyone who is thirsty—here is water! Come, you that have no money—buy corn and eat! Come! Buy wine and milk—it will cost you nothing! Why spend money on what does not satisfy? Why spend your wages and still be hungry? Listen to me and do what I say, and you will enjoy the best food of all.

Listen now, my people, and come to me; come to me, and you will have life! I will make a lasting covenant with you and give you the blessings I promised to David. I made him a leader and commander of nations, and through him I showed them my power. Now you will summon foreign nations; at one time they did not know you, but now they will come running to join you! I, the Lord your God, the holy God of Israel, will make all this happen; I will give you honour and glory.

Isaiah   Turn to the Lord and pray to him, now that he is near. Let the wicked leave their way of life and change their way of thinking. Let them turn to the Lord, our God; he is merciful and quick to forgive. [The Lord says:]

The Lord
(with dignity)   My thoughts are not like yours, and my ways are different from yours. As high as the heavens are above the earth, so high are my ways and thoughts above yours.

My word is like the snow and the rain that come down from the sky to water the earth. They make the crops grow and provide seed for sowing and food to eat. So also will be the word that I

→

639

speak—it will not fail to do what I plan for it; it will do everything I send it to do.

[You will leave Babylon with joy; you will be led out of the city in peace. The mountains and hills will burst into singing, and the trees will shout for joy. Cypress-trees will grow where now there are briars; myrtle-trees will come up in place of thorns. This will be a sign that will last for ever, a reminder of what I, the Lord, have done.]

Cast	[This is] the word of the Lord.
All	**Thanks be to God.**

Cast: **Isaiah, The Lord.**

God's people will include all nations
From Isaiah 56.1–8

Isaiah	The Lord says to his people:
The Lord	Do what is just and right, for soon I will save you. I will bless those who always observe the Sabbath and do not misuse it. I will bless those who do nothing evil.
Isaiah	A foreigner who has joined the Lord's people should not say, 'The Lord will not let me worship with his people.' And the Lord says to those foreigners who become part of his people, who love him and serve him, who observe the Sabbath and faithfully keep his covenant:
The Lord	I will bring you to Zion, my sacred hill, give you joy in my house of prayer, and accept the sacrifices you offer on my altar. My Temple will be called a house of prayer for the people of all nations.
Isaiah	The Sovereign Lord, who has brought his people Israel home from exile, has promised that he will bring still other people to join them.

Cast	[This is] the word of the Lord.
All	**Thanks be to God.**

Cast: **Isaiah, The Lord.**

True fasting
Isaiah 58.1–9

Isaiah	The Lord says:
The Lord	Shout as loud as you can! Tell my people Israel about their sins! They worship me every day, claiming that they are eager to know my ways and obey my laws. They say they want me to give them just laws and that they take pleasure in worshipping me.
Isaiah	The people ask:

Person 1	Why should we fast if the Lord never notices?
Person 2	Why should we go without food if he pays no attention?
Isaiah	The Lord says to them:
The Lord	The truth is that at the same time as you fast, you pursue your own interests and oppress your workers. Your fasting makes you violent, and you quarrel and fight. Do you think this kind of fasting will make me listen to your prayers? When you fast, you make yourselves suffer; you bow your heads low like a blade of grass, and spread out sackcloth and ashes to lie on. Is that what you call fasting? Do you think I will be pleased with *that*?
	The kind of fasting I want is this: Remove the chains of oppression and the yoke of injustice, and let the oppressed go free. Share your food with the hungry and open your homes to the homeless poor. Give clothes to those who have nothing to wear, and do not refuse to help your own relatives.
	Then my favour will shine on you like the morning sun, and your wounds will be quickly healed. I will always be with you to save you; my presence will protect you on every side. When you pray, I will answer you. When you call to me, I will respond.
Cast	[This is] the word of the Lord.
All	**Thanks be to God.**

Cast: **Isaiah, The Lord, Person 1, Person 2.**

The prophet condemns the people's sins
Isaiah 59.1–19

Isaiah	Don't think that the Lord is too weak to save you or too deaf to hear your call for help! It is because of your *sins* that he doesn't hear you. It is your sins that *separate* you from God when you try to worship him. You are guilty of lying, violence, and murder. You go to court, but you haven't got justice on your side. You depend on lies to win your case. You carry out your plans to hurt others. The evil plots you make are as deadly as the eggs of a poisonous snake. Crush an egg, out comes a snake! But your plots will do you no good—they are as useless as clothing made of cobwebs! You are always planning something evil, and you can hardly wait to do it. You never hesitate to murder innocent people. You leave ruin and destruction wherever you go, and no one is safe when you are about. Everything you do is unjust. You follow a crooked path, and no one who walks that path will ever be safe. The people say:
Person 1	Now we know why God does not save us from those who oppress us.
Person 2	We hope for light to walk by, but there is only darkness, and we grope about like blind people.
Person 3	We stumble at noon, as if it were night, as if we were in the dark world of the dead.

Person 4	We are frightened and distressed.
Person 1	We long for God to save us from oppression and wrong, but nothing happens.
Person 2	Lord, our crimes against you are many. Our sins accuse us. We are well aware of them all.
Person 4	We have rebelled against you, rejected you, and refused to follow you.
Person 2	We have oppressed others and turned away from you.
Person 4	Our thoughts are false; our words are lies.
Person 3	Justice is driven away, and right cannot come near. Truth stumbles in the public square, and honesty finds no place there.
Person 1	There is so little honesty that anyone who stops doing evil finds himself the victim of crime.
Isaiah	The Lord has seen this, and he is displeased that there is no justice. He is astonished to see that there is no one to help the oppressed. So he will use his own power to rescue them and to win the victory. He will wear justice like a coat of armour and saving power like a helmet. He will clothe himself with the strong desire to set things right and to punish and avenge the wrongs that people suffer. He will punish his enemies according to what they have done, even those who live in distant lands. From east to west everyone will fear him and his great power. He will come like a rushing river, like a strong wind.
Cast	[This is] the word of the Lord.
All	**Thanks be to God.**

Cast: **Isaiah, Person 1** (practical), **Person 2** (educated), **Person 3** (poetic), **Person 4** (conscientious). (Persons 1–4 can be the same.)

The future glory of Jerusalem
Isaiah 60.1–6

Voice 1	Arise, Jerusalem, and shine like the sun.
Voice 2	The glory of the Lord is shining on you!
Voice 1	Other nations will be covered by darkness.
Voice 2	But on you the light of the Lord will shine.
Voice 3	The brightness of his presence will be with you.
Voice 1	Nations will be drawn to your light.
Voice 2	And kings to the dawning of your new day.
Voice 1	Look around you and see what is happening: your people are gathering to come home!
Voice 2	Your sons will come from far away.
Voice 3	Your daughters will be carried like children.

Voice 1	You will see this and be filled with joy.
Voice 2	You will tremble with excitement.
Voice 3	The wealth of the nations will be brought to you; from across the sea their riches will come.
Voice 1	Great caravans of camels will come, from Midian and Ephah.
Voice 2	They will come from Sheba, bringing gold and incense.
Voice 3	People will tell the good news of what the Lord has done!
Cast	[This is] the word of the Lord.
All	**Thanks be to God.**

Cast: **Voice 1, Voice 2, Voice 3.**

The good news of deliverance
Isaiah 61.1–11

Isaiah   The Sovereign Lord has filled me with his spirit. He has chosen me and sent me to bring good news to the poor, to heal the broken-hearted, to announce release to captives and freedom to those in prison. He has sent me to proclaim that the time has come when the Lord will save his people and defeat their enemies. He has sent me to comfort all who mourn, to give to those who mourn in Zion joy and gladness instead of grief, a song of praise instead of sorrow. They will be like trees that the Lord himself has planted. They will all do what is right, and God will be praised for what he has done. They will rebuild cities that have long been in ruins.

My people, foreigners will serve you. They will take care of your flocks and farm your land and tend your vineyards. And you will be known as the priests of the Lord, the servants of our God. You will enjoy the wealth of the nations and be proud that it is yours. Your shame and disgrace are ended. You will live in your own land, and your wealth will be doubled; your joy will last for ever.

The Lord says:

The Lord   I love justice and I hate oppression and crime. I will faithfully reward my people and make an eternal covenant with them. They will be famous among the nations; everyone who sees them will know that they are a people whom I have blessed.

Isaiah   Jerusalem rejoices because of what the Lord has done. She is like a bride dressed for her wedding. God has clothed her with salvation and victory. As surely as seeds sprout and grow, the Sovereign Lord will save his people, and all the nations will praise him.

Cast   [This is] the word of the Lord.
All   **Thanks be to God.**

Cast: **Isaiah, The Lord.**

New names
From Isaiah 62.1–12

Isaiah	I will speak out to encourage Jerusalem; I will not be silent until she is saved, and her victory shines like a torch in the night. Jerusalem, the nations will see you victorious! All their kings will see your glory. You will be called by a new name, a name given by the Lord himself. You will be like a beautiful crown for the Lord. No longer will you be called:
Sad voice	'Forsaken'—
Isaiah	Or your land be called:
Sad voice	'The Deserted Wife.'
Isaiah	Your new name will be:
Joyful voice	'God Is Pleased with Her.'
Isaiah	Your land will be called:
Joyful voice	'Happily Married'—
Isaiah	Because the Lord is pleased with you and will be like a husband to your land. Like a young man taking a virgin as his bride, he who formed you will marry you. As a groom is delighted with his bride, so your God will delight in you.
	[People of Jerusalem, go out of the city and build a road for your returning people! Prepare a highway; clear it of stones! Put up a signal so that the nations can know that the Lord is announcing to all the earth:
The Lord	Tell the people of Jerusalem that the Lord is coming to save you, bringing with him the people he has rescued.]
Isaiah	You will be called:
Joyful voice	'God's Holy People,' 'The People the Lord Has Saved.'
Isaiah	Jerusalem will be called:
Joyful voice	'The City That God Loves,' 'The City That God Did Not Forsake.'
Cast	[This is] the word of the Lord.
All	**Thanks be to God.**

Cast: **Isaiah, Sad voice, Joyful voice, [The Lord].**

The Lord's victory over the nations
Isaiah 63.1–6

Person 1	Who is this coming from the city of Bozrah in Edom?
Person 2	Who is this so splendidly dressed in red, marching along in power and strength?
Person 3	It is the Lord, powerful to save, coming to announce his victory.

Person 1	Why is his clothing so red?—
Person 2	Like that of a man who tramples grapes to make wine?
Isaiah	The Lord answers:
The Lord	I have trampled the nations like grapes, and no one came to help me. I trampled them in my anger, and their blood has stained all my clothing. I decided that the time to save my people had come; it was time to punish their enemies. I was amazed when I looked and saw that there was no one to help me. But my anger made me strong, and I won the victory myself. In my anger I trampled whole nations and shattered them. I poured out their life-blood on the ground.
Cast	[This is] the word of the Lord.
All	**Thanks be to God.**

Cast: **Person 1, Person 2, Person 3, Isaiah, The Lord.**

The Lord's goodness to Israel
Isaiah 63.7–14

Isaiah	I will tell of the Lord's unfailing love; I praise him for all he has done for us. He has richly blessed the people of Israel because of his mercy and constant love. The Lord said:
The Lord	They are my people; they will not deceive me.
Isaiah	And so he saved them from all their suffering. It was not an angel, but the Lord himself who saved them. In his love and compassion he rescued them. He had always taken care of them in the past, but they rebelled against him and made his holy spirit sad. So the Lord became their enemy and fought against them.
	But then they remembered the past, the days of Moses, the servant of the Lord, and they asked:
Person 1	Where now is the Lord, who saved the leaders of his people from the sea?
Person 2	Where is the Lord, who gave his spirit to Moses?
Person 3	Where is the Lord, who by his power did great things through Moses, dividing the waters of the sea and leading his people through the deep water, to win everlasting fame for himself?
Isaiah	Led by the Lord, they were as sure-footed as wild horses, and never stumbled. As cattle are led into a fertile valley, so the Lord gave his people rest. He led his people and brought honour to his name.
Cast	[This is] the word of the Lord.
All	**Thanks be to God.**

Cast: **Isaiah, The Lord, Person 1, Person 2, Person 3** (Persons 1–3 can be the same).

JEREMIAH

The call to Jeremiah
Jeremiah 1.1–10

Announcer	This book is the account of what was said by Jeremiah son of Hilkiah, one of the priests of the town of Anathoth in the territory of Benjamin.
	The Lord spoke to Jeremiah in the thirteenth year that Josiah son of Amon was king of Judah, and he spoke to him again when Josiah's son Jehoiakim was king. After that, the Lord spoke to him many times, until the eleventh year of the reign of Zedekiah son of Josiah. In the fifth month of that year the people of Jerusalem were taken into exile.
Jeremiah	The Lord said to me:
The Lord	I chose you before I gave you life, and before you were born I selected you to be a prophet to the nations.
Jeremiah	I answered:
Young Jeremiah	Sovereign Lord, I don't know how to speak; I am too young.
[Jeremiah	But the Lord said to me:]
The Lord	Do not say that you are too young, but go to the people I send you to, and tell them everything I command you to say. Do not be afraid of them, for I will be with you to protect you. I, the Lord, have spoken!
Jeremiah	Then the Lord stretched out his hand, touched my lips, and said to me:
The Lord	Listen, I am giving you the words you must speak. Today I give you authority over nations and kingdoms to uproot and to pull down, to destroy and to overthrow, to build and to plant.
Cast	[This is] the word of the Lord.
All	**Thanks be to God.**

Cast: **Announcer, Jeremiah, The Lord, Young Jeremiah.**

Jeremiah's two visions
Jeremiah 1.11–19

Jeremiah	The Lord asked me:
The Lord	Jeremiah, what do you see?
Jeremiah	I answered:
Young Jeremiah	A branch of an almond-tree.

[Jeremiah	The Lord said:]**
The Lord	You are right, and I am watching to see that my words come true. (PAUSE)
Jeremiah	Then the Lord spoke to me again [He asked]:
The Lord	What else do you see?
[Jeremiah	I answered:]
Young Jeremiah	I see a pot boiling in the north, and it is about to tip over this way.
The Lord	Destruction will boil over from the north on all who live in this land, because I am calling all the nations in the north to come. Their kings will set up their thrones at the gates of Jerusalem and round its walls, and also round the other cities of Judah. I will punish my people because they have sinned; they have abandoned me, have offered sacrifices to other gods, and have made idols and worshipped them.
	Get ready, Jeremiah; go and tell them everything I command you to say. Do not be afraid of them now, or I will make you even more afraid when you are with them. Listen, Jeremiah! Everyone in this land—the kings of Judah, the officials, the priests, and the people—will be against you. But today I am giving you the strength to resist them; you will be like a fortified city, an iron pillar, and a bronze wall. They will not defeat you, for I will be with you to protect you. (PAUSE) I, the Lord, have spoken!
Cast	[This is] the word of the Lord.
All	**Thanks be to God.**

Cast: **Jeremiah, The Lord, Young Jeremiah.**

God's care for Israel
Jeremiah 2.1–13

Jeremiah	The Lord told me to proclaim this message to everyone in Jerusalem:
The Lord	I remember how faithful you were when you were young, how you loved me when we were first married; you followed me through the desert, through a land that had not been sown. Israel, you belonged to me alone; you were my sacred possession. I sent suffering and disaster on everyone who hurt you. I, the Lord, have spoken.
Jeremiah	Listen to the Lord's message, you descendants of Jacob, you tribes of Israel [The Lord says]:
The Lord	What accusation did your ancestors bring against me? What made them turn away from me? They worshipped worthless idols and became worthless themselves. They did not care about me, even though I rescued them from Egypt and led them through the wilderness: a land of deserts and sand-dunes, a dry and dangerous land where no one lives and no one will even travel.

→

647

I brought them into a fertile land, to enjoy its harvests and its other good things. But instead they ruined my land; they defiled the country I had given them. The priests did not ask, 'Where is the Lord?' My own priests did not know me. The rulers rebelled against me; the prophets spoke in the name of Baal and worshipped useless idols. And so I, the Lord, will state my case against my people again. I will bring charges against their descendants.

(urgently)   Go west to the island of Cyprus, and send someone eastwards to the land of Kedar. You will see that nothing like this has ever happened before. No other nation has ever changed its gods, even though they were not real. But my people have exchanged me, the God who brought them honour, for gods that can do nothing for them.

(severely)   And so I command the sky to shake with horror, to be amazed and astonished, for my people have committed two sins: they have turned away from me, the spring of fresh water, and they have dug cisterns, cracked cisterns that can hold no water at all.

Cast	[This is] the word of the Lord.
All	**Thanks be to God.**

Cast: **Jeremiah, The Lord.**

Israel refuses to worship the Lord
From Jeremiah 2.20–25

Jeremiah   The Sovereign Lord says:

The Lord   Israel, long ago you rejected my authority; you refused to obey me and worship me. On every high hill and under every green tree you worshipped fertility gods. I planted you like a choice vine from the very best seed. But look what you have become! You are like a rotten, worthless vine. Even if you washed with the strongest soap, I would still see the stain of your guilt. How can you say you have not defiled yourself, that you have never worshipped Baal? Look how you sinned in the valley; see what you have done. But you say:

Person   No! I can't turn back. I have loved foreign gods and will go after them.

Cast	[This is] the word of the Lord.
All	**Thanks be to God.**

Cast: **Jeremiah, The Lord, Person.**

Israel deserves to be punished
From Jeremiah 2.31—3.5

Jeremiah   The Lord says:

The Lord   People of Israel, listen to what I am saying. Have I been like a desert to you, like a dark and dangerous land? Why, then, do you say that you will do as you please, that you will never come back to me? Does a young woman forget her jewellery, or a bride her wedding-dress? But my people have forgotten me for more days than can be counted. But in spite of all this, you say:

Person 1   I am innocent.

Person 2   Surely the Lord is no longer angry with me.

The Lord   But I, the Lord, will punish you because you deny that you have sinned. You have cheapened yourself by turning to the gods of other nations. You will be disappointed by Egypt, just as you were by Assyria. You will turn away from Egypt, hanging your head in shame. I, the Lord, have rejected those you trust; you will not gain anything from them.

And now you say to me:

Person 1   You are my father, and you have loved me ever since I was a child.

Person 2   You won't always be angry; you won't be cross with me for ever.

The Lord   Israel, that is what you said, but you did all the evil you could.

Cast   [This is] the word of the Lord.
All   **Thanks be to God.**

Cast: **Jeremiah, The Lord, Person 1, Person 2** (can be the same as Person 1).

Israel must repent
From Jeremiah 3.11—22

Jeremiah   The Lord told me that, even though Israel had turned away from him, she had proved to be better than unfaithful Judah. He told me to go and say to Israel:

The Lord   Unfaithful Israel, come back to me. I am merciful and will not be angry; I will not be angry with you for ever. Only admit that you are guilty and that you have rebelled against the Lord, your God. Confess that under every green tree you have given your love to foreign gods and that you have not obeyed my commands. I, the Lord, have spoken.

Jeremiah   The Lord says:

The Lord   Israel, I wanted to accept you as my son
and give you a delightful land,
the most beautiful land in all the world.
I wanted you to call me father,
and never again turn away from me.

$\rightarrow$

> But like an unfaithful wife,
> you have not been faithful to me.
> I, the Lord, have spoken.

Jeremiah   A noise is heard on the hill-tops: it is the people of Israel crying and pleading, because they have lived sinful lives and have forgotten the Lord their God.

(calling)   Return, all of you who have turned away from the Lord; he will heal you and make you faithful.

Cast   [This is] the word of the Lord.
All   **Thanks be to God.**

Cast: **Jeremiah, The Lord.**

The idolatry of God's people
Jeremiah 3.19—4.4

Jeremiah   The Lord says:

The Lord   Israel, I wanted to accept you as my son and give you a delightful land, the most beautiful land in all the world. I wanted you to call me father, and never again turn away from me. But like an unfaithful wife, you have not been faithful to me. I, the Lord, have spoken.

Jeremiah   A noise is heard on the hill-tops: it is the people of Israel crying and pleading, because they have lived sinful lives and have forgotten the Lord their God. Return, all of you who have turned away from the Lord; he will heal you and make you faithful. [You say:]

Person 1   Yes, we are coming to the Lord, because he is our God.

Person 2 (sadly)   We were not helped at all by our pagan worship on the hill-tops.

Person 1   Help for Israel comes only from the Lord our God.

Person 2   But the worship of Baal, the god of shame, has made us lose flocks and herds, sons and daughters—everything that our ancestors have worked for since ancient times.

Person 1   We should lie down in shame and let our disgrace cover us.

Person 2   We and our ancestors have always sinned against the Lord our God; we have never obeyed his commands.

[Jeremiah   The Lord says:]

The Lord   People of Israel, if you want to turn, then turn back to me. If you are faithful to me and remove the idols I hate, it will be right for you to swear by my name. Then all the nations will ask me to bless them, and they will praise me.

Jeremiah   The Lord says to the people of Judah and Jerusalem:

The Lord   Plough up your unploughed fields; do not sow your seeds among thorns. Keep your covenant with me, your Lord, and dedicate yourselves to me, you people of Judah and Jerusalem. If you don't, my anger will burn like fire because of the evil things you have done. It will burn, and there will be no one to put it out.

Cast	[This is] the word of the Lord.
All	**Thanks be to God.**

Cast: **Jeremiah, The Lord, Person 1, Person 2.** (This reading overlaps with the previous one).

A call to repentance
Jeremiah 4.1–4

Jeremiah	The Lord says:
The Lord	People of Israel, if you want to turn, then turn back to me. If you are faithful to me and remove the idols I hate, it will be right for you to swear by my name. Then all the nations will ask me to bless them, and they will praise me.
Jeremiah	The Lord says to the people of Judah and Jerusalem:
The Lord	Plough up your unploughed fields; do not sow your seeds among thorns. Keep your covenant with me, your Lord, and dedicate yourselves to me, you people of Judah and Jerusalem. If you don't, my anger will burn like fire because of the evil things you have done. It will burn, and there will be no one to put it out.
Cast	[This is] the word of the Lord.
All	**Thanks be to God.**

Cast: **Jeremiah, The Lord.** (This reading is included in the previous one).

Judah is threatened with invasion
From Jeremiah 4.5–18

Voice 1	Blow the trumpet throughout the land!
Voice 2	Shout loud and clear!
Voice 3	Tell the people of Judah and Jerusalem to run to the fortified cities.
Voice 1	Point the way to Zion!
Voice 2	Run for safety! Don't delay!
Voice 1	The Lord is bringing disaster and great destruction from the north.
Voice 2	Like a lion coming from its hiding place, a destroyer of nations has set out. He is coming to destroy Judah.
Voice 3	The cities of Judah will be left in ruins, and no one will live in them.
Voice 1	So put on sackcloth, and weep and wail because the fierce anger of the Lord has not turned away from Judah.

Jeremiah	The Lord said:
The Lord	On that day kings and officials will lose their courage; priests will be shocked and prophets will be astonished.
Jeremiah	Then I said:
Young Jeremiah	Sovereign Lord, you have completely deceived the people of Jerusalem! You have said there would be peace, but a sword is at their throats.
Jeremiah	The time is coming when the people of Jerusalem will be told that a scorching wind is blowing in from the desert towards them. It will not be a gentle wind that only blows away the chaff—the wind that comes at the Lord's command will be much stronger than that! It is the Lord himself who is pronouncing judgement on his people.
Voice 1	Look, the enemy is coming like clouds.
Voice 2	His war-chariots are like a whirlwind, and his horses are faster than eagles.
Voice 3	We are lost!
Voice 1–3	We are doomed!
Jeremiah	Jerusalem, wash the evil from your heart, so that you may be saved. How long will you go on thinking sinful thoughts?
	Judah, you have brought this on yourself by the way you have lived and by the things you have done. Your sin has caused this suffering; it has stabbed you through the heart.
Cast	[This is] the word of the Lord.
All	**Thanks be to God.**

Cast: **Voice 1, Voice 2, Voice 3, Jeremiah, The Lord, Young Jeremiah** (can be the same as Jeremiah).

Jeremiah's sorrow for his people
Jeremiah 4.19–22

Jeremiah	The pain! I can't bear the pain! My heart! My heart is beating wildly! I can't keep quiet; I hear the trumpets and the shouts of battle. One disaster follows another; the whole country is left in ruins. Suddenly our tents are destroyed; their curtains are torn to pieces. How long must I see the battle raging and hear the blasts of trumpets? The Lord says:
The Lord	My people are stupid; they don't know me. They are like foolish children; they have no understanding. They are experts at doing what is evil, but failures at doing what is good.
Cast	[This is] the word of the Lord.
All	**Thanks be to God.**

Cast: **Jeremiah, The Lord.** (This reading can be linked with the previous one, or with the next).

Jeremiah's vision of the coming destruction
Jeremiah 4.23–31

Voice 1	I looked at the earth—it was a barren waste; at the sky—there was no light.
Voice 2	I looked at the mountains—they were shaking, and the hills were rocking to and fro.
Voice 3	I saw that there were no people; even the birds had flown away.
Voices 1–3	The fertile land had become a desert; its cities were in ruins because of the Lord's fierce anger.
Voice 3	The Lord has said that the whole earth will become a wilderness, but that he will not completely destroy it.
Voice 1	The earth will mourn; the sky will grow dark.
Voice 2	The Lord has spoken and will not change his mind.
Voice 3	He has made his decision and will not turn back.
Voice 1	At the noise of the horsemen and bowmen everyone will run away.
Voice 2	Some will run to the forest, others will climb up among the rocks.
Voice 3	Every town will be left empty, and no one will live in them again.
Voices 1–3	Jerusalem, you are doomed!
Voice 1	Why do you dress in scarlet?
Voice 2	Why do you put on jewellery and paint your eyes?
Voice 1	You are making yourself beautiful for nothing!
Voice 2	Your lovers have rejected you and want to kill you.
Voice 1	I heard a cry, like a woman in labour, a scream like a woman bearing her first child. It was the cry of Jerusalem gasping for breath, stretching out her hand and saying:
Voice 3	I am doomed! They are coming to kill me!
Cast	[This is] the word of the Lord.
All	**Thanks be to God.**

Cast: **Voice 1** (preferably male), **Voice 2**, **Voice 3** (preferably female).

The sin of Jerusalem
Jeremiah 5.1–11

Jeremiah	People of Jerusalem, run through your streets! Look around! See for yourselves! Search the market-places! Can you find one person who does what is right and tries to be faithful to God? If you can, the Lord will forgive Jerusalem. Even though you claim to worship the Lord, you do not mean what you say. Surely the Lord looks for faithfulness. He struck you, but you paid no attention; he crushed you, but you refused to learn. You were stubborn and would not turn from your sins. (PAUSE) Then I thought:
Young Jeremiah	These are only the poor and ignorant. They behave foolishly; they don't know what their God requires, what the Lord wants them to do. I will go to the people in power, and talk with them. Surely they know what their God requires, what the Lord wants them to do.
Jeremiah	But all of them have rejected the Lord's authority and refuse to obey him. That is why lions from the forest will kill them; wolves from the desert will tear them to pieces, and leopards will prowl through their towns. If those people go out, they will be torn apart because their sins are numerous and time after time they have turned from God. The Lord asked:
The Lord	Why should I forgive the sins of my people? They have abandoned me and have worshipped gods that are not real. I fed my people until they were full, but they committed adultery and spent their time with prostitutes. They were like well-fed stallions wild with desire, each lusting for his neighbour's wife. Shouldn't I punish them for these things and take revenge on a nation such as this? I will send enemies to cut down my people's vineyards, but not to destroy them completely. I will tell them to strip away the branches, because those branches are not mine. The people of Israel and Judah have betrayed me completely. (PAUSE) I, the Lord, have spoken!
Cast	[This is] the word of the Lord.
All	**Thanks be to God.**

Cast: **Jeremiah, Young Jeremiah, The Lord.**

The Lord rejects Israel
Jeremiah 5.12–19

Jeremiah	The Lord's people have denied him and have said:
Person 1	He won't *really* do anything.
Person 2	*We* won't have hard times.
Person 1	We won't have war or famine.
Person 2	The prophets are nothing but windbags.

Person 1	They have no message from the Lord.
Jeremiah	The Lord God Almighty said to me:
The Lord	Jeremiah, because these people have said such things, I will make my words like a fire in your mouth. The people will be like wood, and the fire will burn them up.
Jeremiah	People of Israel, the Lord is bringing a nation from afar to attack you. It is a strong and ancient nation, a nation whose language you do not know. Their bowmen are mighty soldiers who kill without mercy. They will devour your crops and your food; they will kill your sons and your daughters. They will slaughter your flocks and your herds and destroy your vines and fig-trees. The fortified cities in which you trust will be destroyed by their army. The Lord says:
The Lord	Yet even in those days I will not completely destroy my people. When they ask why I did all these things, tell them, Jeremiah, that just as they turned away from me and served foreign gods in their own land, so they will serve strangers in a land that is not theirs.
Cast	[This is] the word of the Lord.
All	**Thanks be to God.**

Cast: **Jeremiah, Person 1, Person 2,** (can be the same as Person 1), **The Lord.**

Jerusalem is surrounded by enemies
Jeremiah 6.1–8

Jeremiah	People of Benjamin, run for safety! Escape from Jerusalem! Sound the trumpet in Tekoa and build a signal fire in Beth Haccherem. Disaster and destruction are about to come from the north. The city of Zion is beautiful, but it will be destroyed; kings will camp there with their armies. They will pitch their tents round the city, and each one will camp wherever he wants. [They will say:]
King 1	Prepare to attack Jerusalem!
King 2	Get ready!
King 3	We'll attack at noon!
Jeremiah	But then they will say:
King 1	It's too late, the day is almost over, and the evening shadows are growing long.
King 2	We'll attack by night.
King 3	We'll destroy the city's fortresses.
Jeremiah	The Lord Almighty has ordered these kings to cut down trees and build mounds in order to besiege Jerusalem [He has said]:
The Lord (to Jeremiah)	I will punish this city because it is full of oppression. As a well keeps its water fresh, so Jerusalem keeps its evil fresh. I hear violence and destruction in the city; sickness and wounds are all I see.

$\rightarrow$

(calling)	People of Jerusalem, let these troubles be a warning to you, or else I will abandon you; I will turn your city into a desert, a place where no one lives.
Cast	[This is] the word of the Lord.
All	**Thanks be to God.**

Cast: **Jeremiah, King 1, King 2, King 3, The Lord.**

Rebellious Israel
Jeremiah 6.9–15

Jeremiah	The Lord Almighty said to me:
The Lord	Israel will be stripped clean like a vineyard from which every grape has been picked. So you must rescue everyone you can while there is still time.
Jeremiah	I answered:
Young Jeremiah (petulantly)	Who would listen to me if I spoke to them and warned them? (PAUSE) They are stubborn and refuse to listen to your message; they laugh at what you tell me to say.
(angrily)	Your anger against them burns in me too, Lord, and I can't hold it in any longer.
Jeremiah	Then the Lord said to me:
The Lord	Pour out my anger on the children in the streets and on the gatherings of the young men. Husbands and wives will be taken away, and even the very old will not be spared. Their houses will be given to others, and so will their fields and their wives. I am going to punish the people of this land. Everyone, great and small, tries to make money dishonestly; even prophets and priests cheat the people. They act as if my people's wounds were only scratches. They say:
A prophet (complacently)	All is well—
The Lord	When all is not well. (PAUSE) Were they ashamed because they did these disgusting things? No, they were not at all ashamed; they don't even know how to blush. And so they will fall as others have fallen; when I punish them, that will be the end of them. (PAUSE) I, the Lord, have spoken!
Cast	[This is] the word of the Lord.
All	**Thanks be to God.**

Cast: **Jeremiah, The Lord, Young Jeremiah** (can be the same as Jeremiah), **A prophet.**

Israel rejects God's way
Jeremiah 6.16–21

Jeremiah	The Lord said to his people:
The Lord	Stand at the crossroads and look. Ask for the ancient paths and where the best road is. Walk on it, and you will live in peace.

Jeremiah	But they said:
Persons 1 and **2**	No!
Person 1	We will not!
Jeremiah	Then the Lord appointed watchmen to listen for the trumpet's warning. But they said:
Persons 1 and **2**	We will not listen.
Jeremiah	So the Lord said:
The Lord	Listen, you nations, and learn what is going to happen to my people. Listen, earth! As punishment for all their schemes I am bringing ruin on these people, because they have rejected my teaching and have not obeyed my words. What do I care about the incense they bring me from Sheba, or the spices from a distant land? I will not accept their offerings or be pleased with their sacrifices. And so I will make these people stumble and fall. Fathers and sons will die, and so will friends and neighbours.
Cast	[This is] the word of the Lord.
All	**Thanks be to God.**

Cast: **Jeremiah, The Lord, Person 1, Person 2.**

Invasion from the North
Jeremiah 6.22–30

Jeremiah	The Lord says:
The Lord	People are coming from a country in the north; a mighty nation far away is preparing for war. They have taken up their bows and swords; they are cruel and merciless. They sound like the roaring sea, as they ride their horses. They are ready for battle against Jerusalem.
Jeremiah	The people of Jerusalem say:
Person 1 (frightened)	We have heard the news, and our hands hang limp.
Person 2	We are seized by anguish and pain like a woman in labour.
Person 1	We dare not go to the countryside or walk on the roads, because our enemies are armed and terror is all round us.
Jeremiah	The Lord says to his people:
The Lord	Put on sackcloth and roll in ashes. Mourn with bitter tears as you would for an only son, because the one who comes to destroy you will suddenly attack. Jeremiah, test my people, as you would test metal, and find out what they are like. They are all stubborn rebels, hard as bronze and iron. They are all corrupt, going round and spreading gossip. The furnace burns fiercely, but the waste metals do not melt and run off. It is useless to go on refining my people, because those who are evil are not taken away. They will be called worthless dross, because I, the Lord, have rejected them.
Cast	[This is] the word of the Lord.
All	**Thanks be to God.**

Cast: **Jeremiah, The Lord, Person 1, Person 2** (can be the same as Person 1).

Jeremiah preaches in the Temple
Jeremiah 7.1–15

Jeremiah The Lord sent me to the gate of the Temple where the people of Judah went in to worship. He told me to stand there and announce what the Lord Almighty, the God of Israel, had to say to them:

The Lord Change the way you are living and the things you are doing, and I will let you go on living here. Stop believing those deceitful words:

Persons 1 and **2** We are safe!

Person 1
(proudly) This is the Lord's Temple!

Person 2 This is the Lord's Temple!

Persons 1 and **2** This is the Lord's Temple!

The Lord Change the way you are living and stop doing the things you are doing. Be fair in your treatment of one another. Stop taking advantage of aliens, orphans, and widows. Stop killing innocent people in this land. Stop worshipping other gods, for that will destroy you. If you change, I will let you go on living here in the land which I gave your ancestors as a permanent possession.

Look, you put your trust in deceitful words. You steal, murder, commit adultery, tell lies under oath, offer sacrifices to Baal, and worship gods that you had not known before. You do these things I hate, and then you come and stand in my presence, in my own Temple, and say:

Persons 1 and **2**
(complacently) We are safe!

The Lord Do you think that my Temple is a hiding place for robbers? I have seen what you are doing. Go to Shiloh, the first place where I chose to be worshipped, and see what I did to it because of the sins of my people Israel. You have committed all these sins, and even though I spoke to you over and over again, you refused to listen. You would not answer when I called you. And so, what I did to Shiloh I will do to this Temple of mine, in which you trust. Here in this place that I gave to your ancestors and to you, I will do the same thing that I did to Shiloh. I will drive you out of my sight as I drove out your relatives, the people of Israel. (PAUSE) I, the Lord, have spoken!

Cast [This is] the word of the Lord.
All **Thanks be to God.**

Cast: **Jeremiah, The Lord, Person 1, Person 2** (can be the same as Person 1).

Sin and punishment
From Jeremiah 8.4–17

Jeremiah	The Lord told me to say to his people:
The Lord	When someone falls down, doesn't he get back up? If someone misses the road, doesn't he turn back? Why then, my people, do you turn away from me without ever turning back? You cling to your idols and refuse to return to me. I listened carefully, but you did not speak the truth. Not one of you has been sorry for his wickedness; not one of you has asked:
Person 1 (penitently)	What have I done wrong?
The Lord	[Everyone keeps on going his own way, like a horse rushing into battle. Even storks know when it is time to return; doves, swallows, and thrushes know when it is time to migrate. But,] my people, you do not know the laws by which I rule you. How can you say that you are wise, and that you know my laws? Look, the laws have been changed by dishonest scribes. Your wise men are put to shame; they are confused and trapped. They have rejected my words; what wisdom have they got now? [So I will give their fields to new owners and their wives to other men.] Everyone, great and small, tries to make money dishonestly. Even prophets and priests cheat the people. They act as if my people's wounds were only scratches [They say]:
Prophet(s) (complacently)	All is well— (PAUSE).
The Lord	When all is *not* well. I wanted to gather my people, as a man gathers his harvest; but they are like a vine with no grapes, like a fig-tree with no figs; even the leaves have withered. Therefore, I have allowed outsiders to take over the land.
Jeremiah	God's people ask:
Person 1	Why are we sitting still?
Person 2	Come on, we will run to the fortified cities, and die there.
Person 3	The Lord our God has condemned us to die; he has given us poison to drink, because we have sinned against him.
Person 2	We hoped for peace and a time of healing, but it was no use; terror came instead.
Person 1	Our enemies are already in the city of Dan; we hear the snorting of their horses.
Person 3	The whole land trembles when their horses neigh.
Person 2	Our enemies have come to destroy our land and everything in it, our city and all its people.
Jeremiah	The Lord says:

659

The Lord	Watch out! I am sending snakes among you, poisonous snakes that cannot be charmed, and they will bite you.
Cast	[This is] the word of the Lord.
All	**Thanks be to God.**

Cast: **Jeremiah, The Lord, Person 1, Prophet(s), Person 2, Person 3** (Persons 1–3 can be the same).

Jeremiah's sorrow for his people
Jeremiah 8.18—9.16

Jeremiah	My sorrow cannot be healed; I am sick at heart. Listen! Throughout the land I hear my people crying out:
Person 1	Is the Lord no longer in Zion?
Person 2	Is Zion's king no longer there? (PAUSE)
Jeremiah	The Lord, their king, replies:
The Lord	Why have you made me angry by worshipping your idols and by bowing down to your useless foreign gods?
Jeremiah	The people cry out:
Person 1	The summer is gone.
Person 2	The harvest is over.
Persons 1 and **2**	But we have not been saved.
Jeremiah	My heart has been crushed because my people are crushed; I mourn; I am completely dismayed. Is there no medicine in Gilead? Are there no doctors there? Why, then, have my people not been healed? I wish my head were a well of water, and my eyes a fountain of tears, so that I could cry day and night for my people who have been killed. I wish I had a place to stay in the desert where I could get away from my people. They are all unfaithful, a mob of traitors. They are always ready to tell lies; dishonesty instead of truth rules the land. [The Lord says:]
The Lord	My people do one evil thing after another, and do not acknowledge me as their God.
Jeremiah	Everyone must be on guard against his friend, and no one can trust his brother; for every brother is as deceitful as Jacob, and everyone slanders his friends. They all mislead their friends, and no one tells the truth; they have taught their tongues to lie and will not give up their sinning. They do one violent thing after another, and one deceitful act follows another.
	The Lord says that his people reject him. [Because of this the Lord Almighty says:]
The Lord	I will refine my people like metal and put them to the test. My people have done evil—what else can I do with them? Their tongues are like deadly arrows; they always tell lies. Everyone speaks friendly words to his neighbour, but is really setting a trap for him. Will I not punish them for these things? Will I not take revenge on a nation like this? I, the Lord, have spoken.

Jeremiah	I said:
	'I will mourn for the mountains
	and weep for the pastures,
	because they have dried up,
	and no one travels through them.
	The sound of livestock is no longer heard;
	birds and wild animals have fled and gone.'
	The Lord says:
The Lord	I will make Jerusalem a pile of ruins, a place where jackals live; the cities of Judah will become a desert, a place where no one lives.
Jeremiah	I asked: 'Lord, why is the land devastated and dry as a desert, so that no one travels through it? Who is wise enough to understand this? To whom have you explained it so that he can tell others?'
	The Lord answered:
The Lord	This has happened because my people have abandoned the teaching that I gave them. They have not obeyed me or done what I told them. Instead, they have been stubborn and have worshipped the idols of Baal as their fathers taught them to do. So then, listen to what I, the Lord Almighty, the God of Israel, will do: I will give my people bitter plants to eat and poison to drink. I will scatter them among nations that neither they nor their ancestors have heard about, and I will send armies against them until I have completely destroyed them.
Cast	[This is] the word of the Lord.
All	**Thanks be to God.**

Cast: **Jeremiah, Person 1, Person 2** (can be the same as Person 1), **The Lord.**

The people of Jerusalem cry out for help
Jeremiah 9.17–24

Jeremiah	The Lord Almighty said:
The Lord	Think about what is happening!
	Call for the mourners to come,
	for the women who sing funeral songs.
Jeremiah	The people said:
Person 1	Tell them to hurry and sing a funeral song for us—
Person 2	Until our eyes fill with tears,
	and our eyelids are wet from crying.
Jeremiah	Listen to the sound of crying in Zion:
Person 1	We are ruined!
Person 2	We are completely disgraced!
Person 1	We must leave our lands.
Person 2	Our homes have been torn down.

Jeremiah	I said:
Young Jeremiah	Listen to the Lord, you women, and pay attention to his words. Teach your daughters how to mourn, and your friends how to sing a funeral song. Death has come in through our windows and entered our palaces; it has cut down the children in the streets and the young men in the market-places. Dead bodies are scattered everywhere, like piles of manure on the fields, like corn cut and left behind by the reapers, corn that no one gathers. This is what the Lord has told me to say.
Jeremiah	The Lord says:
The Lord	Wise men should not boast of their wisdom, nor strong men of their strength, nor rich men of their wealth. If anyone wants to boast, he should boast that he knows and understands me, because my love is constant, and I do what is just and right. These are the things that please me. (PAUSE) I, the Lord, have spoken!
Cast	[This is] the word of the Lord.
All	**Thanks be to God.**

Cast: **Jeremiah, The Lord, Person 1, Person 2** (can be the same as Person 1), **Young Jeremiah.**

Idolatry and true worship
Jeremiah 10.1–11

Jeremiah	People of Israel, listen to the message that the Lord has for you. He says:
The Lord	Do not follow the ways of other nations; do not be disturbed by unusual sights in the sky, even though other nations are terrified. The religion of these people is worthless. A tree is cut down in the forest; it is carved by the tools of the woodcarver, and decorated with silver and gold. It is fastened down with nails to keep it from falling over. Such idols are like scarecrows in a field of melons; they cannot speak; they have to be carried because they cannot walk. Do not be afraid of them: they can cause you no harm, and they can do you no good.
Jeremiah (to The Lord)	Lord, there is no one like you; you are mighty, and your name is great and powerful. Who would not honour you, the king of all nations? You deserve to be honoured. There is no one like you among all the wise men of the nations or among any of their kings. All of them are stupid and foolish. What can they learn from wooden idols? Their idols are covered with silver from Spain and with gold from Uphaz, all the work of artists; they are dressed in violet and purple cloth woven by skilled weavers. But you, Lord, are the true God, you are the living God and the eternal king. When you are angry, the world trembles; the nations cannot endure your anger.
(to audience)	You people must tell them that the gods who did not make the

earth and the sky will be destroyed. They will no longer exist anywhere on earth.

Cast	[This is] the word of the Lord.
All	**Thanks be to God.**

Cast: **Jeremiah, The Lord.**

A hymn of praise to God
Jeremiah 10.12–16

Voice 1
The Lord made the earth by his power;
by his wisdom he created the world
and stretched out the heavens.

Voice 2
At his command the waters above the sky roar;
he brings clouds from the ends of the earth.

Voice 1
He makes lightning flash in the rain
and sends the wind from his storeroom.

Voice 3
At the sight of this, men feel stupid and senseless;
those who make idols are disillusioned,
because the gods they make are false and lifeless.

They are worthless and should be despised;
they will be destroyed when the Lord comes to deal with them.

Voice 2
The God of Jacob is not like them;
he is the one who made everything,
and he has chosen Israel to be his very own people.

Voices 1–3
The Lord Almighty is his name.

Cast	[This is] the word of the Lord.
All	**Thanks be to God.**

Cast: **Voice 1, Voice 2, Voice 3.**

The coming exile
Jeremiah 10.17–25

Jeremiah
People of Jerusalem, you are under siege! Gather up your belongings. The Lord is going to throw you out of this land; he is going to crush you until not one of you is left. The Lord has spoken. The people of Jerusalem cried out:

Voice 1
How badly we are hurt!

Voice 2
Our wounds will not heal.

Voice 1
And we thought this was something we could endure!

Voice 2
Our tents are ruined; the ropes that held them have broken.

Voice 1
Our children have all gone away.

Voice 2
There is no one left to put up our tents again.

Voice 1	There is no one to hang their curtains.
Jeremiah	I answered:
Young Jeremiah (to Voices 1 and 2)	Our leaders are stupid; they do not ask the Lord for guidance. This is why they have failed, and our people have been scattered. (PAUSE)
(to audience)	Listen! News has come! There is a great commotion in a nation to the north; its army will turn the cities of Judah into a desert, a place where jackals live.
Jeremiah	Lord, I know that no one is the master of his own destiny; no person has control over his own life. Correct your people, Lord; but do not be too hard on us or punish us when you are angry; that would be the end of us. Turn your anger on the nations that do not worship you and on the people who reject you. They have killed your people; they have destroyed us completely and left our country in ruins.
Cast	[This is] the word of the Lord.
All	**Thanks be to God.**

Cast: **Jeremiah, Voice 1, Voice 2, Young Jeremiah.**

Jeremiah and the covenant
Jeremiah 11.1–17

Jeremiah	The Lord said to me:
The Lord	Listen to the terms of the covenant. Tell the people of Judah and of Jerusalem that I, the Lord God of Israel, have placed a curse on everyone who does not obey the terms of this covenant. It is the covenant I made with their ancestors when I brought them out of Egypt, the land that was like a blazing furnace to them. I told them to obey me and to do everything that I had commanded. I told them that if they obeyed, they would be my people and I would be their God. Then I would keep the promise I made to their ancestors that I would give them the rich and fertile land which they now have.
Jeremiah	[I said,] 'Yes, Lord.' (PAUSE)
	[Then the Lord said to me:]
The Lord	Go to the cities of Judah and to the streets of Jerusalem. Proclaim my message there and tell the people to listen to the terms of the covenant and to obey them. When I brought their ancestors out of Egypt, I solemnly warned them to obey me, and I have kept on warning the people until this day. But they did not listen or obey. Instead, everyone continued to be as stubborn and evil as ever. I had commanded them to keep the covenant, but they refused. So I brought on them all the punishments described in it.
Jeremiah	Then the Lord said to me:

The Lord
The people of Judah and of Jerusalem are plotting against me. They have gone back to the sins of their ancestors, who refused to do what I said; they have worshipped other gods. Both Israel and Judah have broken the covenant that I made with their ancestors. So now, I, the Lord, warn them that I am going to bring destruction on them, and they will not escape. And when they cry out to me for help, I will not listen to them. Then the people of Judah and of Jerusalem will go to the gods to whom they offer sacrifices and will cry out to them for help. But those gods will not be able to save them when this destruction comes. The people of Judah have as many gods as they have cities, and the inhabitants of Jerusalem have set up as many altars for sacrifices to that disgusting god Baal as there are streets in the city.

Jeremiah, don't pray to me or plead with me on behalf of these people. When they are in trouble and call to me for help, I will not listen to them.

Jeremiah
The Lord says:

The Lord
(to Jeremiah)
The people I love are doing evil things. What right have they to be in my Temple? Do they think they can prevent disaster by making promises and by offering animal sacrifices? Will that make them happy? I once called them a leafy olive-tree, full of beautiful fruit; but now, with a roar like thunder I will set its leaves on fire and break its branches.

(to audience)
I, the Lord Almighty, planted Israel and Judah; but now I threaten them with disaster. They have brought this on themselves because they have done wrong; they have made me angry by offering sacrifices to Baal.

Cast
[This is] the word of the Lord.

All
Thanks be to God.

Cast: **Jeremiah, The Lord.**

A plot against Jeremiah's life
Jeremiah 11.18–23

Jeremiah
The Lord informed me of the plots that my enemies were making against me. I was like a trusting lamb taken out to be killed, and I did not know that it was against me that they were planning evil things. [They were saying:]

Enemy 1
(maliciously)
Let's chop down the tree while it is still healthy:

Enemy 2
Let's kill him so that no one will remember him any more.

Jeremiah
Then I prayed:

Young Jeremiah
Almighty Lord, you are a just judge; you test people's thoughts and feelings. I have placed my cause in your hands; so let me watch you take revenge on these people.

Jeremiah	The men of Anathoth wanted me killed, and they told me that they would kill me if I kept on proclaiming the Lord's message. So the Lord Almighty said:
The Lord	I will punish them! Their young men will be killed in war; their children will die of starvation. I have set a time for bringing disaster on the people of Anathoth, and when that time comes, none of them will survive.
Cast	[This is] the word of the Lord.
All	**Thanks be to God.**

Cast: **Jeremiah, Enemy 1, Enemy 2,** (can be the same as Enemy 1), **Young Jeremiah, The Lord.**

Jeremiah questions the Lord
Jeremiah 12.1–6

Jeremiah (to The Lord)	Lord, if I argued my case with you, you would prove to be right. Yet I must question you about matters of justice. Why are wicked men so prosperous? Why do dishonest men succeed? You plant them, and they take root; they grow and bear fruit. They always speak well of you, yet they do not really care about you. But, Lord, you know me; you see what I do, and how I love you. Drag these evil men away like sheep to be butchered; guard them until it is time for them to be slaughtered.
(musing)	How long will our land be dry, and the grass in every field be withered? Animals and birds are dying because of the wickedness of our people, people who say, 'God doesn't see what we are doing.' (PAUSE)
	The Lord said:
The Lord	Jeremiah, if you get tired racing against men, how can you race against horses? If you can't even stand up in open country, how will you manage in the jungle by the Jordan? Even your brothers, members of your own family, have betrayed you; they join in the attacks against you. Do not trust them, even though they speak friendly words.
Cast	[This is] the word of the Lord.
All	**Thanks be to God.**

Cast: **Jeremiah, The Lord.**

Jeremiah condemns disobedience
Jeremiah 13.1–11

Jeremiah	The Lord told me to go and buy myself some linen shorts and to put them on; but he told me not to put them in water. So I bought them and put them on. Then the Lord spoke to me again, and said:
The Lord	Go to the River Euphrates and hide the shorts in a hole in the rocks.

Jeremiah	So I went and hid them near the Euphrates.
	Some time later the Lord told me to go back to the Euphrates and get the shorts. So I went back, and when I found the place where I had hidden them, I saw that they were ruined and were no longer any good.
	Then the Lord spoke to me again:
The Lord	This is how I will destroy the pride of Judah and the great pride of Jerusalem. These evil people have refused to obey me. They have been as stubborn and wicked as ever, and have worshipped and served other gods. So then, they will become like these shorts that are no longer any good. Just as shorts fit tightly round the waist, so I intended all the people of Israel and Judah to hold tightly to me. I did this so that they would be my people and would bring praise and honour to my name; but they would not obey me.
Cast	[This is] the word of the Lord.
All	**Thanks be to God.**

Cast: **Jeremiah, The Lord.**

Jeremiah warns against pride
Jeremiah 13.15–27

Jeremiah	People of Israel, the Lord has spoken! Be humble and listen to him. Honour the Lord, your God, before he brings darkness, and you stumble on the mountains; before he turns into deep darkness the light you hoped for. If you will not listen, I will cry in secret because of your pride; I will cry bitterly, and my tears will flow because the Lord's people have been taken away as captives.
	The Lord said to me:
The Lord	Tell the king and his mother to come down from their thrones, because their beautiful crowns have fallen from their heads. The towns of southern Judah are under siege; no one can get through to them. All the people of Judah have been taken away into exile.
Jeremiah	Jerusalem, look! Your enemies are coming down from the north! Where are the people entrusted to your care, your people you were so proud of? What will you say when people you thought were your friends conquer you and rule over you? You will be in pain like a woman giving birth. If you ask why all this has happened to you—why your clothes have been torn off and you have been raped—it is because your sin is so terrible. Can a black man change the colour of his skin, or a leopard remove its spots? If they could, then you that do nothing but evil could learn to do what is right. The Lord will scatter you like straw that is blown away by the desert wind. He has said that this will be your fate. This is what he has decided to do with you, because you have

→

forgotten him and have trusted in false gods. The Lord himself will strip off your clothes and expose you to shame. He has seen you do the things he hates. He has seen you go after pagan gods on the hills and in the fields, like a man lusting after his neighbour's wife or like a stallion after a mare. People of Jerusalem, you are doomed! When will you ever be pure?

Cast	[This is] the word of the Lord.
All	**Thanks be to God.**

Cast: **Jeremiah, The Lord.**

The terrible drought
Jeremiah 14.1–18

Jeremiah	The Lord said to me concerning the drought:
The Lord	Judah is in mourning; its cities are dying, its people lie on the ground in sorrow, and Jerusalem cries out for help. The rich people send their servants for water; they go to the cisterns, but find no water; they come back with their jars empty. Discouraged and confused, they hide their faces. Because there is no rain and the ground is dried up, the farmers are sick at heart; they hide their faces. In the field the mother deer abandons her new-born fawn because there is no grass. The wild donkeys stand on the hilltops and pant for breath like jackals; their eyesight fails them because they have no food. My people cry out to me:
Person 1	Even though our sins accuse us, help us, Lord, as you have promised.
Person 2	We have turned away from you many times.
Person 3	We have sinned against you.
Person 1	You are Israel's only hope.
Person 2	You are the one who saves us from disaster.
Person 1	Why are you like a stranger in our land, like a traveller who stays for only one night?
Person 3	Why are you like a man taken by surprise, like a soldier powerless to help?
Person 2	Surely, Lord, you are with us!
Person 3	We are your people—
Persons 1–3	Do not abandon us.
Jeremiah	The Lord says about these people:
The Lord	They love to run away from me, and they will not control themselves. So I am not pleased with them. I will remember the wrongs they have done and punish them because of their sins.
Jeremiah	The Lord said to me:

The Lord	Do not ask me to help these people. Even if they fast, I will not listen to their cry for help; and even if they offer me burnt-offerings and grain-offerings, I will not be pleased with them. Instead, I will kill them in war and by starvation and disease.
Jeremiah	Then I said:
Young Jeremiah	Sovereign Lord, you know that the prophets are telling the people that there will be no war or starvation, because you have promised, they say, that there will be only peace in our land.
Jeremiah	But the Lord replied:
The Lord	The prophets are telling lies in my name; I did not send them, nor did I give them any orders or speak one word to them. The visions they talk about have not come from me; their predictions are worthless things that they have imagined. I, the Lord, tell you what I am going to do to those prophets whom I did not send but who speak in my name and say war and starvation will not strike this land—I will kill them in war and by starvation. The people to whom they have said these things will be killed in the same way. Their bodies will be thrown out into the streets of Jerusalem, and there will be no one to bury them. This will happen to all of them—including their wives, their sons, and their daughters. I will make them pay for their wickedness.
Jeremiah	The Lord commanded me to tell the people about my sorrow [and to say]:
Young Jeremiah	May my eyes flow with tears day and night, may I never stop weeping, for my people are deeply wounded and are badly hurt. When I go out into the fields, I see the bodies of men killed in war; when I go into the towns, I see people starving to death. Prophets and priests carry on their work, but they don't know what they are doing.
Cast	[This is] the word of the Lord.
All	**Thanks be to God.**

Cast: **Jeremiah, The Lord, Person 1, Person 2, Person 3, Young Jeremiah.**

The people plead with the Lord
Jeremiah 14.19–22

Voice 1	Lord, have you completely rejected Judah?
Voice 2	Do you hate the people of Zion?
Voice 3	Why have you hurt us so badly that we cannot be healed?
Voice 1	We looked for peace, but nothing good happened.
Voice 2	We hoped for healing, but terror came instead.
Voice 3	We have sinned against you, Lord; we confess our own sins and the sins of our ancestors.
Voice 1	Remember your promises and do not despise us; do not bring disgrace on Jerusalem, the place of your glorious throne.

Voice 2	Do not break the covenant you made with us.
Voice 3	None of the idols of the nations can send rain; the sky by itself cannot make showers fall.
Voice 1	We have put our hope in you, O Lord our God, because you are the one who does these things.
Cast **All**	[This is] the word of the Lord. **Thanks be to God.**

Cast: **Voice 1, Voice 2, Voice 3.**

Doom for the people of Judah
Jeremiah 15.1–4

Jeremiah	The people pleaded with the Lord. Then the Lord said to me:
The Lord	Even if Moses and Samuel were standing here pleading with me, I would not show these people any mercy. Make them go away; make them get out of my sight. When they ask you where they should go, tell them that I have said:
	Some are doomed to die by disease—
Voice 1	That's where they will go!
The Lord	Others are doomed to die in war—
Voice 2	That's where they will go!
The Lord	Some are doomed to die of starvation—
Voice 1	That's where they will go!
The Lord	Others are doomed to be taken away as prisoners—
Voices 1 and 2	That's where they will go!
The Lord	I, the Lord, have decided that four terrible things will happen to them:
Voice 1	They will be killed in war.
Voice 2	Their bodies will be dragged off by dogs.
Voice 1	Birds will eat them.
Voice 2	And wild animals will devour what is left over.
The Lord	I will make all the people of the world horrified at them because of what Hezekiah's son Manasseh did in Jerusalem when he was king of Judah.
Cast **All**	[This is] the word of the Lord. **Thanks be to God.**

Cast: **Jeremiah, The Lord, Voice 1, Voice 2** (can be the same as Voice 1).

Jeremiah complains to the Lord
Jeremiah 15.10–21

Jeremiah   What an unhappy man I am! Why did my mother bring me into the world? I have to quarrel and argue with everyone in the land. I have not lent any money or borrowed any; yet everyone curses me. Lord, may all their curses come true if I have not served you well, if I have not pleaded with you on behalf of my enemies when they were in trouble and distress.

The Lord said to me:

The Lord   I will send enemies to carry away the wealth and treasures of my people, in order to punish them for the sins they have committed throughout the land. I will make them serve their enemies in a land they know nothing about, because my anger is like fire, and it will burn for ever.

Jeremiah   Then I said:

Young Jeremiah   Lord, you understand. Remember me and help me. Let me have revenge on those who persecute me. Do not be so patient with them that they succeed in killing me. Remember that it is for your sake that I am insulted. You spoke to me, and I listened to every word. I belong to you, Lord God Almighty, and so your words filled my heart with joy and happiness. I did not spend my time with other people, laughing and having a good time. In obedience to your orders I stayed by myself and was filled with anger. Why do I keep on suffering? Why are my wounds incurable? Why won't they heal? Do you intend to disappoint me like a stream that goes dry in the summer?

Jeremiah   To this the Lord replied:

The Lord   If you return, I will take you back, and you will be my servant again. If instead of talking nonsense you proclaim a worthwhile message, you will be my prophet again. The people will come back to you, and you will not need to go to them. I will make you like a solid bronze wall as far as they are concerned. They will fight against you, but they will not defeat you. I will be with you to protect you and keep you safe. I will rescue you from the power of wicked and violent men. (PAUSE) I, the Lord, have spoken!

Cast   [This is] the word of the Lord.
All   **Thanks be to God.**

Cast: **Jeremiah, The Lord, Young Jeremiah.**

Jeremiah's prayer of confidence in the Lord
Jeremiah 16.19–21

Jeremiah   Lord, you are the one who protects me and gives me strength; you help me in times of trouble. Nations will come to you from the ends of the earth and say:

Person 1	Our ancestors had nothing but false gods—
Person 2	Nothing but useless idols.
Person 1	Can a man make his *own* gods?
Person 2	No, if he did, they would not really be gods.
Jeremiah	The Lord says:
The Lord	So then, once and for all I will make the nations know my power and my might; they will know that I am the Lord.
Cast	[This is] the word of the Lord.
All	**Thanks be to God.**

Cast: **Jeremiah, Person 1, Person 2** (can be the same as Person 1), **The Lord.**

Various sayings
Jeremiah 17.5–17

Jeremiah	The Lord says:
The Lord	I will condemn the person who turns away from me and puts his trust in man, in the strength of mortal man. He is like a bush in the desert, which grows in the dry wilderness, on salty ground where nothing else grows. Nothing good ever happens to him.
	But I will bless the person who puts his trust in me. He is like a tree growing near a stream and sending out roots to the water. It is not afraid when hot weather comes, because its leaves stay green; it has no worries when there is no rain; it keeps on bearing fruit.
	Who can understand the human heart? There is nothing else so deceitful; it is too sick to be healed. I, the Lord, search the minds and test the hearts of men. I treat each one according to the way he lives, according to what he does.
Jeremiah (to audience)	The person who gets money dishonestly is like a bird that hatches eggs it didn't lay. In the prime of life he will lose his riches, and in the end he is nothing but a fool.
	Our Temple is like a glorious throne, standing on a high mountain from the beginning.
(praying)	Lord, you are Israel's hope; all who abandon you will be put to shame. They will disappear like names written in the dust, because they have abandoned you, the Lord, the spring of fresh water.
	Lord, heal me and I will be completely well; rescue me and I will be perfectly safe. You are the one I praise!
	The people say:
Person 1	Where are those threats the Lord made against us?
Person 2	Let him carry them out now!

Jeremiah	But, Lord, I never urged you to bring disaster on them; I did not wish a time of trouble for them. Lord, you know this; you know what I have said. Do not be a terror to me; you are my place of safety when trouble comes.
Cast	[This is] the word of the Lord.
All	**Thanks be to God.**

Cast: **Jeremiah, The Lord, Person 1, Person 2** (can be the same as Person 1).

A plot against Jeremiah
From Jeremiah 18.18—19.11

Jeremiah	The people said:
Person 1	Let's do something about Jeremiah!
Person 2	There will always be priests to instruct us, wise men to give us counsel, and prophets to proclaim God's message.
Person 1	Let's bring charges against him—
Person 2	And stop listening to what he says.
Jeremiah	So I prayed:
Young Jeremiah	Lord, hear what I am saying and listen to what my enemies are saying about me. Is evil the payment for good? Yet they have dug a pit for me to fall in. Remember how I came to you and spoke on their behalf, so that you would not deal with them in anger. But now, Lord, they have dug a pit for me to fall in and have set traps to catch me. But, Lord, you know all their plots to kill me.
Jeremiah	The Lord told me to go and buy a clay jar. He also told me to take some of the elders of the people and some of the older priests, and to go through Potsherd Gate out to the Valley of Hinnom. There I was to proclaim the message that he would give me. The Lord told me to say:
The Lord	Kings of Judah and people of Jerusalem, listen to what I, the Lord Almighty, the God of Israel, have to say. I am going to bring such a disaster on this place that everyone who hears about it will be stunned. I am going to do this because the people have abandoned me and defiled this place by offering sacrifices here to other gods—gods that neither they nor their ancestors nor the kings of Judah have known anything about. They have filled this place with the blood of innocent people, and they have built altars for Baal in order to burn their children in the fire as sacrifices. I never commanded them to do this; it never even entered my mind. So then, the time will come when this place will no longer be called Topheth or the Valley of Hinnom. Instead, it will be known as the Valley of Slaughter. I will bring such terrible destruction on this city that everyone who passes by will be shocked and amazed. The enemy will surround the city and try to kill its people. The siege will be so terrible that the people inside the city will eat one another and even their own children.

Jeremiah	Then the Lord told me to break the jar in front of the men who had gone with me and to tell them that the Lord Almighty had said, 'I will break this people and this city, and it will be like this broken clay jar that cannot be put together again.'
Cast	[This is] the word of the Lord.
All	**Thanks be to God.**

Cast: **Jeremiah, Person 1, Person 2** (can be the same as Person 1), **Young Jeremiah, The Lord.**

The clay jar
Jeremiah 19.10–15

Jeremiah	The Lord told me to break a clay jar in front of the men who had gone with me and to tell them that the Lord Almighty had said:
The Lord	I will break this people and this city, and it will be like this broken clay jar that cannot be put together again. People will bury their dead even in Topheth because there will be nowhere else to bury them. I promise that I will make this city and its inhabitants like Topheth. The houses of Jerusalem, the houses of the kings of Judah, and indeed all the houses on whose roofs incense has been burnt to the stars and where wine has been poured out as an offering to other gods—they will all be as unclean as Topheth.
Jeremiah	Then I left Topheth, where the Lord had sent me to proclaim his message. I went and stood in the court of the Temple and told all the people that the Lord Almighty, the God of Israel, had said:
The Lord	I am going to bring on this city and on every nearby town all the punishment that I said I would, because you are stubborn and will not listen to what I say.
Cast	[This is] the word of the Lord.
All	**Thanks be to God.**

Cast: **Jeremiah, The Lord** (This reading overlaps with the previous one).

Jeremiah's conflict with Pashhur
Jeremiah 20.1–6

Jeremiah	When the priest Pashhur son of Immer, who was the chief officer of the Temple, heard me proclaim the Lord's message, he ordered me to be beaten and placed in chains near the upper Benjamin Gate in the Temple. The next morning, after Pashhur had released me from the chains, I said to him:
Young Jeremiah	The Lord did not name you Pashhur. The name he has given you is 'Terror Everywhere.' The Lord himself has said:
The Lord	I am going to make you a terror to yourself and to your friends, and you will see them all killed by the swords of their enemies. I am going to put all the people of Judah under the power of the king of Babylonia; he will take some away as prisoners to his country and put others to death. I will also let their enemies

plunder all the wealth of this city and seize all its possessions and property, even the treasures of the kings of Judah, and carry everything off to Babylonia. As for you, Pashhur, you and all your family will also be captured and taken off to Babylonia. There you will die and be buried, along with all your friends to whom you have told so many lies.

Cast	[This is] the word of the Lord.
All	**Thanks be to God.**

Cast: **Jeremiah, Young Jeremiah, The Lord.**

Jeremiah complains to the Lord
Jeremiah 20.7–13

Jeremiah	Lord, you have deceived me, and I was deceived. You are stronger than I am, and you have overpowered me. Everyone jeers at me; they mock me all day long. Whenever I speak, I have to cry out and shout:
Voice	Violence! Destruction!
Jeremiah	Lord, I am ridiculed and scorned all the time because I proclaim your message. But when I say:
Voice	I will forget the Lord and no longer speak in his name—
Jeremiah	Then your message is like a fire burning deep within me. I try my best to hold it in, but can no longer keep it back. I hear everybody whispering:
Person 1	Terror is everywhere!
Person 2	Let's report him to the authorities!
Jeremiah	Even my close friends wait for my downfall. [They say:]
Friend 1	Perhaps he can be tricked.
Friend 2	Then we can catch him and get revenge. (PAUSE)
Jeremiah	But you, Lord, are on my side, strong and mighty, and those who persecute me will fail. They will be disgraced for ever, because they cannot succeed. Their disgrace will never be forgotten. But, Almighty Lord, you test men justly; you know what is in their hearts and minds. So let me see you take revenge on my enemies, for I have placed my cause in your hands. Sing to the Lord! Praise the Lord! He rescues the oppressed from the power of evil men.
Cast	[This is] the word of the Lord.
All	**Thanks be to God.**

Cast: **Jeremiah, Voice, Person 1, Person 2** (can be the same as Person 1), **Friend 1, Friend 2** (Friends 1 and 2 can be the same as Persons 1 and 2).

Jerusalem's defeat is predicted
Jeremiah 21.1–10

Jeremiah King Zedekiah of Judah sent Pashhur son of Malchiah and the priest Zephaniah son of Maaseiah to me with this request:

Pashhur Please speak to the Lord for us, because King Nebuchadnezzar of Babylonia and his army are besieging the city. Maybe the Lord will perform one of his miracles for us and force Nebuchadnezzar to retreat.

Jeremiah Then the Lord spoke to me, and I told the men who had been sent to me to tell Zedekiah that the Lord, the God of Israel, had said:

The Lord Zedekiah, I am going to defeat your army that is fighting against the king of Babylonia and his army. I will pile up your soldiers' weapons in the centre of the city. I will fight against you with all my might, my anger, my wrath, and my fury. I will kill everyone living in this city; people and animals alike will die of a terrible disease. But as for you, your officials, and the people who survive the war, the famine, and the disease—I will let all of you be captured by King Nebuchadnezzar and by your enemies, who want to kill you. Nebuchadnezzar will put you to death. He will not spare any of you or show mercy or pity to any of you. I, the Lord, have spoken.

Jeremiah Then the Lord told me to say to the people:

The Lord Listen! I, the Lord, am giving you a choice between the way that leads to life and the way that leads to death. Anyone who stays in the city will be killed in war or by starvation or disease. But whoever goes out and surrenders to the Babylonians, who are now attacking the city, will not be killed; he will at least escape with his life. I have made up my mind not to spare this city, but to destroy it. It will be given over to the king of Babylonia and he will burn it to the ground. (PAUSE) I, the Lord, have spoken!

Cast [This is] the word of the Lord.
All **Thanks be to God.**

Cast: **Jeremiah, Pashhur, The Lord.**

Judgement on the royal house of Judah
Jeremiah 21.11—22.9

Jeremiah The Lord told me to give this message to the royal house of Judah, the descendants of David:

The Lord Listen to what I, the Lord, am saying. See that justice is done every day. Protect the person who is being cheated from the one who is cheating him. If you don't, the evil you are doing will make my anger burn like a fire that cannot be put out. You, Jerusalem, are sitting high above the valleys, like a rock rising above the plain. But I will fight against you. You say that no one can attack you or break through your defences. But I will punish you for what you have done. I will set your palace on fire, and the fire will burn down everything round it. I, the Lord, have spoken.

Jeremiah   The Lord told me to go to the palace of the king of Judah, the descendant of David, and there tell the king, his officials, and the people of Jerusalem to listen to what the Lord had said:

The Lord   I, the Lord, command you to do what is just and right. Protect the person who is being cheated from the one who is cheating him. Do not ill-treat or oppress foreigners, orphans, or widows; and do not kill innocent people in this holy place. If you really do as I have commanded, then David's descendants will continue to be kings. And they, together with their officials and their people, will continue to pass through the gates of this palace in chariots and on horses. But if you do not obey my commands, then I swear to you that this palace will fall into ruins. I, the Lord, have spoken.

To me, Judah's royal palace is as beautiful as the land of Gilead and as the Lebanon Mountains; but I will make it a desolate place where no one lives. I am sending men to destroy it. They will all bring their axes, cut down its beautiful cedar pillars, and throw them into the fire.

Afterwards many foreigners will pass by and ask one another why I, the Lord, have done such a thing to this great city. Then they will answer that it is because you have abandoned your covenant with me, your God, and have worshipped and served other gods.

Cast   [This is] the word of the Lord.
All   **Thanks be to God.**

Cast: **Jeremiah, The Lord.**

Jeremiah's message concerning the king of Judah
Jeremiah 22.10–19

Jeremiah   People of Judah, do not weep for King Josiah; do not mourn his death. But weep bitterly for Joahaz, his son; they are taking him away, never to return, never again to see the land where he was born. The Lord says concerning Josiah's son Joahaz, who succeeded his father as king of Judah:

The Lord   He has gone away from here, never to return. He will die in the country where they have taken him, and he will never again see this land.

Jeremiah   Doomed is the man who builds his house by injustice and enlarges it by dishonesty; who makes his countrymen work for nothing and does not pay their wages. Doomed is the man who says:

Jehoiakim
(pretentiously)   I will build myself a mansion with spacious rooms upstairs.

Jeremiah   So he puts windows in his house, panels it with cedar, and paints it red. Does it make you a better king if you build houses of cedar, finer than those of others? Your father enjoyed a full life. He was

→

677

always just and fair, and he prospered in everything he did. He gave the poor a fair trial, and all went well with him. That is what it means to know the Lord. But you can only see your selfish interests; you kill the innocent and violently oppress your people. The Lord has spoken.

So then, the Lord says about Josiah's son Jehoiakim, king of Judah:

The Lord   No one will mourn his death or say, 'How terrible, my friend, how terrible!' No one will weep for him or cry, 'My lord! My king!' With the funeral honours of a donkey, he will be dragged away and thrown outside Jerusalem's gates.

Cast   [This is] the word of the Lord.
All   **Thanks be to God.**

Cast: **Jeremiah, The Lord, Jehoiakim.**

God's judgement on Jehoiachin
Jeremiah 22.24–30

Jeremiah   The Lord said to King Jehoiachin, son of King Jehoiakim of Judah:

The Lord   As surely as I am the living God, even if you were the signet-ring on my right hand, I would pull you off and give you to people you are afraid of, people who want to kill you. I will give you to King Nebuchadnezzar of Babylonia and his soldiers. I am going to force you and your mother into exile. You will go to a country where neither of you was born, and both of you will die there. You will long to see this country again, but you will never return.

Jeremiah   I said:

Young Jeremiah   Has King Jehoiachin become like a broken jar that is thrown away and that no one wants? Is that why he and his children have been taken into exile to a land they know nothing about?

Jeremiah   O land, land, land! Listen to what the Lord has said:

The Lord   This man is condemned to lose his children, to be a man who will never succeed. He will have no descendants who will rule in Judah as David's successors. (PAUSE) I, the Lord, have spoken!

Cast   [This is] the word of the Lord.
All   **Thanks be to God.**

Cast: **Jeremiah, The Lord, Young Jeremiah.**

Hope for the future
Jeremiah 23.1–6 [7–8]

Jeremiah   How terrible will be the Lord's judgement on those rulers who destroy and scatter his people! This is what the Lord, the God of Israel, says about the rulers who were supposed to take care of his people:

The Lord	You have not taken care of my people; you have scattered them and driven them away. Now I am going to punish you for the evil you have done. I will gather the rest of my people from the countries where I have scattered them, and I will bring them back to their homeland. They will have many children and increase in number. I will appoint rulers to take care of them. My people will no longer be afraid or terrified, and I will not punish them again. I, the Lord, have spoken.
Jeremiah	The Lord says:
The Lord	The time is coming when I will choose as king a righteous descendant of David. That king will rule wisely and do what is right and just throughout the land. When he is king, the people of Judah will be safe, and the people of Israel will live in peace. He will be called:
Persons	The Lord Our Salvation.
[Jeremiah	The Lord says:
The Lord	The time is coming, when people will no longer swear by me as the living God who brought the people of Israel out of the land of Egypt. Instead, they will swear by me as the living God who brought the people of Israel out of a northern land and out of all the other countries where I had scattered them. Then they will live in their own land.]
Cast	[This is] the word of the Lord.
All	**Thanks be to God.**

Cast: **Jeremiah, The Lord, Persons** (2 or more, can be the same as The Lord). (See also Appendix: Christmas Readings, New Testament page 405.)

Jeremiah's message about the prophets
Jeremiah 23.9–15

Jeremiah	My heart is crushed, and I am trembling. Because of the Lord, because of his holy words, I am like a man who is drunk, a man who has had too much wine. The land is full of people unfaithful to the Lord; they live wicked lives and misuse their power. Because of the Lord's curse the land mourns and the pastures are dry. (PAUSE)
	The Lord says:
The Lord	The prophets and the priests are godless; I have caught them doing evil in the Temple itself. The paths they follow will be slippery and dark; I will make them stumble and fall. I am going to bring disaster on them; the time of their punishment is coming. I, the Lord, have spoken. I have seen the sin of Samaria's prophets: they have spoken in the name of Baal and have led my people astray. But I have seen the prophets in Jerusalem do even worse: they commit adultery and tell lies; they help people to do wrong, so that no one stops doing what is evil. To me, they are all as bad as the people of Sodom and Gomorrah.

Jeremiah	So then, this is what the Lord Almighty, says about the prophets of Jerusalem:
The Lord	I will give them bitter plants to eat and poison to drink, because they have spread ungodliness throughout the land.
Cast	[This is] the word of the Lord.
All	**Thanks be to God.**

Cast: **Jeremiah, The Lord.**

Two baskets of figs
Jeremiah 24.1–10

Jeremiah	The Lord showed me two baskets of figs placed in front of the Temple—
Commentator (interrupting)	This was after King Nebuchadnezzar of Babylonia had taken away Jehoiakim's son, King Jehoiachin of Judah, as a prisoner from Jerusalem to Babylonia, together with the leaders of Judah, the craftsmen, and the skilled workers—
Jeremiah	The first basket contained good figs, those that ripen early; the other one contained bad figs, too bad to eat. Then the Lord said to me:
The Lord	Jeremiah, what do you see?
Jeremiah	I answered:
Young Jeremiah	Figs. The good ones are very good, and the bad ones are very bad, too bad to eat.
Jeremiah	So the Lord said to me:
The Lord	I, the Lord, the God of Israel, consider that the people who were taken away to Babylonia are like these good figs, and I will treat them with kindness. I will watch over them and bring them back to this land. I will build them up and not tear them down; I will plant them and not pull them up. I will give them the desire to know that I am the Lord. Then they will be my people, and I will be their God, because they will return to me with all their heart.
	As for King Zedekiah of Judah, the politicians round him, and the rest of the people of Jerusalem who have stayed in this land or moved to Egypt—I, the Lord, will treat them all like these figs that are too bad to be eaten. I will bring such a disaster on them that all the nations of the world will be terrified. People will mock them, make jokes about them, ridicule them, and use their name as a curse everywhere I scatter them. I will bring war, starvation, and disease on them until there is not one of them left in the land that I gave to them and their ancestors.
Cast	[This is] the word of the Lord.
All	**Thanks be to God.**

Cast: **Jeremiah, Commentator, The Lord, Young Jeremiah.**

God's judgement on the nations
From Jeremiah 25.15–31

Jeremiah	The Lord, the God of Israel, said to me:
The Lord	Here is a wine cup filled with my anger. Take it to all the nations to whom I send you, and make them drink from it. When they drink from it, they will stagger and go out of their minds because of the war I am sending against them.
Jeremiah	So I took the cup from the Lord's hand, gave it to all the nations to whom the Lord had sent me, and made them drink from it. Jerusalem and all the towns of Judah, together with its kings and leaders, were made to drink from it, so that they would become a desert, a terrible and shocking sight, and so that people would use their name as a curse—as they still do.
	Here is the list of all the others who had to drink from the cup:
Reader	The king of Egypt, his officials and leaders; all the Egyptians and all the foreigners in Egypt; all the kings of the land of Uz; all the kings of the Philistine cities; all the people of Edom, Moab, and Ammon; all the kings of Tyre and Sidon; all the kings of the Mediterranean lands; the cities of Dedan, Tema, and Buz; all the kings of Arabia; all the kings of the desert tribes; all the kings of Zimri, Elam, and Media; all the kings of the north.
Jeremiah	Every nation on the face of the earth had to drink from it. Last of all, the king of Babylonia will drink from it.
	Then the Lord said to me:
The Lord	Tell the people that I, the Lord Almighty, the God of Israel, am commanding them to drink until they are drunk and vomit, until they fall down and cannot get up, because of the war that I am sending against them. And if they refuse to take the cup from your hand and drink from it, then tell them that the Lord Almighty has said that they will still have to drink from it. I will begin my work of destruction in my own city. Do they think they will go unpunished? No, they will be punished, for I am going to send war on all the people on earth. I, the Lord Almighty, have spoken.
	You, Jeremiah, must proclaim everything I have said. You must tell these people:
Reader	The Lord will roar from heaven and thunder from the heights of heaven. He will roar against his people; he will shout like a man treading grapes. Everyone on earth will hear him,

→

681

and the sound will echo to the ends of the earth.
The Lord has a case against the nations.
He will bring all people to trial
and put the wicked to death.

Cast	
(with flourish)	The Lord has spoken!

Cast	[This is] the word of the Lord.
All	**Thanks be to God.**

Cast: **Jeremiah, The Lord, Reader.**

Jeremiah is brought to trial
Jeremiah 26.1–16

Jeremiah	Soon after Jehoiakim son of Josiah became king of Judah, the Lord said to me:
The Lord	Stand in the court of the Temple and proclaim all I have commanded you to say to the people who come from the towns of Judah to worship there. Do not leave out anything. Perhaps the people will listen and give up their evil ways. If they do, then I will change my mind about the destruction I plan to bring on them for all their wicked deeds.
Jeremiah	The Lord told me to say to the people:
The Lord	I, the Lord, have said that you must obey me by following the teaching that I gave you, and by paying attention to the words of my servants, the prophets, whom I have kept on sending to you. You have never obeyed what they said. If you continue to disobey, then I will do to this Temple what I did to Shiloh, and all the nations of the world will use the name of this city as a curse.
Jeremiah	The priests, the prophets, and all the people heard me saying these things in the Temple, and as soon as I had finished all that the Lord had commanded me to speak, they seized me and shouted:
Priest	You ought to be killed for this!
Prophet	Why have you said in the Lord's name that this Temple will become like Shiloh—
Priest	And that this city will be destroyed and no one will live in it?
Jeremiah	Then the people crowded round me. When the leaders of Judah heard what had happened, they hurried from the royal palace to the Temple and took their places at the New Gate. Then the priests and the prophets said to the leaders and to the people:
Priest	This man deserves to be sentenced to death because he has spoken against our city.
Prophet	You heard him with your own ears.
Jeremiah	Then I said:

Young Jeremiah The Lord sent me to proclaim everything that you heard me say against this Temple and against this city. You must change the way you are living and the things you are doing, and must obey the Lord your God. If you do, he will change his mind about the destruction that he said he would bring on you. As for me, I am in your power! Do with me whatever you think is fair and right. But be sure of this: if you kill me, you and the people of this city will be guilty of killing an innocent man, because it is the Lord who sent me to give you this warning.

Jeremiah Then the leaders and the people said to the priests and the prophets:

Leader This man spoke to us in the name of the Lord our God; he should not be put to death.

Cast [This is] the word of the Lord.
All **Thanks be to God.**

Cast: **Jeremiah, The Lord, Priest, Prophet** (can be the same as Priest), **Young Jeremiah, Leader.**

Jeremiah wears an ox yoke
Jeremiah 27.1–22

Jeremiah Soon after Josiah's son Zedekiah became king of Judah, the Lord told me to make myself a yoke out of leather straps and wooden crossbars and to put it on my neck. Then the Lord told me to send a message to the kings of Edom, Moab, Ammon, Tyre, and Sidon through their ambassadors who had come to Jerusalem to see King Zedekiah. The Lord Almighty, the God of Israel, told me to command them to tell their kings that the Lord had said:

The Lord By my great power and strength I created the world, mankind, and all the animals that live on the earth; and I give it to anyone I choose. I am the one who has placed all these nations under the power of my servant, King Nebuchadnezzar of Babylonia, and I have made even the wild animals serve him. All nations will serve him, and they will serve his son and his grandson until the time comes for his own nation to fall. Then his nation will serve powerful nations and great kings.

But if any nation or kingdom will not submit to his rule, then I will punish that nation by war, starvation, and disease until I have let Nebuchadnezzar destroy it completely. Do not listen to your prophets or to anyone who claims he can predict the future, either by dreams or by calling up the spirits of the dead or by magic. They all tell you not to submit to the king of Babylonia. They are deceiving you and will cause you to be taken far away from your country. I will drive you out, and you will be destroyed. But if any nation submits to the king of Babylonia and serves him, then I will let it stay on in its own land, to farm it and live there. I, the Lord, have spoken.

Jeremiah I said the same thing to King Zedekiah of Judah:

Young Jeremiah	Submit to the king of Babylonia. Serve him and his people, and you will live. Why should you and your people die in war or of starvation or disease? That is what the Lord has said will happen to any nation that does not submit to the king of Babylonia. Do not listen to the prophets who tell you not to surrender to him. They are deceiving you. The Lord himself has said that he did not send them and that they are lying to you in his name. And so he will drive you out, and you will be killed, you and the prophets who are telling you these lies.
Jeremiah	Then I told the priests and the people that the Lord had said:
The Lord	Do not listen to the prophets who say that the temple treasures will soon be brought back from Babylonia. They are lying to you. Don't listen to them! Submit to the king of Babylonia and you will live! Why should this city become a pile of ruins? If they are really prophets and if they have my message, let them ask me, the Lord Almighty, not to allow the treasures that remain in the Temple and in the royal palace to be taken to Babylonia.
Commentator	When King Nebuchadnezzar took away to Babylonia the king of Judah, Jehoiachin son of Jehoiakim, and the leading men of Judah and Jerusalem, he left the columns, the bronze tank, the carts, and some of the other temple treasures.
The Lord	Listen to what I, the Lord Almighty, the God of Israel, say about the treasures that are left in the Temple and in the royal palace in Jerusalem: they will be taken to Babylonia and will remain there until I turn my attention to them. Then I will bring them back and restore them to this place. (PAUSE) I, the Lord, have spoken!
Cast	[This is] the word of the Lord.
All	**Thanks be to God.**

Cast: **Jeremiah, The Lord, Young Jeremiah, Commentator.**

Jeremiah and the prophet Hananiah
Jeremiah 28.1–17

Jeremiah	In the fifth month of the fourth year that Zedekiah was king, Hananiah son of Azzur, a prophet from the town of Gibeon, spoke to me in the Temple. In the presence of the priests and of the people he told me that the Lord Almighty, the God of Israel, had said:
The Lord	I have broken the power of the king of Babylonia. Within two years I will bring back to this place all the temple treasures that King Nebuchadnezzar took to Babylonia. I will also bring back the king of Judah, Jehoiachin son of Jehoiakim, along with all the people of Judah who went into exile in Babylonia. Yes, I will break the power of the king of Babylonia. I, the Lord, have spoken.
	Then in the presence of the priests and of all the people who were standing in the Temple, I said to Hananiah:

684

Young Jeremiah	Wonderful! I hope the Lord will do this! I certainly hope he will make your prophecy come true and will bring back from Babylonia all the temple treasures and all the people who were taken away as prisoners. But listen to what I say to you and to the people. The prophets who spoke long ago, before my time and yours, predicted that war, starvation, and disease would come to many nations and powerful kingdoms. But a prophet who predicts peace can only be recognized as a prophet whom the Lord has truly sent when that prophet's predictions come true.
Jeremiah	Then Hananiah took the yoke off my neck, broke it in pieces, and said in the presence of all the people:
Hananiah	The Lord has said that this is how he will break the yoke that King Nebuchadnezzar has put on the neck of all the nations; and he will do this within two years.
Jeremiah	Then I left. (PAUSE)
	Some time after this the Lord told me to go and say to Hananiah:
Young Jeremiah	The Lord has said that you may be able to break a wooden yoke, but he will replace it with an iron yoke. The Lord Almighty, the God of Israel, has said that he will put an iron yoke on all these nations and that they will serve King Nebuchadnezzar of Babylonia. The Lord has said that he will make even the wild animals serve Nebuchadnezzar.
Jeremiah	Then I told Hananiah this, and added:
Young Jeremiah	Listen, Hananiah! The Lord did not send you, and you are making these people believe a lie. And so the Lord himself says that he is going to get rid of you. Before this year is over you will die because you have told the people to rebel against the Lord.
Jeremiah	And Hananiah died in the seventh month of that same year.
Cast	[This is] the word of the Lord.
All	**Thanks be to God.**

Cast: **Jeremiah, The Lord** (can be the same as Hananiah), **Young Jeremiah, Hananiah.**

Jeremiah's letter to the Jews in Babylonia
Jeremiah 29.1–23

Jeremiah	I wrote a letter to the priests, the prophets, the leaders of the people, and to all the others whom Nebuchadnezzar had taken away as prisoners from Jerusalem to Babylonia. I wrote it after King Jehoiachin, his mother, the palace officials, the leaders of Judah and of Jerusalem, the craftsmen, and the skilled workmen had been taken into exile. I gave the letter to Elasah son of Shaphan and to Gemariah son of Hilkiah, whom King Zedekiah of Judah was sending to King Nebuchadnezzar of Babylonia. It said:
Young Jeremiah	The Lord Almighty, the God of Israel, says to all those people whom he allowed Nebuchadnezzar to take away as prisoners from Jerusalem to Babylonia:

The Lord Build houses and settle down. Plant gardens and eat what you grow in them. Marry and have children. Then let your children get married, so that they also may have children. You must increase in numbers and not decrease. Work for the good of the cities where I have made you go as prisoners. Pray to me on their behalf, because if they are prosperous, you will be prosperous too. I, the Lord, the God of Israel, warn you not to let yourselves be deceived by the prophets who live among you or by any others who claim they can predict the future. Do not pay any attention to their dreams. They are telling you lies in my name. I did not send them. I, the Lord Almighty, have spoken.

Young Jeremiah The Lord says:

The Lord When Babylonia's seventy years are over, I will show my concern for you and keep my promise to bring you back home. I alone know the plans I have for you, plans to bring you prosperity and not disaster, plans to bring about the future you hope for. Then you will call to me. You will come and pray to me, and I will answer you. You will seek me, and you will find me because you will seek me with all your heart. Yes, I say, you will find me, and I will restore you to your land. I will gather you from every country and from every place to which I have scattered you, and I will bring you back to the land from which I had sent you away into exile. I, the Lord, have spoken.

Young Jeremiah You say that the Lord has given you prophets in Babylonia. Listen to what the Lord says about the king who rules the kingdom that David ruled and about the people of this city, that is, your relatives who were not taken away as prisoners with you. The Lord Almighty says:

The Lord I am bringing war, starvation, and disease on them, and I will make them like figs that are too rotten to be eaten. I will pursue them with war, starvation, and disease, and all the nations of the world will be horrified at what they see. Everywhere I scatter them, people will be shocked and terrified at what has happened to them. People will mock them and use their name as a curse. This will happen to them because they did not obey the message that I kept on sending to them through my servants the prophets. They refused to listen. All of you whom I sent into exile in Babylonia, listen to what I, the Lord, say.

Young Jeremiah The Lord Almighty, the God of Israel, has spoken about Ahab son of Kolaiah and Zedekiah son of Maaseiah, who are telling you lies in his name. He has said that he will hand them over to the power of King Nebuchadnezzar of Babylonia, who will put them to death before your eyes. When the people who were taken away as prisoners from Jerusalem to Babylonia want to bring a curse on someone, they will say:

Prisoner May the Lord treat you like Zedekiah and Ahab, whom the king of Babylonia roasted alive!

Young Jeremiah This will be their fate because they are guilty of terrible sins—they have committed adultery and have told lies in the Lord's name.

This was against the Lord's will; he knows what they have done, and he is a witness against them.

Jeremiah
(with flourish) The Lord has spoken!

Cast [This is] the word of the Lord.
All **Thanks be to God.**

Cast: **Jeremiah, Young Jeremiah, The Lord, Prisoner** (can be the same as Young Jeremiah).

The letter of Shemaiah
Jeremiah 29.24–32

Jeremiah The Lord Almighty, the God of Israel, gave me a message for Shemaiah of Nehelam, who had sent a letter in his own name to all the people of Jerusalem and to the priest Zephaniah son of Maaseiah and to all the other priests. In this letter, Shemaiah wrote to Zephaniah:

Shemaiah The Lord made you a priest in place of Jehoiada, and you are now the chief officer in the Temple. It is your duty to see that every madman who pretends to be a prophet is placed in chains with an iron collar round his neck. Why haven't you done this to Jeremiah of Anathoth, who has been speaking as a prophet to the people? He must be stopped because he told the people in Babylonia that they would be prisoners there a long time and should build houses, settle down, plant gardens, and eat what they grow.

Jeremiah Zephaniah read the letter to me, and then the Lord told me to send to all the prisoners in Babylon this message about Shemaiah:

The Lord I, the Lord, will punish Shemaiah and all his descendants. I did not send him, but he spoke to you as if he were a prophet, and he made you believe lies. He will have no descendants among you. He will not live to see the good things that I am going to do for my people, because he told them to rebel against me. (PAUSE) I, the Lord, have spoken!

Cast [This is] the word of the Lord.
All **Thanks be to God.**

Cast: **Jeremiah, Shemaiah, The Lord.**

The Lord's promises to his people (i)
Jeremiah 30.1–11

Jeremiah The Lord, the God of Israel, said to me:

The Lord Write down in a book everything that I have told you, because the time is coming when I will restore my people, Israel and Judah. I will bring them back to the land that I gave their ancestors, and they will take possession of it again. I, the Lord, have spoken.

Jeremiah The Lord says to the people of Israel and Judah:

The Lord	I heard a cry of terror, a cry of fear and not of peace. Now stop and think! Can a *man* give birth to a child? Why then do I see every man with his hands on his stomach like a woman in labour? Why is everyone so pale? A terrible day is coming; no other day can compare with it— a time of distress for my people, but they will survive.
Jeremiah	The Lord Almighty says:
The Lord	When that day comes, I will break the yoke that is round their necks and remove their chains, and they will no longer be the slaves of foreigners. Instead, they will serve me, the Lord their God, and a descendant of David, whom I will enthrone as king.
Singer	My people, do not be afraid; people of Israel, do not be terrified. I will rescue you from that distant land, from the land where you are prisoners. You will come back home and live in peace; you will be secure, and no one will make you afraid. I will come to you and save you. I will destroy all the nations where I have scattered you, but I will not destroy you. I will not let you go unpunished; but when I punish you, I will be fair.
The Lord (with flourish)	I, the Lord, have spoken!
Cast	[This is] the word of the Lord.
All	**Thanks be to God.**

Cast: **Jeremiah, The Lord, Singer** (can be the same as The Lord).

The Lord's promises to his people (ii)
Jeremiah 30.18–24

Jeremiah	The Lord says:
The Lord	I will restore my people to their land and have mercy on every family; Jerusalem will be rebuilt, and its palace restored. The people who live there will sing praise; they will shout for joy. By my blessing they will increase in numbers; my blessing will bring them honour. I will restore the nation's ancient power and establish it firmly again; I will punish all who oppress them. Their ruler will come from their own nation, their prince from their own people. He will approach me when I invite him, for who would dare come uninvited? They will be my people, and I will be their God. (PAUSE) I, the Lord, have spoken!

Jeremiah	The Lord's anger is a storm, a furious wind that will rage over the heads of the wicked. It will not end until he has done all that he intends to do. In days to come his people will understand this clearly.
Cast	[This is] the word of the Lord.
All	**Thanks be to God.**

Cast: **Jeremiah, The Lord.**

Israel's return home
From Jeremiah 31.1–14

Jeremiah	The Lord says:
The Lord	The time is coming when I will be the God of all the tribes of Israel, and they will be my people. In the desert I showed mercy to those people who had escaped death. When the people of Israel longed for rest, I appeared to them from far away. People of Israel, I have always loved you, so I continue to show you my constant love. Once again I will rebuild you. Once again you will take up your tambourines and dance joyfully. Once again you will plant vineyards on the hills of Samaria, and those who plant them will eat what the vineyards produce. Yes, the time is coming when watchmen will call out on the hills of Ephraim:
Watchman 1 & 2	Let's go up to Zion—
Watchman 1	To the Lord our God.
Jeremiah	The Lord says:
The Lord	Sing with joy for Israel, the greatest of the nations. Sing your song of praise.
Singer	The Lord has saved his people; he has rescued all who are left.
The Lord	I will bring them from the north and gather them from the ends of the earth. The blind and the lame will come with them, pregnant women and those about to give birth. They will come back a great nation. My people will return weeping, praying as I lead them back. I will guide them to streams of water, on a smooth road where they will not stumble. I am like a father to Israel, and Ephraim is my eldest son.
Jeremiah	The Lord says:
The Lord	Nations, listen to me, and proclaim my words on the far-off shores. I scattered my people, but I will gather them and guard them as a shepherd guards his flock. I have set Israel's people free and have saved them from a mighty nation. They will come and sing for joy on Mount Zion and be delighted with my gifts—gifts of corn and wine and olive-oil, gifts of sheep and cattle. They will be like a well-watered garden; they will have everything they need. Then the girls will dance and be happy, and men, young and old, will rejoice. I will comfort them and turn their mourning

$\rightarrow$

into joy, their sorrow into gladness. I will fill the priests with the richest food and satisfy all the needs of my people. I, the Lord, have spoken.

Cast	[This is] the word of the Lord.
All	**Thanks be to God.**

Cast: **Jeremiah, The Lord, Watchman 1, Watchman 2** (can be the same as Watchman 1), **Singer.**

The Lord's mercy on Israel
Jeremiah 31.15–22

Jeremiah	The Lord says:
The Lord	A sound is heard in Ramah, the sound of bitter weeping. Rachel is crying for her children; they are gone, and she refuses to be comforted. Stop your crying and wipe away your tears. All that you have done for your children will not go unrewarded; they will return from the enemy's land. There is hope for your future; your children will come back home. I, the Lord, have spoken.
	I hear the people of Israel say in grief:
Person 1	Lord, we were like an untamed animal, but you taught us to obey.
Person 2	Bring us back; we are ready to return to you, the Lord our God.
Person 1	We turned away from you, but soon we wanted to return.
Person 2	After you had punished us, we hung our heads in grief.
Person 3	We were ashamed and disgraced, because we sinned when we were young.
The Lord	Israel, you are my dearest son, the child I love best. Whenever I mention your name, I think of you with love. My heart goes out to you; I will be merciful.
(urgently)	Set up signs and mark the road; find again the way by which you left. Come back, people of Israel, come home to the towns you left. How long will you hesitate, faithless people? I have created something new and different, as different as a woman protecting a man.

Cast	[This is] the word of the Lord.
All	**Thanks be to God.**

Cast: **Jeremiah, The Lord, Person 1, Person 2, Person 3** (Persons 1–3 can be the same).

The future prosperity of God's people
Jeremiah 31.23–37 [38–40]

Jeremiah	The Lord Almighty, the God of Israel, says:
The Lord	When I restore the people to their land, they will once again say in the land of Judah and in its towns:
Singer	May the Lord bless the sacred hill of Jerusalem, the holy place where he lives.

The Lord	People will live in Judah and in all its towns, and there will be farmers, and shepherds with their flocks. I will refresh those who are weary and will satisfy with food everyone who is weak from hunger. So then, people will say:
Person	I went to sleep and woke up refreshed.
The Lord	I, the Lord, say that the time is coming when I will fill the land of Israel and Judah with people and animals. And just as I took care to uproot, to pull down, to overthrow, to destroy, and to demolish them, so I will take care to plant them and to build them up. When that time comes, people will no longer say:
Person	The parents ate the sour grapes, but the children got the sour taste.
The Lord	Instead, whoever eats sour grapes will have his *own* teeth set on edge; and everyone will die because of his *own* sin.
Jeremiah	The Lord says:
The Lord	The time is coming when I will make a new covenant with the people of Israel and with the people of Judah. It will not be like the old covenant that I made with their ancestors when I took them by the hand and led them out of Egypt. Although I was like a husband to them, they did not keep that covenant. The new covenant that I will make with the people of Israel will be this: I will put my law within them and write it on their hearts. I will be their God, and they will be my people. None of them will have to teach his fellow-countryman to know the Lord, because all will know me, from the least to the greatest. I will forgive their sins and I will no longer remember their wrongs. I, the Lord, have spoken.
Singer	The Lord provides the sun for light by day, the moon and the stars to shine at night. He stirs up the sea and makes it roar; his name is the Lord Almighty. He promises that as long as the natural order lasts, so long will Israel be a nation. If one day the sky could be measured and the foundations of the earth explored, only then would he reject the people of Israel because of all they have done.
Jeremiah	The Lord has spoken! (PAUSE) [The Lord says:
The Lord	The time is coming when all Jerusalem will be rebuilt as my city, from Hananel Tower west to the Corner Gate. And the boundary line will continue from there on the west to the hill of Gareb and then round to Goah. The entire valley, where the dead are buried and refuse is thrown, and all the fields above the brook of Kidron as far as the Horse Gate to the east, will be sacred to me. The city will never again be torn down or destroyed.]
Cast	[This is] the word of the Lord.
All	**Thanks be to God.**

Cast: **Jeremiah, The Lord, Singer, Person.**

Jeremiah buys a field
Jeremiah 32.1–15

Jeremiah The Lord spoke to me in the tenth year that Zedekiah was king of Judah, which was also the eighteenth year of King Nebuchadnezzar of Babylonia. At that time the army of the king of Babylonia was attacking Jerusalem, and I was locked up in the courtyard of the royal palace. King Zedekiah had imprisoned me there and had accused me of announcing that the Lord had said:

The Lord I am going to let the king of Babylonia capture this city, and King Zedekiah will not escape. He will be handed over to the king of Babylonia; he will see him face to face and will speak to him in person. Zedekiah will be taken to Babylonia, and he will remain there until I deal with him. Even if he fights the Babylonians, he will not be successful. I, the Lord, have spoken.

Jeremiah The Lord told me that Hanamel, my uncle Shallum's son, would come to me with the request to buy his field at Anathoth in the territory of Benjamin, because I was his nearest relative and had the right to buy it for myself. Then, just as the Lord had said, Hanamel came to me there in the courtyard and asked me to buy the field. So I knew that the Lord had really spoken to me. I bought the field from Hanamel and weighed out the money to him; the price came to seventeen pieces of silver. I signed and sealed the deed, had it witnessed, and weighed out the money on scales. Then I took both copies of the deed of purchase—the sealed copy containing the contract and its conditions, and the open copy—and gave them to Baruch, the son of Neriah and grandson of Mahseiah. I gave them to him in the presence of Hanamel and of the witnesses who had signed the deed of purchase and of the men who were sitting in the courtyard. Before them all I said to Baruch:

Young Jeremiah The Lord Almighty, the God of Israel, has ordered you to take these deeds, both the sealed deed of purchase and the open copy, and to place them in a clay jar, so that they may be preserved for years to come. The Lord Almighty, the God of Israel, has said that houses, fields, and vineyards will again be bought in this land.

Cast [This is] the word of the Lord.
All **Thanks be to God.**

Cast: **Jeremiah, The Lord, Young Jeremiah.**

Jeremiah's prayer
Jeremiah 32.16–35

Jeremiah After I had given the deed of purchase to Baruch, I prayed:

Young Jeremiah Sovereign Lord, you made the earth and the sky by your great power and might; nothing is too difficult for you. You have shown constant love to thousands, but you also punish people for the sins of their parents. You are a great and powerful God; you are the Lord Almighty. You make wise plans and do mighty things; you see everything that people do, and you reward them according to their actions. Long ago, you performed miracles and wonders in Egypt, and you have continued to perform them to this day, both in Israel and among all the other nations, so that you are now known everywhere. By means of miracles and wonders that terrified our enemies, you used your power and might to bring your people Israel out of Egypt. You gave them this rich and fertile land, as you had promised their ancestors. But when they came into this land and took possession of it, they did not obey your commands or live according to your teaching; they did nothing that you had ordered them to do. And so you brought all this destruction on them.

The Babylonians have built siege mounds round the city to capture it, and they are attacking. War, starvation, and disease will make the city fall into their hands. You can see that all you have said has come true. Yet, Sovereign Lord, you are the one who ordered me to buy the field in the presence of witnesses, even though the city is about to be captured by the Babylonians.

Jeremiah   Then the Lord said to me:

The Lord   I am the Lord, the God of all mankind. Nothing is too difficult for me. I am going to give this city over to King Nebuchadnezzar of Babylonia and his army; they will capture it and set it on fire. They will burn it down, together with the houses where people have made me angry by burning incense to Baal on the roof-tops and by pouring out wine-offerings to other gods. From the very beginning of their history the people of Israel and the people of Judah have displeased me and made me angry by what they have done. The people of this city have made me angry and furious from the day it was built. I have decided to destroy it because of all the evil that has been done by the people of Judah and Jerusalem, together with their kings and leaders, their priests and prophets. They turned their backs on me; and though I kept on teaching them, they would not listen and learn. They even placed their disgusting idols in the Temple built for my worship, and they have defiled it. They have built altars to Baal in the Valley of Hinnom, to sacrifice their sons and daughters to the god Molech. I did not command them to do this, and it did not even enter my mind that they would do such a thing and make the people of Judah sin.

Cast   [This is] the word of the Lord.
All   **Thanks be to God.**

Cast: **Jeremiah, Young Jeremiah, The Lord.**

Another promise of hope
Jeremiah 33.1–11

Jeremiah   While I was in prison in the palace courtyard, the Lord's message came to me again. The Lord, who made the earth, who formed it and set it in place, spoke to me [He whose name is the Lord said]:

The Lord   Call to me, and I will answer you; I will tell you wonderful and marvellous things that you know nothing about. I, the Lord, the God of Israel, say that the houses of Jerusalem and the royal palace of Judah will be torn down as a result of the siege and the attack. Some will fight against the Babylonians, who will fill the houses with the corpses of those whom I am going to strike down in my anger and fury. I have turned away from this city because of the evil things that its people have done. But I will heal this city and its people and restore them to health. I will show them abundant peace and security. I will make Judah and Israel prosperous, and I will rebuild them as they were before. I will purify them from the sins that they have committed against me, and I will forgive their sins and their rebellion. Jerusalem will be a source of joy, honour, and pride to me; and every nation in the world will fear and tremble when they hear about the good things that I do for the people of Jerusalem and about the prosperity that I bring to the city.

[Jeremiah   The Lord said:]

The Lord   People are saying:

Person 1   This place is like a desert.

Person 2   It has no people or animals living in it.

The Lord   They are right; the towns of Judah and the streets of Jerusalem are empty; no people or animals live there. But in these places you will hear again the shouts of gladness and joy and the happy sounds of wedding feasts. You will hear people sing as they bring thank-offerings to my Temple [they will say]:

Person 1   Give thanks to the Lord Almighty.

Person 2   Because he is good.

Persons 1 and 2   His love is eternal.

The Lord   I will make this land as prosperous as it was before. I, the Lord, have spoken!

Cast   [This is] the word of the Lord.
All   **Thanks be to God.**

Cast: **Jeremiah, The Lord, Person 1, Person 2** (can be the same as Person 1).

The coming king
From Jeremiah 33.1,2,14–26

Jeremiah   While I was in prison in the palace courtyard, the Lord's message came to me again. The Lord, who made the earth, who formed it and set it in place, spoke to me. He whose name is the Lord said:

The Lord   The time is coming when I will fulfil the promise that I made to the people of Israel and Judah. At that time I will choose as king a righteous descendant of David. That king will do what is right and just throughout the land. The people of Judah and of Jerusalem will be rescued and will live in safety. The city will be called:

Herald (calling)   The Lord Our Salvation.

The Lord   I, the Lord, promise that there will always be a descendant of David to be king of Israel and that there will always be priests from the tribe of Levi to serve me and to offer burnt-offerings, grain-offerings, and sacrifices.

Jeremiah   The Lord said to me:

The Lord   I have made a covenant with the day and with the night, so that they always come at their proper times; and that covenant can never be broken. In the same way I have made a covenant with my servant David that he would always have a descendant to be king, and I have made a covenant with the priests from the tribe of Levi that they would always serve me; and those covenants can never be broken. I will choose one of David's descendants to rule over the descendants of Abraham, Isaac, and Jacob. I will be merciful to my people and make them prosperous again.

Cast   [This is] the word of the Lord.
All   **Thanks be to God.**

Cast: **Jeremiah, The Lord, Herald.**

A message for Zedekiah
Jeremiah 34.1–7

Jeremiah   The Lord spoke to me when King Nebuchadnezzar of Babylonia and his army, supported by troops from all the nations and races that were subject to him, were attacking Jerusalem and its nearby towns. The Lord, the God of Israel, told me to go and say to King Zedekiah of Judah:

The Lord   I, the Lord, will hand this city over to the king of Babylonia, and he will burn it down. You will not escape; you will be captured and handed over to him. You will see him face to face and talk to him in person; then you will go to Babylonia. Zedekiah, listen to what I say about you. You will not be killed in battle. You will die in peace, and as people burnt incense when they buried your ancestors, who were kings before you, in the same way they will burn incense for you. They will mourn over you and say:

Mourners	Our king is dead!
The Lord	I, the Lord, have spoken.
Jeremiah	Then I gave this message to King Zedekiah in Jerusalem while the army of the king of Babylonia was attacking the city. The army was also attacking Lachish and Azekah, the only other fortified cities left in Judah.
Cast	[This is] the word of the Lord.
All	**Thanks be to God.**

Cast: **Jeremiah, The Lord, Mourners** (preferably two or more).

Deceitful treatment of slaves
Jeremiah 34.8–22

Jeremiah   King Zedekiah and the people of Jerusalem had made an agreement to set free their Hebrew slaves, both male and female, so that no one would have a fellow-Israelite as a slave. All the people and their leaders agreed to free their slaves and never to enslave them again. They did set them free, but later they changed their minds, took them back, and forced them to become slaves again.

Then the Lord, the God of Israel, told me to say to the people:

The Lord   I made a covenant with your ancestors when I rescued them from Egypt and set them free from slavery. I told them that every seven years they were to set free any Hebrew slave who had served them for six years. But your ancestors would not pay any attention to me or listen to what I said. Just a few days ago you changed your minds and did what pleased me. All of you agreed to set your fellow-Israelites free, and you made a covenant in my presence, in the Temple where I am worshipped. But then you changed your minds again and dishonoured me. All of you took back the slaves whom you had set free as they desired, and you forced them into slavery again. So now, I, the Lord, say that you have disobeyed me: you have not given your fellow-Israelites their freedom. Very well, then, I will give you freedom: the freedom to die by war, disease, and starvation. I will make every nation in the world horrified at what I do to you. The officials of Judah and of Jerusalem, together with the palace officials, the priests, and all the leaders, made a covenant with me by walking between the two halves of a bull that they had cut in two. But they broke the covenant and did not keep its terms. So I will do to these people what they did to the bull. I will hand them over to their enemies, who want to kill them, and their corpses will be eaten by birds and wild animals. I will also hand over King Zedekiah of Judah and his officials to those who want to kill them. I will hand them over to the Babylonian army, which has stopped its attack against you. I will give the order, and they will return to this city. They will attack it, capture it, and burn it down. I will make the towns of Judah like a desert where no one lives. I, the Lord, have spoken.

Cast	[This is] the word of the Lord.
All	**Thanks be to God.**

Cast: **Jeremiah, The Lord.**

Jeremiah and the Rechabites
Jeremiah 35.1–19

Jeremiah	When Jehoiakim son of Josiah was king of Judah, the Lord said to me:
The Lord	Go to the members of the Rechabite clan and talk to them. Then bring them into one of the rooms in the Temple and offer them some wine.
Jeremiah	So I took the entire Rechabite clan—Jaazaniah the son of another Jeremiah, who was Habazziniah's son, and all his brothers and sons—and brought them to the Temple. I took them into the room of the disciples of the prophet Hanan son of Igdaliah. This room was above the room of Maaseiah son of Shallum, an important official in the Temple, and near the rooms of the other officials. Then I placed cups and bowls full of wine before the Rechabites, and I said to them:
Young Jeremiah	Have some wine.
[Jeremiah	But they answered:]
Rechabites 1 & 2	We do not drink wine.
Rechabite 1	Our ancestor Jonadab son of Rechab told us that neither we nor our descendants were ever to drink any wine.
Rechabite 2	He also told us not to build houses or farm the land, and not to plant vineyards or buy them. He commanded us always to live in tents, so that we might remain in this land where we live like strangers. We have obeyed all the instructions that Jonadab gave us.
Rechabite 1	We ourselves never drink wine, and neither do our wives, our sons, or our daughters.
Rechabite 2	We do not build houses for homes—we live in tents—and we own no vineyards, fields, or corn.
Rechabite 1	We have fully obeyed everything that our ancestor Jonadab commanded us. But when King Nebuchadnezzar invaded the country, we decided to come to Jerusalem to get away from the Babylonian and Syrian armies.
Rechabite 2	That is why we are living in Jerusalem.
Jeremiah	Then the Lord Almighty, the God of Israel, told me to go and say to the people of Judah and Jerusalem:

The Lord	I, the Lord, ask you why you refuse to listen to me and to obey my instructions. Jonadab's descendants have obeyed his command not to drink wine, and to this very day none of them drink any. But I have kept on speaking to you, and you have not obeyed me. I have continued to send you all my servants the prophets, and they have told you to give up your evil ways and to do what is right. They warned you not to worship and serve other gods, so that you could go on living in the land that I gave you and your ancestors. But you would not listen to me or pay attention to me. Jonadab's descendants have obeyed the command that their ancestor gave them, but you people have not obeyed me. So now, I, the Lord Almighty, the God of Israel, will bring on you people of Judah and of Jerusalem all the destruction that I promised. I will do this because you would not listen when I spoke to you, and you would not answer when I called you.
Jeremiah	Then I told the Rechabite clan that the Lord Almighty, the God of Israel, had said:
The Lord	You have obeyed the command that your ancestor Jonadab gave you; you have followed all his instructions, and you have done everything he commanded you. So I, the Lord Almighty, the God of Israel, promise that Jonadab son of Rechab will always have a male descendant to serve me.
Cast	[This is] the word of the Lord.
All	**Thanks be to God.**

Cast: **Jeremiah, The Lord, Young Jeremiah, Rechabite 1, Rechabite 2.**

Baruch reads the scroll in the Temple
Jeremiah 36.1–10

Jeremiah	In the fourth year that Jehoiakim son of Josiah was king of Judah, the Lord said to me:
The Lord	Get a scroll and write on it everything that I have told you about Israel and Judah and all the nations. Write everything that I have told you from the time I first spoke to you, when Josiah was king, up to the present. Perhaps when the people of Judah hear about all the destruction that I intend to bring on them, they will turn from their evil ways. Then I will forgive their wickedness and their sins.
Jeremiah	So I called Baruch son of Neriah and dictated to him everything that the Lord had said to me. And Baruch wrote it all down on a scroll. Then I gave Baruch the following instructions:
Young Jeremiah	I am no longer allowed to go into the Temple. But I want you to go there the next time the people are fasting. You are to read the scroll aloud, so that they will hear everything that the Lord has said to me and that I have dictated to you. Do this where everyone can hear you, including the people of Judah who have come in from their towns. Perhaps they will pray to the Lord and turn from their evil ways, because the Lord has threatened this people with his terrible anger and fury.
Jeremiah	So Baruch read the Lord's words in the Temple exactly as I had told him to do. (PAUSE)

In the ninth month of the fifth year that Jehoiakim was king of Judah, the people fasted to gain the Lord's favour. The fast was kept by all who lived in Jerusalem and by all who came there from the towns of Judah. Then, while all the people were listening, Baruch read from the scroll everything that I had said. He did this in the Temple, from the room of Gemariah son of Shaphan, the court secretary. His room was in the upper court near the entrance of the New Gate of the Temple.

Cast	[This is] the word of the Lord.
All	**Thanks be to God.**

Cast: **Jeremiah, The Lord, Young Jeremiah.**

The scroll is read to the officials
Jeremiah 36.11–19

Jeremiah	Micaiah, the son of Gemariah and grandson of Shaphan, heard Baruch read from the scroll what the Lord had said. Then he went to the royal palace, to the room of the court secretary, where all the officials were in session. Elishama, the court secretary, Delaiah son of Shemaiah, Elnathan son of Achbor, Gemariah son of Shaphan, Zedekiah son of Hananiah, and all the other officials were there. Micaiah told them everything that he had heard Baruch read to the people. Then the officials sent Jehudi to tell Baruch to bring the scroll that he had read to the people. Baruch brought them the scroll. They said:
Official 1	Sit down.
Official 2	Read the scroll to us.
Jeremiah	So Baruch did. (PAUSE) After he had read it, they turned to one another in alarm, and said to Baruch:
Official 1	We must report this to the king.
Jeremiah	They asked him:
Official 2	Tell us, now, how did you come to write all this?
Official 1	Did Jeremiah dictate it to you?
Jeremiah	Baruch answered:
Baruch	Jeremiah dictated every word of it to me, and I wrote it down in ink on this scroll.
Jeremiah	Then they said to him:
Official 1	You and Jeremiah must go and hide.
Official 2	Don't let anyone know where you are.
Cast	[This is] the word of the Lord.
All	**Thanks be to God.**

Cast: **Jeremiah, Official 1, Official 2** (can be the same as Official 1), **Baruch.**

The king burns the scroll
Jeremiah 36.20–32

Jeremiah

The officials put the scroll—on which was written everything the Lord had said to me—in the room of Elishama, the court secretary, and went to the king's court, where they reported everything to the king. Then the king sent Jehudi to get the scroll. He took it from the room of Elishama and read it to the king and all the officials who were standing round him. It was winter and the king was sitting in his winter palace in front of the fire. As soon as Jehudi finished reading three or four columns, the king cut them off with a small knife and threw them into the fire. He kept doing this until the entire scroll was burnt up. But neither the king nor any of his officials who heard all this was afraid or showed any sign of sorrow. Although Elnathan, Delaiah, and Gemariah begged the king not to burn the scroll, he paid no attention to them. Then he ordered Prince Jerahmeel, together with Seraiah son of Azriel and Shelemiah son of Abdeel, to arrest me and my secretary Baruch. But the Lord had hidden us. (PAUSE)

After King Jehoiakim had burnt the scroll that I had dictated to Baruch, the Lord told me to take another scroll and write on it everything that had been on the first one. The Lord told me to say to the king:

The Lord

You have burnt the scroll, and you have asked Jeremiah why he wrote that the king of Babylonia would come and destroy this land and kill its people and its animals. So now, I, the Lord, say to you, King Jehoiakim, that no descendant of yours will ever rule over David's kingdom. Your corpse will be thrown out where it will be exposed to the sun during the day and to the frost at night. I will punish you, your descendants, and your officials because of the sins all of you commit. Neither you nor the people of Jerusalem and of Judah have paid any attention to my warnings, and so I will bring on all of you the disaster that I have threatened.

Jeremiah

Then I took another scroll and gave it to my secretary Baruch, and he wrote down everything that I dictated. He wrote everything that had been on the first scroll and similar messages that I dictated to him.

Cast   [This is] the word of the Lord.
All   **Thanks be to God.**

Cast: **Jeremiah, The Lord.**

Jeremiah receives Zedekiah's request
Jeremiah 37.1–10

Jeremiah

King Nebuchadnezzar of Babylonia made Zedekiah son of Josiah king of Judah in the place of Jehoiachin son of Jehoiakim. But neither Zedekiah nor his officials nor the people obeyed the message which the Lord had given me.

King Zedekiah sent Jehucal son of Shelemiah and the priest Zephaniah son of Maaseiah to ask me to pray to the Lord our God on behalf of our nation. I had not yet been put in prison and was still moving about freely among the people. The Babylonian army had been besieging Jerusalem, but when they heard that the Egyptian army had crossed the Egyptian border, they retreated.

Then the Lord, the God of Israel, told me to say to Zedekiah:

The Lord   The Egyptian army is on its way to help you, but it will return home. Then the Babylonians will come back, attack the city, capture it, and burn it down. I, the Lord, warn you not to deceive yourselves into thinking that the Babylonians will not come back, because they will. Even if you defeat the whole Babylonian army, so that only wounded men are left, lying in their tents, those men would still get up and burn this city to the ground.

Cast   [This is] the word of the Lord.
All   **Thanks be to God.**

Cast: **Jeremiah, The Lord.**

Jeremiah is arrested and imprisoned
Jeremiah 37.11–21

Jeremiah   The Babylonian army retreated from Jerusalem because the Egyptian army was approaching. So I started to leave Jerusalem and go to the territory of Benjamin to take possession of my share of the family property. But when I reached the Benjamin Gate, the officer in charge of the soldiers on duty there, a man by the name of Irijah, the son of Shelemiah and grandson of Hananiah, stopped me [and said]:

Irijah   You are deserting to the Babylonians!

Jeremiah   I answered:

Young Jeremiah   That's not so! I'm not deserting.

Jeremiah   But Irijah would not listen to me. Instead, he arrested me and took me to the officials. They were furious with me and ordered me to be beaten and locked up in the house of Jonathan, the court secretary, whose house had been made into a prison. I was put in an underground cell and kept there a long time. (PAUSE)

Later on King Zedekiah sent for me, and there in the palace he asked me privately:

Zedekiah   Is there any message from the Lord?

[Jeremiah   I answered:]

Young Jeremiah   There is. You will be handed over to the king of Babylonia.

[Jeremiah   Then I asked:]

Young Jeremiah   What crime have I committed against you or your officials or this people, to make you put me in prison? What happened to your

$\rightarrow$

prophets who told you that the king of Babylonia would not attack you or the country? And now, Your Majesty, I beg you to listen to me and do what I ask. Please do not send me back to the prison in Jonathan's house. If you do, I will surely die there.

Jeremiah So King Zedekiah ordered me to be locked up in the palace courtyard. I stayed there, and each day I was given a loaf of bread from the bakeries until all the bread in the city was gone.

Cast [This is] the word of the Lord.
All **Thanks be to God.**

Cast: **Jeremiah, Irijah, Young Jeremiah, Zedekiah.**

Jeremiah in a dry well
Jeremiah 38.1–13; 39.15–18

Jeremiah Shephatiah son of Mattan, Gedaliah son of Pashhur, Jehucal son of Shelemiah, and Pashhur son of Malchiah heard that I was telling the people that the Lord had said:

The Lord Whoever stays on in the city will die in war or of starvation or disease. But whoever goes out and surrenders to the Babylonians will not be killed; he will at least escape with his life.

Jeremiah I was also telling them that the Lord had said:

The Lord I am going to give the city to the Babylonian army, and they will capture it.

Jeremiah Then the officials went to the king and said:

Officials 1 and 2
(to Zedekiah) This man must be put to death.

Official 1 By talking like this he is making the soldiers in the city lose their courage, and he is doing the same thing to everyone else left in the city.

Official 2 He is not trying to help the people; he only wants to hurt them.

Jeremiah King Zedekiah answered:

Zedekiah
(to Officials) Very well, then, do what you wish with him; I can't stop you.

Jeremiah So they took me and let me down by ropes into Prince Malchiah's well, which was in the palace courtyard. There was no water in the well, only mud, and I sank down in it. (PAUSE)

However, Ebedmelech the Sudanese, a eunuch who worked in the royal palace, heard that they had put me in the well. At that time the king was holding court at the Benjamin Gate. So Ebedmelech went there and said to the king:

Ebedmelech
(to Zedekiah) Your Majesty, what these men have done is wrong. They have put Jeremiah in the well, where he is sure to die of starvation, since there is no more food in the city.

Jeremiah Then the king ordered Ebedmelech to take with him three men and to pull me out of the well before I died. So Ebedmelech went with the men to the palace storeroom and got some worn-out clothing which he let down to me by ropes. He told me to put the rags under my arms, so that the ropes wouldn't hurt me. I did this, and they pulled me up out of the well. After that I was kept in the courtyard.

While I was still imprisoned in the palace courtyard, the Lord told me to tell Ebedmelech the Sudanese that the Lord Almighty, the God of Israel, had said:

The Lord (to Ebedmelech)	Just as I said I would, I am going to bring upon this city destruction and not prosperity. And when this happens, you will be there to see it. But I, the Lord, will protect you, and you will not be handed over to the men you are afraid of. I will keep you safe, and you will not be put to death. You will escape with your life because you have put your trust in me. (PAUSE) I, the Lord, have spoken!
Cast	[This is] the word of the Lord.
All	**Thanks be to God.**

Cast: **Jeremiah, The Lord, Official 1, Official 2, Zedekiah, Ebedmelech.**

Zedekiah asks Jeremiah's advice
Jeremiah 38.14—28

Jeremiah	King Zedekiah had me brought to him at the third entrance to the Temple, and he said:
Zedekiah (to Young Jeremiah)	I am going to ask you a question, and I want you to tell me the whole truth.
Jeremiah	I answered:
Young Jeremiah (to Zedekiah)	If I tell you the truth, you will put me to death, and if I give you advice, you won't pay any attention.
Jeremiah	So King Zedekiah promised me in secret:
Zedekiah	I swear by the living God, the God who gave us life, that I will not put you to death or hand you over to the men who want to kill you.
Jeremiah	Then I told Zedekiah that the Lord Almighty, the God of Israel, had said:
The Lord	If you surrender to the king of Babylonia's officers, your life will be spared, and this city will not be burnt down. Both you and your family will be spared. But if you do not surrender, then this city will be handed over to the Babylonians, who will burn it down, and you will not escape from them.
Jeremiah	But the king answered:
Zedekiah	I am afraid of our countrymen who have deserted to the Babylonians. I may be handed over to them and tortured.
Jeremiah	I said:

703

Young Jeremiah	You will not be handed over to them. I beg you to obey the Lord's message; then all will go well with you, and your life will be spared. But the Lord has shown me in a vision what will happen if you refuse to surrender. In it I saw all the women left in Judah's royal palace being led out to the king of Babylonia's officers. Listen to what they were saying as they went:
Woman 1	The king's best friends misled him, they overruled him.
Woman 2	And now that his feet have sunk in the mud, his friends have left him.
Jeremiah	Then I added:
Young Jeremiah	All your women and children will be taken out to the Babylonians, and you yourself will not escape from them. You will be taken prisoner by the king of Babylonia, and this city will be burnt to the ground.
Jeremiah	Zedekiah replied:
Zedekiah	Don't let anyone know about this conversation, and your life will not be in danger. If the officials hear that I have talked with you, they will come and ask you what we said. They will promise not to put you to death if you tell them everything. Just tell them you were begging me not to send you back to prison to die there.
Jeremiah	Then all the officials came and questioned me, and I told them exactly what the king had told me to say. There was nothing else they could do, because no one had overheard the conversation. And I was kept in the palace courtyard until the day Jerusalem was captured.
Cast	[This is] the word of the Lord.
All	**Thanks be to God.**

Cast: **Jeremiah, Zedekiah, Young Jeremiah, The Lord, Woman 1, Woman 2.**

Jeremiah's release
Jeremiah 39.11–14; 40.1–6

Jeremiah	King Nebuchadnezzar commanded Nebuzaradan, the commanding officer, to give the following order:
Nebuchadnezzar	Go and find Jeremiah and take good care of him. Do not harm him, but do for him whatever he wants.
Jeremiah	So Nebuzaradan, together with the high officials Nebushazban and Nergal Sarezer and all the other officers of the king of Babylonia, brought me from the palace courtyard. They put me under the care of Gedaliah, the son of Ahikam and grandson of Shaphan, who was to see that I got home safely. And so I stayed there among the people. (PAUSE) The Lord spoke to me after Nebuzaradan, the commanding officer, had set me free at Ramah. I had been taken there in chains, along with all the other people from Jerusalem and Judah who were being taken away as prisoners to Babylonia.

The commanding officer took me aside [and said]:

Nebuzaradan The Lord your God threatened this land with destruction, and now he has done what he said he would. All this happened because your people sinned against the Lord and disobeyed him. Now, I am taking the chains off your wrists and setting you free. If you want to go to Babylonia with me, you may do so, and I will take care of you. But if you don't want to go, you don't have to. You have the whole country to choose from, and you may go wherever you wish.

Jeremiah When I did not answer, Nebuzaradan said:

Nebuzaradan Go back to Gedaliah, the son of Ahikam and grandson of Shaphan, whom the king of Babylonia has made governor of the towns of Judah. You may stay with him and live among the people, or you may go anywhere you think you should.

Jeremiah Then he gave me a present and some food to take with me, and let me go on my way. I went to stay with Gedaliah in Mizpah and lived among the people who were left in the land.

Cast [This is] the word of the Lord.
All **Thanks be to God.**

Cast: **Jeremiah, Nebuchadnezzar, Nebuzaradan.**

Gedaliah, governor of Judah
Jeremiah 40.7–12

Jeremiah Some of the Judaean officers and soldiers had not surrendered. They heard that the king of Babylonia had made Gedaliah governor of the land and had placed him in charge of all those who had not been taken away to Babylonia—the poorest people in the land. So Ishmael son of Nethaniah, Johanan son of Kareah, Seraiah son of Tanhumeth, the sons of Ephai from Netophah, and Jezaniah from Maacah went with their men to Gedaliah at Mizpah. Gedaliah said to them:

Gedaliah I give you my word that there is no need for you to be afraid to surrender to the Babylonians. Settle down in this land, serve the king of Babylonia, and all will go well with you. I myself will stay in Mizpah and be your representative when the Babylonians come here. But you can gather and store up wine, fruit, and olive-oil, and live in the villages you occupy.

Jeremiah Meanwhile, all the Israelites who were in Moab, Ammon, Edom, and other countries, heard that the king of Babylonia had allowed some Israelites to stay on in Judah and that he had made Gedaliah their governor. So they left the places where they had been scattered, and returned to Judah. They came to Gedaliah at Mizpah, and there they gathered in large amounts of wine and fruit.

Cast [This is] the word of the Lord.
All **Thanks be to God.**

Cast: **Jeremiah, Gedaliah.**

Gedaliah is murdered
From Jeremiah 40.13—41.18

Jeremiah	Johanan and the leaders of the soldiers who had not surrendered came to Gedaliah at Mizpah [and said to him]:
Johanan	Don't you know that King Baalis of Ammon has sent Ishmael to murder you?
Jeremiah	But Gedaliah did not believe it. Then Johanan said privately to him:
Johanan (to Gedaliah)	Let me go and kill Ishmael, and no one will know who did it. Why should he be allowed to murder you? That would cause all the Jews who have gathered round you to be scattered, and it would bring disaster on all the people who are left in Judah.
Jeremiah	But Gedaliah answered:
Gedaliah (to Johanan)	Don't do it! What you are saying about Ishmael is not true!
Jeremiah	In the seventh month of that year, Ishmael, the son of Nethaniah and grandson of Elishama, a member of the royal family and one of the king's chief officers, went to Mizpah with ten men to see Gedaliah. While they were all eating a meal together, Ishmael and the ten men with him pulled out their swords and killed Gedaliah. Ishmael also killed all the Israelites who were with Gedaliah at Mizpah and the Babylonian soldiers who happened to be there.
	The next day, before anyone knew about Gedaliah's murder, eighty men arrived from Shechem, Shiloh, and Samaria. They had shaved off their beards, torn their clothes, and gashed themselves. They were taking corn and incense to offer in the Temple. So Ishmael went out from Mizpah to meet them, weeping as he went. When he came to them, he said:
Ishmael	Please come in to see Gedaliah.
Jeremiah	As soon as they were inside the city, Ishmael and his men killed them and threw their bodies in a well.
	But there were ten men in the group who said to Ishmael:
Man 1	Please don't kill us!
Man 2	We have wheat, barley, olive-oil, and honey hidden in the fields.
Jeremiah	So he spared them. The well into which Ishmael threw the bodies of the men he had killed was the large one that King Asa had dug when he was being attacked by King Baasha of Israel. Ishmael filled the well with the bodies. Then he made prisoners of the king's daughters and all the rest of the people in Mizpah, whom Nebuzaradan the commanding officer had placed under the care of Gedaliah. Ishmael took them prisoner and started off in the direction of the territory of Ammon.

Johanan and all the army leaders with him heard of the crime that Ishmael had committed. They were afraid of the Babylonians because Ishmael had murdered Gedaliah, whom the king of Babylonia had made governor of the land. So they set out for Egypt, in order to get away from the Babylonians. On the way, they stopped at Chimham, near Bethlehem.

Cast	[This is] the word of the Lord.
All	**Thanks be to God.**

Cast: **Jeremiah, Johanan, Gedaliah, Ishmael, Man 1, Man 2.**

The people ask Jeremiah to pray for them
Jeremiah 42.1–22

Jeremiah	All the army leaders, including Johanan son of Kareah and Azariah son of Heshaiah, came with people of every class and said to me:
Leader 1	Please do what we ask you!
Leader 2	Pray to the Lord our God for us.
Leader 1	Pray for all of us who have survived. Once there were many of us; but now only a few of us are left, as you can see.
Leader 2	Pray that the Lord our God will show us the way we should go and what we should do.
Jeremiah	I answered:
Young Jeremiah	Very well, then. I will pray to the Lord our God, just as you have asked, and whatever he says, I will tell you. I will not keep back anything from you.
Leader 1	May the Lord be a true and faithful witness against us if we do not obey all the commands that the Lord our God gives you for us.
Leader 2	Whether it pleases us or not, we will obey the Lord our God, to whom we are asking you to pray.
Leader 1	All will go well with us if we obey him.
Jeremiah	Ten days later the Lord spoke to me; so I called together Johanan, all the army leaders who were with him, and all the other people. I said to them:
Young Jeremiah	The Lord, the God of Israel, to whom you sent me with your request has said:
The Lord	If you are willing to go on living in this land, then I will build you up and not tear you down; I will plant you and not pull you up. The destruction I brought on you has caused me great sorrow. Stop being afraid of the king of Babylonia. I am with you, and I will rescue you from his power. Because I am merciful, I will make him have mercy on you and let you go back home. I, the Lord, have spoken.

Young Jeremiah	But you people who are left in Judah must not disobey the Lord your God and refuse to live in this land. You must not say:
[Person]	No, we will go and live in Egypt, where we won't face war any more or hear the call to battle or go hungry.
Young Jeremiah	If you say this, then the Lord Almighty, the God of Israel, says:
The Lord	If you are determined to go and live in Egypt, then the war that you fear will overtake you, and the hunger you dread will follow you, and you will die there in Egypt. All the people who are determined to go and live in Egypt will die either in war or of starvation or disease. Not one of them will survive, not one will escape the disaster that I am going to bring on them.
Young Jeremiah	The Lord, the God of Israel, says:
The Lord	Just as my anger and fury were poured out on the people of Jerusalem, so my fury will be poured out on you if you go to Egypt. You will be a horrifying sight; people will treat you with scorn and use your name as a curse. You will never see this place again.
Jeremiah	Then I continued:
Young Jeremiah	The Lord has told you people who are left in Judah not to go to Egypt. And so I warn you now that you are making a fatal mistake. You asked me to pray to the Lord our God for you, and you promised that you would do everything that he commands. And now I have told you, but you are disobeying everything that the Lord our God sent me to tell you. So then, remember this: you will die in war or of starvation or disease in the land where you want to go and live.
Cast All	[This is] the word of the Lord. **Thanks be to God.**

Cast: **Jeremiah, Leader 1, Leader 2, Young Jeremiah, The Lord, Person** (can be the same as Young Jeremiah).

Jeremiah is taken to Egypt
Jeremiah 43.1–13

Jeremiah	I finished telling the people everything that the Lord their God had sent me to tell them. Then Azariah son of Hoshaiah and Johanan son of Kareah and all the other arrogant men said to me:
Azariah	You are lying. The Lord our God did not send you to tell us not to go and live in Egypt. Baruch son of Neriah has stirred you up against us, so that the Babylonians will gain power over us and can either kill us or take us away to Babylonia.
Jeremiah	So neither Johanan nor any of the army officers nor any of the people would obey the Lord's command to remain in the land of Judah. (PAUSE) Then Johanan and all the army officers took everybody left in Judah away to Egypt, together with all the people who had returned from the nations where they had been

scattered: the men, the women, the children, and the king's daughters. They took everyone whom Nebuzaradan the commanding officer had left under the care of Gedaliah, including Baruch and me. They disobeyed the Lord's command and went into Egypt as far as the city of Tahpanhes. (PAUSE)

There the Lord said to me:

The Lord Get some large stones and bury them in the mortar of the pavement in front of the entrance to the government building here in the city, and let some of the Israelites see you do it. Then tell them that I, the Lord Almighty, the God of Israel, am going to bring my servant King Nebuchadnezzar of Babylonia to this place, and he will put his throne over these stones that you buried, and will spread the royal tent over them. Nebuchadnezzar will come and defeat Egypt. Those people who are doomed to die of disease will die of disease, those doomed to be taken away as prisoners will be taken away as prisoners, and those doomed to be killed in war will be killed in war. I will set fire to the temples of Egypt's gods, and the king of Babylonia will either burn their gods or carry them off. As a shepherd picks his clothes clean of lice, so the king of Babylonia will pick the land of Egypt clean and then leave victorious. He will destroy the sacred stone monuments at Heliopolis in Egypt and will burn down the temples of the Egyptian gods.

Cast [This is] the word of the Lord.
All **Thanks be to God.**

Cast: **Jeremiah, Azariah, The Lord.**

The Lord's message to the Israelites in Egypt
Jeremiah 44.1–30

Jeremiah The Lord spoke to me concerning all the Israelites living in Egypt, in the cities of Migdol, Tahpanhes, and Memphis, and in the southern part of the country. The Lord Almighty, the God of Israel, said:

The Lord You yourselves have seen the destruction I brought on Jerusalem and all the other cities of Judah. Even now they are still in ruins, and no one lives in them because their people had done evil and had made me angry. They offered sacrifices to other gods and served gods that neither they nor you nor your ancestors ever worshipped. I kept sending you my servants the prophets, who told you not to do this terrible thing that I hate. But you would not listen or pay any attention. You would not give up your evil practice of sacrificing to other gods. So I poured out my anger and fury on the towns of Judah and on the streets of Jerusalem, and I set them on fire. They were left in ruins and became a horrifying sight, as they are today.

And so I, the Lord Almighty, the God of Israel, now ask why you are doing such an evil thing to yourselves. Do you want to bring

→

709

destruction on men and women, children and babies, so that none of your people will be left? Why do you make me angry by worshipping idols and by sacrificing to other gods here in Egypt, where you have come to live? Are you doing this just to destroy yourselves, so that every nation on earth will treat you with scorn and use your name as a curse? Have you forgotten all the wicked things that have been done in the towns of Judah and in the streets of Jerusalem by your ancestors, by the kings of Judah and their wives, and by you and your wives? But to this day you have not humbled yourselves. You have not honoured me or lived according to all the laws that I gave you and your ancestors.

So then, I, the Lord Almighty, the God of Israel, will turn against you and destroy all Judah. As for the people of Judah who are left and are determined to go and live in Egypt, I will see to it that all of them are destroyed. All of them, great and small, will die in Egypt, either in war or of starvation. They will be a horrifying sight; people will treat them with scorn and use their name as a curse. I will punish those who live in Egypt, just as I punished Jerusalem—with war, starvation, and disease. None of the people of Judah who are left and have come to Egypt to live will escape or survive. Not one of them will return to Judah, where they long to live once again. No one will return except a few refugees.

Jeremiah	Then all the men who knew that their wives offered sacrifices to other gods, and all the women who were standing there, including the Israelites who lived in southern Egypt—a large crowd in all—said to me:
Man 1	We refuse to listen to what you have told us in the name of the Lord.
Man 2	We will do everything that we said we would. We will offer sacrifices to our goddess, the Queen of Heaven, and we will pour out wine-offerings to her, just as we and our ancestors, our king and our leaders, used to do in the towns of Judah and in the streets of Jerusalem.
Man 3	Then we had plenty of food, we were prosperous, and had no troubles. But ever since we stopped sacrificing to the Queen of Heaven and stopped pouring out wine-offerings to her, we have had nothing, and our people have died in war and of starvation.
Jeremiah	And the women added:
Woman	When we baked cakes shaped like the Queen of Heaven, offered sacrifices to her, and poured out wine-offerings to her, our husbands approved of what we were doing.
Jeremiah	Then I said to all the men and the women who had answered me in this way:
Young Jeremiah	As for the sacrifices which you and your ancestors, your kings and your leaders, and the people of the land offered in the towns of Judah and in the streets of Jerusalem—do you think that the Lord did not know about them or that he forgot them? This very day your land lies in ruins and no one lives in it. It has become a

horrifying sight, and people use its name as a curse because the Lord could no longer endure your wicked and evil practices. This present disaster has come on you because you offered sacrifices to other gods and sinned against the Lord by not obeying all his commands.

Jeremiah I told all the people, especially the women, what the Lord Almighty, the God of Israel, was saying to the people of Judah living in Egypt:

The Lord Both you and your wives have made solemn promises to the Queen of Heaven. You promised that you would offer sacrifices to her and pour out wine-offerings to her, and you have kept your promises. Very well, then! Keep your promises! Carry out your vows! But now listen to the vow that I, the Lord, have made in my mighty name to all you Israelites in Egypt: Never again will I let any of you use my name to make a vow by saying, 'I swear by the living Sovereign Lord!' I will see to it that you will not prosper, but will be destroyed. All of you will die, either in war or of disease, until not one of you is left. But a few of you will escape death and return from Egypt to Judah. Then the survivors will know whose words have come true, mine or theirs. I, the Lord, will give you proof that I will punish you in this place and that my promise to bring destruction on you will come true. I will hand over King Hophra of Egypt to his enemies who want to kill him, just as I handed over King Zedekiah of Judah to King Nebuchadnezzar of Babylonia, who was his enemy and wanted to kill him.

Cast [This is] the word of the Lord.
All **Thanks be to God.**

Cast: **Jeremiah, The Lord, Man 1, Man 2, Man 3, Woman, Young Jeremiah.**

God's promise to Baruch
Jeremiah 45.1–5

Jeremiah In the fourth year that Jehoiakim son of Josiah was king of Judah, Baruch wrote down what I had dictated to him. Then I told him that the Lord, the God of Israel, had said:

The Lord Baruch, you are saying:

Baruch I give up! The Lord has added sorrow to my troubles. I am worn out from groaning, and I can't find any rest!

The Lord But I, the Lord, am tearing down what I have built and pulling up what I have planted. I will do this to the entire earth. Are you looking for special treatment for yourself? Don't do it. I am bringing disaster on all mankind, but you will at least escape with your life, wherever you go. (PAUSE) I, the Lord, have spoken!

Cast [This is] the word of the Lord.
All **Thanks be to God.**

Cast: **Jeremiah, The Lord, Baruch.**

Egypt's defeat at Carchemish
Jeremiah 46.1–10

Jeremiah	The Lord spoke to me about the nations, beginning with Egypt. This is what he said about the army of King Neco of Egypt, which King Nebuchadnezzar of Babylonia defeated at Carchemish near the River Euphrates in the fourth year that Jehoiakim was king of Judah:
The Lord	The Egyptian officers shout:
Officer 1	Get your shields ready and march into battle!
Officer 2	Harness your horses and mount them!
Officer 1	Fall in line and put on your helmets!
Officer 2	Sharpen your spears!
Officer 1	Put on your armour!
Jeremiah	The Lord asks:
The Lord	But what do I see?
Narrator 1	They are turning back in terror. Their soldiers are beaten back.
Narrator 2	Overcome with fear, they run as fast as they can and do not look back.
Narrator 1	Those who run fast cannot get away.
Narrator 2	The soldiers cannot escape.
Narrator 1	In the north, by the Euphrates, they stumble and fall.
Narrator 2	Who is this that rises like the Nile, like a river flooding its banks?
Narrator 1	It is Egypt, rising like the Nile, like a river flooding its banks. Egypt said:
Egyptian	I will rise and cover the world; I will destroy cities and the people who live there.
Officer 1	Command the horses to go and the chariots to roll!
Officer 2	Send out the soldiers:
Narrator 2	Men from Sudan and Libya, carrying shields, and skilled bowmen from Lydia.
Jeremiah	This is the day of the Sovereign Lord Almighty: today he will take revenge; today he will punish his enemies.
Cast	[This is] the word of the Lord.
All	**Thanks be to God.**

Cast: **Jeremiah, The Lord, Officer 1, Officer 2, Narrator 1, Narrator 2, Egyptian** (at a distance).

The coming of Nebuchadnezzar
From Jeremiah 46.13–28

Jeremiah	When King Nebuchadnezzar of Babylonia came to attack Egypt, the Lord spoke to me.
The Lord	Proclaim it in the towns of Egypt, in Migdol, Memphis, and Tahpanhes:
Herald (calling)	Get ready to defend yourselves; all you have will be destroyed in war! Why has your mighty god Apis fallen? The Lord has struck him down!
The Lord	Your soldiers have stumbled and fallen; each one says to the other:
Soldier	Hurry! Let's go home to our people and escape the enemy's sword!
The Lord	Give the king of Egypt a new name—
Herald	Noisy Braggart Who Missed His Chance.
The Lord	I, the Lord Almighty, am king. I am the living God. As Mount Tabor towers above the mountains and Mount Carmel stands high above the sea, so will be the strength of the one who attacks you. Get ready to be taken prisoner, you people of Egypt! Memphis will be made a desert, a ruin where no one lives. Egypt is like a splendid cow, attacked by a stinging fly from the north. The people of Egypt are put to shame; they are conquered by the people of the north. I, the Lord, have spoken. My people, do not be afraid, people of Israel, do not be terrified. I will rescue you from that distant land, from the land where you are prisoners. You will come back home and live in peace; you will be secure, and no one will make you afraid. I will come to you and save you.
Cast	[This is] the word of the Lord.
All	**Thanks be to God.**

Cast: **Jeremiah, The Lord, Herald, Soldier.**

The Lord's message about Philistia
Jeremiah 47.1—48.9

Jeremiah	Before the king of Egypt attacked Gaza, the Lord spoke to me about Philistia. He said:
The Lord	Look! Waters are rising in the north and will rush like a river in flood. They will cover the land and everything on it, cities and the people who live there. People will call out for help; everyone on earth will cry bitterly. They will hear the hoof beats of horses, the clatter of chariots, the rumble of wheels. Fathers will not turn back for their children; their hands will hang limp at their sides. The time has come to destroy Philistia, to cut off from Tyre and Sidon all the help that remains. I, the Lord, will destroy the

→

Philistines, all who came from the shores of Crete. Great sorrow has come to the people of Gaza, and Ashkelon's people are silent. How long will the rest of Philistia mourn? You cry out:

Victim Sword of the Lord! How long will you go on slashing? Go back to your scabbard, stay there and rest!

The Lord But how can it rest, when I have given it work to do? I have commanded it to attack Ashkelon and the people who live on the coast.

Jeremiah This is what the Lord Almighty said about Moab:

The Lord Pity the people of Nebo—their town is destroyed! Kiriathaim is captured, its mighty fortress torn down, and its people put to shame; the splendour of Moab is gone. The enemy have captured Heshbon and plot to destroy the nation of Moab. The town of Madmen will be silenced; armies will march against it. The people of Horonaim cry out, 'Violence! Destruction!' Moab has been destroyed; listen to the children crying. Hear the sound of their sobs along the road up to Luhith, the cries of distress on the way down to Horonaim. They say:

Moabite Quick, run for your lives! Run like a wild desert donkey!

The Lord Moab, you trusted in your strength and your wealth, but now even you will be conquered; your god Chemosh will go into exile, along with his princes and priests. Not a town will escape the destruction; both valley and plain will be ruined. I, the Lord, have spoken. Set up a tombstone for Moab; it will soon be destroyed. Its towns will be left in ruins, and no one will live there again.

Cast [This is] the word of the Lord.
All **Thanks be to God.**

Cast: **Jeremiah, The Lord, Victim, Moabite.**

The cities of Moab are destroyed
From Jeremiah 48.11–25

Jeremiah The Lord said:

The Lord Moab has always lived secure and has never been taken into exile. Moab is like wine left to settle undisturbed and never poured from jar to jar. Its flavour has never been ruined, and it tastes as good as ever.

So now, the time is coming when I will send people to pour Moab out like wine. They will empty its wine-jars and break them in pieces. Then the Moabites will be disillusioned with their god Chemosh, just as the Israelites were disillusioned with Bethel, a god in whom they trusted.

Singer 1 Men of Moab, why do you claim to be heroes,
brave soldiers tested in war?
Moab and its cities are destroyed;
its finest young men have been slaughtered.

The Lord	I am the king, the Lord Almighty, and I have spoken. Moab's doom approaches; its ruin is coming soon.
Singer 2	Mourn for that nation, you that live near by, all of you that know its fame.
Singer 1	Its powerful rule has been broken; its glory and might are no more.
Singer 2	You that live in Dibon, come down from your place of honour and sit on the ground in the dust; Moab's destroyer is here and has left its forts in ruins.
Singer 1	You that live in Aroer, stand by the road and wait; ask those who are running away, find out from them what has happened.
The Lord	They will answer:
Refugee 1	Moab has fallen; weep for it; it is disgraced.
Refugee 2	Announce along the River Arnon that Moab is destroyed!
The Lord	Moab's might has been crushed; its power has been destroyed. (PAUSE) I, the Lord, have spoken!
Cast	[This is] the word of the Lord.
All	**Thanks be to God.**

Cast: **Jeremiah, The Lord, Singer 1, Singer 2, Refugee 1** (can be the same as Singer 1)**, Refugee 2** (can be the same as Singer 2).

The Lord's judgement on Edom
Jeremiah 49.7–22

Jeremiah	This is what the Lord Almighty said about Edom:
The Lord	Have the people of Edom lost their good judgement? Can their advisers no longer tell them what to do? Has all their wisdom disappeared? People of Dedan, turn and run! Hide! I am going to destroy Esau's descendants, because the time has come for me to punish them. When men pick grapes, they leave a few on the vines, and when robbers come at night, they take only what they want. But I have stripped Esau's descendants completely and uncovered their hiding places, so that they can no longer hide. All the people of Edom are destroyed. Not one of them is left. Leave your orphans with me, and I will take care of them. Your widows can depend on me.
	If even those who did not deserve to be punished had to drink from the cup of punishment, do you think that you will go unpunished? No, you must drink from the cup! I myself have sworn that the city of Bozrah will become a horrifying sight and a desert; people will jeer at it and use its name as a curse. All the nearby villages will be in ruins for ever. I, the Lord, have spoken.

Jeremiah	I said:
Young Jeremiah	Edom, I have received a message from the Lord. He has sent a messenger to tell the nations to assemble their armies and to get ready to attack you. The Lord is going to make you weak, and no one will respect you. Your pride has deceived you. No one fears you as much as you think they do. You live on the rocky cliffs, high on top of the mountain; but even though you live as high up as an eagle, the Lord will bring you down. The Lord has spoken.
Jeremiah	The Lord said:
The Lord	The destruction that will come on Edom will be so terrible that everyone who passes by will be shocked and terrified. The same thing will happen to Edom as happened to Sodom and Gomorrah, when they and the near by towns were destroyed. No one will ever live there again. I, the Lord, have spoken. Like a lion coming out of the thick woods along the Jordan up to the green pasture land, I will come and make the Edomites run away suddenly from their country. Then the leader I choose will rule the nation. Who can be compared to me? Who would dare challenge me? What ruler could oppose me? So listen to the plan that I have made against the people of Edom, and to what I intend to do to the people of the city of Teman. Even their children will be dragged off, and everyone will be horrified. When Edom falls, there will be such a noise that the entire earth will shake, and the cries of alarm will be heard as far away as the Gulf of Aqaba. The enemy will attack Bozrah like an eagle swooping down with outspread wings. On that day Edom's soldiers will be as frightened as a woman in labour.

Cast	[This is] the word of the Lord.
All	**Thanks be to God.**

Cast: **Jeremiah, The Lord, Young Jeremiah.**

God speaks of Israel's return
Jeremiah 50.4–10

The Lord	When the time of my judgement comes, the people of both Israel and Judah will come weeping, looking for me, their God. They will ask the way to Zion and then go in that direction. They will make an eternal covenant with me and never break it.
	My people are like sheep whose shepherds have let them get lost in the mountains. They have wandered like sheep from one mountain to another, and they have forgotten where their home is. They are attacked by all who find them. Their enemies say:
Enemy 1	They sinned against the Lord, and so what we have done is not wrong.
Enemy 2	Their ancestors trusted in the Lord, and they themselves should have remained faithful to him.

The Lord	People of Israel, run away from Babylonia! Leave the country! Be the first to leave! I am going to stir up a group of strong nations in the north and make them attack Babylonia. They will line up in battle against the country and conquer it. They are skilful hunters, shooting arrows that never miss the mark. Babylonia will be looted, and those who loot it will take everything they want. (PAUSE) I, the Lord, have spoken!
Cast	[This is] the word of the Lord.
All	**Thanks be to God.**

Cast: **The Lord, Enemy 1, Enemy 2.**

Further judgements on Babylonia
From Jeremiah 51.8–14

Jeremiah	The Lord says:
The Lord	Babylonia has suddenly fallen and is destroyed! Mourn over it! Get medicine for its wounds, and perhaps it can be healed. Foreigners living there said:
Foreigner 1	We tried to help Babylonia, but it was too late.
Foreigner 2	Let's leave her now and go back home.
Foreigner 1	God has punished Babylonia with all his might and has destroyed it completely.
Jeremiah	The Lord says:
The Lord	My people shout:
Person 1	The Lord has shown that we are in the right.
Person 2	Let's go and tell the people in Jerusalem what the Lord our God has done.
Jeremiah	The Lord has stirred up the kings of Media, because he intends to destroy Babylonia. That is how he will take revenge for the destruction of his Temple.
	The attacking officers command:
Officer 1	Sharpen your arrows!
Officer 2	Get your shields ready!
Officer 3	Give the signal to attack Babylon's walls.
Officer 1	Strengthen the guard!
Officer 2	Post the sentries!
Officer 3	Place men in ambush!
Jeremiah	The Lord has done what he said he would do to the people of Babylonia. That country has many rivers and rich treasures, but its time is up, and its thread of life is cut. The Lord Almighty has

→

717

sworn by his own life that he will bring many men to attack Babylonia like a swarm of locusts, and they will shout with victory.

Cast	[This is] the word of the Lord.
All	**Thanks be to God.**

Cast: **Jeremiah, The Lord** (can be the same as Jeremiah), **Foreigner 1, Foreigner 2** (can be the same as Foreigner 1, **Person 1, Person 2** (can be the same as Person 1), **Officer 1, Officer 2** (can be the same as Officer 1), **Officer 3.**

A hymn of praise to God
Jeremiah 51.15–19

Singer 1	The Lord made the earth by his power; by his wisdom he created the world and stretched out the heavens.
Singer 2	At his command the waters above the sky roar; he brings clouds from the ends of the earth.
Singer 3	He makes lightning flash in the rain and sends the wind from his storeroom.
Singer 1	At the sight of this, men feel stupid and senseless; those who make idols are disillusioned because the gods they make are false and lifeless.
Singer 2	They are worthless and should be despised; they will be destroyed when the Lord comes to deal with them.
Singer 3	The God of Jacob is not like them; he is the one who made everything, and he has chosen Israel to be his very own people.
Singers 1–3 (with flourish)	The Lord Almighty is his name!
Cast	[This is] the word of the Lord.
All	**Thanks be to God.**

Cast: **Singer 1, Singer 2, Singer 3.**

Babylonia
Jeremiah 51.20–35

Jeremiah	The Lord says:
The Lord	Babylonia, you are my hammer, my weapon of war. I used you to crush nations and kingdoms, to shatter horses and riders, to shatter chariots and their drivers, to kill men and women, to slay old and young, to kill boys and girls, to slaughter shepherds and their flocks, to slaughter ploughmen and their horses, to crush rulers and high officials.

[Jeremiah	The Lord says:]
The Lord	You will see me repay Babylonia and its people for all the evil they did to Jerusalem. Babylonia, you are like a mountain that destroys the whole world, but I, the Lord, am your enemy. I will take hold of you, level you to the ground, and leave you in ashes. None of the stones from your ruins will ever be used again for building. You will be like a desert for ever. (PAUSE) I, the Lord, have spoken.
Voice 1	Give the signal to attack!
Voice 2	Blow the trumpet so that the nations can hear!
Voice 1	Prepare the nations for war against Babylonia!
Voice 2	Tell the kingdoms of Ararat, Minni, and Ashkenaz to attack.
Voice 1	Appoint an officer to lead the attack.
Voice 2	Bring up the horses like a swarm of locusts.
Voice 1	Prepare the nations for war against Babylonia.
Voice 2	Send for the kings of Media, their leaders and officials, and the armies of all the countries they control.
Jeremiah	The earth trembles and shakes because the Lord is carrying out his plan to make Babylonia a desert, where no one lives. The Babylonian soldiers have stopped fighting and remain in their forts. They have lost their courage and have become like women. The city gates are broken down, and the houses are on fire. Messenger after messenger runs to tell the king of Babylonia that his city has been broken into from every side. The enemy have captured the river-crossing and have set the fortresses on fire. The Babylonian soldiers have panicked.
The Lord	Soon the enemy will cut them down and trample them like corn on a threshing-place. I, the Lord Almighty, the God of Israel, have spoken.
Singer	The king of Babylonia cut Jerusalem up and ate it. He emptied the city like a jar; like a monster he swallowed it. He took what he wanted and threw the rest away.
Jeremiah	Let the people of Zion say:
Person 1	May Babylonia be held responsible for the violence done to us!
Jeremiah	Let the people of Jerusalem say:
Person 2	May Babylonia be held responsible for what we have suffered!
Cast **All**	[This is] the word of the Lord. **Thanks be to God.**

Cast: **Jeremiah, The Lord, Voice 1, Voice 2** (can be the same as Voice 1)**, Singer, Person 1, Person 2.**

God's message to the Israelites in Babylonia
Jeremiah 51.50–53

Jeremiah	The Lord says to his people in Babylonia:
The Lord	You have escaped death! Now go! Don't wait! Though you are far from home, think about me, your Lord, and remember Jerusalem. You say—
Person 1	We've been disgraced and made ashamed.
Person 2	We feel completely helpless because foreigners have taken over the holy places in the Temple.
The Lord	So then, I say that the time is coming when I will deal with Babylon's idols, and the wounded will groan throughout the country. Even if Babylon could climb to the sky and build a strong fortress there, I would still send people to destroy it. I, the Lord, have spoken.
Cast	[This is] the word of the Lord.
All	**Thanks be to God.**

Cast: **Jeremiah, The Lord, Person 1, Person 2** (can be the same as Person 1).

Jeremiah's message is sent to Babylonia
Jeremiah 51.59–64

Jeremiah	King Zedekiah's personal attendant was Seraiah, the son of Neriah and grandson of Mahseiah. In the fourth year that Zedekiah was king of Judah, Seraiah was going to Babylonia with him, and I gave him some instructions. I wrote in a book an account of all the destruction that would come on Babylonia, as well as all these other things about Babylonia. I told Seraiah:
Young Jeremiah	When you get to Babylon, be sure to read aloud to the people everything that is written here. Then pray—
Seraiah	Lord, you have said that you would destroy this place, so that there would be no living creature in it, neither man nor animal, and it would be like a desert for ever.
Young Jeremiah	Seraiah, when you finish reading this book to the people, then tie it to a stone and throw it into the River Euphrates, and say:
Seraiah	This is what will happen to Babylonia—it will sink and never rise again, because of the destruction that the Lord is going to bring on it.
Jeremiah (with flourish)	The words of Jeremiah end here!
Cast	[This is] the word of the Lord.
All	**Thanks be to God.**

Cast: **Jeremiah, Young Jeremiah, Seraiah.**

LAMENTATIONS

The sorrows of Jerusalem
From Lamentations 1.1–20

Voice 1   How lonely lies Jerusalem, once so full of people!
Once honoured by the world, she is now like a widow;
the noblest of cities has fallen into slavery.

Voice 2   All night long she cries; tears run down her cheeks.
Of all her former friends, not one is left to comfort her.
Her allies have betrayed her and all are now against her.

Voice 3   Judah's people are helpless slaves, forced away from home.
They live in other lands, with no place to call their own—
surrounded by enemies, with no way to escape.

Voice 1   No one comes to the Temple now to worship on the holy days.
The girls who sang there suffer, and the priests can only groan.
The city gates stand empty, and Zion is in agony.

Voice 2   Her enemies succeeded; they hold her in their power.
The Lord has made her suffer for all her many sins;
her children have been captured and taken away.

Voice 3   The splendour of Jerusalem is a thing of the past.
Her leaders are like deer that are weak from hunger,
whose strength is almost gone as they flee from the hunters.

Voice 1   A lonely ruin now, Jerusalem recalls her ancient splendour.
When she fell to the enemy, there was no one to help her;
her conquerors laughed at her downfall.

Voice 2   Her honour is gone; she is naked and held in contempt.
She groans and hides her face in shame.
Jerusalem made herself filthy with terrible sin.

Voice 3   Her uncleanness was easily seen,
but she showed no concern for her fate.
Her downfall was terrible; no one can comfort her.
Her enemies have won, and she cries to the Lord for mercy.

Voice 1   Her enemies robbed her of all her treasures.
She saw them enter the Temple itself,
where the Lord had forbidden Gentiles to go.

Voice 2   Her people groan as they look for something to eat;
they exchange their treasures for food to keep themselves alive.

The city cries:

City 1 and **2**   Look at me, Lord!

City 1   See me in my misery.

Voice 2   She cries to everyone who passes by:

City 1 and **2**	Look at me!
City 2	No one has ever had pain like mine, pain that the Lord brought on me in the time of his anger.
City 1	He sent fire from above, a fire that burnt inside me. He set a trap for me and brought me to the ground. Then he abandoned me and left me in constant pain.
City 2	He took note of all my sins and tied them all together; he hung them round my neck, and I grew weak beneath the weight. The Lord gave me to my foes, and I was helpless against them.
City 1	That is why my eyes are overflowing with tears. No one can comfort me; no one can give me courage. I stretch out my hands, but no one will help me.
City 2	But the Lord is just, for I have disobeyed him. Look, O Lord, at my agony, at the anguish of my soul! My heart is broken in sorrow for my sins.
Cast	[This is] the word of the Lord.
All	**Thanks be to God.**

Cast: **Voice 1, Voice 2, Voice 3, City 1, City 2.** (City 1 and 2: preferably female voices).

The Lord's punishment of Jerusalem
From Lamentations 2.1–19

Voice 1	The Lord in his anger has covered Zion with darkness. Its heavenly splendour he has turned into ruins. On the day of his anger he abandoned even his Temple.
Voice 2	He smashed to pieces the Temple where we worshipped him; he has put an end to holy days and Sabbaths. King and priest alike have felt the force of his anger.
Voice 1	The Lord rejected his altar and deserted his holy Temple; he allowed the enemy to tear down its walls. They shouted in victory where once we had worshipped in joy.
Voice 2	The Lord was determined that the walls of Zion should fall; he measured them off to make sure of total destruction. The towers and walls now lie in ruins together.
Voice 1	The gates lie buried in rubble, their bars smashed to pieces. The king and the noblemen now are in exile. The Law is no longer taught, and the prophets have no visions from the Lord.
Voice 2	My eyes are worn out with weeping; my soul is in anguish. O Jerusalem, beloved Jerusalem, what can I say? How can I comfort you? No one has ever suffered like this.
Voice 1	Your prophets had nothing to tell you but lies; their preaching deceived you by never exposing your sin. They made you think you did not need to repent.

Voice 2	People passing by the city look at you in scorn.
	They shake their heads and laugh at the ruins of Jerusalem:
Person 1	Is *this* that lovely city?
Person 2	Is *this* the pride of the world?
Voice 2	All your enemies mock you and glare at you with hate.
	They curl their lips and sneer:
Enemy 1	We have destroyed it!
Enemy 2	This is the day we have waited for!
Voice 1	The Lord has finally done what he threatened to do:
	he has destroyed us without mercy, as he warned us long ago.
	He gave our enemies victory, gave them joy at our downfall.
Voice 2	O Jerusalem, let your very walls cry out to the Lord!
	Let your tears flow like rivers night and day;
	pour out your heart and beg him for mercy.
Cast	[This is] the word of the Lord.
All	**Thanks be to God.**

Cast: **Voice 1, Voice 2, Person 1, Person 2, Enemy 1, Enemy 2.**

Repentance and hope (i)
From Lamentations 3.22–42

Voice 1	The Lord's unfailing love and mercy still continue,
	fresh as the morning, as sure as the sunrise.
	The Lord is all I have, and so I put my hope in him.
Voice 2	The Lord is good to everyone who trusts in him,
	so it is best for us to wait in patience—to wait for him to save us—
	and it is best to learn this patience in our youth.
Voice 1	The Lord is merciful and will not reject us for ever.
	He may bring us sorrow, but his love for us is sure and strong.
	He takes no pleasure in causing us grief or pain.
Voice 2	The Lord knows when our spirits are crushed in prison;
	he knows when we are denied the rights he gave us;
	when justice is perverted in court, he knows.
Voice 1	The will of the Lord alone is always carried out.
	Good and evil alike take place at his command.
	Why should we ever complain when we are punished for our sin?
Voice 2	Let us examine our ways and turn back to the Lord.
	Let us open our hearts to God in heaven and pray:
Voices 1 and 2	We have sinned and rebelled—
Voice 1	And you, O Lord, have not forgiven us.
Cast	[This is] the word of the Lord.
All	**Thanks be to God.**

Cast: **Voice 1, Voice 2.**

Repentance and hope (ii)
From Lamentations 3.52–58

Voice 1   I was trapped like a bird by enemies who had no cause to hate me.
They threw me alive into a pit
and closed the opening with a stone.
Water began to close over me, and I thought death was near.

Voice 2   From the bottom of the pit, O Lord, I cried out to you,
And when I begged you to listen to my cry, you heard.
You answered me and told me not to be afraid.

Voices 1 and 2   You came to my rescue, Lord—

Voice 1   And saved my life.

Cast   [This is] the word of the Lord.
All   **Thanks be to God.**

Cast: **Voice 1, Voice 2.**

Jerusalem after its fall
From Lamentations 4.1–18

Voice 1   Our glittering gold has grown dull;
the stones of the Temple lie scattered in the streets.

Voice 2   The Lord turned loose the full force of his fury;
he lit a fire in Zion that burnt it to the ground.

Voice 1   No one anywhere, not even rulers of foreign nations,
believed that any invader could enter Jerusalem's gates.

Voice 2   But it happened because her prophets sinned
and her priests were guilty of causing the death of innocent people.
Her leaders wandered through the streets like blind men,
so stained with blood that no one would touch them.

Voice 1   People shouted:

Person 1   Go away!

Person 2   You're defiled!

Person 1   Don't touch me!

Voice 1   So they wandered from nation to nation, welcomed by no one.

Voice 2   The Lord had no more concern for them;
he scattered them himself.
He showed no regard for our priests and leaders.

Voice 1   We looked until we could look no longer for help that never came.
We kept waiting for help from a nation that had none to give.

Voices 1 and 2   Our days were over; the end had come.

Cast   [This is] the word of the Lord.
All   **Thanks be to God.**

Cast: **Voice 1, Voice 2, Person 1, Person 2.**

A prayer for mercy
From Lamentations 5.1–22

Voice 1	Remember, O Lord, what has happened to us.
Voice 2	Look at us, and see our disgrace.
Voice 1	Happiness has gone out of our lives.
Voice 2	Grief has taken the place of our dances.
Voice 1	Nothing is left of all we were proud of.
Voice 2	We sinned, and now we are doomed.
Voice 1	We are sick at our very hearts.
Voice 2	We can hardly see through our tears.
Voice 1	But you, O Lord, are king for ever, and will rule to the end of time.
Voices 1 and 2	Bring us back to you, Lord! Bring us back!
Voice 2	Restore our ancient glory.
Voice 1	Or have you rejected us for ever?
Voice 2	Is there no limit to your anger?
Cast	[This is] the word of the Lord.
All	**Thanks be to God.**

Cast: **Voice 1, Voice 2.**

EZEKIEL

Ezekiel's first vision of God
God's throne
Ezekiel 1.1–28

Ezekiel On the fifth day of the fourth month of the thirtieth year, I, Ezekiel the priest, son of Buzi, was living with the Jewish exiles by the River Chebar in Babylonia. The sky opened, and I saw a vision of God.

Chronicler It was the fifth year since King Jehoiachin had been taken into exile.

Ezekiel There in Babylonia beside the River Chebar, I heard the Lord speak to me and I felt his power. I looked up and saw a storm coming from the north.

Voice 1 Lightning was flashing from a huge cloud, and the sky round it was glowing. Where the lightning was flashing, something shone like bronze.

Ezekiel At the centre of the storm, I saw what looked like four living creatures in human form.

Voice 2 But each of them had four faces and four wings. Their legs were straight, and they had hoofs like those of a bull. They shone like polished bronze. In addition to their four faces and four wings, they each had four human hands, one under each wing. Two wings of each creature were spread out so that the creatures formed a square with their wing tips touching. When they moved, they moved as a group without turning their bodies.

Voice 3 Each living creature had four different faces: a human face in front, a lion's face at the right, a bull's face at the left, and an eagle's face at the back. Two wings of each creature were raised so that they touched the tips of the wings of the creatures next to it, and their other two wings were folded against their bodies. Each creature faced all four directions, and so the group could go wherever they wished, without having to turn.

Voice 1 Among the creatures there was something that looked like a blazing torch, constantly moving. The fire would blaze up and shoot out flashes of lightning. The creatures themselves darted to and fro with the speed of lightning.

Ezekiel As I was looking at the four creatures, I saw four wheels touching the ground, one beside each of them.

Voice 2 All four wheels were alike; each one shone like a precious stone, and each had another wheel intersecting it at right angles, so that the wheels could move in any of the four directions. The rims of the wheels were covered with eyes.

Voice 3 Whenever the creatures moved, the wheels moved with them,

726

and if the creatures rose up from the earth, so did the wheels. The creatures went wherever they wished, and the wheels did exactly what the creatures did, because the creatures controlled them. So every time the creatures moved or stopped or rose in the air, the wheels did exactly the same.

Voice 1 Above the heads of the creatures there was something that looked like a dome made of dazzling crystal. There under the dome stood the creatures, each stretching out two wings towards the ones next to it and covering its body with the other two wings.

Ezekiel I heard the noise their wings made in flight.

Voice 2 It sounded like the roar of the sea, like the noise of a huge army, like the voice of Almighty God.

Voice 3 When they stopped flying, they folded their wings, but there was still a sound coming from above the dome over their heads.

Voice 1 Above the dome there was something that looked like a throne made of sapphire, and sitting on the throne was a figure that looked like a man.

Voice 2 The figure seemed to be shining like bronze in the middle of a fire.

Voice 3 It shone all over with a bright light that had in it all the colours of the rainbow.

Voices 1–3 This was the dazzling light that shows the presence of the Lord. (PAUSE)

Ezekiel When I saw this, I fell face downwards on the ground.

Cast [This is] the word of the Lord.
All **Thanks be to God.**

Cast: **Ezekiel, Chronicler, Voice 1, Voice 2, Voice 3.**

God calls Ezekiel to be a prophet
From Ezekiel 1.(1) 26—3.15

Ezekiel On the fifth day of the fourth month of the thirtieth year, I, Ezekiel the priest, son of Buzi, was living with the Jewish exiles by the River Chebar in Babylonia. The sky opened, and I saw a vision of God.

There was something that looked like a throne made of sapphire, and sitting on the throne was a figure that looked like a man. The figure seemed to be shining like bronze in the middle of a fire. It shone all over with a bright light that had in it all the colours of the rainbow. This was the dazzling light that shows the presence of the Lord. When I saw this, I fell face downwards on the ground. (PAUSE) Then I heard a voice saying:

God Mortal man, stand up. I want to talk to you.

Ezekiel While the voice was speaking, God's spirit entered me and raised me to my feet, and I heard the voice continue:

God	Mortal man, I am sending you to the people of Israel. They have rebelled and turned against me and are still rebels, just as their ancestors were. They are stubborn and do not respect me, so I am sending you to tell them what I, the Sovereign Lord, am saying to them. Whether those rebels listen to you or not, they will know that a prophet has been among them. But you, mortal man, must not be afraid of them or of anything they say. They will defy and despise you; it will be like living among scorpions. Still, don't be afraid of those rebels or of anything they say. You will tell them whatever I tell you to say, whether they listen or not.
Ezekiel	God said:
God	Mortal man, listen to what I tell you. Don't be rebellious like them. Open your mouth and eat what I am going to give you.
Ezekiel	I saw a hand stretched out towards me, and it was holding a scroll. The hand unrolled the scroll, and I saw that there was writing on both sides—cries of grief were written there, and wails and groans. God said:
God	Mortal man, eat this scroll; then go and speak to the people of Israel.
Ezekiel	So I opened my mouth, and he gave me the scroll to eat. He said:
God	Mortal man, eat this scroll that I give you; fill your stomach with it.
Ezekiel	I ate it, and it tasted as sweet as honey. Then God said:
God	Mortal man, go to the people of Israel and say to them whatever I tell you to say. I am not sending you to a nation that speaks a difficult foreign language, but to the Israelites. If I sent you to great nations that spoke difficult languages you didn't understand, they would listen to you. But none of the people of Israel will be willing to listen; they will not even listen to me. All of them are stubborn and defiant. Now I will make you as stubborn and as tough as they are. I will make you as firm as a rock, as hard as a diamond; don't be afraid of those rebels.
	Mortal man, pay close attention and remember everything I tell you. Then go to your countrymen who are in exile and tell them what I, the Sovereign Lord, am saying to them, whether they pay attention to you or not.
Ezekiel	Then God's spirit lifted me up, and I heard behind me the loud roar of a voice that said:
Voice (loudly)	Praise the glory of the Lord in heaven above!
Ezekiel	I heard the wings of the creatures beating together in the air, and the noise of the wheels, as loud as an earthquake. The power of the Lord came on me with great force, and as his spirit carried me off, I felt bitter and angry.
	So I came to Tel Abib beside the River Chebar, where the exiles were living, and for seven days I stayed there, overcome by what I had seen and heard.
Cast	[This is] the word of the Lord.
All	**Thanks be to God.**

Cast: **Ezekiel, God, Voice.**

Ezekiel will be unable to talk
Ezekiel 3.22–27

Ezekiel   I felt the powerful presence of the Lord and heard him say to me:

The Lord   Get up and go out into the valley. I will talk to you there.

Ezekiel   So I went out into the valley, and there I saw the glory of the Lord, just as I had seen it beside the River Chebar. I fell face downwards on the ground, but God's spirit entered me and raised me to my feet. The Lord said to me:

The Lord   Go home and shut yourself up in the house. You will be tied with ropes, mortal man, and you will not be able to go out in public. I will paralyse your tongue so that you won't be able to warn these rebellious people. Then, when I speak to you again and give you back the power of speech, you will tell them what I, the Sovereign Lord, am saying. Some of them will listen, but some will ignore you, for they are a nation of rebels.

Cast   [This is] the word of the Lord.
All   **Thanks be to God.**

Cast: **Ezekiel, The Lord.**

Ezekiel acts out the siege of Jerusalem
From Ezekiel 4.1–17

Ezekiel   God said:

The Lord   Mortal man, get a brick, put it in front of you, and scratch lines on it to represent the city of Jerusalem. Then, to represent a siege, put trenches, earthworks, camps, and battering-rams all round it. Take an iron pan and set it up like a wall between you and the city. Face the city. It is under siege, and you are the one besieging it. This will be a sign to the nation of Israel.

Then lie down on your left side, and I will place on you the guilt of the nation of Israel. For 390 days you will stay there and suffer because of their guilt. I have sentenced you to one day for each year their punishment will last. When you finish that, turn over on your right side and suffer for the guilt of Judah for forty days—one day for each year of their punishment.

Fix your eyes on the siege of Jerusalem. Shake your fist at the city and prophesy against it. I will tie you up so that you cannot turn from one side to the other until the siege is over.

Now take some wheat, barley, beans, peas, millet, and spelt. Mix them all together and make bread. That is what you are to eat during the 390 days you are lying on your left side. You will be allowed 230 grammes of bread a day, and it will have to last until the next day. You will also have a limited amount of water to drink, two cups a day.

Ezekiel	The Lord said:
The Lord	The Israelites will have to eat food which the Law forbids, when I scatter them to foreign countries.
Ezekiel	But I replied:
Young Ezekiel	No, Sovereign Lord! I have never defiled myself. From childhood on I have never eaten meat from any animal that died a natural death or was killed by wild animals. I have never eaten any food considered unclean.
Ezekiel	So God said:
The Lord	Very well. But I am going to cut off the supply of bread for Jerusalem. The people there will be distressed and anxious as they measure out the food they eat and the water they drink. They will run out of bread and water; they will be in despair, and they will waste away because of their sins.
Cast	[This is] the word of the Lord.
All	**Thanks be to God.**

Cast: **Ezekiel, The Lord, Young Ezekiel.**

The end is near for Israel
Ezekiel 7.1–14

Ezekiel	The Lord spoke to me. He said:
The Lord	Mortal man, this is what I, the Sovereign Lord, am saying to the land of Israel: This is the end for the whole land! Israel, the end has come. You will feel my anger, because I am judging you for what you have done. I will pay you back for all your disgusting conduct. I will not spare you or show you any mercy. I am going to punish you for the disgusting things you have done, so that you will know that I am the Lord.
Ezekiel	This is what the Sovereign Lord is saying:
The Lord	One disaster after another is coming on you. It's all over. This is the end. You are finished. The end is coming for you people who live in the land. The time is near when there will be no more celebrations at the mountain shrines, only confusion. Very soon now you will feel all the force of my anger. I am judging you for what you have done, and I will pay you back for all your disgusting conduct. I will not spare you or show you any mercy. I am going to punish you for the disgusting things you have done, so that you will know that I am the Lord, and that I am the one who punishes you.
Ezekiel	The day of disaster is coming for Israel. Violence is flourishing. Pride is at its height. Violence produces more wickedness. Nothing of theirs will remain, nothing of their wealth, their splendour, or their glory.
	The time is coming. The day is near when buying and selling will have no more meaning, because God's punishment will fall on

everyone alike. No merchant will live long enough to get back what he has lost, because God's anger is on everyone. Those who are evil cannot survive. The trumpet sounds, and everyone gets ready. But no one goes off to war, for God's anger will fall on everyone alike.

| Cast | [This is] the word of the Lord. |
| All | **Thanks be to God.** |

Cast: **Ezekiel, The Lord.**

Punishment for Israel's sins
Ezekiel 7.15–27

Ezekiel

There is fighting in the streets, and sickness and hunger in the houses. Anyone who is out in the country will die in the fighting, and anyone in the city will be a victim of sickness and hunger. Some will escape to the mountains like doves frightened from the valleys. All of them will moan over their sins. Everyone's hands will be weak, and their knees will shake. They will put on sackcloth and they will tremble all over. Their heads will be shaved, and they will all be disgraced. They will throw their gold and silver away in the streets like refuse, because neither silver nor gold can save them when the Lord pours out his fury. They cannot use it to satisfy their desires or fill their stomachs. Gold and silver led them into sin. Once they were proud of their beautiful jewels, but they used them to make disgusting idols. That is why the Lord has made their wealth repulsive to them.

The Lord says:

The Lord

I will let foreigners rob them, and law-breakers will take all their wealth and defile it. I will not interfere when my treasured Temple is profaned, when robbers break into it and defile it.

Everything is in confusion—the land is full of murders and the cities are full of violence. I will bring the most evil nations here and let them have your homes. Your strongest men will lose their confidence when I let the nations profane the places where you worship. Despair is coming. You will look for peace and never find it. One disaster will follow another, and a steady stream of bad news will pour in. You will beg the prophets to reveal what they foresee. The priests will have nothing to teach the people, and the elders will have no advice to give. The king will mourn, the prince will give up hope, and the people will shake with fear.

I will punish you for all you have done, and will judge you in the same way as you have judged others. This will show you that I am the Lord.

| Cast | [This is] the word of the Lord. |
| All | **Thanks be to God.** |

Cast: **Ezekiel, The Lord.**

Idolatry in Jerusalem
Ezekiel 8.1–18

Ezekiel	On the fifth day of the sixth month of the sixth year of our exile, the leaders of the exiles from Judah were sitting in my house with me. Suddenly the power of the Sovereign Lord came on me. I looked up and saw a vision of a fiery human form. From the waist down his body looked like fire, and from the waist up he was shining like polished bronze. He stretched out what seemed to be a hand and seized me by the hair. Then in this vision God's spirit lifted me high in the air and took me to Jerusalem. He took me to the inner entrance of the north gate of the Temple, where there was an idol that was an outrage to God. There I saw the dazzling light that shows the presence of Israel's God, just as I had seen it when I was by the River Chebar. God said to me:
God	Mortal man, look towards the north.
Ezekiel	I looked, and there near the altar by the entrance of the gateway I saw the idol that was an outrage to God. God said to me:
God	Mortal man, do you see what is happening? Look at the disgusting things the people of Israel are doing here, driving me farther and farther away from my holy place. You will see even more disgraceful things than this.
Ezekiel	He took me to the entrance of the outer courtyard and showed me a hole in the wall. He said:
God	Mortal man, break through the wall here.
Ezekiel	I broke through it and found a door. He said to me:
God	Go in and look at the evil, disgusting things they are doing there.
Ezekiel	So I went in and looked. The walls were covered with drawings of snakes and other unclean animals, and of the other things which the Israelites were worshipping. Seventy Israelite leaders were there, including Jaazaniah son of Shaphan. Each one was holding an incense-burner, and smoke was rising from the incense. God asked me:
God	Mortal man, do you see what the Israelite leaders are doing in secret? They are all worshipping in a room full of images. Their excuse is:
Jaazaniah	The Lord doesn't see us!
Pelatiah	He has abandoned the country.
Ezekiel	Then the Lord said to me:
God	You are going to see them do even more disgusting things than that.
Ezekiel	So he took me to the inner courtyard of the Temple. There near the entrance of the sanctuary, between the altar and the passage,

were about twenty-five men. They had turned their backs to the sanctuary and were bowing low towards the east, worshipping the rising sun. The Lord said to me:

God	Mortal man, do you see that? These people of Judah are not satisfied with merely doing all the disgusting things you have seen here and with spreading violence throughout the country. No, they must come and do them here in the Temple itself and make me even more angry. Look how they insult me in the most offensive way possible! They will feel all the force of my anger. I will not spare them or show them any mercy. They will shout prayers to me as loud as they can, but I will not listen to them.
Cast	[This is] the word of the Lord.
All	**Thanks be to God.**

Cast: **Ezekiel, God, Jaazaniah, Pelatiah** (can be the same as Jaazaniah).

Jerusalem is punished
Ezekiel 9.1–11

Ezekiel	I heard God shout:
God (calling)	Come here, you men who are going to punish the city. Bring your weapons with you.
Ezekiel	At once six men came from the outer north gate of the Temple, each one carrying a weapon. With them was a man dressed in linen clothes, carrying something to write with. They all came and stood by the bronze altar. Then the dazzling light of the presence of the God of Israel rose up from the winged creatures, where it had been, and moved to the entrance of the Temple. The Lord called to the man dressed in linen:
God	Go through the whole city of Jerusalem and put a mark on the forehead of everyone who is distressed and troubled because of all the disgusting things being done in the city.
Ezekiel	And I heard God say to the other men:
God	Follow him through the city, and kill. Spare no one; have mercy on no one. Kill the old men, young men, young women, mothers, and children. But don't touch anyone who has the mark on his forehead. Start here at my Temple.
Ezekiel	So they began with the leaders who were standing there at the Temple. God said to them:
God	Defile the Temple. Fill its courtyards with corpses. Get to work!
Ezekiel	So they began to kill the people in the city. While the killing was going on, I was there alone. I threw myself face downwards on the ground and shouted:
Young Ezekiel	Sovereign Lord, are you so angry with Jerusalem that you are going to kill everyone left in Israel?

God	The people of Israel and Judah are guilty of terrible sins. They have committed murder all over the land and have filled Jerusalem with crime. They say that I, the Lord, have abandoned their country and that I don't see them. But I will not have pity on them; I will do to them what they have done to others.
Ezekiel	Then the man wearing linen clothes returned and reported to the Lord:
Man	I have carried out your orders.
Cast	[This is] the word of the Lord.
All	**Thanks be to God.**

Cast: **Ezekiel, God, Young Ezekiel, Man.**

Jerusalem is condemned
Ezekiel 11.1–13

Ezekiel	God's spirit lifted me up and took me to the east gate of the Temple. There near the gate I saw twenty-five men, including Jaazaniah son of Azzur and Pelatiah son of Benaiah, two leaders of the nation. God said to me:
God	Mortal man, these men make evil plans and give bad advice in this city. They say:
Man	We will soon be building houses again. The city is like a cooking-pot, and we are like the meat in it, but at least it protects us from the fire.
God	Now then, denounce them, mortal man.
Ezekiel	The spirit of the Lord took control of me, and the Lord told me to give the people this message:
Young Ezekiel [OR **The Lord**]	People of Israel, I know what you are saying and what you are planning. You have murdered so many people here in the city that the streets are full of corpses. So this is what I, the Sovereign Lord, am saying to you. This city is indeed a cooking-pot, but what is the meat? The corpses of those you have killed! You will not be here—I will throw you out of the city! Are you afraid of swords? I will bring men with swords to attack you. I will take you out of the city and hand you over to foreigners. I have sentenced you to death, and you will be killed in battle in your own country. Then everyone will know that I am the Lord. This city will not protect you as a pot protects the meat in it. I will punish you wherever you may be in the land of Israel. You will know that I am the Lord and that while you were keeping the laws of the neighbouring nations, you were breaking *my* laws and disobeying *my* commands.
Ezekiel	While I was prophesying, Pelatiah dropped dead. I threw myself face downwards on the ground and shouted:
Young Ezekiel	No, Sovereign Lord! Are you going to kill everyone left in Israel?
Cast	[This is] the word of the Lord.
All	**Thanks be to God.**

Cast: **Ezekiel, God, Man, Young Ezekiel, [The Lord].**

God's promise to the exiles
Ezekiel 11.14–25

Ezekiel	The Lord spoke to me:
The Lord	Mortal man, the people who live in Jerusalem are talking about you and your fellow-Israelites who are in exile. [They say:]
Person 1	The exiles are too far away to worship the Lord.
Person 2	He has given us possession of the land.
The Lord	Now tell your fellow-exiles what I am saying. I am the one who sent them to live in far-off nations and scattered them in other countries. Yet, for the time being I will be present with them in the lands where they have gone.
	So tell them what I, the Sovereign Lord, am saying. I will gather them out of the countries where I scattered them, and will give the land of Israel back to them. When they return, they are to get rid of all the filthy, disgusting idols they find. I will give them a new heart and a new mind. I will take away their stubborn heart of stone and will give them an obedient heart. Then they will keep my laws and faithfully obey all my commands. They will be my people, and I will be their God. But I will punish the people who love to worship filthy, disgusting idols. I will punish them for what they have done.
Herald (with flourish)	The Sovereign Lord has spoken. (PAUSE)
Ezekiel	The living creatures in my vision began to fly, and the wheels went with them. The dazzling light of the presence of the God of Israel was over them. Then the dazzling light left the city and moved to the mountain east of it. In the vision the spirit of God lifted me up and brought me back to the exiles in Babylonia. Then the vision faded, and I told the exiles everything that the Lord had shown me.
Cast	[This is] the word of the Lord.
All	**Thanks be to God.**

Cast: **Ezekiel, The Lord, Person 1, Person 2, Herald** (can be the same as The Lord).

God's glory leaves Jerusalem
Ezekiel 11.22—12.16

Ezekiel	The living creatures in my vision began to fly, and the wheels went with them. The dazzling light of the presence of the God of Israel was over them. Then the dazzling light left the city and moved to the mountain east of it. In the vision the spirit of God lifted me up and brought me back to the exiles in Babylonia. Then the vision faded, and I told the exiles everything that the Lord had shown me.

→

The Lord spoke to me:

The Lord Mortal man, you are living among rebellious people. They have eyes, but they see nothing; they have ears, but they hear nothing, because they are rebellious.

Now, mortal man, pack a bundle just as a refugee would, and start out before nightfall. Let everyone see you leaving and going to another place. Maybe those rebels will notice you. While it is still daylight, pack your bundle for exile, so that they can see you, and then let them watch you leave in the evening as if you were going into exile. While they are watching, break a hole through the wall of your house and take your pack out through it. Let them watch you putting your pack on your shoulder and going out into the dark with your eyes covered, so that you can't see where you are going. What you do will be a warning to the Israelites.

Ezekiel I did what the Lord told me to do. That day I packed a bundle as a refugee would, and that evening as it was getting dark I dug a hole in the wall with my hands and went out. While everyone watched, I put the pack on my shoulder and left. The next morning the Lord spoke to me:

The Lord Mortal man, now that those Israelite rebels are asking you what you're doing, tell them what I, the Sovereign Lord, am saying to them. This message is for the prince ruling in Jerusalem and for all the people who live there. Tell them that what you have done is a sign of what will happen to them—they will be refugees and captives. The prince who is ruling them will shoulder his pack in the dark and escape through a hole that they dig for him in the wall. He will cover his eyes and not see where he is going. But I will spread out my net and trap him in it. Then I will take him to the city of Babylon, where he will die without having seen it. I will scatter in every direction all the members of his court and his advisers and bodyguard, and people will search for them to kill them. When I scatter them among the other nations and in foreign countries, they will know that I am the Lord. I will let a few of them survive the war, the famine, and the diseases, so that there among the nations they will realize how disgusting their actions have been and will acknowledge that I am the Lord.

Cast [This is] the word of the Lord.
All **Thanks be to God.**

Cast: **Ezekiel, The Lord.** (This reading overlaps with the previous one.)

A popular proverb and an unpopular message
Ezekiel 12. 21–28

Ezekiel The Lord spoke to me. He said:

The Lord Mortal man, why do the people of Israel repeat this proverb:

Israelite Time goes by, and predictions come to nothing!

The Lord Now tell them what I, the Sovereign Lord, have to say about that.

I will put an end to that proverb. It won't be repeated in Israel any more. Tell them instead:

[Voice] The time has come, and the predictions are coming *true*!

Ezekiel The Sovereign Lord says:

The Lord Among the people of Israel there will be no more false visions or misleading prophecies. I, the Lord, will speak to them, and what I say will be done. There will be no more delay. In your own lifetime, you rebels, I will do what I have warned you I would do.

(with flourish) I have spoken!

Ezekiel The Lord said to me:

The Lord Mortal man, the Israelites think that your visions and prophecies are about the distant future. So tell them that I, the Sovereign Lord, am saying:

[Voice] There will be no more delay.

The Lord What I have said will be done. I, the Sovereign Lord, have spoken!

Cast [This is] the word of the Lord.
All **Thanks be to God.**

Cast: **Ezekiel, The Lord, Israelite, Voice** (can be the same as The Lord).

A parable about a vine
Ezekiel 15.1–8

Ezekiel The Lord spoke to me [He said]:

The Lord Mortal man, how does a vine compare with a tree? What good is a branch of a grapevine compared with the trees of the forest? Can you use it to make anything? Can you even make a peg out of it to hang things on? It is only good for building a fire. And when the ends are burnt up and the middle is charred, can you make anything out of it? It was useless even before it was burnt. Now that the fire has burnt it and charred it, it is even more useless.

Ezekiel Now this is what the Sovereign Lord is saying:

The Lord Just as a vine is taken from the forest and burnt, so I will take the people who live in Jerusalem and will punish them. They have escaped one fire, but now fire will burn them up. When I punish them, you will know that I am the Lord. They have been unfaithful to me, and so I will make the country a wilderness.

Ezekiel
(with flourish) The Sovereign Lord has spoken!

Cast [This is] the word of the Lord.
All **Thanks be to God.**

Cast: **Ezekiel, The Lord.**

God requires repentance
Ezekiel 18.1–4, 20–32

Ezekiel	The Lord spoke to me and said:
The Lord	What is this proverb people keep repeating in the land of Israel?
Israelite	The parents ate the sour grapes, but the children got the sour taste.
Ezekiel	The Sovereign Lord says:
The Lord	As surely as I am the living God you will not repeat this proverb in Israel any more. The life of every person belongs to me, the life of the parent as well as that of the child. The person who sins is the one who will die. A son is not to suffer because of his father's sins, nor a father because of the sins of his son. A good man will be rewarded for doing good, and an evil man will suffer for the evil he does. If an evil man stops sinning and keeps my laws, if he does what is right and good, he will not die; he will certainly live. All his sins will be forgiven, and he will live, because he did what is right.
Ezekiel	The Sovereign Lord asks:
The Lord	Do you think I enjoy seeing an evil man die? No, I would rather see him repent and live. But if a righteous man stops doing good and starts doing all the evil, disgusting things that evil men do, will he go on living? No! None of the good he did will be remembered. He will die because of his unfaithfulness and his sins. But you say:
Israelite	What the Lord does isn't right.
The Lord	Listen to me, you Israelites. Do you think my way of doing things isn't right? It is *your* way that isn't right. When a righteous man stops doing good and starts doing evil and then dies, he dies because of the evil he has done. When an evil man stops sinning and does what is right and good, he *saves* his life. He realizes what he is doing and stops sinning, so he will certainly not die, but go on living. And you Israelites say:
Israelite	What the Lord does isn't right.
The Lord	You think my way isn't right, do you? It is *your* way that isn't right. Now I, the Sovereign Lord, am telling you Israelites that I will judge each of you by what he has done. Turn away from all the evil you are doing, and don't let your sin destroy you. Give up all the evil you have been doing, and get yourselves new minds and hearts. Why do you Israelites want to die? I do not want anyone to die.
Ezekiel	The Sovereign Lord says:
The Lord	Turn away from your sins and live.
Cast	[This is] the word of the Lord.
All	**Thanks be to God.**

Cast: **Ezekiel, The Lord, Israelite.**

The death of the prophet's wife
Ezekiel 24.15–27

Ezekiel	The Lord spoke to me:
The Lord	Mortal man, with one blow I am going to take away the person you love most. You are not to complain or cry or shed any tears. Don't let your sobbing be heard. Do not go bareheaded or barefoot as a sign of mourning. Don't cover your face or eat the food that mourners eat.
Ezekiel	Early in the day I was talking with the people. That evening my wife died, and the next day I did as I had been told. (PAUSE)
	The people asked me:
Person	Why are you acting like this?
Ezekiel	So I said to them:
Young Ezekiel	The Lord spoke to me and told me to give you Israelites this message: You are proud of the strength of the Temple. You like to look at it and to visit it, but the Lord is going to profane it. And the younger members of your families who are left in Jerusalem will be killed in war. Then you will do what I have done. You will not cover your faces or eat the food that mourners eat. You will not go bareheaded or barefoot or mourn or cry. You will waste away because of your sins, and you will groan to one another. Then I will be a sign to you; you will do everything I have done. The Lord says that when this happens, you will know that he is the Sovereign Lord.
Ezekiel	The Lord said:
The Lord	Now, mortal man, I will take away from them the strong Temple that was their pride and joy, which they liked to look at and to visit. And I will take away their sons and daughters. On the day that I do this, someone who escapes the destruction will come and tell you about it. That same day you will get back the power of speech which you had lost, and you will talk with him. In this way you will be a sign to the people, and they will know that I am the Lord.
Cast	[This is] the word of the Lord.
All	**Thanks be to God.**

Cast: **Ezekiel, The Lord, Person, Young Ezekiel.**

Prophecy against Tyre
From Ezekiel 26.1–22

Ezekiel	On the first day of the month of the eleventh year of our exile in Babylon, the Lord spoke to me:
The Lord	Mortal man, this is what the people in the city of Tyre are cheering about. They shout:
Person 1	Jerusalem is shattered!

739

Person 2	Her commercial power is gone!
Person 1	She won't be our rival any more!
The Lord	Now then, this is what I, the Sovereign Lord, am saying: I am your enemy, city of Tyre. I will bring many nations to attack you, and they will come like the waves of the sea. They will destroy your city walls and tear down your towers. Then I will sweep away all the dust and leave only a bare rock. Fishermen will dry their nets on it, there where it stands in the sea. I, the Sovereign Lord, have spoken. The nations will plunder Tyre, and with their swords they will kill those who live in her towns on the mainland. Then Tyre will know that I am the Lord.
Ezekiel	The Sovereign Lord has this to say to the city of Tyre:
The Lord	When you are being conquered, the people who live along the coast will be terrified at the screams of those who are slaughtered. All the kings of the seafaring nations will come down from their thrones. They will take off their robes and their embroidered clothes and sit trembling on the ground. They will be so terrified at your fate that they will not be able to stop trembling. They will sing this funeral song for you:
Kings 1 and **2**	The famous city is destroyed!
King 1	Her ships have been swept from the seas.
King 2	The people of this city ruled the seas and terrified all who lived on the coast.
King 1	Now, on the day it has fallen, the islands are trembling,
King 2	And their people are shocked at such destruction.
Ezekiel	The Sovereign Lord says:
The Lord	I will make you as desolate as ruined cities where no one lives. I will cover you with the water of the ocean depths. I will send you down to the world of the dead to join the people who lived in ancient times. I will make you stay in that underground world among eternal ruins, keeping company with the dead. As a result you will never again be inhabited and take your place in the land of the living. I will make you a terrifying example, and that will be the end of you. People may look for you, but you will never be found.
Ezekiel (with flourish)	The Sovereign Lord has spoken!
Cast **All**	[This is] the word of the Lord. **Thanks be to God.**

Cast: **Ezekiel, The Lord, Person 1, Person 2, King 1, King 2.**

Egypt is compared to a cedar tree
From Ezekiel 31.1–18

Ezekiel On the first day of the third month of the eleventh year of our exile in Babylon, the Lord spoke to me:

The Lord Mortal man, say to the king of Egypt and all his people—

Singer How powerful you are!
What can I compare you to?
You are like a cedar in Lebanon,
with beautiful, shady branches,
a tree so tall it reaches the clouds.
There was water to make it grow,
and underground rivers to feed it.
They watered the place where the tree was growing
and sent streams to all the trees of the forest.
Because it was well-watered,
it grew taller than other trees.
Its branches grew thick and long.
Every kind of bird built nests in its branches;
the wild animals bore their young in its shelter;
the nations of the world rested in its shade.
How beautiful the tree was—
so tall, with such long branches.
Its roots reached down to the deep-flowing streams.
No cedar in God's garden could compare with it.
No fir-tree ever had such branches,
and no plane-tree such boughs.
No tree in God's own garden was so beautiful.
I made it beautiful, with spreading branches.
It was the envy of every tree in Eden, the garden of God.

The Lord Now then, I, the Sovereign Lord, will tell you what is going to happen to that tree that grew until it reached the clouds. As it grew taller it grew proud; so I have rejected it and will let a foreign ruler have it. He will give that tree what it deserves for its wickedness. Ruthless foreigners will cut it down and leave it.

Ezekiel The Sovereign Lord says:

The Lord The tree is the king of Egypt and all his people. Not even the trees in Eden were so tall and impressive. But now, like the trees of Eden, it will go down to the world of the dead and join the ungodly and those killed in battle. (PAUSE) I have spoken!

Cast [This is] the word of the Lord.
All **Thanks be to God.**

Cast: **Ezekiel, The Lord, Singer.**

Individual responsibility
From Ezekiel 33.10–19

Ezekiel	The Lord spoke to me [He said]:
The Lord	Mortal man, repeat to the Israelites what they are saying—
Israelite 1	We are burdened with our sins and the wrongs we have done.
Israelite 2	We are wasting away.
Israelites 1 and **2**	How can we live?
The Lord	Tell them that as surely as I, the Sovereign Lord, am the living God, I do not enjoy seeing a sinner die. I would rather see him stop sinning and live. If an evil man stops sinning and does what is right and good—for example, if he returns the security he took for a loan or gives back what he stole—if he stops sinning and follows the laws that give life, he will not die, but live. I will forgive the sins he has committed, and he will live because he has done what is right and good.
(deliberately)	When an evil man gives up sinning and does what is right and good, he has saved his life.
Cast	[This is] the word of the Lord.
All	**Thanks be to God.**

Cast: **Ezekiel, The Lord, Israelite 1, Israelite 2** (can be the same as Israelite 1).

Jerusalem's fall and Israel's peril
Ezekiel 33.21–29

Ezekiel	On the fifth day of the tenth month of the twelfth year of our exile in Babylon, a man who had escaped from Jerusalem came and told me that the city had fallen. The evening before he came, I had felt the powerful presence of the Lord. When the man arrived the next morning, the Lord gave me back the power of speech. (PAUSE)
	The Lord spoke to me:
The Lord	Mortal man, the people who are living in the ruined cities of the land of Israel are saying—
Person 1	Abraham was only one man, and he was given the whole land.
Person 2	There are many of us, so now the land is ours.
The Lord	Tell them what I, the Sovereign Lord, am saying: You eat meat with the blood still in it. You worship idols. You commit murder. What makes you think that the land belongs to you? You rely on your swords. Your actions are disgusting. Everyone commits adultery. What makes you think that the land is yours?
	Tell them that I, the Sovereign Lord, warn them that as surely as I am the living God, the people who live in the ruined cities will be killed. Those living in the country will be eaten by wild animals. Those hiding in the mountains and in caves will die of disease. I

will make the country a desolate waste, and the power they were so proud of will come to an end. The mountains of Israel will be so wild that no one will be able to travel through them. When I punish the people for their sins and make the country a waste, then they will know that I am the Lord.

| Cast | [This is] the word of the Lord. |
| All | **Thanks be to God.** |

Cast: **Ezekiel, The Lord, Person 1, Person 2.**

The results of the prophet's message
Ezekiel 33.30–33

Ezekiel	The Lord said:
The Lord	Mortal man, your people are talking about you when they meet by the city walls or in the doorways of their houses. They say to one another:
Person	Let's go and hear what word has come from the Lord now.
The Lord	So my people crowd in to hear what you have to say, but they don't do what you tell them to do. Loving words are on their lips, but they continue their greedy ways. To them you are nothing more than an entertainer singing love songs or playing a harp. They listen to all your words and don't obey a single one of them. But when all your words come true—and they will come true—then they will know that a prophet has been among them.

| Cast | [This is] the word of the Lord. |
| All | **Thanks be to God.** |

Cast: **Ezekiel, The Lord, Person.**

The shepherds of Israel
Ezekiel 34.1–10

Ezekiel	The Lord spoke to me:
The Lord	Mortal man, denounce the rulers of Israel. Prophesy to them, and tell them what I, the Sovereign Lord, say to them:
Voice of Ezekiel	You are doomed, you shepherds of Israel! You take care of yourselves, but never tend the sheep. You drink the milk, wear clothes made from the wool, and kill and eat the finest sheep. But you never *tend* the sheep. You have not taken care of the weak ones, healed those that are sick, bandaged those that are hurt, brought back those that wandered off, or looked for those that were lost. Instead, you treated them cruelly. Because the sheep had no shepherd, they were scattered, and wild animals killed and ate them.

743

The Lord	So my sheep wandered over the high hills and the mountains. They were scattered over the face of the earth, and no one looked for them or tried to find them.
	Now, you shepherds, listen to what I, the Lord, am telling you. As surely as I am the living God, you had better listen to me. My sheep have been attacked by wild animals that killed and ate them because there was no shepherd. My shepherds did not try to find the sheep. They were taking care of themselves and not the sheep. So listen to me, you shepherds. I, the Sovereign Lord, declare that I am your enemy. I will take my sheep away from you and never again let you be their shepherds; never again will I let you take care only of yourselves. I will rescue my sheep from you and not let you eat them.
Cast	[This is] the word of the Lord.
All	**Thanks be to God.**

Cast: **Ezekiel, The Lord, Voice of Ezekiel.**

The good shepherd
Ezekiel 34.11–31

Voice 1	I, the Sovereign Lord, tell you that I myself will look for my sheep and take care of them in the same way as a shepherd takes care of his sheep that were scattered and are brought together again.
Voice 2	I will bring them back from all the places where they were scattered on that dark, disastrous day.
Voice 3	I will take them out of foreign countries, gather them together, and bring them back to their own land.
Voice 1	I will lead them back to the mountains and the streams of Israel and will feed them in pleasant pastures.
Voice 2	I will let them graze in safety in the mountain meadows and the valleys and in all the green pastures of the land of Israel.
Voice 3	I myself will be the shepherd of my sheep, and I will find them a place to rest.
Voices 1–3	I, the Sovereign Lord, have spoken.
Voice 1	I will look for those that are lost, bring back those that wander off, bandage those that are hurt, and heal those that are sick.
Voice 2	But those that are fat and strong I will destroy, because I am a shepherd who does what is right.
Voice 3	Now then, my flock, I, the Sovereign Lord, tell you that I will judge each of you and separate the good from the bad, the sheep from the goats.
Voice 1	Some of you are not satisfied with eating the best grass; you even trample down what you don't eat!

Voice 2	You drink the clear water, and muddy what you don't drink!
Voice 3	My other sheep have to eat the grass you trample down, and drink the water you muddy.
Voice 1	So now, I, the Sovereign Lord, tell you that I will judge between you strong sheep and the weak sheep.
Voice 2	You pushed the sick ones aside and butted them away from the flock.
Voice 3	But I will rescue my sheep and not let them be ill-treated any more.
Voice 1	I will judge each of my sheep and separate the good from the bad.
Voice 2	I will give them a king like my servant David to be their one shepherd, and he will take care of them.
Voice 3	I, the Lord, will be their God, and a king like my servant David will be their ruler.
Voices 1–3	I have spoken.
Voice 1	I will make a covenant with them that guarantees their security.
Voice 2	I will get rid of all the dangerous animals in the land, so that my sheep can live safely in the fields and sleep in the forests.
Voice 3	I will bless them and let them live round my sacred hill.
Voice 1	There I will bless them with showers of rain when they need it. The trees will bear fruit, the fields will produce crops, and everyone will live in safety on his own land. When I break my people's chains and set them free from those who made them slaves, then they will know that I am the Lord.
Voice 2	The heathen nations will not plunder them any more, and the wild animals will not kill and eat them. They will live in safety, and no one will terrify them.
Voice 3	I will give them fertile fields and put an end to hunger in the land. The other nations will not sneer at them any more. Everyone will know that I protect Israel and that they are my people.
Voices 1–3	I, the Sovereign Lord, have spoken.
Voice 1	The Sovereign Lord says:
Voice 2	You, my sheep, the flock that I feed, are my people, and I am your God.
Cast	[This is] the word of the Lord.
All	**Thanks be to God.**

Cast: **Voice 1, Voice 2, Voice 3.**

The valley of dry bones
From Ezekiel 37.1–14

Ezekiel I felt the powerful presence of the Lord, and his spirit took me and set me down in a valley where the ground was covered with bones. He led me all round the valley, and I could see that there were very many bones and that they were very dry. [He said to me:]

The Lord Mortal man, can these bones come back to life?

Ezekiel [I replied:] Sovereign Lord, only you can answer that! [He said:]

The Lord Prophesy to the bones. Tell these dry bones to listen to the word of the Lord. Tell them that I, the Sovereign Lord, am saying to them, 'I am going to put breath into you and bring you back to life. I will give you sinews and muscles, and cover you with skin. I will put breath into you and bring you back to life. Then you will know that I am the Lord.'

Ezekiel So I prophesied as I had been told. While I was speaking, I heard a rattling noise, and the bones began to join together. While I watched, the bones were covered with sinews and muscles, and then with skin. But there was no breath in the bodies.

God said to me:

The Lord Mortal man, prophesy to the wind. Tell the wind that the Sovereign Lord commands it to come from every direction, to breathe into these dead bodies, and to bring them back to life.

Ezekiel So I prophesied as I had been told. Breath entered the bodies, and they came to life and stood up. There were enough of them to form an army.

God said to me:

The Lord Mortal man, the people of Israel are like these bones. They say that they are dried up, without any hope and with no future. So prophesy to my people Israel and tell them that I, the Sovereign Lord, am going to open their graves. I am going to take them out and bring them back to the land of Israel. When I open the graves where my people are buried and bring them out, they will know that I am the Lord. I will put my breath in them, bring them back to life, and let them live in their own land. Then they will know that I am the Lord.

(deliberately) I have promised that I would do this—and I will. (PAUSE) I, the Lord, have spoken!

Cast [This is] the word of the Lord.
All **Thanks be to God.**

Cast: **Ezekiel, The Lord.**

Ezekiel is taken to the Temple
From Ezekiel 40.1—41.22 [41.23—42.14]

Ezekiel It was the tenth day of the new year, which was the twenty-fifth year after we had been taken into exile and the fourteenth year after Jerusalem was captured. On that day I felt the powerful presence of the Lord, and he carried me away. In a vision God took me to the land of Israel and put me on a high mountain. I saw in front of me a group of buildings that looked like a city. He took me closer, and I saw a man who shone like bronze. He was holding a linen tape-measure and a measuring-rod and was standing by a gateway. He said to me:

Man Watch, mortal man. Listen carefully and pay close attention to everything I show you, because this is why you were brought here. You are to tell the people of Israel everything you see.

Ezekiel What I saw was the Temple, and there was a wall round it. The man took his measuring-rod, which was three metres long, and measured the wall. It was three metres high and three metres thick.

The man took me through the gateway into the courtyard. There were thirty rooms built against the outer wall, and in front of them there was an area paved with stones, which extended round the courtyard.

Then the man measured the gateway on the north side that led into the outer courtyard.

Next, the man took me to the south side, and there we saw another gateway. He measured it, and it was the same as the others.

The man took me through the east gateway into the inner courtyard. He measured the gateway, and it was the same size as the others.

Then the man took me to the north gateway. He measured it, and it was the same size as the others.

The man measured the inner courtyard, and it was fifty metres square. The Temple was on the west side, and in front of it was an altar.

Next, the man took me into the central room, the Holy Place.

This room was beyond the central room. Then he said to me:

Man This is the Most Holy Place.

Ezekiel The man measured the outside of the Temple, and it was fifty metres long. And from the back of the Temple, across the open space to the far side of the building to the west, the distance was also fifty metres. The distance across the front of the Temple, including the open space on either side was also fifty metres. He measured the length of the building to the west, including its corridors on both sides, and it was also fifty metres.

→

The entrance room of the Temple, the Holy Place, and the Most Holy Place were all panelled with wood from the floor to the windows. These windows could be covered. The inside walls of the Temple, up as high as above the doors, were completely covered with carvings of palm-trees and winged creatures. Palm-trees alternated with creatures, one following the other, all the way round the room. Each creature had two faces: a human face that was turned towards the palm-tree on one side, and a lion's face that was turned towards the tree on the other side. It was like this all round the wall, from the floor to above the doors. The door-posts of the Holy Place were square.

In front of the entrance of the Most Holy Place there was something that looked like a wooden altar. It was one and a half metres high and one metre wide. Its corner-posts, its base, and its sides were all made of wood. The man said to me:

Man   This is the table which stands in the presence of the Lord.

[Ezekiel   There was a door at the end of the passage leading to the Holy Place and one also at the end of the passage leading to the Most Holy Place. They were double doors that swung open in the middle. There were palm-trees and winged creatures carved on the doors of the Holy Place, just as there were on the walls. And there was a wooden covering over the outside of the doorway of the entrance room. At the sides of this room there were windows, and the walls were decorated with palm-trees.

The man said to me:

Man   Both these buildings are holy. In them the priests who enter the Lord's presence eat the holiest offerings. Because the rooms are holy, the priests will place the holiest offerings there: the grain-offerings and the sacrifices offered for sin or as repayment-offerings. When priests have been in the Temple and want to go to the outer courtyard, they must leave in these rooms the holy clothing they wore while serving the Lord. They must put on other clothes before going out to the area where the people gather.]

Cast   [This is] the word of the Lord.
All   **Thanks be to God.**

Cast: **Ezekiel, Man.**

The Lord returns to the Temple
Ezekiel 43.1–9

Ezekiel   In my vision the man took me to the gate of the Temple that faces east, and there I saw coming from the east the dazzling light of the presence of the God of Israel. God's voice sounded like the roar of the sea, and the earth shone with the dazzling light. This vision was like the one I had seen when God came to destroy Jerusalem, and the one I saw by the River Chebar. Then I threw myself face downwards on the ground. The dazzling light passed through the east gate and went into the Temple.

The Lord's spirit lifted me up and took me into the inner courtyard, where I saw that the Temple was filled with the glory of the Lord. The man stood beside me there, and I heard the Lord speak to me out of the Temple:

The Lord   Mortal man, here is my throne. I will live here among the people of Israel and rule over them for ever. Neither the people of Israel nor their kings will ever again disgrace my holy name by worshipping other gods or by burying the corpses of their kings in this place. The kings built the thresholds and door-posts of their palace right against the thresholds and door-posts of my Temple, so that there was only a wall between us. They disgraced my holy name by all the disgusting things they did, and so in my anger I destroyed them. Now they must stop worshipping other gods and remove the corpses of their kings. If they do, I will live among them for ever.

Cast   [This is] the word of the Lord.
All   **Thanks be to God.**

Cast: **Ezekiel, The Lord.**

Rules for admission to the Temple
Ezekiel 44.1–5

Ezekiel   In my vision the man led me to the outer gate at the east side of the Temple area. The gate was closed, and the Lord said to me:

The Lord   This gate will stay closed and will never be opened. No human being is allowed to use it, because I, the Lord God of Israel, have entered through it. It is to remain closed. The ruling prince, however, may go there to eat a holy meal in my presence. He is to enter and leave the gateway through the entrance room at the inner end.

Ezekiel   Then the man took me through the north gate to the front of the Temple. As I looked, I saw that the Temple of the Lord was filled with the dazzling light of his presence. I threw myself face downwards on the ground, and the Lord said to me:

The Lord   Mortal man, pay attention to everything you see and hear. I am going to tell you the rules and regulations for the Temple. Note carefully which persons are allowed to go in and out of the Temple and which persons are not.

Cast   [This is] the word of the Lord.
All   **Thanks be to God.**

Cast: **Ezekiel, The Lord.**

The stream flowing from the Temple
Ezekiel 47.1–12

Ezekiel In my vision the man led me back to the entrance of the Temple. Water was coming out from under the entrance and flowing east, the direction the Temple faced. It was flowing down from under the south part of the Temple past the south side of the altar. The man then took me out of the temple area by way of the north gate and led me round to the gate that faces east. A small stream of water was flowing out at the south side of the gate. With his measuring-rod the man measured five hundred metres downstream to the east and told me to wade through the stream there. The water came only to my ankles. Then he measured another five hundred metres, and the water came up to my knees. Another five hundred metres further down, the water was up to my waist. He measured five hundred metres more, and there the stream was so deep I could not wade through it. It was too deep to cross except by swimming. He said to me:

Man Mortal man, note all this carefully.

Ezekiel Then the man took me back to the bank of the river, and when I got there I saw that there were very many trees on each bank. He said to me:

Man This water flows through the land to the east and down into the Jordan Valley and to the Dead Sea. When it flows into the Dead Sea, it replaces the salt water of that sea with fresh water. Wherever the stream flows, there will be all kinds of animals and fish. The stream will make the water of the Dead Sea fresh, and wherever it flows, it will bring life. From the Springs of Engedi all the way to the Springs of Eneglaim, there will be fishermen on the shore of the sea, and they will spread out their nets there to dry. There will be as many different kinds of fish there as there are in the Mediterranean Sea. But the water in the marshes and ponds along the shore will not be made fresh. They will remain there as a source of salt. On each bank of the stream all kinds of trees will grow to provide food. Their leaves will never wither, and they will never stop bearing fruit. They will have fresh fruit every month, because they are watered by the stream that flows from the Temple. The trees will provide food, and their leaves will be used for healing people.

Cast [This is] the word of the Lord.
All **Thanks be to God.**

Cast: **Ezekiel, Man.**

DANIEL

The young men at Nebuchadnezzar's court
Daniel 1.1–21

Narrator 1	In the third year that Jehoiakim was king of Judah, King Nebuchadnezzar of Babylonia attacked Jerusalem and surrounded the city.
Narrator 2	The Lord let him capture King Jehoiakim and seize some of the temple treasures. He took some prisoners back with him to the temple of his gods in Babylon, and put the captured treasures in the temple storerooms.
Narrator 1	The king ordered Ashpenaz, his chief official, to select from among the Israelite exiles some young men of the royal family and of the noble families. They had to be handsome, intelligent, well-trained, quick to learn, and free from physical defects, so that they would be qualified to serve in the royal court. Ashpenaz was to teach them to read and write the Babylonian language.
Narrator 2	The king also gave orders that every day they were to be given the same food and wine as the members of the royal court. After three years of this training they were to appear before the king.
Narrator 1	Among those chosen were Daniel, Hananiah, Mishael, and Azariah, all of whom were from the tribe of Judah. The chief official gave them new names: Belteshazzar, Shadrach, Meshach, and Abednego.
Narrator 2	Daniel made up his mind not to let himself become ritually unclean by eating the food and drinking the wine of the royal court, so he asked Ashpenaz to help him, and God made Ashpenaz sympathetic to Daniel. Ashpenaz, however, was afraid of the king, so he said to Daniel:
Ashpenaz	The king has decided what you are to eat and drink, and if you don't look as fit as the other young men, he may kill me.
Narrator 2	So Daniel went to the guard whom Ashpenaz had placed in charge of him and his three friends. He said:
Daniel	Test us for ten days. Give us vegetables to eat and water to drink. Then compare us with the young men who are eating the food of the royal court, and base your decision on how we look.
Narrator 2	He agreed to let them try it for ten days.
Narrator 1	When the time was up, they looked healthier and stronger than all those who had been eating the royal food. So from then on the guard let them continue to eat vegetables instead of what the king provided.

Narrator 2	God gave the four young men knowledge and skill in literature and philosophy. In addition, he gave Daniel skill in interpreting visions and dreams.
Narrator 1	At the end of the three years set by the king, Ashpenaz took all the young men to Nebuchadnezzar. The king talked with them all, and Daniel, Hananiah, Mishael, and Azariah impressed him more than any of the others.
Narrator 2	So they became members of the king's court. No matter what question the king asked, or what problem he raised, these four knew ten times more than any fortune-teller or magician in his whole kingdom.
Narrator 1	Daniel remained at the royal court until Cyrus the emperor of Persia conquered Babylonia.
Cast	[This is] the word of the Lord.
All	**Thanks be to God.**

Cast: **Narrator 1, Narrator 2, Ashpenaz, Daniel.**

Nebuchadnezzar's dream
Daniel 2.1–13

Narrator	In the second year that Nebuchadnezzar was king, he had a dream. It worried him so much that he couldn't sleep, so he sent for his fortune-tellers, magicians, sorcerers, and wizards to come and explain the dream to him. When they came and stood before the king, he said to them:
Nebuchadnezzar	I'm worried about a dream I have had. I want to know what it means.
Narrator	They answered the king in Aramaic:
Adviser	May Your Majesty live for ever! Tell us your dream, and we will explain it to you.
Narrator	The king said to them:
Nebuchadnezzar	I have made up my mind that you must tell me the dream and then tell me what it means. If you can't, I'll have you torn limb from limb and make your houses a pile of ruins. But if you can tell me both the dream and its meaning, I will reward you with gifts and great honour. Now then, tell me what the dream was and what it means.
Narrator	They answered the king again:
Adviser	If Your Majesty will only tell us what the dream was, we will explain it.
Narrator	At that, the king exclaimed:
Nebuchadnezzar	Just as I thought! You are trying to gain time, because you see that I have made up my mind to give all of you the same punishment if you don't tell me the dream. You have agreed among yourselves

	to go on telling me lies because you hope that in time things will change. Tell me what the dream was, and then I will know that you can also tell me what it means.
Narrator	The advisers replied:
Adviser	There is no one on the face of the earth who can tell Your Majesty what you want to know. No king, not even the greatest and most powerful, has ever made such a demand of his fortune-tellers, magicians, and wizards. What Your Majesty is asking for is so difficult that no one can do it for you except the gods, and they do not live among human beings.
Narrator	At that, the king flew into a rage and ordered the execution of all the royal advisers in Babylon. So the order was issued for all of them to be killed, including Daniel and his friends.
Cast	[This is] the word of the Lord.
All	**Thanks be to God.**

Cast: **Narrator, Nebuchadnezzar, Adviser.**

God shows Daniel what the dream means
Daniel 2.14–23

Narrator	[Then] Daniel went to Arioch, commander of the king's bodyguard, who had been ordered to carry out the execution of all the royal advisers. Choosing his words carefully, he asked Arioch why the king had issued such a harsh order. So Arioch told Daniel what had happened. Daniel went at once and obtained royal permission for more time, so that he could tell the king what the dream meant. Then Daniel went home and told his friends Hananiah, Mishael, and Azariah what had happened. He told them to pray to the God of heaven for mercy and to ask him to explain the mystery to them so that they would not be killed along with the other advisers in Babylon. Then that same night the mystery was revealed to Daniel in a vision, and he praised the God of heaven:
Daniel	God is wise and powerful! Praise him for ever and ever. He controls the times and the seasons; he makes and unmakes kings; it is he who gives wisdom and understanding. He reveals things that are deep and secret; he knows what is hidden in darkness, and he himself is surrounded by light. I praise you and honour you, God of my ancestors. You have given me wisdom and strength; you have answered my prayer and shown us what to tell the king.
Cast	[This is] the word of the Lord.
All	**Thanks be to God.**

Cast: **Narrator, Daniel.**

Daniel tells the king the dream and explains it
Daniel 2.24–49

Narrator   [So] Daniel went to Arioch, whom the king had commanded to execute the royal advisers. He said to him:

Daniel   Don't put them to death. Take me to the king, and I will tell him what his dream means.

Narrator   At once Arioch took Daniel into King Nebuchadnezzar's presence and told the king:

Arioch   I have found one of the Jewish exiles, who can tell Your Majesty the meaning of your dream.

Narrator   The king said to Daniel:

King   Can you tell me what I dreamt and what it means?

Narrator   Daniel replied:

Daniel   Your Majesty, there is no wizard, magician, fortune-teller, or astrologer who can tell you that. But there is a God in heaven, who reveals mysteries. He has informed Your Majesty what will happen in the future. Now I will tell you the dream, the vision you had while you were asleep.

While Your Majesty was sleeping, you dreamt about the future; and God, who reveals mysteries, showed you what is going to happen. Now, this mystery was revealed to me, not because I am wiser than anyone else, but so that Your Majesty may learn the meaning of your dream and understand the thoughts that have come to you.

Your Majesty, in your vision you saw standing before you a giant statue, bright and shining, and terrifying to look at. Its head was made of the finest gold; its chest and arms were made of silver; its waist and hips of bronze; its legs of iron, and its feet partly of iron and partly of clay. While you were looking at it, a great stone broke loose from a cliff without anyone touching it, struck the iron and clay feet of the statue, and shattered them. At once the iron, clay, bronze, silver, and gold crumbled and became like the dust on a threshing-place in summer. The wind carried it all away, leaving not a trace. But the stone grew to be a mountain that covered the whole earth.

This was the dream. Now I will tell Your Majesty what it means. Your Majesty, you are the greatest of all kings. The God of heaven has made you emperor and given you power, might, and honour. He has made you ruler of all the inhabited earth and ruler over all the animals and birds. You are the head of gold. After you there will be another empire, not as great as yours, and after that a third, an empire of bronze, which will rule the whole earth. And then there will be a fourth empire, as strong as iron, which shatters and breaks everything. And just as iron shatters everything, it will shatter and crush all the earlier empires. You also saw that the feet and the toes were partly clay and partly iron. This means that it will be a divided empire. It will have something of the strength of iron, because there was iron mixed with the clay. The toes—partly iron and partly clay—mean that part of the empire will be strong and part of it weak. You also saw that the iron was mixed with the clay. This means that the rulers of that empire will try to unite their families by intermarriage, but they will not be able to, any more than iron can mix with clay. At the time of those rulers the God of heaven will establish a kingdom that will never end. It will never be conquered, but will completely destroy all those empires, and then last for ever. You saw how a stone broke loose from a cliff without anyone touching it and how it struck the statue made of iron, bronze, clay, silver, and gold. The great God is telling Your Majesty what will happen in the future. I have told you exactly what you dreamt, and have given you its true meaning.

Narrator   Then King Nebuchadnezzar bowed to the ground and gave orders for sacrifices and offerings to be made to Daniel. The king said:

King   Your God is the greatest of all gods, the Lord over kings, and the one who reveals mysteries. I know this because you have been able to explain this mystery.

Narrator   Then he gave Daniel a high position, presented him with many splendid gifts, put him in charge of the province of Babylon, and made him the head of all the royal advisers. At Daniel's request the king put Shadrach, Meshach, and Abednego in charge of the affairs of the province of Babylon; Daniel, however, remained at the royal court.

Cast   [This is] the word of the Lord.
All   **Thanks be to God.**

Cast: **Narrator, Daniel, Arioch, King.**

Nebuchadnezzar commands everyone to worship a gold statue
Daniel 3.1–7

Narrator   King Nebuchadnezzar had a gold statue made, twenty-seven metres high and nearly three metres wide, and he had it set up in the plain of Dura in the province of Babylon. Then the king gave orders for all his officials to come together—the princes, governors, lieutenant-governors, commissioners, treasurers, judges, magistrates, and all the other officials of the provinces. They were to attend the dedication of the statue which King Nebuchadnezzar had set up. When all these officials gathered for the dedication and stood in front of the statue, a herald announced in a loud voice:

Herald   People of all nations, races, and languages! You will hear the
(calling)   sound of the trumpets, followed by the playing of oboes, lyres, zithers, and harps; and then all the other instruments will join in.

$\rightarrow$

As soon as the music starts, you are to bow down and worship the gold statue that King Nebuchadnezzar has set up. Anyone who does not bow down and worship will immediately be thrown into a blazing furnace.

Narrator   And so, as soon as they heard the sound of the instruments, the people of all the nations, races, and languages bowed down and worshipped the gold statue which King Nebuchadnezzar had set up.

Cast   [This is] the word of the Lord.
All   **Thanks be to God.**

Cast: **Narrator, Herald.**

Daniel's three friends are accused of disobedience
Daniel 3.7–18

Narrator   [Peoples of all nations, races, and languages bowed down and worshipped the gold statue which King Nebuchadnezzar had set up.] It was then that some Babylonians took the opportunity to denounce the Jews. They said to King Nebuchadnezzar:

Babylonian   May Your Majesty live for ever! Your Majesty has issued an order that as soon as the music starts, everyone is to bow down and worship the gold statue, and that anyone who does not bow down and worship it is to be thrown into a blazing furnace. There are some Jews whom you put in charge of the province of Babylon—Shadrach, Meshach, and Abednego—who are disobeying Your Majesty's orders. They do not worship your god or bow down to the statue you set up.

Narrator   At that, the king flew into a rage and ordered the three men to be brought before him. He said to them:

King
(angrily)   Shadrach, Meshach, and Abednego, is it true that you refuse to worship my god and to bow down to the gold statue I have set up? Now then, as soon as you hear the sound of the trumpets, oboes, lyres, zithers, harps, and all the other instruments, bow down and worship the statue. If you do not, you will immediately be thrown into a blazing furnace. Do you think there is any god who can save you?

Narrator   Shadrach, Meshach, and Abednego answered:

Shadrach   Your Majesty, we will not try to defend ourselves. If the God whom we serve is able to save us from the blazing furnace and from your power, then he will. But even if he doesn't, Your Majesty may be sure that we will not worship your god, and we will not bow down to the gold statue that you have set up.

Cast   [This is] the word of the Lord.
All   **Thanks be to God.**

Cast: **Narrator, Babylonian, King, Shadrach.** (This reading overlaps with the previous one.)

Daniel's three friends in the furnace
Daniel 3.19–30

Narrator
[Then] Nebuchadnezzar lost his temper, and his face turned red with anger at Shadrach, Meshach, and Abednego who refused to worship his god or bow down to the statue he had set up. He ordered his men to heat the furnace seven times hotter than usual. And he commanded the strongest men in his army to tie the three men up and throw them into the blazing furnace. So they tied them up, fully dressed—shirts, robes, caps, and all—and threw them into the blazing furnace. Now because the king had given strict orders for the furnace to be made extremely hot, the flames burnt up the guards who took the men to the furnace. Then Shadrach, Meshach, and Abednego, still tied up, fell into the heart of the blazing fire.

Suddenly Nebuchadnezzar leapt to his feet in amazement [He asked his officials]:

Nebuchadnezzar
Didn't we tie up three men and throw them into the blazing furnace?

Officials 1 & 2
Yes, we did, Your Majesty.

Nebuchadnezzar
Then why do I see four men walking about in the fire? They are not tied up, and they show no sign of being hurt—and the fourth one looks like an angel.

Narrator
So Nebuchadnezzar went up to the door of the blazing furnace [and called out]:

Nebuchadnezzar
(calling)
Shadrach! Meshach! Abednego! Servants of the Supreme God! Come out!

Narrator
And they came out at once. All the princes, governors, lieutenant-governors, and other officials of the king gathered to look at the three men, who had not been harmed by the fire. Their hair was not singed, their clothes were not burnt, and there was no smell of smoke on them.

[Narrator
The king said:]

Nebuchadnezzar
(amazed)
Praise the God of Shadrach, Meshach, and Abednego! He sent his angel and rescued these men who serve and trust him. They disobeyed my orders and risked their lives rather than bow down and worship any god except their own. (PAUSE)

And now I command that if anyone of any nation, race, or language speaks disrespectfully of the God of Shadrach, Meshach, and Abednego, he is to be torn limb from limb, and his house is to be made a pile of ruins. There is no other god who can rescue like this.

Narrator	And the king promoted Shadrach, Meshach, and Abednego to higher positions in the province of Babylon.
Cast	[This is] the word of the Lord.
All	**Thanks be to God.**

Cast: **Narrator, Nebuchadnezzar, Official 1, Official 2.**

Nebuchadnezzar's second dream
Daniel 4.1–18

Narrator	King Nebuchadnezzar sent the following message to the people of all nations, races, and languages in the world:
Messenger	[Greetings!] Listen to my account of the wonders and miracles which the Supreme God has shown me.
Singer	How great are the wonders God shows us! How powerful are the miracles he performs! God is king for ever; he will rule for all time.
Messenger	I was living comfortably in my palace, enjoying great prosperity. But I had a frightening dream and saw terrifying visions while I was asleep. I ordered all the royal advisers in Babylon to be brought to me so that they could tell me what the dream meant. Then all the fortune-tellers, magicians, wizards, and astrologers were brought in, and I told them my dream, but they could not explain it to me. Then Daniel came in. The spirit of the holy gods is in him, so I told him what I had dreamt. I said to him:
Nebuchadnezzar	Daniel, chief of the fortune-tellers, I know that the spirit of the holy gods is in you, and that you understand all mysteries. This is my dream. Tell me what it means.
	While I was asleep, I had a vision of a huge tree in the middle of the earth. It grew bigger and bigger until it reached the sky and could be seen by everyone in the world. Its leaves were beautiful, and it was loaded down with fruit—enough for the whole world to eat. Wild animals rested in its shade, birds built nests in its branches, and every kind of living being ate its fruit.
	While I was thinking about the vision, I saw coming down from heaven an angel, alert and watchful. He proclaimed in a loud voice:
Angel	Cut the tree down and chop off its branches; strip off its leaves and scatter its fruit. Drive the animals from under it and the birds out of its branches. But leave the stump in the ground with a band of iron and bronze round it. Leave it there in the field with the grass.
	Now let the dew fall on this man, and let him live with the animals and the plants. For seven years he will not have a human mind, but the mind of an animal. This is the decision of the alert and

watchful angels. So then, let all people everywhere know that the Supreme God has power over human kingdoms and that he can give them to anyone he chooses—even to the least important of men.

Nebuchadnezzar This is the dream I had. Now, Daniel, tell me what it means. None of my royal advisers could tell me, but you can, because the spirit of the holy gods is in you.

Cast [This is] the word of the Lord.
All **Thanks be to God.**

Cast: **Narrator, Messenger, Singer, Nebuchadnezzar, Angel.**

Daniel explains the dream
Daniel 4.19–33

Narrator Daniel, was so alarmed at the implications of King Nebuchadnezzar's dream that he could not say anything. The king said to him:

Nebuchadnezzar Daniel, don't let the dream and its message alarm you.

Narrator Daniel replied:

Daniel Your Majesty, I wish that the dream and its explanation applied to your enemies and not to you. The tree, so tall that it reached the sky, could be seen by everyone in the world. Its leaves were beautiful, and it had enough fruit on it to feed the whole world. Wild animals rested under it, and birds made their nests in its branches. Your Majesty, you are the tree, tall and strong. You have grown so great that you reach the sky, and your power extends over the whole world. While Your Majesty was watching, an angel came down from heaven and said:

Angel Cut the tree down and destroy it, but leave the stump in the ground. Wrap a band of iron and bronze round it, and leave it there in the field with the grass. Let the dew fall on this man, and let him live there with the animals for seven years.

Daniel This, then, is what it means, Your Majesty, and this is what the Supreme God has declared will happen to you. You will be driven away from human society and will live with wild animals. For seven years you will eat grass like an ox, and sleep in the open air, where the dew will fall on you. Then you will admit that the Supreme God controls all human kingdoms, and that he can give them to anyone he chooses. The angel ordered the stump to be left in the ground. This means that you will become king again when you acknowledge that God rules all the world. So then, Your Majesty, follow my advice. Stop sinning, do what is right, and be merciful to the poor. Then you will continue to be prosperous.

Narrator All this did happen to King Nebuchadnezzar. Only twelve months later, while he was walking about on the roof of his royal palace in Babylon, he said:

Nebuchadnezzar	Look how great Babylon is! I built it as my capital city to display my power and might, my glory and majesty.
Narrator	Before the words were out of his mouth, a voice spoke from heaven:
Voice	King Nebuchadnezzar, listen to what I say! Your royal power is now taken away from you. You will be driven away from human society, live with wild animals, and eat grass like an ox for seven years. Then you will acknowledge that the Supreme God has power over human kingdoms and that he can give them to anyone he chooses.
Narrator	The words came true immediately. Nebuchadnezzar was driven out of human society and ate grass like an ox. The dew fell on his body, and his hair grew as long as eagles' feathers and his nails as long as birds' claws.
Cast	[This is] the word of the Lord.
All	**Thanks be to God.**

Cast: **Narrator, Nebuchadnezzar, Daniel, Angel, Voice.**

Nebuchadnezzar praises God
Daniel 4.34–37

[Narrator	King Nebuchadnezzar said:]
Nebuchadnezzar	When the seven years had passed I looked up at the sky, and my sanity returned. I praised the Supreme God and gave honour and glory to the one who lives for ever.
Singer	He will rule for ever, and his kingdom will last for all time. He looks on the people of the earth as nothing; angels in heaven and people on earth are under his control. No one can oppose his will or question what he does.
Nebuchadnezzar	When my sanity returned, my honour, my majesty, and the glory of my kingdom were given back to me. My officials and my noblemen welcomed me, and I was given back my royal power, with even greater honour than before. And now, I, Nebuchadnezzar, praise, honour, and glorify the King of Heaven. Everything he does is right and just, and he can humble anyone who acts proudly.
Cast	[This is] the word of the Lord.
All	**Thanks be to God.**

Cast: **[Narrator,] Nebuchadnezzar, Singer.**

Belshazzar's banquet
Daniel 5.1–12

Narrator	One night King Belshazzar invited a thousand noblemen to a great banquet, and they drank wine together. While they were

drinking, Belshazzar gave orders to bring in the gold and silver cups and bowls which his father Nebuchadnezzar had carried off from the Temple in Jerusalem. The king sent for them so that he, his noblemen, his wives, and his concubines could drink out of them. At once the gold cups and bowls were brought in, and they all drank wine out of them and praised gods made of gold, silver, bronze, iron, wood, and stone.

Suddenly a human hand appeared and began writing on the plaster wall of the palace, where the light from the lamps was shining most brightly. And the king saw the hand as it was writing. He turned pale and was so frightened that his knees began to shake. He shouted for someone to bring in the magicians, wizards, and astrologers. When they came in, the king said to them:

Belshazzar
(anxiously)

Anyone who can read this writing and tell me what it means will be dressed in robes of royal purple, wear a gold chain of honour round his neck, and be the third in power in the kingdom.

Narrator

The royal advisers came forward, but none of them could read the writing or tell the king what it meant. In his distress King Belshazzar grew even paler, and his noblemen had no idea what to do. The queen mother heard the noise made by the king and his noblemen and entered the banqueting-hall. She said:

Queen

May Your Majesty live for ever! Please do not be so disturbed and look so pale. There is a man in your kingdom who has the spirit of the holy gods in him. When your father was king, this man showed good sense, knowledge, and wisdom like the wisdom of the gods. And King Nebuchadnezzar, your father, made him chief of the fortune-tellers, magicians, wizards, and astrologers. He has unusual ability and is wise and skilful in interpreting dreams, solving riddles, and explaining mysteries; so send for this man Daniel, whom the king named Belteshazzar, and he will tell you what all this means.

Cast
All

[This is] the word of the Lord.
Thanks be to God.

Cast: **Narrator, Belshazzar, Queen.**

Daniel explains the writing
Daniel 5.13–31

Narrator

Daniel was brought into King Belshazzar's presence, and the king said to him:

Belshazzar

Are you Daniel, that Jewish exile whom my father the king brought here from Judah? I have heard that the spirit of the holy gods is in you and that you are skilful and have knowledge and wisdom. The advisers and magicians were brought in to read this writing and tell me what it means, but they could not discover the meaning. Now I have heard that you can find hidden meanings and explain mysteries. If you can read this writing and tell me

→

what it means, you will be dressed in robes of royal purple, wear a gold chain of honour round your neck, and be the third in power in the kingdom.

Narrator   Daniel replied:

Daniel   Keep your gifts for yourself or give them to someone else. I will read for Your Majesty what has been written and tell you what it means. (PAUSE)

The Supreme God made your father Nebuchadnezzar a great king and gave him dignity and majesty. He was so great that people of all nations, races, and languages were afraid of him and trembled. If he wanted to kill someone, he did; if he wanted to keep someone alive, he did. He honoured or disgraced anyone he wanted to. But because he became proud, stubborn, and cruel, he was removed from his royal throne and lost his place of honour. He was driven away from human society, and his mind became like that of an animal. He lived with wild donkeys, ate grass like an ox, and slept in the open air with nothing to protect him from the dew. Finally he admitted that the Supreme God controls all human kingdoms and can give them to anyone he chooses. But you, his son, have not humbled yourself, even though you knew all this. You acted against the Lord of heaven and brought in the cups and bowls taken from his Temple. You, your noblemen, your wives, and your concubines drank wine out of them and praised gods made of gold, silver, bronze, iron, wood, and stone—gods that cannot see or hear and that do not know anything. But you did not honour the God who determines whether you live or die and who controls everything you do. That is why God has sent the hand to write these words. This is what was written:

Voice   'Number, number, weight, divisions.'

Daniel   And this is what it means:

Voice   Number—

Daniel   God has numbered the days of your kingdom and brought it to an end.

Voice   Weight—

Daniel   You have been weighed on the scales and found to be too light.

Voice   Divisions—

Daniel   Your kingdom is divided up and given to the Medes and Persians.

Narrator   Immediately Belshazzar ordered his servants to dress Daniel in a robe of royal purple and to hang a gold chain of honour round his neck. And he made him the third in power in the kingdom. That same night Belshazzar, the king of Babylonia, was killed; and Darius the Mede, who was then sixty-two years old, seized the royal power.

Cast   [This is] the word of the Lord.
All   **Thanks be to God.**

Cast: **Narrator, Belshazzar, Daniel, Voice.**

Daniel's courage
Daniel 6.1–23

Narrator	King Darius decided to appoint a hundred and twenty governors to hold office throughout his empire. In addition, he chose Daniel and two others to supervise the governors and to look after the king's interests. Daniel soon showed that he could do better work than the other supervisors or the governors. Because he was so outstanding, the king considered putting him in charge of the whole empire. Then the other supervisors and the governors tried to find something wrong with the way Daniel administered the empire, but they couldn't, because Daniel was reliable and did not do anything wrong or dishonest. They said to one another:
Enemy 1	We are not going to find anything of which to accuse Daniel.
Enemy 2	Unless it is something in connection with his religion.
Narrator	So they went to see the king and said:
Enemies 1 and 2	King Darius, may Your Majesty live for ever!
Enemy 1	All of us who administer your empire—the supervisors, the governors, the lieutenant-governors, and the other officials—have agreed that Your Majesty should issue an order and enforce it strictly.
Enemy 2	Give orders that for thirty days no one be permitted to request anything from any god or from any man except from Your Majesty.
Enemy 1	Anyone who violates this order is to be thrown into a pit filled with lions.
Enemy 2	So let Your Majesty issue this order and sign it, and it will be in force, a law of the Medes and Persians, which cannot be changed.
Narrator	And so King Darius signed the order. (PAUSE) When Daniel learnt that the order had been signed, he went home. In an upstairs room of his house there were windows that faced towards Jerusalem. There, just as he had always done, he knelt down at the open windows and prayed to God three times a day.
	When Daniel's enemies observed him praying to God, all of them went together to the king to accuse Daniel. They said:
Enemies 1 and 2	Your Majesty—
Enemy 2	You signed an order that for the next thirty days anyone who requested anything from any god or from any man except you, would be thrown into a pit filled with lions.
Narrator	The king replied:
Darius	Yes, a strict order, a law of the Medes and Persians, which cannot be changed.
Enemy 2	Daniel, one of the exiles from Judah, does not respect Your Majesty or obey the order you issued.

Enemy 1	He prays regularly three times a day.
Narrator	When the king heard this, he was upset and did his best to find some way to rescue Daniel. He kept trying until sunset. Then the men came back to the king and said to him:
Enemy 2	Your Majesty knows that according to the laws of the Medes and Persians no order which the king issues can be changed.
Narrator	So the king gave orders for Daniel to be arrested and he was thrown into the pit filled with lions. He said to Daniel:
Darius	May your God, whom you serve so loyally, rescue you.
Narrator	A stone was put over the mouth of the pit, and the king placed his own royal seal and the seal of his noblemen on the stone, so that no one could rescue Daniel. Then the king returned to the palace and spent a sleepless night, without food or any form of entertainment. (PAUSE)
	At dawn the king got up and hurried to the pit. When he got there, he called out anxiously:
Darius (calling)	Daniel, servant of the living God! Was the God you serve so loyally able to save you from the lions?
Narrator	Daniel answered:
Daniel (calling)	May Your Majesty live for ever! God sent his angel to shut the mouths of the lions so that they would not hurt me. He did this because he knew that I was innocent and because I have not wronged you, Your Majesty.
Narrator	The king was overjoyed and gave orders for Daniel to be pulled up out of the pit. So they pulled him up and saw that he had not been hurt at all, for he trusted God.
Cast All	[This is] the word of the Lord. **Thanks be to God.**

Cast: **Narrator, Enemy 1, Enemy 2, Darius, Daniel** (preferably unseen).

King Darius writes
Daniel 6.25–28

Narrator	King Darius wrote to the people of all nations, races, and languages on earth:
Darius	[Greetings!] I command that throughout my empire everyone should fear and respect Daniel's God.
Singer	He is a living God, and he will rule for ever. His kingdom will never be destroyed, and his power will never come to an end. He saves and rescues; he performs wonders and miracles in heaven and on earth. He saved Daniel from being killed by the lions.

Narrator	Daniel prospered during the reign of Darius and the reign of Cyrus the Persian.
Cast All	[This is] the word of the Lord. **Thanks be to God.**

Cast: **Narrator, Darius, Singer.**

Daniel's vision of the four beasts
Daniel 7.1–8

Voice 1	In the first year that Belshazzar was king of Babylonia, I had a dream and saw a vision in the night. I wrote the dream down, and this is the record of what I saw that night:
Voice 2	Winds were blowing from all directions and lashing the surface of the ocean. Four huge beasts came up out of the ocean, each one different from the others. The first one looked like a lion, but had wings like an eagle. While I was watching, the wings were torn off. The beast was lifted up and made to stand like a man. And then a human mind was given to it. (PAUSE)
Voice 3	The second beast looked like a bear standing on its hind legs. It was holding three ribs between its teeth, and a voice said to it:
Voice 1	Go on, eat as much meat as you can!
Voice 2	While I was watching, another beast appeared. It looked like a leopard, but on its back there were four wings, like the wings of a bird, and it had four heads. It had a look of authority about it.
Voice 3	As I was watching, a fourth beast appeared. It was powerful, horrible, terrifying. With its huge iron teeth it crushed its victims, and then it trampled on them. Unlike the other beasts, it had ten horns.
Voice 1	While I was staring at the horns, I saw a little horn coming up among the others. It tore out three of the horns that were already there. This horn had human eyes and a mouth that was boasting proudly.
Cast All	[This is] the word of the Lord. **Thanks be to God.**

Cast: **Voice 1, Voice 2, Voice 3.**

The vision of the One who has been living for ever
Daniel 7.(1) 9–14

Voice 1	[In the first year that Belshazzar was king of Babylonia, I had a dream and saw a vision in the night.]
	While I was looking, thrones were put in place.
Voice 2	One who had been living for ever sat down on one of the thrones. His clothes were white as snow, and his hair was like pure wool.

→

	His throne, mounted on fiery wheels, was blazing with fire, and a stream of fire was pouring out from it.
Voice 3	There were many thousands of people there to serve him, and millions of people stood before him. The court began its session, and the books were opened.
[Voice 1	While I was looking, I could still hear the little horn bragging and boasting.
Voice 2	As I watched, the fourth beast was killed, and its body was thrown into the flames and destroyed.
Voice 3	The other beasts had their power taken away, but they were permitted to go on living for a limited time.]
Voice 1	During this vision in the night, I saw what looked like a human being. He was approaching me, surrounded by clouds, and he went to the one who had been living for ever and was presented to him. He was given authority, honour, and royal power, so that the people of all nations, races, and languages would serve him.
Voices 1 and **2**	His authority would last for ever, and his kingdom would never end.
Cast	[This is] the word of the Lord.
All	**Thanks be to God.**

Cast: **Voice 1, Voice 2, Voice 3.** (This reading overlaps with the previous one).

The visions are explained
Daniel 7.15–28

Daniel	The visions I saw alarmed me, and I was deeply disturbed. I went up to one of those standing there and asked him to explain it all. So he told me the meaning. He said:
Witness	These four huge beasts are four empires which will arise on earth. And the people of the Supreme God will receive royal power and keep it for ever and ever.
Daniel	Then I wanted to know more about the fourth beast, which was not like any of the others—the terrifying beast which crushed its victims with its bronze claws and iron teeth and then trampled on them. And I wanted to know about the ten horns on its head and the horn that had come up afterwards and had made three of the horns fall. It had eyes and a mouth and was boasting proudly. It was more terrifying than any of the others. While I was looking, that horn made war on God's people and conquered them. Then the one who had been living for ever came and pronounced judgement in favour of the people of the Supreme God. The time had arrived for God's people to receive royal power. This is the explanation I was given:
Witness	The fourth beast is a fourth empire that will be on the earth and will be different from all other empires. It will crush the whole earth and trample it down. The ten horns are ten kings who will

rule that empire. Then another king will appear; he will be very different from the earlier ones and will overthrow three kings. He will speak against the Supreme God and oppress God's people. He will try to change their religious laws and festivals, and God's people will be under his power for three and a half years. Then the heavenly court will sit in judgement, take away his power, and destroy him completely. The power and greatness of all the kingdoms on earth will be given to the people of the Supreme God. Their royal power will never end and all rulers on earth will serve and obey them.

Daniel
This is the end of the account. I was so frightened that I turned pale, and I kept everything to myself.

Cast [This is] the word of the Lord.
All **Thanks be to God.**

Cast: **Daniel, Witness.**

Daniel's vision of disaster
From Daniel 8.1–14

Daniel
In the third year that Belshazzar was king, I saw a second vision. In the vision I saw a ram that had two long horns, one of which was longer and newer than the other. I watched the ram butting with his horns to the west, the north, and the south. No animal could stop him or escape his power. He did as he pleased and grew arrogant.

The little horn, whose power extended towards the south and the east and towards the Promised Land grew strong enough to attack the army of heaven, the stars themselves, and it threw some of them to the ground and trampled on them. It even defied the Prince of the heavenly army, stopped the daily sacrifices offered to him, and desecrated the Temple. People sinned there instead of offering the proper daily sacrifices, and true religion was thrown to the ground. The horn was successful in everything it did. Then I heard one angel ask another:

Angel 1
How long will these things that were seen in the vision continue? How long will an awful sin replace the daily sacrifices? How long will the army of heaven and the Temple be trampled on?

Daniel
I heard the other angel answer:

Angel 2
It will continue for 1,150 days, during which evening and morning sacrifices will not be offered. Then the Temple will be restored.

Cast [This is] the word of the Lord.
All **Thanks be to God.**

Cast: **Daniel, Angel 1, Angel 2.**

The angel Gabriel explains the vision
From Daniel 8.15–27

Daniel	I was trying to understand what the vision meant, when suddenly someone was standing in front of me. I heard a voice call out over the River Ulai:
Voice	Gabriel, explain to him the meaning of what he saw.
Daniel	Gabriel came and stood beside me, and I was so terrified that I fell to the ground. He said to me:
Gabriel	Mortal man, understand the meaning. The vision has to do with the end of the world.
Daniel	While he was talking, I fell to the ground unconscious. But he took hold of me, raised me to my feet, and said:
Gabriel	I am showing you what the result of God's anger will be. The vision refers to the time of the end. When the end of those kingdoms is near and they have become so wicked that they must be punished, there will be a stubborn, vicious, and deceitful king. He will grow strong—but not by his own power. He will cause terrible destruction and be successful in everything he does. He will bring destruction on powerful men and on God's own people. Because he is cunning, he will succeed in his deceitful ways. He will be proud of himself and destroy many people without warning. He will even defy the greatest King of all, but he will be destroyed without the use of any human power. This vision about the evening and morning sacrifices which has been explained to you will come true. But keep it secret now, because it will be a long time before it does come true.
Daniel	I was depressed and ill for several days. Then I got up and went back to the work that the king had assigned to me, but I was puzzled by the vision and could not understand it.
Cast	[This is] the word of the Lord.
All	**Thanks be to God.**

Cast: **Daniel, Voice, Gabriel.**

Daniel prays for his people
Daniel 9.1–19

Daniel	Darius the Mede, who was the son of Xerxes, ruled over the kingdom of Babylonia. In the first year of his reign, I was studying the sacred books and thinking about the seventy years that Jerusalem would be in ruins, according to what the Lord had told the prophet Jeremiah. And I prayed earnestly to the Lord God, pleading with him, fasting, wearing sackcloth, and sitting in ashes. I prayed to the Lord my God and confessed the sins of my people. I said:
Voices 1 and **2**	Lord God, you are great, and we honour you.
Voice 3	You are faithful to your covenant and show constant love to those who love you and do what you command.

Voice 1	We have sinned.
Voice 2	We have been evil.
Voice 3	We have done wrong.
Voice 1	We have rejected what you commanded us to do and have turned away from what you showed us was right.
Voice 2	We have not listened to your servants the prophets, who spoke in your name to our kings, our rulers, our ancestors, and our whole nation.
Voice 3	You, Lord, always do what is right, but we have always brought disgrace on ourselves.
Voice 1	This is true of all of us who live in Judaea and in Jerusalem and of all the Israelites whom you scattered in countries near and far because they were unfaithful to you. Our kings, our rulers, and our ancestors have acted shamefully and sinned against you, Lord. You are merciful and forgiving, although we have rebelled against you.
Voice 2	We did not listen to you, O Lord our God, when you told us to live according to the laws which you gave us through your servants the prophets.
Voice 3	All Israel broke your laws and refused to listen to what you said. We sinned against you, and so you brought on us the curses that are written in the Law of Moses, your servant.
Voice 1	You did what you said you would do to us and our rulers. You punished Jerusalem more severely than any other city on earth, giving us all the punishment described in the Law of Moses.
Voice 2	But even now, O Lord our God, we have not tried to please you by turning from our sins or by following your truth.
Voice 3	You, O Lord our God, were prepared to punish us, and you did, because you always do what is right, and we did not listen to you.
Voice 1	O Lord our God, you showed your power by bringing your people out of Egypt, and your power is still remembered.
Voices 2 and **3**	We have sinned; we have done wrong.
Voice 1	You have defended us in the past, so do not be angry with Jerusalem any longer. It is your city, your sacred hill. All the people in the neighbouring countries look down on Jerusalem and on your people because of our sins and the evil our ancestors did.
Daniel	O God, hear my prayer and pleading. Restore your Temple, which has been destroyed; restore it so that everyone will know that you are God.
Voice 1	Listen to us, O God!
Voice 2	Look at us, and see the trouble we are in and the suffering of the city that bears your name.
Voice 3	We are praying to you because you are merciful, not because we have done right.
Voice 1	Lord, hear us.
Voice 2	Lord, forgive us.

Voice 3	Lord, listen to us, and act!
Daniel	In order that everyone will know that you are God, do not delay! This city and these people are yours.
Cast	[This is] the word of the Lord.
All	**Thanks be to God.**

Cast: **Daniel, Voice 1, Voice 2, Voice 3.**

Gabriel explains the prophecy
Daniel 9.20–27

Daniel	I went on praying, confessing my sins and the sins of my people Israel, and pleading with the Lord my God to restore his holy Temple. While I was praying, Gabriel, whom I had seen in the earlier vision, came flying down to where I was. It was the time for the evening sacrifice to be offered. [He explained:]
Gabriel	Daniel, I have come here to help you understand the prophecy. When you began to plead with God, he answered you. He loves you, and so I have come to tell you the answer. Now pay attention while I explain the vision.
	Seven times seventy years is the length of time God has set for freeing your people and your holy city from sin and evil. Sin will be forgiven and eternal justice established, so that the vision and the prophecy will come true, and the holy Temple will be rededicated. Note this and understand it: From the time the command is given to rebuild Jerusalem, until God's chosen leader comes, seven times seven years will pass. Jerusalem will be rebuilt with streets and strong defences, and will stand for seven times sixty-two years, but this will be a time of troubles. And at the end of that time God's chosen leader will be killed unjustly. The city and the Temple will be destroyed by the invading army of a powerful ruler. The end will come like a flood, bringing the war and destruction which God has prepared. That ruler will have a firm agreement with many people for seven years, and when half this time is past, he will put an end to sacrifices and offerings. The Awful Horror will be placed on the highest point of the Temple and will remain there until the one who put it there meets the end which God has prepared for him.
Cast	[This is] the word of the Lord.
All	**Thanks be to God.**

Cast: **Daniel, Gabriel.**

Daniel's vision by the River Tigris
Daniel 10.1–19

Narrator	In the third year that Cyrus was emperor of Persia, a message was revealed to Daniel, who is also called Belteshazzar. The message was true but extremely hard to understand. It was explained to him in a vision.
Daniel	At that time, I was mourning for three weeks. I did not eat any

rich food or any meat, drink any wine, or comb my hair until the three weeks were past. On the twenty-fourth day of the first month of the year, I was standing on the bank of the mighty River Tigris. I looked up and saw someone who was wearing linen clothes and a belt of fine gold. His body shone like a jewel. His face was as bright as a flash of lightning, and his eyes blazed like fire. His arms and legs shone like polished bronze, and his voice sounded like the roar of a great crowd.

I was the only one who saw the vision. The men who were with me did not see anything, but they were terrified and ran and hid. I was left there alone, watching this amazing vision. I had no strength left, and my face was so changed that no one could have recognized me. When I heard his voice, I fell to the ground unconscious and lay there face downwards. Then a hand took hold of me and raised me to my hands and knees; I was still trembling. The angel said to me:

Angel — Daniel, God loves you. Stand up and listen carefully to what I am going to say. I have been sent to you.

Daniel — When he had said this, I stood up, still trembling. Then he said:

Angel — Daniel, don't be afraid. God has heard your prayers ever since the first day you decided to humble yourself in order to gain understanding. I have come in answer to your prayer. The angel prince of the kingdom of Persia opposed me for twenty-one days. Then Michael, one of the chief angels, came to help me, because I had been left there alone in Persia. I have come to make you understand what will happen to your people in the future. This is a vision about the future.

Daniel — When he said this, I stared at the ground, speechless. Then the angel, who looked like a man, stretched out his hand and touched my lips. I said to him:

Young Daniel — Sir, this vision makes me so weak that I can't stop trembling. I am like a slave standing before his master. How can I talk to you? I have no strength or breath left in me.

Daniel — Once more he took hold of me, and I felt stronger. He said:

Angel — God loves you, so don't let anything worry you or frighten you.

Daniel — When he had said this, I felt even stronger and said:

Young Daniel — Sir, tell me what you have to say.

Cast — [This is] the word of the Lord.
All — **Thanks be to God.**

Cast: **Narrator, Daniel, Angel, Young Daniel.**

The time of the end
From Daniel 12.1–13

Daniel   In my vision, the angel wearing linen clothes said:

Angel   The great angel Michael, who guards your people, will appear. Then there will be a time of troubles, the worst since nations first came into existence. When that time comes, all the people of your nation whose names are written in God's book will be saved. Many of those who have already died will live again: some will enjoy eternal life, and some will suffer eternal disgrace. The wise leaders will shine with all the brightness of the sky. And those who have taught many people to do what is right will shine like the stars for ever.

Daniel   He said to me:

Angel   And now, Daniel, close the book and put a seal on it until the end of the world. Meanwhile, many people will waste their efforts trying to understand what is happening.

Daniel   Then I saw two men standing by a river, one on each bank. One of them asked the angel who was standing further upstream:

Man   How long will it be until these amazing events come to an end?

Daniel   The angel raised both hands towards the sky and made a solemn promise in the name of the Eternal God. I heard him say:

Angel   It will be three and a half years. When the persecution of God's people ends, all these things will have happened.

Daniel   I heard what he said, but I did not understand it. So I asked:

Young Daniel   But, sir, how will it all end?

Daniel   He answered:

Angel   You must go now, Daniel, because these words are to be kept secret and hidden until the end comes. Many people will be purified. Those who are wicked will not understand but will go on being wicked; only those who are wise will understand. And you, Daniel, be faithful to the end. Then you will die, but you will rise to receive your reward at the end of time.

Cast   [This is] the word of the Lord.
All   **Thanks be to God.**

Cast: **Daniel, Angel, Man, Young Daniel** (can be the same as Daniel).

HOSEA

Hosea's wife and children
Hosea 1.1–9 [10—2.1]

Narrator   This is the message which the Lord gave Hosea son of Beeri during the time that Uzziah, Jotham, Ahaz, and Hezekiah were kings of Judah, and Jeroboam son of Jehoash was king of Israel.

When the Lord first spoke to Israel through Hosea, he said to Hosea:

The Lord   Go and get married; your wife will be unfaithful, and your children will be just like her. In the same way, my people have left me and become unfaithful.

Narrator   So Hosea married a woman named Gomer, the daughter of Diblaim. After the birth of their first child, a son, the Lord said to Hosea:

The Lord   Name him 'Jezreel,' because it will not be long before I punish the king of Israel for the murders that his ancestor Jehu committed at Jezreel. I am going to put an end to Jehu's dynasty. And in the Valley of Jezreel I will at that time destroy Israel's military power.

Narrator   Gomer had a second child—this time it was a girl. The Lord said to Hosea:

The Lord   Name her 'Unloved,' because I will no longer show love to the people of Israel or forgive them. But to the people of Judah I will show love. I, the Lord their God, will save them, but I will not do it by war—with swords or bows and arrows or with horses and horsemen.

Narrator   After Gomer had weaned her daughter, she became pregnant again and had another son. The Lord said to Hosea:

The Lord   Name him 'Not-My-People,' because the people of Israel are not my people, and I am not their God. (PAUSE)

[Narrator   The people of Israel will become like the sand of the sea, more than can be counted or measured. Now God says to them:

The Lord   You are not my people.

Narrator   But the day is coming when he will say to them:

The Lord   You are the children of the living God!

Narrator   The people of Judah and the people of Israel will be reunited. They will choose for themselves a single leader, and once again they will grow and prosper in their land. Yes, the day of Jezreel will be a great day! So call your fellow-Israelites 'God's People' and 'Loved-by-the-Lord'.]

Cast   [This is] the word of the Lord.
All   **Thanks be to God.**

Cast: **Narrator, The Lord.**

The Lord's punishment for unfaithful Israel
Hosea 2.2–13

Prophet   My children, plead with your mother—though she is no longer a wife to me, and I am no longer her husband. Plead with her to stop her adultery and prostitution. If she does not, I will strip her as naked as she was on the day she was born. I will make her like a dry and barren land, and she will die of thirst. I will not show mercy to her children; they are the children of a shameless prostitute. She herself said:

Israel   I will go to my lovers—they give me food and water, wool and linen, olive-oil and wine.

Prophet   So I am going to fence her in with thorn-bushes and build a wall to block her way. She will run after her lovers but will not catch them. She will look for them but will not find them. Then she will say:

Israel   I am going back to my first husband—I was better off then than I am now.

Prophet   She would never acknowledge that I am the one who gave her the corn, the wine, the olive-oil, and all the silver and gold that she used in the worship of Baal. So at harvest time I will take back my gifts of corn and wine, and will take away the wool and the linen I gave her for clothing. I will strip her naked in front of her lovers, and no one will be able to save her from my power. I will put an end to all her festivities—her annual and monthly festivals and her Sabbath celebrations—all her religious meetings. I will destroy her grapevines and her fig-trees, which she said her lovers gave her for serving them. I will turn her vineyards and orchards into a wilderness; wild animals will destroy them. I will punish her for the times that she forgot me when she burnt incense to Baal and put on her jewellery to go chasing after her lovers. (PAUSE) The Lord has spoken!

Cast   [This is] the word of the Lord.
All   **Thanks be to God.**

Cast: **Prophet, Israel.**

The Lord's love for his people
Hosea 2.14–23

Prophet   I am going to take your mother into the desert again; there I will win her back with words of love. I will give back to her the vineyards she had and make Trouble Valley a door of hope. She will respond to me there as she did when she was young, when she came from Egypt. Then once again she will call me her husband— she will no longer call me her Baal. I will never let her speak the name of Baal again. At that time I will make a covenant with all the wild animals and birds, so that they will not harm my people. I will also remove all weapons of war from the land, all swords and bows, and will let my people live in peace and safety.

Poet	Israel, I will make you my wife;
	I will be true and faithful;
	I will show you constant love and mercy
	and make you mine for ever.
	I will keep my promise and make you mine,
	and you will acknowledge me as Lord.
	At that time I will answer the prayers of my people Israel.
	I will make rain fall on the earth,
	and the earth will produce corn and grapes and olives.
	I will establish my people in the land and make them prosper.
	I will show love to those who were called 'Unloved',
	and to those who were called 'Not-My-People'.
	I will say, 'You are my people,' and they will answer,
	'You are our God.'
Cast	[This is] the word of the Lord.
All	**Thanks be to God.**

Cast: **Prophet, Poet.**

Hosea's reconciliation with his wife
Hosea 3.1–5

Hosea	The Lord said to me:
The Lord	Go, show your love to your wife again, though she is loved by another and is an adulteress. Love her as the Lord loves the Israelites, though they turn to other gods and love the sacred raisin cakes.
Hosea	So I bought her for fifteen shekels of silver and about a homer and a lethek of barley. Then I told her:
Young Hosea	You are to live with me for many days; you must not be a prostitute or be intimate with any man, and I will live with you.
Hosea	For the Israelites will live for many days without king or prince, without sacrifice or sacred stones, without ephod or idol. Afterwards the Israelites will return and seek the Lord their God and David their king. They will come trembling to the Lord and to his blessings in the last days.
Cast	[This is] the word of the Lord.
All	**Thanks be to God.**

Cast: **Hosea, The Lord, Young Hosea.**

Judgement is coming
From Hosea 5.1–15

Hosea	The Lord says:
The Lord	Listen to this, you priests! Pay attention, people of Israel! Listen, you that belong to the royal family! You are supposed to judge with justice—so judgement will fall on you! You have become a

→

	trap and I will punish all of you. I know what Israel is like—she cannot hide from *me*. She has been unfaithful, and her people are unfit to worship me.
Hosea	The evil that the people have done prevents them from returning to their God. Idolatry has a powerful hold on them, and they do not acknowledge the Lord. The arrogance of the people of Israel cries out against them. Their sins make them stumble and fall, and the people of Judah fall with them. They take their sheep and cattle to offer as sacrifices to the Lord, but it does them no good. They cannot find him, for he has left them. They have been unfaithful to the Lord; their children do not belong to him. So now they and their lands will soon be destroyed.
Commander 1	Blow the war trumpets in Gibeah!
Commander 2	Sound the alarm in Ramah!
Commander 1	Raise the war-cry at Bethaven!
Commander 2	Into battle, men of Benjamin!
Hosea	The day of punishment is coming, and Israel will be ruined. People of Israel, this will surely happen! The Lord says:
The Lord	I will abandon my people until they have suffered enough for their sins and come looking for me. Perhaps in their suffering they will try to find me.
Cast	[This is] the word of the Lord.
All	**Thanks be to God.**

Cast: **Hosea, The Lord, Commander 1, Commander 2.**

The people's insincere repentance
Hosea 6.1–6 [7—7.2]

Prophet	The people say:
Persons 1 and **2**	Let's return to the Lord!
Person 1	He has hurt us, but he will be sure to heal us.
Person 2	He has wounded us, but he will bandage our wounds, won't he?
Person 1	In two or three days he will revive us, and we will live in his presence.
Person 2	Let us try to know the Lord. He will come to us as surely as the day dawns, as surely as the spring rains that water the earth.
Prophet	But the Lord says:
The Lord	Israel and Judah, what am I going to do with you? Your love for me disappears as quickly as morning mist; it is like dew, that vanishes early in the day. That is why I have sent my prophets to you with my message of judgement and destruction. What I want from you is plain and clear: I want your constant love, not your animal sacrifices. I would rather have my people know me than burn offerings to me.

[But as soon as they entered the land at Adam, they broke the covenant I had made with them. Gilead is a city full of evil men and murderers. The priests are like a gang of robbers who wait in ambush for a man. Even on the road to the holy place at Shechem they commit murder. And they do all this evil deliberately! I have seen a horrible thing in Israel: my people have defiled themselves by worshipping idols. And as for you, people of Judah, I have set a time to punish you also for what you are doing. Whenever I want to heal my people Israel and make them prosperous again, all I can see is their wickedness and the evil they do. They cheat one another; they break into houses and steal; they rob people in the streets. It never enters their heads that I will remember all this evil; but their sins surround them, and I cannot avoid seeing them.]

Cast	[This is] the word of the Lord.
All	**Thanks be to God.**

Cast: **Prophet, Person 1, Person 2** (can be the same as Person 1), **The Lord.**

The prophet speaks about Israel
Hosea 10.1–8

Prophet The people of Israel were like a grapevine that was full of grapes. The more prosperous they were, the more altars they built. The more productive their land was, the more beautiful they made the sacred stone pillars they worship. The people whose hearts are deceitful must now suffer for their sins. God will break down their altars and destroy their sacred pillars. These people will soon be saying:

Person 1 We have no king because we did not fear the Lord.

Person 2 But what could a king do for us anyway?

Prophet They utter empty words and make false promises and useless treaties. Justice has become injustice, growing like poisonous weeds in a ploughed field.

The people who live in the city of Samaria will be afraid and will mourn the loss of the gold bull at Bethel. They and the priests who serve the idol will weep over it. They will wail when it is stripped of its golden splendour. The idol will be carried off to Assyria as tribute to the great emperor. Israel will be disgraced and put to shame because of the advice she followed. Her king will be carried off, like a chip of wood on water. The hilltop shrines of Aven, where the people of Israel worship idols, will be destroyed. Thorns and weeds will grow up over their altars. The people will call out to the mountains:

Persons 1 and 2 Hide us!

Prophet And to the hills:

Persons 1 and 2 Cover us!

Cast	[This is] the word of the Lord.
All	**Thanks be to God.**

Cast: **Prophet, Person 1, Person 2.**

God's love for his rebellious people
Hosea 11.1–9

Voice 1
When Israel was a child, I loved him
and called him out of Egypt as my son.

Voice 2
But the more I called to him,
the more he turned away from me.
My people sacrificed to Baal;
they burnt incense to idols.

Voice 1
Yet I was the one who taught Israel to walk.
I took my people up in my arms.

Voice 2
But they did not acknowledge that I took care of them.

Voice 1
I drew them to me with affection and love.
I picked them up and held them to my cheek;
I bent down to them and fed them.

Voice 2
They refuse to return to me, and so they must return to Egypt,
and Assyria will rule them. War will sweep through their cities
and break down the city gates. It will destroy my people because
they do what they themselves think best. They insist on turning
away from me. They will cry out because of the yoke that is on
them, but no one will lift it from them.

Voice 1
How can I give you up, Israel?
How can I abandon you?
Could I ever destroy you as I did Admah,
or treat you as I did Zeboiim?
My heart will not let me do it!
My love for you is too strong.
I will not punish you in my anger;
I will not destroy Israel again.
For I am God and not man.
I, the Holy One, am with you.
I will not come to you in anger.

Cast
[This is] the word of the Lord.
All
Thanks be to God.

Cast: **Voice 1** (caring), **Voice 2** (warning).

Further words of judgement
Hosea 12.7–14

Prophet
The Lord says:

The Lord
The people of Israel are as dishonest as the Canaanites; they love
to cheat their customers with false scales. They say:

Israelites 1 & 2
We are rich.

Israelite 1
We've made a fortune.

Israelite 2
And no one can accuse us of getting rich dishonestly.

The Lord	But I, the Lord your God who led you out of Egypt, I will make you live in tents again, as you did when I came to you in the desert. I spoke to the prophets and gave them many visions, and through the prophets I gave my people warnings. Yet idols are worshipped in Gilead, and those who worship them will die. Bulls are sacrificed in Gilgal, and the altars there will become piles of stone in the open fields.
Prophet	Our ancestor Jacob had to flee to Mesopotamia, where, in order to get a wife, he worked for another man and took care of his sheep. The Lord sent a prophet to rescue the people of Israel from slavery in Egypt and to take care of them. The people of Israel have made the Lord bitterly angry; they deserve death for their crimes. The Lord will punish them for the disgrace they have brought on him.
Cast	[This is] the word of the Lord.
All	**Thanks be to God.**

Cast: **Prophet, The Lord, Israelite 1, Israelite 2** (can be the same as Israelite 1).

Final judgement on Israel
Hosea 13.1–9

Prophet	In the past, when the tribe of Ephraim spoke, the other tribes of Israel were afraid; they looked up to Ephraim. But the people sinned by worshipping Baal, and for this they will die. They still keep on sinning by making metal images to worship—idols of silver, designed by human minds, made by human hands. And then they say,
Person	Offer sacrifices to them!
Prophet	How can men kiss those idols—idols in the shape of bulls! And so these people will disappear like morning mist, like the dew that vanishes early in the day. They will be like chaff which the wind blows from the threshing-place, like smoke from a chimney. (PAUSE) The Lord says:
The Lord	I am the Lord your God, who led you out of Egypt. You have no God but me. I alone am your saviour. I took care of you in a dry, desert land. But when you entered the good land, you became full and satisfied, and then you grew proud and forgot me. So I will attack you like a lion. Like a leopard I will lie in wait along your path. I will attack you like a bear that has lost her cubs, and I will tear you open. Like a lion I will devour you on the spot, and will tear you to pieces like a wild animal. I will destroy you, people of Israel! Then who can help you?
Cast	[This is] the word of the Lord.
All	**Thanks be to God.**

Cast: **Prophet, Person, The Lord.**

The fruit of repentance
Hosea 14.1–9

Prophet	Return to the Lord your God, people of Israel. Your sin has made you stumble and fall. Return to the Lord, and let this prayer be your offering to him:
Israelite 1	Forgive all our sins and accept our prayer, and we will praise you as we have promised.
Israelite 2	Assyria can never save us, and war-horses cannot protect us.
Israelite 1	We will never again say to our idols that they are our God.
Israelite 2	O Lord, you show mercy to those who have no one else to turn to.
Prophet	The Lord says:

The Lord
I will bring my people back to me.
I will love them with all my heart;
no longer am I angry with them.
I will be to the people of Israel
like rain in a dry land.
They will blossom like flowers;
they will be firmly rooted
like the trees of Lebanon.
They will be alive with new growth,
and beautiful like olive-trees.
They will be fragrant
like the cedars of Lebanon.
Once again they will live under my protection.
They will flourish like a garden
and be fruitful like a vineyard.
They will be as famous as the wine of Lebanon.
The people of Israel will have nothing more to do with idols;
I will answer their prayers and take care of them;
like an evergreen tree I will shelter them;
I am the source of all their blessings.

Prophet
May those who are wise understand what is written here, and may they take it to heart. The Lord's ways are right, and righteous people live by following them, but sinners stumble and fall because they ignore them.

Cast [This is] the word of the Lord.
All **Thanks be to God.**

Cast: **Prophet, Israelite 1, Israelite 2** (can be the same as Israelite 1), **The Lord.**

JOEL

The people mourn the destruction of the crops
Joel 1.1–20

Voice 1   This is the Lord's message to Joel son of Pethuel:

Voice 2   Pay attention, you older people; everyone in Judah, listen. Has anything like this ever happened in your time or the time of your fathers? Tell your children about it; they will tell their children, who in turn will tell the next generation. Swarm after swarm of locusts settled on the crops; what one swarm left, the next swarm devoured.

Voice 3   Wake up and weep, you drunkards; cry, you wine-drinkers; the grapes for making new wine have been destroyed. An army of locusts has attacked our land; they are powerful and too many to count; their teeth are as sharp as those of a lion. They have destroyed our grapevines and chewed up our fig-trees. They have stripped off the bark, till the branches are white.

Voice 1   Cry, you people, like a girl who mourns the death of the man she was going to marry. There is no corn or wine to offer in the Temple; the priests mourn because they have no offerings for the Lord. The fields are bare; the ground mourns because the corn is destroyed, the grapes are dried up, and the olive-trees are withered.

Voice 2   Grieve, you farmers; cry, you that take care of the vineyards, because the wheat, the barley, yes all the crops are destroyed. The grapevines and fig-trees have withered; all the fruit-trees have wilted and died. The joy of the people is gone.

Voice 3   Put on sackcloth and weep, you priests who serve at the altar! Go into the Temple and mourn all night! There is no corn or wine to offer your God. Give orders for a fast; call an assembly! Gather the leaders and all the people of Judah into the Temple of the Lord your God and cry out to him. The day of the Lord is near; the day when the Almighty brings destruction. What terror that day will bring!

Voice 1   We look on helpless as our crops are destroyed. There is no joy in the Temple of our God. The seeds die in the dry earth. There is no grain to be stored, and so the empty granaries are in ruins. The cattle are bellowing in distress because there is no pasture for them; the flocks of sheep also suffer.

Voice 2   I cry out to you, Lord, because the pastures and trees are dried up, as though a fire had burnt them. Even the wild animals cry out to you because the streams have become dry.

Cast   [This is] the word of the Lord.
All   **Thanks be to God.**

Cast: **Voice 1, Voice 2, Voice 3.**

The locusts as a warning of the Day of the Lord
Joel 2.1–11

Voices 1 and **2**	Blow the trumpet!
Voice 3	Sound the alarm on Zion, God's sacred hill.
Voice 1	Tremble, people of Judah!
Voice 2	The day of the Lord is coming soon.
Voice 3	It will be a dark and gloomy day.
Voices 1 and **2**	A black and cloudy day.
Voice 1	The great army of locusts advances like darkness spreading over the mountains.
Voice 2	There has never been anything like it, and there never will be again.
Voice 3	Like fire they eat up the plants.
Voice 1	In front of them the land is like the Garden of Eden.
Voice 2	But behind them it is a barren desert.
Voices 1 and **3**	Nothing escapes them.
Voice 1	They look like horses.
Voice 2	They run like war-horses.
Voice 1	They leap on the tops of the mountains.
Voice 2	They rattle like chariots.
Voice 3	They crackle like dry grass on fire.
Voice 1	They are lined up like a great army ready for battle.
Voice 2	As they approach, everyone is terrified—
Voices 1 and **3**	Every face turns pale.
Voice 3	They attack like warriors.
Voice 1	They climb the walls like soldiers.
Voice 3	They all keep marching straight ahead and do not change direction or get in each other's way.
Voice 1	They swarm through defences, and nothing can stop them.
Voice 2	They rush against the city.
Voice 1	They run over the walls.
Voice 2	They climb up the houses—
Voice 1	And go in through the windows like thieves.
Voices 1 and **2**	The earth shakes as they advance.
Voices 2 and **3**	The sky trembles.

Voice 2	The sun and the moon grow dark—
Voice 3	And the stars no longer shine.
Voice 1	The Lord thunders commands to his army.
Voice 2	The troops that obey him are many and mighty.
Voices 1–3	How terrible is the day of the Lord!
Voice 3	Who will survive it?
Cast	[This is] the word of the Lord.
All	**Thanks be to God.**

Cast: **Voice 1, Voice 2, Voice 3.**

A call to repentance
Joel 2.12–17

Joel	The Lord says:
The Lord	But even now, repent sincerely and return to me with fasting and weeping and mourning. Let your broken heart show your sorrow; tearing your clothes is not enough.
Joel	Come back to the Lord your God. He is kind and full of mercy; he is patient and keeps his promise; he is always ready to forgive and not punish. Perhaps the Lord your God will change his mind and bless you with abundant crops. Then you can offer him corn and wine.
(calling)	Blow the trumpet on Mount Zion; give orders for a fast and call an assembly! Gather the people together; prepare them for a sacred meeting; bring the old people; gather the children and the babies too. Even newly married couples must leave their room and come. The priests, serving the Lord between the altar and the entrance of the Temple, must weep and pray:
Priest 1	Have pity on your people, Lord.
Priest 2	Do not let other nations despise us and mock us by saying—
Priests 1 and 2	Where is your God?
Cast	[This is] the word of the Lord.
All	**Thanks be to God.**

Cast: **Joel, The Lord, Priest 1, Priest 2** (can be the same as Priest 1).

God restores fertility to the land
From Joel 2.18–27

Joel	When the people assembled and the priests wept and prayed, then the Lord showed concern for his land; he had mercy on his people. He answered them:

The Lord	Now I am going to give you corn and wine and olive-oil, and you will be satisfied. Other nations will no longer despise you. I will remove the locust army that came from the north and will drive some of them into the desert. Their front ranks will be driven into the Dead Sea, their rear ranks into the Mediterranean. Their dead bodies will stink. I will destroy them because of all they have done to you.
Joel	Fields, don't be afraid, but be joyful and glad because of all the Lord has done for you. Animals, don't be afraid. The pastures are green; the trees bear their fruit, and there are plenty of figs and grapes. Be glad, people of Zion, rejoice at what the Lord your God has done for you. He has given you the right amount of autumn rain; he has poured down the winter rain for you and the spring rain as before.
The Lord	The threshing-places will be full of corn; the pits beside the presses will overflow with wine and olive-oil. I will give you back what you lost in the years when swarms of locusts ate your crops. It was I who sent this army against you.
Joel	Now you will have plenty to eat, and be satisfied. You will praise the Lord your God, who has done wonderful things for you.
The Lord	Then, Israel, you will know that I am among you, and that I, the Lord, am your God and there is no other. My people will never be despised again.
Cast	[This is] the word of the Lord.
All	**Thanks be to God.**

Cast: **Joel, The Lord.**

The Day of the Lord
Joel 2.28–32

The Lord	I will pour out my spirit on everyone: your sons and daughters will proclaim my message; your old men will have dreams, and your young men will see visions. At that time I will pour out my spirit even on servants, both men and women. (PAUSE)
	I will give warnings of that day in the sky and on the earth; there will be bloodshed, fire, and clouds of smoke.
Joel	The sun will be darkened, and the moon will turn red as blood before the great and terrible day of the Lord comes. But all who ask the Lord for help will be saved. As the Lord has said:
The Lord	Some in Jerusalem will escape; those whom I choose will survive.
Cast	[This is] the word of the Lord.
All	**Thanks be to God.**

Cast: **The Lord, Joel.**

God will judge the nations
Joel 3.9–15

The Lord	Make this announcement among the nations:
Heralds 1 and **2**	Prepare for war.
Herald 1	Call your warriors:
Herald 2	Gather all your soldiers and march!
Herald 1	Hammer the points of your ploughs into swords and your pruning-knives into spears.
Herald 2	Even the weak must fight.
Herald 1	Hurry and come, all you surrounding nations, and gather in the valley.
Joel	Send down, O Lord, your army to attack them.
The Lord	The nations must get ready and come to the Valley of Judgement. There I, the Lord, will sit to judge all the surrounding nations. They are very wicked; cut them down like corn at harvest time; crush them as grapes are crushed in a full winepress until the wine runs over.
Joel	Thousands and thousands are in the Valley of Judgement. It is there that the day of the Lord will soon come. The sun and the moon grow dark, and the stars no longer shine.
Cast	[This is] the word of the Lord.
All	**Thanks be to God.**

Cast: **The Lord, Herald 1, Herald 2** (Heralds 1 and 2 can be the same as The Lord)**, Joel.**

AMOS

God's judgement
Amos 1.1—2.8

Narrator   These are the words of Amos, a shepherd from the town of Tekoa. Two years before the earthquake, when Uzziah was king of Judah and Jeroboam son of Jehoash was king of Israel, God revealed to Amos all these things about Israel. Amos said:

Amos   The Lord roars from Mount Zion; his voice thunders from Jerusalem. The pastures dry up, and the grass on Mount Carmel turns brown. (PAUSE)

(with flourish)   The Lord says:

The Lord   The people of Damascus have sinned again and again, and for this I will certainly punish them. They treated the people of Gilead with savage cruelty. So I will send fire upon the palace built by King Hazael and I will burn down the fortresses of King Benhadad. I will smash the city gates of Damascus and remove the inhabitants of the Valley of Aven and the ruler of Betheden. The people of Syria will be taken away as prisoners to the land of Kir.

Amos
(with flourish)   The Lord says:

The Lord   The people of Gaza have sinned again and again, and for this I will certainly punish them. They carried off a whole nation and sold them as slaves to the people of Edom. So I will send fire upon the city walls of Gaza and burn down its fortresses. I will remove the rulers of the cities of Ashdod and Ashkelon. I will punish the city of Ekron, and all the Philistines who are left will die.

Amos
(with flourish)   The Lord says:

The Lord   The people of Tyre have sinned again and again, and for this I will certainly punish them. They carried off a whole nation into exile in the land of Edom, and did not keep the treaty of friendship they had made. So I will send fire upon the city walls of Tyre and burn down its fortresses.

Amos
(with flourish)   The Lord says:

The Lord   The people of Edom have sinned again and again, and for this I will certainly punish them. They hunted down their brothers, the Israelites, and showed them no mercy. Their anger had no limits, and they never let it die. So I will send fire upon the city of Teman and burn down the fortresses of Bozrah.

Amos
(with flourish)   The Lord says:

786

The Lord	The people of Ammon have sinned again and again, and for this I will certainly punish them. In their wars for more territory they even ripped open pregnant women in Gilead. So I will send fire upon the city walls of Rabbah and burn down its fortresses. Then there will be shouts on the day of battle, and the fighting will rage like a storm. Their king and his officers will go into exile.
Amos (with flourish)	The Lord says:
The Lord	The people of Moab have sinned again and again, and for this I will certainly punish them. They dishonoured the bones of the king of Edom by burning them to ashes. I will send fire upon the land of Moab and burn down the fortresses of Kerioth. The people of Moab will die in the noise of battle while soldiers are shouting and trumpets are sounding. I will kill the ruler of Moab and all the leaders of the land.
Amos (with flourish)	The Lord says:
The Lord	The people of Judah have sinned again and again, and for this I will certainly punish them. They have despised my teachings and have not kept my commands. They have been led astray by the same false gods that their ancestors served. So I will send fire upon Judah and burn down the fortresses of Jerusalem.
Amos (with flourish)	The Lord says:
The Lord	The people of Israel have sinned again and again, and for this I will certainly punish them. They sell into slavery honest men who cannot pay their debts, poor men who cannot repay even the price of a pair of sandals. They trample down the weak and helpless and push the poor out of the way. A man and his father have intercourse with the same slave-girl, and so profane my holy name. At every place of worship men sleep on clothing that they have taken from the poor as security for debts. In the temple of their God they drink wine which they have taken from those who owe them money.
`Cast	[This is] the word of the Lord.
All	**Thanks be to God.**

Cast: Narrator, **Amos, The Lord.**

Judgement upon Israel
Amos 2.9—3.2

Amos (with flourish)	The Lord says:
The Lord	My people, it was for your sake that I totally destroyed the Amorites, men who were as tall as cedar-trees and as strong as oaks. I brought you out of Egypt, led you through the desert for

→

forty years, and gave you the land of the Amorites to be your own. I chose some of your sons to be prophets, and some of your young men to be Nazirites. Isn't this true, people of Israel? I, the Lord, have spoken.

But you made the Nazirites drink wine, and ordered the prophets not to speak my message. And now I will crush you to the ground, and you will groan like a cart loaded with corn. Not even fast runners will escape; strong men will lose their strength, and soldiers will not be able to save their own lives. Bowmen will not stand their ground, fast runners will not get away, and men on horses will not escape with their lives. On that day even the bravest soldiers will drop their weapons and run.

Amos The Lord has spoken. People of Israel, listen to this message which the Lord has spoken about you, the entire nation that he brought out of Egypt:

The Lord Of all the nations on earth, you are the only one I have known and cared for. That is what makes your sins so terrible, and that is why I must punish you for them.

Cast [This is] the word of the Lord.
All **Thanks be to God.**

Cast: **Amos, The Lord.**

The prophet's task
Amos 3.3–8

Voice 1 Do two men start travelling together without arranging to meet?

Voice 2 Does a lion roar in the forest unless he has found a victim?

Voice 1 Does a young lion growl in his den unless he has caught something?

Voice 2 Does a bird get caught in a trap if the trap has not been baited?

Voice 1 Does a trap spring unless something sets it off?

Voice 2 Does the war trumpet sound in a city without making the people afraid?

Voice 1 Does disaster strike a city unless the Lord sends it? (PAUSE)

The Sovereign Lord never does anything without revealing his plan to his servants, the prophets.

Voice 2 When a lion roars, who can avoid being afraid?

Voice 1 When the Sovereign Lord speaks, who can avoid proclaiming his message?

Cast [This is] the word of the Lord.
All **Thanks be to God.**

Cast: **Voice 1, Voice 2.**

788

The doom of Samaria
Amos 3.9—4.3

Amos Announce to those who live in the palaces of Egypt and Ashdod:

Herald Gather together in the hills surrounding Samaria and see the great disorder and the crimes being committed there.

Amos
(with flourish) The Lord says:

The Lord These people fill their mansions with things taken by crime and violence. They don't even know how to be honest. And so an enemy will surround their land, destroy their defences, and plunder their mansions.

Amos
(with flourish) The Lord says:

The Lord As a shepherd recovers only two legs or an ear of a sheep that a lion has eaten, so only a few will survive of Samaria's people, who now recline on luxurious couches. Listen now, and warn the descendants of Jacob.

Amos
(with flourish) The Sovereign Lord Almighty says:

The Lord On the day when I punish the people of Israel for their sins, I will destroy the altars of Bethel. The corners of every altar will be broken off and will fall to the ground. I will destroy winter houses and summer houses. The houses decorated with ivory will fall in ruins; every large house will be destroyed.

Amos Listen to this, you women of Samaria, who grow fat like the well-fed cows of Bashan, who ill-treat the weak, oppress the poor, and demand that your husbands keep you supplied with liquor! As the Sovereign Lord is holy, he has promised:

The Lord The days will come when they will drag you away with hooks; every one of you will be like a fish on a hook. You will be dragged to the nearest break in the wall and thrown out.

Cast [This is] the word of the Lord.
All **Thanks be to God.**

Cast: **Amos, Herald** (can be the same as Amos), **The Lord.**

Israel's failure to learn
Amos 4.4–13

Amos The Sovereign Lord says:

Voice 1 People of Israel, go to the holy place in Bethel and sin, if you must!

Voice 2 Go to Gilgal and sin with all your might!

Voice 3	Go ahead and bring animals to be sacrificed morning after morning, and bring your tithes every third day.
Voice 1	Go ahead and offer your bread in thanksgiving to God, and boast about the extra offerings you bring! This is the kind of thing you love to do.
	I was the one who brought famine to all your cities, yet you did not come back to me.
Voice 2	I held back the rain when your crops needed it most.
Voice 3	I sent rain on one city, but not on another. Rain fell on one field, but another field dried up. Weak with thirst, the people of several cities went to a city where they hoped to find water, but there was not enough to drink.
Voice 1	Still you did not come back to me.
Voice 2	I sent a scorching wind to dry up your crops. The locusts ate up all your gardens and vineyards, your fig-trees and olive-trees.
Voice 1	Still you did not come back to me.
Voice 3	I sent a plague on you like the one I sent on Egypt. I killed your young men in battle and took your horses away. I filled your nostrils with the stink of dead bodies in your camps.
Voice 1	Still you did not come back to me.
Voice 2	I destroyed some of you as I destroyed Sodom and Gomorrah. Those of you who survived were like a burning stick saved from a fire.
Voice 1	Still you did not come back to me:
Amos	The Lord says:
Voices 1–3	So then, people of Israel, I am going to punish you. And because I am going to do this, get ready to face my judgement!
Amos (slowly)	God is the one who made the mountains and created the winds. He makes his thoughts known to us; he changes day into night. He walks on the heights of the earth. This is his name: the Lord God Almighty!
Cast	[This is] the word of the Lord.
All	**Thanks be to God.**

Cast: **Amos, Voice 1, Voice 2, Voice 3.**

A call to repentance
Amos 5.1–9

Amos	Listen, people of Israel, to this funeral song which I sing over you:
Singer	Virgin Israel has fallen, never to rise again! She lies abandoned on the ground, and no one helps her up.

Amos (with flourish)	The Sovereign Lord says:
The Lord	A city in Israel sends out a thousand soldiers, but only a hundred return; another city sends out a hundred, but only ten come back.
Amos	The Lord says to the people of Israel:
The Lord	Come to me, and you will live. Do not go to Beersheba to worship. Do not try to find me at Bethel—Bethel will come to nothing. Do not go to Gilgal—her people are doomed to exile.
Amos	Go to the Lord, and you will live. If you do not go, he will sweep down like fire on the people of Israel. The fire will burn up the people of Bethel, and no one will be able to put it out. You are doomed, you that twist justice and cheat people out of their rights!
Singer	The Lord made the stars, the Pleiades and Orion. He turns darkness into daylight, and day into night. He calls for the waters of the sea and pours them out on the earth. His name is the Lord. He brings destruction on the mighty and their strongholds.
Cast	[This is] the word of the Lord.
All	**Thanks be to God.**

Cast: **Amos, Singer, The Lord.**

The Day of the Lord
Amos 5.10–27

Amos	You people hate anyone who challenges injustice and speaks the whole truth in court. You have oppressed the poor and robbed them of their grain. And so you will not live in the fine stone houses you build or drink wine from the beautiful vineyards you plant. I know how terrible your sins are and how many crimes you have committed. You persecute good men, take bribes, and prevent the poor from getting justice in the courts. And so, keeping quiet in such evil times is the clever thing to do!
	Make it your aim to do what is right, not what is evil, so that you may live. Then the Lord God Almighty really will be with you, as you claim he is. Hate what is evil, love what is right, and see that justice prevails in the courts. Perhaps the Lord will be merciful to the people of this nation who are still left alive.
	And so the Sovereign Lord Almighty says:
The Lord	There will be wailing and cries of sorrow in the city streets. Even farmers will be called to mourn the dead along with those who are paid to mourn. There will be wailing in all the vineyards. All this will take place because I am coming to punish you.

Amos	The Lord has spoken. How terrible it will be for you who long for the day of the Lord! What good will that day do you? For you it will be a day of darkness and not of light. It will be like a man who runs from a lion and meets a bear! Or like a man who comes home and puts his hand on the wall—only to be bitten by a snake! The day of the Lord will bring darkness and not light; it will be a day of gloom, without any brightness.
(with flourish)	The Lord says:
The Lord	I hate your religious festivals; I cannot stand them! When you bring me burnt-offerings and grain-offerings, I will not accept them; I will not accept the animals you have fattened to bring me as offerings. Stop your noisy songs; I do not want to listen to your harps. Instead, let justice flow like a stream, and righteousness like a river that never goes dry.
	People of Israel, I did not demand sacrifices and offerings during those forty years that I led you through the desert. But now, because you have worshipped images of Sakkuth, your king god, and of Kaiwan, your star god, you will have to carry those images when I take you into exile in a land beyond Damascus.
Amos (with flourish)	So says the Lord, whose name is Almighty God!
Cast **All**	[This is] the word of the Lord. **Thanks be to God.**

Cast: **Amos, The Lord.**

The destruction of Israel
Amos 6.1–14

Amos	How terrible it will be for you that have such an easy life in Zion and for you that feel safe in Samaria—you great men of this great nation Israel, you to whom the people go for help! Go and look at the city of Calneh. Then go on to the great city of Hamath and on down to the Philistine city of Gath. Were they any better than the kingdoms of Judah and Israel? Was their territory larger than yours? You refuse to admit that a day of disaster is coming, but what you do only brings that day closer. How terrible it will be for you that stretch out on your luxurious couches, feasting on veal and lamb! You like to compose songs, as David did, and play them on harps. You drink wine by the bowlful and use the finest perfumes, but you do not mourn over the ruin of Israel. So you will be the first to go into exile. Your feasts and banquets will come to an end.
(deliberately)	The Sovereign Lord Almighty has given this solemn warning:
The Lord	I hate the pride of the people of Israel; I despise their luxurious mansions. I will give their capital city and everything in it to the enemy.

Amos	If there are ten men left in a family, they will die. The dead man's relative, the one in charge of the funeral, will take the body out of the house. The relative will call to whoever is still left in the house:
Voice 1	Is anyone else there with you?
Amos	A voice will answer:
Voice 2	No!
Amos	Then the relative will say:
Voice 1	Be quiet! We must be careful not even to mention the Lord's name.
Amos	When the Lord gives the command, houses large and small will be smashed to pieces. Do horses gallop on rocks? Do men plough the sea with oxen? Yet you have turned justice into poison, and right into wrong.
	You boast about capturing the town of Lodebar. You boast:
Voices 1 and **2**	We were strong enough to take Karnaim.
Amos (with flourish)	The Lord God Almighty himself says:
The Lord	People of Israel, I am going to send a foreign army to occupy your country. It will oppress you from Hamath Pass in the north to the brook of the Arabah in the south.
Cast	[This is] the word of the Lord.
All	**Thanks be to God.**

Cast: **Amos, The Lord, Voice 1, Voice 2.**

Amos' visions
Amos 7.1–9

Amos	I had a vision from the Sovereign Lord. In it I saw him create a swarm of locusts just after the king's share of the hay had been cut and the grass was starting to grow again. In my vision I saw the locusts eat up every green thing in the land, and then I said:
Young Amos	Sovereign Lord, forgive your people! How can they survive? They are so small and weak!
Amos	The Lord changed his mind:
The Lord	What you saw will not take place.
Amos	I had another vision from the Sovereign Lord. In it I saw him preparing to punish his people with fire. The fire burnt up the great ocean under the earth, and started to burn up the land. Then I said:
Young Amos	Stop, Sovereign Lord! How can your people survive? They are so small and weak!
Amos	The Lord changed his mind again:

The Lord	This will not take place either.
Amos	I had another vision from the Lord. In it I saw him standing beside a wall that had been built with the help of a plumb-line, and there was a plumb-line in his hand. [He asked me:]
The Lord	Amos, what do you see?
Young Amos	A plumb-line.
The Lord	I am using it to show that my people are like a wall that is out of line. I will not change my mind again about punishing them. The places where Isaac's descendants worship will be destroyed. The holy places of Israel will be left in ruins. I will bring the dynasty of King Jeroboam to an end.
Cast	[This is] the word of the Lord.
All	**Thanks be to God.**

Cast: **Amos, Young Amos, The Lord.**

Amos and Amaziah
Amos 7.10–17

Narrator	Amaziah, the priest of Bethel, sent a report to King Jeroboam of Israel:
Amaziah (as if writing a letter)	Amos is plotting against you among the people. His speeches will destroy the country. This is what he says: 'Jeroboam will die in battle, and the people of Israel will be taken away from their land into exile.'
Narrator	Amaziah then said to Amos:
Amaziah (to Amos)	That's enough, prophet! Go on back to Judah and do your preaching there. Let *them* pay you for it. Don't prophesy here at Bethel any more. This is the king's place of worship, the national temple.
[**Narrator**	Amos answered:]
Amos	I am not the kind of prophet who prophesies for pay. I am a herdsman, and I take care of fig-trees. But the Lord took me from my work as a shepherd and ordered me to come and prophesy to his people Israel. So now listen to what the Lord says. You tell me to stop prophesying, to stop raving against the people of Israel. And so, Amaziah, the Lord says to you, 'Your wife will become a prostitute on the streets, and your children will be killed in war. Your land will be divided up and given to others, and you yourself will die in a heathen country. And the people of Israel will certainly be taken away from their own land into exile.'
Cast	[This is] the word of the Lord.
All	**Thanks be to God.**

Cast: **Narrator, Amaziah, Amos.**

A vision of a basket of fruit
Amos 8.1–3

Amos	I had a vision from the Sovereign Lord. In it I saw a basket of fruit. The Lord asked:
The Lord	Amos, what do you see?
Young Amos	A basket of fruit.
[Amos	The Lord said to me:]
The Lord	The end has come for my people Israel. I will not change my mind again about punishing them. On that day the songs in the palace will become cries of mourning. There will be dead bodies everywhere. They will be thrown out in silence.
Cast	[This is] the word of the Lord.
All	**Thanks be to God.**

Cast: **Amos, The Lord, Young Amos.**

Israel's doom
Amos 8.4–14

Amos	Listen to this, you that trample on the needy and try to destroy the poor of the country. You say among yourselves:
Israelite 1	We can hardly wait for the holy days to be over so that we can sell our corn.
Israelite 2	When will the Sabbath end, so that we can start selling again?
Israelite 1	Then we can overcharge, use false measures, and tamper with the scales to cheat our customers.
Israelite 2	We can sell worthless wheat at a high price.
Israelite 1	We'll find a poor man who can't pay his debts, not even the price of a pair of sandals, and we'll buy him as a slave.
Amos (with flourish)	The Lord, the God of Israel, has sworn:
The Lord	I will never forget their evil deeds. And so the earth will quake, and everyone in the land will be in distress. The whole country will be shaken; it will rise and fall like the River Nile. The time is coming when I will make the sun go down at noon and the earth grow dark in daytime. I, the Sovereign Lord, have spoken. I will turn your festivals into funerals and change your glad songs into cries of grief. I will make you shave your heads and wear sackcloth, and you will be like parents mourning for their only son. That day will be bitter to the end.
	The time is coming when I will send famine on the land. People will be hungry, but not for bread; they will be thirsty, but not for water. They will hunger and thirst for a message from the Lord.

→

I, the Sovereign Lord, have spoken. People will wander from the Dead Sea to the Mediterranean and then on from the north to the east. They will look everywhere for a message from the Lord, but they will not find it. On that day even healthy young men and women will collapse from thirst. Those who swear by the idols of Samaria, who say, 'By the god of Dan,' or, 'By the god of Beersheba'—those people will fall and not rise again.

Cast	[This is] the word of the Lord.
All	**Thanks be to God.**

Cast: **Amos, Israelite 1, Israelite 2** (can be the same as Israelite 1)**, The Lord.**

The Lord's judgements
Amos 9.1–10

Amos	I saw the Lord standing by the altar.
(with flourish)	He gave the command:
The Lord	Strike the tops of the temple columns so hard that the whole porch will shake. Break them off and let them fall on the heads of the people. I will kill the rest of the people in war. No one will get away; not one will escape. Even if they dig their way down to the world of the dead, I will catch them. Even if they climb up to heaven, I will bring them down. If they hide on the top of Mount Carmel, I will search for them and catch them. If they hide from me at the bottom of the sea, I will command the sea-monster to bite them. If they are taken away into captivity by their enemies, I will order them to be put to death. I am determined to destroy them, not to help them.
Singer 1	The Sovereign Lord Almighty touches the earth, and it quakes; all who live there mourn. The whole world rises and falls like the River Nile.
Singer 2	The Lord builds his home in the heavens, and over the earth he puts the dome of the sky. He calls for the waters of the sea and pours them out on the earth.
Singers 1 and **2**	His name is the Lord! (PAUSE)
Amos (with flourish)	The Lord says:
The Lord	People of Israel, I think as much of the people of Sudan as I do of you. I brought the Philistines from Crete and the Syrians from Kir, just as I brought you from Egypt. I, the Sovereign Lord, am watching this sinful kingdom of Israel, and I will destroy it from the face of the earth. But I will not destroy all the descendants of Jacob.
	I will give the command and shake the people of Israel like corn

in a sieve. I will shake them among the nations to remove all who are worthless. The sinners among my people will be killed in war—all those who say, 'God will not let any harm come near us.'

Cast	[This is] the word of the Lord.
All	**Thanks be to God.**

Cast: **Amos, The Lord, Singer 1, Singer 2** (Singers can be the same as Amos).

The future restoration of Israel
Amos 9.11–15

Amos
(with flourish)   The Lord says:

The Lord   A day is coming when I will restore the kingdom of David, which is like a house fallen into ruins. I will repair its walls and restore it. I will rebuild it and make it as it was long ago. And so the people of Israel will conquer what is left of the land of Edom and all the nations that were once mine.

Amos
(with flourish)   So says the Lord, who will cause this to happen!

The Lord says:

The Lord   The days are coming
when corn will grow faster than it can be harvested,
and grapes will grow faster than the wine can be made.
The mountains will drip with sweet wine,
and the hills will flow with it.
I will bring my people back to their land.
They will rebuild their ruined cities and live there;
they will plant vineyards and drink the wine;
they will plant gardens and eat what they grow.
I will plant my people on the land I gave them,
and they will not be pulled up again.

Amos
(with flourish)   The Lord your God has spoken!

Cast	[This is] the word of the Lord.
All	**Thanks be to God.**

Cast: **Amos, The Lord.**

OBADIAH

The Lord will punish Edom
Obadiah 1–14

Announcer	This is the prophecy of Obadiah: it is what the Sovereign Lord said about the nation of Edom:
Obadiah	The Lord has sent his messenger to the nations, and we have heard his message:
The Lord	Get ready! Let us go to war against Edom!
Obadiah	The Lord says to Edom:
The Lord	I will make you weak; everyone will despise you. Your pride has deceived you. Your capital is a fortress of solid rock; your home is high in the mountains, and so you say to yourself:
Edomite	Who can ever pull me down?
The Lord	Even though you make your home as high as an eagle's nest, so that it seems to be among the stars, yet I will pull you down. When thieves come at night, they take only what they want. When people gather grapes, they always leave a few. But your enemies have wiped you out completely. Descendants of Esau, your treasures have been looted. Your allies have deceived you; they have driven you from your country. People who were at peace with you have now conquered you. Those friends who ate with you have laid a trap for you; they say of you:
Friend	Where is all that cleverness he had?
The Lord	On the day I punish Edom, I will destroy their clever men and wipe out all their wisdom. The fighting men of Teman will be terrified, and every soldier in Edom will be killed. Because you robbed and killed your brothers, the descendants of Jacob, you will be destroyed and dishonoured for ever. You stood aside on that day when enemies broke down their gates.

You were as bad as those strangers
who carried off Jerusalem's wealth
and divided it among themselves.
You should not have gloated
over the misfortune of your brothers in Judah.
You should not have been glad
on the day of their ruin.
You should not have laughed at them
in their distress.
You should not have entered the city of my people
to gloat over their suffering
and to seize their riches
on the day of their disaster.
You should not have stood at the crossroads
to catch those trying to escape.
You should not have handed them over to the enemy
on the day of their distress.

Cast	[This is] the word of the Lord.
All	**Thanks be to God.**

Cast: **Announcer, Obadiah, The Lord, Edomite, Friend.**

JONAH

Jonah disobeys the Lord
From Jonah 1.1–17

Narrator	One day, the Lord spoke to Jonah son of Amittai:
The Lord	Go to Nineveh, that great city, and speak out against it; I am aware how wicked its people are.
Narrator	Jonah, however, set out in the opposite direction in order to get away from the Lord.
	He went to Joppa, where he found a ship about to go to Spain. He paid his fare and went aboard with the crew to sail to Spain, where he would be away from the Lord. But the Lord sent a strong wind on the sea, and the storm was so violent that the ship was in danger of breaking up. The sailors were terrified and cried out for help, each one to his own god. Then, in order to lessen the danger, they threw the cargo overboard.
	Meanwhile, Jonah had gone below and was lying in the ship's hold, sound asleep. The captain found him there [and said to him:]
Captain	What are you doing asleep? Get up and pray to your god for help. Maybe he will feel sorry for us and spare our lives.
Narrator	The sailors said to one another:
Sailors 1 and **2**	Let's draw lots—
Sailor 2	And find out who is to blame for getting us into this danger.
Narrator	They did so, and Jonah's name was drawn. So they said to him:
Sailor 2	Now then, tell us! Who is to blame for this?
Sailor 1	What are you doing here?
Sailor 2	What country do you come from?
Sailor 1	What is your nationality?
[Narrator	Jonah answered:]
Jonah	I am a Hebrew, I worship the Lord, the God of heaven, who made land and sea.
Narrator	Jonah went on to tell them that he was running away from the Lord. The sailors were terrified [and said to him]:
Sailor 2	That was an awful thing to do!
Narrator	The storm was getting worse all the time, so the sailors asked him:
Sailor 1	What should we do to you to stop the storm?
[Narrator	Jonah answered:]

Jonah	Throw me into the sea, and it will calm down. I know it is my fault that you are caught in this violent storm.
Narrator	Instead, the sailors tried to get the ship to shore, rowing with all their might. But the storm was getting worse and worse, and they got nowhere. So they cried out to the Lord:
Sailor 2	O Lord, we pray, don't punish us with death for taking this man's life!
Sailor 1	You, O Lord, are responsible for all this.
Sailor 2	It is your doing.
Narrator	Then they picked Jonah up and threw him into the sea, (PAUSE) and it calmed down at once. This made the sailors so afraid of the Lord that they offered a sacrifice and promised to serve him.
	At the Lord's command a large fish swallowed Jonah, and he was inside the fish for three days and nights.
Cast	[This is] the word of the Lord.
All	**Thanks be to God.**

Cast: **Narrator, The Lord, Captain, Sailor 1, Sailor 2** (can be the same as Captain)**, Jonah.**

Jonah's prayer
Jonah 2.1–10

Narrator	From deep inside the fish Jonah prayed to the Lord his God:
Jonah	In my distress, O Lord, I called to you,

In my distress, O Lord, I called to you,
and you answered me.
From deep in the world of the dead
I cried for help, and you heard me.
You threw me down into the depths,
to the very bottom of the sea,
where the waters were all round me,
and all your mighty waves rolled over me.
I thought I had been banished from your presence
and would never see your holy Temple again.
The water came over me and choked me;
the sea covered me completely,
and seaweed was wrapped round my head.
I went down to the very roots of the mountains,
into the land whose gates lock shut for ever.
But you, O Lord my God,
brought me back from the depths alive.
When I felt my life slipping away,
then, O Lord, I prayed to you,
and in your holy Temple you heard me.
Those who worship worthless idols
have abandoned their loyalty to you.
But I will sing praises to you;
I will offer you a sacrifice
and do what I have promised.

→

801

	Salvation comes from the Lord!
Narrator	Then the Lord ordered the fish to spew Jonah up on the beach . . . and it did.
Cast	[This is] the word of the Lord.
All	**Thanks be to God.**

Cast: **Narrator, Jonah.**

Jonah obeys the Lord
Jonah 3.1–10

Narrator	Once again the Lord spoke to Jonah:
The Lord	Go to Nineveh, that great city, and proclaim to the people the message I have given you.
Narrator	So Jonah obeyed the Lord and went to Nineveh, a city so large that it took three days to walk through it. Jonah started through the city, and after walking a whole day, he proclaimed:
Jonah (calling)	In forty days Nineveh will be destroyed!
Narrator	The people of Nineveh believed God's message. So they decided that everyone should fast, and all the people, from the greatest to the least, put on sackcloth to show that they had repented. When the king of Nineveh heard about it, he got up from his throne, took off his robe, put on sackcloth, and sat down in ashes. He sent out a proclamation to the people of Nineveh:
King	This is an order from the king and his officials: No one is to eat anything; all persons, cattle, and sheep are forbidden to eat or drink. All persons and animals must wear sackcloth. Everyone must pray earnestly to God and must give up his wicked behaviour and his evil actions. Perhaps God will change his mind; perhaps he will stop being angry, and we will not die!
Narrator	God saw what they did; he saw that they had given up their wicked behaviour. So he changed his mind and did not punish them as he had said he would.
Cast	[This is] the word of the Lord.
All	**Thanks be to God.**

Cast: **Narrator, The Lord, Jonah, King.**

Jonah's anger and God's mercy
Jonah 4.1–11

Narrator	Jonah was very unhappy that God had not punished the people of Nineveh, and he became angry.
Jonah (angry)	Lord, didn't I say before I left home that this is just what you would do? That's why I did my best to run away to Spain! I knew

that you are a loving and merciful God, always patient, always kind, and always ready to change your mind and not punish. Now, Lord, let me die. I am better off dead than alive.

Narrator   The Lord answered:

The Lord   What right have you to be angry?

Narrator   Jonah went out east of the city and sat down. He made a shelter for himself and sat in its shade, waiting to see what would happen to Nineveh. Then the Lord God made a plant grow up over Jonah to give him some shade, so that he would be more comfortable. Jonah was extremely pleased with the plant. But at dawn the next day, at God's command, a worm attacked the plant, and it died. After the sun had risen, God sent a hot east wind, and Jonah was about to faint from the heat of the sun beating down on his head. So he wished he were dead. He said:

Jonah (petulant)   I am better off dead than alive.

Narrator   But God said to him:

The Lord
(conciliatory)   What right have you to be angry about the plant?

Jonah (bitter)   I have every right to be angry—angry enough to die!

The Lord   This plant grew up in one night and disappeared the next; you didn't do anything for it, and you didn't make it grow—yet you feel sorry for it! How much more, then, should I have pity on Nineveh, that great city. After all, it has more than 120,000 innocent children in it, as well as many animals!

Cast   [This is] the word of the Lord.
All   **Thanks be to God.**

Cast: **Narrator, Jonah, The Lord.**

MICAH

An introduction to Micah
Micah 1.1–9

Narrator   During the time that Jotham, Ahaz, and Hezekiah were kings of Judah, the Lord gave this message to Micah, who was from the town of Moresheth. The Lord revealed to Micah all these things about Samaria and Jerusalem.

Micah   Hear this, all you nations;
                   listen to this, all who live on earth!
                   The Sovereign Lord will testify against you.
                   Listen! He speaks from his heavenly temple.
                   The Lord is coming from his holy place;
                   he will come down and walk on the tops of the mountains.
                   Then the mountains will melt under him
                   like wax in a fire;
                   they will pour down into the valleys
                   like water pouring down a hill. (PAUSE)

                   All this will happen because the people of Israel have sinned and rebelled against God.

Questioner   Who is to blame for Israel's rebellion?

Micah   Samaria, the capital city itself!

Questioner   Who is guilty of idolatry in Judah?

Micah   Jerusalem itself! So the Lord says:

The Lord   I will make Samaria a pile of ruins in the open country, a place for planting grapevines. I will pour the rubble of the city down into the valley, and will lay bare the city's foundations. All its precious idols will be smashed to pieces, everything given to its temple prostitutes will be destroyed by fire, and all its images will become a desolate heap. Samaria acquired these things for its fertility rites, and now her enemies will carry them off for temple prostitutes elsewhere.

Narrator   Then Micah said:

Micah   Because of this I will mourn and lament. To show my sorrow, I will walk about barefoot and naked. I will howl like a jackal and wail like an ostrich. Samaria's wounds cannot be healed, and Judah is about to suffer in the same way; destruction has reached the gates of Jerusalem itself, where my people live.

Cast   [This is] the word of the Lord.
All   **Thanks be to God.**

Cast: **Narrator, Micah, Questioner** (can be the same as Narrator), **The Lord.**

The fate of those who oppress the poor
Micah 2.1–13

Micah   How terrible it will be for those who lie awake and plan evil! When morning comes, as soon as they have the chance, they do the evil they planned. When they want fields, they seize them; when they want houses, they take them. No man's family or property is safe.

And so the Lord says:

The Lord   I am planning to bring disaster on you, and you will not be able to escape it. You are going to find yourselves in trouble, and then you will not walk so proudly any more. When that time comes, people will use your story as an example of disaster, and they will sing this song of despair about your experience:

Singers 1 and **2**   We are completely ruined!

Singer 1   The Lord has taken our land away—

Singer 2   And given it to those who took us captive.

Micah   So then, when the time comes for the land to be given back to the Lord 's people, there will be no share for any of you.

The people preach at me and say:

Persons 1 and **2**   Don't preach at us.

Person 1   Don't preach about all that. God is not going to disgrace us.

Person 2   Do you think the people of Israel are under a *curse*?

Person 1   Has the Lord lost his patience? Would he *really* do such things?

Person 2   Doesn't he speak kindly to those who do right?

Micah   The Lord replies:

The Lord   You attack my people like enemies. Men return from battle, thinking they are safe at home, but there you are, waiting to steal the coats off their backs. You drive the women of my people out of the homes they love, and you have robbed their children of my blessings for ever. Get up and go; there is no safety here any more. Your sins have doomed this place to destruction.

These people want the kind of prophet who goes about full of lies and deceit and says, 'I prophesy that wine and liquor will flow for you.'

But I will gather you together, all you people of Israel that are left. I will bring you together like sheep returning to the fold. Like a pasture full of sheep, your land will once again be filled with many people.

Micah   God will open the way for them and lead them out of exile. They will break out of the city gates and go free. Their king, the Lord himself, will lead them out.

Cast   [This is] the word of the Lord.
All   **Thanks be to God.**

Cast: **Micah, The Lord, Singer 1, Singer 2** (can be the same as Singer 1), **Person 1, Person 2** (can be the same as Person 1).

Micah denounces Israel's leaders
Micah 3.1–12

Micah   Listen, you rulers of Israel! You are supposed to be concerned about justice, yet you hate what is good and you love what is evil. You skin my people alive and tear the flesh off their bones. You eat my people up. You strip off their skin, break their bones, and chop them up like meat for the pot. The time is coming when you will cry out to the Lord, but he will not answer you. He will not listen to your prayers, for you have done evil.

My people are deceived by prophets who promise peace to those who pay them, but threaten war for those who don't. To these prophets the Lord says:

The Lord   Prophets, your day is almost over; the sun is going down on you. Because you mislead my people, you will have no more prophetic visions, and you will not be able to predict anything.

Micah   Those who predict the future will be disgraced by their failure. They will all be humiliated because God does not answer them.

But as for me, the Lord fills me with his spirit and power, and gives me a sense of justice and the courage to tell the people of Israel what their sins are. Listen to me, you rulers of Israel, you that hate justice and turn right into wrong. You are building God's city, Jerusalem, on a foundation of murder and injustice. The city's rulers govern for bribes, the priests interpret the Law for pay, the prophets give their revelations for money—and they all claim that the Lord is with them:

Person 1   No harm will come to us,

Person 2   The Lord is with us.

Micah   And so, because of you, Zion will be ploughed like a field, Jerusalem will become a pile of ruins, and the Temple hill will become a forest.

Cast   [This is] the word of the Lord.
All   **Thanks be to God.**

Cast: **Micah, The Lord, Person 1, Person 2.**

The Lord's universal reign of peace
Micah 4.1–4 [5] (NIV)

Micah   In the last days the mountain of the Lord's Temple will be established
as chief among the mountains;
it will be raised above the hills,
and peoples will stream to it.

Many nations will come and say:

Person 1   Come, let us go up to the mountain of the Lord,
to the house of the God of Jacob.

Person 2   He will teach us his ways,
so that we may walk in his paths.

Micah	The law will go out from Zion,
	the word of the Lord from Jerusalem.
	He will judge between many peoples
	and will settle disputes for strong nations far and wide.
	They will beat their swords into ploughshares
	and their spears into pruning hooks.
	Nation will not take up sword against nation,
	nor will they train for war any more.
	Every man will sit under his own vine
	and under his own fig-tree,
	and no one will make them afraid—
Cast	The Lord Almighty has spoken!
[Micah	All the nations may walk
	in the name of their gods—
Cast	We will walk in the name of the Lord
	our God for ever and ever.]
Cast	[This is] the word of the Lord.
All	**Thanks be to God.**

Cast: **Micah, Person 1, Person 2.**

The Lord's universal reign of peace
Micah 4.1–4 [5] (GNB)

Micah	In days to come
	the mountain where the Temple stands
	will be the highest one of all,
	towering above all the hills.
	Many nations will come streaming to it,
	and their people will say:
Person 1	Let us go up the hill of the Lord,
	to the Temple of Israel's God,
	for he will teach us what he wants us to do.
Person 2	We will walk in the paths he has chosen,
	for the Lord's teaching comes from Jerusalem;
	from Zion he speaks to his people.
Micah	He will settle disputes among the nations,
	among the great powers near and far.
	They will hammer their swords into ploughs
	and their spears into pruning-knives.
	Nations will never again go to war,
	never prepare for battle again.
	Everyone will live in peace
	among his own vineyards and fig-trees,
	and no one will make him afraid.
Cast	The Lord Almighty has promised this.

[Micah	Each nation worships and obeys its own god—
Cast	But we will worship and obey the Lord our God for ever and ever.]

Cast	[This is] the word of the Lord.
All	**Thanks be to God.**

Cast: **Micah, Person 1, Person 2.**

Israel will return from exile
Micah 4.6—5.1

The Lord	The time is coming—
Micah (with flourish)	Says the Lord . . .
The Lord	when I will gather together the people I punished, those who have suffered in exile. They are crippled and far from home, but I will make a new beginning with those who are left, and they will become a great nation. I will rule over them on Mount Zion from that time on and for ever.
Micah	And you, Jerusalem, where God, like a shepherd, watches over his people, will once again be the capital of the kingdom that was yours.
	Why do you cry out so loudly? Why are you suffering like a woman in labour? Is it because you have no king, and your counsellors are dead? Twist and groan, people of Jerusalem, like a woman giving birth, for now you will have to leave the city and live in the open country. You will have to go to Babylon, but there the Lord will save you from your enemies. Many nations have gathered to attack you. [They say:]
Attacker 1	Jerusalem must be destroyed!
Attacker 2	We will see this city in ruins!
Micah	But these nations do not know what is in the Lord's mind. They do not realize that they have been gathered together to be punished in the same way that corn is brought in to be threshed.
	The Lord says:
The Lord	People of Jerusalem, go and punish your enemies! I will make you as strong as a bull with iron horns and bronze hoofs. You will crush many nations, and the wealth they got by violence you will present to me, the Lord of the whole world.
Micah	People of Jerusalem, gather your forces! We are besieged! They are attacking the leader of Israel!
Cast	[This is] the word of the Lord.
All	**Thanks be to God.**

Cast: **The Lord, Micah, Attacker 1, Attacker 2.**

God promises a ruler from Bethlehem
Micah 5.2–5

Micah
(with flourish)   The Lord says:

The Lord   Bethlehem Ephrathah, you are one of the smallest towns in Judah, but out of you I will bring a ruler for Israel, whose family line goes back to ancient times.

Micah   So the Lord will abandon his people to their enemies until the woman who is to give birth has her son. Then his fellow-countrymen who are in exile will be reunited with their own people. When he comes, he will rule his people with the strength that comes from the Lord and with the majesty of the Lord God himself. His people will live in safety because people all over the earth will acknowledge his greatness (PAUSE) and he will bring peace.

Cast   [This is] the word of the Lord.
All   **Thanks be to God.**

Cast: **Micah, The Lord.** (See also Appendix: Christmas Readings, New Testament page 405.)

Deliverance and punishment
Micah 5.5—6.5

Micah   When the Assyrians invade our country and break through our defences, we will send our strongest leaders to fight them. By force of arms they will conquer Assyria, the land of Nimrod, and they will save us from the Assyrians when they invade our territory.

The people of Israel who survive will be like refreshing dew sent by the Lord for many nations, like showers on growing plants. They will depend on God, not man. Those who are left among the nations will be like a lion hunting for food in a forest or a pasture: he gets in among the sheep, pounces on them, and tears them to pieces—and there is no hope of rescue. Israel will conquer her enemies and destroy them all.

(with flourish)   The Lord says:

The Lord   At that time I will take away your horses and destroy your chariots. I will destroy the cities in your land and tear down all your defences. I will destroy the magic charms you use and leave you without any fortune-tellers. I will destroy your idols and sacred stone pillars; no longer will you worship the things that you yourselves have made. I will pull down the images of the goddess Asherah in your land and destroy your cities. And in my great anger I will take revenge on all nations that have not obeyed me.

Micah
(to audience)   Listen to the Lord's case against Israel.   →

(to the Lord)	Arise, O Lord, and present your case; let the mountains and the hills hear what you say.
(calling)	You mountains, you everlasting foundations of the earth, listen to the Lord's case! The Lord has a case against his people. He is going to bring an accusation against Israel.
(with flourish)	The Lord says:
The Lord	My people, what have I done to you? How have I been a burden to you? Answer me. I brought you out of Egypt; I rescued you from slavery; I sent Moses, Aaron, and Miriam to lead you. My people, remember what King Balak of Moab planned to do to you and how Balaam son of Beor answered him. Remember the things that happened on the way from the camp at Acacia to Gilgal. Remember these things and you will realize what I did in order to save you.

Cast	[This is] the word of the Lord.
All	**Thanks be to God.**

Cast: **Micah, The Lord.**

What the Lord requires
Micah 6.6–16

Micah	What shall I bring to the Lord, the God of heaven, when I come to worship him? Shall I bring the best calves to burn as offerings to him? Will the Lord be pleased if I bring him thousands of sheep or endless streams of olive-oil? Shall I offer him my first-born child to pay for my sins? No, the Lord has told us what is good. What he requires of us is this: to do what is just, to show constant love, and to live in humble fellowship with our God. It is wise to fear the Lord.
(with flourish)	He calls to the city:
The Lord	Listen, you people who assemble in the city! In the houses of evil men are treasures which they got dishonestly. They use false measures, a thing that I hate. How can I forgive men who use false scales and weights? Your rich men exploit the poor, and all of you are liars. So I have already begun your ruin and destruction because of your sins. You will eat, but not be satisfied—in fact you will still be hungry. You will carry things off, but you will not be able to save them; anything you do save I will destroy in war. You will sow corn, but not harvest the crop. You will press oil from olives, but never be able to use it. You will make wine, but never drink it. This will happen because you have followed the evil practices of King Omri and of his son, King Ahab. You have continued their policies, and so I will bring you to ruin, and everyone will despise you. People everywhere will treat you with contempt.

Cast	[This is] the word of the Lord.
All	**Thanks be to God.**

Cast: **Micah, The Lord.**

NAHUM

The Lord's judgement
Nahum 1.2–10

Voice 1 The Lord God tolerates no rivals;
he punishes those who oppose him.
In his anger he pays them back.

Voice 2 The Lord does not easily become angry,
but he is powerful
and never lets the guilty go unpunished.

Voice 3 Where the Lord walks, storms arise;
the clouds are the dust raised by his feet!

Voice 1 He commands the sea, and it dries up!
He makes the rivers go dry.
The fields of Bashan wither,
Mount Carmel turns brown,
and the flowers of Lebanon fade.

Voice 2 Mountains quake in the presence of the Lord;
hills melt before him.

Voice 3 The earth shakes when the Lord appears;
the world and all its people tremble.

Voice 1 When he is angry, who can survive?

Voice 2 Who can survive his terrible fury?

Voice 3 He pours out his flaming anger;
rocks crumble to dust before him.

Voice 1 The Lord is good;
he protects his people in times of trouble;
he takes care of those who turn to him.

Voice 2 Like a great rushing flood he completely destroys his enemies;
he sends to their death those who oppose him.

Voice 3 What are you plotting against the Lord?

Voice 1 He will destroy you.

Voice 2 No one opposes him more than once.

Voice 3 Like tangled thorns and dry straw,
you drunkards will be burnt up!

Cast [This is] the word of the Lord.
All **Thanks be to God.**

Cast: **Voice 1, Voice 2, Voice 3.**

The Lord's anger against Nineveh
Nahum 1.11–15

Nahum   From you, Nineveh, there came a man full of wicked schemes, who plotted against the Lord. This is what the Lord says to his people Israel:

The Lord   Even though the Assyrians are strong and numerous, they will be destroyed and disappear. My people, I made you suffer, but I will not do it again. I will now end Assyria's power over you and break the chains that bind you.

Nahum   This is what the Lord has decreed about the Assyrians:

The Lord   They will have no descendants to carry on their name. I will destroy the idols that are in the temples of their gods. I am preparing a grave for the Assyrians—they don't deserve to live!

Nahum   Look, a messenger is coming over the mountains with good news! He is on his way to announce the victory! People of Judah, celebrate your festivals and give God what you solemnly promised him. The wicked will never invade your land again. They have been totally destroyed!

Cast   [This is] the word of the Lord.
All   **Thanks be to God.**

Cast: **Nahum, The Lord.**

The fall of Nineveh
Nahum 2.1–13

Nahum   Nineveh, you are under attack!
The power that will shatter you has come.

Voice 1   Man the defences!

Voice 2   Guard the road!

Voice 3   Prepare for battle!

Nahum   The Lord is about to restore the glory of Israel, as it was before her enemies plundered her.

Voice 1   The enemy soldiers carry red shields
and wear uniforms of red.

Voice 2   They are preparing to attack!

Voice 3   Their chariots flash like fire!

Voice 1   Their horses prance!

Voice 2   Chariots dash wildly through the streets,
rushing to and fro through the city squares.

Voice 3   They flash like torches
and dart about like lightning.

Voice 1	The officers are summoned; they stumble as they press forward.
Voice 2	The attackers rush to the wall and set up the shield for the battering-ram.
Voice 3	The gates by the river burst open; the palace is filled with terror.
Voice 1	The queen is taken captive—
Voice 2	Her servants moan like doves and beat their breasts in sorrow.
Voice 3	Like water from a broken dam the people rush from Nineveh!
Nahum	The cry rings out:
Voices 1 and **2**	Stop! Stop!
Voice 3 (slowly)	But no one turns back.
Voice 1	Plunder the silver!
Voice 2	Plunder the gold!
Voice 3	The city is full of treasure!
Voice 1	Nineveh is destroyed!
Voice 2	Deserted!
Voice 3	Desolate!
Voices 1–3 (slowly)	Hearts melt with fear—
Voice 1	Knees tremble.
Voice 2	Strength is gone—
Voice 3	Faces grow pale.
Voice 1	Where now is the city that was like a den of lions?
Voice 2	The place where young lions were fed.
Voice 3	Where the lion and the lioness would go and their cubs would be safe.
Voice 1	The lion killed his prey and tore it to pieces for his mate and her cubs; he filled his den with torn flesh. (PAUSE)
Nahum (with flourish)	The Lord Almighty says:
The Lord	*I* am your enemy! I will burn up your chariots. Your soldiers will be killed in war, and I will take away everything that you took from others. The demands of your envoys will no longer be heard.
Cast	[This is] the word of the Lord.
All	**Thanks be to God.**

Cast: **Nahum, Voice 1, Voice 2, Voice 3, The Lord.**

HABAKKUK

Habakkuk complains of injustice
Habakkuk 1.1–17

Announcer	This is the message that the Lord revealed to the prophet Habakkuk:
Habakkuk	O Lord, how long must I call for help before you listen, before you save us from violence? Why do you make me see such trouble? How can you endure to look on such wrongdoing? Destruction and violence are all round me, and there is fighting and quarrelling everywhere. The law is weak and useless, and justice is never done. Evil men get the better of the righteous, and so justice is perverted.
Announcer	Then the Lord said to his people:
The Lord	Keep watching the nations round you, and you will be astonished at what you see. I am going to do something that you will not believe when you hear about it. I am bringing the Babylonians to power, those fierce, restless people. They are marching out across the world to conquer other lands. They spread fear and terror, and in their pride they are a law to themselves.
	Their horses are faster than leopards, fiercer than hungry wolves. Their horsemen come riding from distant lands; their horses paw the ground. They come swooping down like eagles attacking their prey.
	Their armies advance in violent conquest, and everyone is terrified as they approach. Their captives are as numerous as grains of sand. They treat kings with contempt and laugh at high officials. No fortress can stop them—they pile up earth against it and capture it. Then they sweep on like the wind and are gone, these men whose power is their god.
Habakkuk	Lord, from the very beginning you are God. You are my God, holy and eternal. Lord, my God and protector, you have chosen the Babylonians and made them strong so that they can punish us. But how can you stand these treacherous, evil men? Your eyes are too holy to look at evil, and you cannot stand the sight of people doing wrong. So why are you silent while they destroy people who are more righteous than they are?
	How can you treat people like fish or like a swarm of insects that have no ruler to direct them? The Babylonians catch people with hooks, as though they were fish. They drag them off in nets and shout for joy over their catch! They even worship their nets and offer sacrifices to them, because their nets provide them with the best of everything.

Are they going to use their swords for ever and keep on destroying nations without mercy?

Cast [This is] the word of the Lord.
All **Thanks be to God.**

Cast: **Announcer, Habakkuk, The Lord.**

Habakkuk receives the Lord's answer
Habakkuk 2.1–4

Habakkuk I will climb my watch-tower and wait to see what the Lord will tell me to say and what answer he will give to my complaint. (PAUSE)

The Lord gave me this answer:

The Lord Write down clearly on clay tablets what I reveal to you, so that it can be read at a glance. Put it in writing, because it is not yet time for it to come true. But the time is coming quickly, and what I show you will come true. It may seem slow in coming, but wait for it; it will certainly take place, and it will not be delayed. And this is the message:

Messenger Those who are evil will not survive, but those who are righteous will live because they are faithful to God.

Cast [This is] the word of the Lord.
All **Thanks be to God.**

Cast: **Habakkuk, The Lord, Messenger.**

Doom on the unrighteous
From Habakkuk 2.5–14

Habakkuk Wealth is deceitful. Greedy men are proud and restless—like death itself they are never satisfied. That is why they conquer nation after nation for themselves. The conquered people will taunt their conquerors and show their scorn for them. They will say:

Person 1 You take what isn't yours, but you are doomed!

Person 2 How long will you go on getting rich by forcing your debtors to pay up?

Habakkuk But before you know it, you that have conquered others will be in debt yourselves and be forced to pay interest. Enemies will come and make you tremble. They will plunder you! You have plundered the people of many nations, but now those who have survived will plunder you because of the murders you have committed and because of your violence against the people of the world and its cities.

Persons 1 and 2 You are doomed!

Habakkuk	You have made your family rich with what you took by violence, and have tried to make your own home safe from harm and danger! But your schemes have brought shame on your family; by destroying many nations you have only brought ruin on yourself. Even the stones of the walls cry out against you, and the rafters echo the cry:
Persons 1 and **2**	You are doomed!
Habakkuk	The Lord Almighty has done this. But the earth will be as full of the knowledge of the Lord's glory as the seas are full of water.
Cast	[This is] the word of the Lord.
All	**Thanks be to God.**

Cast: **Habakkuk, Person 1, Person 2.**

Idols
Habakkuk 2.18–20

Habakkuk	What's the use of an idol? It is only something that a man has made, and it tells you nothing but lies. What good does it do for its maker to trust it—a god that can't even talk! You are doomed!
	You say to a piece of wood:
Person	Wake up!
Habakkuk	Or to a block of stone:
Person	Get up!
Habakkuk	Can an idol reveal anything to you? It may be covered with silver and gold, but there is no life in it. (PAUSE)
	The Lord is in his holy Temple: let everyone on earth be silent in his presence!
Cast	[This is] the word of the Lord.
All	**Thanks be to God.**

Cast: **Habakkuk, Person.**

A prayer of Habakkuk
From Habakkuk 3.1–19

Announcer	This is a prayer of the prophet Habakkuk:
Voice 1	O Lord, I have heard of what you have done, and I am filled with awe. Now do again in our times the great deeds you used to do. Be merciful, even when you are angry.
Voice 2	God is coming again— the holy God is coming from the hills of Paran. His splendour covers the heavens;

and the earth is full of his praise.
He comes with the brightness of lightning;
light flashes from his hand,
there where his power is hidden.
He sends disease before him
and commands death to follow him.
When he stops, the earth shakes;
at his glance the nations tremble.
The eternal mountains are shattered;
the everlasting hills sink down,
the hills where he walked in ancient times.

Voice 1
Was it the rivers that made you angry, Lord?
Was it the sea that made you furious?
You rode upon the clouds;
the storm cloud was your chariot,
as you brought victory to your people.
You got ready to use your bow,
ready to shoot your arrows.
Your lightning split open the earth.
When the mountains saw you, they trembled;
water poured down from the skies.
The waters under the earth roared,
and their waves rose high.
At the flash of your speeding arrows
and the gleam of your shining spear,
the sun and the moon stood still.
You marched across the earth in anger;
you trampled the sea with your horses,
and the mighty waters foamed.

Voice 2
I hear all this, and I tremble;
my lips quiver with fear.
My body goes limp,
and my feet stumble beneath me. (PAUSE)

I will quietly wait for the time to come
when God will punish those who attack us.

Voice 1
Even though the fig-trees have no fruit
and no grapes grow on the vines,
even though the olive-crop fails
and the fields produce no corn,
even though the sheep all die
and the cattle-stalls are empty,
I will still be joyful and glad,
because the Lord God is my saviour.
The Sovereign Lord gives me strength.
He makes me sure-footed as a deer,
and keeps me safe on the mountains.

Cast [This is] the word of the Lord.
All **Thanks be to God.**

Cast: **Announcer, Voice 1, Voice 2.**

ZEPHANIAH

The day of the Lord's judgement
Zephaniah 1.1–18

Announcer   This is the message that the Lord gave to Zephaniah during the time that Josiah son of Amon was king of Judah—Zephaniah was descended from King Hezekiah through Amariah, Gedaliah, and Cushi.

Zephaniah   The Lord said:

The Lord   I am going to destroy everything on earth, all human beings and animals, birds and fish. I will bring about the downfall of the wicked. I will destroy all mankind, and no survivors will be left. I, the Lord, have spoken.

I will punish the people of Jerusalem and of all Judah. I will destroy the last trace of the worship of Baal there, and no one will even remember the pagan priests who serve him. I will destroy anyone who goes up on the roof and worships the sun, the moon, and the stars. I will also destroy those who worship me and swear loyalty to me, but then take oaths in the name of the god Molech. I will destroy those who have turned back and no longer follow me, those who do not come to me or ask me to guide them.

Zephaniah   The day is near when the Lord will sit in judgement; so be silent in his presence. The Lord is preparing to sacrifice his people and has invited enemies to plunder Judah. [The Lord says:]

The Lord   On that day of slaughter I will punish the officials, the king's sons, and all who practise foreign customs. I will punish all who worship like pagans and who steal and kill in order to fill their master's house with loot.

[Zephaniah   Again the Lord says:]

The Lord   On that day you will hear the sound of crying at the Fish Gate in Jerusalem. You will hear wailing in the newer part of the city and a great crashing sound in the hills. Wail and cry when you hear this, you that live in the lower part of the city, because all the merchants will be dead!

At that time I will take a lamp and search Jerusalem. I will punish the people who are self-satisfied and confident, who say to themselves:

Person   The Lord never does anything, one way or the other.

The Lord   Their wealth will be looted and their houses destroyed. They will never live in the houses they are building or drink wine from the vineyards they are planting.

Zephaniah   The great day of the Lord is near—very near and coming fast!

That will be a bitter day, for even the bravest soldiers will cry out in despair! It will be a day of fury, a day of trouble and distress, a day of ruin and destruction, a day of darkness and gloom, a black and cloudy day, a day filled with the sound of war-trumpets and the battle-cry of soldiers attacking fortified cities and high towers.

[The Lord says:]

The Lord I will bring such disasters on mankind that everyone will grope about like a blind man. They have sinned against me, and now their blood will be poured out like water, and their dead bodies will lie rotting on the ground.

Zephaniah On the day when the Lord shows his fury, not even all their silver and gold will save them. The whole earth will be destroyed by the fire of his anger. He will put an end—a sudden end—to everyone who lives on earth.

Cast [This is] the word of the Lord.
All **Thanks be to God.**

Cast: **Announcer, Zephaniah, The Lord, Person.**

The doom of the nations around Israel
Zephaniah 2.1–11

Zephaniah
(sternly) Shameless nation, come to your senses before you are driven away like chaff blown by the wind, before the burning anger of the Lord comes upon you, before the day when he shows his fury.

(kindly) Turn to the Lord, all you humble people of the land, who obey his commands. Do what is right, and humble yourselves before the Lord. Perhaps *you* will escape punishment on the day when the Lord shows his anger.

(sternly) No one will be left in the city of Gaza. Ashkelon will be deserted. The people of Ashdod will be driven out in half a day, and the people of Ekron will be driven from their city. You Philistines are doomed, you people who live along the coast. The Lord has passed sentence on you. He will destroy you, and not one of you will be left. Your land by the sea will become open fields with shepherds' huts and sheep pens.

(kindly) The people of Judah who survive will occupy your land. They will pasture their flocks there and sleep in the houses of Ashkelon. The Lord their God will be with them and make them prosper again.

The Lord Almighty says:

The Lord I have heard the people of Moab and Ammon insulting and taunting my people, and boasting that they would seize their land. As surely as I am the living Lord, the God of Israel, I swear that Moab and Ammon are going to be destroyed like Sodom and Gomorrah. They will become a place of salt pits and everlasting ruin, overgrown with weeds. Those of my people who survive will plunder them and take their land.

Zephaniah	That is how the people of Moab and Ammon will be punished for their pride and arrogance and for insulting the people of the Lord Almighty. The Lord will terrify them. He will reduce the gods of the earth to nothing, and then every nation will worship him, each in its own land.
Cast	[This is] the word of the Lord.
All	**Thanks be to God.**

Cast: **Zephaniah, The Lord.**

Jerusalem's sin and redemption
Zephaniah 3.1–13

Zephaniah (sternly)	Jerusalem is doomed, that corrupt, rebellious city that oppresses its own people. It has not listened to the Lord or accepted his discipline. It has not put its trust in the Lord or asked for his help. Its officials are like roaring lions; its judges are like hungry wolves, too greedy to leave a bone until morning. The prophets are irresponsible and treacherous; the priests defile what is sacred, and twist the law of God to their own advantage.
(gently)	But the Lord is still in the city; he does what is right and never what is wrong. Every morning without fail, he brings justice to his people. And yet the unrighteous people there keep on doing wrong and are not ashamed.
(with flourish)	The Lord says:
The Lord	I have wiped out whole nations; I have destroyed their cities and left their walls and towers in ruins. The cities are deserted; the streets are empty—no one is left. I thought that then my people would have reverence for me and accept my discipline, that they would never forget the lesson I taught them. But soon they were behaving as badly as ever.
Zephaniah	Again, the Lord says:
The Lord	Just wait. Wait for the day when I rise to accuse the nations. I have made up my mind to gather nations and kingdoms, in order to let them feel the force of my anger. The whole earth will be destroyed by the fire of my fury.
	Then I will change the people of the nations, and they will pray to me alone and not to other gods. They will all obey me. Even from distant Sudan my scattered people will bring offerings to me. At that time you, my people, will no longer need to be ashamed that you rebelled against me. I will remove everyone who is proud and arrogant, and you will never again rebel against me on my sacred hill. I will leave there a humble and lowly people, who will come to me for help. The people of Israel who survive will do no wrong to anyone, tell no lies, nor try to deceive. They will be prosperous and secure, afraid of no one.
Cast	[This is] the word of the Lord.
All	**Thanks be to God.**

Cast: **Zephaniah, The Lord.**

A song of joy
Zephaniah 3.14–20

Zephaniah Sing and shout for joy, people of Israel!
Rejoice with all your heart, Jerusalem!
The Lord has ended your punishment;
he has removed all your enemies.
The Lord, the king of Israel, is with you;
there is no reason now to be afraid.
The time is coming when they will say to Jerusalem:

Person 1 Do not be afraid, city of Zion!

Person 2 Do not let your hands hang limp!

Person 1 The Lord your God is with you;
his power gives you victory.

Person 2 The Lord will take delight in you,
and in his love he will give you new life.

Person 1 He will sing and be joyful over you,
as joyful as people at a festival.

Zephaniah The Lord says:

The Lord I have ended the threat of doom
and taken away your disgrace.

The time is coming!
I will punish your oppressors;
I will rescue all the lame
and bring the exiles home.
I will turn their shame to honour,
and all the world will praise them.

The time is coming!
I will bring your scattered people home;
I will make you famous throughout the world
and make you prosperous once again.

Zephaniah
(with flourish) The Lord has spoken!

Cast [This is] the word of the Lord.
All **Thanks be to God.**

Cast: **Zephaniah, Person 1, Person 2** (can be the same as Person 1), **The Lord.**

HAGGAI

The Lord's command to rebuild the temple
Haggai 1.1–15

Narrator During the second year that Darius was emperor of Persia, on the first day of the sixth month, the Lord spoke through the prophet Haggai. The message was for the governor of Judah, Zerubbabel son of Shealtiel, and for the High Priest, Joshua son of Jehozadak.

The Lord Almighty said to Haggai:

The Lord These people say that this is not the right time to rebuild the Temple.

Narrator The Lord then gave this message to the people through the prophet Haggai:

Haggai My people, why should you be living in well-built houses while my Temple lies in ruins? Don't you see what is happening to you? You have sown much corn, but have harvested very little. You have food to eat, but not enough to make you full. You have wine to drink, but not enough to get drunk on! You have clothing, but not enough to keep you warm. And the working man cannot earn enough to live on. Can't you see why this has happened? Now go up into the hills, get timber, and rebuild the Temple; then I will be pleased and will be worshipped as I should be.

You hoped for large harvests, but they turned out to be small. And when you brought the harvest home, I blew it away. Why did I do that? Because my Temple lies in ruins while every one of you is busy working on his own house. That is why there is no rain and nothing can grow. I have brought drought on the land—on its hills, cornfields, vineyards, and olive orchards—on every crop the ground produces, on men and animals, on everything you try to grow.

Narrator Then Zerubbabel and Joshua and all the people who had returned from the exile in Babylonia, did what the Lord their God told them to do. They were afraid and obeyed the prophet Haggai, the Lord's messenger. Then Haggai gave the Lord's message to the people:

Haggai and **The Lord** I will be with you—that is my promise.

Narrator The Lord inspired everyone to work on the Temple: Zerubbabel, the governor of Judah; Joshua, the High Priest, and all the people who had returned from the exile. They began working on the Temple of the Lord Almighty, their God, on the twenty-fourth day of the sixth month of the second year that Darius was emperor.

Cast [This is] the word of the Lord.
All **Thanks be to God.**

Cast: **Narrator, The Lord, Haggai** (can be the same as The Lord).

The splendour of the new Temple
Haggai 2.1–9

Narrator On the twenty-first day of the seventh month of the second year that Darius was emperor, the Lord spoke again through the prophet Haggai. He told Haggai to speak to Zerubbabel, the governor of Judah, to Joshua, the High Priest, and to the people, and to say to them:

The Lord Is there anyone among you who can still remember how splendid the Temple used to be? How does it look to you now? It must seem like nothing at all. But now don't be discouraged, any of you. Do the work, for I am with you. When you came out of Egypt, I promised that I would always be with you. I am still with you, so do not be afraid.

Before long I will shake heaven and earth, land and sea. I will overthrow all the nations, and their treasures will be brought here, and the Temple will be filled with wealth. All the silver and gold of the world is mine. The new Temple will be more splendid than the old one, and there I will give my people prosperity and peace.

Haggai
(with flourish) The Lord Almighty has spoken!

Cast [This is] the word of the Lord.
All **Thanks be to God.**

Cast: **Narrator, The Lord, Haggai.**

The prophet consults the priests
Haggai 2.10–14

Narrator On the twenty-fourth day of the ninth month of the second year that Darius was emperor, the Lord Almighty spoke again to the prophet Haggai. He said:

The Lord Ask the priests for a ruling on this question: Suppose someone takes a piece of consecrated meat from a sacrifice and carries it in a fold of his robe. If he then lets his robe touch any bread, cooked food, wine, olive-oil, or any kind of food at all, will it make that food consecrated also?

Narrator When the question was asked, the priests answered:

Priest(s) No.

Narrator Then Haggai asked:

Haggai Suppose a man is defiled because he has touched a dead body. If he then touches any of these foods, will that make them defiled too?

Narrator The priests answered:

Priest(s) Yes.

Haggai	The Lord says that the same thing applies to the people of this nation and to everything they produce; and so everything they offer on the altar is defiled.

Cast	[This is] the word of the Lord.
All	**Thanks be to God.**

Cast: **Narrator, The Lord, Priest(s), Haggai.**

The Lord promises his blessing
Haggai 2.15–23

Narrator	The Lord says:
The Lord	Can't you see what has happened to you? Before you started to rebuild the Temple, you would go to a heap of corn expecting to find two hundred kilogrammes, but there would be only a hundred. You would go to draw a hundred litres of wine from a vat, but find only forty. I sent scorching winds and hail to ruin everything you tried to grow, but still you did not repent. Today is the twenty-fourth day of the ninth month, the day that the foundation of the Temple has been completed. See what is going to happen from now on. Although there is no corn left, and the grapevines, fig-trees, pomegranates, and olive-trees have not yet produced, yet from now on I will bless you.
Narrator	On that same day, the twenty-fourth of the month, the Lord gave Haggai a second message for Zerubbabel, the governor of Judah:
The Lord	I am about to shake heaven and earth and overthrow kingdoms and end their power. I will overturn chariots and their drivers; the horses will die, and their riders will kill one another. On that day I will take you, Zerubbabel my servant, and I will appoint you to rule in my name. You are the one I have chosen.
Haggai (with flourish)	The Lord Almighty has spoken!

Cast	[This is] the word of the Lord.
All	**Thanks be to God.**

Cast: **Narrator, The Lord, Haggai.**

ZECHARIAH

Zechariah's vision of the horses
Zechariah 1.7–17

Zechariah	In the second year that Darius was emperor, on the twenty-fourth day of the eleventh month—the month of Shebat—the Lord gave me a message in a vision at night. I saw an angel of the Lord riding a red horse. He had stopped among some myrtle-trees in a valley, and behind him were other horses—red, dappled, and white. I asked him:
Young Zechariah	Sir, what do these horses mean?
[Zechariah	He answered:]
Angel	I will show you what they mean. The Lord sent them to go and inspect the earth.
Zechariah	They reported to the angel:
Rider	We have been all over the world and have found that the whole world lies helpless and subdued.
Zechariah	Then the angel said:
Angel	Almighty Lord, you have been angry with Jerusalem and the cities of Judah for seventy years now. How much longer will it be before you show them mercy?
Zechariah	The Lord answered the angel with comforting words, and the angel told me to proclaim what the Lord Almighty had said:
The Lord	I have a deep love and concern for Jerusalem, my holy city, and I am very angry with the nations that enjoy quiet and peace. For while I was holding back my anger against my people, those nations made the sufferings of my people worse. So I have come back to Jerusalem to show mercy to the city. My Temple will be restored, and the city will be rebuilt.
Zechariah	The angel also told me to proclaim:
Young Zechariah	The Lord Almighty says that his cities will be prosperous again and that he will once again help Jerusalem and claim the city as his own.
Cast	[This is] the word of the Lord.
All	**Thanks be to God.**

Cast: **Zechariah, Young Zechariah, Angel, Rider, The Lord.**

The vision of the horns
Zechariah 1.18–21

Zechariah	In another vision I saw four ox horns. I asked the angel that had been speaking to me:
Young Zechariah	What do these horns mean?
[Zechariah	He answered:]
Angel	They stand for the world powers that have scattered the people of Judah, Israel, and Jerusalem.
Zechariah	Then the Lord showed me four workmen with hammers. [I asked:]
Young Zechariah	What have these men come to do?
[Zechariah	He answered:]
The Angel	They have come to terrify and overthrow the nations that completely crushed the land of Judah and scattered its people.
Cast	[This is] the word of the Lord.
All	**Thanks be to God.**

Cast: **Zechariah, Young Zechariah, Angel.**

The vision of the measuring-line
Zechariah 2.1–5

Zechariah	In a vision I saw a man with a measuring-line in his hand. I asked:
Young Zechariah	Where are you going?
[Zechariah	He answered:]
Man	To measure Jerusalem, to see how long and how wide it is.
Zechariah	Then I saw the angel who had been speaking to me step forward, and another angel came to meet him. The first one said to the other:
Angel	Run and tell that young man with the measuring-line that there are going to be so many people and so much livestock in Jerusalem that it will be too big to have walls. The Lord has promised that he himself will be a wall of fire round the city to protect it and that he will live there in all his glory.
Cast	[This is] the word of the Lord.
All	**Thanks be to God.**

Cast: **Zechariah, Young Zechariah, Man, Angel.**

The exiles are called to come home
Zechariah 2.6–13

Zechariah	The Lord said to his people:
The Lord	I scattered you in all directions. But now, you exiles, escape from Babylonia and return to Jerusalem. Anyone who strikes you strikes what is most precious to me.
Zechariah	So the Lord Almighty sent me with this message for the nations that had plundered his people:
Young Zechariah	The Lord himself will fight against you, and you will be plundered by the people who were once your servants.
Zechariah	When this happens, everyone will know that the Lord Almighty sent me. (PAUSE)
	[The Lord said:]
The Lord	Sing for joy, people of Jerusalem! I am coming to live among you!
Zechariah	At that time many nations will come to the Lord and become his people. He will live among you, and you will know that he has sent me to you. Once again Judah will be the special possession of the Lord in his sacred land, and Jerusalem will be the city he loves most of all. (PAUSE)
	Be silent, everyone, in the presence of the Lord, for he is coming from his holy dwelling-place.
Cast	[This is] the word of the Lord.
All	**Thanks be to God.**

Cast: **Zechariah, The Lord, Young Zechariah.**

The prophet's vision of the High Priest
Zechariah 3.1–10

Zechariah	In a vision the Lord showed me the High Priest Joshua standing before the angel of the Lord. And there beside Joshua stood Satan, ready to bring an accusation against him. The angel of the Lord said to Satan:
Angel	May the Lord condemn you, Satan! May the Lord, who loves Jerusalem, condemn you. This man is like a stick snatched from the fire.
Zechariah	Joshua was standing there, wearing filthy clothes. The angel said to his heavenly attendants:
Angel	Take away the filthy clothes this man is wearing.
Zechariah	Then he said to Joshua:
Angel	I have taken away your sin and will give you new clothes to wear.

Zechariah	He commanded the attendants to put a clean turban on Joshua's head. They did so, and then they put the new clothes on him while the angel of the Lord stood there.
	Then the angel told Joshua that the Lord Almighty had said:
The Lord	If you obey my laws and perform the duties I have assigned to you, then you will continue to be in charge of my Temple and its courts, and I will hear your prayers, just as I hear the prayers of the angels who are in my presence. Listen then, Joshua, you who are the High Priest; and listen, you fellow-priests of his, you that are the sign of a good future: I will reveal my servant, who is called The Branch! I am placing in front of Joshua a single stone with seven facets. I will engrave an inscription on it, and in a single day I will take away the sin of this land. When that day comes, each of you will invite his neighbour to come and enjoy peace and security, surrounded by your vineyards and fig-trees.
Cast	[This is] the word of the Lord.
All	**Thanks be to God.**

Cast: **Zechariah, Angel, The Lord.**

The vision of the lamp-stand
From Zechariah 4.1–14

Zechariah	The angel who had been speaking to me came again and roused me as if I had been sleeping [He asked]:
Angel	What do you see?
Zechariah	I answered:
Young Zechariah	A lamp-stand made of gold. At the top is a bowl for the oil. On the lamp-stand are seven lamps, each one with places for seven wicks. There are two olive-trees beside the lamp-stand, one on each side of it.
Zechariah	Then I asked the angel:
Young Zechariah	What do these things stand for, sir?
Angel	Don't you know?
Young Zechariah	No, I don't, sir.
[Zechariah	The angel said to me:]
Angel	The seven lamps are the seven eyes of the Lord, which see all over the earth.
Young Zechariah	What do the two olive-trees on either side of the lamp-stand mean? And what is the meaning of the two olive branches beside the two gold pipes from which the olive-oil pours?

Angel	Don't you know?
Young Zechariah	No, I don't, sir.
Angel	These are the two men whom God has chosen and anointed to serve him, the Lord of the whole earth.
Cast	[This is] the word of the Lord.
All	**Thanks be to God.**

Cast: **Zechariah, Angel, Young Zechariah.** (As in the Good News Bible, verses 6–10a are moved to the next reading in order to retain the natural order of the narrative.)

God's promise to Zerubbabel
Zechariah 4.6–10

Zechariah	The angel told me to give Zerubbabel this message from the Lord:
The Lord	You will succeed, not by military might or by your own strength, but by my spirit. Obstacles as great as mountains will disappear before you. You will rebuild the Temple, and as you put the last stone in place, the people will shout:
Persons 1	Beautiful!
Persons 1 and 2	Beautiful!
Zechariah	Another message came to me from the Lord [He said:]
The Lord	Zerubbabel has laid the foundation of the Temple, and he will finish the building. When this happens, my people will know that it is I who sent you to them. They are disappointed because so little progress is being made. But they will see Zerubbabel continuing to build the Temple, and they will be glad.
Cast	[This is] the word of the Lord.
All	**Thanks be to God.**

Cast: **Zechariah, The Lord, Person 1, Person 2** (can be the same as Person 1). (As in the Good News Bible, verses 6–10 are moved after verses 10b–14 in order to retain the natural order of the narrative.)

Zechariah's visions
Zechariah 5.1—6.8

Zechariah	I looked again, and this time I saw a scroll flying through the air. The angel asked me what I saw. I answered:
Young Zechariah	A scroll flying through the air; it is nine metres long and four and a half metres wide.
Zechariah	Then he said to me:
Angel	On it is written the curse that is to go out over the whole land. On one side of the scroll it says that every thief will be removed from the land; and on the other side it says that everyone who tells lies under oath will also be taken away. The Lord Almighty says that

→

	he will send this curse out, and it will enter the house of every thief and the house of everyone who tells lies under oath. It will remain in their houses and leave them in ruins.
Zechariah	The angel appeared again [and said:]
Angel	Look! Something else is coming!
Young Zechariah	What is it?
Angel	It is a basket, and it stands for the sin of the whole land.
Zechariah	The basket had a lid made of lead. As I watched, the lid was raised, and there in the basket sat a woman! [The angel said:]
Angel	This woman represents wickedness.
Zechariah	Then he pushed her down into the basket and put the lid back down. I looked up and saw two women flying towards me with powerful wings like those of a stork. They picked up the basket and flew off with it. I asked the angel:
Young Zechariah	Where are they taking it?
[Zechariah	He answered:]
Angel	To Babylonia, where they will build a temple for it. When the temple is finished, the basket will be placed there to be worshipped.
Zechariah	I had another vision. This time I saw four chariots coming out from between two bronze mountains. The first chariot was pulled by red horses, the second by black horses, the third by white horses, and the fourth by dappled horses. Then I asked the angel:
Young Zechariah	Sir, what do these chariots mean?
Angel	These are the four winds; they have just come from the presence of the Lord of all the earth.
Zechariah	The chariot pulled by the black horses was going north to Babylonia, the white horses were going to the west, and the dappled horses were going to the country in the south. As the dappled horses came out, they were impatient to go and inspect the earth. The angel said:
Angel	Go and inspect the earth!
Zechariah	And they did. Then the angel cried out to me:
Angel	The horses that went north to Babylonia have calmed down the Lord's anger.
Cast **All**	[This is] the word of the Lord. **Thanks be to God.**

Cast: **Zechariah, Young Zechariah, Angel.**

The command to crown Joshua
Zechariah 6.9–15

Zechariah	The Lord gave me this message. He said:
The Lord	Take the gifts given by the exiles Heldai, Tobijah, and Jedaiah, and go at once to the home of Josiah son of Zephaniah. All these men have returned from exile in Babylonia. Make a crown out of the silver and gold they have given, and put it on the head of the High Priest, Joshua son of Jehozadak. Tell him that the Lord Almighty says, 'The man who is called The Branch will flourish where he is and rebuild the Lord's Temple. He is the one who will build it and receive the honour due to a king, and he will rule his people. A priest will stand by his throne, and they will work together in peace and harmony.' The crown will be a memorial in the Lord's Temple in honour of Heldai, Tobijah, Jedaiah, and Josiah.
Zechariah	Men who live far away will come and help to rebuild the Temple of the Lord. And when it is rebuilt, you will know that the Lord Almighty sent me to you. This will all happen if you fully obey the commands of the Lord your God.
Cast	[This is] the word of the Lord.
All	**Thanks be to God.**

Cast: **Zechariah, The Lord.**

The Lord condemns insincere fasting
Zechariah 7.1–7

Zechariah	In the fourth year that Darius was emperor, on the fourth day of the ninth month—the month of Kislev—the Lord gave me a message.
	The people of Bethel had sent Sharezer and Regemmelech and their men to the Temple of the Lord Almighty to pray for the Lord's blessing and to ask the priests and the prophets this question:
Questioner	Should we continue to mourn because of the destruction of the Temple, by fasting in the fifth month as we have done for so many years now?
Zechariah	This is the message of the Lord that came to me:
The Lord	Tell the people of the land and the priests that when they fasted and mourned in the fifth and seventh months during these seventy years, it was not in honour of me. And when they ate and drank, it was for their own satisfaction.
Zechariah	This is what the Lord said through the earlier prophets at the time when Jerusalem was prosperous and filled with people and when there were many people living not only in the towns round the city but also in the southern region and in the western foothills.
Cast	[This is] the word of the Lord.
All	**Thanks be to God.**

Cast: **Zechariah, Questioner, The Lord.**

Disobedience, the cause of exile
Zechariah 7.8–14

Narrator	The Lord gave this message to Zechariah:
The Lord	Long ago I gave these commands to my people—
Voice	You must see that justice is done, and must show kindness and mercy to one another. Do not oppress widows, orphans, foreigners who live among you, or anyone else in need. And do not plan ways of harming one another.
The Lord	But my people stubbornly refused to listen. They closed their minds and made their hearts as hard as rock. Because they would not listen to the teaching which I sent through the prophets who lived long ago, I became very angry. Because they did not listen when I spoke, I did not answer when they prayed. Like a storm I swept them away to live in foreign countries. This good land was left a desolate place, with no one living in it.
Cast	[This is] the word of the Lord.
All	**Thanks be to God.**

Cast: **Narrator, The Lord, Voice.**

The Lord promises to restore Jerusalem (i)
From Zechariah 8.1–13

Narrator	The Lord Almighty gave this message to Zechariah:
The Lord	I have longed to help Jerusalem because of my deep love for her people, a love which has made me angry with her enemies. I will return to Jerusalem, my holy city, and live there. It will be known as the faithful city, and the hill of the Lord Almighty will be called the sacred hill. Once again old men and women, so old that they use a stick when they walk, will be sitting in the city squares. And the streets will again be full of boys and girls playing.
	My people will sow their crops in peace. Their vines will bear grapes, the earth will produce crops, and there will be plenty of rain. I will give all these blessings to the people of my nation who survive.
	People of Judah and Israel! In the past foreigners have cursed one another by saying:
Foreigner 1	May the same disasters fall on you that fell on Judah and Israel!
The Lord	But I will save you, and then those foreigners will say to one another:
Foreigner 2	May you receive the same blessings that came to Judah and Israel!
The Lord	So have courage and don't be afraid.
Cast	[This is] the word of the Lord.
All	**Thanks be to God.**

Cast: **Narrator, The Lord, Foreigner 1, Foreigner 2.**

The Lord promises to restore Jerusalem (ii)
Zechariah 8.14–23

Narrator The Lord Almighty says:

The Lord When your ancestors made me angry, I planned disaster for them and did not change my mind, but carried out my plans. But now I am planning to bless the people of Jerusalem and Judah. So don't be afraid. These are the things you should do: Speak the truth to one another. In the courts, give *real* justice—the kind that brings peace. Do not plan ways of harming one another. Do not give false testimony under oath. I hate lying, injustice, and violence.

Narrator The Lord Almighty gave this message to Zechariah:

The Lord The fasts held in the fourth, fifth, seventh, and tenth months will become festivals of joy and gladness for the people of Judah. You must love truth and peace.

Narrator The Lord Almighty says:

The Lord The time is coming when people from many cities will come to Jerusalem. Those from one city will say to those from another—

Foreigner 1 We are going to worship the Lord Almighty and pray for his blessing.

Foreigner 2 Come with us!

The Lord Many peoples and powerful nations will come to Jerusalem to worship the Lord Almighty, and to pray for his blessing. In those days ten foreigners will come to one Jew and say:

Foreigner 1 We want to share in your destiny, because we have heard that God is with you.

Cast [This is] the word of the Lord.
All **Thanks be to God.**

Cast: **Narrator, The Lord, Foreigner 1, Foreigner 2.**

Judgement on neighbouring nations
Zechariah 9.1–8

Zechariah This is the Lord's message:

He has decreed punishment for the land of Hadrach and for the city of Damascus. Not only the tribes of Israel, but also the capital of Syria belong to the Lord. Hamath, which borders on Hadrach, also belongs to him, and so do the cities of Tyre and Sidon, with all their skill. Tyre has built fortifications for herself and has piled up so much silver and gold that it is as common as dirt! But the Lord will take away everything she has. He will throw her wealth into the sea, and the city will be burnt to the ground. →

The city of Ashkelon will see this and be afraid. The city of Gaza will see it and suffer great pain. So will Ekron, and her hopes will be shattered. Gaza will lose her king, and Ashkelon will be left deserted. People of mixed race will live in Ashdod. The Lord says:

The Lord   I will humble all these proud Philistines. They will no longer eat meat with blood in it, or other forbidden food. All the survivors will become part of my people and be like a clan in the tribe of Judah. Ekron will become part of my people, as the Jebusites did. I will guard my land and keep armies from passing through it. I will not allow tyrants to oppress my people any more. I have seen how my people have suffered.

Cast   [This is] the word of the Lord.
All   **Thanks be to God.**

Cast: **Zechariah, The Lord.**

The future king
Zechariah 9.9–10

Voice 1   Rejoice, rejoice, people of Zion!

Voice 2   Shout for joy, you people of Jerusalem!

Voices 1 and 2   Look, your king is coming to you!

Zechariah   He comes triumphant and victorious,
                     but humble and riding on a donkey—
                     on a colt, the foal of a donkey.

(with flourish)   The Lord says:

The Lord   I will remove the war-chariots from Israel and take the horses from Jerusalem; the bows used in battle will be destroyed. Your king will make peace among the nations; he will rule from sea to sea, from the River Euphrates to the ends of the earth.

Cast   [This is] the word of the Lord.
All   **Thanks be to God.**

Cast: **Voice 1, Voice 2, Zechariah** (can be the same as Voices 1 and 2)**, The Lord.**

The restoration of God's people
From Zechariah 9.11–17

Zechariah
(with flourish)   The Lord says:

The Lord   Because of my covenant with you that was sealed by the blood of sacrifices, I will set your people free—free from the waterless pit of exile. Return, you exiles who now have hope; return to your place of safety. I tell you now, I will repay you twice over with blessing for all you have suffered. I will use Judah like a soldier's bow and Israel like the arrows. I will use the men of Zion like a sword, to fight the men of Greece.

Zechariah	When that day comes, the Lord will save his people, as a shepherd saves his flock from danger. They will shine in his land like the jewels of a crown. How good and beautiful the land will be! The young people will grow strong on its corn and wine.
Cast	[This is] the word of the Lord.
All	**Thanks be to God.**

Cast: **Zechariah, The Lord.**

The Lord promises deliverance
From Zechariah 10.1–12

Zechariah	Ask the Lord for rain in the spring of the year. It is the Lord who sends rain-clouds and showers, making the fields green for everyone. People consult idols and fortune-tellers, but the answers they get are lies and nonsense. Some interpret dreams, but only mislead you; the comfort they give is useless. So the people wander about like lost sheep. They are in trouble because they have no leader.
(with flourish)	The Lord says:
The Lord	I am angry with those foreigners who rule my people, and I am going to punish them. The people of Judah are mine, and I, the Lord Almighty, will take care of them. They will be my powerful war-horses. From among them will come rulers, leaders, and commanders to govern my people. The people of Judah will be victorious like soldiers who trample their enemies into the mud of the streets. They will fight because the Lord is with them, and they will defeat even the enemy horsemen.
Singer 1	I will make the people of Judah strong; I will rescue the people of Israel. I will have compassion on them and bring them all back home. They will be as though I had never rejected them. I am the Lord their God; I will answer their prayers.
Singer 2	I will call my people and gather them together. I will rescue them and make them as numerous as they used to be.
Singer 1	Though I have scattered them among the nations, yet in far-off places they will remember me. They and their children will survive and return home together. From Egypt and Assyria I will bring them home and settle them in their own country. I will settle them in Gilead and Lebanon also; the whole land will be filled with people.
Singer 2	When they pass through their sea of trouble, I, the Lord, will strike the waves, and the depths of the Nile will go dry.

→

Proud Assyria will be humbled,
and mighty Egypt will lose her power.
I will make my people strong;
they will worship and obey me.

Zechariah
(with flourish)   The Lord has spoken!

Cast	[This is] the word of the Lord.
All	**Thanks be to God.**

Cast: **Zechariah, The Lord, Singer 1, Singer 2** (can be the same as Singer 1).

The two shepherds
From Zechariah 11.4–17

Zechariah   The Lord my God said to me:

The Lord   Act the part of the shepherd of a flock of sheep that are going to be butchered. Their owners kill them and go unpunished. They sell the meat and say—

Owners 1 and **2**   Praise the Lord!

Owner 2   We are rich!

The Lord   Even their own shepherds have no pity on them.

Zechariah   Those who bought and sold the sheep hired me, and I became the shepherd of the sheep that were going to be butchered. I took two sticks: one I called 'Favour', and the other 'Unity'. And I took care of the flock. I lost patience with three other shepherds, who hated me, and I got rid of them all in a single month. Then I said to the flock:

Young Zechariah   I will not be your shepherd any longer. Let those who are to die, die. Let those who are to be destroyed, be destroyed. Those who are left will destroy one another.

Zechariah   Then I took the stick called 'Favour' and broke it, to cancel the covenant which the Lord had made with all the nations. So the covenant was cancelled on that day. Those who bought and sold the sheep were watching me, and they knew that the Lord was speaking through what I did. I said to them:

Young Zechariah   If you are willing, give me my wages. But if not, keep them.

Zechariah   So they paid me thirty pieces of silver as my wages. The Lord said to me:

The Lord   Put them in the temple treasury.

Zechariah   So I took the thirty pieces of silver—the magnificent sum they thought I was worth—and put them in the temple treasury. Then I broke the second stick, the one called 'Unity', and the unity of Judah and Israel was shattered.

Then the Lord said to me:

The Lord   Once again act the part of a shepherd, this time a worthless one. I have put a shepherd in charge of my flock, but he does not help the sheep that are threatened by destruction; nor does he look for the lost, or heal those that are hurt, or feed the healthy. Instead, he eats the meat of the fattest sheep and tears off their hoofs. That worthless shepherd is doomed! He has abandoned his flock. War will totally destroy his power. His arm will wither, and his right eye will go blind.

Cast   [This is] the word of the Lord.
All   **Thanks be to God.**

Cast: **Zechariah, The Lord, Owner 1, Owner 2** (can be the same as Owner 1), **Young Zechariah.**

MALACHI

The Lord's love for Israel
Malachi 1.1–5

Announcer	This is the message that the Lord gave Malachi to tell the people of Israel.
Malachi	The Lord says to his people:
The Lord	I have always loved you.
Malachi	But they reply:
Person 1	How have you shown your love for us?
Malachi	The Lord answers:
The Lord	Esau and Jacob were brothers, but I have loved Jacob and his descendants, and have hated Esau and his descendants. I have devastated Esau's hill-country and abandoned the land to jackals.
Malachi	If Esau's descendants, the Edomites, say, 'Our towns have been destroyed, but we will rebuild them,' then the Lord will reply, '*Let* them rebuild—I will tear them down again. People will call them 'The evil country' and 'The nation with whom the Lord is angry for ever.' The people of Israel are going to see this with their own eyes, and they will say:
Persons 1 and **2**	The Lord is mighty—
Person 2	Even outside the land of Israel!
Cast	[This is] the word of the Lord.
All	**Thanks be to God.**

Cast: **Announcer, Malachi, The Lord, Person 1, Person 2** (can be the same as Person 1).

The Lord reprimands the priests
Malachi 1.6–14

Malachi	The Lord Almighty says to the priests:
The Lord	A son honours his father, and a servant honours his master. I am your father—why don't you honour me? I am your master—why don't you respect me? You despise me, and yet you ask:
Priest 1	*How* have we despised you?
The Lord	This is how—by offering worthless food on my altar. (PAUSE) Then you ask:
Priest 2	How have we failed to respect you?
The Lord	I will tell you—by showing contempt for my altar. When you bring a blind or sick or lame animal to sacrifice to me, do you think

there's nothing wrong with that? Try giving an animal like that to the governor! Would he be pleased with you or grant you any favours?

Malachi Now, you priests, try asking God to be good to us. He will not answer your prayer, and it will be your fault. The Lord Almighty says:

The Lord I wish one of you would close the temple doors so as to prevent you from lighting useless fires on my altar. I am not pleased with you; I will not accept the offerings you bring me. People from one end of the world to the other honour me. Everywhere they burn incense to me and offer acceptable sacrifices. All of them honour me! But you dishonour me when you say that my altar is worthless and when you offer on it food that you despise. You say:

Priests 1 and **2** How tired we are of all this!

The Lord And you turn up your nose at me. As your offering to me you bring a stolen animal or one that is lame or sick. Do you think I will accept that from you? A curse on the cheat who sacrifices a worthless animal to me, when he has in his flock a good animal that he promised to give me! For I am a great king, and people of all nations fear me.

Cast [This is] the word of the Lord.
All **Thanks be to God.**

Cast: **Malachi, The Lord, Priest 1, Priest 2** (can be the same as Priest 1).

The people's unfaithfulness to God
From Malachi 2.10–16

Speaker 1 Don't we all have the same father?

Speaker 2 Didn't the same God create us all?

Speaker 1 Then why do we break our promises to one another?

Speaker 2 And why do we despise the covenant that God made with our ancestors?

Speaker 1 You ask why he no longer accepts your offerings.

Speaker 2 It is because he knows you have broken your promise to the wife you married when you were young.

Speaker 1 She was your partner, and you have broken your promise to her, although you promised before God that you would be faithful to her.

Speaker 2 Didn't God make you one body and spirit with her? What was his purpose in this?

Speaker 1 It was that you should have children who are truly God's people. So make sure that none of you breaks his promise to his wife.

Speaker 2 The Lord God of Israel says:

The Lord	I hate divorce. I hate it when one of you does such a cruel thing to his wife. Make sure that you do not break your promise to be faithful to your wife.
Cast	[This is] the word of the Lord.
All	**Thanks be to God.**

Cast: **Speaker 1, Speaker 2, The Lord.**

The Day of Judgement is near
Malachi 2.17—3.6

Malachi	You have tired the Lord out with your talk. But you ask:
Persons 1 and **2**	How have we tired him?
Malachi	By saying:
Person 1	The Lord Almighty thinks all evildoers are good; in fact he likes them.
Malachi	Or by asking:
Person 2	Where is the God who is supposed to be just?
Malachi	The Lord Almighty answers:
The Lord	I will send my messenger to prepare the way for me. Then the Lord you are looking for will suddenly come to his Temple. The messenger you long to see will come and proclaim my covenant.
Malachi	But who will be able to endure the day when he comes? Who will be able to survive when he appears? He will be like strong soap, like a fire that refines metal. He will come to judge like one who refines and purifies silver. As a metal-worker refines silver and gold, so the Lord's messenger will purify the priests, so that they will bring to the Lord the right kind of offerings. Then the offerings which the people of Judah and Jerusalem bring to the Lord will be pleasing to him, as they used to be in the past.
(with flourish)	The Lord Almighty says:
The Lord	I will appear among you to judge, and I will testify at once against those who practise magic, against adulterers, against those who give false testimony, those who cheat employees out of their wages, and those who take advantage of widows, orphans, and foreigners—against all who do not respect me. (PAUSE) I am the Lord, and I do not change!
Cast	[This is] the word of the Lord.
All	**Thanks be to God.**

Cast: **Malachi, Person 1, Person 2** (can be the same as Person 1)**, The Lord.**

The Lord calls for tithes
Malachi 3.6–12

The Lord   I am the Lord, and I do not change. And so you, the descendants of Jacob, are not yet completely lost. You, like your ancestors before you, have turned away from my laws and have not kept them. Turn back to me, and I will turn to you. But you ask:

Person(s)   What must we do to turn back to you?

The Lord   I ask you, is it right for a person to cheat God? Of course not, yet you are cheating me. You ask:

Person(s)   How?

The Lord   In the matter of tithes and offerings. (PAUSE) A curse is on all of you because the whole nation is cheating me.

Bring the full amount of your tithes to the Temple, so that there will be plenty of food there. Put me to the test and you will see that I will open the windows of heaven and pour out on you in abundance all kinds of good things. I will not let insects destroy your crops, and your grapevines will be loaded with grapes. Then the people of all nations will call you happy, because your land will be a good place to live in.

Cast   [This is] the word of the Lord.
All   **Thanks be to God.**

Cast: **The Lord, Person(s).**

God's promise of mercy
Malachi 3.13–18

Malachi   The Lord says:

The Lord   You have said terrible things about me. But you ask:

Person(s)   What have we said about you?

The Lord   You have said:

Person   It's useless to serve God. What's the use of doing what he says or of trying to show the Lord Almighty that we are sorry for what we have done? As we see it, proud people are the ones who are happy. Evil men not only prosper, but they test God's patience with their evil deeds and get away with it.

Malachi   Then the people who feared the Lord spoke to one another, and the Lord listened and heard what they said. In his presence, there was written down in a book a record of those who feared the Lord and respected him. The Lord Almighty says:

The Lord	They will be my people. On the day when I act, they will be my very own. I will be merciful to them, as a father is merciful to the son who serves him. Once again my people will see the difference between what happens to the righteous and to the wicked, to the person who serves me and the one who does not.
Cast	[This is] the word of the Lord.
All	**Thanks be to God.**

Cast: **Malachi, The Lord, Person(s).**

The Day of the Lord is coming
Malachi 4.1–6

Malachi	The Lord Almighty says:
The Lord	The day is coming when all proud and evil people will burn like straw. On that day they will burn up, and there will be nothing left of them. But for you who obey me, my saving power will rise on you like the sun and bring healing like the sun's rays. You will be as free and happy as calves let out of a stall. On the day when I act, you will overcome the wicked, and they will be like dust under your feet. Remember the teachings of my servant Moses, the laws and commands which I gave him at Mount Sinai for all the people of Israel to obey. But before the great and terrible day of the Lord comes, I will send you the prophet Elijah. He will bring fathers and children together again; otherwise I would have to come and destroy your country.
Cast	[This is] the word of the Lord.
All	**Thanks be to God.**

Cast: **Malachi, The Lord.**

NEW TESTAMENT

THE GOSPEL OF
MATTHEW

Joseph, and Jesus' birth
Matthew 1.18–25

Narrator	This is how the birth of Jesus Christ came about: His mother Mary was pledged to be married to Joseph, but before they came together, she was found to be with child through the Holy Spirit. Because Joseph her husband was a righteous man and did not want to expose her to public disgrace, he had in mind to divorce her quietly.
	But after he had considered this, an angel of the Lord appeared to him in a dream:
Angel	Joseph son of David, do not be afraid to take Mary home as your wife, because what is conceived in her is from the Holy Spirit. She will give birth to a son, and you are to give him the name Jesus, because he will save his people from their sins.
Narrator	All this took place to fulfil what the Lord had said through the prophet:
Prophet	The virgin will be with child and will give birth to a son, and they will call him Immanuel—
Narrator	Which means 'God with us'. (PAUSE) When Joseph woke up, he did what the angel of the Lord had commanded him and took Mary home as his wife. But he had no union with her until she gave birth to a son. And he gave him the name Jesus.

Cast	[This is] the word of the Lord. OR This is the Gospel of Christ / *This is the Gospel of the Lord.*
All	**Thanks be to God.** **Praise to Christ our Lord** / *Praise to you, Lord Jesus Christ.*

Cast: **Narrator, Angel, Prophet.** (See also Appendix: Christmas Readings, page 407.)

Visitors from the east
Matthew 2.1–11 [12]

Narrator	After Jesus was born in Bethlehem in Judaea, during the time of King Herod, Magi from the east came to Jerusalem and asked:
Magi	Where is the one who has been born king of the Jews? We saw his star in the east and have come to worship him.
Narrator	When King Herod heard this he was disturbed, and all Jerusalem with him. When he had called together all the people's chief priests and teachers of the law, he asked them where the Christ was to be born. They replied:
Chief priest	In Bethlehem in Judaea.
Teacher	For this is what the prophet has written:
Prophet	But you, Bethlehem, in the land of Judah,

→

are by no means least among the rulers of Judah;
for out of you will come a ruler
who will be the shepherd of my people Israel.

Narrator   Then Herod called the Magi secretly and found out from them the exact time the star had appeared. He sent them to Bethlehem [and said]:

Herod   Go and make a careful search for the child. As soon as you find him, report to me, so that I too may go and worship him.

Narrator   After they had heard the king, they went on their way, and the star they had seen in the east went ahead of them until it stopped over the place where the child was. When they saw the star, they were overjoyed. On coming to the house, they saw the child with his mother Mary, and they bowed down and worshipped him. Then they opened their treasures and presented him with gifts of gold and of incense and of myrrh. [And having been warned in a dream not to go back to Herod, they returned to their country by another route.]

Cast   [This is] the word of the Lord.   OR   This is the Gospel of Christ / *This is the Gospel of the Lord.*
All   **Thanks be to God.**   **Praise to Christ our Lord** / *Praise to you, Lord Jesus Christ.*

Cast: **Narrator, Magi, Chief priest, Teacher** (can be the same as Chief priest), **Prophet, Herod.** (See also Appendix: Christmas Readings, page 409.)

The escape into Egypt
Matthew 2.13–18

Narrator   When the Magi had gone, an angel of the Lord appeared to Joseph in a dream:

Angel   Get up. Take the child and his mother and escape to Egypt. Stay there until I tell you, for Herod is going to search for the child to kill him.

Narrator   So he got up, took the child and his mother during the night and left for Egypt, where he stayed until the death of Herod. And so was fulfilled what the Lord had said through the prophet:

Prophet   Out of Egypt I called my son.

Narrator   When Herod realised that he had been outwitted by the Magi, he was furious, and he gave orders to kill all the boys in Bethlehem and its vicinity who were two years old and under, in accordance with the time he had learned from the Magi. Then what was said through the prophet Jeremiah was fulfilled:

Jeremiah   A voice is heard in Ramah,
weeping and great mourning,
Rachel weeping for her children
and refusing to be comforted,
because they are no more.

Cast   [This is] the word of the Lord.   OR   This is the Gospel of Christ / *This is the Gospel of the Lord.*
All   **Thanks be to God.**   **Praise to Christ our Lord** / *Praise to you, Lord Jesus Christ.*

Cast: **Narrator, Angel, Prophet, Jeremiah.** (See also Appendix: Christmas Readings, page 409.)

The return from Egypt
Matthew 2.19–23

Narrator   After Herod died, an angel of the Lord appeared in a dream to Joseph in Egypt:

Angel   Get up, take the child and his mother, and go back to the land of Israel, because those who tried to kill the child are dead.

Narrator   So Joseph got up, took the child and his mother, and went back to Israel.

But when Joseph heard that Archelaus had succeeded his father Herod as king of Judaea, he was afraid to go there. He was given more instructions in a dream, so he went to the province of Galilee and made his home in a town named Nazareth. And so what the prophets had said came true:

Prophet   He will be called a Nazarene.

Cast   [This is] the word of the Lord.   OR   This is the Gospel of Christ / *This is the Gospel of the Lord.*
All   **Thanks be to God.**   **Praise to Christ our Lord** / *Praise to you, Lord Jesus Christ.*

Cast: **Narrator, Angel, Prophet.** (See also Appendix: Christmas Readings, page 410.)

The preaching of John the Baptist
Matthew 3.1–12

Narrator   John the Baptist came to the desert of Judaea and started preaching.

John   Turn away from your sins, because the Kingdom of heaven is near!

Narrator   John was the man the prophet Isaiah was talking about when he said:

Isaiah   Someone is shouting in the desert,
'Prepare a road for the Lord;
make a straight path for him to travel!'

Narrator   John's clothes were made of camel's hair; he wore a leather belt round his waist, and his food was locusts and wild honey. People came to him from Jerusalem, from the whole province of Judaea, and from all the country near the River Jordan. They confessed their sins, and he baptized them in the Jordan. (PAUSE)

When John saw many Pharisees and Sadducees coming to him to be baptized, he said to them:

John   You snakes—who told you that you could escape from the punishment God is about to send? Do those things that will show that you have turned from your sins. And don't think you can escape punishment by saying that Abraham is your ancestor. I tell you that God can take these stones and make descendants for Abraham! The axe is ready to cut down the trees at the roots; every tree that does not bear good fruit will be cut down and

→

thrown in the fire. I baptize you with water to show that you have repented, but the one who will come after me will baptize you with the Holy Spirit and fire. He is much greater than I am; and I am not good enough even to carry his sandals. He has his winnowing shovel with him to thresh out all the grain. He will gather his wheat into his barn, but he will burn the chaff in a fire that never goes out.

Cast [This is] the word of the Lord. OR This is the Gospel of Christ / *This is the Gospel of the Lord.*
All **Thanks be to God.** **Praise to Christ our Lord** / *Praise to you, Lord Jesus Christ.*

Cast: **Narrator, John, Isaiah.**

The baptism of Jesus
Matthew 3.13–17

Narrator Jesus arrived from Galilee and came to John at the Jordan to be baptized by him. But John tried to make him change his mind:

John I ought to be baptized by you, and yet you have come to me!

[Narrator But Jesus answered him:]

Jesus Let it be so for now. For in this way we shall do all that God requires.

Narrator So John agreed. (PAUSE)

As soon as Jesus was baptized, he came up out of the water. Then heaven was opened to him, and he saw the Spirit of God coming down like a dove and alighting on him. Then a voice said from heaven:

Voice This is my own dear Son, with whom I am pleased.

Cast [This is] the word of the Lord. OR This is the Gospel of Christ / *This is the Gospel of the Lord.*
All **Thanks be to God.** **Praise to Christ our Lord** / *Praise to you, Lord Jesus Christ.*

Cast: **Narrator, John, Jesus, Voice.**

The temptation of Jesus
Matthew 4.1–11

Narrator The Spirit led Jesus into the desert to be tempted by the Devil. After spending forty days and nights without food, Jesus was hungry. Then the Devil came to him and said:

The Devil If you are God's Son, order these stones to turn into bread.

[Narrator But Jesus answered:]

Jesus The scripture says, 'Man cannot live on bread alone, but needs every word that God speaks.'

Narrator Then the Devil took Jesus to Jerusalem, the Holy City, set him on the highest point of the Temple, and said to him:

4

The Devil	If you are God's Son, throw yourself down, for the scripture says, 'God will give orders to his angels about you; they will hold you up with their hands, so that not even your feet will be hurt on the stones.'
Jesus	But the scripture also says, 'Do not put the Lord your God to the test.'
Narrator	Then the Devil took Jesus to a very high mountain and showed him all the kingdoms of the world in all their greatness.
The Devil	All this I will give you, if you kneel down and worship me.
Jesus	Go away, Satan! The scripture says, 'Worship the Lord your God and serve only him!'
Narrator	Then the Devil left Jesus; and angels came and helped him.

Cast	[This is] the word of the Lord. OR	This is the Gospel of Christ / *This is the Gospel of the Lord.*
All	**Thanks be to God.**	**Praise to Christ our Lord** / *Praise to you, Lord Jesus Christ.*

Cast: **Narrator, The Devil, Jesus.**

Jesus begins his work in Galilee
Matthew 4.12–25

Narrator	When Jesus heard that John had been put in prison, he went away to Galilee. He did not stay in Nazareth, but went to live in Capernaum, a town by Lake Galilee, in the territory of Zebulun and Naphtali. This was done to make what the prophet Isaiah had said come true:
Isaiah	Land of Zebulun and land of Naphtali, on the road to the sea, on the other side of the Jordan, Galilee, land of the Gentiles! The people who live in darkness will see a great light. On those who live in the dark land of death the light will shine.
Narrator	From that time Jesus began to preach his message:
Jesus	Turn away from your sins, because the Kingdom of heaven is near!
Narrator	As Jesus walked along the shore of Lake Galilee, he saw two brothers who were fishermen, Simon—called Peter—and his brother Andrew, catching fish in the lake with a net. [Jesus said to them:]
Jesus	Come with me, and I will teach you to catch men.
Narrator	At once they left their nets and went with him. (PAUSE)
	He went on and saw two other brothers, James and John, the sons of Zebedee. They were in their boat with their father Zebedee, getting their nets ready. Jesus called them, and at once they left the boat and their father, and went with him. (PAUSE) →

5

Jesus went all over Galilee, teaching in the synagogues, preaching the Good News about the Kingdom, and healing people who had all kinds of disease and sickness. The news about him spread through the whole country of Syria, so that people brought to him all those who were sick, suffering from all kinds of diseases and disorders: people with demons, and epileptics, and paralytics— and Jesus healed them all. Large crowds followed him from Galilee and the Ten Towns, from Jerusalem, Judaea, and the land on the other side of the Jordan.

Cast	[This is] the word of the Lord. OR	This is the Gospel of Christ / *This is the Gospel of the Lord.*
All	**Thanks be to God.**	**Praise to Christ our Lord** / *Praise to you, Lord Jesus Christ.*

Cast: **Narrator, Isaiah, Jesus.**

Jesus makes up his team
From John 1 and Matthew 4 and 9

Narrator	Jesus decided to go to Galilee. He found Philip [and said]:
Jesus	Come with me!
Narrator	Philip found Nathanael [and told him]:
Philip	We have found the one whom Moses wrote about in the book of the Law, and whom the prophets also wrote about. He is Jesus son of Joseph, from Nazareth.
[Narrator	Nathanael asked:]
Nathanael	Can anything good come from Nazareth?
Philip	Come and see.
Narrator	When Jesus saw Nathanael coming to him, he said about him:
Jesus	Here is a real Israelite; there is nothing false in him!
Nathanael	How do you know me?
Jesus	I saw you when you were under the fig-tree before Philip called you.
Nathanael	Teacher, you are the Son of God! You are the King of Israel.
Narrator	As Jesus walked along the shore of Lake Galilee, he saw two brothers who were fishermen, Simon—called Peter—and his brother Andrew, catching fish in the lake with a net. [Jesus said to them:]
Jesus	Come with me, and I will teach you to catch men.
Narrator	At once they left their nets and went with him. (PAUSE)
	He went on and saw two other brothers, James and John, the sons of Zebedee. They were in their boat with their father Zebedee, getting their nets ready. Jesus called them, and at once they left the boat and their father, and went with him.
	As Jesus walked along, he saw a tax collector, named Matthew, sitting in his office. [He said to him:]

Jesus	Follow me.
Narrator	Matthew got up and followed him. (PAUSE)
	While Jesus was having a meal in Matthew's house, many tax collectors and other outcasts came and joined Jesus and his disciples at the table. Some Pharisees saw this and asked his disciples:
Pharisee	Why does your teacher eat with such people?
Narrator	Jesus heard them [and answered]:
Jesus	People who are well do not need a doctor, but only those who are sick. I have not come to call respectable people, but outcasts.

Cast	[This is] the word of the Lord.	OR	This is the Gospel of Christ / *This is the Gospel of the Lord.*
All	**Thanks be to God.**		**Praise to Christ our Lord** / *Praise to you, Lord Jesus Christ.*

Cast: **Narrator, Jesus, Philip, Nathanael, Pharisee.**

The Beatitudes
Matthew 5.3–12

Jesus	Happy are those who know they are spiritually poor:
Students	The Kingdom of heaven belongs to them!
Jesus	Happy are those who mourn:
Students	God will comfort them!
Jesus	Happy are those who are humble:
Students	They will receive what God has promised!
Jesus	Happy are those whose greatest desire is to do what God requires:
Students	God will satisfy them fully!
Jesus	Happy are those who are merciful to others:
Students	God will be merciful to them!
Jesus	Happy are the pure in heart:
Students	They will see God!
Jesus	Happy are those who work for peace:
Students	God will call them his children!
Jesus	Happy are those who are persecuted because they do what God requires:
Students	The Kingdom of heaven belongs to them!
Jesus	Happy are you when people insult you and persecute you and tell all kinds of evil lies against you because you are my followers. Be happy and glad, for a great reward is kept for you in heaven. This is how the prophets who lived before you were persecuted.

Cast	[This is] the word of the Lord.	OR	This is the Gospel of Christ / *This is the Gospel of the Lord.*
All	**Thanks be to God.**		**Praise to Christ our Lord** / *Praise to you, Lord Jesus Christ.*

Cast: **Jesus, Students.** (This reading is set out to reflect classic rabbinical teaching method.)

Jesus' teaching about anger
Matthew 5.21–24

Jesus	You have heard that people were told in the past:
Rabbi	Do not commit murder; anyone who does will be brought to trial.
Jesus	But now I tell you: whoever is angry with his brother will be brought to trial, whoever calls his brother:
Brother	You good-for-nothing!
Jesus	Will be brought before the Council, and whoever calls his brother:
Brother	Worthless fool!
Jesus	. . . will be in danger of going to the fire of hell. So if you are about to offer your gift to God at the altar and there you remember that your brother has something against you, leave your gift there in front of the altar, go at once and make peace with your brother, and then come back and offer your gift to God.

Cast	[This is] the word of the Lord. OR	This is the Gospel of Christ / *This is the Gospel of the Lord.*
All	**Thanks be to God.**	**Praise to Christ our Lord** / *Praise to you, Lord Jesus Christ.*

Cast: **Jesus, Rabbi, Brother.**

Jesus' teaching about adultery and divorce
Matthew 5.27–32

Jesus	You have heard that it was said:
Rabbi	Do not commit adultery.
Jesus	But now I tell you: anyone who looks at a woman and wants to possess her is guilty of committing adultery with her in his heart. So if your right eye causes you to sin, take it out and throw it away! It is much better for you to lose a part of your body than to have your whole body thrown into hell. If your right hand causes you to sin, cut it off and throw it away! It is much better for you to lose one of your limbs than for your whole body to go to hell. (PAUSE) It was also said:
Rabbi	Anyone who divorces his wife must give her a written notice of divorce.
Jesus	But now I tell you: if a man divorces his wife, for any cause other than her unfaithfulness, then he is guilty of making her commit adultery if she marries again; and the man who marries her commits adultery also.

Cast	[This is] the word of the Lord. OR	This is the Gospel of Christ / *This is the Gospel of the Lord.*
All	**Thanks be to God.**	**Praise to Christ our Lord** / *Praise to you, Lord Jesus Christ.*

Cast: **Jesus, Rabbi.**

Jesus' teaching about vows
Matthew 5.33–37

Jesus   You have also heard that people were told in the past:

Rabbi   Do not break your promise, but do what you have vowed to the Lord to do.

Jesus   But now I tell you: do not use any vow when you make a promise. Do not swear by heaven, for it is God's throne; nor by earth, for it is the resting place for his feet; nor by Jerusalem, for it is the city of the great King. Do not even swear by your head, because you cannot make a single hair white or black. Just say 'Yes' or 'No'— anything else you say comes from the Evil One.

Cast	[This is] the word of the Lord. OR	This is the Gospel of Christ / *This is the Gospel of the Lord.*
All	**Thanks be to God.**	**Praise to Christ our Lord** / *Praise to you, Lord Jesus Christ.*

Cast: **Jesus, Rabbi.**

Jesus' teaching on prayer and fasting
Matthew 6.5–18 (GNB)

Jesus   When you pray, do not be like the hypocrites! They love to stand up and pray in the houses of worship and on the street corners, so that everyone will see them. I assure you, they have already been paid in full. But when you pray, go to your room, close the door, and pray to your Father, who is unseen. And your Father, who sees what you do in private, will reward you.

When you pray, do not use a lot of meaningless words, as the pagans do, who think their gods will hear them because their prayers are long. Do not be like them. Your Father already knows what you need before you ask him. This, then, is how you should pray:

Leader   Our Father in heaven:

Students   May your holy name be honoured;

Leader   May your Kingdom come;

Students   May your will be done on earth as it is in heaven.

Give us today the food we need.

Leader   Forgive us the wrongs we have done,

Students   As we forgive the wrongs that others have done to us.

Leader   Do not bring us to hard testing,

Students   But keep us safe from the Evil One.

Jesus	If you forgive others the wrongs they have done to you, your Father in heaven will also forgive you. But if you do not forgive others, then your Father will not forgive the wrongs you have done.
	[And when you fast, do not put on a sad face as the hypocrites do. They neglect their appearance so that everyone will see that they are fasting. I assure you, they have already been paid in full. When you go without food, wash your face and comb your hair, so that others cannot know that you are fasting—only your Father, who is unseen, will know. And your Father, who sees what you do in private, will reward you.]

Cast	[This is] the word of the Lord.	OR	This is the Gospel of Christ / *This is the Gospel of the Lord.*
All	**Thanks be to God.**		**Praise to Christ our Lord** / *Praise to you, Lord Jesus Christ.*

Cast: **Jesus, Leader** (can be the same as Jesus), **Students** (two or more). (This reading is arranged to reflect the rabbinic style of teaching. For a straightforward treatment see page 154.)

Jesus' teaching on prayer and fasting
Matthew 6.5–18 (NIV)

Jesus	When you pray, do not be like the hypocrites, for they love to pray standing in the synagogues and on the street corners to be seen by men. I tell you the truth, they have received their reward in full. When you pray, go into your room, close the door and pray to your Father, who is unseen. Then your Father, who sees what is done in secret, will reward you. And when you pray, do not keep on babbling like pagans, for they think they will be heard because of their many words. Do not be like them, for your Father knows what you need before you ask him. This, then, is how you should pray:
Leader	Our Father in heaven,
Students	Hallowed be your name,
Leader	Your kingdom come,
Students	Your will be done on earth as it is in heaven.
	Give us today our daily bread.
Leader	Forgive us our debts,
Students	As we also have forgiven our debtors.
Leader	And lead us not into temptation,
Students	But deliver us from the evil one.
Jesus	For if you forgive men when they sin against you, your heavenly Father will also forgive you. But if you do not forgive men their sins, your Father will not forgive your sins. (PAUSE)
	[When you fast, do not look sombre as the hypocrites do, for they disfigure their faces to show men they are fasting. I tell you the truth, they have received their reward in full. But when you fast,

put oil on your head and wash your face, so that it will not be obvious to men that you are fasting, but only to your Father, who is unseen; and your Father, who sees what is done in secret, will reward you.]

Cast	[This is] the word of the Lord.	OR	This is the Gospel of Christ / *This is the Gospel of the Lord.*
All	**Thanks be to God.**		**Praise to Christ our Lord** / *Praise to you, Lord Jesus Christ.*

Cast: **Jesus, Leader** (can be the same as Jesus), **Students** (two or more). (This reading is arranged to reflect the rabbinic style of teaching. For a straightforward treatment see page 154.)

Jesus' teaching about God and possessions
Matthew 6.24–34

Jesus No one can be a slave of two masters; he will hate one and love the other; he will be loyal to one and despise the other. You cannot serve both God and money. This is why I tell you not to be worried about the food and drink you need in order to stay alive, or about clothes for your body. After all, isn't life worth more than food? And isn't the body worth more than clothes? Look at the birds: they do not sow seeds, gather a harvest and put it in barns; yet your Father in heaven takes care of them! Aren't you worth more than birds?

Can any of you live a bit longer by worrying about it? And why worry about clothes? Look how the wild flowers grow: they do not work or make clothes for themselves. But I tell you that not even King Solomon with all his wealth had clothes as beautiful as one of these flowers. It is God who clothes the wild grass—grass that is here today and gone tomorrow, burnt up in the oven. Won't he be all the more sure to clothe you? How little faith you have! So do not start worrying:

Person 1 Where will my food come from?

Person 2 Or my drink?

Person 3 Or my clothes?

Commentator These are the things the pagans are always concerned about.

Jesus Your Father in heaven knows that you need all these things. Instead, be concerned above everything else with the Kingdom of God and with what he requires of you, and he will provide you with all these things. So do not worry about tomorrow; it will have enough worries of its own. There is no need to add to the troubles each day brings.

Cast	[This is] the word of the Lord.	OR	This is the Gospel of Christ / *This is the Gospel of the Lord.*
All	**Thanks be to God.**		**Praise to Christ our Lord** / *Praise to you, Lord Jesus Christ.*

Cast: **Jesus, Person 1, Person 2, Person 3** (can be the same as Persons 1 and 2), **Commentator** (can be the same as Jesus).

Jesus' warning about judging others
Matthew 7.1–5

Jesus   Do not judge others, so that God will not judge you, for God will judge you in the same way as you judge others, and he will apply to you the same rules you apply to others. Why, then, do you look at the speck in your brother's eye, and pay no attention to the log in your own eye? How dare you say to your brother:

Person   Please, let me take that speck out of your eye.

Jesus   When you have a log in your own eye? You hypocrite! First take the log out of your own eye, and then you will be able to see clearly to take the speck out of your brother's eye.

Cast   [This is] the word of the Lord.   OR   This is the Gospel of Christ / *This is the Gospel of the Lord.*
All   **Thanks be to God.**   **Praise to Christ our Lord** / *Praise to you, Lord Jesus Christ.*

Cast: **Jesus, Person.**

I never knew you
Matthew 7.21–23

Jesus   Not everyone who calls me:

Person 1   Lord!

Person 2   Lord!

Jesus   Will enter the Kingdom of heaven, but only those who do what my Father in heaven wants them to do. When Judgement Day comes, many will say to me:

Person 1   Lord!

Person 2   Lord!

Person 1   In your name we spoke God's message.

Person 2   By your name we drove out many demons.

Person 1   And performed many miracles!

Jesus   Then I will say to them:

Jesus as Judge   I never knew you. Get away from me, you wicked people!

Cast   [This is] the word of the Lord.   OR   This is the Gospel of Christ / *This is the Gospel of the Lord.*
All   **Thanks be to God.**   **Praise to Christ our Lord** / *Praise to you, Lord Jesus Christ.*

Cast: **Jesus, Person 1, Person 2, Jesus as Judge** (can be the same as Jesus).

Jesus' parable of the two house-builders
Matthew 7.24–29

Voice 1	Anyone who hears these words of mine and obeys them is like a wise man who built his house on rock.
Voice 2	The rain poured down, the rivers overflowed, and the wind blew hard against that house. But it did not fall, because it was built on rock.
Voice 1	But anyone who hears these words of mine and does not obey them is like a foolish man who built his house on sand.
Voice 2	The rain poured down, the rivers overflowed, the wind blew hard against that house, and it fell. And what a terrible fall that was!
Narrator	When Jesus finished saying these things, the crowd was amazed at the way he taught. He wasn't like the teachers of the Law; instead, he taught with authority.

Cast	[This is] the word of the Lord.	OR	This is the Gospel of Christ / *This is the Gospel of the Lord.*
All	**Thanks be to God.**		**Praise to Christ our Lord** / *Praise to you, Lord Jesus Christ.*

Cast: **Voice 1, Voice 2, Narrator.**

Jesus heals people
Matthew 8.1–13 [14–17]

Narrator	When Jesus came down from the hill, large crowds followed him. Then a man suffering from leprosy came to him, and knelt down before him.
Man	Sir, if you want to, you can make me clean.
Narrator	Jesus stretched out his hand and touched him.
Jesus	I do want to. Be clean!
Narrator	At once the man was healed of his disease.
Jesus	Listen! Don't tell anyone, but go straight to the priest and let him examine you; then in order to prove to everyone that you are cured, offer the sacrifice that Moses ordered. (PAUSE)
Narrator	When Jesus entered Capernaum, a Roman officer met him and begged for help:
Officer	Sir, my servant is sick in bed at home, unable to move and suffering terribly.
Jesus	I will go and make him well.
Officer	Oh no, sir. I do not deserve to have you come into my house. Just give the order, and my servant will get well. I, too, am a man under the authority of superior officers, and I have soldiers under me. I order this one, 'Go!' and he goes; and I order that one, 'Come!' and he comes; and I order my slave, 'Do this!' and he does it.

Narrator	When Jesus heard this, he was surprised and said to the people following him:
Jesus (to crowd)	I tell you, I have never found anyone in Israel with faith like this. I assure you that many will come from the east and the west and sit down with Abraham, Isaac, and Jacob at the feast in the Kingdom of heaven. But those who should be in the Kingdom will be thrown out into the darkness, where they will cry and grind their teeth.
Jesus (to Officer)	Go home, and what you believe will be done for you.
Narrator	And the officer's servant was healed that very moment. (PAUSE)
	[Jesus went to Peter's home, and there he saw Peter's mother-in-law sick in bed with a fever. He touched her hand; the fever left her, and she got up and began to wait on him. (PAUSE)
	When evening came, people brought to Jesus many who had demons in them. Jesus drove out the evil spirits with a word and healed all who were sick. He did this to make what the prophet Isaiah had said come true:
Isaiah	He himself took our sickness and carried away our diseases.]

Cast	[This is] the word of the Lord.	OR	This is the Gospel of Christ / *This is the Gospel of the Lord.*
All	**Thanks be to God.**		**Praise to Christ our Lord** / *Praise to you, Lord Jesus Christ.*

Cast: **Narrator, Man, Jesus, Officer, [Isaiah** (can be the same as Narrator)].

The would-be followers of Jesus
Matthew 8.18–22

Narrator	When Jesus noticed the crowd round him, he ordered his disciples to go to the other side of the lake. A teacher of the Law came to him. [He said:]
Lawyer	Teacher, I am ready to go with you wherever you go.
[Narrator	Jesus answered him:]
Jesus (to Lawyer)	Foxes have holes, and birds have nests, but the Son of Man has nowhere to lie down and rest.
Narrator	Another man, who was a disciple, said:
Disciple	Sir, first let me go back and bury my father.
Narrator	Jesus answered:
Jesus (to Disciple)	Follow me, and let the dead bury their own dead.

Cast	[This is] the word of the Lord.	OR	This is the Gospel of Christ / *This is the Gospel of the Lord.*
All	**Thanks be to God.**		**Praise to Christ our Lord** / *Praise to you, Lord Jesus Christ.*

Cast: **Narrator, Lawyer, Jesus, Disciple.**

Jesus calms a storm
Matthew 8.23–27

Narrator   Jesus got into a boat, and his disciples went with him. Suddenly a fierce storm hit the lake, and the boat was in danger of sinking. But Jesus was asleep. The disciples went to him and woke him up:

Disciples   Save us, Lord! We are about to die!

[Narrator   Jesus answered:]

Jesus   Why are you so frightened? How little faith you have!

Narrator   Then Jesus got up and ordered the winds and the waves to stop, and there was a great calm. Everyone was amazed.

Disciples   What kind of man is this? Even the winds and the waves obey him!

Cast   [This is] the word of the Lord.   OR   This is the Gospel of Christ / *This is the Gospel of the Lord.*
All   **Thanks be to God.**   **Praise to Christ our Lord** / *Praise to you, Lord Jesus Christ.*

Cast: **Narrator, Disciples, Jesus.**

Jesus rids two men of demons
Matthew 8.28–34

Narrator   When Jesus came to the territory of Gadara on the other side of the lake, he was met by two men who came out of the burial caves there. These men had demons in them and were so fierce that no one dared travel on that road. At once they screamed:

Man 1   What do you want with us, you Son of God?

Man 2   Have you come to punish us before the right time?

Narrator   Not far away there was a large herd of pigs feeding. So the demons begged Jesus:

Demon   If you are going to drive us out, send us into that herd of pigs.

[Narrator   Jesus told them:]

Jesus   Go!

Narrator   So they left and went off into the pigs. The whole herd rushed down the side of the cliff into the lake and was drowned. (PAUSE)

The men who had been taking care of the pigs ran away and went into the town, where they told the whole story and what had happened to the men with the demons. So everyone from the town went out to meet Jesus; and when they saw him, they begged him to leave their territory.

Cast   [This is] the word of the Lord.   OR   This is the Gospel of Christ / *This is the Gospel of the Lord.*
All   **Thanks be to God.**   **Praise to Christ our Lord** / *Praise to you, Lord Jesus Christ.*

Cast: **Narrator, Man 1, Man 2, Demon, Jesus.**

Jesus heals a paralysed man
Matthew 9.1–8

Narrator Jesus got into the boat and went back across the lake to his own town, where some people brought to him a paralysed man, lying on a bed. When Jesus saw how much faith they had, he said to the paralysed man:

Jesus Courage, my son! Your sins are forgiven.

Narrator Then some teachers of the Law said to themselves:

Lawyer This man is speaking blasphemy!

Narrator Jesus perceived what they were thinking [so he said]:

Jesus
(to Lawyer) Why are you thinking such evil things? Is it easier to say, 'Your sins are forgiven,' or to say, 'Get up and walk'? I will prove to you, then, that the Son of Man has authority on earth to forgive sins.

[Narrator So he said to the paralysed man:]

Jesus (to man) Get up, pick up your bed, and go home!

Narrator The man got up and went home. When the people saw it, they were afraid, and praised God for giving such authority to men.

Cast [This is] the word of the Lord. OR This is the Gospel of Christ / *This is the Gospel of the Lord.*
All **Thanks be to God.** **Praise to Christ our Lord** / *Praise to you, Lord Jesus Christ.*

Cast: **Narrator, Jesus, Lawyer.**

Jesus calls Matthew
Matthew 9.9–13

Narrator As Jesus walked along, he saw a tax collector, named Matthew, sitting in his office. [He said to him:]

Jesus Follow me.

Narrator Matthew got up and followed him. While Jesus was having a meal in Matthew's house, many tax collectors and other outcasts came and joined Jesus and his disciples at the table. Some Pharisees saw this and asked his disciples:

Pharisee Why does your teacher eat with such people?

Narrator Jesus heard them [and answered]:

Jesus People who are well do not need a doctor, but only those who are sick. Go and find out what is meant by the scripture that says:

Hosea It is kindness that I want, not animal sacrifices.

Jesus I have not come to call respectable people, but outcasts.

Cast [This is] the word of the Lord. OR This is the Gospel of Christ / *This is the Gospel of the Lord.*
All **Thanks be to God.** **Praise to Christ our Lord** / *Praise to you, Lord Jesus Christ.*

Cast: **Narrator, Jesus, Pharisee, Hosea** (can be the same as Jesus). (See also comprehensive text on pages 6 and 201.)

The question about fasting
Matthew 9.14–17

Narrator   The followers of John the Baptist came to Jesus [asking]:

Person   Why is it that we and the Pharisees fast often, but your disciples don't fast at all?

[Narrator   Jesus answered:]

Jesus   Do you expect the guests at a wedding party to be sad as long as the bridegroom is with them? Of course not! But the day will come when the bridegroom will be taken away from them, and then they will fast.

No one patches up an old coat with a piece of new cloth, for the new patch will shrink and make an even bigger hole in the coat. Nor does anyone pour new wine into used wineskins, for the skins will burst, the wine will pour out, and the skins will be ruined. Instead, new wine is poured into fresh wineskins, and both will keep in good condition.

Cast   [This is] the word of the Lord.   OR   This is the Gospel of Christ / *This is the Gospel of the Lord.*
All   **Thanks be to God.**   **Praise to Christ our Lord** / *Praise to you, Lord Jesus Christ.*

Cast: **Narrator, Person, Jesus.**

The official's daughter, and the woman who touched Jesus' cloak
Matthew 9.18–26

Narrator   A Jewish official came to Jesus and knelt down before him. [He said:]

Official   My daughter has just died; but come and place your hands on her, and she will live.

Narrator   So Jesus got up and followed him, and his disciples went along with him. (PAUSE)

A woman who had suffered from severe bleeding for twelve years came up behind Jesus [and said to herself]:

Woman   If I only touch his cloak, I will get well.

Narrator   She touched the edge of his cloak. Jesus turned round and saw her [and said]:

Jesus   Courage, my daughter! Your faith has made you well.

Narrator   At that very moment the woman became well. (PAUSE)

Then Jesus went into the official's house. He saw the musicians for the funeral and the people all stirred up [and said:]

Jesus   Get out, everybody! The little girl is not dead—she is only sleeping!

Narrator   Then they all laughed at him. But as soon as the people had been put out, Jesus went into the girl's room and took hold of her hand, and she got up. The news about this spread all over that part of the country.

Cast   [This is] the word of the Lord.   OR   This is the Gospel of Christ / *This is the Gospel of the Lord.*
All   **Thanks be to God.**   **Praise to Christ our Lord** / *Praise to you, Lord Jesus Christ.*

Cast: **Narrator, Official, Woman, Jesus.**

Jesus heals more people
Matthew 9.27–38

Narrator	As Jesus walked along, two blind men started following him. [They shouted:]
Blind man 1 (shouting)	Son of David!
Blind man 2 (shouting)	Take pity on us!
Narrator	When Jesus had gone indoors, the two blind men came to him, and he asked them:
Jesus	Do you believe that I can heal you?
Blind men 1 and **2**	Yes, sir!
Narrator	Then Jesus touched their eyes.
Jesus	Let it happen, then, just as you believe!
Narrator	And their sight was restored. (PAUSE) Jesus spoke sternly to them:
Jesus	Don't tell this to anyone!
Narrator	But they left and spread the news about Jesus all over that part of the country. (PAUSE)
	As the men were leaving, some people brought to Jesus a man who could not talk because he had a demon. But as soon as the demon was driven out, the man started talking, and everyone was amazed.
Person	We have never seen anything like this in Israel!
Narrator	But the Pharisees said:
Pharisee	It is the chief of the demons who gives him the power to drive out demons. (PAUSE)
Narrator	Jesus went round visiting all the towns and villages. He taught in the synagogues, preached the Good News about the Kingdom, and healed people with every kind of disease and sickness. As he saw the crowds, his heart was filled with pity for them, because they were worried and helpless, like sheep without a shepherd. [So he said to his disciples:]
Jesus	The harvest is large, but there are few workers to gather it in. Pray to the owner of the harvest that he will send out workers to gather in his harvest.

Cast	[This is] the word of the Lord.	OR	This is the Gospel of Christ / *This is the Gospel of the Lord.*
All	**Thanks be to God.**		**Praise to Christ our Lord** / *Praise to you, Lord Jesus Christ.*

Cast: **Narrator**, **Blind man 1**, **Blind man 2** (can be the same as Blind man 1), **Jesus**, **Person**, **Pharisee**.

The twelve apostles
Matthew 10.1–8 [8–15]

Narrator	Jesus called his twelve disciples together and gave them authority to drive out evil spirits and to heal every disease and every sickness. These are the names of the twelve apostles: first, Simon—
Commentator	Called Peter.
Narrator	And his brother Andrew; James and his brother John, the sons of Zebedee; Philip and Bartholomew; Thomas and Matthew—
Commentator	The tax collector.
Narrator	James son of Alphaeus, and Thaddaeus; Simon the Patriot, and Judas Iscariot—
Commentator	Who betrayed Jesus.
Narrator	These twelve men were sent out by Jesus with the following instructions:
Jesus	Do not go to any Gentile territory or any Samaritan towns. Instead, you are to go to the lost sheep of the people of Israel. Go and preach:
Disciple(s)	The Kingdom of heaven is near!
Jesus	Heal the sick, bring the dead back to life, heal those who suffer from dreaded skin-diseases, and drive out demons.
	[You have received without paying, so give without being paid. Do not carry any gold, silver, or copper money in your pockets; do not carry a beggar's bag for the journey or an extra shirt or shoes or a stick. A worker should be given what he needs. When you come to a town or village, go in and look for someone who is willing to welcome you, and stay with him until you leave that place. When you go into a house, say:
Disciple(s)	Peace be with you.
Jesus	If the people in that house welcome you, let your greeting of peace remain; but if they do not welcome you, then take back your greeting. And if some home or town will not welcome you or listen to you, then leave that place and shake the dust off your feet. I assure you that on the Judgement Day God will show more mercy to the people of Sodom and Gomorrah than to the people of that town!]

Cast	[This is] the word of the Lord.	OR	This is the Gospel of Christ / *This is the Gospel of the Lord.*
All	**Thanks be to God.**		**Praise to Christ our Lord** / *Praise to you, Lord Jesus Christ.*

Cast: **Narrator, Commentator, Jesus, Disciple(s).**

The cost of following Jesus
Matthew 10.32–39

Jesus Whoever acknowledges me before men, I will also acknowledge him before my Father in heaven. But whoever disowns me before men, I will disown him before my Father in heaven. Do not suppose that I have come to bring peace to the earth. I did not come to bring peace, but a sword. For I have come to turn:

Micah A man against his father,
a daughter against her mother,
a daughter-in-law against her mother-in-law—
a man's enemies will be the members of his own household.

Jesus Anyone who loves his father or mother more than me is not worthy of me; anyone who loves his son or daughter more than me is not worthy of me; and anyone who does not take his cross and follow me is not worthy of me. Whoever finds his life will lose it, and whoever loses his life for my sake will find it.

Cast [This is] the word of the Lord.   OR   This is the Gospel of Christ / *This is the Gospel of the Lord.*
All **Thanks be to God.**   **Praise to Christ our Lord** / *Praise to you, Lord Jesus Christ.*

Cast: **Jesus, Micah.**

The messengers from John the Baptist
Matthew 11.1–10

Narrator When Jesus finished giving instructions to his twelve disciples, he left that place and went off to teach and preach in the towns near there.

When John the Baptist heard in prison about the things that Christ was doing, he sent some of his disciples to him. [They asked Jesus:]

Disciple 1 Tell us, are you the one John said was going to come—

Disciple 2 Or should we expect someone else?

Jesus
(to Disciples) Go back and tell John what you are hearing and seeing: the blind can see, the lame can walk, those who suffer from leprosy are made clean, the deaf hear, the dead are brought back to life, and the Good News is preached to the poor. How happy are those who have no doubts about me!

Narrator While John's disciples were leaving, Jesus spoke about him to the crowds:

Jesus
(to crowd) When you went out to John in the desert, what did you expect to see? A blade of grass bending in the wind? What did you go out to see? A man dressed up in fancy clothes? People who dress like that live in palaces! Tell me, what did you go out to see? A prophet? Yes indeed, but you saw much more than a prophet. For John is the one of whom the scripture says: 'God said, I will send my messenger ahead of you to open the way for you.'

Cast [This is] the word of the Lord.   OR   This is the Gospel of Christ / *This is the Gospel of the Lord.*
All **Thanks be to God.**   **Praise to Christ our Lord** / *Praise to you, Lord Jesus Christ.*

Cast: **Narrator, Disciple 1, Disciple 2, Jesus.**

Jesus speaks of John the Baptist
Matthew 11.11–19

Jesus I assure you that John the Baptist is greater than any man who has ever lived. But he who is least in the Kingdom of heaven is greater than John. From the time John preached his message until this very day the Kingdom of heaven has suffered violent attacks, and violent men try to seize it. Until the time of John all the prophets and the Law of Moses spoke about the Kingdom; and if you are willing to believe their message, John is Elijah, whose coming was predicted. Listen, then, if you have ears! Now, to what can I compare the people of this day? They are like children sitting in the market-place. One group shouts to the other:

Child 1 We played wedding music for you,

Child 2 But you wouldn't dance!

Child 3 We sang funeral songs,

Child 4 But you wouldn't cry!

Jesus When John came, he fasted and drank no wine, and everyone said:

Person 1 He has a demon in him!

Jesus When the Son of Man came, he ate and drank, and everyone said:

Person 2 Look at this man!

Person 1 He is a glutton and a drinker—

Person 2 A friend of tax collectors and other outcasts!

Jesus God's wisdom, however, is shown to be true by its results.

Cast [This is] the word of the Lord.   OR   This is the Gospel of Christ / *This is the Gospel of the Lord.*
All **Thanks be to God.**   **Praise to Christ our Lord** / *Praise to you, Lord Jesus Christ.*

Cast: **Jesus, Child 1, Child 2** (can be the same as Child 1), **Child 3, Child 4** (can be the same as Child 3), **Person 1, Person 2** (can be the same as Person 1).

The unbelieving towns
Matthew 11.20–24

Narrator The people in the towns where Jesus had performed most of his miracles did not turn from their sins, so he reproached those towns.

Jesus How terrible it will be for you, Chorazin! How terrible for you too, Bethsaida! If the miracles which were performed in you had been performed in Tyre and Sidon, the people there would long ago have put on sackcloth and sprinkled ashes on themselves, to show that they had turned from their sins! I assure you that on the Judgement Day God will show more mercy to the people of Tyre and Sidon than to you! And as for you, Capernaum! Did you want to lift yourself up to heaven? You will be thrown down to hell! If →

21

the miracles which were performed in you had been performed in Sodom, it would still be in existence today! You can be sure that on the Judgement Day God will show more mercy to Sodom than to you!

Cast	[This is] the word of the Lord. OR	This is the Gospel of Christ / *This is the Gospel of the Lord.*
All	**Thanks be to God.**	**Praise to Christ our Lord** / *Praise to you, Lord Jesus Christ.*

Cast: **Narrator, Jesus.**

Come to me and rest
Matthew 11.25–30

Narrator   Jesus said:

Jesus
(in prayer)   Father, Lord of heaven and earth! I thank you because you have shown to the unlearned what you have hidden from the wise and learned. Yes, Father, this was how you wanted it to happen. (PAUSE)

Jesus
(to disciples)   My Father has given me all things. No one knows the Son except the Father, and no one knows the Father except the Son and those to whom the Son chooses to reveal him. (PAUSE)

Jesus
(to crowd)   Come to me, all of you who are tired from carrying heavy loads, and I will give you rest. Take my yoke and put it on you, and learn from me, because I am gentle and humble in spirit; and you will find rest. For the yoke I will give you is easy, and the load I will put on you is light.

Cast	[This is] the word of the Lord. OR	This is the Gospel of Christ / *This is the Gospel of the Lord.*
All	**Thanks be to God.**	**Praise to Christ our Lord** / *Praise to you, Lord Jesus Christ.*

Cast: **Narrator, Jesus.**

The question about the Sabbath
Matthew 12.1–14

Narrator   Jesus was walking through some cornfields on the Sabbath. His disciples were hungry, so they began to pick ears of corn and eat the grain. When the Pharisees saw this, they said to Jesus:

Pharisee   Look, it is against our Law for your disciples to do this on the Sabbath!

[Narrator   Jesus answered:]

Jesus   Have you never read what David did that time when he and his men were hungry? He went into the house of God, and he and his men ate the bread offered to God, even though it was against the Law for them to eat it—only the priests were allowed to eat that bread. Or have you not read in the Law of Moses that every Sabbath the priests in the Temple actually break the Sabbath law, yet they are not guilty? I tell you that there is something here greater than the Temple. The scripture says, 'It is kindness that I want, not animal sacrifices.' If you really knew what this means, you would not condemn people who are not guilty; for the Son of Man is Lord of the Sabbath.

Narrator   Jesus left that place and went to a synagogue, where there was a man who had a paralysed hand. Some people were there who wanted to accuse Jesus of doing wrong, so they asked him:

Pharisee   Is it against our Law to heal on the Sabbath?

Jesus   What if one of you has a sheep and it falls into a deep hole on the Sabbath? Will he not take hold of it and lift it out? And a man is worth much more than a sheep! So then, our Law does allow us to help someone on the Sabbath.

[Narrator   Then he said to the man with the paralysed hand:]

Jesus   Stretch out your hand.

Narrator   He stretched it out, and it became well again, just like the other one. Then the Pharisees left and made plans to kill Jesus.

Cast	[This is] the word of the Lord. OR	This is the Gospel of Christ / *This is the Gospel of the Lord.*
All	**Thanks be to God.**	**Praise to Christ our Lord** / *Praise to you, Lord Jesus Christ.*

Cast: **Narrator, Pharisee, Jesus.**

God's chosen servant
Matthew 12.15–21

Narrator   When Jesus heard about the plot against him, he went away from that place; and large crowds followed him. He healed all those who were ill and gave them orders not to tell others about him. He did this so as to make what God had said through the prophet Isaiah come true:

Isaiah   Here is my servant, whom I have chosen,
the one I love, and with whom I am pleased.
I will send my Spirit upon him,
and he will announce my judgement to the nations.
He will not argue or shout,
or make loud speeches in the streets.
He will not break off a bent reed,
or put out a flickering lamp.
He will persist until he causes justice to triumph,
and in him all peoples will put their hope.

Cast	[This is] the word of the Lord. OR	This is the Gospel of Christ / *This is the Gospel of the Lord.*
All	**Thanks be to God.**	**Praise to Christ our Lord** / *Praise to you, Lord Jesus Christ.*

Cast: **Narrator, Isaiah.**

Jesus and Beelzebul
From Matthew 12.22–32

Narrator Some people brought to Jesus a man who was blind and could not talk because he had a demon. Jesus healed the man, so that he was able to talk and see. The crowds were all amazed at what Jesus had done [and asked]:

Person(s) Could he be the Son of David?

Narrator When the Pharisees heard this, they replied:

Pharisee He drives out demons only because their ruler Beelzebul gives him power to do so.

Narrator Jesus knew what they were thinking, so he said to them:

Jesus Any country that divides itself into groups which fight each other will not last very long. And any town or family that divides itself into groups which fight each other will fall apart. So if one group is fighting another in Satan's kingdom, this means that it is already divided into groups and will soon fall apart! You say that I drive out demons because Beelzebul gives me the power to do so. Well, then, who gives your followers the power to drive them out? What your own followers do proves that you are wrong! No, it is not Beelzebul, but God's Spirit, who gives me the power to drive out demons, which proves that the Kingdom of God has already come upon you.

I tell you that people can be forgiven any sin and any evil thing they say; but whoever says evil things against the Holy Spirit will not be forgiven. Anyone who says something against the Son of Man can be forgiven; but whoever says something against the Holy Spirit will not be forgiven—now or ever.

Cast	[This is] the word of the Lord. OR	This is the Gospel of Christ / *This is the Gospel of the Lord.*
All	**Thanks be to God.**	**Praise to Christ our Lord** / *Praise to you, Lord Jesus Christ.*

Cast: **Narrator, Person(s), Pharisee, Jesus.**

The demand for a miracle
Matthew 12.38–41 [42]

Narrator Some teachers of the Law and some Pharisees spoke up:

Pharisee Teacher, we want to see you perform a miracle.

[Narrator Jesus exclaimed:]

Jesus How evil and godless are the people of this day! You ask me for a miracle? No! The only miracle you will be given is the miracle of the prophet Jonah. In the same way that Jonah spent three days and nights in the big fish, so will the Son of Man spend three days and nights in the depths of the earth. On Judgement Day the people of Nineveh will stand up and accuse you, because they turned from their sins when they heard Jonah preach; and I tell you that there is something here greater than Jonah!

[On Judgement Day the Queen of Sheba will stand up and accuse you, because she travelled all the way from her country to listen to King Solomon's wise teaching; and I assure you that there is something here greater than Solomon!]

Cast	[This is] the word of the Lord. OR	This is the Gospel of Christ / *This is the Gospel of the Lord.*
All	**Thanks be to God.**	**Praise to Christ our Lord** / *Praise to you, Lord Jesus Christ.*

Cast: **Narrator, Pharisee, Jesus.** (This reading is short, and may be linked with the previous one, in which case it is desirable to omit the line in square brackets.)

The return of the evil spirit
Matthew 12.43–45

Jesus   When an evil spirit goes out of a person, it travels over dry country looking for a place to rest. If it can't find one, it says to itself:

Evil spirit   I will go back to my house.

Jesus   So it goes back and finds the house empty, clean, and all tidy. Then it goes out and brings along seven other spirits even worse than itself, and they come and live there. So when it is all over, that person is in a worse state than he was at the beginning.

Jesus (slowly)   This is what will happen to the evil people of this day.

Cast	[This is] the word of the Lord. OR	This is the Gospel of Christ / *This is the Gospel of the Lord.*
All	**Thanks be to God.**	**Praise to Christ our Lord** / *Praise to you, Lord Jesus Christ.*

Cast: **Jesus, Evil spirit.**

Jesus' mother and brothers
Matthew 12.46–50

Narrator   Jesus was still talking to the people when his mother and brothers arrived. They stood outside, asking to speak with him:

Person 1   Look, your mother and brothers are standing outside.

Person 2   They want to speak with you.

[Narrator   Jesus answered:]

Jesus   Who is my mother? Who are my brothers?

Narrator   Then he pointed to his disciples.

Jesus   Look! Here are my mother and my brothers! Whoever does what my Father in heaven wants him to do is my brother, my sister, and my mother.

Cast	[This is] the word of the Lord. OR	This is the Gospel of Christ / *This is the Gospel of the Lord.*
All	**Thanks be to God.**	**Praise to Christ our Lord** / *Praise to you, Lord Jesus Christ.*

Cast: **Narrator, Person 1, Person 2** (can be same as Person 1)**, Jesus.**

The parable of the sower
Matthew 13.1–9, 18–23*

Narrator   Jesus left the house and went to the lake-side, where he sat down to teach. The crowd that gathered round him was so large that he got into a boat and sat in it, while the crowd stood on the shore. He used parables to tell them many things.

Story-teller   Once there was a man who went out to sow corn.

Interpreter   Listen, then, and learn what the parable of the sower means.

Story-teller   As he scattered the seed in the field, some of it fell along the path, and the birds came and ate it up.

Interpreter   Those who hear the message about the Kingdom but do not understand it are like the seeds that fell along the path. The Evil One comes and snatches away what was sown in them. (PAUSE)

Story-teller   Some of it fell on rocky ground, where there was little soil. The seeds soon sprouted, because the soil wasn't deep. But when the sun came up, it burnt the young plants; and because the roots had not grown deep enough, the plants soon dried up.

Interpreter   The seeds that fell on rocky ground stand for those who receive the message gladly as soon as they hear it. But it does not sink deep into them, and they don't last long. So when trouble or persecution comes because of the message, they give up at once. (PAUSE)

Story-teller   Some of the seed fell among thorn bushes, which grew up and choked the plants.

Interpreter   The seeds that fell among thorn bushes stand for those who hear the message; but the worries about this life and the love for riches choke the message, and they don't bear fruit. (PAUSE)

Story-teller   But some seeds fell in good soil, and the plants produced corn; some produced a hundred grains, others sixty, and others thirty.

Interpreter   And the seeds sown in the good soil stand for those who hear the message and understand it: they bear fruit, some as much as a hundred, others sixty, and others thirty.

Narrator   And Jesus concluded, 'Listen, then, if you have ears!'

Cast [This is] the word of the Lord.   OR   This is the Gospel of Christ / *This is the Gospel of the Lord.*
All   **Thanks be to God.**   **Praise to Christ our Lord** / *Praise to you, Lord Jesus Christ.*

Cast: **Narrator, Story-teller, Interpreter.** (*The parable of the sower is set out sequentially where it occurs at Mark 4.1–9 and Luke 8.4–15. Here, parable and interpretation are intermixed for teaching purposes.)

The purpose of the parables
Matthew 13.10–17

Narrator	The disciples came to Jesus and asked him:
Disciple	Why do you use parables when you talk to the people?
Jesus	The knowledge about the secrets of the Kingdom of heaven has been given to you, but not to them. For the person who has something will be given more, so that he will have more than enough; but the person who has nothing will have taken away from him even the little he has. The reason I use parables in talking to them is that they look, but do not see, and they listen, but do not hear or understand. So the prophecy of Isaiah applies to them:
Isaiah	This people will listen and listen, but not understand; they will look and look, but not see, because their minds are dull, and they have stopped up their ears and have closed their eyes. Otherwise, their eyes would see, their ears would hear, their minds would understand, and they would turn to me, says God, and I would heal them.
Jesus	As for you, how fortunate you are! Your eyes see and your ears hear. I assure you that many prophets and many of God's people wanted very much to see what you see, but they could not, and to hear what you hear, but they did not.

Cast	[This is] the word of the Lord.	OR	This is the Gospel of Christ / *This is the Gospel of the Lord.*
All	**Thanks be to God.**		**Praise to Christ our Lord** / *Praise to you, Lord Jesus Christ.*

Cast: **Narrator, Disciple, Isaiah, Jesus.**

Jesus' parable of the weeds
Matthew 13.24–30, 37–43

Story-teller	The Kingdom of heaven is like this. A man sowed good seed in his field.
Interpreter	The man who sowed the good seed is the Son of Man; the field is the world; the good seed is the people who belong to the Kingdom.
Story-teller	One night, when everyone was asleep, an enemy came and sowed weeds among the wheat and went away.
Interpreter	The weeds are the people who belong to the Evil One; and the enemy who sowed the weeds is the Devil.
Story-teller	When the plants grew and the ears of corn began to form, then the weeds showed up. The man's servants came to him [and said]:
Servant	Sir, it was good seed you sowed in your field; where did the weeds come from?
[Story-teller	He answered:]
Man	It was some enemy who did this.

Servant	Do you want us to go and pull up the weeds?
Man	No, because as you gather the weeds you might pull up some of the wheat along with them. Let the wheat and the weeds both grow together until harvest. Then I will tell the harvest workers to pull up the weeds first, tie them in bundles and burn them, and then to gather in the wheat and put it in my barn.
Interpreter	The harvest is the end of the age, and the harvest workers are angels. Just as the weeds are gathered up and burnt in the fire, so the same thing will happen at the end of the age: the Son of Man will send out his angels to gather up out of his Kingdom all those who cause people to sin and all others who do evil things, and they will throw them into the fiery furnace where they will cry and grind their teeth. Then God's people will shine like the sun in their Father's Kingdom. Listen, then, if you have ears!

Cast	[This is] the word of the Lord. OR	This is the Gospel of Christ / *This is the Gospel of the Lord.*
All	**Thanks be to God.**	**Praise to Christ our Lord** / *Praise to you, Lord Jesus Christ.*

Cast: **Story-teller, Interpreter, Servant, Man.**

Parables of the Kingdom
Matthew 13.31–35, 44–52

Narrator	Jesus told another parable: the parable of the mustard seed.
Jesus	The Kingdom of heaven is like this. A man takes a mustard seed and sows it in his field. It is the smallest of all seeds, but when it grows up, it is the biggest of all plants. It becomes a tree, so that birds come and make their nests in its branches.

Narrator	Jesus told them still another parable: the parable of the yeast.
Jesus	The Kingdom of heaven is like this. A woman takes some yeast and mixes it with forty litres of flour until the whole batch of dough rises.
Narrator	Jesus used parables to tell all these things to the crowds; he would not say a thing to them without using a parable. He did this to make what the prophet had said come true:
Psalmist	I will use parables when I speak to them; I will tell them things unknown since the creation of the world.

Narrator	The parable of the hidden treasure. (PAUSE)
Jesus	The Kingdom of heaven is like this. A man happens to find a treasure hidden in a field. He covers it up again, and is so happy that he goes and sells everything he has, and then goes back and buys that field.

Narrator	The parable of the pearl. (PAUSE)

28

Jesus	The Kingdom of heaven is like this. A man is looking for fine pearls, and when he finds one that is unusually fine, he goes and sells everything he has, and buys that pearl.

———

Narrator	The parable of the net. (PAUSE)
Jesus	The Kingdom of heaven is like this. Some fishermen throw their net out in the lake and catch all kinds of fish. When the net is full, they pull it to shore and sit down to divide the fish: the good ones go into their buckets, the worthless ones are thrown away. It will be like this at the end of the age: the angels will go out and gather up the evil people from among the good and will throw them into the fiery furnace, where they will cry and grind their teeth.

———

Narrator	New truths and old. (PAUSE) [Jesus asked them]:
Jesus	Do you understand these things?
Disciple(s)	Yes.
Jesus	This means, then, that every teacher of the Law who becomes a disciple in the Kingdom of heaven is like the owner of a house who takes new and old things out of his storeroom.

Cast	[This is] the word of the Lord. OR This is the Gospel of Christ / *This is the Gospel of the Lord.*
All	**Thanks be to God.** **Praise to Christ our Lord** / *Praise to you, Lord Jesus Christ.*

Cast: **Narrator, Jesus, Psalmist** (can be same as Narrator or can be same as Jesus), **Disciple(s).**

Jesus is rejected at Nazareth
Matthew 13.53–58

Narrator	Jesus went back to his home town. He taught in the synagogue, and those who heard him were amazed.
Person 1	Where did he get such wisdom?
Person 2	And what about his miracles?
Person 3	Isn't he the carpenter's son?
Person 1	Isn't Mary his mother?
Person 2	And aren't James, Joseph, Simon, and Judas his brothers?
Person 1	Aren't all his sisters living here?
Person 3	Where did he get all this?
Narrator	And so they rejected him. (PAUSE) Jesus said to them:
Jesus	A prophet is respected everywhere except in his home town and by his own family.
Narrator	Because they did not have faith, he did not perform many miracles there.

Cast	[This is] the word of the Lord. OR This is the Gospel of Christ / *This is the Gospel of the Lord.*
All	**Thanks be to God.** **Praise to Christ our Lord** / *Praise to you, Lord Jesus Christ.*

Cast: **Narrator, Person 1** (preferably female), **Person 2, Person 3, Jesus.**

The death of John the Baptist
Matthew 14.1–12

Narrator Herod, the ruler of Galilee, heard about Jesus. He told his officials:

Herod He is really John the Baptist, who has come back to life. That is why he has this power to perform miracles.

Narrator For Herod had earlier ordered John's arrest, and he had him chained and put in prison. He had done this because of Herodias, his brother Philip's wife. For some time John the Baptist had told Herod:

John It isn't right for you to be married to Herodias!

Narrator Herod wanted to kill him, but he was afraid of the Jewish people, because they considered John to be a prophet. (PAUSE)

On Herod's birthday the daughter of Herodias danced in front of the whole group. Herod was so pleased that he promised her:

Herod I swear that I will give you anything you ask for!

Narrator At her mother's suggestion she asked him:

Daughter Give me here and now the head of John the Baptist on a dish!

Narrator The king was sad, but because of the promise he had made in front of all his guests he gave orders that her wish be granted. So he had John beheaded in prison. The head was brought in on a dish and given to the girl, who took it to her mother. John's disciples came, carried away his body, and buried it; then they went and told Jesus.

Cast [This is] the word of the Lord.   OR   This is the Gospel of Christ / *This is the Gospel of the Lord.*
All   **Thanks be to God.**   **Praise to Christ our Lord** / *Praise to you, Lord Jesus Christ.*

Cast: **Narrator, Herod, John, Daughter.**

Jesus feeds five thousand
Matthew 14.13–21

Narrator When Jesus heard the news about John the Baptist's death, he left there in a boat and went to a lonely place by himself. The people heard about it, so they left their towns and followed him by land. Jesus got out of the boat, and when he saw the large crowd, his heart was filled with pity for them, and he healed those who were ill.

That evening his disciples came to him [and said]:

Disciple 1	It is already very late, and this is a lonely place. Send the people away and let them go to the villages to buy food for themselves.
[Narrator	Jesus answered:]
Jesus	They don't have to leave. *You* give them something to eat!
Disciple 2	All we have here are five loaves and two fish.
Jesus	Then bring them here to me.
Narrator	Jesus ordered the people to sit down on the grass; then he took the five loaves and the two fish, looked up to heaven, and gave thanks to God. He broke the loaves and gave them to the disciples, and the disciples gave them to the people.
	Everyone ate and had enough. Then the disciples took up twelve baskets full of what was left over. The number of men who ate was about five thousand, not counting the women and children.

Cast	[This is] the word of the Lord.	OR	This is the Gospel of Christ / *This is the Gospel of the Lord.*
All	**Thanks be to God.**		**Praise to Christ our Lord** / *Praise to you, Lord Jesus Christ.*

Cast: **Narrator, Disciple 1, Jesus, Disciple 2** (can be the same as Disciple 1).

Jesus walks on the water
Matthew 14.22–33

Narrator	Jesus made the disciples get into the boat and go on ahead to the other side of the lake, while he sent the people away. After sending the people away, he went up a hill by himself to pray. (PAUSE) When evening came, Jesus was there alone; and by this time the boat was far out in the lake, tossed about by the waves, because the wind was blowing against it. (PAUSE)
	Between three and six o'clock in the morning Jesus came to the disciples, walking on the water. When they saw him walking on the water, they were terrified.
Disciple	It's a ghost!
Narrator	And they screamed with fear. Jesus spoke to them at once:
Jesus	Courage! It is I. Don't be afraid!
Narrator	Then Peter spoke up:
Peter	Lord, if it is really you, order me to come out on the water to you.
Jesus	Come!
Narrator	So Peter got out of the boat and started walking on the water to Jesus. But when he noticed the strong wind, he was afraid and started to sink down in the water. [He cried:]
Peter	Save me, Lord!
Narrator	At once Jesus reached out and grabbed hold of him.
Jesus	How little faith you have! Why did you doubt?

31

Narrator	They both got into the boat, and the wind died down. Then the disciples in the boat worshipped Jesus.
Disciple	Truly you are the Son of God!

Cast	[This is] the word of the Lord. OR This is the Gospel of Christ / *This is the Gospel of the Lord.*
All	**Thanks be to God.** **Praise to Christ our Lord** / *Praise to you, Lord Jesus Christ.*

Cast: **Narrator, Disciple, Jesus, Peter.**

The teaching of the ancestors
Matthew 15.1–9

Narrator	Some Pharisees and teachers of the Law came from Jerusalem to Jesus [and asked him]:
Pharisee	Why is it that your disciples disobey the teaching handed down by our ancestors?
Lawyer	They don't wash their hands in the proper way before they eat!
[Narrator	Jesus answered:]
Jesus	And why do you disobey God's command and follow your own teaching? For God said, 'Respect your father and your mother,' and 'Whoever curses his father or his mother is to be put to death.' But you teach that if a person has something he could use to help his father or mother, but says, 'This belongs to God,' he does not need to honour his father. In this way you disregard God's command, in order to follow your own teaching. You hypocrites! How right Isaiah was when he prophesied about you:
Isaiah	These people, says God, honour me with their words, but their heart is really far away from me. It is no use for them to worship me, because they teach man-made rules as though they were my laws!

Cast	[This is] the word of the Lord. OR This is the Gospel of Christ / *This is the Gospel of the Lord.*
All	**Thanks be to God.** **Praise to Christ our Lord** / *Praise to you, Lord Jesus Christ.*

Cast: **Narrator, Pharisee, Lawyer** (can be the same as Pharisee), **Jesus, Isaiah.**

The things that make a person unclean
Matthew 15.10–20

Narrator	Jesus called the crowd to him [and said to them]:
Jesus (to crowd)	Listen and understand! It is not what goes into a person's mouth that makes him ritually unclean; rather, what comes out of it makes him unclean.
Narrator	Then the disciples came to him [and said]:
Disciple	Do you know that the Pharisees had their feelings hurt by what you said?

Jesus (to disciples)	Every plant which my Father in heaven did not plant will be pulled up. Don't worry about them! They are blind leaders of the blind; and when one blind man leads another, both fall into a ditch.
[Narrator	Peter spoke up:]
Peter	Explain this saying to us.
Jesus	You are still no more intelligent than the others. Don't you understand? Anything that goes into a person's mouth goes into his stomach and then on out of his body. But the things that come out of the mouth come from the heart, and these are the things that make a person ritually unclean. For from his heart come the evil ideas which lead him to kill, commit adultery, and do other immoral things; to rob, lie, and slander others. These are the things that make a person unclean. But to eat without washing your hands as they say you should—this doesn't make a person unclean.

| Cast | [This is] the word of the Lord.   OR | This is the Gospel of Christ / *This is the Gospel of the Lord.* |
| All | **Thanks be to God.** | **Praise to Christ our Lord** / *Praise to you, Lord Jesus Christ.* |

Cast: **Narrator, Jesus, Disciple, Peter** (can be the same as Disciple, in which case words in brackets may be omitted).

A woman's faith
Matthew 15.21–28

Narrator	Jesus went off to the territory near the cities of Tyre and Sidon. A Canaanite woman who lived in that region came to him:
Woman (crying out)	Son of David! Have mercy on me, sir! My daughter has a demon and is in a terrible condition.
Narrator	But Jesus did not say a word to her. His disciples came to him [and begged him]:
Disciple 1	Send her away!
Disciple 2	She is following us and making all this noise!
[Narrator	Then Jesus replied:]
Jesus	I have been sent only to the lost sheep of the people of Israel.
Narrator	At this the woman came and fell at his feet:
Woman	Help me, sir!
Jesus	It isn't right to take the children's food and throw it to the dogs.
Woman	That's true, sir, but even the dogs eat the leftovers that fall from their masters' table.
Jesus	You are a woman of great faith! What you want will be done for you.
Narrator	And at that very moment her daughter was healed.

| Cast | [This is] the word of the Lord.   OR | This is the Gospel of Christ / *This is the Gospel of the Lord.* |
| All | **Thanks be to God.** | **Praise to Christ our Lord** / *Praise to you, Lord Jesus Christ.* |

Cast: **Narrator, Woman, Disciple 1, Disciple 2** (can be the same as Disciple 1), **Jesus.**

Jesus heals and feeds many people
Matthew 15.29–38

Narrator Jesus went along by Lake Galilee. He climbed a hill and sat down. Large crowds came to him, bringing with them the lame, the blind, the crippled, the dumb, and many other sick people, whom they placed at Jesus' feet; and he healed them. The people were amazed as they saw the dumb speaking, the crippled made whole, the lame walking, and the blind seeing; and they praised the God of Israel. (PAUSE)

Jesus called his disciples to him:

Jesus I feel sorry for these people, because they have been with me for three days and now have nothing to eat. I don't want to send them away without feeding them, for they might faint on their way home.

[Narrator The disciples asked him:]

Disciple Where will we find enough food in this desert to feed this crowd?

Jesus How much bread have you?

Disciple Seven loaves and a few small fish.

Narrator So Jesus ordered the crowd to sit down on the ground. Then he took the seven loaves and the fish, gave thanks to God, broke them, and gave them to the disciples; and the disciples gave them to the people. They all ate and had enough. Then the disciples took up seven baskets full of pieces left over. The number of men who ate was four thousand, not counting the women and children.

Then Jesus sent the people away, got into a boat, and went to the territory of Magadan.

Cast [This is] the word of the Lord. OR This is the Gospel of Christ / *This is the Gospel of the Lord.*
All **Thanks be to God.** **Praise to Christ our Lord** / *Praise to you, Lord Jesus Christ.*

Cast: **Narrator, Jesus, Disciple.**

The demand for a miracle
Matthew 16.1–4

Narrator Some Pharisees and Sadducees who came to Jesus wanted to trap him, so they asked him to perform a miracle for them, to show that God approved of him. But Jesus answered:

Jesus When the sun is setting, you say:

Person 1 We are going to have fine weather, because the sky is red.

Jesus And early in the morning you say:

Person 2 It is going to rain, because the sky is red and dark.

Jesus You can predict the weather by looking at the sky, but you cannot interpret the signs concerning these times! How evil and godless are the people of this day! You ask me for a miracle? No! The only miracle you will be given is the miracle of Jonah.

Narrator So he left them and went away.

Cast [This is] the word of the Lord.   OR   This is the Gospel of Christ / *This is the Gospel of the Lord.*
All   **Thanks be to God.**   **Praise to Christ our Lord** / *Praise to you, Lord Jesus Christ.*

Cast: **Narrator, Jesus, Person 1, Person 2** (can be the same as Person 1).

The yeast of the Pharisees and Sadducees
Matthew 16.5–12

Narrator When the disciples crossed over to the other side of the lake, they forgot to take any bread. Jesus said to them:

Jesus Take care; be on your guard against the yeast of the Pharisees and Sadducees.

Narrator They started discussing among themselves:

Disciple He says this because we didn't bring any bread.

Narrator Jesus knew what they were saying, so he asked them:

Jesus Why are you discussing among yourselves about not having any bread? How little faith you have! Don't you understand yet? Don't you remember when I broke the five loaves for the five thousand men? How many baskets did you fill? And what about the seven loaves for the four thousand men? How many baskets did you fill? How is it that you don't understand that I was not talking to you about bread? Guard yourselves from the yeast of the Pharisees and Sadducees!

Narrator Then the disciples understood that he was not warning them to guard themselves from the yeast used in bread but from the teaching of the Pharisees and Sadducees.

Cast [This is] the word of the Lord.   OR   This is the Gospel of Christ / *This is the Gospel of the Lord.*
All   **Thanks be to God.**   **Praise to Christ our Lord** / *Praise to you, Lord Jesus Christ.*

Cast: **Narrator, Jesus, Disciple.**

Peter's declaration about Jesus
Matthew 16.13–20

Narrator Jesus went to the territory near the town of Caesarea Philippi, where he asked his disciples:

Jesus Who do people say the Son of Man is?

[Narrator They answered:]

Disciple 1 Some say John the Baptist.

Disciple 2 Others say Elijah.

Disciple 3	Others say Jeremiah or some other prophet.
Jesus	What about you? Who do you say I am?
Narrator	Simon Peter answered:
Peter	You are the Messiah, the Son of the living God.
Jesus	Good for you, Simon son of John! For this truth did not come to you from any human being, but it was given to you directly by my Father in heaven. And so I tell you, Peter: you are a rock, and on this rock foundation I will build my church, and not even death will ever be able to overcome it. I will give you the keys of the Kingdom of heaven; what you prohibit on earth will be prohibited in heaven, and what you permit on earth will be permitted in heaven.
Narrator	Then Jesus ordered his disciples not to tell anyone that he was the Messiah.

Cast	[This is] the word of the Lord. OR	This is the Gospel of Christ / *This is the Gospel of the Lord.*
All	**Thanks be to God.**	**Praise to Christ our Lord** / *Praise to you, Lord Jesus Christ.*

Cast: **Narrator, Jesus, Disciple 1, Disciple 2, Disciple 3** (can be the same as Disciple 1), **Peter** (can be the same as Disciple 2).

Jesus speaks about his suffering and death
Matthew 16.21–28

Narrator	From that time on Jesus began to say plainly to his disciples:
Jesus	I must go to Jerusalem and suffer much from the elders, the chief priests, and the teachers of the Law. I will be put to death, but three days later I will be raised to life.
Narrator	Peter took him aside and began to rebuke him.
Peter	God forbid it, Lord! That must never happen to you!
[Narrator	Jesus turned around and said to Peter:]
Jesus (to Peter)	Get away from me, Satan! You are an obstacle in my way, because these thoughts of yours don't come from God, but from man.
Narrator	Then Jesus said to his disciples:
Jesus	If anyone wants to come with me, he must forget self, carry his cross, and follow me. For whoever wants to save his own life will lose it; but whoever loses his life for my sake will find it. Will a person gain anything if he wins the whole world but loses his life? Of course not! There is nothing he can give to regain his life. For the Son of Man is about to come in the glory of his Father with his angels, and then he will reward each one according to his deeds. I assure you that there are some here who will not die until they have seen the Son of Man come as King.

Cast	[This is] the word of the Lord. OR	This is the Gospel of Christ / *This is the Gospel of the Lord.*
All	**Thanks be to God.**	**Praise to Christ our Lord** / *Praise to you, Lord Jesus Christ.*

Cast: **Narrator, Jesus, Peter.**

The Transfiguration
Matthew 17.1–13

Narrator
Jesus took with him Peter and the brothers James and John and led them up a high mountain where they were alone. As they looked on, a change came over Jesus: his face was shining like the sun, and his clothes were dazzling white. Then the three disciples saw Moses and Elijah talking with Jesus. So Peter spoke up:

Peter
Lord, how good it is that we are here! If you wish, I will make three tents here, one for you, one for Moses, and one for Elijah.

Narrator
While he was talking, a shining cloud came over them, and a voice from the cloud said:

Voice
This is my own dear Son, with whom I am pleased—listen to him!

Narrator
When the disciples heard the voice, they were so terrified that they threw themselves face downwards on the ground. Jesus came to them and touched them.

Jesus
Get up! Don't be afraid!

Narrator
So they looked up and saw no one there but Jesus.

As they came down the mountain, Jesus ordered them:

Jesus
Don't tell anyone about this vision you have seen until the Son of Man has been raised from death.

Narrator
Then the disciples asked Jesus:

Disciple
Why do the teachers of the Law say that Elijah has to come first?

Jesus
Elijah is indeed coming first, and he will get everything ready. But I tell you that Elijah has already come and people did not recognize him, but treated him just as they pleased. In the same way they will also ill-treat the Son of Man.

Narrator
Then the disciples understood that he was talking to them about John the Baptist.

Cast [This is] the word of the Lord. OR	This is the Gospel of Christ / *This is the Gospel of the Lord.*
All **Thanks be to God.**	**Praise to Christ our Lord** / *Praise to you, Lord Jesus Christ.*

Cast: **Narrator, Peter, Voice, Jesus, Disciple.**

Jesus heals a boy with a demon
Matthew 17.14–20

Narrator
When they returned to the crowd, a man came to Jesus and knelt before him:

Man
Sir, have mercy on my son! He is an epileptic and has such terrible fits that he often falls in the fire or into water. I brought him to your disciples, but they could not heal him.

[Narrator
Jesus answered:]

Jesus	How unbelieving and wrong you people are! How long must I stay with you? How long do I have to put up with you? Bring the boy here to me!
Narrator	Jesus gave a command to the demon, and it went out of the boy, and at that very moment he was healed.
	Then the disciples came to Jesus in private:
Disciple	Why couldn't we drive the demon out?
Jesus	It was because you haven't enough faith. I assure you that if you have faith as big as a mustard seed, you can say to this hill, 'Go from here to there!' and it will go. You could do anything!

Cast	[This is] the word of the Lord. OR This is the Gospel of Christ / *This is the Gospel of the Lord.*
All	**Thanks be to God.** **Praise to Christ our Lord** / *Praise to you, Lord Jesus Christ.*

Cast: **Narrator, Man, Jesus, Disciple.**

Who is the greatest?
Matthew 18.1–5, 10; 19.13–15

Narrator	The disciples came to Jesus [asking]:
Disciple	Who is the greatest in the Kingdom of heaven?
Narrator	So Jesus called a child and made him stand in front of them. [He said:]
Jesus	I assure you that unless you change and become like children, you will never enter the Kingdom of heaven. The greatest in the Kingdom of heaven is the one who humbles himself and becomes like this child. And whoever welcomes in my name one such child as this, welcomes me. See that you don't despise any of these little ones. Their angels in heaven, I tell you, are always in the presence of my Father in heaven.
Narrator	Some people brought children to Jesus for him to place his hands on them and to pray for them, but the disciples scolded the people. [Jesus said:]
Jesus	Let the children come to me and do not stop them, because the Kingdom of heaven belongs to such as these.
Narrator	He placed his hands on them and then went away.

Cast	[This is] the word of the Lord. OR This is the Gospel of Christ / *This is the Gospel of the Lord.*
All	**Thanks be to God.** **Praise to Christ our Lord** / *Praise to you, Lord Jesus Christ.*

Cast: **Narrator, Disciple, Jesus.**

The parable of the unforgiving servant
Matthew 18.21–35

Narrator	Peter came to Jesus [and asked:]
Peter	Lord, if my brother keeps on sinning against me, how many times do I have to forgive him? Seven times?

[Narrator	Jesus answered:]
Jesus	No, not seven times, but seventy times seven, because the Kingdom of heaven is like this. Once there was a king who decided to check on his servants' accounts. He had just begun to do so when one of them was brought in who owed him millions of pounds. The servant did not have enough to pay his debt, so the king ordered him to be sold as a slave, with his wife and his children and all that he had, in order to pay the debt. The servant fell on his knees before the king. [He begged:]
Servant	Be patient with me and I will pay you everything!
Jesus	The king felt sorry for him, so he forgave him the debt and let him go. Then the man went out and met one of his fellow-servants who owed him a few pounds. He grabbed him and started choking him. [He said:]
Servant (roughly)	Pay back what you owe me!
Jesus	His fellow-servant fell down and begged him:
Fellow-servant (pleading)	Be patient with me, and I will pay you back!
Jesus	But he refused; instead, he had him thrown into jail until he should pay the debt. When the other servants saw what had happened, they were very upset and went to the king and told him everything. So he called the servant in.
King	You worthless slave! I forgave you the whole amount you owed me, just because you asked me to. You should have had mercy on your fellow-servant, just as I had mercy on you.
Jesus	The king was very angry, and he sent the servant to jail to be punished until he should pay back the whole amount.
[Narrator	And Jesus concluded:]
Jesus (looking round)	That is how my Father in heaven will treat every one of you unless you forgive your brother from your heart.

Cast	[This is] the word of the Lord.	OR	This is the Gospel of Christ / *This is the Gospel of the Lord.*
All	**Thanks be to God.**		**Praise to Christ our Lord** / *Praise to you, Lord Jesus Christ.*

Cast: **Narrator, Peter, Jesus, Servant, Fellow-servant, King.**

Jesus teaches about divorce
Matthew 19.1–12

Narrator	Jesus left Galilee and went to the territory of Judaea on the other side of the River Jordan. Large crowds followed him, and he healed them there.
	Some Pharisees came to him and tried to trap him.

Pharisee 1	Does our Law allow a man to divorce his wife for whatever reason he wishes?
[Narrator	Jesus answered:]
Jesus	Haven't you read the scripture that says that in the beginning the Creator made people male and female? And God said:
God	For this reason a man will leave his father and mother and unite with his wife, and the two will become one.
Jesus	So they are no longer two, but one. Man must not separate, then, what God has joined together.
[Narrator	The Pharisees asked him:]
Pharisee 2	Why, then, did Moses give the law for a man to hand his wife a divorce notice and send her away?
Jesus	Moses gave you permission to divorce your wives because you are so hard to teach. But it was not like that at the time of creation. I tell you, then, that any man who divorces his wife for any cause other than her unfaithfulness, commits adultery if he marries some other woman.
Narrator	His disciples said to him:
Disciple	If this is how it is between a man and his wife, it is better not to marry.
Jesus	This teaching does not apply to everyone, but only to those to whom God has given it. For there are different reasons why men cannot marry: some, because they were born that way; others, because men made them that way; and others do not marry for the sake of the Kingdom of heaven. Let him who can accept this teaching do so.

Cast	[This is] the word of the Lord. OR	This is the Gospel of Christ / *This is the Gospel of the Lord.*
All	**Thanks be to God.**	**Praise to Christ our Lord** / *Praise to you, Lord Jesus Christ.*

Cast: **Narrator, Pharisee 1, Jesus, God** (can be the same as Jesus), **Pharisee 2, Disciple.**

Jesus blesses little children
Matthew 19.13–15

Narrator	Some people brought children to Jesus for him to place his hands on them and to pray for them, but the disciples scolded the people. Jesus said:
Jesus	Let the children come to me and do not stop them, because the Kingdom of heaven belongs to such as these. (PAUSE)
Narrator	He placed his hands on them and then went away.

Cast	[This is] the word of the Lord. OR	This is the Gospel of Christ / *This is the Gospel of the Lord.*
All	**Thanks be to God.**	**Praise to Christ our Lord** / *Praise to you, Lord Jesus Christ.*

Cast: **Narrator, Jesus.**

The rich young man
Matthew 19.16–30

Narrator Once a man came to Jesus. [He asked:]

Man Teacher, what good thing must I do to receive eternal life?

[Narrator Jesus answered:]

Jesus Why do you ask me concerning what is good? There is only One who is good. Keep the commandments if you want to enter life.

Man What commandments?

Jesus Do not commit murder; do not commit adultery; do not steal; do not accuse anyone falsely; respect your father and your mother; and love your neighbour as you love yourself.

Man I have obeyed all these commandments. What else do I need to do?

Jesus If you want to be perfect, go and sell all you have and give the money to the poor, and you will have riches in heaven; then come and follow me.

Narrator When the young man heard this, he went away sad, because he was very rich.

Jesus then said to his disciples:

Jesus I assure you: it will be very hard for rich people to enter the Kingdom of heaven. I repeat: it is much harder for a rich person to enter the Kingdom of God than for a camel to go through the eye of a needle.

Narrator When the disciples heard this, they were completely amazed. [They asked:]

Disciple Who, then, can be saved?

Narrator Jesus looked straight at them [and answered]:

Jesus
(looking hard) This is impossible for man, but for God everything is possible.

Narrator Then Peter spoke up:

Peter Look, we have left everything and followed you. What will we have?

Jesus You can be sure that when the Son of Man sits on his glorious throne in the New Age, then you twelve followers of mine will also sit on thrones, to rule the twelve tribes of Israel. And everyone who has left houses or brothers or sisters or father or mother or children or fields for my sake, will receive a hundred times more and will be given eternal life. But many who now are first will be last, and many who now are last will be first.

Cast [This is] the word of the Lord. OR This is the Gospel of Christ / *This is the Gospel of the Lord.*
All **Thanks be to God.** **Praise to Christ our Lord** / *Praise to you, Lord Jesus Christ.*

Cast: **Narrator, Man, Jesus, Disciple, Peter.**

Jesus tells the parable of the workers in the vineyard
Matthew 20.1–16

Jesus The Kingdom of heaven is like this. Once there was a man who went out early in the morning to hire some men to work in his vineyard. He agreed to pay them the regular wage, a silver coin a day, and sent them to work in his vineyard. He went out again to the market place at nine o'clock and saw some men standing there doing nothing [so he told them]:

Owner You also go and work in the vineyard, and I will pay you a fair wage.

Jesus So they went. (PAUSE) Then at twelve o'clock and again at three o'clock he did the same thing. It was nearly five o'clock when he went to the market place and saw some other men still standing there. [He asked them:]

Owner Why are you wasting the whole day here doing nothing?

[Jesus They answered:]

Man 3 No one hired us.

Owner Well, then, you also go and work in the vineyard.

Jesus When evening came, the owner told his foreman:

Owner Call the workers and pay them their wages, starting with those who were hired last and ending with those who were hired first.

Jesus The men who had begun to work at five o'clock were paid a silver coin each. So when the men who were the first to be hired came to be paid, they thought they would get more; but they too were given a silver coin each. They took their money and started grumbling against the employer. [They said:]

Man 1
(grumbling) These men who were hired last worked only one hour.

Man 2 While we put up with a whole day's work in the hot sun.

Man 1 Yet you paid them the same as you paid us!

Owner
(to Man 1) Listen, friend, I have not cheated you. After all, you agreed to do a day's work for one silver coin. Now take your pay and go home. I want to give this man who was hired last as much as I have given you. Don't I have the right to do as I wish with my own money? Or are you jealous because I am generous? (PAUSE)

Jesus (looking round) So those who are last will be first, and those who are first will be last.

Cast	[This is] the word of the Lord.　OR	This is the Gospel of Christ / *This is the Gospel of the Lord.*
All	**Thanks be to God.**	**Praise to Christ our Lord** / *Praise to you, Lord Jesus Christ.*

Cast: **Jesus** (as Narrator), **Owner, Man 3, Man 1, Man 2** (can be the same as **Man 1**).

Jesus speaks a third time about his death
Matthew 20.17–19

Narrator As Jesus was going up to Jerusalem, he took the twelve disciples aside and spoke to them privately, as they walked along. He told them:

Jesus Listen, we are going up to Jerusalem, where the Son of Man will be handed over to the chief priests and the teachers of the Law. They will condemn him to death and then hand him over to the Gentiles, who will mock him, whip him, and crucify him; but three days later he will be raised to life.

Cast [This is] the word of the Lord.   OR   This is the Gospel of Christ / *This is the Gospel of the Lord.*
All   **Thanks be to God.**   **Praise to Christ our Lord** / *Praise to you, Lord Jesus Christ.*

Cast: **Narrator, Jesus.**

A mother's request
Matthew 20.20–28

Narrator The wife of Zebedee came to Jesus with her two sons, bowed before him, and asked him a favour. [Jesus asked her:]

Jesus What do you want?

Wife Promise me that these two sons of mine will sit at your right and your left when you are King.

[Narrator Jesus answered the sons:]

Jesus (to the Sons) You don't know what you are asking for. Can you drink the cup of suffering that I am about to drink?

[Narrator They answered:]

Sons We can.

Jesus You will indeed drink from my cup, but I do not have the right to choose who will sit at my right and my left. These places belong to those for whom my Father has prepared them.

Narrator When the other ten disciples heard about this they became angry with the two brothers. So Jesus called them all together.

Jesus You know that the rulers of the heathen have power over them, and the leaders have complete authority. This, however, is not the way it shall be among you. If one of you wants to be great, he must be the servant of the rest; and if one of you wants to be first, he must be your slave—like the Son of Man, who did not come to be served, but to serve and to give his life to redeem many people.

Cast [This is] the word of the Lord.   OR   This is the Gospel of Christ / *This is the Gospel of the Lord.*
All   **Thanks be to God.**   **Praise to Christ our Lord** / *Praise to you, Lord Jesus Christ.*

Cast: **Narrator, Jesus, Wife, Sons** (two).

Jesus heals two blind men
Matthew 20.29–34

Narrator   As Jesus and his disciples were leaving Jericho, a large crowd was following. Two blind men who were sitting by the road heard that Jesus was passing by, so they began to shout:

Blind man 1   Son of David!

Blind man 2   Take pity on us, sir!

Narrator   The crowd scolded them and told them to be quiet. But they shouted even more loudly:

Blind men 1 & 2   Son of David! Take pity on us, sir!

Narrator   Jesus stopped and called them.

Jesus   What do you want me to do for you?

Blind man 1   Sir, we want you to give us our sight!

Narrator   Jesus had pity on them and touched their eyes; at once they were able to see, and they followed him.

Cast   [This is] the word of the Lord.   OR   This is the Gospel of Christ / *This is the Gospel of the Lord.*
All   **Thanks be to God.**   **Praise to Christ our Lord** / *Praise to you, Lord Jesus Christ.*

Cast: **Narrator, Blind man 1, Blind man 2, Jesus.**

The triumphant entry into Jerusalem
Matthew 21.1–11

Narrator   As Jesus and his disciples approached Jerusalem, they came to Bethphage at the Mount of Olives. There Jesus sent two of the disciples on ahead with these instructions:

Jesus   Go to the village there ahead of you, and at once you will find a donkey tied up with her colt beside her. Untie them and bring them to me. And if anyone says anything, tell him, 'The Master needs them'; and then he will let them go at once.

Narrator   This happened in order to make what the prophet had said come true:

Zechariah   Tell the city of Zion,
Look, your king is coming to you!
He is humble and rides on a donkey
and on a colt, the foal of a donkey.

Narrator   So the disciples went and did what Jesus had told them to do: they brought the donkey and the colt, threw their cloaks over them, and Jesus got on. A large crowd of people spread their cloaks on the road while others cut branches from the trees and spread them on the road. The crowds walking in front of Jesus and those walking behind began to shout:

Person 1   Praise to David's Son!

Person 2	God bless him who comes in the name of the Lord!
Person 3	Praise God!
Narrator	When Jesus entered Jerusalem, the whole city was thrown into an uproar. [The people asked:]
Persons 1 and	Who is he?
Person 3	This is the prophet Jesus, from Nazareth in Galilee.

Cast [This is] the word of the Lord.   OR   This is the Gospel of Christ / *This is the Gospel of the Lord.*
All   **Thanks be to God.**   **Praise to Christ our Lord** / *Praise to you, Lord Jesus Christ.*

Cast: **Narrator, Jesus, Zechariah** (can be the same as Narrator), **Person 1, Person 2, Person 3.**

The house of prayer
Matthew 21.12–16 [17]

Narrator	Jesus went into the Temple and drove out all those who were buying and selling there. He overturned the tables of the money-changers and the stools of those who sold pigeons [and said to them]:
Jesus	It is written in the Scriptures that God said, 'My Temple will be called a house of prayer.' But you are making it a hideout for thieves!
Narrator	The blind and the crippled came to him in the Temple, and he healed them. The chief priests and the teachers of the Law became angry when they saw the wonderful things he was doing and the children shouting in the Temple:
Children	Praise to David's Son!
Narrator	So they asked Jesus:
Chief priest (to Jesus)	Do you hear what they are saying?
Jesus	Indeed I do. Haven't you ever read this scripture? 'You have trained children and babies to offer perfect praise.'
[Narrator	Jesus left them and went out of the city to Bethany, where he spent the night.]

Cast [This is] the word of the Lord.   OR   This is the Gospel of Christ / *This is the Gospel of the Lord.*
All   **Thanks be to God.**   **Praise to Christ our Lord** / *Praise to you, Lord Jesus Christ.*

Cast: **Narrator, Jesus, Children** (at least two), **Chief priest.**

Jesus curses the fig-tree
Matthew 21.18–22

Narrator	On his way back to the city early next morning, Jesus was hungry. He saw a fig-tree by the side of the road and went to it, but found nothing on it except leaves. So he said to the tree:
Jesus	You will never again bear fruit!
Narrator	At once the fig-tree dried up.

→

The disciples saw this and were astounded.

Disciple How did the fig-tree dry up so quickly?

Jesus I assure you that if you believe and do not doubt, you will be able to do what I have done to this fig-tree. And not only this, but you will even be able to say to this hill, 'Get up and throw yourself in the sea,' and it will. If you believe, you will receive whatever you ask for in prayer.

Cast [This is] the word of the Lord. OR This is the Gospel of Christ / *This is the Gospel of the Lord.*
All **Thanks be to God.** **Praise to Christ our Lord** / *Praise to you, Lord Jesus Christ.*

Cast: **Narrator, Jesus, Disciple.**

The question about Jesus' authority
Matthew 21.23–27

Narrator Jesus came back to the Temple; and as he taught, the chief priests and the elders came to him [and asked]:

Chief priest 1 What right have you to do these things?

Chief priest 2 Who gave you this right?

[Narrator Jesus answered them:]

Jesus I will ask you just one question, and if you give me an answer, I will tell you what right I have to do these things. Where did John's right to baptize come from: was it from God or from man?

Narrator They started to argue among themselves:

Chief priest 1 What shall we say?

Chief priest 2 If we answer, 'From God,' he will say to us, 'Why, then, did you not believe John?'

Chief priest 1 But if we say, 'From man,' we are afraid of what the people might do, because they are all convinced that John was a prophet. (PAUSE)

[Narrator So they answered Jesus:]

Chief priests 1 and 2 We don't know.

Jesus Neither will I tell you, then, by what right I do these things.

Cast [This is] the word of the Lord. OR This is the Gospel of Christ / *This is the Gospel of the Lord.*
All **Thanks be to God.** **Praise to Christ our Lord** / *Praise to you, Lord Jesus Christ.*

Cast: **Narrator, Chief priest 1, Jesus, Chief priest 2.**

The parable of the two sons
Matthew 21.28–32

Jesus Now, what do you think? There was once a man who had two sons. He went to the elder one [and said]:

Father Son, go and work in the vineyard today.

46

[Jesus	He answered:]
Elder son	I don't want to.
Jesus	But later he changed his mind and went. (PAUSE) Then the father went to the other son and said the same thing. He answered:
Younger son	Yes, sir.
Jesus	But he did not go. (PAUSE) Which one of the two did what his father wanted?
Person	The elder one.
Jesus	I tell you: the tax collectors and the prostitutes are going into the Kingdom of God ahead of you. For John the Baptist came to you showing you the right path to take, and you would not believe him; but the tax collectors and the prostitutes believed him. Even when you saw this, you did not later change your minds and believe him.

Cast	[This is] the word of the Lord.	OR	This is the Gospel of Christ / *This is the Gospel of the Lord.*
All	**Thanks be to God.**		**Praise to Christ our Lord** / *Praise to you, Lord Jesus Christ.*

Cast: **Jesus, Father, Elder son, Younger son, Person.**

The parable of the tenants and the vineyard
Matthew 21.33–46

Narrator	Jesus said:
Jesus	Listen to another parable.
	There was once a landowner who planted a vineyard, put a fence around it, dug a hole for the winepress, and built a watch-tower. Then he let out the vineyard to tenants and went on a journey. When the time came to gather the grapes, he sent his slaves to the tenants to receive his share of the harvest. The tenants seized his slaves, beat one, killed another, and stoned another. Again the man sent other slaves, more than the first time, and the tenants treated them the same way. Last of all he sent his son to them [and said]:
Landowner	Surely they will respect my son.
Jesus	But when the tenants saw the son, they said to themselves:
Tenant 1	This is the owner's son.
Tenant 2	Come on, let's kill him, and we will get his property!
Jesus	So they seized him, threw him out of the vineyard, and killed him. (PAUSE)
	Now, when the owner of the vineyard comes, what will he do to those tenants?
Person 1	He will certainly kill those evil men—
Person 2	And let the vineyard out to other tenants—
Person 1	Who will give him his share of the harvest at the right time.
Jesus	Haven't you ever read what the Scriptures say?

Psalmist	The stone which the builders rejected as worthless turned out to be the most important of all. This was done by the Lord; what a wonderful sight it is!
Jesus	And so I tell you, the Kingdom of God will be taken away from you and given to a people who will produce the proper fruits.
Narrator	The chief priests and the Pharisees heard Jesus' parables and knew that he was talking about them, so they tried to arrest him. But they were afraid of the crowds, who considered Jesus to be a prophet.

Cast	[This is] the word of the Lord. OR This is the Gospel of Christ / *This is the Gospel of the Lord.*
All	**Thanks be to God.** **Praise to Christ our Lord** / *Praise to you, Lord Jesus Christ.*

Cast: **Narrator, Jesus, Landowner, Tenant 1, Tenant 2, Person 1, Person 2** (can be the same as Person 1), **Psalmist** (can be the same as Jesus).

Jesus tells the parable of the wedding feast
Matthew 22.1—14

[Narrator	Jesus again used parables in talking to the people.]
Jesus	The Kingdom of heaven is like this. Once there was a king who prepared a wedding feast for his son. He sent his servants to tell the invited guests to come to the feast, but they did not want to come. So he sent other servants with this message for the guests:
King	My feast is ready now; my bullocks and prize calves have been butchered, and everything is ready. Come to the wedding feast!
Jesus	But the invited guests paid no attention and went about their business: one went to his farm, another to his shop, while others grabbed the servants, beat them, and killed them.
	The king was very angry; so he sent his soldiers, who killed those murderers and burnt down their city. Then he called his servants [and said to them]:
King	My wedding feast is ready, but the people I invited did not deserve it. Now go to the main streets and invite to the feast as many people as you find.
Jesus	So the servants went out into the streets and gathered all the people they could find, good and bad alike; and the wedding hall was filled with people. (PAUSE)
	The king went in to look at the guests and saw a man who was not wearing wedding clothes. [The king asked him:]
King	Friend, how did you get in here without wedding clothes?
Jesus	But the man said nothing. Then the king told the servants:
King	Tie him up hand and foot, and throw him outside in the dark. There he will cry and grind his teeth.

[Narrator   And Jesus concluded:]

Jesus (slowly)   Many are invited, but few are chosen.

Cast	[This is] the word of the Lord.	OR	This is the Gospel of Christ / *This is the Gospel of the Lord.*
All	**Thanks be to God.**		**Praise to Christ our Lord** / *Praise to you, Lord Jesus Christ.*

Cast: **[Narrator], Jesus, King.**

The question about paying taxes
Matthew 22.15–22

Narrator   The Pharisees went off and made a plan to trap Jesus with questions. Then they sent to him some of their disciples and some members of Herod's party. [They said:]

Spy 1   Teacher, we know that you tell the truth.

Spy 2   You teach the truth about God's will for man, without worrying about what people think, because you pay no attention to a man's status.

Spy 1   Tell us, then, what do you think? Is it against our Law to pay taxes to the Roman Emperor, or not?'

Narrator   Jesus, however, was aware of their evil plan:

Jesus   You hypocrites! Why are you trying to trap me? Show me the coin for paying the tax!

Narrator   They brought him the coin. (PAUSE)

Jesus   Whose face and name are these?

Spies 1 and 2   The Emperor's.

Jesus   Well, then, pay the Emperor what belongs to the Emperor, and pay God what belongs to God.

Narrator   When they heard this, they were amazed; and they left him and went away.

Cast	[This is] the word of the Lord.	OR	This is the Gospel of Christ / *This is the Gospel of the Lord.*
All	**Thanks be to God.**		**Praise to Christ our Lord** / *Praise to you, Lord Jesus Christ.*

Cast: **Narrator, Spy 1, Spy 2, Jesus.**

The question about rising from death
Matthew 22.23–33

Narrator   Some Sadducees came to Jesus and claimed that people will not rise from death.

Sadducee 1   Teacher, Moses said that if a man who has no children dies, his brother must marry the widow so that they can have children who will be considered the dead man's children.

Sadducee 2   Now, there were seven brothers who used to live here. The eldest got married and died without having children, so he left his widow to his brother.

Sadducee 1	The same thing happened to the second brother, to the third, and finally to all seven.
Sadducee 2	Last of all, the woman died.
Sadducee 1	Now, on the day when the dead rise to life, whose wife will she be?
Sadducee 2	All of them had married her.
[Narrator	Jesus answered them:]
Jesus	How wrong you are! It is because you don't know the Scriptures or God's power. For when the dead rise to life, they will be like the angels in heaven and will not marry. Now, as for the dead rising to life: haven't you ever read what God has told you? [He said:]
Voice	I am the God of Abraham, the God of Isaac, and the God of Jacob.
Jesus	He is the God of the living, not of the dead.
Narrator	When the crowds heard this, they were amazed at his teaching.

Cast   [This is] the word of the Lord.   OR   This is the Gospel of Christ / *This is the Gospel of the Lord.*
All   **Thanks be to God.**   **Praise to Christ our Lord** / *Praise to you, Lord Jesus Christ.*

Cast: **Narrator, Sadducee 1, Sadducee 2, Jesus, Voice** (can be the same as Jesus).

The great commandment
Matthew 22.34–40

Narrator	When the Pharisees heard that Jesus had silenced the Sadducees, they came together, and one of them, a teacher of the Law, tried to trap him with a question.
Pharisee	Teacher, which is the greatest commandment in the Law?
[Narrator	Jesus answered:]
Jesus	'Love the Lord your God with all your heart, with all your soul, and with all your mind.' This is the greatest and the most important commandment. The second most important commandment is like it: 'Love your neighbour as you love yourself.' The whole Law of Moses and the teachings of the prophets depend on these two commandments.

Cast   [This is] the word of the Lord.   OR   This is the Gospel of Christ / *This is the Gospel of the Lord.*
All   **Thanks be to God.**   **Praise to Christ our Lord** / *Praise to you, Lord Jesus Christ.*

Cast: **Narrator, Pharisee, Jesus.**

The question about the Messiah
Matthew 22.41–46

Narrator	When some Pharisees gathered together, Jesus asked them:
Jesus	What do you think about the Messiah? Whose descendant is he?
[Narrator	They answered:]

Pharisee	He is David's descendant.
Jesus	Why, then, did the Spirit inspire David to call him 'Lord'? David said:
Psalmist	The Lord said to my Lord, 'Sit here on my right until I put your enemies under your feet.'
Jesus	If, then, David called him 'Lord', how can the Messiah be David's descendant?
Narrator	No one was able to give Jesus any answer, and from that day on no one dared to ask him any more questions.

Cast	[This is] the word of the Lord. OR	This is the Gospel of Christ / *This is the Gospel of the Lord.*
All	**Thanks be to God.**	**Praise to Christ our Lord** / *Praise to you, Lord Jesus Christ.*

Cast: **Narrator, Jesus, Pharisee, Psalmist,** (can be the same as Jesus).

Jesus warns against the teachers of the Law and the Pharisees (i)
Matthew 23.1–12

Narrator	Jesus spoke to the crowds and to his disciples:
Jesus	The teachers of the Law and the Pharisees are the authorized interpreters of Moses' Law. So you must obey and follow everything they tell you to do; do not, however, imitate their actions, because they don't practise what they preach. They tie on to people's backs loads that are heavy and hard to carry, yet they aren't willing even to lift a finger to help them carry those loads. They do everything so that people will see them. Look at the straps with scripture verses on them which they wear on their foreheads and arms, and notice how large they are! Notice also how long are the tassels on their cloaks! They love the best places at feasts and the reserved seats in the synagogues; they love to be greeted with respect in the market-places and to be called:
Persons 1 and **2** (ingratiatingly)	Teacher!
Jesus	You must not be called 'Teacher', because you are all brothers of one another and have only one Teacher. And you must not call anyone here on earth:
Person 1	Father!
Jesus	Because you have only the one Father in heaven. Nor should you be called:
Person 2	Leader!
Jesus	Because your one and only leader is the Messiah. The greatest one among you must be your servant. (PAUSE) Whoever makes himself great will be humbled, and whoever humbles himself will be made great.

Cast	[This is] the word of the Lord. OR	This is the Gospel of Christ / *This is the Gospel of the Lord.*
All	**Thanks be to God.**	**Praise to Christ our Lord** / *Praise to you, Lord Jesus Christ.*

Cast: **Narrator, Jesus, Person 1, Person 2.**

Jesus warns against the teachers of the Law and the Pharisees (ii)
Matthew 23.[1], 13–22

[**Narrator**   Jesus spoke to the crowds and to his disciples:]

Jesus   How terrible for you, teachers of the Law and Pharisees! You hypocrites! You lock the door to the Kingdom of heaven in people's faces, and you yourselves don't go in, nor do you allow in those who are trying to enter! How terrible for you, teachers of the Law and Pharisees! You hypocrites! You sail the seas and cross whole countries to win one convert; and when you succeed, you make him twice as deserving of going to hell as you yourselves are! How terrible for you, blind guides! (PAUSE)

[You teach:]

Lawyer   If someone swears by the Temple, he isn't bound by his vow.

Pharisee   But if he swears by the gold in the Temple, he is bound.

Jesus   Blind fools! Which is more important, the gold or the Temple which makes the gold holy? (PAUSE)

[You also teach:]

Lawyer   If someone swears by the altar, he isn't bound by his vow.

Pharisee   But if he swears by the gift on the altar, he is bound.

Jesus   How blind you are! Which is the more important, the gift or the altar which makes the gift holy? So then, when a person swears by the altar, he is swearing by it and by all the gifts on it; and when he swears by the Temple, he is swearing by it and by God, who lives there; and when someone swears by heaven, he is swearing by God's throne and by him who sits on it.

Cast   [This is] the word of the Lord.   OR   This is the Gospel of Christ / *This is the Gospel of the Lord.*
All   **Thanks be to God.**   **Praise to Christ our Lord** / *Praise to you, Lord Jesus Christ.*

Cast: [**Narrator**] (should be omitted when this reading continues from the previous one), **Jesus, Lawyer, Pharisee.**

Jesus' love for Jerusalem
Matthew 23.37–39

Jesus   Jerusalem, Jerusalem! You kill the prophets and stone the messengers God has sent you! How many times have I wanted to put my arms round all your people, just as a hen gathers her chicks under her wings, but you would not let me! And so your Temple will be abandoned and empty. From now on, I tell you, you will never see me again until you say:

Persons   God bless him who comes in the name of the Lord.

Cast   [This is] the word of the Lord.   OR   This is the Gospel of Christ / *This is the Gospel of the Lord.*
All   **Thanks be to God.**   **Praise to Christ our Lord** / *Praise to you, Lord Jesus Christ.*

Cast: **Jesus, Persons** (three or more).

Jesus speaks of troubles to come
Matthew 24.1–14

Narrator   Jesus was going away from the Temple when his disciples came to him to call his attention to its buildings.

Jesus   Yes, you may well look at all these. I tell you this: not a single stone here will be left in its place; every one of them will be thrown down.

Narrator   As Jesus sat on the Mount of Olives, the disciples came to him in private. [They asked:]

Disciple 1
(to Jesus)   Tell us when all this will be—

Disciple 2   And what will happen to show that it is the time for your coming and the end of the age.

Jesus   Be on your guard, and do not let anyone deceive you. Many men, claiming to speak for me, will come and say, 'I am the Messiah!' and they will deceive many people. You are going to hear the noise of battles close by and the news of battles far away; but do not be troubled. Such things must happen, but they do not mean that the end has come. Countries will fight each other, kingdoms will attack one another. There will be famines and earthquakes everywhere.

All these things are like the first pains of childbirth.

Then you will be arrested and handed over to be punished and be put to death. All mankind will hate you because of me. Many will give up their faith at that time; they will betray one another and hate one another. Then many false prophets will appear and deceive many people. Such will be the spread of evil that many people's love will grow cold. But whoever holds out to the end will be saved. And this Good News about the Kingdom will be preached through all the world for a witness to all mankind; and then the end will come.

Cast   [This is] the word of the Lord.   OR   This is the Gospel of Christ / *This is the Gospel of the Lord.*
All   **Thanks be to God.**   **Praise to Christ our Lord** / *Praise to you, Lord Jesus Christ.*

Cast: **Narrator, Jesus, Disciple 1, Disciple 2** (can be the same as Disciple 1).

Jesus speaks of things to come
Matthew 24.15–27

Jesus   You will see 'The Awful Horror' of which the prophet Daniel spoke. It will be standing in the holy place.

Narrator   Be sure to understand what this means!

Jesus   Then those who are in Judaea must run away to the hills. A man who is on the roof of his house must not take the time to go down and get his belongings from the house. A man who is in the field

→

must not go back to get his cloak. How terrible it will be in those days for women who are pregnant and for mothers with little babies! Pray to God that you will not have to run away during the winter or on a Sabbath! For the trouble at that time will be far more terrible than any there has ever been, from the beginning of the world to this very day. Nor will there ever be anything like it again. But God has already reduced the number of days; had he not done so, nobody would survive. For the sake of his chosen people, however, God will reduce the days. (PAUSE)

Then, if anyone says to you:

Person 1   Look, here is the Messiah!

Jesus   Or:

Person 2   There he is!

Jesus   Do not believe him. For false Messiahs and false prophets will appear; they will perform great miracles and wonders in order to deceive even God's chosen people, if possible. Listen! I have told you this before the time comes. (PAUSE)

Or, if people should tell you:

Person 1   Look, he is out in the desert!

Jesus   Don't go there; or if they say:

Person 2   Look, he is hiding here!

Jesus   Don't believe it. For the Son of Man will come like the lightning which flashes across the whole sky from the east to the west.

Cast	[This is] the word of the Lord.	OR	This is the Gospel of Christ / *This is the Gospel of the Lord.*
All	**Thanks be to God.**		**Praise to Christ our Lord** / *Praise to you, Lord Jesus Christ.*

Cast: **Jesus, Narrator** (can be the same as Jesus), **Person 1, Person 2.**

The coming of the Son of Man
Matthew 24.29–31

Reader 1   Soon after the trouble of those days, the sun will grow dark.

Reader 2   The moon will no longer shine.

Reader 3   The stars will fall from heaven.

Reader 4   And the powers in space will be driven from their courses.

Reader 1   Then the sign of the Son of Man will appear in the sky.

Reader 2   And all the peoples of earth will weep as they see the Son of Man coming on the clouds of heaven with power and great glory.

Reader 3	The great trumpet will sound.
Reader 4	And he will send out his angels to the four corners of the earth.
Reader 1	And they will gather his chosen people from one end of the world to the other.

Cast   [This is] the word of the Lord.   OR   This is the Gospel of Christ / *This is the Gospel of the Lord.*
All   **Thanks be to God.**   **Praise to Christ our Lord** / *Praise to you, Lord Jesus Christ.*

Cast: **Reader 1, Reader 2, Reader 3, Reader 4.**

Jesus teaches the lesson of the fig-tree
Matthew 24.32–35

Reader 1	Let the fig-tree teach you a lesson.
Reader 2	When its branches become green and tender and it starts putting out leaves, you know that summer is near.
Reader 1	In the same way, when you see all these things, you will know that the time is near, ready to begin.
Reader 2	Remember that all these things will happen before the people now living have all died.
Reader 1	Heaven and earth will pass away, but my words will never pass away.

Cast   [This is] the word of the Lord.   OR   This is the Gospel of Christ / *This is the Gospel of the Lord.*
All   **Thanks be to God.**   **Praise to Christ our Lord** / *Praise to you, Lord Jesus Christ.*

Cast: **Reader 1, Reader 2.**

No one knows the day and hour
Matthew 24.36–44

Reader 1	No one knows when that day and hour will come—neither the angels in heaven nor the Son; the Father alone knows.
Reader 2	The coming of the Son of Man will be like what happened in the time of Noah. In the days before the flood people ate and drank, men and women married, up to the very day Noah went into the boat; yet they did not realize what was happening until the flood came and swept them all away. That is how it will be when the Son of Man comes.
Reader 1	At that time two men will be working in a field: one will be taken away, the other will be left behind. Two women will be at a mill grinding meal: one will be taken away, the other will be left behind.
Reader 2	Be on your guard, then, because you do not know what day your Lord will come. If the owner of a house knew the time when the thief would come, he can be sure that he would stay awake and not let the thief break into his house.

Reader 1	So then, you also must always be ready, because the Son of Man will come at an hour when you are not expecting him.

Cast	[This is] the word of the Lord.	OR	This is the Gospel of Christ / *This is the Gospel of the Lord.*
All	**Thanks be to God.**		**Praise to Christ our Lord** / *Praise to you, Lord Jesus Christ.*

Cast: **Reader 1, Reader 2.**

The parable of the ten girls
Matthew 25.1–13

Jesus	The Kingdom of heaven will be like this. Once there were ten girls who took their oil lamps and went out to meet the bridegroom. Five of them were foolish, and the other five were wise. The foolish ones took their lamps but did not take any extra oil with them, while the wise ones took containers full of oil for their lamps. The bridegroom was late in coming, so the girls began to nod and fall asleep. It was already midnight when the cry rang out:
Voice	Here is the bridegroom! Come and meet him!
Jesus	The ten girls woke up and trimmed their lamps. Then the foolish ones said to the wise ones:
Foolish girl 1	Let us have some of your oil.
Foolish girl 2	Our lamps are going out.
Jesus	The wise ones answered:
Wise girl 1	No, indeed, there is not enough for you and for us.
Wise girl 2	Go to the shop and buy some for yourselves.
Jesus	So the foolish girls went off to buy some oil; and while they were gone, the bridegroom arrived. The five girls who were ready went in with him to the wedding feast, and the door was closed. Later the other girls arrived.
Foolish girl 1 (crying out)	Sir!
Foolish girl 2 (crying out)	Sir!
Foolish girls 1 and 2	Let us in!
Jesus	The bridegroom answered:
Bridegroom	Certainly not! I don't know you!
Jesus	Be on your guard, then, because you do not know the day or the hour.

Cast	[This is] the word of the Lord.	OR	This is the Gospel of Christ / *This is the Gospel of the Lord.*
All	**Thanks be to God.**		**Praise to Christ our Lord** / *Praise to you, Lord Jesus Christ.*

Cast: **Jesus, Voice** (at a distance), **Foolish girl 1, Foolish girl 2, Wise girl 1, Wise girl 2** (can be the same as Wise girl 1), **Bridegroom** (can be the same as Voice).

Jesus tells the parable of the three servants
Matthew 25.14–30

Jesus The Kingdom of heaven will be like this. Once there was a man who was about to go on a journey; he called his servants and put them in charge of his property. He gave to each one according to his ability: to one he gave five thousand gold coins, to another he gave two thousand, and to another he gave one thousand. Then he left on his journey. The servant who had received five thousand coins went at once and invested his money and earned another five thousand. In the same way the servant who had received two thousand coins earned another two thousand. But the servant who had received one thousand coins went off, dug a hole in the ground, and hid his master's money. (PAUSE)

After a long time the master of those servants came back and settled accounts with them. The servant who had received five thousand coins came in and handed over the other five thousand.

Servant 1 You gave me five thousand coins, sir. Look! Here are another five thousand that I have earned.

Jesus His master said:

Master Well done, you good and faithful servant! You have been faithful in managing small amounts, so I will put you in charge of large amounts. Come on in and share my happiness! (PAUSE)

Jesus Then the servant who had been given two thousand coins came in.

Servant 2 You gave me two thousand coins, sir. Look! Here are another two thousand that I have earned.

Master Well done, you good and faithful servant! You have been faithful in managing small amounts, so I will put you in charge of large amounts. Come on in and share my happiness! (PAUSE)

Jesus Then the servant who had received one thousand coins came in.

Servant 3 Sir, I know you are a hard man; you reap harvests where you did not sow, and you gather crops where you did not scatter seed. I was afraid, so I went off and hid your money in the ground. Look! Here is what belongs to you!

Master You bad and lazy servant! You knew, did you, that I reap harvests where I did not sow, and gather crops where I did not scatter seed? Well, then, you should have deposited my money in the bank, and I would have received it all back with interest when I returned. Now, take the money away from him and give it to the one who has ten thousand coins.

Jesus (slowly) For to every person who has something, even more will be given, and he will have more than enough; but the person who has nothing, even the little that he has will be taken away from him.

Master As for this useless servant—throw him outside in the darkness; there he will cry and grind his teeth.

Cast [This is] the word of the Lord.   OR   This is the Gospel of Christ / *This is the Gospel of the Lord.*
All **Thanks be to God.**   **Praise to Christ our Lord** / *Praise to you, Lord Jesus Christ.*

Cast: **Jesus, Servant 1, Master, Servant 2, Servant 3.**

The final judgement
Matthew 25.31–46

Jesus	When the Son of Man comes as King and all the angels with him, he will sit on his royal throne, and the people of all the nations will be gathered before him. Then he will divide them into two groups, just as a shepherd separates the sheep from the goats. He will put the righteous people on his right and the others on his left. Then the King will say to the people on his right:
The King	Come, you that are blessed by my Father! Come and possess the kingdom which has been prepared for you ever since the creation of the world. I was hungry and you fed me, thirsty and you gave me a drink; I was a stranger and you received me in your homes, naked and you clothed me; I was sick and you took care of me, in prison and you visited me.
Jesus	The righteous will then answer him:
Righteous person 1	When, Lord, did we ever see you hungry and feed you, or thirsty and give you a drink?
Righteous person 2	When did we ever see you a stranger and welcome you in our homes, or naked and clothe you?
Righteous person 1	When did we ever see you sick or in prison, and visit you?
The King (to Righteous person)	I tell you, whenever you did this for one of the least important of these brothers of mine, you did it for me!
Jesus	Then he will say to those on his left:
The King (to Person under a curse)	Away from me, you that are under God's curse! Away to the eternal fire which has been prepared for the Devil and his angels! I was hungry but you would not feed me, thirsty but you would not give me a drink; I was a stranger but you would not welcome me in your homes, naked but you would not clothe me; I was sick and in prison but you would not take care of me.
Jesus	Then they will answer him:
Person under a curse	When, Lord, did we ever see you hungry or thirsty or a stranger or naked or sick or in prison, and would not help you?
Jesus	The King will reply:
The King	I tell you, whenever you refused to help one of these least important ones, you refused to help me.
Jesus	These, then, will be sent off to eternal punishment, but the righteous will go to eternal life.

Cast	[This is] the word of the Lord.	OR	This is the Gospel of Christ / *This is the Gospel of the Lord.*
All	**Thanks be to God.**		**Praise to Christ our Lord** / *Praise to you, Lord Jesus Christ.*

Cast: **Jesus, The King, Righteous person 1, Righteous person 2** (can be the same as Righteous person 1), **Person under a curse.**

The plot against Jesus
Matthew 26.1–5, 14–16

Narrator   When Jesus had finished teaching all these things, he said to his disciples:

Jesus   In two days, as you know, it will be the Passover Festival, and the Son of Man will be handed over to be crucified. (PAUSE)

Narrator   Then the chief priests and the elders met together in the palace of Caiaphas, the High Priest, and made plans to arrest Jesus secretly and put him to death. [They said:]

Chief priest   We must not do it during the festival or the people will riot.

Narrator   Then one of the twelve disciples—the one named Judas Iscariot— went to the chief priests [and asked]:

Judas Iscariot   What will you give me if I betray Jesus to you?

Narrator   They counted out thirty silver coins and gave them to him. From then on Judas was looking for a good chance to hand Jesus over to them.

Cast   [This is] the word of the Lord.   OR   This is the Gospel of Christ / *This is the Gospel of the Lord.*
All   **Thanks be to God.**   **Praise to Christ our Lord** / *Praise to you, Lord Jesus Christ.*

Cast: **Narrator, Jesus, Chief priest, Judas Iscariot.**

Jesus is anointed at Bethany
Matthew 26.6–13

Narrator   Jesus was in Bethany at the house of Simon, a man who had suffered from leprosy. While Jesus was eating, a woman came to him with an alabaster jar filled with an expensive perfume, which she poured on his head. The disciples saw this and became angry.

Disciple 1   Why all this waste?

Disciple 2   This perfume could have been sold for a large amount and the money given to the poor!

Narrator   Jesus knew what they were saying [so he said to them]:

Jesus   Why are you bothering this woman? It is a fine and beautiful thing that she has done for me. You will always have poor people with you, but you will not always have me. What she did was to pour this perfume on my body to get me ready for burial. Now, I assure you that wherever this gospel is preached all over the world, what she has done will be told in memory of her.

Cast   [This is] the word of the Lord.   OR   This is the Gospel of Christ / *This is the Gospel of the Lord.*
All   **Thanks be to God.**   **Praise to Christ our Lord** / *Praise to you, Lord Jesus Christ.*

Cast: **Narrator, Disciple 1, Disciple 2** (can be the same as Disciple 1)**, Jesus.**

Jesus eats the Passover meal with his disciples
Matthew 26.17–25

Narrator	On the first day of the Festival of Unleavened Bread the disciples came to Jesus [and asked him]:
Disciple	Where do you want us to get the Passover meal ready for you?
[Narrator	He said to them:]
Jesus	Go to a certain man in the city, and tell him: 'The Teacher says, My hour has come; my disciples and I will celebrate the Passover at your house.' (PAUSE)
Narrator	The disciples did as Jesus had told them and prepared the Passover meal. (PAUSE)
	When it was evening, Jesus and the twelve disciples sat down to eat. During the meal Jesus said:
Jesus	I tell you, one of you will betray me.
Narrator	The disciples were very upset and began to ask him, one after the other:
Disciple	Surely, Lord, you don't mean me?
Jesus	One who dips his bread in the dish with me will betray me. The Son of Man will die as the Scriptures say he will, but how terrible for that man who betrays the Son of Man! It would have been better for that man if he had never been born!
Narrator	Judas, the traitor, spoke up.
Judas	Surely, Teacher, you don't mean me?
Jesus (slowly)	So you say.

Cast [This is] the word of the Lord. OR   This is the Gospel of Christ / *This is the Gospel of the Lord.*
All   **Thanks be to God.**   **Praise to Christ our Lord** / *Praise to you, Lord Jesus Christ.*

Cast: **Narrator, Disciple, Jesus, Judas.**

The Lord's Supper
Matthew 26.26–30 (GNB)

Narrator	While they were eating, Jesus took a piece of bread, gave a prayer of thanks, broke it, and gave it to his disciples. [He said:]
Jesus	Take and eat it; this is my body.
Narrator	Then he took a cup, gave thanks to God, and gave it to them. [He said:]
Jesus	Drink it, all of you; this is my blood, which seals God's covenant, my blood poured out for many for the forgiveness of sins. (PAUSE)
	I tell you, I will never again drink this wine until the day I drink the new wine with you in my Father's Kingdom.
Narrator	Then they sang a hymn and went out to the Mount of Olives.

Cast [This is] the word of the Lord. OR   This is the Gospel of Christ / *This is the Gospel of the Lord.*
All   **Thanks be to God.**   **Praise to Christ our Lord** / *Praise to you, Lord Jesus Christ.*

Cast: **Narrator, Jesus.**

The Lord's Supper
Matthew 26.26–30 (NIV)

Narrator   While they were eating, Jesus took bread, gave thanks and broke it, and gave it to his disciples [saying]:

Jesus   Take and eat; this is my body.

Narrator   Then he took the cup, gave thanks and offered it to them [saying]:

Jesus   Drink from it, all of you. This is my blood of the covenant, which is poured out for many for the forgiveness of sins. I tell you, I will not drink of this fruit of the vine from now on until that day when I drink it anew with you in my Father's kingdom.

Narrator   When they had sung a hymn, they went out to the Mount of Olives.

Cast	[This is] the word of the Lord.	OR	This is the Gospel of Christ / *This is the Gospel of the Lord.*
All	**Thanks be to God.**		**Praise to Christ our Lord** / *Praise to you, Lord Jesus Christ.*

Cast: **Narrator, Jesus.**

Jesus predicts Peter's denial
Matthew 26.31–35

Narrator   Jesus said to his disciples:

Jesus   This very night all of you will run away and leave me, for the scripture says:

Zechariah   God will kill the shepherd, and the sheep of the flock will be scattered.

Jesus   But after I am raised to life, I will go to Galilee ahead of you.

Narrator   Peter spoke up [and said to Jesus]:

Peter
(to Jesus)   I will never leave you, even though all the rest do!

Jesus   I tell you that before the cock crows tonight, you will say three times that you do not know me.

Peter   I will never say that, even if I have to die with you! (PAUSE)

Narrator   And all the other disciples said the same thing.

Cast	[This is] the word of the Lord.	OR	This is the Gospel of Christ / *This is the Gospel of the Lord.*
All	**Thanks be to God.**		**Praise to Christ our Lord** / *Praise to you, Lord Jesus Christ.*

Cast: **Narrator, Jesus, Zechariah** (can be the same as Jesus)**, Peter.**

Jesus prays in Gethsemane
Matthew 26.36–46

Narrator Jesus went with his disciples to a place called Gethsemane, and he said to them:

Jesus Sit here while I go over there and pray.

Narrator He took with him Peter and the two sons of Zebedee. Grief and anguish came over him.

Jesus The sorrow in my heart is so great that it almost crushes me. Stay here and keep watch with me.

Narrator He went a little farther on, threw himself face downwards on the ground, and prayed:

Jesus My Father, if it is possible, take this cup of suffering from me! Yet not what I want, but what you want.

Narrator Then he returned to the three disciples and found them asleep; and he said to Peter:

Jesus How is it that you three were not able to keep watch with me even for one hour? Keep watch and pray that you will not fall into temptation. The spirit is willing, but the flesh is weak.

Narrator Once more Jesus went away and prayed:

Jesus My Father, if this cup of suffering cannot be taken away unless I drink it, your will be done.

Narrator He returned once more (PAUSE) and found the disciples asleep; they could not keep their eyes open. (PAUSE)

Again Jesus left them, went away, and prayed the third time, saying the same words. Then he returned to the disciples [and said]:

Jesus Are you still sleeping and resting? Look! The hour has come for the Son of Man to be handed over to the power of sinful men. Get up, let us go. Look, here is the man who is betraying me!

Cast [This is] the word of the Lord. OR This is the Gospel of Christ / *This is the Gospel of the Lord.*
All **Thanks be to God.** **Praise to Christ our Lord** / *Praise to you, Lord Jesus Christ.*

Cast: **Narrator, Jesus.**

The arrest of Jesus
Matthew 26.47–56

Narrator Jesus was still speaking when Judas, one of the twelve disciples, arrived. With him was a large crowd armed with swords and clubs and sent by the chief priests and the elders. The traitor had given the crowd a signal:

Judas Iscariot The man I kiss is the one you want. Arrest him!

Narrator Judas went straight to Jesus [and said]:

Judas Iscariot Peace be with you, Teacher.

Narrator And he kissed him. Jesus answered:

Jesus Be quick about it, friend!

Narrator Then they came up, arrested Jesus, and held him tight. One of those who were with Jesus drew his sword and struck at the High Priest's slave, cutting off his ear.

[Jesus said to him:]

Jesus Put your sword back in its place. All who take the sword will die by the sword. Don't you know that I could call on my Father for help, and at once he would send me more than twelve armies of angels? But in that case, how could the Scriptures come true which say that this is what must happen?

Narrator Then Jesus spoke to the crowd:

Jesus Did you have to come with swords and clubs to capture me, as though I were an outlaw? Every day I sat down and taught in the Temple, and you did not arrest me. But all this has happened in order to make what the prophets wrote in the Scriptures come true.

Narrator Then all the disciples left him and ran away.

Cast	[This is] the word of the Lord.	OR	This is the Gospel of Christ / *This is the Gospel of the Lord.*
All	**Thanks be to God.**		**Praise to Christ our Lord** / *Praise to you, Lord Jesus Christ.*

Cast: **Narrator, Judas Iscariot, Jesus.**

Jesus before the Council
Matthew 26.57–68

Narrator Those who had arrested Jesus took him to the house of Caiaphas, the High Priest, where the teachers of the Law and the elders had gathered together. Peter followed from a distance, as far as the courtyard of the High Priest's house. He went into the courtyard and sat down with the guards to see how it would all come out. The chief priests and the whole Council tried to find some false evidence against Jesus to put him to death, but they could not find any, even though many people came forward and told lies about him. Finally two men stepped up [and said]:

Man 1	This man said, 'I am able to tear down God's Temple—
Man 2	And three days later build it up again.'
Narrator	The High Priest stood up and said to Jesus:
High Priest (to Jesus)	Have you no answer to give to this accusation against you?
Narrator	But Jesus kept quiet. (PAUSE) Again the High Priest spoke to him:
High Priest	In the name of the living God I now put you on oath: tell us if you are the Messiah, the Son of God.
[Narrator	Jesus answered him:]
Jesus	So you say. But I tell all of you: from this time on you will see the Son of Man sitting on the right of the Almighty and coming on the clouds of heaven!
Narrator	At this the High Priest tore his clothes [and said]:
High Priest	Blasphemy! We don't need any more witnesses! You have just heard his blasphemy! What do you think?
Man 1	He is guilty.
Man 2	He must die.
Narrator	Then they spat in his face and beat him. [And those who slapped him said:]
Man 1 (cynically)	Prophesy for us, Messiah!
Man 2	Guess who hit you!

Cast	[This is] the word of the Lord.	OR	This is the Gospel of Christ / *This is the Gospel of the Lord.*
All	**Thanks be to God.**		**Praise to Christ our Lord** / *Praise to you, Lord Jesus Christ.*

Cast: **Narrator, Man 1, Man 2, High Priest, Jesus.**

Peter denies Jesus
Matthew 26.69–75

Narrator	Peter was sitting outside in the courtyard when one of the High Priest's servant-girls came to him [and said]:
Girl 1	You, too, were with Jesus of Galilee.
Narrator	But he denied it in front of them all:
Peter	I don't know what you are talking about.
Narrator	He went on out to the entrance of the courtyard. (PAUSE) Another servant-girl saw him and said to the men there:
Girl 2 (to Men)	He was with Jesus of Nazareth.
Narrator	Again Peter denied it:
Peter	I swear that I don't know that man!

Narrator	After a little while the men standing there came to Peter:
Man 1	Of course you are one of them.
Man 2	After all, the way you speak gives you away!
[Narrator	Then Peter said:]
Peter	I swear that I am telling the truth! May God punish me if I am not! I do not know that man!
Narrator	Just then a cock crowed, and Peter remembered what Jesus had told him:
Voice of Jesus (far away)	Before the cock crows, you will say three times that you do not know me.
Narrator	He went out and wept bitterly.

Cast	[This is] the word of the Lord.	OR	This is the Gospel of Christ / *This is the Gospel of the Lord.*
All	**Thanks be to God.**		**Praise to Christ our Lord** / *Praise to you, Lord Jesus Christ.*

Cast: **Narrator, Girl 1, Peter, Girl 2, Man 1, Man 2, Voice of Jesus** (far away).

Jesus is taken to Pilate
Matthew 27.1–2, 11–14

Narrator	Early in the morning all the chief priests and the elders made their plans against Jesus to put him to death. They put him in chains, led him off, and handed him over to Pilate, the Roman governor.
	Jesus stood before the Roman governor, who questioned him.
Pilate	Are you the king of the Jews?
[Narrator	Jesus answered:]
Jesus	So you say.
Narrator	But Jesus said nothing in response to the accusations of the chief priests and elders.
	[So Pilate said to him:]
Pilate	Don't you hear all these things they accuse you of?
Narrator	But Jesus refused to answer a single word, with the result that the Governor was greatly surprised.

Cast	[This is] the word of the Lord.	OR	This is the Gospel of Christ / *This is the Gospel of the Lord.*
All	**Thanks be to God.**		**Praise to Christ our Lord** / *Praise to you, Lord Jesus Christ.*

Cast: **Narrator, Pilate, Jesus.**

The death of Judas
Matthew 27.3–10

Narrator	When Judas, the traitor, learnt that Jesus had been condemned, he repented and took back the thirty silver coins to the chief priests and the elders:
Judas	I have sinned by betraying an innocent man to death!
[Narrator	They answered:]
Chief priest	What do we care about that?
Elder	That is your business!
Narrator	Judas threw the coins down in the Temple and left; then he went off and hanged himself.
	The chief priests picked up the coins and said:
Elder	This is blood money.
Chief priest	It is against our Law to put it in the temple treasury.
Narrator	After reaching an agreement about it, they used the money to buy Potter's Field, as a cemetery for foreigners. That is why that field is called 'Field of Blood' to this very day. Then what the prophet Jeremiah had said came true:
Jeremiah	They took the thirty silver coins, the amount the people of Israel had agreed to pay for him, and used the money to buy the potter's field, as the Lord had commanded me.

Cast	[This is] the word of the Lord. OR	This is the Gospel of Christ / *This is the Gospel of the Lord.*
All	**Thanks be to God.**	**Praise to Christ our Lord** / *Praise to you, Lord Jesus Christ.*

Cast: **Narrator, Judas, Chief priest, Elder, Jeremiah** (distant voice).

Jesus is sentenced to death
From Matthew 27.15–26

Narrator	At every Passover Festival the Roman governor was in the habit of setting free any one prisoner the crowd asked for. At that time there was a well-known prisoner named Jesus Barabbas. So when the crowd gathered, Pilate asked them:
Pilate	Which one do you want me to set free for you? Jesus Barabbas, or Jesus called the Messiah?
Narrator	He knew very well that the Jewish authorities had handed Jesus over to him because they were jealous.
	While Pilate was sitting in the judgement hall, his wife sent him a message:
Pilate's wife	Have nothing to do with that innocent man, because in a dream last night I suffered much on account of him.
Narrator	The chief priests and the elders persuaded the crowd to ask Pilate to set Barabbas free and have Jesus put to death. But Pilate asked the crowd:
Pilate	Which one of these two do you want me to set free for you?

Person 1 (calling)	Barabbas!
Pilate	What, then, shall I do with Jesus called the Messiah?
Person 2 (calling)	Crucify him!
[Narrator	But Pilate asked:]
Pilate	What crime has he committed?
Narrator	Then they started shouting at the top of their voices:
Persons 1 and **2**	Crucify him!
Narrator	When Pilate saw that it was no use to go on, but that a riot might break out, he took some water, and washed his hands in front of the crowd.
Pilate	I am not responsible for the death of this man! This is your doing!
[Narrator	The whole crowd answered:]
Person 1	Let the responsibility for his death fall on us—
Person 2	And our children!
Narrator	Then Pilate set Barabbas free for them; and after he had had Jesus whipped, he handed him over to be crucified.

Cast [This is] the word of the Lord. OR This is the Gospel of Christ / *This is the Gospel of the Lord.*
All **Thanks be to God.** **Praise to Christ our Lord** / *Praise to you, Lord Jesus Christ.*

Cast: **Narrator, Pilate, Pilate's wife, Person 1, Person 2.**

Jesus is crucified
Matthew 27.27–44

Narrator	Pilate's soldiers took Jesus into the governor's palace, and the whole company gathered round him. They stripped off his clothes and put a scarlet robe on him. Then they made a crown out of thorny branches and placed it on his head, and put a stick in his right hand; then they knelt before him and mocked him.
Soldier(s)	Long live the King of the Jews!
Narrator	They spat on him, and took the stick and hit him over the head. When they had finished mocking him, they took the robe off and put his own clothes back on him. Then they led him out to crucify him. (PAUSE) As they were going out, they met a man from Cyrene named Simon, and the soldiers forced him to carry Jesus' cross. They came to a place called Golgotha, which means:
Voice (slowly)	The Place of the Skull.
Narrator	There they offered Jesus wine mixed with a bitter substance; but after tasting it, he would not drink it. →

They crucified him and then divided his clothes among them by throwing dice. After that they sat there and watched him. Above his head they put the written notice of the accusation against him:

Voice   This is Jesus, the King of the Jews.

Narrator   Then they crucified two bandits with Jesus, one on his right and the other on his left. (PAUSE)

People passing by shook their heads and hurled insults at Jesus:

Person 1   You were going to tear down the Temple and build it up again in three days!

Person 2   Save yourself if you are God's Son!

Person 1   Come on down from the cross!

Narrator   In the same way the chief priests and the teachers of the Law and the elders jeered at him:

Priest
(cynically)   He saved others, but he cannot save himself!

Lawyer
(with sarcasm)   Isn't he the king of Israel?

Elder (mocking)   If he comes down off the cross now, we will believe in him!

Priest
(challenging)   He trusts in God and claims to be God's Son. Well, then, let us see if God wants to save him now!

Narrator
(slowly)   Even the bandits who had been crucified with him insulted him in the same way.

Cast	[This is] the word of the Lord.	OR	This is the Gospel of Christ / *This is the Gospel of the Lord.*
All	**Thanks be to God.**		**Praise to Christ our Lord** / *Praise to you, Lord Jesus Christ.*

Cast: **Narrator, Soldier(s), Voice** (can be the same as Narrator), **Person 1, Person 2, Priest, Lawyer, Elder.**

The death of Jesus
Matthew 27.45–56

Narrator   At noon the whole country was covered with darkness, which lasted for three hours. At about three o'clock Jesus cried out with a loud shout:

Jesus   Eli, Eli, lema sabachthani? My God, my God, why did you abandon me?

Narrator   Some of the people standing there heard him [and said]:

Person 1   He is calling for Elijah!

Narrator   One of them ran up at once, took a sponge, soaked it in cheap wine, put it on the end of a stick, and tried to make him drink it. But the others said:

Person 2   Wait, let us see if Elijah is coming to save him!

Narrator   Jesus again gave a loud cry and breathed his last. (PAUSE)

Then the curtain hanging in the Temple was torn in two from top to bottom. The earth shook, the rocks split apart, the graves broke open, and many of God's people who had died were raised to life. They left the graves, and after Jesus rose from death, they went into the Holy City, where many people saw them. When the army officer and the soldiers with him who were watching Jesus saw the earthquake and everything else that happened, they were terrified [and said]:

Officer   He really *was* the Son of God!

Narrator   There were many women there, looking on from a distance, who had followed Jesus from Galilee and helped him. Among them were Mary Magdalene, Mary the mother of James and Joseph, and the wife of Zebedee.

Cast   [This is] the word of the Lord.   OR   This is the Gospel of Christ / *This is the Gospel of the Lord.*
All   **Thanks be to God.**   **Praise to Christ our Lord** / *Praise to you, Lord Jesus Christ.*

Cast: **Narrator, Jesus, Person 1, Person 2, Officer.**

The burial of Jesus
Matthew 27.57–66

Narrator   When it was evening, a rich man from Arimathea arrived; his name was Joseph, and he also was a disciple of Jesus. He went into the presence of Pilate and asked for the body of Jesus. Pilate gave orders for the body to be given to Joseph. So Joseph took it, wrapped it in a new linen sheet, and placed it in his own tomb, which he had just recently dug out of solid rock. Then he rolled a large stone across the entrance to the tomb and went away. Mary Magdalene and the other Mary were sitting there, facing the tomb. (PAUSE)

The next day, which was a Sabbath, the chief priests and the Pharisees met with Pilate [and said]:

Priest   Sir, we remember that while that liar was still alive he said, 'I will be raised to life three days later.' Give orders, then, for his tomb to be carefully guarded until the third day, so that his disciples will not be able to go and steal the body, and then tell the people that he was raised from death. This last lie would be even worse than the first one.

Narrator   Pilate told them:

Pilate   Take a guard, go and make the tomb as secure as you can.

Narrator   So they left and made the tomb secure by putting a seal on the stone and leaving the guard on watch.

Cast   [This is] the word of the Lord.   OR   This is the Gospel of Christ / *This is the Gospel of the Lord.*
All   **Thanks be to God.**   **Praise to Christ our Lord** / *Praise to you, Lord Jesus Christ.*

Cast: **Narrator, Priest, Pilate.**

The Resurrection
Matthew 28.1–10

Narrator After the Sabbath, as Sunday morning was dawning, Mary Magdalene and the other Mary went to look at the tomb. Suddenly there was a violent earthquake; an angel of the Lord came down from heaven, rolled the stone away, and sat on it. His appearance was like lightning, and his clothes were white as snow. The guards were so afraid that they trembled and became like dead men. The angel spoke to the women:

Angel You must not be afraid. I know you are looking for Jesus, who was crucified. He is not here; he has been raised, just as he said. Come here and see the place where he was lying.

Go quickly now, and tell his disciples, 'He has been raised from death, and now he is going to Galilee ahead of you; there you will see him!' Remember what I have told you.

Narrator So they left the tomb in a hurry, afraid and yet filled with joy, and ran to tell his disciples. Suddenly Jesus met them:

Jesus Peace be with you.

Narrator They came up to him, took hold of his feet, and worshipped him.

Jesus Do not be afraid. Go and tell my brothers to go to Galilee, and there they will see me.

Cast	[This is] the word of the Lord. OR	This is the Gospel of Christ / *This is the Gospel of the Lord.*
All	**Thanks be to God.**	**Praise to Christ our Lord** / *Praise to you, Lord Jesus Christ.*

Cast: **Narrator, Angel, Jesus.**

The report of the guard
Matthew 28.11–15

Narrator While the women went on their way, some of the soldiers guarding the tomb went back to the city and told the chief priests everything that had happened. The chief priests met with the elders and made their plan: they gave a large sum of money to the soldiers and said:

Priest You are to say that his disciples came during the night and stole his body while you were asleep. And if the Governor should hear of this, we will convince him that you are innocent, and you will have nothing to worry about.

Narrator The guards took the money and did what they were told to do. And so that is the report spread round by the Jews to this very day.

Cast	[This is] the word of the Lord. OR	This is the Gospel of Christ / *This is the Gospel of the Lord.*
All	**Thanks be to God.**	**Praise to Christ our Lord** / *Praise to you, Lord Jesus Christ.*

Cast: **Narrator, Priest.** (This reading is short and preferably linked with the preceding one).

Jesus appears to his disciples
Matthew 28.16–20

Narrator	The eleven disciples went to the hill in Galilee where Jesus had told them to go. When they saw him, they worshipped him, even though some of them doubted. Jesus drew near [and said to them]:
Jesus	I have been given all authority in heaven and on earth. Go, then, to all peoples everywhere and make them my disciples: baptize them in the name of the Father, the Son and the Holy Spirit, and teach them to obey everything I have commanded you. And I will be with you always, to the end of the age.

Cast [This is] the word of the Lord. OR This is the Gospel of Christ / *This is the Gospel of the Lord.*
All **Thanks be to God.** **Praise to Christ our Lord** / *Praise to you, Lord Jesus Christ.*

Cast: **Narrator, Jesus.**

71

THE GOSPEL OF
MARK

The preaching of John the Baptist
Mark 1.1–8

Narrator	This is the Good News about Jesus Christ, the Son of God. It began as the prophet Isaiah had written:
Prophet	God said, 'I will send my messenger ahead of you to clear the way for you.' Someone is shouting in the desert, 'Get the road ready for the Lord; make a straight path for him to travel!'
Narrator	So John appeared in the desert, baptizing and preaching.
John	Turn away from your sins and be baptized, and God will forgive your sins.
Narrator	Many people from the province of Judaea and the city of Jerusalem went out to hear John. They confessed their sins, and he baptized them in the River Jordan. (PAUSE)
	John wore clothes made of camel's hair, with a leather belt round his waist, and his food was locusts and wild honey. He announced to the people:
John	The man who will come after me is much greater than I am. I am not good enough even to bend down and untie his sandals. *I* baptize you with water, but *he* will baptize you with the Holy Spirit.

Cast	[This is] the word of the Lord. OR	This is the Gospel of Christ / *This is the Gospel of the Lord.*
All	**Thanks be to God.**	**Praise to Christ our Lord** / *Praise to you, Lord Jesus Christ.*

Cast: **Narrator, Prophet, John.**

The baptism and temptation of Jesus
Mark 1.9–12

Narrator	[*Not long afterwards] Jesus came from Nazareth in the province of Galilee, and was baptized by John in the Jordan. As soon as Jesus came up out of the water, he saw heaven opening and the Spirit coming down on him like a dove. And a voice came from heaven:
Voice	You are my own dear Son. I am pleased with you.
Narrator	At once the Spirit made him go into the desert, where he stayed forty days, being tempted by Satan. Wild animals were there also, but angels came and helped him.

Cast	[This is] the word of the Lord. OR	This is the Gospel of Christ / *This is the Gospel of the Lord.*
All	**Thanks be to God.**	**Praise to Christ our Lord** / *Praise to you, Lord Jesus Christ.*

Cast: **Narrator, Voice.** (*This link is retained when the reading is used with the previous one.)

Jesus calls four fishermen
Mark 1.14–20

Narrator	After John had been put in prison, Jesus went to Galilee and preached the Good News from God:
Jesus	The right time has come, and the Kingdom of God is near! Turn away from your sins and believe the Good News!
Narrator	As Jesus walked along the shore of Lake Galilee, he saw two fishermen, Simon and his brother Andrew, catching fish with a net. Jesus said to them:
Jesus	Come with me, and I will teach you to catch men.
Narrator	At once they left their nets and went with him. (PAUSE)
	He went a little farther on and saw two other brothers, James and John, the sons of Zebedee. They were in their boat getting their nets ready. As soon as Jesus saw them, he called them; they left their father Zebedee in the boat with the hired men and went with Jesus.

Cast [This is] the word of the Lord.   OR   This is the Gospel of Christ / *This is the Gospel of the Lord.*
All   **Thanks be to God.**   **Praise to Christ our Lord** / *Praise to you, Lord Jesus Christ.*

Cast: **Narrator, Jesus.**

A man with an evil spirit
Mark 1.21–28

Narrator	Jesus and his disciples came to the town of Capernaum, and on the next Sabbath Jesus went to the synagogue and began to teach. The people who heard him were amazed at the way he taught, for he wasn't like the teachers of the Law; instead, he taught with authority.
	Just then a man with an evil spirit in him came into the synagogue and screamed:
Man	What do you want with us, Jesus of Nazareth? Are you here to destroy us? I know who you are—you are God's holy messenger!
Narrator	Jesus ordered the spirit:
Jesus	Be quiet, and come out of the man!
Narrator	The evil spirit shook the man hard, gave a loud scream, and came out of him. The people were all so amazed that they started saying to one another:
Person 1	What is this?
Person 2	Is it some kind of new teaching?
Person 1	This man has authority to give orders to the evil spirits.
Person 2	And they obey him!
Narrator	And so the news about Jesus spread quickly everywhere in the province of Galilee.

Cast [This is] the word of the Lord.   OR   This is the Gospel of Christ / *This is the Gospel of the Lord.*
All   **Thanks be to God.**   **Praise to Christ our Lord** / *Praise to you, Lord Jesus Christ.*

Cast: **Narrator, Man, Jesus, Person 1, Person 2.**

Jesus preaches in Galilee
From Mark 1.35–45

Narrator   Long before daylight, Jesus got up and left the house. He went out of the town to a lonely place, where he prayed. But Simon and his companions went out searching for him. [They said:]

Disciple   Everyone is looking for you.

[Narrator   But Jesus answered:]

Jesus   We must go on to the other villages round here. I have to preach in them also, because that is why I came.

Narrator   So he travelled all over Galilee, preaching in the synagogues and driving out demons. (PAUSE)

A man suffering from leprosy came to Jesus, knelt down, and begged him for help.

Man   If you want to, you can make me clean.

Narrator   Jesus was filled with pity, and stretched out his hand and touched him.

Jesus   I do want to. Be clean!

Narrator   At once the disease left the man, and he was clean. Then Jesus spoke sternly to him [and sent him away at once]:

Jesus   Listen, don't tell anyone about this. But go straight to the priest and let him examine you; then in order to prove to everyone that you are cured, offer the sacrifice that Moses ordered.

Narrator   But the man went away and began to spread the news everywhere. Indeed, he talked so much that Jesus could not go into a town publicly. Instead, he stayed out in lonely places, and people came to him from everywhere.

Cast	[This is] the word of the Lord. OR	This is the Gospel of Christ / *This is the Gospel of the Lord.*
All	**Thanks be to God.**	**Praise to Christ our Lord** / *Praise to you, Lord Jesus Christ.*

Cast: **Narrator, Disciple, Jesus, Man.**

Jesus heals a paralysed man
Mark 2.1–12

Narrator   Jesus went back to Capernaum, and the news spread that he was at home. So many people came together that there was no room left, not even out in front of the door. Jesus was preaching the message to them when four men arrived, carrying a paralysed man to Jesus. Because of the crowd, however, they could not get the man to him. So they made a hole in the roof right above the place where Jesus was. When they had made an opening, they let the man down, lying on his mat. Seeing how much faith they had, Jesus said to the paralysed man:

Jesus	My son, your sins are forgiven.
Narrator	Some teachers of the Law who were sitting there thought to themselves:
Lawyer 1	How does he dare to talk like this?
Lawyer 2	This is blasphemy!
Lawyer 3	God is the only one who can forgive sins!
Narrator	At once Jesus knew what they were thinking [so he said to them]:
Jesus	Why do you think such things? Is it easier to say to this paralysed man, 'Your sins are forgiven', or to say, 'Get up, pick up your mat, and walk'? I will prove to you, then, that the Son of Man has authority on earth to forgive sins.
Narrator	So he said to the paralysed man:
Jesus	I tell you, get up, pick up your mat, and go home!
Narrator	While they all watched, the man got up, picked up his mat, and hurried away. They were all completely amazed and praised God [saying]:
Person	We have never seen anything like this!

Cast	[This is] the word of the Lord. OR This is the Gospel of Christ / *This is the Gospel of the Lord.*
All	**Thanks be to God.**	**Praise to Christ our Lord** / *Praise to you, Lord Jesus Christ.*

Cast: **Narrator, Jesus, Lawyer 1, Lawyer 2, Lawyer 3, Person** (can be the same as Lawyer 1 OR Lawyers 1 and 2 can be the same).

Jesus calls Matthew Levi
From Mark 2.13–17

Narrator	Jesus went back again to the shore of Lake Galilee. A crowd came to him, and he started teaching them. As he walked along, he saw a tax collector, Levi son of Alphaeus, sitting in his office. [Jesus said to him:]
Jesus	Follow me.
Narrator	Levi got up and followed him. (PAUSE)
	Later on Jesus was having a meal in Levi's house. A large number of tax collectors and other outcasts were following Jesus, and many of them joined him and his disciples at the table. Some teachers of the Law, who were Pharisees, saw that Jesus was eating with these outcasts and tax collectors [so they asked his disciples]:
Pharisee	Why does he eat with such people?
Narrator	Jesus heard them [and answered]:
Jesus	People who are well do not need a doctor, but only those who are sick. I have not come to call respectable people, but outcasts.

Cast	[This is] the word of the Lord. OR This is the Gospel of Christ / *This is the Gospel of the Lord.*
All	**Thanks be to God.**	**Praise to Christ our Lord** / *Praise to you, Lord Jesus Christ.*

Cast: **Narrator, Jesus, Pharisee.**

The question about fasting
Mark 2.18–22

Narrator   On one occasion the followers of John the Baptist and the Pharisees were fasting. Some people came to Jesus [and asked him]:

Person   Why is it that the disciples of John the Baptist and the disciples of the Pharisees fast, but yours do not?

[Narrator   Jesus answered:]

Jesus   Do you expect the guests at a wedding party to go without food? Of course not! As long as the bridegroom is with them, they will not do that. But the day will come when the bridegroom will be taken away from them, and then they will fast.

No one uses a piece of new cloth to patch up an old coat, because the new patch will shrink and tear off some of the old cloth, making an even bigger hole. Nor does anyone pour new wine into used wineskins, because the wine will burst the skins, and both the wine and the skins will be ruined. Instead, new wine must be poured into fresh wineskins.

Cast   [This is] the word of the Lord.   OR   This is the Gospel of Christ / *This is the Gospel of the Lord.*
All   **Thanks be to God.**   **Praise to Christ our Lord** / *Praise to you, Lord Jesus Christ.*

Cast: **Narrator, Person, Jesus.**

The question about the Sabbath
Mark 2.23–28

Narrator   Jesus was walking through some cornfields on the Sabbath. As his disciples walked along with him, they began to pick the ears of corn. So the Pharisees said to Jesus:

Pharisee   Look, it is against our Law for your disciples to do that on the Sabbath!

[Narrator   Jesus answered:]

Jesus
(to Pharisee)   Have you never read what David did that time when he needed something to eat? He and his men were hungry, so he went into the house of God and ate the bread offered to God. This happened when Abiathar was the High Priest. According to our Law only the priests may eat this bread—but David ate it and even gave it to his men.

The Sabbath was made for the good of man; man was not made for the Sabbath. So the Son of Man is Lord even of the Sabbath.

Cast   [This is] the word of the Lord.   OR   This is the Gospel of Christ / *This is the Gospel of the Lord.*
All   **Thanks be to God.**   **Praise to Christ our Lord** / *Praise to you, Lord Jesus Christ.*

Cast: **Narrator, Pharisee, Jesus.**

The man with a paralysed hand
Mark 3.1–6

Narrator	Jesus went back to the synagogue, where there was a man who had a paralysed hand. Some people were there who wanted to accuse Jesus of doing wrong; so they watched him closely to see whether he would heal the man on the Sabbath. Jesus said to the man:
Jesus	Come up here to the front.
Narrator	Then he asked the people:
Jesus	What does our Law allow us to do on the Sabbath? To help or to harm? To save a man's life or to destroy it?
Narrator	But they did not say a thing. Jesus was angry as he looked round at them, but at the same time he felt sorry for them, because they were so stubborn and wrong. Then he said to the man:
Jesus	Stretch out your hand.
Narrator	He stretched it out, and it became well again. So the Pharisees left the synagogue and met at once with some members of Herod's party, (SLOWLY) and they made plans to kill Jesus.

Cast   [This is] the word of the Lord.   OR   This is the Gospel of Christ / *This is the Gospel of the Lord.*
All   **Thanks be to God.**   **Praise to Christ our Lord** / *Praise to you, Lord Jesus Christ.*

Cast: **Narrator, Jesus.**

A crowd by the lake
Mark 3.7–12

Narrator 1	Jesus and his disciples went away to Lake Galilee, and a large crowd followed him.
Narrator 2	They had come from Galilee, from Judaea, from Jerusalem, from the territory of Idumea, from the territory on the east side of the Jordan, and from the region round the cities of Tyre and Sidon.
Narrator 1	All these people came to Jesus because they had heard of the things he was doing.
Narrator 2	The crowd was so large that Jesus told his disciples to get a boat ready for him, so that the people would not crush him.
Narrator 1	He had healed many people, and all those who were ill kept pushing their way to him in order to touch him.
Narrator 2	And whenever the people who had evil spirits in them saw him, they would fall down before him and scream:
Person (loudly)	You are the Son of God!
Narrator 2	Jesus sternly ordered the evil spirits not to tell anyone who he was.

Cast   [This is] the word of the Lord.   OR   This is the Gospel of Christ / *This is the Gospel of the Lord.*
All   **Thanks be to God.**   **Praise to Christ our Lord** / *Praise to you, Lord Jesus Christ.*

Cast: **Narrator 1, Narrator 2** (can be the same as Narrator 1 when this reading is linked to the previous one), **Person.**

Jesus chooses the twelve apostles
Mark 3.13–19

Narrator	Jesus went up a hill and called to himself the men he wanted. They came to him, and he chose twelve, whom he named apostles. [He told them:]
Jesus	I have chosen you to be with me. I will also send you out to preach, and you will have authority to drive out demons.
Narrator	These are the twelve he chose: Simon—
Commentator	Jesus gave him the name Peter.
Narrator	James and his brother John—
Commentator	The sons of Zebedee. Jesus gave them the name Boanerges, which means 'Men of Thunder'.
Narrator	Andrew, Philip, Bartholomew, Matthew, Thomas, James—
Commentator	The son of Alphaeus.
Narrator	Thaddaeus, Simon—
Commentator	The Patriot.
Narrator	And Judas Iscariot—
Commentator	Who betrayed Jesus.

Cast	[This is] the word of the Lord.	OR	This is the Gospel of Christ / *This is the Gospel of the Lord.*
All	**Thanks be to God.**		**Praise to Christ our Lord** / *Praise to you, Lord Jesus Christ.*

Cast: **Narrator, Jesus, Commentator.**

Jesus and Beelzebul
Mark 3.20–30

Narrator	Jesus went home. Again such a large crowd gathered that Jesus and his disciples had no time to eat. When his family heard about it, they set out to take charge of him, because people were saying:
Person	He's gone mad!
Narrator	Some teachers of the Law who had come from Jerusalem were saying:
Lawyer 1	He has Beelzebul in him!
Lawyer 2	It is the chief of the demons who gives him the power to drive them out.
Narrator	So Jesus called them to him and spoke to them in parables:

78

Jesus	How can Satan drive out Satan? If a country divides itself into groups which fight each other, that country will fall apart. If a family divides itself into groups which fight each other, that family will fall apart. So if Satan's kingdom divides into groups, it cannot last, but will fall apart and come to an end.
	No one can break into a strong man's house and take away his belongings unless he first ties up the strong man; then he can plunder his house.
	I assure you that people can be forgiven all their sins and all the evil things they may say. But whoever says evil things against the Holy Spirit will never be forgiven, because he has committed an eternal sin.
Narrator	Jesus said this because some people were saying, 'He has an evil spirit in him.'

Cast   [This is] the word of the Lord.   OR   This is the Gospel of Christ / *This is the Gospel of the Lord.*
All   **Thanks be to God.**   **Praise to Christ our Lord** / *Praise to you, Lord Jesus Christ.*

Cast: **Narrator, Person, Lawyer 1, Lawyer 2** (can be the same as Lawyer 1), **Jesus.**

Jesus' mother and brothers
Mark 3.31–35

Narrator	Jesus' mother and brothers arrived. They stood outside the house and sent in a message, asking for him. A crowd was sitting round Jesus, and they said to him:
Person 1	Look, your mother and your brothers and sisters are outside.
Person 2	They want you.
Narrator	Jesus answered:
Jesus	Who is my mother? Who are my brothers?
Narrator	He looked at the people sitting round him.
Jesus	Look! Here are my mother and my brothers! Whoever does what God wants him to do is my brother, my sister, my mother.

Cast   [This is] the word of the Lord.   OR   This is the Gospel of Christ / *This is the Gospel of the Lord.*
All   **Thanks be to God.**   **Praise to Christ our Lord** / *Praise to you, Lord Jesus Christ.*

Cast: **Narrator, Person 1, Person 2** (can be the same as Person 1), **Jesus.**

The parable of the sower
From Mark 4.1–20

Narrator	Jesus began to teach beside Lake Galilee. The crowd that gathered round him was so large that he got into a boat and sat in it. The boat was out in the water and the crowd stood on the shore at the water's edge. He used parables to teach them many things:

Jesus	Listen! Once there was a man who went out to sow corn. As he scattered the seed in the field, some of it fell along the path, and the birds came and ate it up. Some of it fell on rocky ground, where there was little soil. The seeds soon sprouted, because the soil wasn't deep. Then, when the sun came up, it burnt the young plants; and because the roots had not grown deep enough, the plants soon dried up. Some of the seed fell among thorn bushes, which grew up and choked the plants, and they didn't produce any corn. But some seeds fell in good soil, and the plants sprouted, grew, and produced corn: some had thirty grains, others sixty, and others a hundred.
Narrator	And Jesus concluded:
Jesus	Listen, then, if you have ears!
Narrator	When Jesus was alone, some of those who had heard him came to him with the twelve disciples and asked him to explain the parables. [Jesus answered:]
Jesus	You have been given the secret of the Kingdom of God. But the others, who are on the outside, hear all things by means of parables, so that, as Isaiah says:
Isaiah	They may look and look, yet not see; they may listen and listen, yet not understand. For if they did, they would turn to God, and he would forgive them.
[Narrator	Then Jesus asked them:]
Jesus	Don't you understand this parable? How, then, will you ever understand any parable? The sower sows God's message. Some people are like the seeds that fall along the path; as soon as they hear the message, Satan comes and takes it away.
	Other people are like the seeds that fall on rocky ground. As soon as they hear the message, they receive it gladly. But it does not sink deep into them, and they don't last long. So when trouble or persecution comes because of the message, they give up at once.
	Other people are like the seeds sown among the thorn bushes. These are the ones who hear the message, but the worries about this life, the love for riches, and all other kinds of desires crowd in and choke the message, and they don't bear fruit.
	But other people are like the seeds sown in good soil. They hear the message, accept it, and bear fruit: some thirty, some sixty, and some a hundred.

Cast	[This is] the word of the Lord.	OR	This is the Gospel of Christ / *This is the Gospel of the Lord.*
All	**Thanks be to God.**		**Praise to Christ our Lord** / *Praise to you, Lord Jesus Christ.*

Cast: **Narrator, Jesus, Isaiah.** (See two quite different dramatisations of this parable at Matthew 13.1 and Luke 8.4.)

Parables of the Kingdom
Mark 4.21–34

Narrator   Jesus said:

Jesus   Does anyone ever bring in a lamp and put it under a bowl or under the bed? Doesn't he put it on the lampstand? Whatever is hidden away will be brought out into the open, and whatever is covered up will be uncovered. Listen, then, if you have ears!

Narrator   Jesus also said to them:

Jesus   Pay attention to what you hear! The same rules you use to judge others will be used by God to judge you—but with even greater severity. The person who has something will be given more, and the person who has nothing will have taken away from him even the little he has.

Narrator   Jesus went on to say:

Jesus   The Kingdom of God is like this. A man scatters seed in his field. He sleeps at night, is up and about during the day, and all the while the seeds are sprouting and growing. Yet he does not know how it happens. The soil itself makes the plants grow and bear fruit; first the tender stalk appears, then the ear, and finally the ear full of corn. When the corn is ripe, the man starts cutting it with his sickle, because harvest time has come. (PAUSE)

Narrator   Jesus asked his followers:

Jesus   What shall we say the Kingdom of God is like? What parable shall we use to explain it? It is like this. A man takes a mustard seed, the smallest seed in the world, and plants it in the ground. After a while it grows up and becomes the biggest of all plants. It puts out such large branches that the birds come and make their nests in its shade.

Narrator   Jesus preached his message to the people, using many other parables like these; he told them as much as they could understand. He would not speak to them without using parables, but when he was alone with his disciples, he would explain everything to them.

Cast   [This is] the word of the Lord.   OR   This is the Gospel of Christ / *This is the Gospel of the Lord.*
All   **Thanks be to God.**   **Praise to Christ our Lord** / *Praise to you, Lord Jesus Christ.*

Cast: **Narrator, Jesus.**

Jesus calms a storm
Mark 4.35–41 [6.45–51]

Narrator   Jesus said to his disciples:

Jesus   Let us go across to the other side of the lake.

Narrator   So they left the crowd; the disciples got into the boat in which Jesus was already sitting, and they took him with them. Other boats were there too. Suddenly a strong wind blew up, and the waves began to spill over into the boat, so that it was about to fill with water. Jesus was in the back of the boat, sleeping with his head on a pillow. The disciples woke him up:

Disciples 1 & 2	Teacher!
Disciple 1	Don't you care that we are about to die?
Narrator	Jesus stood up and commanded the wind:
Jesus	Be quiet!
Narrator	And he said to the waves:
Jesus	Be still!
Narrator	The wind died down, and there was a great calm. Then Jesus said to his disciples:
Jesus	Why are you frightened? Have you still no faith?
Narrator	But they were terribly afraid and said to one another:
Disciple 1	Who is this man?
Disciple 2	Even the wind and the waves obey him!
[Narrator	On another occasion Jesus made his disciples get into the boat and go ahead of him to Bethsaida, on the other side of the lake, while he sent the crowd away. After saying good-bye to the people he went away to a hill to pray. When evening came, the boat was in the middle of the lake, while Jesus was alone on land. He saw that his disciples were straining at the oars, because they were rowing against the wind; so some time between three and six o'clock in the morning he came to them, walking on the water. He was going to pass them by, but they saw him walking on the water:
Disciples 1 & 2 (hoarse whisper)	It's a ghost!
Narrator	They were all terrified when they saw him, and screamed.
Jesus	Courage! It is I. Don't be afraid!
Narrator	Then he got into the boat with them, and the wind died down. The disciples were completely amazed.]

Cast	[This is] the word of the Lord. OR	This is the Gospel of Christ / *This is the Gospel of the Lord.*
All	**Thanks be to God.**	**Praise to Christ our Lord** / *Praise to you, Lord Jesus Christ.*

Cast: **Narrator, Jesus, Disciple 1, Disciple 2** (can be the same as Disciple 1).

Jesus heals a man with evil spirits
Mark 5.1–20

Narrator	Jesus and his disciples arrived on the other side of Lake Galilee, in the territory of Gerasa. As soon as Jesus got out of the boat, he was met by a man who came out of the burial caves there. This man had an evil spirit in him and lived among the tombs. Nobody could keep him chained up any more; many times his feet and hands had been chained, but every time he broke the chains and smashed the irons on his feet. He was too strong for anyone to control him. Day and night he wandered among the tombs and through the hills, screaming and cutting himself with stones.
	He was some distance away when he saw Jesus; so he ran, fell on his knees before him, and screamed in a loud voice:

Man	Jesus, Son of the Most High God! What do you want with me? For God's sake, I beg you, don't punish me!
Narrator	He said this because Jesus was saying:
[Jesus]	Evil spirit, come out of this man!
Narrator	So Jesus asked him:
Jesus	What is your name?
Man	My name is 'Mob'—there are so many of us!
Narrator	And he kept begging Jesus not to send the evil spirits out of that region. (PAUSE)
	There was a large herd of pigs near by, feeding on a hillside. So the spirits begged Jesus:
A spirit	Send us to the pigs, and let us go into them.
Narrator	He let them go, and the evil spirits went out of the man and entered the pigs. The whole herd—about two thousand pigs in all—rushed down the side of the cliff into the lake and was drowned. (PAUSE)
	The men who had been taking care of the pigs ran away and spread the news in the town and among the farms. People went out to see what had happened, and when they came to Jesus, they saw the man who used to have the mob of demons in him. He was sitting there, clothed and in his right mind; and they were all afraid. Those who had seen it told the people what happened to the man with the demons, and about the pigs. So they asked Jesus to leave their territory.
	As Jesus was getting into the boat, the man who had had the demons begged him:
Man	Let me go with you!
Narrator	But Jesus would not let him:
Jesus	Go back home to your family and tell them how much the Lord has done for you and how kind he has been to you.
Narrator	So the man left and went all through the Ten Towns, telling what Jesus had done for him. And all who heard it were amazed.

Cast	[This is] the word of the Lord.	OR	This is the Gospel of Christ / *This is the Gospel of the Lord.*
All	**Thanks be to God.**		**Praise to Christ our Lord** / *Praise to you, Lord Jesus Christ.*

Cast: **Narrator, Man, Jesus, A spirit.**

Jairus' daughter and the woman who touched Jesus' cloak
Mark 5.21–43

Narrator	Jesus went back across to the other side of the lake. There at the lakeside a large crowd gathered round him. Jairus, an official of the local synagogue, arrived, and when he saw Jesus, he threw himself down at his feet and begged him earnestly:
Jairus	My little daughter is very ill. Please come and place your hands on her, so that she will get well and live!

Narrator	Then Jesus started off with him. So many people were going along with Jesus that they were crowding him from every side.
	There was a woman who had suffered terribly from severe bleeding for twelve years, even though she had been treated by many doctors. She had spent all her money, but instead of getting better she got worse all the time. She had heard about Jesus, so she came in the crowd behind him, saying to herself:
Woman	If I just touch his clothes, I will get well.
Narrator	She touched his cloak, and her bleeding stopped at once; and she had the feeling inside herself that she was healed of her trouble. At once Jesus knew that power had gone out of him, so he turned round in the crowd [and asked]:
Jesus	Who touched my clothes?
Narrator	His disciples answered:
Disciple 1	You see how the people are crowding you!
Disciple 2	Why do you ask who touched you?
Narrator	But Jesus kept looking round to see who had done it. The woman realized what had happened to her, so she came, trembling with fear, knelt at his feet, and told him the whole truth. [Jesus said to her:]
Jesus	My daughter, your faith has made you well. Go in peace, and be healed of your trouble.
Narrator	While Jesus was saying this, some messengers came from Jairus' house [and told him]:
Messenger (to Jairus)	Your daughter has died. Why bother the Teacher any longer?
Narrator	Jesus paid no attention to what they said [but told him]:
Jesus (to Jairus)	Don't be afraid, only believe.
Narrator	Then he did not let anyone else go on with him except Peter and James and his brother John. They arrived at Jairus' house, where Jesus saw the confusion and heard all the loud crying and wailing. [He went in and said to them:]
Jesus	Why all this confusion? Why are you crying? The child is not dead—she is only sleeping!
Narrator	They laughed at him, so he put them all out, took the child's father and mother and his three disciples, and went into the room where the child was lying. He took her by the hand:
Jesus	Talitha, koum. Little girl, I tell you to get up!
Narrator	She got up at once and started walking around—she was twelve years old. When this happened, they were completely amazed. But Jesus gave them strict orders not to tell anyone, and he said:
Jesus	Give her something to eat.

Cast	[This is] the word of the Lord.	OR	This is the Gospel of Christ / *This is the Gospel of the Lord.*
All	**Thanks be to God.**		**Praise to Christ our Lord** / *Praise to you, Lord Jesus Christ.*

Cast: **Narrator, Jairus, Woman, Jesus, Disciple 1, Disciple 2** (can be the same as Jairus), **Messenger.**

Jesus is rejected at Nazareth
Mark 6.1–6

Narrator   Jesus went back to his home town, followed by his disciples. On the Sabbath he began to teach in the synagogue. Many people were there; and when they heard him, they were all amazed.

Person 1   Where did he get all this?

Person 2   What wisdom is this that has been given him?

Person 1   How does he perform miracles?

Person 2   Isn't he the carpenter, the son of Mary?

Person 1   And the brother of James, Joseph, Judas, and Simon?

Person 2   Aren't his sisters living here?

Narrator   And so they rejected him. (PAUSE)

[Jesus said to them:]

Jesus (to Persons 1 & 2)   A prophet is respected everywhere except in his own home town and by his relatives and his family.

Narrator   He was not able to perform any miracles there, except that he placed his hands on a few sick people and healed them. He was greatly surprised, because the people did not have faith.

Cast   [This is] the word of the Lord.   OR   This is the Gospel of Christ / *This is the Gospel of the Lord.*
All   **Thanks be to God.**   **Praise to Christ our Lord** / *Praise to you, Lord Jesus Christ.*

Cast: **Narrator, Person 1, Person 2, Jesus.**

Jesus sends out the twelve disciples
Mark 6.6–13

Narrator   Jesus went to the villages, teaching the people. He called the twelve disciples together and sent them out two by two. He gave them authority over the evil spirits and ordered them:

Jesus   Don't take anything with you on your journey except a stick—no bread, no beggar's bag, no money in your pockets. Wear sandals, but don't carry an extra shirt. Wherever you are welcomed, stay in the same house until you leave that place. If you come to a town where people do not welcome you or will not listen to you, leave it and shake the dust off your feet. That will be a warning to them!

Narrator   So they went out and preached that people should turn away from their sins. They drove out many demons, and rubbed olive-oil on many sick people and healed them.

Cast   [This is] the word of the Lord.   OR   This is the Gospel of Christ / *This is the Gospel of the Lord.*
All   **Thanks be to God.**   **Praise to Christ our Lord** / *Praise to you, Lord Jesus Christ.*

Cast: **Narrator, Jesus.**

The death of John the Baptist
Mark 6.14–29

Narrator Now King Herod heard about Jesus, because his reputation had spread everywhere. Some people were saying:

Person 1 John the Baptist has come back to life! That is why he has this power to perform miracles.

Narrator Others, however, said:

Person 2 He is Elijah.

Narrator Others said:

Person 1 He is a prophet, like one of the prophets of long ago.

Narrator When Herod heard it, he said:

Herod
(frightened) He is John the Baptist! I had his head cut off, but he has come back to life!

Narrator Herod himself had ordered John's arrest, and he had him chained and put in prison. Herod did this because of Herodias, whom he had married, even though she was the wife of his brother Philip. John the Baptist kept telling Herod:

John It isn't right for you to be married to your brother's wife!

Narrator So Herodias held a grudge against John and wanted to kill him, but she could not because of Herod. Herod was afraid of John because he knew that John was a good and holy man, and so he kept him safe. He liked to listen to him, even though he became greatly disturbed every time he heard him.

Finally Herodias got her chance. It was on Herod's birthday, when he gave a feast for all the chief government officials, the military commanders, and the leading citizens of Galilee. The daughter of Herodias came in and danced, and pleased Herod and his guests. So the king said to the girl:

Herod What would you like to have? I will give you anything you want.

Narrator With many vows he said to her:

Herod I swear that I will give you anything you ask for, even as much as half my kingdom!

Narrator So the girl went out and asked her mother:

Girl What shall I ask for?

[Narrator She answered:]

Herodias
(with malice) The head of John the Baptist.

Narrator	The girl hurried back at once to the king and demanded:
Girl	I want you to give me here and now the head of John the Baptist on a dish!
Narrator	This made the king very sad, but he could not refuse her because of the vows he had made in front of all his guests. So he sent off a guard at once with orders to bring John's head. The guard left, went to the prison, and cut John's head off; then he brought it on a dish and gave it to the girl, who gave it to her mother. When John's disciples heard about this, they came and took away his body, and buried it.

Cast	[This is] the word of the Lord. OR This is the Gospel of Christ / *This is the Gospel of the Lord.*
All	**Thanks be to God.** **Praise to Christ our Lord** / *Praise to you, Lord Jesus Christ.*

Cast: **Narrator, Person 1, Person 2, Herod, John** (the Baptist, can be the same as Narrator), **Girl, Herodias.**

Jesus feeds five thousand
Mark 6.30–44

Narrator	The apostles returned and met with Jesus, and told him all they had done and taught. There were so many people coming and going that Jesus and his disciples didn't even have time to eat. So he said to them:
Jesus	Let us go off by ourselves to some place where we will be alone and you can rest for a while.
Narrator	So they started out in a boat by themselves for a lonely place. (PAUSE)

Many people, however, saw them leave and knew at once who they were; so they went from all the towns and ran ahead by land and arrived at the place ahead of Jesus and his disciples. When Jesus got out of the boat, he saw this large crowd, and his heart was filled with pity for them, because they were like sheep without a shepherd. So he began to teach them many things. When it was getting late, his disciples came to him. |
Disciple 1	It is already very late, and this is a lonely place.
Disciple 2	Send the people away.
Disciple 1	Let them go to the nearby farms and villages in order to buy themselves something to eat.
Jesus	You yourselves give them something to eat.
Disciple 1	Do you want us to go and spend two hundred silver coins on bread in order to feed them?
Jesus	How much bread have you got? Go and see.
Narrator	When they found out, they told him:
Disciple 2	Five loaves and also two fish.
Narrator	Jesus then told his disciples to make all the people divide into groups and sit down on the green grass. So the people sat down in rows, in groups of a hundred and groups of fifty. Then Jesus took the five loaves and the two fish, looked up to heaven, and gave

→

thanks to God. He broke the loaves and gave them to his disciples to distribute to the people. He also divided the two fish among them all. Everyone ate and had enough. Then the disciples took up twelve baskets full of what was left of the bread and the fish.

The number of men who were fed was five thousand.

Cast	[This is] the word of the Lord.	OR	This is the Gospel of Christ / *This is the Gospel of the Lord.*
All	**Thanks be to God.**		**Praise to Christ our Lord** / *Praise to you, Lord Jesus Christ.*

Cast: **Narrator, Jesus, Disciple 1, Disciple 2.**

Jesus walks on the water
Mark 6.45–56

Narrator Jesus made his disciples get into the boat and go ahead of him to Bethsaida, on the other side of the lake, while he sent the crowd away. After saying good-bye to the people he went away to a hill to pray. When evening came, the boat was in the middle of the lake, while Jesus was alone on land. He saw that his disciples were straining at the oars, because they were rowing against the wind; so some time between three and six o'clock in the morning he came to them, walking on the water. He was going to pass them by, but they saw him walking on the water:

Disciples 1 & 2
(hoarse whisper) It's a ghost!

Narrator They were all terrified when they saw him, and screamed.

Jesus Courage! It is I. Don't be afraid!

Narrator Then he got into the boat with them, and the wind died down. The disciples were completely amazed, because they had not understood the real meaning of the feeding of the five thousand; their minds could not grasp it.

They crossed the lake and came to land at Gennesaret, where they tied up the boat. As they left the boat, people recognized Jesus at once. So they ran throughout the whole region; and wherever they heard he was, they brought to him sick people lying on their mats. And everywhere Jesus went, to villages, towns, or farms, people would take those who were ill to the market-places and beg him to let them at least touch the edge of his cloak; and all who touched it were made well.

Cast	[This is] the word of the Lord.	OR	This is the Gospel of Christ / *This is the Gospel of the Lord.*
All	**Thanks be to God.**		**Praise to Christ our Lord** / *Praise to you, Lord Jesus Christ.*

Cast: **Narrator, Disciple 1, Disciple 2** (can be the same as Disciple 1)**, Jesus.** (See also composite version on page 81).

The teaching of the ancestors
Mark 7.1–13

Narrator Some Pharisees and teachers of the Law who had come from Jerusalem gathered round Jesus. They noticed that some of his disciples were eating their food with hands that were ritually unclean—that is, they had not washed them in the way the Pharisees said people should.

For the Pharisees, as well as the rest of the Jews, follow the teaching they received from their ancestors: they do not eat unless they wash their hands in the proper way; nor do they eat anything that comes from the market unless they wash it first. And they follow many other rules which they have received, such as the proper way to wash cups, pots, copper bowls, and beds.

So the Pharisees and the teachers of the Law asked Jesus:

Lawyer   Why is it that your disciples do not follow the teaching handed down by our ancestors, but instead eat with ritually unclean hands?

[Narrator   Jesus answered them:]

Jesus   How right Isaiah was when he prophesied about you! You are hypocrites, just as he wrote:

Isaiah   These people, says God, honour me with their words,
but their heart is really far away from me.
It is no use for them to worship me,
because they teach man-made rules
as though they were God's laws!

Jesus   You put aside God's command and obey the teachings of men. You have a clever way of rejecting God's law in order to uphold your own teaching. For Moses commanded:

Moses   Respect your father and your mother. Whoever curses his father or his mother is to be put to death.

Jesus   But you teach that if a person has something he could use to help his father or mother, but says, 'This is Corban'—

Narrator (aside)   Which means, it belongs to God—

Jesus   He is excused from helping his father or mother. In this way the teaching you pass on to others cancels out the word of God. And there are many other things like this that you do.

Cast   [This is] the word of the Lord.   OR   This is the Gospel of Christ / *This is the Gospel of the Lord.*
All   **Thanks be to God.**   **Praise to Christ our Lord** / *Praise to you, Lord Jesus Christ.*

Cast: **Narrator, Lawyer, Jesus, Isaiah, Moses.**

The things that make a person unclean
Mark 7.14–23

Narrator   Jesus called the crowd to him once more.

Jesus   Listen to me, all of you, and understand. There is nothing that goes into a person from the outside which can make him ritually unclean. Rather, it is what comes out of a person that makes him unclean. Listen, then, if you have ears.

Narrator   When he left the crowd and went into the house, his disciples asked him to explain this saying.

Jesus	You are no more intelligent than the others. Don't you understand? Nothing that goes into a person from the outside can really make him unclean, because it does not go into his heart but into his stomach and then goes on out of the body.
Narrator	In saying this, Jesus declared that all foods are fit to be eaten.
Jesus	It is what comes out of a person that makes him unclean. For from the inside, from a person's heart, come the evil ideas which lead him to do immoral things, to rob, kill, commit adultery, be greedy, and do all sorts of evil things; deceit, indecency, jealousy, slander, pride, and folly— all these evil things come from inside a person and make him unclean.

Cast	[This is] the word of the Lord. OR	This is the Gospel of Christ / *This is the Gospel of the Lord.*
All	**Thanks be to God.**	**Praise to Christ our Lord** / *Praise to you, Lord Jesus Christ.*

Cast: **Narrator, Jesus.**

A woman's faith
Mark 7.24–30

Narrator	Jesus left and went away to the territory near the city of Tyre. He went into a house and did not want anyone to know he was there, but he could not stay hidden. A woman, whose daughter had an evil spirit in her, heard about Jesus and came to him at once and fell at his feet. The woman was a Gentile, born in the region of Phoenicia in Syria. She begged Jesus to drive the demon out of her daughter. But Jesus answered:
Jesus	Let us first feed the children. It isn't right to take the children's food and throw it to the dogs.
Woman	Sir, even the dogs under the table eat the children's left-overs!
Jesus	Because of that answer, go back home, where you will find that the demon has gone out of your daughter!
Narrator	She went home and found her child lying on the bed; the demon had indeed gone out of her.

Cast	[This is] the word of the Lord. OR	This is the Gospel of Christ / *This is the Gospel of the Lord.*
All	**Thanks be to God.**	**Praise to Christ our Lord** / *Praise to you, Lord Jesus Christ.*

Cast: **Narrator, Jesus, Woman.**

Jesus heals a deaf-mute
Mark 7.31–37

Narrator	Jesus left the neighbourhood of Tyre and went on through Sidon to Lake Galilee, going by way of the territory of the Ten Towns. Some people brought him a man who was deaf and could hardly speak, and they begged Jesus to place his hands on him. So Jesus took him off alone, away from the crowd, put his fingers in the man's ears, spat, and touched the man's tongue. Then Jesus looked up to heaven, gave a deep groan, and said to the man:

Jesus	Ephphatha! Open up!
Narrator	At once the man was able to hear, his speech impediment was removed, and he began to talk without any trouble. Then Jesus ordered the people not to speak of it to anyone; but the more he ordered them not to, the more they spoke. And all who heard were completely amazed.
Person 1	How well he does everything!
Person 2	He even causes the deaf to hear and the dumb to speak!

Cast [This is] the word of the Lord.　　OR　　This is the Gospel of Christ / *This is the Gospel of the Lord.*
All　**Thanks be to God.**　　　　　　　　　　　　**Praise to Christ our Lord** / *Praise to you, Lord Jesus Christ.*

Cast: **Narrator, Jesus, Person 1, Person 2** (can be the same as Person 1).

Jesus feeds four thousand
Mark 8.1–10

Narrator	Another large crowd came together. When the people had nothing left to eat, Jesus called the disciples to him:
Jesus	I feel sorry for these people, because they have been with me for three days and now have nothing to eat. If I send them home without feeding them, they will faint as they go, because some of them have come a long way.
Narrator	His disciples asked him:
Disciple	Where in this desert can anyone find enough food to feed all these people?
Jesus	How much bread have you got?
Disciple	Seven loaves.
Narrator	He ordered the crowd to sit down on the ground. Then he took the seven loaves, gave thanks to God, broke them, and gave them to his disciples to distribute to the crowd; and the disciples did so. They also had a few small fish. Jesus gave thanks for these and told the disciples to distribute them too. Everybody ate and had enough—there were about four thousand people. Then the disciples took up seven baskets full of pieces left over. Jesus sent the people away and at once got into a boat with his disciples and went to the district of Dalmanutha.

Cast [This is] the word of the Lord.　　OR　　This is the Gospel of Christ / *This is the Gospel of the Lord.*
All　**Thanks be to God.**　　　　　　　　　　　　**Praise to Christ our Lord** / *Praise to you, Lord Jesus Christ.*

Cast: **Narrator, Jesus, Disciple.**

The Pharisees ask for a miracle
Mark 8.11–21

Narrator	Some Pharisees came to Jesus and started to argue with him. They wanted to trap him, so they asked him to perform a miracle to show that God approved of him. But Jesus gave a deep groan [and said]:
Jesus	Why do the people of this day ask for a miracle? No, I tell you! No such proof will be given to these people!

Narrator	He left them, got back into the boat, and started across to the other side of the lake. (PAUSE)
	The disciples had forgotten to bring enough bread and had only one loaf with them in the boat. Jesus warned them:
Jesus	Take care, and be on your guard against the yeast of the Pharisees and the yeast of Herod.
Narrator	They started discussing among themselves:
Disciple (aside)	He says this because we haven't any bread.
Narrator	Jesus knew what they were saying [so he asked them]:
Jesus	Why are you discussing about not having any bread? Don't you know or understand yet? Are your minds so dull? You have eyes—can't you see? You have ears—can't you hear? Don't you remember when I broke the five loaves for the five thousand people? How many baskets full of leftover pieces did you take up?'
Disciple	Twelve.
Jesus	And when I broke the seven loaves for the four thousand people, how many baskets full of leftover pieces did you take up?
Disciple	Seven.
Jesus	And you *still* don't understand?

Cast	[This is] the word of the Lord.	OR	This is the Gospel of Christ / *This is the Gospel of the Lord.*
All	**Thanks be to God.**		**Praise to Christ our Lord** / *Praise to you, Lord Jesus Christ.*

Cast: **Narrator, Jesus, Disciple.**

Jesus heals a blind man at Bethsaida
Mark 8.22–26

Narrator	They came to Bethsaida, where some people brought a blind man to Jesus and begged him to touch him. Jesus took the blind man by the hand and led him out of the village. After spitting on the man's eyes, Jesus placed his hands on him and asked him:
Jesus	Can you see anything?
Narrator	The man looked up and said:
Man	Yes, I can see people, but they look like trees walking about.
Narrator	Jesus again placed his hands on the man's eyes. This time the man looked intently, his eyesight returned, and he saw everything clearly. Jesus then sent him home with the order:
Jesus	Don't go back into the village.

Cast	[This is] the word of the Lord.	OR	This is the Gospel of Christ / *This is the Gospel of the Lord.*
All	**Thanks be to God.**		**Praise to Christ our Lord** / *Praise to you, Lord Jesus Christ.*

Cast: **Narrator, Jesus, Man.**

Peter's declaration about Jesus
Mark 8.27–30

Narrator	Jesus and his disciples went away to the villages near Caesarea Philippi. On the way he asked his disciples:
Jesus	Tell me, who do people say I am?
Disciple	Some say that you are John the Baptist; others say that you are Elijah, while others say that you are one of the prophets.
Jesus	What about you? Who do you say I am?
Narrator	Peter answered:
Peter	You are the Messiah.
[Narrator	Then Jesus ordered them:]
Jesus (to disciples)	Do not tell anyone about me.

Cast [This is] the word of the Lord.   OR   This is the Gospel of Christ / *This is the Gospel of the Lord.*
All   **Thanks be to God.**   **Praise to Christ our Lord** / *Praise to you, Lord Jesus Christ.*

Cast: **Narrator, Jesus, Disciple, Peter.**

Jesus speaks about his suffering and death
Mark 8.31–38

Narrator	Jesus began to teach his disciples:
Jesus	The Son of Man must suffer much and be rejected by the elders, the chief priests, and the teachers of the Law. He will be put to death, but three days later he will rise to life.
Narrator	He made this very clear to them. So Peter took him aside and began to rebuke him. But Jesus turned round, looked at his disciples, and rebuked Peter:
Jesus	Get away from me, Satan. Your thoughts don't come from God but from man!
Narrator	Then Jesus called the crowd and his disciples to him.
Jesus	If anyone wants to come with me, he must forget self, carry his cross, and follow me. For whoever wants to save his own life will lose it; but whoever loses his life for me and for the gospel will save it. Does a person gain anything if he wins the whole world but loses his life? Of course not! There is nothing he can give to regain his life. If a person is ashamed of me and of my teaching in this godless and wicked day, then the Son of Man will be ashamed of him when he comes in the glory of his Father with the holy angels.

Cast [This is] the word of the Lord.   OR   This is the Gospel of Christ / *This is the Gospel of the Lord.*
All   **Thanks be to God.**   **Praise to Christ our Lord** / *Praise to you, Lord Jesus Christ.*

Cast: **Narrator, Jesus.**

The Transfiguration
Mark 9.2–13

Narrator   Six days later Jesus took with him Peter, James, and John, and led them up a high mountain, where they were alone. As they looked on, a change came over Jesus, and his clothes became shining white—whiter than anyone in the world could wash them. Then the three disciples saw Elijah and Moses talking with Jesus. Peter spoke up:

Peter   Teacher, how good it is that we are here! We will make three tents, one for you, one for Moses, and one for Elijah.

Narrator   He and the others were so frightened that he did not know what to say. Then a cloud appeared and covered them with its shadow, and a voice came from the cloud:

Voice   This is my own dear Son—listen to him!

Narrator   They took a quick look round but did not see anyone else; only Jesus was with them. (PAUSE)

As they came down the mountain, Jesus ordered them:

Jesus   Don't tell anyone what you have seen, until the Son of Man has risen from death.

Narrator   They obeyed his order, but among themselves they started discussing the matter:

Disciple 1   What does this 'rising from death' mean?

Narrator   And they asked Jesus:

Disciple 2   Why do the teachers of the Law say that Elijah has to come first?

Jesus   Elijah is indeed coming first in order to get everything ready. Yet why do the Scriptures say that the Son of Man will suffer much and be rejected? I tell you, however, that Elijah has already come and that people treated him just as they pleased, as the Scriptures say about him.

Cast	[This is] the word of the Lord. OR	This is the Gospel of Christ / *This is the Gospel of the Lord.*
All	**Thanks be to God.**	**Praise to Christ our Lord** / *Praise to you, Lord Jesus Christ.*

Cast: **Narrator, Peter, Voice** (at a distance), **Jesus, Disciple 1, Disciple 2.**

Jesus heals a boy with an evil spirit
Mark 9.14–29

Narrator   When they joined the rest of the disciples, they saw a large crowd round them and some teachers of the Law arguing with them. When the people saw Jesus, they were greatly surprised, and ran to him and greeted him. Jesus asked his disciples:

Jesus   What are you arguing with them about?

Narrator   A man in the crowd answered:

94

Father	Teacher, I brought my son to you because he has an evil spirit in him and cannot talk. Whenever the spirit attacks him, it throws him to the ground, and he foams at the mouth, grits his teeth, and becomes stiff all over. I asked your disciples to drive the spirit out, but they could not.
Jesus	How unbelieving you people are! How long must I stay with you? How long do I have to put up with you? Bring the boy to me!
Narrator	They brought him to Jesus.
	As soon as the spirit saw Jesus, it threw the boy into a fit, so that he fell on the ground and rolled round, foaming at the mouth. [Jesus asked the father:]
Jesus	How long has he been like this?
Father	Ever since he was a child. Many times the evil spirit has tried to kill him by throwing him in the fire and into water. Have pity on us and help us, if you possibly can!
Jesus	Yes, if you yourself can! Everything is possible for the person who has faith.
Father (crying out)	I *do* have faith, but not enough. Help me to have more!
Narrator	Jesus noticed that the crowd was closing in on them, so he gave a command to the evil spirit:
Jesus	Deaf and dumb spirit, I order you to come out of the boy and never go into him again!
Narrator	The spirit screamed, threw the boy into a bad fit, and came out. The boy looked like a corpse, and everyone said:
Father and **Disciple**	He is dead!
Narrator	But Jesus took the boy by the hand and helped him to rise, and he stood up. (PAUSE)
	After Jesus had gone indoors, his disciples asked him privately:
Disciple	Why couldn't we drive the spirit out?
Jesus	Only prayer can drive this kind out; nothing else can.

Cast	[This is] the word of the Lord. OR	This is the Gospel of Christ / *This is the Gospel of the Lord.*
All	**Thanks be to God.**	**Praise to Christ our Lord** / *Praise to you, Lord Jesus Christ.*

Cast: **Narrator, Jesus, Father, Disciple.**

Jesus and his disciples
Mark 9.30–41

Jesus speaks again about his suffering and death (Mark 9.30–32)

Narrator	Jesus and his disciples left that place and went on through Galilee. Jesus did not want anyone to know where he was, because he was teaching his disciples:

95

Jesus	The Son of Man will be handed over to men who will kill him. Three days later, however, he will rise to life.
Narrator	But they did not understand what this teaching meant, and they were afraid to ask him. (PAUSE)

Who is the greatest? (Mark 9.33–37)

Narrator	They came to Capernaum, and after going indoors Jesus asked his disciples:
Jesus	What were you arguing about on the road?
Narrator	But they would not answer him, because on the road they had been arguing among themselves about who was the greatest. Jesus sat down and called the twelve disciples:
Jesus	Whoever wants to be first must place himself last of all and be the servant of all.
Narrator	Then he took a child and made him stand in front of them. He put his arms round him.
Jesus	Whoever welcomes in my name one of the children, welcomes me; and whoever welcomes me, welcomes not only me but also the one who sent me.

Whoever is not against us is for us (Mark 9.38–41)

Narrator	John said to Jesus:
John	Teacher, we saw a man who was driving out demons in your name, and we told him to stop, because he doesn't belong to our group.
Jesus	Do not try to stop him, because no one who performs a miracle in my name will be able soon afterwards to say evil things about me. For whoever is not against us is for us. I assure you that anyone who gives you a drink of water because you belong to me will certainly receive his reward.

Cast	[This is] the word of the Lord.	OR	This is the Gospel of Christ / *This is the Gospel of the Lord.*
All	**Thanks be to God.**		**Praise to Christ our Lord** / *Praise to you, Lord Jesus Christ.*

Cast: **Narrator, Jesus, John.**

Jesus' teaching about temptations to sin
Mark 9.42–50

Teacher	If anyone should cause one of these little ones to lose his faith in me, it would be better for that person to have a large millstone tied round his neck and be thrown into the sea.
Reader 1	If your hand makes you lose your faith, cut it off!
Teacher	It is better for you to enter life without a hand than to keep both hands and go off to hell, to the fire that never goes out.
Reader 2	If your foot makes you lose your faith, cut it off!

Teacher	It is better for you to enter life without a foot than to keep both feet and be thrown into hell.
Reader 3	If your eye makes you lose your faith, take it out!
Teacher	It is better for you to enter the Kingdom of God with only one eye than to keep both eyes and be thrown into hell.
Isaiah	There 'the worms that eat them never die, and the fire that burns them is never put out.'
Teacher	Everyone will be purified by fire as a sacrifice is purified by salt.
Readers 1 and 2	Salt is good;
Reader 3	But if it loses its saltiness, how can you make it salty again?
Teacher	Have the salt of friendship among yourselves, and live in peace with one another.

Cast	[This is] the word of the Lord.	OR	This is the Gospel of Christ / *This is the Gospel of the Lord.*
All	**Thanks be to God.**		**Praise to Christ our Lord** / *Praise to you, Lord Jesus Christ.*

Cast: **Teacher, Reader 1, Reader 2, Reader 3, Isaiah.**

Jesus teaches about divorce
Mark 10.1–12

Narrator	Jesus went to the province of Judaea, and crossed the River Jordan. Crowds came flocking to him again, and he taught them, as he always did.
	Some Pharisees came to him and tried to trap him:
Pharisee	Tell us, does our Law allow a man to divorce his wife?
Narrator	Jesus answered with a question:
Jesus	What law did Moses give you?
Pharisee	Moses gave permission for a man to write a divorce notice and send his wife away.
Jesus	Moses wrote this law for you because you are so hard to teach. But in the beginning, at the time of creation, 'God made them male and female,' as the scripture says. 'And for this reason a man will leave his father and mother and unite with his wife, and the two will become one.' So they are no longer two, but one. Man must not separate, then, what God has joined together.
Narrator	When they went back into the house, the disciples asked Jesus about this matter. He said to them:
Jesus	A man who divorces his wife and marries another woman commits adultery against his wife. In the same way, a woman who divorces her husband and marries another man commits adultery.

Cast	[This is] the word of the Lord.	OR	This is the Gospel of Christ / *This is the Gospel of the Lord.*
All	**Thanks be to God.**		**Praise to Christ our Lord** / *Praise to you, Lord Jesus Christ.*

Cast: **Narrator, Pharisee, Jesus.**

Jesus blesses little children
Mark 10.[1], 13–16

Narrator   Jesus crossed the river Jordan. Crowds came flocking to him again, and he taught them, as he always did.

Some people brought children to Jesus for him to place his hands on them, but the disciples scolded the people. When Jesus noticed this, he was angry and said to his disciples:

Jesus   Let the children come to me, and do not stop them, because the Kingdom of God belongs to such as these. I assure you that whoever does not receive the Kingdom of God like a child will never enter it.

Narrator   Then he took the children in his arms, placed his hands on each of them, and blessed them.

Cast	[This is] the word of the Lord.	OR	This is the Gospel of Christ / *This is the Gospel of the Lord.*
All	**Thanks be to God.**		**Praise to Christ our Lord** / *Praise to you, Lord Jesus Christ.*

Cast: **Narrator, Jesus.**

The rich man
Mark 10.17–31

Narrator   As Jesus was starting on his way again, a man ran up and knelt before him.

Man   Good Teacher, what must I do to receive eternal life?

[Narrator   Jesus asked him:]

Jesus   Why do you call me good? No one is good except God alone. You know the commandments: 'Do not commit murder; do not commit adultery; do not steal; do not accuse anyone falsely; do not cheat; respect your father and your mother.'

Man   Teacher, ever since I was young, I have obeyed all these commandments.

Narrator   Jesus looked straight at him with love:

Jesus   You need only one thing. Go and sell all you have and give the money to the poor, and you will have riches in heaven; then come and follow me.

Narrator   When the man heard this, gloom spread over his face, and he went away sad, because he was very rich. (PAUSE)

Jesus looked round at his disciples:

Jesus   How hard it will be for rich people to enter the Kingdom of God!

Narrator	The disciples were shocked at these words [but Jesus went on to say:]
Jesus	My children, how hard it is to enter the Kingdom of God! It is much harder for a rich person to enter the Kingdom of God than for a camel to go through the eye of a needle.
Narrator	At this the disciples were completely amazed [and asked one another]:
Disciple (aside)	Who, then, can be saved?
Narrator	Jesus looked straight at them and answered:
Jesus	This is impossible for man, but not for God; everything is possible for God.
Narrator	Then Peter spoke up:
Peter	Look, we have left everything and followed you.
Jesus	Yes, and I tell you that anyone who leaves home or brothers or sisters or mother or father or children or fields for me and for the gospel, will receive much more in this present age. He will receive a hundred times more houses, brothers, sisters, mothers, children and fields—and persecutions as well; and in the age to come he will receive eternal life. But many who now are first will be last, and many who now are last will be first.

Cast [This is] the word of the Lord.   OR   This is the Gospel of Christ / *This is the Gospel of the Lord.*
All   **Thanks be to God.**   **Praise to Christ our Lord** / *Praise to you, Lord Jesus Christ.*

Cast: **Narrator, Man, Jesus, Disciple, Peter.**

Jesus speaks about his death
Mark 10.32–34

Narrator	Jesus and his disciples were now on the road going up to Jerusalem. Jesus was going ahead of the disciples, who were filled with alarm; the people who followed behind were afraid. Once again Jesus took the twelve disciples aside and spoke of the things that were going to happen to him:
Jesus	Listen, we are going up to Jerusalem where the Son of Man will be handed over to the chief priests and the teachers of the Law. They will condemn him to death and then hand him over to the Gentiles, who will mock him, spit on him, whip him, and kill him; but three days later he will rise to life.

Cast [This is] the word of the Lord.   OR   This is the Gospel of Christ / *This is the Gospel of the Lord.*
All   **Thanks be to God.**   **Praise to Christ our Lord** / *Praise to you, Lord Jesus Christ.*

Cast: **Narrator, Jesus.**

99

The request of James and John
Mark 10.35–45

Narrator	James and John, the sons of Zebedee, came to Jesus. [They said:]
James	Teacher, we want you to do for us whatever we ask.
[Narrator	Jesus asked:]
Jesus	What do you want me to do for you?
John	Let one of us sit at your right and the other at your left in your glory.
Jesus	You don't know what you are asking. Can you drink the cup I drink or be baptized with the baptism I am baptized with?
James and **John**	We can.
Jesus	You will drink the cup I drink and be baptized with the baptism I am baptized with, but to sit at my right or left is not for me to grant. These places belong to those for whom they have been prepared.
Narrator	When the ten heard about this, they became indignant with James and John. Jesus called them together:
Jesus	You know that those who are regarded as rulers of the Gentiles lord it over them, and their high officials exercise authority over them. Not so with you. Instead, whoever wants to become great among you must be your servant, and whoever wants to be first must be slave of all. For even the Son of Man did not come to be served, but to serve, and to give his life as a ransom for many.

Cast [This is] the word of the Lord. OR This is the Gospel of Christ / *This is the Gospel of the Lord.*
All **Thanks be to God.** **Praise to Christ our Lord** / *Praise to you, Lord Jesus Christ.*

Cast: **Narrator, James, Jesus, John.**

Jesus heals blind Bartimaeus
Mark 10.46–52

Narrator	They came to Jericho, and as Jesus was leaving with his disciples and a large crowd, a blind beggar named Bartimaeus son of Timaeus was sitting by the road. When he heard that it was Jesus of Nazareth, he began to shout:
Bartimaeus	Jesus! Son of David! Take pity on me!
Narrator	Many of the people scolded him and told him to be quiet. But he shouted even more loudly:
Bartimaeus	Son of David, take pity on me!
Narrator	Jesus stopped.
Jesus	Call him.
Narrator	So they called the blind man:

Person 1	Cheer up!
Person 2	Get up, he is calling you.
Narrator	He threw off his cloak, jumped up, and came to Jesus. [Jesus asked him:]
Jesus	What do you want me to do for you?
Bartimaeus	Teacher, I want to see again.
Jesus	Go, your faith has made you well.
Narrator	At once he was able to see and followed Jesus on the road.

Cast	[This is] the word of the Lord. OR	This is the Gospel of Christ / *This is the Gospel of the Lord.*
All	**Thanks be to God.**	**Praise to Christ our Lord** / *Praise to you, Lord Jesus Christ.*

Cast: **Narrator, Bartimaeus, Jesus, Person 1, Person 2** (can be the same as Person 1).

The triumphant entry into Jerusalem
From Mark 11.1–11

Narrator	As they approached Jerusalem, near the towns of Bethphage and Bethany, they came to the Mount of Olives. Jesus sent two of his disciples on ahead with these instructions:
Jesus	Go to the village there ahead of you. As soon as you get there, you will find a colt tied up that has never been ridden. Untie it and bring it here. And if someone asks you why you are doing that, tell him that the Master needs it and will send it back at once.
Narrator	So they went and found a colt out in the street, tied to the door of a house. As they were untying it, some of the bystanders asked them:
Bystanders 1 and 2	What are you doing—
Bystander 1	Untying that colt?
Narrator	They answered just as Jesus had told them, and the men let them go. They brought the colt to Jesus, threw their cloaks over the animal, and Jesus got on. Many people spread their cloaks on the road, while others cut branches in the fields and spread them on the road. The people who were in front and those who followed behind began to shout:
Persons 1 and 2	Praise God!
Person 1	God bless him who comes in the name of the Lord!
Person 2	God bless the coming kingdom of King David, our father!
Persons 1 and 2	Praise God!
Narrator	Jesus entered Jerusalem, went into the Temple, and looked round at everything. But since it was already late in the day, he went out to Bethany with the twelve disciples.

Cast	[This is] the word of the Lord. OR	This is the Gospel of Christ / *This is the Gospel of the Lord.*
All	**Thanks be to God.**	**Praise to Christ our Lord** / *Praise to you, Lord Jesus Christ.*

Cast: **Narrator, Jesus, Bystander 1, Bystander 2** (can be the same as Bystander 1), **Person 1, Person 2** (can be the same as Bystander 2).

Jesus and the fig-tree
Mark 11.12–14, 20–26

Narrator The next day, as they were coming back from Bethany, Jesus was hungry. He saw in the distance a fig-tree covered with leaves, so he went to see if he could find any figs on it. But when he came to it, he found only leaves, because it was not the right time for figs. Jesus said to the fig-tree:

Jesus No one shall ever eat figs from you again!

Narrator And his disciples heard him. (PAUSE)

Early next morning, as they walked along the road, they saw the fig-tree. It was dead all the way down to its roots. Peter remembered what had happened:

Peter Look, Teacher, the fig-tree you cursed has died!

Jesus Have faith in God. I assure you that whoever tells this hill to get up and throw itself in the sea and does not doubt in his heart, but believes that what he says will happen, it will be done for him. For this reason I tell you: When you pray and ask for something, believe that you have received it, and you will be given whatever you ask for. And when you stand and pray, forgive anything you may have against anyone, so that your Father in heaven will forgive the wrongs you have done.

Cast [This is] the word of the Lord.　　OR　　This is the Gospel of Christ / *This is the Gospel of the Lord.*
All　　**Thanks be to God.**　　　　　　　　　　**Praise to Christ our Lord** / *Praise to you, Lord Jesus Christ.*

Cast: **Narrator, Jesus, Peter.**

Jesus goes to the Temple
Mark 11.15–19, 27–33

Narrator When they arrived in Jerusalem, Jesus went to the Temple and began to drive out all those who were buying and selling. He overturned the tables of the money-changers and the stools of those who sold pigeons, and he would not let anyone carry anything through the temple courtyards. He then taught the people:

Jesus It is written in the Scriptures that God said, 'My Temple will be called a house of prayer for the people of all nations.' But you have turned it into a hideout for thieves!

Narrator The chief priests and the teachers of the Law heard of this, so they began looking for some way to kill Jesus. They were afraid of him, because the whole crowd was amazed at his teaching.

When evening came, Jesus and his disciples left the city. (PAUSE)

Next morning they arrived once again in Jerusalem. As Jesus was walking in the Temple, the chief priests, the teachers of the Law, and the elders came to him and asked him:

Lawyer 1   What right have you to do these things?

Lawyer 2   Who gave you this right?

Jesus   I will ask you just one question, and if you give me an answer, I will tell you what right I have to do these things. Tell me, where did John's right to baptize come from: was it from God or from man?

Narrator   They started to argue among themselves:

Lawyer 1   What shall we say?

Lawyer 2   If we answer, 'From God,' he will say, 'Why, then, did you not believe John?'

Lawyer 1   But if we say, 'From man . . .'

Narrator   They were afraid of the people, because everyone was convinced that John had been a prophet. So their answer to Jesus was:

Lawyer 1   We don't know.

Jesus (firmly)   Neither will I tell you, then, by what right I do these things.

Cast	[This is] the word of the Lord. OR	This is the Gospel of Christ / *This is the Gospel of the Lord.*
All	**Thanks be to God.**	**Praise to Christ our Lord** / *Praise to you, Lord Jesus Christ.*

Cast: **Narrator, Jesus, Lawyer 1, Lawyer 2.**

The parable of the tenants in the vineyard
Mark 12.1–12

Narrator   Jesus spoke to them in parables:

Jesus   Once there was a man who planted a vineyard, put a fence round it, dug a hole for the winepress, and built a watch-tower. Then he let out the vineyard to tenants and left home on a journey. When the time came to gather the grapes, he sent a slave to the tenants to receive from them his share of the harvest. The tenants seized the slave, beat him, and sent him back without a thing. Then the owner sent another slave; the tenants beat him over the head and treated him shamefully. The owner sent another slave, and they killed him; and they treated many others the same way, beating some and killing others. The only one left to send was the man's own dear son. Last of all, then, he sent his son to the tenants. He said:

Owner   I am sure they will respect my son.

Jesus   But those tenants said to one another:

Tenant 1   This is the owner's son.

Tenant 2	Come on, let's kill him, and his property will be ours!
Jesus	So they seized the son and killed him and threw his body out of the vineyard.
[Narrator	Jesus asked:]
Jesus	What, then, will the owner of the vineyard do? He will come and kill those men and hand the vineyard over to other tenants. Surely you have read this scripture?
Psalmist	The stone which the builders rejected as worthless turned out to be the most important of all. This was done by the Lord; what a wonderful sight it is!
Narrator	The Jewish leaders tried to arrest Jesus, because they knew that he had told this parable against *them*. But they were afraid of the crowd, so they left him and went away.

Cast	[This is] the word of the Lord.	OR	This is the Gospel of Christ / *This is the Gospel of the Lord.*
All	**Thanks be to God.**		**Praise to Christ our Lord** / *Praise to you, Lord Jesus Christ.*

Cast: **Narrator, Jesus, Owner, Tenant 1, Tenant 2, Psalmist.**

The question about paying taxes
Mark 12.13–17

Narrator	Some Pharisees and some members of Herod's party were sent to Jesus to trap him with questions. [They came to him and said:]
Herodian	Teacher, we know that you tell the truth, without worrying about what people think.
Pharisee	You pay no attention to a man's status, but teach the truth about God's will for man.
Herodian	Tell us, is it against our Law to pay taxes to the Roman Emperor?
Pharisee	Should we pay them or not?
Narrator	But Jesus saw through their trick.
Jesus	Why are you trying to trap me? Bring a silver coin, and let me see it.
Narrator	They brought him one. (PAUSE)
Jesus	Whose face and name are these?
Pharisee and **Herodian**	The Emperor's.
Jesus	Well, then, pay the Emperor what belongs to the Emperor, and pay God what belongs to God.
Narrator	And they were amazed at Jesus.

Cast	[This is] the word of the Lord.	OR	This is the Gospel of Christ / *This is the Gospel of the Lord.*
All	**Thanks be to God.**		**Praise to Christ our Lord** / *Praise to you, Lord Jesus Christ.*

Cast: **Narrator, Herodian, Pharisee, Jesus.**

The question about rising from death
Mark 12.18–27

Narrator	Some Sadducees, who say that people will not rise from death, came to Jesus:
Sadducee 1	Teacher, Moses wrote this law for us:
Sadducee 2	If a man dies and leaves a wife but no children, that man's brother must marry the widow so that they can have children who will be considered the dead man's children.
Sadducee 1	Once there were seven brothers; the eldest got married and died without having children.
Sadducee 2	Then the second one married the woman, and he also died without having children.
Sadducee 1	The same thing happened to the third brother, and then to the rest.
Sadducee 2	All seven brothers married the woman and died without having children.
Sadducee 1	Last of all, the woman died.
Sadducee 2	Now, when all the dead rise to life on the day of resurrection, whose wife will she be? All seven of them had married her.
Narrator	Jesus answered them:
Jesus	How wrong you are! And do you know why? It is because you don't know the Scriptures or God's power. For when the dead rise to life, they will be like the angels in heaven and will not marry. Now, as for the dead being raised: haven't you ever read in the Book of Moses the passage about the burning bush? There it is written that God said to Moses, 'I am the God of Abraham, the God of Isaac, and the God of Jacob.' He is the God of the living, not of the dead. You are completely wrong!

Cast	[This is] the word of the Lord.　　OR	This is the Gospel of Christ / *This is the Gospel of the Lord.*
All	**Thanks be to God.**	**Praise to Christ our Lord** / *Praise to you, Lord Jesus Christ.*

Cast: **Narrator, Sadducee 1, Sadducee 2** (can be the same as Sadducee 1), **Jesus.**

The great commandment
Mark 12.28–34

Narrator	A teacher of the Law was there who heard the discussion. He saw that Jesus had given the Sadducees a good answer, so he came to him with a question:
Lawyer	Which commandment is the most important of all?
[Narrator	Jesus replied:]

Jesus	The most important one is this, 'Listen, Israel! The Lord our God is the only Lord. Love the Lord your God with all your heart, with all your soul, with all your mind, and with all your strength.' The second most important commandment is this: 'Love your neighbour as you love yourself.' There is no other commandment more important than these two.
Lawyer	Well done, Teacher! It is true, as you say, that only the Lord is God and that there is no other god but he. And man must love God with all his heart and with all his mind and with all his strength; and he must love his neighbour as he loves himself. It is more important to obey these two commandments than to offer animals and other sacrifices to God.
Narrator	Jesus noticed how wise his answer was, and so he told him:
Jesus	You are not far from the Kingdom of God.
Narrator	After this nobody dared to ask Jesus any more questions.

Cast [This is] the word of the Lord.   OR   This is the Gospel of Christ / *This is the Gospel of the Lord.*
All   **Thanks be to God.**   **Praise to Christ our Lord** / *Praise to you, Lord Jesus Christ.*

Cast: **Narrator, Lawyer, Jesus.**

Jesus teaches in the Temple
Mark 12.35–40

Narrator	As Jesus was teaching in the Temple, he asked the question:
Jesus	How can the teachers of the Law say that the Messiah will be the descendant of David? The Holy Spirit inspired David to say:
David	The Lord said to my Lord: Sit here on my right until I put your enemies under your feet.
Jesus	David himself called him 'Lord'; so how can the Messiah be David's descendant?
Narrator	A large crowd was listening to Jesus gladly. As he taught them, he said:
Jesus	Watch out for the teachers of the Law, who like to walk around in their long robes and be greeted with respect in the market-place, who choose the reserved seats in the synagogues and the best places at feasts. They take advantage of widows and rob them of their homes, and then make a show of saying long prayers. Their punishment will be all the worse!

Cast [This is] the word of the Lord.   OR   This is the Gospel of Christ / *This is the Gospel of the Lord.*
All   **Thanks be to God.**   **Praise to Christ our Lord** / *Praise to you, Lord Jesus Christ.*

Cast: **Narrator, Jesus, David** (can be the same as Jesus).

The widow's offering
Mark 12.41–44

Narrator   As Jesus sat near the Temple treasury, he watched the people as they dropped in their money. Many rich men dropped in a lot of money; then a poor widow came along and dropped in two little copper coins, worth about a penny. He called his disciples together.

Jesus   I tell you that this poor widow put more in the offering box than all the others. For the others put in what they had to spare of their riches; but she, poor as she is, put in all she had—she gave all she had to live on.

Cast   [This is] the word of the Lord.   OR   This is the Gospel of Christ / *This is the Gospel of the Lord.*
All   **Thanks be to God.**   **Praise to Christ our Lord** / *Praise to you, Lord Jesus Christ.*

Cast: **Narrator, Jesus.**

Jesus speaks of troubles
Mark 13.1–13

Narrator   As Jesus was leaving the Temple, one of his disciples said:

Disciple   Look, Teacher! What wonderful stones and buildings!

[Narrator   Jesus answered:]

Jesus   You see these great buildings? Not a single stone here will be left in its place; every one of them will be thrown down. (PAUSE)

Narrator   Jesus was sitting on the Mount of Olives, across from the Temple, when Peter, James, John, and Andrew came to him in private:

Disciple   Tell us when this will be, and tell us what will happen to show that the time has come for all these things to take place.

Jesus   Be on guard, and don't let anyone deceive you. Many men, claiming to speak for me, will come and say, 'I am he!' and they will deceive many people. And don't be troubled when you hear the noise of battles close by and news of battles far away. Such things must happen, but they do not mean that the end has come. Countries will fight each other; kingdoms will attack one another. There will be earthquakes everywhere, and there will be famines. These things are like the first pains of childbirth.

You yourselves must be on guard. You will be arrested and taken to court. You will be beaten in the synagogues; you will stand before rulers and kings for my sake to tell them the Good News. But before the end comes, the gospel must be preached to all peoples. And when you are arrested and taken to court, do not worry beforehand about what you are going to say; when the time comes, say whatever is then given to you. For the words you speak will not be yours; they will come from the Holy Spirit. Men will hand over their own brothers to be put to death, and fathers will do the same to their children. Children will turn against their parents and have them put to death. Everyone will hate you because of me. But whoever holds out to the end will be saved.

Cast	[This is] the word of the Lord.	OR	This is the Gospel of Christ / *This is the Gospel of the Lord.*
All	**Thanks be to God.**		**Praise to Christ our Lord** / *Praise to you, Lord Jesus Christ.*

Cast: **Narrator, Disciple, Jesus.**

Jesus speaks of the Awful Horror
Mark 13.14–23

Jesus You will see 'The Awful Horror' standing in the place where he should not be.

Narrator [Note to the reader:] be sure to understand what this means!

Jesus Then those who are in Judaea must run away to the hills. A man who is on the roof of his house must not lose time by going down into the house to get anything to take with him. A man who is in the field must not go back to the house for his cloak. How terrible it will be in those days for women who are pregnant and for mothers with little babies! Pray to God that these things will not happen in the winter! For the trouble of those days will be far worse than any the world has ever known from the very beginning when God created the world until the present time. Nor will there ever be anything like it again. But the Lord has reduced the number of those days; if he had not, nobody would survive. For the sake of his chosen people, however, he has reduced those days.

Then, if anyone says to you:

Person 1 Look, here is the Messiah!

Jesus Or,

Person 2 Look, there he is!

Jesus Do not believe him. For false Messiahs and false prophets will appear. They will perform miracles and wonders in order to deceive even God's chosen people, if possible. Be on your guard! I have told you everything before the time comes.

Cast	[This is] the word of the Lord.	OR	This is the Gospel of Christ / *This is the Gospel of the Lord.*
All	**Thanks be to God.**		**Praise to Christ our Lord** / *Praise to you, Lord Jesus Christ.*

Cast: **Jesus, Narrator, Person 1, Person 2.**

Jesus' warnings about the end
Mark 13.24–37

Teacher 1 In the days after that time of trouble the sun will grow dark, the moon will no longer shine, the stars will fall from heaven, and the powers in space will be driven from their courses. Then the Son of Man will appear, coming in the clouds with great power and glory. He will send the angels out to the four corners of the earth to gather God's chosen people from one end of the world to the other.

Teacher 2   Let the fig-tree teach you a lesson. When its branches become green and tender and it starts putting out leaves, you know that summer is near. In the same way, when you see these things happening, you will know that the time is near, ready to begin. Remember that all these things will happen before the people now living have all died. Heaven and earth will pass away, but my words will never pass away.

Teacher 1   No one knows, however, when that day or hour will come—neither the angels in heaven, nor the Son; only the Father knows. Be on watch, be alert, for you do not know when the time will come.

Teacher 2   It will be like a man who goes away from home on a journey and leaves his servants in charge, after giving to each one his own work to do and after telling the doorkeeper to keep watch. Be on guard, then, because you do not know when the master of the house is coming—it might be in the evening or at midnight or before dawn or at sunrise. If he comes suddenly, he must not find you asleep.

[Teacher 1   What I say to you, then, I say to all:]

Teachers 1 and **2**   Watch!

Cast   [This is] the word of the Lord.   OR   This is the Gospel of Christ / *This is the Gospel of the Lord.*
All   **Thanks be to God.**   **Praise to Christ our Lord** / *Praise to you, Lord Jesus Christ.*

Cast: **Teacher 1, Teacher 2.**

Jesus in danger
Mark 14.1–11

The plot against Jesus (Mark 14.1–2)

Narrator   It was now two days before the Festival of Passover and Unleavened Bread. The chief priests and the teachers of the Law were looking for a way to arrest Jesus secretly and put him to death:

Priest   We must not do it during the festival.

Lawyer   The people might riot.

Jesus is anointed at Bethany (Mark 14.3–9)

Narrator   Jesus was in Bethany at the house of Simon, a man who had suffered from a dreaded skin-disease. While Jesus was eating, a woman came in with an alabaster jar full of very expensive perfume made of pure nard. She broke the jar and poured the perfume on Jesus' head. Some of the people there became angry:

Person 1   What was the use of wasting the perfume?

Person 2	It could have been sold for more than three hundred silver coins and the money given to the poor!
Narrator	And they criticized her harshly. But Jesus said:
Jesus	Leave her alone! Why are you bothering her? She has done a fine and beautiful thing for me. You will always have poor people with you, and any time you want to, you can help them. But you will not always have me. She did what she could; she poured perfume on my body to prepare it ahead of time for burial. Now, I assure you that wherever the gospel is preached all over the world, what she has done will be told in memory of her.

Judas agrees to betray Jesus (Mark 14.10–11)

Narrator	Then Judas Iscariot, one of the twelve disciples, went off to the chief priests in order to betray Jesus to them. They were pleased to hear what he had to say, and promised to give him money. So Judas started looking for a good chance to hand Jesus over to them.

Cast	[This is] the word of the Lord. OR	This is the Gospel of Christ / *This is the Gospel of the Lord.*
All	**Thanks be to God.**	**Praise to Christ our Lord** / *Praise to you, Lord Jesus Christ.*

Cast: **Narrator, Priest, Lawyer** (can be the same as Priest), **Person 1, Person 2** (can be the same as Person 1), **Jesus.**

Jesus eats the Passover meal
Mark 14.12–21

Narrator	On the first day of the Festival of Unleavened Bread, the day the lambs for the Passover meal were killed, Jesus' disciples asked him:
Disciple	Where do you want us to go and get the Passover meal ready for you?
Narrator	Then Jesus sent two of them with these instructions:
Jesus	Go into the city, and a man carrying a jar of water will meet you. Follow him to the house he enters, and say to the owner of the house: 'The Teacher says, Where is the room where my disciples and I will eat the Passover meal?' Then he will show you a large upstairs room, prepared and furnished, where you will get everything ready for us.
Narrator	The disciples left, went to the city, and found everything just as Jesus had told them; and they prepared the Passover meal. (PAUSE) When it was evening, Jesus came with the twelve disciples. While they were at the table eating, Jesus said:
Jesus	I tell you that one of you will betray me—one who is eating with me.
Narrator	The disciples were upset and began to ask him, one after the other:

Disciple	Surely you don't mean me, do you?
Jesus	It will be one of you twelve, one who dips his bread in the dish with me. The Son of Man will die as the Scriptures say he will; but how terrible for that man who betrays the Son of Man! It would have been better for that man if he had never been born!

Cast	[This is] the word of the Lord.	OR	This is the Gospel of Christ / *This is the Gospel of the Lord.*
All	**Thanks be to God.**		**Praise to Christ our Lord** / *Praise to you, Lord Jesus Christ.*

Cast: **Narrator, Disciple, Jesus.**

The Lord's Supper
Mark 14.22–26 (GNB)

Narrator	While they were eating, Jesus took a piece of bread, gave a prayer of thanks, broke it, and gave it to his disciples. [He said:]
Jesus	Take it, this is my body.
Narrator	Then he took a cup, gave thanks to God, and handed it to them; and they all drank from it. [Jesus said:]
Jesus	This is my blood which is poured out for many, my blood which seals God's covenant. I tell you, I will never again drink this wine until the day I drink the new wine in the Kingdom of God.
Narrator	Then they sang a hymn and went out to the Mount of Olives.

Cast	[This is] the word of the Lord.	OR	This is the Gospel of Christ / *This is the Gospel of the Lord.*
All	**Thanks be to God.**		**Praise to Christ our Lord** / *Praise to you, Lord Jesus Christ.*

Cast: **Narrator, Jesus.**

The Lord's Supper
Mark 14.22–26 (NIV)

Narrator	While they were eating, Jesus took bread, gave thanks and broke it, and gave it to his disciples [saying]:
Jesus	Take it; this is my body.
Narrator	Then he took a cup, gave thanks and offered it to them, and they all drank from it. [He said:]
Jesus	This is my blood of the covenant, which is poured out for many. I tell you the truth, I will not drink again of the fruit of the vine until that day when I drink it anew in the kingdom of God.
Narrator	When they had sung a hymn, they went out to the Mount of Olives.

Cast	[This is] the word of the Lord.	OR	This is the Gospel of Christ / *This is the Gospel of the Lord.*
All	**Thanks be to God.**		**Praise to Christ our Lord** / *Praise to you, Lord Jesus Christ.*

Cast: **Narrator, Jesus.**

Jesus predicts Peter's denial
Mark 14.27–31

Narrator	Jesus said to them:
Jesus	All of you will run away and leave me, for the scripture says, 'God will kill the shepherd, and the sheep will all be scattered.' But after I am raised to life, I will go to Galilee ahead of you.
Narrator	Peter answered:
Peter	I will never leave you, even though all the rest do!
Jesus (to Peter)	I tell you that before the cock crows twice tonight, you will say three times that you do not know me.
Peter (insistently)	I will never say that, even if I have to die with you!
Narrator	And all the other disciples said the same thing.

Cast	[This is] the word of the Lord. OR	This is the Gospel of Christ / *This is the Gospel of the Lord.*
All	**Thanks be to God.**	**Praise to Christ our Lord** / *Praise to you, Lord Jesus Christ.*

Cast: **Narrator, Jesus, Peter.**

Jesus prays in the garden of Gethsemane
Mark 14.32–42

Narrator	They came to a place called Gethsemane, and Jesus said to his disciples:
Jesus	Sit here while I pray.
Narrator	He took Peter, James, and John with him. Distress and anguish came over him:
Jesus	The sorrow in my heart is so great that it almost crushes me. Stay here and keep watch.
Narrator	He went a little farther on, threw himself on the ground, and prayed that, if possible, he might not have to go through that time of suffering:
Jesus	Father, my Father! All things are possible for you. Take this cup of suffering away from me. (PAUSE) Yet not what I want, but what you want.
Narrator	Then he returned and found the three disciples asleep. He said to Peter:
Jesus	Simon, are you asleep? Weren't you able to stay awake even for one hour?
[Narrator	And he said to them:]
Jesus (looking round)	Keep watch, and pray that you will not fall into temptation. The spirit is willing, but the flesh is weak.
Narrator	He went away once more and prayed, saying the same words.

112

(PAUSE)Then he came back to the disciples and found them asleep; they could not keep their eyes open. And they did not know what to say to him. (PAUSE) When he came back the third time . . . [he said to them:]

Jesus   Are you still sleeping and resting? Enough! The hour has come! Look, the Son of Man is now being handed over to the power of sinful men. Get up, let us go. Look, here is the man who is betraying me!

Cast   [This is] the word of the Lord.   OR   This is the Gospel of Christ / *This is the Gospel of the Lord.*
All   **Thanks be to God.**   **Praise to Christ our Lord** / *Praise to you, Lord Jesus Christ.*

Cast: **Narrator, Jesus.**

The arrest of Jesus
Mark 14.43–52

Narrator   Jesus was still speaking when Judas, one of the twelve disciples, arrived. With him was a crowd armed with swords and clubs, and sent by the chief priests, the teachers of the Law, and the elders. The traitor had given the crowd a signal:

Judas   The man I kiss is the one you want. Arrest him and take him away under guard.

Narrator   As soon as Judas arrived, he went up to Jesus . . .

Judas   Teacher!

Narrator   . . . and kissed him. So they arrested Jesus and held him tight. But one of those standing there drew his sword and struck at the High Priest's slave, cutting off his ear. Then Jesus spoke up:

Jesus   Did you have to come with swords and clubs to capture me, as though I were an outlaw? Day after day I was with you teaching in the Temple, and you did not arrest me. But the Scriptures must come true.

Narrator   Then all the disciples left him and ran away. (PAUSE)

A certain young man, dressed only in a linen cloth, was following Jesus. They tried to arrest him, but he ran away naked, leaving the cloth behind.

Cast   [This is] the word of the Lord.   OR   This is the Gospel of Christ / *This is the Gospel of the Lord.*
All   **Thanks be to God.**   **Praise to Christ our Lord** / *Praise to you, Lord Jesus Christ.*

Cast: **Narrator, Judas, Jesus.**

Jesus before the Council
Mark 14.53–65

Narrator   Jesus was taken to the High Priest's house, where all the chief priests, the elders, and the teachers of the Law were gathering. Peter followed from a distance and went into the

→

113

courtyard of the High Priest's house. There he sat down with the guards, keeping himself warm by the fire. The chief priests and the whole Council tried to find some evidence against Jesus in order to put him to death, but they could not find any. Many witnesses told lies against Jesus, but their stories did not agree.

Then some men stood up and told this lie against Jesus:

Man   We heard him say, 'I will tear down this Temple which men have made, and after three days I will build one that is not made by men.'

Narrator   Not even they, however, could make their stories agree.

The High Priest stood up in front of them all and questioned Jesus:

High Priest   Have you no answer to the accusation they bring against you?

Narrator   But Jesus kept quiet and would not say a word. Again the High Priest questioned him:

High Priest   Are you the Messiah, the Son of the Blessed God?

[Narrator   Jesus answered:]

Jesus   I am, and you will all see the Son of Man seated on the right of the Almighty and coming with the clouds of heaven!

Narrator   The High Priest tore his robes:

High Priest   We don't need any more witnesses! You heard his blasphemy. What is your decision?

Narrator   They all voted against him: he was guilty and should be put to death.

Some of them began to spit on Jesus, and they blindfolded him and hit him [They said]:

Man   Guess who hit you!

Narrator   And the guards took him and slapped him.

Cast   [This is] the word of the Lord.   OR   This is the Gospel of Christ / *This is the Gospel of the Lord.*
All   **Thanks be to God.**   **Praise to Christ our Lord** / *Praise to you, Lord Jesus Christ.*

Cast: **Narrator, Man, High Priest, Jesus.**

Peter denies Jesus
Mark 14.66–72

Narrator   Peter was still down in the courtyard when one of the High Priest's servant-girls came by. When she saw Peter warming himself, she looked straight at him [and said]:

Girl   You, too, were with Jesus of Nazareth.

Peter
(denying)   I don't know . . . I don't understand what you are talking about.

114

Narrator	And he went out into the passage. Just then a cock crowed. (PAUSE)
	The servant-girl saw him there and began to repeat to the bystanders:
Girl	He is one of them!
Narrator	But Peter denied it again. (PAUSE)
	A little while later the bystanders accused Peter again:
Bystander	You can't deny that you are one of them, because you, too, are from Galilee.
Peter	I swear that I am telling the truth! May God punish me if I am not! I do not know the man you are talking about!
Narrator	Just then a cock crowed a second time, and Peter remembered how Jesus had said to him, 'Before the cock crows twice, you will say three times that you do not know me.' And he broke down and cried.

Cast	[This is] the word of the Lord.	OR	This is the Gospel of Christ / *This is the Gospel of the Lord.*
All	**Thanks be to God.**		**Praise to Christ our Lord** / *Praise to you, Lord Jesus Christ.*

Cast: **Narrator, Girl, Peter, Bystander.**

Jesus is brought before Pilate
Mark 15.1–15

Narrator	Early in the morning the chief priests met hurriedly with the elders, the teachers of the Law, and the whole Council, and made their plans. They put Jesus in chains, led him away, and handed him over to Pilate. Pilate questioned him:
Pilate	Are you the king of the Jews?
[Narrator	Jesus answered:]
Jesus	So you say.
Narrator	The chief priests were accusing Jesus of many things, so Pilate questioned him again:
Pilate	Aren't you going to answer? Listen to all their accusations!
Narrator	Again Jesus refused to say a word, and Pilate was amazed. (PAUSE)
	At every Passover Festival Pilate was in the habit of setting free any one prisoner the people asked for. At that time a man named Barabbas was in prison with the rebels who had committed murder in the riot. When the crowd gathered and began to ask Pilate for the usual favour, he asked them:
Pilate (calling)	Do you want me to set free for you the king of the Jews?
Narrator	He knew very well that the chief priests had handed Jesus over to him because they were jealous.

→

115

But the chief priests stirred up the crowd to ask, instead, for Pilate to set Barabbas free for them. Pilate spoke again to the crowd:

Pilate   What, then, do you want me to do with the one you call the king of the Jews?

[Narrator   They shouted back:]

Crowd   Crucify him!

Pilate   But what crime has he committed?

[Narrator   They shouted all the louder:]

Crowd   Crucify him!

Narrator   Pilate wanted to please the crowd, so he set Barabbas free for them. Then he had Jesus whipped and handed him over to be crucified.

Cast   [This is] the word of the Lord.   OR   This is the Gospel of Christ / *This is the Gospel of the Lord.*
All   **Thanks be to God.**   **Praise to Christ our Lord** / *Praise to you, Lord Jesus Christ.*

Cast: **Narrator, Pilate, Jesus, Crowd** (two or more persons).

Jesus is crucified
From Mark 15.16–32

Narrator   The soldiers took Jesus inside to the courtyard of the governor's palace and called together the rest of the company. They put a purple robe on Jesus, made a crown out of thorny branches, and put it on his head. Then they began to salute him:

Soldier(s)   Long live the King of the Jews!

Narrator   They beat him over the head with a stick, spat on him, fell on their knees, and bowed down to him. When they had finished mocking him, they took off the purple robe and put his own clothes back on him. Then they led him out to crucify him. (PAUSE)

On the way they met a man named Simon, who was coming into the city from the country, and the soldiers forced him to carry Jesus' cross. (Simon was from Cyrene and was the father of Alexander and Rufus.) They took Jesus to a place called Golgotha, which means 'The Place of the Skull'. There they tried to give him wine mixed with a drug called myrrh, but Jesus would not drink it. Then they crucified him and divided his clothes among themselves, throwing dice to see who would get which piece of clothing. It was nine o'clock in the morning when they crucified him. The notice of the accusation against him said:

Voice of Pilate
(slowly)   The King of the Jews.

Narrator	They also crucified two bandits with Jesus, one on his right and the other on his left.
	People passing by shook their heads and hurled insults at Jesus:
Persons 1 and **2**	Aha!
Person 1	You were going to tear down the Temple and build it up again in three days!
Person 2	Now come down from the cross and save yourself!
Narrator	In the same way the chief priests and the teachers of the Law jeered at Jesus, saying to each other:
Lawyer 1	He saved others, but he cannot save himself!
Lawyer 2	Let us see the Messiah, the king of Israel, come down from the cross now, and we will believe in him!
Narrator	And the two who were crucified with Jesus insulted him also.

Cast	[This is] the word of the Lord.	OR	This is the Gospel of Christ / *This is the Gospel of the Lord.*
All	**Thanks be to God.**		**Praise to Christ our Lord** / *Praise to you, Lord Jesus Christ.*

Cast: **Narrator, Soldier(s)** (one or more persons – can be supplemented by Lawyers 1 and 2), **Voice of Pilate, Person 1, Person 2, Lawyer 1, Lawyer 2.**

The death of Jesus
Mark 15.33–39

Narrator	At noon the whole country was covered with darkness, which lasted for three hours. At three o'clock Jesus cried out with a loud shout:
Jesus	Eloi, Eloi, lema sabachthani?
Narrator	Which means: My God, my God, why did you abandon me? Some of the people there heard him [and said:]
Person 1	Listen, he is calling for Elijah!
Narrator	One of them ran up with a sponge, soaked it in cheap wine, and put it on the end of a stick. Then he held it up to Jesus' lips [and said]:
Person 2	Wait! Let us see if Elijah is coming to bring him down from the cross! (PAUSE)
Narrator	With a loud cry Jesus died. (PAUSE)
	The curtain hanging in the Temple was torn in two, from top to bottom. The army officer who was standing there in front of the cross saw how Jesus had died. [He said:]
Officer	This man was really the Son of God!

Cast	[This is] the word of the Lord.	OR	This is the Gospel of Christ / *This is the Gospel of the Lord.*
All	**Thanks be to God.**		**Praise to Christ our Lord** / *Praise to you, Lord Jesus Christ.*

Cast: **Narrator, Jesus, Person 1, Person 2, Officer.**

The people round Jesus—his burial
Mark 15.40–47

Narrator 1	Some women were there, looking on from a distance. Among them were Mary Magdalene, Mary the mother of the younger James and of Joseph, and Salome. They had followed Jesus while he was in Galilee and had helped him. Many other women who had come to Jerusalem with him were there also.
Narrator 2	It was towards evening when Joseph of Arimathea arrived. He was a respected member of the Council, who was waiting for the coming of the Kingdom of God. It was Preparation day—
Commentator	That is, the day before the Sabbath.
Narrator 2	So Joseph went boldly into the presence of Pilate and asked him for the body of Jesus. Pilate was surprised to hear that Jesus was already dead. He called the army officer and asked him if Jesus had been dead a long time. After hearing the officer's report, Pilate told Joseph he could have the body. Joseph bought a linen sheet, took the body down, wrapped it in the sheet, and placed it in a tomb which had been dug out of solid rock. Then he rolled a large stone across the entrance to the tomb.
Narrator 1	Mary Magdalene and Mary the mother of Joseph were watching and saw where the body of Jesus was placed.

Cast   [This is] the word of the Lord.   OR   This is the Gospel of Christ / *This is the Gospel of the Lord.*
All   **Thanks be to God.**   **Praise to Christ our Lord** / *Praise to you, Lord Jesus Christ.*

Cast: **Narrator 1, Narrator 2, Commentator** (can be the same as Narrator 1).

The Resurrection
Mark 16.1–8

Narrator	After the Sabbath was over, Mary Magdalene, Mary the mother of James, and Salome bought spices to go and anoint the body of Jesus. Very early on Sunday morning, at sunrise, they went to the tomb. On the way they said to one another:
Mary	Who will roll away the stone for us from the entrance to the tomb?
Narrator	It was a very large stone. (PAUSE) Then they looked up and saw that the stone had already been rolled back. So they entered the tomb, where they saw a young man sitting on the right, wearing a white robe—and they were alarmed. He said:
Young man	Don't be alarmed. I know you are looking for Jesus of Nazareth, who was crucified. He is not here—he has been raised! Look, here is the place where they put him. (PAUSE) Now go and give this message to his disciples, including Peter: 'He is going to Galilee ahead of you; there you will see him, just as he told you.'
Narrator	So they went out and ran from the tomb, distressed and terrified. They said nothing to anyone, because they were afraid.

Cast   [This is] the word of the Lord.   OR   This is the Gospel of Christ / *This is the Gospel of the Lord.*
All   **Thanks be to God.**   **Praise to Christ our Lord** / *Praise to you, Lord Jesus Christ.*

Cast: **Narrator, Mary, Young man.**

Jesus appears to his disciples and is taken up to heaven
Mark 16.9–20

Narrator 1	After Jesus rose from death early on Sunday, he appeared first to Mary Magdalene, from whom he had driven out seven demons. She went and told his companions. They were mourning and crying; and when they heard her say that Jesus was alive and that she had seen him, they did not believe her.
Narrator 2	After this, Jesus appeared in a different manner to two of them while they were on their way to the country. They returned and told the others, but they would not believe it.
Narrator 1	Last of all, Jesus appeared to the eleven disciples as they were eating. He scolded them, because they did not have faith and because they were too stubborn to believe those who had seen him alive. He said to them:
Jesus	Go throughout the whole world and preach the gospel to all mankind. Whoever believes and is baptized will be saved; whoever does not believe will be condemned. Believers will be given the power to perform miracles: they will drive out demons in my name; they will speak in strange tongues; if they pick up snakes or drink any poison, they will not be harmed; they will place their hands on sick people, who will get well.
Narrator 2	After the Lord Jesus had talked with them, he was taken up to heaven and sat at the right side of God. The disciples went and preached everywhere, and the Lord worked with them and proved that their preaching was true by the miracles that were performed.

Cast	[This is] the word of the Lord.	OR	This is the Gospel of Christ / *This is the Gospel of the Lord.*
All	**Thanks be to God.**		**Praise to Christ our Lord** / *Praise to you, Lord Jesus Christ.*

Cast: **Narrator 1, Narrator 2, Jesus.**

THE GOSPEL OF
LUKE

The birth of John the Baptist is announced
Luke 1.5–25

Narrator 1	During the time when Herod was king of Judaea, there was a priest named Zechariah, who belonged to the priestly order of Abijah. His wife's name was Elizabeth; she also belonged to a priestly family.
Narrator 2	They both lived good lives in God's sight and obeyed fully all the Lord's laws and commands. They had no children because Elizabeth could not have any, and she and Zechariah were both very old. (PAUSE)
Narrator 1	One day Zechariah was doing his work as a priest in the Temple, taking his turn in the daily service.
Narrator 2	According to the custom followed by the priests, he was chosen by lot to burn incense on the altar.
Narrator 1	So he went into the Temple of the Lord, while the crowd of people outside prayed during the hour when the incense was burnt. An angel of the Lord appeared to him, standing on the right of the altar where the incense was burnt. When Zechariah saw him, he was alarmed and felt afraid. But the angel said to him:
Angel	Don't be afraid, Zechariah! God has heard your prayer, and your wife Elizabeth will bear you a son. You are to name him John. How glad and happy you will be, and how happy many others will be when he is born! He will be a great man in the Lord's sight. He must not drink any wine or strong drink. From his very birth he will be filled with the Holy Spirit, and he will bring back many of the people of Israel to the Lord their God. He will go ahead of the Lord, strong and mighty like the prophet Elijah. He will bring fathers and children together again; he will turn disobedient people back to the way of thinking of the righteous; he will get the Lord's people ready for him.
Narrator 1	Zechariah said to the angel:
Zechariah	How shall I know if this is so? I am an old man, and my wife is old also.
Angel	I am Gabriel. I stand in the presence of God, who sent me to speak to you and tell you this good news. But you have not believed my message, which will come true at the right time. Because you have not believed, you will be unable to speak; you will remain silent until the day my promise to you comes true.
Narrator 2	In the meantime the people were waiting for Zechariah and wondering why he was spending such a long time in the Temple.

Narrator 1	When he came out, he could not speak to them, and so they knew that he had seen a vision in the Temple. Unable to say a word, he made signs to them with his hands.
Narrator 2	When his period of service in the Temple was over, Zechariah went back home. Some time later his wife Elizabeth became pregnant and did not leave the house for five months. She said:
Elizabeth	Now at last the Lord has helped me. He has taken away my public disgrace!

Cast	[This is] the word of the Lord.	OR	This is the Gospel of Christ / *This is the Gospel of the Lord.*
All	**Thanks be to God.**		**Praise to Christ our Lord** / *Praise to you, Lord Jesus Christ.*

Cast: **Narrator 1, Narrator 2, Angel, Zechariah, Elizabeth.**

The birth of Jesus is announced to Mary
Luke 1.26–38

Narrator	In the sixth month, God sent the angel Gabriel to Nazareth, a town in Galilee, to a virgin pledged to be married to a man named Joseph, a descendant of David. The virgin's name was Mary. The angel went to her [and said]:
Angel	Greetings, you who are highly favoured! The Lord is with you.
Narrator	Mary was greatly troubled at his words and wondered what kind of greeting this might be. [But the angel said to her:]
Angel	Do not be afraid, Mary, you have found favour with God. You will be with child and give birth to a son, and you are to give him the name Jesus. He will be great and will be called the Son of the Most High. The Lord God will give him the throne of his father David, and he will reign over the house of Jacob for ever; his kingdom will never end.
[Narrator	Mary asked the angel:]
Mary	How will this be, since I am a virgin?
Angel	The Holy Spirit will come upon you, and the power of the Most High will overshadow you. So the holy one to be born will be called the Son of God.

[Even Elizabeth your relative is going to have a child in her old age, and she who was said to be barren is in sixth month. For nothing is impossible with God.] |
[Narrator	Mary answered:]
Mary	I am the Lord's servant. May it be to me as you have said.
Narrator	Then the angel left her.

Cast	[This is] the word of the Lord.	OR	This is the Gospel of Christ / *This is the Gospel of the Lord.*
All	**Thanks be to God.**		**Praise to Christ our Lord** / *Praise to you, Lord Jesus Christ.*

Cast: **Narrator, Angel, Mary.** (See also Appendix: Christmas Readings, page 405.)

Mary visits Elizabeth
Luke 1.39–56

Narrator Mary got ready and hurried off to a town in the hill-country of Judaea. She went into Zechariah's house and greeted Elizabeth. When Elizabeth heard Mary's greeting, the baby moved within her. Elizabeth was filled with the Holy Spirit [and said in a loud voice]:

Elizabeth You are the most blessed of all women, and blessed is the child you
(delighted) will bear! Why should this great thing happen to me, that my Lord's mother comes to visit me? For as soon as I heard your greeting, the baby within me jumped with gladness. How happy you are to believe that the Lord's message to you will come true!

Narrator Mary said:

Mary My heart praises the Lord;
my soul is glad because of God my Saviour,
for he has remembered me, his lowly servant!
From now on all people will call me happy,
because of the great things the Mighty God has done for me.
His name is holy;
from one generation to another
he shows mercy to those who honour him.
He has stretched out his mighty arm
and scattered the proud with all their plans.
He has brought down mighty kings from their thrones,
and lifted up the lowly.
He has filled the hungry with good things,
and sent the rich away with empty hands.
He has kept the promise he made to our ancestors,
and has come to the help of his servant Israel.
He has remembered to show mercy to Abraham
and to all his descendants for ever!

[Narrator Mary stayed about three months with Elizabeth and then went back home.]

Cast [This is] the word of the Lord. OR This is the Gospel of Christ / *This is the Gospel of the Lord.*
All **Thanks be to God.** **Praise to Christ our Lord** / *Praise to you, Lord Jesus Christ.*

Cast: **Narrator, Elizabeth, Mary.** (See also Appendix: Christmas Readings, page 406.)

The birth of John the Baptist
Luke 1.57–80

Narrator The time came for Elizabeth to have her baby, and she gave birth to a son. Her neighbours and relatives heard how wonderfully good the Lord had been to her, and they all rejoiced with her. (PAUSE)

When the baby was a week old, they came to circumcise him, and they were going to name him Zechariah, after his father. But his mother said:

Elizabeth	No! His name is to be John.
[Narrator	They said to her:]
Relative	But you have no relatives with that name!
Narrator	Then they made signs to his father, asking him what name he would like the boy to have. Zechariah asked for a writing tablet and wrote:
Zechariah*	His name is John.
Narrator	How surprised they all were! At that moment Zechariah was able to speak again, and he started praising God. The neighbours were all filled with fear, and the news about these things spread through all the hill-country of Judaea. Everyone who heard of it thought about it and asked:
Relative	What is this child going to be?
Narrator	For it was plain that the Lord's power was upon him. John's father Zechariah was filled with the Holy Spirit, and he spoke God's message:
Zechariah	Let us praise the Lord, the God of Israel! He has come to the help of his people and has set them free. He has provided for us a mighty Saviour, a descendant of his servant David. He promised through his holy prophets long ago that he would save us from our enemies, from the power of all those who hate us. He said he would show mercy to our ancestors and remember his sacred covenant. With a solemn oath to our ancestor Abraham he promised to rescue us from our enemies and allow us to serve him without fear, so that we might be holy and righteous before him all the days of our life. You, my child, will be called a prophet of the Most High God. You will go ahead of the Lord to prepare his road for him, to tell his people that they will be saved by having their sins forgiven. Our God is merciful and tender. He will cause the bright dawn of salvation to rise on us and to shine from heaven on all those who live in the dark shadow of death, to guide our steps into the path of peace.
Narrator	The child grew and developed in body and spirit. He lived in the desert until the day when he appeared publicly to the people of Israel.

Cast	[This is] the word of the Lord. OR	This is the Gospel of Christ / *This is the Gospel of the Lord.*
All	**Thanks be to God.**	**Praise to Christ our Lord** / *Praise to you, Lord Jesus Christ.*

Cast: **Narrator, Elizabeth, Relative, Zechariah** (*At this point it is better if Zechariah does not speak, but holds up a previously written placard with the words 'His name is John').

The birth of Jesus
Luke 2.1–7

Narrator   The Emperor Augustus ordered a census to be taken throughout the Roman Empire.

Commentator   When this first census took place, Quirinius was the governor of Syria.

Narrator   Everyone, then, went to register himself, each to his own town.

Joseph went from the town of Nazareth in Galilee to the town of Bethlehem in Judaea, the birthplace of King David.

Commentator   Joseph went there because he was a descendant of David.

Narrator   He went to register with Mary, who was promised in marriage to him. She was pregnant, and while they were in Bethlehem, the time came for her to have her baby. She gave birth to her first son, wrapped him in strips of cloth and laid him in a manger— there was no room for them to stay in the inn.

Cast [This is] the word of the Lord. OR	This is the Gospel of Christ / *This is the Gospel of the Lord.*
All **Thanks be to God.**	**Praise to Christ our Lord** / *Praise to you, Lord Jesus Christ.*

Cast: **Narrator, Commentator.** (See also Appendix: Christmas Readings, page 407.)

The angels announce the birth of Jesus
Luke 2.8–14

Narrator   There were shepherds living out in the fields near Bethlehem, keeping watch over their flocks at night. An angel of the Lord appeared to them, and the glory of the Lord shone around them, and they were terrified. But the angel said to them:

Angel   Do not be afraid. I bring you good news of great joy that will be for all the people. Today in the town of David a Saviour has been born to you; he is Christ the Lord. This will be a sign to you: You will find a baby wrapped in cloths and lying in a manger.

Narrator   Suddenly a great company of the heavenly host appeared with the angel, praising God.

Chorus   Glory to God in the highest
(joyfully)   and on earth peace to all on whom his favour rests.

Cast [This is] the word of the Lord. OR	This is the Gospel of Christ / *This is the Gospel of the Lord.*
All **Thanks be to God.**	**Praise to Christ our Lord** / *Praise to you, Lord Jesus Christ.*

Cast: **Narrator, Angel, Chorus** (three or more, including Angel). (See also Appendix: Christmas Readings, page 408.)

The shepherds find the baby
Luke 2.15–20

Narrator   When the angels had left them and gone into heaven, the shepherds said to one another:

Shepherd 1   Let's go to Bethlehem—

Shepherd 2   And see this thing that has happened—

Shepherd 3   Which the Lord has told us about.

Narrator   So they hurried off and found Mary and Joseph, and the baby, who was lying in the manger. When they had seen him, they spread the word concerning what had been told them about this child, and all who heard it were amazed at what the shepherds said to them. (PAUSE) But Mary treasured up all these things and pondered them in her heart. The shepherds returned, glorifying and praising God for all the things they had heard and seen, which were just as they had been told.

Cast	[This is] the word of the Lord. OR This is the Gospel of Christ / *This is the Gospel of the Lord.*
All	**Thanks be to God.** **Praise to Christ our Lord** / *Praise to you, Lord Jesus Christ.*

Cast: **Narrator, Shepherd 1, Shepherd 2, Shepherd 3** (can be the same as Shepherd 1 and/or Shepherd 2). (See also Appendix: Christmas Readings, page 408.)

Jesus is presented in the Temple
Luke 2.22–38

Narrator   The time came for Joseph and Mary to perform the ceremony of purification, as the Law of Moses commanded. So they took the child to Jerusalem to present him to the Lord, as it is written in the law of the Lord:

Lawyer   Every first-born male is to be dedicated to the Lord.

Narrator   They also went to offer a sacrifice of a pair of doves or two young pigeons, as required by the law of the Lord. (PAUSE)

At that time there was a man named Simeon living in Jerusalem. He was a good, God-fearing man and was waiting for Israel to be saved. The Holy Spirit was with him and had assured him that he would not die before he had seen the Lord's promised Messiah. Led by the Spirit, Simeon went into the Temple. When the parents brought the child Jesus into the Temple to do for him what the Law required, Simeon took the child in his arms and gave thanks to God:

Simeon   Now, Lord, you have kept your promise,
and you may let your servant go in peace.
With my own eyes I have seen your salvation,
which you have prepared in the presence of all peoples:
A light to reveal your will to the Gentiles
and bring glory to your people Israel.

Narrator	The child's father and mother were amazed at the things Simeon said about him. Simeon blessed them and said to Mary, his mother:
Simeon	This child is chosen by God for the destruction and the salvation of many in Israel. He will be a sign from God which many people will speak against and so reveal their secret thoughts. And sorrow, like a sharp sword, will break your own heart.
Narrator	There was a very old prophetess, a widow named Anna, daughter of Phanuel of the tribe of Asher. She had been married for only seven years and was now eighty-four years old. She never left the Temple; day and night she worshipped God, fasting and praying. That very same hour she arrived and gave thanks to God and spoke about the child to all who were waiting for God to set Jerusalem free.

Cast	[This is] the word of the Lord. OR	This is the Gospel of Christ / *This is the Gospel of the Lord.*
All	**Thanks be to God.**	**Praise to Christ our Lord** / *Praise to you, Lord Jesus Christ.*

Cast: **Narrator, Lawyer, Simeon.** (See also Appendix: Christmas Readings, page 410.)

Jesus as a boy
From Luke 2.39–52

Narrator	When Joseph and Mary had finished doing all that was required by the law of the Lord, they returned to their home town of Nazareth in Galilee. The child Jesus grew and became strong; he was full of wisdom, and God's blessings were upon him. (PAUSE)
	Every year the parents of Jesus went to Jerusalem for the Passover Festival. When Jesus was twelve years old, they went to the festival as usual. When the festival was over, they started back home, but the boy Jesus stayed in Jerusalem. His parents did not know this; they thought that he was with the group, so they travelled a whole day and then started looking for him among their relatives and friends. They did not find him, so they went back to Jerusalem looking for him. On the third day they found him in the Temple, sitting with the Jewish teachers, listening to them and asking questions. All who heard him were amazed at his intelligent answers. His parents were astonished when they saw him, and his mother said to him:
Mary	My son, why have you done this to us? Your father and I have been terribly worried trying to find you.
[Narrator	He answered them:]
Jesus	Why did you have to look for me? Didn't you know that I had to be in my Father's house?
Narrator	But they did not understand his answer. So Jesus went back with them to Nazareth, where he was obedient to them. His mother treasured all these things in her heart. Jesus grew both in body and in wisdom, gaining favour with God and men.

Cast	[This is] the word of the Lord. OR	This is the Gospel of Christ / *This is the Gospel of the Lord.*
All	**Thanks be to God.**	**Praise to Christ our Lord** / *Praise to you, Lord Jesus Christ.*

Cast: **Narrator, Mary, Jesus** (as a boy).

The preaching of John the Baptist
Luke 3.1–14

Narrator [It was the fifteenth year of the rule of the Emperor Tiberius; Pontius Pilate was governor of Judaea, Herod was ruler of Galilee, and his brother Philip was ruler of the territory of Iturea and Trachonitis; Lysanias was ruler of Abilene, and Annas and Caiaphas were high priests. At that time] the word of God came to John son of Zechariah in the desert. So John went throughout the whole territory of the River Jordan, preaching:

John Turn away from your sins and be baptized, and God will forgive your sins. As it is written in the book of the prophet Isaiah:

Isaiah Someone is shouting in the desert:
'Get the road ready for the Lord;
make a straight path for him to travel!
Every valley must be filled up,
every hill and mountain levelled off.
The winding roads must be made straight,
and the rough paths made smooth.
All mankind will see God's salvation!'

Narrator Crowds of people came out to John to be baptized by him. He said to them:

John You snakes! Who told you that you could escape from the punishment God is about to send? Do those things that will show that you have turned from your sins. And don't start saying among yourselves that Abraham is your ancestor. I tell you that God can take these stones and make descendants for Abraham! The axe is ready to cut down the trees at the roots; every tree that does not bear good fruit will be cut down and thrown in the fire.

Narrator The people asked him:

Person What are we to do, then?

John Whoever has two shirts must give one to the one who has none, and whoever has food must share it.

Narrator Some tax collectors came to be baptized, and they asked him:

Tax collector Teacher, what are we to do?

John Don't collect more than is legal.

Narrator Some soldiers also asked him:

Soldier What about us? What are we to do?

John Don't take money from anyone by force or accuse anyone falsely. Be content with your pay.

Cast [This is] the word of the Lord.   OR   This is the Gospel of Christ / *This is the Gospel of the Lord.*
All **Thanks be to God.**   **Praise to Christ our Lord** / *Praise to you, Lord Jesus Christ.*

Cast: **Narrator, John, Isaiah, Person, Tax collector, Soldier.**

John the Baptist and the baptism of Jesus
Luke 3.15–22

Narrator People's hopes began to rise, and they began to wonder whether John perhaps might be the Messiah. So John said to all of them:

John I baptize you with water, but someone is coming who is much greater than I am. I am not good enough even to untie his sandals. He will baptize you with the Holy Spirit and fire. He has his winnowing shovel with him, to thresh out all the grain and gather the wheat into his barn; but he will burn the chaff in a fire that never goes out.

Narrator In many different ways John preached the Good News to the people and urged them to change their ways. But John reprimanded Herod, the governor, because he had married Herodias, his brother's wife, and had done many other evil things. Then Herod did an even worse thing by putting John in prison. (PAUSE)

After all the people had been baptized, Jesus also was baptized. While he was praying, heaven was opened, and the Holy Spirit came down upon him in bodily form like a dove. And a voice came from heaven:

Voice You are my own dear Son. I am pleased with you.

Cast [This is] the word of the Lord. OR This is the Gospel of Christ / *This is the Gospel of the Lord.*
All **Thanks be to God.** **Praise to Christ our Lord** / *Praise to you, Lord Jesus Christ.*

Cast: **Narrator, John, Voice** (from a distance).

The temptation of Jesus
Luke 4.1–15

Narrator Jesus returned from the Jordan full of the Holy Spirit and was led by the Spirit into the desert, where he was tempted by the Devil for forty days. In all that time he ate nothing, so that he was hungry when it was over. The Devil said to him:

Devil If you are God's Son, order this stone to turn into bread.

[Narrator But Jesus answered:]

Jesus The scripture says, 'Man cannot live on bread alone.'

Narrator Then the Devil took him up and showed him in a second all the kingdoms of the world.

Devil I will give you all this power and all this wealth. It has all been handed over to me, and I can give it to anyone I choose. All this will be yours, then, if you worship me.

Jesus The scripture says, 'Worship the Lord your God and serve only him!'

Narrator Then the Devil took him to Jerusalem and set him on the highest point of the Temple.

Devil	If you are God's Son, throw yourself down from here. For the scripture says: 'God will order his angels to take good care of you.'
	It also says: 'They will hold you up with their hands so that not even your feet will be hurt on the stones.'
Jesus	The scripture says: 'Do not put the Lord your God to the test.'
Narrator	When the Devil finished tempting Jesus in every way, he left him for a while.
	Then Jesus returned to Galilee, and the power of the Holy Spirit was with him. The news about him spread throughout all that territory. He taught in the synagogues and was praised by everyone.

Cast	[This is] the word of the Lord.	OR This is the Gospel of Christ / *This is the Gospel of the Lord.*
All	**Thanks be to God.**	**Praise to Christ our Lord** / *Praise to you, Lord Jesus Christ.*

Cast: **Narrator, Devil, Jesus.**

Jesus is rejected at Nazareth
Luke 4.16–30

Narrator	Jesus went to Nazareth, where he had been brought up, and on the Sabbath he went as usual to the synagogue. He stood up to read the Scriptures and was handed the book of the prophet Isaiah. He unrolled the scroll and found the place where it is written:
Jesus	The Spirit of the Lord is upon me, because he has chosen me to bring good news to the poor. He has sent me to proclaim liberty to the captives and recovery of sight to the blind; to set free the oppressed and announce that the time has come when the Lord will save his people.
Narrator	Jesus rolled up the scroll, gave it back to the attendant, and sat down. All the people in the synagogue had their eyes fixed on him.
Jesus	This passage of scripture has come true today, as you heard it being read.
Narrator	They were all well impressed with him and marvelled at the eloquent words that he spoke.
Worshipper	Isn't he the son of Joseph?
Jesus	I am sure that you will quote this proverb to me, 'Doctor, heal yourself.' You will also tell me to do here in my home town the same things you heard were done in Capernaum. I tell you this, a prophet is never welcomed in his home town. (PAUSE)
	Listen to me: it is true that there were many widows in Israel during the time of Elijah, when there was no rain for three and a half years and a severe famine spread throughout the whole land.

→

Yet Elijah was not sent to anyone in Israel, but only to a widow living in Zarephath in the territory of Sidon. And there were many people suffering from a dreaded skin-disease who lived in Israel during the time of the prophet Elisha; yet not one of them was healed, but only Naaman the Syrian.

Narrator   When the people in the synagogue heard this, they were filled with anger. They rose up, dragged Jesus out of the town, and took him to the top of the hill on which their town was built. They meant to throw him over the cliff, but he walked through the middle of the crowd and went his way.

Cast	[This is] the word of the Lord. OR	This is the Gospel of Christ / *This is the Gospel of the Lord.*
All	**Thanks be to God.**	**Praise to Christ our Lord** / *Praise to you, Lord Jesus Christ.*

Cast: **Narrator, Jesus, Worshipper.**

A man with an evil spirit
Luke 4.31–37

Narrator   Jesus went to Capernaum, a town in Galilee, where he taught the people on the Sabbath. They were all amazed at the way he taught, because he spoke with authority. In the synagogue was a man who had the spirit of an evil demon in him; he screamed out in a loud voice:

Man (loudly)   Ah! What do you want with us, Jesus of Nazareth? Are you here to destroy us? I know who you are: you are God's holy messenger!

Narrator   Jesus ordered the spirit:

Jesus (firmly)   Be quiet and come out of the man!

Narrator   The demon threw the man down in front of them and went out of him without doing him any harm. The people were all amazed.

Person 1   What kind of words are these?

Person 2   With authority and power this man gives orders to the evil spirits.

Person 1   And they come out!

Narrator   And the report about Jesus spread everywhere in that region.

Cast	[This is] the word of the Lord. OR	This is the Gospel of Christ / *This is the Gospel of the Lord.*
All	**Thanks be to God.**	**Praise to Christ our Lord** / *Praise to you, Lord Jesus Christ.*

Cast: **Narrator, Man, Jesus, Person 1, Person 2.**

Jesus heals and preaches
Luke 4.38–44

Narrator   Jesus left the synagogue and went to Simon's house. Simon's mother-in-law was sick with a high fever, and they spoke to Jesus about her. He went and stood at her bedside and ordered the fever to leave her. The fever left her, and she got up at once and began to wait on them. After sunset all who had friends who were sick with various diseases brought them to Jesus; he placed his hands on every one of them and healed them all. Demons also went out from many people, screaming:

Demon   You are the Son of God!

Narrator   Jesus gave the demons an order and would not let them speak, because they knew that he was the Messiah. (PAUSE)

At daybreak Jesus left the town and went off to a lonely place. The people started looking for him, and when they found him, they tried to keep him from leaving. But he said to them:

Jesus   I must preach the Good News about the Kingdom of God in other towns also, because that is what God sent me to do.

Narrator   So he preached in the synagogues throughout the country.

Cast	[This is] the word of the Lord. OR	This is the Gospel of Christ / *This is the Gospel of the Lord.*
All	**Thanks be to God.**	**Praise to Christ our Lord** / *Praise to you, Lord Jesus Christ.*

Cast: **Narrator, Demon, Jesus.**

Jesus calls the first disciples
Luke 5.1–11

Narrator   One day Jesus was standing on the shore of Lake Gennesaret while the people pushed their way up to him to listen to the word of God. He saw two boats pulled up on the beach; the fishermen had left them and were washing the nets. Jesus got into one of the boats—it belonged to Simon—and asked him to push off a little from the shore. Jesus sat in the boat and taught the crowd. (PAUSE)

When he finished speaking, he said to Simon:

Jesus   Push the boat out further to the deep water, and you and your partners let down your nets for a catch.

[Narrator   Simon answered:]

Simon   Master, we worked hard all night long and caught nothing. But if you say so, I will let down the nets.

Narrator   They let them down and caught such a large number of fish that the nets were about to break. So they motioned to their partners in the other boat to come and help them. They came and filled both boats so full of fish that the boats were about to sink. When Simon Peter saw what had happened, he fell on his knees before Jesus.

Simon   Go away from me, Lord! I am a sinful man!

Narrator   He and the others with him were all amazed at the large number of fish they had caught. The same was true of Simon's partners, James and John, the sons of Zebedee. [Jesus said to Simon:]

Jesus (to Simon)   Don't be afraid; from now on you will be catching men.

Narrator   They pulled the boats up on the beach, left everything, and followed Jesus.

Cast	[This is] the word of the Lord.
All	**Thanks be to God.**

Cast: **Narrator, Jesus, Simon.**

The man with leprosy
Luke 5.12–16

Narrator	While Jesus was in one of the towns, a man came along who was covered with leprosy. When he saw Jesus, he fell with his face to the ground and begged him:
Man	Lord, if you are willing, you can make me clean.
Narrator	Jesus reached out his hand and touched the man [He said]:
Jesus	I *am* willing. Be clean!
Narrator	And immediately the leprosy left him. Then Jesus ordered him:
Jesus	Don't tell anyone, but go, show yourself to the priest and offer the sacrifices that Moses commanded for your cleansing, as a testimony to them.
Narrator	Yet the news about him spread all the more, so that crowds of people came to hear him and to be healed of their sicknesses. But Jesus often withdrew to lonely places and prayed.

Cast [This is] the word of the Lord.   OR   This is the Gospel of Christ / *This is the Gospel of the Lord.*
All   **Thanks be to God.**   **Praise to Christ our Lord** / *Praise to you, Lord Jesus Christ.*

Cast: **Narrator, Man, Jesus.**

Jesus heals a paralysed man
Luke 5.17–26

Narrator	One day when Jesus was teaching, some Pharisees and teachers of the Law were sitting there who had come from every town in Galilee and Judaea and from Jerusalem. The power of the Lord was present for Jesus to heal the sick. Some men came carrying a paralysed man on a bed, and they tried to take him into the house and put him in front of Jesus. Because of the crowd, however, they could find no way to take him in. So they carried him up on the roof, made an opening in the tiles, and let him down on his bed into the middle of the group in front of Jesus. When Jesus saw how much faith they had, he said to the man:
Jesus	Your sins are forgiven, my friend.
Narrator	The teachers of the Law and the Pharisees began to say to themselves:
Lawyer	Who is this man who speaks such blasphemy!
Pharisee	God is the only one who can forgive sins!
Narrator	Jesus knew their thoughts and said to them:

Jesus	Why do you think such things? Is it easier to say, 'Your sins are forgiven you,' or to say, 'Get up and walk'? I will prove to you, then, that the Son of Man has authority on earth to forgive sins.
Narrator	So he said to the paralysed man:
Jesus	I tell you, get up, pick up your bed, and go home!
Narrator	At once the man got up in front of them all, took the bed he had been lying on, and went home, praising God. They were all completely amazed! Full of fear, they praised God:
Person	What marvellous things we have seen today!

Cast	[This is] the word of the Lord.	OR	This is the Gospel of Christ / *This is the Gospel of the Lord.*
All	**Thanks be to God.**		**Praise to Christ our Lord** / *Praise to you, Lord Jesus Christ.*

Cast: **Narrator, Jesus, Lawyer, Pharisee** (can be the same as Lawyer), **Person.**

Jesus calls Levi
Luke 5.27–32

Narrator	Jesus went out and saw a tax collector named Levi, sitting in his office. [Jesus said to him:]
Jesus	Follow me.
Narrator	Levi got up, left everything, and followed him. (PAUSE) Then Levi had a big feast in his house for Jesus, and among the guests was a large number of tax collectors and other people. Some Pharisees and some teachers of the Law who belonged to their group complained to Jesus' disciples. [They asked:]
Pharisee	Why do you eat and drink with tax collectors and other outcasts?
[Narrator	Jesus answered them:]
Jesus	People who are well do not need a doctor, but only those who are sick. I have not come to call respectable people to repent, but outcasts.

Cast	[This is] the word of the Lord.	OR	This is the Gospel of Christ / *This is the Gospel of the Lord.*
All	**Thanks be to God.**		**Praise to Christ our Lord** / *Praise to you, Lord Jesus Christ.*

Cast: **Narrator, Jesus, Pharisee.** (Words in brackets may be omitted – especially if this reading is linked to the previous one so that the identity of Jesus is established.)

The question about fasting
Luke 5.33–39

Narrator	Some people said to Jesus:
Person 1	The disciples of John fast frequently and offer prayers.
Person 2	And the disciples of the Pharisees do the same.
Person 1	But your disciples eat and drink.

Jesus	Do you think you can make the guests at a wedding party go without food as long as the bridegroom is with them? Of course not! But the day will come when the bridegroom will be taken away from them, and then they will fast.
Narrator	Jesus also told them this parable:
Jesus	No one tears a piece off a new coat to patch up an old coat. If he does, he will have torn the new coat, and the piece of new cloth will not match the old. Nor does anyone pour new wine into used wineskins, because the new wine will burst the skins, the wine will pour out, and the skins will be ruined. Instead, new wine must be poured into fresh wineskins! And no one wants new wine after drinking old wine. 'The old is better,' he says.

Cast	[This is] the word of the Lord.	OR	This is the Gospel of Christ / *This is the Gospel of the Lord.*
All	**Thanks be to God.**		**Praise to Christ our Lord** / *Praise to you, Lord Jesus Christ.*

Cast: **Narrator, Person 1, Person 2** (can be the same as Person 1), **Jesus.**

The question about the Sabbath
Luke 6.1–11

Narrator	Jesus was walking through some cornfields on the Sabbath. His disciples began to pick the ears of corn, rub them in their hands, and eat the grain. Some Pharisees asked:
Pharisee	Why are you doing what our Law says you cannot do on the Sabbath?
[Narrator	Jesus answered them:]
Jesus	Haven't you read what David did when he and his men were hungry? He went into the house of God, took the bread offered to God, ate it, and gave it also to his men. Yet it is against our Law for anyone except the priests to eat that bread. The Son of Man is Lord of the Sabbath.
Narrator	On another Sabbath Jesus went into a synagogue and taught. A man was there whose right hand was paralysed. Some teachers of the Law and some Pharisees wanted a reason to accuse Jesus of doing wrong, so they watched him closely to see if he would heal on the Sabbath. But Jesus knew their thoughts and said to the man:
Jesus	Stand up and come here to the front.
Narrator	The man got up and stood there. Then Jesus said to them:
Jesus	I ask you: What does our Law allow us to do on the Sabbath? To help or to harm? To save a man's life or destroy it?
Narrator	He looked around at them all; then he said to the man:
Jesus	Stretch out your hand.
Narrator	He did so, and his hand became well again. They were filled with rage and began to discuss among themselves what they could do to Jesus.

Cast	[This is] the word of the Lord.	OR	This is the Gospel of Christ / *This is the Gospel of the Lord.*
All	**Thanks be to God.**		**Praise to Christ our Lord** / *Praise to you, Lord Jesus Christ.*

Cast: **Narrator, Pharisee, Jesus.**

Jesus chooses the twelve apostles
Luke 6.12–19

Narrator 1	Jesus went up a hill to pray and spent the whole night there praying to God. When day came, he called his disciples to him and chose twelve of them, whom he named apostles: Simon—
Narrator 2	whom he named Peter.
Narrator 1	And Andrew—
Narrator 2	his brother.
Narrator 1	James and John, Philip and Bartholomew, Matthew and Thomas, James—
Narrator 2	son of Alphaeus.
Narrator 1	And Simon—
Narrator 2	who was called the Patriot.
Narrator 1	Judas—
Narrator 2	son of James.
Narrator 1	And Judas Iscariot—
Narrator 2	who became the traitor.
Narrator 1	When Jesus had come down from the hill with the apostles, he stood on a level place with a large number of his disciples.
Narrator 2	A large crowd of people was there from all over Judaea and from Jerusalem and from the coastal cities of Tyre and Sidon.
Narrator 1	They had come to hear him and to be healed of their diseases.
Narrator 2	Those who were troubled by evil spirits also came and were healed.
Narrator 1	All the people tried to touch him, for power was going out from him and healing them all.

Cast	[This is] the word of the Lord.	OR	This is the Gospel of Christ / *This is the Gospel of the Lord.*
All	**Thanks be to God.**		**Praise to Christ our Lord** / *Praise to you, Lord Jesus Christ.*

Cast: **Narrator 1, Narrator 2.**

Happiness and sorrow
Luke 6.20–26

Narrator	Jesus looked at his disciples and said:
Jesus	Happy are you poor—
Students	The Kingdom of God is yours!
Jesus	Happy are you who are hungry now—

135

Students	You will be filled!
Jesus	Happy are you who weep now—
Students	You will laugh!
Jesus	Happy are you when people hate you, reject you, insult you, and say that you are evil, all because of the Son of Man! Be glad when that happens, and dance for joy, because a great reward is kept for you in heaven. For their ancestors did the very same things to the prophets. But how terrible for you who are rich now;
Students	You have had your easy life!
Jesus	How terrible for you who are full now—
Students	You will go hungry!
Jesus	How terrible for you who laugh now—
Students	You will mourn and weep!
Jesus	How terrible when all people speak well of you; their ancestors said the very same things about the false prophets.

Cast	[This is] the word of the Lord.	OR	This is the Gospel of Christ / *This is the Gospel of the Lord.*
All	**Thanks be to God.**		**Praise to Christ our Lord** / *Praise to you, Lord Jesus Christ.*

Cast: **Narrator, Jesus** (can be the same as Narrator)**, Students** (two or more – the dramatised reading reflects the classic rabbinic way of teaching and learning this form of instruction)**.**

Love for enemies
Luke 6.27–36

Jesus	I tell you who hear me: Love your enemies,
Students	Do good to those who hate you.
Jesus	Bless those who curse you—
Students	Pray for those who ill-treat you.
Jesus	If anyone hits you on one cheek—
Students	Let him hit the other one too.
Jesus	If someone takes your coat—
Students	Let him have your shirt as well.
Jesus	Give to everyone who asks you for something—
Students	And when someone takes what is yours, do not ask for it back.
Jesus	Do for others just what you want them to do for you. (PAUSE)
	If you love only the people who love you, why should you receive a blessing?
Students	Even sinners love those who love them!

Jesus	And if you do good only to those who do good to you, why should you receive a blessing?
Students	Even sinners do that!
Jesus	And if you lend only to those from whom you hope to get it back, why should you receive a blessing?
Students	Even sinners lend to sinners, to get back the same amount!
Jesus	No! Love your enemies—
Students	And do good to them.
Jesus	Lend—
Students	And expect nothing back.
Jesus	You will then have a great reward—
Students	And you will be sons of the Most High God.
Jesus	For he is good to the ungrateful and the wicked. Be merciful just as your Father is merciful.

Cast	[This is] the word of the Lord.	OR	This is the Gospel of Christ / *This is the Gospel of the Lord.*
All	**Thanks be to God.**		**Praise to Christ our Lord** / *Praise to you, Lord Jesus Christ.*

Cast: **Jesus, Students** (two or more—the dramatised reading reflects the classic rabbinic way of teaching and learning this form of instruction).

Judging others
Luke 6.37–42

Jesus	Do not judge others—
Students	And God will not judge you.
Jesus	Do not condemn others—
Students	And God will not condemn you.
Jesus	Forgive others—
Students	And God will forgive you.
Jesus	Give to others—
Students	And God will give to you.
Jesus	Indeed, you will receive a full measure, a generous helping, poured into your hands —all that you can hold. The measure you use for others is the one that God will use for you.
Narrator	And Jesus told them this parable:
Jesus	One blind man cannot lead another one; if he does, both will fall into a ditch. No pupil is greater than his teacher; but every pupil, when he has completed his training, will be like his teacher. (PAUSE)
	Why do you look at the speck in your brother's eye, but pay no attention to the log in your own eye? How can you say to your brother:

Voice	Please, brother, let me take that speck out of your eye!
Jesus	Yet you cannot even see the log in your own eye? You hypocrite! First take the log out of your own eye, and then you will be able to see clearly to take the speck out of your brother's eye.

Cast [This is] the word of the Lord.   OR   This is the Gospel of Christ / *This is the Gospel of the Lord.*
All **Thanks be to God.** **Praise to Christ our Lord** / *Praise to you, Lord Jesus Christ.*

Cast: **Jesus, Students** (two or more—the dramatised reading reflects the classic rabbinic way of teaching and learning this form of instruction), **Narrator** (can be the same as one of the Students), **Voice** (can be the same as one of the Students).

Jesus' analogy of a tree and its fruit
Luke 6.43–45

Reader 1	A healthy tree does not bear bad fruit.
Reader 2	Nor does a poor tree bear good fruit.
Reader 1	Every tree is known by the fruit it bears; you do not pick figs from thorn bushes.
Reader 2	Or gather grapes from bramble bushes.
Reader 1	A good person brings good out of the treasure of good things in his heart.
Reader 2	A bad person brings bad out of his treasure of bad things.
Readers 1 and **2**	For the mouth speaks what the heart is full of.

Cast [This is] the word of the Lord.   OR   This is the Gospel of Christ / *This is the Gospel of the Lord.*
All **Thanks be to God.** **Praise to Christ our Lord** / *Praise to you, Lord Jesus Christ.*

Cast: **Reader 1** (encouraging, happy voice), **Reader 2** (serious, warning voice).

The two house-builders
Luke 6.46–49

Narrator 1	Jesus said: Why do you call me:
Narrators 1 & **2**	Lord, Lord,
Narrator 1	And yet don't do what I tell you? Anyone who comes to me and listens to my words and obeys them—I will show you what he is like. He is like a man who, in building his house, dug deep and laid the foundation on rock. The river overflowed and hit that house but could not shake it, because it was well built.
Narrator 2	But anyone who hears my words and does not obey them is like a man who built his house without laying a foundation; when the flood hit that house it fell at once—and what a terrible crash that was!

Cast [This is] the word of the Lord.   OR   This is the Gospel of Christ / *This is the Gospel of the Lord.*
All **Thanks be to God.** **Praise to Christ our Lord** / *Praise to you, Lord Jesus Christ.*

Cast: **Narrator 1, Narrator 2.**

Jesus heals a Roman officer's servant
Luke 7.1–10

Narrator   Jesus went to Capernaum. A Roman officer there had a servant who was very dear to him; the man was sick and about to die. When the officer heard about Jesus, he sent some Jewish elders to ask him to come and heal his servant. They came to Jesus and begged him earnestly:

Elder 1   This man really deserves your help.

Elder 2   He loves our people and he himself built a synagogue for us.

Narrator   So Jesus went with them. He was not far from the house when the officer sent friends to tell him:

Friend   Sir, don't trouble yourself. I do not deserve to have you come into my house, neither do I consider myself worthy to come to you in person. Just give the order, and my servant will get well. I, too, am a man placed under the authority of superior officers, and I have soldiers under me. I order this one, 'Go!' and he goes; I order that one, 'Come!' and he comes; and I order my slave, 'Do this!' and he does it.

Narrator   Jesus was surprised when he heard this; he turned round and said to the crowd following him:

Jesus   I tell you, I have never found faith like this, not even in Israel!

Narrator   The messengers went back to the officer's house and found his servant well.

Cast [This is] the word of the Lord.   OR   This is the Gospel of Christ / *This is the Gospel of the Lord.*
All   **Thanks be to God.**   **Praise to Christ our Lord** / *Praise to you, Lord Jesus Christ.*

Cast: **Narrator, Elder 1, Elder 2** (can be the same as Elder 1)**, Friend, Jesus.**

Jesus raises a widow's son
Luke 7.11–17

Narrator   Jesus went to a town called Nain, accompanied by his disciples and a large crowd. Just as he arrived at the gate of the town, a funeral procession was coming out. The dead man was the only son of a woman who was a widow, and a large crowd from the town was with her. When the Lord saw her, his heart was filled with pity for her [and he said to her]:

Jesus   Don't cry.

Narrator   Then he walked over and touched the coffin, and the men carrying it stopped. [Jesus said:]

Jesus   Young man! Get up, I tell you!

Narrator   The dead man sat up and began to talk, and Jesus gave him back to his mother. They all were filled with fear and praised God:

Person 1	A great prophet has appeared among us!
Person 2	God has come to save his people!
Narrator	This news about Jesus went out through all the country and the surrounding territory.

| Cast | [This is] the word of the Lord.   OR | This is the Gospel of Christ / *This is the Gospel of the Lord.* |
| All | **Thanks be to God.** | **Praise to Christ our Lord** / *Praise to you, Lord Jesus Christ.* |

Cast: **Narrator, Jesus, Person 1, Person 2.**

The messengers from John the Baptist
Luke 7.18–35

Narrator	John the Baptist called two of his disciples and sent them to the Lord to ask him, 'Are you the one John said was going to come, or should we expect someone else?'
	When they came to Jesus, they said:
Disciple 1	John the Baptist sent us to ask if you are the one he said was going to come.
Disciple 2	Or if we should expect someone else?
Narrator	At that very time Jesus cured many people of their sicknesses, diseases, and evil spirits, and gave sight to many blind people. He answered John's messengers:
Jesus	Go back and tell John what you have seen and heard: the blind can see, the lame can walk, those who suffer from leprosy are made clean, the deaf can hear, the dead are raised to life, and the Good News is preached to the poor. How happy are those who have no doubts about me!
Narrator	After John's messengers had left, Jesus began to speak about him to the crowds:
Jesus	When you went out to John in the desert, what did you expect to see? A blade of grass bending in the wind? What did you go out to see? A man dressed up in fancy clothes? People who dress like that and live in luxury are found in palaces! Tell me, what did you go out to see? A prophet? Yes indeed, but you saw much more than a prophet. For John is the one of whom the scripture says:
Malachi	God said, I will send my messenger ahead of you to open the way for you.
Jesus	I tell you, John is greater than any man who has ever lived. But he who is least in the Kingdom of God is greater than John.
Narrator	All the people heard him; they and especially the tax collectors were the ones who had obeyed God's righteous demands and had been baptized by John. But the Pharisees and the teachers of the Law rejected God's purpose for themselves and refused to be baptized by John.

Jesus	Now to what can I compare the people of this day? What are they like? They are like children sitting in the market-place. One group shouts to the other:
Person 1	We played wedding music for you, but you wouldn't dance!
Person 2	We sang funeral songs, but you wouldn't cry!
Jesus	John the Baptist came, and he fasted and drank no wine, and you said:
Person 3	He has a demon in him!
Jesus	The Son of Man came, and he ate and drank, and you said:
Person 4	Look at this man! He is a glutton and a drinker, a friend of tax collectors and other outcasts!
Jesus	God's wisdom, however, is shown to be true by all who accept it.

Cast	[This is] the word of the Lord. OR This is the Gospel of Christ / *This is the Gospel of the Lord.*
All	**Thanks be to God.**	**Praise to Christ our Lord** / *Praise to you, Lord Jesus Christ.*

Cast: **Narrator, Disciple 1, Disciple 2** (can be the same as Disciple 1)**, Jesus, Malachi, Person 1, Person 2** (both preferably children)**, Person 3, Person 4.**

Jesus at the home of Simon the Pharisee
Luke 7.36–50

Narrator	A Pharisee invited Jesus to have dinner with him, and Jesus went to his house and sat down to eat. In that town was a woman who lived a sinful life. She heard that Jesus was eating in the Pharisee's house, so she brought an alabaster jar full of perfume and stood behind Jesus, by his feet, crying and wetting his feet with her tears. Then she dried his feet with her hair, kissed them, and poured the perfume on them. When the Pharisee saw this, he said to himself:
Simon	If this man really were a prophet, he would know who this woman is who is touching him; he would know what kind of sinful life she lives!
Narrator	Jesus spoke up and said to him:
Jesus	Simon, I have something to tell you.
Simon	Yes, Teacher, tell me.
Jesus	There were two men who owed money to a money-lender. One owed him five hundred silver coins, and the other owed him fifty. Neither of them could pay him back, so he cancelled the debts of both. Which one, then, will love him more?
Simon	I suppose that it would be the one who was forgiven more.
Jesus	You are right.
Narrator	Then he turned to the woman, and said to Simon:
Jesus (to Simon)	Do you see this woman? I came into your home, and you gave me no water for my feet, but she has washed my feet with her tears

→

and dried them with her hair. You did not welcome me with a kiss, but she has not stopped kissing my feet since I came. You provided no olive-oil for my head, but she has covered my feet with perfume. I tell you, then, the great love she has shown proves that her many sins have been forgiven. But whoever has been forgiven little shows only a little love.

Narrator   Then Jesus said to the woman:

Jesus   Your sins are forgiven.

Narrator   The others sitting at the table began to say to themselves:

Person 1   Who is this?

Person 2   He even forgives sins?

Narrator   But Jesus said to the woman:

Jesus   Your faith has saved you; go in peace.

Cast	[This is] the word of the Lord.	OR	This is the Gospel of Christ / *This is the Gospel of the Lord.*
All	**Thanks be to God.**		**Praise to Christ our Lord** / *Praise to you, Lord Jesus Christ.*

Cast: **Narrator, Simon** (the Pharisee)**, Jesus, Person 1, Person 2** (can be the same as Person 1).

The parable of the sower
Luke 8.4–15

Narrator   People kept coming to Jesus from one town after another; and when a great crowd gathered, Jesus told this parable:

Speaker 1   Once there was a man who went out to sow corn.

Speaker 2   As he scattered the seed in the field, some of it fell along the path, where it was stepped on, and the birds ate it up.

Speaker 1   Some of it fell on rocky ground, and when the plants sprouted, they dried up because the soil had no moisture.

Speaker 2   Some of the seed fell among thorn bushes, which grew up with the plants and choked them.

Speaker 1   And some seeds fell in good soil; the plants grew and produced corn, a hundred grains each.

Narrator   And Jesus concluded—'Listen, then, if you have ears!' His disciples asked Jesus what this parable meant, and he answered — The knowledge of the secrets of the Kingdom of God has been given to you, but to the rest it comes by means of parables, so that they may look but not see, and listen but not understand. This is what the parable means:

Speaker 2   The seed is the word of God.

Speaker 1   The seeds that fell along the path stand for those who hear; but the Devil comes and takes the message away from their hearts in order to keep them from believing and being saved.

Speaker 2	The seeds that fell on rocky ground stand for those who hear the message and receive it gladly. But it does not sink deep into them; they believe only for a while but when the time of testing comes, they fall away.
Speaker 1	The seeds that fell among thorn bushes stand for those who hear; but the worries and riches and pleasures of this life crowd in and choke them, and their fruit never ripens.
Speaker 2	The seeds that fell in good soil stand for those who hear the message and retain it in a good and obedient heart, and they persist until they bear fruit.

Cast	[This is] the word of the Lord.	OR	This is the Gospel of Christ / *This is the Gospel of the Lord.*
All	**Thanks be to God.**		**Praise to Christ our Lord** / *Praise to you, Lord Jesus Christ.*

Cast: **Narrator, Speaker 1, Speaker 2.** (See two quite different dramatisations of this parable at Matthew 13.1 and Mark 4.1.)

A lamp under a bowl
Luke 8.16–18

Speaker 1	No one lights a lamp and covers it with a bowl or puts it under a bed.
Speaker 2	Instead, he puts it on the lampstand, so that people will see the light as they come in.
Speaker 1	Whatever is hidden away will be brought out into the open.
Speaker 2	And whatever is covered up will be found and brought to light.
Speaker 1	Be careful, then, how you listen; because whoever has something will be given more.
Speaker 2	But whoever has nothing will have taken away from him even the little he thinks he has.

Cast	[This is] the word of the Lord.	OR	This is the Gospel of Christ / *This is the Gospel of the Lord.*
All	**Thanks be to God.**		**Praise to Christ our Lord** / *Praise to you, Lord Jesus Christ.*

Cast: **Speaker 1, Speaker 2.**

Jesus' mother and brothers
Luke 8.19–21

Narrator	Jesus' mother and brothers came to him, but were unable to join him because of the crowd. Someone said to Jesus:
Person	Your mother and brothers are standing outside and want to see you.
Narrator	Jesus said to them all:
Jesus	My mother and brothers are those who hear the word of God and obey it.

Cast	[This is] the word of the Lord.	OR	This is the Gospel of Christ / *This is the Gospel of the Lord.*
All	**Thanks be to God.**		**Praise to Christ our Lord** / *Praise to you, Lord Jesus Christ.*

Cast: **Narrator, Person, Jesus.**

Jesus calms a storm
Luke 8.22–25

Narrator	One day Jesus got into a boat with his disciples and said to them:
Jesus	Let us go across to the other side of the lake.
Narrator	So they started out. As they were sailing, Jesus fell asleep. Suddenly a strong wind blew down on the lake, and the boat began to fill with water, so that they were all in great danger. The disciples went to Jesus and woke him up [saying]:
Disciple 1 (calling)	Master, Master!
Disciple 2	We are about to die!
Narrator	Jesus got up and gave an order to the wind and the stormy water; they died down, and there was a great calm. Then he said to the disciples:
Jesus	Where is your faith?
Narrator	But they were amazed and afraid, and said to one another:
Disciple 1 (amazed)	Who is this man?
Disciple 2	He gives orders to the winds and waves, and they obey him!

Cast	[This is] the word of the Lord.	OR	This is the Gospel of Christ / *This is the Gospel of the Lord.*
All	**Thanks be to God.**		**Praise to Christ our Lord** / *Praise to you, Lord Jesus Christ.*

Cast: **Narrator, Jesus, Disciple 1, Disciple 2.**

Jesus heals a man with demons
Luke 8.26–39

Narrator	Jesus and his disciples sailed on over to the territory of Gerasa, which is across the lake from Galilee. As Jesus stepped ashore, he was met by a man from the town who had demons in him. For a long time this man had gone without clothes and would not stay at home, but spent his time in the burial caves. When he saw Jesus, he gave a loud cry, threw himself down at his feet, and shouted:
Mob	Jesus, Son of the Most High God! What do you want with me? I beg you, don't punish me!
Narrator	He said this because Jesus had ordered the evil spirit to go out of him. Many times it had seized him, and even though he was kept a prisoner, his hands and feet fastened with chains, he would break the chains and be driven by the demon out into the desert. Jesus asked him:
Jesus	What is your name?
Narrator	Because many demons had gone into him, he answered:
Mob	My name is 'Mob'.

144

Narrator	The demons begged Jesus not to send them into the abyss. (PAUSE)
	There was a large herd of pigs near by, feeding on a hillside. So the demons begged Jesus to let them go into the pigs, and he let them. They went out of the man and into the pigs. The whole herd rushed down the side of the cliff into the lake and was drowned. (PAUSE)
	The men who had been taking care of the pigs saw what happened, so they ran off and spread the news in the town and among the farms. People went out to see what had happened, and when they came to Jesus, they found the man from whom the demons had gone out sitting at the feet of Jesus, clothed and in his right mind; and they were all afraid. Those who had seen it told the people how the man had been cured. Then all the people from that territory asked Jesus to go away, because they were terribly afraid. So Jesus got into the boat and left. The man from whom the demons had gone out begged Jesus:
Mob	Let me go with you.
Narrator	But Jesus sent him away:
Jesus	Go back home and tell what God has done for you.
Narrator	The man went through the town, telling what Jesus had done for him.

Cast	[This is] the word of the Lord.	OR	This is the Gospel of Christ / *This is the Gospel of the Lord.*
All	**Thanks be to God.**		**Praise to Christ our Lord** / *Praise to you, Lord Jesus Christ.*

Cast: **Narrator, Mob, Jesus.**

Jairus' daughter, and the woman who touched Jesus' cloak
Luke 8.40–56

Narrator	When Jesus returned to the other side of the lake, the people welcomed him, because they had all been waiting for him. Then a man named Jairus arrived; he was an official in the local synagogue. He threw himself down at Jesus' feet and begged him to go to his home, because his only daughter, who was twelve years old, was dying.
	As Jesus went along, the people were crowding him from every side. Among them was a woman who had suffered from severe bleeding for twelve years; she had spent all she had on doctors, but no one had been able to cure her. She came up in the crowd behind Jesus and touched the edge of his cloak, and her bleeding stopped at once. Jesus asked:
Jesus	Who touched me?
Narrator	Everyone denied it, and Peter said:
Peter	Master, the people are all round you and crowding in on you.
Jesus	Someone touched me, for I knew it when power went out of me.

145

Narrator	The woman saw that she had been found out, so she came trembling and threw herself at Jesus' feet. There in front of everybody, she told him why she had touched him and how she had been healed at once. Jesus said to her:
Jesus	My daughter, your faith has made you well. Go in peace.
Narrator	While Jesus was saying this, a messenger came from the official's house. [He told Jairus:]
Messenger	Your daughter has died; don't bother the Teacher any longer.
Narrator	But Jesus heard it and said to Jairus:
Jesus	Don't be afraid; only believe, and she will be well. (PAUSE)
Narrator	When he arrived at the house, he would not let anyone go in with him except Peter, John, and James, and the child's father and mother. Everyone there was crying and mourning for the child. Jesus said:
Jesus	Don't cry; the child is not dead—she is only sleeping!
Narrator	They all laughed at him, because they knew that she was dead. But Jesus took her by the hand and called out:
Jesus	Get up, my child!
Narrator	Her life returned, and she got up at once, and Jesus ordered them to give her something to eat. Her parents were astounded, but Jesus commanded them not to tell anyone what had happened.

Cast	[This is] the word of the Lord.	OR	This is the Gospel of Christ / *This is the Gospel of the Lord.*
All	**Thanks be to God.**		**Praise to Christ our Lord** / *Praise to you, Lord Jesus Christ.*

Cast: **Narrator, Jesus, Peter, Messenger.**

Jesus sends out the twelve disciples
Luke 9.1–10

Narrator	Jesus called the twelve disciples together and gave them power and authority to drive out all demons and to cure diseases. Then he sent them out to preach the Kingdom of God and to heal the sick, after saying to them:
Jesus	Take nothing with you for the journey: no stick, no beggar's bag, no food, no money, not even an extra shirt. Wherever you are welcomed, stay in the same house until you leave that town; wherever people don't welcome you, leave that town and shake the dust off your feet as a warning to them.
Narrator	The disciples left and travelled through all the villages, preaching the Good News and healing people everywhere. (PAUSE)
	When Herod, the ruler of Galilee, heard about all the things that were happening, he was very confused, because some people were saying that John the Baptist had come back to life. Others were saying that Elijah had appeared, and still others that one of the prophets of long ago had come back to life. Herod said:

Herod   I had John's head cut off; but who is this man I hear these things about?

Narrator   And he kept trying to see Jesus.

The apostles came back and told Jesus everything they had done.

Cast	[This is] the word of the Lord. OR	This is the Gospel of Christ / *This is the Gospel of the Lord.*
All	**Thanks be to God.**	**Praise to Christ our Lord** / *Praise to you, Lord Jesus Christ.*

Cast: **Narrator, Jesus, Herod.**

Jesus feeds five thousand
Luke 9.10–17

Narrator   Jesus took the disciples with him, and they went off by themselves to a town called Bethsaida. When the crowds heard about it, they followed him. He welcomed them, spoke to them about the Kingdom of God, and healed those who needed it. (PAUSE)

When the sun was beginning to set, the twelve disciples came to him [and said]:

Disciple 1   Send the people away so that they can go to the villages and farms round here—

Disciple 2   And find food and lodging—

Disciple 1   Because this is a lonely place.

[Narrator   But Jesus said to them:]

Jesus   You yourselves give them something to eat.

Disciple 2   All we have are five loaves and two fish.

Disciple 1   Do you want us to go and buy food for this whole crowd?

Narrator   There were about five thousand men there. (PAUSE) Jesus said to his disciples:

Jesus   Make the people sit down in groups of about fifty each.

Narrator   After the disciples had done so, Jesus took the five loaves and two fish, looked up to heaven, thanked God for them, broke them, and gave them to the disciples to distribute to the people. They all ate and had enough, and the disciples took up twelve baskets of what was left over.

Cast	[This is] the word of the Lord. OR	This is the Gospel of Christ / *This is the Gospel of the Lord.*
All	**Thanks be to God.**	**Praise to Christ our Lord** / *Praise to you, Lord Jesus Christ.*

Cast: **Narrator, Disciple 1, Disciple 2, Jesus.**

Peter's declaration about Jesus
Luke 9.18–27

Narrator	One day when Jesus was praying alone, the disciples came to him. He asked them:
Jesus	Who do the crowds say I am?
Narrator	They answered:
Disciple 1	Some say that you are John the Baptist.
Disciple 2	Others say that you are Elijah.
Disciple 3	Others say that one of the prophets of long ago has come back to life.
Jesus	What about you? Who do you say I am?
Narrator	Peter answered:
Peter	You are God's Messiah.
Narrator	Then Jesus gave them strict orders not to tell this to anyone. He also said to them:
Jesus (to disciples)	The Son of Man must suffer much and be rejected by the elders, the chief priests, and the teachers of the Law. He will be put to death, but three days later he will be raised to life.
Narrator	And he said to them all:
Jesus (calling)	If anyone wants to come with me, he must forget self, take up his cross every day, and follow me. For whoever wants to save his own life will lose it, but whoever loses his life for my sake will save it. Will a person gain anything if he wins the whole world but is himself lost or defeated? Of course not! If a person is ashamed of me and of my teaching, then the Son of Man will be ashamed of him when he comes in his glory and in the glory of the Father and of the holy angels. I assure you that there are some here who will not die until they have seen the Kingdom of God.

Cast	[This is] the word of the Lord. OR This is the Gospel of Christ / *This is the Gospel of the Lord.*
All	**Thanks be to God.** **Praise to Christ our Lord** / *Praise to you, Lord Jesus Christ.*

Cast: **Narrator, Jesus, Disciple 1, Disciple 2, Disciple 3** (can be the same as Disciple 1), **Peter** (can be the same as Disciple 2).

The Transfiguration
From Luke 9.28–36

Narrator	Jesus took Peter, John, and James with him and went up a hill to pray. While he was praying, his face changed its appearance, and his clothes became dazzling white. Suddenly two men were there talking with him. They were Moses and Elijah, who appeared in heavenly glory and talked with Jesus about the way in which he would soon fulfil God's purpose by dying in Jerusalem. Peter and his companions were sound asleep, but they woke up and saw Jesus' glory and the two men who were standing with him. As the men were leaving Jesus, Peter said to him:

Peter	Master, how good it is that we are here! We will make three tents, one for you, one for Moses, and one for Elijah.
Narrator	He did not really know what he was saying. While he was still speaking, a cloud appeared and covered them with its shadow; and the disciples were afraid as the cloud came over them. There was a voice from the cloud:
Voice	This is my Son, whom I have chosen—listen to him!
Narrator	When the voice stopped, there was Jesus all alone. The disciples kept quiet about all this, and told no one at that time anything they had seen.

Cast	[This is] the word of the Lord. OR	This is the Gospel of Christ / *This is the Gospel of the Lord.*
All	**Thanks be to God.**	**Praise to Christ our Lord** / *Praise to you, Lord Jesus Christ.*

Cast: **Narrator, Peter, Voice.**

Jesus heals a boy with an evil spirit
Luke 9.37–45

Narrator	[The next day] Jesus and the three disciples went down from the hill, and a large crowd met Jesus. A man shouted from the crowd:
Man	Teacher! I beg you, look at my son—my only son! A spirit attacks him with a sudden shout and throws him into a fit, so that he foams at the mouth; it keeps on hurting him and will hardly let him go! I begged your disciples to drive it out, but they couldn't.
[Narrator	Jesus answered:]
Jesus (to all)	How unbelieving and wrong you people are! How long must I stay with you? How long do I have to put up with you?
[Narrator	Then he said to the man:]
Jesus (to the man)	Bring your son here.
Narrator	As the boy was coming, the demon knocked him to the ground and threw him into a fit. Jesus gave a command to the evil spirit, healed the boy, and gave him back to his father. All the people were amazed at the mighty power of God. (PAUSE)
	The people were still marvelling at everything Jesus was doing, when he said to his disciples:
Jesus	Don't forget what I am about to tell you! The Son of Man is going to be handed over to the power of men.
Narrator	But the disciples did not know what this meant. It had been hidden from them so that they could not understand it, and they were afraid to ask him about the matter.

Cast	[This is] the word of the Lord. OR	This is the Gospel of Christ / *This is the Gospel of the Lord.*
All	**Thanks be to God.**	**Praise to Christ our Lord** / *Praise to you, Lord Jesus Christ.*

Cast: **Narrator, Man, Jesus.**

Jesus and his disciples
Luke 9.46–56

Narrator   An argument broke out among the disciples as to which one of them was the greatest. Jesus knew what they were thinking, so he took a child and stood him by his side. [He said to them:]

Jesus   Whoever welcomes this child in my name, welcomes me; and whoever welcomes me, also welcomes the one who sent me. For he who is least among you all is the greatest. (PAUSE)

Narrator   John spoke up:

John   Master, we saw a man driving out demons in your name, and we told him to stop, because he doesn't belong to our group.

Jesus   Do not try to stop him, because whoever is not against you is for you. (PAUSE)

Narrator   As the time drew near when Jesus would be taken up to heaven, he made up his mind and set out on his way to Jerusalem. He sent messengers ahead of him, who went into a village in Samaria to get everything ready for him. But the people there would not receive him, because it was clear that he was on his way to Jerusalem. When the disciples James and John saw this, they said:

James   Lord, do you want us to call fire down from heaven . . .

John   . . . to destroy them?

Narrator   Jesus turned and rebuked them. Then Jesus and his disciples went on to another village.

Cast   [This is] the word of the Lord.   OR   This is the Gospel of Christ / *This is the Gospel of the Lord.*
All   **Thanks be to God.**   **Praise to Christ our Lord** / *Praise to you, Lord Jesus Christ.*

Cast: **Narrator, Jesus, John, James** (can be the same as John).

The would-be followers of Jesus
Luke 9.57–62

Narrator   As they went on their way, a man said to Jesus:

Man 1   I will follow you wherever you go.

Narrator   Jesus said to him:

Jesus   Foxes have holes, and birds have nests, but the Son of Man has nowhere to lie down and rest.

Narrator   He said to another man:

Jesus   Follow me.

[Narrator   But that man said:]

Man 2   Sir, first let me go back and bury my father.

Jesus   Let the dead bury their own dead. You go and proclaim the Kingdom of God.

[Narrator	Another man said:]**
Man 3	I will follow you, sir; but first let me go and say good-bye to my family.
Jesus	Anyone who starts to plough and then keeps looking back is of no use to the Kingdom of God.

Cast	[This is] the word of the Lord. OR This is the Gospel of Christ / *This is the Gospel of the Lord.*
All	**Thanks be to God.** **Praise to Christ our Lord** / *Praise to you, Lord Jesus Christ.*

Cast: **Narrator, Man 1, Jesus, Man 2, Man 3.**

Jesus sends out the seventy-two men
Luke 10.1–20

Narrator	[After this] the Lord chose another seventy-two men and sent them out two by two, to go ahead of him to every town and place where he himself was about to go. [He said to them:]
Jesus	There is a large harvest, but few workers to gather it in. Pray to the owner of the harvest that he will send out workers to gather in his harvest. Go! I am sending you like lambs among wolves. Don't take a purse or a beggar's bag or shoes; don't stop to greet anyone on the road. Whenever you go into a house, first say, 'Peace be with this house.' If a peace-loving man lives there, let your greeting of peace remain on him; if not, take back your greeting of peace. Stay in that same house, eating and drinking whatever they offer you, for a worker should be given his pay. Don't move round from one house to another. Whenever you go into a town and are made welcome, eat what is set before you, heal the sick in that town, and say to the people there, 'The Kingdom of God has come near you.' But whenever you go into a town and are not welcomed, go out in the streets and say, 'Even the dust from your town that sticks to our feet we wipe off against you. But remember that the Kingdom of God has come near you!' I assure you that on Judgement Day God will show more mercy to Sodom than to that town! (PAUSE)
Narrator	Jesus exclaimed:
Jesus	How terrible it will be for you, Chorazin! How terrible for you too, Bethsaida! If the miracles which were performed in you had been performed in Tyre and Sidon, the people there would long ago have sat down, put on sackcloth, and sprinkled ashes on themselves, to show that they had turned from their sins! God will show more mercy on Judgement Day to Tyre and Sidon than to you. And as for you, Capernaum! Did you want to lift yourself up to heaven? You will be thrown down to hell!
Narrator	Jesus said to his disciples:
Jesus	Whoever listens to you listens to me; whoever rejects you rejects me; and whoever rejects me rejects the one who sent me.
Narrator	The seventy-two men came back in great joy. [They said:]

Man	Lord, even the demons obeyed us when we gave them a command in your name!
Jesus	I saw Satan fall like lightning from heaven. Listen! I have given you authority, so that you can walk on snakes and scorpions and overcome all the power of the Enemy, and nothing will hurt you. But don't be glad because the evil spirits obey you; rather be glad because your names are written in heaven.

Cast   [This is] the word of the Lord.   OR   This is the Gospel of Christ / *This is the Gospel of the Lord.*
All   **Thanks be to God.**   **Praise to Christ our Lord** / *Praise to you, Lord Jesus Christ.*

Cast: **Narrator, Jesus, Man.**

Jesus rejoices
Luke 10.21–24

Narrator	Jesus was filled with joy by the Holy Spirit [and said]:
Jesus (in prayer)	Father, Lord of heaven and earth! I thank you because you have shown to the unlearned what you have hidden from the wise and learned. Yes, Father, this was how you wanted it to happen. (PAUSE)
(to all)	My Father has given me all things. No one knows who the Son is except the Father, and no one knows who the Father is except the Son and those to whom the Son chooses to reveal him.
Narrator	Then Jesus turned to the disciples [and said to them privately]:
Jesus (confiding)	How fortunate you are to see the things you see! I tell you many prophets and kings wanted to see what you see, but they could not, and to hear what you hear, but they did not.

Cast   [This is] the word of the Lord.   OR   This is the Gospel of Christ / *This is the Gospel of the Lord.*
All   **Thanks be to God.**   **Praise to Christ our Lord** / *Praise to you, Lord Jesus Christ.*

Cast: **Narrator, Jesus.**

The parable of the good Samaritan
Luke 10.25–37

Narrator	A teacher of the Law came up and tried to trap Jesus.
Lawyer	Teacher, what must I do to receive eternal life?
[Narrator	Jesus answered him:]
Jesus	What do the Scriptures say? How do you interpret them?
Lawyer	'Love the Lord your God with all your heart, with all your soul, with all your strength, and with all your mind'; and 'Love your neighbour as you love yourself.'
Jesus	You are right; do this and you will live.
Narrator	But the teacher of the Law wanted to justify himself, so he asked Jesus:

Lawyer (pertly)	Who is my neighbour?
Jesus	There was once a man who was going down from Jerusalem to Jericho when robbers attacked him, stripped him, and beat him up, leaving him half dead. It so happened that a priest was going down that road; but when he saw the man, he walked on by, on the other side. In the same way a Levite also came along, went over and looked at the man, and then walked on by, on the other side. But a Samaritan who was travelling that way came upon the man, and when he saw him, his heart was filled with pity. He went over to him, poured oil and wine on his wounds and bandaged them; then he put the man on his own animal and took him to an inn, where he took care of him. The next day he took out two silver coins and gave them to the innkeeper.
Samaritan	Take care of him, and when I come back this way, I will pay you whatever else you spend on him.
Narrator	And Jesus concluded:
Jesus	In your opinion, which one of these three acted like a neighbour towards the man attacked by the robbers?
Narrator	The teacher of the Law answered:
Lawyer	The one who was kind to him.
Jesus	You go, then, and do the same.

Cast	[This is] the word of the Lord.	OR This is the Gospel of Christ / *This is the Gospel of the Lord.*
All	**Thanks be to God.**	**Praise to Christ our Lord** / *Praise to you, Lord Jesus Christ.*

Cast: **Narrator, Lawyer, Jesus, Samaritan.**

Jesus visits Martha and Mary
Luke 10.38–42

Narrator	As Jesus and his disciples went on their way, he came to a village where a woman named Martha welcomed him in her home. She had a sister named Mary, who sat down at the feet of the Lord and listened to his teaching. Martha was upset over all the work she had to do, so she came and said:
Martha	Lord, don't you care that my sister has left me to do all the work by myself? Tell her to come and help me!
[Narrator	The Lord answered her:]
Jesus	Martha, Martha! You are worried and troubled over so many things, but just one is needed. Mary has chosen the right thing, and it will not be taken away from her.

Cast	[This is] the word of the Lord.	OR This is the Gospel of Christ / *This is the Gospel of the Lord.*
All	**Thanks be to God.**	**Praise to Christ our Lord** / *Praise to you, Lord Jesus Christ.*

Cast: **Narrator, Martha, Jesus.**

The Lord's Prayer
Luke 11.1–4 (GNB)

Narrator	One day Jesus was praying in a certain place. When he had finished, one of his disciples said to him:
Disciple	Lord, teach us to pray, just as John taught his disciples.
Narrator	Jesus said to them:
Jesus	When you pray, say this: 'Father: May your holy name be honoured; may your Kingdom come. Give us day by day the food we need. Forgive us our sins, for we forgive everyone who does us wrong. And do not bring us to hard testing.'

Cast	[This is] the word of the Lord.	OR	This is the Gospel of Christ / *This is the Gospel of the Lord.*
All	**Thanks be to God.**		**Praise to Christ our Lord** / *Praise to you, Lord Jesus Christ.*

Cast: **Narrator, Disciple, Jesus.**

The Lord's Prayer
Luke 11.1–4 (NIV)

Narrator	One day Jesus was praying in a certain place. When he finished, one of his disciples said to him:
Disciple	Lord, teach us to pray, just as John taught his disciples.
Narrator	He said to them:
Jesus	When you pray, say: 'Father, Hallowed be your name, your kingdom come. Give us each day our daily bread. Forgive us our sins, for we also forgive everyone who sins against us. And lead us not into temptation.'

Cast	[This is] the word of the Lord.	OR	This is the Gospel of Christ / *This is the Gospel of the Lord.*
All	**Thanks be to God.**		**Praise to Christ our Lord** / *Praise to you, Lord Jesus Christ.*

Cast: **Narrator, Disciple, Jesus.**

Jesus' teaching on prayer
Luke 11.5–13

Jesus	Suppose one of you should go to a friend's house at midnight and say to him:
Disciple	Friend, let me borrow three loaves of bread. A friend of mine who

is on a journey has just come to my house, and I haven't got any food for him!

Jesus   And suppose your friend should answer from inside:

Friend   Don't bother me! The door is already locked, and my children
(off-stage)   and I are in bed. I can't get up and give you anything.

Jesus   Well, what then? I tell you that even if he will not get up and give you the bread because you are his friend, yet he will get up and give you everything you need because you are not ashamed to keep on asking. And so I say to you: Ask, and you will receive; seek, and you will find; knock, and the door will be opened to you.

Student   For everyone who asks will receive, and he who seeks will find, and the door will be opened to anyone who knocks.

Jesus   Would any of you who are fathers give your son a snake when he asks for fish?

Student   Or would you give him a scorpion when he asks for an egg?

Jesus   Bad as you are, you know how to give good things to your children. How much more, then, will the Father in heaven give the Holy Spirit to those who ask him!

Cast   [This is] the word of the Lord.   OR   This is the Gospel of Christ / *This is the Gospel of the Lord.*
All   **Thanks be to God.**   **Praise to Christ our Lord** / *Praise to you, Lord Jesus Christ.*

Cast: **Jesus, Disciple, Friend, Student** (can be the same as Disciple).

Jesus and Beelzebul
Luke 11.14–22 [23]

Narrator   Jesus was driving out a demon that could not talk; and when the demon went out, the man began to talk. The crowds were amazed, but some of the people said:

Person   It is Beelzebul, the chief of the demons, who gives him the power to drive them out.

Narrator   Others wanted to trap Jesus, so they asked him to perform a miracle to show that God approved of him. But Jesus knew what they were thinking [so he said to them]:

Jesus   Any country that divides itself into groups which fight each other will not last very long; a family divided against itself falls apart. So if Satan's kingdom has groups fighting each other, how can it last? You say that I drive out demons because Beelzebul gives me the power to do so. If this is how I drive them out, how do your followers drive them out? Your own followers prove that you are wrong! No, it is rather by means of God's power that I drive out demons, and this proves that the Kingdom of God has already come to you.

When a strong man, with all his weapons ready, guards his own house, all his belongings are safe. But when a stronger man attacks him and defeats him, he carries away all the weapons the →

owner was depending on and divides up what he stole.

[Anyone who is not for me is really against me; anyone who does not help me gather is really scattering.]

Cast	[This is] the word of the Lord.	OR	This is the Gospel of Christ / *This is the Gospel of the Lord.*
All	**Thanks be to God.**		**Praise to Christ our Lord** / *Praise to you, Lord Jesus Christ.*

Cast: **Narrator, Person, Jesus.**

The return of the evil spirit
Luke 11.24–28

Narrator   Jesus said:

Jesus   When an evil spirit goes out of a person, it travels over dry country looking for a place to rest. If it can't find one, it says to itself, 'I will go back to my house.' So it goes back and finds the house clean and tidy. Then it goes out and brings seven other spirits even worse than itself, and they come and live there. So when it is all over, that person is in a worse state than he was at the beginning.

Narrator   When Jesus had said this, a woman spoke up from the crowd:

Woman   How happy is the woman who bore you and nursed you!

[Narrator   But Jesus answered:]

Jesus   Rather, how happy are those who hear the word of God and obey it!

Cast	[This is] the word of the Lord.	OR	This is the Gospel of Christ / *This is the Gospel of the Lord.*
All	**Thanks be to God.**		**Praise to Christ our Lord** / *Praise to you, Lord Jesus Christ.*

Cast: **Narrator, Jesus, Woman.**

Jesus talks of light
Luke 11.33–36

Speaker 1   No one lights a lamp and then hides it or puts it under a bowl;

Speaker 2   Instead, he puts it on the lampstand, so that people may see the light as they come in. Your eyes are like a lamp for the body. When your eyes are sound, your whole body is full of light;

Speaker 1   But when your eyes are no good, your whole body will be in darkness.

Speaker 2   Make certain, then, that the light in you is not darkness. If your whole body is full of light, with no part of it in darkness, it will be bright all over, as when a lamp shines on you with its brightness.

Cast	[This is] the word of the Lord.	OR	This is the Gospel of Christ / *This is the Gospel of the Lord.*
All	**Thanks be to God.**		**Praise to Christ our Lord** / *Praise to you, Lord Jesus Christ.*

Cast: **Speaker 1** (serious voice), **Speaker 2** (cheerful voice).

Jesus accuses the Pharisees and the teachers of the Law
Luke 11.37—12.3

Speaker 1	When Jesus finished speaking, a Pharisee invited him to eat with him; so he went in and sat down to eat. The Pharisee was surprised when he noticed that Jesus had not washed before eating. So the Lord said to him:
Speaker 2	Now then, you Pharisees clean the outside of your cup and plate, but inside you are full of violence and evil. Fools! Did not God, who made the outside, also make the inside? But give what is in your cups and plates to the poor, and everything will be ritually clean for you.
Speaker 1	How terrible for you Pharisees!
Speaker 2	You give God a tenth of the seasoning herbs, such as mint and rue and all the other herbs, but you neglect justice and love for God. These you should practise, without neglecting the others.
Speaker 1	How terrible for you Pharisees!
Speaker 2	You love the reserved seats in the synagogues and to be greeted with respect in the market-places.
Speaker 1	How terrible for you!
Speaker 2	You are like unmarked graves which people walk on without knowing it.
Speaker 1	One of the teachers of the Law said to him:
Lawyer	Teacher, when you say this, you insult us too!
Speaker 1	Jesus answered:
Jesus	How terrible also for you teachers of the Law!
Speaker 2	You put loads on people's backs which are hard to carry, but you yourselves will not stretch out a finger to help them carry those loads.
Speaker 1	How terrible for you!
Speaker 2	You make fine tombs for the prophets—the very prophets your ancestors murdered. You yourselves admit, then, that you approve of what your ancestors did; they murdered the prophets, and you build their tombs. For this reason the Wisdom of God said:
Voice	I will send them prophets and messengers; they will kill some of them and persecute others.
Speaker 2	So the people of this time will be punished for the murder of all the prophets killed since the creation of the world, from the murder of Abel to the murder of Zechariah, who was killed between the altar and the Holy Place. Yes, I tell you, the people of this time will be punished for them all!
Speaker 1	How terrible for you teachers of the Law!

Speaker 2   You have kept the key that opens the door to the house of knowledge; you yourselves will not go in, and you stop those who are trying to go in!

Speaker 1   When Jesus left that place, the teachers of the Law and the Pharisees began to criticize him bitterly and ask him questions about many things, trying to lay traps for him and catch him saying something wrong. (PAUSE)

As thousands of people crowded together, so that they were stepping on each other, Jesus said first to his disciples:

Speaker 2   Be on guard against the yeast of the Pharisees—I mean their hypocrisy. Whatever is covered up will be uncovered, and every secret will be made known. So then, whatever you have said in the dark will be heard in broad daylight, and whatever you have whispered in private in a closed room will be shouted from the housetops.

Cast   [This is] the word of the Lord.   OR   This is the Gospel of Christ / *This is the Gospel of the Lord.*
All   **Thanks be to God.**   **Praise to Christ our Lord** / *Praise to you, Lord Jesus Christ.*

Cast: **Speaker 1, Speaker 2, Lawyer, Jesus, Voice.**

Confessing and rejecting Christ
Luke 12.4–12

Speaker 1   I tell you, my friends, do not be afraid of those who kill the body but cannot afterwards do anything worse.

Speaker 2   I will show you whom to fear: fear God, who, after killing, has the authority to throw into hell. Believe me, he is the one you must fear!

Speaker 1   Aren't five sparrows sold for two pennies? Yet not one sparrow is forgotten by God.

Speaker 2   Even the hairs of your head have all been counted. So do not be afraid; you are worth much more than many sparrows!

Speaker 1   I assure you that whoever declares publicly that he belongs to me, the Son of Man will do the same for him before the angels of God.

Speaker 2   But whoever rejects me publicly, the Son of Man will also reject him before the angels of God.

Speaker 1   Anyone who says a word against the Son of Man can be forgiven.

Speaker 2   But whoever says evil things against the Holy Spirit will not be forgiven.

Speaker 1   When they bring you to be tried in the synagogues or before governors or rulers, do not be worried about how you will defend yourself or what you will say.

Speaker 2   For the Holy Spirit will teach you at that time what you should say.

Cast   [This is] the word of the Lord.   OR   This is the Gospel of Christ / *This is the Gospel of the Lord.*
All   **Thanks be to God.**   **Praise to Christ our Lord** / *Praise to you, Lord Jesus Christ.*

Cast: **Speaker 1, Speaker 2.**

The parable of the rich man (longer version)
Luke 12.13–21

Narrator	A man in the crowd said to Jesus:
Man (angrily)	Teacher, tell my brother to divide with me the property our father left us.
[Narrator	Jesus answered him:]
Jesus (to the Man)	My friend, who gave me the right to judge or to divide the property between you two?
Narrator	And he went on to say to them all:
Jesus (to everyone)	Watch out and guard yourselves from every kind of greed; because a person's true life is not made up of the things he owns, no matter how rich he may be.
Narrator	Then Jesus told them this parable:
Jesus	There was once a rich man who had land which bore good crops. He began to think to himself:
Rich man	I haven't anywhere to keep all my crops. What can I do? (PAUSE TO THINK)
	This is what I will do; I will tear down my barns and build bigger ones, where I will store my corn and all my other goods. Then I will say to myself, 'Lucky man! You have all the good things you need for many years. Take life easy, eat, drink, and enjoy yourself!'
Jesus	But God said to him:
God	You fool! This very night you will have to give up your life; then who will get all these things you have kept for yourself?
Narrator	And Jesus concluded:
Jesus	This is how it is with those who pile up riches for themselves but are not rich in God's sight.

Cast	[This is] the word of the Lord. OR This is the Gospel of Christ / *This is the Gospel of the Lord.*
All	**Thanks be to God.** **Praise to Christ our Lord** / *Praise to you, Lord Jesus Christ.*

Cast: **Narrator, Man, Jesus, Rich man, God.**

The parable of the rich man (shorter version)
Luke 12.16–21

Jesus	There was once a rich man who had land which bore good crops. He began to think to himself:
Rich man	I haven't anywhere to keep all my crops. What can I do?
Jesus	He told himself:
Rich man	This is what I will do; I will tear down my barns and build bigger ones, where I will store my corn and all my other goods. Then I

159 →

will say to myself, 'Lucky man! You have all the good things you need for many years. Take life easy, eat, drink, and enjoy yourself!'

Jesus   But God said to him:

God   You fool! This very night you will have to give up your life; then who will get all these things you have kept for yourself?

Jesus   This is how it is with those who pile up riches for themselves but are not rich in God's sight.

Cast   [This is] the word of the Lord.   OR   This is the Gospel of Christ / *This is the Gospel of the Lord.*
All   **Thanks be to God.**   **Praise to Christ our Lord** / *Praise to you, Lord Jesus Christ.*

Cast: **Jesus, Rich man, God.**

Jesus' teaching about trust in God
Luke 12.22–31

Narrator   Jesus said to the disciples:

Teacher   And so I tell you not to worry about the food you need to stay alive or about the clothes you need for your body. Life is much more important than food, and the body much more important than clothes.

Voice 1   Look at the crows: they don't sow seeds or gather a harvest; they don't have store-rooms or barns; God feeds them! You are worth so much more than birds!

Voice 2   Can any of you live a bit longer by worrying about it? If you can't manage even such a small thing, why worry about the other things?

Voice 1   Look how the wild flowers grow: they don't work or make clothes for themselves. But I tell you that not even King Solomon with all his wealth had clothes as beautiful as one of these flowers.

Voice 2   It is God who clothes the wild grass—grass that is here today and gone tomorrow, burnt up in the oven. Won't he be all the more sure to clothe you? How little faith you have!

Teacher   So don't be all upset, always concerned about what you will eat and drink.

Narrator   For the pagans of this world are always concerned about all these things.

Teacher   Your Father knows that you need these things. Instead, be concerned with his Kingdom, and he will provide you with these things.

Cast   [This is] the word of the Lord.   OR   This is the Gospel of Christ / *This is the Gospel of the Lord.*
All   **Thanks be to God.**   **Praise to Christ our Lord** / *Praise to you, Lord Jesus Christ.*

Cast: **Narrator, Teacher, Voice 1, Voice 2.**

Watchful and faithful servants
Luke 12.22, 35–48

Narrator   Jesus said to the disciples:

Jesus   Be ready for whatever comes, dressed for action and with your lamps lit, like servants who are waiting for their master to come back from a wedding feast. When he comes and knocks, they will open the door for him at once. How happy are those servants whose master finds them awake and ready when he returns! I tell you, he will take off his coat, ask them to sit down, and will wait on them. How happy they are if he finds them ready, even if he should come at midnight or even later! And you can be sure that if the owner of a house knew the time when the thief would come, he would not let the thief break into his house. And you, too, must be ready, because the Son of Man will come at an hour when you are not expecting him.

Narrator   Peter said:

Peter   Lord does this parable apply to us, or do you mean it for everyone?

Narrator   The Lord answered:

Jesus   Who, then, is the faithful and wise servant? He is the one that his master will put in charge, to run the household and give the other servants their share of the food at the proper time. How happy that servant is if his master finds him doing this when he comes home! Indeed, I tell you, the master will put that servant in charge of all his property. But if that servant says to himself that his master is taking a long time to come back and if he begins to beat the other servants, both the men and the women, and eats and drinks and gets drunk, then the master will come back one day when the servant does not expect him and at a time he does not know. The master will cut him in pieces and make him share the fate of the disobedient.

The servant who knows what his master wants him to do, but does not get himself ready and do it, will be punished with a heavy whipping. But the servant who does not know what his master wants, and yet does something for which he deserves a whipping, will be punished with a light whipping. Much is required from the person to whom much is given; much more is required from the person to whom much more is given.

Cast   [This is] the word of the Lord.   OR   This is the Gospel of Christ / *This is the Gospel of the Lord.*
All   **Thanks be to God.**   **Praise to Christ our Lord** / *Praise to you, Lord Jesus Christ.*

Cast: **Narrator, Jesus, Peter.**

Jesus tells the parable of the unfruitful fig-tree
Luke 13.6–9

[Narrator Jesus told them this parable:]

Jesus There was once a man who had a fig-tree growing in his vineyard. He went to look for figs on it but found none. So he said to his gardener:

Man Look, for three years I have been coming here looking for figs on this fig-tree, and I haven't found any. Cut it down! Why should it go on using up the soil?

Jesus But the gardener answered:

Gardener Leave it alone, sir, just one more year; I will dig round it and put in some manure. Then if the tree bears figs next year, so much the better; if not, then you can have it cut down.

Cast [This is] the word of the Lord. OR This is the Gospel of Christ / *This is the Gospel of the Lord.*
All **Thanks be to God.**   **Praise to Christ our Lord** / *Praise to you, Lord Jesus Christ.*

Cast: **[Narrator,] Jesus, Man, Gardener.**

Jesus heals a crippled woman on the Sabbath
Luke 13.10–17

Narrator One Sabbath Jesus was teaching in a synagogue. A woman there had an evil spirit that had made her ill for eighteen years; she was bent over and could not straighten up at all. When Jesus saw her, he called out to her:

Jesus Woman, you are free from your illness!

Narrator He placed his hands on her, and at once she straightened herself up and praised God. (PAUSE)

He called out to her:the synagogue was angry that Jesus had healed on the Sabbath, so he spoke up and said to the people:

Official There are six days in which we should work; so come during those days and be healed, but not on the Sabbath!

[Narrator The Lord answered him:]

Jesus You hypocrites! Any one of you would untie his ox or his donkey from the stall and take it out to give it water on the Sabbath. Now here is this descendant of Abraham whom Satan has kept bound up for eighteen years; should she not be released on the Sabbath?

Narrator His answer made his enemies ashamed of themselves, while the people rejoiced over all the wonderful things that he did.

Cast [This is] the word of the Lord. OR This is the Gospel of Christ / *This is the Gospel of the Lord.*
All **Thanks be to God.**   **Praise to Christ our Lord** / *Praise to you, Lord Jesus Christ.*

Cast: **Narrator, Jesus, Official.**

The parables of the mustard seed and the yeast
Luke 13.18–21

Speaker 1	Jesus asked, 'What is the Kingdom of God like? What shall I compare it with?'
Speaker 2	It is like this. A man takes a mustard seed and sows it in his field. The plant grows and becomes a tree, and the birds make their nests in its branches.
Speaker 1	Again Jesus asked, 'What shall I compare the Kingdom of God with?'
Speaker 2	It is like this. A woman takes some yeast and mixes it with forty litres of flour until the whole batch of dough rises.

Cast [This is] the word of the Lord.   OR   This is the Gospel of Christ / *This is the Gospel of the Lord.*
All   **Thanks be to God.**   **Praise to Christ our Lord** / *Praise to you, Lord Jesus Christ.*

Cast: **Speaker 1, Speaker 2.**

The narrow door
Luke 13.22–30

Narrator	Jesus went through towns and villages, teaching the people and making his way towards Jerusalem. Someone asked him:
Person	Sir, will just a few people be saved?
Narrator	Jesus answered:
Jesus	Do your best to go in through the narrow door; because many people will surely try to go in but will not be able. The master of the house will get up and close the door; then when you stand outside and begin to knock on the door and say:
Person	Open the door for us, sir!
Jesus	He will answer you:
Master	I don't know where you come from!
Jesus	Then you will answer:
Person	We ate and drank with you; you taught in our town!
Jesus	But he will say again:
Master	I don't know where you come from. Get away from me, all you wicked people! (PAUSE)
Jesus	How you will cry and grind your teeth when you see Abraham, Isaac, and Jacob, and all the prophets in the Kingdom of God, while you are thrown out! People will come from the east and the west, from the north and the south, and sit down at the feast in the Kingdom of God. Then those who are now last will be first, and those who are now first will be last.

Cast [This is] the word of the Lord.   OR   This is the Gospel of Christ / *This is the Gospel of the Lord.*
All   **Thanks be to God.**   **Praise to Christ our Lord** / *Praise to you, Lord Jesus Christ.*

Cast: **Narrator, Person, Jesus, Master.**

Jesus' love for Jerusalem
Luke 13.31–35

Narrator	Some Pharisees came to Jesus and said to him:
Pharisee 1	You must get out of here and go somewhere else—
Pharisee 2	Because Herod wants to kill you.
[Narrator	Jesus answered them:]
Jesus (sternly)	Go and tell that fox: 'I am driving out demons and performing cures today and tomorrow, and on the third day I shall finish my work.' Yet I must be on my way today, tomorrow, and the next day; it is not right for a prophet to be killed anywhere except in Jerusalem. (PAUSE)
(sadly)	Jerusalem, Jerusalem! You kill the prophets, you stone the messengers God has sent you! How many times have I wanted to put my arms round all your people, just as a hen gathers her chicks under her wings, but you would not let me! And so your Temple will be abandoned. I assure you that you will not see me until the time comes when you say, 'God bless him who comes in the name of the Lord.'

Cast   [This is] the word of the Lord.   OR   This is the Gospel of Christ / *This is the Gospel of the Lord.*
All   **Thanks be to God.**   **Praise to Christ our Lord** / *Praise to you, Lord Jesus Christ.*

Cast: **Narrator, Pharisee 1, Pharisee 2** (can be the same as Pharisee 1)**, Jesus.**

Jesus heals a sick man
Luke 14.1–6

Narrator	One Sabbath Jesus went to eat a meal at the home of one of the leading Pharisees; and people were watching Jesus closely. A man whose legs and arms were swollen came to Jesus, and Jesus asked the teachers of the Law and the Pharisees:
Jesus	Does our Law allow healing on the Sabbath or not?
Narrator	But they would not say anything. Jesus took the man, healed him, and sent him away. Then he said to them:
Jesus	If any one of you had a son or an ox that happened to fall in a well on a Sabbath, would you not pull him out at once on the Sabbath itself?
Narrator	But they were not able to answer him about this.

Cast   [This is] the word of the Lord.   OR   This is the Gospel of Christ / *This is the Gospel of the Lord.*
All   **Thanks be to God.**   **Praise to Christ our Lord** / *Praise to you, Lord Jesus Christ.*

Cast: **Narrator, Jesus.**

Humility and hospitality
Luke 14.7–14

Narrator	Jesus noticed how some of the guests were choosing the best places, so he told this parable to all of them:
Jesus	When someone invites you to a wedding feast, do not sit down in the best place. It could happen that someone more important than you has been invited, and your host, who invited both of you, would have to come and say to you:
Host	Let him have this place.
Jesus	Then you would be embarrassed and have to sit in the lowest place. Instead, when you are invited, go and sit in the lowest place, so that your host will come to you and say:
Host	Come on up, my friend, to a better place.
Jesus	This will bring you honour in the presence of all the other guests. For everyone who makes himself great will be humbled, and everyone who humbles himself will be made great.
Narrator	Then Jesus said to his host:
Jesus	When you give a lunch or a dinner, do not invite your friends or your brothers or your relatives or your rich neighbours—for they will invite you back, and in this way you will be paid for what you did. When you give a feast, invite the poor, the crippled, the lame, and the blind; and you will be blessed, because they are not able to pay you back. God will repay you on the day the good people rise from death.

Cast	[This is] the word of the Lord.	OR	This is the Gospel of Christ / *This is the Gospel of the Lord.*
All	**Thanks be to God.**		**Praise to Christ our Lord** / *Praise to you, Lord Jesus Christ.*

Cast: **Narrator, Jesus, Host.**

The parable of the great feast
Luke 14.15–24

Narrator	One of the men sitting at table said to Jesus:
Man	How happy are those who will sit down at the feast in the Kingdom of God!
[Narrator	Jesus said to him:]
Jesus	There was once a man who was giving a great feast to which he invited many people. When it was time for the feast, he sent his servant to tell his guests:
Servant	Come, everything is ready!
Jesus	But they all began, one after another, to make excuses. The first one told the servant:
Guest 1	I have bought a field and must go and look at it; please accept my apologies.

Jesus	Another one said:
Guest 2	I have bought five pairs of oxen and am on my way to try them out; please accept my apologies.
Jesus	Another one said:
Guest 3	I have just got married, and for that reason I cannot come.
Jesus	The servant went back and told all this to his master. The master was furious and said to his servant:
Master	Hurry out to the streets and alleys of the town, and bring back the poor, the crippled, the blind, and the lame.
Jesus	Soon the servant said:
Servant	Your order has been carried out, sir, but there is room for more.
Jesus	So the master said to the servant:
Master	Go out to the country roads and lanes and make people come in, so that my house will be full. I tell you all that none of those men who were invited will taste my dinner!

Cast	[This is] the word of the Lord.	OR	This is the Gospel of Christ / *This is the Gospel of the Lord.*
All	**Thanks be to God.**		**Praise to Christ our Lord** / *Praise to you, Lord Jesus Christ.*

Cast: **Narrator, Man, Jesus, Servant, Guest 1, Guest 2, Guest 3, Master.**

The cost of being a disciple
Luke 14.25–33

Narrator	Once when large crowds of people were going along with Jesus, he turned and said to them:
Jesus	Whoever comes to me cannot be my disciple unless he loves me more than he loves his father and his mother, his wife and his children, his brothers and his sisters, and himself as well. Whoever does not carry his own cross and come after me cannot be my disciple.
	If one of you is planning to build a tower, he sits down first and works out what it will cost, to see if he has enough money to finish the job. If he doesn't, he will not be able to finish the tower after laying the foundation; and all who see what happened will laugh at him:
Person (jeering)	This man began to build but can't finish the job!
Jesus	If a king goes out with ten thousand men to fight another king who comes against him with twenty thousand men, he will sit down first and decide if he is strong enough to face that other king. If he isn't, he will send messengers to meet the other king, to ask for terms of peace while he is still a long way off.
[Narrator	Jesus concluded:]
Jesus	In the same way, none of you can be my disciple unless he gives up everything he has.

Cast	[This is] the word of the Lord.	OR	This is the Gospel of Christ / *This is the Gospel of the Lord.*
All	**Thanks be to God.**		**Praise to Christ our Lord** / *Praise to you, Lord Jesus Christ.*

Cast: **Narrator, Jesus, Person.**

The lost sheep and the lost coin
Luke 15.1–10

Narrator   One day when many tax collectors and other outcasts came to listen to Jesus, the Pharisees and the teachers of the Law started grumbling:

Pharisee   This man welcomes outcasts.

Lawyer   And even eats with them!

Narrator   So Jesus told them this parable:

Jesus   Suppose one of you has a hundred sheep and loses one of them—what does he do? He leaves the other ninety-nine sheep in the pasture and goes looking for the one that got lost until he finds it. When he finds it, he is so happy that he puts it on his shoulders and carries it back home. Then he calls his friends and neighbours together and says to them:

Shepherd   I am so happy I found my lost sheep. Let us celebrate!

Jesus   In the same way, I tell you, there will be more joy in heaven over one sinner who repents than over ninety-nine respectable people who do not need to repent. (PAUSE)

Or suppose a woman who has ten silver coins loses one of them—what does she do? She lights a lamp, sweeps her house, and looks carefully everywhere until she finds it. When she finds it, she calls her friends and neighbours together [and says to them]:

Woman   I am so happy I found the coin I lost. Let us celebrate!

Jesus   In the same way, I tell you, the angels of God rejoice over one sinner who repents.

Cast   [This is] the word of the Lord.   OR   This is the Gospel of Christ / *This is the Gospel of the Lord.*
All   **Thanks be to God.**   **Praise to Christ our Lord** / *Praise to you, Lord Jesus Christ.*

Cast: **Narrator, Pharisee, Lawyer** (can be the same as Pharisee), **Jesus, Shepherd, Woman.**

Jesus tells the parable of the lost son
Luke 15.11–32

Jesus   There was once a man who had two sons. The younger one said to him:

Younger son   Father, give me my share of the property now.

Jesus   So the man divided his property between his two sons. After a few days the younger son sold his part of the property and left home with the money. He went to a country far away, where he wasted his money in reckless living. He spent everything he had. Then a severe famine spread over that country, and he was left without a thing. So he went to work for one of the citizens of that country, who sent him out to his farm to take care of the pigs. He wished

→

	he could fill himself with the bean pods the pigs ate, but no one gave him anything to eat. At last he came to his senses.
Younger son	All my father's hired workers have more than they can eat, and here I am about to starve! (WITH RESOLVE) I will get up and go to my father and say, Father, I have sinned against God and against you. I am no longer fit to be called your son; treat me as one of your hired workers.
Jesus	So he got up and started back to his father. (PAUSE)
	He was still a long way from home when his father saw him; his heart was filled with pity, and he ran, threw his arms round his son, and kissed him. The son said:
Younger son	Father, I have sinned against God and against you. I am no longer fit to be called your son.
Jesus	But the father called his servants:
Father	Hurry! Bring the best robe and put it on him. Put a ring on his finger and shoes on his feet. Then go and get the prize calf and kill it, and let us celebrate with a feast! For this son of mine was dead, but now he is alive; he was lost, but now he has been found.
Jesus	And so the feasting began. (PAUSE)
	In the meantime the elder son was out in the field. On his way back, when he came close to the house, he heard the music and dancing. So he called one of the servants and asked him:
Elder son	What's going on?
[Jesus	The servant answered:]
Servant	Your brother has come back home, and your father has killed the prize calf, because he got him back safe and sound.
Jesus	The elder brother was so angry that he would not go into the house; so his father came out and begged him to come in. But he answered his father:
Elder son	Look, all these years I have worked for you like a slave, and I have never disobeyed your orders. What have you given me? Not even a goat for me to have a feast with my friends! But this son of yours wasted all your property on prostitutes, and when he comes back home, you kill the prize calf for him!
[Jesus	The father answered:]
Father	My son, you are always here with me, and everything I have is yours. But we had to celebrate and be happy, because your brother was dead, but now he is alive; he was lost, but now he has been found.

Cast	[This is] the word of the Lord.	OR	This is the Gospel of Christ / *This is the Gospel of the Lord.*
All	**Thanks be to God.**		**Praise to Christ our Lord** / *Praise to you, Lord Jesus Christ.*

Cast: **Jesus, Younger son, Father, Elder son, Servant.**

Jesus tells the parable of the shrewd manager
Luke 16.1–8

Jesus   There was once a rich man who had a servant who managed his property. The rich man was told that the manager was wasting his master's money, so he called him in.

Master   What is this I hear about you? Present me with a complete account of your handling of my property, because you cannot be my manager any longer.

Jesus   The servant said to himself:

Manager   My master is going to dismiss me from my job. What shall I do? I am not strong enough to dig ditches, and I am ashamed to beg. Now I know what I will do! Then when my job is gone, I shall have friends who will welcome me in their homes.

Jesus   So he called in all the people who were in debt to his master. He asked the first one:

Manager
(to Debtor 1)   How much do you owe my master?

Debtor 1   One hundred barrels of olive-oil.

Jesus   The manager told him:

Manager   Here is your account; sit down and write fifty.

[Jesus   Then he asked another one:]

Manager
(to Debtor 2)   And you—how much do *you* owe?

Debtor 2   A thousand sacks of wheat.

Manager   Here is your account, write eight hundred.

Jesus   As a result the master of this dishonest manager praised him for doing such a shrewd thing; because the people of this world are much more shrewd in handling their affairs than the people who belong to the light.

Cast   [This is] the word of the Lord.   OR   This is the Gospel of Christ / *This is the Gospel of the Lord.*
All   **Thanks be to God.**   **Praise to Christ our Lord** / *Praise to you, Lord Jesus Christ.*

Cast: **Jesus, Master, Manager, Debtor 1, Debtor 2.**

More of Jesus' teaching on stewardship
Luke 16.9–12

Teacher   Use worldly wealth to gain friends for yourselves, so that when it is gone, you will be welcomed into eternal dwellings.

Voice 1   Whoever can be trusted with very little can also be trusted with much.

Voice 2   Whoever is dishonest with very little will also be dishonest with much.

Voice 1 So if you have not been trustworthy in handling worldly wealth, who will trust you with true riches?

Voice 2 And if you have not been trustworthy with someone else's property, who will give you property of your own?

Cast	[This is] the word of the Lord. OR This is the Gospel of Christ / *This is the Gospel of the Lord.*
All	**Thanks be to God.** **Praise to Christ our Lord** / *Praise to you, Lord Jesus Christ.*

Cast: **Teacher, Voice 1, Voice 2.**

Some sayings of Jesus
Luke 16.13–15

Narrator Jesus said:

Jesus No servant can be the slave of two masters; he will hate one and love the other; he will be loyal to one and despise the other. You cannot serve both God and money.

Narrator When the Pharisees heard all this, they sneered at Jesus, because they loved money. Jesus said to them:

Jesus You are the ones who make yourselves look right in other people's sight, but God knows your hearts. For the things that are considered of great value by man are worth nothing in God's sight.

Cast	[This is] the word of the Lord. OR This is the Gospel of Christ / *This is the Gospel of the Lord.*
All	**Thanks be to God.** **Praise to Christ our Lord** / *Praise to you, Lord Jesus Christ.*

Cast: **Narrator, Jesus.**

The rich man and Lazarus
Luke 16.19–31

Narrator 1 There was once a rich man who dressed in the most expensive clothes and lived in great luxury every day.

Narrator 2 There was also a poor man named Lazarus, covered with sores, who used to be brought to the rich man's door, hoping to eat the bits of food that fell from the rich man's table. Even the dogs would come and lick his sores. (PAUSE) The poor man died and was carried by the angels to sit beside Abraham at the feast in heaven.

Narrator 1 The rich man died and was buried, and in Hades, where he was in great pain, he looked up and saw Abraham, far away, with Lazarus at his side. So he called out:

Rich man
(calling) Father Abraham! Take pity on me, and send Lazarus to dip his finger in some water and cool my tongue, because I am in great pain in this fire!

Narrator 2 But Abraham said:

Abraham Remember, my son, that in your lifetime you were given all the good things, while Lazarus got all the bad things. But now he is

170

enjoying himself here, while you are in pain. Besides all that, there is a deep pit lying between us, so that those who want to cross over from here to you cannot do so, nor can anyone cross over to us from where you are.

Rich man   Then I beg you, father Abraham, send Lazarus to my father's house, where I have five brothers. Let him go and warn them so that they, at least, will not come to this place of pain.

Abraham   Your brothers have Moses and the prophets to warn them; your brothers should listen to what they say.

Rich man   That is not enough, father Abraham! But if someone were to rise from death and go to them, then they would turn from their sins.

Abraham   If they will not listen to Moses and the prophets, they will not be convinced even if someone were to rise from death.

Cast   [This is] the word of the Lord.   OR   This is the Gospel of Christ / *This is the Gospel of the Lord.*
All   **Thanks be to God.**   **Praise to Christ our Lord** / *Praise to you, Lord Jesus Christ.*

Cast: **Narrator 1, Narrator 2, Rich man, Abraham.**

Jesus talks about sin, faith, and service
Luke 17.1–10

Narrator   Jesus said to his disciples:

Jesus   Things that make people fall into sin are bound to happen, but how terrible for the one who makes them happen! It would be better for him if a large millstone were tied round his neck and he were thrown into the sea than for him to cause one of these little ones to sin. So watch what you do!

If your brother sins, rebuke him, and if he repents, forgive him. If he sins against you seven times in one day, and each time he comes to you saying:

Voice   I repent.

Jesus   You must forgive him.

Narrator   The apostles said to the Lord:

Apostle   Make our faith greater.

Narrator   The Lord answered:

Jesus   If you had faith as big as a mustard seed, you could say to this mulberry tree:

Voice   Pull yourself up by the roots and plant yourself in the sea!

Jesus   And it would obey you. (PAUSE)

Suppose one of you has a servant who is ploughing or looking after the sheep. When he comes in from the field, do you tell him to hurry and eat his meal? Of course not! Instead, you say to him:

Voice	Get my supper ready, then put on your apron and wait on me while I eat and drink; after that you may have your meal.
Jesus	The servant does not deserve thanks for obeying orders, does he? It is the same with you; when you have done all you have been told to do, say:
Voice	We are ordinary servants; we have only done our duty.

Cast	[This is] the word of the Lord. OR This is the Gospel of Christ / *This is the Gospel of the Lord.*
All	**Thanks be to God.** **Praise to Christ our Lord** / *Praise to you, Lord Jesus Christ.*

Cast: **Narrator, Jesus, Voice, Apostle.**

Jesus heals ten men of leprosy
Luke 17.11–19

Narrator	Now on his way to Jerusalem, Jesus travelled along the border between Samaria and Galilee. As he was going into a village, ten men who had leprosy met him. They stood at a distance and called out in a loud voice:
Man 1	Jesus!
Man 2	Master!
Man 1	Have pity on us!
Narrator	Jesus saw them.
Jesus	Go, show yourselves to the priests.
Narrator	And as they went, they were cleansed. One of them, when he saw he was healed, came back, praising God in a loud voice. He threw himself at Jesus' feet and thanked him—and he was a Samaritan. Jesus asked:
Jesus	Were not all ten cleansed? Where are the other nine? Was no-one found to return and give praise to God except this foreigner?
[Narrator	Then he said to him:]
Jesus (to the Man)	Rise and go; your faith has made you well.

Cast	[This is] the word of the Lord. OR This is the Gospel of Christ / *This is the Gospel of the Lord.*
All	**Thanks be to God.** **Praise to Christ our Lord** / *Praise to you, Lord Jesus Christ.*

Cast: **Narrator, Man 1, Man 2, Jesus.**

The coming of the Kingdom
From Luke 17.20–24, 31–37

Narrator	Some Pharisees asked Jesus when the Kingdom of God would come. His answer was:
Jesus	The Kingdom of God does not come in such a way as to be seen. No one will say, 'Look, here it is!' or, 'There it is!'; because the Kingdom of God is within you.

Narrator	Then he said to the disciples:
Jesus	The time will come when you will wish you could see one of the days of the Son of Man, but you will not see it. There will be those who will say to you:
Person 1	Look, over there!
Person 2	Look, over here!
Jesus	But don't go out looking for it. As the lightning flashes across the sky and lights it up from one side to the other, so will the Son of Man be in his day. On that day the man who is on the roof of his house must not go down into the house to get his belongings; in the same way the man who is out in the field must not go back to the house. Remember Lot's wife! Whoever tries to save his own life will lose it; whoever loses his life will save it. On that night, I tell you, there will be two people sleeping in the same bed: one will be taken away, the other will be left behind. Two women will be grinding corn together: one will be taken away, the other will be left behind.
Narrator	The disciples asked him:
Disciple(s)	Where, Lord?
Jesus	Wherever there is a dead body, the vultures will gather.

Cast	[This is] the word of the Lord. OR This is the Gospel of Christ / *This is the Gospel of the Lord.*
All	**Thanks be to God.** **Praise to Christ our Lord** / *Praise to you, Lord Jesus Christ.*

Cast: **Narrator, Jesus, Person 1, Person 2** (Persons 1 and 2 can be the same as Jesus), **Disciple(s).**

The parable of the widow and the judge
Luke 18.1–8

Narrator	Jesus told his disciples a parable to teach them that they should always pray and never become discouraged.
Jesus	In a certain town there was a judge who neither feared God nor respected man. And there was a widow in that same town who kept coming to him and pleading for her rights, saying:
Widow	Help me against my opponent!
Jesus	For a long time the judge refused to act, but at last he said to himself:
Judge	Even though I don't fear God or respect man, yet because of all the trouble this widow is giving me, I will see to it that she gets her rights. If I don't, she will keep on coming and finally wear me out!
[Narrator	And the Lord continued:]

173

Jesus	Listen to what that corrupt judge said. Now, will God not judge in favour of his own people who cry to him day and night for help? Will he be slow to help them? I tell you, he will judge in their favour and do it quickly. But will the Son of Man find faith on earth when he comes?

Cast	[This is] the word of the Lord.	OR	This is the Gospel of Christ / *This is the Gospel of the Lord.*
All	**Thanks be to God.**		**Praise to Christ our Lord** / *Praise to you, Lord Jesus Christ.*

Cast: **Narrator, Jesus, Widow, Judge.**

The parable of the Pharisee and the tax collector
Luke 18.9–14

Narrator	Jesus told this parable to people who were sure of their own goodness and despised everybody else:
Jesus	Once there were two men who went up to the Temple to pray: one was a Pharisee, the other a tax collector.
	The Pharisee stood apart by himself and prayed:
Pharisee (haughtily)	I thank you, God, that I am not greedy, dishonest, or an adulterer, like everybody else. I thank you that I am not like that tax collector over there. I fast two days a week, and I give you a tenth of all my income.
Jesus	But the tax collector stood at a distance and would not even raise his face to heaven, but beat on his breast and said:
Tax collector (humbly)	God, have pity on me, a sinner!
Jesus	I tell you, the tax collector, and not the Pharisee, was in the right with God when he went home. For everyone who makes himself great will be humbled, and everyone who humbles himself will be made great.

Cast	[This is] the word of the Lord.	OR	This is the Gospel of Christ / *This is the Gospel of the Lord.*
All	**Thanks be to God.**		**Praise to Christ our Lord** / *Praise to you, Lord Jesus Christ.*

Cast: **Narrator, Jesus, Pharisee, Tax collector.**

Jesus blesses little children
Luke 18.15–17

Narrator	Some people brought their infants to Jesus for him to place his hands on them. The disciples saw them and scolded them for doing so, but Jesus called the children to him and said:
Jesus	Let the children come to me and do not stop them, because the Kingdom of God belongs to such as these. Remember this! Whoever does not receive the Kingdom of God like a child will never enter it.

Cast	[This is] the word of the Lord.	OR	This is the Gospel of Christ / *This is the Gospel of the Lord.*
All	**Thanks be to God.**		**Praise to Christ our Lord** / *Praise to you, Lord Jesus Christ.*

Cast: **Narrator, Jesus.**

The rich man
Luke 18.18–30

Narrator A Jewish leader asked Jesus:

Leader Good Teacher, what must I do to receive eternal life?

[Narrator Jesus asked him:]

Jesus Why do you call me good? No one is good except God alone. You know the commandments: 'Do not commit adultery; do not commit murder; do not steal; do not accuse anyone falsely; respect your father and your mother.'

Leader Ever since I was young, I have obeyed all these commandments.

Jesus There is still one more thing you need to do. Sell all you have and give the money to the poor, and you will have riches in heaven; then come and follow me.

Narrator But when the man heard this, he became very sad, because he was very rich. (PAUSE)

Jesus saw that he was sad.

Jesus How hard it is for rich people to enter the Kingdom of God! It is much harder for a rich person to enter the Kingdom of God than for a camel to go through the eye of a needle.

Narrator The people who heard him asked:

Person Who, then, can be saved?

Jesus What is impossible for man is possible for God.

Narrator Then Peter said:

Peter Look! We have left our homes to follow you.

Jesus Yes, and I assure you that anyone who leaves home or wife or brothers or parents or children for the sake of the Kingdom of God will receive much more in this present age and eternal life in the age to come.

Cast	[This is] the word of the Lord. OR	This is the Gospel of Christ / *This is the Gospel of the Lord.*
All	**Thanks be to God.**	**Praise to Christ our Lord** / *Praise to you, Lord Jesus Christ.*

Cast: **Narrator, Leader, Jesus, Person, Peter.**

Jesus speaks about his death
Luke 18.31–34

Narrator Jesus took the twelve disciples aside [and said to them]:

Jesus Listen! We are going to Jerusalem where everything the prophets wrote about the Son of Man will come true. He will be handed over to the Gentiles, who will mock him, insult him, and spit on him. They will whip him and kill him, but three days later he will rise to life.

| Narrator | But the disciples did not understand any of these things; the meaning of the words was hidden from them, and they did not know what Jesus was talking about. |

Cast: **Narrator, Jesus.**

Jesus heals a blind beggar
Luke 18.35–43

Narrator	As Jesus was coming near Jericho, there was a blind man sitting by the road, begging. When he heard the crowd passing by, he asked:
Blind man	What is this?
[Narrator	They told him:]
Person	Jesus of Nazareth is passing by.
Blind man (crying out)	Jesus! Son of David! Take pity on me!
Narrator	The people in front scolded him and told him to be quiet. But he shouted even more loudly:
Blind man (crying out)	Son of David! Take pity on me!'
Narrator	So Jesus stopped and ordered the blind man to be brought to him. When he came near, Jesus asked him:
Jesus	What do you want me to do for you?
Blind man	Sir, I want to see again.
Jesus	Then see! Your faith has made you well.
Narrator	At once he was able to see, and he followed Jesus, giving thanks to God. When the crowd saw it, they all praised God.

Cast: **Narrator, Blind man, Person, Jesus.**

Jesus and Zacchaeus
From Luke 19.1–10

| Narrator | Jesus went on into Jericho and was passing through. There was a chief tax collector there named Zacchaeus, who was rich. He was trying to see who Jesus was, but he was a little man and could not see Jesus because of the crowd. So he ran ahead of the crowd and climbed a sycomore tree to see Jesus, who was going to pass that way. When Jesus came to that place, he looked up. |

Jesus	Hurry down, Zacchaeus, because I must stay in your house today.
Narrator	Zacchaeus hurried down and welcomed him with great joy. (PAUSE)
	All the people who saw it started grumbling:
Grumbling person	This man has gone as a guest to the home of a sinner!
Narrator	Zacchaeus stood up [and said to the Lord]:
Zacchaeus (to Jesus)	Listen, sir! I will give half my belongings to the poor, and if I have cheated anyone, I will pay him back four times as much.
Jesus (to Zacchaeus)	Salvation has come to this house today, for this man, also, is a descendant of Abraham. The Son of Man came to seek and to save the lost.

Cast	[This is] the word of the Lord. OR	This is the Gospel of Christ / *This is the Gospel of the Lord.*
All	**Thanks be to God.**	**Praise to Christ our Lord** / *Praise to you, Lord Jesus Christ.*

Cast: **Narrator, Jesus, Grumbling person, Zacchaeus.**

Jesus tells the parable of the gold coins
Luke 19.12–26

[Narrator	Jesus told them a parable. He was now almost at Jerusalem, and they supposed that the Kingdom of God was just about to appear. So he said:]
Jesus	There was once a man of high rank who was going to a country far away to be made king, after which he planned to come back home. Before he left, he called his ten servants and gave them each a gold coin and told them:
King	See what you can earn with this while I am gone.
Jesus	Now his countrymen hated him, and so they sent messengers after him to say:
Messenger	We don't want this man to be our king.
Jesus	The man was made king and came back. At once he ordered his servants to appear before him, in order to find out how much they had earned. The first one came and said:
Servant 1	Sir, I have earned ten gold coins with the one you gave me.
King (to Servant 1)	Well done; you are a good servant! Since you were faithful in small matters, I will put you in charge of ten cities.
Jesus	The second servant came and said:
Servant 2	Sir, I have earned five gold coins with the one you gave me.
King (to Servant 2)	You will be in charge of five cities.
Jesus	Another servant came and said:
Servant 3	Sir, here is your gold coin; I kept it hidden in a handkerchief. I was afraid of you, because you are a hard man. You take what is not yours and reap what you did not sow.

King (to Servant 3)	You bad servant! I will use your own words to condemn you! You know that I am a hard man, taking what is not mine and reaping what I have not sown. Well, then, why didn't you put my money in the bank? Then I would have received it back with interest when I returned.
Jesus	Then he said to those who were standing there:
King	Take the gold coin away from him and give it to the servant who has ten coins.
[Jesus	But they said to him:]
Person	Sir, he already has ten coins!
[Jesus	The king replied:]
King (to Person)	I tell you, that to every person who has something, even more will be given; but the person who has nothing, even the little that he has will be taken away from him.

Cast **All**	[This is] the word of the Lord. OR This is the Gospel of Christ / *This is the Gospel of the Lord.* **Thanks be to God.** **Praise to Christ our Lord** / *Praise to you, Lord Jesus Christ.*

Cast: [**Narrator**], **Jesus, King, Messenger, Servant 1, Servant 2, Servant 3, Person** (can be the same as Servant 2).

The triumphant approach to Jerusalem
Luke 19.28–40

Narrator	As Jesus came near Bethphage and Bethany at the Mount of Olives, he sent two disciples ahead with these instructions:
Jesus	Go to the village there ahead of you; as you go in, you will find a colt tied up that has never been ridden. Untie it and bring it here. If someone asks you why you are untying it, tell him that the Master needs it.
Narrator	They went on their way and found everything just as Jesus had told them. As they were untying the colt, its owners said to them:
Owner	Why are you untying it?
Narrator	They answered:
Disciple	The Master needs it.
Narrator	And they took the colt to Jesus. Then they threw their cloaks over the animal and helped Jesus get on. As he rode on, people spread their cloaks on the road. (PAUSE) When he came near Jerusalem, at the place where the road went down the Mount of Olives, the large crowd of his disciples began to thank God and praise him in loud voices for all the great things that they had seen:
Person 1 (calling)	God bless the king who comes in the name of the Lord!
Person 2	Peace in heaven and glory to God!

Narrator	Then some of the Pharisees in the crowd spoke to Jesus.
Pharisee	Teacher, command your disciples to be quiet!
Jesus	I tell you that if they keep quiet, the stones themselves will start shouting.

Cast   [This is] the word of the Lord.   OR   This is the Gospel of Christ / *This is the Gospel of the Lord.*
All   **Thanks be to God.**   **Praise to Christ our Lord** / *Praise to you, Lord Jesus Christ.*

Cast: **Narrator, Jesus, Owner, Disciple, Person 1** (can be the same as Disciple), **Person 2** (can be the same as Owner), **Pharisee.**

Jesus weeps over Jerusalem and goes to the Temple
Luke 19.41–48

Narrator	Jesus came closer to the city, and when he saw it, he wept over it [saying]:
Jesus	If you only knew today what is needed for peace! But now you cannot see it! The time will come when your enemies will surround you with barricades, blockade you, and close in on you from every side. They will completely destroy you and the people within your walls; not a single stone will they leave in its place, because you did not recognize the time when God came to save you!
Narrator	Then Jesus went into the Temple and began to drive out the merchants [saying to them]:
Jesus (firmly)	It is written in the Scriptures that God said, 'My Temple will be called a house of prayer.' But you have turned it into a hideout for thieves!
Narrator	Every day Jesus taught in the Temple. The chief priests, the teachers of the Law, and the leaders of the people wanted to kill him, but they could not find a way to do it, because all the people kept listening to him, not wanting to miss a single word.

Cast   [This is] the word of the Lord.   OR   This is the Gospel of Christ / *This is the Gospel of the Lord.*
All   **Thanks be to God.**   **Praise to Christ our Lord** / *Praise to you, Lord Jesus Christ.*

Cast: **Narrator, Jesus.**

The question about Jesus' authority
Luke 20.1–8

Narrator	One day when Jesus was in the Temple teaching the people and preaching the Good News, the chief priests and the teachers of the Law, together with the elders, came and said to him:
Priest	Tell us, what right have you to do these things?
Teacher	Who gave you this right?
[Narrator	Jesus answered them:]

Jesus	Now let me ask you a question. Tell me, did John's right to baptize come from God or from man?
Narrator	They started to argue among themselves:
Priest	What shall we say?
Teacher	If we say, 'From God,' he will say, 'Why, then, did you not believe John?'
Priest	But if we say, 'From man,' this whole crowd here will stone us, because they are convinced that John was a prophet.
[Narrator	So they answered:]
Teacher	We don't know where it came from.
Jesus	Neither will I tell you, then, by what right I do these things.

Cast   [This is] the word of the Lord.   OR   This is the Gospel of Christ / *This is the Gospel of the Lord.*
All   **Thanks be to God.**   **Praise to Christ our Lord** / *Praise to you, Lord Jesus Christ.*

Cast: **Narrator, Priest, Teacher, Jesus.**

The parable of the tenants in the vineyard
Luke 20.9–18

Narrator	Then Jesus told the people this parable:
Jesus	There was once a man who planted a vineyard, let it out to tenants, and then left home for a long time. When the time came to gather the grapes, he sent a slave to the tenants to receive from them his share of the harvest. But the tenants beat the slave and sent him back without a thing. So he sent another slave; but the tenants beat him also, treated him shamefully, and sent him back without a thing. Then he sent a third slave; the tenants wounded him, too, and threw him out. Then the owner of the vineyard said:
Owner	What shall I do? I will send my own dear son; surely they will respect him!
Jesus	But when the tenants saw him, they said to one another:
Tenant 1	This is the owner's son.
Tenant 2	Let's kill him, and his property will be ours!
Jesus	So they threw him out of the vineyard and killed him. What, then, will the owner of the vineyard do to the tenants? He will come and kill those men, and hand the vineyard over to other tenants.
Narrator	When the people heard this, they said:
Person	Surely not!
Narrator	Jesus looked at them and asked:
Jesus	What, then, does this scripture mean?

Psalmist	The stone which the builders rejected as worthless turned out to be the most important of all.
Jesus	Everyone who falls on that stone will be cut to pieces; and if that stone falls on someone, it will crush him to dust.

Cast	[This is] the word of the Lord.	OR	This is the Gospel of Christ / *This is the Gospel of the Lord.*
All	**Thanks be to God.**		**Praise to Christ our Lord** / *Praise to you, Lord Jesus Christ.*

Cast: **Narrator, Jesus, Owner, Tenant 1, Tenant 2, Person, Psalmist** (can be the same as Jesus).

The question about paying taxes
Luke 20.19–26

Narrator	The teachers of the Law and the chief priests tried to arrest Jesus on the spot, because they knew that he had told this parable against them; but they were afraid of the people. So they looked for an opportunity. They bribed some men to pretend they were sincere, and they sent them to trap Jesus with questions, so that they could hand him over to the authority and power of the Roman Governor.
Spy 1 (cunning tone)	Teacher, we know that what you say and teach is right.
Spy 2	We know that you pay no attention to a man's status, but teach the truth about God's will for man.
Spy 1 (quickly)	Tell us, is it against our Law for us to pay taxes to the Roman Emperor, or not?
Narrator	But Jesus saw through their trick [and said to them]:
Jesus	Show me a silver coin. Whose face and name are these on it?
Spies 1 and **2**	The Emperor's.
Jesus	Well, then, pay the Emperor what belongs to the Emperor, and pay God what belongs to God.
Narrator	There before the people they could not catch him out in anything, so they kept quiet, amazed at his answer.

Cast	[This is] the word of the Lord.	OR	This is the Gospel of Christ / *This is the Gospel of the Lord.*
All	**Thanks be to God.**		**Praise to Christ our Lord** / *Praise to you, Lord Jesus Christ.*

Cast: **Narrator, Spy 1, Spy 2, Jesus.**

The question about rising from death
Luke 20.27–40 [40–47]

Narrator	Some Sadducees, who say that people will not rise from death, came to Jesus and said:
Sadducee 1	Teacher, Moses wrote this law for us:
[Moses]	If a man dies and leaves a wife but no children, that man's brother must marry the widow so that they can have children who will be considered the dead man's children.

Sadducee 1	Once there were seven brothers; the eldest got married and died without having children.
Sadducee 2	Then the second one married the woman.
Sadducee 1	And then the third.
Sadducee 2	The same thing happened to all seven—they died without having children.
Sadducee 1	Last of all, the woman died.
Sadducee 2	Now, on the day when the dead rise to life, whose wife will she be?
Sadducee 1	All seven of them had married her.
[Narrator	Jesus answered them:]
Jesus	The men and women of this age marry, but the men and women who are worthy to rise from death and live in the age to come will not then marry. They will be like angels and cannot die. They are the sons of God, because they have risen from death. And Moses clearly proves that the dead are raised to life. In the passage about the burning bush he speaks of the Lord as:
[Moses]	The God of Abraham, the God of Isaac, and the God of Jacob.
Jesus	He is the God of the living, not of the dead, for to him all are alive.
Narrator	Some of the teachers of the Law spoke up:
Lawyer	A good answer, Teacher!
Narrator	For they did not dare ask him any more questions. (PAUSE)
[Jesus	How can it be said that the Messiah will be the descendant of David? For David himself says in the book of Psalms:
Psalmist	The Lord said to my Lord: Sit here on my right until I put your enemies as a footstool under your feet.
Jesus	David called him 'Lord'; how, then, can the Messiah be David's descendant?
Narrator	As all the people listened to him, Jesus said to his disciples:
Jesus	Be on your guard against the teachers of the Law, who like to walk about in their long robes and love to be greeted with respect in the market-place; who choose the reserved seats in the synagogues and the best places at feasts; who take advantage of widows and rob them of their homes, and then make a show of saying long prayers! Their punishment will be all the worse!]

Cast	[This is] the word of the Lord.	OR	This is the Gospel of Christ / *This is the Gospel of the Lord.*
All	**Thanks be to God.**		**Praise to Christ our Lord** / *Praise to you, Lord Jesus Christ.*

Cast: **Narrator, Sadducee 1, [Moses], Sadducee 2** (can be the same as Sadducee 1), **Jesus, Lawyer** (can be the same as Moses), **Psalmist** (can be the same as Sadducee).

The widow's offering
Luke 21.1–4

Narrator	Jesus looked round and saw rich men dropping their gifts in the temple treasury, and he also saw a very poor widow dropping in two little copper coins. [He said:]
Jesus	I tell you that this poor widow put in more than all the others. For the others offered their gifts from what they had to spare of their riches; but she, poor as she is, gave all she had to live on.

Cast	[This is] the word of the Lord.	OR	This is the Gospel of Christ / *This is the Gospel of the Lord.*
All	**Thanks be to God.**		**Praise to Christ our Lord** / *Praise to you, Lord Jesus Christ.*

Cast: **Narrator, Jesus.**

Jesus speaks of the future (i)
Luke 21.5–19

Narrator	Some of the disciples were talking about the Temple, how beautiful it looked with its fine stones and the gifts offered to God. Jesus said:
Jesus	All this you see—the time will come when not a single stone here will be left in its place; every one will be thrown down.
Disciple	Teacher, when will this be? And what will happen in order to show that the time has come for it to take place?
Jesus	Be on guard; don't be deceived. Many men, claiming to speak for me, will come and say:
Man 1	I am he!
Man 2	The time has come!
Jesus	But don't follow them. Don't be afraid when you hear of wars and revolutions; such things must happen first, but they do not mean that the end is near. (PAUSE) Countries will fight each other; kingdoms will attack one another. There will be terrible earthquakes, famines, and plagues everywhere; there will be strange and terrifying things coming from the sky. Before all these things take place, however, you will be arrested and persecuted; you will be handed over to be tried in synagogues and be put in prison; you will be brought before kings and rulers for my sake. This will be your chance to tell the Good News. Make up your minds beforehand not to worry about how you will defend yourselves, because I will give you such words and wisdom that none of your enemies will be able to refute or contradict what you say. You will be handed over by your parents, your brothers, your relatives, and your friends; and some of you will be put to death. Everyone will hate you because of me. But not a single hair from your heads will be lost. Stand firm, and you will save yourselves.

Cast	[This is] the word of the Lord.	OR	This is the Gospel of Christ / *This is the Gospel of the Lord.*
All	**Thanks be to God.**		**Praise to Christ our Lord** / *Praise to you, Lord Jesus Christ.*

Cast: **Narrator, Jesus, Disciple, Man 1, Man 2** (Man 1 and Man 2 can be the same as Jesus).

Jesus speaks of the future (ii)
Luke 21.20–28

Speaker 3   When you see Jerusalem surrounded by armies, then you will know that she will soon be destroyed.

Speaker 1   Then those who are in Judaea must run away to the hills.

Speaker 2   Those who are in the city must leave.

Speaker 3   And those who are out in the country must not go into the city.

Speaker 1   For those will be—

Speakers 1 & 2
(slowly)   The Days of Punishment.

Speaker 3   To make all that the Scriptures say come true.

Speaker 1   How terrible it will be in those days for women who are pregnant and for mothers with little babies!

Speaker 2   Terrible distress will come upon this land, and God's punishment will fall on this people.

Speaker 1   Some will be killed by the sword,

Speaker 2   And others will be taken as prisoners to all countries.

Speaker 3   And the heathen will trample over Jerusalem until their time is up.

Speaker 1   There will be strange things happening to the sun, the moon, and the stars.

Speaker 2   On earth whole countries will be in despair, afraid of the roar of the sea and the raging tides.

Speaker 3   People will faint from fear as they wait for what is coming over the whole earth, for the powers in space will be driven from their courses.

Speaker 1   Then the Son of Man will appear, coming in a cloud with great power and glory.

Speaker 2   When these things begin to happen—

Speakers 1–3   Stand up and raise your heads, because your salvation is near.

Cast	[This is] the word of the Lord. OR	This is the Gospel of Christ / *This is the Gospel of the Lord.*
All	**Thanks be to God.**	**Praise to Christ our Lord** / *Praise to you, Lord Jesus Christ.*

Cast: **Speaker 3, Speaker 1, Speaker 2.**

The lesson of the fig-tree
Luke 21.29–38

Narrator   Jesus told his disciples this parable:

Speaker 1   Think of the fig-tree and all the other trees.

Speaker 2   When you see their leaves beginning to appear, you know that summer is near.

Speaker 3   In the same way, when you see these things happening, you will know that the Kingdom of God is about to come.

Speaker 1   Remember that all these things will take place before the people now living have all died.

Speaker 2   Heaven and earth will pass away, but my words will never pass away.

Speakers 1–3   Be on your guard!

Speaker 1   Don't let yourselves become occupied with too much feasting and drinking and with the worries of this life, or that Day may suddenly catch you like a trap.

Speaker 2   For it will come upon all people everywhere on earth.

Speaker 3   Be on the alert and pray always that you will have the strength to go safely through all those things that will happen and to stand before the Son of Man.

Narrator   Jesus spent those days teaching in the Temple, and when evening came, he would go out and spend the night on the Mount of Olives. Early each morning all the people went to the Temple to listen to him.

Cast   [This is] the word of the Lord.   OR   This is the Gospel of Christ / *This is the Gospel of the Lord.*
All   **Thanks be to God.**   **Praise to Christ our Lord** / *Praise to you, Lord Jesus Christ.*

Cast: **Narrator, Speaker 1, Speaker 2, Speaker 3.**

The plot against Jesus
Luke 22.1–13

Narrator   The time was near for the Festival of Unleavened Bread, which is called the Passover. The chief priests and the teachers of the Law were afraid of the people, and so they were trying to find a way of putting Jesus to death secretly.

Then Satan entered Judas, called Iscariot, who was one of the twelve disciples. So Judas went off and spoke with the chief priests and the officers of the temple guard about how he could betray Jesus to them. They were pleased and offered to pay him money. Judas agreed to it and started looking for a good chance to hand Jesus over to them without the people knowing about it. (PAUSE)

The day came during the Festival of Unleavened Bread when the lambs for the Passover meal were to be killed. Jesus sent off Peter and John with these instructions:

185

Jesus	Go and get the Passover meal ready for us to eat.
Peter	Where do you want us to get it ready?
Jesus	As you go into the city, a man carrying a jar of water will meet you. Follow him into the house that he enters, and say to the owner of the house: 'The Teacher says to you, Where is the room where my disciples and I will eat the Passover meal?' He will show you a large furnished room upstairs, where you will get everything ready.
Narrator	They went off and found everything just as Jesus had told them, and they prepared the Passover meal.

Cast	[This is] the word of the Lord.	OR	This is the Gospel of Christ / *This is the Gospel of the Lord.*
All	**Thanks be to God.**		**Praise to Christ our Lord** / *Praise to you, Lord Jesus Christ.*

Cast: **Narrator, Jesus, Peter.**

The Lord's Supper
From Luke 22.14–20 [21–23] (GNB)

Narrator	When the hour came, Jesus took his place at the table with the apostles. [He said to them:]
Jesus	I have wanted so much to eat this Passover meal with you before I suffer! For I tell you, I will never eat it until it is given its full meaning in the Kingdom of God.
Narrator	Then Jesus took a cup, gave thanks to God, and said:
Jesus	Take this and share it among yourselves. I tell you that from now on I will not drink this wine until the Kingdom of God comes.
Narrator	Then he took a piece of bread, gave thanks to God, broke it, and gave it to them, saying:
Jesus	This is my body, which is given for you. Do this in memory of me.
Narrator	In the same way, he gave them the cup after the supper, saying:
Jesus	This cup is God's new covenant, sealed with my blood, which is poured out for you.
	[But, look! The one who betrays me is here at the table with me! The Son of Man will die as God has decided, but how terrible for that man who betrays him!
Narrator	Then they began to ask among themselves which one of them it could be who was going to do this.]

Cast	[This is] the word of the Lord.	OR	This is the Gospel of Christ / *This is the Gospel of the Lord.*
All	**Thanks be to God.**		**Praise to Christ our Lord** / *Praise to you, Lord Jesus Christ.*

Cast: **Narrator, Jesus.**

The Lord's Supper
22.14–20 [21–23] (NIV)

Narrator	When the hour came, Jesus and his apostles reclined at the table. [And he said to them:]
Jesus	I have eagerly desired to eat this Passover with you before I suffer. For I tell you, I will not eat it again until it finds fulfilment in the kingdom of God.

Narrator	After taking the cup, he gave thanks [and said:]
Jesus	Take this and divide it among you. For I tell you I will not drink again of the fruit of the vine until the kingdom of God comes.
Narrator	And he took the bread, gave thanks and broke it, and gave it to them.
Jesus	This is my body given for you; do this in remembrance of me.
Narrator	In the same way, after the supper he took the cup.
Jesus	This cup is the new covenant in my blood, which is poured out for you. [But the hand of him who is going to betray me is with mine on the table. The Son of Man will go as it has been decreed, but woe to that man who betrays him.
Narrator	They began to question among themselves which of them it might be who would do this.]

Cast   [This is] the word of the Lord.   OR   This is the Gospel of Christ / *This is the Gospel of the Lord.*
All   **Thanks be to God.**   **Praise to Christ our Lord** / *Praise to you, Lord Jesus Christ.*

Cast: **Narrator, Jesus.**

The argument about greatness
Luke 22.24–34

Narrator	An argument broke out among the disciples as to which one of them should be thought of as the greatest. Jesus said to them:
Jesus	The kings of the pagans have power over their people, and the rulers claim the title 'Friends of the People'. But this is not the way it is with you; rather, the greatest one among you must be like the youngest, and the leader must be like the servant. Who is greater, the one who sits down to eat or the one who serves him? The one who sits down, of course. But I am among you as one who serves.
	You have stayed with me all through my trials; and just as my Father has given me the right to rule, so I will give you the same right. You will eat and drink at my table in my Kingdom, and you will sit on thrones to rule over the twelve tribes of Israel. (PAUSE)
(to Peter)	Simon, Simon! Listen! Satan has received permission to test all of you, to separate the good from the bad, as a farmer separates the wheat from the chaff. But I have prayed for you, Simon, that your faith will not fail. And when you turn back to me, you must strengthen your brothers.
[Narrator	Peter answered:]
Peter	Lord, I am ready to go to prison with you and to die with you!
Jesus	I tell you, Peter, the cock will not crow tonight until you have said three times that you do not know me.

Cast   [This is] the word of the Lord.   OR   This is the Gospel of Christ / *This is the Gospel of the Lord.*
All   **Thanks be to God.**   **Praise to Christ our Lord** / *Praise to you, Lord Jesus Christ.*

Cast: **Narrator, Jesus, Peter.**

Jesus prays on the Mount of Olives
Luke 22.35–53

Narrator	Jesus asked his disciples:
Jesus	When I sent you out that time without purse, bag, or shoes, did you lack anything?
Disciple	Not a thing.
Jesus	But now, whoever has a purse or a bag must take it; and whoever has no sword must sell his coat and buy one. For I tell you that the scripture which says, 'He shared the fate of criminals,' must come true about me, because what was written about me is coming true.
Disciple	Look! Here are two swords, Lord!
Jesus	That is enough!
Narrator	Jesus left the city and went, as he usually did, to the Mount of Olives; and the disciples went with him. When he arrived at the place, he said to them:
Jesus	Pray that you will not fall into temptation.
Narrator	Then he went off from them about the distance of a stone's throw and knelt down and prayed.
Jesus	Father, if you will, take this cup of suffering away from me. Not my will, however, but your will be done.
Narrator	An angel from heaven appeared to him and strengthened him. In great anguish he prayed even more fervently; his sweat was like drops of blood falling to the ground. (PAUSE)
	Rising from his prayer, he went back to the disciples and found them asleep, worn out by their grief.
Jesus	Why are you sleeping? Get up and pray that you will not fall into temptation.
Narrator	Jesus was still speaking when a crowd arrived, led by Judas, one of the twelve disciples. He came up to Jesus to kiss him.
Jesus	Judas, is it with a kiss that you betray the Son of Man?
Narrator	When the disciples who were with Jesus saw what was going to happen, they asked:
Disciple	Shall we use our swords, Lord?
Narrator	And one of them struck the High Priest's slave and cut off his right ear.
Jesus	Enough of this!
Narrator	Jesus touched the man's ear and healed him. Then Jesus said to the chief priests and the officers of the temple guard and the elders who had come there to get him:

Jesus	Did you have to come with swords and clubs, as though I were an outlaw? I was with you in the Temple every day, and you did not try to arrest me. But this is your hour to act, when the power of darkness rules.

Cast	[This is] the word of the Lord.	OR	This is the Gospel of Christ / *This is the Gospel of the Lord.*
All	**Thanks be to God.**		**Praise to Christ our Lord** / *Praise to you, Lord Jesus Christ.*

Cast: **Narrator, Jesus, Disciple.**

Peter denies Jesus
Luke 22.54–62

Narrator	They arrested Jesus and took him away into the house of the High Priest; and Peter followed at a distance. A fire had been lit in the centre of the courtyard, and Peter joined those who were sitting round it. When one of the servant-girls saw him sitting there at the fire, she looked straight at him:
Girl	This man too was with Jesus!
[Narrator	But Peter denied it:]
Peter	Woman, I don't even know him!
Narrator	After a little while a man noticed Peter.
Man 1	You are one of them, too!
[Narrator	But Peter answered:]
Peter	Man, I am not!
Narrator	And about an hour later another man insisted strongly:
Man 2	There isn't any doubt that this man was with Jesus, because he also is a Galilean!
[Narrator	But Peter answered:]
Peter	Man, I don't know what you are talking about!
Narrator	At once, while he was still speaking, a cock crowed. The Lord turned round and looked straight at Peter, and Peter remembered that the Lord had said to him:
Jesus	Before the cock crows tonight, you will say three times that you do not know me.
Narrator	Peter went out and wept bitterly.

Cast	[This is] the word of the Lord.	OR	This is the Gospel of Christ / *This is the Gospel of the Lord.*
All	**Thanks be to God.**		**Praise to Christ our Lord** / *Praise to you, Lord Jesus Christ.*

Cast: **Narrator, Girl, Peter, Man 1, Man 2, Jesus** (can be the same as Narrator).

Jesus is brought before the Council
Luke 22.63–71

Narrator	The men who were guarding Jesus mocked him and beat him. They blindfolded him and asked him:
Guard	Who hit you? Guess!
Narrator	And they said many other insulting things to him. (PAUSE)

→

When day came, the elders, the chief priests, and the teachers of the Law met together, and Jesus was brought before the Council.

Lawyer Tell us, are you the Messiah?

[Narrator Jesus answered:]

Jesus If I tell you, you will not believe me; and if I ask you a question, you will not answer. But from now on the Son of Man will be seated on the right of Almighty God.

Lawyer Are you, then, the Son of God?

Jesus You say that I am.

Lawyer We don't need any witnesses! We ourselves have heard what he said!

Cast	[This is] the word of the Lord.　OR	This is the Gospel of Christ / *This is the Gospel of the Lord.*
All	**Thanks be to God.**	**Praise to Christ our Lord** / *Praise to you, Lord Jesus Christ.*

Cast: **Narrator, Guard, Lawyer, Jesus.**

Jesus is brought before Pilate
Luke 23.1–12

Narrator The whole group rose up and took Jesus before Pilate, where they began to accuse him:

Leader 1 We caught this man misleading our people.

Leader 2 Telling them not to pay taxes to the Emperor.

Leader 1 And claiming that he himself is the Messiah, a king.

[Narrator Pilate asked him:]

Pilate
(to Jesus) Are you the king of the Jews?

[Narrator Jesus answered:]

Jesus So you say.

Narrator Then Pilate said to the chief priests and the crowds:

Pilate I find no reason to condemn this man.

Narrator But they insisted even more strongly:

Leader 1 With his teaching he is starting a riot among the people all through Judaea.

Leader 2 He began in Galilee and now has come here.

[Narrator When Pilate heard this, he asked:]

Pilate Is this man a Galilean?

Narrator When he learnt that Jesus was from the region ruled by Herod, he sent him to Herod, who was also in Jerusalem at that time. [Herod was very pleased when he saw Jesus, because he had heard about him and had been wanting to see him for a long time. He was hoping to see Jesus perform some miracle. So Herod asked Jesus many questions, but Jesus made no answer.]

The chief priests and the teachers of the Law stepped forward and made strong accusations against Jesus. Herod and his soldiers mocked Jesus and treated him with contempt; then they put a fine robe on him and sent him back to Pilate. [On that very day Herod and Pilate became friends; before this they had been enemies.]

Cast	[This is] the word of the Lord.	OR	This is the Gospel of Christ / *This is the Gospel of the Lord.*
All	**Thanks be to God.**		**Praise to Christ our Lord** / *Praise to you, Lord Jesus Christ.*

Cast: **Narrator, Leader 1, Leader 2** (can be the same as Leader 1), **Pilate, Jesus.**

Jesus is sentenced to death
Luke 23.13–25

Narrator Pilate called together the chief priests, the leaders, and the people:

Pilate You brought this man to me and said that he was misleading the people. Now, I have examined him here in your presence, and I have not found him guilty of any of the crimes you accuse him of. Nor did Herod find him guilty, for he sent him back to us. There is nothing this man has done to deserve death. So I will have him whipped and let him go.

Narrator At every Passover Festival Pilate had to set free one prisoner for them.

[The whole crowd cried out:]

Persons 1 and **2** Kill him!

Person 2 Set Barabbas free for us!

Narrator Barabbas had been put in prison for a riot that had taken place in the city, and for murder. Pilate wanted to set Jesus free, so he appealed to the crowd again. But they shouted back:

Person 1 Crucify him!

Persons 1 and **2** Crucify him!

Narrator Pilate said to them the third time:

Pilate But what crime has he committed? I cannot find anything he has done to deserve death! I will have him whipped and set him free.

Narrator But they kept on shouting at the top of their voices that Jesus should be crucified, and finally their shouting succeeded. So Pilate passed the sentence on Jesus that they were asking for. He set free the man they wanted, the one who had been put in prison for riot and murder, and he handed Jesus over for them to do as they wished.

Cast	[This is] the word of the Lord.	OR	This is the Gospel of Christ / *This is the Gospel of the Lord.*
All	**Thanks be to God.**		**Praise to Christ our Lord** / *Praise to you, Lord Jesus Christ.*

Cast: **Narrator, Pilate, Person 1, Person 2.**

Jesus is crucified
Luke 23.26–32

Narrator The soldiers led Jesus away, and as they were going, they met a man from Cyrene named Simon who was coming into the city from the country. They seized him, put the cross on him, and made him carry it behind Jesus.

A large crowd of people followed him; among them were some women who were weeping and wailing for him. Jesus turned to them and said:

Jesus Women of Jerusalem! Don't cry for me, but for yourselves and your children. For the days are coming when people will say, 'How lucky are the women who never had children, who never bore babies, who never nursed them!' That will be the time when people will say to the mountains, 'Fall on us!' and to the hills, 'Hide us!' For if such things as these are done when the wood is green, what will happen when it is dry?

Narrator Two other men, both of them criminals, were also led out to be put to death with Jesus.

Cast [This is] the word of the Lord.   OR   This is the Gospel of Christ / *This is the Gospel of the Lord.*
All **Thanks be to God.**   **Praise to Christ our Lord** / *Praise to you, Lord Jesus Christ.*

Cast: **Narrator, Jesus.**

The way Jesus died
Luke 23.33–43

Narrator When they came to the place called 'The Skull', they crucified Jesus there, and the two criminals, one on his right and the other on his left. Jesus said:

Jesus Forgive them, Father! They don't know what they are doing.

Narrator They divided his clothes among themselves by throwing dice. The people stood there watching while the Jewish leaders jeered at him:

Leader 1 He saved others; let him save himself—

Leader 2 If he is the Messiah whom God has chosen!

Narrator The soldiers also mocked him: they came up to him and offered him cheap wine, and said:

Soldier Save yourself if you are the king of the Jews!

Narrator Above him were written these words:

Pilate This is the King of the Jews.

Narrator	One of the criminals hanging there hurled insults at him:
Criminal 1	Aren't you the Messiah? Save yourself and us!
Narrator	The other one, however, rebuked him, saying:
Criminal 2	Don't you fear God? You received the same sentence he did. Ours, however, is only right, because we are getting what we deserve for what we did; but he has done no wrong.
Narrator	And he said to Jesus:
Criminal 2	Remember me, Jesus, when you come as King!
[Narrator	Jesus said to him:]
Jesus	I promise you that today you will be in Paradise with me.

Cast	[This is] the word of the Lord. OR This is the Gospel of Christ / *This is the Gospel of the Lord.*
All	**Thanks be to God.** **Praise to Christ our Lord** / *Praise to you, Lord Jesus Christ.*

Cast: **Narrator, Jesus, Leader 1, Leader 2** (can be the same as Leader 1), **Soldier, Pilate, Criminal 1, Criminal 2.**

The death of Jesus
Luke 23.44–49

Narrator	It was about twelve o'clock when the sun stopped shining and darkness covered the whole country until three o'clock; and the curtain hanging in the Temple was torn in two. Jesus cried out in a loud voice:
Jesus	Father! In your hands I place my spirit!
Narrator	He said this and died. (PAUSE)
	The army officer saw what had happened, and he praised God, saying:
Officer	Certainly he was a good man!
Narrator	When the people who had gathered there to watch the spectacle saw what happened, they all went back home, beating their breasts in sorrow. All those who knew Jesus personally, including the women who had followed him from Galilee, stood at a distance to watch.

Cast	[This is] the word of the Lord. OR This is the Gospel of Christ / *This is the Gospel of the Lord.*
All	**Thanks be to God.** **Praise to Christ our Lord** / *Praise to you, Lord Jesus Christ.*

Cast: **Narrator, Jesus, Officer.**

The burial of Jesus
Luke 23.50–56

Narrator 1	There was a man named Joseph from Arimathea, a town in Judaea. He was a good and honourable man, who was waiting for the coming of the Kingdom of God. Although he was a member of the Council, he had not agreed with their decision and action.

→

He went into the presence of Pilate and asked for the body of Jesus. Then he took the body down, wrapped it in a linen sheet, and placed it in a tomb which had been dug out of solid rock and which had never been used. It was Friday, and the Sabbath was about to begin.

Narrator 2   The women who had followed Jesus from Galilee went with Joseph and saw the tomb and how Jesus' body was placed in it. Then they went back home and prepared the spices and perfumes for the body.

Narrator 1   On the Sabbath they rested, as the Law commanded.

Cast	[This is] the word of the Lord. OR	This is the Gospel of Christ / *This is the Gospel of the Lord.*
All	**Thanks be to God.**	**Praise to Christ our Lord** / *Praise to you, Lord Jesus Christ.*

Cast: **Narrator 1, Narrator 2.**

The Resurrection
Luke 24.1–12

Narrator   Very early on Sunday morning the women went to the tomb, carrying the spices they had prepared. They found the stone rolled away from the entrance to the tomb, so they went in; but they did not find the body of the Lord Jesus. They stood there puzzled about this, when suddenly two men in bright shining clothes stood by them. Full of fear, the women bowed down to the ground, as the men said to them:

Man 1   Why are you looking among the dead for one who is alive?

Man 2   He is not here; he has been raised.

Man 1   Remember what he said to you while he was in Galilee:

Man 2   'The Son of Man must be handed over to sinful men, and be crucified.'

Man 1   'And three days later rise to life.'

Narrator   Then the women remembered his words, returned from the tomb, and told all these things to the eleven disciples and all the rest. The women were Mary Magdalene, Joanna, and Mary the mother of James; they and the other women with them told these things to the apostles. But the apostles thought that what the women said was nonsense, and they did not believe them. But Peter got up and ran to the tomb; he bent down and saw the linen wrappings but nothing else. Then he went back home amazed at what had happened.

Cast	[This is] the word of the Lord. OR	This is the Gospel of Christ / *This is the Gospel of the Lord.*
All	**Thanks be to God.**	**Praise to Christ our Lord** / *Praise to you, Lord Jesus Christ.*

Cast: **Narrator, Man 1, Man 2.**

On the road to Emmaus
Luke 24.13–35

Narrator	Now that same day two of them were going to a village called Emmaus, about seven miles from Jerusalem. They were talking with each other about everything that had happened. As they talked and discussed these things with each other, Jesus himself came up and walked along with them; but they were kept from recognising him. He asked them:
Jesus	What are you discussing together as you walk along?
Narrator	They stood still, their faces downcast. One of them, named Cleopas, asked him:
Cleopas	Are you only a visitor to Jerusalem and do not know the things that have happened there in these days?
Jesus	What things?
Cleopas	About Jesus of Nazareth.
Companion	He was a prophet, powerful in word and deed before God and all the people.
Cleopas	The chief priests and our rulers handed him over to be sentenced to death, and they crucified him.
Companion	But we had hoped that he was the one who was going to redeem Israel.
Cleopas	And what is more, it is the third day since all this took place.
Companion	In addition, some of our women amazed us. They went to the tomb early this morning but didn't find his body.
Cleopas	They came and told us that they had seen a vision of angels, who said he was alive.
Companion	Then some of our companions went to the tomb and found it just as the women had said.
Cleopas	But him they did not see.
Jesus	How foolish you are, and how slow of heart to believe all that the prophets have spoken! Did not the Christ have to suffer these things and then enter his glory?
Narrator	And beginning with Moses and all the Prophets, he explained to them what was said in all the Scriptures concerning himself. (PAUSE) As they approached the village to which they were going, Jesus acted as if he were going further. But they urged him strongly:
Companion	Stay with us, for it is nearly evening.
Cleopas	The day is almost over.
Narrator	So he went in to stay with them. (PAUSE) When he was at the table with them, he took bread, gave thanks, broke it and began to give

it to them. Then their eyes were opened and they recognised him, and he disappeared from their sight. (PAUSE) They asked each other:

Cleopas   Were not our hearts burning within us while he talked with us on the road . . .

Companion   . . . and opened the Scriptures to us?

Narrator   They got up and returned at once to Jerusalem. There they found the Eleven and those with them, assembled together and saying:

Disciple 1   It is true!

Disciple 2   The Lord has risen.

Disciple 1   And has appeared to Simon.

Narrator   Then the two told what had happened on the way, and how Jesus was recognised by them when he broke the bread.

Cast   [This is] the word of the Lord.   OR   This is the Gospel of Christ / *This is the Gospel of the Lord.*
All   **Thanks be to God.**   **Praise to Christ our Lord** / *Praise to you, Lord Jesus Christ.*

Cast: **Narrator, Jesus, Cleopas, Companion, Disciple 1, Disciple 2.**

Jesus appears to his disciples and is taken up to heaven
Luke 24.36–53

Narrator   Suddenly the Lord himself stood among his disciples [and said to them]:

Jesus   Peace be with you.

Narrator   They were terrified, thinking that they were seeing a ghost.

Jesus   Why are you alarmed? Why are these doubts coming up in your minds? Look at my hands and my feet, and see that it is I myself. Feel me, and you will know, for a ghost doesn't have flesh and bones, as you can see I have.

Narrator   He said this and showed them his hands and his feet. They still could not believe, they were so full of joy and wonder; so he asked them:

Jesus   Have you anything here to eat?

Narrator   They gave him a piece of cooked fish, which he took and ate in their presence. (PAUSE)

Jesus   These are the very things I told you about while I was still with you: everything written about me in the Law of Moses, the writings of the prophets, and the Psalms had to come true.

Narrator   Then he opened their minds to understand the Scriptures:

Jesus   This is what is written: the Messiah must suffer and must rise from death three days later, and in his name the message about repentance and the forgiveness of sins must be preached to all nations, beginning in Jerusalem. You are witnesses of these things. And I myself will send upon you what my Father has promised. But you must wait in the city until the power from above comes down upon you.

Narrator   Then he led them out of the city as far as Bethany, where he raised his hands and blessed them. As he was blessing them, he departed from them and was taken up into heaven. They worshipped him and went back into Jerusalem, filled with great joy, and spent all their time in the Temple giving thanks to God.

Cast	[This is] the word of the Lord. OR	This is the Gospel of Christ / *This is the Gospel of the Lord.*
All	**Thanks be to God.**	**Praise to Christ our Lord** / *Praise to you, Lord Jesus Christ.*

Cast: **Narrator, Jesus.**

THE GOSPEL OF
JOHN

The Word became flesh
John 1.1–14 [15–18]

Voice 1	In the beginning was the Word, and the Word was with God, and the Word was God. He was with God in the beginning.
Voice 2	Through him all things were made; without him nothing was made that has been made.
Voice 1	In him was life, and that life was the light of men. The light shines in the darkness, but the darkness has not understood it.
Voice 3	There came a man who was sent from God; his name was John. He came as a witness to testify concerning that light, so that through him all men might believe.
Voice 4	He himself was not the light; he came only as a witness to the light.
Voice 2	The true light that gives light to every man was coming into the world.
Voice 1	He was in the world, and though the world was made through him, the world did not recognise him.
Voice 2	He came to that which was his own, but his own did not receive him. Yet to all who received him, to those who believed in his name, he gave the right to become children of God—
Voice 4	Children born not of natural descent, nor of human decision or a husband's will, but born of God.
Voice 1	The Word became flesh and made his dwelling among us. We have seen his glory, the glory of the One and Only, who came from the Father, full of grace and truth.
[Voice 3	John testifies concerning him. He cries out, saying:
John the Baptist	This was he of whom I said, 'He who comes after me has surpassed me because he was before me.'
Voice 2	From the fulness of his grace we have all received one blessing after another.
Voice 3	For the law was given through Moses; grace and truth came through Jesus Christ.
Voice 1	No-one has ever seen God, but God the One and Only, who is at the Father's side, has made him known.]

Cast	[This is] the word of the Lord. OR This is the Gospel of Christ / *This is the Gospel of the Lord.*
All	**Thanks be to God.** **Praise to Christ our Lord** / *Praise to you, Lord Jesus Christ.*

Cast: **Voice 1, Voice 2, Voice 3, Voice 4, [John the Baptist]**. (See also Appendix: Christmas Readings, page 411.)

John—the messenger
From John 1.6–36

Narrator	God sent his messenger, a man named John, who came to tell people about the light, so that all should hear the message and believe. He himself was not the light; he came to tell about the light. This was the real light—the light that comes into the world and shines on all mankind.
	John spoke about him. He cried out:
John	This is the one I was talking about when I said, 'He comes after me, but he is greater than I am, because he existed before I was born.'
Narrator	The Jewish authorities in Jerusalem sent some priests and Levites to John, to ask him:
Lawyer	Who are you?
Narrator	John did not refuse to answer, but spoke out openly and clearly:
John	I am not the Messiah.
Lawyer	Who are you, then?
Priest	Are you Elijah?
John	No, I am not.
Lawyer	Are you the Prophet?
John	No.
Lawyer	Then tell us who you are.
Priest	We have to take an answer back to those who sent us.
Lawyer	What do you say about yourself?
Narrator	John answered by quoting the prophet Isaiah:
John	I am 'the voice of someone shouting in the desert: Make a straight path for the Lord to travel!'
Narrator	The messengers, who had been sent by the Pharisees, then asked John:
Priest	If you are not the Messiah nor Elijah nor the Prophet, why do you baptize?
John	I baptize with water, but among you stands the one you do not know. He is coming after me, but I am not good enough even to untie his sandals.
Narrator	All this happened in Bethany on the east side of the River Jordan, where John was baptizing. (PAUSE)
	The next day John saw Jesus coming to him.
John	There is the Lamb of God, who takes away the sin of the world! This is the one I was talking about when I said, 'A man is coming

→

after me, but he is greater than I am, because he existed before I was born.' I did not know who he would be, but I came baptizing with water in order to make him known to the people of Israel.

Narrator   And John gave this testimony:

John   I saw the Spirit come down like a dove from heaven and stay on him. I still did not know that he was the one, but God, who sent me to baptize with water, had said to me, 'You will see the Spirit come down and stay on a man; he is the one who baptizes with the Holy Spirit.' I have seen it and I tell you that he is the Son of God. (PAUSE)

Narrator   The next day John was standing there again with two of his disciples, when he saw Jesus walking by. [He said:]

John   There is the Lamb of God!

Cast   [This is] the word of the Lord.   OR   This is the Gospel of Christ / *This is the Gospel of the Lord.*
All   **Thanks be to God.**   **Praise to Christ our Lord** / *Praise to you, Lord Jesus Christ.*

Cast: **Narrator, John, Lawyer, Priest** (can be the same as Lawyer). (See also Appendix: Christmas Readings, page 411).

The first disciples of Jesus
John 1.38–51

Narrator   Jesus turned and saw two of John's disciples following him.

Jesus   What are you looking for?

Disciple and
   Andrew   Where do you live, Rabbi?

Narrator   This word means 'Teacher'.

Jesus   Come and see.

Narrator   It was then about four o'clock in the afternoon. So they went with him and saw where he lived, and spent the rest of that day with him. (PAUSE)

          One of them was Andrew, Simon Peter's brother. At once he found his brother Simon [and told him]:

Andrew   We have found the Messiah.

Narrator   This word means 'Christ'. Then he took Simon to Jesus. Jesus looked at him [and said]:

Jesus   Your name is Simon son of John, but you will be called Cephas.

Narrator   This is the same as Peter and means 'a rock'. (PAUSE) The next day Jesus decided to go to Galilee. He found Philip [and said to him]:

Jesus   Come with me!

Narrator   Philip was from Bethsaida, the town where Andrew and Peter lived—Philip found Nathanael [and told him]:

Philip	We have found the one whom Moses wrote about in the book of the Law and whom the prophets also wrote about. He is Jesus son of Joseph, from Nazareth.
[Narrator	Nathanael asked:]
Nathanael	Can anything good come from Nazareth?
Philip	Come and see.
Narrator	When Jesus saw Nathanael coming to him, he said about him:
Jesus	Here is a real Israelite; there is nothing false in him!
Nathanael	How do you know me?
Jesus	I saw you when you were under the fig-tree before Philip called you.
Nathanael	Teacher, you are the Son of God! You are the King of Israel!
Jesus	Do you believe just because I told you I saw you when you were under the fig-tree? You will see much greater things than this!
Jesus (to the disciples)	I am telling you the truth: you will see heaven open and God's angels going up and coming down on the Son of Man.

Cast	[This is] the word of the Lord.	OR	This is the Gospel of Christ / *This is the Gospel of the Lord.*
All	**Thanks be to God.**		**Praise to Christ our Lord** / *Praise to you, Lord Jesus Christ.*

Cast: **Narrator, Jesus, Disciple, Andrew** (can be the same as Disciple), **Philip, Nathanael.** (See also composite reading below.)

Jesus makes up his team
From John 1, Matthew 4 and 9

Narrator	Jesus decided to go to Galilee. He found Philip [and said]:
Jesus	Come with me!
Narrator	Philip found Nathanael [and told him]:
Philip	We have found the one whom Moses wrote about in the book of the Law and whom the prophets also wrote about. He is Jesus son of Joseph, from Nazareth.
[Narrator	Nathanael asked:]
Nathanael	Can anything good come from Nazareth?
Philip	Come and see.
Narrator	When Jesus saw Nathanael coming to him, he said about him:
Jesus	Here is a real Israelite; there is nothing false in him!
Nathanael	How do you know me?
Jesus	I saw you when you were under the fig-tree before Philip called you.
Nathanael	Teacher, you are the Son of God! You are the King of Israel!
Narrator	As Jesus walked along the shore of Lake Galilee, he saw two brothers who were fishermen, Simon—called Peter—and his brother Andrew, catching fish in the lake with a net. [Jesus said to them:]

Jesus	Come with me, and I will teach you to catch men.
Narrator	At once they left their nets and went with him. (PAUSE)
	He went on and saw two other brothers, James and John, the sons of Zebedee. They were in their boat with their father Zebedee, getting their nets ready. Jesus called them, and at once they left the boat and their father, and went with him.
	As Jesus walked along, he saw a tax collector, named Matthew, sitting in his office. [He said to him:]
Jesus	Follow me.
Narrator	Matthew got up and followed him. (PAUSE)
	While Jesus was having a meal in Matthew's house, many tax collectors and other outcasts came and joined Jesus and his disciples at the table. Some Pharisees saw this and asked his disciples:
Pharisee	Why does your teacher eat with such people?
Narrator	Jesus heard them [and answered]:
Jesus	People who are well do not need a doctor, but only those who are sick. I have not come to call respectable people, but outcasts.

Cast	[This is] the word of the Lord.	OR	This is the Gospel of Christ / *This is the Gospel of the Lord.*
All	**Thanks be to God.**		**Praise to Christ our Lord** / *Praise to you, Lord Jesus Christ.*

Cast: **Narrator, Jesus, Philip, Nathanael, Pharisee.** (See page 200 for Johannine version only.)

Jesus changes water to wine
From John 2.1–11

Narrator	On the third day a wedding took place at Cana in Galilee. Jesus' mother was there, and Jesus and his disciples had also been invited to the wedding. When the wine was gone, Jesus' mother said to him:
Mary	They have no more wine.
Jesus	Dear woman, why do you involve me? My time has not yet come.
Narrator	His mother said to the servants:
Mary	Do whatever he tells you.
Narrator	Nearby stood six stone water jars, the kind used by the Jews for ceremonial washing, each holding from twenty to thirty gallons. Jesus spoke to the servants:
Jesus	Fill the jars with water.
Narrator	So they filled them to the brim.
Jesus	Now draw some out and take it to the master of the banquet.
Narrator	They did so, and the master of the banquet tasted the water that had been turned into wine. He did not realise where it had come

from, though the servants who had drawn the water knew. Then he called the bridegroom aside:

Master   Everyone brings out the choice wine first and then the cheaper wine after the guests have had too much to drink; but you have saved the best till now.

Narrator   This, the first of his miraculous signs, Jesus performed in Cana of Galilee. He thus revealed his glory, and his disciples put their faith in him.

Cast	[This is] the word of the Lord. OR	This is the Gospel of Christ / *This is the Gospel of the Lord.*
All	**Thanks be to God.**	**Praise to Christ our Lord** / *Praise to you, Lord Jesus Christ.*

Cast: **Narrator, Mary, Jesus, Master.**

Jesus goes to the Temple
John 2.13–22 [23–25]

Narrator   It was almost time for the Passover Festival, so Jesus went to Jerusalem. There in the Temple he found men selling cattle, sheep, and pigeons, and also the money-changers sitting at their tables. So he made a whip from cords and drove all the animals out of the Temple, both the sheep and the cattle; he overturned the tables of the money-changers and scattered their coins; and he ordered the men who sold the pigeons:

Jesus   Take them out of here! Stop making my Father's house a market-place!

Narrator   His disciples remembered that the scripture says:

Psalmist   My devotion to your house, O God, burns in me like a fire.

Narrator   The Jewish authorities replied with a question:

Lawyer   What miracle can you perform to show us that you have the right to do this?

Jesus   Tear down this Temple, and in three days I will build it again.

Lawyer   Are you going to build it again in three days? It has taken forty-six years to build this Temple!

Narrator   But the temple Jesus was speaking about was his body. So when he was raised from death, his disciples remembered that he had said this, and they believed the scripture and what Jesus had said.

[While Jesus was in Jerusalem during the Passover Festival, many believed in him as they saw the miracles he performed. But Jesus did not trust himself to them, because he knew them all. There was no need for anyone to tell him about them, because he himself knew what was in their hearts.]

Cast	[This is] the word of the Lord. OR	This is the Gospel of Christ / *This is the Gospel of the Lord.*
All	**Thanks be to God.**	**Praise to Christ our Lord** / *Praise to you, Lord Jesus Christ.*

Cast: **Narrator, Jesus, Psalmist** (can be the same as Narrator), **Lawyer.**

Jesus and Nicodemus
John 3.1–17 [18–21]

Narrator	There was a Jewish leader named Nicodemus, who belonged to the party of the Pharisees. One night he went to Jesus.
Nicodemus	Rabbi, we know that you are a teacher sent by God. No one could perform the miracles you are doing unless God were with him.
[Narrator	Jesus answered:]
Jesus	I am telling you the truth: no one can see the Kingdom of God unless he is born again.
Nicodemus	How can a grown man be born again? He certainly cannot enter his mother's womb and be born a second time!
Jesus	I am telling you the truth, no one can enter the Kingdom of God unless he is born of water and the Spirit. A person is born physically of human parents, but he is born spiritually of the Spirit. Do not be surprised because I tell you that you must all be born again. The wind blows wherever it wishes; you hear the sound it makes, but you do not know where it comes from or where it is going. It is like that with everyone who is born of the Spirit.
Nicodemus	How can this be?
Jesus	You are a great teacher in Israel, and you don't know this? I am telling you the truth: we speak of what we know and report what we have seen, yet none of you is willing to accept our message. You do not believe me when I tell you about the things of this world; how will you ever believe me, then, when I tell you about the things of heaven? No one has ever gone up to heaven except the Son of Man, who came down from heaven. As Moses lifted up the bronze snake on a pole in the desert, in the same way the Son of Man must be lifted up, so that everyone who believes in him may have eternal life. For God loved the world so much that he gave his only Son, so that everyone who believes in him may not die but have eternal life. For God did not send his Son into the world to be its judge, but to be its saviour.
	[Whoever believes in the Son is not judged; but whoever does not believe has already been judged, because he has not believed in God's only Son. This is how the judgement works: the light has come into the world, but people love the darkness rather than the light, because their deeds are evil. Anyone who does evil things hates the light and will not come to the light because he does not want his evil deeds to be shown up. But whoever does what is true comes to the light in order that the light may show that what he did was in obedience to God.]

Cast	[This is] the word of the Lord. OR	This is the Gospel of Christ / *This is the Gospel of the Lord.*
All	**Thanks be to God.**	**Praise to Christ our Lord** / *Praise to you, Lord Jesus Christ.*

Cast: **Narrator, Nicodemus, Jesus.**

Jesus and John
John 3.22–30 [31–36]

Narrator	Jesus and his disciples went to the province of Judaea, where he spent some time with them and baptized. John also was baptizing in Aenon, not far from Salim, because there was plenty of water in that place. People were going to him, and he was baptizing them.
[Commentator	This was before John had been put in prison.]
Narrator	Some of John's disciples began arguing with a Jew about the matter of ritual washing. So they went to John.
Disciple 1	Teacher, you remember the man who was with you on the east side of the Jordan.
Disciple 2	The one you spoke about?
Disciple 1	Well, *he* is baptizing now—
Disciple 2	And everyone is going to him!
Narrator	John answered:
John the Baptist	No one can have anything unless God gives it to him. You yourselves are my witnesses that I said, 'I am not the Messiah, but I have been sent ahead of him.' The bridegroom is the one to whom the bride belongs; but the bridegroom's friend, who stands by and listens, is glad when he hears the bridegroom's voice. This is how my own happiness is made complete. He must become more important while I become less important.

[He who comes from above is greater than all. He who is from the earth belongs to the earth and speaks about earthly matters, but he who comes from heaven is above all. He tells what he has seen and heard, yet no one accepts his message. But whoever accepts his message confirms by this that God is truthful. The one whom God has sent speaks God's words, because God gives him the fullness of his Spirit. The Father loves his Son and has put everything in his power. Whoever believes in the Son has eternal life; whoever disobeys the Son will not have life, but will remain under God's punishment.] |

Cast	[This is] the word of the Lord.	OR	This is the Gospel of Christ / *This is the Gospel of the Lord.*
All	**Thanks be to God.**		**Praise to Christ our Lord** / *Praise to you, Lord Jesus Christ.*

Cast: **Narrator, [Commentator,] Disciple 1, Disciple 2, John the Baptist.**

Jesus and the Samaritan woman
From John 4.5–42

Narrator	In Samaria Jesus came to a town named Sychar, which was not far from the field that Jacob had given to his son Joseph. Jacob's well was there, and Jesus, tired out by the journey, sat down by the well. It was about noon. A Samaritan woman came to draw some water, and Jesus said to her:

Jesus	Give me a drink of water.
Narrator	His disciples had gone into town to buy food. Now Jews will not use the same cups and bowls that Samaritans use.
	[So the woman answered:]
Woman	You are a Jew, and I am a Samaritan—so how can you ask me for a drink?
Jesus	If only you knew what God gives and who it is that is asking you for a drink, you would ask him, and he would give you life-giving water.
Woman	Sir, you haven't got a bucket, and the well is deep. Where would you get that life-giving water? It was our ancestor Jacob who gave us this well; he and his sons and his flocks all drank from it. You don't claim to be greater than Jacob, do you?
Jesus	Whoever drinks this water will be thirsty again, but whoever drinks the water that I will give him will never be thirsty again. The water that I will give him will become in him a spring which will provide him with life-giving water and give him eternal life.
Woman	Sir, give me that water! Then I will never be thirsty again, nor will I have to come here to draw water.
Jesus	Go and call your husband, and come back.
Woman	I haven't got a husband.
Jesus	You are right when you say you haven't got a husband. You have been married to five men, and the man you live with now is not really your husband. You have told me the truth.
[Woman	I see you are a prophet, sir. My Samaritan ancestors worshipped God on this mountain, but you Jews say that Jerusalem is the place where we should worship God.
Jesus	Believe me, woman, the time will come when people will not worship the Father either on this mountain or in Jerusalem. You Samaritans do not really know whom you worship; but we Jews know whom we worship, because it is from the Jews that salvation comes. But the time is coming and is already here, when by the power of God's Spirit people will worship the Father as he really is, offering him the true worship that he wants. God is Spirit, and only by the power of his Spirit can people worship him as he really is.
Woman	I know that the Messiah will come, and when he comes, he will tell us everything. (PAUSE)
Jesus (slowly)	I am he, I who am talking with you.
Narrator	At that moment Jesus' disciples returned, and they were greatly surprised to find him talking with a woman. But none of them said to her, 'What do you want?' or asked him, 'Why are you talking with her?' (PAUSE)]
	Then the woman left her water jar, went back to the town, and said to the people there:

Woman	Come and see the man who told me everything I have ever done. Could he be the Messiah?
Narrator	So they left the town and went to Jesus. Many of the Samaritans in that town believed in Jesus because the woman had said:
[Woman]	He told me everything I have ever done.
Narrator	So when the Samaritans came to him, they begged him to stay with them, and Jesus stayed there two days. Many more believed because of his message, and they said to the woman:
Person 1	We believe now, not because of what you said, but because we ourselves have heard him.
Person 2	And we know that he really is the Saviour of the world.

Cast	[This is] the word of the Lord. OR This is the Gospel of Christ / *This is the Gospel of the Lord.*
All	**Thanks be to God.** **Praise to Christ our Lord** / *Praise to you, Lord Jesus Christ.*

Cast: **Narrator, Jesus, Woman, Person 1, Person 2 (can be the same as Person 1).**

Jesus heals an official's son
John 4.43–54

Narrator	After spending two days in Samaria, Jesus left and went to Galilee. For he himself had said:
[Jesus]	A prophet is not respected in his own country.
Narrator	When he arrived in Galilee, the people there welcomed him, because they had gone to the Passover Festival in Jerusalem and had seen everything that he had done during the festival. (PAUSE)
	Then Jesus went back to Cana in Galilee, where he had turned the water into wine. A government official was there whose son was ill in Capernaum. When he heard that Jesus had come from Judaea to Galilee, he went to him and asked him to go to Capernaum and heal his son, who was about to die. Jesus said to him:
Jesus	None of you will ever believe unless you see miracles and wonders.
[Narrator	The official replied:]
Official	Sir, come with me before my child dies.
Jesus	Go, your son will live!
Narrator	The man believed Jesus' words and went. On his way home his servants met him with this news:
Servant 1	Your boy is going to live!
Narrator	He asked them what time it was when his son got better. [And they answered:]
Servant 2	It was one o'clock yesterday afternoon when the fever left him.

Narrator	Then the father remembered that it was at that very hour when Jesus had told him, 'Your son will live.' So he and all his family believed.
	This was the second miracle that Jesus performed after coming from Judaea to Galilee.

Cast	[This is] the word of the Lord. OR This is the Gospel of Christ / *This is the Gospel of the Lord.*
All	**Thanks be to God.** **Praise to Christ our Lord** / *Praise to you, Lord Jesus Christ.*

Cast: **Narrator, Jesus, Official, Servant 1, Servant 2** (can be the same as Servant 1).

The healing at the pool
From John 5.1–18

Narrator	Jesus went to Jerusalem for a religious festival. Near the Sheep Gate in Jerusalem there is a pool with five porches; in Hebrew it is called Bethzatha. A large crowd of sick people were lying in the porches—the blind, the lame, and the paralysed. A man was there who had been ill for thirty-eight years. Jesus saw him lying there, and he knew that the man had been ill for such a long time; so he asked him:
Jesus	Do you want to get well?
[Narrator	The sick man answered:]
Man	Sir, I have no one here to put me in the pool when the water is stirred up; while I am trying to get in, somebody else gets there first.
Jesus	Get up, pick up your mat, and walk.
Narrator	Immediately the man got well; he picked up his mat and started walking. (PAUSE)
	The day this happened was a Sabbath, so the Jewish authorities told the man who had been healed:
Lawyer 1	This is a Sabbath—
Lawyer 2	It is against our Law for you to carry your mat.
Man	The man who made me well told me to pick up my mat and walk.
Lawyer 1	Who is the man who told you to do this?
Narrator	But the man who had been healed did not know who Jesus was, for there was a crowd in that place, and Jesus had slipped away. (PAUSE)
	Afterwards, Jesus found him in the Temple.
Jesus	Listen, you are well now; so stop sinning or something worse may happen to you.
Narrator	Then the man left and told the Jewish authorities that it was Jesus who had healed him. So they began to persecute Jesus, because he had done this healing on a Sabbath. Jesus answered them:
Jesus (to Lawyers)	My Father is always working, and I too must work.

| Narrator | This saying made the Jewish authorities all the more determined to kill him; not only had he broken the Sabbath law, but he had said that God was his own Father and in this way had made himself equal with God. |

| Cast | [This is] the word of the Lord.   OR   This is the Gospel of Christ / *This is the Gospel of the Lord.* |
| All | **Thanks be to God.**   **Praise to Christ our Lord** / *Praise to you, Lord Jesus Christ.* |

Cast: **Narrator, Jesus, Man, Lawyer 1, Lawyer 2** (can be the same as Lawyer 1).

Jesus feeds five thousand
John 6.1–15

Narrator	Jesus went across Lake Galilee—or, Lake Tiberias, as it is also called. A large crowd followed him, because they had seen his miracles of healing those who were ill. Jesus went up a hill and sat down with his disciples. The time for the Passover Festival was near. Jesus looked round and saw that a large crowd was coming to him, so he asked Philip:
Jesus	Where can we buy enough food to feed all these people?
Narrator	He said this to test Philip; actually he already knew what he would do. [Philip answered:]
Philip	For everyone to have even a little, it would take more than two hundred silver coins to buy enough bread.
Narrator	Another of his disciples, Andrew, who was Simon Peter's brother, said:
Andrew	There is a boy here who has five loaves of barley bread and two fish. But they will certainly not be enough for all these people.
Jesus	Make the people sit down.
Narrator	There was a lot of grass there. So all the people sat down; there were about five thousand men. Jesus took the bread, gave thanks to God, and distributed it to the people who were sitting there. He did the same with the fish, and they all had as much as they wanted. When they were all full, he said to his disciples:
Jesus	Gather the pieces left over; let us not waste any.
Narrator	So they gathered them all up and filled twelve baskets with the pieces left over from the five barley loaves which the people had eaten. (PAUSE)
	Seeing this miracle that Jesus had performed, the people there said:
Persons 1 and 2	Surely this is the Prophet who was to come into the world!
Narrator	Jesus knew that they were about to come and seize him in order to make him king by force; so he went off again to the hills by himself.

| Cast | [This is] the word of the Lord.   OR   This is the Gospel of Christ / *This is the Gospel of the Lord.* |
| All | **Thanks be to God.**   **Praise to Christ our Lord** / *Praise to you, Lord Jesus Christ.* |

Cast: **Narrator, Jesus, Philip, Andrew, Person 1, Person 2** (Persons 1 and 2 can be the same as Philip and Andrew).

Jesus walks on the water
John 6.16–24

Narrator 1   When evening came, his disciples went down to the lake, where they got into a boat and set off across the lake for Capernaum.

Narrator 2   By now it was dark, and Jesus had not yet joined them. A strong wind was blowing and the waters grew rough.

Narrator 1   When they had rowed three or three and a half miles, they saw Jesus approaching the boat, walking on the water; and they were terrified. But he said to them:

Jesus   It is I; don't be afraid.

Narrator 1   Then they were willing to take him into the boat, and immediately the boat reached the shore where they were heading.

Narrator 2   The next day the crowd that had stayed on the opposite shore of the lake realised that only one boat had been there, and that Jesus had not entered it with his disciples, but that they had gone away alone.

Narrator 1   Then some boats from Tiberias landed near the place where the people had eaten the bread after the Lord had given thanks. Once the crowd realised that neither Jesus nor his disciples were there, they got into the boats and went to Capernaum in search of Jesus.

Cast	[This is] the word of the Lord. OR	This is the Gospel of Christ / *This is the Gospel of the Lord.*
All	**Thanks be to God.**	**Praise to Christ our Lord** / *Praise to you, Lord Jesus Christ.*

Cast: **Narrator 1, Narrator 2, Jesus.**

Jesus the bread of life
John 6.25–35

Narrator   When the people found Jesus on the other side of the lake, they said to him:

Person 1   Teacher!

Person 2   When did you get here?

Jesus   I am telling you the truth: you are looking for me because you ate the bread and had all you wanted, not because you understood my miracles. Do not work for food that goes bad; instead, work for the food that lasts for eternal life. This is the food which the Son of Man will give you, because God, the Father, has put his mark of approval on him.

Person 1   What can we do in order to do what God wants?

Jesus   What God wants you to do is to believe in the one he sent.

Person 2   What miracle will you perform so that we may see it and believe you?

Person 1	What will you do? Our ancestors ate manna in the desert, just as the scripture says, 'He gave them bread from heaven to eat.'
Jesus	I am telling you the truth. What Moses gave you was not the bread from heaven; it is my Father who gives you the real bread from heaven. For the bread that God gives is he who comes down from heaven and gives life to the world.
Persons 1 and **2**	Sir, give us this bread always.
Jesus	I am the bread of life. He who comes to me will never be hungry; he who believes in me will never be thirsty.

Cast	[This is] the word of the Lord. OR This is the Gospel of Christ / *This is the Gospel of the Lord.*
All	**Thanks be to God.** **Praise to Christ our Lord** / *Praise to you, Lord Jesus Christ.*

Cast: **Narrator, Person 1, Person 2, Jesus.**

Life-giving bread
From John 6.41–51 [52–55]

Narrator	The people started grumbling about Jesus, because he said:
Jesus	I am the bread that came down from heaven.
Narrator	So they said:
Person 1	This man is Jesus son of Joseph, isn't he?
Person 2	We know his father and mother.
Person 1	How, then, does he now say he came down from heaven?
[Narrator	Jesus answered:]
Jesus	No one can come to me unless the Father who sent me draws him to me; and I will raise him to life on the last day. He who believes has eternal life. I am the bread of life. Your ancestors ate manna in the desert, but they died. But the bread that comes down from heaven is of such a kind that whoever eats it will not die. I am the living bread that came down from heaven. If anyone eats this bread, he will live for ever. The bread that I will give him is my flesh, which I give so that the world may live.
[Narrator	This started an angry argument among them.
Person 2	How can this man give us his flesh to eat?
Narrator	Jesus said to them:
Jesus	I am telling you the truth: if you do not eat the flesh of the Son of Man and drink his blood, you will not have life in yourselves. Whoever eats my blood has eternal life, and I will raise him to life on the last day. For my flesh is the real food; my blood is the real drink.]

Cast	[This is] the word of the Lord. OR This is the Gospel of Christ / *This is the Gospel of the Lord.*
All	**Thanks be to God.** **Praise to Christ our Lord** / *Praise to you, Lord Jesus Christ.*

Cast: **Narrator, Jesus, Person 1, Person 2.**

The words of eternal life
From John 6.56–69 [70–71]

Narrator	Jesus said this as he taught in the synagogue in Capernaum:
Jesus	Whoever eats my flesh and drinks my blood lives in me, and I live in him. The living Father sent me, and because of him I live also. In the same way whoever eats me will live because of me. This, then, is the bread that came down from heaven; it is not like the bread that your ancestors ate, but then later died. The one who eats this bread will live for ever.
Narrator	Many of his followers heard this and said:
Follower 1	This teaching is too hard—
Follower 2	Who can listen to it?
Narrator	Without being told, Jesus knew that they were grumbling about this, so he said to them:
Jesus	Does this make you want to give up? Suppose, then, that you should see the Son of Man go back up to the place where he was before? What gives life is God's Spirit; man's power is of no use at all. The words I have spoken to you bring God's life-giving Spirit. Yet some of you do not believe. This is the very reason I told you that no one can come to me unless the Father makes it possible for him to do so.
Narrator	Because of this, many of Jesus' followers turned back and would not go with him any more. So he asked the twelve disciples:
Jesus	And you—would you also like to leave?
Narrator	Simon Peter answered him:
Peter	Lord, to whom would we go? You have the words that give eternal life. And now we believe and know that you are the Holy One who has come from God.
[Narrator	Jesus replied:
Jesus	I chose the twelve of you, didn't I? Yet one of you is a devil!
Narrator	He was talking about Judas, the son of Simon Iscariot. For Judas, even though he was one of the twelve disciples, was going to betray him.]

Cast	[This is] the word of the Lord. OR This is the Gospel of Christ / *This is the Gospel of the Lord.*
All	**Thanks be to God.** **Praise to Christ our Lord** / *Praise to you, Lord Jesus Christ.*

Cast: **Narrator, Jesus, Follower 1, Follower 2, Peter** (can be the same as Follower 1).

Jesus and his brothers
John 7.1–10 [11–13]

Narrator	Jesus went around in Galilee, purposely staying away from Judaea because the Jews there were waiting to take his life.

	But when the Jewish Feast of Tabernacles was near, Jesus' brothers said to him:
Brother 1	You ought to leave here and go to Judea, so that your disciples may see the miracles you do.
Brother 2	No-one who wants to become a public figure acts in secret. Since you are doing these things, show yourself to the world.
Narrator	For even his own brothers did not believe in him. Therefore Jesus told them:
Jesus	The right time for me has not yet come; for you any time is right. The world cannot hate you, but it hates me because I testify that what it does is evil. You go to the Feast. I am not yet going up to this Feast, because for me the right time has not yet come.
Narrator	Having said this, he stayed in Galilee. However, after his brothers had left for the Feast, he went also, not publicly, but in secret.
	[Now at the Feast the Jews were watching for him and asking:
Person 1	Where is that man?
Narrator	Among the crowds there was widespread whispering about him. Some said:
Person 2	He is a good man.
Narrator	Others replied:
Person 1	No, he deceives the people.
Narrator	But no-one would say anything publicly about him for fear of the Jews.]

Cast	[This is] the word of the Lord.	OR	This is the Gospel of Christ / *This is the Gospel of the Lord.*
All	**Thanks be to God.**		**Praise to Christ our Lord** / *Praise to you, Lord Jesus Christ.*

Cast: **Narrator, Brother 1, Brother 2, Jesus, [Person 1** (harsh voice), **Person 2** (appreciative voice)]. (The bracketed section should be omitted if the next reading is also to be used.)

Jesus at the Festival of Shelters
From John 7.11–31

Narrator	The Jewish authorities were looking for Jesus at the festival. They asked:
Ruler	Where is he?
Narrator	There was much whispering about him in the crowd. [Some people said:]
Person 1 (positive voice)	He is a good man.
[Narrator	Others said:]
Person 2 (critical voice)	No, he is misleading the people.

Narrator	But no one talked about him openly, because they were afraid of the Jewish authorities. (PAUSE)
	The festival was nearly half over when Jesus went to the Temple and began teaching. The Jewish authorities were greatly surprised.
Ruler	How does this man know so much when he has never had any training?
[Narrator	Jesus answered:]
Jesus	What I teach is not my own teaching, but it comes from God, who sent me. Whoever is willing to do what God wants will know whether what I teach comes from God or whether I speak on my own authority. A person who speaks on his own authority is trying to gain glory for himself. But he who wants glory for the one who sent him is honest, and there is nothing false in him. (PAUSE)
Person 1	Isn't this the man the authorities are trying to kill?
Person 2	Look! He is talking in public, and they say nothing against him!
Person 1	Can it be that they really know that he is the Messiah?
Person 2	But when the Messiah comes, no one will know where he is from. And we all know where this man comes from.
Narrator	Jesus taught in the Temple. [He said in a loud voice:]
Jesus (loudly)	Do you really know me and know where I am from? I have not come on my own authority. He who sent me, however, is truthful. You do not know him, but I know him, because I come from him and he sent me.
Narrator	Then they tried to seize him, but no one laid a hand on him, because his hour had not yet come. But many in the crowd believed in him and said:
Person 1	When the Messiah comes, will he perform more miracles than this man has?

Cast	[This is] the word of the Lord. OR This is the Gospel of Christ / *This is the Gospel of the Lord.*
All	**Thanks be to God.** **Praise to Christ our Lord** / *Praise to you, Lord Jesus Christ.*

Cast: **Narrator, Ruler, Person 1, Person 2** (can be the same as Ruler), **Jesus.**

Guards are sent to arrest Jesus
John 7.32–36, 45–52

Narrator	The Pharisees heard the crowd whispering these things about Jesus, so they and the chief priests sent some guards to arrest him. Jesus said:
Jesus	I shall be with you a little while longer, and then I shall go away to him who sent me. You will look for me, but you will not find me, because you cannot go where I will be.
Narrator	The Jewish authorities said among themselves:

Leader 1	Where is he about to go so that we shall not find him?
Leader 2	Will he go to the Greek cities where our people live, and teach the Greeks?
Leader 1	He says that we will look for him but will not find him, and that we cannot go where he will be.
Leader 2	What does he mean?
Narrator	When the guards went back, the chief priests and Pharisees asked them:
Pharisee 1	Why did you not bring him?
Narrator	The guards answered:
Guard	Nobody has ever talked like this man!
Pharisee 1	Did he fool you, too?
Pharisee 2	Have you ever known one of the authorities or one Pharisee to believe in him?
Pharisee 1	This crowd does not know the Law of Moses, so they are under God's curse!
Narrator	One of the Pharisees there was Nicodemus, the man who had gone to see Jesus before. He said to the others:
Nicodemus	According to our Law we cannot condemn a man before hearing him and finding out what he has done.
Pharisee 1	Well, are you also from Galilee?
Pharisee 2	Study the Scriptures and you will learn that no prophet ever comes from Galilee.

Cast	[This is] the word of the Lord.	OR	This is the Gospel of Christ / *This is the Gospel of the Lord.*
All	**Thanks be to God.**		**Praise to Christ our Lord** / *Praise to you, Lord Jesus Christ.*

Cast: **Narrator, Jesus, Leader 1, Leader 2, Pharisee 1, Guard, Pharisee 2, Nicodemus.**

Streams of life-giving water
John 7.37–44

Narrator	On the last and most important day of the festival Jesus stood up and said in a loud voice:
Jesus	Whoever is thirsty should come to me and drink. As the scripture says:
[Scripture]	Whoever believes in me, streams of life-giving water will pour out from his heart.
Narrator	Jesus said this about the Spirit, which those who believed in him were going to receive. At that time the Spirit had not yet been given, because Jesus had not been raised to glory.
	Some of the people in the crowd heard him say this [and said:]
Person 1	This man is *really* the Prophet!

215

[Narrator	Others said:]
Person 2	He is the *Messiah!*
[Narrator	But others said:]
Person 3	The Messiah will not come from Galilee! The scripture says that the Messiah will be a descendant of King David and will be born in Bethlehem, the town where David lived.
Narrator	So there was a division in the crowd because of Jesus. Some wanted to seize him, but no one laid a hand on him.

Cast	[This is] the word of the Lord. OR	This is the Gospel of Christ / *This is the Gospel of the Lord.*
All	**Thanks be to God.**	**Praise to Christ our Lord** / *Praise to you, Lord Jesus Christ.*

Cast: **Narrator, Jesus, [Scripture], Person 1, Person 2, Person 3.**

The woman caught in adultery
John 8.2–11

Narrator	Early the next morning Jesus went back to the Temple. All the people gathered round him, and he sat down and began to teach them. The teachers of the Law and the Pharisees brought in a woman who had been caught committing adultery, and they made her stand before them all.
Pharisee	Teacher, this woman was caught in the very act of committing adultery.
Lawyer	In our Law Moses commanded that such a woman must be stoned to death.
Pharisee	Now, what do you say?
Narrator	They said this to trap Jesus, so that they could accuse him. But he bent over and wrote on the ground with his finger. (LONG PAUSE)
	As they stood there asking him questions, he straightened himself up:
Jesus	Whichever one of you has committed no sin may throw the first stone at her.
Narrator	Then he bent over again and wrote on the ground. When they heard this, they all left, one by one, the older ones first. Jesus was left alone, with the woman still standing there. He straightened himself up:
Jesus (to the woman)	Where are they? Is there no one left to condemn you?
Woman	No one, sir.
Jesus	Well, then, I do not condemn you either. Go, but do not sin again.

Cast	[This is] the word of the Lord. OR	This is the Gospel of Christ / *This is the Gospel of the Lord.*
All	**Thanks be to God.**	**Praise to Christ our Lord** / *Praise to you, Lord Jesus Christ.*

Cast: **Narrator, Pharisee, Lawyer** (can be the same as Pharisee)**, Jesus, Woman.**

Jesus the light of the world
John 8.12–20

Narrator	Jesus spoke to the Pharisees again:
Jesus	I am the light of the world. Whoever follows me will have the light of life and will never walk in darkness.
Narrator	The Pharisees said to him:
Pharisee 1	Now you are testifying on your own behalf—
Pharisee 2	What you say proves nothing.
Jesus	No, even though I do testify on my own behalf, what I say is true, because I know where I came from and where I am going. You do not know where I came from or where I am going. You make judgements in a purely human way; I pass judgement on no one. But if I were to do so, my judgement would be true, because I am not alone in this; the Father who sent me is with me. It is written in your Law that when two witnesses agree, what they say is true. I testify on my own behalf, and the Father who sent me also testifies on my behalf.
Pharisee 2	Where is your father?
Jesus	You know neither me nor my Father. If you knew me, you would know my Father also.
Narrator	Jesus said all this as he taught in the Temple, in the room where the offering boxes were placed. And no one arrested him, because his hour had not come.

Cast	[This is] the word of the Lord. OR	This is the Gospel of Christ / *This is the Gospel of the Lord.*
All	**Thanks be to God.**	**Praise to Christ our Lord** / *Praise to you, Lord Jesus Christ.*

Cast: **Narrator, Jesus, Pharisee 1, Pharisee 2.**

You cannot go where I am going
John 8.21–30

Narrator	Jesus said to them:
Jesus	I will go away; you will look for me, but you will die in your sins. You cannot go where I am going.
Narrator	So the Jewish authorities said:
Lawyer 1	He says that we cannot go where he is going.
Lawyer 2	Does this mean that he will kill himself?
Jesus	You belong to this world here below, but I come from above. You are from this world, but I am not from this world. That is why I told you that you will die in your sins. And you will die in your sins if you do not believe that 'I Am Who I Am'.
Lawyer 1	Who are you?

Jesus	What I have told you from the very beginning. I have much to say about you, much to condemn you for. The one who sent me, however, is truthful, and I tell the world only what I have heard from him.
Narrator	They did not understand that Jesus was talking to them about the Father. So he said to them:
Jesus	When you lift up the Son of Man, you will know that 'I Am Who I Am'; then you will know that I do nothing on my own authority, but I say only what the Father has instructed me to say. And he who sent me is with me; he has not left me alone, because I always do what pleases him.
Narrator	Many who heard Jesus say these things believed in him.

Cast	[This is] the word of the Lord. OR This is the Gospel of Christ / *This is the Gospel of the Lord.*
All	**Thanks be to God.** **Praise to Christ our Lord** / *Praise to you, Lord Jesus Christ.*

Cast: **Narrator, Jesus, Lawyer 1, Lawyer 2** (can be the same as Lawyer 1).

Are you a slave, or free?
John 8.31–36

Narrator	Jesus said to those who believed in him:
Jesus	If you obey my teaching, you are really my disciples; you will know the truth, and the truth will set you free.
[Narrator	They answered:]
Believer 1	We are the descendants of Abraham, and we have *never* been anybody's slaves—
Believer 2	What do you mean, then, by saying, 'You will be *free*'?
Jesus	I am telling you the truth: everyone who sins is a slave of sin. A slave does not belong to a family permanently, but a son belongs there for ever. If the Son sets you free, then you will be really free.

Cast	[This is] the word of the Lord. OR This is the Gospel of Christ / *This is the Gospel of the Lord.*
All	**Thanks be to God.** **Praise to Christ our Lord** / *Praise to you, Lord Jesus Christ.*

Cast: **Narrator, Jesus, Believer 1, Believer 2** (can be the same as Believer 1).

Jesus and Abraham
John 8.37–59

Narrator	Jesus said to the Pharisees:
Jesus	I know you are Abraham's descendants. Yet you are trying to kill me, because you will not accept my teaching. I talk about what my Father has shown me, but you do what your father has told you.
[Narrator	They answered him:]
Pharisee 1	Our father is Abraham.

Jesus	If you really were Abraham's children, you would do the same things that he did. All I have ever done is to tell you the truth I heard from God, yet you are trying to kill me. Abraham did nothing like this! You are doing what your father did.
Pharisee 2	God himself is the only Father we have, and we are his true sons.
Jesus	If God really were your Father, you would love me, because I came from God and now I am here. I did not come on my own authority, but he sent me. Why do you not understand what I say? It is because you cannot bear to listen to my message. You are the children of your father, the Devil, and you want to follow your father's desires. From the very beginning he was a murderer and has never been on the side of truth, because there is no truth in him. When he tells a lie, he is only doing what is natural to him, because he is a liar and the father of all lies. But I tell the truth, and that is why you do not believe me. Which one of you can prove that I am guilty of sin? If I tell the truth, then why do you not believe me? He who comes from God listens to God's words. You, however, are not from God, and that is why you will not listen.
Pharisee 1	Were we not right in saying that you are a Samaritan and you have a demon in you?
Jesus	I have no demon. I honour my Father, but you dishonour me. I am not seeking honour for myself. But there *is* one who is seeking it and who judges in my favour. I am telling you the truth: whoever obeys my teaching will never die.
Pharisee 1	Now we are certain that you have a demon!
Pharisee 2	Abraham died, and the prophets died, yet you say that whoever obeys your teaching will never die.
Pharisee 1	Our father Abraham died; you do not claim to be greater than Abraham, do you? And the prophets also died. Who do you think you are?
Jesus	If I were to honour myself, that honour would be worth nothing. The one who honours me is my Father—the very one you say is your God. You have never known him, but I know him. If I were to say that I do not know him, I would be a liar like you. But I do know him, and I obey his word. Your father Abraham rejoiced that he was to see the time of my coming; he saw it and was glad.
Pharisee 1	You are not even fifty years old—and you have seen Abraham?
Jesus	I am telling you the truth. Before Abraham was born, 'I Am'.
Narrator	Then they picked up stones to throw at him, but Jesus hid himself and left the Temple.

Cast	[This is] the word of the Lord.	OR	This is the Gospel of Christ / *This is the Gospel of the Lord.*
All	**Thanks be to God.**		**Praise to Christ our Lord** / *Praise to you, Lord Jesus Christ.*

Cast: **Narrator, Jesus, Pharisee 1, Pharisee 2.**

Jesus and the man born blind (i)
John 9.1–12

Narrator	As Jesus was walking along, he saw a man who had been born blind. His disciples asked him:
Disciple 1	Teacher, whose sin caused him to be born blind?
Disciple 2	Was it his own or his parents' sin?
[Narrator	Jesus answered:]
Jesus	His blindness has nothing to do with his sins or his parents' sins. He is blind so that God's power might be seen at work in him. As long as it is day, we must keep on doing the work of him who sent me; night is coming when no one can work. While I am in the world, I am the light for the world.
Narrator	After he said this, Jesus spat on the ground and made some mud with the spittle; he rubbed the mud on the man's eyes [and said]:
Jesus	Go and wash your face in the Pool of Siloam.
Narrator	This name means 'Sent'. So the man went, washed his face, and came back seeing. (PAUSE)
	His neighbours, then, and the people who had seen him begging before this, asked:
Person 1	Isn't this the man who used to sit and beg?
[Narrator	Some said:]
Person 2	He *is* the one.
[Narrator	But others said:]
Person 3	No he isn't; he just looks like him.
[Narrator	So the man himself said:]
Man	I *am* the man.
[Narrator	They asked him:]
Person 2	How is it that you can now see?
Man	The man called Jesus made some mud, rubbed it on my eyes, and told me to go to Siloam and wash my face. So I went, and as soon as I washed, I could see.
Person 1	Where is he?
Man	I don't know.

Cast	[This is] the word of the Lord.	OR	This is the Gospel of Christ / *This is the Gospel of the Lord.*
All	**Thanks be to God.**		**Praise to Christ our Lord** / *Praise to you, Lord Jesus Christ.*

Cast: **Narrator, Disciple 1, Disciple 2, Jesus, Person 1, Person 2, Person 3, Man.**

Jesus and the man born blind (ii)
From John 9.13–25

Narrator	[Then] they took to the Pharisees the man who had been blind. The day that Jesus made the mud and cured him of his blindness was a Sabbath. The Pharisees, then, asked the man again how he had received his sight. [He told them:]
Man	He put some mud on my eyes; I washed my face, and now I can see.
[Narrator	Some of the Pharisees said:]
Pharisee 1	The man who did this cannot be from God, for he does not obey the Sabbath law.
[Narrator	Others, however, said:]
Pharisee 2	How could a man who is a sinner perform such miracles as these? (PAUSE)
Narrator	There was a division among them. So the Pharisees asked the man once more:
Pharisee 1	You say he cured you of your blindness—well, what do you say about him?
Man	He is a prophet.
Narrator	The Jewish authorities, however, were not willing to believe that he had been blind and could now see, until they called his parents.
Pharisee 1	Is this your son?
Pharisee 2	You say that he was born blind; how is it, then, that he can now see?
Father	We know that he is our son, and we know that he was born blind.
Mother	But we do not know how it is that he is now able to see—
Father	Nor do we know who cured him of his blindness.
Mother	Ask him; he is old enough, and he can answer for himself!
[Narrator	His parents said this because they were afraid of the Jewish authorities, who had already agreed that anyone who said he believed that Jesus was the Messiah would be expelled from the synagogue. That is why his parents said, 'He is old enough; ask him!']
	A second time they called back the man who had been born blind.
Pharisee 2	Promise before God that you will tell the truth!
Pharisee 1	We know that this man who cured you is a sinner.
Man	I do not know if he is a sinner or not. One thing I do know: I was blind, and now I see.

Cast	[This is] the word of the Lord.	OR	This is the Gospel of Christ / *This is the Gospel of the Lord.*
All	**Thanks be to God.**		**Praise to Christ our Lord** / *Praise to you, Lord Jesus Christ.*

Cast: **Narrator, Man, Pharisee 1, Pharisee 2, Father, Mother.**

Jesus and the man born blind (iii)
John 9.26–34

Narrator	The Pharisees asked [the man born blind whom Jesus had made to see]:
Pharisee 1	What did Jesus do to you?
Pharisee 2	How did he cure you of your blindness?
Narrator	He answered:
Man	I have already told you, and you would not listen. Why do you want to hear it again? Maybe you, too, would like to be his disciples?
Narrator	They cursed him and said:
Pharisee 1	You are that fellow's disciple; but we are Moses' disciples.
Pharisee 2	We know that God spoke to Moses.
Pharisee 1	As for that fellow, however, we do not even know where he comes from!
Man	What a strange thing that is! You do not know where he comes from, but he cured me of my blindness! We know that God does not listen to sinners; he does listen to people who respect him and do what he wants them to do. Since the beginning of the world nobody has ever heard of anyone giving sight to a person born blind. Unless this man came from God, he would not be able to do a thing.
Pharisee 1	You were born and brought up in sin—and *you* are trying to teach *us*?
Narrator	And they expelled him from the synagogue.

Cast [This is] the word of the Lord.   OR   This is the Gospel of Christ / *This is the Gospel of the Lord.*
All   **Thanks be to God.**   **Praise to Christ our Lord** / *Praise to you, Lord Jesus Christ.*

Cast: **Narrator, Pharisee 1, Pharisee 2, Man.**

Spiritual blindness
John 9.35–41

Narrator	[When he heard what had happened] Jesus found the man born blind whom he had made to see and asked him:
Jesus	Do you believe in the Son of Man?
Man	Tell me who he is, sir, so that I can believe in him!
Jesus	You have already seen him, and he is the one who is talking with you now.
Man	I believe, Lord!
Narrator	The man knelt down before Jesus.

Jesus	I came to this world to judge, so that the blind should see and those who see should become blind.
Narrator	Some Pharisees who were there with him heard him say this [and asked him:]
Pharisee	Surely you don't mean that we are blind, too?
Jesus	If you were blind, then you would not be guilty; but since you claim that you can see, this means that you are still guilty.

Cast	[This is] the word of the Lord.	OR	This is the Gospel of Christ / *This is the Gospel of the Lord.*
All	**Thanks be to God.**		**Praise to Christ our Lord** / *Praise to you, Lord Jesus Christ.*

Cast: **Narrator, Jesus, Man, Pharisee.**

The parable of the shepherd
John 10.1–10

Narrator	Jesus said:
Jesus	I am telling you the truth: the man who does not enter the sheepfold by the gate, but climbs in some other way, is a thief and a robber. The man who goes in through the gate is the shepherd of the sheep. The gatekeeper opens the gate for him; the sheep hear his voice as he calls his own sheep by name, and he leads them out. When he has brought them out, he goes ahead of them, and the sheep follow him, because they know his voice. They will not follow someone else; instead, they will run away from such a person, because they do not know his voice.
Narrator	Jesus told them this parable, but they did not understand what he meant. So Jesus said again:
Jesus	I am telling you the truth: I am the gate for the sheep. All others who came before me are thieves and robbers, but the sheep did not listen to them. I am the gate. Whoever comes in by me will be saved; he will come in and go out and find pasture. The thief comes only in order to steal, kill, and destroy. I have come in order that you might have life—life in all its fullness.

Cast	[This is] the word of the Lord.	OR	This is the Gospel of Christ / *This is the Gospel of the Lord.*
All	**Thanks be to God.**		**Praise to Christ our Lord** / *Praise to you, Lord Jesus Christ.*

Cast: **Narrator, Jesus.**

Jesus the Good Shepherd
John 10.[11–13] 14–21

Narrator	Jesus said:
Jesus	[I am the good shepherd, who is willing to die for the sheep. When the hired man, who is not a shepherd and does not own the sheep, sees a wolf coming, he leaves the sheep and runs away; so the wolf snatches the sheep and scatters them. The hired man runs away because he is only a hired man and does not care about the sheep.]

→

I am the good shepherd. As the Father knows me and I know the Father, in the same way I know my sheep and they know me. And I am willing to die for them. There are other sheep which belong to me that are not in this sheepfold. I must bring them, too; they will listen to my voice, and they will become one flock with one shepherd.

The Father loves me because I am willing to give up my life, in order that I may receive it back again. No one takes my life away from me. I give it up of my own free will. I have the right to give it up, and I have the right to take it back. This is what my Father has commanded me to do.

Narrator	Again there was a division among the people because of these words. [Many of them were saying:]
Person 1	He has a demon!
Person 2	He is mad!
Person 1	Why do you listen to him?
[Narrator	But others were saying:]
Person 3	A man with a demon could not talk like this!
Person 4	How could a demon give sight to blind people?

Cast   [This is] the word of the Lord.   OR   This is the Gospel of Christ / *This is the Gospel of the Lord.*
All   **Thanks be to God.**   **Praise to Christ our Lord** / *Praise to you, Lord Jesus Christ.*

Cast: **Narrator, Jesus, Person 1, Person 2, Person 3, Person 4.**

Jesus is rejected
John 10.22–42

Narrator	It was winter, and the Festival of the Dedication of the Temple was being celebrated in Jerusalem. Jesus was walking in Solomon's Porch in the Temple, when the people gathered round him [and asked]:
Person 1	How long are you going to keep us in suspense?
Person 2	Tell us the plain truth: are you the Messiah?
Jesus	I have already told you, but you would not believe me. The things I do by my Father's authority speak on my behalf; but you will not believe, for you are not my sheep. My sheep listen to my voice; I know them, and they follow me. I give them eternal life, and they shall never die. No one can snatch them away from me. What my Father has given me is greater than everything, and no one can snatch them away from the Father's care. The Father and I are one.
Narrator	Then the people again picked up stones to throw at him. [Jesus said to them:]

Jesus (urgently)	I have done many good deeds in your presence which the Father gave me to do; for which one of these do you want to stone me?
Person 1	We do not want to stone you because of any good deeds, but because of your blasphemy!
Person 2	You are only a man, but you are trying to make yourself God!
Jesus	It is written in your own Law that God said, 'You are gods.' We know that what the scripture says is true for ever; and God called those people gods, the people to whom his message was given. As for me, the Father chose me and sent me into the world. How, then, can you say that I blaspheme because I said that I am the Son of God? Do not believe me, then, if I am not doing the things my Father wants me to do. But if I do them, even though you do not believe me, you should at least believe my deeds, in order that you may know once and for all that the Father is in me and that I am in the Father.
Narrator	Once more they tried to seize Jesus, but he slipped out of their hands. (PAUSE) Jesus then went back again across the River Jordan to the place where John had been baptizing, and he stayed there. Many people came to him. [They said:]
Person 3	John performed no miracles, but everything he said about this man was true.
Narrator	And many people there believed in him.

Cast	[This is] the word of the Lord. OR This is the Gospel of Christ / *This is the Gospel of the Lord.*
All	**Thanks be to God.** **Praise to Christ our Lord** / *Praise to you, Lord Jesus Christ.*

Cast: **Narrator, Person 1, Person 2, Jesus, Person 3**

Jesus the resurrection and the life
From John 11.1–44

Narrator	A man named Lazarus, who lived in Bethany, was ill. Bethany was the town where Mary and her sister Martha lived. This Mary was the one who poured the perfume on the Lord's feet and wiped them with her hair; it was her brother Lazarus who was ill. The sisters sent Jesus a message:
Mary	Lord, your dear friend is ill.
Narrator	When Jesus heard it, he said:
Jesus	The final result of this illness will not be the death of Lazarus; this has happened in order to bring glory to God, and it will be the means by which the Son of God will receive glory.
Narrator	Jesus loved Martha and her sister and Lazarus. Yet when he received the news that Lazarus was ill, he stayed where he was for two more days. Then he said to the disciples:
Jesus	Let us go back to Judaea. Our friend Lazarus has fallen asleep, but I will go and wake him up.(PAUSE)

Narrator	When Jesus arrived, he found that Lazarus had been buried four days before. When Martha heard that Jesus was coming, she went out to meet him, but Mary stayed in the house. Martha said to Jesus:
Martha	If you had been here, Lord, my brother would not have died! But I know that even now God will give you whatever you ask him for.
Jesus	Your brother will rise to life.
Martha	I know that he will rise to life on the last day.
Jesus	I am the resurrection and the life. Whoever believes in me will live, even though he dies; and whoever lives and believes in me will never die. Do you believe this?
Martha	Yes, Lord! I do believe that you are the Messiah, the Son of God, who was to come into the world.
Narrator	After Martha said this, she went back and called her sister Mary privately:
Martha	The Teacher is here, and is asking for you.
Narrator	When Mary heard this, she got up and hurried out to meet him. The people who were in the house with Mary, comforting her, followed her when they saw her get up and hurry out. They thought that she was going to the grave to weep there. (PAUSE)
	Mary arrived where Jesus was, and as soon as she saw him, she fell at his feet and said:
Mary	Lord, if you had been here, my brother would not have died!
Narrator	Jesus saw her weeping, and he saw how the people who were with her were weeping also; his heart was touched, and he was deeply moved.
Jesus	Where have you buried him?
Mary & **Martha**	Come and see, Lord.
Narrator (slowly)	Jesus wept.
	The people said:
Person 1	See how much he loved him!
Narrator	But some of them said:
Person 2	He gave sight to the blind man, didn't he? Could he not have kept Lazarus from dying?
Narrator	Deeply moved once more, Jesus went to the tomb, which was a cave with a stone placed at the entrance. [Jesus ordered:]
Jesus	Take the stone away!
Martha	There will be a bad smell, Lord. He has been buried four days!
Jesus	Didn't I tell you that you would see God's glory if you believed?
Narrator	They took the stone away. Jesus looked up and said:
Jesus	I thank you, Father, that you listen to me. I know that you always listen to me, but I say this for the sake of the people here, so that they will believe that you sent me. (PAUSE)
(loudly)	Lazarus, come out!

Narrator	He came out, his hands and feet wrapped in grave clothes, and with a cloth round his face. Jesus told them:
Jesus	Untie him, and let him go.

Cast	[This is] the word of the Lord. OR	This is the Gospel of Christ / *This is the Gospel of the Lord.*
All	**Thanks be to God.**	**Praise to Christ our Lord** / *Praise to you, Lord Jesus Christ.*

Cast: **Narrator, Mary, Jesus, Martha, Person 1, Person 2.**

The plot against Jesus
John 11.45–57

Narrator	Many of the people who had come to visit Mary saw what Jesus did and they believed in him. But some of them returned to the Pharisees and told them what Jesus had done. So the Pharisees and the chief priests met with the Council and said:
Pharisee	What shall we do?
Chief priest	Look at all the miracles this man is performing!
Counsellor	If we let him go on in this way, everyone will believe in him, and the Roman authorities will take action and destroy our Temple and our nation!
Narrator	One of them, named Caiaphas, who was High Priest that year, said:
Caiaphas	What fools you are! Don't you realize that it is better for you to let one man die for the people, instead of having the whole nation destroyed?
Narrator	Actually, he did not say this of his own accord; rather, as he was High Priest that year, he was prophesying that Jesus was going to die for the Jewish people, and not only for them, but also to bring together into one body all the scattered people of God. From that day on the Jewish authorities made plans to kill Jesus. So Jesus did not travel openly in Judaea, but left and went to a place near the desert, to a town named Ephraim, where he stayed with the disciples. The time for the Passover Festival was near, and many people went up from the country to Jerusalem to perform the ritual of purification before the festival. They were looking for Jesus, and as they gathered in the Temple, they asked one another:
Person	What do you think? Surely he will not come to the festival, will he?
Narrator	The chief priests and the Pharisees had given orders that if anyone knew where Jesus was, he must report it, so that they could arrest him.

Cast	[This is] the word of the Lord. OR	This is the Gospel of Christ / *This is the Gospel of the Lord.*
All	**Thanks be to God.**	**Praise to Christ our Lord** / *Praise to you, Lord Jesus Christ.*

Cast: **Narrator, Pharisee, Chief priest, Counsellor, Caiaphas, Person.**

Mary anoints Jesus
John 12.1–8 [9–11]

Narrator   Six days before the Passover, Jesus went to Bethany, the home of Lazarus, the man he had raised from death. They prepared a dinner for him there, which Martha helped to serve; Lazarus was one of those who were sitting at the table with Jesus. Then Mary took half a litre of a very expensive perfume made of pure nard, poured it on Jesus' feet, and wiped them with her hair. The sweet smell of the perfume filled the whole house. One of Jesus' disciples, Judas Iscariot—the one who was going to betray him—said:

Judas   Why wasn't this perfume sold for three hundred silver coins and the money given to the poor?

Narrator   He said this, not because he cared about the poor, but because he was a thief. He carried the money bag and would help himself from it.

But Jesus said:

Jesus   Leave her alone! Let her keep what she has for the day of my burial. You will always have poor people with you, but you will not always have me.

[Narrator   A large number of people heard that Jesus was in Bethany, so they went there, not only because of Jesus but also to see Lazarus, whom Jesus had raised from death. So the chief priests made plans to kill Lazarus too, because on his account many Jews were rejecting them and believing in Jesus.]

Cast   [This is] the word of the Lord.   OR   This is the Gospel of Christ / *This is the Gospel of the Lord.*
All   **Thanks be to God.**   **Praise to Christ our Lord** / *Praise to you, Lord Jesus Christ.*

Cast: **Narrator, Judas, Jesus.**

The triumphant entry into Jerusalem
John 12.12–19

Narrator   The large crowd that had come to the Passover Festival heard that Jesus was coming to Jerusalem. So they took branches of palm-trees and went out to meet him, shouting:

Persons 1 and 2   Praise God!

Person 1   God bless him who comes in the name of the Lord!

Person 2   God bless the King of Israel!

Narrator   Jesus found a donkey and rode on it, just as the scripture says:

Zechariah   Do not be afraid, city of Zion!
Here comes your king,
riding on a young donkey.

Narrator	His disciples did not understand this at the time; but when Jesus had been raised to glory, they remembered that the scripture said this about him and that they had done this for him.
	The people who had been with Jesus when he called Lazarus out of the grave and raised him from death had reported what had happened. That was why the crowd met him—because they heard that he had performed this miracle. The Pharisees then said to one another:
Pharisee 1	You see, we are not succeeding at all!
Pharisee 2	Look, the whole world is following him!

Cast	[This is] the word of the Lord.	OR	This is the Gospel of Christ / *This is the Gospel of the Lord.*
All	**Thanks be to God.**		**Praise to Christ our Lord** / *Praise to you, Lord Jesus Christ.*

Cast: **Narrator, Person 1, Person 2, Zechariah** (can be the same as Narrator)**, Pharisee 1, Pharisee 2** (can be the same as Pharisee 1).

Some Greeks seek Jesus
John 12.20–26

Narrator	Some Greeks were among those who had gone to Jerusalem to worship during the festival. They went to Philip—he was from Bethsaida in Galilee—and said:
Greeks 1 and 2	Sir—
Greek 2	We want to see Jesus.
Narrator	Philip went and told Andrew, and the two of them went and told Jesus. Jesus answered them:
Jesus	The hour has now come for the Son of Man to receive great glory. I am telling you the truth: a grain of wheat remains no more than a single grain unless it is dropped into the ground and dies. If it does die, then it produces many grains. Whoever loves his own life will lose it; whoever hates his own life in this world will keep it for life eternal. Whoever wants to serve me must follow me, so that my servant will be with me where I am. And my Father will honour anyone who serves me.

Cast	[This is] the word of the Lord.	OR	This is the Gospel of Christ / *This is the Gospel of the Lord.*
All	**Thanks be to God.**		**Praise to Christ our Lord** / *Praise to you, Lord Jesus Christ.*

Cast: **Narrator, Greek 1, Greek 2** (can be the same as Greek 1)**, Jesus.**

Jesus speaks about his death
John 12.27–36

Jesus	Now my heart is troubled—and what shall I say? Shall I say, 'Father, do not let this hour come upon me'? But that is why I came—so that I might go through this hour of suffering. Father, bring glory to your name!
Narrator	Then a voice spoke from heaven:

Voice	I have brought glory to it, and I will do so again.
Narrator	The crowd standing there heard the voice, and some of them said it was thunder, while others said:
Person 1	An angel spoke to him!
Narrator	But Jesus said to them:
Jesus	It was not for my sake that this voice spoke, but for yours. Now is the time for this world to be judged; now the ruler of this world will be overthrown. When I am lifted up from the earth, I will draw everyone to me.
Narrator	In saying this he indicated the kind of death he was going to suffer.
	The crowd answered:
Person 1	Our Law tells us that the Messiah will live for ever.
Person 2	How, then, can you say that the Son of Man must be lifted up?
Person 1	Who is this Son of Man?
Jesus	The light will be among you a little longer. Continue on your way while you have the light, so that the darkness will not come upon you; for the one who walks in the dark does not know where he is going. Believe in the light, then, while you have it, so that you will be the people of the light.

Cast	[This is] the word of the Lord.	OR	This is the Gospel of Christ / *This is the Gospel of the Lord.*
All	**Thanks be to God.**		**Praise to Christ our Lord** / *Praise to you, Lord Jesus Christ.*

Cast: **Jesus, Narrator, Voice, Person 1, Person 2.**

The unbelief of the people
John 12.36–43

Narrator	Jesus went off and hid himself from the crowd. Even though he had performed all these miracles in their presence, they did not believe in him, so that what the prophet Isaiah had said might come true:
Isaiah	Lord, who believed the message we told? To whom did the Lord reveal his power?
Narrator	And so they were not able to believe, because Isaiah also said:
Isaiah	God has blinded their eyes and closed their minds, so that their eyes would not see, and their minds would not understand, and they would not turn to me, says God, for me to heal them.

| Narrator | Isaiah said this because he saw Jesus' glory and spoke about him. Even then, many of the Jewish authorities believed in Jesus; but because of the Pharisees they did not talk about it openly, so as not to be expelled from the synagogue. They loved the approval of men rather than the approval of God. |

| Cast | [This is] the word of the Lord.   OR   This is the Gospel of Christ / *This is the Gospel of the Lord.* |
| All | **Thanks be to God.** **Praise to Christ our Lord** / *Praise to you, Lord Jesus Christ.* |

Cast: **Narrator, Isaiah.**

Jesus washes his disciples' feet
From John 13.1–15 [16–20]

Narrator	It was now the day before the Passover Festival. Jesus knew that the hour had come for him to leave this world and go to the Father. He had always loved those in the world who were his own, and he loved them to the very end.
	Jesus and his disciples were at supper. The Devil had already put into the heart of Judas, the son of Simon Iscariot, the thought of betraying Jesus. Jesus knew that the Father had given him complete power; he knew that he had come from God and was going to God. So he rose from the table, took off his outer garment, and tied a towel round his waist. Then he poured some water into a basin and began to wash the disciples' feet and dry them with the towel round his waist. He came to Simon Peter who said to him:
Peter	Are you going to wash my feet, Lord?
[Narrator	Jesus answered him:]
Jesus	You do not understand now what I am doing, but you will understand later.
Peter	Never at any time will you wash my feet!
Jesus	If I do not wash your feet, you will no longer be my disciple.
Peter	Lord, do not wash only my feet, then! Wash my hands and head, too!
Jesus	Anyone who has had a bath is completely clean and does not have to wash himself, except for his feet. All of you are clean—all except one.
Narrator	Jesus already knew who was going to betray him; that is why he said, 'All of you, except one, are clean.' (PAUSE)
	After Jesus had washed their feet, he put his outer garment back on and returned to his place at the table:
Jesus	Do you understand what I have just done to you? You call me Teacher and Lord, and it is right that you do so, because that is what I am. I, your Lord and Teacher, have just washed your feet. You, then, should wash one another's feet. I have set an example for you, so that you will do just what I have done for you.

→

231

[I am telling you the truth: no slave is greater than his master, and no messenger is greater than the one who sent him. Now that you know this truth, how happy you will be if you put it into practice! I am not talking about all of you; I know those I have chosen. But the scripture must come true that says, 'The man who shared my food turned against me.' I tell you this now before it happens, so that when it does happen, you will believe that 'I Am Who I Am.' I am telling you the truth: whoever receives anyone I send receives me also; and whoever receives me receives him who sent me.]

Cast	[This is] the word of the Lord.	OR	This is the Gospel of Christ / *This is the Gospel of the Lord.*
All	**Thanks be to God.**		**Praise to Christ our Lord** / *Praise to you, Lord Jesus Christ.*

Cast: **Narrator, Peter, Jesus.**

Jesus predicts his betrayal
John 13.21–30

Narrator Jesus was deeply troubled [and declared openly]:

Jesus I am telling you the truth: one of you is going to betray me.

Narrator The disciples looked at one another, completely puzzled about whom he meant. One of the disciples, the one whom Jesus loved, was sitting next to Jesus. Simon Peter motioned to him:

Peter
(to John) Ask him whom he is talking about.

Narrator So that disciple moved closer to Jesus' side.

John
(to Jesus) Who is it, Lord?

Jesus I will dip some bread in the sauce and give it to him; he is the man.

Narrator So he took a piece of bread, dipped it, and gave it to Judas, the son of Simon Iscariot. As soon as Judas took the bread, Satan entered him. Jesus said to him:

Jesus Be quick about what you are doing!

Narrator None of the others at the table understood why Jesus said this to him. Since Judas was in charge of the money bag, some of the disciples thought that Jesus had told him to go and buy what they needed for the festival, or to give something to the poor. Judas accepted the bread and went out at once. (PAUSE) It was night.

Cast	[This is] the word of the Lord.	OR	This is the Gospel of Christ / *This is the Gospel of the Lord.*
All	**Thanks be to God.**		**Praise to Christ our Lord** / *Praise to you, Lord Jesus Christ.*

Cast: **Narrator, Jesus, Peter, John.**

Jesus predicts Peter's denial
John 13.31–38

Narrator When Judas was gone, Jesus said:

Jesus Now is the Son of Man glorified and God is glorified in him. If God is glorified in him, God will glorify the Son in himself, and will glorify him at once.

My children, I will be with you only a little longer. You will look for me, and just as I told the Jews, so I tell you now: Where I am going, you cannot come.

A new command I give you: Love one another. As I have loved you, so you must love one another. By this all men will know that you are my disciples; if you love one another.

[Narrator Simon Peter asked him:]

Peter Lord, where are you going?

Jesus Where I am going, you cannot follow now, but you will follow later.

Peter Lord, why can't I follow you now? I will lay down my life for you.

Jesus Will you really lay down your life for me? I tell you the truth, Peter, before the cock crows you will disown me three times!

Cast [This is] the word of the Lord.   OR   This is the Gospel of Christ / *This is the Gospel of the Lord.*
All **Thanks be to God.**   **Praise to Christ our Lord** / *Praise to you, Lord Jesus Christ.*

Cast: **Narrator, Jesus, Peter.**

Jesus the way to the Father
John 14.1–11

Narrator Jesus told his disciples:

Jesus Do not be worried and upset. Believe in God and believe also in me. There are many rooms in my Father's house, and I am going to prepare a place for you. I would not tell you this if it were not so. And after I go and prepare a place for you, I will come back and take you to myself, so that you will be where I am. You know the way that leads to the place where I am going.

Narrator Thomas said to him:

Thomas Lord, we do not know where you are going; so how can we know the way to get there?

Jesus I am the way, the truth, and the life; no one goes to the Father except by me. Now that you have known me, you will know my Father also, and from now on you do know him and you have seen him.

Narrator Philip said to him:

Philip Lord, show us the Father; that is all we need.

$\rightarrow$

233

Jesus	For a long time I have been with you all; yet you do not know me, Philip? Whoever has seen me has seen the Father. Why, then, do you say, 'Show us the Father'? Do you not believe, Philip, that I am in the Father and the Father is in me? The words that I have spoken to you do not come from me. The Father, who remains in me, does his own work. Believe me when I say that I am in the Father and the Father is in me. If not, believe because of the things I do.

Cast	[This is] the word of the Lord.	OR	This is the Gospel of Christ / *This is the Gospel of the Lord.*
All	**Thanks be to God.**		**Praise to Christ our Lord** / *Praise to you, Lord Jesus Christ.*

Cast: **Narrator, Jesus, Thomas, Philip.**

Jesus talks to his disciples
From John 14.1–26 [27–31]

Jesus	Believe in God and believe also in me. There are many rooms in my Father's house, and I am going to prepare a place for you. I would not tell you this if it were not so. And after I go and prepare a place for you, I will come back and take you to myself, so that you will be where I am. You know the way that leads to the place where I am going.
Thomas	Lord, we do not know where you are going; so how can we know the way to get there?
Jesus	I am the way, the truth, and the life; no one goes to the Father except by me. Now that you have known me, you will know my Father also, and from now on you do know him and you have seen him.
Philip	Lord, show us the Father; that is all we need.
Jesus	For a long time I have been with you all; yet you do not know me, Philip? Whoever has seen me has seen the Father. Why, then, do you say, 'Show us the Father'? Do you not believe, Philip, that I am in the Father and the Father is in me? The words that I have spoken to you do not come from me. The Father, who remains in me, does his own work. Believe me when I say that I am in the Father and the Father is in me. And I will do whatever you ask for in my name, so that the Father's glory will be shown through the Son. If you ask me for anything in my name, I will do it.
	I will ask the Father, and he will give you another Helper, who will stay with you for ever. He is the Spirit who reveals the truth about God. When I go, you will not be left all alone; I will come back to you. When that day comes, you will know that I am in my Father and that you are in me, just as I am in you.
	My Father will love whoever loves me; I too will love him and reveal myself to him.
Judas	Lord, how can it be that you will reveal yourself to us and not to the world?

Jesus	Whoever loves me will obey my teaching. My Father will love him, and my Father and I will come to him and live with him.
	I have told you this while I am still with you. The Helper, the Holy Spirit, whom the Father will send in my name, will teach you everything and make you remember all that I have told you.
	[Peace is what I leave with you; it is my own peace that I give you. I do not give it as the world does. Do not be worried and upset; do not be afraid. You heard me say to you, 'I am leaving, but I will come back to you.' If you loved me, you would be glad that I am going to the Father; for he is greater than I. I have told you this now before it all happens, so that when it does happen, you will believe. I cannot talk with you much longer, because the ruler of this world is coming. He has no power over me, but the world must know that I love the Father; that is why I do everything he commands me.
	Come, let us go from this place.]

Cast	[This is] the word of the Lord. OR This is the Gospel of Christ / *This is the Gospel of the Lord.*
All	**Thanks be to God.** **Praise to Christ our Lord** / *Praise to you, Lord Jesus Christ.*

Cast: **Jesus, Thomas, Philip, Judas** (Thomas, Philip and Judas can all be the same).

Sadness and gladness
John 16.16–24

Narrator	Jesus was talking to his disciples:
Jesus	In a little while you will not see me any more, and then a little while later you will see me.
Narrator	Some of his disciples asked among themselves:
Disciple 1	What does this mean?
Disciple 2	He tells us that in a little while we will not see him, and then a little while later we will see him.
Disciple 1	And he also says, 'It is because I am going to the Father.'
Disciple 2	What does this 'a little while' mean?
Disciple 1	We don't know what he is talking about!
Narrator	Jesus knew that they wanted to question him, so he said to them:
Jesus	I said, 'In a little while you will not see me, and then a little while later you will see me.' Is this what you are asking about among yourselves? I am telling you the truth: you will cry and weep, but the world will be glad; you will be sad, but your sadness will turn into gladness. When a woman is about to give birth, she is sad because her hour of suffering has come; but when the baby is born, she forgets her suffering, because she is happy that a baby has been born into the world. That is how it is with you: now you are sad, but I will see you again, and your hearts will be filled with gladness, the kind of gladness that no one can take away from you.

→

When that day comes, you will not ask me for anything. I am telling you the truth: the Father will give you whatever you ask in my name; ask and you will receive, so that your happiness may be complete.

Cast	[This is] the word of the Lord. OR	This is the Gospel of Christ / *This is the Gospel of the Lord.*
All	**Thanks be to God.**	**Praise to Christ our Lord** / *Praise to you, Lord Jesus Christ.*

Cast: **Narrator, Jesus, Disciple 1, Disciple 2.**

Jesus speaks of victory over the world
John 16.25–33

[Narrator Jesus said to his disciples:]

Jesus I have used figures of speech to tell you these things. But the time will come when I will not use figures of speech, but will speak to you plainly about the Father. When that day comes, you will ask him in my name; and I do not say that I will ask him on your behalf, for the Father himself loves you. He loves you because you love me and have believed that I came from God. I did come from the Father, and I came into the world; and now I am leaving the world and going to the Father.

[Narrator Then his disciples said to him:]

Disciple 1 Now you are speaking plainly, without using figures of speech.

Disciple 2 We know now that you know everything; you do not need someone to ask you questions.

Disciple 1 This makes us believe that you came from God.

Jesus Do you believe now? The time is coming, and is already here, when all of you will be scattered, each one to his own home, and I will be left all alone. But I am not really alone, because the Father is with me. I have told you this so that you will have peace by being united to me. The world will make you suffer. But be brave! I have defeated the world!

Cast	[This is] the word of the Lord. OR	This is the Gospel of Christ / *This is the Gospel of the Lord.*
All	**Thanks be to God.**	**Praise to Christ our Lord** / *Praise to you, Lord Jesus Christ.*

Cast: **[Narrator], Jesus, Disciple 1, Disciple 2.**

Jesus' arrest
John 18.1–13

Narrator Jesus left with his disciples and went across the brook called Kidron. There was a garden in that place, and Jesus and his disciples went in. Judas, the traitor, knew where it was, because many times Jesus had met there with his disciples. So Judas went to the garden, taking with him a group of Roman soldiers, and some temple guards sent by the chief priests and the Pharisees; they were armed and carried lanterns and torches. Jesus knew everything that was going to happen to him, so he stepped forward [and asked them:]

Jesus	Who is it you are looking for?
Soldier 1	Jesus of Nazareth.
Jesus	I am he.
Narrator	Judas, the traitor, was standing there with them. When Jesus said to them, 'I am he,' they moved back and fell to the ground. Again Jesus asked them:
Jesus	Who is it you are looking for?
Soldier 2	Jesus of Nazareth.
Jesus	I have already told you that I am he. If, then, you are looking for me, let these others go.
Narrator	He said this so that what he had said might come true: 'Father, I have not lost even one of those you gave me.'
	Simon Peter, who had a sword, drew it and struck the High Priest's slave, cutting off his right ear. The name of the slave was Malchus. [Jesus said to Peter:]
Jesus	Put your sword back in its place! Do you think that I will not drink the cup of suffering which my Father has given me?
Narrator	Then the Roman soldiers with their commanding officer and the Jewish guards arrested Jesus, bound him, and took him away.

Cast	[This is] the word of the Lord.	OR	This is the Gospel of Christ / *This is the Gospel of the Lord.*
All	**Thanks be to God.**		**Praise to Christ our Lord** / *Praise to you, Lord Jesus Christ.*

Cast: **Narrator, Jesus, Soldier 1, Soldier 2** (can be the same as Soldier 1).

Peter denies Jesus
John 18.[12–14] 15–27

Narrator	[The Roman soldiers with their commanding officer and the Jewish guards arrested Jesus and bound him. They took him first to Annas. He was the father-in-law of Caiaphas, who was High Priest that year. It was Caiaphas who had advised the Jewish authorities that it was better that one man should die for all the people.]
	Simon Peter and another disciple followed Jesus. That other disciple was well known to the High Priest, so he went with Jesus into the courtyard of the High Priest's house, while Peter stayed outside by the gate. Then the other disciple went back out, spoke to the girl at the gate, and brought Peter inside. The girl at the gate said to Peter:
Girl (to Peter)	Aren't you also one of the disciples of that man?
Peter	No, I am not.
Narrator	It was cold, so the servants and guards had built a charcoal fire and were standing round it, warming themselves. So Peter went over and stood with them, warming himself. (PAUSE) →

The High Priest questioned Jesus about his disciples and about his teaching. Jesus answered:

Jesus I have always spoken publicly to everyone; all my teaching was done in the synagogues and in the Temple, where all the people come together. I have never said anything in secret. Why, then, do you question me? Question the people who heard me. Ask them what I told them—they know what I said.

Narrator When Jesus said this, one of the guards there slapped him:

Guard How dare you talk like that to the High Priest!

Jesus If I have said anything wrong, tell everyone here what it was. But if I am right in what I have said, why do you hit me?

Narrator Then Annas sent him, still bound, to Caiaphas the High Priest. (PAUSE)

Peter was still standing there keeping himself warm. [So the others said to him:]

Person 1
(to Peter) Aren't you also one of the disciples of that man?

[Narrator But Peter denied it:]

Peter No, I am not.

Narrator One of the High Priest's slaves, a relative of the man whose ear Peter had cut off, spoke up:

Person 2
(to Peter) Didn't I see you with him in the garden?

Peter No!

Narrator
(slowly) And at once a cock crowed.

Cast	[This is] the word of the Lord.	OR	This is the Gospel of Christ / *This is the Gospel of the Lord.*
All	**Thanks be to God.**		**Praise to Christ our Lord** / *Praise to you, Lord Jesus Christ.*

Cast: **Narrator, Girl, Peter, Jesus, Guard, Person 1, Person 2.**

Jesus is brought before Pilate
From John 18.28—19.16

Narrator Early in the morning Jesus was taken from Caiaphas' house to the governor's palace. The Jewish authorities did not go inside the palace, for they wanted to keep themselves ritually clean, in order to be able to eat the Passover meal. So Pilate went outside to them:

Pilate What do you accuse this man of?

Priest We would not have brought him to you if he had not committed a crime.

Pilate Then you yourselves take him and try him according to your own law.

Person 1	We are not allowed to put anyone to death. (PAUSE)
Narrator	Pilate went back into the palace and called Jesus.
Pilate	Are you the King of the Jews?
[Narrator	Jesus answered:]
Jesus	Does this question come from you or have others told you about me?
Pilate	Do you think I am a Jew? It was your own people and the chief priests who handed you over to me. What have you done?
Jesus	My kingdom does not belong to this world; if my kingdom belonged to this world, my followers would fight to keep me from being handed over to the Jewish authorities. No, my kingdom does not belong here!
Pilate	Are you a king, then? (PAUSE)
Jesus	You say that I am a king. I was born and came into the world for this one purpose, to speak about the truth. Whoever belongs to the truth listens to me.
Pilate (slowly)	And what is truth? (PAUSE)
Narrator	Then Pilate went back outside to the people.
Pilate	I cannot find any reason to condemn him. But according to the custom you have, I always set free a prisoner for you during the Passover. Do you want me to set free for you the King of the Jews?
Person 1	No, not him!
Person 2	We want Barabbas!
Narrator (slowly)	Barabbas was a bandit (PAUSE)
	Then Pilate took Jesus and had him whipped. The soldiers made a crown out of thorny branches and put it on his head; then they put a purple robe on him and came to him.
Soldiers 1 and **2**	Long live the King of the Jews!
Narrator	And they went up and slapped him.
	Pilate went out once more and said to the crowd:
Pilate	Look, I will bring him out here to you to let you see that I cannot find any reason to condemn him.
Narrator	So Jesus came out, wearing the crown of thorns and the purple robe.
Pilate	Look! Here is the man!
Narrator	When the chief priests and the temple guards saw him, they shouted:
Priest	Crucify him!
Soldiers 1 and **2**	Crucify him!
Pilate	You take him, then, and crucify him. I find no reason to condemn him.

239

Person 1	We have a law that says he ought to die, because he claimed to be the Son of God.
Narrator	When Pilate heard this, he was even more afraid. He went back into the palace [and asked Jesus]:
Pilate	Where do you come from?
Narrator	But Jesus did not answer. (PAUSE)
Pilate	You will not speak to me? Remember, I have the authority to set you free and also to have you crucified.
Jesus	You have authority over me only because it was given to you by God. So the man who handed me over to you is guilty of a worse sin.
Narrator	When Pilate heard this, he tried to find a way to set Jesus free. But the crowd shouted back:
Person 2	If you set him free, that means that you are not the Emperor's friend!
Person 1	Anyone who claims to be a king is a rebel against the Emperor!
Narrator	When Pilate heard these words, he took Jesus outside and sat down on the judge's seat in the place called 'The Stone Pavement'. In Hebrew the name is 'Gabbatha'. It was then almost noon of the day before the Passover. [Pilate said to the people:]
Pilate (to all)	Here is your king!
Persons 1 and **2**	Kill him!
Soldiers 1 and **2**	Kill him!
Priest	Crucify him!
Pilate	Do you want me to crucify your king?
Priest	The only king we have is the Emperor!
Narrator	Then Pilate handed Jesus over to them to be crucified.

Cast [This is] the word of the Lord.   OR   This is the Gospel of Christ / *This is the Gospel of the Lord.*
All   **Thanks be to God.**   **Praise to Christ our Lord** / *Praise to you, Lord Jesus Christ.*

Cast: **Narrator, Pilate, Priest, Person 1, Jesus, Person 2** (can be the same as Person 1)**, Soldier 1, Soldier 2** (Soldiers 1 and 2 can also be Persons 1 and 2).

Jesus is crucified
John 19.17–30

Narrator	Jesus went out, carrying his cross, and came to 'The Place of the Skull', as it is called. In Hebrew it is called 'Golgotha'. There they crucified him; and they also crucified two other men, one on each side, with Jesus between them. Pilate wrote a notice and had it put on the cross.
Pilate	Jesus of Nazareth, the King of the Jews.

Narrator	Many people read it, because the place where Jesus was crucified was not far from the city. The notice was written in Hebrew, Latin, and Greek. The chief priests said to Pilate:
Priest	Do not write 'The King of the Jews', but rather, 'This man said, I am the King of the Jews.'
Pilate	What I have written stays written.
Narrator	After the soldiers had crucified Jesus, they took his clothes and divided them into four parts, one part for each soldier. They also took the robe, which was made of one piece of woven cloth without any seams in it. [The soldiers said to one another:]
Soldier 1 (to Soldier 2)	Let's not tear it.
Soldier 2 (to Soldier 1)	Let's throw dice to see who will get it.
Narrator	This happened in order to make the scripture come true:
Psalmist	They divided my clothes among themselves and gambled for my robe.
Narrator	And this is what the soldiers did. (PAUSE) Standing close to Jesus' cross were his mother, his mother's sister, Mary the wife of Clopas, and Mary Magdalene. Jesus saw his mother and the disciple he loved standing there; so he said to his mother:
Jesus	He is your son.
Narrator	Then he said to the disciple:
Jesus	She is your mother.
Narrator	From that time the disciple took her to live in his home. (PAUSE) Jesus knew that by now everything had been completed; and in order to make the scripture come true, he said:
Jesus	I am thirsty.
Narrator	A bowl was there, full of cheap wine; so a sponge was soaked in the wine, put on a stalk of hyssop, and lifted up to his lips. Jesus drank the wine and said:
Jesus	It is finished! (PAUSE)
Narrator	Then he bowed his head and died.

Cast	[This is] the word of the Lord. OR This is the Gospel of Christ / *This is the Gospel of the Lord.*
All	**Thanks be to God.** **Praise to Christ our Lord** / *Praise to you, Lord Jesus Christ.*

Cast: **Narrator, Pilate, Priest, Soldier 1, Soldier 2, Psalmist** (can be the same as Priest), **Jesus.**

The burial of Jesus
John 19.31–42

Narrator The Jewish authorities asked Pilate to allow them to break the legs of the men who had been crucified, and to take the bodies down from the crosses. They requested this because it was Friday, and they did not want the bodies to stay on the crosses on the Sabbath, since the coming Sabbath was especially holy. So the soldiers went and broke the legs of the first man and then of the other man who had been crucified with Jesus. But when they came to Jesus, they saw that he was already dead, so they did not break his legs. One of the soldiers, however, plunged his spear into Jesus' side, and at once blood and water poured out.

Witness The one who saw this happen has spoken of it, so that you also may believe. What he said is true, and he knows that he speaks the truth.

Narrator This was done to make the scripture come true:

Scripture 1 Not one of his bones will be broken.

Narrator And there is another scripture that says:

Scripture 2 People will look at him whom they pierced.

Narrator After this, Joseph, who was from the town of Arimathea, asked Pilate if he could take Jesus' body.

Witness Joseph was a follower of Jesus, but in secret, because he was afraid of the Jewish authorities.

Narrator Pilate told him he could have the body, so Joseph went and took it away. Nicodemus, who at first had gone to see Jesus at night, went with Joseph, taking with him about thirty kilogrammes of spices, a mixture of myrrh and aloes. The two men took Jesus' body and wrapped it in linen with the spices according to the Jewish custom of preparing a body for burial. There was a garden in the place where Jesus had been put to death, and in it there was a new tomb where no one had ever been buried. Since it was the day before the Sabbath and because the tomb was close by, they placed Jesus' body there.

Cast [This is] the word of the Lord.   OR   This is the Gospel of Christ / *This is the Gospel of the Lord.*
All **Thanks be to God.**   **Praise to Christ our Lord** / *Praise to you, Lord Jesus Christ.*

Cast: **Narrator, Witness, Scripture 1, Scripture 2** (can be the same as Scripture 1).

The empty tomb
John 20.1–18

Narrator Early on Sunday morning, while it was still dark, Mary Magdalene went to the tomb and saw that the stone had been taken away from the entrance. She went running to Simon Peter and the other disciple, whom Jesus loved.

Mary They have taken the Lord from the tomb, and we don't know where they have put him!

Narrator	Then Peter and the other disciple went to the tomb. The two of them were running, but the other disciple ran faster than Peter and reached the tomb first. He bent over and saw the linen wrappings, but he did not go in. Behind him came Simon Peter, and he went straight into the tomb. He saw the linen wrappings lying there and the cloth which had been round Jesus' head. It was not lying with the linen wrappings but was rolled up by itself. Then the other disciple, who had reached the tomb first, also went in; he saw and believed. They still did not understand the scripture which said that he must rise from death. Then the disciples went back home. (PAUSE)
	Mary stood crying outside the tomb. While she was still crying, she bent over and looked in the tomb and saw two angels there dressed in white, sitting where the body of Jesus had been, one at the head and the other at the feet. [They asked her:]
Angel(s)	Woman, why are you crying?
Mary	They have taken my Lord away, and I do not know where they have put him!
Narrator	Then she turned round and saw Jesus standing there; but she did not know that it was Jesus.
Jesus	Woman, why are you crying? Who is it that you are looking for?
Narrator	She thought he was the gardener.
Mary	If you took him away, sir, tell me where you have put him, and I will go and get him.
Jesus	Mary!
Mary	Rabboni! Teacher!
Jesus	Do not hold on to me, because I have not yet gone back up to the Father. But go to my brothers and tell them that I am returning to him who is my Father and their Father, my God and their God.
Narrator	So Mary Magdalene went and told the disciples that she had seen the Lord and related to them what he had told her.

Cast	[This is] the word of the Lord. OR	This is the Gospel of Christ / *This is the Gospel of the Lord.*
All	**Thanks be to God.**	**Praise to Christ our Lord** / *Praise to you, Lord Jesus Christ.*

Cast: **Narrator, Mary, Angel(s), Jesus.**

Jesus appears to his disciples
John 20.19–23

Narrator	It was late that Sunday evening, and the disciples were gathered together behind locked doors, because they were afraid of the Jewish authorities. Then Jesus came and stood among them. [He said:]
Jesus	Peace be with you.
Narrator	After saying this, he showed them his hands and his side. The disciples were filled with joy at seeing the Lord. [Jesus said to them again:]

Jesus	Peace be with you. As the Father sent me, so I send you.
Narrator	Then he breathed on them [and said]:
Jesus	Receive the Holy Spirit. If you forgive people's sins, they are forgiven; if you do not forgive them, they are not forgiven.

| Cast | [This is] the word of the Lord.   OR   This is the Gospel of Christ / *This is the Gospel of the Lord.* |
| All | **Thanks be to God.** | **Praise to Christ our Lord** / *Praise to you, Lord Jesus Christ.* |

Cast: **Narrator, Jesus.**

Jesus and Thomas
John 20.24–29

Narrator	One of the twelve disciples, Thomas (called the Twin), was not with them when Jesus came. So the other disciples told him:
Disciple(s)	We have seen the Lord!
[Narrator	Thomas said to them:]
Thomas	Unless I see the scars of the nails in his hands and put my finger on those scars and my hand in his side, I will not believe.
Narrator	A week later the disciples were together again indoors, and Thomas was with them. The doors were locked, but Jesus came and stood among them [and said]:
Jesus	Peace be with you.
[Narrator	Then he said to Thomas:]
Jesus (to Thomas)	Put your finger here, and look at my hands; then stretch out your hand and put it in my side. Stop your doubting, and believe!
Thomas	My Lord and my God!
Jesus	Do you believe because you see me? How happy are those who believe without seeing me!

| Cast | [This is] the word of the Lord.   OR   This is the Gospel of Christ / *This is the Gospel of the Lord.* |
| All | **Thanks be to God.** | **Praise to Christ our Lord** / *Praise to you, Lord Jesus Christ.* |

Cast: **Narrator, Disciple(s), Thomas, Jesus.**

Jesus appears to seven disciples
John 21.1–14

Narrator	Jesus appeared once more to his disciples at Lake Tiberias. This is how it happened. Simon Peter, Thomas—called the Twin, Nathanael—the one from Cana in Galilee, the sons of Zebedee, and two other disciples of Jesus were all together. Simon Peter said to the others:
Peter	I am going fishing.
Disciple	We will come with you.
Narrator	So they went out in a boat, but all that night they did not catch a

thing. As the sun was rising, Jesus stood at the water's edge, but the disciples did not know that it was Jesus. [Then he asked them:]

Jesus (calling) Young men, haven't you caught anything?

Disciple Not a thing.

Jesus (calling) Throw your net out on the right side of the boat, and you will catch some.

Narrator So they threw the net out and could not pull it back in, because they had caught so many fish. The disciple whom Jesus loved said to Peter:

John It is the Lord!

Narrator When Peter heard that it was the Lord, he wrapped his outer garment round him—for he had taken his clothes off—and jumped into the water. The other disciples came to shore in the boat, pulling the net full of fish. They were not very far from land, about a hundred metres away. When they stepped ashore, they saw a charcoal fire there with fish on it and some bread. [Then Jesus said to them:]

Jesus Bring some of the fish you have just caught.

Narrator Simon Peter went aboard and dragged the net ashore full of big fish, a hundred and fifty-three in all; even though there were so many, still the net did not tear. [Jesus said to them:]

Jesus Come and eat.

Narrator None of the disciples dared ask him, 'Who are you?' because they knew it was the Lord. So Jesus went over, took the bread, and gave it to them; he did the same with the fish.

This, then, was the third time Jesus appeared to the disciples after he was raised from death.

Cast [This is] the word of the Lord. OR This is the Gospel of Christ / *This is the Gospel of the Lord.*
All **Thanks be to God.** **Praise to Christ our Lord** / *Praise to you, Lord Jesus Christ.*

Cast: **Narrator, Peter, Disciple, Jesus, John** (can be the same as Disciple).

Jesus and Peter
John 21.15–22

Narrator After they had eaten, Jesus said to Simon Peter:

Jesus Simon son of John, do you love me more than these others do?

Peter Yes, Lord, you know that I love you.

Jesus Take care of my lambs. (PAUSE) Simon son of John, do you love me?

Peter Yes, Lord, you know that I love you.

Jesus Take care of my sheep. (PAUSE) Simon son of John, do you love me?

Narrator	Peter was sad because Jesus asked him the third time, 'Do you love me?'
Peter	Lord, you know everything; you know that I love you!
Jesus	Take care of my sheep. (PAUSE)
	I am telling you the truth: when you were young, you used to get ready and go anywhere you wanted to; but when you are old, you will stretch out your hands and someone else will bind you and take you where you don't want to go.
Narrator	In saying this, Jesus was indicating the way in which Peter would die and bring glory to God. (PAUSE) Then Jesus said to him:
Jesus	Follow me!
Narrator	Peter turned round and saw behind him that other disciple, whom Jesus loved—the one who had leaned close to Jesus at the meal and had asked, 'Lord, who is going to betray you?' When Peter saw him, he asked Jesus:
Peter	Lord, what about this man?
Jesus	If I want him to live until I come, what is that to you? Follow me!

Cast	[This is] the word of the Lord.	OR	This is the Gospel of Christ / *This is the Gospel of the Lord.*
All	**Thanks be to God.**		**Praise to Christ our Lord** / *Praise to you, Lord Jesus Christ.*

Cast: **Narrator, Jesus, Peter.**

Conclusion to the Gospel of John
John 20.30–31; 21.24–25

Voice 1	In his disciples' presence Jesus performed many other miracles which are not written down in this book. But these have been written in order that you may believe that Jesus is the Messiah, the Son of God, and that through your faith in him you may have life.
Voice 2	That disciple whom Jesus loved spoke of these things, the one who also wrote them down; and we know that what he said is true.
Voice 1	Now, there are many other things that Jesus did. If they were all written down one by one, I suppose that the whole world could not hold the books that would be written.

Cast	[This is] the word of the Lord.	OR	This is the Gospel of Christ / *This is the Gospel of the Lord.*
All	**Thanks be to God.**		**Praise to Christ our Lord** / *Praise to you, Lord Jesus Christ.*

Cast: **Voice 1, Voice 2.**

ACTS

Jesus is taken up to heaven
From Acts 1.4–11

Narrator	When his apostles came together, Jesus gave them this order:
Jesus	Do not leave Jerusalem, but wait for the gift I told you about, the gift my Father promised. John baptized with water, but in a few days you will be baptized with the Holy Spirit.
Narrator	When the apostles met together with Jesus, they asked him:
Apostle	Lord, will you at this time give the Kingdom back to Israel?
Jesus	The times and occasions are set by my Father's own authority, and it is not for you to know when they will be. But when the Holy Spirit comes upon you, you will be filled with power, and you will be witnesses for me in Jerusalem, in all Judaea and Samaria, and to the ends of the earth.
Narrator	After saying this, he was taken up to heaven as they watched him, and a cloud hid him from their sight. They still had their eyes fixed on the sky as he went away, when two men dressed in white suddenly stood beside them and said:
Angel	Galileans, why are you standing there looking up at the sky? This Jesus, who was taken from you into heaven, will come back in the same way that you saw him go to heaven.
Cast	[This is] the word of the Lord.
All	**Thanks be to God.**

Cast: **Narrator, Jesus, Apostle, Angel.**

Judas' successor
From Acts 1.12–26

Narrator	The apostles went back to Jerusalem from the Mount of Olives, which is about a kilometre away from the city. They entered the city and went up to the room where they were staying: Peter, John, James and Andrew, Philip and Thomas, Bartholomew and Matthew, James son of Alphaeus, Simon the Patriot, and Judas son of James. They gathered frequently to pray as a group, together with the women and with Mary the mother of Jesus and with his brothers.
	A few days later there was a meeting of the believers, about a hundred and twenty in all, and Peter stood up to speak:
Peter	My brothers, the scripture had to come true in which the Holy Spirit, speaking through David, made a prediction about Judas, who was the guide for those who arrested Jesus. Judas was a member of our group, for he had been chosen to have a part in our work.

Narrator	With the money that Judas got for his evil act he bought a field, where he fell to his death. All the people living in Jerusalem heard about it, and so in their own language they call that field Akeldama, which means 'Field of Blood'.
Peter	For it is written in the book of Psalms:
Voice	May his house become empty; may no one live in it.
Peter	It is also written:
Voice	May someone else take his place of service.
Peter	So then, someone must join us as a witness to the resurrection of the Lord Jesus. He must be one of the men who were in our group during the whole time that the Lord Jesus travelled about with us, beginning from the time John preached his message of baptism until the day Jesus was taken up from us to heaven.
Narrator	So they proposed two men: Joseph, who was called Barsabbas, also known as Justus, and Matthias. Then they prayed:
Peter	Lord, you know the thoughts of everyone, so show us which of these two you have chosen to serve as an apostle in the place of Judas, who left to go to the place where he belongs.
Narrator	Then they drew lots to choose between the two men, and the one chosen was Matthias, who was added to the group of eleven apostles.
Cast	[This is] the word of the Lord.
All	**Thanks be to God.**

Cast: **Narrator, Peter, Voice** (can be the same as Peter).

The coming of the Holy Spirit
From Acts 2.1–21

Narrator	When the day of Pentecost came, all the believers were gathered together in one place. Suddenly there was a noise from the sky which sounded like a strong wind blowing, and it filled the whole house where they were sitting. Then they saw what looked like tongues of fire which spread out and touched each person there. They were all filled with the Holy Spirit and began to talk in other languages, as the Spirit enabled them to speak. There were Jews living in Jerusalem, religious men who had come from every country in the world. When they heard this noise, a large crowd gathered. They were all excited, because each one of them heard the believers speaking in his own language. [In amazement and wonder they exclaimed:]
Person 1 (amazed)	These people who are talking like this are Galileans! How is it, then, that all of us hear them speaking in our own native languages about the great things that God has done?

Narrator	Amazed and confused, they kept asking each other:
Persons 1 and **2**	What does this mean?
Narrator	Others made fun of the believers:
Person 2	These people are drunk!
Narrator	Then Peter stood up with the other eleven apostles and in a loud voice began to speak to the crowd:
Peter	Fellow-Jews and all of you who live in Jerusalem, listen to me and let me tell you what this means. These people are not drunk, as you suppose; it is only nine o'clock in the morning. Instead, this is what the prophet Joel spoke about:
Joel	This is what I will do in the last days, God says: I will pour out my Spirit on everyone. Your sons and daughters will proclaim my message; your young men will see visions, and your old men will have dreams. Yes, even on my servants, both men and women, I will pour out my Spirit in those days, and they will proclaim my message. I will perform miracles in the sky above and wonders on the earth below. There will be blood, fire, and thick smoke; the sun will be darkened, and the moon will turn red as blood, before the great and glorious Day of the Lord comes. And then, whoever calls out to the Lord for help will be saved.
Cast	[This is] the word of the Lord.
All	**Thanks be to God.**

Cast: **Narrator, Person 1, Person 2, Peter, Joel** (can be the same as Peter).

Peter speaks of Christ the Son of David
Acts 2.22–35

Peter	Listen to these words, fellow-Israelites! Jesus of Nazareth was a man whose divine authority was clearly proven to you by all the miracles and wonders which God performed through him. You yourselves know this, for it happened here among you. In accordance with his own plan God had already decided that Jesus would be handed over to you; and you killed him by letting sinful men crucify him. But God raised him from death, setting him free from its power, because it was impossible that death should hold him prisoner. For David said about him:
David	I saw the Lord before me at all times; he is near me, and I will not be troubled. And so I am filled with gladness, and my words are full of joy.

→

And I, mortal though I am,
will rest assured in hope,
because you will not abandon me in the world of the dead;
you will not allow your faithful servant to rot in the grave.
You have shown me the paths that lead to life,
and your presence will fill me with joy.

Peter   My brothers, I must speak to you plainly about our famous ancestor King David. He died and was buried, and his grave is here with us to this very day. He was a prophet, and he knew what God had promised him: God had made a vow that he would make one of David's descendants a king, just as David was. David saw what God was going to do in the future, and so he spoke about the resurrection of the Messiah [when he said]:

David   He was not abandoned in the world of the dead;
his body did not rot in the grave.

Peter   God has raised this very Jesus from death, and we are all witnesses to this fact. He has been raised to the right-hand side of God, his Father, and has received from him the Holy Spirit, as he had promised. What you now see and hear is his gift that he has poured out on us. For it was not David who went up into heaven; rather he said:

David   The Lord said to *my Lord*:
Sit here at my right
until I put your enemies as a footstool under your feet.

Cast   [This is] the word of the Lord.
All   **Thanks be to God.**

Cast: **Peter, David.**

The early church
Acts 2.36–47

Narrator   Peter said:

Peter   All the people of Israel, then, are to know for sure that this Jesus, whom you crucified, is the one that God has made Lord and Messiah!

Narrator   When the people heard this, they were deeply troubled and said to Peter and the other apostles:

Person   What shall we do, brothers?

Peter   Each one of you must turn away from his sins and be baptized in the name of Jesus Christ, so that your sins will be forgiven; and you will receive God's gift, the Holy Spirit. For God's promise was made to you and your children, and to all who are far away—all whom the Lord our God calls to himself.

Narrator   Peter made his appeal to them and with many other words he urged them:

Peter	Save yourselves from the punishment coming on this wicked people!
Narrator	Many of them believed his message and were baptized, and about three thousand people were added to the group that day. They spent their time in learning from the apostles, taking part in the fellowship, and sharing in the fellowship meals and the prayers. (PAUSE)
	Many miracles and wonders were being done through the apostles, and everyone was filled with awe. All the believers continued together in close fellowship and shared their belongings with one another. They would sell their property and possessions, and distribute the money among all, according to what each one needed. Day after day they met as a group in the Temple, and they had their meals together in their homes, eating with glad and humble hearts, praising God, and enjoying the good will of all the people. And every day the Lord added to their group those who were being saved.
Cast	[This is] the word of the Lord.
All	**Thanks be to God.**

Cast: **Narrator, Peter, Person.**

A lame man is healed
Acts 3.1–10 [11–16]

Narrator	One day Peter and John went to the Temple at three o'clock in the afternoon, the hour for prayer. There at the Beautiful Gate, as it was called, was a man who had been lame all his life. Every day he was carried to the gate to beg for money from the people who were going into the Temple. When he saw Peter and John going in, he begged them to give him something. They looked straight at him, and Peter said:
Peter	Look at us!
Narrator	So he looked at them, expecting to get something from them. But Peter said to him:
Peter	I have no money at all, but I give you what I have: in the name of Jesus Christ of Nazareth I order you to get up and walk!
Narrator	Then he took him by his right hand and helped him up. At once the man's feet and ankles became strong; he jumped up, stood on his feet, and started walking around. Then he went into the Temple with them, walking and jumping and praising God. The people there saw him walking and praising God, and when they recognized him as the beggar who had sat at the Beautiful Gate, they were all surprised and amazed at what had happened to him.
	[As the man held on to Peter and John in Solomon's Porch, as it was called, the people were amazed and ran to them. When Peter saw the people, he said to them:

251

Peter	Fellow-Israelites, why are you surprised at this, and why do you stare at us? Do you think that it was by means of our own power or godliness that we made this man walk? The God of Abraham, Isaac, and Jacob, the God of our ancestors, has given divine glory to his Servant Jesus. But you handed him over to the authorities, and you rejected him in Pilate's presence, even after Pilate had decided to set him free. He was holy and good, but you rejected him, and instead you asked Pilate to do you the favour of turning loose a murderer. You killed the one who leads to life, but God raised him from death—and we are witnesses to this. It was the power of his name that gave strength to this lame man. What you see and know was done by faith in his name; it was faith in Jesus that has made him well, and you can all see.]
Cast	[This is] the word of the Lord.
All	**Thanks be to God.**

Cast: **Narrator, Peter.**

Peter's message in the Temple
Acts 3.17–26

Peter	My brothers, I know that what you and your leaders did to Jesus was due to your ignorance. God announced long ago through all the prophets that his Messiah had to suffer; and he made it come true in this way. Repent, then, and turn to God, so that he will forgive your sins. If you do, times of spiritual strength will come from the Lord, and he will send Jesus, who is the Messiah he has already chosen for you. He must remain in heaven until the time comes for all things to be made new, as God announced through his holy prophets who lived long ago. For Moses said:
Moses	The Lord your God will send you a prophet, just as he sent me, and he will be one of your own people. You are to obey everything that he tells you to do. Anyone who does not obey that prophet shall be separated from God's people and destroyed.
Peter	And all the prophets who had a message, including Samuel and those who came after him, also announced what has been happening these days. The promises of God through his prophets are for you, and you share in the covenant which God made with your ancestors. As he said to Abraham:
God	Through your descendants I will bless all the people on earth.
Peter	And so God chose his Servant and sent him first to you, to bless you by making every one of you turn away from his wicked ways.
Cast	[This is] the word of the Lord.
All	**Thanks be to God.**

Cast: **Peter, Moses, God.**

Peter and John before the Council
Acts 4.1–22

Narrator After healing the man in Solomon's porch of the Temple, Peter and John were still speaking to the people when some priests, the officer in charge of the temple guards, and some Sadducees arrived. They were annoyed because the two apostles were teaching the people that Jesus had risen from death, which proved that the dead will rise to life. So they arrested them and put them in jail until the next day, since it was already late. But many who heard the message believed; and the number of men grew to about five thousand.

The next day the Jewish leaders, the elders, and the teachers of the Law gathered in Jerusalem. They met with the High Priest Annas and with Caiaphas, John, Alexander, and the others who belonged to the High Priest's family. They made the apostles stand before them and asked them:

Elder 1 How did you do this?

Elder 2 What power have you got?

Elder 1 Whose name did you use?

Narrator Peter, full of the Holy Spirit, answered them:

Peter Leaders of the people and elders: if we are being questioned today about the good deed done to the lame man and how he was healed, then you should all know, and all the people of Israel should know, that this man stands here before you completely well through the power of the name of Jesus Christ of Nazareth— whom you crucified and whom God raised from death. Jesus is the one of whom the scripture says:

Psalmist The stone that you the builders despised
turned out to be the most important of all.

Peter Salvation is to be found through him alone; in all the world there is no one else whom God has given who can save us.

Narrator The members of the Council were amazed to see how bold Peter and John were and to learn that they were ordinary men of no education. They realized then that they had been companions of Jesus. But there was nothing that they could say, because they saw the man who had been healed standing there with Peter and John. So they told them to leave the Council room, and then they started discussing among themselves:

Elder 1 What shall we do with these men?

Elder 2 Everyone in Jerusalem knows that this extraordinary miracle has been performed by them, and we cannot deny it. But to keep this matter from spreading any further among the people, let us warn these men never again to speak to anyone in the name of Jesus.

Narrator	So they called them back in and told them that on no condition were they to speak or to teach in the name of Jesus. But Peter and John answered them:
Peter	You yourselves judge which is right in God's sight—to obey you or to obey God. For we cannot stop speaking of what we ourselves have seen and heard.
Narrator	So the Council warned them even more strongly and then set them free. They saw that it was impossible to punish them, because the people were all praising God for what had happened. The man on whom this miracle of healing had been performed was over forty years old.
Cast	[This is] the word of the Lord.
All	**Thanks be to God.**

Cast: **Narrator, Elder 1, Elder 2, Peter, Psalmist** (can be the same as Peter).

The believers pray for boldness
Acts 4.23–31

Narrator	As soon as Peter and John were set free, they returned to their group and told them what the chief priests and the elders had said. When the believers heard it, they all joined together in prayer to God:
Believer 1	Master and Creator of heaven, earth, and sea, and all that is in them! By means of the Holy Spirit you spoke through our ancestor David, your servant, when he said:
David	Why were the Gentiles furious; why did people make their useless plots? The kings of the earth prepared themselves, and the rulers met together against the Lord and his Messiah.
Believer 1	For indeed Herod and Pontius Pilate met together in this city with the Gentiles and the people of Israel against Jesus, your holy Servant, whom you made Messiah. They gathered to do everything that you by your power and will had already decided would happen.
Believer 2	Now, Lord, take notice of the threats they have made, and allow us, your servants, to speak your message with all boldness. Stretch out your hand to heal, and grant that wonders and miracles may be performed through the name of your holy Servant Jesus.
Narrator	When they finished praying, the place where they were meeting was shaken. They were all filled with the Holy Spirit and began to proclaim God's message with boldness.
Cast	[This is] the word of the Lord.
All	**Thanks be to God.**

Cast: **Narrator, Believer 1, Believer 2** (can be the same as Believer 1), **David.**

The believers share their possessions
Acts 4.32–37

Voice 1   The group of believers was one in mind and heart.

Voice 2   No one said that any of his belongings was his own, but they all shared with one another everything they had.

Voice 1   With great power the apostles gave witness to the resurrection of the Lord Jesus, and God poured rich blessings on them all.

Voice 2   There was no one in the group who was in need. Those who owned fields or houses would sell them, bring the money received from the sale, and hand it over to the apostles; and the money was distributed to each one according to his need.

Voice 1   And so it was that Joseph, a Levite born in Cyprus, whom the apostles called Barnabas—which means 'One who Encourages'—sold a field he owned, brought the money, and handed it over to the apostles.

Cast   [This is] the word of the Lord.
All   **Thanks be to God.**

Cast: **Voice 1, Voice 2.**

Ananias and Sapphira
Acts 5.1–11

Narrator   There was a man named Ananias, who with his wife Sapphira sold some property that belonged to them. But with his wife's agreement he kept part of the money for himself and handed the rest over to the apostles. Peter said to him:

Peter   Ananias, why did you let Satan take control of you and make you lie to the Holy Spirit by keeping part of the money you received for the property? Before you sold the property, it belonged to you; and after you sold it, the money was yours. Why, then, did you decide to do such a thing? You have not lied to men—you have lied to God!

Narrator   As soon as Ananias heard this, he fell down dead; and all who heard about it were terrified. The young men came in, wrapped up his body, carried him out, and buried him. (PAUSE)

About three hours later his wife, not knowing what had happened, came in. Peter asked her:

Peter   Tell me, was this the full amount you and your husband received for your property?

[Narrator   She answered:]

Sapphira   Yes, the full amount.

Peter   Why did you and your husband decide to put the Lord's Spirit to the test? The men who buried your husband are now at the door, and they will carry you out too!

255

Narrator	At once she fell down at his feet and died. The young men came in and saw that she was dead, so they carried her out and buried her beside her husband. The whole church and all the others who heard of this were terrified.
Cast	[This is] the word of the Lord.
All	**Thanks be to God.**

Cast: **Narrator, Peter, Sapphira.**

The apostles are persecuted
Acts 5.12–26

Narrator	Many miracles and wonders were being performed among the people by the apostles. All the believers met together in Solomon's Porch. Nobody outside the group dared to join them, even though the people spoke highly of them. But more and more people were added to the group—a crowd of men and women who believed in the Lord. As a result of what the apostles were doing, sick people were carried out into the streets and placed on beds and mats so that at least Peter's shadow might fall on some of them as he passed by. And crowds of people came in from the towns around Jerusalem, bringing those who were ill or who had evil spirits in them; and they were all healed.
	The High Priest and all his companions, members of the local party of the Sadducees, became extremely jealous of the apostles; so they decided to take action. They arrested the apostles and put them in the public jail. But that night an angel of the Lord opened the prison gates and led the apostles out. [He said to them:]
Angel	Go and stand in the Temple, and tell the people all about this new life.
Narrator	The apostles obeyed, and at dawn they entered the Temple and started teaching. The High Priest and his companions called together all the Jewish elders for a full meeting of the Council; then they sent orders to the prison to have the apostles brought before them. But when the officials arrived, they did not find the apostles in prison, so they returned to the Council [and reported]:
Official	When we arrived at the jail, we found it locked up tight and all the guards on watch at the gates; but when we opened the gates, we found no one inside!
Narrator	When the chief priests and the officer in charge of the temple guards heard this, they wondered what had happened to the apostles. Then a man came in and told them:
Man	Listen! The men you put in prison are in the Temple teaching the people!
Narrator	So the officer went off with his men and brought the apostles back. They did not use force, however, because they were afraid that the people might stone them.
Cast	[This is] the word of the Lord.
All	**Thanks be to God.**

Cast: **Narrator, Angel, Official, Man.**

The apostles before the Council
Acts 5.27–42

Narrator The officer and his men brought the apostles in, made them stand before the Council, and the High Priest questioned them.

High Priest We gave you strict orders not to teach in the name of this man; but see what you have done! You have spread your teaching all over Jerusalem and you want to make us responsible for his death!

[Narrator Peter and the other apostles replied:]

Peter We must obey God, not men. The God of our ancestors raised Jesus from death, after you had killed him by nailing him to a cross. God raised him to his right-hand side as Leader and Saviour, to give the people of Israel the opportunity to repent and have their sins forgiven. We are witnesses to these things—we and the Holy Spirit, who is God's gift to those who obey him.

Narrator When the members of the Council heard this, they were so furious that they wanted to have the apostles put to death. But one of them, a Pharisee named Gamaliel, who was a teacher of the Law and was highly respected by all the people, stood up in the Council. He ordered the apostles to be taken out for a while, and then he said to the Council:

Gamaliel Fellow-Israelites, be careful what you do to these men. You remember that Theudas appeared some time ago, claiming to be somebody great, and about four hundred men joined him. But he was killed, all his followers were scattered, and his movement died out. After that, Judas the Galilean appeared during the time of the census; he drew a crowd after him, but he also was killed and all his followers were scattered. And so in this case, I tell you, do not take any action against these men. Leave them alone! If what they have planned and done is of human origin, it will disappear, but if it comes from God, you cannot possibly defeat them. You could find yourselves fighting against God!

Narrator The Council followed Gamaliel's advice. They called the apostles in, had them whipped, and ordered them never again to speak in the name of Jesus; and then they set them free. As the apostles left the Council, they were happy, because God had considered them worthy to suffer disgrace for the sake of Jesus. And every day in the Temple and in people's homes they continued to teach and preach the Good News about Jesus the Messiah.

Cast [This is] the word of the Lord.
All **Thanks be to God.**

Cast: **Narrator, High Priest, Peter, Gamaliel.**

The seven helpers
Acts 6.1–7

Narrator   As the number of disciples kept growing, there was a quarrel between the Greek-speaking Jews and the native Jews. The Greek-speaking Jews claimed that their widows were being neglected in the daily distribution of funds. So the twelve apostles called the whole group of believers together [and said]:

Apostle   It is not right for us to neglect the preaching of God's word in order to handle finances. So then, brothers, choose seven men among you who are known to be full of the Holy Spirit and wisdom, and we will put them in charge of this matter. We ourselves, then, will give our full time to prayer and the work of preaching.

Narrator   The whole group was pleased with the apostles' proposal, so they chose Stephen, a man full of faith and the Holy Spirit, and Philip, Prochorus, Nicanor, Timon, Parmenas, and Nicolaus, a Gentile from Antioch who had earlier been converted to Judaism. The group presented them to the apostles, who prayed and placed their hands on them. And so the word of God continued to spread. The number of disciples in Jerusalem grew larger and larger, and a great number of priests accepted the faith.

Cast   [This is] the word of the Lord.
All   **Thanks be to God.**

Cast: **Narrator, Apostle.**

The arrest and martyrdom of Stephen
From Acts 6.8—8.1

Narrator   Stephen, a man richly blessed by God and full of power, performed great miracles and wonders among the people. But he was opposed by some men who were members of the synagogue of the Freedmen—as it was called—which included Jews from Cyrene and Alexandria. They and other Jews from the provinces of Cilicia and Asia started arguing with Stephen. But the Spirit gave Stephen such wisdom that when he spoke, they could not refute him. So they bribed some men to say:

Man 1   We heard him speaking against Moses.

Man 2   And against God!

Narrator   In this way they stirred up the people, the elders, and the teachers of the Law. They seized Stephen and took him before the Council. Then they brought in some men to tell lies about him:

Man 3   This man is always talking against our sacred Temple and the Law of Moses.

Man 4   We heard him say that this Jesus of Nazareth will tear down the Temple and change all the customs which have come down to us from Moses!

Narrator	All those sitting in the Council fixed their eyes on Stephen and saw that his face looked like the face of an angel. (PAUSE)
	The High Priest asked Stephen:
High Priest	Is this true?
Narrator	Stephen answered:
Stephen	Brothers and fathers, listen to me! The Most High God does not live in houses built by men; as the prophet says:
Isaiah	Heaven is my throne, says the Lord, and the earth is my footstool. What kind of house would you build for me? Where is the place for me to live in? Did not I myself make all these things?
Stephen	How stubborn you are! How heathen your hearts, how deaf you are to God's message! You are just like your ancestors: you too have always resisted the Holy Spirit! Was there any prophet that your ancestors did not persecute? They killed God's messengers, who long ago announced the coming of his righteous Servant. And now you have betrayed and murdered him. You are the ones who received God's law, that was handed down by angels—yet you have not obeyed it!
Narrator	As the members of the Council listened to Stephen, they became furious and ground their teeth at him in anger. But Stephen, full of the Holy Spirit, looked up to heaven and saw God's glory and Jesus standing there:
Stephen	Look! I see heaven opened and the Son of Man standing at the right-hand side of God!
Narrator	With a loud cry the members of the Council covered their ears with their hands. Then they all rushed at him at once, threw him out of the city, and stoned him. The witnesses left their cloaks in the care of a young man named Saul. They kept on stoning Stephen as he called out to the Lord:
Stephen	Lord Jesus, receive my spirit!
Narrator	He knelt down and cried out in a loud voice:
Stephen	Lord! Do not remember this sin against them!
Narrator	He said this and died. And Saul approved of his murder.
Cast	[This is] the word of the Lord.
All	**Thanks be to God.**

Cast: **Narrator, Man 1, Man 2, Man 3** (can be the same as Man 1), **Man 4** (can be the same as Man 2), **High Priest, Stephen, Isaiah.**

The Church is persecuted and scattered
Acts 8.1–25

Narrator	On the day of Stephen's death a great persecution broke out against the church at Jerusalem, and all except the apostles were

→

259

scattered throughout Judaea and Samaria. Godly men buried Stephen and mourned deeply for him. But Saul began to destroy the church. Going from house to house, he dragged off men and women and put them in prison. Those who had been scattered preached the word wherever they went. Philip went down to a city in Samaria and proclaimed the Christ there. When the crowds heard Philip and saw the miraculous signs he did, they all paid close attention to what he said. With shrieks, evil spirits came out of many, and many paralytics and cripples were healed. So there was great joy in that city.

Now for some time a man named Simon had practised sorcery in the city and amazed all the people of Samaria. He boasted that he was someone great, and all the people, both high and low, gave him their attention and exclaimed:

Person   This man is the divine power known as the Great Power.

Narrator   They followed him because he had amazed them for a long time with his magic. But when they believed Philip as he preached the good news of the kingdom of God and the name of Jesus Christ, they were baptized, both men and women. Simon himself believed and was baptized. And he followed Philip everywhere, astonished by the great signs and miracles he saw. When the apostles in Jerusalem heard that Samaria had accepted the word of God, they sent Peter and John to them. When they arrived, they prayed for them that they might receive the Holy Spirit, because the Holy Spirit had not yet come upon any of them; they had simply been baptized into the name of the Lord Jesus. Then Peter and John placed their hands on them, and they received the Holy Spirit.

When Simon saw that the Spirit was given at the laying on of the apostles' hands, he offered them money.

Simon   Give me also this ability so that everyone on whom I lay my hands may receive the Holy Spirit.

Narrator   Peter answered:

Peter   May your money perish with you, because you thought you could buy the gift of God with money! You have no part or share in this ministry, because your heart is not right before God. Repent of this wickedness and pray to the Lord. Perhaps he will forgive you for having such a thought in your heart. For I see that you are full of bitterness and captive to sin.

Simon   Pray to the Lord for me so that nothing you have said may happen to me.

Narrator   When they had testified and proclaimed the word of the Lord, Peter and John returned to Jerusalem, preaching the gospel in many Samaritan villages.

Cast   [This is] the word of the Lord.
All   **Thanks be to God.**

Cast: **Narrator, Person, Simon, Peter.**

Philip and the Ethiopian official
From Acts 8.26–40

Narrator   An angel of the Lord said to Philip:

Angel   Get ready and go south to the road that goes from Jerusalem to Gaza.

Narrator   This road is not used nowadays. So Philip got ready and went. Now an Ethiopian eunuch, who was an important official in charge of the treasury of the queen of Ethiopia, was on his way home. He had been to Jerusalem to worship God and was going back home in his carriage. As he rode along, he was reading from the book of the prophet Isaiah. The Holy Spirit said to Philip:

Holy Spirit   Go over to that carriage and stay close to it.

Narrator   Philip ran over and heard him reading from the book of the prophet Isaiah. He asked him:

Philip   Do you understand what you are reading?

Ethiopian   How can I understand unless someone explains it to me?

Narrator   And he invited Philip to climb up and sit in the carriage with him. The passage of scripture which he was reading was this:

Isaiah   Like a sheep that is taken to be slaughtered,
like a lamb that makes no sound when its wool is cut off,
he did not say a word.
He was humiliated, and justice was denied him.
No one will be able to tell about his descendants,
because his life on earth has come to an end.

[Narrator   The official asked Philip:]

Ethiopian   Tell me, of whom is the prophet saying this? Of himself or of someone else?

Narrator   Then Philip began to speak; starting from this passage of scripture, he told him the Good News about Jesus. As they travelled down the road, they came to a place where there was some water, and the official said:

Ethiopian   Here is some water. What is to keep me from being baptized?

Narrator   The official ordered the carriage to stop, and both Philip and the official went down into the water, and Philip baptized him. When they came up out of the water, the Spirit of the Lord took Philip away. The official did not see him again, but continued on his way, full of joy. Philip found himself in Azotus; he went on to Caesarea, and on the way he preached the Good News in every town.

Cast   [This is] the word of the Lord.
All   **Thanks be to God.**

Cast: **Narrator, Angel, Holy Spirit, Philip, Ethiopian, Isaiah.**

The conversion of Saul
Acts 9.1–8

Narrator   Saul kept up his violent threats of murder against the followers of the Lord. He went to the High Priest and asked for letters of introduction to the synagogues in Damascus, so that if he should find there any followers of the Way of the Lord, he would be able to arrest them, both men and women, and bring them back to Jerusalem.

As Saul was coming near the city of Damascus, suddenly a light from the sky flashed round him. He fell to the ground and heard a voice [saying to him]:

The Lord   Saul, Saul! Why do you persecute me?

[Narrator   He asked:]

Saul   Who are you, Lord?

The Lord   I am Jesus, whom you persecute. But get up and go into the city, where you will be told what you must do.

Narrator   The men who were travelling with Saul had stopped, not saying a word; they heard the voice but could not see anyone. Saul got up from the ground and opened his eyes, but could not see a thing. So they took him by the hand and led him into Damascus.

Cast   [This is] the word of the Lord.
All   **Thanks be to God.**

Cast: **Narrator, The Lord, Saul.**

Saul meets Ananias
Acts 9.9–19

Narrator   For three days Saul was not able to see, and during that time he did not eat or drink anything. There was a Christian in Damascus named Ananias. He had a vision, in which the Lord spoke to him:

The Lord   Ananias!

[Narrator   He answered:]

Ananias   Here I am, Lord.

The Lord   Get ready and go to Straight Street, and at the house of Judas ask for a man from Tarsus named Saul. He is praying, and in a vision he has seen a man named Ananias come in and place his hands on him so that he might see again.

Ananias   Lord, many people have told me about this man and about all the terrible things he has done to your people in Jerusalem. And he has come to Damascus with authority from the chief priests to arrest all who worship you.

The Lord	Go, because I have chosen him to serve me, to make my name known to Gentiles and kings and to the people of Israel. And I myself will show him all that he must suffer for my sake.
Narrator	So Ananias went, entered the house where Saul was, and placed his hands on him.
Ananias	Brother Saul, the Lord has sent me—Jesus himself, who appeared to you on the road as you were coming here. He sent me so that you might see again and be filled with the Holy Spirit.
Narrator	At once something like fish scales fell from Saul's eyes, and he was able to see again. He stood up and was baptized; and after he had eaten, his strength came back.
Cast	[This is] the word of the Lord.
All	**Thanks be to God.**

Cast: **Narrator, The Lord, Ananias.**

Saul preaches in Damascus
Acts 9.19–25

Narrator	Saul stayed for a few days with the believers in Damascus. He went straight to the synagogues and began to preach that Jesus was the Son of God. All who heard him were amazed:
Hearer 1	Isn't he the one who in Jerusalem was killing those who worship that man Jesus?
Hearer 2	And didn't he come here for the very purpose of arresting those people and taking them back to the chief priests?
Narrator	But Saul's preaching became even more powerful, and his proofs that Jesus was the Messiah were so convincing that the Jews who lived in Damascus could not answer him. (PAUSE) After many days had gone by, the Jews met together and made plans to kill Saul, but he was told of their plan. Day and night they watched the city gates in order to kill him. But one night Saul's followers took him and let him down through an opening in the wall, lowering him in a basket.
Cast	[This is] the word of the Lord.
All	**Thanks be to God.**

Cast: **Narrator, Hearer 1, Hearer 2.**

Saul in Jerusalem
Acts 9.26–31

Narrator 1	Saul went to Jerusalem and tried to join the disciples.
Narrator 2	But they would not believe that he was a disciple, and they were all afraid of him.

263

Narrator 1	Then Barnabas came to his help and took him to the apostles. He explained to them how Saul had seen the Lord on the road and that the Lord had spoken to him.
Narrator 2	He also told them how boldly Saul had preached in the name of Jesus in Damascus.
Narrator 1	And so Saul stayed with them and went all over Jerusalem, preaching boldly in the name of the Lord. He also talked and disputed with the Greek-speaking Jews, but they tried to kill him.
Narrator 2	When the believers found out about this, they took Saul to Caesarea and sent him away to Tarsus.
Narrator 1	And so it was that the church throughout Judaea, Galilee, and Samaria had a time of peace. Through the help of the Holy Spirit it was strengthened and grew in numbers, as it lived in reverence for the Lord.
Cast **All**	[This is] the word of the Lord. **Thanks be to God.**

Cast: **Narrator 1, Narrator 2.**

Peter in Lydda and Joppa
Acts 9.32–43

Narrator	Peter travelled everywhere, and on one occasion he went to visit God's people who lived in Lydda. There he met a man named Aeneas, who was paralysed and had not been able to get out of bed for eight years. [Peter said to him:]
Peter	Aeneas, Jesus Christ makes you well. Get up and make your bed.
Narrator	At once Aeneas got up. All the people living in Lydda and Sharon saw him, and they turned to the Lord. (PAUSE) In Joppa there was a woman named Tabitha, who was a believer. Her name in Greek is Dorcas, meaning 'a deer'. She spent all her time doing good and helping the poor. At that time she became ill and died. Her body was washed and laid in a room upstairs. Joppa was not very far from Lydda, and when the believers in Joppa heard that Peter was in Lydda, they sent two men to him with the message:
Man	Please hurry and come to us.
Narrator	So Peter got ready and went with them. When he arrived, he was taken to the room upstairs, where all the widows crowded round him, crying and showing him all the shirts and coats that Dorcas had made while she was alive. Peter put them all out of the room, and knelt down and prayed; then he turned to the body and said:
Peter	Tabitha, get up!
Narrator	She opened her eyes, and when she saw Peter, she sat up. Peter reached over and helped her get up. Then he called all the

believers, including the widows, and presented her alive to them. The news about this spread all over Joppa, and many people believed in the Lord. Peter stayed on in Joppa for many days with a tanner of leather named Simon.

Cast	[This is] the word of the Lord.
All	**Thanks be to God.**

Cast: **Narrator, Peter, Man.**

Peter and Cornelius
Acts 10.1–48

Narrator There was a man in Caesarea named Cornelius, who was a captain in the Roman regiment called 'The Italian Regiment'. He was a religious man; he and his whole family worshipped God. He also did much to help the Jewish poor people and was constantly praying to God. It was about three o'clock one afternoon when he had a vision, in which he clearly saw an angel of God come in and say to him:

Angel Cornelius!

Narrator He stared at the angel in fear and said:

Cornelius What is it, sir?

Angel God is pleased with your prayers and works of charity, and is ready to answer you. And now send some men to Joppa for a certain man whose full name is Simon Peter. He is a guest in the home of a tanner of leather named Simon, who lives by the sea.

Narrator Then the angel went away, and Cornelius called two of his house servants and a soldier, a religious man who was one of his personal attendants. He told them what had happened and sent them off to Joppa.

The next day, as they were on their way and coming near Joppa, Peter went up on the roof of the house about noon in order to pray. He became hungry and wanted something to eat; while the food was being prepared, he had a vision. He saw heaven opened and something coming down that looked like a large sheet being lowered by its four corners to the earth. In it were all kinds of animals, reptiles, and wild birds. A voice said to him:

The Lord Get up, Peter; kill and eat!

[Narrator But Peter said:]

Peter Certainly not, Lord! I have never eaten anything ritually unclean or defiled.

The Lord Do not consider anything unclean that God has declared clean.

Narrator This happened three times, and then the thing was taken back up into heaven. While Peter was wondering about the meaning of this vision, the men sent by Cornelius had learnt where Simon's house was, and they were now standing in front of the gate. They called out and asked:

Man 1	Is there a guest here by the name of Simon Peter?
Narrator	Peter was still trying to understand what the vision meant, when the Spirit said:
The Spirit	Listen! Three men are here looking for you. So get ready and go down, and do not hesitate to go with them, for I have sent them.
Narrator	So Peter went down and said to the men:
Peter	I am the man you are looking for. Why have you come?
[Narrator	They answered:]
Man 1	Captain Cornelius sent us. He is a good man who worships God and is highly respected by all the Jewish people.
Man 2	An angel of God told him to invite you to his house, so that he could hear what you have to say.
Narrator	Peter invited the men in and persuaded them to spend the night there. (PAUSE)
	The next day he got ready and went with them; and some of the believers from Joppa went along with him. The following day he arrived in Caesarea, where Cornelius was waiting for him, together with relatives and close friends that he had invited. As Peter was about to go in, Cornelius met him, fell at his feet, and bowed down before him. But Peter made him rise:
Peter	Stand up! I myself am only a man.
Narrator	Peter kept on talking to Cornelius as he went into the house, where he found many people gathered. He said to them:
Peter (to the people)	You yourselves know very well that a Jew is not allowed by his religion to visit or associate with Gentiles. But God has shown me that I must not consider any person ritually unclean or defiled.
(to Cornelius)	And so when you sent for me, I came without any objection. I ask you, then, why did you send for me?
[Narrator	Cornelius said:]
Cornelius	It was about this time three days ago that I was praying in my house at three o'clock in the afternoon. Suddenly a man dressed in shining clothes stood in front of me and said:
Angel	Cornelius! God has heard your prayer and has taken notice of your works of charity. Send someone to Joppa for a man whose full name is Simon Peter. He is a guest in the home of Simon the tanner of leather, who lives by the sea.
Cornelius	And so I sent for you at once, and you have been good enough to come. Now we are all here in the presence of God, waiting to hear anything that the Lord has instructed you to say.
[Narrator	Peter began to speak:]
Peter	I now realize that it is true that God treats everyone on the same basis. Whoever worships him and does what is right is acceptable to him, no matter what race he belongs to. You know the message

he sent to the people of Israel, proclaiming the Good News of peace through Jesus Christ, who is Lord of all. You know of the great event that took place throughout the land of Israel, beginning in Galilee after John preached his message of baptism. You know about Jesus of Nazareth and how God poured out on him the Holy Spirit and power. He went everywhere, doing good and healing all who were under the power of the Devil, for God was with him. We are witnesses of everything that he did in the land of Israel and in Jerusalem. Then they put him to death by nailing him to a cross. But God raised him from death three days later and caused him to appear, not to everyone, but only to the witnesses that God had already chosen, that is, to us who ate and drank with him after he rose from death. And he commanded us to preach the gospel to the people and to testify that he is the one whom God has appointed judge of the living and the dead. All the prophets spoke about him, saying that everyone who believes in him will have his sins forgiven through the power of his name.

Narrator While Peter was still speaking, the Holy Spirit came down on all those who were listening to his message. The Jewish believers who had come from Joppa with Peter were amazed that God had poured out his gift of the Holy Spirit on the Gentiles also. For they heard them speaking in strange tongues and praising God's greatness. Peter spoke up:

Peter These people have received the Holy Spirit, just as we also did. Can anyone, then, stop them from being baptized with water?

Narrator So he ordered them to be baptized in the name of Jesus Christ.

Cast [This is] the word of the Lord.
All **Thanks be to God.**

Cast: **Narrator, Angel** (male voice), **Cornelius, The Lord, Peter, Man 1, The Spirit** (can be the same as The Lord), **Man 2** (can be the same as Man 1).

Peter's report to the church at Jerusalem
Acts 11.1–18

Narrator The apostles and the other believers throughout Judaea heard that the Gentiles also had received the word of God. When Peter went to Jerusalem, those who were in favour of circumcising Gentiles criticized him:

Apostle 1 You were a guest in the home of uncircumcised Gentiles.

Apostle 2 You even ate with them!

Narrator So Peter gave them a complete account of what had happened from the very beginning:

Peter While I was praying in the city of Joppa, I had a vision. I saw something coming down that looked like a large sheet being lowered by its four corners from heaven, and it stopped next to me. I looked closely inside and saw domesticated and wild animals, reptiles, and wild birds. Then I heard a voice [saying to me]:

The Lord	Get up, Peter; kill and eat!
Peter	But I said, 'Certainly not, Lord! No ritually unclean or defiled food has ever entered my mouth.' The voice spoke again from heaven:
The Lord	Do not consider anything unclean that God has declared clean.
Peter	This happened three times, and finally the whole thing was drawn back up into heaven. At that very moment three men who had been sent to me from Caesarea arrived at the house where I was staying. The Spirit told me to go with them without hesitation. These six fellow-believers from Joppa accompanied me to Caesarea, and we all went into the house of Cornelius. He told us how he had seen an angel standing in his house, who said to him:
Angel	Send someone to Joppa for a man whose full name is Simon Peter. He will speak words to you by which you and all your family will be saved.
Peter	And when I began to speak, the Holy Spirit came down on them just as on us at the beginning. Then I remembered what the Lord had said:
The Lord	John baptized with water, but you will be baptized with the Holy Spirit.
Peter	It is clear that God gave those Gentiles the same gift that he gave us when we believed in the Lord Jesus Christ; who was I, then, to try to stop God!
Narrator	When they heard this, they stopped their criticism and praised God [saying]:
Apostle 1	Then God has given to the Gentiles also the opportunity to repent and live!
Cast	[This is] the word of the Lord.
All	**Thanks be to God.**

Cast: **Narrator, Apostle 1, Apostle 2** (can be the same as Apostle 1)**, Peter, The Lord** (preferably unseen)**, Angel.**

The church at Antioch
Acts 11.19–30

Narrator 1	Some of the believers who were scattered by the persecution which took place when Stephen was killed went as far as Phoenicia, Cyprus, and Antioch, telling the message to Jews only.
Narrator 2	But other believers, men from Cyprus and Cyrene, went to Antioch and proclaimed the message to Gentiles also, telling them the Good News about the Lord Jesus. The Lord's power was with them, and a great number of people believed and turned to the Lord. The news about this reached the church in Jerusalem, so they sent Barnabas to Antioch.
Narrator 1	When he arrived and saw how God had blessed the people, he was glad and urged them all to be faithful and true to the Lord with all their hearts.

Narrator 3	Barnabas was a good man, full of the Holy Spirit and faith, and many people were brought to the Lord.
Narrator 1	Then Barnabas went to Tarsus to look for Saul. When he found him, he took him to Antioch, and for a whole year the two met with the people of the church and taught a large group. It was at Antioch that the believers were first called Christians.
Narrator 2	About that time some prophets went from Jerusalem to Antioch. One of them, named Agabus, stood up and by the power of the Spirit predicted that a severe famine was about to come over all the earth.
Narrator 3	It came when Claudius was emperor.
Narrator 2	The disciples decided that each of them would send as much as he could to help their fellow-believers who lived in Judaea. They did this, then, and sent the money to the church elders by Barnabas and Saul.
Cast	[This is] the word of the Lord.
All	**Thanks be to God.**

Cast: **Narrator 1, Narrator 2, Narrator 3.**

Peter is set free from prison
From Acts 12.1–19

Narrator	King Herod began to persecute some members of the church. He had James, the brother of John, put to death by the sword. When he saw that this pleased the Jews, he went on to arrest Peter. After his arrest Peter was put in jail, where he was handed over to be guarded by four groups of four soldiers each. Herod planned to put him on trial in public after Passover. So Peter was kept in jail, but the people of the church were praying earnestly to God for him.
	The night before Herod was going to bring him out to the people, Peter was sleeping between two guards. He was tied with two chains, and there were guards on duty at the prison gate. Suddenly an angel of the Lord stood there, and a light shone in the cell. The angel shook Peter by the shoulder and woke him up:
Angel	Hurry! Get up!
Narrator	At once the chains fell off Peter's hands.
Angel	Fasten your belt and put on your sandals.
[Narrator	Peter did so, (PAUSE) and the angel said:]
Angel	Put your cloak round you and come with me.
Narrator	Peter followed him out of the prison, not knowing, however, if what the angel was doing was real; he thought he was seeing a vision. They passed by the first guard post and then the second, and came at last to the iron gate leading into the city. The gate opened for them by itself, and they went out. They walked down a street, and suddenly the angel left Peter. Then Peter realized what had happened to him:

Peter	Now I know that it is really true! The Lord sent his angel to rescue me from Herod's power and from everything the Jewish people expected to happen.
Narrator	Aware of his situation, he went to the home of Mary, the mother of John Mark, where many people had gathered and were praying. Peter knocked at the outside door, and a servant-girl named Rhoda came to answer it. She recognized Peter's voice and was so happy that she ran back in without opening the door, and announced that Peter was standing outside. [They told her:]
Person 1	You are mad!
Narrator	But she insisted that it was true. [So they answered:]
Person 2	It is his angel.
Narrator	Meanwhile Peter kept on knocking. At last they opened the door, and when they saw him, they were amazed. He motioned with his hand for them to be quiet, and he explained to them how the Lord had brought him out of prison. [He said:]
Peter	Tell this to James and the rest of the believers.
Narrator	Then he left and went somewhere else.
	When morning came, there was a tremendous confusion among the guards—what had happened to Peter? Herod gave orders to search for him, but they could not find him. So he had the guards questioned and ordered them to be put to death. After this, Herod left Judaea and spent some time in Caesarea.
Cast	[This is] the word of the Lord.
All	**Thanks be to God.**

Cast: **Narrator, Angel, Peter, Person 1, Person 2** (can be the same as Person 1).

The death of Herod
Acts 12.20–25

Narrator	Herod was very angry with the people of Tyre and Sidon, so they went in a group to see him. First they convinced Blastus, the man in charge of the palace, that he should help them. Then they went to Herod and asked him for peace, because their country got its food supplies from the king's country. On a chosen day Herod put on his royal robes, sat on his throne, and made a speech to the people.
	They shouted:
Person 1	It isn't a man speaking—
Persons 1 and 2	It's a god!
Narrator	At once the angel of the Lord struck Herod down, because he did not give honour to God. He was eaten by worms and died. Meanwhile the word of God continued to spread and grow.

Barnabas and Saul finished their mission and returned from Jerusalem, taking John Mark with them.

Cast	[This is] the word of the Lord.
All	**Thanks be to God.**

Cast: **Narrator, Person 1, Person 2** (can be the same as Person 1).

Barnabas and Saul are chosen and sent
Acts 13.1–3

Narrator	In the church at Antioch there were some prophets and teachers: Barnabas, Simeon—
Commentator	Called the Black.
Narrator	Lucius—
Commentator	From Cyrene.
Narrator	Manaen—
Commentator	Who had been brought up with Herod the governor.
Narrator	And Saul. While they were serving the Lord and fasting, the Holy Spirit said to them:
Holy Spirit	Set apart for me Barnabas and Saul, to do the work to which I have called them:
Narrator	They fasted and prayed, placed their hands on them, and sent them off.
Cast	[This is] the word of the Lord.
All	**Thanks be to God.**

Cast: **Narrator, Commentator, Holy Spirit.**

Barnabas and Saul in Cyprus
Acts 13.4–12

Narrator	Having been sent by the Holy Spirit, Barnabas and Saul went to Seleucia and sailed from there to the island of Cyprus. When they arrived at Salamis, they preached the word of God in the synagogues. They had John Mark with them to help in the work. They went all the way across the island to Paphos, where they met a certain magician named Bar-Jesus, a Jew who claimed to be a prophet. He was a friend of the governor of the island, Sergius Paulus, who was an intelligent man. The governor called Barnabas and Saul before him because he wanted to hear the word of God. But they were opposed by the magician Elymas— that is his name in Greek—who tried to turn the governor away from the faith. Then Saul—also known as Paul—was filled with the Holy Spirit; he looked straight at the magician:
Paul	You son of the Devil! You are the enemy of everything that is good. You are full of all kinds of evil tricks, and you always keep trying to turn the Lord's truths into lies! The Lord's hand will come down on you now; you will be blind and will not see the light of day for a time.

Narrator	At once Elymas felt a dark mist cover his eyes, and he walked about trying to find someone to lead him by the hand. When the governor saw what had happened, he believed; for he was greatly amazed at the teaching about the Lord.
Cast	[This is] the word of the Lord.
All	**Thanks be to God.**

Cast: **Narrator, Paul.**

Paul preaches in Antioch in Pisidia
From Acts 13.13–28

Narrator	Paul and his companions sailed from Paphos and came to Perga, a city in Pamphylia, where John Mark left them and went back to Jerusalem. They went on from Perga and arrived in Antioch in Pisidia, and on the Sabbath they went into the synagogue and sat down. After the reading from the Law of Moses and from the writings of the prophets, the officials of the synagogue sent them a message:
Official	Brothers, we want you to speak to the people if you have a message of encouragement for them.
Narrator	Paul stood up, motioned with his hand, and began to speak:
Paul	Fellow-Israelites and all Gentiles here who worship God: hear me! The God of the people of Israel chose our ancestors and made the people a great nation. God made David their king. This is what God said about him:
Voice	I have found that David son of Jesse is the kind of man I like, a man who will do all I want him to do.
Paul	It was Jesus, a descendant of David, whom God made the Saviour of the people of Israel, as he had promised. Before Jesus began his work, John preached to all the people of Israel that they should turn from their sins and be baptized. And as John was about to finish his mission, he said to the people:
John	Who do you think I am? I am not the one you are waiting for. But listen! He is coming after me, and I am not good enough to take his sandals off his feet.
Paul	My fellow-Israelites, descendants of Abraham, and all Gentiles here who worship God: it is to us that this message of salvation has been sent! For the people who live in Jerusalem and their leaders did not know that he is the Saviour, nor did they understand the words of the prophets that are read every Sabbath. Yet they made the prophets' words come true by condemning Jesus. And even though they could find no reason to pass the death sentence on him, they asked Pilate to have him put to death.
Cast	[This is] the word of the Lord.
All	**Thanks be to God.**

Cast: **Narrator, Official, Paul, Voice, John.**

Paul preaches in Antioch (continued)
Acts 13.29–52

Paul   After the people who live in Jerusalem and their leaders had done everything that the Scriptures say about Jesus, they took him down from the cross and placed him in a tomb. But God raised him from death, and for many days he appeared to those who had travelled with him from Galilee to Jerusalem. They are now witnesses for him to the people of Israel. And we are here to bring the Good News to you: what God promised our ancestors he would do, he has now done for us, who are their descendants, by raising Jesus to life. As it is written in the second Psalm:

Voice   You are my Son;
today I have become your Father.

Paul   And this is what God said about raising him from death, never to rot away in the grave:

Voice   I will give you the sacred and sure blessings
that I promised to David.

Paul   As indeed he says in another passage:

Voice   You will not allow your devoted servant to rot in the grave.

Paul   For David served God's purposes in his own time, and then he died, was buried with his ancestors, and his body rotted in the grave. But this did not happen to the one whom God raised from death. We want you to know, my fellow-Israelites, that it is through Jesus that the message about forgiveness of sins is preached to you; and that everyone who believes in him is set free from all the sins from which the Law of Moses could not set you free. Take care, then, so that what the prophets said may not happen to you:

Voice   Look, you scoffers! Be astonished and die!
For what I am doing today
is something that you will not believe,
even when someone explains it to you!

Narrator   As Paul and Barnabas were leaving the synagogue, the people invited them to come back the next Sabbath and tell them more about these things. After the people had left the meeting, Paul and Barnabas were followed by many Jews and by many Gentiles who had been converted to Judaism. The apostles spoke to them and encouraged them to keep on living in the grace of God. (PAUSE)

The next Sabbath nearly everyone in the town came to hear the word of the Lord. When the Jews saw the crowds, they were filled with jealousy; they disputed what Paul was saying and insulted him. But Paul and Barnabas spoke out even more boldly:

Paul	It was necessary that the word of God should be spoken first to you. But since you reject it and do not consider yourselves worthy of eternal life, we will leave you and go to the Gentiles. For this is the commandment that the Lord has given us:
Voice	I have made you a light for the Gentiles, so that all the world may be saved.
Narrator	When the Gentiles heard this, they were glad and praised the Lord's message; and those who had been chosen for eternal life became believers. (PAUSE)
	The word of the Lord spread everywhere in that region. But the Jews stirred up the leading men of the city and the Gentile women of high social standing who worshipped God. They started a persecution against Paul and Barnabas and threw them out of their region. The apostles shook the dust off their feet in protest against them and went on to Iconium. The believers in Antioch were full of joy and the Holy Spirit.
Cast All	[This is] the word of the Lord. **Thanks be to God.**

Cast: **Paul, Voice, Narrator.**

In Iconium
Acts 14.1–7

Narrator 1	Paul and Barnabas went to the synagogue and spoke in such a way that a great number of Jews and Gentiles became believers.
Narrator 2	But the Jews who would not believe stirred up the Gentiles and turned them against the believers.
Narrator 1	The apostles stayed there for a long time, speaking boldly about the Lord, who proved that their message about his grace was true by giving them the power to perform miracles and wonders.
Narrator 2	The people of the city were divided: some were for the Jews, others for the apostles. Then some Gentiles and Jews, together with their leaders, decided to ill-treat the apostles and stone them. When the apostles learnt about it, they fled to the cities of Lystra and Derbe in Lycaonia and to the surrounding territory.
Narrators 1 and 2	There they preached the Good News.
Cast All	[This is] the word of the Lord. **Thanks be to God.**

Cast: **Narrator 1** (excited voice), **Narrator 2** (serious voice).

Paul and Barnabas in Lystra and Derbe
Acts 14.8–20

Narrator In Lystra there was a man who had been lame from birth and had never been able to walk. He sat there and listened to Paul's words. Paul saw that he believed and could be healed, so he looked straight at him:

Paul (loudly) Stand up straight on your feet!

Narrator The man jumped up and started walking around. When the crowds saw what Paul had done, they started shouting in their own Lycaonian language:

Person 1 The gods have become like men.

Person 2 They have come down to us!

Narrator They gave Barnabas the name Zeus, and Paul the name Hermes, because he was the chief speaker. The priest of the god Zeus, whose temple stood just outside the town, brought bulls and flowers to the gate, for he and the crowds wanted to offer sacrifice to the apostles.

When Barnabas and Paul heard what they were about to do, they tore their clothes and ran into the middle of the crowd [shouting:]

Barnabas Why are you doing this? We ourselves are only human beings like you!

Paul We are here to announce the Good News.

Barnabas To turn you away from these worthless things to the living God, who made heaven, earth, sea, and all that is in them.

Paul In the past he allowed all people to go their own way. But he has always given evidence of his existence by the good things he does: he gives you rain from heaven and crops at the right times; he gives you food and fills your hearts with happiness.

Narrator Even with these words the apostles could hardly keep the crowd from offering a sacrifice to them. (PAUSE)

Some Jews came from Antioch in Pisidia and from Iconium; they won the crowd over to their side, stoned Paul and dragged him out of the town, thinking that he was dead. But when the believers gathered round him, he got up and went back into the town. The next day he and Barnabas went to Derbe.

Cast [This is] the word of the Lord.
All **Thanks be to God.**

Cast: **Narrator, Paul, Person 1, Person 2** (can be the same as Person 1), **Barnabas.**

Paul and Barnabas return to Antioch in Syria
Acts 14.21–26

Narrator   Paul and Barnabas preached the Good News in Derbe and won many disciples. Then they went back to Lystra, to Iconium, and on to Antioch in Pisidia. They strengthened the believers and encouraged them to remain true to the faith. They taught:

Paul   We must pass through many troubles to enter the Kingdom of God.

Narrator   In each church they appointed elders, and with prayers and fasting they commended them to the Lord, in whom they had put their trust. (PAUSE)

After going through the territory of Pisidia, they came to Pamphylia. There they preached the message in Perga and then went to Attalia, and from there they sailed back to Antioch, the place where they had been commended to the care of God's grace for the work they had now completed.

Cast   [This is] the word of the Lord.
All   **Thanks be to God.**

Cast: **Narrator, Paul.**

The meeting in Jerusalem
Acts 14.27—15.21

Narrator   When Paul and Barnabas arrived in Antioch, they gathered the people of the church together and told them about all that God had done with them and how he had opened the way for the Gentiles to believe. And they stayed a long time there with the believers. Some men came from Judaea to Antioch and started teaching the believers:

Man   You cannot be saved unless you are circumcised as the Law of Moses requires.

Narrator   Paul and Barnabas got into a fierce argument with them about this, so it was decided that Paul and Barnabas and some of the others in Antioch should go to Jerusalem and see the apostles and elders about this matter. They were sent on their way by the church; and as they went through Phoenicia and Samaria, they reported how the Gentiles had turned to God; this news brought great joy to all the believers. (PAUSE)

When they arrived in Jerusalem, they were welcomed by the church, the apostles, and the elders, to whom they told all that God had done through them. But some of the believers who belonged to the party of the Pharisees stood up:

Believer 1   The Gentiles must be circumcised.

Believer 2   And told to obey the Law of Moses.

Narrator   The apostles and the elders met together to consider this question. After a long debate Peter stood up:

Peter	My brothers, you know that a long time ago God chose me from among you to preach the Good News to the Gentiles, so that they could hear and believe. And God, who knows the thoughts of everyone, showed his approval of the Gentiles by giving the Holy Spirit to them, just as he had to us. He made no difference between us and them; he forgave their sins because they believed. So then, why do you now want to put God to the test by laying a load on the backs of the believers which neither our ancestors nor we ourselves were able to carry? No! We believe and are saved by the grace of the Lord Jesus, just as they are.
Narrator	The whole group was silent as they heard Barnabas and Paul report all the miracles and wonders that God had performed through them among the Gentiles. When they had finished speaking, James spoke up:
James	Listen to me, my brothers! Simon has just explained how God first showed his care for the Gentiles by taking from among them a people to belong to him. The words of the prophets agree completely with this. As the scripture says:
Amos	After this I will return, says the Lord, and restore the kingdom of David. I will rebuild its ruins and make it strong again. And so all the rest of mankind will come to me, all the Gentiles whom I have called to be my own. So says the Lord, who made this known long ago.
James	It is my opinion that we should not trouble the Gentiles who are turning to God. Instead, we should write a letter telling them not to eat any food that is ritually unclean because it has been offered to idols; to keep themselves from sexual immorality; and not to eat any animal that has been strangled, or any blood. For the Law of Moses has been read for a very long time in the synagogues every Sabbath, and his words are preached in every town.
Cast	[This is] the word of the Lord.
All	**Thanks be to God.**

Cast: **Narrator, Man, Believer 1, Believer 2** (can be the same as Believer 1), **Peter, James, Amos.**

The letter to the Gentile believers
Acts 15.22–33

Narrator	The apostles and the elders, together with the whole church, decided to choose some men from the group and send them to Antioch with Paul and Barnabas. They chose two men who were highly respected by the believers, Judas, called Barsabbas, and Silas, and they sent the following letter by them:
Apostle	We, the apostles and the elders, your brothers, send greetings to all our brothers of Gentile birth who live in Antioch, Syria, and Cilicia. We have heard that some men who went from our group have troubled and upset you by what they said; they had not,

→

277

however, received any instruction from us. And so we have met together and have all agreed to choose some messengers and send them to you. They will go with our dear friends Barnabas and Paul, who have risked their lives in the service of our Lord Jesus Christ. We send you, then, Judas and Silas, who will tell you in person the same things we are writing. The Holy Spirit and we have agreed not to put any other burden on you besides these necessary rules: eat no food that has been offered to idols; eat no blood; eat no animal that has been strangled; and keep yourselves from sexual immorality. You will do well if you take care not to do these things. With our best wishes.

Narrator The messengers were sent off and went to Antioch, where they gathered the whole group of believers and gave them the letter. When the people read it, they were filled with joy by the message of encouragement. Judas and Silas, who were themselves prophets, spoke a long time with them, giving them courage and strength. After spending some time there, they were sent off in peace by the believers and went back to those who had sent them.

Cast [This is] the word of the Lord.
All **Thanks be to God.**

Cast: **Narrator, Apostle.**

Paul and Barnabas separate
Acts 15.35–41

Narrator Paul and Barnabas spent some time in Antioch, and together with many others they taught and preached the word of the Lord. (PAUSE)

Some time later Paul said to Barnabas:

Paul Let us go back and visit our brothers in every town where we preached the word of the Lord, and let us find out how they are getting on.

Narrator Barnabas wanted to take John Mark with them, but Paul did not think it was right to take him, because he had not stayed with them to the end of their mission, but had turned back and left them in Pamphylia. There was a sharp argument, and they separated: Barnabas took Mark and sailed off for Cyprus, while Paul chose Silas and left, commended by the believers to the care of the Lord's grace. He went through Syria and Cilicia, strengthening the churches.

Cast [This is] the word of the Lord.
All **Thanks be to God.**

Cast: **Narrator, Paul.**

Paul and Silas in Troas and in Philippi
Acts 16.6–15

Narrator Paul and Silas travelled through the region of Phrygia and Galatia because the Holy Spirit did not let them preach the message in the province of Asia. When they reached the border of Mysia, they tried to go into the province of Bithynia, but the Spirit of Jesus did not allow them. So they travelled right on through Mysia and went to Troas. That night Paul had a vision in which he saw a Macedonian standing and begging him:

Macedonian Come over to Macedonia and help us!

Luke As soon as Paul had this vision, we got ready to leave for Macedonia, because we decided that God had called us to preach the Good News to the people there.

We left by ship from Troas and sailed straight across to Samothrace, and the next day to Neapolis. From there we went inland to Philippi, a city of the first district of Macedonia; it is also a Roman colony. We spent several days there. On the Sabbath we went out of the city to the river-side, where we thought there would be a place where Jews gathered for prayer. We sat down and talked to the women who gathered there. One of those who heard us was Lydia from Thyatira, who was a dealer in purple cloth. She was a woman who worshipped God, and the Lord opened her mind to pay attention to what Paul was saying. After she and the people of her house had been baptized, she invited us:

Lydia Come and stay in my house if you have decided that I am a true believer in the Lord.

Luke And she persuaded us to go.

Cast [This is] the word of the Lord.
All **Thanks be to God.**

Cast: **Narrator, Macedonian, Luke** (can be the same as Narrator), **Lydia.**

Paul and Silas in prison at Philippi
Acts 16.16–24

Luke One day as we were going to the place of prayer, we were met by a slave-girl who had an evil spirit that enabled her to predict the future. She earned a lot of money for her owners by telling fortunes. She followed Paul and us, shouting:

Slave-girl These men are servants of the Most High God! They announce to you how you can be saved!

Luke She did this for many days, until Paul became so upset that he turned round and said to the spirit:

Paul In the name of Jesus Christ I order you to come out of her!

Luke The spirit went out of her that very moment. (PAUSE)

→

279

When her owners realized that their chance of making money was gone, they seized Paul and Silas and dragged them to the authorities in the public square. They brought them before the Roman officials [and said]:

Owner   These men are Jews, and they are causing trouble in our city. They are teaching customs that are against our law; we are Roman citizens, and we cannot accept these customs or practise them.

Luke   And the crowd joined in the attack against Paul and Silas. Then the officials tore the clothes off Paul and Silas and ordered them to be whipped. After a severe beating, they were thrown into jail, and the jailer was ordered to lock them up tight. Upon receiving this order, the jailer threw them into the inner cell and fastened their feet between heavy blocks of wood.

Cast   [This is] the word of the Lord.
All   **Thanks be to God.**

Cast: **Luke, Slave-girl, Paul, Owner.**

A baptism in Philippi
Acts 16.25–34

Narrator   About midnight Paul and Silas were praying and singing hymns to God, and the other prisoners were listening to them. Suddenly there was a violent earthquake, which shook the prison to its foundations. At once all the doors opened, and the chains fell off all the prisoners. The jailer woke up, and when he saw the prison doors open, he thought that the prisoners had escaped; so he pulled out his sword and was about to kill himself. But Paul shouted at the top of his voice:

Paul (loudly)   Don't harm yourself! We are all here!

Narrator   The jailer called for a light, rushed in, and fell trembling at the feet of Paul and Silas. Then he led them out [and asked]:

Jailer   Sirs, what must I do to be saved?

Paul   Believe in the Lord Jesus, and you will be saved—you and your family.

Narrator   Then they preached the word of the Lord to him and to all the others in his house. At that very hour of the night the jailer took them and washed their wounds; and he and all his family were baptized at once. Then he took Paul and Silas up into his house and gave them some food to eat. He and his family were filled with joy, because they now believed in God.

Cast   [This is] the word of the Lord.
All   **Thanks be to God.**

Cast: **Narrator, Paul, Jailer.**

After the earthquake
Acts 16.35–40

Narrator	When it was daylight, the magistrates sent their officers to the jailer with the order:
Officer	Release those men.
Narrator	The jailer told Paul:
Jailer	The magistrates have ordered that you and Silas be released. Now you can leave. Go in peace.
Narrator	But Paul said to the officers:
Paul	They beat us publicly without a trial, even though we are Roman citizens, and threw us into prison. And now do they want to get rid of us quietly? No! Let them come themselves and escort us out.
Narrator	The officers reported this to the magistrates, and when they heard that Paul and Silas were Roman citizens, they were alarmed. They came to appease them and escorted them from the prison, requesting them to leave the city. After Paul and Silas came out of the prison, they went to Lydia's house, where they met with the brothers and encouraged them. Then they left.
Cast	[This is] the word of the Lord.
All	**Thanks be to God.**

Cast: **Narrator, Officer, Jailer, Paul.**

Paul and Silas in Thessalonica
Acts 17.1–10

Narrator	They came to Thessalonica, where there was a Jewish synagogue. As his custom was, Paul went into the synagogue, and on three Sabbath days he reasoned with them from the Scriptures, explaining and proving that the Christ had to suffer and rise from the dead:
Paul	This Jesus I am proclaiming to you is the Christ.
Narrator	Some of the Jews were persuaded and joined Paul and Silas, as did a large number of God-fearing Greeks and not a few prominent women. But the Jews were jealous; so they rounded up some bad characters from the market-place, formed a mob and started a riot in the city. They rushed to Jason's house in search of Paul and Silas in order to bring them out to the crowd. But when they did not find them, they dragged Jason and some other brothers before the city officials [shouting]:
Person (loudly)	These men who have caused trouble all over the world have now come here, and Jason has welcomed them into his house. They are all defying Caesar's decrees, saying that there is another king, one called Jesus.

Narrator	When they heard this, the crowd and the city officials were thrown into turmoil. Then they put Jason and the others on bail and let them go. As soon as it was night, the brothers sent Paul and Silas away to Berea.
Cast	[This is] the word of the Lord.
All	**Thanks be to God.**

Cast: **Narrator, Paul, Person.**

Paul and Silas in Berea
Acts 17.10–15

Narrator 1	When Paul and Silas arrived in Berea, they went to the synagogue.
Narrator 2	The people there were more open-minded than the people in Thessalonica. They listened to the message with great eagerness, and every day they studied the Scriptures to see if what Paul said was really true.
Narrator 1	Many of them believed; and many Greek women of high social standing and many Greek men also believed.
Narrator 2	But when the Jews in Thessalonica heard that Paul had preached the word of God in Berea also, they came there and started exciting and stirring up the mob.
Narrator 1	At once the believers sent Paul away to the coast.
Narrator 2	But both Silas and Timothy stayed in Berea.
Narrator 1	The men who were taking Paul went with him as far as Athens and then returned to Berea with instructions from Paul that Silas and Timothy should join him as soon as possible.
Cast	[This is] the word of the Lord.
All	**Thanks be to God.**

Cast: **Narrator 1, Narrator 2.**

Paul in Athens
Acts 17.16–34

Narrator	While Paul was waiting in Athens for Silas and Timothy, he was greatly upset when he noticed how full of idols the city was. So he held discussions in the synagogue with the Jews and with the Gentiles who worshipped God, and also in the public square every day with the people who happened to pass by. Certain Epicurean and Stoic teachers also debated with him. Some of them asked:
Teacher 1	What is this ignorant show-off trying to say?
Narrator	Others answered:
Teacher 2	He seems to be talking about foreign gods.

Narrator	They said this because Paul was preaching about Jesus and the resurrection. So they took Paul, brought him before the city council, the Areopagus, and said:
Teacher 1	We would like to know what this new teaching is that you are talking about.
Teacher 2	Some of the things we hear you say sound strange to us, and we would like to know what they mean.
Narrator	For all the citizens of Athens and the foreigners who lived there liked to spend all their time telling and hearing the latest new thing.
	Paul stood up in front of the city council and said:
Paul	I see that in every way you Athenians are very religious. For as I walked through your city and looked at the places where you worship, I found an altar on which is written, 'To an Unknown God'. That which you worship, then, even though you do not know it, is what I now proclaim to you. God, who made the world and everything in it, is Lord of heaven and earth and does not live in man-made temples. Nor does he need anything that we can supply by working for him, since it is he himself who gives life and breath and everything else to everyone. From one man he created all races of mankind and made them live throughout the whole earth. He himself fixed beforehand the exact times and the limits of the places where they would live. He did this so that they would look for him, and perhaps find him as they felt about for him. Yet God is actually not far from any one of us; as someone has said:
Voice 2	In him we live and move and exist.
Paul	It is as some of your poets have said:
Voice 1	We too are his children.
Paul	Since we are God's children, we should not suppose that his nature is anything like an image of gold or silver or stone, shaped by the art and skill of man. God has overlooked the times when people did not know him, but now he commands all of them everywhere to turn away from their evil ways. For he has fixed a day in which he will judge the whole world with justice by means of a man he has chosen. He has given proof of this to everyone by raising that man from death!
Narrator	When they heard Paul speak about a raising from death, some of them made fun of him, but others said:
Teacher 2	We want to hear you speak about this again.
Narrator	And so Paul left the meeting. Some men joined him and believed, among whom was Dionysius, a member of the council; there was also a woman named Damaris, and some other people.
Cast	[This is] the word of the Lord.
All	**Thanks be to God.**

Cast: **Narrator, Teacher 1, Teacher 2, Paul, Voice 2** (can be the same as Teacher 2), **Voice 1** (can be the same as Teacher 1).

Paul in Corinth
Acts 18.1–17

Narrator	Paul left Athens and went on to Corinth. There he met a Jew named Aquila, born in Pontus, who had recently come from Italy with his wife Priscilla, for the Emperor Claudius had ordered all the Jews to leave Rome. Paul went to see them, and stayed and worked with them, because he earned his living by making tents, just as they did. He held discussions in the synagogue every Sabbath, trying to convince both Jews and Greeks.
	When Silas and Timothy arrived from Macedonia, Paul gave his whole time to preaching the message, testifying to the Jews that Jesus is the Messiah. When they opposed him and said evil things about him, he protested by shaking the dust from his clothes and saying to them:
Paul (firmly)	If you are lost, you yourselves must take the blame for it! I am not responsible. From now on I will go to the Gentiles.
Narrator	So he left them and went to live in the house of a Gentile named Titius Justus, who worshipped God; his house was next to the synagogue. Crispus, who was the leader of the synagogue, believed in the Lord, together with all his family; and many other people in Corinth heard the message, believed, and were baptized.
	One night Paul had a vision in which the Lord said to him:
The Lord	Do not be afraid, but keep on speaking and do not give up, for I am with you. No one will be able to harm you, for many in this city are my people.
Narrator	So Paul stayed there for a year and a half, teaching the people the word of God. (PAUSE)
	When Gallio was made the Roman governor of Achaia, the Jews got together, seized Paul, and took him into court. [They said:]
Jew	This man is trying to persuade people to worship God in a way that is against the law!
Narrator	Paul was about to speak, when Gallio said to the Jews:
Gallio	If this were a matter of some evil crime or wrong that has been committed, it would be reasonable for me to be patient with you Jews. But since it is an argument about words and names and your own law, you yourselves must settle it. I will not be the judge of such things!
Narrator	And he drove them out of the court. They all seized Sosthenes, the leader of the synagogue, and beat him in front of the court. But that did not bother Gallio a bit.
Cast	[This is] the word of the Lord.
All	**Thanks be to God.**

Cast: **Narrator, Paul, The Lord, Jew, Gallio.**

Paul returns to Antioch
Acts 18.18–23

Narrator   Paul stayed on with the believers in Corinth for many days, then left them and sailed off with Priscilla and Aquila for Syria. Before sailing from Cenchreae he had his head shaved because of a vow he had taken. They arrived in Ephesus, where Paul left Priscilla and Aquila. He went into the synagogue and held discussions with the Jews. The people asked him to stay longer, but he would not consent. Instead, he told them as he left:

Paul   If it is the will of God, I will come back to you.

Narrator   And so he sailed from Ephesus. (PAUSE)

When he arrived at Caesarea, he went to Jerusalem and greeted the church, and then went to Antioch. After spending some time there, he left and went through the region of Galatia and Phrygia, strengthening all the believers.

Cast   [This is] the word of the Lord.
All   **Thanks be to God.**

Cast: **Narrator, Paul.**

Apollos
Acts 18.24–28

Narrator 1   Meanwhile a Jew named Apollos, a native of Alexandria, came to Ephesus.

Narrator 2   He was a learned man, with a thorough knowledge of the Scriptures. He had been instructed in the way of the Lord, and he spoke with great fervour and taught about Jesus accurately, though he knew only the baptism of John. He began to speak boldly in the synagogue.

Narrator 1   When Priscilla and Aquila heard him, they invited him to their home and explained to him the way of God more adequately.

Narrator 2   When Apollos wanted to go to Achaia, the brothers encouraged him and wrote to the disciples there to welcome him. On arriving, he was a great help to those who by grace had believed. For he vigorously refuted the Jews in public debate, proving from the Scriptures that Jesus was the Christ.

Cast   [This is] the word of the Lord.
All   **Thanks be to God.**

Cast: **Narrator 1, Narrator 2.**

Paul in Ephesus
Acts 19.1–10

Narrator	Paul arrived in Ephesus. There he found some disciples [and asked them:]
Paul	Did you receive the Holy Spirit when you became believers?
[Narrator	They answered:]
Believer 1	We have not even heard that there *is* a Holy Spirit.
Paul	Well, then, what kind of baptism did you receive?
Believer 2	The baptism of John.
Paul	The baptism of John was for those who turned from their sins; and he told the people of Israel to believe in the one who was coming after him—that is, in Jesus.
Narrator	When they heard this, they were baptized in the name of the Lord Jesus. Paul placed his hands on them, and the Holy Spirit came upon them; they spoke in strange tongues and also proclaimed God's message. They were about twelve men in all.
	Paul went into the synagogue and during three months spoke boldly with the people, holding discussions with them and trying to convince them about the Kingdom of God. But some of them were stubborn and would not believe, and before the whole group they said evil things about the Way of the Lord. So Paul left them and took the believers with him, and every day he held discussions in the lecture hall of Tyrannus. This went on for two years, so that all the people who lived in the province of Asia, both Jews and Gentiles, heard the word of the Lord.
Cast	[This is] the word of the Lord.
All	**Thanks be to God.**

Cast: **Narrator, Paul, Believer 1, Believer 2.**

The sons of Sceva
Acts 19.11–20

Narrator	God was performing unusual miracles through Paul. Even handkerchiefs and aprons he had used were taken to those who were ill, and their diseases were driven away, and the evil spirits would go out of them. Some Jews who travelled round and drove out evil spirits also tried to use the name of the Lord Jesus to do this. They said to the evil spirits:
Jew	I command you in the name of Jesus, whom Paul preaches.
Narrator	Seven brothers, who were the sons of a Jewish High Priest named Sceva, were doing this. But the evil spirit said to them:
Evil spirit	I know Jesus, and I know about Paul; but you—who are you?
Narrator	The man who had the evil spirit in him attacked them with such violence that he overpowered them all. They ran away from his house, wounded and with their clothes torn off. All the Jews and

Gentiles who lived in Ephesus heard about this; they were all filled with fear, and the name of the Lord Jesus was given greater honour. Many of the believers came, publicly admitting and revealing what they had done. Many of those who had practised magic brought their books together and burnt them in public. They added up the price of the books, and the total came to fifty thousand silver coins. In this powerful way the word of the Lord kept spreading and growing stronger.

Cast	[This is] the word of the Lord.
All	**Thanks be to God.**

Cast: **Narrator, Jew, Evil spirit.**

The riot in Ephesus
Acts 19.21–41

Narrator Paul made up his mind to travel through Macedonia and Achaia and go on to Jerusalem. He said:

Paul After I go there, I must also see Rome.

Narrator So he sent Timothy and Erastus, two of his helpers, to Macedonia, while spent more time in the province of Asia.

It was at this time that there was serious trouble in Ephesus because of the Way of the Lord. A certain silversmith named Demetrius made silver models of the temple of the goddess Artemis, and his business brought a great deal of profit to the workers. So he called them all together with others whose work was like theirs.

Demetrius Men, you know that our prosperity comes from this work. Now, you can see and hear for yourselves what this fellow Paul is doing. He says that man-made gods are not gods at all, and he has succeeded in convincing many people, both here in Ephesus and in nearly the whole province of Asia. There is the danger, then, that this business of ours will get a bad name. Not only that, but there is also the danger that the temple of the great goddess Artemis will come to mean nothing and that her greatness will be destroyed—the goddess worshipped by everyone in Asia and in all the world!

Narrator As the crowd heard these words, they became furious [and started shouting]:

Person(s)
(shouting) Great is Artemis of Ephesus!

Narrator The uproar spread throughout the whole city. The mob seized Gaius and Aristarchus, two Macedonians who were travelling with Paul, and rushed with them to the theatre. Paul himself wanted to go before the crowd, but the believers would not let him. Some of the provincial authorities, who were his friends, also sent him a message begging him not to show himself in the theatre. Meanwhile the whole meeting was in an uproar: some

→

people were shouting one thing, others were shouting something else, because most of them did not even know why they had come together. Some of the people concluded that Alexander was responsible, since the Jews made him go up to the front. Then Alexander motioned with his hand for the people to be silent, and he tried to make a speech of defence. But when they recognized that he was a Jew, they all shouted together the same thing for two hours:

Person(s) Great is Artemis of Ephesus!

Narrator At last the town clerk was able to calm the crowd.

Town Clerk Fellow-Ephesians! Everyone knows that the city of Ephesus is the keeper of the temple of the great Artemis and of the sacred stone that fell down from heaven. Nobody can deny these things. So then, you must calm down and not do anything reckless. You have brought these men here even though they have not robbed temples or said evil things about our goddess. If Demetrius and his workers have an accusation against anyone, we have the authorities and the regular days for court; charges can be made there. But if there is something more that you want, it will have to be settled in a legal meeting of citizens. For after what has happened today, there is the danger that we will be accused of a riot. There is no excuse for all this uproar, and we would not be able to give a good reason for it.

Narrator After saying this, he dismissed the meeting.

Cast [This is] the word of the Lord.
All **Thanks be to God.**

Cast: **Narrator, Paul, Demetrius, Person(s), Town Clerk.**

Paul's last visit to Troas
Acts 20.7–12 [13–16]

Luke On Saturday evening we gathered together for the fellowship meal. Paul spoke to the people and kept on speaking until midnight, since he was going to leave the next day. Many lamps were burning in the upstairs room where we were meeting. A young man named Eutychus was sitting in the window, and as Paul kept on talking, Eutychus got sleepier and sleepier, until he finally went sound asleep and fell from the third storey to the ground. When they picked him up, he was dead. But Paul went down and threw himself on him and hugged him. [He said:]

Paul Don't worry, he is still alive!

Luke Then he went back upstairs, broke bread, and ate. After talking with them for a long time, even until sunrise, Paul left. They took the young man home alive and were greatly comforted.

[We went on ahead to the ship and sailed off to Assos, where we were going to take Paul aboard. He had told us to do this, because he was going there by land. When he met us in Assos, we took him aboard and went on to Mitylene. We sailed from there and arrived off Chios the next day. A day later we came to Samos, and the following day we reached Miletus. Paul had decided to sail on past Ephesus, so as not to lose any time in the province of Asia. He was in a hurry to arrive in Jerusalem by the day of Pentecost, if at all possible.]

Cast	[This is] the word of the Lord.
All	**Thanks be to God.**

Cast: **Luke, Paul.**

Paul's farewell speech to the elders of Ephesus
Acts 20.17–24 [25–31] 32–38

Narrator
From Miletus Paul sent a message to Ephesus, asking the elders of the church to meet him. When they arrived, he said to them:

Paul
You know how I spent the whole time I was with you, from the first day I arrived in the province of Asia. With all humility and many tears I did my work as the Lord's servant during the hard times that came to me because of the plots of the Jews. You know that I did not hold back anything that would be of help to you as I preached and taught in public and in your homes. To Jews and Gentiles alike I gave solemn warning that they should turn from their sins to God and believe in our Lord Jesus. And now, in obedience to the Holy Spirit I am going to Jerusalem, not knowing what will happen to me there. I only know that in every city the Holy Spirit has warned me that prison and troubles wait for me. But I reckon my own life to be worth nothing to me; I only want to complete my mission and finish the work that the Lord Jesus gave me to do, which is to declare the Good News about the grace of God.

[I have gone about among all of you, preaching the Kingdom of God. And now I know that none of you will ever see me again. So I solemnly declare to you this very day: if any of you should be lost, I am not responsible. For I have not held back from announcing to you the whole purpose of God. So keep watch over yourselves and over all the flock which the Holy Spirit has placed in your care. Be shepherds of the church of God, which he made his own through the sacrificial death of his Son. I know that after I leave, fierce wolves will come among you, and they will not spare the flock. The time will come when some men from your own group will tell lies to lead the believers away after them. Watch, then, and remember that with many tears, day and night, I taught every one of you for three years.]

And now I commend you to the care of God and to the message of his grace, which is able to build you up and give you the blessings God has for all his people. I have not wanted anyone's silver or gold or clothing. You yourselves know that I have worked with these hands of mine to provide everything that my companions and I have needed. I have shown you in all things that by working hard in this way we must help the weak, remembering the words that the Lord Jesus himself said, 'There is more happiness in giving than in receiving.'

289

| Narrator | When Paul finished, he knelt down with them and prayed. They were all crying as they hugged him and kissed him good-bye. They were especially sad because he had said that they would never see him again. And so they went with him to the ship. |

| Cast | [This is] the word of the Lord. |
| All | **Thanks be to God.** |

Cast: **Narrator, Paul.**

Paul goes to Jerusalem
Acts 21.3–16

Luke	We went ashore at Tyre, where the ship was going to unload its cargo. There we found some believers and stayed with them a week. By the power of the Spirit they told Paul not to go to Jerusalem. But when our time with them was over, we left and went on our way. All of them, together with their wives and children, went with us out of the city to the beach, where we all knelt and prayed. Then we said good-bye to one another, and we went on board the ship while they went back home.
	We continued our voyage, sailing from Tyre to Ptolemais, where we greeted the believers and stayed with them for a day. On the following day we left and arrived in Caesarea. There we stayed at the house of Philip the evangelist, one of the seven men who had been chosen as helpers in Jerusalem. He had four unmarried daughters who proclaimed God's message. We had been there for several days when a prophet named Agabus arrived from Judaea. He came to us, took Paul's belt, tied up his own feet and hands with it, and said:
Agabus	This is what the Holy Spirit says: 'The owner of this belt will be tied up in this way by the Jews in Jerusalem, and they will hand him over to the Gentiles.'
Luke	When we heard this, we and the others there begged Paul not to go to Jerusalem. But he answered:
Paul	What are you doing, crying like this and breaking my heart? I am ready not only to be tied up in Jerusalem but even to die there for the sake of the Lord Jesus.
Luke	We could not convince him, so we gave up [and said]:
Young Luke	May the Lord's will be done.
Luke	After spending some time there, we got our things ready and left for Jerusalem. Some of the disciples from Caesarea also went with us and took us to the house of the man we were going to stay with—Mnason, from Cyprus, who had been a believer since the early days.

| Cast | [This is] the word of the Lord. |
| All | **Thanks be to God.** |

Cast: **Luke, Agabus, Paul, Young Luke** (can be the same as Luke).

Paul visits James
From Acts 21.17–26

Luke   When we arrived in Jerusalem, the believers welcomed us warmly. The next day Paul went with us to see James; and all the church elders were present. Paul greeted them and gave a complete report of everything that God had done among the Gentiles through his work. After hearing him, they all praised God. [Then they said:]

Elder 1   Brother Paul, you can see how many thousands of Jews have become believers, and how devoted they all are to the Law.

Elder 2   They have been told that you have been teaching all the Jews who live in Gentile countries to abandon the Law of Moses, telling them not to circumcise their children or follow the Jewish customs.

Elder 1   They are sure to hear that you have arrived. What should be done, then?

Elder 2   This is what we want you to do. There are four men here who have taken a vow. Go along with them and join them in the ceremony of purification. And pay their expenses; then they will be able to shave their heads.

Elder 1   In this way everyone will know that there is no truth in any of the things that they have been told about you, but that you yourself live in accordance with the Law of Moses.

Luke   So Paul took the men and the next day performed the ceremony of purification with them. Then he went into the Temple and gave notice of how many days it would be until the end of the period of purification, when a sacrifice would be offered for each one of them.

Cast   [This is] the word of the Lord.
All   **Thanks be to God.**

Cast: **Luke, Elder 1, Elder 2.**

Paul is arrested in the Temple
Acts 21.27—22.2

Narrator   [Just when the seven days were about to come to an end] some Jews from the province of Asia saw Paul in the Temple. They stirred up the whole crowd and seized Paul. [They shouted:]

Jew 1 (loudly)   Men of Israel!

Jews 1 and 2   Help!

Jew 2   This is the man who goes everywhere teaching everyone against the people of Israel, the Law of Moses, and this Temple.

Jew 1   And now he has even brought some Gentiles into the Temple and defiled this holy place!

291

Narrator	They said this because they had seen Trophimus from Ephesus with Paul in the city, and they thought that Paul had taken him into the Temple.
	Confusion spread through the whole city, and the people all ran together, seized Paul, and dragged him out of the Temple. At once the Temple doors were closed. The mob was trying to kill Paul, when a report was sent up to the commander of the Roman troops that all Jerusalem was rioting. At once the commander took some officers and soldiers and rushed down to the crowd. When the people saw him with the soldiers, they stopped beating Paul. The commander went over to Paul, arrested him, and ordered him to be bound with two chains. [Then he asked:]
Commander	Who is this man, and what has he done?
Narrator	Some in the crowd shouted one thing, others something else. There was such confusion that the commander could not find out exactly what had happened, so he ordered his men to take Paul up into the fort. They got as far as the steps with him, and then the soldiers had to carry him because the mob was so wild. They were all coming after him and screaming:
Jews 1 and **2**	Kill him!
Narrator	As the soldiers were about to take Paul into the fort, he spoke to the commander:
Paul	May I say something to you?
Commander	You speak Greek, do you? (PAUSE) Then you are not that Egyptian fellow who some time ago started a revolution and led four thousand armed terrorists out into the desert?
Paul	I am a Jew, born in Tarsus in Cilicia, a citizen of an important city. Please let me speak to the people.
Narrator	The commander gave him permission, so Paul stood on the steps and motioned with his hand for the people to be silent. When they were quiet, Paul spoke to them in Hebrew:
Paul	My fellow-Israelites, listen to me as I make my defence before you!
Narrator	When they heard him speaking to them in Hebrew, they became even quieter; and Paul began to speak . . .
Cast **All**	[This is] the word of the Lord. **Thanks be to God.**

Cast: **Narrator, Jew 1, Jew 2, Commander, Paul.**

Paul tells his story
Acts 22.3–16

Paul	I am a Jew, born in Tarsus in Cilicia, but brought up here in Jerusalem as a student of Gamaliel. I received strict instruction in the Law of our ancestors and was just as dedicated to God as are all of you who are here today. I persecuted to the death the people who followed this Way. I arrested men and women and threw them into prison. The High Priest and the whole Council can prove that I am telling the truth. I received from them letters written to fellow-Jews in Damascus, so I went there to arrest these people and bring them back in chains to Jerusalem to be punished.
	As I was travelling and coming near Damascus, about midday a bright light from the sky flashed suddenly round me. I fell to the ground and heard a voice:
Voice	Saul, Saul! Why do you persecute me?
Paul	I asked:
Young Paul	Who are you, Lord?
Voice	I am Jesus of Nazareth, whom you persecute.
Paul	The men with me saw the light, but did not hear the voice of the one who was speaking to me. I asked:
Young Paul	What shall I do, Lord?
Paul	And the Lord said to me:
Voice	Get up and go into Damascus, and there you will be told everything that God has determined for you to do.
Paul	I was blind because of the bright light, and so my companions took me by the hand and led me into Damascus.
	In that city was a man named Ananias, a religious man who obeyed our Law and was highly respected by all the Jews living there. He came to me and stood by me:
Ananias	Brother Saul, see again!
Paul	At that very moment I saw again and looked at him.
Ananias	The God of our ancestors has chosen you to know his will, to see his righteous Servant, and to hear him speaking with his own voice. For you will be a witness for him to tell everyone what you have seen and heard. And now, why wait any longer? Get up and be baptized and have your sins washed away by praying to him.
Cast	[This is] the word of the Lord.
All	**Thanks be to God.**

Cast: **Paul, Voice, Young Paul, Ananias.**

Paul tells of his call to preach to the Gentiles
Acts 22.17–29

Paul While I was praying in the Temple, I had a vision, in which I saw the Lord as he said to me:

The Lord Hurry and leave Jerusalem quickly, because the people here will not accept your witness about me.

Paul [I answered:] Lord, they know very well that I went to the synagogues and arrested and beat those who believe in you. And when your witness Stephen was put to death, I myself was there, approving of his murder and taking care of the cloaks of his murderers. [The Lord said to me:]

The Lord Go, for I will send you far away to the Gentiles.

Narrator The people listened to Paul until he said this; but then they started shouting at the top of their voices:

Person 1 Away with him!

Person 2 Kill him!

Person 3 He's not fit to live!

Narrator They were screaming, waving their clothes, and throwing dust up in the air. The Roman commander ordered his men to take Paul into the fort, and he told them to whip him in order to find out why the Jews were screaming like this against him. But when they had tied him up to be whipped, Paul said to the officer standing there:

Paul Is it lawful for you to whip a Roman citizen who hasn't even been tried for any crime?

Narrator When the officer heard this, he went to the commander and asked him:

Officer
(alarmed) What are you doing? That man is a Roman citizen!

Narrator So the commander went to Paul and asked him:

Commander Tell me, are you a Roman citizen?

Paul Yes.

Commander
(ruefully) I became one by paying a large amount of money.

Paul But I am one by birth.

Narrator At once the men who were going to question Paul drew back from him; and the commander was frightened when he realized that Paul was a Roman citizen and that he had put him in chains.

Cast [This is] the word of the Lord.
All **Thanks be to God.**

Cast: **Paul, The Lord, Narrator, Person 1, Person 2, Person 3** (can be the same as Person 1), **Officer, Commander.**

Paul before the Council
Acts 22.30—23.11

Narrator   The commander wanted to find out for certain what the Jews were accusing Paul of; so the next day he had Paul's chains taken off and ordered the chief priests and the whole Council to meet. Then he took Paul and made him stand before them. Paul looked straight at the Council:

Paul   My fellow-Israelites! My conscience is perfectly clear about the way in which I have lived before God to this very day.

Narrator   The High Priest Ananias ordered those who were standing close to Paul to strike him on the mouth.

Paul   God will certainly strike you—you whitewashed wall! You sit there to judge me according to the Law, yet you break the Law by ordering them to strike me!

[Narrator   The men close to Paul said to him:]

Man   You are insulting God's High Priest!

Paul   My fellow-Israelites, I did not know that he was the High Priest. The scripture says, 'You must not speak evil of the ruler of your people.'

Narrator   When Paul saw that some of the group were Sadducees and the others were Pharisees, he called out in the Council:

Paul   Fellow-Israelites! I am a Pharisee, the son of Pharisees. I am on trial here because of the hope I have that the dead will rise to life!

Narrator   As soon as he said this, the Pharisees and Sadducees started to quarrel, and the group was divided. For the Sadducees say that people will not rise from death and that there are no angels or spirits; but the Pharisees believe in all three. The shouting became louder, and some of the teachers of the Law who belonged to the party of the Pharisees stood up and protested strongly:

Pharisee 1   We cannot find anything wrong with this man!

Pharisee 2   Perhaps a spirit or an angel really did speak to him!

Narrator   The argument became so violent that the commander was afraid that Paul would be torn to pieces. So he ordered his soldiers to go down into the group, get Paul away from them, and take him into the fort. (PAUSE)

That night the Lord stood by Paul and said:

The Lord   Don't be afraid! You have given your witness for me here in Jerusalem, and you must also do the same (PAUSE) in Rome.

Cast   [This is] the word of the Lord.
All   **Thanks be to God.**

Cast: **Narrator, Paul, Man, Pharisee 1, Pharisee 2** (can be the same as Pharisee 1)**, The Lord.**

The plot against Paul's life
Acts 23.12—22

Narrator The next morning after the Lord stood by Paul and spoke to him, some Jews met together and made a plan. They took a vow that they would not eat or drink anything until they had killed Paul. There were more than forty who planned this together. Then they went to the chief priests and elders.

Conspirator We have taken a solemn vow together not to eat a thing until we have killed Paul. Now then, you and the Council send word to the Roman commander to bring Paul down to you, pretending that you want to get more accurate information about him. But we will be ready to kill him before he ever gets here.

Narrator But the son of Paul's sister heard about the plot; so he went to the fort and told Paul. Then Paul called one of the officers:

Paul Take this young man to the commander; he has something to tell him.

Narrator The officer took him and led him to the commander.

Officer (to Commander) The prisoner Paul called me and asked me to bring this young man to you, because he has something to say to you.

Narrator The commander took him by the hand and led him off by himself.

Commander What have you got to tell me?

Narrator He said:

Paul's nephew The Jewish authorities have agreed to ask you tomorrow to take Paul down to the Council, pretending that the Council wants to get more accurate information about him. But don't listen to them, because there are more than forty men who will be hiding and waiting for him. They have taken a vow not to eat or drink until they have killed him. They are now ready to do it and are waiting for your decision.

Commander Don't tell anyone that you have reported this to me.

Narrator And he sent the young man away.

Cast [This is] the word of the Lord.
All **Thanks be to God.**

Cast: **Narrator, Conspirator, Paul, Officer, Commander, Paul's nephew.**

Paul is sent to Governor Felix
Acts 23.23—35

Narrator The commander called two of his officers:

Commander Get two hundred soldiers ready to go to Caesarea, together with seventy horsemen and two hundred spearmen, and be ready to leave by nine o'clock tonight. Provide some horses for Paul to ride and get him safely through to the governor Felix.

Narrator Then the commander wrote a letter that went like this:

Commander	Claudius Lysias to His Excellency, the governor Felix: Greetings. The Jews seized this man and were about to kill him. I learnt that he was a Roman citizen, so I went with my soldiers and rescued him. I wanted to know what they were accusing him of, so I took him down to their Council. I found out that he had not done anything for which he deserved to die or be put in prison; the accusation against him had to do with questions about their own law. And when I was informed that there was a plot against him, at once I decided to send him to you. I have told his accusers to make their charges against him before you.
Narrator	The soldiers carried out their orders. They got Paul and took him that night as far as Antipatris. The next day the foot-soldiers returned to the fort and left the horsemen to go on with him. They took him to Caesarea, delivered the letter to the governor, and handed Paul over to him. The governor read the letter and asked Paul what province he was from. When he found out that he was from Cilicia, he said:
Governor	I will hear you when your accusers arrive.
Narrator	Then he gave orders for Paul to be kept under guard in the governor's headquarters.
Cast	[This is] the word of the Lord.
All	**Thanks be to God.**

Cast: **Narrator, Commander, Governor.**

Paul is accused by the Jews
Acts 24.1–23

Narrator	[Five days later] the High Priest Ananias went to Caesarea with some elders and a lawyer named Tertullus. They appeared before Felix and made their charges against Paul. Then Paul was called in, and Tertullus began to make his accusation, as follows:
Tertullus	Your Excellency! Your wise leadership has brought us a long period of peace, and many necessary reforms are being made for the good of our country. We welcome this everywhere and at all times, and we are deeply grateful to you. I do not want to take up too much of your time, however, so I beg you to be kind and listen to our brief account. We found this man to be a dangerous nuisance; he starts riots among the Jews all over the world and is a leader of the party of the Nazarenes. He also tried to defile the Temple, and we arrested him. We planned to judge him according to our own Law, but Lysias the commander came, and with great violence took him from us. Then Lysias gave orders that his accusers should come before you. If you question this man, you yourself will be able to learn from him all the things that we are accusing him of.
Narrator	The Jews joined in the accusation and said that all this was true. The governor then motioned to Paul to speak, and Paul said:

297

Paul	I know that you have been a judge over this nation for many years, and so I am happy to defend myself before you. As you can find out for yourself, it was no more than twelve days ago that I went to Jerusalem to worship. The Jews did not find me arguing with anyone in the Temple, nor did they find me stirring up the people, either in the synagogues or anywhere else in the city. Nor can they give you proof of the accusations they now bring against me. I do admit this to you: I worship the God of our ancestors by following that Way which they say is false. But I also believe in everything written in the Law of Moses and the books of the prophets. I have the same hope in God that these themselves have, namely, that all people, both the good and the bad, will rise from death. And so I do my best always to have a clear conscience before God and man.
	After being away from Jerusalem for several years, I went there to take some money to my own people and to offer sacrifices. It was while I was doing this that they found me in the Temple after I had completed the ceremony of purification. There was no crowd with me and no disorder. But some Jews from the province of Asia were there; they themselves ought to come before you and make their accusations if they have anything against me. Or let these men here tell what crime they found me guilty of when I stood before the Council—except for the one thing I called out when I stood before them: 'I am being tried by you today for believing that the dead will rise to life.'
Narrator	Then Felix, who was well informed about the Way, brought the hearing to a close:
Felix	When Lysias the commander arrives, I will decide your case.
Narrator	He ordered the officer in charge of Paul to keep him under guard, but to give him some freedom and allow his friends to provide for his needs.
Cast	[This is] the word of the Lord.
All	**Thanks be to God.**

Cast: **Narrator, Tertullus, Paul, Felix.**

Paul before Felix and Drusilla
Acts 24.24–27

Narrator	Felix came to Caesarea with his wife Drusilla, who was Jewish. He sent for Paul and listened to him as he talked about faith in Christ Jesus. But as Paul went on discussing about goodness, self-control, and the coming Day of Judgement, Felix was afraid:
Felix (nervously)	You may leave now. I will call you again when I get the chance.

Narrator	At the same time he was hoping that Paul would give him some money; and for this reason he would often send for him and talk with him. After two years had passed, Porcius Festus succeeded Felix as governor. Felix wanted to gain favour with the Jews so he left Paul in prison.
Cast	[This is] the word of the Lord.
All	**Thanks be to God.**

Cast: **Narrator, Felix.**

Paul appeals to the Emperor
Acts 25.1–12

Narrator	Three days after Festus arrived in the province, he went from Caesarea to Jerusalem, where the chief priests and the Jewish leaders brought their charges against Paul. They begged Festus to do them the favour of bringing Paul to Jerusalem, for they had made a plot to kill him on the way. Festus answered:
Festus	Paul is being kept a prisoner in Caesarea, and I myself will be going back there soon. Let your leaders go to Caesarea with me and accuse the man if he has done anything wrong.
Narrator	Festus spent another eight or ten days with them and then went to Caesarea. On the next day he sat down in the court of judgement and ordered Paul to be brought in. When Paul arrived, the Jews who had come from Jerusalem stood round him and started making many serious charges against him, which they were not able to prove. But Paul defended himself:
Paul	I have done nothing wrong against the Law of the Jews or against the Temple or against the Roman Emperor.
Narrator	But Festus wanted to gain favour with the Jews. [So he asked Paul:]
Festus	Would you be willing to go to Jerusalem and be tried on these charges before me there?
Paul	I am standing before the Emperor's own court of judgement, where I should be tried. I have done no wrong to the Jews, as you yourself well know. If I have broken the law and done something for which I deserve the death penalty, I do not ask to escape it. But if there is no truth in the charges they bring against me, no one can hand me over to them. I appeal to the Emperor.
Narrator	Then Festus, after conferring with his advisers, answered:
Festus	You have appealed to the Emperor, so to the Emperor you will go.
Cast	[This is] the word of the Lord.
All	**Thanks be to God.**

Cast: **Narrator, Festus, Paul.**

Paul before Agrippa and Bernice
Acts 25.13–27

Narrator   Some time later King Agrippa and Bernice came to Caesarea to pay a visit of welcome to Festus. After they had been there several days, Festus explained Paul's situation to the king:

Festus   There is a man here who was left a prisoner by Felix; and when I went to Jerusalem, the Jewish chief priests and elders brought charges against him and asked me to condemn him. But I told them that we Romans are not in the habit of handing over any man accused of a crime before he has met his accusers face to face and has had the chance of defending himself against the accusation. When they came here, then, I lost no time, but on the very next day I sat in the court and ordered the man to be brought in. His opponents stood up, but they did not accuse him of any of the evil crimes that I thought they would. All they had were some arguments with him about their own religion and about a man named Jesus, who has died; but Paul claims that he is alive. I was undecided about how I could get information on these matters, so I asked Paul if he would be willing to go to Jerusalem and be tried there on these charges. But Paul appealed; he asked to be kept under guard and to let the Emperor decide his case. So I gave orders for him to be kept under guard until I could send him to the Emperor.

Narrator   Agrippa said to Festus:

Agrippa   I would like to hear this man myself.

Festus   You will hear him tomorrow.

Narrator   The next day Agrippa and Bernice came with great pomp and ceremony and entered the audience hall with the military chiefs and the leading men of the city. Festus gave the order, and Paul was brought in. Festus said:

Festus   King Agrippa and all who are here with us: You see this man against whom all the Jewish people, both here and in Jerusalem, have brought complaints to me. They scream that he should not live any longer. But I could not find that he had done anything for which he deserved the death sentence. And since he himself made an appeal to the Emperor, I have decided to send him. But I have nothing definite about him to write to the Emperor. So I have brought him here before you— and (TO AGRIPPA) especially before *you*, King Agrippa!—so that, after investigating his case, I may have something to write. For it seems unreasonable to me to send a prisoner without clearly indicating the charges against him.

Cast   [This is] the word of the Lord.
All   **Thanks be to God.**

Cast: **Narrator, Festus, Agrippa.**

Paul defends himself before Agrippa
From Acts 26.1–18

Narrator	Agrippa said to Paul:
Agrippa	You have permission to speak on your own behalf.
Narrator	Paul stretched out his hand and defended himself:
Paul	King Agrippa! I consider myself fortunate that today I am to defend myself before you from all the things the Jews accuse me of, particularly since you know so well all the Jewish customs and disputes. I ask you, then, to listen to me with patience.

All the Jews know how I have lived ever since I was young. They know how I have spent my whole life, at first in my own country and then in Jerusalem. They have always known, if they are willing to testify, that from the very first I have lived as a member of the strictest party of our religion, the Pharisees. And now I stand here to be tried because of the hope I have in the promise that God made to our ancestors— the very thing that the twelve tribes of our people hope to receive, as they worship God day and night. And it is because of this hope, Your Majesty, that I am being accused by the Jews! Why do you who are here find it impossible to believe that God raises the dead? I myself thought that I should do everything I could against the cause of Jesus of Nazareth. That is what I did in Jerusalem. I received authority from the chief priests and put many of God's people in prison; and when they were sentenced to death, I also voted against them. Many times I had them punished in the synagogues and tried to make them deny their faith. I was so furious with them that I even went to foreign cities to persecute them.

It was for this purpose that I went to Damascus with authority and orders from the chief priests. It was on the road at midday, Your Majesty, that I saw a light much brighter than the sun, coming from the sky and shining round me and the men travelling with me. All of us fell to the ground, and I heard a voice say to me in Hebrew:

Voice	Saul, Saul! Why are you persecuting me? You are hurting yourself by hitting back, like an ox kicking against its owner's stick.
Paul	'Who are you, Lord?' [I asked. And the Lord answered:]
Voice	I am Jesus, whom you persecute. But get up and stand on your feet. I have appeared to you to appoint you as my servant. You are to tell others what you have seen of me today and what I will show you in the future. I will rescue you from the people of Israel and from the Gentiles to whom I will send you. You are to open their eyes and turn them from the darkness to the light and from the power of Satan to God, so that through their faith in me they will have their sins forgiven and receive their place among God's chosen people.
Cast	[This is] the word of the Lord.
All	**Thanks be to God.**

Cast: **Narrator, Agrippa, Paul, Voice.**

Paul tells of his work
Acts 26.19–32

Paul
King Agrippa, I did not disobey the vision I had from heaven. First in Damascus and in Jerusalem and then in all Judaea and among the Gentiles, I preached that they must repent of their sins and turn to God and do the things that would show they had repented. It was for this reason that the Jews seized me while I was in the Temple, and they tried to kill me. But to this very day I have been helped by God, and so I stand here giving my witness to all, to small and great alike. What I say is the very same thing which the prophets and Moses said was going to happen: that the Messiah must suffer and be the first one to rise from death, to announce the light of salvation to the Jews and to the Gentiles.

Narrator
As Paul defended himself in this way, Festus shouted at him:

Festus
You are mad, Paul! Your great learning is driving you mad!

Paul
I am not mad, Your Excellency! I am speaking the sober truth. King Agrippa! I can speak to you with all boldness, because you know about these things. I am sure that you have taken notice of every one of them, for this thing has not happened hidden away in a corner. King Agrippa, do you believe the prophets? I know that you do!

[Narrator
Agrippa said to Paul:]

Agrippa
In this short time do you think you will make me a Christian?

Paul
Whether a short time or a long time, my prayer to God is that you and all the rest of you who are listening to me today might become what I am—except, of course, for these chains!

Narrator
Then the king, the governor, Bernice, and all the others got up, and after leaving they said to each other:

Agrippa (to companion)
This man has not done anything for which he should die—

Companion
Or be put in prison.

Narrator
And Agrippa said to Festus:

Agrippa
This man could have been released if he had not appealed to the Emperor.

Cast
[This is] the word of the Lord.
All
Thanks be to God.

Cast: **Paul, Narrator, Festus, Agrippa, Companion** (female as Bernice, or can be the same as Agrippa).

Paul sails for Rome
Acts 27.1–12

Luke
When it was decided that we should sail to Italy, they handed Paul and some other prisoners over to Julius, an officer in the Roman regiment called 'The Emperor's Regiment'. We went aboard a

ship from Adramyttium, which was ready to leave for the seaports of the province of Asia, and we sailed away. Aristarchus, a Macedonian from Thessalonica, was with us. The next day we arrived at Sidon. Julius was kind to Paul and allowed him to go and see his friends, to be given what he needed. We went on from there, and because the winds were blowing against us, we sailed on the sheltered side of the island of Cyprus. We crossed over the sea off Cilicia and Pamphylia and came to Myra in Lycia. There the officer found a ship from Alexandria that was going to sail for Italy, so he put us aboard.

We sailed slowly for several days and with great difficulty finally arrived off the town of Cnidus. The wind would not let us go any further in that direction, so we sailed down the sheltered side of the island of Crete, passing by Cape Salmone. We kept close to the coast and with great difficulty came to a place called Safe Harbours, not far from the town of Lasea. We spent a long time there, until it became dangerous to continue the voyage, for by now the Day of Atonement was already past. So Paul gave them this advice:

Paul   Men, I see that our voyage from here on will be dangerous; there will be great damage to the cargo and to the ship, and loss of life as well.

Luke   But the army officer was convinced by what the captain and the owner of the ship said, and not by what Paul said. The harbour was not a good one to spend the winter in; so most of the men were in favour of putting out to sea and trying to reach Phoenix, if possible, in order to spend the winter there. Phoenix is a harbour in Crete that faces south-west and north-west.

Cast   [This is] the word of the Lord.
All   **Thanks be to God.**

Cast: **Luke, Paul.** (Please note overlap with the next reading.)

The storm
Acts 27.9–38

Luke   We spent a long time at Safe Harbours, until it became dangerous to continue the voyage, for by now the Day of Atonement was already past. So Paul gave them this advice:

Paul   Men, I see that our voyage from here on will be dangerous; there will be great damage to the cargo and to the ship, and loss of life as well.

Luke   But the army officer was convinced by what the captain and the owner of the ship said, and not by what Paul said. The harbour was not a good one to spend the winter in; so most of the men were in favour of putting out to sea and trying to reach Phoenix, if possible, in order to spend the winter there. Phoenix is a harbour in Crete that faces south-west and north-west.   →

(Luke)   A soft wind from the south began to blow, and the men thought that they could carry out their plan, so they pulled up anchor and sailed as close as possible along the coast of Crete. But soon a very strong wind—the one called 'North-easter'—blew down from the island. It hit the ship, and since it was impossible to keep the ship headed into the wind, we gave up trying and let it be carried along by the wind. We got some shelter when we passed to the south of the little island of Cauda. There, with some difficulty, we managed to make the ship's boat secure. They pulled it aboard and then fastened some ropes tight round the ship. They were afraid that it might run into the sandbanks off the coast of Libya, so they lowered the sail and let the ship be carried by the wind. The violent storm continued, so on the next day they began to throw some of the ship's cargo overboard, and on the following day they threw part of the ship's equipment overboard. For many days we could not see the sun or the stars and the wind kept on blowing very hard. We finally gave up all hope of being saved.

After the men had gone a long time without food, Paul stood before them:

Paul   Men, you should have listened to me and not have sailed from Crete; then we would have avoided all this damage and loss. But now I beg you, take heart! Not one of you will lose his life; only the ship will be lost. For last night an angel of the God to whom I belong and whom I worship came to me and said, 'Don't be afraid, Paul! You must stand before the Emperor. And God in his goodness to you has spared the lives of all those who are sailing with you.' So take heart, men! For I trust in God that it will be just as I was told. But we will be driven ashore on some island.

Luke   It was the fourteenth night, and we were being driven about in the Mediterranean by the storm. About midnight the sailors suspected that we were getting close to land. So they dropped a line with a weight tied to it and found that the water was forty metres deep; a little later they did the same and found that it was thirty metres deep. They were afraid that the ship would go on the rocks, so they lowered four anchors from the back of the ship and prayed for daylight. Then the sailors tried to escape from the ship; they lowered the boat into the water and pretended that they were going to put out some anchors from the front of the ship. But Paul said to the army officer and soldiers:

Paul   If the sailors don't stay on board, you have no hope of being saved.

Luke   So the soldiers cut the ropes that held the boat and let it go.

Just before dawn, Paul begged them all to eat some food:

Paul   You have been waiting for fourteen days now, and all this time you have not eaten anything. I beg you, then, eat some food; you need it in order to survive. Not even a hair of your heads will be lost.

Luke	After saying this, Paul took some bread, gave thanks to God before them all, broke it, and began to eat. They took heart, and every one of them also ate some food. There was a total of 276 of us on board. After everyone had eaten enough, they lightened the ship by throwing all the wheat into the sea.
Cast	[This is] the word of the Lord.
All	**Thanks be to God.**

Cast: **Luke, Paul.** (Please note overlap with the previous reading.)

The shipwreck
Acts 27.39–44

Narrator 1	When day came, the sailors did not recognize the coast, but they noticed a bay with a beach and decided that, if possible, they would run the ship aground there.
Narrator 2	So they cut off the anchors and let them sink in the sea, and at the same time they untied the ropes that held the steering oars.
Narrator 1	Then they raised the sail at the front of the ship so that the wind would blow the ship forward, and we headed for shore.
Narrator 2	But the ship hit a sandbank and went aground; the front part of the ship got stuck and could not move, while the back part was being broken to pieces by the violence of the waves.
Narrator 1	The soldiers made a plan to kill all the prisoners, in order to keep them from swimming ashore and escaping.
Narrator 2	But the army officer wanted to save Paul, so he stopped them from doing this.
Narrator 1	Instead, he ordered all the men who could swim to jump overboard first and swim ashore.
Narrator 2	The rest were to follow, holding on to the planks or to some broken pieces of the ship.
Narrator 1	And this was how we all got safely ashore.
Cast	[This is] the word of the Lord.
All	**Thanks be to God.**

Cast: **Narrator 1, Narrator 2** (if used with previous and/or subsequent readings, both Narrators are the same as Luke).

Paul in Malta—and on to Rome
Acts 28.1–10 [11–15]

Luke	When we were safely ashore, we learnt that the island was called Malta. The natives there were very friendly to us. It had started to rain and was cold, so they lit a fire and made us all welcome. Paul gathered up a bundle of sticks and was putting them on the fire when a snake came out on account of the heat and fastened itself to his hand. The natives saw the snake hanging on Paul's hand and said to one another:

Person 1	This man must be a murderer, but Fate will not let him live—
Person 2	Even though he escaped from the sea.
Luke	But Paul shook the snake off into the fire without being harmed at all. They were waiting for him to swell up or suddenly fall down dead. But after waiting for a long time and not seeing anything unusual happening to him, they changed their minds:
Persons 1 and **2**	He is a god!
Luke	Not far from that place were some fields that belonged to Publius, the chief official of the island. He welcomed us kindly and for three days we were his guests. Publius' father was in bed, sick with fever and dysentery. Paul went into his room, prayed, placed his hands on him, and healed him. When this happened, all the other sick people on the island came and were healed. They gave us many gifts, and when we sailed, they put on board what we needed for the voyage. (PAUSE)
	[After three months we sailed away on a ship from Alexandria, called 'The Twin Gods', which had spent the winter in the island. We arrived in the city of Syracuse and stayed there for three days. From there we sailed on and arrived in the city of Rhegium. The next day a wind began to blow from the south, and in two days we came to the town of Puteoli. We found some believers there who asked us to stay with them a week. And so we came to Rome. The believers in Rome heard about us and came as far as the towns of Market of Appius and Three Inns to meet us. When Paul saw them, he thanked God and was greatly encouraged.]
Cast	[This is] the word of the Lord.
All	**Thanks be to God.**

Cast: **Luke, Person 1, Person 2.**

Paul in Rome
Acts 28.16–31

Narrator	In Rome, Paul was allowed to live by himself with a soldier guarding him. After three days Paul called the local Jewish leaders to a meeting. [When they had gathered, he said to them:]
Paul	My fellow-Israelites, even though I did nothing against our people or the customs that we received from our ancestors, I was made a prisoner in Jerusalem and handed over to the Romans. After questioning me, the Romans wanted to release me, because they found that I had done nothing for which I deserved to die. But when the Jews opposed this, I was forced to appeal to the Emperor, even though I had no accusation to make against my own people. That is why I asked to see you and talk with you. As a matter of fact, I am bound in chains like this for the sake of him for whom the people of Israel hope.
[Narrator	They said to him:]

Jewish leader We have not received any letters from Judaea about you, nor have any of our people come from there with any news or anything bad to say about you. But we would like to hear your ideas, because we know that everywhere people speak against this party to which you belong.

Narrator So they fixed a date with Paul, and a large number of them came that day to the place where Paul was staying. From morning till night he explained to them his message about the Kingdom of God, and he tried to convince them about Jesus by quoting from the Law of Moses and the writings of the prophets. Some of them were convinced by his words, but others would not believe. So they left, disagreeing among themselves, after Paul had said this one thing:

Paul How well the Holy Spirit spoke through the prophet Isaiah to your ancestors, [for he said]:

Isaiah Go and say to this people:
You will listen and listen, but not understand;
you will look and look, but not see,
because this people's minds are dull,
and they have stopped up their ears
and closed their eyes.
Otherwise, their eyes would see,
their ears would hear,
their minds would understand,
and they would turn to me, says God,
and I would heal them.

Paul You are to know, then, that God's message of salvation has been sent to the Gentiles. They will listen!

Narrator For two years Paul lived in a place he rented for himself, and there he welcomed all who came to see him. He preached about the Kingdom of God and taught about the Lord Jesus Christ, speaking with all boldness and freedom.

Cast [This is] the word of the Lord.
All **Thanks be to God.**

Cast: **Narrator, Paul, Jewish leader, Isaiah.**

ROMANS

Is God being just?
Romans 2.28—3.8

Question   Who is a real Jew, truly circumcised?

Answer   It is not the man who is a Jew on the outside, whose circumcision
is a physical thing. Rather, the real Jew is the person who is a Jew
on the inside, that is, whose heart has been circumcised, and this
is the work of God's Spirit, not of the written Law. Such a person
receives his praise from God, not from man.

Question   Have the Jews then any advantage over the Gentiles? Or is there
any value in being circumcised?

Answer   Much, indeed, in every way! In the first place, God trusted his
message to the Jews.

Question   But what if some of them were not faithful? Does this mean that
God will not be faithful?

Answer   Certainly not! God must be true, even though every man is a liar.
As the scripture says:

Psalmist   You must be shown to be right when you speak;
you must win your case when you are being tried.

Question   But what if our doing wrong serves to show up more clearly God's
doing right? Can we say that God does wrong when he punishes
us? [This would be the natural question to ask.]

Answer   By no means! If God is not just, how can he judge the world?

Question   But what if my untruth serves God's glory by making his truth
stand out more clearly? Why should I still be condemned as a
sinner? Why not say, then, 'Let us do evil so that good may come'?

Answer   Some people, indeed, have insulted me by accusing me of saying
this very thing! They will be condemned, as they should be.

Cast   [This is] the word of the Lord.
All   **Thanks be to God.**

Cast: **Question, Answer, Psalmist** (can be the same as Answer).

How God puts us right with him
Romans 3.9–26

Paul   Well then, are we Jews in any better condition than the Gentiles?
Not at all! I have already shown that Jews and Gentiles alike are all
under the power of sin. As the Scriptures say:

308

Psalmist	There is no one who is righteous, no one who is wise or who worships God. All have turned away from God; they have all gone wrong; no one does what is right, not even one. Their words are full of deadly deceit; wicked lies roll off their tongues, and dangerous threats, like snake's poison, from their lips; their speech is filled with bitter curses.
Isaiah	They are quick to hurt and kill; they leave ruin and destruction wherever they go. They have not known the path of peace—
Psalmist	Nor have they learnt reverence for God.
Paul	Now we know that everything in the Law applies to those who live under the Law, in order to stop all human excuses and bring the whole world under God's judgement. For no one is put right in God's sight by doing what the Law requires; what the Law does is to make man know that he has sinned. But now God's way of putting people right with himself has been revealed. It has nothing to do with law, even though the Law of Moses and the prophets gave their witness to it. God puts people right through their faith in Jesus Christ. God does this to all who believe in Christ, because there is no difference at all: everyone has sinned and is far away from God's saving presence. But by the free gift of God's grace all are put right with him through Christ Jesus, who sets them free. God offered him, so that by his sacrificial death he should become the means by which people's sins are forgiven through their faith in him.
Cast	[This is] the word of the Lord.
All	**Thanks be to God.**

Cast: **Paul, Psalmist, Isaiah.**

Faith and law
Romans 3.26–31

Question	In the past God was patient and overlooked people's sins; but in the present time he deals with their sins, in order to demonstrate his righteousness. In this way God shows that he himself is righteous and that he puts right everyone who believes in Jesus. What, then, can we boast about?
Answer	Nothing!
Question	And what is the reason for this? Is it that we obey the Law?
Answer	No, but that we *believe*. For we conclude that a person is put right with God only through *faith*, and not by doing what the Law commands.
Question	Or is God the God of the Jews only? Is he not the God of the Gentiles also?

Answer	Of course he is. God is one, and he will put the Jews right with himself on the basis of *their* faith, and will put the Gentiles right through *their* faith.
Question	Does this mean that by this faith we do away with the Law?
Answer	No, not at all; instead, we uphold the Law.
Cast	[This is] the word of the Lord.
All	**Thanks be to God.**

Cast: **Question, Answer.**

The example of Abraham
Romans 4.1–12

Question	What shall we say, then, of Abraham, the father of our race? What was his experience?
Answer	If he was put right with God by the things he *did*, he would have something to boast about—but not in God's sight. The scripture says:
Reader	Abraham believed God, and because of his *faith* God accepted him as righteous.
Answer	A person who works is paid his wages, but they are not regarded as a gift; they are something that he has earned. But the person who depends on his faith, not on his deeds, and who believes in the God who declares the guilty to be innocent, it is his *faith* that God takes into account in order to put him right with himself. This is what David meant when he spoke of the happiness of the person whom God accepts as righteous, apart from anything that person does:
Reader	Happy are those whose wrongs are forgiven, whose sins are pardoned! Happy is the person whose sins the Lord will not keep account of!
Question	Does this happiness that David spoke of belong only to those who are circumcised?
Answer	No indeed! It belongs also to those who are not circumcised. For we have quoted the scripture:
Reader	Abraham believed God, and because of his faith God accepted him as righteous.
Question	When did this take place? Was it before or after Abraham was circumcised?
Answer	It was before, not after. He was circumcised later, and his circumcision was a sign to show that because of his faith God had accepted him as righteous before he had been circumcised. And so Abraham is the spiritual father of all who believe in God and are accepted as righteous by him, even though they are not circumcised. He is also the father of those who are circumcised, that is, of those who, in addition to being circumcised, also live the same life of faith that our father Abraham lived before he was circumcised.
Cast	[This is] the word of the Lord.
All	**Thanks be to God.**

Cast: **Question, Answer, Reader.**

God's promise is received through faith
From Romans 4.13–25

Paul
When God promised Abraham and his descendants that the world would belong to him, he did so, not because Abraham obeyed the Law, but because he believed and was accepted as righteous by God. For if what God promises is to be given to those who obey the Law, then man's faith means nothing and God's promise is worthless. The Law brings down God's anger; but where there is no law, there is no disobeying of the law.

And so the promise was based on faith, in order that the promise should be guaranteed as God's free gift to all of Abraham's descendants—not just to those who obey the Law, but also to those who believe as Abraham did. For Abraham is the spiritual father of us all; as the scripture says:

Genesis
I have made you father of many nations.

Paul
So the promise is good in the sight of God, in whom Abraham believed—the God who brings the dead to life and whose command brings into being what did not exist. Abraham believed and hoped, even when there was no reason for hoping, and so became:

Genesis
The father of many nations.

Paul
Just as the scripture says:

Genesis
Your descendants will be as many as the stars.

Paul
He was then almost one hundred years old; but his faith did not weaken when he thought of his body, which was already practically dead, or of the fact that Sarah could not have children. His faith did not leave him, and he did not doubt God's promise; his faith filled him with power, and he gave praise to God. He was absolutely sure that God would be able to do what he had promised. That is why Abraham, through faith was:

Genesis
Accepted as righteous by God.

Paul
The words:

Genesis
He was accepted as righteous . . .

Paul
. . . were not written for him alone. They were written also for us who are to be accepted as righteous, who believe in him who raised Jesus our Lord from death. Because of our sins he was handed over to die, and he was raised to life in order to put us right with God.

Cast   [This is] the word of the Lord.
All   **Thanks be to God.**

Cast: **Paul, Genesis.**

311

Right with God
Romans 5.1–11

Voice 1 Now that we have been put right with God through faith, we have peace with God through our Lord Jesus Christ. He has brought us by faith into this experience of God's grace, in which we now live. And so we boast of the hope we have of sharing God's glory!

Voice 2 We also boast of our troubles, because we know that trouble produces endurance, endurance brings God's approval, and his approval creates hope.

Voice 1 This hope does not disappoint us, for God has poured out his love into our hearts by means of the Holy Spirit, who is God's gift to us. For when we were still helpless, Christ died for the wicked at the time that God chose.

Voice 2 It is a difficult thing for someone to die for a righteous person. It may even be that someone might dare to die for a good person. But God has shown us how much he loves us—it was while we were still sinners that Christ died for us!

Voice 1 By his sacrificial death we are now put right with God; how much more, then, will we be saved by him from God's anger!

Voice 2 We were God's enemies, but he made us his friends through the death of his Son. Now that we are God's friends, how much more will we be saved by Christ's life!

Voice 1 But that is not all; we rejoice because of what God has done through our Lord Jesus Christ, who has now made us God's friends.

Cast [This is] the word of the Lord.
All **Thanks be to God.**

Cast: **Voice 1** (enthusiastic), **Voice 2** (serious).

Dead to sin
From Romans 6.1–23

Question What shall we say, then? Should we continue to live in sin so that God's grace will increase?

Answer Certainly not! We have died to sin—how then can we go on living in it? Sin must no longer rule in your mortal bodies, so that you obey the desires of your natural self. Nor must you surrender any part of yourselves to sin to be used for wicked purposes. Instead, give yourselves to God, as those who have been brought from death to life, and surrender your whole being to him to be used for righteous purposes. Sin must not be your master; for you do not live under law but under God's grace.

Question What, then? Shall we sin, because we are not under law but under God's grace?

Answer	By no means! Surely you know that when you surrender yourselves as slaves to obey someone, you are in fact the slaves of the master you obey—either of sin, which results in death, or of obedience, which results in being put right with God. But thanks be to God! For though at one time you were slaves to sin, you have obeyed with all your heart the truths found in the teaching you received. But now you have been set free from sin and are the slaves of God. Your gain is a life fully dedicated to him, and the result is eternal life. For sin pays its wage—death; but God's free gift is eternal life in union with Christ Jesus our Lord.
Cast	[This is] the word of the Lord.
All	**Thanks be to God.**

Cast: **Question, Answer.**

Law and sin
Romans 7.6–13

Answer	Now we are free from the Law, because we died to that which once held us prisoners. No longer do we serve in the old way of a written law, but in the new way of the Spirit.
Question	Shall we say, then, that the Law itself is sinful?
Answer	Of course not! But it was the Law that made me know what sin is. If the Law had not said, 'Do not desire what belongs to someone else,' I would not have known such a desire. But by means of that commandment sin found its chance to stir up all kinds of selfish desires in me. Apart from law, sin is a dead thing. I myself was once alive apart from law; but when the commandment came, sin sprang to life, and I died. And the commandment which was meant to bring life, in my case brought death. Sin found its chance, and by means of the commandment it deceived me and killed me. So then, the Law itself is holy, and the commandment is holy, right, and good.
Question	But does this mean that what is good caused my death?
Answer	By no means! It was sin that did it; by using what is good, sin brought death to me, in order that its true nature as sin might be revealed. And so, by means of the commandment sin is shown to be even more terribly sinful.
Cast	[This is] the word of the Lord.
All	**Thanks be to God.**

Cast: **Answer, Question.**

Life in the Spirit
Romans 8.1–11

Voice 1	There is no condemnation now for those who live in union with Christ Jesus. For the law of the Spirit, which brings us life in union with Christ Jesus, has set me free from the law of sin and death.

→

What the Law could not do, because human nature was weak, God did. He condemned sin in human nature by sending his own Son, who came with a nature like man's sinful nature, to do away with sin. God did this so that the righteous demands of the Law might be fully satisfied in us who live according to the Spirit, and not according to human nature.

Voice 2   Those who live as their human nature tells them to, have their minds controlled by what human nature wants.

Voice 1   Those who live as the Spirit tells them to, have their minds controlled by what the Spirit wants.

Voice 2   To be controlled by human nature results in death.

Voice 1   To be controlled by the Spirit results in life and peace.

Voice 2   And so a person becomes an enemy of God when he is controlled by his human nature; for he does not obey God's law, and in fact he cannot obey it. Those who obey their human nature cannot please God.

Voice 1   But you do not live as your human nature tells you to; instead, you live as the Spirit tells you to—if, in fact, God's Spirit lives in you.

Voice 2   Whoever does not have the Spirit of Christ does not belong to him.

Voice 1   But if Christ lives in you, the Spirit is life for you because you have been put right with God, even though your bodies are going to die because of sin. If the Spirit of God, who raised Jesus from death, lives in you, then he who raised Christ from death will also give life to your mortal bodies by the presence of his Spirit in you.

Cast   [This is] the word of the Lord.
All   **Thanks be to God.**

Cast: **Voice 1** (triumphant), **Voice 2** (serious).

Led by God's Spirit
Romans 8.14–17

Reader   Those who are led by God's Spirit are God's sons. For the Spirit that God has given you does not make you slaves and cause you to be afraid; instead, the Spirit makes you God's children, and by the Spirit's power we cry out to God:

Person 1   Father!
Person 2   My Father!

Reader   God's Spirit joins himself to our spirits to declare that we are God's children.

Person 1   Since we are his children, we will possess the blessings he keeps for his people.

Person 2   And we will also possess with Christ what God has kept for him.

Person 1   For if we share Christ's suffering, we will also share his glory.

Cast   [This is] the word of the Lord.
All   **Thanks be to God.**

Cast: **Reader, Person 1, Person 2.**

God's love in Christ
Romans 8.28–39

Answer	We know that in all things God works for good with those who love him, those whom he has called according to his purpose. Those whom God had already chosen he also set apart to become like his Son, so that the Son would be the first among many brothers. And so those whom God set apart, he called; and those he called, he put right with himself, and he shared his glory with them.
Question	In view of all this, what can we say? If God is for us, who can be against us?
Answer	Certainly not God, who did not even keep back his own Son, but offered him for us all! He gave us his Son—will he not also freely give us all things?
Question	Who will accuse God's chosen people?
Answer	God himself declares them not guilty!
Question	Who, then, will condemn them?
Answer	Not Christ Jesus, who died, or rather, who was raised to life and is at the right-hand side of God, pleading with him for us!
Question	Who, then, can separate us from the love of Christ? Can trouble do it, or hardship or persecution or hunger or poverty or danger or death? As the scripture says:
Psalmist	For your sake we are in danger of death at all times; we are treated like sheep that are going to be slaughtered.
Answer	No, in all these things we have complete victory through him who loved us! For I am certain that nothing can separate us from his love: neither death nor life, neither angels nor other heavenly rulers or powers, neither the present nor the future, neither the world above nor the world below—there is nothing in all creation that will ever be able to separate us from the love of God which is ours through Christ Jesus our Lord.
Cast All	[This is] the word of the Lord. **Thanks be to God.**

Cast: **Answer, Question, Psalmist** (can be the same as Question).

God and his people
Romans 9.6–18

Paul	I am not saying that the promise of God has failed; for not all the people of Israel are the people of God. Nor are all Abraham's descendants the children of God. God said to Abraham:
God	It is through Isaac that you will have the descendants I promised you.

Paul	This means that the children born *in the usual way* are not the children of God; instead, the children born *as a result of God's promise* are regarded as the true descendants. For God's promise was made in these words:
God	At the right time I will come back, and Sarah will have a son.
Paul	And this is not all. For Rebecca's two sons had the same father, our ancestor Isaac. But in order that the choice of one son might be completely the result of God's own purpose, God said to her:
God	The elder will serve the younger.
Paul	He said this before they were born, before they had done anything either good or bad; so God's choice was based on his call, and not on anything they had done. As the scripture says:
God	I loved Jacob, but I hated Esau.
Questioner	Shall we say, then, that God is unjust?
Paul	Not at all. For he said to Moses:
God	I will have mercy on anyone I wish; I will take pity on anyone I wish.
Paul	So then, everything depends, not on what man wants or does, but only on God's mercy. For the scripture says to the king of Egypt:
God	I made you king in order to use you to show my power and to spread my fame over the whole world.
Paul	So then, God has mercy on anyone he wishes, and he makes stubborn anyone he wishes.
Cast	[This is] the word of the Lord.
All	**Thanks be to God.**

Cast: **Paul, God, Questioner** (can be the same as Paul).

God's anger and mercy
Romans 9.19–29

Paul	One of you will say to me:
Questioner	If this is so, how can God find fault with anyone? Who can resist God's will?
Paul	But who are you, my friend, to answer God back? A clay pot does not ask the man who made it, 'Why did you make me like this?' After all, the man who makes the pots has the right to use the clay as he wishes, and to make two pots from the same lump of clay, one for special occasions and the other for ordinary use.
	And the same is true of what God has done. He wanted to show his anger and to make his power known. But he was very patient in enduring those who were the objects of his anger, who were doomed to destruction. And he also wanted to reveal his abundant glory, which was poured out on us who are the objects of his mercy, those of us whom he has prepared to receive his

glory. For we are the people he called, not only from among the Jews but also from among the Gentiles. This is what he says in the book of Hosea:

God	The people who were not mine I will call 'My People.' The nation that I did not love I will call 'My Beloved.' And in the very place where they were told, 'You are not my people,' there they will be called the sons of the living God.
Paul	And Isaiah exclaims about Israel:
Isaiah	Even if the people of Israel are as many as the grains of sand by the sea, yet only a few of them will be saved; for the Lord will quickly settle his full account with the world.
Paul	It is as Isaiah had said before:
Isaiah	If the Lord Almighty had not left us some descendants, we would have become like Sodom, we would have been like Gomorrah.
Cast	[This is] the word of the Lord.
All	**Thanks be to God.**

Cast: **Paul, Questioner, God, Isaiah.**

Salvation is for all
Romans 10.5–21

Paul	Moses wrote this about being put right with God by obeying the Law:
Reader	Whoever obeys the commands of the Law will live.
Paul	But what the scripture says about being put right with God through faith is this:
Reader	You are not to ask yourself, 'Who will go up into heaven?'
Paul	That is, to bring Christ down.
Reader	Nor are you to ask, 'Who will go down into the world below?'
Paul	That is, to bring Christ up from death. What it says is this:
Reader	God's message is near you, on your lips and in your heart.
Paul	That is, the message of faith that we preach. (PAUSE) If you confess that Jesus is Lord and believe that God raised him from death, you will be saved. For it is by our faith that we are put right with God; it is by our confession that we are saved. The scripture says:
Reader	Whoever believes in him will not be disappointed.
Paul	This includes everyone, because there is no difference between Jews and Gentiles; God is the same Lord of all and richly blesses all who call to him. As the scripture says:

Reader	Everyone who calls out to the Lord for help will be saved.
Paul	But how can they call to him for help if they have not believed? And how can they believe if they have not heard the message? And how can they hear if the message is not proclaimed? And how can the message be proclaimed if the messengers are not sent out? As the scripture says:
Reader	How wonderful is the coming of messengers who bring good news!
Paul	But not all have accepted the Good News. Isaiah himself said:
Reader	Lord, who believed our message?
Paul	So then, faith comes from hearing the message, and the message comes through preaching Christ. But I ask: Is it true that they did not hear the message? Of course they did—for as the scripture says:
Reader	The sound of their voice went out to all the world; their words reached the ends of the earth.
Paul	Again I ask: Did the people of Israel not understand? Moses himself is the first one to answer:
Reader	I will use a so-called nation to make my people jealous; and by means of a nation of fools I will make my people angry.
Paul	And Isaiah is even bolder when he says:
Reader	I was found by those who were not looking for me; I appeared to those who were not asking for me.
Paul	But concerning Israel he says:
Reader	All day long I held out my hands to welcome a disobedient and rebellious people.
Cast	[This is] the word of the Lord.
All	**Thanks be to God.**

Cast: **Paul, Reader.** (A shorter version of this dramatised reading follows.)

The message of salvation
Romans 10.8–17

Deuteronomy	God's message is near you, on your lips and in your heart.
Paul	That is, the message of faith that we preach. If you confess that Jesus is Lord and believe that God raised him from death, you will be saved. For it is by our faith that we are put right with God; it is by our confession that we are saved. [The scripture says:]
Isaiah	Whoever believes in him will not be disappointed.
Paul	This includes everyone, because there is no difference between Jews and Gentiles; God is the same Lord of all and richly blesses all who call to him. [As the scripture says:]

Joel	Everyone who calls out to the Lord for help will be saved.
Paul	But how can they call to him for help if they have not believed? And how can they believe if they have not heard the message? And how can they hear if the message is not proclaimed? And how can the message be proclaimed if the messengers are not sent out?
	[As the scripture says:]
Isaiah	How wonderful is the coming of messengers who bring good news!
Paul	But not all have accepted the Good News. [Isaiah himself said:]
Isaiah	Lord, who believed our message?
Paul	So then, faith comes from hearing the message, and the message comes through preaching Christ.
Cast	[This is] the word of the Lord.
All	**Thanks be to God.**

Cast: **Deuteronomy, Paul, Isaiah, Joel** (Deuteronomy, Isaiah, and Joel can be the same). (For a fuller version of this reading see page 317 above.)

God's mercy on Israel
Romans 11.1–12

Question	I ask, then: Did God reject his own people?
Answer	Certainly not! I myself am an Israelite, a descendant of Abraham, a member of the tribe of Benjamin. God has not rejected his people, whom he chose from the beginning. You know what the scripture says in the passage where Elijah pleads with God against Israel:
Reader	Lord, they have killed your prophets and torn down your altars; I am the only one left, and they are trying to kill me.
Question	What answer did God give him?
Reader	I have kept for myself seven thousand men who have not worshipped the false god Baal.
Answer	It is the same way now: there is a small number left of those whom God has chosen because of his grace. His choice is based on his grace, not on what they have done. For if God's choice were based on what people do, then his grace would not be real grace.
Question	What then?
Answer	The people of Israel did not find what they were looking for. It was only the small group that God chose who found it; the rest grew deaf to God's call. As the scripture says:
Reader	God made their minds and hearts dull; to this very day they cannot see or hear.
Answer	And David says:

Reader	May they be caught and trapped at their feasts; may they fall, may they be punished! May their eyes be blinded so that they cannot see; and make them bend under their troubles at all times.
Question	I ask, then: When the Jews stumbled, did they fall to their ruin?
Answer	By no means! Because they sinned, salvation has come to the Gentiles, to make the Jews jealous of them. The sin of the Jews brought rich blessings to the world, and their spiritual poverty brought rich blessings to the Gentiles. Then, how much greater the blessings will be when the complete number of Jews is included!
Cast	[This is] the word of the Lord.
All	**Thanks be to God.**

Cast: **Question, Answer, Reader.**

God's mercy on all
Romans 11.25–36

Paul	There is a secret truth, my brothers, which I want you to know, for it will keep you from thinking how wise you are. It is that the stubbornness of the people of Israel is not permanent, but will last only until the complete number of Gentiles comes to God. And this is how all Israel will be saved. As the scripture says:
Isaiah	The Saviour will come from Zion and remove all wickedness from the descendants of Jacob.
Jeremiah	I will make this covenant with them when I take away their sins.
Paul	Because they reject the Good News, the Jews are God's enemies for the sake of you Gentiles. But because of God's choice, they are his friends because of their ancestors. For God does not change his mind about whom he chooses and blesses. As for you Gentiles, you disobeyed God in the past; but now you have received God's mercy because the Jews were disobedient. In the same way, because of the mercy that you have received, the Jews now disobey God, in order that they also may now receive God's mercy. For God has made all people prisoners of disobedience, so that he might show mercy to them all.
Isaiah	How great are God's riches! How deep are his wisdom and knowledge! Who can explain his decisions? Who can understand his ways?
Paul	As the scripture says:
Isaiah	Who knows the mind of the Lord? Who is able to give him advice?
Job	Who has ever given him anything, so that he had to pay it back?

Paul	For all things were created by him, and all things exist through him and for him. To God be the glory for ever! Amen.
Cast	[This is] the word of the Lord.
All	**Thanks be to God.**

Cast: **Paul, Isaiah, Jeremiah, Job.** (Please note: this reading overlaps with the next.)

Life in God's service
Romans 11.33—12.2

Paul	How great are God's riches! How deep are his wisdom and knowledge! Who can explain his decisions? Who can understand his ways? As the scripture says:
Reader	Who knows the mind of the Lord? Who is able to give him advice? Who has ever given him anything, so that he had to pay it back?
Paul	For all things were created by him, and all things exist through him and for him. To God be the glory for ever!
Paul and **Reader**	Amen.
Paul	So then, my brothers, because of God's great mercy to us I appeal to you: Offer yourselves as a living sacrifice to God, dedicated to his service and pleasing to him. This is the true worship that you should offer. Do not conform yourselves to the standards of this world, but let God transform you inwardly by a complete change of your mind. Then you will be able to know the will of God— what is good and is pleasing to him and is perfect.
Cast	[This is] the word of the Lord.
All	**Thanks be to God.**

Cast: **Paul, Reader.** (This reading overlaps with the previous reading.)

One body
Romans 12.4–13

Person 1	We have many parts in the one body, and all these parts have different functions.
Person 2	In the same way, though we are many, we are one body in union with Christ, and we are all joined to each other as different parts of one body.
Person 3	So we are to use our different gifts in accordance with the grace that God has given us.
Person 1	If our gift is to speak God's message, we should do it according to the faith that we have.
Person 2	If it is to serve, we should serve.

Person 3	If it is to teach, we should teach.
Person 1	If it is to encourage others, we should do so.
Person 2	Whoever shares with others should do it generously.
Person 3	Whoever has authority should work hard.
Person 1	Whoever shows kindness to others should do it cheerfully.
Teacher	Love must be completely sincere. Hate what is evil, hold on to what is good. Love one another warmly as Christian brothers, and be eager to show respect for one another. Work hard and do not be lazy. Serve the Lord with a heart full of devotion. Let your hope keep you joyful, be patient in your troubles, and pray at all times. Share your belongings with your needy fellow-Christians, and open your homes to strangers.
Cast	[This is] the word of the Lord.
All	**Thanks be to God.**

Cast: **Person 1, Person 2, Person 3, Teacher** (may be divided between Persons 1–3).

About revenge
Romans 12.14–21

Paul	Ask God to bless those who persecute you—yes, ask him to bless, not to curse. Be happy with those who are happy, weep with those who weep. Have the same concern for everyone. Do not be proud, but accept humble duties. Do not think of yourselves as wise.
	If someone has done you wrong, do not repay him with a wrong. Try to do what everyone considers to be good. Do everything possible on your part to live in peace with everybody. Never take revenge, my friends, but instead let God's anger do it. For the scripture says:
Reader	I will take revenge, I will pay back, says the Lord.
Paul	Instead, as the scripture says:
Reader	If your enemy is hungry, feed him; if he is thirsty, give him a drink; for by doing this you will make him burn with shame.
Paul	Do not let evil defeat you; instead, conquer evil with good.
Cast	[This is] the word of the Lord.
All	**Thanks be to God.**

Cast: **Paul, Reader.**

Duties towards one another
Romans 13.8–10 [11–14]

Paul	Be under obligation to no one—the only obligation you have is to love one another. Whoever does this has obeyed the Law. The commandments:

322

Reader	Do not commit adultery; do not commit murder; do not steal; do not desire what belongs to someone else:
Paul	All these, and any others besides, are summed up in the one command:
Reader	Love your neighbour as you love yourself.
Paul	If you love someone, you will never do him wrong; to love, then, is to obey the whole Law.
	[You must do this, because you know that the time has come for you to wake up from your sleep. For the moment when we will be saved is closer now than it was when we first believed. The night is nearly over, day is almost here. Let us stop doing the things that belong to the dark, and let us take up weapons for fighting in the light. Let us conduct ourselves properly, as people who live in the light of day—no orgies or drunkenness, no immorality or indecency, no fighting or jealousy. But take up the weapons of the Lord Jesus Christ, and stop paying attention to your sinful nature and satisfying its desires.]
Cast	[This is] the word of the Lord.
All	**Thanks be to God.**

Cast: **Paul, Reader.**

Good news for the Gentiles
Romans 15.7–13

Paul	Accept one another, then, for the glory of God, as Christ has accepted you. For I tell you that Christ's life of service was on behalf of the Jews, to show that God is faithful, to make his promises to their ancestors come true, and to enable even the Gentiles to praise God for his mercy. As the scripture says:
Reader	And so I will praise you among the Gentiles; I will sing praises to you.
Paul	Again it says:
Reader	Rejoice, Gentiles, with God's people!
Paul	And again:
Reader	Praise the Lord, all Gentiles; praise him, all peoples!
Paul	And again, Isaiah says:
Reader	A descendant of Jesse will appear; he will come to rule the Gentiles, and they will put their hope in him.
Paul	May God, the source of hope, fill you with all joy and peace by means of your faith in him, so that your hope will continue to grow by the power of the Holy Spirit.
Cast	[This is] the word of the Lord.
All	**Thanks be to God.**

Cast: **Paul, Reader.**

1 CORINTHIANS

Divisions in the Church
1 Corinthians 1.10–17

Paul
By the authority of our Lord Jesus Christ I appeal to all of you, my brothers, to agree in what you say, so that there will be no divisions among you. Be completely united, with only one thought and one purpose. For some people from Chloe's family have told me quite plainly, my brothers, that there are quarrels among you. Let me put it this way—each one of you says something different:

Person 1
I follow Paul.

Person 2
I follow Apollos.

Person 3
I follow Peter. (PAUSE)

Person 4
(emphatically)
I follow Christ.

Paul
Christ has been divided into groups! Was it Paul who died on the cross for you? Were you baptized as Paul's disciples? I thank God that I did not baptize any of you except Crispus and Gaius. No one can say, then, that you were baptized as my disciples.

(as an afterthought)
Oh yes, I also baptized Stephanas and his family; but I can't remember whether I baptized anyone else.

Christ did not send me to baptize. He sent me to tell the Good News, and to tell it without using the language of human wisdom, in order to make sure that Christ's death on the cross is not robbed of its power.

Cast
[This is] the word of the Lord.

All
Thanks be to God.

Cast: **Paul, Person 1, Person 2, Person 3** (can be the same as Person 1), **Person 4** (can be the same as Person 2).

Use your bodies for God's glory
1 Corinthians 6.12–20

Paul
Someone will say:

Person 1
I am allowed to do anything.

Paul
Yes; but not everything is good for you. I could say that I am allowed to do anything, but I am not going to let anything make me its slave. Someone else will say:

Person 2
Food is for the stomach, and the stomach is for food.

Paul	Yes; but God will put an end to both. The body is not to be used for sexual immorality, but to serve the Lord; and the Lord provides for the body. God raised the Lord from death, and he will also raise us by his power.
	You know that your bodies are parts of the body of Christ. Shall I take a part of Christ's body and make it part of the body of a prostitute? Impossible! Or perhaps you don't know that the man who joins his body to a prostitute becomes physically one with her? The scripture says quite plainly:
Scripture	The two will become one body.
Paul	But he who joins himself to the Lord becomes spiritually one with him. Avoid immorality. Any other sin a man commits does not affect his body; but the man who is guilty of sexual immorality sins against his own body. Don't you know that your body is the temple of the Holy Spirit, who lives in you and who was given to you by God? You do not belong to yourselves but to God; he bought you for a price. So use your bodies for God's glory.
Cast	[This is] the word of the Lord.
All	**Thanks be to God.**

Cast: **Paul, Person 1, Person 2, Scripture** (can be the same as Paul).

The Lord's Supper
1 Corinthians 11.23–26 (GNB)

Paul	I received from the Lord the teaching that I passed on to you: that the Lord Jesus, on the night he was betrayed, took a piece of bread, gave thanks to God and broke it. He said:
Jesus	This is my body, which is for you. Do this in memory of me.
Paul	In the same way, after the supper he took the cup [and said]:
Jesus	This cup is God's new covenant, sealed with my blood. Whenever you drink it, do so in memory of me.
Paul	This means that every time you eat this bread and drink from this cup you proclaim the Lord's death until he comes.
Cast	[This is] the word of the Lord.
All	**Thanks be to God.**

Cast: **Paul, Jesus.**

The Lord's Supper
1 Corinthians 11.23–26 (NIV)

Paul	I received from the Lord what I also passed on to you: The Lord Jesus, on the night he was betrayed, took bread, and when he had given thanks he broke it [and said]:
Jesus	This is my body, which is for you; do this in remembrance of me.
Paul	In the same way, after supper he took the cup [saying]:

Jesus	This cup is the new covenant in my blood; do this, whenever you drink it, in remembrance of me.
Paul	For whenever you eat this bread and drink this cup, you proclaim the Lord's death until he comes.
Cast	[This is] the word of the Lord.
All	**Thanks be to God.**

Cast: **Paul, Jesus.**

One body with many parts
From 1 Corinthians 12.12–27

Paul	Christ is like a single body, which has many parts; it is still one body, even though it is made up of different parts. In the same way, all of us, whether Jews or Gentiles, whether slaves or free, have been baptized into the one body by the same Spirit, and we have all been given the one Spirit to drink.
	For the body itself is not made up of only one part, but of many parts. If the foot were to say:
Foot	Because I am not a hand, I don't belong to the body.
Paul	That would not keep it from being a part of the body. And if the ear were to say:
Ear	Because I am not an eye, I don't belong to the body.
Paul	That would not keep it from being a part of the body. If the whole body were just an eye, how could it hear? And if it were only an ear, how could it smell? As it is, however, God put every different part in the body just as he wanted it to be. There would not be a body if it were all only one part! As it is, there are many parts but one body.
	So then, the eye cannot say to the hand:
Eye	I don't need you!
Paul	Nor can the head say to the feet:
Head	Well, I don't need *you!*
Paul	On the contrary, we cannot do without the parts of the body that seem to be weaker.
Cast	All of you are Christ's body, and each one is a part of it.
Cast	[This is] the word of the Lord.
All	**Thanks be to God.**

Cast: **Paul, Foot, Ear, Eye, Head.**

Love
1 Corinthians 12.31—13.13

Reader 1	Now I will show you the most excellent way.
Reader 2	If I speak in the tongues of men and of angels, but have not love, I am only a resounding gong or a clanging cymbal.
Reader 3	If I have the gift of prophecy and can fathom all mysteries and all knowledge, and if I have a faith that can move mountains, but have not love, I am nothing.
Reader 4	If I give all I possess to the poor and surrender my body to the flames, but have not love, I gain nothing. (PAUSE)
Reader 1	Love is patient, love is kind. It does not envy, it does not boast, it is not proud.
Reader 2	It is not rude, it is not self-seeking, it is not easily angered, it keeps no record of wrongs.
Reader 3	Love does not delight in evil but rejoices with the truth. It always protects, always trusts, always hopes, always perseveres.
Reader 4	Love never fails.
Reader 1	But where there are prophecies, they will cease.
Reader 2	Where there are tongues, they will be stilled.
Reader 3	Where there is knowledge, it will pass away.
Reader 4	For we know in part and we prophesy in part, but when perfection comes, the imperfect disappears.
Reader 1	When I was a child, I talked like a child, I thought like a child, I reasoned like a child. When I became a man, I put childish ways behind me.
Reader 2	Now we see but a poor reflection; then we shall see face to face.
Reader 3	Now I know in part; then I shall know fully, even as I am fully known. (PAUSE)
Reader 4	And now these three remain:
Reader 1 (slowly)	Faith. (PAUSE)
Reader 2	Hope. (PAUSE)
Reader 3	And love.
Reader 4	But the greatest of these is love.
Cast	[This is] the word of the Lord.
All	**Thanks be to God.**

Cast: **Reader 1, Reader 2, Reader 3, Reader 4.**

Tongues
1 Corinthians 14.18–25

Paul I thank God that I speak in strange tongues much more than any of you. But in church worship I would rather speak five words that can be understood, in order to teach others, than speak thousands of words in strange tongues.

Do not be like children in your thinking, my brothers; be children so far as evil is concerned, but be grown-up in your thinking. In the Scriptures it is written:

Scripture By means of men speaking strange languages
I will speak to my people, says the Lord.
I will speak through lips of foreigners,
but even then my people will not listen to me.

Paul So then, the gift of speaking in strange tongues is proof for unbelievers, not for believers, while the gift of proclaiming God's message is proof for believers, not for unbelievers.

If, then, the whole church meets together and everyone starts speaking in strange tongues—and if some ordinary people or unbelievers come in, won't they say that you are all crazy? But if everyone is proclaiming God's message when some unbeliever or ordinary person comes in, he will be convinced of his sin by what he hears. He will be judged by all he hears, his secret thoughts will be brought into the open, and he will bow down and worship God, confessing:

Person Truly God is here among you!

Cast [This is] the word of the Lord.
All **Thanks be to God.**

Cast: **Paul, Scripture, Person.**

The Resurrection of Christ
1 Corinthians 15.1–11

Paul Now I want to remind you, my brothers, of the Good News which I preached to you, which you received, and on which your faith stands firm. That is the gospel, the message that I preached to you. You are saved by the gospel if you hold firmly to it—unless it was for nothing that you believed.

I passed on to you what I received, which is of the greatest importance—that:

Young Paul Christ died for our sins, as written in the Scriptures; that he was buried and that he was raised to life three days later, as written in the Scriptures; that he appeared to Peter and then to all twelve apostles. Then he appeared to more than five hundred of his followers at once, most of whom are still alive, although some have died. Then he appeared to James, and afterwards to all the apostles.

Paul   Last of all he appeared also to me—even though I am like someone whose birth was abnormal. For I am the least of all the apostles—I do not even deserve to be called an apostle, because I persecuted God's church. But by God's grace I am what I am, and the grace that he gave me was not without effect. On the contrary, I have worked harder than any of the other apostles, although it was not really my own doing, but God's grace working with me. So then, whether it came from me or from them, this is what we all preach, and this is what you believe.

Cast   [This is] the word of the Lord.
All   **Thanks be to God.**

Cast: **Paul, Young Paul** (or, perhaps, Peter—see Galatians 1.18).

The resurrection body
From 1 Corinthians 15.35–57

Paul   Someone will ask:

Person   How can the dead be raised to life? What kind of body will they have?

Paul   When you sow a seed in the ground, it does not sprout to life unless it dies. And what you sow is a bare seed, perhaps a grain of wheat or some other grain, not the full-bodied plant that will later grow up. God provides that seed with the body he wishes; he gives each its own proper body. There is, of course, a physical body, so there has to be a spiritual body. For the scripture says:

Scripture   The first man, Adam, was created a living being.

Paul   But the last Adam is the life-giving Spirit. It is not the spiritual that comes first, but the physical, and then the spiritual. The first Adam, made of earth, came from the earth; the second Adam came from heaven. Those who belong to the earth are like the one who was made of earth; those who are of heaven are like the one who came from heaven. Just as we wear the likeness of the man made of earth, so we will wear the likeness of the Man from heaven.

What I mean, brothers, is that what is made of flesh and blood cannot share in God's Kingdom, and what is mortal cannot possess immortality.

Listen to this secret truth: we shall not all die, but when the last trumpet sounds, we shall all be changed in an instant, as quickly as the blinking of an eye. For when the trumpet sounds, the dead will be raised, never to die again, and we shall all be changed. For what is mortal must be changed into what is immortal; what will die must be changed into what cannot die. So when this takes place, and the mortal has been changed into the immortal, then the scripture will come true:

Scripture   Death is destroyed; victory is complete!
Where, Death, is your victory?
Where, Death, is your power to hurt?

Paul   Death gets its power to hurt from sin, and sin gets its power from the Law. But thanks be to God who gives us the victory through our Lord Jesus Christ!

Cast   [This is] the word of the Lord.
All   **Thanks be to God.**

Cast: **Paul, Person, Scripture.**

2 CORINTHIANS

Warning against pagan influences
2 Corinthians 6.14—7.1

Paul Do not try to work together as equals with unbelievers, for it cannot be done. How can right and wrong be partners? How can light and darkness live together? How can Christ and the Devil agree? What does a believer have in common with an unbeliever? How can God's temple come to terms with pagan idols? For we are the temple of the living God! As God himself has said:

Scripture I will make my home with my people
and live among them;
I will be their God,
and they shall be my people.

Paul And so the Lord says:

Scripture You must leave them
and separate yourselves from them.
Have nothing to do with what is unclean,
and I will accept you.
I will be your father,
and you shall be my sons and daughters,
says the Lord Almighty.

Paul All these promises are made to us, my dear friends. So then, let us purify ourselves from everything that makes body or soul unclean, and let us be completely holy by living in awe of God.

Cast [This is] the word of the Lord.
All **Thanks be to God.**

Cast: **Paul, Scripture.**

Christian giving
From 2 Corinthians 8.7–15; 9.6–15

Reader 1 You are so rich in all you have: in faith, speech, and knowledge, in your eagerness to help and in your love for us. And so we want you to be generous also in this service of love.

Reader 2 I am not laying down any rules. But by showing how eager others are to help, I am trying to find out how real your own love is.

Reader 3 You know the grace of our Lord Jesus Christ; rich as he was, he made himself poor for your sake, in order to make you rich by means of his poverty.

Reader 1 If you are eager to give, God will accept your gift on the basis of what you have to give, not on what you haven't.

Reader 2	I am not trying to relieve others by putting a burden on you; but since you have plenty at this time, it is only fair that you should help those who are in need. Then, when you are in need and they have plenty, they will help you. In this way both are treated equally. As the scripture says:
Reader 3	The one who gathered much did not have too much, and the one who gathered little did not have too little.
Reader 2	Remember that the person who sows few seeds will have a small crop; the one who sows many seeds will have a large crop.
Reader 1	Each one should give, then, as he has decided, not with regret or out of a sense of duty; for God loves the one who gives gladly.
Reader 2	And God is able to give you more than you need, so that you will always have all you need for yourselves and more than enough for every good cause. As the scripture says:
Reader 3	He gives generously to the needy; his kindness lasts for ever.
Readers 1–3	Let us give thanks to God for his priceless gift!
Cast	[This is] the word of the Lord.
All	**Thanks be to God.**

Cast: **Reader 1, Reader 2, Reader 3.**

Paul's authority
From 2 Corinthians 10.7–18

Paul	You are looking at the outward appearance of things. Is there someone there who reckons himself to belong to Christ? Well, let him think again about himself, because we belong to Christ just as much as he does. For I am not ashamed, even if I have boasted somewhat too much about the authority that the Lord has given us—authority to build you up, not to tear you down. I do not want it to appear that I am trying to frighten you with my letters. Someone will say:
Corinthian	Paul's letters are severe and strong, but when he is with us in person, he is weak, and his words are nothing!
Paul	Such a person must understand that there is no difference between what we write in our letters when we are away and what we will do when we are there with you.
	Of course we would not dare to classify ourselves or compare ourselves with those who rate themselves so highly. How stupid they are! They make up their own standards to measure themselves by, and they judge themselves by their own standards! As for us, however, our boasting will not go beyond certain limits; it will stay within the limits of the work which God has set for us, and this includes our work among you. But as the scripture says:

Scripture	Whoever wants to boast must boast about what the Lord has done.
Paul	For it is when the Lord thinks well of a person that he is really approved, and not when he thinks well of himself.
Cast	[This is] the word of the Lord.
All	**Thanks be to God.**

Cast: **Paul, Corinthian, Scripture.**

Paul's vision and revelation
From 2 Corinthians 12.1–10

Paul	I *have* to boast, even though it doesn't do any good. But I will now talk about visions and revelations given me by the Lord. If I wanted to boast, I would not be a fool, because I would be telling the truth. But I will not boast, because I do not want anyone to have a higher opinion of me than he has as a result of what he has seen me do and heard me say. To keep me from being puffed up with pride because of the many wonderful things I saw, I was given a painful physical ailment, which acts as Satan's messenger to beat me and keep me from being proud. Three times I prayed to the Lord about this and asked him to take it away. But his answer was:
The Lord (slowly)	My grace is all you need, for my power is greatest when you are weak.
Paul	I am most happy, then, to be proud of my weaknesses, in order to feel the protection of Christ's power over me. I am content with weaknesses, insults, hardships, persecutions, and difficulties for Christ's sake. For when I am weak, then I am strong.
Cast	[This is] the word of the Lord.
All	**Thanks be to God.**

Cast: **Paul, The Lord.**

GALATIANS

Law or faith
Galatians 3.1–14

Paul   You foolish Galatians! Who put a spell on you? Before your very eyes you had a clear description of the death of Jesus Christ on the cross! Tell me this one thing: did you receive God's Spirit by doing what the Law requires or by hearing the gospel and believing it? How can you be so foolish! You began by God's Spirit; do you now want to finish by your own power? Did all your experience mean nothing at all? Surely it meant something! Does God give you the Spirit and work miracles among you because you do what the Law requires or because you hear the gospel and believe it?

Consider the experience of Abraham; as the scripture says:

Reader   He believed God, and because of his faith God accepted him as righteous.

Paul   You should realize then, that the real descendants of Abraham are the people who have faith. The scripture predicted that God would put the Gentiles right with himself through faith. And so the scripture announced the Good News to Abraham:

Reader   Through you God will bless all mankind.

Paul   Abraham believed and was blessed; so all who believe are blessed as he was. Those who depend on obeying the Law live under a curse. For the scripture says:

Reader   Whoever does not always obey everything that is written in the book of the Law is under God's curse!

Paul   Now, it is clear that no one is put right with God by means of the Law, because the scripture says:

Reader   Only the person who is put right with God through faith shall live.

Paul   But the Law has nothing to do with faith. Instead, as the scripture says:

Reader   Whoever *does* everything the Law requires will live.

Paul   But by becoming a curse for us Christ has redeemed us from the curse that the Law brings; for the scripture says:

Reader   Anyone who is hanged on a tree is under God's curse.

Paul   Christ did this in order that the blessing which God promised to Abraham might be given to the Gentiles by means of Christ Jesus, so that through faith we might receive the Spirit promised by God.

Cast   [This is] the word of the Lord.
All   **Thanks be to God.**

Cast: **Paul, Reader.**

God's law and his promises
From Galatians 3.17–22 [23–29]

Paul The Law cannot break that covenant and cancel God's promise. For if God's gift depends on the Law, then it no longer depends on his promise. However, it was because of his promise that God gave that gift to Abraham.

Questioner What, then, was the purpose of the Law?

Paul It was added in order to show what wrongdoing is, and it was meant to last until the coming of Abraham's descendant, to whom the promise was made. The Law was handed down by angels, with a man acting as a go-between. But a go-between is not needed when only one person is involved; and God is one.

Questioner Does this mean that the Law is against God's promises?

Paul No, not at all! For if mankind had received a law that could bring life, then everyone could be put right with God by obeying it. But the scripture says that the whole world is under the power of sin; and so the gift which is promised on the basis of faith in Jesus Christ is given to those who believe.

[But before the time for faith came, the Law kept us all locked up as prisoners until this coming faith should be revealed. And so the Law was in charge of us until Christ came, in order that we might then be put right with God through faith. Now that the time for faith is here, the Law is no longer in charge of us.

It is through faith that all of you are God's sons in union with Christ Jesus. You were baptized into union with Christ, and now you are clothed, so to speak, with the life of Christ himself. So there is no difference between Jews and Gentiles, between slaves and free men, between men and women; you are all one in union with Christ Jesus. If you belong to Christ, then you are the descendants of Abraham and will receive what God has promised.]

Cast [This is] the word of the Lord.
All **Thanks be to God.**

Cast: **Paul, Questioner.**

The example of Hagar and Sarah
Galatians 4.21–31

Paul Let me ask those of you who want to be subject to the Law: do you not hear what the Law says? It says that Abraham had two sons, one by a slave-woman, the other by a free woman. His son by the slave-woman was born in the usual way, but his son by the free woman was born as a result of God's promise. These things can be understood as a figure: the two women represent two covenants.

→

The one whose children are born in slavery is Hagar, and she represents the covenant made at Mount Sinai. Hagar, who stands for Mount Sinai in Arabia, is a figure of the present city of Jerusalem, in slavery with all its people. But the heavenly Jerusalem is free, and she is our mother. For the scripture says:

Reader   Be happy, you childless woman!
Shout and cry with joy, you who never felt the pains of childbirth!
For the woman who was deserted will have more children
than the woman whose husband never left her.

Paul   Now, you, my brothers, are God's children as a result of his promise, just as Isaac was. At that time the son who was born in the usual way persecuted the one who was born because of God's Spirit; and it is the same now. But what does the scripture say? [It says:]

Reader   Send the slave-woman and her son away; for the son of the slave-woman will not have a part of the father's property along with the son of the free woman.

Paul   So then, my brothers, we are not the children of a slave-woman but of a free woman.

Cast   [This is] the word of the Lord.
All   **Thanks be to God.**

Cast: **Paul, Reader.**

EPHESIANS

Spiritual blessings in Christ
Ephesians 1.2–14

Voices 1 and **2**	May God our Father and the Lord Jesus Christ give you grace and peace.
Voice 1	Let us give thanks to the God and Father of our Lord Jesus Christ! For in our union with Christ he has blessed us by giving us every spiritual blessing in the heavenly world.
Voice 2	Even before the world was made, God had already chosen us to be his through our union with Christ, so that we would be holy and without fault before him.
Voice 1	Because of his love God had already decided that through Jesus Christ he would make us his sons—this was his pleasure and purpose.
Voices 1 and **2**	Let us praise God for his glorious grace.
Voice 2	For the free gift he gave us in his dear Son!
Voice 1	For by the sacrificial death of Christ we are set free, that is, our sins are forgiven.
Voice 2	How great is the grace of God, which he gave to us in such large measure!
Voice 1	In all his wisdom and insight God did what he had purposed, and made known to us the secret plan he had already decided to complete by means of Christ. This plan, which God will complete when the time is right, is to bring all creation together, everything in heaven and on earth, with Christ as head.
Voice 2	All things are done according to God's plan and decision; and God chose us to be his own people in union with Christ because of his own purpose, based on what he had decided from the very beginning.
Voices 1 and **2**	Let us, then, who were the first to hope in Christ, praise God's glory!
Voice 1	And you also became God's people when you heard the true message, the Good News that brought you salvation. You believed in Christ, and God put his stamp of ownership on you by giving you the Holy Spirit he had promised.
Voice 2	The Spirit is the guarantee that we shall receive what God has promised his people, and this assures us that God will give complete freedom to those who are his.
Voices 1 and **2**	Let us praise his glory!
Cast	[This is] the word of the Lord.
All	**Thanks be to God.**

Cast: **Voice 1, Voice 2.**

God's power and the church
Ephesians 1.19–23; 3.20–21

Voice 1 The power working in us is the same as the mighty strength which he used when he raised Christ from death and seated him at his right side in the heavenly world.

Voice 2 Christ rules there above all heavenly rulers, authorities, powers, and lords; he has a title superior to all titles of authority in this world and in the next.

Voice 3 God put all things under Christ's feet and gave him to the church as supreme Lord over all things.

Voice 1 The church is Christ's body, the completion of him who himself completes all things everywhere.

Voice 2 To him who by means of his power working in us is able to do so much more than we can ever ask for, or even think of:

Voice 3 To God be the glory in the church and in Christ Jesus for all time, for ever and ever!

Voices 1–3 Amen.

Cast [This is] the word of the Lord.
All **Thanks be to God.**

Cast: **Voice 1, Voice 2, Voice 3.**

From death to life
Ephesians 2.1–10

Voice 1 In the past you were spiritually dead because of your disobedience and sins. At that time you followed the world's evil way; you obeyed the ruler of the spiritual powers in space, the spirit who now controls the people who disobey God.

Voice 2 Actually all of us were like them and lived according to our natural desires, doing whatever suited the wishes of our own bodies and minds. In our natural condition we, like everyone else, were destined to suffer God's anger. But God's mercy is so abundant, and his love for us is so great, that while we were spiritually dead in our disobedience he brought us to life with Christ.

Voice 1 It is by God's grace that you have been saved.

Voice 2 In our union with Christ Jesus he raised us up with him to rule with him in the heavenly world. He did this to demonstrate for all time to come the extraordinary greatness of his grace in the love he showed us in Christ Jesus.

Voice 1 For it is by God's grace that you have been saved through faith. It is not the result of your own efforts, but God's gift, so that no one can boast about it.

Voice 2	God has made us what we are, and in our union with Christ Jesus he has created us for a life of good deeds, which he has already prepared for us to do.
Cast	[This is] the word of the Lord.
All	**Thanks be to God.**

Cast: **Voice 1** (authoritative), **Voice 2** (grateful).

Gifts and unity in the church
Ephesians 4.1–16

Voice 1	Live a life that measures up to the standard God set when he called you.
Voice 2	Be always humble, gentle, and patient. Show your love by being tolerant with one another.
Voice 3	Do your best to preserve the unity which the Spirit gives by means of the peace that binds you together.
Voice 1	There is one body and one Spirit, just as there is one hope to which God has called you.
Voice 2	There is one Lord, one faith, one baptism.
Voice 3	There is one God and Father of all mankind, who is Lord of all, works through all, and is in all.
Voice 1	Each one of us has received a special gift in proportion to what Christ has given. As the scripture says:
Psalmist	When he went up to the very heights, he took many captives with him; he gave gifts to mankind.
Voice 2	Now, what does 'he went up' mean?
Voice 1	It means that first he came down to the lowest depths of the earth.
Voice 3	So the one who came down is the same one who went up, above and beyond the heavens, to fill the whole universe with his presence.
Voice 1	It was he who 'gave gifts to mankind'; he appointed some to be apostles, others to be prophets, others to be evangelists, others to be pastors and teachers. He did this to prepare all God's people for the work of Christian service, in order to build up the body of Christ.
Voice 2	And so we shall all come together to that oneness in our faith and in our knowledge of the Son of God.
Voice 3	We shall become mature people, reaching to the very height of Christ's full stature. Then we shall no longer be children, carried by the waves and blown about by every shifting wind of the teaching of deceitful men, who lead others into error by the tricks they invent.

Voice 1	Instead, by speaking the truth in a spirit of love, we must grow up in every way to Christ, who is the head.
Voice 2	Under his control all the different parts of the body fit together, and the whole body is held together by every joint with which it is provided.
Voice 3	So when each separate part works as it should, the whole body grows and builds itself up through love.
Cast	[This is] the word of the Lord.
All	**Thanks be to God.**

Cast: **Voice 1, Voice 2, Voice 3, Psalmist** (can be the same as Voice 3).

Christian do's and don'ts (i)
Ephesians 4.22–32

Don't	Get rid of your old self, which made you live as you used to—the old self that was being destroyed by its deceitful desires.
Do	Your hearts and minds must be made completely new, and you must put on the new self, which is created in God's likeness and reveals itself in the true life that is upright and holy.
Don't	No more lying, then!
Do	Everyone must tell the truth to his fellow-believer, because we are all members together in the body of Christ.
Don't	If you become angry, do not let your anger lead you into sin, and do not stay angry all day. Don't give the Devil a chance. The man who used to rob must stop robbing.
Do	He must start working, in order to earn an honest living for himself and to be able to help the poor.
Don't	Do not use harmful words.
Do	Only helpful words, the kind that build up and provide what is needed, so that what you say will do good to those who hear you.
Don't	Do not make God's Holy Spirit sad.
Do	The Spirit is God's mark of ownership on you, a guarantee that the Day will come when God will set you free.
Don't	Get rid of all bitterness, passion, and anger. No more shouting or insults, no more hateful feelings of any sort.
Do	Instead, be kind and tender-hearted to one another, and forgive one another, as God has forgiven you through Christ.
Cast	[This is] the word of the Lord.
All	**Thanks be to God.**

Cast: **Don't** (a negative voice), **Do** (a positive voice).

Christian do's and don'ts (ii)
From Ephesians 5.3–20

Don't   Since you are God's people, it is not right that any matters of sexual immorality or indecency or greed should even be mentioned among you. Nor is it fitting for you to use language which is obscene, profane, or vulgar.

Do   Rather you should give thanks to God.

Don't   You may be sure that no one who is immoral, indecent, or greedy—for greed is a form of idolatry—will ever receive a share in the Kingdom of Christ and of God. (PAUSE)

Do not let anyone deceive you with foolish words; it is because of these very things that God's anger will come upon those who do not obey him. So have nothing at all to do with such people.

Do   You yourselves used to be in the darkness, but since you have become the Lord's people, you are in the light. So you must live like people who belong to the light, for it is the light that brings a rich harvest of every kind of goodness, righteousness, and truth. Try to learn what pleases the Lord.

Don't   Have nothing to do with the worthless things that people do, things that belong to the darkness.

Do   Instead, bring them out to the light. And when all things are brought out to the light, then their true nature is clearly revealed; for anything that is clearly revealed becomes light.

Don't   Don't live like ignorant people, but like wise people.

Do   Make good use of every opportunity you have, because these are evil days.

Don't   Don't be fools, then.

Do   But try to find out what the Lord wants you to do.

Don't   Do not get drunk with wine, which will only ruin you.

Do   Instead, be filled with the Spirit. (PAUSE) Speak to one another with the words of psalms, hymns, and sacred songs; sing hymns and psalms to the Lord with praise in your hearts. In the name of our Lord Jesus Christ, always give thanks for everything to God the Father.

Cast   [This is] the word of the Lord.
All   **Thanks be to God.**

Cast: **Don't** (a negative voice), **Do** (a positive voice).

The Christian family
From Ephesians 5.1—6.12

Minister /Leader

Be imitators of God, therefore, as dearly loved children and live a life of love, just as Christ loved us and gave himself up for us as a fragrant offering and sacrifice to God. Speak to one another with psalms, hymns and spiritual songs. Sing and make music in your heart to the Lord, always giving thanks to God the Father for everything, in the name of our Lord Jesus Christ. Submit to one another out of reverence for Christ.

Wife

Wives, submit to your husbands as to the Lord. For the husband is the head of the wife as Christ is the head of the church, his body, of which he is the Saviour. Now as the church submits to Christ, so also wives should submit to their husbands in everything.

Husband

Husbands, love your wives, just as Christ loved the church and gave himself up for her to make her holy, cleansing her by the washing with water through the word, and to present her to himself as a radiant church, without stain or wrinkle or any other blemish, but holy and blameless. In this same way, husbands ought to love their wives as their own bodies. He who loves his wife loves himself. After all, no-one ever hated his own body, but he feeds and cares for it, just as Christ does the church.

Minister /Leader

For this reason a man will leave his father and mother and be united to his wife, and the two will become one flesh. This is a profound mystery—but I am talking about Christ and the church. However, each one of you also must love his wife as he loves himself, and the wife must respect her husband.

Child

Children, obey your parents in the Lord, for this is right. 'Honour your father and mother'—which is the first commandment with a promise—'that it may go well with you and that you may enjoy long life on the earth.'

Father

Fathers, do not exasperate your children; instead, bring them up in the training and instruction of the Lord.

Minister /Leader

Finally, be strong in the Lord and in his mighty power. Put on the full armour of God so that you can take your stand against the Devil's schemes. For our struggle is not against flesh and blood, but against the rulers, against the authorities, against the powers of this dark world and against the spiritual forces of evil in the heavenly realms.

Cast [This is] the word of the Lord.
All **Thanks be to God.**

Cast: **Minister/Leader, Wife, Husband, Child, Father.**

The whole armour of God
Ephesians 6.10–18

Voice 1   Build up your strength in union with the Lord and by means of his mighty power.

Voice 2   Put on all the armour that God gives you, so that you will be able to stand up against the Devil's evil tricks.

Voice 1   For we are not fighting against human beings but against the wicked spiritual forces in the heavenly world, the rulers, authorities, and cosmic powers of this dark age.

Voice 2   So put on God's armour now!

Voice 1   Then when the evil day comes, you will be able to resist the enemy's attacks; and after fighting to the end, you will still hold your ground.

Voice 2   So stand ready—

Voice 3   With truth as a belt tight round your waist.

Voice 2   With righteousness as your breastplate.

Voice 3   And as your shoes, the readiness to announce the Good News of peace.

Voice 2   At all times carry faith as a shield; for with it you will be able to put out all the burning arrows shot by the Evil One.

Voice 3   And accept salvation as a helmet—

Voice 2   And the word of God as the sword which the Spirit gives you.

Voice 1   Do all this in prayer, asking for God's help. Pray on every occasion, as the Spirit leads. For this reason keep alert and never give up.

Cast   [This is] the word of the Lord.
All   **Thanks be to God.**

Cast: **Voice 1, Voice 2** (urgent), **Voice 3** (can be the same as Voice 1).

PHILIPPIANS

Christ's humility and greatness
Philippians 2.1–11

Paul   Your life in Christ makes you strong, and his love comforts you. You have fellowship with the Spirit, and you have kindness and compassion for one another. I urge you, then, to make me completely happy by having the same thoughts, sharing the same love, and being one in soul and mind. Don't do anything from selfish ambition or from a cheap desire to boast, but be humble towards one another, always considering others better than yourselves. And look out for one another's interests, not just for your own. The attitude you should have is the one that Christ Jesus had:

Singer 1   He always had the nature of God.

Singer 2   But he did not think that by force he should try to become equal with God. Instead of this, of his own free will he gave up all he had, and took the nature of a servant.

Singer 1   He became like man and appeared in human likeness.

Singer 2   He was humble and walked the path of obedience all the way to death—his death on the cross.

Singer 3   For this reason God raised him to the highest place above.

Singer 4   And gave him the name that is greater than any other name.

Singer 3   And so, in honour of the name of Jesus all beings in heaven, on earth, and in the world below will fall on their knees.

Singer 4   And all will openly proclaim:

Singers 1–4   Jesus Christ is Lord—

Singer 4   To the glory of God the Father.

Cast   [This is] the word of the Lord.
All   **Thanks be to God.**

Cast: **Paul, Singer 1, Singer 2, Singer 3, Singer 4.** (See also Appendix: Christmas Readings, page 411.)

COLOSSIANS

The supremacy of Christ
Colossians 1.15–20

Voice 1 Christ is the image of the invisible God, the firstborn over all creation.

Voice 2 By him all things were created—

Voice 3 Things in heaven and on earth, visible and invisible, whether thrones or powers or rulers or authorities.

Voice 1 All things were created by him and for him.

Voice 2 He is before all things, and in him all things hold together.

Voice 3 And he is the head of the body, the church.

Voice 1 He is the beginning and the firstborn from among the dead, so that in everything he might have the supremacy.

Voice 2 For God was pleased to have all his fulness dwell in him, and through him to reconcile to himself all things.

Voice 3 Whether things on earth or things in heaven—

Voice 1 By making peace through his blood, shed on the cross.

Cast [This is] the word of the Lord.
All **Thanks be to God.**

Cast: **Voice 1, Voice 2, Voice 3.** (See also Appendix: Christmas Readings, page 411.)

God's chosen people
Colossians 3.12–17 [3.18—4.1]

Voice 1 As God's chosen people, holy and dearly loved, clothe yourselves with compassion, kindness, humility, gentleness and patience.

Voice 2 Bear with each other and forgive whatever grievances you may have against one another—

Voice 1 Forgive as the Lord forgave you.

Voice 2 And over all these virtues put on love, which binds them all together in perfect unity.

Voice 1 Let the peace of Christ rule in your hearts, since as members of one body you were called to peace.

Voices 1 and **2**
(slowly) And be thankful. (PAUSE)

Voice 1 Let the word of Christ dwell in you richly as you teach and admonish one another with all wisdom, and as you sing psalms, hymns and spiritual songs with gratitude in your hearts to God.

Voice 2	And whatever you do, whether in word or deed, do it all in the name of the Lord Jesus, giving thanks to God the Father through him.
[Voice 3	Wives, submit to your husbands, as is fitting in the Lord.
Voice 1	Husbands, love your wives and do not be harsh with them.
Voice 2	Children, obey your parents in everything, for this pleases the Lord.
Voice 3	Fathers, do not embitter your children, or they will become discouraged.
Voice 1	Slaves, obey your earthly masters in everything; and do it, not only when their eye is on you and to win their favour, but with sincerity of heart and reverence for the Lord.
Voice 2	Whatever you do, work at it with all your heart, as working for the Lord, not for men, since you know that you will receive an inheritance from the Lord as a reward. It is the Lord Christ you are serving.
Voice 1	Anyone who does wrong will be repaid for his wrong, and there is no favouritism.
Voice 3	Masters, provide your slaves with what is right and fair, because you know that you also have a Master in heaven.]
Cast	[This is] the word of the Lord.
All	**Thanks be to God.**

Cast: **Voice 1, Voice 2, [Voice 3** (preferably female)].

1 THESSALONIANS

The Lord's coming
1 Thessalonians 4.13–18

Voice 1   We want you to know the truth about those who have died, so that you will not be sad, as are those who have no hope.

Voice 2   We believe that Jesus died and rose again, and so we believe that God will take back with Jesus those who have died believing in him.

Voice 1   What we are teaching you now is the Lord's teaching: we who are alive on the day the Lord comes will not go ahead of those who have died.

Voice 1   There will be the shout of command, the archangel's voice, the sound of God's trumpet, and the Lord himself will come down from heaven.

Voice 1   Those who have died believing in Christ will rise to life first.

Voice 2   Then we who are living at that time will be gathered up along with them in the clouds to meet the Lord in the air.

Voice 1   And so we will always be with the Lord. So then—

Voices 1 and 2   Encourage one another with these words.

Cast   [This is] the word of the Lord.
All   **Thanks be to God.**

Cast: **Voice 1, Voice 2.**

Instructions to the church
From 1 Thessalonians 5.12–28

Voice 1   [Now we ask you . . . to] respect those who work hard among you, who are over you in the Lord and who admonish you.

Voice 2   Hold them in the highest regard in love because of their work.

Voice 3   Live in peace with each other.

Voice 1   And we urge you . . .

Voice 2   Warn those who are idle.

Voice 3   Encourage the timid.

Voice 1   Help the weak.

Voice 2   Be patient with everyone.

Voice 3   Make sure that nobody pays back wrong for wrong, but always try to be kind to each other and to everyone else.

Voice 1	Be joyful always.
Voice 2	Pray continually; give thanks in all circumstances—
Voice 3	For this is God's will for you in Christ Jesus.
Voice 1	Do not put out the Spirit's fire; do not treat prophecies with contempt.
Voice 2	Test everything.
Voice 3	Hold on to the good.
Voice 1	Avoid every kind of evil.
Voice 2	May God himself, the God of peace, sanctify you through and through.
Voice 3	May your whole spirit, soul and body be kept blameless at the coming of our Lord Jesus Christ.
Voice 1	The one who calls you is faithful and he will do it.
Voices 1–3	The grace of our Lord Jesus Christ be with you.
Cast	[This is] the word of the Lord.
All	**Thanks be to God.**

Cast: **Voice 1, Voice 2, Voice 3.**

348

2 THESSALONIANS

Blessings

2 Thessalonians 1.2,11; 2.16–17; 3.5,16,18

Voice 1   May God our Father and the Lord Jesus Christ give you grace and peace.

Voice 2   May he fulfil by his power all your desire for goodness, and complete your work of faith.

Voice 3   May our Lord Jesus himself and God our Father, who loved us and in his grace gave us unfailing courage and a firm hope, encourage you and strengthen you to always do and say what is good.

Voice 2   May the Lord lead you into a greater understanding of God's love and the endurance that is given by Christ.

Voice 1   May the Lord himself, who is our source of peace, give you peace at all times and in every way.

Voices 1–3 May the grace of our Lord Jesus Christ be with you all.

Cast   [This is] the word of the Lord.
All   **Thanks be to God.**

Cast: **Voice 1, Voice 2, Voice 3.**

349

1 TIMOTHY

Leaders in the Church
1 Timothy 3.1–13

Voice 1	This is a true saying:
Voice 3	If a man is eager to be a church leader, he desires an excellent work.
Voice 1	A church leader must be without fault.
Voice 2	He must have only one wife, be sober, self-controlled, and orderly.
Voice 1	He must welcome strangers in his home.
Voice 2	He must be able to teach.
Voice 1	He must not be a drunkard or a violent man, but gentle and peaceful.
Voice 2	He must not love money.
Voice 1	He must be able to manage his own family well and make his children obey him with all respect.
Voice 3	For if a man does not know how to manage his own family, how can he take care of the church of God?
Voice 1	He must be mature in the faith, so that he will not swell up with pride and be condemned, as the Devil was.
Voice 2	He should be a man who is respected by the people outside the church, so that he will not be disgraced and fall into the Devil's trap.
Voice 1	Church helpers must also have a good character and be sincere.
Voice 2	They must not drink too much wine or be greedy for money.
Voice 1	They should hold to the revealed truth of the faith with a clear conscience.
Voice 2	They should be tested first, and then, if they pass the test, they are to serve.
Voice 3	Their wives also must be of good character and must not gossip; they must be sober and honest in everything.
Voice 1	A church helper must have only one wife, and be able to manage his children and family well.
Voice 2	Those helpers who do their work well win for themselves a good standing and are able to speak boldly about their faith in Christ Jesus.
Cast	[This is] the word of the Lord.
All	**Thanks be to God.**

Cast: **Voice 1, Voice 2, Voice 3.**

The great secret
From 1 Timothy 3.14–16

Paul As I write this letter to you, I hope to come and see you soon. But if I am delayed, this letter will let you know how we should conduct ourselves in God's household, which is the church of the living God, the pillar and support of the truth. No one can deny how great is the secret of our religion:

Voice 1 He appeared in human form.

Voice 2 He was shown to be right by the Spirit.

Voice 3 He was seen by angels.

Voice 1 He was preached among the nations.

Voice 2 He was believed in throughout the world.

Voice 3 He was taken up to heaven.

Cast [This is] the word of the Lord.
All **Thanks be to God.**

Cast: **Paul, Voice 1, Voice 2, Voice 3.**

A good servant of Christ Jesus
From 1 Timothy 4.6—5.21

Voice 1 Feed yourself spiritually on the words of faith and of the true teaching which you have followed. But keep away from those godless legends, which are not worth telling.

Voice 2 Keep yourself in training for a godly life. Physical exercise has some value, but spiritual exercise is valuable in every way, because it promises life both for the present and for the future. We struggle and work hard, because we have placed our hope in the living God, who is the Saviour of all and especially of those who believe.

Voice 3 Do not let anyone look down on you because you are young, but be an example for the believers in your speech, your conduct, your love, faith, and purity.

Voice 1 Give your time and effort to the public reading of the Scriptures and to preaching and teaching. Do not neglect the spiritual gift that is in you, which was given to you when the prophets spoke and the elders laid their hands on you. Practise these things and devote yourself to them, in order that your progress may be seen by all. Watch yourself and watch your teaching. Keep on doing these things, because if you do, you will save both yourself and those who hear you.

Voice 2 Do not rebuke an older man, but appeal to him as if he were your father. Treat the younger men as your brothers, the older women as mothers, and the younger women as sisters, with all purity.

Voice 3	Show respect for widows who really are all alone. Do not add any widow to the list of widows unless she is over sixty years of age. In addition, she must have been married only once and have a reputation for good deeds: a woman who brought up her children well, received strangers in her home, performed humble duties for fellow-Christians, helped people in trouble, and devoted herself to doing good.
Voice 1	Do not listen to an accusation against an elder unless it is brought by two or more witnesses.
Voice 2	Rebuke publicly all those who commit sins, so that the rest may be afraid.
Voice 3	In the presence of God and of Christ Jesus and of the holy angels I solemnly call upon you to obey these instructions without showing any prejudice or favour to anyone in anything you do.
Cast	[This is] the word of the Lord.
All	**Thanks be to God.**

Cast: **Voice 1, Voice 2, Voice 3.**

2 TIMOTHY

A loyal soldier of Christ Jesus
From 2 Timothy 1.2—2.13

Voices 1–3   May God the Father and Christ Jesus our Lord give you grace, mercy, and peace.

Paul   Hold firmly to the true words that I taught you, as the example for you to follow, and remain in the faith and love that are ours in union with Christ Jesus. Through the power of the Holy Spirit, who lives in us, keep the good things that have been entrusted to you.

Be strong through the grace that is ours in union with Christ Jesus. Take your part in suffering, as a loyal soldier of Christ Jesus.

Voice 1   A soldier on active service wants to please his commanding officer and so does not get mixed up in the affairs of civilian life.

Voice 2   An athlete who runs in a race cannot win the prize unless he obeys the rules.

Paul   Because I preach the Good News, I suffer and I am even chained like a criminal. But the word of God is not in chains, and so I endure everything for the sake of God's chosen people, in order that they too may obtain the salvation that comes through Christ Jesus and brings eternal glory. This is a true saying:

Voice 1   If we have died with him—
We shall also live with him.

Voice 1   If we continue to endure—

Voices 2 and 3   We shall also rule with him.

Voice 1   If we deny him—

Voices 2 and 3   He also will deny us.

Voice 1   If we are not faithful—

Voices 2 and 3   He remains faithful . . .

Voice 3   . . . because he cannot be false to himself.

Cast   [This is] the word of the Lord.
All   **Thanks be to God.**

Cast: **Voice 1, Voice 2, Voice 3, Paul** (can be the same as Voice 3).

TITUS

The grace of Christ
From Titus 2.11—3.7

Voice 1   The grace of God that brings salvation has appeared to all. It teaches us to say:

Voices 1–3   No!

Voice 1   . . . to ungodliness and worldly passions, and to live self-controlled, upright and godly lives in this present age, while we wait for the blessed hope—

Voice 2   The glorious appearing of our great God and Saviour, Jesus Christ, who gave himself for us to redeem us from all wickedness—

Voice 3   And to purify for himself a people that are his very own, eager to do what is good.

Voice 1   At one time we too were foolish . . .

Voice 2   Disobedient . . .

Voice 3   Deceived and enslaved by all kinds of passions and pleasures.

Voice 1   We lived in malice and envy, being hated and hating one another.

Voice 2   But when the kindness and love of God our Saviour appeared, he saved us—

Voice 3   Not because of righteous things we had done, but because of his mercy.

Voice 2   He saved us through the washing of rebirth and renewal by the Holy Spirit, whom he poured out on us generously through Jesus Christ our Saviour.

Voice 1   So that, having been justified by his grace, we might become heirs having the hope of eternal life.

Cast   [This is] the word of the Lord.
All   **Thanks be to God.**

Cast: **Voice 1, Voice 2, Voice 3.**

PHILEMON

Thanksgiving and prayer
Philemon 3–7, 25

Voices 1–3	Grace to you and peace from God our Father and the Lord Jesus Christ.
Voice 1	I always thank my God as I remember you in my prayers, because I hear about your faith in the Lord Jesus and your love for all the saints.
Voice 2	I pray that you may be active in sharing your faith, so that you will have a full understanding of every good thing we have in Christ.
Voice 3	Your love has given me great joy and encouragement, because you, brother, have refreshed the hearts of the saints.
Voices 1–3	May the grace of the Lord Jesus Christ be with your spirit.
Cast	[This is] the word of the Lord.
All	**Thanks be to God.**

Cast: **Voice 1, Voice 2, Voice 3.**

HEBREWS

God's word through his Son
Hebrews 1.1–14

Narrator   In the past, God spoke to our ancestors many times and in many ways through the prophets, but in these last days he has spoken to us through his Son. He is the one through whom God created the universe, the one whom God has chosen to possess all things at the end. He reflects the brightness of God's glory and is the exact likeness of God's own being, sustaining the universe with his powerful word. After achieving forgiveness for the sins of mankind, he sat down in heaven at the right-hand side of God, the Supreme Power.

The Son was made greater than the angels, just as the name that God gave him is greater than theirs. For God never said to any of his *angels*:

God   You are my Son;
today I have become your Father.

Narrator   Nor did God say about any *angel*:

God   I will be his Father,
and he will be my Son.

Narrator   But when God was about to send his first-born *Son* into the world, he said:

God   All God's angels must worship him.

Narrator   But about the *angels* God said:

God   God makes his angels winds,
and his servants flames of fire.

Narrator   About the *Son*, however, God said:

God   Your kingdom, O God, will last for ever and ever!
You rule over your people with justice.
You love what is right and hate what is wrong.
That is why God, your God, has chosen you
and has given you the joy of an honour far greater
than he gave to your companions.

Narrator   He also said:

God   You, Lord, in the beginning created the earth,
and with your own hands you made the heavens.
They will disappear, but you will remain;
they will all wear out like clothes.
You will fold them up like a coat,
and they will be changed like clothes.
But you are always the same,
and your life never ends.

Narrator   God never said to any of his *angels*:

God	Sit here on my right until I put your enemies as a footstool under your feet.
Narrator	What *are* the angels, then? They are spirits who serve God, and are sent by him to help those who are to receive salvation.
Cast	[This is] the word of the Lord.
All	**Thanks be to God.**

Cast: **Narrator, God.** (See also Appendix: Christmas Readings, page 411.)

The one who leads us to salvation
Hebrews 2.5–18 (NIV)

Narrator	It is not to angels that God has subjected the world to come, about which we are speaking. But there is a place where someone has testified:
Psalmist	What is man that you are mindful of him, the son of man that you care for him? You made him a little lower than the angels; you crowned him with glory and honour and put everything under his feet.
Narrator	In putting everything under him, God left nothing that is not subject to him. Yet at present we do not see everything subject to him. But we see Jesus, who was made a little lower than the angels, now crowned with glory and honour because he suffered death, so that by the grace of God he might taste death for everyone.

In bringing many sons to glory, it was fitting that God, for whom and through whom everything exists, should make the author of their salvation perfect through suffering. Both the one who makes men holy and those who are made holy are of the same family. So Jesus is not ashamed to call them brothers. [He says:] |
Psalmist	I will declare your name to my brothers; in the presence of the congregation I will sing your praises.
Narrator	And again:
Isaiah	I will put my trust in him.
Narrator	And again he says:
Isaiah	Here am I, and the children God has given me.
Narrator	Since the children have flesh and blood, he too shared in their humanity so that by his death he might destroy him who holds the power of death—that is, the Devil—and free those who all their lives were held in slavery by their fear of death. For surely it is not angels he helps, but Abraham's descendants. For this reason he had to be made like his brothers in every way, in order that he might become a merciful and faithful high priest in service to God, and that he might make atonement for the sins of the people. Because he himself suffered when he was tempted, he is able to help those who are being tempted.
Cast	[This is] the word of the Lord.
All	**Thanks be to God.**

Cast: **Narrator, Psalmist, Isaiah.**

The one who leads us to salvation
Hebrews 2.5–18 (GNB)

Narrator God has not placed the angels as rulers over the new world to come—the world of which we speak. Instead, as it is said somewhere in the Scriptures:

Psalmist What is man, O God, that you should think of him;
mere man, that you should care for him?
You made him for a little while lower than the angels;
you crowned him with glory and honour,
and made him ruler over all things.

Narrator It says that God made man 'ruler over all things'; this clearly includes everything. We do not, however, see man ruling over all things now. But we do see Jesus, who for a little while was made lower than the angels, so that through God's grace he should die for everyone. We see him now crowned with glory and honour because of the death he suffered. It was only right that God, who creates and preserves all things, should make Jesus perfect through suffering, in order to bring many sons to share his glory. For Jesus is the one who leads them to salvation. He purifies people from their sins, and both he and those who are made pure all have the same Father. That is why Jesus is not ashamed to call them his brothers. [He says to God:]

Psalmist I will tell my brothers what you have done;
I will praise you in their meeting.

Narrator He also says:

Isaiah I will put my trust in God.

Narrator And he also says:

Isaiah Here I am with the children that God has given me.

Narrator Since the children, as he calls them, are people of flesh and blood, Jesus himself became like them and shared their human nature. He did this so that through his death he might destroy the Devil, who has the power over death, and in this way set free those who were slaves all their lives because of their fear of death. For it is clear that it is not the angels that he helps. Instead, as the scripture says:

Scripture He helps the descendants of Abraham.

Narrator This means that he had to become like his brothers in every way, in order to be their faithful and merciful high priest in his service to God, so that the people's sins would be forgiven. And now he can help those who are tempted, because he himself was tempted and suffered.

Cast [This is] the word of the Lord.
All **Thanks be to God.**

Cast: **Narrator, Psalmist, Isaiah, Scripture** (can be the same as Psalmist).

A rest for God's people
Hebrews 3.7—4.2, 12–13

Narrator As the Holy Spirit says:

Psalmist If you hear God's voice *today*,
do not be stubborn,
as your ancestors were when they rebelled against God,
as they were that day in the desert when they put him to the test.
There they put me to the test and tried me, says God,
although they had seen what I did for forty years.
And so I was angry with those people and said,
'They are always disloyal
and refuse to obey my commands.'
I was angry and made a solemn promise:
'They will never enter the land
where I would have given them rest!'

Narrator My fellow-believers, be careful that no one among you has a heart so evil and unbelieving that he will turn away from the living God. Instead, in order that none of you be deceived by sin and become stubborn, you must help one another every day, as long as the word 'Today' in the scripture applies to us. For we are all partners with Christ if we hold firmly to the end the confidence we had at the beginning.

This is what the scripture says:

Psalmist If you hear God's voice *today*,
do not be stubborn, as your ancestors were
when they rebelled against God.

Narrator Who were the people who heard God's voice and rebelled against him? All those who were led out of Egypt by Moses. With whom was God angry for forty years? With the people who sinned, who fell down dead in the desert. When God made his solemn promise:

Psalmist They will never enter the land where I would have given them rest.

Narrator Of whom was he speaking? Of those who rebelled. We see, then, that they were not able to enter the land, because they did not believe.

Now, God has offered us the promise that we may receive that rest he spoke about. Let us take care, then, that none of you will be found to have failed to receive that promised rest. For we have heard the Good News, just as they did. They heard the message, but it did them no good, because when they heard it, they did not accept it with faith.

The word of God is alive and active, sharper than any double-edged sword. It cuts all the way through, to where soul and spirit

→

meet, to where joints and marrow come together. It judges the desires and thoughts of man's heart. There is nothing that can be hidden from God; everything in all creation is exposed and lies open before his eyes. And it is to him that we must all give an account of ourselves.

Cast	[This is] the word of the Lord.
All	**Thanks be to God.**

Cast: **Narrator, Psalmist.**

Jesus the great High Priest
Hebrews 4.14—5.10

Voice 1	Let us, then, hold firmly to the faith we profess. For we have a great High Priest who has gone into the very presence of God—Jesus, the Son of God. Our High Priest is not one who cannot feel sympathy for our weaknesses.
Voice 2	On the contrary, we have a High Priest who was tempted in every way that we are, but did not sin.
Voice 1	Let us have confidence, then, and approach God's throne, where there is grace.
Voice 2	There we will receive mercy and find grace to help us just when we need it.
Voice 1	Every high priest is chosen from his fellow-men and appointed to serve God on their behalf, to offer sacrifices and offerings for sins. Since he himself is weak in many ways, he is able to be gentle with those who are ignorant and make mistakes. And because he is himself weak, he must offer sacrifices not only for the sins of the people but also for his own sins.
Voice 2	No one chooses for himself the honour of being a high priest. It is only by God's call that a man is made a high priest—just as Aaron was.
Voice 1	In the same way, Christ did not take upon himself the honour of being a high priest. Instead, God said to him:
God	You are my Son; today I have become your Father.
Voice 2	He also said in another place:
God	You will be a priest for ever, in the priestly order of Melchizedek.
Voice 1	In his life on earth Jesus made his prayers and requests with loud cries and tears to God, who could save him from death. Because he was humble and devoted, God heard him.
Voice 2	But even though he was God's Son, he learnt through his sufferings to be obedient.

Voice 1	When he was made perfect, he became the source of eternal salvation for all those who obey him.
Voice 2	And God declared him to be high priest, in the priestly order of Melchizedek.
Cast	[This is] the word of the Lord.
All	**Thanks be to God.**

Cast: **Voice 1, Voice 2, God.**

God's sure promise
Hebrews 6.13–19

Narrator 1	When God made his promise to Abraham, he made a vow to do what he had promised. Since there was no one greater than himself, he used his own name when he made his vow. He said:
God	I promise you that I will bless you and give you many descendants. (PAUSE)
Narrator 2	Abraham was patient, and so he received what God had promised.
Narrator 1	When a person makes a vow, he uses the name of someone greater than himself, and the vow settles all arguments. To those who were to receive what he promised, God wanted to make it very clear that he would never change his purpose; so he added his vow to the promise. (PAUSE)
Narrator 2	There are these two things, then, that cannot change and about which God cannot lie. So we who have found safety with him are greatly encouraged to hold firmly to the hope placed before us.
Narrator 1	We have this hope as an anchor for our lives.
Cast	[This is] the word of the Lord.
All	**Thanks be to God.**

Cast: **Narrator 1, God, Narrator 2.**

Another priest, like Melchizedek
Hebrews 7.15–28

Narrator	A different priest has appeared, who is like Melchizedek. He was made a priest, not by human rules and regulations, but through the power of a life which has no end. For the scripture says:
Psalmist	You will be a priest for ever, in the priestly order of Melchizedek.
Narrator	The old rule, then, is set aside, because it was weak and useless. For the Law of Moses could not make anything perfect. And now a better hope has been provided through which we come near to God. In addition, there is also God's vow. There was no such vow when the others were made priests. But Jesus became a priest by means of a vow when God said to him:

Psalmist The Lord has made a solemn promise
and will not take it back:
'You will be a priest for ever.'

Narrator This difference, then, also makes Jesus the guarantee of a better covenant. There is another difference: there were many of those other priests, because they died and could not continue their work. But Jesus lives on for ever, and his work as priest does not pass on to someone else. And so he is able, now and always, to save those who come to God through him, because he lives for ever to plead with God for them. Jesus, then, is the High Priest that meets our needs. He is holy; he has no fault or sin in him; he has been set apart from sinners and raised above the heavens. He is not like other high priests; he does not need to offer sacrifices every day for his own sins first and then for the sins of the people. He offered one sacrifice, once and for all, when he offered himself. The Law of Moses appoints men who are imperfect to be high priests; but God's promise made with the vow, which came later than the Law, appoints the Son, who has been made perfect for ever.

Cast [This is] the word of the Lord.
All **Thanks be to God.**

Cast: **Narrator, Psalmist.**

Jesus our High Priest
Hebrews 8.3–13

Narrator Every High Priest is appointed to present offerings and animal sacrifices to God, and so our High Priest must also have something to offer. If he were on earth, he would not be a priest at all, since there are priests who offer the gifts required by the Jewish Law. The work they do as priests is really only a copy and a shadow of what is in heaven. It is the same as it was with Moses. When he was about to build the Covenant Tent, God said to him:

Voice of God Be sure to make everything according to the pattern you were shown on the mountain.

Narrator But now, Jesus has been given priestly work which is superior to theirs, just as the covenant which he arranged between God and his people is a better one, because it is based on promises of better things.

If there had been nothing wrong with the first covenant, there would have been no need for a second one. But God finds fault with his people when he says:

Jeremiah The days are coming, says the Lord,
when I will draw up a new covenant with the people of Israel
and with the people of Judah.

362

It will not be like the covenant that I made with their ancestors
on the day I took them by the hand and led them out of Egypt.
They were not faithful to the covenant I made with them,
and so I paid no attention to them.

Now, this is the covenant that I will make with the people of Israel
in the days to come, says the Lord:
I will put my laws in their minds
and write them on their hearts.
I will be their God,
and they will be my people.
None of them will have to teach his fellow-citizen
or say to his fellow-countryman,
'Know the Lord.'
For they will all know me,
from the least to the greatest.
I will forgive their sins
and will no longer remember their wrongs.

Narrator   By speaking of a new covenant, God has made the first one old;
and anything that becomes old and worn out will soon disappear.

Cast   [This is] the word of the Lord.
All   **Thanks be to God.**

Cast: **Narrator, Voice of God, Jeremiah.**

Christ's sacrifice takes away sins
Hebrews 10.1–18

Narrator   The Jewish Law is not a full and faithful model of the real things;
it is only a faint outline of the good things to come. The same
sacrifices are offered for ever, year after year. How can the Law,
then, by means of these sacrifices make perfect the people who
come to God? If the people worshipping God had really been
purified from their sins, they would not feel guilty of sin any
more, and all sacrifices would stop. As it is, however, the sacrifices
serve year after year to remind people of their sins. For the blood
of bulls and goats can never take away sins.

For this reason, when Christ was about to come into the world, he
said to God:

Christ   You do not want sacrifices and offerings,
but you have prepared a body for me.
You are not pleased with animals burnt whole on the altar
or with sacrifices to take away sins.
Then I said, 'Here I am,
to do your will, O God,
just as it is written of me in the book of the Law.'

Narrator   First he said:

Christ	You neither want nor are you pleased with sacrifices and offerings or with animals burnt on the altar and the sacrifices to take away sins.
Narrator	He said this even though all these sacrifices are offered according to the Law. Then he said:
Christ	Here I am, O God, to do your will.
Narrator	So God does away with all the old sacrifices and puts the sacrifice of Christ in their place. Because Jesus Christ did what God wanted him to do, we are all purified from sin by the offering that he made of his own body once and for all.
	Every Jewish priest performs his services every day and offers the same sacrifices many times; but these sacrifices can never take away sins. Christ, however, offered one sacrifice for sins, an offering that is effective for ever, and then he sat down at the right-hand side of God. There he now waits until God puts his enemies as a footstool under his feet. With one sacrifice, then, he has made perfect for ever those who are purified from sin.
	And the Holy Spirit also gives us his witness. First he says:
Holy Spirit	This is the covenant that I will make with them in the days to come, says the Lord, 'I will put my laws in their hearts and write them on their minds.'
Narrator	And then he says:
Holy Spirit	I will not remember their sins and evil deeds any longer.
Narrator	So when these have been forgiven, an offering to take away sins is no longer needed.
Cast All	[This is] the word of the Lord. **Thanks be to God.**

Cast: **Narrator, Christ, Holy Spirit.**

Let us come near to God
From Hebrews 10.19–39

Voice 1	We have, then, my brothers, complete freedom to go into the Most Holy Place by means of the death of Jesus. He opened for us a new way, a living way, through the curtain—that is, through his own body.
Voice 2	We have a great priest in charge of the house of God. So let us come near to God with a sincere heart and a sure faith, with hearts that have been purified from a guilty conscience and with bodies washed with clean water.
Voice 1	Let us hold on firmly to the hope we profess, because we can trust God to keep his promise.
Voice 2	Let us be concerned for one another, to help one another to show love and to do good.

Voice 1	Let us not give up the habit of meeting together, as some are doing. Instead, let us encourage one another all the more, since you see that the Day of the Lord is coming nearer.
	[For there is no longer any sacrifice that will take away sins if we purposely go on sinning after the truth has been made known to us.
Voice 2	Instead, all that is left is to wait in fear for the coming Judgement and the fierce fire which will destroy those who oppose God! For we know who said:
Voice 3	I will take revenge, I will repay.
Voice 2	And who also said:
Voice 3	The Lord will judge his people.
Voice 1	It is a terrifying thing to fall into the hands of the living God!]
Voice 2	Remember how it was with you in the past. In those days, after God's light had shone on you, you suffered many things, yet were not defeated by the struggle. Do not lose your courage, then, because it brings with it a great reward. You need to be patient, in order to do the will of God and receive what he promises. For, as the scripture says:
Voice 3	Just a little while longer, and he who is coming will come; he will not delay. My righteous people, however, will believe and live; but if any of them turns back, I will not be pleased with him.
Voice 1	We are not people who turn back and are lost. Instead, we have faith and are saved.
Cast	[This is] the word of the Lord.
All	**Thanks be to God.**

Cast: **Voice 1, Voice 2, Voice 3.**

Faith (i)
Hebrews 11.1–16

Voice 1	To have faith is to be sure of the things we hope for, to be certain of the things we cannot see.
Voice 2	It was by their faith that people of ancient times won God's approval.
Voice 3	It is by faith that we understand that the universe was created by God's word, so that what can be seen was made out of what cannot be seen.
Voice 1	It was faith that made Abel offer to God a better sacrifice than Cain's. Through his faith he won God's approval as a righteous man, because God himself approved of his gifts. By means of his faith Abel still speaks, even though he is dead.

Voice 2	It was faith that kept Enoch from dying. Instead, he was taken up to God, and nobody could find him, because God had taken him up. The scripture says that before Enoch was taken up, he had pleased God. No one can please God without faith, for whoever comes to God must have faith that God exists and rewards those who seek him.
Voice 3	It was faith that made Noah hear God's warnings about things in the future that he could not see. He obeyed God and built a boat in which he and his family were saved. As a result, the world was condemned, and Noah received from God the righteousness that comes by faith.
Voice 1	It was faith that made Abraham obey when God called him to go out to a country which God had promised to give him. He left his own country without knowing where he was going.
Voice 2	By faith he lived as a foreigner in the country that God had promised him. He lived in tents, as did Isaac and Jacob, who received the same promise from God. For Abraham was waiting for the city which God has designed and built, the city with permanent foundations.
Voice 3	It was faith that made Abraham able to become a father, even though he was too old and Sarah herself could not have children. He trusted God to keep his promise. Though Abraham was practically dead, from this one man came as many descendants as there are stars in the sky, as many as the numberless grains of sand on the sea-shore.
Voice 1	It was in faith that all these persons died. They did not receive the things God had promised, but from a long way off they saw them and welcomed them, and admitted openly that they were foreigners and refugees on earth. Those who say such things make it clear that they are looking for a country of their own. They did not keep thinking about the country they had left; if they had, they would have had the chance to return. Instead, it was a better country they longed for, the heavenly country. And so God is not ashamed for them to call him their God, because he has prepared a city for them.
Cast	[This is] the word of the Lord.
All	**Thanks be to God.**

Cast: **Voice 1, Voice 2, Voice 3.**

Faith (ii)
Hebrews 11.17–33

Voice 1	It was faith that made Abraham offer his son Isaac as a sacrifice when God put Abraham to the test. Abraham was the one to whom God had made the promise, yet he was ready to offer his only son as a sacrifice. God had said to him, 'It is through Isaac that you will have the descendants I promised.' Abraham reckoned that God was able to raise Isaac from death—and, so to speak, Abraham did receive Isaac back from death.

Voice 2	It was faith that made Isaac promise blessings for the future to Jacob and Esau. It was faith that made Jacob bless each of the sons of Joseph just before he died. He leaned on the top of his walking-stick and worshipped God.
Voice 3	It was faith that made Joseph, when he was about to die, speak of the departure of the Israelites from Egypt, and leave instructions about what should be done with his body.
Voice 1	It was faith that made the parents of Moses hide him for three months after he was born. They saw that he was a beautiful child, and they were not afraid to disobey the king's order.
Voice 2	It was faith that made Moses, when he had grown up, refuse to be called the son of the king's daughter. He preferred to suffer with God's people rather than to enjoy sin for a little while. He reckoned that to suffer scorn for the Messiah was worth far more than all the treasures of Egypt, for he kept his eyes on the future reward.
Voice 3	It was faith that made Moses leave Egypt without being afraid of the king's anger. As though he saw the invisible God, he refused to turn back. It was faith that made him establish the Passover and order the blood to be sprinkled on the doors, so that the Angel of Death would not kill the first-born sons of the Israelites.
Voice 1	It was faith that made the Israelites able to cross the Red Sea as if on dry land; when the Egyptians tried to do it, the water swallowed them up.
Voice 2	It was faith that made the walls of Jericho fall down after the Israelites had marched round them for seven days. It was faith that kept the prostitute Rahab from being killed with those who disobeyed God, for she gave the Israelite spies a friendly welcome.
Voice 3	Should I go on? There isn't enough time for me to speak of Gideon, Barak, Samson, Jephthah, David, Samuel, and the prophets. Through faith they fought whole countries and won. They did what was right and received what God had promised.
Cast	[This is] the word of the Lord.
All	**Thanks be to God.**

Cast: **Voice 1, Voice 2, Voice 3.** (This reading overlaps with the following reading.)

Faith (iii)
Hebrews 11.32—12.2

Voice 1	Gideon, Barak, Samson, Jephthah, David, Samuel and the prophets through faith conquered kingdoms, administered justice, and gained what was promised; they shut the mouths of lions, quenched the fury of the flames, and escaped the edge of the sword; their weakness was turned to strength; and they became powerful in battle and routed foreign armies.
Voice 2	Women received back their dead, raised to life again. Others were tortured and refused to be released, so that they might gain a better resurrection. Some faced jeers and flogging, while still

$\rightarrow$

others were chained and put in prison. They were stoned; they were sawn in two; they were put to death by the sword. They went about in sheepskins and goatskins, destitute, persecuted and ill-treated— the world was not worthy of them. They wandered in deserts and mountains, and in caves and holes in the ground.

Voice 3   These were all commended for their faith, yet none of them received what had been promised. God had planned something better for us so that only together with us would they be made perfect.

Voice 1   Therefore, since we are surrounded by such a great cloud of witnesses, let us throw off everything that hinders and the sin that so easily entangles, and let us run with perseverance the race marked out for us. Let us fix our eyes on Jesus, the author and perfecter of our faith, who for the joy set before him endured the cross, scorning its shame, and sat down at the right hand of the throne of God.

Cast   [This is] the word of the Lord.
All   **Thanks be to God.**

Cast: **Voice 1, Voice 2, Voice 3.** (This reading overlaps with the previous reading.)

Love shown in practice
Hebrews 12.3–11

Voice 1   Consider him who endured such opposition from sinful men, so that you will not grow weary and lose heart.

Voice 2   In your struggle against sin, you have not yet resisted to the point of shedding your blood.

Voice 3   And you have forgotten that word of encouragement that addresses you as sons:

Scripture   My son, do not make light of the Lord's discipline,
and do not lose heart when he rebukes you,
because the Lord disciplines those he loves,
and he punishes everyone he accepts as a son.

Voice 3   Endure hardship as discipline; God is treating you as sons. For what son is not disciplined by his father?

Voice 2   If you are not disciplined—and everyone undergoes discipline— then you are illegitimate children and not true sons.

Voice 1   Moreover, we have all had human fathers who disciplined us and we respected them for it. How much more should we submit to the Father of our spirits and live!

Voice 3   Our fathers disciplined us for a little while as they thought best; but God disciplines us for our good, that we may share in his holiness.

Voice 1   No discipline seems pleasant at the time, but painful. Later on, however, it produces a harvest of righteousness and peace for those who have been trained by it.

Cast   [This is] the word of the Lord.
All   **Thanks be to God.**

Cast: **Voice 1, Voice 2, Voice 3, Scripture.**

A warning against refusing God
From Hebrews 12.14–29

Voice 1   Try to be at peace with everyone, and try to live a holy life, because no one will see the Lord without it.

Voice 2   Guard against turning back from the grace of God.

Voice 3   You have not come, as the people of Israel came, to what you can feel, to Mount Sinai with its blazing fire, the darkness and the gloom, the storm, the blast of a trumpet, and the sound of a voice. When the people heard the voice, they begged not to hear another word, because they could not bear the order which said:

Exodus   If even an animal touches the mountain, it must be stoned to death.

Voice 3   The sight was so terrifying that Moses said:

Moses   I am trembling and afraid!

Voice 1   Instead, you have come to Mount Zion and to the city of the living God, the heavenly Jerusalem, with its thousands of angels.

Voice 2   You have come to the joyful gathering of God's first-born sons, whose names are written in heaven.

Voice 3   You have come to God, who is the judge of all mankind, and to the spirits of good people made perfect.

Voice 1   You have come to Jesus, who arranged the new covenant, and to the sprinkled blood that promises much better things than does the blood of Abel.

Voice 2   Be careful, then, and do not refuse to hear him who speaks.

Voice 3   Those who refused to hear the one who gave the divine message on earth did not escape. How much less shall we escape, then, if we turn away from the one who speaks from heaven!

Voice 1   His voice shook the earth at that time, but now he has promised:

Haggai   I will once more shake not only the earth but heaven as well.

Voice 1   The words 'once more' plainly show that the created things will be shaken and removed, so that the things that cannot be shaken will remain.

Voice 2   Let us be thankful, then, because we receive a kingdom that cannot be shaken.

Voice 3   Let us be grateful and worship God in a way that will please him, with reverence and awe; because:

Voices 1–3   Our God is indeed a destroying fire.

Cast   [This is] the word of the Lord.
All   **Thanks be to God.**

Cast: **Voice 1, Voice 2, Voice 3, Exodus, Moses** (can be the same as Exodus), **Haggai** (can be the same as Exodus).

How to please God
From Hebrews 13.1–21

Voice 1   Keep on loving one another as Christians.

Voice 2   Remember to welcome strangers in your homes. There were some who did that and welcomed angels without knowing it.

Voice 3   Remember those who are in prison, as though you were in prison with them.

Voice 1   Remember those who are suffering, as though you were suffering as they are.

Voice 2   Marriage is to be honoured by all, and husbands and wives must be faithful to each other. God will judge those who are immoral and those who commit adultery.

Voice 3   Keep your lives free from the love of money, and be satisfied with what you have. For God has said:

God   I will never leave you; I will never abandon you.

Voice 2   Let us be bold, then, and say:

Voices 1 and 2   The Lord is my helper,
I will not be afraid.
What can anyone do to me?

Voice 1   Remember your former leaders, who spoke God's message to you. Think back on how they lived and died, and imitate their faith. Jesus Christ is the same yesterday, today, and for ever.

Voice 2   There is no permanent city for us here on earth; we are looking for the city which is to come. Let us, then, always offer praise to God as our sacrifice through Jesus, which is the offering presented by lips that confess him as Lord.

Voice 3   Do not forget to do good and to help one another, because these are the sacrifices that please God.

Voice 1   Obey your leaders and follow their orders. They watch over your souls without resting, since they must give God an account of their service. If you obey them, they will do their work gladly; if not, they will do it with sadness, and that would be of no help to you.

Voice 2   May the God of peace provide you with every good thing you need in order to do his will, and may he, through Jesus Christ, do in us what pleases him.

Voice 3   And to Christ be the glory for ever and ever!

Voices 1 and 2   Amen.

Cast   [This is] the word of the Lord.
All   **Thanks be to God.**

Cast: **Voice 1, Voice 2, Voice 3, God** (can be the same as Voice 1).

JAMES

Warning against prejudice
James 2.1–13

James   My brothers, as believers in our Lord Jesus Christ, the Lord of glory, you must never treat people in different ways according to their outward appearance. Suppose a rich man wearing a gold ring and fine clothes comes to your meeting, and a poor man in ragged clothes also comes. If you show more respect to the well-dressed man and say to him:

Person   Have this best seat here.

James   But say to the poor man:

Person   Stand over there, or sit here on the floor by my feet.

James   Then you are guilty of creating distinctions among yourselves and of making judgements based on evil motives. (PAUSE)

Listen, my dear brothers! God chose the poor people of this world to be rich in faith and to possess the kingdom which he promised to those who love him. But you dishonour the poor! Who are the ones who oppress you and drag you before the judges? The rich! They are the ones who speak evil of that good name which has been given to you. (PAUSE)

You will be doing the right thing if you obey the law of the Kingdom, which is found in the scripture:

Scripture   Love your neighbour as you love yourself.

James   But if you treat people according to their outward appearance, you are guilty of sin, and the Law condemns you as a law-breaker. Whoever breaks one commandment is guilty of breaking them all. For the same one who said:

Scripture   Do not commit adultery.

James   Also said:

Scripture   Do not commit murder.

James   Even if you do not commit adultery, you have become a law-breaker if you commit murder. Speak and act as people who will be judged by the law that sets us free. For God will not show mercy when he judges the person who has not been merciful; but mercy triumphs over judgement.

Cast   [This is] the word of the Lord.
All   **Thanks be to God.**

Cast: **James, Person, Scripture.**

Faith and actions
James 2.14–26

James	What good is it for someone to say that he has faith if his actions do not prove it? Can that faith save him? Suppose there are brothers or sisters who need clothes and don't have enough to eat. What good is there in your saying to them:
Person 1	God bless you!
Person 2	Keep warm and eat well!
James	. . . if you don't give them the necessities of life? So it is with faith: if it is alone and includes no actions, then it is dead. But someone will say:
Person 1	One person has faith, another has actions.
James	My answer is, 'Show me how anyone can have faith without actions. I will show you my faith by my actions.' Do you believe that there is only one God? Good! The demons also believe—and tremble with fear. You fool! Do you want to be shown that faith without actions is useless? How was our ancestor Abraham put right with God? It was through his actions, when he offered his son Isaac on the altar. Can't you see? His faith and his actions worked together; his faith was made perfect through his actions. And the scripture came true that said:
Scripture	Abraham believed God, and because of his faith God accepted him as righteous.
James	And so Abraham was called God's friend. You see, then, that it is by his actions that a person is put right with God, and not by his faith alone. It was the same with the prostitute Rahab. She was put right with God through her actions, by welcoming the Israelite spies and helping them to escape by a different road. So then, as the body without the spirit is dead, so also faith without actions is dead.
Cast	[This is] the word of the Lord.
All	**Thanks be to God.**

Cast: **James, Person 1, Person 2,** (can be the same as Person 1), **Scripture.**

Friendship with the world
James 4.1–10

James	Where do all the fights and quarrels among you come from? They come from your desires for pleasure, which are constantly fighting within you. You want things, but you cannot have them, so you are ready to kill; you strongly desire things, but you cannot get them, so you quarrel and fight. You do not have what you want because you do not ask God for it. And when you ask, you do not receive it, because your motives are bad; you ask for things to use for your own pleasures. Unfaithful people! Don't you know

that to be the world's friend means to be God's enemy? Whoever wants to be the world's friend makes himself God's enemy. Don't think that there is no truth in the scripture that says:

Scripture   The spirit that God placed in us is filled with fierce desires.

James   But the grace that God gives is even stronger. As the scripture says:

Scripture   God resists the proud, but gives grace to the humble.

James   So then, submit to God. Resist the Devil, and he will run away from you. Come near to God, and he will come near to you. Wash your hands, you sinners! Purify your hearts, you hypocrites! Be sorrowful, cry, and weep; change your laughter into crying, your joy into gloom! Humble yourselves before the Lord, and he will lift you up.

Cast   [This is] the word of the Lord.
All   **Thanks be to God.**

Cast: **James, Scripture.**

A warning against boasting
James 4.13–17

James   Now listen to me, you that say:

Voice 1
(confident)   Today or tomorrow we will travel to a certain city, where we will stay a year and go into business and make a lot of money.

James   You don't even know what your life tomorrow will be! You are like a puff of smoke, which appears for a moment and then disappears. What you should say is this:

Voice 2
(humble)   If the Lord is willing, we will live and do this or that.

James   But now you are proud, and you boast; all such boasting is wrong. So then, the person who does not do the good he knows he should do is guilty of sin.

Cast   [This is] the word of the Lord.
All   **Thanks be to God.**

Cast: **James, Voice 1, Voice 2.**

1 PETER

A living hope
1 Peter 1.3–12

Voices 1 and **2**	Let us give thanks to the God and Father of our Lord Jesus Christ!
Voice 1	Because of his great mercy he gave us new life by raising Jesus Christ from death.
Voice 2	This fills us with a living hope, and so we look forward to possessing the rich blessings that God keeps for his people.
Voice 1	He keeps them for you in heaven, where they cannot decay or spoil or fade away.
Voice 2	They are for you, who through faith are kept safe by God's power for the salvation which is ready to be revealed at the end of time.
Voice 3	Be glad about this, even though it may now be necessary for you to be sad for a while because of the many kinds of trials you suffer.
Voice 1	Their purpose is to prove that your faith is genuine. Even gold, which can be destroyed, is tested by fire; and so your faith, which is much more precious than gold, must also be tested, so that it may endure.
Voice 3	Then you will receive praise and glory and honour on the Day when Jesus Christ is revealed.
Voice 1	You love him, although you have not seen him.
Voice 2	And you believe in him, although you do not now see him.
Voice 1	So you rejoice with a great and glorious joy which words cannot express, because you are receiving the salvation of your souls, which is the purpose of your faith in him.
Voice 2	It was concerning this salvation that the prophets made careful search and investigation, and they prophesied about this gift which God would give you.
Voice 3	They tried to find out when the time would be and how it would come. This was the time to which Christ's Spirit in them was pointing, in predicting the sufferings that Christ would have to endure and the glory that would follow.
Voice 2	God revealed to these prophets that their work was not for their own benefit, but for yours, as they spoke about those things which you have now heard from the messengers who announced the Good News by the power of the Holy Spirit sent from heaven.
Voice 1	These are things which even the angels would like to understand.
Cast	[This is] the word of the Lord.
All	**Thanks be to God.**

Cast: **Voice 1, Voice 2, Voice 3** (can be the same as Voice 1).

A call to holy living
1 Peter 1.13–25

Voice 1 Have your minds ready for action.

Voice 2 Keep alert and set your hope completely on the blessing which will be given you when Jesus Christ is revealed.

Voice 1 Be obedient to God, and do not allow your lives to be shaped by those desires you had when you were still ignorant.

Voice 2 Instead, be holy in all that you do, just as God who called you is holy. The scripture says:

Scripture Be holy because I am holy.

Voice 1 You call him Father, when you pray to God, who judges all people by the same standard, according to what each one has done; so then, spend the rest of your lives here on earth in reverence for him.

Voice 2 For you know what was paid to set you free from the worthless manner of life handed down by your ancestors. It was not something that can be destroyed, such as silver or gold; it was the costly sacrifice of Christ, who was like a lamb without defect or flaw.

Voice 1 He had been chosen by God before the creation of the world and was revealed in these last days for your sake.

Voice 2 Through him you believe in God, who raised him from death and gave him glory; and so your faith and hope are fixed on God. (PAUSE)

Voice 1 Now that by your obedience to the truth you have purified yourselves and have come to have a sincere love for your fellow-believers, love one another earnestly with all your heart. For through the living and eternal word of God you have been born again as the children of a parent who is immortal, not mortal. As the scripture says:

Scripture All mankind are like grass,
and all their glory is like wild flowers.
The grass withers, and the flowers fall,
but the word of the Lord remains for ever.

Voices 1 and 2 This word is the Good News that was proclaimed to you.

Cast [This is] the word of the Lord.
All **Thanks be to God.**

Cast: **Voice 1, Voice 2, Scripture.**

The living stone and the holy nation
1 Peter 2.1–10

Peter Rid yourselves, then, of all evil; no more lying or hypocrisy or jealousy or insulting language. Be like new-born babies, always thirsty for the pure spiritual milk, so that by drinking it you may grow up and be saved. As the scripture says:

Psalmist	You have found out for yourselves how kind the Lord is.
Peter	Come to the Lord, the living stone rejected by man as worthless but chosen by God as valuable. Come as living stones, and let yourselves be used in building the spiritual temple, where you will serve as holy priests to offer spiritual and acceptable sacrifices to God through Jesus Christ. For the scripture says:
Isaiah	I chose a valuable stone, which I am placing as the cornerstone in Zion; and whoever believes in him will never be disappointed.
Peter	This stone is of great value for you that believe; but for those who do not believe:
Psalmist	The stone which the builders rejected as worthless turned out to be the most important of all.
Peter	And another scripture says:
Isaiah	This is the stone that will make people stumble, the rock that will make them fall.
Peter	They stumbled because they did not believe in the word; such was God's will for them. But you are the chosen race, the King's priests, the holy nation, God's own people, chosen to proclaim the wonderful acts of God, who called you out of darkness into his own marvellous light. At one time you were not God's people, but now you are his people; at one time you did not know God's mercy, but now you have received his mercy.
Cast **All**	[This is] the word of the Lord. **Thanks be to God.**

Cast: **Peter, Psalmist, Isaiah.**

The example of Christ's suffering
1 Peter 2.21–25

Voice 1	Christ himself suffered for you and left you an example, so that you would follow in his steps.
Voice 2	He committed no sin, and no one has ever heard a lie come from his lips.
Voice 1	When he was insulted, he did not answer back with an insult:
Voice 2	When he suffered, he did not threaten, but placed his hopes in God, the righteous Judge.
Voices 1 and **2**	Christ himself carried our sins in his body to the cross, so that we might die to sin and live for righteousness.
Voice 2	It is by his wounds that you have been healed.

Voice 1 You were like sheep that had lost their way, but now you have been brought back to follow the Shepherd and Keeper of your souls.

Cast [This is] the word of the Lord.
All **Thanks be to God.**

Cast: **Voice 1, Voice 2.**

Suffering for doing right
1 Peter 3.8–18

Peter You must all have the same attitude and the same feelings; love one another as brothers, and be kind and humble with one another. Do not pay back evil with evil or cursing with cursing; instead, pay back with a blessing, because a blessing is what God promised to give you when he called you. As the scripture says:

Psalmist Whoever wants to enjoy life
and wishes to see good times,
must keep from speaking evil
and stop telling lies.
He must turn away from evil and do good;
he must strive for peace with all his heart.
For the Lord watches over the righteous
and listens to their prayers;
but he opposes those who do evil.

Peter Who will harm you if you are eager to do what is good? But even if you should suffer for doing what is right, how happy you are! Do not be afraid of anyone, and do not worry. But have reverence for Christ in your hearts, and honour him as Lord. Be ready at all times to answer anyone who asks you to explain the hope you have in you, but do it with gentleness and respect. Keep your conscience clear, so that when you are insulted, those who speak evil of your good conduct as followers of Christ will be ashamed of what they say. For it is better to suffer for doing good, if this should be God's will, than for doing evil. For Christ died for sins once and for all, a good man on behalf of sinners, in order to lead you to God.

Cast [This is] the word of the Lord.
All **Thanks be to God.**

Cast: **Peter, Psalmist.**

2 PETER

Eye-witnesses of Christ's glory
2 Peter 1.16–21

Voice 1 We have not depended on made-up stories in making known to you the mighty coming of our Lord Jesus Christ.

Voices 1 and 2 With our own eyes we saw his greatness.

Voice 2 We were there when he was given honour and glory by God the Father, when the voice came to him from the Supreme Glory, saying:

God This is my own dear Son, with whom I am pleased!

Voice 2 We ourselves heard this voice coming from heaven, when we were with him on the holy mountain.

Voice 1 So we are even more confident of the message proclaimed by the prophets. You will do well to pay attention to it, because it is like a lamp shining in a dark place until the Day dawns and the light of the morning star shines in your hearts.

Voice 2 Above all else, however, remember that no one can explain by himself a prophecy in the Scriptures. For no prophetic message ever came just from the will of man, but men were under the control of the Holy Spirit as they spoke the message that came from God.

Cast [This is] the word of the Lord.
All **Thanks be to God.**

Cast: **Voice 1, Voice 2, God.**

Judgement
2 Peter 3.3–9

Teacher You must understand that in these last days some people will appear whose lives are controlled by their own lusts. They will mock you and will ask:

Person 1 He promised to come, didn't he?

Persons 1 and 2 Where is he?

Person 2 Our fathers have already died, but everything is still the same as it was since the creation of the world!

Teacher They purposely ignore the fact that long ago God gave a command, and the heavens and earth were created. The earth was formed out of water and by water, and it was also by water, the water of the flood, that the old world was destroyed. But the heavens and the earth that now exist are being preserved by the same command of God, in order to be destroyed by fire. They are being kept for the day when godless people will be judged and destroyed. But do not forget one thing, my dear friends! There is no difference in the Lord's sight between one day and a thousand years; to him the two are the same. The Lord is not slow to do what he has promised, as some think. Instead, he is patient with you, because he does not want anyone to be destroyed, but wants all to turn away from their sins.

Cast	[This is] the word of the Lord.
All	**Thanks be to God.**

Cast: **Teacher, Person 1, Person 2.**

The Lord's coming
From 2 Peter 3.10–18

Voice 1	The Day of the Lord will come like a thief.
Voice 2	On that Day the heavens will disappear with a shrill noise.
Voice 1	The heavenly bodies will burn up and be destroyed.
Voice 2	And the earth with everything in it will vanish. (PAUSE)
Voice 1	Since all these things will be destroyed in this way, what kind of people should you be?
Voice 2	Your lives should be holy and dedicated to God, as you wait for the Day of God and do your best to make it come soon—the Day when the heavens will burn up and be destroyed, and the heavenly bodies will be melted by the heat.
Voice 1	But we wait for what God has promised: new heavens and a new earth, where righteousness will be at home.
Voice 2	And so, my friends, as you wait for that Day, do your best to be pure and faultless in God's sight and to be at peace with him. Continue to grow in the grace and knowledge of our Lord and Saviour Jesus Christ.
Voices 1 and **2**	To him be the glory, now and for ever! Amen.

Cast	[This is] the word of the Lord.
All	**Thanks be to God.**

Cast: **Voice 1, Voice 2.**

1 JOHN

The Word of life
1 John 1.1–3

Voice 1 The Word of life has existed from the very beginning.

Voice 2 We have heard it, and we have seen it with our eyes.

Voice 1 Yes, we have seen it, and our hands have touched it.

Voice 2 When this life became visible, we saw it; so we speak of it and tell you about the eternal life which was with the Father and was made known to us.

Voice 1 What we have seen and heard we announce to you also, so that you will join with us in the fellowship that we have with the Father and with his Son Jesus Christ.

Cast [This is] the word of the Lord.
All **Thanks be to God.**

Cast: **Voice 1, Voice 2.**

God is light
1 John 1.5–10

Voice 1 Now the message that we have heard from God's Son and announce is this:

Voices 1 and **2** God is light, and there is no darkness at all in him.

Voice 2 If, then, we say that we have fellowship with him, yet at the same time live in the darkness, we are lying both in our words and in our actions.

Voice 1 But if we live in the light—just as he is in the light—then we have fellowship with one another, and the blood of Jesus, his Son, purifies us from every sin.

Voice 2 If we say that we have no sin, we deceive ourselves, and there is no truth in us.

Voice 1 But if we confess our sins to God, he will keep his promise and do what is right: he will forgive us our sins and purify us from all our wrongdoing.

Voice 2 If we say that we have not sinned, we make God out to be a liar, and his word is not in us.

Cast [This is] the word of the Lord.
All **Thanks be to God.**

Cast: **Voice 1** (encouraging voice), **Voice 2** (warning voice).

Christ our helper
1 John 2.1–6

Voice 1   If anyone does sin, we have someone who pleads with the Father on our behalf—Jesus Christ, the righteous one.

Voice 2   And Christ himself is the means by which our sins are forgiven, and not our sins only, but also the sins of everyone.

Voice 1   If we obey God's commands, then we are sure that we know him.

Voice 2   If someone says that he knows him, but does not obey his commands, such a person is a liar and there is no truth in him.

Voice 1   But whoever obeys his word is the one whose love for God has really been made perfect.

Voice 2   This is how we can be sure that we are in union with God: whoever says that he remains in union with God should live just as Jesus Christ did.

Cast   [This is] the word of the Lord.
All   **Thanks be to God.**

Cast: **Voice 1, Voice 2.**

God is love
1 John 4.7–21

Voice 1   Dear friends, let us love one another, because love comes from God.

Voice 2   Whoever loves is a child of God and knows God.

Voice 3   Whoever does not love does not know God.

Voices 1 and **2**   For God *is* love.

Voice 1   God showed his love for us by sending his only Son into the world, so that we might have life through him. This is what love is:

Voice 3   It is not that we have loved God—

Voice 2   But that he loved us and sent his Son to be the means by which our sins are forgiven.

Voice 1   Dear friends, if this is how God loved us, then we should love one another. (PAUSE)

Voice 3   No one has ever seen God.

Voice 2   But if we love one another, God lives in union with us, and his love is made perfect in us. (PAUSE)

Voice 1   We are sure that we live in union with God and that he lives in union with us, because he has given us his Spirit.

Voice 2   And we have seen and tell others that the Father sent his Son to be the Saviour of the world.

Voice 1	If anyone declares that Jesus is the Son of God, he lives in union with God and God lives in union with him.
Voice 2	And we ourselves know and believe the love which God has for us. (PAUSE)
Voice 1	God is love, and whoever lives in love lives in union with God and God lives in union with him.
Voice 2	Love is made perfect in us in order that we may have courage on Judgement Day; and we will have it because our life in this world is the same as Christ's. There is no fear in love; perfect love drives out all fear.
Voice 3	So then, love has not been made perfect in anyone who is afraid, because fear has to do with punishment.
Voice 1	We love because God first loved us.
Voice 3	If someone says he loves God, but hates his brother, he is a liar. For he cannot love God, whom he has not seen, if he does not love his brother, whom he has seen.
Voice 1	The command that Christ has given us is this:
Voices 2 and **3**	Whoever loves God must love his brother also.
Cast	[This is] the word of the Lord.
All	**Thanks be to God.**

Cast: **Voice 1** (authoritative voice), **Voice 2** (encouraging voice), **Voice 3** (warning voice).

The witness about Jesus Christ
1 John 5.6–12

Voice 1	Jesus Christ is the one who came with the water of his baptism and the blood of his death.
Voice 2	He came not only with the water—
Voice 3	But with both the water and the blood.
Voice 1	And the Spirit himself testifies that this is true, because the Spirit is truth.
Voice 2	There are three witnesses:
Voice 1	The Spirit . . .
Voice 2	The water . . .
Voice 3	And the blood.
Voices 1–3	And all three give the same testimony.
Voice 2	We believe man's testimony.
Voice 3	But God's testimony is much stronger, and he has given this testimony about his Son.

Voice 1	So whoever believes in the Son of God has this testimony in his own heart.
Voice 2	But whoever does not believe God, has made him out to be a liar, because he has not believed what God has said about his Son.
Voice 3	The testimony is this:
Voices 1–3	God has given us eternal life—
Voice 1	And this life has its source in his Son.
Voice 3	Whoever has the Son has this life.
Voice 2	Whoever does not have the Son of God does not have life.
Cast	[This is] the word of the Lord.
All	**Thanks be to God.**

Cast: **Voice 1** (authoritative voice), **Voice 2** (warning voice), **Voice 3** (encouraging voice).

JUDE

Greetings and doxology
From Jude

Voice 1	To those who have been called—
Voice 2	Who are loved by God the Father.
Voice 3	And kept by Jesus Christ:
Voice 1	Mercy, peace and love be yours in full measure.
Voice 2	To him who is able to keep you from falling
Voice 3	And to present you before his glorious presence without fault and with great joy—
Voice 1	To the only God our Saviour—
Voice 2	Be glory
Voice 3	Majesty
Voice 1	Power
Voice 2	Authority
Voice 3	Through Jesus Christ our Lord
Voice 1	Before all ages,
Voices 1 and **2**	Now
Voices 2 and **3**	and for evermore!
Voices 1–3	Amen.

Cast	[This is] the word of the Lord.
All	**Thanks be to God.**

Cast: **Voice 1, Voice 2, Voice 3.**

REVELATION

The revelation to John: introduction
Revelation 1.1–3

Voice 1   This book is the record of the events that Jesus Christ revealed.

Voice 2   God gave him this revelation in order to show his servants what must happen very soon.

Voice 1   Christ made these things known to his servant John by sending his angel to him, and John has told all that he has seen.

Voice 2   This is his report concerning the message from God and the truth revealed by Jesus Christ.

Voice 3   Happy is the one who reads this book, and happy are those who listen to the words of this prophetic message and obey what is written in this book!

Voices 1–3   For the time is near when all these things will happen.

Cast   [This is] the word of the Lord.
All   **Thanks be to God.**

Cast: **Voice 1, Voice 2, Voice 3.**

Greetings to the seven churches
Revelation 1.4–8

Reader   From John to the seven churches in the province of Asia:

John   Grace and peace be yours from God, who is, who was, and who is to come, and from the seven spirits in front of his throne, and from Jesus Christ, the faithful witness, the first to be raised from death and who is also the ruler of the kings of the world.

He loves us, and by his sacrificial death he has freed us from our sins and made us a kingdom of priests to serve his God and Father. To Jesus Christ be the glory and power for ever and ever! Amen.

Look, he is coming on the clouds! Everyone will see him, including those who pierced him. All peoples on earth will mourn over him. So shall it be!

Voice   I am the first and the last.

John   So says the Lord God Almighty, who is, who was, and who is to come.

Cast   [This is] the word of the Lord.
All   **Thanks be to God.**

Cast: **Reader, John, Voice,** (can be the same as Reader).

The glory of the Son of Man
Revelation 1.9–20

John   I am John, your brother, and as a follower of Jesus I am your partner in patiently enduring the suffering that comes to those who belong to his Kingdom. I was put on the island of Patmos because I had proclaimed God's word and the truth that Jesus revealed. On the Lord's day the Spirit took control of me, and I heard a loud voice, that sounded like a trumpet, speaking behind me. It said:

Voice   Write down what you see, and send the book to the churches in these seven cities: Ephesus, Smyrna, Pergamum, Thyatira, Sardis, Philadelphia, and Laodicea.

John   I turned round to see who was talking to me, and I saw seven gold lampstands, and among them there was what looked like a human being, wearing a robe that reached to his feet, and a gold belt round his chest. His hair was white as wool, or as snow, and his eyes blazed like fire; his feet shone like brass that has been refined and polished, and his voice sounded like a roaring waterfall. He held seven stars in his right hand, and a sharp two-edged sword came out of his mouth. His face was as bright as the midday sun. When I saw him, I fell down at his feet like a dead man. He placed his right hand on me and said:

Voice   Don't be afraid! I am the first and the last. I am the living one! I was dead, but now I am alive for ever and ever. I have authority over death and the world of the dead. Write, then, the things you see, both the things that are now and the things that will happen afterwards. This is the secret meaning of the seven stars that you see in my right hand, and of the seven gold lamp-stands: the seven stars are the angels of the seven churches, and the seven lamp-stands are the seven churches.

Cast   [This is] the word of the Lord.
All   **Thanks be to God.**

Cast: **John, Voice.**

The message to Ephesus
Revelation 2.1–7

Voice 1   To the angel of the church in Ephesus write:

Voice 2   This is the message from the one who holds the seven stars in his right hand and who walks among the seven gold lamp-stands:

Voice 3   I know what you have done; I know how hard you have worked and how patient you have been. I know that you cannot tolerate evil men and that you have tested those who say they are apostles but are not, and have found out that they are liars. You are patient, you have suffered for my sake, and you have not given up. But this is what I have against you: you do not love me now as you did at first. Think how far you have fallen! Turn from your sins and do what you did at first! If you don't turn from your sins, I will come to you and take your lamp-stand from its place. But this is what you have in your favour: you hate what the Nicolaitans do, as much as I do.

Voice 1   If you have ears, then, listen to what the Spirit says to the churches!

Voice 3   To those who win the victory I will give the right to eat the fruit of the tree of life that grows in the Garden of God.

Cast   [This is] the word of the Lord.
All   **Thanks be to God.**

Cast: **Voice 1, Voice 2, Voice 3.**

The message to Smyrna
Revelation 2.8–11

Voice 1   To the angel of the church in Smyrna write:

Voice 2   This is the message from the one who is the first and the last, who died and lived again.

Voice 3   I know your troubles; I know that you are poor—but really you are rich! I know the evil things said against you by those who claim to be Jews but are not; they are a group that belongs to Satan! Don't be afraid of anything you are about to suffer. Listen! The Devil will put you to the test by having some of you thrown into prison, and your troubles will last ten days. Be faithful to me, even if it means death, and I will give you life as your prize of victory.

Voice 1   If you have ears, then, listen to what the Spirit says to the churches!

Voice 2   Those who win the victory will not be hurt by the second death.

Cast   [This is] the word of the Lord.
All   **Thanks be to God.**

Cast: **Voice 1, Voice 2, Voice 3.**

The message to Pergamum
Revelation 2.12–17

Voice 1   To the angel of the church in Pergamum write:

Voice 2   This is the message from the one who has the sharp two-edged sword.

Voice 3   I know where you live, there where Satan has his throne. You are true to me, and you did not abandon your faith in me even during the time when Antipas, my faithful witness, was killed there where Satan lives. But there are a few things I have against you: there are some among you who follow the teaching of Balaam, who taught Balak how to lead the people of Israel into sin by

→

persuading them to eat food that had been offered to idols and to practise sexual immorality. In the same way you have people among you who follow the teaching of the Nicolaitans. Now turn from your sins! If you don't, I will come to you soon and fight against those people with the sword that comes out of my mouth.

Voices 1 and **2**   If you have ears, then, listen to what the Spirit says to the churches!

Voice 3   To those who win the victory I will give some of the hidden manna. I will also give each of them a white stone on which is written a new name that no one knows except the one who receives it.

Cast   [This is] the word of the Lord.
All   **Thanks be to God.**

Cast: **Voice 1, Voice 2, Voice 3.**

The message to Sardis
Revelation 3.1–6

Voice 1   To the angel of the church in Sardis write:

Voice 2   This is the message from the one who has the seven spirits of God and the seven stars.

Voice 3   I know what you are doing; I know that you have the reputation of being alive, even though you are dead! So wake up, and strengthen what you still have before it dies completely. For I find that what you have done is not yet perfect in the sight of my God. Remember, then, what you were taught and what you heard; obey it and turn from your sins. If you do not wake up, I will come upon you like a thief, and you will not even know the time when I will come. But a few of you there in Sardis have kept your clothes clean. You will walk with me, clothed in white, because you are worthy to do so. Those who win the victory will be clothed like this in white, and I will not remove their names from the book of the living. In the presence of my Father and of his angels I will declare openly that they belong to me.

Voices 1 and **2**   If you have ears, then, listen to what the Spirit says to the churches!

Cast   [This is] the word of the Lord.
All   **Thanks be to God.**

Cast: **Voice 1, Voice 2, Voice 3.**

The message to Laodicea
Revelation 3.14–22

Voice 1   To the angel of the church in Laodicea write:

Voice 2   This is the message from the Amen, the faithful and true witness, who is the origin of all that God has created:

Voice 3	I know what you have done; I know that you are neither cold nor hot. How I wish you were either one or the other! But because you are lukewarm, neither hot nor cold, I am going to spit you out of my mouth! You say:
Laodicean	I am rich and well off; I have all I need.
Voice 3	But you do not know how miserable and pitiful you are! You are poor, naked, and blind. I advise you, then, to buy gold from me, pure gold, in order to be rich. Buy also white clothing to dress yourself and cover up your shameful nakedness. Buy also some ointment to put on your eyes, so that you may see. I rebuke and punish all whom I love. Be in earnest, then, and turn from your sins. Listen! I stand at the door and knock; if anyone hears my voice and opens the door, I will come into his house and eat with him, and he will eat with me. To those who win the victory I will give the right to sit beside me on my throne, just as I have been victorious and now sit by my Father on his throne.
Voices 1 and **2**	If you have ears, then, listen to what the Spirit says to the churches!
Cast	[This is] the word of the Lord.
All	**Thanks be to God.**

Cast: **Voice 1, Voice 2, Voice 3, Laodicean.**

Worship in heaven
Revelation 4.1–11

John	I had another vision and saw an open door in heaven. And the voice that sounded like a trumpet, which I had heard speaking to me before said:
Voice	Come up here, and I will show you what must happen after this.
John	At once the Spirit took control of me. There in heaven was a throne with someone sitting on it. His face gleamed like such precious stones as jasper and carnelian, and all round the throne there was a rainbow the colour of an emerald. In a circle round the throne were twenty-four other thrones, on which were seated twenty-four elders dressed in white and wearing crowns of gold. From the throne came flashes of lightning, rumblings, and peals of thunder. In front of the throne seven lighted torches were burning, which are the seven spirits of God. Also in front of the throne there was what looked like a sea of glass, clear as crystal.
	Surrounding the throne on each of its sides, were four living creatures covered with eyes in front and behind. The first one looked like a lion; the second looked like a bull; the third had a face like a man's face; and the fourth looked like an eagle in flight. Each one of the four living creatures had six wings, and they were covered with eyes, inside and out. Day and night they never stop singing:

Chorus	Holy, holy, holy, is the Lord God Almighty, who was, who is, and who is to come.
John	The four living creatures sing songs of glory and honour and thanks to the one who sits on the throne, who lives for ever and ever. When they do so, the twenty-four elders fall down before the one who sits on the throne, and worship him who lives for ever and ever. They throw their crowns down in front of the throne and say:
Chorus	Our Lord and God! You are worthy to receive glory, honour, and power. For you created all things, and by your will they were given existence and life.
Cast	[This is] the word of the Lord.
All	**Thanks be to God.**

Cast: **John, Voice, Chorus** (two or more).

The scroll and the Lamb
Revelation 5.1–14

John	I saw a scroll in the right hand of the one who sits on the throne; it was covered with writing on both sides and was sealed with seven seals. And I saw a mighty angel, who announced in a loud voice:
Angel	Who is worthy to break the seals and open the scroll?
John	But there was no one in heaven or on earth or in the world below who could open the scroll and look inside it. I cried bitterly because no one could be found who was worthy to open the scroll or look inside it. Then one of the elders said to me:
Elder	Don't cry. Look! The Lion from Judah's tribe, the great descendant of David, has won the victory, and he can break the seven seals and open the scroll.
John	Then I saw a Lamb standing in the centre of the throne, surrounded by the four living creatures and the elders. The Lamb appeared to have been killed. It had seven horns and seven eyes, which are the seven spirits of God that have been sent throughout the whole earth. The Lamb went and took the scroll from the right hand of the one who sits on the throne. As he did so, the four living creatures and the twenty-four elders fell down before the Lamb. Each had a harp and gold bowls filled with incense, which are the prayers of God's people. They sang a new song:
Chorus	You are worthy to take the scroll and to break open its seals. For you were killed, and by your sacrificial death you bought for God people from every tribe, language, nation, and race. You have made them a kingdom of priests to serve our God, and they shall rule on earth.

John	Again I looked, and I heard angels, thousands and millions of them! They stood round the throne, the four living creatures, and the elders, and sang in a loud voice:
Chorus	The Lamb who was killed is worthy to receive power, wealth, wisdom, and strength, honour, glory, and praise!
John	And I heard every creature in heaven, on earth, in the world below, and in the sea—all living beings in the universe—and they were singing:
Chorus	To him who sits on the throne and to the Lamb, be praise and honour, glory and might, for ever and ever!
John	The four living creatures answered:
Four creatures	Amen!
John	And the elders fell down and worshipped.
Cast **All**	[This is] the word of the Lord. **Thanks be to God.**

Cast: **John, Angel, Elder, Chorus** (two or more—one can be the same as Elder), **Four creatures** (two—one can be the same as Angel, plus two of the Chorus).

The seals
Revelation 6.1–17

John	Then I saw the Lamb break open the first of the seven seals, and I heard one of the four living creatures say in a voice that sounded like thunder:
Creature 1	Come!
John	I looked, and there was a white horse. Its rider held a bow, and he was given a crown. He rode out as a conqueror to conquer. (PAUSE) Then the Lamb broke open the second seal; and I heard the second living creature say:
Creature 2	Come!
John	Another horse came out, a red one. Its rider was given the power to bring war on the earth, so that men should kill each other. He was given a large sword. (PAUSE) Then the Lamb broke open the third seal; and I heard the third living creature say:
Creature 3	Come!
John	I looked, and there was a black horse. Its rider held a pair of scales in his hand. I heard what sounded like a voice coming from among the four living creatures, which said:
Voice	A litre of wheat for a day's wages, and three litres of barley for a day's wages. But do not damage the olive-trees and the vineyards! (PAUSE)
John	Then the Lamb broke open the fourth seal; and I heard the fourth living creature say:

Creature 4	Come!
John	I looked and there was a pale-coloured horse. Its rider was named Death, and Hades followed close behind. They were given authority over a quarter of the earth, to kill by means of war, famine, disease, and wild animals. (PAUSE) Then the Lamb broke open the fifth seal. I saw underneath the altar the souls of those who had been killed because they had proclaimed God's word and had been faithful in their witnessing. They shouted in a loud voice:
Martyrs 1 and **2**	Almighty Lord, holy and true!
Martyr 1	How long will it be until you judge the people on earth?
Martyr 2	And punish them for killing us?
John	Each of them was given a white robe, and they were told to rest a little while longer, until the complete number of their fellow-servants and brothers had been killed, as they had been. (PAUSE) And I saw the Lamb break open the sixth seal. There was a violent earthquake, and the sun became black like coarse black cloth, and the moon turned completely red like blood. The stars fell down to the earth, like unripe figs falling from the tree when a strong wind shakes it. The sky disappeared like a scroll being rolled up, and every mountain and island was moved from its place. Then the kings of the earth, the rulers and the military chiefs, the rich and the powerful, and all other men, slave and free, hid themselves in caves and under rocks on the mountains. They called out to the mountains and to the rocks:
Rulers 1 and **2**	Fall on us!
Ruler 1	Hide us from the eyes of the one who sits on the throne.
Ruler 2	And from the anger of the Lamb!
Ruler 1	The terrible day of their anger is here.
Ruler 2	Who can stand against it?
Cast	[This is] the word of the Lord.
All	**Thanks be to God.**

Cast: **John, Creature 1, Creature 2, Creature 3, Voice, Creature 4, Martyr 1, Martyr 2** (Martyrs 1 and 2 can be the same as Creatures 1 and 2), **Ruler 1, Ruler 2** (Rulers 1 and 2 can be the same as Creatures 3 and 4).

The 144,000 people of Israel
Revelation 7.1–8

John	After this I saw four angels standing at the four corners of the earth, holding back the four winds so that no wind should blow on the earth or the sea or against any tree. And I saw another angel coming up from the east with the seal of the living God. He called out in a loud voice to the four angels to whom God had given the power to damage the earth and the sea:
Angel	Do not harm the earth, the sea, or the trees, until we mark the servants of our God with a seal on their foreheads.

burn them, because the Lamb, who is in the centre of the throne, will be their shepherd, and he will guide them to springs of life-giving water. And God will wipe away every tear from their eyes.

Cast	[This is] the word of the Lord.
All	**Thanks be to God.**

Cast: **John, Voice 1, Voice 2, Voice 3, Elder** (can be the same as Voice 3).

The angel and the little scroll
Revelation 10.1–11

John   Then I saw another mighty angel coming down out of heaven. He was wrapped in a cloud and had a rainbow round his head; his face was like the sun, and his legs were like pillars of fire. He had a small scroll open in his hand. He put his right foot on the sea and his left foot on the land, and called out in a loud voice that sounded like the roar of lions. After he had called out, the seven thunders answered with a roar. As soon as they spoke, I was about to write. But I heard a voice speak from heaven:

Voice   Keep secret what the seven thunders have said; do not write it down!

John   Then the angel that I saw standing on the sea and on the land raised his right hand to heaven and took a vow in the name of God, who lives for ever and ever, who created heaven, earth, and the sea, and everything in them. The angel said:

Angel   There will be no more delay! But when the seventh angel blows his trumpet, then God will accomplish his secret plan, as he announced to his servants, the prophets.

John   Then the voice that I had heard speaking from heaven spoke to me again:

Voice   Go and take the open scroll which is in the hand of the angel standing on the sea and on the land.

John   I went to the angel and asked him to give me the little scroll. He said to me:

Angel   Take it and eat it; it will turn sour in your stomach, but in your mouth it will be sweet as honey.

John   I took the little scroll from his hand and ate it, and it tasted sweet as honey in my mouth. But after I swallowed it, it turned sour in my stomach.

Voice   Once again you must proclaim God's message about many nations, races, languages, and kings.

Cast	[This is] the word of the Lord.
All	**Thanks be to God.**

Cast: **John, Voice, Angel.**

394

The seventh trumpet
Revelation 11.15–19

John   The seventh angel sounded his trumpet, and there were loud voices in heaven, which said:

Elder 1   The kingdom of the world has become—

Elders 1 and **2**   The kingdom of our Lord and of his Christ,

Elder 2   And he will reign for ever and ever.

John   And the twenty-four elders, who were seated on their thrones before God, fell on their faces and worshipped God, saying:

Elder 1   We give thanks to you, Lord God Almighty,
the One who is and who was,
because you have taken your great power
and have begun to reign.

Elder 2   The nations were angry;
and your wrath has come.

Elder 1   The time has come for judging the dead,
and for rewarding your servants the prophets
and your saints and those who reverence your name,
both small and great—
and for destroying those who destroy the earth.

John   Then God's temple in heaven was opened, and within his temple was seen the ark of his covenant. And there came flashes of lightning, rumblings, peals of thunder, an earthquake and a great hailstorm.

Cast   [This is] the word of the Lord.
All   **Thanks be to God.**

Cast: **John, Elder 1, Elder 2.**

The two beasts
Revelation 13.1–10 [11–12, 15–18]

John   Then I saw a beast coming up out of the sea. It had ten horns and seven heads; on each of its horns there was a crown, and on each of its heads there was a name that was insulting to God. The beast looked like a leopard, with feet like a bear's feet and a mouth like a lion's mouth. The dragon gave the beast his own power, his throne, and his vast authority. One of the heads of the beast seemed to have been fatally wounded, but the wound had healed. The whole earth was amazed and followed the beast. Everyone worshipped the dragon because he had given his authority to the beast. They worshipped the beast also, saying:

Worshipper   Who is like the beast? Who can fight against it?

John   The beast was allowed to make proud claims which were insulting to God, and it was permitted to have authority for forty-two months. It began to curse God, his name, the place where he lives, and all those who live in heaven. It was allowed to fight against God's people and to defeat them, and it was given authority over every tribe, nation, language, and race. All people living on earth will worship it, except those whose names were written before the creation of the world in the book of the living which belongs to the Lamb that was killed.

Voice Listen, then, if you have ears! Whoever is meant to be captured will surely be captured; whoever is meant to be killed by the sword will surely be killed by the sword. This calls for endurance and faith on the part of God's people.

[John Then I saw another beast, which came up out of the earth. It had two horns like a lamb's horns, and it spoke like a dragon. It used the vast authority of the first beast in its presence. It forced the earth and all who live on it to worship the first beast, whose wound had healed. The second beast was allowed to breathe life into the image of the first beast, so that the image could talk and put to death all those who would not worship it. The beast forced all the people, small and great, rich and poor, slave and free, to have a mark placed on their right hands or on their foreheads. No one could buy or sell unless he had this mark, that is, the beast's name or the number that stands for the name. This calls for wisdom. Whoever is intelligent can work out the meaning of the number of the beast, because the number stands for a man's name. Its number is 666.]

Cast [This is] the word of the Lord.
All **Thanks be to God.**

Cast: **John, Worshipper, Voice.**

The three angels
Revelation 14.6–13

John I saw an angel flying high in the air, with an eternal message of Good News to announce to the peoples of the earth, to every race, tribe, language, and nation. He said in a loud voice:

Angel 1 Honour God and praise his greatness! For the time has come for him to judge mankind. Worship him who made heaven, earth, sea, and the springs of water!

John A second angel followed the first one, saying:

Angel 2 She has fallen! Great Babylon has fallen! She made all peoples drink her wine—the strong wine of her immoral lust!

John A third angel followed the first two, saying in a loud voice:

Angel 3 Whoever worships the beast and its image and receives the mark on his forehead or on his hand will himself drink God's wine, the wine of his fury, which he has poured at full strength into the cup of his anger! All who do this will be tormented in fire and sulphur before the holy angels and the Lamb. The smoke of the fire that torments them goes up for ever and ever. There is no relief day or night for those who worship the beast and its image, for anyone who has the mark of its name.

John   This calls for endurance on the part of God's people, those who obey God's commandments and are faithful to Jesus. (PAUSE) Then I heard a voice from heaven saying:

Voice   Write this: Happy are those who from now on die in the service of the Lord!

John   The Spirit answers:

Spirit   Yes indeed! They will enjoy rest from their hard work, because the results of their service go with them.

Cast   [This is] the word of the Lord.
All   **Thanks be to God.**

Cast: **John, Angel 1, Angel 2, Angel 3, Voice, Spirit.**

The harvest of the earth
Revelation 14.14–19

John   Then I looked, and there was a white cloud, and sitting on the cloud was what looked like a human being, with a crown of gold on his head and a sharp sickle in his hand. Then another angel came out from the temple and cried out in a loud voice to the one who was sitting on the cloud:

Angel 1   Use your sickle and reap the harvest, because the time has come; the earth is ripe for the harvest!

John   Then the one who sat on the cloud swung his sickle on the earth, and the earth's harvest was reaped. Then I saw another angel come out of the temple in heaven, and he also had a sharp sickle. Then another angel, who is in charge of the fire, came from the altar. He shouted in a loud voice to the angel who had the sharp sickle:

Angel 2   Use your sickle, and cut the grapes from the vineyard of the earth, because the grapes are ripe!

John   So the angel swung his sickle on the earth, cut the grapes from the vine, and threw them into the winepress of God's furious anger.

Cast   [This is] the word of the Lord.
All   **Thanks be to God.**

Cast: **John, Angel 1, Angel 2.**

The angels with the last plagues
Revelation 15.1–8

John   Then I saw in the sky another mysterious sight, great and amazing. There were seven angels with seven plagues, which are the last ones, because they are the final expression of God's anger. Then I saw what looked like a sea of glass mixed with fire. I also saw those who had won the victory over the beast and its image and over the one whose name is represented by a number. They were standing by the sea of glass, holding harps that God had given them and singing the song of Moses, the servant of God, and the song of the Lamb:

Saint 1   Lord God Almighty,
how great and wonderful are your deeds!

Saint 2   King of the nations,
how right and true are your ways!

Saint 3   Who will not stand in awe of you, Lord?

Saint 1   Who will refuse to declare your greatness?

Saint 2   You alone are holy.

Saint 3   All the nations will come
and worship you,
because your just actions are seen by all.

John   After this I saw the temple in heaven open, with the Tent of God's presence in it. The seven angels who had the seven plagues came out of the temple, dressed in clean shining linen and with gold belts tied around their chests. Then one of the four living creatures gave the seven angels seven gold bowls full of the anger of God, who lives for ever and ever. The temple was filled with smoke from the glory and power of God, and no one could go into the temple until the seven plagues brought by the seven angels had come to an end.

Cast   [This is] the word of the Lord.
All   **Thanks be to God.**

Cast: **John, Saint 1, Saint 2, Saint 3.**

The fall of Babylon
From Revelation 18.1–19

John   After this I saw another angel coming down out of heaven. He had great authority, and his splendour brightened the whole earth. He cried out in a loud voice:

Angel   She has fallen! Great Babylon has fallen! She is now haunted by demons and unclean spirits; all kinds of filthy and hateful birds live in her. For all the nations have drunk her wine—the strong wine of her immoral lust. The kings of the earth practised sexual immorality with her, and the businessmen of the world grew rich from her unrestrained lust.

John   Then I heard another voice from heaven, saying:

Voice
Come out, my people! Come out from her!
You must not take part in her sins;
you must not share in her punishment!
For her sins are piled up as high as heaven,
and God remembers her wicked ways.
Because of this, in one day she will be struck with plagues—
disease, grief, and famine.
And she will be burnt with fire,
because the Lord God, who judges her, is mighty.

John
The kings of the earth who took part in her immorality and lust will cry and weep over the city when they see the smoke from the flames that consume her. They stand a long way off, because they are afraid of sharing in her suffering. They say:

King 1
How terrible!

King 2
How awful!

King 1
This great and mighty city Babylon—

King 2
In just one hour you have been punished!

John
The businessmen of the earth also cry and mourn for her, because no one buys their goods any longer; no one buys their gold, silver, precious stones, and pearls; their goods of linen, purple cloth, silk, and scarlet cloth; all kinds of rare woods and all kinds of objects made of ivory and of expensive wood, of bronze, iron, and marble; and cinnamon, spice, incense, myrrh, and frankincense; wine and oil, flour and wheat, cattle and sheep, horses and carriages, slaves, and even human lives. The businessmen say to her:

Businessman 1
All the good things you longed to own have disappeared.

Businessman 2
All your wealth and glamour are gone, and you will never find them again!

John
The businessmen, who became rich from doing business in that city, will stand a long way off, because they are afraid of sharing in her suffering. They will cry and mourn, and say:

Businessman 1
How terrible!

Businessman 2
How awful for the great city!

Businessman 1
She used to dress herself in linen, purple, and scarlet, and cover herself with gold ornaments, precious stones, and pearls!

Businessman 2
And in one hour she has lost all this wealth!

John
All the ships' captains and passengers, the sailors and all others who earn their living on the sea, stood a long way off, and cried out as they saw the smoke from the flames that consumed her:

Sailor 1
How terrible!

Sailor 2
How awful for the great city!

Sailor 1	She is the city where all who have ships sailing the seas became rich on her wealth!
Sailor 2	And in one hour she has lost everything!
Cast	[This is] the word of the Lord.
All	**Thanks be to God.**

Cast: **John, Angel, Voice, King 1, King 2, Businessman 1** (can be the same as Angel)**, Businessman 2** (can be the same as Voice)**, Sailor 1** (can be the same as King 1)**, Sailor 2** (can be the same as King 2)**.**

The wedding-feast of the Lamb
Revelation 19.5–10

John	There came from the throne the sound of a voice, saying:
Voice	Praise our God, all his servants and all people, both great and small, who have reverence for him!
John	Then I heard what sounded like a large crowd, like the sound of a roaring waterfall, like loud peals of thunder. I heard them say:
Saints 1 and **2**	Praise God!
Saint 1	For the Lord, our Almighty God, is King!
Saint 2	Let us rejoice and be glad!
Saint 1	Let us praise his greatness!
Saint 2	For the time has come for the wedding of the Lamb.
Saint 1	His bride has prepared herself for it. She has been given clean shining linen to wear.
John	The linen is the good deeds of God's people. Then the angel said to me:
Angel	Write this: Happy are those who have been invited to the wedding-feast of the Lamb.
John	And the angel added:
Angel	These are the true words of God.
John	I fell down at his feet to worship him, but he said to me:
Angel	Don't do it! I am a fellow-servant of yours and of your brothers, all those who hold to the truth that Jesus revealed. Worship God!
John	For the truth that Jesus revealed is what inspires the prophets.
Cast	[This is] the word of the Lord.
All	**Thanks be to God.**

Cast: **John, Voice, Saint 1, Saint 2, Angel.**

The rider on the white horse
Revelation 19.11–16

John	I saw heaven open, and there was a white horse. Its rider is called Faithful and True; it is with justice that he judges and fights his battles. His eyes were like a flame of fire, and he wore many crowns on his head. He had a name written on him, but no one except himself knows what it is. The robe he wore was covered with blood. His name is:

Voice (slowly)	The Word of God.
John	The armies of heaven followed him, riding on white horses and dressed in clean white linen. Out of his mouth came a sharp sword, with which he will defeat the nations. He will rule over them with a rod of iron, and he will trample out the wine in the winepress of the furious anger of the Almighty God. On his robe and on his thigh was written the name:
Voice (boldly)	King of kings and Lord of lords.
Cast	[This is] the word of the Lord.
All	**Thanks be to God.**

Cast: **John, Voice.**

The new heaven and the new earth
Revelation 21.1–7 [8]

John	Then I saw a new heaven and a new earth. The first heaven and the first earth disappeared, and the sea vanished. And I saw the Holy City, the new Jerusalem, coming down out of heaven from God, prepared and ready, like a bride dressed to meet her husband. I heard a loud voice speaking from the throne:
Voice	Now God's home is with mankind! He will live with them, and they shall be his people. God himself will be with them, and he will be their God. He will wipe away all tears from their eyes. There will be no more death, no more grief or crying or pain. The old things have disappeared.
John	Then the one who sits on the throne said:
God	And now I make all things new!
John	He also said to me:
God	Write this, because these words are true and can be trusted.
John	And he said:
God	It is done! I am the first and the last, the beginning and the end. To anyone who is thirsty I will give the right to drink from the spring of the water of life without paying for it. Whoever wins the victory will receive this from me: I will be his God, and he will be my son. [But cowards, traitors, perverts, murderers, the immoral, those who practise magic, those who worship idols, and all liars— the place for them is the lake burning with fire and sulphur, which is the second death.]
Cast	[This is] the word of the Lord.
All	**Thanks be to God.**

Cast: **John, Voice, God.**

The coming of Jesus
Revelation 22.6–17, [18–19] 20–21

John	The angel said to me:
Angel	These words are true and can be trusted. And the Lord God, who gives his Spirit to the prophets, has sent his angel to show his servants what must happen very soon.
John	Jesus says:
Jesus	Listen! I am coming soon! Happy are those who obey the prophetic words in this book!
John	I, John, have heard and seen all these things. And when I finished hearing and seeing them, I fell down at the feet of the angel who had shown me these things, and I was about to worship him. But he said to me:
Angel	Don't do it! I am a fellow-servant of yours and of your brothers the prophets and of all those who obey the words in this book. Worship God! Do not keep the prophetic words of this book a secret, because the time is near when all this will happen. Whoever is evil must go on doing evil, and whoever is filthy must go on being filthy; whoever is good must go on doing good, and whoever is holy must go on being holy.
John	Jesus says:
Jesus	Listen! I am coming soon! I will bring my rewards with me, to give to each one according to what he has done. I am the first and the last, the beginning and the end.
John	Happy are those who wash their robes clean and so have the right to eat the fruit from the tree of life and to go through the gates into the city. But outside the city are the perverts and those who practise magic, the immoral and the murderers, those who worship idols and those who are liars both in words and deeds.
Jesus	I, Jesus, have sent my angel to announce these things to you in the churches. I am descended from the family of David; I am the bright morning star.
John	The Spirit and the Bride say:
Voices 1 and **2**	Come!
John	Everyone who hears this must also say:
Cast (except Jesus)	Come!
John	Come, whoever is thirsty; accept the water of life as a gift, whoever wants it.
	[I, John, solemnly warn everyone who hears the prophetic words of this book: if anyone adds anything to them, God will add to his punishment the plagues described in this book. And if anyone takes anything away from the prophetic words of this book, God

will take away from him his share of the fruit of the tree of life and of the Holy City, which are described in this book.]

He who gives his testimony to all this says:

Jesus	Yes indeed! I am coming soon!
John	So be it.
Cast (except Jesus)	Come, Lord Jesus!
John	May the grace of the Lord Jesus be with everyone.

Cast	[This is] the word of the Lord.
All	**Thanks be to God.**

Cast: **John, Angel, Jesus, Voice 1, Voice 2** (can be the same as Angel).

APPENDIX

CAST OF READERS
for the dramatised Christmas Readings

Sometimes the dramatised Christmas Readings will be used in public at a crowded service where there is little space for a large cast, or where amplification of the cast is needed but only a single directional microphone is available. In such circumstances it will be as well to keep those participating to a minimum. The cast list below (not in order of appearance) is arranged in groupings to allow each reader to take more than one part in the series, but not in the same reading. This is the minimum configuration which also takes into account a male-female balance of voices. Where such a balance is not possible, please ignore the instructions in brackets.

First Reader (strong female voice)
Narrator—except in 'Mary visits Elizabeth'
Narrator 1—in 'The shepherds find the baby'
Elizabeth

Second Reader (older male voice)
Commentator
Shepherd 1
Teacher 1
Simeon
Hebrews

Third Reader (male voice)
Isaiah
Prophet
Chorus
Magi 1
Colossians

Fourth Reader (male voice)
Jeremiah
Chorus
Magi 2
John
Narrator—in 'Mary visits Elizabeth'
Narrator 2—in 'The shepherds find the baby'

Fifth Reader (authoritative male voice)

Micah
Angel
Shepherd 2
Herod
Philippians

Sixth Reader (female voice)

Numbers
Mary
Chorus
Teacher 2
2 Corinthians

If this cast list is used, bracketed footnotes which begin 'can be the same as . . .' should be ignored.

Suggested carols to match the Christmas readings will be found at the back of our *Carols for Today* (music edition, from Hodder & Stoughton/Hope Publishing Company). Carols to match the Christmas themes will be found indexed at the back of our *Carol Praise* (music edition, from Marshall Pickering/Hope Publishing Company).

CHRISTMAS READINGS

The prophets promise the Saviour
Numbers 24.16–17; Isaiah 7.14; Jeremiah 23. 5–6; Micah 5.2, 4; Isaiah 9.6

Numbers The oracle of one who hears the words of God, who has knowledge from the Most High: I see him, but not now; I behold him, but not near. A star will come out of Jacob; a sceptre will rise out of Israel.

Isaiah The Lord himself will give you a sign: The virgin will be with child and will give birth to a son, and will call him Immanuel.

Jeremiah 'The days are coming,' declares the Lord, 'when I will raise up to David a righteous Branch, a King who will reign wisely and do what is just and right in the land. This is the name by which he will be called: The Lord Our Righteousness.'

Micah Bethlehem Ephrathah, though you are small among the clans of Judah, out of you will come for me one who will be ruler over Israel, whose origins are from of old, from ancient times. He will stand and shepherd his flock in the strength of the Lord, in the majesty of the name of the Lord his God.

Isaiah To us a child is born, to us a son is given, and the government will be on his shoulders. And he will be called Wonderful Counsellor, Mighty God, Everlasting Father, Prince of Peace.

Cast [This is] the word of the Lord.
All **Thanks be to God.**

Cast: **Numbers, Isaiah, Jeremiah, Micah.**

Mary hears the news
From Luke 1.26–38

Narrator In the sixth month, God sent the angel Gabriel to Nazareth, a town in Galilee, to a virgin pledged to be married to a man named Joseph, a descendant of David. The virgin's name was Mary. The angel went to her [and said]:

Angel Greetings, you who are highly favoured! The Lord is with you.

Narrator Mary was greatly troubled at his words and wondered what kind of greeting this might be. But the angel said to her:

Angel Do not be afraid, Mary, you have found favour with God. You will be with child and give birth to a son, and you are to give him the name Jesus. He will be great and will be called the Son of the Most High. The Lord God will give him the throne of his father David, and he will reign over the house of Jacob for ever; his kingdom will never end.

[Narrator	Mary asked the angel:]
Mary	How will this be, since I am a virgin?
Angel	The Holy Spirit will come upon you, and the power of the Most High will overshadow you. So the holy one to be born will be called the Son of God.
[Narrator	Mary answered:]
Mary	I am the Lord's servant. May it be to me as you have said.
Narrator	Then the angel left her.
Cast	[This is] the word of the Lord.
All	**Thanks be to God.**

Cast: **Narrator, Angel, Mary.**

Mary visits Elizabeth*
Luke 1.39–55 (56)

Narrator	Mary got ready and hurried off to a town in the hill-country of Judaea. She went into Zechariah's house and greeted Elizabeth. When Elizabeth heard Mary's greeting, the baby moved within her. Elizabeth was filled with the Holy Spirit [and said in a loud voice]:
Elizabeth (delighted)	You are the most blessed of all women, and blessed is the child you will bear! Why should this great thing happen to me, that my Lord's mother comes to visit me? For as soon as I heard your greeting, the baby within me jumped with gladness. How happy you are to believe that the Lord's message to you will come true!
Narrator	Mary said:
Mary	My heart praises the Lord; my soul is glad because of God my Saviour, for he has remembered me, his lowly servant! From now on all people will call me happy, because of the great things the Mighty God has done for me. His name is holy; from one generation to another he shows mercy to those who honour him. He has stretched out his mighty arm and scattered the proud with all their plans. He has brought down mighty kings from their thrones, and lifted up the lowly. He has filled the hungry with good things, and sent the rich away with empty hands. He has kept the promise he made to our ancestors, and has come to the help of his servant Israel. He has remembered to show mercy to Abraham and to all his descendants for ever!

[Narrator	Mary stayed about three months with Elizabeth and then went back home.]
Cast	[This is] the word of the Lord.
All	**Thanks be to God.**

Cast: **Narrator, Elizabeth, Mary.** (*This reading can be omitted from the series.)

Joseph learns the truth
Matthew 1.18–25

Narrator	This is how the birth of Jesus Christ came about. His mother Mary was pledged to be married to Joseph, but before they came together, she was found to be with child through the Holy Spirit. Because Joseph her husband was a righteous man and did not want to expose her to public disgrace, he had in mind to divorce her quietly.
	But after he had considered this, an angel of the Lord appeared to him in a dream [and said]:
Angel	Joseph son of David, do not be afraid to take Mary home as your wife, because what is conceived in her is from the Holy Spirit. She will give birth to a son, and you are to give him the name Jesus, because he will save his people from their sins.
Narrator	All this took place to fulfil what the Lord had said through the prophet:
Prophet	The virgin will be with child and will give birth to a son, and they will call him Immanuel—
Narrator	Which means 'God with us'. (PAUSE) When Joseph woke up, he did what the angel of the Lord had commanded him and took Mary home as his wife. But he had no union with her until she gave birth to a son. And he gave him the name Jesus.
Cast	[This is] the word of the Lord.
All	**Thanks be to God.**

Cast: **Narrator, Angel, Prophet.**

Jesus is born*
Luke 2.1–7

Narrator	The Emperor Augustus ordered a census to be taken throughout the Roman Empire.
Commentator	When this first census took place, Quirinius was the governor of Syria. Everyone, then, went to register himself, each to his own town.
Narrator	Joseph went from the town of Nazareth in Galilee to the town of Bethlehem in Judaea, the birthplace of King David.
Commentator	Joseph went there because he was a descendant of David.
Narrator	He went to register with Mary, who was promised in marriage to him. She was pregnant, and while they were in Bethlehem, the

→

time came for her to have her baby. She gave birth to her first son, wrapped him in strips of cloth and laid him in a manger.

Commentator   There was no room for them to stay in the inn.

Cast   [This is] the word of the Lord.
All   **Thanks be to God.**

Cast: **Narrator, Commentator.** (*This reading can be omitted from the series.)

The angels announce the birth
Luke 2.8–14

Narrator   There were shepherds living out in the fields near Bethlehem, keeping watch over their flocks at night. An angel of the Lord appeared to them, and the glory of the Lord shone around them, and they were terrified. But the angel said to them:

Angel   Do not be afraid. I bring you good news of great joy that will be for all the people. Today in the town of David a Saviour has been born to you; he is Christ the Lord. This will be a sign to you: You will find a baby wrapped in strips of cloth and lying in a manger.

Narrator   Suddenly a great company of the heavenly host appeared with the angel, praising God:

Chorus   Glory to God in the highest
(cheerfully)   and on earth peace to all on whom his favour rests.

Cast   [This is] the word of the Lord.
All   **Thanks be to God.**

Cast: **Narrator, Angel, Chorus** (three or more, including Angel).

The shepherds find the baby
Luke 2.15–20

Narrator 1   When the angels had left them and gone into heaven, the shepherds said to one another:

Shepherds 1 & 2   Let's go to Bethlehem!

Shepherd 1   And see this thing that has happened—

Shepherd 2   Which the Lord has told us about.

Narrator 1   So they hurried off and found Mary and Joseph, and the baby, who was lying in the manger.

Narrator 2   When they had seen him, they spread the word concerning what had been told them about this child, and all who heard it were amazed at what the shepherds said to them.

Narrator 1   But Mary treasured up all these things and pondered them in her heart.

Narrator 2   The shepherds returned, glorifying and praising God for all the things they had heard and seen, which were just as they had been told.

Cast   [This is] the word of the Lord.
All   **Thanks be to God.**

Cast: **Narrator 1, Shepherd 1, Shepherd 2** (can be the same as Shepherd 1), **Narrator 2** (can be the same as Narrator 1).

The wise men follow the star
From Matthew 2.1–11

Narrator	After Jesus was born in Bethlehem in Judaea, during the time of King Herod, Magi from the east came to Jerusalem and asked:
Magi	Where is the one who has been born king of the Jews? We saw his star in the east and have come to worship him.
Narrator	When King Herod heard this, he was disturbed, and all Jerusalem with him. When he had called together all the people's chief priests and teachers of the law, he asked them:
Herod	Where will the Christ be born?
[Narrator	They replied:]
Teachers 1 and 2	In Bethlehem in Judaea.
Teacher 2	For this is what the prophet has written:
Prophet	Bethlehem, in the land of Judah, out of you will come a ruler who will be the shepherd of my people Israel.
Narrator	Then Herod called the Magi secretly and found out from them the exact time the star had appeared. He sent them to Bethlehem [and said]:
Herod	Go and make a careful search for the child. As soon as you find him, report to me, so that I too may go and worship him.
Narrator	After they had heard the king, they went on their way, and the star they had seen in the east went ahead of them until it stopped over the place where the child was. When they saw the star, they were overjoyed. On coming to the house, they saw the child with his mother Mary, and they bowed down and worshipped him. Then they opened their treasures and presented him with gifts of gold and of incense and of myrrh.
Cast	[This is] the word of the Lord.
All	**Thanks be to God.**

Cast: **Narrator, Magi, Herod, Teacher 1, Teacher 2** (can be the same as Teacher 1), **Prophet** (can be the same as Teacher 1).

The child escapes the sword
From Matthew 2.13–18

Narrator	When the Magi had gone, an angel of the Lord appeared to Joseph in a dream:
Angel	Get up. Take the child and his mother and escape to Egypt. Stay there until I tell you, for Herod is going to search for the child to kill him.
Narrator	So Joseph got up, took the child and his mother during the night and left for Egypt, where he stayed until the death of Herod. And so was fulfilled what the Lord had said through the prophet:
Prophet	Out of Egypt I called my son.
Narrator	When Herod realised that he had been outwitted by the Magi, he was furious, and he gave orders to kill all the boys in Bethlehem

$\rightarrow$

and its vicinity who were two years old and under, in accordance with the time he had learned from the Magi. Then what was said through the prophet Jeremiah was fulfilled:

Jeremiah
A voice is heard in Ramah,
weeping and great mourning,
Rachel weeping for her children
and refusing to be comforted,
because they are no more.

Cast [This is] the word of the Lord.
All **Thanks be to God.**

Cast: **Narrator, Angel, Prophet, Jeremiah** (can be the same as Prophet).

The family return from Egypt*
Matthew 2.19–23

Narrator
After Herod died, an angel of the Lord appeared in a dream to Joseph in Egypt:

Angel
Get up, take the child and his mother, and go back to the land of Israel, because those who tried to kill the child are dead.

Narrator
So Joseph got up, took the child and his mother, and went back to Israel.

But when Joseph heard that Archelaus had succeeded his father Herod as king of Judaea, he was afraid to go there. He was given more instructions in a dream, so he went to the province of Galilee and made his home in a town named Nazareth. And so what the prophets had said came true:

Prophet
He will be called a Nazarene.

Cast [This is] the word of the Lord.
All **Thanks be to God.**

Cast: **Narrator, Angel, Prophet.** (*This reading can be omitted from the series.)

Simeon recognises the Messiah
From Luke 2.25–32

Narrator
There was a man in Jerusalem called Simeon, who was righteous and devout. He was waiting for the consolation of Israel, and the Holy Spirit was upon him. It had been revealed to him by the Holy Spirit that he would not die before he had seen the Lord's Christ. Moved by the Spirit, he went into the temple courts. When the parents brought in the child Jesus to do for him what the custom of the Law required, Simeon took him in his arms and praised God [saying]:

Simeon
Sovereign Lord, as you have promised,
you now dismiss your servant in peace.
For my eyes have seen your salvation,
which you have prepared in the sight of all people,
a light for revelation to the Gentiles
and for the glory to your people Israel.

Narrator	The child's father and mother marvelled at what was said about him. Then Simeon blessed them and said to Mary, his mother:
Simeon	This child is destined to cause the falling and rising of many in Israel, and to be a sign that will be spoken against, so that the thoughts of many hearts will be revealed. And a sword will pierce your own soul too.
Cast	[This is] the word of the Lord.
All	**Thanks be to God.**

Cast: **Narrator, Simeon.**

The apostles explain the meaning

John 1.1, 3, 14; Colossians 1.15, 17; Hebrews 1.1–3; 2 Corinthians 4.6; 8.9; Philippians 2.6–7; John 1.11–12

John	In the beginning was the Word, and the Word was with God, and the Word was God. Through him all things were made. The Word became flesh and lived for a while among us. We have seen his glory, the glory of the one and only Son, who came from the Father, full of grace and truth.
Colossians	Christ is the image of the invisible God, the first-born over all creation. He is before all things, and in him all things hold together.
Hebrews	In the past God spoke to our forefathers through the prophets, but in these last days he has spoken to us by his Son, who is the radiance of his glory and the exact representation of his being.
2 Corinthians	God, who said, 'Let light shine out of darkness,' made his light shine in our hearts to give us the light of the knowledge of the glory of God in the face of Christ. You know the grace of our Lord Jesus Christ, that though he was rich, yet for your sakes he became poor, so that you through his poverty might become rich.
Philippians	Christ Jesus, being in very nature God, did not consider equality with God something to be grasped, but made himself nothing, taking the very nature of a servant, being made in human likeness.
John	He came to that which was his own, but his own did not receive him. Yet to all who received him, to those who believed in his name, he gave the right to become children of God.
Cast	[This is] the word of the Lord.
All	**Thanks be to God.**

Cast: **John, Colossians, Hebrews, 2 Corinthians, Philippians.**

Narrator   One realises that one marvelled at what was said about
             him. Then Simeon blessed them and said to Mary, his mother,

Simeon   'This child is destined to cause the falling and rising of many in
             Israel, and to be a sign that will be spoken against, so that the
             thoughts of many hearts will be revealed. And a sword will pierce
             your own soul too.'

Carl   This is the word of the Lord.
All   Thanks be to God.

The apostles explain its meaning

John 1:1-5, 14; Colossians 1:15-17; Hebrews 1:1-3; 2 Corinthians 4:6;
Philippians 2:6-7; John 1:11-13

John   In the beginning was the Word, and the Word was with God, and
             the Word was God. Through him all things were made. The
             Word became flesh and lived for a while among us. We have seen
             his glory, the glory of the one and only Son, who came from the
             Father, full of grace and truth.

Colossians   Christ is the image of the invisible God, the first-born over all
             creation. He is before all things, and in him all things hold
             together.

Hebrews   In the past God spoke to our forefathers through the prophets
             but in these last days he has spoken to us by his Son, who is the
             radiance of his glory and the exact representation of his being.

2 Corinthians God, who said, 'Let light shine out of darkness', made his light
             shine in our hearts to give us the light of the knowledge of the
             glory of God in the face of Christ. You know the grace of our Lord
             Jesus Christ, that though he was rich, yet for your sakes he
             became poor, so that you through his poverty might become rich.

Philippians Christ Jesus, being in very nature God, did not consider equality
             with God something to be grasped, but made himself nothing,
             taking the very nature of a servant, being made in human
             likeness.

John   He came to that which was his own, but his own did not receive
             him. Yet to all who received him, to those who believed in his
             name, he gave the right to become children of God.

Carl   This is the word of the Lord.
All   Thanks be to God.

INDEXES

INDEXES.

INDEX TO
SEASONAL AND LITURGICAL MATERIAL

Italics indicate New Testament page numbers

This index also corresponds with the sequence of the Editor's
Church Family Worship and *Prayers for the People*.
From page 420 it provides every two months four to five appropriate themes for worship.

THROUGHOUT THE YEAR

JANUARY–FEBRUARY

New Year/Thanksgiving for the Old Year

The Wise Men/The Escape to Egypt/Epiphany

MARCH–APRIL

Mothering Sunday/The Family

MAY–JUNE

JULY–AUGUST

The Worldwide Church/The Church's Mission

2 Peter 1.16–21: Eye-witnesses of Christ's glory—*378*
Revelation 5.1–14: The scroll and the Lamb—*390*
Revelation 7.9–17: The enormous crowd—*393*

Revelation 15.1–8: The angels with the last plagues—*398*
Revelation 19.5–10: The wedding-feast of the Lamb—*400*

SEPTEMBER–OCTOBER

The Caring Church/Healing

Genesis 4.1–16: Cain and Abel—5
Leviticus 19.1–37: Laws of holiness and justice—105
Numbers 21.4–9: The snake made of bronze—121
Ruth 1.6–22: Naomi and Ruth return to Bethlehem—203
1 Samuel 17.55–18.5: David is presented to Saul—240
2 Samuel 9.1–13: David and Mephibosheth—274
2 Kings 4.8–37: Elisha and the rich woman from Shunem—348
Nehemiah 5.1–13: Oppression of the poor—440
Psalm 15.1–5: What God requires—486
Psalm 41.1–13: The prayer for health—500
Psalm 52.1–9: God's judgement and grace—508
Psalm 82.1–8: God, the supreme ruler—521
Psalm 122.1–8: In praise of Jerusalem—552
Isaiah 61.1–11: The good news of deliverance—643
Amos 5.10–27: The Day of the Lord—791

Matthew 7.24–29: Jesus' parable of the two house-builders—*13*
Matthew 8.1–17: Jesus heals people—*13*
Matthew 8.1–13, 14–17: Jesus heals people—*13*
Matthew 9.9–13: Jesus calls Matthew—*16*
Matthew 9.9–13: Jesus calls Matthew—*16*
Matthew 9.27–38: Jesus heals more people—*18*
Matthew 10.1–15: The twelve apostles—*19*
Matthew 12.15–21: God's chosen servant—*23*
Matthew 12.43–45: The return of the evil spirit—*25*
Matthew 15.29–38: Jesus heals and feeds many people—*34*
Matthew 22.34–40: The great commandment—*50*
Matthew 25.31–46: The final judgement—*58*
Mark 1.21–28: A man with an evil spirit—*73*
Mark 2.1–12: Jesus heals a paralysed man—*74*
Mark 3.1–6: The man with a paralysed hand—*77*
Mark 3.7–12: A crowd by the lake—*77*
Mark 5.1–20: Jesus heals a man with evil spirits—*82*
Mark 8.22–26: Jesus heals a blind man at Bethsaida—*92*
Mark 9.14–29: Jesus heals a boy with an evil spirit—*94*
Mark 12.28–34: The great commandment—*105*
Luke 4.31–37: A man with an evil spirit—*130*
Luke 4.38–44: Jesus heals and preaches—*130*
Luke 5.12–16: The man with leprosy—*132*
Luke 5.17–26: Jesus heals a paralysed man—*132*
Luke 6.27–36: Love for enemies—*136*
Luke 6.37–42: Judging others—*137*
Luke 10.25–37: The parable of the good Samaritan—*152*
Luke 16.19–31: The rich man and Lazarus—*170*
Luke 17.1–10: Jesus talks about sin, faith, and service—*171*

John 5.1–18: The healing at the pool—*208*
John 9.1–12: Jesus and the man born blind (i)—*220*
John 9.26–34: Jesus and the man born blind (iii)—*222*
John 13.1–15, 16–20: Jesus washes his disciples' feet—*231*
Acts 3.1–16: A lame man is healed—*251*
Acts 6.1–7: The seven helpers—*258*
Acts 6.1–7: The seven helpers—*258*
Acts 11.19–30: The church at Antioch—*268*
Romans 12.4–13: One body—*321*
Romans 12.14–21: About revenge—*322*
Romans 13.8–14: Duties towards one another—*322*
1 Corinthians 12.31–13.13: Love—*327*
2 Corinthians 8.7–15, 9.6–15: Christian giving—*331*
2 Corinthians 12.1–10: Paul's vision and revelation—*333*
Philippians 2.1–11: Christ's humility and greatness—*344*
James 2.1–13: Warning against prejudice—*371*
James 2.14–26: Faith and actions—*372*
1 Peter 1.3–12: A living hope—*374*
1 Peter 3.8–18: Suffering for doing right—*376*
1 John 4.7–21: God is love—*381*

God's Gifts to the Church/Renewal

Genesis 40.1–23: Joseph interprets the prisoners' dreams—50
Exodus 18.13–26: The appointment of judges—94
Leviticus 8.1–36: The ordination of Aaron and his sons—103
Deuteronomy 1.6–18: Moses appoints judges—129
Deuteronomy 31.1–8: Joshua becomes Moses' successor—143
Deuteronomy 31.14–29: The Lord's last instruction to Moses—144
1 Samuel 10.1–2, 9–16: Samuel and Saul—223
1 Kings 12.1–24: The northern tribes revolt—319
2 Chronicles 15.1–15: Asa's reforms—404
Psalm 134.1–3: A call to praise the Lord—557
Psalm 150.1–6: Praise the Lord—564
Isaiah 5.1–7: The song of the vineyard—591
Isaiah 27.2–6: Restoration—613
Isaiah 43.14–21: Escape from Babylon—628
Isaiah 61.1–11: The good news of deliverance—643
Isaiah 62.1–12: New names—644
Ezekiel 34.1–10: The shepherds of Israel—743
Ezekiel 34.11–31: The good shepherd—744
Ezekiel 37.1–14: The valley of dry bones—746

Matthew 10.1–15: The twelve apostles—*19*
Luke 16.9–12: More of Jesus' teaching on stewardship—*169*
Luke 19.12–26: Jesus tells the parable of the gold coins—*177*

Harvest

NOVEMBER–DECEMBER

Christian Conflict and Character/Our Work, Schools

Heaven/God's Peace

Christ's Coming/Judgement

Christmas

INDEX TO
SELECTED MAJOR THEMES

Italics indicate New Testament page numbers

A full thematic index to the Psalms (including the Liturgical Version in *The Dramatised Bible*)
may be found in the Editor's *Psalms for Today.*

INDEX TO
CHARACTERS

Italics indicate New Testament page numbers

INDEX TO
THE DRAMATISED VERSIONS

Italics indicate New Testament page numbers

THE OLD TESTAMENT

Proverbs

Ecclesiastes

Song of Songs

Isaiah

Jeremiah

THE NEW TESTAMENT

Mark

John	And I was told that the number of those who were marked with God's seal on their foreheads was 144,000. They were from the twelve tribes of Israel, twelve thousand from each tribe: Judah, Reuben, Gad, Asher, Naphtali, Manasseh, Simeon, Levi, Issachar, Zebulun, Joseph, and Benjamin.
Cast	[This is] the word of the Lord.
All	**Thanks be to God.**

Cast: **John, Angel.**

The enormous crowd
Revelation 7.9–17

John	I looked, and there was an enormous crowd—no one could count all the people! They were from every race, tribe, nation, and language, and they stood in front of the throne and of the Lamb, dressed in white robes and holding palm branches in their hands. They called out in a loud voice:
Voices 1 and 2	Salvation comes from our God, who sits on the throne, and from the Lamb!
John	All the angels stood round the throne, the elders, and the four living creatures. Then they threw themselves face downwards in front of the throne and worshipped God, saying:
Voices 2 and 3	Amen!
Voice 1	Praise
Voice 2	Glory
Voice 3	Wisdom
Voice 1	Thanksgiving
Voice 2	Honour
Voice 3	Power
Voice 1	Might
Voice 2 and 3	Belong to our God for ever and ever!
Voices 1–3	Amen!
John	One of the elders asked me:
Elder	Who are these people dressed in white robes, and where do they come from?
John	I don't know, sir. You do.
Elder	These are the people who have come safely through the terrible persecution. They have washed their robes and made them white with the blood of the Lamb. That is why they stand before God's throne and serve him day and night in his temple. He who sits on the throne will protect them with his presence. Never again will they hunger or thirst; neither sun nor any scorching heat will

→